PAPER MONEY
of the
UNITED STATES

A COMPLETE ILLUSTRATED GUIDE WITH VALUATIONS

Sixteenth Edition

*Large Size Notes, Fractional Currency, Small Size Notes, Encased Postage Stamps
from the First Year of Paper Money, 1861, to the Present
Confederate Notes
A Complete Listing of Colonial and Continental Currency from 1690 to 1788*

The standard reference work on paper money

by
ARTHUR L. FRIEDBERG
AND
IRA S. FRIEDBERG

based on the original work by
ROBERT FRIEDBERG (1912-1963)

THE COIN & CURRENCY INSTITUTE, INC.

P.O. Box 1057, Clifton, N.J. 07014

(973) 471-1441 • E-mail: coincurin@aol.com

PAPER MONEY OF THE UNITED STATES

A Complete Illustrated Guide With Valuations

Copyright 1953, 1955, 1959, 1962, 1964, 1968, 1972, 1975, 1978 by The Coin and Currency Institute, Inc., assigned to Arthur L. Friedberg and Ira S. Friedberg.
Copyright 1981, 1986, 1989, 1992, 1995, 1998, 2001 by Arthur L. Friedberg and Ira S. Friedberg.

Library of Congress Catalog Card No. 86-070306
ISBN 0-87184-516-4
ISSN 1099-9981

SPECIAL NOTICE

Permission is hereby granted for the free use of the numbering system employed in this book by any newspaper, magazine or periodical; and also by any coin dealer, currency dealer or stamp dealer in any advertisement, circular, price list or auction catalogue issued for free distribution, and not offered for sale. This permission is granted only when proper acknowledgment is made by the user of this numbering system of its source. This proper acknowledgment shall consist of mention of the title of this book, or the name of the author, or both, and shall appear whenever and wherever this numbering system is used. However, written permission shall be required when this numbering system is used in any publication that is offered for sale. Licenses for commercial use are available from the publisher.

OTHER BOOKS PUBLISHED BY
THE COIN & CURRENCY INSTITUTE

GOLD COINS OF THE WORLD
COINS OF THE BRITISH WORLD
APPRAISING AND SELLING YOUR COINS
SO-CALLED DOLLARS
AMERICA'S FOREIGN COINS
MODERN WORLD COINS
CURRENT COINS OF THE WORLD

A publication of
THE COIN & CURRENCY INSTITUTE, INC.

Printed in the United States of America

SIXTEENTH EDITION

Associate Editor
Arthur S. Goldenberg

ACKNOWLEDGEMENTS

Our thanks to the following who have helped to make the many editions of *Paper Money of the United States* possible:

The Honorable Secretary of the Treasury
The Assistant Secretary of the Treasury
The Chief, U.S. Secret Service
The Director, Bureau of Engraving and Printing
The Comptroller of the Currency
U.S. Treasury Department, Fiscal Service

The National Archives, Fiscal Branch
The Federal Reserve Bank of Chicago
The Federal Reserve Bank of San Francisco
The American Numismatic Society of N.Y.
The Chase Manhattan Bank Museum of Moneys of the World
The American Numismatic Association

And to the following for their long continuing assistance, giving unselfishly of their time and numismatic experience, and who have contributed to the completeness or accuracy of this book by furnishing information on unpublished notes, by offering valuable suggestions or by rendering technical assistance. Contributors to the present edition are denoted by an asterisk (*) following their name: -

William T. Anton, Jr. *
Thomas C. Bain, (dec'd)
R.J. Balbaton
Douglas B. Ball *
Harry J. Barnett
Aubrey E. Bebee (dec'd)
Q. David Bowers
Walter Breen (dec'd)
Vernon L. Brown (dec'd)
Robert Burgraff
Amon G. Carter, Jr. (dec'd)
Carlson R. Chambliss *
Thomas Conklin
Grover C. Criswell, Jr. (dec'd)
Pat Cyrgalis *
John F. Dahringer
Forrest W. Daniel
Charles Deibel
Thomas Denly *
William H. Dillisten (dec'd)
William P. Donlon (dec'd)
Brian Duckworth *
William R. Fisher
Kevin Foley
Dennis Forgue *
Jack Friedberg (dec'd)
Milton R. Friedberg
David L. Ganz *
Louis A. Geller (dec'd)
Martin Gengerke *
Leonard Glazer *
Nate Gold (dec'd)
Gerald Goldenberg
Stephen L. Goldsmith *
Barbara Gregory *
Bruce R. Hagen*
Robert W. Hearn
James Hodgson
Robert Hoge *
George H. Hubler
Curtis Iversen
Harry E. Jones *
Arthur M. Kagin*
Donald H. Kagin *
Paul Kagin *
Jules J. Karp
Theodore Kemm
David H. Klein
Lyn F. Knight *
David R. Koble *
James Lamb
Arthur Leister

Dana Linett *
Jesse Lipka
Michael P. Marchioni *
Lester Merkin (dec'd)
Steve Michaels
John H. Miller
Allen Mincho *
John H. Morris, Jr.
Stanley Morycz *
Doug Murray *
Charles H. Nehf
Frank Nowak
Susie Nulty *
Dean Oakes *
Chuck O'Donnell (dec'd)
Michelle Orzano *
V.H. Oswald, Sr. *
J. Roy Pennell
Alex Perakis *
Arnold Perl (dec'd)
M. Perlmutter
Jess Peters (dec'd)
W. A. Philpott, Jr. (dec'd)
K.B. Robertson
Thomas B. Ross
Matt H. Rothert (dec'd)
Stanley J. Roy
Sergio Sanchez, Jr. *
David Sarpal
R. F. Schermerhorn (dec'd)
Neil Shafer
Austin M. Sheheen, Jr.
Hugh Shull
James A. Simek *
Lillian Sisselman
Norman Shultz (dec'd)
Leon L. Smith, Jr.
William A.E. Spies
Harvey Stack *
James F. Stiff
Kari Stone *
David Sundman *
James Thompson (dec'd)
Robert L. Vandevender II
M.O. Warns
Mel Weinstein
Ron Weiss *
Louis Werner (dec'd)
Thomas Werner
Herbert Weston
Stephanie Westover *
William Youngerman *
Louis Zara (dec'd)

CONTENTS

PREFACE TO THE SIXTEENTH EDITION

It would not be far off the mark to offer the opinion that since the fifteenth edition of *Paper Money of the United States* was published two years ago, the growth in the field has been exponential. While a closer look shows that not to be so, the increases are still startling. The demand for all forms of American paper money continues undiminished. The base of collectors is growing steadily, aided by a vigorous economy and a preference for this field of collecting over its hard-metal cousin, which oftentimes seems geared only towards investment and packaging and not towards collecting. In fact, one advantage of acquiring paper money today is that it is still living history that may be held in one's hand - unlike so many coins.

Truly rare large size notes, always the bellwether of the market, are stronger than ever. In particular, bright, well-centered, untampered-with specimens, when offered at public auction, have driven bidders into frenzies. An added consequence is that specimens of lesser quality have risen as well to satisfy the demand.

Among the notable recent auction highlights are:
No. 150a. $50 Legal Tender Note 1863. Unc. $176,000.
No. 183c. $500 Legal Tender Note 1863. Crisp Unc. $517,000.
No. 186d. $1,000 Legal Tender Note 1863. Choice AU. $451,000.
No. 212d. $50 Interest Bearing Note 1865. VF. $181,500.
No. 213. $10 Refunding Certificate. 1879. $429,000.
No. 378. $100 Treasury Note 1891. EF. $154,000.
No. 379a. $1,000 Treasury Note 1890. Choice AU. $792,000.
No. 1166b. $20 Gold Certificate 1863. VF-EF. $528,000.
No. 1218d. $1000 Gold Certificate 1882. $935,000.
No. 2230-E. $10,000 Federal Reserve Note 1928. Unc. $126,500.
No. 2231-G. $10,000 Federal Reserve Note 1934. Unc. $82,500.

As prices for large size notes exceeded the collecting budgets of many collectors, small size notes (which have now been in circulation longer than their predecessors) have come more into their own. Many more of these are available in top condition at reasonable prices. Many early small size notes are now experiencing price escalation which at one time would have only been seen on large types.

The collecting of small size notes has been aided by the Bureau of Engraving and Printing's termination of its experiment with web presses. In fact, the web presses have now been dismantled. The result is a limited number of notes (Series 1988-A, 1993 and 1995), from a relatively few Federal Reserve districts, and despite their recency, a number of very rare issues.

Fractional Currency has emerged from the shadows and some scarce types in superior condition have changed hands at prices which would have once been considered fantasies.

The first major redesign of American currency in generations was completed on November 16, 1999 when Treasury Secretary Lawrence H. Summers introduced the new Series 1999 $5 and $10 notes. The new notes are similar in style to the $20, $50 and $100 notes introduced earlier as Series 1996.

The busts of Abraham Lincoln and Alexander Hamilton are still on the Five and Ten Dollar notes, respectively, but both are now framed in larger, off-center portrait frames. While the reverse of the Five Dollar Note is similar to its predecessor, the Ten features a facing view of the Treasury Department. The automobiles have been eliminated rather than modernized. Both notes contain polymer security threads with the words "USA TEN" and "USA FIVE" and they are printed on watermarked paper. Only the Ten Dollar note makes use of color-shifting black/green ink for one of the numerals.

The purpose of the redesign was to deter the counterfeiting of currency which has been made much easier with the wide availability of scanners, color printers and digital technology familiar even to average high school students, let alone professional criminals. It may be reasonable to suspect this currency redesign was not the last.

The United States Currency Collection
of the American Numismatic Association

The Museum of the American Numismatic Association in Colorado Springs, Colorado is one of the world's foremost repositories of coins and paper money. Its holdings range broadly through time and space from the ancient coinages of Greece and Rome through the pocket change used around the world today.

Two collections are of particular interest and importance for readers of this book: The Aubrey and Adeline Bebee Collection of United States Paper Money and the Robert T. Herdegen Collection of Fractional Currency (see page 146).

Aubrey and Adeline Bebee of Omaha, Nebraska are the ANA Museum's foremost benefactors. Among their donations are some of the most valuable coins in the world: the 1804 silver dollar and the 1913 Liberty nickel. Their collection of American paper money is the foremost collection of same in the world. A conservative estimate of its value today would be in excess of $2 million. In terms of consistent quality it surpasses even that of the Federal Reserve Bank of San Francisco, whose notes were featured in this book's last edition, and which continue to be featured prominently in this one.

The Bebee Collection was formed over a period of forty-six years and was donated to the Association in 1987 and 1988. It includes nearly all issues of every denomination of American currency, excluding fractional issues, from the Civil War to the 1980s. Among its most impressive components are some extremely rare uncut sheets of early notes.

Within the overall collection are some remarkable specialized groupings. One is the 1882 $5 "Brown Back" issues of the Second Charter period National Bank notes with examples from nearly every state. Another includes examples of notes showing all of the official government signature combinations which may be found on

"legal tender." Yet another includes examples of the very rare National Bank Notes issued in United States territories.

Wherever possible, notes from the Bebee collection have been used in the illustrations of Large Size Notes in Part One. There is also a special color section (pages 321-340) illustrating highlights from the collection.

In 1953, Aubrey Bebee was one of the original contributors to the first edition of this book. His support and cooperation in every subsequent edition until his passing were invaluable. It is a fitting tribute to the Bebees that their collection is now a part of a book in which they have had an important part.

Highlights from these great collections are always on view at the Museum of the American Numismatic Association in Colorado Springs, Colorado. Many are also available for viewing online at the ANA website, www.money.org.

Aubrey and Adeline Bebee would be pleased to know that their wonderful collection is helping to enhance the knowledge and enjoyment of all those who appreciate numismatics — the fraternity of students and collectors to whom they so generously dedicated this portion of their life's work and love.

GENERAL INFORMATION ON U. S. CURRENCY
1. LEGAL TENDER STATUS

The first United States paper money under the Constitution dates from 1861, when the Demand Notes were issued. From then to now, all currency issued by the United States Government has remained valid.

All the old and obsolete notes described in this book are still legal tender at their face value and will be exchanged by banks or the Government, if the owner so desires, for current paper money.

In some cases, the actual redemption value is higher than the face value, and such notes will be redeemed by the Government at the higher value. These are the Compound Interest Notes, the Interest Bearing Notes and the Refunding Certificates. Please refer to Sections III, IV and V in the text for further information.

Only once in the past has the Government ever recalled any of its paper currency for any reason, or mandated its exchange for other types of paper money. This was in 1933, when the Gold Reserve Act required all holders of Gold Certificates to surrender them for ordinary currency. However, to this day, Gold Certificates will be exchanged like all other notes, even though they are no longer redeemable in actual gold coin.

The exalted position thus occupied by American currency is unique in the annals of world finance. It is doubtful if any nation past or present, can point to such a long, unbroken series of currency issues, the integrity of which has so surely and confidently been maintained. The 3 Cent Fractional Currency Note of 1869 is still able to buy a 3 cent postage stamp, and the 1,000 Dollar Note of 1869 can still purchase its equivalent in the goods and services of today.

Americans can be quite proud of the basic soundness of this country's financial structure that has made all this possible. Collectors of old currency especially, can take a great deal of comfort in the knowledge that their valuable notes are so well fortified against loss of face value by the Government of the United States and its Treasury Department.

2. THE BEGINNINGS OF U.S. CURRENCY
Colonial Notes, Continental Currency, State Bank Notes

Paper money circulated in the United States long before 1861, when the Demand Notes were issued.

Various types of paper money, for example, were in use in all of the American Colonies while they were still under English rule. The issuance of this currency by the Colonies was a matter of urgent necessity since there was a shortage of coins in the growing nation.

Beginning in mid-1775, the Continental Congress authorized the issuance of currency to finance the Revolutionary War. This became known as Continental Currency. The notes were redeemable in Spanish Milled Dollars (a large silver coin of 8 Real denomination struck at any of the Spanish Colonial Mints in Mexico or South America). But the Continental Currency depreciated to a point where it cost more to print than it would buy. The depreciation of these notes is the source of the expression "not worth a Continental."

After the Constitution was ratified, the coinage system of the United States was established. The first coins of the new country were struck in 1793 at the Philadelphia Mint, when copper cents and half cents were issued. From then on until 1861, the Government did not find it necessary to issue paper money as we know it.

However, during this interim, there were periods of war, financial stress and sometimes panic. To meet the drain on the Treasury caused by these events, and to overcome the deficits, the Government from time to time issued Treasury Notes. These notes were actually promissory notes which bore interest and which the Treasury redeemed as quickly as possible. They did not circulate as money, except for the small denomination notes of 1815. The 5, 10, 20 and 50 Dollar notes of 1815 were not interest bearing and did circulate as money for a brief period.

Some of the events which brought forth these Treasury Notes were the War of 1812, the Mexican War of 1846, the "Hard Times" of 1837-1843, the Panic of 1857 and the unsettling situation of 1860 just prior to the impending Civil War.

It was also during the latter part of this interim period (1793-1861) that the United States was virtually blanketed by issues of State Bank Notes. The country at this time was just beginning to prosper and grow, and it soon became apparent that there was insufficient money in actual circulation to meet the demands of trade and commerce.

Consequently, the various States granted charters to many private banks in their jurisdiction, and by the terms of these State Charters the banks were authorized to print and circulate their own currency.

Ostensibly, the backing for this currency was the amount of money on deposit in the Bank -there were none of the restraints that we know today. The tragic consequence of this banking system was that the banks failed with alarming ease. If bank borrowers defaulted on their loans because of poor business, or for other reasons, then the banks had no recourse but to close their doors, since they literally went "broke." When that happened, the currency issued by the banks became worthless paper and a great deal of financial hardship was inflicted on the holders of these bank notes. In the old days, the term "wildcat" was applied both to the banks and their currency. Today, these historical paper mementos are called "Broken Bank Notes." Some of them are of great beauty of design and color and they are widely collected by the present generation of currency collectors.

Soon after the Civil War began, the United States found itself in desperate need for money to finance the war. The only remedy that could be found was in an issue of paper money. Accordingly, Congress passed the Act of July 17, 1861 which permitted the Treasury Department to print and circulate paper money to the extent of 60 million dollars. In the meanwhile, the Government had suspended specie payments. The effect of this suspension was that this new paper money could not be converted into coin, either silver or gold. The public was thus forced to accept this money purely on faith and in a belief that the money would be good.

These first United States Notes are known as Demand Notes. They were followed in 1862 by the Legal Tender Notes and then by all the others as can be seen in the ensuing text.

3. THE TREASURY SEAL

Original Seal   New Seal

The Treasury Seal is a distinguishing feature of American Currency. In one form or another, it has appeared on every piece of paper money issued by the Treasury Department since 1862. The Demand Notes of 1861 are without the seal, as are also the first three issues of Fractional Currency.

The Treasury Seal, one might say, is the final stamp of approval that insures the legality of our currency. Combined with the expressed obligation of the government and the two signatures, it notarizes the contract, so to speak, made between the United States and the holders of its currency.

The Seal appears in several different forms and colors, as will be seen by referring to the illustrations and the text. It may be quite small, or large enough to fill up a substantial part of the note; it may be within a plain circle, or within a circle of rays, spikes or scallops; it may be red, brown, blue, green, gold or yellow. From the viewpoint of collecting, the kind of seal used makes a distinct variety out of a given note. Two notes which otherwise appear similar in design, year and signatures, may differ in the color, shape, or size of the seal.

The design of the Treasury Seal includes a shield on which a scale, representing the emblem of Justice, and a Key, representing the emblem of official authority, appear. These two symbols are separated by a chevron bearing 13 stars symbolic of the 13 original colonies or states. The legend around the seal is "THESAUR. AMER. SEPTENT. SIGIL.," the meaning of which is "The Seal of the Treasury of North America." The Great Seal of the Treasury is older than the Constitution, having been used by the Board of Treasury under the Articles of Confederation. In 1778 the Continental Congress named John Witherspoon, Robert Morris and Richard Henry Lee to design seals for the Treasury and Navy. The committee reported on a design for the Navy the following year but there is no record of a report about one for the Treasury.

The Treasury considers Francis Hopkinson, the Treasurer of Loans, to be the actual creator of its seal. Hopkinson is known to have submitted bills to the Congress in 1780 authorizing the design of departmental seals, including the Board of Treasury. Although it is not certain that he was the designer, the seal is similar to others by him.

After the Constitution was ratified in 1789, the Treasury adopted the same seal. With only slight changes in design, this seal has been in use ever since. In 1968, a major design change was made. The new seal is simpler and less cluttered in appearance than the original. The scale and key were enlarged and five-pointed stars were replaced by the more ornate six-pointed ones. The lover's knot and flowers were removed and the Latin legend was replaced by an inscription in English reading, "The Department of the Treasury." Below is the date of the founding of the Treasury Department, "1789."

The new seal made its first appearance on the $100 United States Note, Series of 1966. It is currently being used on all denominations of U.S. currency.

4. THE GREAT SEAL

Since 1935, the most familiar denomination of paper currency, the One Dollar note, has carried the Great Seal of the United States on its reverse. Appearing on the Seal's obverse, on the right of the note, is the Latin inscription, "E Pluribus Unum," which means, "Out of Many (States), One (Nation)."

The Seal's reverse on the left, bears two inscriptions: Annuit Coeptis, meaning "He (God) Has Favored Our Undertakings," and Novus Ordo Seclorum meaning "A New Order of the Ages." The eye in the triangle is a symbol of the all-seeing eye of God. The pyramid of 13 rows represents the 13 original colonies. The date MDCCLXXVI (1776) refers to the year of the signing of the Declaration of Independence. (The Great Seal appears on notes 1607-1621, and 1900-1925 and 2300).

5. SIGNATURES

Except for the first two issues of Fractional Currency, all our notes bear the engraved facsimile signatures of two Treasury officials.

However, in the case of the Demand Notes of 1861, the names of these Treasury Officials do not appear on the notes, but the two signatures are those of Treasury employees signing for the officials. Please refer to Design Nos. 1, 2 and 3 in the text for the way in which these signatures appear.

From the series of 1862 through the series of 1923, the signatures appearing on our currency are of the Register of the Treasury and of the Treasurer of the United States.

However, on the large Federal Reserve Notes of 1914, and on all small size notes, the Register's name no longer appears but is replaced by the signature of the Secretary of the Treasury, the highest official of the Treasury Department. It is the Secretary's signature that now appears on our currency, alongside that of the Treasurer. There are several issues of currency which bear two other signatures in addition to those described above. These issues are the National Bank Notes, both large and small, and the Federal Reserve Bank Notes, both large and small. On the National Bank Notes, the two additional signatures are of the President and Cashier of the issuing bank; on the Federal Reserve Bank Notes, the two additional signatures are of the Governor and Cashier (or Deputy Governor) of the issuing bank.

There are also two issues that were countersigned by various assistant Treasurers. These are the Silver Certificates of 1878 and some of the Gold Certificates of 1882. All these notes are very rare.

The question is very often asked what the functions of the Register were during the period his signature appeared on our large notes and whether there is still today a Register of the Treasury. The Treasury Department advises that the office of the Register is still in existence and occupied, and that his functions during the issuance of large notes were as follows, "To receive from official agencies all bonds and other public debt securities, both bearer and registered, including collateral issue of interest coupons, representing principal and interest of the public debt when paid and canceled, or otherwise canceled and retired or voided, for any purpose whatever; to audit, hold in custody, and make disposition thereof; to record all bearer securities and other contiguous coupons prepared for issue and all such securities and coupons retired, and to record registered bonds issued and retired; to certify to the Comptroller General of the United States the clearance of the public debt disbursements of the Treasurer of the United States for all redeemed securities whether paid by the Treasurer direct or through the Federal Reserve Banks and charged against the Treasurer's account."

For a complete list of all the Registers and Treasurers, and their years in office concurrently, please refer to the table in the Appendix.

6. DATING U.S. PAPER MONEY

Every piece of United States paper money bears a date. It may be the date of an Act of Congress that authorized the issue or it may be the series year.

However, the year appearing on a given note is not necessarily the year in which it was printed and issued. This can be puzzling to a beginning currency collector, and it is certainly different from the minting of coins, which are usually struck only during the calendar year that appears on the coin.

Refer, for example, to a typical note in the text, let us say, number 234, which bears the date "Series of 1899" and the signatures of Elliott and Burke. This note could obviously not have been printed in 1899 since official public records indicate that the two signers were in office concurrently only from November 21, 1919 to January 5, 1921. Therefore, note number 234 could have been printed only during this period. The last issue of large notes is Series of 1923 with signatures of Woods and Tate, who were in office together for 7 months, 16 days during 1928 and 1929.

The table in the appendix gives a complete chronological listing of the various Treasury Officials who signed our currency. This table also indicates the exact periods of time during which they held office concurrently, so that by referring to this table, it will be quite simple to determine when any note was printed, with the exception of National Bank Notes. See under "The Dates of Issue" in the introduction to large size National Bank Notes on page 74.

7. SIZE

In accordance with Treasury Department regulations, the illustrations in this book are reduced to slightly less than three-fourths the size of the original notes. With certain exceptions, the size of an average large note is 7 by 3 inches.

The Interest Bearing and Compound Interest Notes are slightly larger, especially in their width. The Refunding Certificates are slightly smaller but much wider and measure 6 3/4 by 3 inches.

As will be seen by the illustrations, Fractional Currency is of several sizes. However, these illustrations are uniformly somewhat less than three-fourths the size of the original notes. The actual size of the smallest piece of Fractional Currency is 2 1/2 by 1 5/8 inches and of the largest piece, it is 4 3/8 by 2 1/8 inches.

8. COLOR

The dominant colors of U.S. paper money are black and green. The obverses all bear portraits of famous Americans or allegorical scenes and are printed in black and white, considerably enlivened by colored seals, colored serial numbers and attractive colored embellishments.

The reverses are printed in varying shades of green except for the following classes of currency: The Refunding Certificates of 1879 are printed in black and white; the Silver Certificates of 1878 and 1880 are printed in a brownish black; the National Bank Notes of the First Charter Period are bi-colored, the central painting in black, the borders in green; the first issues of the National Bank Notes of 1882 are printed in brown; the National Gold Bank Notes are bi-colored, the central portion of gold coins in black, the borders in brown; the Gold Certificates are printed in a brilliant golden orange to simulate the color of gold.

The same coloration is typical of Fractional Currency except for certain issues, which are noted in the text. (See notes 1226-1383-a.)

9. ERROR, FREAK NOTES AND UNCUT SHEETS

From time to time, through human or mechanical failure, unusual notes have been printed and issued.

These accidents have taken different forms, and some of these notes are highly prized by collectors. All such notes are of greater or lesser rarity, since the Bureau of Engraving and Printing is most strict in the inspection and release of the finished currency, and will not issue any notes that are imperfect in any way.

Some of the errors that have occurred in the past are as follows: without seal or seal only partly showing; serial numbers missing, incomplete or even different on the same note; a white unprinted portion showing on a note, where the paper had been accidentally folded; the seal or serial numbers upside down or printed on the reverse side of the note; the reverse inverted (a normal note is turned like the page of a book in order to read the reverse); two denominations on the same note.

By far, the most cherished and valuable error notes are those with two denominations, for example, a 5 Dollar obverse and a 10 Dollar reverse. Such notes are extremely rare, are in great demand and bring very high prices on the few occasions when they are offered for sale. An extraordinary error like this is most likely caused during the process of printing, when a sheet which has already been printed on one side is inadvertently removed from its proper place and put with sheets of another denomination, which similarly have so far been printed on only one side.

Although not considered either errors or freaks, uncut sheets of notes are also collected for their unusual appeal. Uncut sheets will most frequently be found among the National Bank Notes, more rarely among the other series. The reason for this is that National Bank Notes were delivered to the banks by the Treasury Department in the form of complete sheets. Once at the banks, the notes had to be signed by the president and cashier, and the separation of the notes became a matter of convenience for the individual bank.

An uncut sheet of American paper money is a seldom seen oddity and is usually a conversation piece. Such an item makes a handsome and impressive addition to any collection of currency.

10. HIGH DENOMINATION NOTES

As will be seen in the text, the Government has issued some notes with a very high face value. These notes are of the denominations of 500, 1,000, 5,000 and 10,000 Dollars.

These high denomination notes are merely mentioned in the text as having once upon a time been issued, since the main concern of numismatists is with the small denomination notes from 1 to 100 Dollars. Although illustrated, the high denomination notes have not been priced, because they represent so much purchasing power and are of such great rarity as to make their collecting purely academic. They are quite beyond the reach of the ordinary collector because of their high face value, and just as much beyond the reach of the millionaire because of their extreme rarity, or because a few issues will be forever unobtainable, the last existing note having already been redeemed by the Treasury.

Although these high denomination notes were available to anyone who wanted them, they were not, as a matter of practice, to be found in ordinary circulation. They were held mainly by banks and clearing houses and were used to settle large cash balances. Several examples of their rarity can be given, as taken from official Treasury records of Dec. 31, 1965.

500 Dollars.	Silver Certificate.	14 pieces extant.
500 Dollars.	National Bank Note.	6 pieces extant.
1,000 Dollars.	Silver Certificate.	8 pieces extant.
1,000 Dollars.	National Bank Note.	10 pieces extant.
1,000 Dollars.	Treasury or Coin Note.	5 pieces extant.
5,000 Dollars.	Legal Tender Note.	None extant.
10,000 Dollars.	Legal Tender Note.	None extant.

The current small size notes were also issued in high denominations up to 10,000 Dollars. (See under Federal Reserve Notes.) The last 5,000 and 10,000 Dollar notes were issued during the tenure of Julian and Morgenthau. The Treasury no longer prints notes with denominations of 500 to 10,000 Dollars, and these are now being slowly retired. The 100 Dollar note has thus become the largest denomination note available.

11. RARITY

As collectors of currency quickly discover, many notes are quite difficult to obtain. Even after years of searching inquiry among all possible sources, some notes will remain elusive enough as to be almost unobtainable.

This rarity can be of two kinds, either of design or of condition. Great rarity is generally a combination of both.

The rarity of design is the more important since the notes involved exist in only one or two varieties, whereas notes of more common design may have numerous varieties of seals or signature combinations, making such designs far easier to acquire. Since most collectors are content with only one note of each distinctive design, the notes of rare design are in great demand and bring high prices.

The rarity of condition is concerned with those notes, irrespective of design, which are extremely difficult to acquire in new condition, although they may be fairly common in circulated state. This factor of condition is of the greatest importance to collectors who wish to build a complete collection of currency, since their aim is the acquisition of notes in the finest possible condition.

Several examples can be cited of notes of rare designs. They are here given in the order of their rarity: All Interest Bearing Notes, Compound Interest Notes and Refunding Certificates; all Demand Notes; all National Gold Bank Notes and all Silver Certificates of 1878 and 1880 (10 to 100 Dollars). Coincidentally, all the foregoing notes also represent the highest rarity of condition since they are practically unknown in new or uncirculated state. The average condition in which these notes appear is only fine.

The following specific notes can also be mentioned as of rare designs: Legal Tender 50 Dollars of 1869, Treasury or Coin 50 Dollars of 1891 and 100 Dollars of 1890 and 1891; Federal Reserve Bank Note 50 Dollars of 1918; all Legal Tender Notes of 1869; the 50 and 100 Dollar Notes of the Legal Tender issues of 1862-1863 and also of the First Charter National Bank Issues of 1863-1875; all notes of the Second Charter National Bank issues of 1882 with the denomination spelled out on the reverse, and all Treasury or Coin Notes of 1890.

Among notes which are of common design but very rare in new condition, note No. 49 is probably the most famous example. This design is quite common but only about five specimens are known of this particular variety.

In addition to the notes of rare condition mentioned in the third paragraph above, the following are also noteworthy as being most difficult to acquire in new condition: All Legal Tender Notes of 1869; all National Bank Notes of the First Charter Period, 1863-1875; and in general all 10, 20, 50, and 100 Dollar notes of all categories from 1862 to 1890 inclusive; also the following specific notes for which please refer to the text: Numbers 19, 21-25, 31, 32, 43, 45, 46, 53, 54, 55, 74-78, 220, 221, 243, 244, 265, 347-349, 353-355, 359-361.

A word is also in order here regarding the so-called Educational Set of notes. Please see design numbers 61, 66 and 70. These notes are of extraordinary beauty and of great historical appeal and although not particularly rare, there has been such a persistent demand for them that they are expected to become very rare in time. Notes in a similar category are those of design number 68. These too have an unusual appeal and enjoy great popularity because of the numismatic reverse which shows a row of five silver Dollars.

12. GRADING AND CONDITION

The condition of a note is its state of preservation—its newness, its crispness, its color, its eye appeal.

The notes in this book have been priced in new, very fine and very good condition. In some cases, where the notes are very rare in new or very fine condition, they have been listed in only fine condition.

The following grading standards apply to paper money:

Gem Uncirculated: A note that is flawless, with the same freshness, crispness and bright color as when first printed. It must be perfectly centered, with full margins, and free of any marks, blemishes or traces of handling.

Choice Uncirculated: An uncirculated note which is fresher and brighter than the norm for its particular issue. Almost as nice as Gem Uncirculated, but not quite there. Must be reasonably well centered.

Uncirculated: A note which shows no trace of circulation. It may not have perfect centering and may have one or more pinholes, counting smudges, or other evidence of improper handling, while still retaining its original crispness.

Sometimes large size notes will be encountered which are obviously uncirculated, but which may have some tiny pin holes. It was customary in the old days to spindle or pin new notes together, and that is why so many uncirculated notes may show tiny pin holes. Such imperfections do not generally impair the choice appearance of a new note, and such notes are to be regarded as being in uncirculated condition, although they generally command slightly lower prices than notes in perfect condition.

About Uncirculated: A bright, crisp note that appears new but upon close examination shows a trace of very light use, such as a corner fold or faint crease. About Uncirculated is a borderline condition, applied to a note which may not be quite uncirculated, but yet is obviously better than an average Extra Fine note. Such notes command a price only slightly below a new note and are highly desirable.

Extra Fine: A note that shows some faint evidence of circulation, although it will still be bright and retain nearly full crispness. It may have two or three minor folds or creases but no tears or stains and no discolorations.

Very Fine: A note that has been in circulation, but not actively or for long. It still retains some crispness and is still choice enough in its condition to be altogether desirable. It may show folds or creases, or some light smudges from the hands of a past generation. Sometimes, Very Fine notes are the best available in certain rare issues, and they should accordingly be cherished just as much as uncirculated notes. See the section on rarity above.

Fine: A fine note shows evidence of much more circulation, has lost its crispness and very fine detail, and creases are more pronounced, although the note is still not seriously soiled or stained.

Very Good: A note that has had considerable wear or circulation and may be limp, soiled or dark in appearance and even have a small tear or two on an edge.

Good: A note that is badly worn, with margin or body tears, frayed margins and missing corners.

In general, discriminating collectors will not acquire Fine or worse notes because they have lost their aesthetic appeal, but this applies only to common notes. A really rare note has a ready market in even poor condition, because it may not otherwise exist, or if it is choice, will have an extremely high price commensurate with its great rarity.

13. VALUATIONS

No book of this nature would be either complete or desirable without an indication of the numismatic or collectors' value of the notes.

All large size notes, fractional currency , and many, particularly older, small size notes, are important collectors' items today, and the valuations given here are offered as a guide for collectors, or for students of the subject. These prices were most carefully prepared, and are based upon recent sales records, supply and demand, rarity, general activity and a thorough analytical study of the market. The prices thus represent an average at or about which the notes would be obtainable from a numismatic dealer when in stock.

The pricing of rare notes always poses a special problem since they come up for sale so seldom and the demand for them is so avid, that any price for a rare note can, at best, be only nominal. Some rare notes in the past have no doubt changed hands at much higher prices than here quoted, and it is conceivable that they will do so again, but as mentioned above, a fair average valuation has been attempted. It must also be borne in mind that many early notes, though not rare in themselves, are of the greatest rarity when in choice uncirculated condition. Such notes are practically priceless and command their own figure when offered.

14. "STAR" NOTES

When a note is found to be imperfect in the course of manufacture, it is replaced with a "star" note, that is a note bearing a star either before or after the serial number. In all other respects, the "star" note is indistinguishable from the regular notes, and, of course, worth the same face value.

On Federal Reserve Notes, the star appears after the serial number. On all other issues, the star precedes the serial number. A "star" note is also used for the 100,000,000th note in a series, since the numbering machines cannot print over eight digits.

"Star" notes are indicated in the Small Size Notes section by an (*) appearing after the catalog number.

15. THE COLLECTING OF UNITED STATES CURRENCY

As shown by the illustrations in the text, large size notes offer the collector an abundance of colorful design, artistic subject matter and historical and educational data.

In the last 30 years or so, the collecting of this currency has increased to such an extent that notes which were once plentiful are now rare, and bring prices out of all proportion to what they brought in 1940. This difference can easily be seen by comparing price lists issued at different times since 1940. This trend is still continuing, and collectors throughout the country are competing with each other for the acquisition of choice notes. More and more, note collecting is becoming an adjunct of coin collecting, and now almost all numismatists collect both.

The designs of large notes, both obverse and reverse, represent the best work of the best engravers of the nineteenth century. It is for good reason indeed that our old notes have so often been called masterpieces of the art of engraving, and beautiful enough to rank with other works of art.

So active has the collecting of large notes been, that there are now no major stocks in existence of choice and rare notes where one can select anything of his choice. In the 1940's, two of the greatest collections of paper money ever formed were broken up and the notes quickly absorbed by countless collectors. The collections referred to were those formed by Colonel Green (son of Hetty Green) and Albert A. Grinnell. The first collection was broken up in 1942 and the second was sold over a period from 1944 to 1946.

There are several ways of collecting large notes. One may collect just one note of each design or all the varieties of seal and signature of each design; or one may collect only the Legal Tender Notes or the Silver Certificates, or some other series; or one may collect the notes of a given denomination such as 1, 2 or 5 Dollar notes, etc.; or one may collect only notes of special artistic value, or of historical interest. In short, the collecting of currency, as in other collecting

fields, is determined purely by personal preference and by purse.

The above paragraphs apply equally to Fractional Currency, which has also enjoyed great popularity in recent years.

By comparison with large notes, the small size currency of today is more standardized. Though it does not have the richness of color and design of the past, the collecting of small size currency nevertheless has its own charms, since the fewer basic designs have many interesting varieties that lend themselves to true numismatic study. Actually, the portraits that first appeared on these notes in 1929 remained unchanged until the late 1990's, but a glance at the illustrations will show many obvious differences in the overall appearance of these notes.

Despite their apparent paucity of design, the small size notes offer a rich paradise of variety and one who undertakes to acquire a complete set of small size notes has set himself upon a monumental task. It is believed that a complete set of uncirculated small size notes has not yet been formed, although it has been tried. Many of the notes just cannot be found in uncirculated condition.

A comparison will quickly show the difference. Large notes were issued from 1861 to 1929, a period of 68 years, which produced about 140 designs and about 1,200 varieties. The issue of small notes from 1929 to 1971 is a period of 42 years which has produced only 7 portrait types but about 1,184 varieties. The above comparisons are for notes up to the 100 Dollars and do not include either the large or small National Bank Notes which were issued by thousands of different banks.

A collection of currency can be kept in either of two standard ways, in bound albums especially made for currency or in individual heavy, transparent envelopes which can be filed upright in a box.

In either case care should be taken that all materials are chemically inert.

16. THE COUNTERFEIT CLAUSE

The counterfeiting of United States paper money is an extremely dangerous offense. Although the penalties upon being convicted are very serious and heavy, nevertheless counterfeiters have indulged in this felony almost since our first notes were made.

In order to publicize the serious nature of counterfeiting and to acquaint the population with the penalties, many issues of our large notes bear an extract from the Criminal Code pertaining to the counterfeiting of United States paper money.

This counterfeit clause first appeared on the National Bank Notes of the First Charter period, and is last seen on the Legal Tender issues of the 1917 series. The punishment has become progressively worse since the 1860's when this clause first appeared.

On the National Bank Notes referred to above, the counterfeit clause reads "Every person making or engraving, or aiding to make

or engrave, or passing or attempting to pass any imitation or alterations of this note, and every person having in possession a plate or impression made in imitation of it, or any paper made in imitation of that on which this note is printed, is by Act of Congress approved June 3, 1864, guilty of felony, and subject to a fine not exceeding one thousand dollars, or imprisonment not exceeding fifteen years, or both."

On the Legal Tender issues of the 1917 series this clause reads, "Counterfeiting or altering this note or passing any counterfeit or alteration of it, or having in possession any false or counterfeit plate or impression of it, or any paper made in imitation of the paper on which it is printed is a felony and is punishable by a $5,000 fine or 15 years' imprisonment at hard labor or both."

17. BIBLIOGRAPHY

The following publications have been consulted:

Behrens. *Paper Money in Maryland 1727-1789.*

Bowen. *Rhode Island Colonial Money and its Counterfeiting 1647-1726.*

Breck. *Historical Sketch of Continental Paper Money.*

Criswell. *Confederate and Southern States Currency.*

Dillistin. *A Descriptive History of National Bank Notes.*

Haseltine. *Paper Money of the Continental Congress.*

Hessler. *The Comprehensive Catalog of U.S. Paper Money.*

Hickman & Oakes. *Standard Catalog of National Bank Notes.*

Kelly. *National Bank Notes.*

Limpert. *United States Paper Money, Old Series, 1861-1923.*

Limpert. *Classified List of U.S. Postage and Fractional Currency.*

Lloyd. *National and Federal Reserve Currency, 1928-1950.*

Newman. *The Early Paper Money of America.*

O'Donnell. *The Standard Handbook of Modern U.S. Paper Money*

Oakes. *Small Size U.S. Paper Money.*

Raymond. *The Standard Paper Money Catalogue.* Various editions.

Steinmetz. *National Bank Notes of the United States, 1863-1935.*

Van Belkum. *National Banks of the Note Issuing Period 1863-1935.*

PART ONE. LARGE SIZE NOTES
I. THE DEMAND NOTES OF 1861

The term "Greenback" for United States paper money originated with the issue of the Demand Notes of 1861. As mentioned earlier in this book, these Demand Notes are the first and earliest issue of United States currency as we know it.

They were issued in denominations of 5, 10 and 20 Dollars only, and were authorized by the Congressional Acts of July 17 and August 5, 1861. All notes bear the first date, "Act of July 17, 1861" and also the additional date of "Aug. 10th, 1861," which is probably the day the notes were first issued to the public.

Demand Notes are unique in United States Currency, in that they alone bear neither the Treasury Seal nor the actual names of the Treasurer and Register of the Treasury. They also have the serial number imprinted only once.

Sixty million dollars in currency was authorized to be issued by the above Acts. This was a very large sum for those days and involved the printing and signing of several million actual notes. At this time, a situation arose which was unprecedented.

The first plates made for the various denominations had blank spaces for two signatures, and below these spaces were engraved "Register of the Treasury" and "Treasurer of the United States."

These two busy and important Treasury officials obviously could not sit down and personally autograph several million notes. Therefore, a large staff of clerks from the Treasury Department was employed to sign their own names for the two officials. The way the plates were worded made it necessary for these clerks to write also the words "For the" in addition to their own name.

It quickly became apparent that this additional wording was both wasteful and inefficient and the plates were at once changed so that the finished printed note read as follows, "For the Register of the Treasury" and "For the Treasurer of the United States."

Compared to the total amount of notes issued, those released to the public before the plates were changed were small in number. Today, only a few survive and they are of the highest rarity and greatest historical interest.

The obligation on the Demand Notes is as follows. "The United States promised to pay to the bearer. . . . . Dollars on demand. . . . Payable by the Assistant Treasurer of the United States at (New York, Philadelphia, Boston, Cincinnati or St. Louis). Receivable in payment of all public dues."

5 Dollar Notes

DESIGN NO. 1

(Notes 1-5a)

Thomas Crawford's statue of Freedom on top of the U.S. Capitol in Washington. Head of Alexander Hamilton, the first Secretary of the Treasury, 1789-1795.

Reverse of Design No. 1.

Printed in green. The green reverses of the Demand Notes are the origin of the term "Greenback" as applied to U.S. paper money in general.

Note illustrated from collection of the American Numismatic Association.

No.	Payable at	Very Good	Very Fine	No.	Payable at	Very Good	Very Fine
1.	New York	950.00	4,000.00	3a.	"For the" handwritten	Unique	—
1a.	"For the" handwritten	2,500.00	Rare	4.	Cincinnati	Rare	—
2.	Philadelphia	900.00	3,750.00	4a.	"For the" handwritten	Unknown	—
2a.	"For the" handwritten	Unknown	—	5.	St. Louis	Very Rare	—
3.	Boston	925.00	3,750.00	5a.	"For the" handwritten	Unique	—

10 Dollar Notes

DESIGN NO. 2

(Notes 6-10a)

Head of Abraham Lincoln, 16th President of the United States, 1861-1865. At top center, an eagle with draped shield. At right, a female allegory representing Art.

Reverse of Design No. 2

Note illustrated from collection of the American Numismatic Association.

No.	Payable at	Very Good	Very Fine	No.	Payable at	Very Good	Very Fine
6.	New York	1,500.00	6,000.00	8a.	"For the" handwritten	Two known	
6a.	"For the" handwritten	Rare	Rare	9.	Cincinnati	Extremely Rare	
7.	Philadelphia	1,500.00	6,000.00	9a.	"For the" handwritten	Unique	
7a.	"For the" handwritten	Extremely Rare		10.	St. Louis	Extremely Rare	
8.	Boston	1,400.00	5,500.00	10a.	"For the" handwritten	Unknown	

20 Dollar Notes

DESIGN NO. 3

(Notes 11-15)

Liberty holding sword and shield.

Reverse of Design No. 3.

Note illustrated, of a canceled specimen, from collection of the American Numismatic Association.

	No.	Payable at	Very Good	
11.		New York	13,500.00	
11a.		"For the" handwritten		Unique
12.		Philadelphia	13,500.00	
12a.		"For the" handwritten		Unknown
13.		Boston	20,000.00	

No.	Payable at	Very Good	
13a.	"For the" handwritten		Unknown
14.	Cincinnati		Unique
14a.	"For the" handwritten		Unknown
15.	St. Louis		Unknown

II. LEGAL TENDER ISSUES (UNITED STATES NOTES)

There are five issues of Legal Tender Notes, which are also called United States Notes.

First Issue. These notes are dated March 10, 1862 and were issued in all denominations from 5 to 1,000 Dollars. The obligation on the obverse of all these notes is, "The United States promise to pay to the bearer...... Dollars.... Payable at the Treasury of the United States at New York." There are two separate obligations on the reverse side of these notes.

First Obligation. Earlier issues have the so-called First Obligation which reads as follows, "This note is a legal tender for all debts, public and private. except duties on imports and interest on the public debt, and is exchangeable for U.S. six per cent twenty year bonds, redeemable at the pleasure of the United States after five years."

Second Obligation. The later issues have so-called Second Obligation, which reads as follows, "This note is a legal tender for all debts, public and private, except duties on imports and interest on the public debt, and is receivable in payment of all loans made to the United States."

Notes of 1862 with the Second Obligation are much rarer than those with the First Obligation.

These notes are without the titles that appear on later issues which have the heading either "Treasury Note" or "United States Note."

Second Issue. These notes are dated August 1, 1862 and were issued in denominations of 1 and 2 Dollars only. The obligation on these notes, both obverse and reverse, is the same as on the notes of the Second Obligation above.

Third Issue. These notes are dated March 10, 1863 and were issued in all denominations from 5 to 1,000 Dollars. The obligations, both obverse and reverse, are the same as on the notes of the Second Obligation of the First Issue.

Fourth Issue. All notes of this issue were printed under authority of the Congressional Act of March 3, 1863. The notes issued were from 1 to 10,000 Dollars and include the series of 1869, 1874, 1878, 1880, 1907, 1917 and 1923. The notes of 1869 are titled "Treasury Notes;" all later issues are titled "United States Notes." However, the obligation on all series is the same. "The United States will pay to bearer...... dollars.... This note is a legal tender at its face value for all debts public and private, except duties on imports and interest on the public debt."

Fifth Issue. This issue consisted only of 10 Dollar notes of the series of 1901. These notes were issued under authority of the Legal Tender Acts of 1862 and 1863. The obligation on these notes is as follows, "The United States of America will pay to the bearer ten dollars ... This note is a Legal Tender for ten dollars subject to the provisions of Section 3588 R.S.... This note is a Legal Tender at its face value for all debts public and private except duties on imports and interest on the public debt."

1 Dollar Notes

DESIGN NO. 4

(Notes 16-17a)

Head of Salmon P. Chase, Secretary of the Treasury under Abraham Lincoln, 1861-1864, and Chief Justice of the U.S. Supreme Court, 1864-1873. He is probably best known to numismatists for his causing the motto "In God We Trust" to be adopted for our national coinage.

Reverse of Design No. 4.

Note illustrated from collection of the American Numismatic Association.

All are Series of 1862, with signatures of Chittenden and Spinner and with small red seal.

No.		Very Good	Very Fine	Unc
16.	National Bank Note Co. printed twice above lower border	110.00	450.00	1,850.00
16a.	As above, with American Bank Note Co. monogram near center at right edge of obverse	200.00	600.00	3,000.00
17.	National Bank Note Co. and American Bank Note Co. printed above lower border	Rare		
17a.	As above, with American Bank Note Co. monogram near center at right edge of obverse	110.00	500.00	2,000.00

DESIGN NO. 5

(Note 18)

Head of George Washington, first President of the United States, 1789-1797. At the left, Christopher Columbus in sight of land. This vignette was designed by Joseph P. Ourdan.

Reverse of Design No. 5.

Note illustrated from collection of the American Numismatic Association.

No.	Series	Signatures		Seal	Very Good	Very Fine	Unc
18.	1869	Allison	Spinner	Large Red	150.00	600.00	2,250.00

DESIGN NO. 6

(Notes 19-39)

Vignettes similar to Design No. 5. Because of color, seal placement or embellishments, there are several distinct types of this design as follows:
  6a. Notes 19-27
  6b. Notes 28-30
  6c. Notes 31-33
  6d. Notes 34-35
  6e. Notes 36-39

Reverse of Design No. 6.

Because of its design, it is known as the "sawhorse reverse."

Note illustrated from collection of the American Numismatic Association.

6a. Red floral ornament around "ONE DOLLAR" at right; seal at left.

No.	Series	Signatures		Seal	Very Good	Very Fine	Unc
19.	1874	Allison	Spinner	Small Red with rays	90.00	200.00	1,750.00
20.	1875	Allison	New	Small Red with rays	85.00	200.00	1,700.00
21.				Same but Series A	250.00	600.00	3,500.00
22				Same but Series B	250.00	600.00	3,500.00
23.				Same but Series C	300.00	700.00	3,000.00
24.				Same but Series D	275.00	700.00	3,500.00
25.				Same but Series E	300.00	1,000.00	4,000.00
26.	1875	Allison	Wyman	Small Red with rays	85.00	200.00	1,400.00
27.	1878	Allison	Gilfillan	Small Red with rays	85.00	200.00	1,400.00

6b. Large seal replaces floral ornament at right; red serial numbers.

No.	Series	Signatures		Seal	Very Good	Very Fine	Unc
28.	1880	Scofield	Gilfillan	Large Brown	85.00	200.00	1,250.00
29.	1880	Bruce	Gilfillan	Large Brown	85.00	200.00	1,250.00
30.	1880	Bruce	Wyman	Large Brown	85.00	200.00	1,250.00

6c. Same as above, except serial numbers are blue.

No.	Series	Signatures		Seal	Very Good	Very Fine	Unc
31.	1880	Rosecrans	Huston	Large Red	200.00	800.00	3,500.00
32.	1880	Rosecrans	Huston	Large Brown	225.00	900.00	3,600.00
33.	1880	Rosecrans	Nebeker	Large Brown	250.00	950.00	4,000.00

6d. Seal is now small and is moved to left side of note; blue serial numbers.

No.	Series	Signatures		Seal	Very Good	Very Fine	Unc
34.	1880	Rosecrans	Nebeker	Small Red, Scalloped	75.00	175.00	1,000.00
35.	1880	Tillman	Morgan	Small Red, Scalloped	75.00	175.00	1,000.00

6e. Serial numbers are red, and are no longer in ornamental frames.

No.	Series	Signatures		Seal	Very Good	Very Fine	Unc
36.	1917	Teehee	Burke	Small Red, Scalloped	35.00	65.00	400.00
37.	1917	Ellliott	Burke	Small Red, Scalloped	35.00	65.00	350.00
37a.	1917	Burke	Elliott	(Signatures Reversed)	95.00	350.00	1,100.00
38.	1917	Elliott	White	Small Red, Scalloped	35.00	65.00	350.00
39.	1917	Speelman	White	Small Red, Scalloped	35.00	65.00	350.00

DESIGN NO. 7

(Note 40)

Head of George Washington.
This was the last large size One Dollar note issued prior to the changeover to small size notes.

Reverse of Design No. 7

The "cogwheel reverse."

Note illustrated from collection of the American Numismatic Association.

No.	Series	Signatures		Seal	Very Good	Very Fine	Unc
40.	1923	Speelman	White	Small Red, Scalloped	35.00	85.00	525.00

2 Dollar Notes

DESIGN NO. 8

(Notes 41-41a)

Head of Alexander Hamilton.

Reverse of Design No. 8

Note illustrated from collection of the American Numismatic Association.

Series of 1862 with signatures of Chittenden and Spinner and with small red seal.

No.		Very Good	Very Fine	Unc
41.	National Bank Note Company printed vertically at left border	200.00	750.00	3,500.00
41a.	American Bank Note Company printed vertically at left border	200.00	750.00	3,500.00

DESIGN NO. 9

(Note 42)

Head of Thomas Jefferson, third President of the United States, 1801-1805. The portrait was engraved by James Smillie. At center, a view of the Capitol.

Reverse of Design No. 9.

42.	1869	Allison	Spinner	Large Red	225.00	900.00	5,000.00

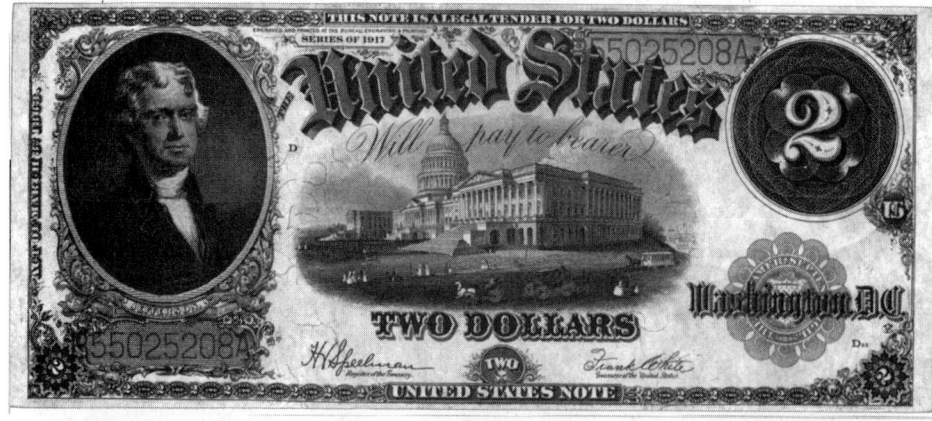

DESIGN NO. 10

(Notes 43-60)

Vignettes similar to Design No. 9. Because of color, seal placement or embellishments, there are several distinct types of the design as follows:
  10a. Notes 43-49
  10b. Notes 50-52
  10c. Notes 53-56
  10d. Notes 57-60

Reverse of Design No. 10.

The "bracelet reverse."

Note illustrated from collection of the American Numismatic Association.

10a. Red floral ornament around "Washington, D.C."; seal at left.

No.	Series	Signatures		Seal	Very Good	Very Fine	Unc
43.	1874	Allison	Spinner	Small Red with rays	175.00	600.00	2,200.00
44.	1875	Allison	New	Small Red with rays	150.00	575.00	1,750.00
45.				Same but Series A	250.00	750.00	4,000.00
46.				Same but Series B	225.00	700.00	3,500.00
47.	1875	Allison	Wyman	Small Red with rays	250.00	750.00	4,000.00
48.	1878	Allison	Gilfillan	Small Red with rays	150.00	575.00	1,750.00
49.	1878	Scofield	Gilfillan	Small Red with rays	2,550.00	7,500.00	20,000.00

10b. Large seal replaces floral ornament at right; red serial numbers.

No.	Series	Signatures		Seal	Very Good	Very Fine	Unc
50.	1880	Scofield	Gilfillan	Large Brown	90.00	200.00	1,200.00
51.	1880	Bruce	Gilfillan	Large Brown	95.00	225.00	1,300.00
52.	1880	Bruce	Wyman	Large Brown	90.00	200.00	1,200.00

10c. Same as above, except serial numbers are blue.

No.	Series	Signatures		Seal	Very Good	Very Fine	Unc
53.	1880	Rosecrans	Huston	Large Red	350.00	1,000.00	8,000.00
54.	1880	Rosecrans	Huston	Large Brown	375.00	1,200.00	8,500.00
55.	1880	Rosecrans	Nebeker	Small Red, Scalloped	90.00	175.00	1,000.00
56.	1880	Tillman	Morgan	Small Red, Scalloped	85.00	135.00	950.00

10d. Same as above, except serial numbers are again red.

No.	Series	Signatures		Seal	Very Good	Very Fine	Unc
57.	1917	Teehee	Burke	Small Red, Scalloped	45.00	85.00	475.00
58.	1917	Elliott	Burke	Small Red, Scalloped	45.00	85.00	475.00
59.	1917	Elliott	White	Small Red, Scalloped	45.00	85.00	475.00
60.	1917	Speelman	White	Small Red, Scalloped	45.00	85.00	450.00

5 Dollar Notes

DESIGN NO.11

(Notes 61-63b)

Obverse is similar to Design No. 1, but Treasury seal has been added and "On Demand" removed.

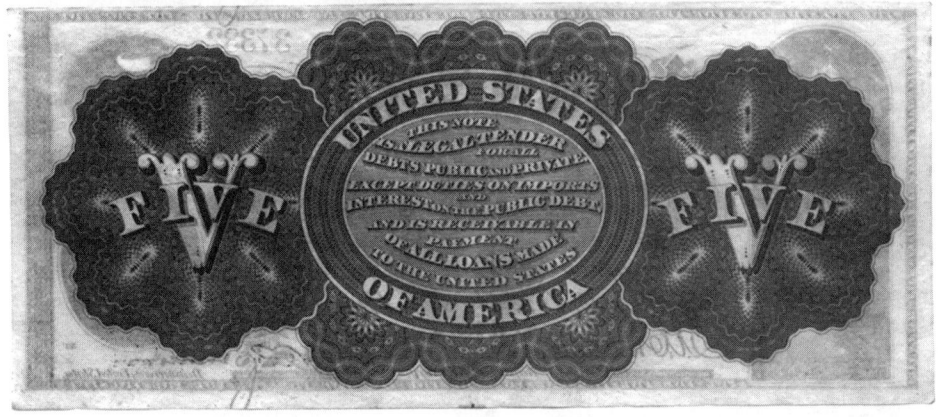

*Reverse of Design No. 11.
The reverse shown is the Second Obligation.*

Note illustrated from collection of the American Numismatic Association.

No.	Act	Signatures	Seal	Very Good	Very Fine	Unc
61.	1862	Chittenden Spinner	Small Red			
	American Bank Note Co. on upper		*border*	Extremely Rare	—	—
61a.	1862	Chittenden Spinner	Small Red, "Series" on obverse			
	American Bank Note Co. on upper		*border*	175.00	500.00	1,750.00
	(The above notes with the First Obligation on reverse.)					
62.	1862	Chittenden Spinner	Small Red	200.00	800.00	4,000.00
63.	1863	Chittenden Spinner	Small Red			
	American Bank Note Co. and National Bank Note Co. on lower border			175.00	600.00	1,850.00
63a.	1863	Chittenden Spinner	Small Red, One Serial No.			
	American Bank Note Co. twice on lower border			125.00	350.00	1,800.00
63b.	1863	Chittenden Spinner	Small Red, Two Serial Nos.			
	American Bank Note Co. twice on lower border			175.00	600.00	2,500.00
	(The above three notes with the Second Obligation on reverse.)					

DESIGN NO. 12

(Note 64)

Head of Andrew Jackson, seventh President of the United States, 1829-1833, from a painting by Thomas Sully, engraved by Alfred Sealey. At center, a Pioneer Family, engraved by Henry Gugler.

Reverse of Design No. 12.

Note illustrated from collection of the American Numismatic Association.

No.	Series	Signatures		Seal	Very Good	Very Fine	Unc
64.	1869	Allison	Spinner	Large Red	200.00	500.00	2,500.00

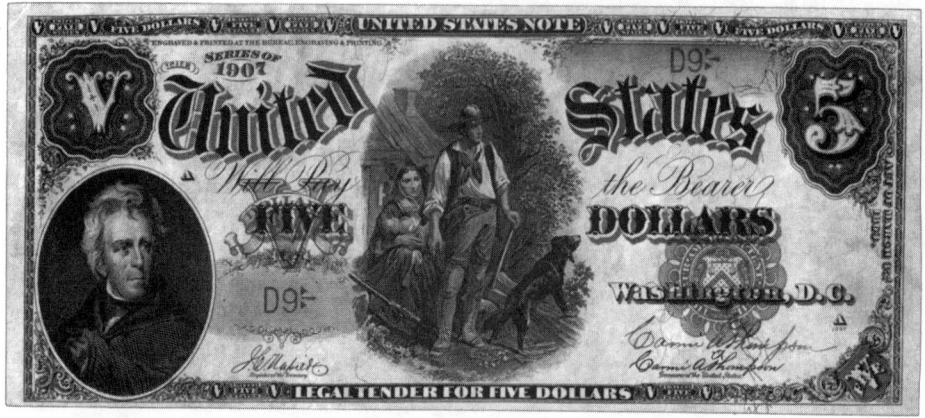

DESIGN NO. 13

(Notes 65-92)

Vignettes similar to Design No. 12. Because of color, seal placement or embellishments, there are several distinct types of this design, as follows:
    13a. Notes 65-69
    13b. Notes 70-72
    13c. Notes 73-82
    13d. Notes 83-92

Reverse of Design No. 13.

Note illustrated from collection of the American Numismatic Association.

13a. Large red floral ornament around "Washington, D.C."; seal at left.

No.	Series	Signatures		Seal	Very Good	Very Fine	Unc
65.	1875	Allison	New	Small Red with rays	80.00	200.00	1,000.00
66.		As above but Series A			150.00	750.00	2,500.00
67.		As above but Series B			75.00	200.00	1,000.00
68.	1875	Allison	Wyman	Small Red with rays	75.00	175.00	1,000.00
69.	1878	Allison	Gilfillan	Small Red with rays	85.00	350.00	1,000.00

13b. Large seal replaces floral ornament at right; red serial numbers.

No.	Series	Signatures		Seal	Very Good	Very Fine	Unc
70.	1880	Scofield	Gilfillan	Large Brown	500.00	1,350.00	Rare
71.	1880	Bruce	Gilfillan	Large Brown	80.00	300.00	1,500.00
72.	1880	Bruce	Wyman	Large Brown	75.00	275.00	1,500.00

13c. Same as above but serial numbers are blue.

No.	Series	Signatures		Seal	Very Good	Very Fine	Unc
73.	1880	Bruce	Wyman	Large Red, plain	125.00	400.00	1,750.00
74.	1880	Rosecrans	Jordan	Large Red, plain	125.00	400.00	1,850.00
75.	1880	Rosecrans	Hyatt	Large Red, plain	135.00	425.00	2,500.00
76.	1880	Rosecrans	Huston	Large Red with spikes	175.00	725.00	3,000.00
77.	1880	Rosecrans	Huston	Large Brown	225.00	1,350.00	4,500.00

No.	Series	Signatures		Seal	Very Good	Very Fine	Unc
78.	1880	Rosecrans	Nebeker	Large Brown	200.00	1,100.00	5,000.00
79.	1880	Rosecrans	Nebeker	Small Red, scalloped	55.00	150.00	1,000.00
80.	1880	Tillman	Morgan	Small Red, scalloped	55.00	150.00	1,000.00
81.	1880	Bruce	Roberts	Small Red, scalloped	55.00	150.00	1,000.00
82.	1880	Lyons	Roberts	Small Red, scalloped	60.00	175.00	1,100.00

13d. Red "V" and "Dollars" added to design at left; Red Serial numbers.

No.	Series	Signatures		Seal	Very Good	Very Fine	Unc
83.	1907	Vernon	Treat	Small Red, scalloped	75.00	100.00	800.00
84.	1907	Vernon	McClung	Small Red, scalloped	75.00	125.00	800.00
85.	1907	Napier	McClung	Small Red, scalloped	75.00	100.00	800.00
86.	1907	Napier	Thompson	Small Red, scalloped	80.00	300.00	2,500.00
87.	1907	Parker	Burke	Small Red, scalloped	75.00	100.00	800.00
88.	1907	Teehee	Burke	Small Red, scalloped	75.00	100.00	800.00
89.	1907	Elliott	Burke	Small Red, scalloped	75.00	150.00	1,000.00
90.	1907	Elliott	White	Small Red, scalloped	75.00	100.00	700.00
91.	1907	Speelman	White	Small Red, scalloped	70.00	100.00	600.00
92.	1907	Woods	White	Small Red, scalloped	75.00	125.00	700.00

10 Dollar Notes

DESIGN NO. 14

(Note 93)

Obverse is similar to Design No. 2, but Treasury Seal has been added and "On Demand" removed

Reverse of Design No. 14. With the First Obligation.

Note illustrated from collection of the American Numismatic Association..

No.	Act	Signatures		Seal	Very Good	Very Fine	Unc
93.	1862	Chittenden	Spinner	Small Red	325.00	1,350.00	6,000.00

DESIGN NO. 14-a.

(Notes 94-95b)

Obverse is similar to Design No. 2, but Treasury Seal has been added and "On Demand" removed. The reverse (shown) is the Second Obligation.

No.	Series	Signatures	Seal	Very Good	Very Fine	Unc
94.	1862	Chittenden Spinner	Small Red	375.00	1,500.00	5,500.00
95.	1863	Chittenden Spinner	Small Red			
		National Bank Note Co. on lower border		350.00	1,300.00	3,500.00
95a.	1863	Chittenden Spinner	Small Red, One Serial No.			
		American Bank Note Co. on lower border		325.00	1,400.00	4,500.00
95b.	1863	Chittenden Spinner	Small Red, Two Serial Nos.			
		American Bank Note Co. on lower border		325.00	1,200.00	4,000.00

DESIGN NO. 15

(Note 96)

Head of Daniel Webster, U.S. Congressman and Senator; Secretary of State in 1841 and from 1850-1852. Engraved by Alfred Sealey. At the right, Indian Princess Pocahontas being presented to England's royal court. This is the first "Jackass note," so-called because the eagle on bottom of the note looks like the head of a jackass when the note is held upside down. All notes from 96-113 are the so-called "Jackass" notes.

Reverse of Design No. 15.

Note illustrated from collection of the American Numismatic Association.

No.	Series	Signatures		Seal	Very Good	Very Fine	Unc
96.	1869	Allison	Spinner	Large Red	235.00	950.00	4,500.00

DESIGN NO. 16

(Notes 97-113)

Vignettes similar to Design No. 15. Because of color, seal placement or embellishments, there are several distinct types of this design as follows:
  16a. Notes 97-99
  16b. Notes 100-102
  16c. Notes 103-113

Reverse of Design No. 16.

Note illustrated from collection of the American Numismatic Association.

16a. Red "TEN" in red ornamental design at right center; seal at left.

No.	Series	Signatures		Seal	Very Good	Very Fine	Unc
97.	1875	Allison	New	Small Red with rays	300.00	850.00	6,000.00
98.		Same as above but Series A			300.00	850.00	6,000.00
99.	1878	Allison	Gilfillan	Small Red with rays	300.00	800.00	5,500.00

16b. Large seal replaces the red "TEN"; red serial numbers.

100.	1880	Scofield	Gilfillan	Large Brown	195.00	700.00	5,000.00
101.	1880	Bruce	Gilfillan	Large Brown	150.00	675.00	4,000.00
102.	1880	Bruce	Wyman	Large Brown	175.00	650.00	4,000.00

16c. Same as above but serial numbers are blue.

103.	1880	Bruce	Wyman	Large Red, plain	195.00	650.00	2,500.00
104.	1880	Rosecrans	Jordan	Large Red, plain	200.00	750.00	4,500.00
105.	1880	Rosecrans	Hyatt	Large Red, plain	200.00	850.00	4,500.00
106.	1880	Rosecrans	Hyatt	Large Red with spikes	175.00	600.00	2,250.00
107.	1880	Rosecrans	Huston	Large Red with spikes	175.00	625.00	2,300.00
108.	1880	Rosecrans	Huston	Large Brown	185.00	700.00	2,500.00
109.	1880	Rosecrans	Nebeker	Large Brown	Extremely Rare	—	—
110.	1880	Rosecrans	Nebeker	Small Red, scalloped	150.00	500.00	1,500.00
111.	1880	Tillman	Morgan	Small Red, scalloped	150.00	500.00	1,500.00
112.	1880	Bruce	Roberts	Small Red, scalloped	160.00	550.00	2,250.00
113.	1880	Lyons	Roberts	Small Red, scalloped	150.00	475.00	1,500.00

DESIGN NO. 17

(Notes 114-122)

Bison between the explorers Meriwether Lewis and William Clark.
There is dispute over whether the bison is Black Diamond, the animal on the reverse of the Indian Head nickel, or Pablo, a bison which resided at the Washington Zoo.

Reverse of Design No. 17

Female figure representing Columbia standing between two pillars and two scrolls.

Note illustrated from collection of the American Numismatic Association.

No.	Series	Signatures		Seal	Very Good	Very Fine	Unc
114.	1901	Lyons	Roberts	Small Red, scalloped	400.00	750.00	3,500.00
115.	1901	Lyons	Treat	Small Red, scalloped	400.00	750.00	3,500.00
116.	1901	Vernon	Treat	Small Red, scalloped	425.00	800.00	3,850.00
117.	1901	Vernon	McClung	Small Red, scalloped	400.00	750.00	3,600.00
118.	1901	Napier	McClung	Small Red, scalloped	400.00	750.00	3,600.00
119.	1901	Parker	Burke	Small Red, scalloped	400.00	750.00	3,600.00
120.	1901	Teehee	Burke	Small Red, scalloped	425.00	800.00	3,850.00
121.	1901	Elliott	White	Small Red, scalloped	400.00	750.00	3,500.00
122.	1901	Speelman	White	Small Red, scalloped	400.00	625.00	3,400.00

DESIGN NO. 18

(Note 123)

Head of Andrew Jackson.
This was the last large size Ten Dollar note issued prior to the introduction of small size currency.

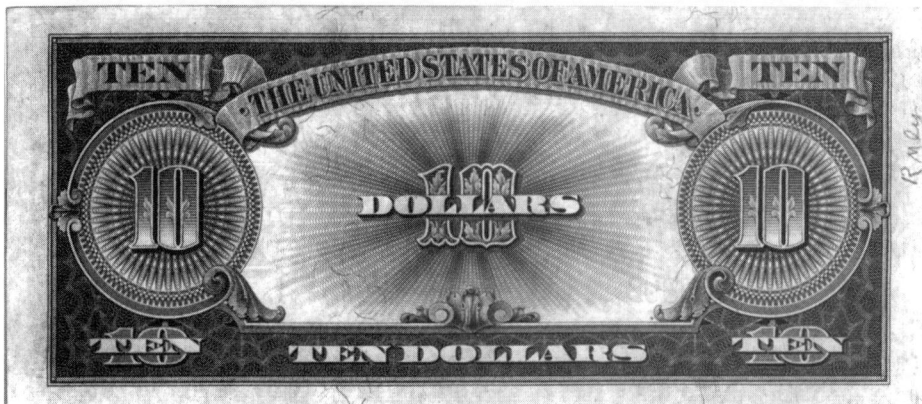

Reverse of Design No. 18.

Note illustrated from collection of the American Numismatic Association.

No.	Series	Signatures		Seal	Very Good	Very Fine	Unc
123.	1923	Speelman	White	Small Red, scalloped	300.00	1,100.00	4,750.00

20 Dollar Notes

DESIGN NO. 19

(Notes 124-126b)

Obverse is similar to Design No. 3, but Treasury Seal has been added and "On Demand" removed. The reverse shown is the First Obligation.

No.	Act	Signatures		Seal	Very Good	Very Fine	Unc
124.	1862	Chittenden	Spinner	Red	950.00	2,500.00	10,000.00
	(The above note with the First Obligation on reverse.)						
125.	1862	Chittenden	Spinner	Red	900.00	2,250.00	9,000.00
126.	1863	Chittenden	Spinner	Red			
	National Bank Note Co. and American Bank Note Co. on lower border				900.00	2,250.00	9,000.00
126a.	1863	Chittenden	Spinner	Red, One Serial No.			
	American Bank Note Co. on lower border				800.00	2,150.00	8,000.00

No.	Act	Signatures	Seal	Very Good	Very Fine	Unc
126b.	1863	Chittenden Spinner	Red, Two Serial Nos.			
		American Bank Note Co. on lower border		800.00	2,000.00	7,500.00

(The above notes with the Second Obligation on reverse.)

DESIGN NO. 20

(Note 127)

Head of Alexander Hamilton.
Victory advancing holding shield and
sword.

Reverse of Design No. 20.

The Arabic numeral 20 is repeated
105 times and the Roman Numeral XX
appears 103 times in the reverse design.

Note illustrated from collection of the
American Numismatic Association.

127.	1869	Allison Spinner	Large Red	850.00	3,500.00	9,500.00

DESIGN NO. 21

(Notes 128-147)

Vignettes similar to Design No. 20.
Because of color, seal placement or
embellishments, there are several distinct
types of this design, as follows:
    21a. Notes 128-129
    21b. Notes 130-145
    21c. Notes 146-147

Reverse of Design No. 21.

Note illustrated from collection of the
American Numismatic Association.

21a. A red "XX" at both right and left center of note.

No.	Series	Signatures		Seal	Very Good	Very Fine	Unc
128.	1875	Allison	New	Small Red with rays	550.00	1,300.00	6,000.00
129.	1878	Allison	Gilfillan	Small Red with rays	500.00	900.00	4,750.00

21b. The pair of red "XX's" is removed; blue serial numbers.

130.	1880	Scofield	Gilfillan	Large Brown	250.00	850.00	4,500.00
131.	1880	Bruce	Gilfillan	Large Brown	250.00	850.00	4,500.00
132.	1880	Bruce	Wyman	Large Brown	250.00	850.00	4,500.00
133.	1880	Bruce	Wyman	Large Red, plain	900.00	2,500.00	9,500.00
134.	1880	Rosecrans	Jordan	Large Red, plain	250.00	850.00	4,000.00
135.	1880	Rosecrans	Hyatt	Large Red, plain	250.00	850.00	4,500.00
136.	1880	Rosecrans	Hyatt	Large Red with spike	175.00	550.00	3,200.00
137.	1880	Rosecrans	Huston	Large Red with spike	175.00	550.00	3,200.00
138.	1880	Rosecrans	Huston	Large Brown	175.00	500.00	3,200.00
139.	1880	Rosecrans	Nebeker	Large Brown	600.00	1,350.00	5,250.00
140.	1880	Rosecrans	Nebeker	Small Red, scalloped	175.00	450.00	2,750.00
141.	1880	Tillman	Morgan	Small Red, scalloped	175.00	400..00	2,750.00
142.	1880	Bruce	Roberts	Small Red, scalloped	175.00	400.00	2,750.00
143.	1880	Lyons	Roberts	Small Red, scalloped	175.00	400.00	2,750.00
144.	1880	Vernon	Treat	Small Red, scalloped	185.00	350.00	3,000.00
145.	1880	Vernon	McClung	Small Red, scalloped	185.00	350.00	3,000.00

21c. Same as above, but red serial numbers.

146.	1880	Teehee	Burke	Small Red, scalloped	200.00	600.00	2,850.00
147.	1880	Elliott	White	Small Red, scalloped	175.00	500.00	2,000.00

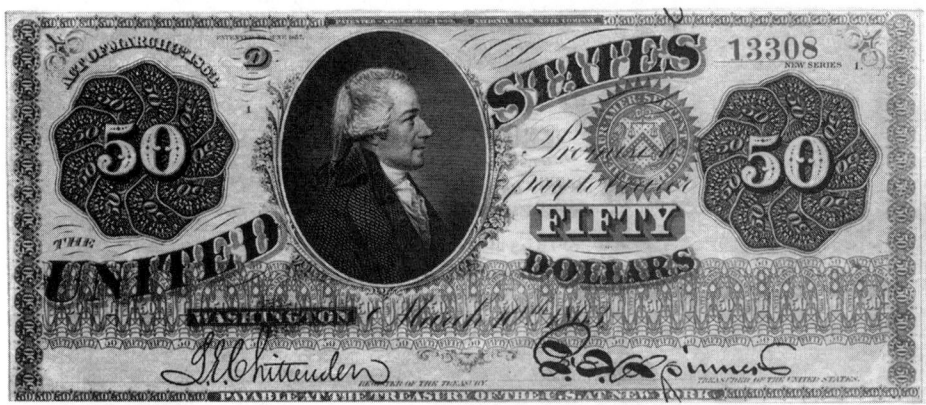

50 Dollar Notes

DESIGN NO. 22

(Notes 148-150a)

Head of Alexander Hamilton.

Reverse of Design No. 22.
The Second Obligation is shown.

Note illustrated from collection of the
American Numismatic Association.

No.	Act	Signatures		Seal	Very Good	Very Fine	Unc
148.	1862	Chittenden	Spinner	Red	3,750.00	11,000.00	Rare

(The above note with the First Obligation on reverse.)

149.	1862	Chittenden	Spinner	Red	Unknown	—	—
150.	1863	Chittenden	Spinner	Red			
	National Bank Note Co. on top border				3,500.00	10,000.00	Rare
150a.	1863	Chittenden	Spinner	Red			
	National Bank Note Co. and American Bank Note Co. on top border				3,500.00	10,000.00	Rare

(The above notes with the Second Obligation on reverse.)

DESIGN NO. 23

(Note 151)

Head of Henry Clay, U.S. Congressman and Senator; Secretary of State from 1825-1829. At the left, a female figure representing Peace, holding a laurel branch and a statue of Mercury.

Reverse of Design No. 23.

This note is extremely rare, with less than three dozen notes reported outstanding on U.S. Treasury books.

Note illustrated from collection of the American Numismatic Association.

151.	1869	Allison	Spinner	Large Red	6,500.00	30,000.00	70,000.00

DESIGN NO. 24

(Notes 152-164)

Head of Benjamin Franklin, 1706-1790, statesman, printer and scientist, and one of the drafters of the Declaration of Independence.
Engraved by Charles Burt from the Duplessis portrait. At the right, Liberty dressed as Columbia. Because of color, seal placement or embellishments, there are several distinct types of this design, as follows:
24a. Notes 152-154
24b. Notes 155-164

Reverse of Design No. 24.

Note illustrated from collection of the American Numismatic Association.

24a. A large red "L" is at both right and left center of note.

No.	Series	Signatures		Seal	Very Good	Very Fine	Unc
152.	1874	Spinner	Allison	Small Red with rays	2,000.00	7,000.00	20,000.00
153.	1875	Wyman	Allison	Small Red with rays	Three known	—	—
154.	1878	Gilfillan	Allison	Small Red with rays	2,250.00	8,000.00	30,000.00

24b. The two red "L's" are removed.

No.	Series	Signatures		Seal	Very Good	Very Fine	Unc
155.	1880	Gilfillan	Bruce	Large Brown	3,250.00	8,500.00	Rare
156.	1880	Wyman	Bruce	Large Brown	2,750.00	7,500.00	Rare
157.	1880	Jordan	Rosecrans	Large Red, plain	3,250.00	8,500.00	Rare
158.	1880	Hyatt	Rosecrans	Large Red, plain	Seven known	—	—
159.	1880	Hyatt	Rosecrans	Large Red, spiked	2,750.00	7,500.00	Rare
160.	1880	Huston	Rosecrans	Large Red, spiked	3,250.00	8,500.00	Rare
161.	1880	Huston	Rosecrans	Large Brown	1,500.00	4,500.00	14,000.00
162.	1880	Tillman	Morgan	Small Red, scalloped	1,500.00	4,500.00	13,000.00
163.	1880	Bruce	Roberts	Small Red, scalloped	6,000.00	Rare	Rare
164.	1880	Lyons	Roberts	Small Red, scalloped	1,500.00	3,850.00	13,000.00

100 Dollar Notes

DESIGN NO. 25

(Notes 165-167b)

Large American eagle.
This was the first note to feature the American eagle.

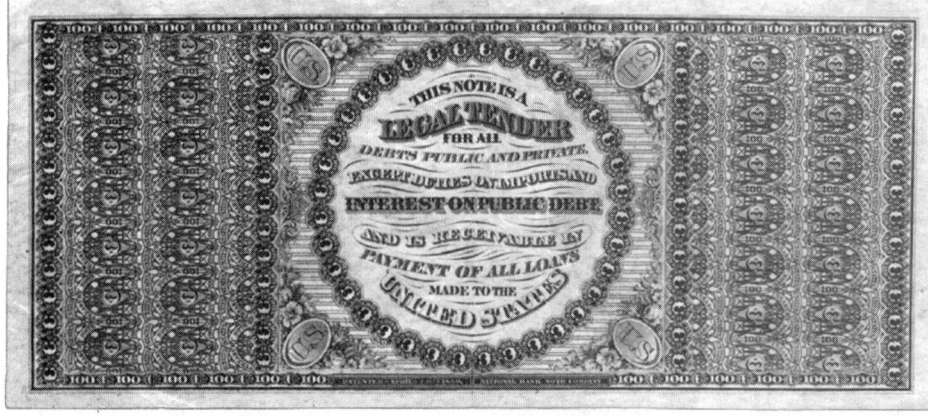

Reverse of Design No. 25.

The Second Obligation is shown.

Note illustrated from collection of the American Numismatic Association.

Act of 1862, with signatures of Chittenden and Spinner and with red seal.

No.	Series	Signatures		Seal	Very Good	Very Fine	Unc
165.		American Bank Note Co. monogram in upper left			4,900.00	13,500.00	Rare
165-a.		As above, No ABNCO monogram			4,900.00	13,000.00	Rar
		(The above two notes with the First Obligation on reverse.)					
166.	1862	Chittenden	Spinner	Red	Unknown	—	—
167.	1863	Chittenden	Spinner	Red, One Serial No.	5,000.00	17,500.00	Rare
		The above two notes with National Bank Note Co. and American Bank Note Co. at top.					
167-a.	1863	Chittenden	Spinner	Red, Two Serial Nos.	4,7500.00	12,500.00	45,000.00
167-b.	1863	Chittenden	Spinner	Red, One Serial No.	Very rare	—	—
		The above two notes with National Bank Note Co. only at top					
		(The above four notes with the Second Obligation on reverse.)					

DESIGN NO. 26

(Note 168)

Head of Abraham Lincoln. At the right, an allegory representing Architecture.

Reverse of Design No. 26.

Note illustrated from collection of the American Numismatic Association.

No.	Series	Signatures		Seal	Very Good	Very Fine	Unc
168.	1869	Allison	Spinner	Large Red	6,500.00	25,000.00	85,000.00

DESIGN NO. 27

(Notes 169-182)

Vignettes similar to Design No. 26. Because of color, seal placement or embellishments, there are several distinct types of this design, as follows:
27a. Notes 169-171
27b. Notes 172-182

Reverse of Design No. 27

Note illustrated from collection of the American Numismatic Association.

27a. Top central floral design printed in red.

No.	Series	Signatures		Seal	Very Good	Very Fine	Unc
169.	1875	Allison	New	Small Red with rays (Series A)	4,250.00	25,000.00	50,000.00
170.	1875	Allison	Wyman	Small Red with rays	5,000.00	12,000.00	Rare
171.	1878	Allison	Gilfillan	Small Red with rays	4,000.00	10,000.00	40,000.00

27b. Top central floral design printed in black.

No.	Series	Signatures		Seal	Very Good	Very Fine	Unc
172.	1880	Bruce	Gilfillan	Large Brown	3,500.00	5,500.00	40,000.00
173.	1880	Bruce	Wyman	Large Brown	3,500.00	5,500.00	40,000.00
174.	1880	Rosecrans	Jordan	Large Red, plain	3,400.00	5,000.00	32,000.00
175.	1880	Rosecrans	Hyatt	Large Red, plain	Very Rare	—	—
176.	1880	Rosecrans	Hyatt	Large Red, spiked	3,500.00	9,500.00	32,000.00
177.	1880	Rosecrans	Huston	Large Red, spiked	3,400.00	9,000.00	18,000.00
178.	1880	Rosecrans	Huston	Large Brown	3,400.00	9,000.00	18,000.00
179.	1880	Tillman	Morgan	Small Red, scalloped	2,750.00	7,000.00	15,000.00
180.	1880	Bruce	Roberts	Small Red, scalloped	3,000.00	7,250.00	16,000.00
181.	1880	Lyons	Roberts	Small Red, scalloped	2,550.00	6,750.00	15,000.00
182.	1880	Napier	McClung	Small Red, scalloped	Unknown	—	—

500 Dollar Notes

DESIGN NO. 28

(Notes 183a-183d)

Head of Albert Gallatin, Secretary of the Treasury under President Thomas Jefferson, 1801-1813.

Reverse of Design No. 28.

The Second Obligation is shown.

No.	Act	Signatures		Seal	
183-a.	1862	Chittenden	Spinner	Red. First obligation	Extremely Rare
183-b.	1862	Chittenden	Spinner	Red. Second obligation	Extremely Rare
183-c.	1863	Chittenden	Spinner	Red. Second obligation, One Serial No.	Extremely Rare
183-d.	1863	Chittenden	Spinner	Red. Second obligation, Two Serial Nos.	Extremely Rare

DESIGN NO. 29

(Note 184)

Head of John Quincy Adams, sixth President of the United States, 1825-1829. Justice seated at left.

Reverse of Design No. 29.

No.	Series	Signatures		Seal	
184.	1869	Allison	Spinner	Large Red	Extremely Rare

DESIGN NO. 30

(Notes 185a-185n)

Head of Major General Joseph King Mansfield, killed in action at the Battle of Antietam, 1862. At the left a female allegory representing Victory.

The series of 1880 is without the two large red "D's" on the obverse, which appear the series of 1874, 1875 and 1878.

Reverse of Design No. 30.

Note illustrated from collection of the American Numismatic Association.

No.	Series	Signatures		Seal	No.	Series	Signatures		Seal
185a.	1874	Allison	Spinner	Small Red, rays	185-h.	1880	Rosecrans	Hyatt	Large Red, plain
185-b.	1875	Allison	New	Small Red, rays	185-i.	1880	Rosecrans	Huston	Large Red, spiked
185-c.	1875	Allison	Wyman	Small Red, rays	185-j.	1880	Rosecrans	Nebeker	Small Red, scalloped
185-d.	1878	Allison	Gilfillan	Small Red, rays	185-k.	1880	Tillman	Morgan	Small Red, scalloped
185-e.	1880	Scofield	Gilfillan	Large Brown	185-l.	1880	Bruce	Roberts	Small Red, scalloped
185-f.	1880	Bruce	Wyman	Large Brown	185-m.	1880	Lyons	Roberts	Small Red, scalloped
185-g.	1880	Rosecrans	Jordan	Large Red, plain	185-n.	1880	Napier	McClung	Small Red, scalloped

(The above notes are Extremely Rare.)

1,000 Dollar Notes

DESIGN NO. 31

(Notes 186a-186e)

Head of Robert Morris, Superintendent of Finance, 1781-1784. He was a signer of the Declaration of Independence.

Reverse of Design No. 31.

The Second Obligation is shown.

This illustration by courtesy of Mr. Amon G. Carter Jr.

No.	Act	Signatures		Seal	
186-a.	1862	Chittenden	Spinner	Red. First Obligation	Unknown
186-b.	1862	Chittenden	Spinner	Red. Second Obligation	Unknown
186-c.	1863	Chittenden	Spinner	Red. Second Obligation, One Serial No.	Extremely Rare
		American Bank Note Co. at right, National Bank Note Co. at left.			
186-d.	1863	Chittenden	Spinner	Red. Second Obligation, One Serial No.	Extremely Rare
		American Bank Note Co. at right only.			
186-e.	1863	Chittenden	Spinner	Red. Second Obligation, Two Serial Nos.	Unique
		American Bank Note Co. at right only.			

DESIGN NO. 31-a.

(Note 186f)

Head of DeWitt Clinton, 1769-1828, Governor of New York, Mayor of New York City, U.S. Senator.

The seated figure is Christopher Columbus.

Reverse of Design No. 31-a.

186-f.	1869	Allison	Spinner	Large Red	Extremely Rare

DESIGN NO. 32

(Notes 187-a–187-l)

*Vignettes similar to
Design No. 31-a.*

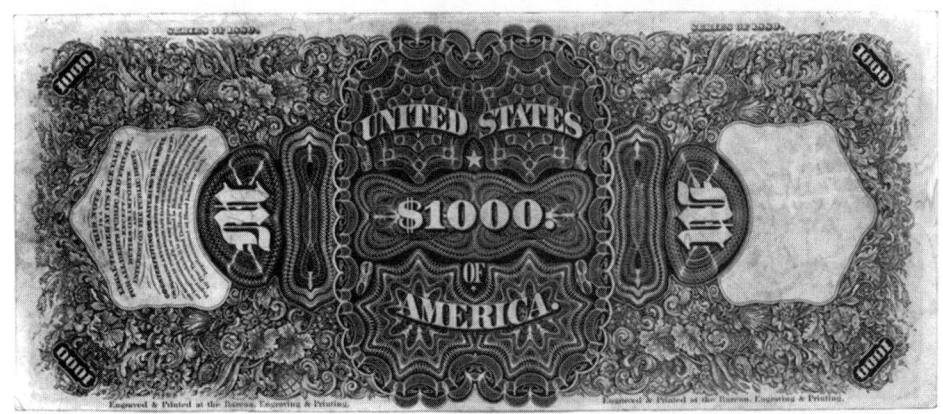

Reverse of Design No. 32.

*Note illustrated from collection of the
American Numismatic Association.*

No.	Series	Signatures		Seal	No.	Series	Signatures		Seal
187-a.	1878	Allison	Gilfillan	Small Red, rays	187-g.	1880	Tillman	Morgan	Small Red, scalloped
187-b.	1880	Bruce	Wyman	Large Brown	187-h.	1880	Tillman	Roberts	Small Red, scalloped
187-c.	1880	Rosecrans	Jordan	Large Red, plain	187-i.	1880	Bruce	Roberts	Small Red, scalloped
187-d.	1880	Rosecrans	Hyatt	Large Red, spiked	187-j.	1880	Lyons	Roberts	Small Red, scalloped
187-e.	1880	Rosecrans	Huston	Large Red, spiked	187-k.	1880	Vernon	Treat	Small Red, scalloped
187-f.	1880	Rosecrans	Nebeker	Large Brown	187-l.	1880	Napier	McClung	Small Red, scalloped

(The above notes are Extremely Rare.)

5,000 Dollar Notes

DESIGN NO. 33

(Note 188)

Head of James Madison, fourth President of the United States, 1809-1813.

Reverse of Design No. 33.

(All specimens of this issue have been redeemed and there are none outstanding. The illustration is of a non-negotiable note furnished the Chinese Government by the Treasury Department.)

No.	Series	Signatures		Seal
188.	1878	Scofield	Gilfillan	Large Brown

10,000 Dollar Notes

DESIGN NO. 34

(Note 189)

Head of Andrew Jackson.

Reverse of Design No. 34.

(All specimens of this issue have been redeemed and none are outstanding. The illustration is of a sample note and was furnished by courtesy of the Bureau of Engraving and Printing.)

189.	1878	Scofield	Gilfillan	Large Brown

III. COMPOUND INTEREST TREASURY NOTES

These notes are really Legal Tender circulating notes, which for a period of three years, bore interest at six per cent, that was compounded twice a year. The Acts of Congress of March 3, 1863 and June 30,1864 authorized the issue by the Treasury Department of these notes. It should be noted that the time of issue was late in the Civil War when the financial position of the Treasury was precarious and the country was almost bankrupt because of the cost of carrying on the war.

Money was very rare and the issue of these Compound Interest Treasury Notes was an attempt to alleviate this pressing problem.

They were issued in denominations of 10, 20, 50, 100, 500 and 1,000 Dollars, and were legal tender at their face value. The date of issue is printed in red on each note and the full interest was payable only at the end of the three year period after date of issue.

The reverse of each denomination shows in tabular form what the interest and redemption value was at the end of each six month period for the three years.

For the redemption value of each denomination, please see the text.

The obverse of each note is surcharged in large gold letters with "Compound Interest Treasury Note" and the numerals of the denomination.

All notes of this issue are very rare today and are seldom seen. The 50 and 100 Dollar notes are of extraordinary rarity. Also, all denominations are extremely rare in really choice condition.

The obligation on these Compound Interest Treasury Notes is as follows, "Three years after date the United States will pay the bearer...... dollars with interest at the rate of six per cent compounded semi-annually ... By Act of Congress, this note is a legal tender for...... dollars but bears interest at six per cent compounded every six months though payable only at maturity as follows ... This sum $...... will be paid the holder for principal and interest at maturity of note three years from date."

All of these notes have a small red treasury seal with spikes and the signatures of either Colby and Spinner or Chittenden and Spinner. The 50 and 100 Dollar notes are of great rarity and have been counterfeited extensively.

10 Dollar Notes

DESIGN NO. 35

(Notes 190-190b)

Head of Salmon P. Chase, Secretary of the Treasury under Abraham Lincoln, 1861-1864. At the center, an eagle. At the right, a female allegory representing Peace.

Reverse of Design No. 35.

Redemption value $11.94.

Note illustrated from collection of the American Numismatic Association.

No.	Act of	Overprint Date	Signatures		Very Good	Fine
190.	1863	June 10, 1864	Chittenden	Spinner	Extremely Rare	—
190-a.	1864	July 15, 1864	Chittenden	Spinner	Extremely Rare	—
190-b.	1864	Aug. 15 - Dec. 15, 1864	Colby	Spinner	1,650.00	2,750.00

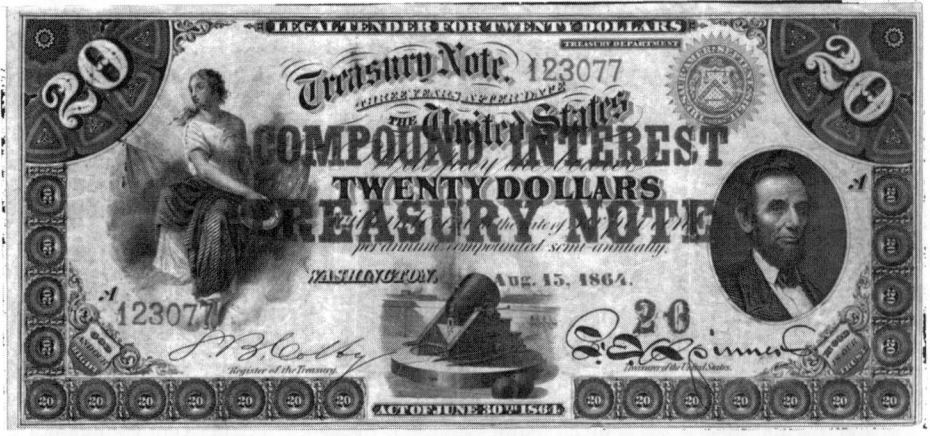

20 Dollar Notes

DESIGN NO. 36

(Notes 191-191a)

Head of Abraham Lincoln. The female allegory at the left represents Victory. At the lower center is a mortar firing.

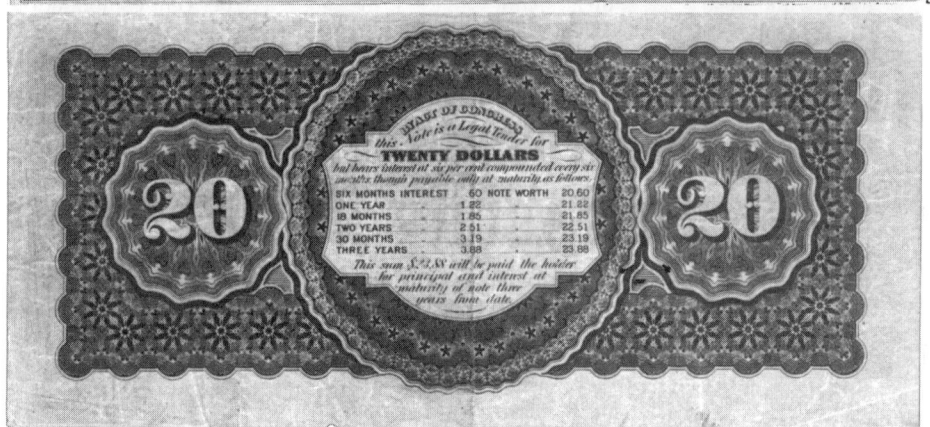

Reverse of Design No. 36.

Redemption value $23.88

Note illustrated from collection of the American Numismatic Association.

No.	Act of	Overprint Date	Signatures		Very Good	Fine
191.	1864	July 15, 1864	Chittenden	Spinner	Extremely Rare	—
191-a.	1864	Aug. 15, 1864 - Oct. 16, 1865	Colby	Spinner	1,750.00	2,750.00

50 Dollar Notes

DESIGN NO. 37

(Notes 192-192b)

Head of Alexander Hamilton. At the left is a female allegory representing Loyalty.

Reverse of Design No. 37.

Redemption value $59.70.

Note illustrated from collection of the American Numismatic Association.

No.	Act of	Overprint Date	Signatures		Value	
192.	1863	June 10, 1864	Chittenden	Spinner	Unique	—
192-a.	1864	July 15, 1864	Chittenden	Spinner	Unknown	—
192-b.	1864	Aug. 15, 1864 - Sept. 1, 1865	Colby	Spinner	12,500.00	Rare

100 Dollar Notes

DESIGN NO. 38

(Notes 193-193b)

Standing figure of George Washington between female allegories representing The Guardian, left, and Justice, right.

Reverse of Design No. 38.

Redemption value $119.40.

No.	Act of	Overprint Date	Signatures		Very Good	Fine
193.	1863	June 10, 1864	Chittenden	Spinner	14,000.00	Rare
193-a.	1864	July 15, 1864	Chittenden	Spinner	Unknown	—
193-b.	1864	Aug. 15, 1864 - Sept. 1, 1865	Colby	Spinner	Extremely Rare	—

500 Dollar Notes

DESIGN NO. 39
(Notes 194-194-b)
Vignettes of the ship New Ironsides and The Standard Bearer.

Redemption value $597.03

No	Act of	Overprint Date	Signatures		
194.	1863	June 10, 1864	Chittenden	Spinner	Unknown
194-a.	1864	July 15, 1864	Chittenden	Spinner	Unknown
194-b.	1864	Aug. 15, 1864 - Oct. 1, 1865	Colby	Spinner	Unknown

1,000 Dollar Notes

DESIGN No. 40
(Notes 195-195-a).
Vignettes of Liberty and Justice.

Redemption value $1,194.06

No.	Act of	Overprint Date	Signatures		
195.	1864	July 15, 1864	Chittenden	Spinner	Unknown
195-a.	1864	Aug. 15, 1864 - Sept. 15, 1865	Colby	Spinner	Unknown

IV. INTEREST BEARING NOTES

The Interest Bearing Notes are the rarest of all issues of American currency. Even advanced collectors after many years of ardent search will not have had the pleasure of seeing one of these notes. Such rarity is only natural for these notes, and applies as well to all three types of American currency which bore interest, the Compound Interest Treasury Notes, the Refunding Certificates and these Interest Bearing Notes. When one considers the perilous state of the nation in those years, the scarcity of money and the general fear, it was a rare person indeed, one either supremely confident or sublimely ignorant, who did not turn in his interest bearing money the moment the interest became payable. That is why so few of these exist today and why so many of the higher values are completely unknown.

Like the Compound Interest Treasury Notes, the Interest Bearing issues were authorized by Congress because of the many financial emergencies during the Civil War years.

There are three separate issues of these notes, the One Year, Two Year and Three Year notes which indicate the length of time for which the interest was computed.

The One Year Notes bore interest at five per cent for one year. They were issued under the Act of Congress of March 3, 1863, The interest became payable to bearer at the end of the year upon presentation of the notes for redemption. They were issued in seven denominations from 10 to 5,000 Dollars. Please see the text for fuller descriptions.

The Two Year Notes bore interest at five per cent for two years. They were also issued under the Act of Congress of March 3, 1863. There were only four denominations of these notes from 50 to 1,000 Dollars. In this case, the interest became payable at the end of two years.

There are three known separate issues of the Three Year Notes. All of these bore interest at 7-3/10 per cent for a period of three years. The three Acts of Congress which authorized these issues are of July 17, 1861, June 30, 1864 and March 3, 1865. This interest of 7-3/10 per cent is the highest ever paid by the Government on its notes. The

Three Year Notes were issued in five denominations from 50 to 5,000 Dollars.

The interest earned on these notes per day is actually stated on the notes. The 50 Dollar note has the clause "Interest one cent per day," the 100 Dollar note, "Two cents per day" and so on for the other denominations.

All Three Year Notes were made payable to order, and there is a line on the obverse for a name, and another line on the reverse for the endorsement of the payee. See Notes 207-212 in the text.

These notes are also distinguished by a feature unique in United States paper money. When first issued to the public, all Three Year Notes had five coupons attached, each coupon bearing the interest for a six month period. At the end of a six month period, one coupon could be detached and the interest on it collected. In this instance, the notes are like bonds. However, since they are Three Year Notes, there should have been six coupons, not five, and therefore the interest for the final six month period was payable only on presentation of the note itself. This method of payment is so stated on the notes.

For example, the full interest on a 100 Dollar Note was $21.90. Each of the five coupons, therefore, had a face value of $3.65 and the final $3.65 was paid when this 100 Dollar note was presented to the Treasury, at which time the holder received $103.65. (See Note 212 in the text.) This partly accounts for the extreme rarity of these notes, since all holders in the past were anxious to collect the interest. The obligations on these various types of Interest Bearing Notes are similar. On the One Year Notes, for example, it reads as follows, "Legal Tender for____ Dollars. One year after date, the United States will pay to bearer Dollars with interest at five per cent ... This note is a legal tender at its face value, excluding interest, for all debts public and private except duties on imports and interest on the public debt."

On the Three Year Notes the obligation is "Three years after date, the United States promise to pay to the order of _____ dollars with 7-3/10 per cent interest payable semi-annually in lawful money." (See note 212 for the convertibility clause.)

A. 60 DAY NOTES. Issued under the Act of March 2, 1861.

The notes of this issue bore interest at 6% for 60 days.

195b.	50 Dollar Note.	One Proof known.
195c.	100 Dollar Note.	One Proof known.
195d.	500 Dollar Note.	One Proof known.

B. ONE YEAR NOTES. Issued under the Act of March 3, 1863.

The notes of this issue bore interest at 5% for a period of one year.

DESIGN NO. 41

(Notes 196-196a)

Head of Salmon P. Chase. At the center is an eagle holding the flag. At the right is a female allegory representing Peace.

Reverse of Design No. 41.

This illustration by courtesy of the Chase Manhattan Bank N.A. of New York.

			Very Good	Fine
196.	10 Dollar Note. Very Rare (about 5 known).	ABN Co.	Rare	Rare
196a.	10 Dollar Note. Rare (about 25 known).	BEP	2,000.00	5,000.00

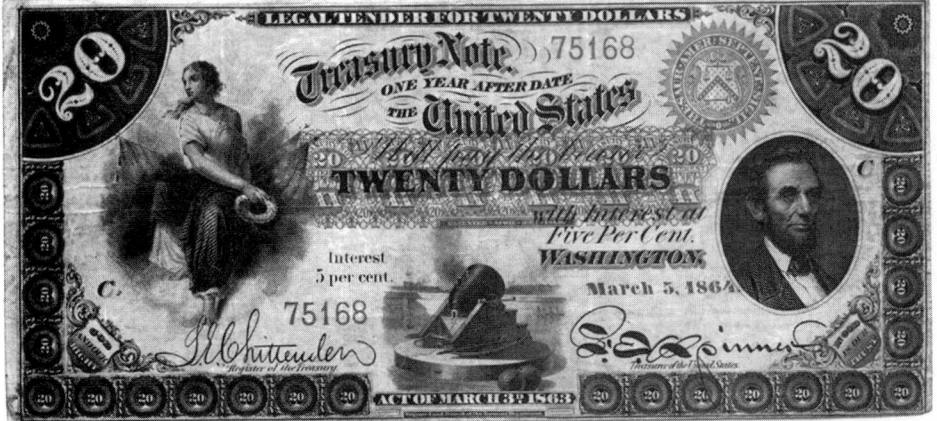

DESIGN NO. 42

(Notes 197-197a)

Head of Abraham Lincoln. The female allegory at the left represents Victory. At the lower center is a mortar firing.

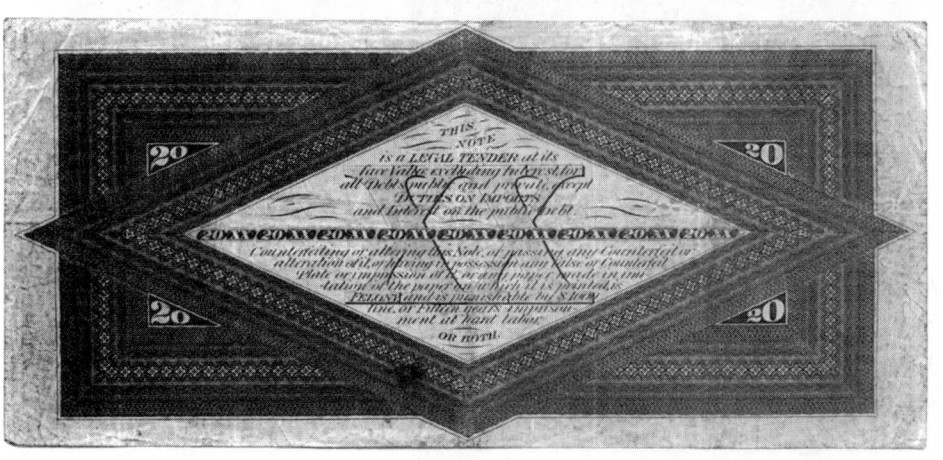

Reverse of Design No. 42.

Note illustrated from collection of the American Numismatic Association..

			Very Good	Fine
197.	20 Dollar Note. Very Rare (about 5 known).	ABN Co.	5,000.00	7,500.00
197a.	20 Dollar Note. Rare (about 20 known).	BEP	3,100.00	5,600.00

DESIGN NO. 43

(Note 198)

Head of Alexander Hamilton. At the left is a female allegory representing Loyalty.

Reverse of Design No. 43.

198.   50 Dollar Note (Three known).   Extremely Rare

DESIGN NO. 44

(Note 199)

Washington standing between female allegories representing The Guardian, left, and Justice, right.

Reverse of Design No. 44.

This illustration by courtesy of Mr. Amon G. Carter Jr.

199.	100 Dollar Note (Two known).	Extremely Rare	
200.	500 Dollar Note. The Ship New Ironsides.	Unknown	**DESIGN NO. 45**
201.	1,000 Dollar Note. Liberty and Justice.	Unknown	**DESIGN NO. 46**
202.	5,000 Dollar Note. Female Allegory.	Unknown	**DESIGN NO. 47**

C. TWO YEAR NOTES. Issued under the Act of March 2, 1861.

The notes of this issue bore interest at 6% for a period of two years.

DESIGN NO. 47-a

(Note 202a)

Female allegory representing Justice flanked by vignettes of Andrew Jackson at left and Salmon P. Chase at right.

Reverse of Design No. 47-a.

Illustration courtesy of Paul Kagin.

202a.	50 Dollar Note.	Unique
202b.	100 Dollar Note.	One Proof known.
202c.	500 Dollar Note.	One Proof known.
202d.	1,000 Dollar Note.	One Proof known.

D. TWO YEAR NOTES. Issued under the Act of March 3, 1863.

The notes of this issue bore interest at 5% for a period of two years.

DESIGN NO. 48

(Note 203)

Allegory of three females representing Caduceus, at the left; Justice, center; and Loyalty.

Reverse of Design No. 48.

203.   50 Dollar Note.   Extremely Rare

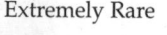

DESIGN NO. 49

(Note 204)

The vignettes show Science and Mechanics, left; the Treasury Building, top center; and Naval Ordnance, right.

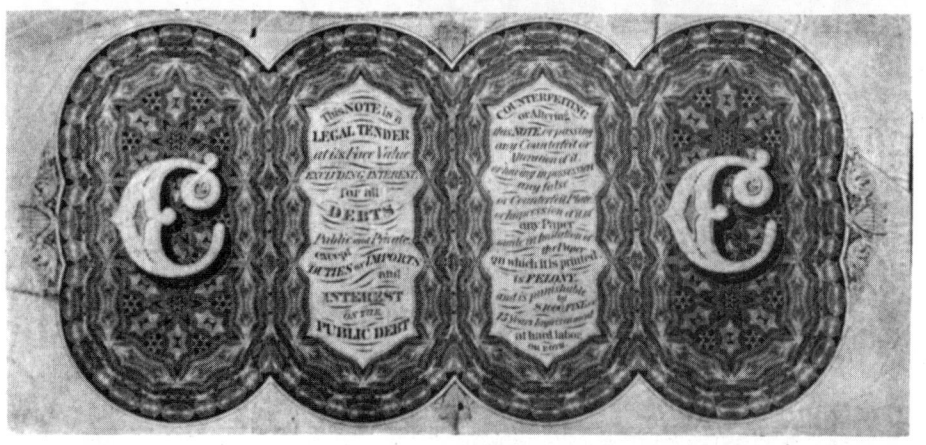

Reverse of Design No. 49.

Illustration by courtesy of the Citizens National Bank, Lebanon, Ky.

The Two-Year Interest Bearing Note of 1864 shown above was discovered in 1961. It had previously been unknown in any collection and it was presumed that no specimens were extant.

204.	100 Dollar Note.		Extremely Rare	
205.	500 Dollar Note.	Liberty and Eagle.	Unknown	**DESIGN NO. 50**
206.	1,000 Dollar Note.	The Ships *Guerriere* and *Constitution*.	Unknown	**DESIGN NO. 51**

E. THREE YEAR NOTES. Issued with 5 coupons attached.

The notes of this issue bore interest at 7-3/10% for a period of three years. For an explanation of the coupons, please refer to the introduction of this section.

1. Notes issued under the Act of July 17, 1861.

DESIGN NO. 52

(Note 207)

With minor variations, the obverse is similar to Design No. 57.

The reverse is as shown and is of a proof or specimen note.

A unique specimen is known of this note with two of the coupons still attached.

207.	50 Dollar Note.	Large eagle.	Extremely Rare
208.	100 Dollar Note.	Head of General Winfield Scott.	Unknown

DESIGN NO. 53

DESIGN NO. 54

(Note 209)

Bust of George Washington in center. Allegorical vignettes representing Justice seated at left; Transportation at right.

Reverse of Design No. 54.

Illustration courtesy of Donald H. Kagin.

209.   500 Dollar Note. Head of George Washington.   Unique

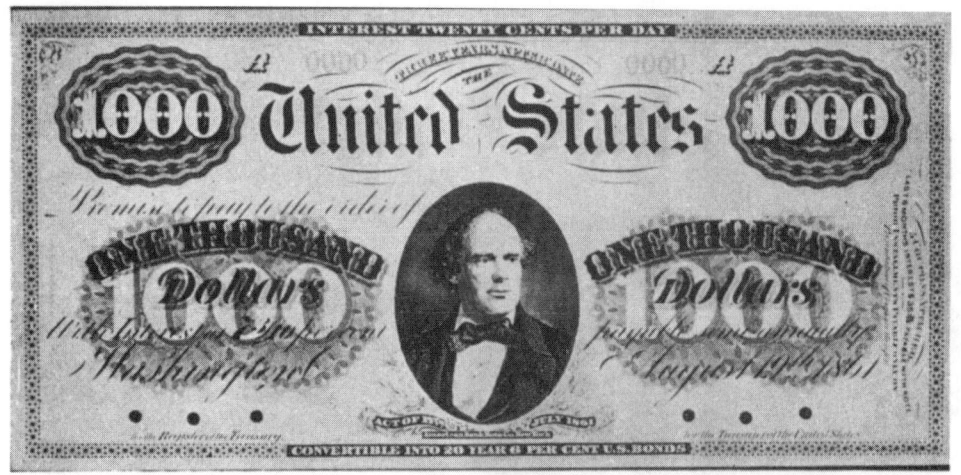

DESIGN NO. 55

(Note 210)

*Head of Salmon P. Chase.
This illustration is of a
proof or specimen note.*

Reverse of Design No. 55.

210.   1,000 Dollar Note.   Unknown

DESIGN NO. 56

(Note 211)

*The female allegory at the left represents
Justice.
At the top center is an Indian female.*

Reverse of Design No. 56.

*This illustration, courtesy of Spink
America, is of a proof or specimen note.
Reduction is to 65% of actual size.*

211.   5,000 Dollar Note.   Unknown

2. Notes issued under the Act of June 30, 1864.

DESIGN NO. 57

(Note 212)

Large eagle.

Reverse of Design No. 57

Illustration courtesy of Donald H. Kagin.

212.   50 Dollar Note.   Extremely Rare

DESIGN NO. 57a.
(Note 212-a)

Bust of General Winfield Scott, General-in-Chief of the Army, 1841-1848 and 1855-1861.

Reverse of Design No. 57a.

Illustration courtesy of Donald H. Kagin.

212-a.   100 Dollar Note   One known   Unique

DESIGN NO. 57-b.

(Note 212-b)

Head of Alexander Hamilton, top center, between a mortar firing, at the left and the figure of George Washington.

Reverse of Design No. 57-b.

212-b.   500 Dollar Note   Extremely Rare
212-c.   1,000 Dollar Note. Probably issued.   Unknown

DESIGN NO. 57-c.

3. Notes issued under the Act of March 3, 1865.

DESIGN NO. 57-d.

(Note 212-d)

With minor variations this obverse is similar to Design No. 57.
This reverse is similar to Design No. 57, except for the large "50" overprinted in gold ink.

This illustration and that of Design No. 57-e are of unique notes. They are the only ones which have survived in their original state of issue, with all 5 coupons still intact. A few other specimens are known of these notes, but some or all of the coupons have been removed.

212-d.   50 Dollar Note.   Extremely Rare

DESIGN NO. 57-e.

(Note 212-e.)

Head of General Winfield Scott, General-in-Chief of the Army from 1841-1848 and l855-1861.

Reverse of Design No. 57-e.

| 212-e. | 100 Dollar Note | Extremely Rare |
| 212-f. | 500 Dollar Note | Extremely Rare |

DESIGN NO. 57-f.

DESIGN NO. 57-g.

(Note 212-g.)

Justice seated. The illustration shows the last of the 5 coupons still attached.

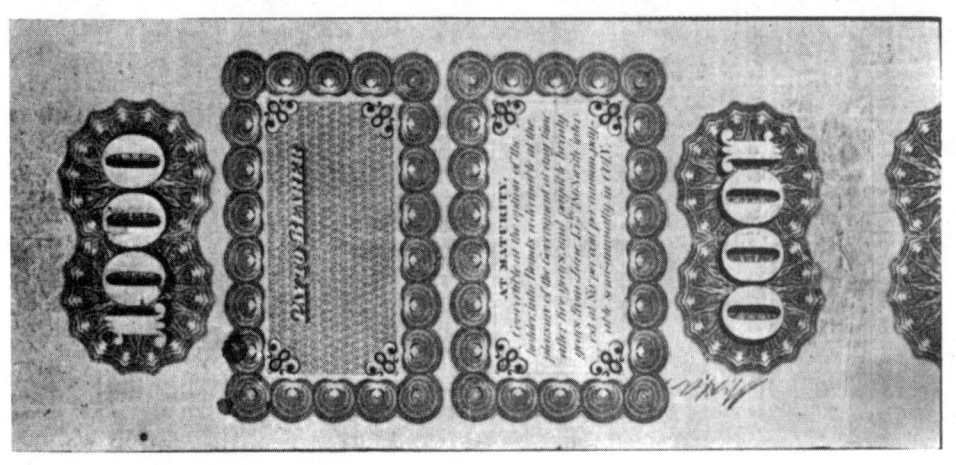

Reverse of Design No. 57-g.

| 212-g. | 1000 Dollar Note | Unique |

V. REFUNDING CERTIFICATES

In order to make government securities more popular and more easily within the reach of the average citizen, Congress passed the Act of February 26, 1879.

This Act made it possible for the Treasury to issue to the public the refunding Certificates of 10 Dollar denomination. These certificates bore interest at the rate of four per cent per year and at the time of issue, it was meant for the interest to accrue indefinitely, as no time limit was set. This was the inducement for the public to keep on holding these notes.

However, in 1907, an Act of Congress stopped the interest on these notes as of July 1 of that year. By that time, the interest alone amounted to $11.30 and therefore the redemption value of these notes today is $21.30, more than double the original face value.

There were two types of these Refunding Certificates. On the first type, the name of the purchaser was written in on the obverse on a line provided for that purpose. The reverse of this type is completely different from the second type (see the illustrations in the text) as it consists of an assignment form for conversion of the note into a four per cent bond. This first type is of the highest rarity as only two specimens are reported extant.

The second type is the one usually seen, as is illustrated in the text. (See Design No. 58-b.)

The obligation on this note is as follows, "This certifies that the sum of Ten Dollars has been deposited with the Treasurer of the United States under Act of February 26th, 1879 convertible with accrued interest at 4 per cent per annum into 4 per cent bonds of the United States issued under the Acts of July 14, 1870 and January 20, 1871 upon presentation at the Office of the Treasurer of the U.S. in sums of $50. or multiples thereof."

Dated April 1, 1879 with signatures of Scofield and Gilfillan and bearing interest at 4 per cent.

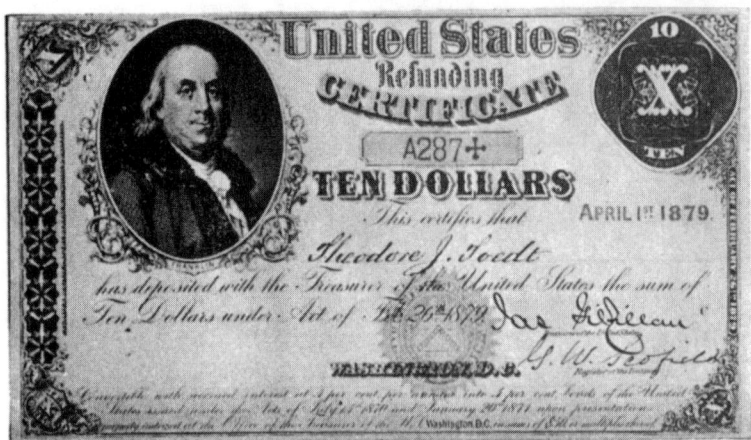

DESIGN NO. 58-a.

(Note 213)

Head of Benjamin Franklin.

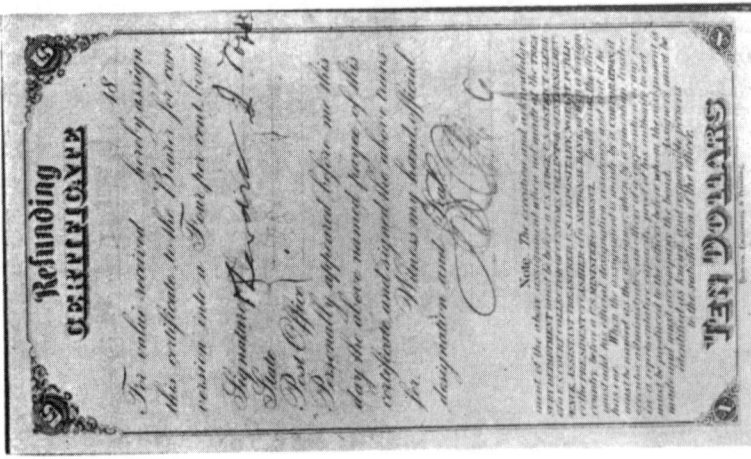

Reverse of Design No. 58-a.

213.   10 Dollar Note. Payable to order.   Extremely Rare

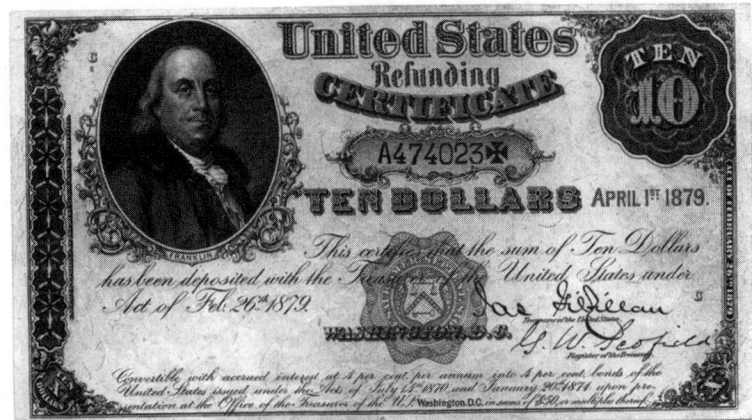

214.   10 Dollar Note. Payable to bearer.

DESIGN NO. 58-b.

(Note 214)

Head of Benjamin Franklin.

Reverse of Design No. 58-b.

Note illustrated from collection of the American Numismatic Association.

Fine	Very Fine	Extra Fine	UNC
950.00	1,750.00	6,500.00	12,500.00

VI. SILVER CERTIFICATES

Like the Legal Tender Notes, the Silver Certificates are extensive and offer many varieties of design and subject matter.

Two Acts of Congress authorized all the Silver Certificates that were issued, the Acts of February 28, 1878 and August 4, 1886. Under these Acts, there were five different issues, as follows:

The first issue consisted of notes from 10 to 1,000 Dollars of the series of 1878 and 1880. These notes are particularly attractive because the reverses are black in color and do not look like conventional paper money. These notes are difficult to find in new condition. They are called on the obverse "Certificate of Deposit," which term does not appear on the later issues.

The obligation on this first issue is as follows, "This certifies that there have been deposited with the Treasurer of the U.S. at Washington, D.C. payable at his office to the bearer on demand - silver Dollars ... This certificate is receivable for customs, taxes and all public dues and when so received may be reissued."

All the notes of the 1878 series are countersigned by various Assistant Treasurers at New York, Washington and San Francisco in order to denote that silver had been deposited at their offices in these cities.

The second issue of Silver Certificates consisted of notes from 1 to 1,000 Dollars of the series of 1886, 1891 and 1908. The notes of the 1886 series are quite popular because of the attractive reverses which are entirely covered with fine, detailed lathe work. Please refer to the text for which denominations exist in any given series.

The third issue consisted only of 1, 2 and 5 Dollar notes of the series of 1896. These notes comprise the famous and ever popular Educational Set. These notes are both the most historical and most artistically designed of all issues of our currency.

The fourth issue consisted only of 1, 2 and 5 Dollar notes of the series of 1899. This issue is notable for the many signature combinations that appear on the notes.

The fifth issue consisted only of 1 and 5 Dollar notes of the series of 1923.

The obligation on the notes of the last four issues is as follows, "This certifies that there have been deposited in the Treasury of the United States (of America) - silver Dollars payable to the bearer on demand ... This certificate is receivable for customs, taxes and all public dues and when so received may be reissued."

1 Dollar Notes

DESIGN NO. 59

(Notes 215-221)

Head of Martha Washington, wife of George Washington.
Engraved by Charles Burt from the Jalabert painting.

Reverse of Design No. 59.

Ornate floral design.

Note illustrated from collection of the American Numismatic Association.

No.	Series	Signatures		Seal	Very Good	Very Fine	Unc
215.	1886	Rosecrans	Jordan	Small Red, plain	160.00	325.00	1,600.00
216.	1886	Rosecrans	Hyatt	Small Red, plain	200.00	375.00	1,750.00
217.	1886	Rosecrans	Hyatt	Large Red	170.00	350.00	1,700.00
218.	1886	Rosecrans	Huston	Large Red	170.00	350.00	1,700.00
219.	1886	Rosecrans	Huston	Large Brown	170.00	350.00	1,725.00
220.	1886	Rosecrans	Nebeker	Large Brown	170.00	350.00	1,800.00
221.	1886	Rosecrans	Nebeker	Small red, scalloped	175.00	360.00	1,700.00

DESIGN NO. 60

(Notes 222-223)

The obverse is similar to Design No. 59.

The reverse is as shown.

No.	Series	Signatures		Seal	Very Good	Very Fine	Unc
222.	1891	Rosecrans	Nebeker	Small Red, scalloped	165.00	300.00	1,500.00
223.	1891	Tillman	Morgan	Small Red, scalloped	165.00	300.00	1,500.00

DESIGN NO. 61

(Notes 224-225)

This is the famous Educational Note, designed by Will H. Low and engraved by Charles Schlecht. History instructing youth: to right, the Constitution; in background, the Washington Monument and the Capitol; around the borders, the names of great Americans in wreaths.

Reverse of Design No. 61.

Heads of George and Martha Washington.
Thomas F. Morris designed the reverse from a portrait of Martha Washington, engraved by Charles Burt in 1878, and a portrait of George Washington, engraved in 1867 by Alfred Sealey.

Note illustrated from collection of the American Numismatic Association.

No.	Series	Signatures		Seal	Very Good	Very Fine	Unc
224.	1896	Tillman	Morgan	Small Red with rays	195.00	475.00	1,500.00
225.	1896	Bruce	Roberts	Small Red with rays	200.00	475.00	1,900.00

DESIGN NO. 62

(Notes 226-236)

Eagle over heads of Presidents Abraham Lincoln and Ulysses S. Grant. Engraved by G.F.C. Smillie.

Reverse of Design No. 62.

Note illustrated from collection of the American Numismatic Association.

No.	Series	Signatures		Seal		Very Good	Very Fine	Unc
226.	1899	Lyons	Roberts	Blue	Date above Serial No.	35.00	75.00	600.00
226-a.	1899	Lyons	Roberts	Blue	Date below Serial No.	52.50	70.00	500.00
227.	1899	Lyons	Treat	Blue	Date below Serial No.	35.00	75.00	850.00
228.	1899	Vernon	Treat	Blue	Date below Serial No.	52.50	70.00	500.00
229.	1899	Vernon	McClung	Blue	Date below Serial No.	52.50	70.00	600.00
229-a.	1899	Vernon	McClung	Blue	Date to right of Seal	65.00	175.00	1,350.00
230.	1899	Napier	McClung	Blue	Date to right of Seal	52.50	70.00	500.00
231.	1899	Napier	Thompson	Blue	Date to right of Seal	40.00	150.00	2,000.00
232.	1899	Parker	Burke	Blue	Date to right of Seal	52.50	70.00	450.00
233.	1899	Teehee	Burke	Blue	Date to right of Seal	52.50	70.00	450.00
234.	1899	Elliott	Burke	Blue	Date to right of Seal	52.50	70.00	450.00
235.	1899	Elliott	White	Blue	Date to right of Seal	52.50	70.00	450.00
236.	1899	Speelman	White	Blue	Date to right of Seal	50.00	70.00	425.00

DESIGN NO. 63

(Notes 237-239)

Head of George Washington, from the painting by Gilbert C. Stuart.

The reverse is similar to Design No. 7.

Note illustrated from collection of the American Numismatic Association.

No.	Series	Signatures		Seal	Very Good	Very Fine	Unc
237.	1923	Speelman	White	Blue	25.00	35.00	100.00
238.	1923	Woods	White	Blue	25.00	37.50	110.00
239.	1923	Woods	Tate	Blue	40.00	70.00	300.00

2 Dollar Notes

DESIGN NO. 64

(Notes 240-244)

Head of General Winfield Scott Hancock, Union general during the Civil War.

Reverse of Design No. 64.

Note illustrated from collection of the American Numismatic Association.

No.	Series	Signatures		Seal	Very Good	Very Fine	Unc
240.	1886	Rosecrans	Jordan	Small Red	200.00	625.00	2,500.00
241.	1886	Rosecrans	Hyatt	Small Red	200.00	625.00	2,750.00
242.	1886	Rosecrans	Hyatt	Large Red	185.00	600.00	2,300.00
243.	1886	Rosecrans	Huston	Large Red	220.00	625.00	2,900.00
244.	1886	Rosecrans	Huston	Large Brown	225.00	650.00	2,900.00

DESIGN NO. 65

(Notes 245-246)

Head of William Windom, Secretary of the Treasury 1881-1884 and 1889-1891.

Reverse of Design No. 65.

Note illustrated from collection of the American Numismatic Association.

No.	Series	Signatures		Seal	Very Good	Very Fine	Unc
245.	1891	Rosecrans	Nebeker	Small Red	160.00	625.00	4,250.00
246.	1891	Tillman	Morgan	Small Red	160.00	600.00	4,000.00

DESIGN NO. 66

(Notes 247-248)

The Second Note of the Educational Series, engraved by Charles Schlecht and G.F.C Smillie after designs by Edwin H. Blashfield (figures) and Thomas F. Morris (frame, background). Science presenting steam and electricity to commerce and manufacture.

Reverse of Design No. 66.

Heads of inventors Robert Fulton and Samuel F.B. Morse.
The portraits are attributed to engraver Lorenzo J. Hatch.

Note illustrated from collection of the American Numismatic Association.

No.	Series	Signatures		Seal	Very Good	Very Fine	Unc
247.	1896	Tillman	Morgan	Small Red	275.00	1,000.00	4,000.00
248.	1896	Bruce	Roberts	Small Red	275.00	1,000.00	4,000.00

DESIGN NO. 67

(Notes 249-258)

Head of George Washington between figures of Mechanics and Agriculture. The engraver was G.F.C. Smillie.

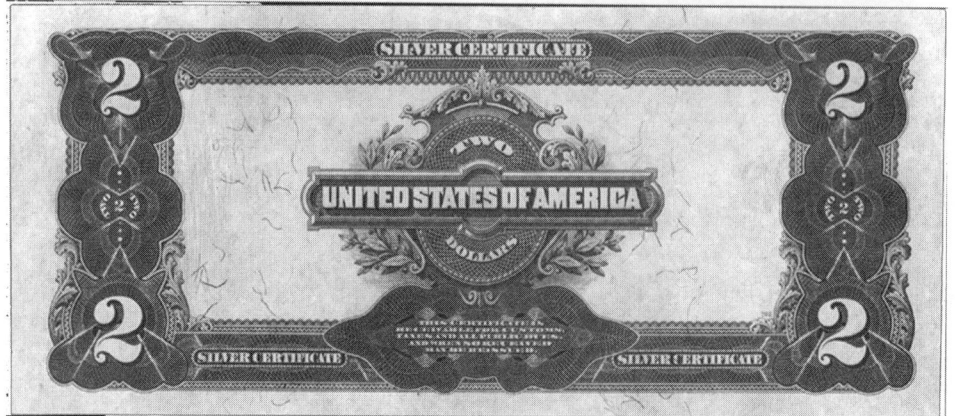

Reverse of Design No. 67.

Note illustrated from collection of the American Numismatic Association.

No.	Series	Signatures		Seal	Very Good	Very Fine	Unc
249.	1899	Lyons	Roberts	Blue	100.00	175.00	750.00
250.	1899	Lyons	Treat	Blue	100.00	175.00	1,500.00
251.	1899	Vernon	Treat	Blue	100.00	175.00	750.00
252.	1899	Vernon	McClung	Blue	100.00	175.00	875.00
253.	1899	Napier	McClung	Blue	100.00	175.00	750.00
254.	1899	Napier	Thompson	Blue	130.00	250.00	2,750.00
255.	1899	Parker	Burke	Blue	100.00	175.00	750.00
256.	1899	Teehee	Burke	Blue	100.00	175.00	750.00
257.	1899	Elliott	Burke	Blue	110.00	180.00	875.00
258.	1899	Speelman	White	Blue	100.00	175.00	750.00

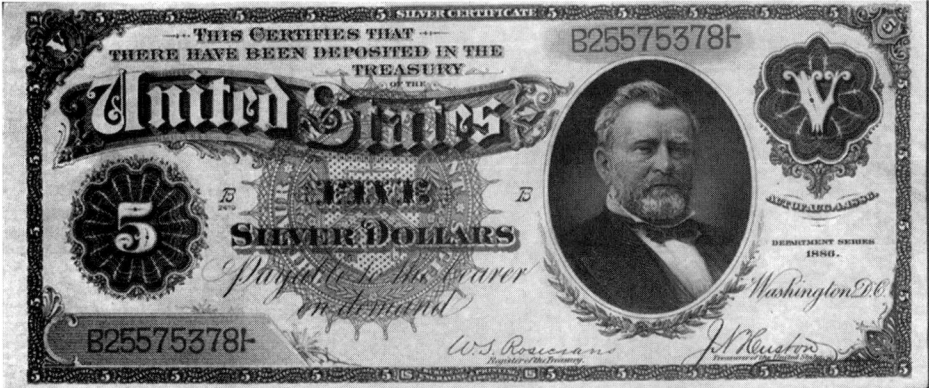

5 Dollar Notes

DESIGN NO. 68

(Notes 259-265)

Head of Ulysses S. Grant, 18th President of the United States, 1869-1873.
The portrait was engraved by Lorenzo J. Hatch.

Reverse of Design No. 68.

5 Silver Dollars, the central one dated 1886, the same year as this series. Portions of the inscription "In God We Trust" are discernible on four of the coins.

Note illustrated from collection of the American Numismatic Association.

No.	Series	Signatures		Seal	Very Good	Very Fine	Unc
259.	1886	Rosecrans	Jordan	Small Red, plain	375.00	1,100.00	7,500.00
260.	1886	Rosecrans	Hyatt	Small Red, plain	350.00	1,100.00	5,000.00
261.	1886	Rosecrans	Hyatt	Large Red	350.00	1,100.00	4,000.00
262.	1886	Rosecrans	Huston	Large Red	350.00	1,100.00	4,000.00
263.	1886	Rosecrans	Huston	Large Brown	350.00	1,100.00	4,000.00
264.	1886	Rosecrans	Nebeker	Large Brown	375.00	1,100.00	4,500.00
265.	1886	Rosecrans	Nebeker	Small Red, scalloped	400.00	1,250.00	10,500.00

DESIGN NO. 69

(Notes 266-267)

The obverse is similar to Design No. 68.

The reverse is as shown.

No.	Series	Signatures		Seal	Very Good	Very Fine	Unc
266.	1891	Rosecrans	Nebeker	Small Red, scalloped	175.00	1,000.00	4,250.00
267.	1891	Tillman	Morgan	Small Red	175.00	1,000.00	4,250.00

DESIGN NO. 70

(Notes 268-270)

The third and last of the Educational Series.
Allegorical group showing electricity as the dominant force in the world.
Engraved by G.F.C. Smillie from a painting by Walter Shirlaw, with border elements designed by Thomas F. Morris.

Reverse of Design No. 70.

Heads of Ulysses S. Grant and Philip Sheridan, Union Army generals during the Civil War.
The portraits of the generals were engraved by Lorenzo J. Hatch, with the remainder engraved by G.F.C. Smillie, after Thomas F. Morris's design.

Note illustrated from collection of the American Numismatic Association.

No.	Series	Signatures		Seal	Very Good	Very Fine	Unc
268.	1896	Tillman	Morgan	Small Red	450.00	1,800.00	7,500.00
269.	1896	Bruce	Roberts	Small Red	450.00	1,800.00	7,500.00
270.	1896	Lyons	Roberts	Small Red	500.00	2,000.00	9,000.00

DESIGN NO. 71

(Notes 271-281)

Head of Ta-to-ka-in-yan-ka, also known as Running Antelope, a member of the Oncpapa tribe of Sioux Indians. George F. C. Smillie engraved the portrait. This is the only issue of U.S. paper money for which a Native American was select-ed as the central feature.

Reverse of Design No. 71.

Note illustrated from collection of the American Numismatic Association.

No.	Series	Signatures		Seal	Very Good	Very Fine	Unc
271.	1899	Lyons	Roberts	Blue	275.00	800.00	2,750.00
272.	1899	Lyons	Treat	Blue	275.00	800.00	2,850.00

No.	Series	Signatures		Seal	Very Good	Very Fine	Unc
273.	1899	Vernon	Treat	Blue	275.00	800.00	2,800.00
274.	1899	Vernon	McClung	Blue	275.00	800.00	2,800.00
275.	1899	Napier	McClung	Blue	275.00	750.00	2,800.00
276.	1899	Napier	Thompson	Blue	350.00	1,500.00	8,500.00
277.	1899	Parker	Burke	Blue	275.00	800.00	2,800.00
278.	1899	Teehee	Burke	Blue	275.00	800.00	2,800.00
279.	1899	Elliott	Burke	Blue	300.00	850.00	2,900.00
280.	1899	Elliott	White	Blue	275.00	800.00	2,800.00
281.	1899	Speelman	White	Blue	275.00	800.00	2,750.00

DESIGN NO. 72

(Note 282)

Head of Abraham Lincoln, after the Matthew Brady photograph of February 9,1864.

This note is known as the "porthole" note because of the circular design around Lincoln's head.

Reverse of Design No. 72.

Note illustrated from collection of the American Numismatic Association.

No.	Series	Signatures		Seal	Very Good	Very Fine	Unc
282.	1923	Speelman	White	Blue	275.00	750.00	2,500.00

10 Dollar Notes

DESIGN NO. 73

(Notes 283-285-a)

Head of Robert Morris, a signer of the Declaration of Independence, and Superintendent of Finance, 1781-1784.

Reverse of Design No. 73.

Printed in brownish black ink.

Note illustrated from collection of the American Numismatic Association.

73. Seal at top of note; large "Ten" underneath.

Countersigned Notes; all with signatures of Scofield and Gilfillan and with large red seal and without the legend "Series of 1878." All have engraved countersignatures except for the notes starred (*) which are autographed.

No.	Series	Countersigned By	Payable At	Deposited With	Fine
283.	1878	W.G. White	New York	Assistant Treasurer of the U.S	Unique
284.	1878	J.C Hopper	New York	Assistant Treasurer of the U.S	Extremely Rare
284-a*.	1878	T. Hillhouse	New York	Assistant Treasurer of the U.S	Unknown
284-b.	1878	T. Hillhouse	New York	Assistant Treasurer of the U.S	Rare
284-c*	1878	R.M. Anthony	San Francisco	Assistant Treasurer of the U.S	Unknown
285*.	1878	A.U. Wyman	Washington, D.C.	Treasurer of the U.S.	Extremely Rare
285-a.	1878	A.U. Wyman	Washington, D.C.	Treasurer of the U.S.	Rare

DESIGN NO. 73-a

(Notes 286-290)
The obverse is as shown. With minor variations, the reverse is similar to Design No. 73.
There are two distinct types of this design, as follows:
    73a. Notes 286-286a
    73b. Notes 287-289
    73c. Note 290

Note illustrated from collection of the American Numismatic Association.

73a. Seal at top of note; large "X" underneath.
Countersigned Notes; all with signatures of Scofield and Gilfillan and with large brown seal.

286.	1880	T. Hillhouse	New York	Assistant Treasurer of the U.S.	4,750.00
286-a.	1880	A.U. Wyman	Washington, D.C.	Treasurer of the U.S.	Unknown

73b. Seal at top of note; large "X" underneath.
Normal notes without a countersigned signature.

No.	Series	Signatures		Seal	Very Good	Very Fine	Unc
287.	1880	Scofield	Gilfillan	Large Brown	550.00	1,950.00	8,500.00
288.	1880	Bruce	Gilfillan	Large Brown	525.00	1,800.00	7,500.00
289.	1880	Bruce	Wyman	Large Brown	525.00	1,800.00	7,500.00

73c. Seal in center of note; without the large brown "X".

290.	1880	Bruce	Wyman	Large Red	650.00	2,500.00	15,000.00

DESIGN NO. 74

(Notes 291-297)

Head of Thomas A. Hendricks, Vice President of the United States from March 4, 1885 to November 25,1885. He died in office.
The portrait was engraved by Charles Schlecht. The so-called "Tombstone Note."

Reverse of Design No. 74.

Note illustrated from collection of the American Numismatic Association.

No.	Series	Signatures		Seal	Very Good	Very Fine	Unc
291.	1886	Rosecrans	Jordan	Small Red, plain	500.00	1,500.00	9,000.00
292.	1886	Rosecrans	Hyatt	Small Red, plain	500.00	1,300.00	8,000.00
293.	1886	Rosecrans	Hyatt	Large Red	400.00	1,300.00	6,500.00
294.	1886	Rosecrans	Huston	Large Red	400.00	1,300.00	7,000.00
295.	1886	Rosecrans	Huston	Large Brown	450.00	1,400.00	7,000.00
296.	1886	Rosecrans	Nebeker	Large Brown	450.00	1,400.00	6,500.00
297.	1886	Rosecrans	Nebeker	Small Red, scalloped	500.00	1,500.00	10,000.00

DESIGN NO. 75

(Notes 298-304)

The obverse is similar to Design No. 74.
The reverse is as shown.
There are two distinct types of this design, as follows:
75a. Notes 298-301
75b. Notes 302-304

75a. With small plate letter only at left center of obverse.

No.	Series	Signatures		Seal	Very Good	Very Fine	Unc
298.	1891	Rosecrans	Nebeker	Small Red	250.00	850.00	6,000.00
299.	1891	Tillman	Morgan	Small Red	240.00	700.00	4,800.00
300.	1891	Bruce	Roberts	Small Red	240.00	700.00	4,800.00
301.	1891	Lyons	Roberts	Small Red	240.00	700.00	4,800.00

75b. Large blue "X" is added to left center of obverse.

No.	Series	Signatures		Seal	Very Good	Very Fine	Unc
302.	1908	Vernon	Treat	Blue	150.00	700.00	4,000.00
303.	1908	Vernon	McClung	Blue	175.00	800.00	4,250.00
304.	1908	Parker	Burke	Blue	150.00	700.00	4,000.00

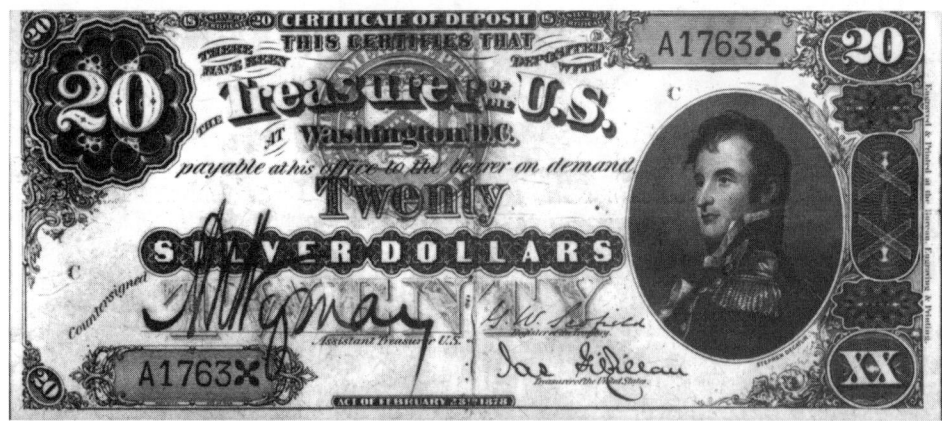

20 Dollar Notes

DESIGN NO. 76

(Notes 305-308)

Head of Captain Stephen Decatur, naval hero of the War of 1812.
There are two distinct types of this design, as follows:
Notes 305-307
Note 308

Reverse of Design No. 76.
Printed in brownish black ink.

Photo courtesy Spink America.

76. Large seal at top of note, with large "Twenty" below on series of 1878; large "XX" below on Series of 1880.
Countersigned Notes; all with signatures of Scofield and Gilfillan and with large red seal except the 1880 series which has a large brown seal. The 1878 countersigned notes are without the legend, "Series of 1878." All have engraved countersignatures except No. 306-b which is autographed.*

No.	Series	Countersigned By	Payable At	Deposited With	Fine
305.	1878	J.C. Hopper	New York	Assistant Treasurer of the U.S.	Extremely Rare
306.	1878	T. Hillhouse	New York	Assistant Treasurer of the U.S.	Rare
306-a.	1878	R.M. Anthony	San Francisco	Assistant Treasurer of the U.S.	Unknown
306-b*	1878	A.U. Wyman	Washington, D.C.	Treasurer of the U.S.	Extremely Rare
307.	1878	A.U. Wyman	Washington	Treasurer of the U.S.	7,500.00
308.	1880	T. Hillhouse	New York	Assistant Treasurer of the U.S.	10,000.00

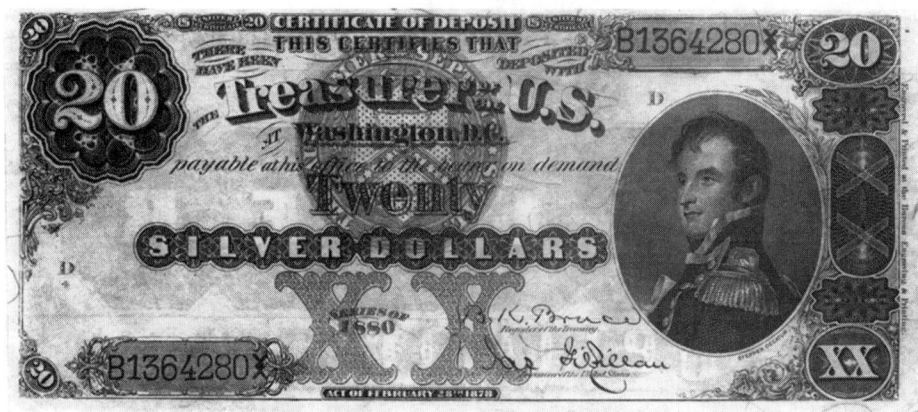

DESIGN NO. 76-a

(Notes 309-312)

Head of Stephen Decatur.
The reverse is similar to Design No. 76.
There are two distinct types of this design, as follows:
76a. Notes 309-311
76b. Note 312

Note illustrated from collection of the American Numismatic Association.

76a. Large seal at top of note with large "XX" below.
Normal notes without a countersigned signature.

No.	Series	Signatures		Seal	Very Good	Very Fine	Unc
309.	1880	Scofield	Gilfillan	Large Brown	1,250.00	4,000.00	15,000.00
310.	1880	Bruce	Gilfillan	Large Brown	1,250.00	4,000.00	15,000.00
311.	1880	Bruce	Wyman	Large Brown	1,250.00	4,000.00	11,000.00

76b. Small seal at bottom of note and without the "XX".

No.	Series	Signatures		Seal	Very Good	Very Fine	Unc
312.	1880	Bruce	Wyman	Small Red	2,000.00	5,500.00	20,000.00

DESIGN NO. 77

(Notes 313-316)

Head of Daniel Manning, Secretary of the Treasury from 1885 to 1887. Lorenzo J. Hatch engraved the portrait. The allegorical figures represent Agriculture and Industry. There are two distinct types of this design as follows:
   77a. Notes 313-315
   77b. Note 316

Reverse of Design No. 77.

Note illustrated from collection of the American Numismatic Association.

77a. Large seal at upper left of note.

No.	Series	Signatures		Seal	Very Good	Very Fine	Unc
313.	1886	Rosecrans	Hyatt	Large Red	1,750.00	5,000.00	25,000.00
314.	1886	Rosecrans	Huston	Large Brown	1,500.00	4,500.00	15,000.00
315.	1886	Rosecrans	Nebeker	Large Brown	1,500.00	4,500.00	20,000.00

77b. Small seal at lower right of note.

No.	Series	Signatures		Seal	Very Good	Very Fine	Unc
316.	1886	Rosecrans	Nebeker	Small Red	1,600.00	4,250.00	15,500.00

DESIGN NO. 78

(Notes 317-322)

The obverse is similar to Design No. 77.
The reverse is as shown.
There are two distinct types of this design, as follows:
   78a. Notes 317-320
   78b. Notes 321-322

78a. The obverse is similar to Design No. 77b.

No.	Series	Signatures		Seal	Very Good	Very Fine	Unc
317.	1891	Rosecrans	Nebeker	Small Red	350.00	1,750.00	7,000.00
318.	1891	Tillman	Morgan	Small Red	350.00	1,750.00	7,000.00
319.	1891	Bruce	Roberts	Small Red	350.00	1,750.00	7,000.00
320.	1891	Lyons	Roberts	Small Red	350.00	1,750.00	7,000.00

78b. A large blue "XX" has been added to left center of note.

No.	Series	Signatures		Seal	Very Good	Very Fine	Unc
321.	1891	Parker	Burke	Blue	325.00	1,400.00	6,000.00
322.	1891	Teehee	Burke	Blue	325.00	1,400.00	6,000.00

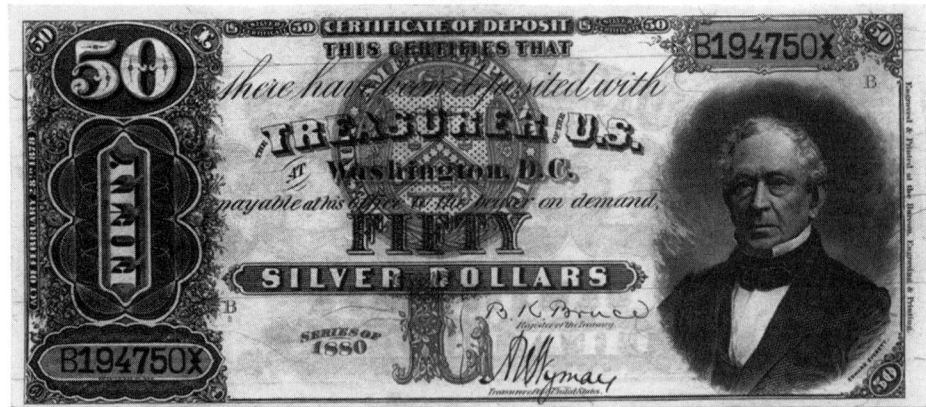

50 Dollar Notes

DESIGN NO. 79

(Notes 323-329)

Head of Edward Everett, Secretary of State under President Fillmore in 1852 and 1853.
There are three distinct types of this design, as follows:
79a. Notes 323-327

79b. Note 328
79c. Note 329

Reverse of Design No. 79.
Printed in brownish black ink.

Note illustrated from collection of the American Numismatic Association.

79a. Large seal at top of note with large "Fifty" below on Series of 1878; large "L" below on Series of 1880.
Countersigned Notes; all three notes with signatures of Scofield and Gilfillan and with large red seal. The 1878 countersigned notes are without the legend "Series of 1878." All have engraved countersignatures except the notes starred (*), which are autographed.

No.	Series	Countersigned By	Payable At	Fine
323*.	1878	W.G. White or J.C. Hopper	New York	Unknown
324.	1878	T. Hillhouse	New York	Extremely Rare
324-a.	1878	R.M. Anthony	San Francisco	Unique
324-b*.	1878	A.U. Wyman	Washington, D.C.	Unknown
324-c.	1878	A.U. Wyman	Washington, D.C.	Extremely Rare

Normal notes without a countersigned signature.

No.	Series	Signatures		Seal	Fine
325.	1880	Scofield	Gilfillan	Large Brown, rays	Unique
326.	1880	Bruce	Gilfillan	Large Brown, rays	Extremely Rare
327.	1880	Bruce	Wyman	Large Brown, rays	Extremely Rare

79b. Large seal in center of note and without the "L" or " Fifty".

328.	1880	Rosecrans	Huston	Large Brown, spikes	7,500.00

79c. Small seal at right center of note.

329.	1880	Rosecrans	Nebeker	Small Red	9,500.00

DESIGN NO. 80

(Notes 330-335)

Head of Edward Everett.

Reverse of Design No. 80.

Note illustrated from collection of the American Numismatic Association.

No.	Series	Signatures		Seal	Very Good	Very Fine	Unc
330.	1891	Rosecrans	Nebeker	Small Red	Rare	—	—
331.	1891	Tillman	Morgan	Small Red	1,250.00	2,750.00	12,500.00
332.	1891	Bruce	Roberts	Small Red	1,250.00	2,750.00	15,000.00
333.	1891	Lyons	Roberts	Small Red	1,300.00	3,000.00	15,000.00
334.	1891	Vernon	Treat	Small Red	1,100.00	2,600.00	10,000.00
335.	1891	Parker	Burke	Blue	1,000.00	2,500.00	9,000.00

100 Dollar Notes

DESIGN NO. 81

(Notes 336-342)

Head of James Monroe, fifth President of the United States, 1817-1825.
There are three distinct types of this design, as follows:
    81a. Notes 336-340
    81b. Note 341
    81c. Note 342

Reverse of Design No. 81.

Printed in brownish black ink.

Note illustrated from collection of the American Numismatic Association.

81a. Large seal at top of note, with large "100" below on Series of 1878; large "C" below on Series of 1880.
Countersigned Notes; all three notes with signatures of Scofield and Gilfillan and with a large red seal. The 1878 countersigned notes are without the legend, "Series of 1878." All have engraved countersignatures except the notes starred (*), which are autographed.

No.	Series	Countersigned By		Payable At	Fine
336.	1878	W.G. White		New York	Unique
336-a.	1878	J.C. Hopper or T. Hillhouse		New York	Unknown
337.*	1878	R.M. Anthony		San Francisco	Unique
337-a.*	1878	A.U. Wyman		Washington, D.C.	Unique
337-b.	1878	A.U. Wyman		Washington, D.C.	Extremely Rare

Normal notes without a countersigned signature.

No.	Series	Signatures		Seal	Fine
338.	1880	Scofield	Gilfillan	Large Brown, rays	Unknown
339.	1880	Bruce	Gilfillan	Large Brown, rays	Extremely Rare
340.	1880	Bruce	Wyman	Large Brown, rays	10,000.00

81b. Large seal in center of note and without the "C" or "100".

341.	1880	Rosecrans	Huston	Large Brown, spikes	9,500.00

81c. Small seal at right bottom of note.

342.	1880	Rosecrans	Nebeker	Small Red	11,000.00

DESIGN NO. 82
(Notes 343-344)

Head of James Monroe.

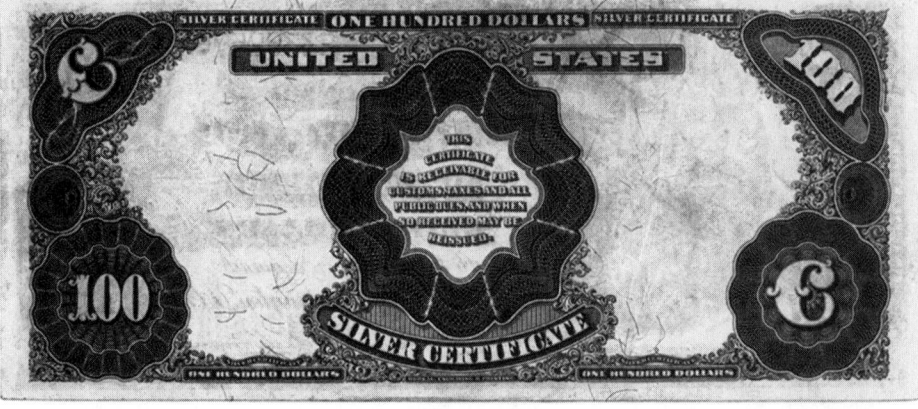

Reverse of Design No. 82.

Note illustrated from collection of the American Numismatic Association.

No.	Series	Signatures		Seal	Very Good	Very Fine	Unc
343.	1891	Rosecrans	Nebeker	Small Red	4,500.00	9,500.00	Rare
344.	1891	Tillman	Morgan	Small Red	4,500.00	9,500.00	Rare

500 Dollar Notes

DESIGN NO. 83

(Notes 345-a - 345-d)

Head of Charles Sumner, 1811-1874, U.S. Senator and Statesman.

Reverse of Design No. 83.

Only 14 notes of this design are outstanding.

Note illustrated from collection of the Federal Reserve Bank of San Francisco.

81d. The 1878 countersigned note is without the legend, "Series of 1878."

No.	Series	Signatures		Seal	
345-a.	1878	Scofield	Gilfillan	Large Red, rays (countersigned)	Unique
345-b.	1880	Scofield	Gilfillan	Large Brown	Unknown
345-c.	1880	Bruce	Gilfillan	Large Brown	Rare
345-d.	1880	Bruce	Wyman	Large Brown	Extremely Rare

1,000 Dollar Notes

DESIGN NO. 84

(Notes 346-a - 346-d)

Head of William L. Marcy, 1786- 1857, Governor of New York, US. Senator, Secretary of War under President Polk and Secretary of State under President Pierce.

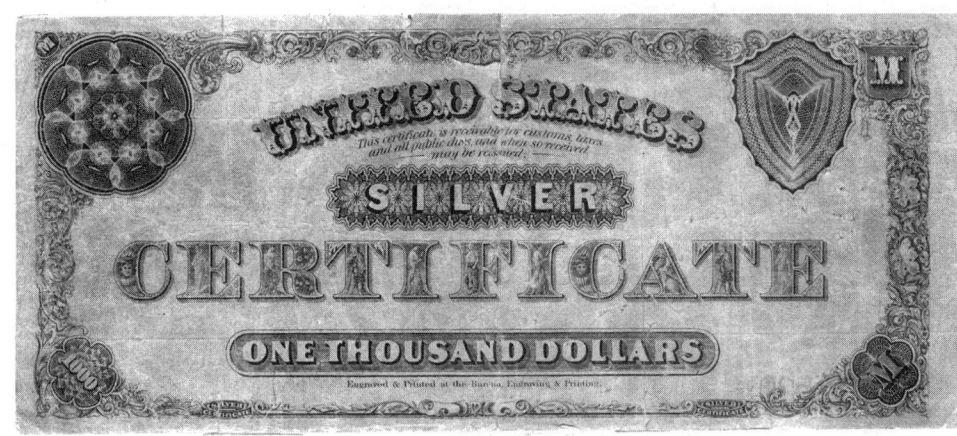

Reverse of Design No. 84.

Only 9 notes are outstanding of this design combined with Design No. 84-a.

Note illustrated from collection of the Federal Reserve Bank of San Francisco.

81e. The 1878 countersigned note is without the legend, "Series of 1878."

No.	Series	Signatures		Seal	
346-a.	1878	Scofield	Gilfillan	Large Red, Rays (countersigned)	Unknown
346-b.	1880	Scofield	Gilfillan	Large Brown	Unknown
346-c.	1880	Bruce	Gilfillan	Large Brown	Unknown
346-d.	1880	Bruce	Wyman	Large Brown	Extremely Rare

DESIGN NO. 84-a

(Note 346-e)

Head of William L. Marcy.

Reverse of Design No. 84-a.

No.	Series	Signatures		Seal	
346-e.	1891	Tillman	Morgan	Small Red	Extremely Rare

VII. TREASURY OR COIN NOTES

These notes were issued as a result of the Legal Tender Act of July 14, 1890. This Act authorized the Secretary of the Treasury to issue these notes in payment for silver bullion purchased by the Treasury Department. The entire issue of these notes thus became backed by metallic reserves. The notes were redeemable in actual coin, but whether silver or gold coin should be paid out was left to the discretion of the Secretary of the Treasury.

The coin notes were issued in denominations of 1, 2, 5, 10, 20, 50, 100, and 1,000 Dollars of the series of 1890 and 1891. A 500 Dollar note with portrait of General Sherman was also authorized and a plate made, but only a proof impression of the note is known; it was not placed in circulation.

The notes of the 1890 Series are especially attractive because of the intricate designs on the reverse. The 1890 notes are all rare today, especially in new condition.

The obligation on the Treasury or Coin Notes is as follows: "The United States of America will pay to bearer - Dollars in coin ... This note is a legal tender at its face value in payment of all debts public and private except when otherwise expressly stipulated in the contract."

1 Dollar Notes

DESIGN NO. 85

(Notes 347-349)

Head of Edwin M. Stanton, Secretary of War under Presidents Abraham Lincoln, 1862-1865, and Andrew Johnson, 1865-1868.

Reverse of Design No. 85.

Note illustrated from collection of the American Numismatic Association.

No.	Series	Signatures		Seal	Very Good	Very Fine	Unc
347.	1890	Rosecrans	Huston	Large Brown	175.00	900.00	4,000.00
348.	1890	Rosecrans	Nebeker	Large Brown	185.00	950.00	4,250.00
349.	1890	Rosecrans	Nebeker	Small Red	200.00	1,100.00	4,500.00

DESIGN NO. 86

(Notes 350-352)

The obverse is similar to Design No. 85.

The reverse is as shown.

No.	Series	Signatures		Seal	Very Good	Very Fine	Unc
350.	1891	Rosecrans	Nebeker	Small Red	125.00	250.00	1,400.00
351.	1891	Tillman	Morgan	Small Red	125.00	250.00	1,200.00
352.	1891	Bruce	Roberts	Small Red	125.00	250.00	1,200.00

2 Dollar Notes

DESIGN NO. 87

(Notes 353-355)

Head of General James McPherson, Union Army general and a hero of the Battle of Vicksburg. Engraved by Charles Burt.

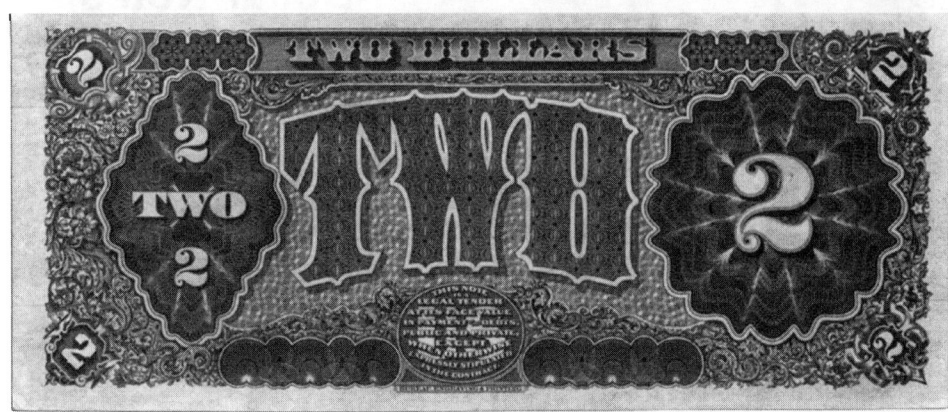

Reverse of Design No. 87.

Note illustrated from collection of the American Numismatic Association.

No.	Series	Signatures		Seal	Very Good	Very Fine	Unc
353.	1890	Rosecrans	Huston	Large Brown	300.00	2,000.00	6,500.00
354.	1890	Rosecrans	Nebeker	Large Brown	300.00	2,500.00	10,000.00
355.	1890	Rosecrans	Nebeker	Small Red	300.00	2,000.00	7,000.00

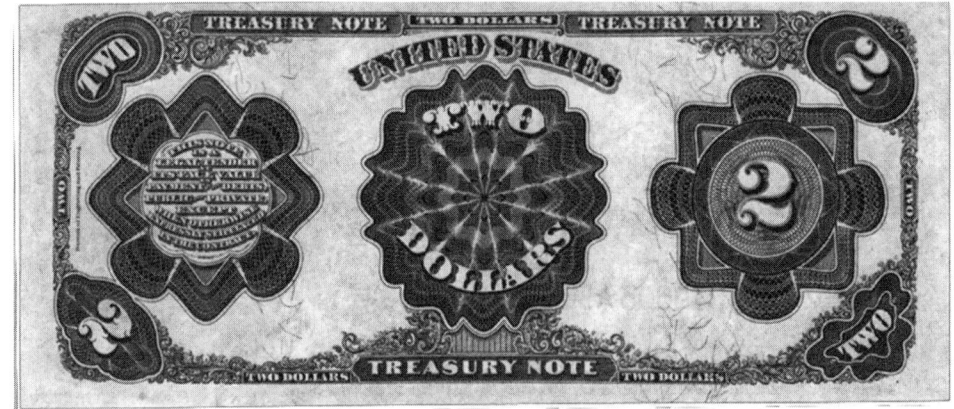

DESIGN NO. 88

(Notes 356-358)

The obverse is similar to Design No. 87.

The reverse is as shown.

No.	Series	Signatures		Seal	Very Good	Very Fine	Unc
356.	1891	Rosecrans	Nebeker	Small Red	150.00	650.00	2,600.00
357.	1891	Tillman	Morgan	Small Red	125.00	600.00	2,550.00
358.	1891	Bruce	Roberts	Small Red	175.00	750.00	3,500.00

5 Dollar Notes

DESIGN NO. 89

(Notes 359-361)

Head of General George H. Thomas, Union Army general famous as "the rock of Chicamauga." His portrait was engraved by Lorenzo J. Hatch.

Reverse of Design No. 89.

Note illustrated from collection of the American Numismatic Association.

No.	Series	Signatures		Seal	Very Good	Very Fine	Unc
359.	1890	Rosecrans	Huston	Large Brown	300.00	1,200.00	4,500.00
360.	1890	Rosecrans	Nebeker	Large Brown	375.00	1,500.00	7,500.00
361.	1890	Rosecrans	Nebeker	Small Red	275.00	1,100.00	4,250.00

DESIGN NO. 90

(Notes 362-365)

The obverse is similar to Design No. 89.

The reverse is as shown.

No.	Series	Signatures		Seal	Very Good	Very Fine	Unc
362.	1891	Rosecrans	Nebeker	Small Red	150.00	600.00	2,200.00
363.	1891	Tillman	Morgan	Small Red	135.00	550.00	1,600.00
364.	1891	Bruce	Roberts	Small Red	135.00	550.00	1,800.00
365.	1891	Lyons	Roberts	Small Red	200.00	750.00	8,500.00

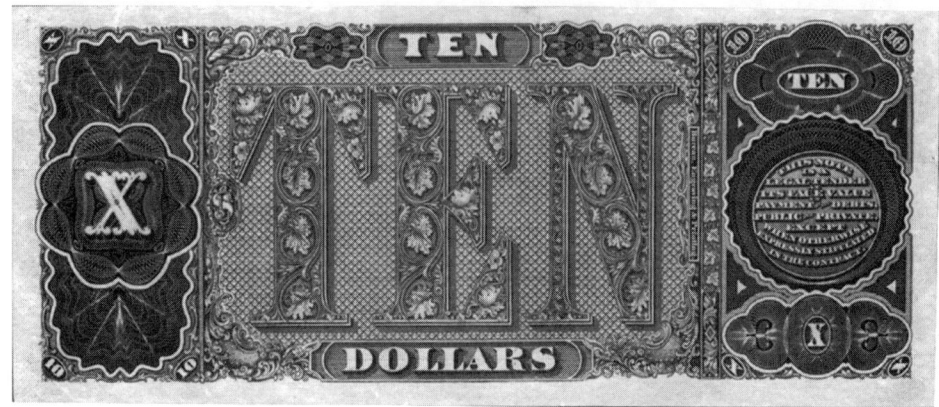

10 Dollar Notes

DESIGN NO. 91

(Notes 366-368)

Head of Philip H. Sheridan. He succeeded Sherman as Commander in Chief of the U.S. Army in 1884.

Reverse of Design No. 91.

Note illustrated from collection of the American Numismatic Association.

No.	Series	Signatures		Seal	Very Good	Very Fine	Unc
366.	1890	Rosecrans	Huston	Large Brown	600.00	2.,000.00	8,000.00
367.	1890	Rosecrans	Nebeker	Large Brown	550.00	1,500.00	6;500.00
368.	1890	Rosecrans	Nebeker	Small Red	500.00	1,400.00	6;000.00

DESIGN NO. 92

(Notes 369-371)

The obverse is similar to Design No. 91.

The reverse is as shown.

No.	Series	Signatures		Seal	Very Good	Very Fine	Unc
369.	1891	Rosecrans	Nebeker	Small Red	275.00	1,000.00	4,500.00
370.	1891	Tillman	Morgan	Small Red	300.00	1,100.00	4,750.00
371.	1891	Bruce	Roberts	Small Red	350.00	1,250.00	7,500.00

20 Dollar Notes

DESIGN NO. 93

(Notes 372-374)

Head of John Marshall, fourth Chief Justice of the United States, who served on the Supreme Court from 1801-1835. He was also Secretary of State from 1800-1801.

Reverse of Design No. 93.

Note illustrated from collection of the American Numismatic Association.

No.	Series	Signatures		Seal	Very Good	Very Fine	Unc
372.	1890	Rosecrans	Huston	Large Brown	2,000.00	4,500.00	17,500.00
373.	1890	Rosecrans	Nebeker	Large Brown	4,000.00	—	—
374.	1890	Rosecrans	Nebeker	Small Red	2,000.00	4,500.00	17,500.00

DESIGN NO. 94

(Notes 375 - 375-a)

The obverse is similar to Design No. 93.

Reverse of Design No. 94.

Note illustrated from collection of the American Numismatic Association.

No.	Series	Signatures		Seal	Very Good	Very Fine	Unc
375.	1891	Tillman	Morgan	Small Red	2,500.00	4,850.00	20,000.00
375-a.	1891	Bruce	Roberts	Small Red	Very Rare	—	—

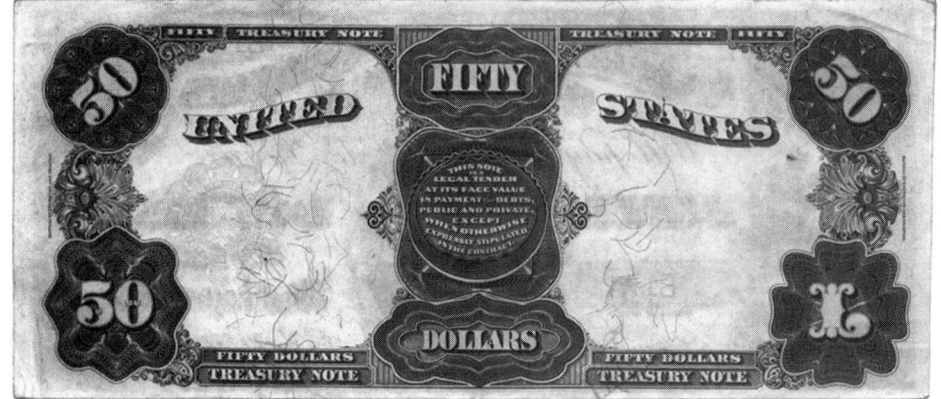

50 Dollar Note

DESIGN NO. 95

(Note 376)

Head of William H. Seward, Secretary of State from 1860-1869. He negotiated the purchase of Alaska from Russia, a transaction which at the time was called "Seward's Folly." This note is extremely rare as only 25 pieces are still reported outstanding on U.S. Treasury books.

Reverse of Design No. 95.

Note illustrated from collection of the American Numismatic Association.

No.	Series	Signatures		Seal	Very Good	Very Fine	Unc
376.	1891	Rosecrans	Nebeker	Small Red	10,000.00	30,000.00	Rare

100 Dollar Notes

DESIGN NO. 96

(Note 377)

Head of Admiral David Glasgow Farragut, 1801-1870, the first man to hold the rank of Admiral in the U.S. Navy.

Reverse of Design No. 96.

This is the famous "Watermelon" note, so called because of the shape of the large zeros.

Note illustrated from collection of the American Numismatic Association.

No.	Series	Signatures		Seal	Very Good	Very Fine	Unc
377.	1890	Rosecrans	Huston	Large Brown	10,000.00	45,000.00	Rare

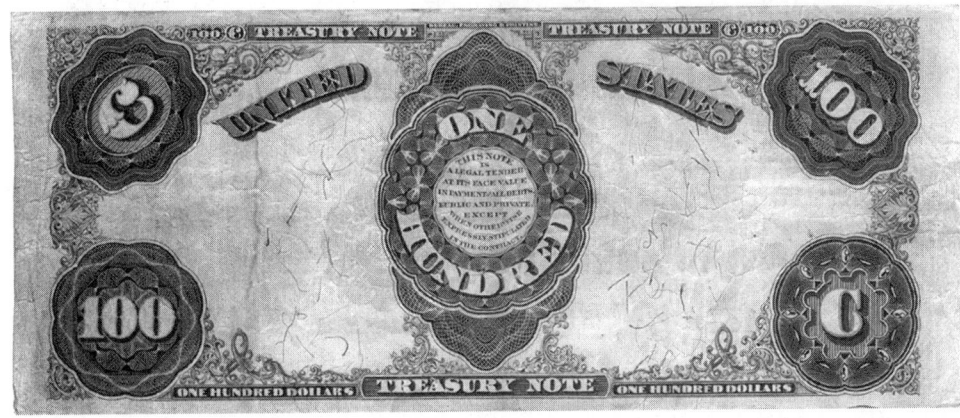

DESIGN NO. 97

(Note 378)

The obverse is similar to Design No. 96.

The reverse is as shown.

No.	Series	Signatures		Seal	Very Good	Very Fine	Unc
378.	1891	Rosecrans	Nebeker	Small Red	15,000.00	50,000.00	Rare

500 Dollar Note

DESIGN NO. 97-a

(Note 379)

Head of General William Tecumseh Sherman, famous for his march to the sea during the Civil War.

Reverse of Design No. 97-a.

The illustration is of a sample note.

Copyrighted photograph courtesy of William T. Anton, Jr. and Morey Perlmutter.

No.	Series	Signatures		
379.	1891	Bruce	Roberts	Unknown

1,000 Dollar Notes

DESIGN NO. 98

(Notes 379-a - 379-b)

Head of General George Gordon Meade, commander of the Union troops at the Battle of Gettysburg.

Reverse of Design No. 98. "The Grand Watermelon."

Only 25 notes are outstanding of this design combined with Design No. 98-a.

Note illustrated from collection of the Federal Reserve Bank of San Francisco.

No.	Series	Signatures		Seal	
379-a.	1890	Rosecrans	Huston	Large Brown	Extremely Rare
379-b.	1890	Rosecrans	Nebeker	Small Red	Two known

DESIGN NO. 98-a

(Notes 379-c - 379-d)

The obverse is similar to Design No. 98.

The reverse is as shown.

Only one specimen is known of each signature variety.

379-c.	1891	Tillman	Morgan	Small Red	Unique
379-d.	1891	Rosecrans	Nebeker	Small Red	Unique

VIII. NATIONAL BANK NOTES

National Bank Notes form the most plentiful and extensive series of American paper money. These notes were issued from 1863 to 1929 by many thousands of banks throughout the country and in our territories, in many denominations and in three Charter Periods.

Indeed, so vast is the extent of the National Bank Notes that no collector can ever hope to complete them. Instead, they are collected either by Treasury signature combination or by locality, that is by state or city of issuing banks.

Origin. National Bank Notes came into being by passage of the National Banking Act of 1863, later supplemented by the Act of June 3, 1864. By the terms of these acts, the government was enabled to grant charters to banks which were then allowed to issue their own notes, but only up to 90% of the par value of the U.S. Government bonds which the banks had previously deposited with the government as security for the notes about to be issued. Each bank had its own charter number, which appeared on all notes issued after 1875. The charter for any bank was valid for a period of twenty years. After that period, a bank could renew the charter for an additional twenty years and continue to keep issuing notes - hence the relationship between the series of 1882 and 1902. A bank's charter began on the day when the Comptroller of Currency presented the bank with its "Certificate of Authority to Commence Business."

These National Bank Notes, although issued by individual banks, are nevertheless conventional United States paper money, fully negotiable, and were produced by the Bureau of Engraving and Printing under the same conditions as regular Treasury issues.

The basic designs on the National Bank Notes are the same for all banks. The only differences are in the name of the bank, the bank charter number, the bank signatures and the coat of arms of the state in which the bank was located.

The issues of National Bank Notes took place during three periods which have been called the First, Second and Third Charter Periods.

The Date on National Bank Notes. All National Bank Notes bear a full date (for example, November 7, 1912) on the face of the note, usually near the name of the city. This date is not necessarily the Charter date of the bank, but is generally somewhat later, and rarely, and surprisingly, even earlier; neither is it the date that the note was issued. The inconsistencies encountered and the many unknown contemporary factors involved in the production of these notes, have made it impossible to determine the exact significance of this date.

The Dates of Issue. Insofar as National Bank Notes are concerned, the dates when they were actually issued are not always consistent with the dates in office of those Treasury Officials whose signatures appear on the notes. (These officials are the Treasurer of the U.S. and the Register of the Treasury). Whereas the original plates bearing their facsimile signatures were no doubt prepared during the period of their combined tenure in the Treasury Department, it was actually the practice of the Bureau of Engraving and Printing to use such plates whenever needed at a later date. As a result, these plates were quite frequently used to print notes long after the particular officials had passed out of office, and perhaps even after their death. That is why it is possible to see notes issued as late as 1922 bearing signatures that could have been originally engraved only in the 1890's. The years when all types of National Bank Notes were actually issued to the public are shown in the following pages where these various types are listed by states.

Production. Until July 1875, National Bank Notes were wholly produced in New York City by the American, Continental or National Bank Note Companies. Their imprints appear on the notes. These three companies engraved and manufactured the plates and accomplished the main printing in their own premises on their own bank note paper. The Treasury Seal and Serial numbers, however, were printed later at the Treasury Department in Washington, D.C.

After March, 1875, the same distinctive paper was required to be used as was then being used for other U.S. currency, and after September of that year, the obverses, or face sides of the notes, began to be printed at the Bureau of Engraving and Printing. The reverses, or backs however, continued to be printed privately in New York by the bank note companies, except for the black portion of the 5 Dollar Note which was let out for printing to the Columbian Bank Note Company in Washington, D.C. (The green portion continued to be printed in New York.)

In January, 1877, all the reverse plates were transferred from New York to Washington, and thereafter the Bureau printed all the reverses as well, except for the black portion of the 5 Dollar Note, which still remained with the Columbian Bank Note Company.

Finally, about October 1877, the entire production of National Bank Notes was assigned permanently to the Bureau of Engraving and Printing.

Charter Numbers. As will be seen later, all National Bank Notes beginning with the series of 1875 bore the charter number of the bank. This charter number was printed prominently either once or twice on the face of each note. Since charter numbers were issued successively in time, it is possible to determine from this number in what year a given bank was chartered. The table in the Appendix gives this information in concise form and at the same time shows how many banks were chartered in each year. In consulting this table, it should be remembered that notes issued from 1929 to 1935 were of the small size, current type.

Serial Numbers. Two serial numbers, unlike each other, appear on the face of each National Bank Note. One is the Treasury Serial Number; the other is the Bank Serial Number. The Treasury Number indicates the running total of such sheets printed on a country-wide basis for all banks; the Bank Number indicates the running total of such sheets printed for the individual Bank. After August 22, 1925, the Treasury Serial Number was discontinued, and its place was taken by a duplicate impression of the Bank Serial Number.

Check or Plate Letters. National Bank Notes were most often printed in sheets of four notes, each note bearing identical serial numbers and differing from each other only by a check or plate letter (or by the denomination of the note). From this check letter it is possible to deduce the original position of the note on the sheet. This check letter appears twice on the face of each note and is usually a script capital letter from A to D. If all four notes on the sheet were of the same denomination, the letters appeared successively as A, B, C, D. If different denominations were printed on each sheet, which was customary, the first note of each denomination began with the check letter A. Some notes of later issues that were printed in large quantities have check letters beyond D. The short table below shows how each denomination was printed on the sheet of four in its most usual combination. The numerals used refer to the denomination:

$$1-1-1-2$$
$$5-5-5-5$$
$$10-10-10-10$$
$$10-10-10-20$$
$$20-20-20-20$$
$$50-50-50-100$$
$$50-100$$

Other combinations exist but they were not as popular with the banks and in some cases sheets consisted of only two notes or of only one note. For example, the 50 and 100 Dollar brown backs of the 1882 series and of the red seal 1902 Series were printed one each on sheets of two notes. In this case, an equal number of each denomination was thus originally issued, unlike the usual combination in which the 50 Dollar note outnumbered the 100 Dollar note three to one. A more detailed listing of plate combinations may be found in "A Descriptive History of National Bank Notes" by William H. Dillistin.

Geographical Letters. In the later period of National Bank history, many thousands of notes were daily being presented to the Treasury Department for redemption. The sorting of these notes was complicated and time consuming and in order to increase sorting efficiency, a so-called geographical letter was printed on notes issued from about 1902 to 1924. These letters, which indicated the geographical region of the issuing bank, were printed in large capital type twice on the face of each note, in both cases near the charter number and in the same color ink as the charter number. The letters used and the various regions are as follows:

N	for banks in New England
E	for banks in the East
S	for banks in the South
M	for banks in the Mid-West
W	for banks in the West
P	for banks in the Pacific region

THE ALDRICH-VREELAND ACT

A knowledge of this Congressional Act is important for a fuller understanding of some of the notes issued during the Second and Third Charter Period. The Act was passed on May 30, 1908 and its provisions were to expire by statute on June 30, 1915. The purpose of the Aldrich-Vreeland Act was to create a supply of emergency money in case further panics occurred. The Panic of 1907 had shown that there was not enough currency in circulation to meet the demands of a financial emergency.

The purpose of the Act was accomplished by permitting National Banks to deposit with the Treasurer of the United States, not only United States bonds, but other securities as well, against the issue of additional circulating notes.

Until then (May 30, 1908) the security for National Bank Notes could consist only of U.S. bonds which the National Banks owned and had deposited as a pledge with the Treasurer of the U.S. in amounts up to 90% of the face value of currency actually issued by the banks. During this period, 1863-1908, all National Bank Notes bore the legend, "Secured by United States bonds deposited with the Treasurer of the United States."

After passage of the Act, the backs of the notes were changed and the security legend on the face of the notes was altered to read as follows, "Secured by United States bonds or other securities." These changes can best be seen by studying the illustrations of the notes of the Aldrich-Vreeland period, 1908-1915, as compared with notes of both earlier and later issues.

Immediately prior to May 30, 1908, two types of National Bank Notes were being issued concurrently; the Second Charter brown backs of the 1882 series and the Third Charter red seals of the 1902 series.

After May 30, 1908, those banks still under the Second Charter Period began to issue notes with the large "1882-1908" on back, replacing the brown backs, and being replaced in 1915 by the type with the denomination on back; those banks under the then existing Third Charter Period, began to issue notes with the small "1902-1908" on back and with a blue seal on face, replacing the red seals and being replaced in 1915 by notes without the "1902-1908" on back.

In accordance with the provisions of the Aldrich-Vreeland Act, National Banks were not permitted after 1915 to pledge "other securities" but once again could use only U.S. bonds to secure their currency. As noted directly above, new notes were issued to mark this legal reversion to type, and this was done so that a quick visual distinction could be made between those notes pledged with "other securities" and those pledged only with U.S. bonds.

Whereas in 1908, all face plates in use had religiously been altered by adding "other securities," the removal of this clause on notes issued after 1915 was only haphazard. Consequently, a certain volume of currency was issued from 1915 to 1929 bearing the anachronistic legend, "Secured by United States bonds or other securities." Such notes of this period are considered scarcer than those without the expression "other securities."

YEARS OF ISSUE OF CHARTER NUMBERS

As mentioned earlier, the Charter Number of the issuing bank was printed prominently on each note, beginning with the Series of 1875 (some notes of the Original Series, 1863-1875, are known with Charter Numbers). The table below shows which Charter Numbers were assigned during each calendar year from 1863 to 1935, (the note issuing period) as well as the number of banks chartered in each of these years. Thus if one knows the Charter Number of a given National Bank, a glance at the table will show in what year this bank was given its original charter. The first bank to be chartered was the First National Bank of Philadelphia, which received Charter No. 1 in June, 1863. The last bank to be chartered was the Roodhouse National Bank of Roodhouse, Illinois which received Charter No. 14,348 in December, 1935. National banks chartered after this date are not included in this list.

Charter Numbers	Assigned During Year	Number of Banks Chartered	Charter Numbers	Assigned During Year	Number of Banks Chartered	Charter Numbers	Assigned During Year	Number of Banks Chartered
1-179	1863	179	3833-3954	1888	122	10306-10472	1913	167
180-682	1864	503	3955-4190	1889	236	10473-10672	1914	200
683-1626	1865	944	4191-4494	1890	304	10673-10810	1915	138
1627-1665	1866	39	4495-4673	1891	179	10811-10932	1916	122
1666-1675	1867	10	4674-4832	1892	159	10933-11126	1917	194
1676-1688	1868	13	4833-4934	1893	102	11127-11282	1918	156
1689-1696	1869	8	4935-4983	1894	49	11283-11570	1919	288
1697-1759	1870	63	4984-5029	1895	46	11571-11903	1920	333
1760-1912	1871	153	5030-5054	1896	25	11904-12082	1921	179
1913-2073	1972	61	5055-5108	1897	54	12083-12287	1922	205
2074-2131	1973	58	5109-5165	1898	57	12288-12481	1923	194
2132-2214	1874	83	5166-5240	1899	75	12482-12615	1924	134
2215-2315	1975	101	5241-5662	1900	422	12616-12866	1925	251
2316-2344	1876	29	5663-6074	1901	412	12867-13022	1926	156
2345-2375	1877	31	6075-6566	1902	492	13023-13159	1927	137
2376-2405	1878	30	6567-7081	1903	514	13160-13269	1928	110
2406-2445	1879	40	7082-7541	1904	460	13270-13412	1929	143
2446-2498	1880	53	7542-8027	1905	486	13413-13516	1930	104
2499-2606	1881	108	8028-8489	1906	462	13517-13586	1931	70
2607-2849	1882	243	8490-8979	1907	490	13587-13654	1932	68
2850-3101	1883	252	8980-9302	1908	323	13655-13920	1933	266
3102-3281	1884	180	9303-9622	1909	320	13921-14317	1934	397
3282-3427	1885	146	9623-9913	1910	291	14318-14348	1935	31
3428-3612	1886	184	9914-10119	1911	206			
3613-3832	1887	220	10120-10305	1912	186			

(The highest Charter Number to appear on a National Bank Note is 14320, on the 10 Dollar Note of the Liberty National Bank & Trust Co. of Louisville, Ky. Chartered banks with later numbers did not issue any notes.)

The Issues of National Bank Notes By States

In the listings that follow, an attempt has been made for the first time in numismatic history to show categorically in what states or territories the various types of National Bank Notes were issued. At the same time the valuations indicate the relative rarity of a given note issued in one state as against the same note issued in another state. This valuation is based on the commonest signature variety of each type in the state of preservation indicated. These valuations are based on the relative quantities of notes known to be in existence, as brought to light by the author's research and experience. Notes issued by banks in small towns are usually scarcer than those of banks in large cities, since they probably issued fewer notes.

The term "rare" in this section indicates that the note in question was issued but that no specimen is as yet known. The term "not issued" indicates that the particular type of note was not issued by any of the banks in the state named, as is shown by the original Registers of the Treasury Department now in the National Archives.

It is the author's opinion that many notes now marked as "rare" will be discovered in time to come, and that, on the other hand, some notes will forever remain unknown.

It should be borne in mind that the Registers for the period 1913 to 1923 cannot be found, probably having been destroyed, and that therefore, the author's findings on four series of notes are partially incomplete and may be subject to some revision (1882 dates on back; 1882 value on back; 1902 dates on back; 1902 blue seal without dates on back).

A better understanding of the Territorial Issues can be gained by reviewing the years when the various note-issuing territories became states: - Arizona 1912 - Colorado 1876 - Idaho 1890 - Montana 1889 - Nebraska 1867 - New Mexico 1912 - Utah 1896 - Washington 1889 - Wyoming 1890 - Dakota Territory became the States of North and South Dakota in 1889 - Indian Territory existed from 1834 to 1907 and Oklahoma Territory from 1890 to 1907, both territories combining to form the State of Oklahoma in 1907 - Hawaii entered territorial status in 1900.

Notes of the First Charter Period

February 25, 1863 to July 11, 1882

(Notes of First Charter type were issued from 1863 to 1902)

Although the charter period was for 20 years, as prescribed by law, notes of First Charter types were actually issued for 40 years, that is until 1902.

This seeming irregularity is due to the fact that a charter was valid for 20 years from the date of a bank's organization and not for 20 years from the date of February 25, 1863. Once a bank was chartered during this period it kept issuing the same type notes for 20 years, notwithstanding that the Second Charter Period may have intervened in the meanwhile. A few examples will suffice to show how the system operated.

Charter No. 1 was given to the First National Bank of Philadelphia in June, 1863. It would have issued typical notes of the First Charter Period for 20 years or until June, 1882. If re-chartered, this bank would then in July, 1882 have begun to issue the brown back notes of the Second Charter Period.

Likewise, a bank chartered in 1873 issued First Charter notes until 1893, and if re-chartered, issued brown backs shortly thereafter.

An extreme example would be the case of any bank chartered in the year 1882 but before July 12th of that year, that is, in the last few months of the First Charter Period. Such a bank would have issued First Charter notes up to 1902. If this bank, however, were chartered in 1882 but before April 12th, its first re-charter notes in 1902 would have been brown backs; but if it had been chartered between April 12 and July 12, 1882, its first re-charter notes in 1902 would have been the red seals of the Third Charter Period, and such a bank would not have issued any notes at all of the Second Charter Period.

There were two series of notes issued under the First Charter Period, the so-called Original Series and the Series of 1875. The notes of the Original Series were issued from 1863 to 1875 and did not bear the charter number of the bank, except for some rare instances. The Series of 1875 came into being as a result of the Act of June 30, 1874, which henceforth required the charter number of the bank to be printed on all National Bank Notes.

The charter numbers were normally printed in red, but a few banks issued 5 Dollar notes with the charter number printed in black in script numerals rather than block numerals. These notes are very rare.

The serial numbers were printed in either red or blue, the records indicating that notes with blue serial numbers are somewhat scarcer.

National Bank Notes were first issued to the public on December 21, 1863, but notes are known dated in November 1863.

These notes were issued in denominations from 1 to 1,000 Dollars, there being two issues: the Original Series and the Series of 1875.

The obligation on notes of the First Charter Period is as follows, "This note is secured by bonds of the United States deposited with the U.S. Treasurer at Washington ... The (name of bank and location) will pay the bearer on demand...... Dollars ... This note is receivable at par in all parts of the United States, in payment of all taxes and excises and all other dues to the United States, except duties on imports, and also for all salaries and other debts and demands owing by the United States to individuals, corporations and associations within the United States, except interest on public debt."

Notes of this period rank among the most beautiful examples of American currency. The obverses bear vignettes pertaining to American history or tradition; the reverses, which are bicolored, show some of the famous paintings on Americana that hang in the Capitol at Washington. All notes of the First Charter Period are very rare in new condition, and when found so, they are of extraordinary beauty and appeal.

1 Dollar Notes

DESIGN NO. 99

(Notes 380-386)

The vignette, titled "Concordia," show-ing two maidens before an altar, was designed by T.A. Liebler and engraved by Charles Burt.

Reverse of Design No. 99.

"Landing of the Pilgrims" engraved by Charles Burt. Borders in green, the painting in black.

Note illustrated from collection of the American Numismatic Association.

No.	Series	Signatures		Seal	Very Good	Very Fine	Extra Fine	Unc
380.	Original	Colby	Spinner	Red with rays	150.00	350.00	600.00	1,600.00
381.	Original	Jeffries	Spinner	Red with rays	850.00	1,750.00	2,250.00	4,750.00
382.	Original	Allison	Spinner	Red with rays	150.00	350.00	600.00	1,600.00
383.	1875	Allison	New	Red with scallops	150.00	350.00	500.00	1,600.00
384.	1875	Allison	Wyman	Red with scallops	135.00	325.00	500.00	1,500.00
385.	1875	Allison	Gilfillan	Red with scallops	135.00	325.00	500.00	1,500.00
386.	1875	Scofield	Gilfillan	Red with scallops	150.00	350.00	600.00	2,000.00

These notes were issued from 1865 to 1878 in sheets of 1-1-1-2 and very rarely 1-1-2-2.

	State	No. of Banks	Fine		State	No. of Banks	Fine		State	No. of Banks	Fine
S-1.	Alabama	5	2,500.00	S-20.	Louisiana	3	900.00	S-39.	Ohio	106	300.00
S-2.	Arizona Terr.	Not issued	----	S-21.	Maine	42	375.00	S-40.	Okla. Terr. & St.	Not issued	----
S-3.	Arkansas	2	Rare	S-22.	Maryland	12	425.00	S-41.	Oregon	Not issued	----
S-4.	California	Not issued	----	S-23.	Massachusetts	177	400.00	S-42.	Pennsylvania	86	300.00
S-5.	Colorado Terr	7	2,000.00	S-24.	Michigan	55	450.00	S-43.	Rhode Island	52	300.00
S-6.	Colorado	Not issued	----	S-25.	Minnesota	28	450.00	S-44.	South Carolina	4	Rare
S-7.	Connecticut	64	300.00	S-26.	Mississippi	Not issued	----	S-45.	South Dakota	Not issued	----
S-8.	Dakota Terr.	1	Rare	S-27.	Missouri	27	350.00	S-46.	Tennessee	15	1,750.00
S-9.	Delaware	5	1,000.00	S-28.	Montana Terr.	2	Rare	S-47.	Texas	4	2,500.00
S-10.	Dist. of Columbia	5	1,250.00	S-29.	Montana State	Not issued	----	S-48.	Utah Terr.	4	2,500.00
S-11.	Florida	Not issued	----	S-30.	Nebraska Terr.	3	Rare	S-49.	Utah	Not issued	----
S-12.	Georgia	5	3,000.00	S-31.	Nebraska	10	900.00	S-50.	Vermont	34	375.00
S-13.	Idaho Terr.	1	Rare	S-32.	Nevada	Not issued	----	S-51.	Virginia	1	Rare
S-14.	Illinois	99	300.00	S-33.	New Hampshire	33	375.00	S-52.	Washington Terr.	Not issued	----
S-15.	Indian Terr.	Not issued	----	S-34.	New Jersey	41	325.00	S-53.	Washington	Not issued	----
S-16.	Indiana	66	300.00	S-35.	New Mexico Terr.	2	Rare	S-54.	West Virginia	5	750.00
S-17.	Iowa	55	425.00	S-36.	New York	228	300.00	S-55.	Wisconsin	30	325.00
S-18.	Kansas	22	425.00	S-37.	North Carolina	6	1,250.00	S-56.	Wyoming Terr.	1	Rare
S-19.	Kentucky	32	400.00	S-38.	North Dakota	Not issued	----	S-57.	Wyoming	Not issued	----

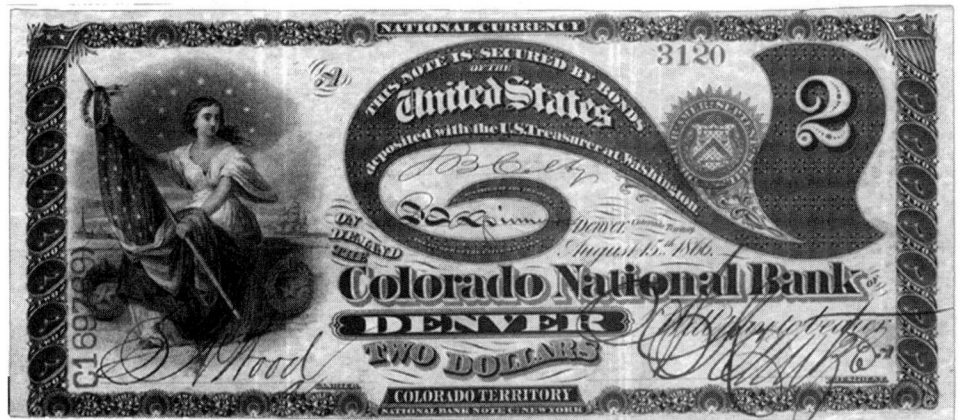

2 Dollar Notes

DESIGN NO. 100

(Notes 387-393)

Woman holding flag.
This is the well known "Lazy 2" note, so called because of the extreme horizontal shape of the 2.

Reverse of Design No. 100.

Sir Walter Raleigh in England, 1585, exhibiting corn and smoking tobacco from America. Borders in green, the painting in black.

Note illustrated from collection of the American Numismatic Association.

No.	Series	Signatures		Seal	Very Good	Very Fine	Extra Fine	Unc
387.	Original	Colby	Spinner	Red with rays	600.00	1,400.00	1,900.00	4,200.00
388.	Original	Jeffries	Spinner	Red with rays	1,600.00	2,700.00	3,300.00	8,000.00
389.	Original	Allison	Spinner	Red with rays	600.00	1,400.00	2,000.00	4,200.00
390.	1875	Allison	New	Red with scallops	550.00	1,300.00	1,900.00	4,000.00
391.	1875	Allison	Wyman	Red with scallops	550.00	1,300.00	1,900.00	4,000.00
392.	1875	Allison	Gilfillan	Red with scallops	650.00	1,300.00	1,900.00	4,000.00
393.	1875	Scofield	Gilfillan	Red with scallops	600.00	1,400.00	2,000.00	4,750.00

These notes were issued from 1865 to 1878 in sheets of 1-1-1-2 and very rarely 1-1-2-2.

	State	No. of Banks	Fine
S-58.	Alabama	5	Rare
S-59.	Arizona Terr.	Not issued	- - - -
S-60.	Arkansas	2	Rare
S-61.	California	Not issued	- - - -
S-62.	Colorado Terr.	7	Rare
S-63.	Colorado	Not issued	- - - -
S-64.	Connecticut	64	850.00
S-65.	Dakota Terr.	1	Rare
S-66.	Delaware	51	850.00
S-67.	Dist. of Columbia	5	4,000.00
S-68.	Florida	Not issued	- - - -
S-69.	Georgia	5	Rare
S-70.	Idaho Terr.	1	Rare
S-71.	Illinois	99	850.00
S-72.	Indian Terr.	Not issued	- - - -
S-73.	Indiana	66	850.00
S-74.	Iowa	56	1,000.00
S-75.	Kansas	22	850.00
S-76.	Kentucky	35	900.00
S-77.	Louisiana	3	Rare
S-78.	Maine	42	1,200.00
S-79.	Maryland	12	1,000.00
S-80.	Massachusetts	177	850.00
S-81.	Michigan	55	900.00
S-82.	Minnesota	28	1,500.00
S-83.	Mississippi	Not issued	- - - -
S-84.	Missouri	27	900.00
S-85.	Montana Terr.	2	Rare
S-86.	Montana State	Not issued	- - - -
S-87.	Nebraska Terr	3	rare
S-88.	Nebraska	10	Rare
S-89.	Nevada	Not issued	- - - -
S-90.	New Hampshire	33	850.00
S-91.	New Jersey	41	950.00
S-92.	New Mexico Terr.	2	Rare
S-93.	New York	228	850.00
S-94.	North Carolina	6	1,750.00
S-95.	North Dakota	Not issued	- - - -
S-96.	Ohio	106	850.00
S-97.	Okla. Terr. & St.	Not issued	- - - -
S-98.	Oregon	Not issued	- - - -
S-99.	Pennsylvania	86	850.00
S-100.	Rhode Island	52	850.00
S-101.	South Carolina	4	Rare
S-102.	South Dakota	Not issued	- - - -
S-103.	Tennessee	15	3,500.00
S-104.	Texas	4	Rare
S-105.	Utah Terr.	4	Rare
S-106.	Utah	Not issued	- - - -
S-107.	Vermont	34	1,000.00
S-108.	Virginia	1	Rare
S-109.	Washington Terr.	Not issued	- - - -
S-110.	Washington	Not issued	- - - -
S-111.	West Virginia	5	Rare
S-112.	Wisconsin	30	900.00
S-113.	Wyoming Terr.	1	Rare
S-114.	Wyoming	Not issued	- - - -

5 Dollar Notes

DESIGN NO. 101

(Notes 394-408-a)

At the left, Christopher Columbus in sight of land. At the right, presentation of an Indian Princess, representing America, to the Old World. Designed by Charles Fenton and engraved by Charles Burt.

Reverse of Design No. 101.

The Landing of Columbus, from a painting by John Vanderlyn. Borders in green, the painting in black.

Note illustrated from collection of the American Numismatic Association.

No.	Series	Signatures		Seal	Very Good	Very Fine	Extra Fine	Unc
394.	Original	Chittenden	Spinner	Red with rays	200.00	475.00	575.00	1,500.00
397.	Original	Colby	Spinner	Red with rays	200.00	475.00	575.00	1,500.00
398.	Original	Jeffries	Spinner	Red with rays	1,000.00	2,000.00	3,000.00	7,000.00
399.	Original	Allison	Spinner	Red with rays	185.00	475.00	550.00	1,400.00
401.	1875	Allison	New	Red with scallops	175.00	450.00	550.00	1,200.00
402.	1875	Allison	Wyman	Red with scallops	175.00	450.00	550.00	1,200.00
403.	1875	Allison	Gilfillan	Red with scallops	175.00	450.00	550.00	1,200.00
404.	1875	Scofield	Gilfillan	Red with scallops	200.00	475.00	575.00	1,250.00
405.	1875	Bruce	Gilfillan	Red with scallops	225.00	500.00	650.00	1,500.00
406.	1875	Bruce	Wyman	Red with scallops	250.00	550.00	750.00	1,700.00
406a.	1875	Bruce	Jordan	Red with scallops	Rare	—	—	—
407.	1875	Rosecrans	Huston	Red with scallops	275.00	600.00	850.00	1,750.00
408.	1875	Rosecrans	Jordan	Red with scallops	250.00	550.00	750.00	1,700.00
408-a.	1875	Rosecrans	Nebeker	Red with scallops	Unique	—	—	—

These notes were issued from 1863 to 1902 in sheets of 5-5-5-5.

	State	No. of Banks	Fine		State	No. of Banks	Fine		State	No. of Banks	Fine
S-115.	Alabama	11	525.00	S-134.	Louisiana	10	500.00	S-153.	Ohio	209	225.00
S-116.	Arizona Terr.	1	Rare	S-135.	Maine	72	300.00	S-154.	Okla. Terr. & St.	Not Issued	- - - -
S-117.	Arkansas	3	7,500.00	S-136.	Maryland	38	275.00	S-155.	Oregon	1	3,000.00
S-118.	California	2	7,500.00	S-137.	Massachusetts	257	225.00	S-156.	Pennsylvania	254	225.00
S-119.	Colorado Terr.	12	1,500.00	S-138.	Michigan	87	275.00	S-157.	Rhode Island	62	250.00
S-120.	Colorado	12	1,000.00	S-139.	Minnesota	41	500.00	S-158.	South Carolina	12	2,500.00
S-121.	Connecticut	89	225.00	S-140.	Mississippi	2	Rare	S-159.	South Dakota	2	Rare
S-122.	Dakota Terr.	12	2,700.00	S-141.	Missouri	44	450.00	S-160.	Tennessee	43	1,000.00
S-123.	Delaware	14	675.00	S-142.	Montana Terr.	9	2,500.00	S-161.	Texas	15	2,750.00
S-124.	Dist. of Columbia	9	1,750.00	S-143.	Montana State	1	2,750.00	S-162.	Utah Terr.	9	2,750.00
S-125.	Florida	1	5,000.00	S-144.	Nebraska Terr.	3	Rare	S-163.	Utah	Not Issued	- - - -
S-126.	Georgia	15	2,500.00	S-145.	Nebraska	14	550.00	S-164.	Vermont	50	450.00
S-127.	Idaho Terr.	1	Rare	S-146.	Nevada	1	Rare	S-165.	Virginia	29	1,000.00
S-128.	Illinois	161	225.00	S-147.	New Hampshire	49	350.00	S-166.	Washington Terr.	2	Rare
S-129.	Indian Terr.	Not Issued	- - - -	S-148.	New Jersey	70	275.00	S-167.	Washington State	1	4,000.00
S-130.	Indiana	117	225.00	S-149.	New Mexico Terr	4	2,250.00	S-168.	West Virginia	21	350.00
S-131.	Iowa	95	225.00	S-150.	New York	365	225.00	S-169.	Wisconsin	59	350.00
S-132.	Kansas	31	300.00	S-151.	North Carolina	12	650.00	S-170.	Wyoming Terr.	3	4,000.00
S-133.	Kentucky	52	300.00	S-152.	North Dakota	2	Rare	S-171.	Wyoming	3	2,500.00

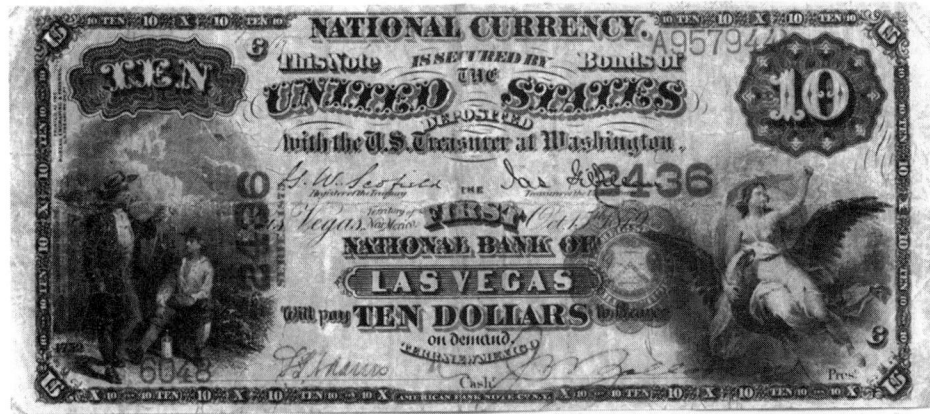

10 Dollar Notes

DESIGN NO. 102

(Notes 409-423-a)

At the left, Benjamin Franklin drawing electricity from the sky with a kite and a key. At right, Liberty soaring on an eagle, clutching lightning in her hand.

Reverse of Design No. 102.

DeSoto discovering the Mississippi in 1541, a painting by W.H. Powell, engraved by Frederick Girsch. Borders in green, the painting in black.

Note illustrated from collection of the American Numismatic Association.

No.	Series	Signatures		Seal	Very Good	Very Fine	Extra Fine	Unc
409.	Original	Chittenden	Spinner	Red with rays	325.00	775.00	1,250.00	3,000.00
412.	Original	Colby	Spinner	Red with rays	300.00	725.00	1,150.00	2,750.00
413.	Original	Jeffries	Spinner	Red with rays	750.00	1,800.00	3,250.00	8,000.00
414.	Original	Allison	Spinner	Red with rays	300.00	725.00	1,000.00	2,750.00
416.	1875	Allison	New	Red with scallops	275.00	675.00	1,150.00	2,250.00
417.	1875	Allison	Wyman	Red with scallops	275.00	675.00	1,150.00	2,250.00
418.	1875	Allison	Gilfillan	Red with scallops	275.00	675.00	1.150.00	2,250.00
419.	1875	Scofield	Gilfillan	Red with scallops	300.00	725.00	1,350.00	3,000.00
420.	1875	Bruce	Gilfillan	Red with scallops	300.00	725.00	1,350.00	3,000.00
421.	1875	Bruce	Wyman	Red with scallops	300.00	725.00	1,350.00	3,000.00
422.	1875	Rosecrans	Huston	Red with scallops	450.00	825.00	1,500.00	3,250.00
423.	1875	Rosecrans	Nebeker	Red with scallops	475.00	875.00	1,500.00	3,500.00
423-a.	1875	Tillman	Morgan	Red with scallops	Unknown	—	—	—

These notes were issued from 1863 to 1902 in sheets of 10-10-10-20 and 10-10-10-10 and rarely in other combinations.

	State	No. of Banks	Fine		State	No. of Banks	Fine		State	No. of Banks	Fine
S-172.	Alabama	7	3,000.00	S-191.	Louisiana	11	1,000.00	S-210.	Ohio	180	450.00
S-173.	Arizona Terr.	Not Issued	- - - -	S-192.	Maine	75	700.00	S-211.	Okla. Terr. & St.	Not Issued	- - - -
S-174.	Arkansas	2	Rare	S-193.	Maryland	41	500.00	S-212.	Oregon	2	2,750.00
S-175.	California	4	6,000.00	S-194.	Massachusetts	238	450.00	S-213.	Pennsylvania	250	450.00
S-176.	Colorado Terr.	5	1,850.00	S-195.	Michigan	63	500.00	S-214.	Rhode Island	62	600.00
S-177.	Colorado	8	1,350.00	S-196.	Minnesota	25	700.00	S-215.	South Carolina	1	4,500.00
S-178.	Connecticut	90	500.00	S-197.	Mississippi	2	Rare	S-216.	South Dakota	2	4,000.00
S-179.	Dakota Terr.	7	2,850.00	S-198.	Missouri	31	700.00	S-217.	Tennessee	45	1,750.00
S-180.	Delaware	13	700.00	S-199.	Montana Terr.	6	2,200.00	S-218.	Texas	20	2,750.00
S-181.	Dist. of Columbia	11	1,750.00	S-200.	Montana State	5	1,850.00	S-219.	Utah Terr.	5	2,350.00
S-182.	Florida	1	Rare	S-201.	Nebraska Terr.	3	Rare	S-220.	Utah State	2	4,500.00
S-183.	Georgia	15	2,500.00	S-202.	Nebraska	11	750.00	S-221.	Vermont	49	600.00
S-184.	Idaho Terr.	1	Rare	S-203.	Nevada	1	Rare	S-222.	Virginia	31	1,100.00
S-185.	Illinois	129	450.00	S-204.	New Hampshire	48	500.00	S-223.	Washington Terr.	Not Issued	- - - -
S-186.	Indian Terr.	Not Issued	- - - -	S-205.	New Jersey	68	450.00	S-224.	Washington State	Not Issued	- - - -
S-187.	Indiana	94	450.00	S-206.	New Mexico Terr.	6	2,450.00	S-225.	West Virginia	21	500.00
S-188.	Iowa	69	500.00	S-207.	New York	327	450.00	S-226.	Wisconsin	27	800.00
S-189.	Kansas	16	700.00	S-208.	North Carolina	12	900.00	S-227.	Wyoming Terr.	3	4,250.00
S-190.	Kentucky	50	400.00	S-209.	North Dakota	7	1,700.00	S-228.	Wyoming	3	3,250.00

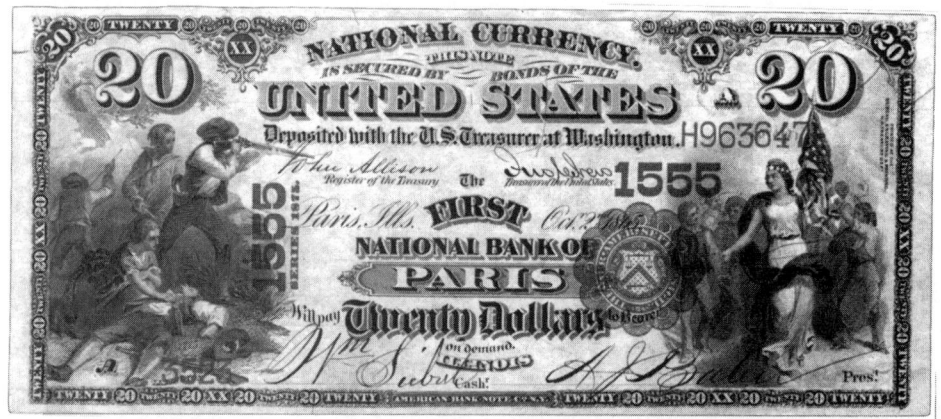

20 Dollar Notes

DESIGN NO. 103

(Notes 424-439)

At the left, the Battle of Lexington, April 19, 1775. At the right Columbia leading procession.

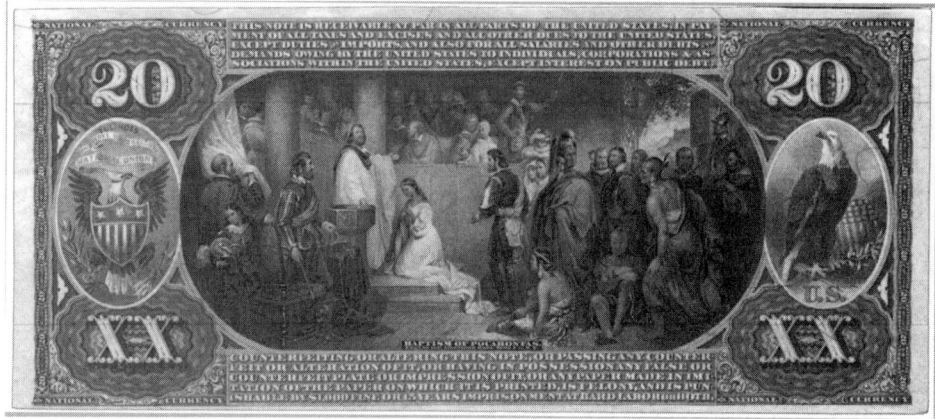

Reverse of Design No. 103.

The Baptism of Pocahontas, painted by John G. Chapman. Borders in green, the painting in black.

Note illustrated from collection of the American Numismatic Association.

No.	Series	Signatures		Seal	Very Good	Very Fine	Ex. Fine	Unc
424.	Original	Chittenden	Spinner	Red with rays	650.00	1,350.00	2,000.00	5,000.00
427.	Original	Colby	Spinner	Red with rays	625.00	1,300.00	1,800.00	4,750.00
428.	Original	Jeffries	Spinner	Red with rays	1,950.00	3,500.00	6,000.00	12,000.00
429.	Original	Allison	Spinner	Red with rays	625.00	1,300.00	1,750.00	4,750.00
431.	1875	Allison	New	Red with scallops	600.00	1,250.00	1,750.00	4,500.00
432.	1875	Allison	Wyman	Red with scallops	600.00	1,250.00	1,750.00	4,500.00
433.	1875	Allison	Gilfillan	Red with scallops	600.00	1,200.00	1,750.00	4,500.00
434.	1875	Scofield	Gilfillan	Red with scallops	600.00	1,200.00	1,750.00	4,500.00
435.	1875	Bruce	Gilfillan	Red with scallops	625.00	1,300.00	1,800.00	4,600.00
436.	1875	Bruce	Wyman	Red with scallops	650.00	1,350.00	2,000.00	5,000.00
437.	1875	Rosecrans	Huston	Red with scallops	600.00	1,400.00	2,100.00	5,000.00
438.	1875	Rosecrans	Nebeker	Red with scallops	600.00	1,450.00	2,250.00	7,000.00
439.	1875	Tillman	Morgan	Red with scallops	600.00	1,450.00	2,250.00	7,000.00

These notes were issued from 1863 to 1902 in sheets of 10-10-10-20 and rarely 10-10-20-20 and 20-20-20-20 as well as a few other rare combinations.

	State	No. of Banks	Fine		State	No. of Banks	Fine		State	No. of Banks	Fine
S-229.	Alabama	7	Rare	S-248.	Louisiana	11	1,350.00	S-267.	Ohio	156	800.00
S-230.	Arizona Terr.	Not Issued	- - - -	S-249.	Maine	73	850.00	S-268.	Okla. Terr. & St.	Not Issued	- - - -
S-231.	Arkansas	2	Rare	S-250.	Maryland	41	800.00	S-269.	Oregon	2	4,500.00
S-232.	California	4	7,500.00	S-251.	Massachusetts	236	800.00	S-270.	Pennsylvania	241	750.00
S-233.	Colorado Terr.	4	2,350.00	S-252.	Michigan	59	850.00	S-271.	Rhode Island	60	750.00
S-234.	Colorado	6	1,850.00	S-253.	Minnesota	23	1,350.00	S-272.	South Carolina	10	Rare
S-235.	Connecticut	87	800.00	S-254.	Mississippi	2	Rare	S-273.	South Dakota	1	Rare
S-236.	Dakota Terr.	7	3,350.00	S-255.	Missouri	29	1,100.00	S-274.	Tennessee	46	2,500.00
S-237.	Delaware	13	1,350.00	S-256.	Montana Terr.	6	2,350.00	S-275.	Texas	20	3,500.00
S-238.	Dist. of Columbia	11	2,750.00	S-257.	Montana State	5	1,850.00	S-276.	Utah Terr.	6	2,600.00
S-239.	Florida	Not Issued	- - - -	S-258.	Nebraska Terr.	3	Rare	S-277.	Utah State	2	2,850.00
S-240.	Georgia	14	4,000.00	S-259.	Nebraska	11	1,100.00	S-278.	Vermont	46	950.00
S-241.	Idaho Terr.	1	Rare	S-260.	Nevada	2	Rare	S-279.	Virginia	29	1,600.00
S-242.	Illinois	122	800.00	S-261.	New Hampshire	47	850.00	S-280.	Washington Terr.	Not Issued	- - - -
S-243.	Indian Terr.	Not Issued	- - - -	S-262.	New Jersey	65	800.00	S-281.	Washington	Not Issued	- - - -
S-244.	Indiana	86	800.00	S-263.	New Mexico Terr.	5	3,300.00	S-282.	West Virginia	21	850.00
S-245.	Iowa	68	1,050.00	S-264.	New York	296	800.00	S-283.	Wisconsin	26	1,050.00
S-246.	Kansas	13	1,050.00	S-265.	North Carolina	13	1,350.00	S-284.	Wyoming Terr.	3	4,700.00
S-247.	Kentucky	51	850.00	S-266.	North Dakota	7	2,100.00	S-285.	Wyoming State	3	3,600.00

50 Dollar Notes

DESIGN NO. 104

(Notes 440-451)

At the left, Washington crossing the Delaware. At the right, Washington at prayer.

Reverse of Design No. 104.

"Embarkation of the Pilgrims," from a mural by Robert W. Weir. Borders in green, the painting in black.

Note illustrated from collection of the American Numismatic Association.

No.	Series	Signatures		Seal	Very Good	Very Fine
440.	Original	Chittenden	Spinner	Red with rays	4,500.00	10,000.00
442.	Original	Colby	Spinner	Red with rays	4,500.00	10,000.00
443.	Original	Allison	Spinner	Red with rays	4,500.00	10,000.00
444.	1875	Allison	New	Red with scallops	4,500.00	10,000.00
444a.	1875	Allison	Wyman	Red with scallops	Rare	—
445.	1875	Allison	Gilfillan	Red with scallops	4,500.00	10,000.00
446.	1875	Scofield	Gilfillan	Red with scallops	4,500.00	10,000.00
447.	1875	Bruce	Gilfillan	Red with scallops	4,500.00	10,000.00
448.	1875	Bruce	Wyman	Red with scallops	4,500.00	10,000.00
449.	1875	Rosecrans	Huston	Red with scallops	4,500.00	10,000.00
450.	1875	Rosecrans	Nebeker	Red with scallops	4,560.00	10,000.00
451.	1875	Tillman	Morgan	Red with scallops	4,500.00	10,000.00

These notes were issued from 1863 to 1901 in sheets of 50-50-50-100 and rarely 50-100 and 100-100
as well as a few other rare combinations.

State	No. of Banks	Fine	State	No. of Banks	Fine	State	No. of Banks	Fine
S-286. Alabama	4	Rare	S-305. Louisiana	9	3,500.00	S-324. Ohio	32	3,250.00
S-287. Arizona Terr.	Not Issued	- - - -	S-306. Maine	27	3,500.00	S-325. Okla. Terr. & St.	Not Issued	- - - -
S-288. Arkansas	Not Issued	- - - -	S-307. Maryland	21	5,000.00	S-326. Oregon	Not Issued	- - - -
S-289. California	1	Rare	S-308. Massachusetts	191	3,250.00	S-327. Pennsylvania	97	3,250.00
S-290. Colorado Terr.	2	Rare	S-309. Michigan	7	4,000.00	S-328. Rhode Island	41	3,300.00
S-291. Colorado State	1	Rare	S-310. Minnesota	5	9,000.00	S-329. South Carolina	4	Rare
S-292. Connecticut	51	3,350.00	S-311. Mississippi	1	Rare	S-330. South Dakota	Not Issued	- - - -
S-293. Dakota Terr.	Not Issued	- - - -	S-312. Missouri	7	Rare	S-331. Tennessee	12	9,000.00
S-294. Delaware	4	3,500.00	S-313. Montana Terr.	1	Rare	S-332. Texas	6	Rare
S-295. Dist. of Columbia	5	6,000.00	S-314. Montana State	Not Issued	- - - -	S-333. Utah Terr.	6	9,000.00
S-296. Florida	Not Issued	- - - -	S-315. Nebraska Terr.	Unknown	- - - -	S-334. Utah State	Not Issued	- - - -
S-297. Georgia	7	Rare	S-316. Nebraska	2	Rare	S-335. Vermont	16	4,000.00
S-298. Idaho Terr.	Not Issued	- - - -	S-317. Nevada	Not Issued	- - - -	S-336. Virginia	11	Rare
S-299. Illinois	19	3,300.00	S-318. New Hampshire	22	3,500.00	S-337. Washington Terr.	Not Issued	- - - -
S-300. Indian Terr.	Not Issued	- - - -	S-319. New Jersey	26	3,300.00	S-338. Washington State	Not Issued	- - - -
S-301. Indiana	16	3,750.00	S-320. New Mexico Terr. 2	Rare		S-339. West Virginia	Not Issued	- - - -
S-302. Iowa	9	3,750.00	S-321. New York	126	3,250.00	S-340. Wisconsin	1	Rare
S-303. Kansas	1	Rare	S-322. North Carolina	1	Rare	S-341. Wyoming Terr.	Not Issued	- - - -
S-304. Kentucky	24	3,500.00	S-323. North Dakota	Not Issued	- - - -	S-342. Wyoming	Not Issued	- - - -

100 Dollar Notes

DESIGN NO. 105

(Notes 452-463)

At the left, Commodore Oliver H. Perry leaving the Lawrence, his flagship, during the battle of Lake Erie, September 10, 1813. At the right, Liberty seated by fasces.

Reverse of Design No. 105.

Thomas Jefferson presenting the Declaration of Independence to John Hancock at the Continental Congress. From a painting by John Trumbull. Borders in green, the painting in black.

Note illustrated from collection of the American Numismatic Association.

No.	Series	Signatures		Seal	Very Good	Very Fine
452.	Original	Chittenden	Spinner	Red with rays	6,000.00	15,000.00
454.	Original	Colby	Spinner	Red with rays	6,000.00	15,000.00
455.	Original	Allison	Spinner	Red with rays	6,000.00	15,000.00
456.	1875	Allison	New	Red with scallops	6,000.00	15,000.00
457.	1875	Allison	Wyman	Red with scallops	6,000.00	15,000.00
458.	1875	Allison	Gilfillan	Red with scallops	6,000.00	15,000.00
459.	1875	Scofield	Gilfillan	Red with scallops	6,000.00	15,000.00
460.	1875	Bruce	Gilfillan	Red with scallops	6,000.00	15,000.00
461.	1875	Bruce	Wyman	Red with scallops	6,000.00	15,000.00
462.	1875	Rosecrans	Huston	Red with scallops	6,000.00	15,000.00
462-a.	1875	Rosecrans	Nebeker	Red with scallops	Rare	—
463.	1875	Tillman	Morgan	Red with scallops	Rare	—

These notes were issued from 1863 to 1901 in sheets of 50-50-50-100 and rarely 50-100 and 100-100 as well as a few other rare combinations.

	State	No. of Banks	Fine		State	No. of Banks	Fine		State	No. of Banks	Fine
S-343.	Alabama	4	9,000.00	S-362.	Louisiana	9	15,000.00	S-381.	Ohio	23	4,000.00
S-344.	Arizona Terr.	Not Issued	- - - -	S-363.	Maine	24	Rare	S-382.	Okla. Terr. & St.	Not Issued	- - - -
S-345.	Arkansas	1	Rare	S-364.	Maryland	19	5,000.00	S-383.	Oregon	Not Issued	- - - -
S-346.	California	1	Rare	S-365.	Massachusetts	171	4,000.00	S-384.	Pennsylvania	87	4,000.00
S-347.	Colorado Terr.	1	Rare	S-366.	Michigan	6	Rare	S-385.	Rhode Island	40	5,000.00
S-348.	Colorado	1	Rare	S-367.	Minnesota	6	Rare	S-386.	South Carolina	3	Rare
S-349.	Connecticut	42	4,100.00	S-368.	Mississippi	1	Rare	S-387.	South Dakota	Not Issued	- - - -
S-350.	Dakota Terr.	Not Issued	- - - -	S-369.	Missouri	5	rare	S-388.	Tennessee	9	Rare
S-351.	Delaware	4	Rare	S-370.	Montana Terr.	1	Rare	S-389.	Texas	4	Rare
S-352.	Dist. of Columbia	5	Rare	S-371.	Montana State	Not Issued	- - - -	S-390.	Utah Terr.	5	Rare
S-353.	Florida	Not Issued	- - - -	S-372.	Nebraska Terr.	Unknown	- - - -	S-391.	Utah State	Not Issued	- - - -
S-354.	Georgia	7	Rare	S-373.	Nebraska	2	Rare	S-392.	Vermont	14	Rare
S-355.	Idaho Terr.	Not Issued	- - - -	S-374.	Nevada	Not Issued	- - - -	S-393.	Virginia	8	Rare
S-356.	Illinois	13	4,000.00	S-375.	New Hampshire	21	Rare	S-394.	Washington Terr.	Not Issued	- - - -
S-357.	Indian Terr.	Not Issued	- - - -	S-376.	New Jersey	25	Rare	S-395.	Washington	Not Issued	- - - -
S-358.	Indiana	15	4,500.00	S-377.	New Mexico Terr.	Not Issued	- - - -	S-396.	West Virginia	Not Issued	- - - -
S-359.	Iowa	9	Rare	S-378.	New York	106	4,000.00	S-397.	Wisconsin	2	Rare
S-360.	Kansas	1	Rare	S-379.	North Carolina	1	6,000.00	S-398.	Wyoming Terr.	Not Issued	- - - -
S-361.	Kentucky	21	5,000.00	S-380.	North Dakota	Not Issued	- - - -	S-399.	Wyoming State	Not Issued	- - - -

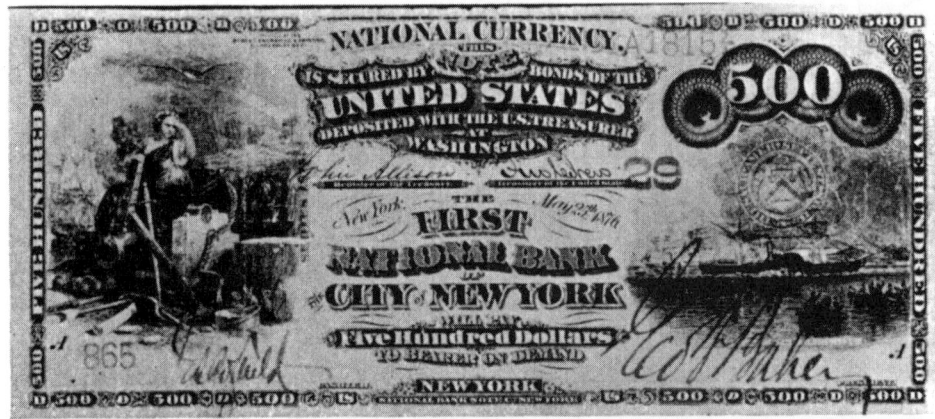

500 Dollar Notes

DESIGN NO. 106

(Notes 464-464-a)

At the left, an allegory representing The Spirit of the Navy. At the right the steamship Sirius arriving in New York harbor in 1838.

Reverse of Design No. 106

The surrender of General John Burgoyne to General Horatio Gates at Saratoga on October 17, 1777. Engraved by Frederick Girsch, from a painting by John Trumbull. Borders in green, the painting in black. The note illustrated is the only specimen known to exist in a collection.

No.	Series	Signatures		Seal	
464.	Original	Colby	Spinner	Red with rays	Extremely Rare
464-a.	1875	Allison	New	Red with scallops	Extremely Rare
	(173 pieces are still outstanding.)				

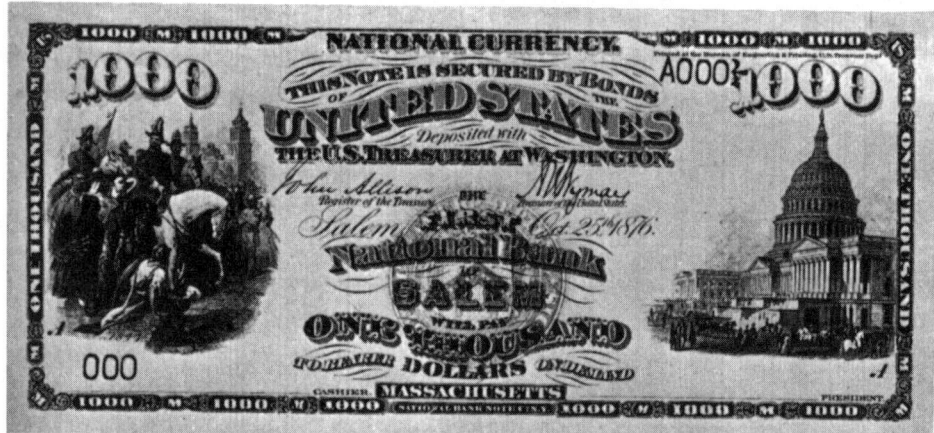

1,000 Dollar Notes

DESIGN NO. 107

(Note 465)

At the left, General Winfield Scott entering Mexico City in 1847 during the Mexican-American War, from a painting by John Trumbull. At the right, the United States Capitol.

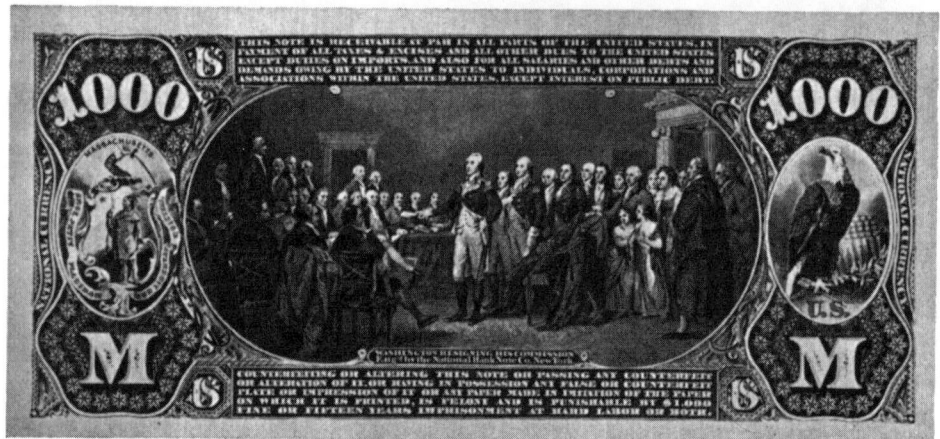

Reverse of Design No. 107

Washington resigning his Commission, from a painting by John Trumbull. Borders in green, the painting in black.

465.   1,000 Dollar National Bank Note. (Unknown, although 21 pieces are still outstanding.)

(The illustration is of a sample note and was furnished by courtesy of the Bureau of Engraving and Printing.)

Notes of the Second Charter Period

July 12, 1882 to April 11, 1902

(Notes of Second Charter types were issued from 1882 to 1922.)

The Congressional Act of July 12, 1882 created the Second Charter Period, the notes of which bear the designation, "Series of 1882." The purpose of the Act was to make it possible for the banks chartered in 1863 and later to renew their charters at the end of their 20 year term, and also to enable newly organized banks to acquire an initial charter. New notes were designed to mark the transition and in all, three types of notes were issued during this period. As was typical of the First Charter Period, and for the same reasons, notes belonging to the Second Charter Period were issued for about 40 years or until 1922. The three types of notes are as follows:

Brown Backs. These were first placed in circulation in 1882 by two classes of banks; by old banks originally chartered in 1863 and then re-chartered in 1882, and by new banks organized and chartered between July 12, 1882 and April 11, 1902. Brown backs were issued from 1882 to 1908, and would no doubt have continued until 1922 had it not been for passage of the Aldrich-Vreeland Act (described on page 76) which resulted in the issuance of the second type. From 1902 to 1908 the brown backs, Series of 1882, were being issued concurrently with the red seals of the Third Charter Period, Series of 1902. The obligation on the notes of these two series is the same as on the First Charter Notes.

Dates on Back. All denominations of this type bear a large "1882-1908" in the central panel on the back which is green. Notes of this type are referred to as "Emergency Money" as they were issued under the provisions of the Aldrich-Vreeland Act. These notes were placed in circulation from June, 1908 to July, 1916, but quite inexplicably, 50 and 100 Dollar notes kept being issued until 1922. The notes of this second type were issued only by those banks that had been issuing brown backs and whose charters were still in force. As a bank's charter expired during this period (1908-1916) it would be re-chartered and would then issue notes of the Third Charter Period,

Series of 1902 with "1902-1908" on back. Understandably, the number of such banks kept decreasing during this nine year period and the notes of this type are today quite scarce. When the Aldrich-Vreeland Act expired in 1915, the third type was issued.

Denomination on Back. All notes of this type bear the denomination of the note, spelled out in large letters in the same panel on the green back formerly occupied by "1882-1908." These notes were placed in circulation from 1916 to 1922 and were issued only by those banks that had been issuing the type with "1882-1908" on back, and whose charters were still in force. By this time (1916 to 1922) the number of such banks had dwindled considerably as charters kept expiring in the ensuing seven years, and the notes of this type were issued by fewer banks and over fewer years than any other types of National Bank Notes before or since. As a class, they are thus the rarest of all National Bank Notes. The 50 and 100 Dollar Notes of this type were issued only over a three year period in a ratio of three 50's to each 100 and at present only about two or three specimens of each note have been discovered. Unfortunately, the least is known about this most interesting series, since the Treasury registers pertaining to the issue and distribution of these notes cannot seem to be found.

As previously stated, the latter two types of green back notes, Dates on Back and Denomination on Back, were in the nature of emergency money. When the decision was made to increase the circulation of National Bank Notes, many of the banks did not own the required amounts of United States Bonds necessary to accomplish this. Therefore, Congress passed a bill enabling the banks to deposit with the Treasurer other types of securities. This addition is so stated on the notes; otherwise the obligation is the same as on previous issues.

First Issue. Series of 1882 with Brown Seal and Brown Back.

5 Dollar Notes

DESIGN NO. 108

(Notes 466-478)

Head of President James Garfield, assassinated seven months after he was elected to the Presidency in 1881.

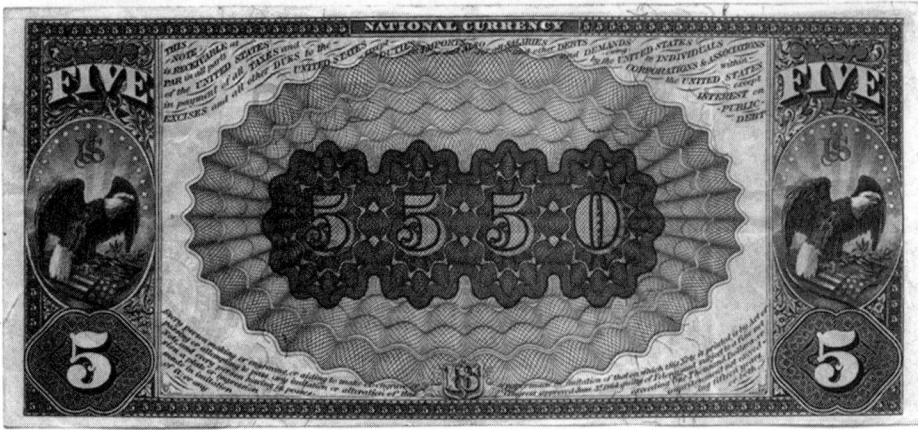

Reverse of Design No. 108.

The charter numbers and surrounding ornament are green, the rest of the reverse is brown. This brown back also appears on Design Nos. 109-112.

Note illustrated from collection of the American Numismatic Association..

No.	Signatures		Very Good	Very Fine	Unc	No.	Signatures		Very Good	Very Fine	Unc
466.	Bruce	Gilfillan	120.00	260.00	800.00	473.	Rosecrans	Morgan	200.00	450.00	1,250.00
467.	Bruce	Wyman	120.00	260.00	800.00	474.	Tillman	Morgan	120.00	260.00	800.00
468.	Bruce	Jordan	130.00	275.00	1,200.00	475.	Tillman	Roberts	120.00	285.00	900.00
469.	Rosecrans	Jordan	120.00	260.00	800.00	476.	Bruce	Roberts	120.00	260.00	800.00
470.	Rosecrans	Hyatt	120.00	260.00	800.00	477.	Lyons	Roberts	120.00	260.00	800.00
471.	Rosecrans	Huston	120.00	260.00	800.00	477-a.	Lyons	Treat	Unknown	—	—
472.	Rosecrans	Nebeker	120.00	260.00	800.00	478.	Vernon	Treat	175.00	300.00	1,200.00

These notes were issued from 1882 to 1909 in sheets of 5-5-5-5.

	State	No. of Banks	Fine		State	No. of Banks	Fine		State	No. of Banks	Fine
S-400.	Alabama	16	400.00	S-420.	Louisiana	18	200.00	S-440.	Oklahoma	13	550.00
S-401.	Arizona Terr.	2	Rare	S-421.	Maine	48	200.00	S-441.	Oregon	11	925.00
S-402.	Arkansas	6	1,750.00	S-422.	Maryland	43	175.00	S-442.	Pennsylvania	274	150.00
S-403.	California	28	200.00	S-423.	Massachusetts	236	150.00	S-443.	Rhode Island	62	175.00
S-404.	Colorado	27	900.00	S-424.	Michigan	68	175.00	S-444.	South Carolina	12	700.00
S-405.	Connecticut	74	175.00	S-425.	Minnesota	63	200.00	S-445.	South Dakota	32	700.00
S-406.	Dakota Terr.	35	2,000.00	S-426.	Mississippi	11	1,500.00	S-446.	Tennessee	30	400.00
S-407.	Delaware	8	1,250.00	S-427.	Missouri	59	200.00	S-447.	Texas	74	400.00
S-408.	Dist. of Columbia	5	150.00	S-428.	Montana Terr.	9	2,250.00	S-448.	Utah Terr.	5	2,000.00
S-409.	Florida	20	2,000.00	S-429.	Montana State	15	850.00	S-449.	Utah	7	700.00
S-410.	Georgia	27	250.00	S-430.	Nebraska	112	175.00	S-450.	Vermont	38	200.00
S-411.	Hawaii Terr.	2	1,250.00	S-431.	Nevada	1	Rare	S-451.	Virginia	29	350.00
S-412.	Idaho Terr.	4	Rare	S-432.	New Hampshire	47	175.00	S-452.	Washington Terr.	13	5,000.00
S-413.	Idaho	8	2,500.00	S-433.	New Jersey	89	150.00	S-453.	Washington State	31	700.00
S-414.	Illinois	105	150.00	S-434.	New Mexico Terr.	7	2,000.00	S-454.	West Virginia	26	175.00
S-415.	Indian Terr.	17	2,000.00	S-435.	New York	274	150.00	S-455.	Wisconsin	57	175.00
S-416.	Indiana	71	150.00	S-436.	North Carolina	18	300.00	S-456.	Wyoming Terr.	2	Rare
S-417.	Iowa	95	175.00	S-437.	North Dakota	14	1,200.00	S-457.	Wyoming	3	3,000.00
S-418.	Kansas	112	200.00	S-438.	Ohio	147	150.00				
S-419.	Kentucky	36	200.00	S-439.	Oklahoma Terr.	15	2,000.00				

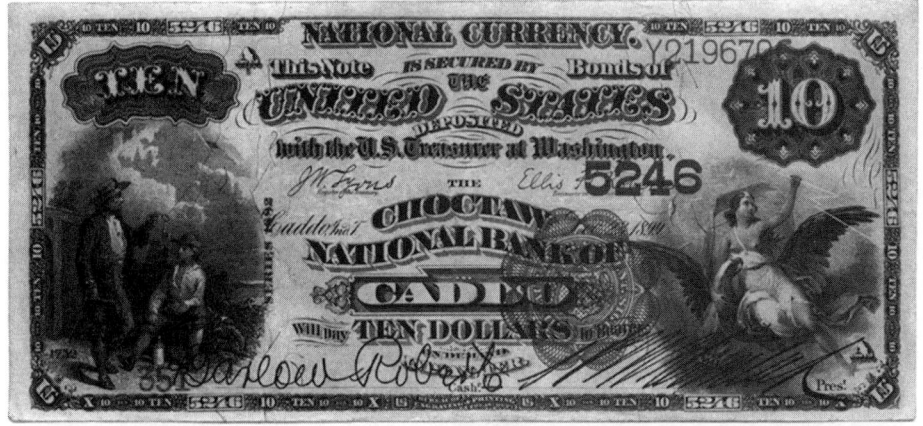

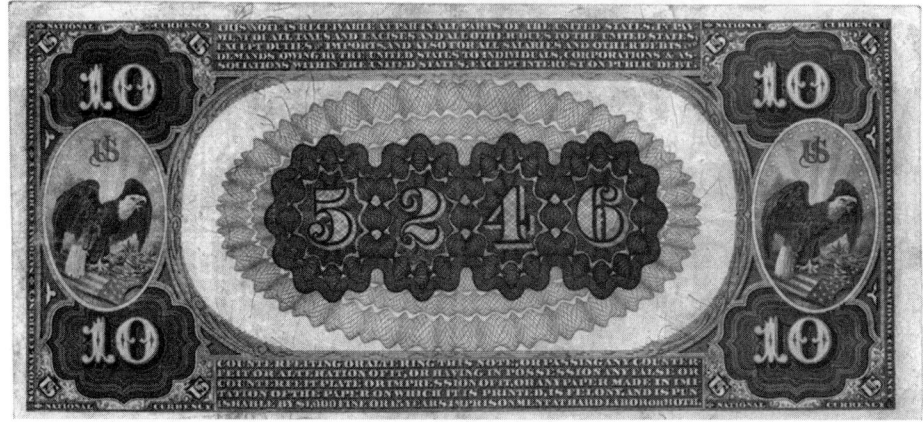

10 Dollar Notes

DESIGN NO. 109

(Notes 479-492)

At the left, Benjamin Franklin drawing electricity from the sky with a kite and a key. At the right, Liberty soaring on an eagle, clutching lightning in her hand.

Reverse of Design No. 109.

The charter numbers and surrounding ornament are green, the rest of the reverse is brown.

Note illustrated from collection of the American Numismatic Association.

No.	Signatures		Very Good	Very Fine	Unc	No.	Signatures		Very Good	Very Fine	Unc
479.	Bruce	Gilfillan	125.00	300.00	900.00	486.	Rosecrans	Morgan	450.00	675.00	3,000.00
480.	Bruce	Wyman	125.00	300.00	900.00	487.	Tillman	Morgan	140.00	325.00	1,000.00
481.	Bruce	Jordan	150.00	350.00	1,200.00	488.	Tillman	Roberts	140.00	325.00	1,300.00
482.	Rosecrans	Jordan	125.00	300.00	900.00	489.	Bruce	Roberts	145.00	325.00	1,000.00
483.	Rosecrans	Hyatt	125.00	300.00	900.00	490.	Lyons	Roberts	145.00	325.00	1,000.00
484.	Rosecrans	Huston	125.00	300.00	900.00	491.	Lyon	Treat	195.00	450.00	1,950.00
485.	Rosecrans	Nebeker	125.00	300.00	900.00	492.	Vernon	Treat	195.00	450.00	1,950.00

These notes were issued from 1882 to 1909 in sheets of 10-10-10-20 and rarely 10-10-10-10.

	State	No. of Banks	Fine		State	No. of Banks	Fine		State	No. of Banks	Fine
S-458.	Alabama	42	425.00	S-479.	Louisiana	26	225.00	S-498.	Oklahoma Territory	62	2,000.00
S-459.	Alaska Territory	1	Rare	S-480.	Maine	81	200.00	S-499.	Oklahoma State	52	575.00
S-460.	Arizona Territory	7	2,500.00	S-481.	Maryland	73	225.00	S-500.	Oregon	38	525.00
S-461.	Arkansas	9	1,750.00	S-482.	Massachusetts	269	200.00	S-501.	Pennsylvania	503	200.00
S-462.	California	47	225.00	S-483.	Michigan	97	225.00	S-502.	Rhode Island	55	225.00
S-463.	Colorado	47	900.00	S-484.	Minnesota	111	225.00	S-503.	South Carolina	29	775.00
S-464.	Connecticut	88	225.00	S-485.	Mississippi	11	1,500.00	S-504.	South Dakota	41	725.00
S-465.	Dakota Terr.	35	2,550.00	S-486.	Missouri	89	250.00	S-505.	Tennessee	52	425.00
S-466.	Delaware	18	525.00	S-487.	Montana Territory	7	2,000.00	S-506.	Texas	314	375.00
S-467.	Dist. of Columbia	12	20.00	S-488.	Montana State	32	775.00	S-507.	Utah Territory	9	2,100.00
S-468.	Florida	16	2,000.00	S-489.	Nebraska	118	225.00	S-508.	Utah State	12	475.00
S-469.	Georgia	44	325.00	S-490.	Nevada	1	Rare	S-509.	Vermont	51	325.00
S-470.	Hawaii Terr.	2	1,250.00	S-491.	New Hampshire	61	225.00	S-510.	Virginia	56	375.00
S-471.	Idaho Terr.	4	Rare	S-492.	New Jersey	120	200.00	S-511.	Washington Terr.	24	5,250.00
S-472.	Idaho	12	1,750.00	S-493.	New Mexico Terr.	17	2,000.00	S-512.	Washington State	59	525.00
S-473.	Illinois	221	175.00	S-494.	New York	367	200.00	S-513.	West Virginia	50	225.00
S-474.	Indian Terr.	53	2,000.00	S-495.	North Carolina	37	325.00	S-514.	Wisconsin	94	225.00
S-475.	Indiana	133	200.00	S-496.	North Dakota	45	1,100.00	S-515.	Wyoming Territory	7	4,250.00
S-476.	Iowa	214	225.00	S-497.	Ohio	288	200.00	S-516.	Wyoming	18	1,500.00
S-477.	Kansas	142	200.00								
S-478.	Kentucky	81	225.00								

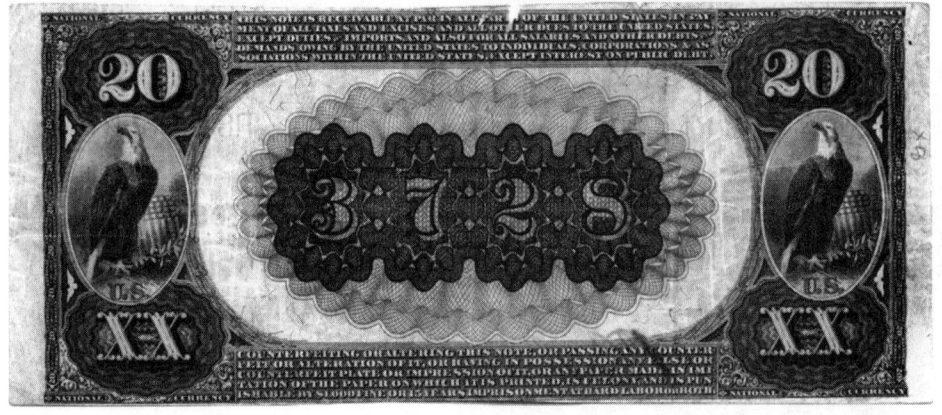

20 Dollar Notes

DESIGN NO. 110

(Notes 493-506)

At the left, the Battle of Lexington, April 19, 1775. At the right Columbia leading procession.

Reverse of Design No. 110.

The charter numbers and surrounding ornament are green, the rest of the reverse is brown.

Note illustrated from collection of the American Numismatic Association.

No.	Signatures		Very Good	Very Fine	Unc	No.	Signatures		Very Good	Very Fine	Unc
493.	Bruce	Gilfillan	175.00	400.00	1,250.00	500.	Rosecrans	Morgan	400.00	950.00	2,750.00
494.	Bruce	Wyman	175.00	400.00	1,250.00	501.	Tillman	Morgan	175.00	400.00	1,250.00
495.	Bruce	Jordan	200.00	425.00	1,500.00	502.	Tillman	Roberts	200.00	400.00	1,500.00
496.	Rosecrans	Jordan	175.00	400.00	1,250.00	503.	Bruce	Roberts	175.00	400.00	1,250.00
497.	Rosecrans	Hyatt	175.00	400.00	1,250.00	504.	Lyons	Roberts	150.00	400.00	1,250.00
498.	Rosecrans	Huston	175.00	400.00	1,250.00	505.	Lyons	Treat	275.00	525.00	1,800.00
499.	Rosecrans	Nebeker	175.00	400.00	1,250.00	506.	Vernon	Treat	200.00	425.00	1,800.00

These notes were issued from 1882 to 1909 in sheets of 10-10-10-20.

State	No. of Banks	Fine	State	No. of Banks	Fine	State	No. of Banks	Fine
S-517. Alabama	41	500.00	S-538. Louisiana	25	350.00	S-557. Oklahoma Terr.	48	2,000.00
S-518. Alaska Territory	1	Rare	S-539. Maine	81	325.00	S-558. Oklahoma	52	600.00
S-519. Arizona Terr.	7	4,000.00	S-540. Maryland	72	325.00	S-559. Oregon	38	750.00
S-520. Arkansas	9	2,250.00	S-541. Massachusetts	254	300.00	S-560. Pennsylvania	485	300.00
S-521. California	47	300.00	S-542. Michigan	97	350.00	S-561. Rhode Island	55	325.00
S-522. Colorado	47	700.00	S-543. Minnesota	109	300.00	S-562. South Carolina	29	750.00
S-523. Connecticut	87	300.00	S-544. Mississippi	11	1,500.00	S-563. South Dakota	41	800.00
S-524. Dakota Terr.	24	3,250.00	S-545. Missouri	88	350.00	S-564. Tennessee	52	450.00
S-525. Delaware	18	900.00	S-546. Montana Terr.	7	2,250.00	S-565. Texas	311	400.00
S-526. Dist. of Columbia	12	300.00	S-547. Montana State	30	900.00	S-566. Utah Terr.	9	2,750.00
S-527. Florida	15	2,250.00	S-548. Nebraska	118	325.00	S-567. Utah State	12	500.00
S-528. Georgia	44	300.00	S-549. Nevada	1	Rare	S-568. Vermont	51	400.00
S-529. Hawaii Terr.	2	900.00	S-550. New Hampshire	61	400.00	S-569. Virginia	56	425.00
S-530. Idaho Terr.	4	Rare	S-551. New Jersey	120	300.00	S-570. Washington Terr.	24	5,000.00
S-531. Idaho	12	1,700.00	S-552. New Mexico Terr.	17	2,200.00	S-571. Washington	59	600.00
S-532. Illinois	221	300.00	S-553. New York	363	300.00	S-572. West Virginia	50	350.00
S-533. Indian Terr.	53	2,500.00	S-554. North Carolina	37	400.00	S-573. Wisconsin	94	350.00
S-534. Indiana	133	300.00	S-555. North Dakota	45	1,250.00	S-574. Wyoming Terr.	7	5,000.00
S-535. Iowa	213	300.00	S-556. Ohio	287	300.00	S-575. Wyoming State	18	1,750.00
S-536. Kansas	142	325.00						
S-537. Kentucky	80	325.00						

50 Dollar Notes

DESIGN NO. 111

(Notes 507-518a)

At the left, Washington crossing the Delaware. At right, Washington at prayer.

Reverse of Design No. 111.

The charter numbers and surrounding ornament are green, the rest of the reverse is brown.

Note illustrated from collection of the American Numismatic Association.

No.	Signatures		Very Good	Very Fine	Unc	No.	Signatures		Very Good	Very Fine	Unc
507.	Bruce	Gilfillan	800.00	1,750.00	6,500.00	514.	Rosecrans	Morgan	950.00	2,000.00	7,000.00
508.	Bruce	Wyman	800.00	1,750.00	6,500.00	515.	Tillman	Morgan	800.00	1,750.00	6,500.00
509.	Bruce	Jordan	900.00	1,750.00	6,750.00	516.	Tillman	Roberts	900.00	1,900.00	6,750.00
510.	Rosecrans	Jordan	800.00	1,750.00	6,500.00	517.	Bruce	Roberts	650.00	1,850.00	6,500.00
511.	Rosecrans	Hyatt	800.00	1,750.00	6,500.00	518.	Lyons	Roberts	650.00	1,850.00	6,500.00
512.	Rosecrans	Huston	800.00	1,750.00	6,500.00	518-a.	Vernon	Treat	1,000.00	2,100.00	7,200.00
513.	Rosecrans	Nebeker	800.00	1,750.00	6,500.00						

These notes were issued from 1882 to 1909 in sheets of 50-100.

	State	No. of Banks	Fine		State	No. of Banks	Fine		State	No. of Banks	Fine
S-576.	Alabama	10	4,000.00	S-596.	Louisiana	10	1,200.00	S-615.	Oklahoma Terr.	7	7,500.00
S-577.	Arizona Terr.	2	Rare	S-597.	Maine	11	1,500.00	S-616.	Oklahoma	5	5,500.00
S-578.	Arkansas	5	Rare	S-598.	Maryland	24	1,100.00	S-617.	Oregon	4	2,000.00
S-579.	California	212	1,300.00	S-599.	Massachusetts	11	1,000.00	S-618.	Pennsylvania	131	1,000.00
S-580.	Colorado	17	2,250.00	S-600.	Michigan	8	1,500.00	S-619.	Rhode Island	9	1,100.00
S-581.	Connecticut	22	1,200.00	S-601.	Minnesota	11	1,750.00	S-620.	South Carolina	3	Rare
S-582.	Dakota Terr.	2	Rare	S-602.	Mississippi	4	Rare	S-621.	South Dakota	4	3,000.00
S-583.	Delaware	8	2,750.00	S-603.	Missouri	19	1,100.00	S-622.	Tennessee	19	1,400.00
S-584.	Dist. of Columbia	4	Rare	S-604.	Montana Terr.	2	Rare	S-623.	Texas	77	1,450.00
S-585.	Florida	7	Rare	S-605.	Montana	3	Rare	S-624.	Utah Terr.	3	Rare
S-586.	Georgia	6	1,600.00	S-606.	Nebraska	24	1,250.00	S-625.	Utah State	1	Rare
S-587.	Hawaii Terr.	1	Rare	S-607.	Nevada	Not Issued	- - - -	S-626.	Vermont	7	3,000.00
S-588.	Idaho Terr.	Not Issued	- - - -	S-608.	New Hampshire	10	1,250.00	S-627.	Virginia	9	4,000.00
S-589.	Idaho	4	6,000.00	S-609.	New Jersey	28	1,050.00	S-628.	Washington Terr.	1	Rare
S-590.	Illinois	63	1,000.00	S-610.	New Mexico Terr.	1	4,500.00	S-629.	Washington	8	1,100.00
S-591.	Indian Terr.	5	7,000.00	S-611.	New York	78	1,000.00	S-630.	West Virginia	2	5,000.00
S-592.	Indiana	27	1,050.00	S-612.	North Carolina	8	1,000.00	S-631.	Wisconsin	6	1,500.00
S-593.	Iowa	42	1,150.00	S-613.	North Dakota	4	6,000.00	S-632.	Wyoming Terr.	Not Issued	- - - -
S-594.	Kansas	30	1,050.00	S-614.	Ohio	53	1,000.00	S-633.	Wyoming	Not Issued	- - - -
S-595.	Kentucky	22	1,100.00								

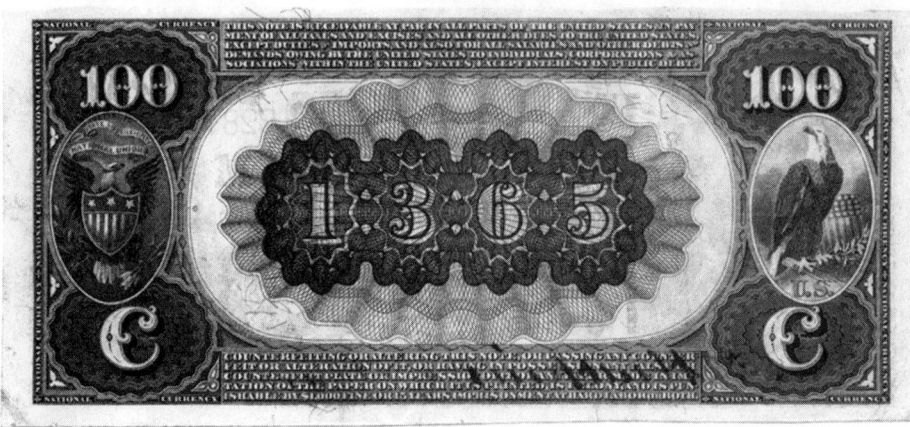

100 Dollar Notes

DESIGN NO. 112

(Notes 519-531)

At the left, Commodore Oliver H. Perry leaving the Lawrence, his flagship, during the battle of Lake Erie, September 10, 1813. At the right, Liberty seated by fasces.

Reverse of Design No. 112.

The charter numbers and surrounding ornament are green, the rest of the reverse is brown.

Note illustrated from collection of the American Numismatic Association.

No.	Signatures		Very Good	Very Fine	Unc	No.	Signatures		Very Good	Very Fine	Unc
519.	Bruce	Gilfillan	950.00	2,100.00	8,500.00	526.	Rosecrans	Morgan	1,100.00	2,350.00	8,500.00
520.	Bruce	Wyman	950.00	2,100.00	8,500.00	527.	Tillman	Morgan	950.00	2,100.00	8,500.00
521.	Bruce	Jordan	950.00	2,100.00	8,500.00	528.	Tillman	Roberts	950.00	2,100.00	8,500.00
522.	Rosecrans	Jordan	950.00	2,100.00	8,500.00	529.	Bruce	Roberts	950.00	2,100.00	8,500.00
523.	Rosecrans	Hyatt	950.00	2,100.00	8,500.00	530.	Lyons	Roberts	950.00	2,100.00	8,500.00
524.	Rosecrans	Huston	950.00	2,100.00	8,500.00	531.	Vernon	Treat	1,100.00	2,500.00	8,750.00
525.	Rosecrans	Nebeker	950.00	2,100.00	8,500.00						

These notes were issued from 1882 to 1909 in sheets of 50-100.

	State	No. of Banks	Fine		State	No. of Banks	Fine		State	No. of Banks	Fine
S-634.	Alabama	10	5,000.00	S-654.	Louisiana	10	1,200.00	S-673.	Oklahoma Terr.	7	7,500.00
S-635.	Arizona Terr.	2	Rare	S-655.	Maine	10	1,600.00	S-674.	Oklahoma	5	5,500.00
S-636.	Arkansas	5	Rare	S-656.	Maryland	24	1,250.00	S-675.	Oregon	4	2,300.00
S-637.	California	21	1,600.00	S-657.	Massachusetts	111	1,200.00	S-676.	Pennsylvania	131	1,200.00
S-638.	Colorado	17	2,250.00	S-658.	Michigan	8	1,600.00	S-677.	Rhode Island	9	1,300.00
S-639.	Connecticut	22	1,400.00	S-659.	Minnesota	11	1,800.00	S-678.	South Carolina	3	Rare
S-640.	Dakota Terr.	2	Rare	S-660.	Mississippi	4	Rare	S-679.	South Dakota	4	3,500.00
S-641.	Delaware	8	3,000.00	S-661.	Missouri	19	1,250.00	S-680.	Tennessee	19	1,500.00
S-642.	Dist. of Columbia	4	Rare	S-662.	Montana Terr.	2	Rare	S-681.	Texas	77	1,700.00
S-643.	Florida	7	Rare	S-663.	Montana	3	Rare	S-682.	Utah Terr.	3	Rare
S-644.	Georgia	6	1,800.00	S-664.	Nebraska	24	1,650.00	S-683.	Utah State	1	Rare
S-645.	Hawaii Terr.	1	Rare	S-665.	Nevada	Not Issued	- - - -	S-684.	Vermont	7	3,500.00
S-646.	Idaho Terr.	Not Issued	- - - -	S-666.	New Hampshire	10	1,300.00	S-685.	Virginia	9	4,500.00
S-647.	Idaho	4	6,000.00	S-667.	New Jersey	28	1,250.00	S-686.	Washington Terr.	1	Rare
S-648.	Illinois	63	1,200.00	S-668.	New Mexico Terr.	1	4,500.00	S-687.	Washington	8	1,250.00
S-649.	Indian Terr.	5	7,000.00	S-669.	New York	78	1,200.00	S-688.	West Virginia	2	5,000.00
S-650.	Indiana	27	1,250.00	S-670.	North Carolina	8	1,400.00	S-689.	Wisconsin	6	1,700.00
S-651.	Iowa	42	1,350.00	S-671.	North Dakota	4	7,000.00	S-690.	Wyoming Terr.	Not Issued	- - - -
S-652.	Kansas	30	1,250.00	S-672.	Ohio	53	1,200.00	S-691.	Wyoming	Not Issued	- - - -
S-653.	Kentucky	22	1,250.00								

Second Issue. Series of 1882 with Blue Seal and with "1882-1908" on Green Back.

5 Dollar Notes

DESIGN NO. 113

(Notes 532-538-b)

Head of President James Garfield, assassinated seven months after he was elected to the Presidency in 1881.

Reverse of Design No. 113.

At the left, head of George Washington. At the right, the U.S. Capitol.

Note illustrated from collection of the American Numismatic Association.

No.	Signatures		Very Good	Very Fine	Unc	No.	Signatures		Very Good	Very Fine	Unc
532.	Rosecrans	Huston	125.00	225.00	800.00	536.	Bruce	Roberts	125.00	250.00	850.00
533.	Rosecrans	Nebeker	125.00	225.00	800.00	537.	Lyons	Roberts	125.00	225.00	800.00
533-a.	Rosecrans	Morgan	300.00	600.00	1,400.00	538.	Vernon	Treat	135.00	250.00	900.00
534.	Tillman	Morgan	125.00	225.00	800.00	538-a.	Vernon	McClung	Unknown	—	—
535.	Tillman	Roberts	135.00	250.00	850.00	538-b.	Napier	McClung	500.00	1,000.00	1,750.00

These notes were issued from 1908 to 1916 in sheets of 5-5-5-5.

	State	No. of Banks	Fine		State	No. of Banks	Fine		State	No. of Banks	Fine
S-692.	Alabama	9	225.00	S-710.	Louisiana	7	225.00	S-727.	North Dakota	5	625.00
S-693.	Arizona Terr.	1	6,000.00	S-711.	Maine	12	325.00	S-728.	Ohio	58	150.00
S-694.	Arizona	1	4,000.00	S-712.	Maryland	19	175.00	S-729.	Oklahoma	31	250.00
S-695.	Arkansas	Not Issued	- - - -	S-713.	Massachusetts	41	150.00	S-730.	Oregon	3	625.00
S-696.	California	14	200.00	S-714.	Michigan	18	200.00	S-731.	Pennsylvania	124	150.00
S-697.	Colorado	9	300.00	S-715.	Minnesota	34	150.00	S-732.	Rhode Island	2	250.00
S-698.	Connecticut	8	200.00	S-716.	Mississippi	1	Rare	S-733.	South Carolina	7	550.00
S-699.	Delaware	3	1,000.00	S-717.	Missouri	23	150.00	S-734.	South Dakota	5	375.00
S-700.	Dist. of Columbia	2	150.00	S-718.	Montana	3	1,050.00	S-735.	Tennessee	13	325.00
S-701.	Florida	7	675.00	S-719.	Nebraska	17	225.00	S-736.	Texas	40	200.00
S-702.	Georgia	16	185.00	S-720.	Nevada	Not Issued	- - - -	S-737.	Utah	7	425.00
S-703.	Hawaii Terr.	2	725.00	S-721.	New Hampshire	14	375.00	S-738.	Vermont	9	275.00
S-704.	Idaho	3	1,250.00	S-722.	New Jersey	36	150.00	S-739.	Virginia	18	175.00
S-705.	Illinois	68	150.00	S-723.	New Mexico Terr.	6	2,500.00	S-740.	Washington	4	475.00
S-706.	Indiana	36	150.00	S-724.	New Mexico State	5	950.00	S-741.	West Virginia	14	175.00
S-707.	Iowa	54	150.00	S-725.	New York	70	150.00	S-742.	Wisconsin	25	175.00
S-708.	Kansas	15	175.00	S-726.	North Carolina	11	325.00	S-743.	Wyoming	1	1,500.00
S-709.	Kentucky	18	175.00								

10 Dollar Notes

DESIGN NO. 114

(Notes 539-548)

At the left, Benjamin Franklin drawing electricity from the sky with a kite and a key. At the right, Liberty soaring on an eagle, clutching lightning in her hand.

Reverse of Design No. 114.

At the left, head of William P. Fessenden, Secretary of the Treasury in 1864. At the right, seated figure representing Mechanics.

Note illustrated from collection of the American Numismatic Association.

No.	Signatures		Very Good	Very Fine	Unc	No.	Signatures		Very Good	Very Fine	Unc
539.	Rosecrans	Huston	125.00	275.00	900.00	544.	Bruce	Roberts	160.00	325.00	1,100.00
540.	Rosecrans	Nebeker	125.00	275.00	900.00	545.	Lyons	Roberts	125.00	275.00	900.00
541.	Rosecrans	Morgan	350.00	775.00	1,400.00	546.	Vernon	Treat	150.00	325.00	1,000.00
542.	Tillman	Morgan	125.00	275.00	900.00	547.	Vernon	McClung	170.00	375.00	1,200.00
543.	Tillman	Roberts	150.00	300.00	1,000.00	548.	Napier	McClung	160.00	350.00	1,100.00

These notes were issued from 1908 to 1922 in sheets of 10-10-10-10 and 10-10-10-20.

	State	No. of Banks	Fine		State	No. of Banks	Fine		State	No. of Banks	Fine
S-744.	Alabama	17	250.00	S-762.	Kentucky	44	175.00	S-780.	North Dakota	26	500.00
S-745.	Alaska Terr.	1	Rare	S-763.	Louisiana	12	200.00	S-781.	Ohio	112	150.00
S-746.	Arizona Terr.	5	6,000.00	S-764.	Maine	20	300.00	S-782.	Oklahoma	85	250.00
S-747.	Arizona State	3	4,000.00	S-765.	Maryland	29	175.00	S-783.	Oregon	10	400.00
S-748.	Arkansas	3	2,500.00	S-766.	Massachusetts	48	150.00	S-784.	Pennsylvania	247	150.00
S-749.	California	20	200.00	S-767.	Michigan	29	175.00	S-785.	Rhode Island	2	275.00
S-750.	Colorado	22	375.00	S-768.	Minnesota	67	150.00	S-786.	South Carolina	10	500.00
S-751.	Connecticut	10	175.00	S-769.	Mississippi	3	700.00	S-787.	South Dakota	20	350.00
S-752.	Delaware	6	800.00	S-770.	Missouri	37	150.00	S-788.	Tennessee	23	300.00
S-753.	Dist. of Columbia	5	150.00	S-771.	Montana	13	500.00	S-789.	Texas	171	150.00
S-754.	Florida	8	500.00	S-772.	Nebraska	43	200.00	S-790.	Utah	9	400.00
S-755.	Georgia	24	175.00	S-773.	Nevada	Not Issued	- - - -	S-791.	Vermont	12	250.00
S-756.	Hawaii Terr.	2	500.00	S-774.	New Hampshire	19	250.00	S-792.	Virginia	33	175.00
S-757.	Idaho	4	1,250.00	S-775.	New Jersey	52	150.00	S-793.	Washington	12	450.00
S-758.	Illinois	133	150.00	S-776.	New Mexico Terr.	8	1,750.00	S-794.	West Virginia	28	175.00
S-759.	Indiana	65	150.00	S-777.	New Mexico State	7	900.00	S-795.	Wisconsin	46	160.00
S-760.	Iowa	130	150.00	S-778.	New York	105	150.00	S-796.	Wyoming	10	500.00
S-761.	Kansas	43	150.00	S-779.	North Carolina	26	250.00				

20 Dollar Notes

DESIGN NO. 115

(Notes 549-557)

At the left, the Battle of Lexington, April 19, 1775. At the right, Columbia leading procession.

Reverse of Design No. 115.

Note illustrated from collection of the American Numismatic Association..

No.	Signatures		Very Good	Very Fine	Unc	No.	Signatures		Very Good	Very Fine	Unc
549.	Rosecrans	Huston	135.00	375.00	1,100.00	554.	Bruce	Roberts	170.00	425.00	1,250.00
550.	Rosecrans	Nebeker	135.00	375.00	1,100.00	555.	Lyons	Roberts	135.00	375.00	1,100.00
551.	Rosecrans	Morgan	400.00	775.00	1,750.00	556.	Vernon	Treat	145.00	400.00	1,200.00
552.	Tillman	Morgan	135.00	375.00	1,100.00	556-a.	Vernon	McClung	Unknown	—	—
553.	Tillman	Roberts	135.00	375.00	1,100.00	557.	Napier	McClung	210.00	625.00	1,500.00

These notes were issued from 1908 to 1916 in sheets of 10-10-10-20.

	State	No. of Banks	Fine		State	No. of Banks	Fine		State	No. of Banks	Fine
S-797.	Alabama	17	350.00	S-815.	Kentucky	44	250.00	S-833.	North Dakota	26	700.00
S-798.	Alaska Terr.	1	Rare	S-816.	Louisiana	11	350.00	S-834.	Ohio	112	200.00
S-799.	Arizona Terr.	5	7,000.00	S-817.	Maine	20	400.00	S-835.	Oklahoma	84	350.00
S-800.	Arizona State	3	5,000.00	S-818.	Maryland	29	250.00	S-836.	Oregon	10	500.00
S-801.	Arkansas	3	3,500.00	S-819.	Massachusetts	48	200.00	S-837.	Pennsylvania	250	200.00
S-802.	California	20	275.00	S-820.	Michigan	29	225.00	S-838.	Rhode Island	2	300.00
S-803.	Colorado	22	450.00	S-821.	Minnesota	66	200.00	S-839.	South Carolina	10	600.00
S-804.	Connecticut	10	250.00	S-822.	Mississippi	3	775.00	S-840.	South Dakota	20	500.00
S-805.	Delaware	6	600.00	S-823.	Missouri	37	200.00	S-841.	Tennessee	23	300.00
S-806.	Dist. of Columbia	5	250.00	S-824.	Montana	13	775.00	S-842.	Texas	169	200.00
S-807.	Florida	8	650.00	S-825.	Nebraska	43	250.00	S-843.	Utah	8	500.00
S-808.	Georgia	22	300.00	S-826.	Nevada	Not Issued	- - - -	S-844.	Vermont	12	350.00
S-809.	Hawaii Terr.	2	750.00	S-827.	New Hampshire	19	325.00	S-845.	Virginia	33	200.00
S-810.	Idaho	4	1,300.00	S-828.	New Jersey	51	200.00	S-846.	Washington	12	500.00
S-811.	Illinois	132	200.00	S-829.	New Mexico Terr.	8	2,100.00	S-847.	West Virginia	28	200.00
S-812.	Indiana	64	200.00	S-830.	New Mexico State	7	950.00	S-848.	Wisconsin	46	200.00
S-813.	Iowa	129	200.00	S-831.	New York	105	200.00	S-849.	Wyoming	10	650.00
S-814.	Kansas	42	200.00	S-832.	North Carolina	26	300.00				

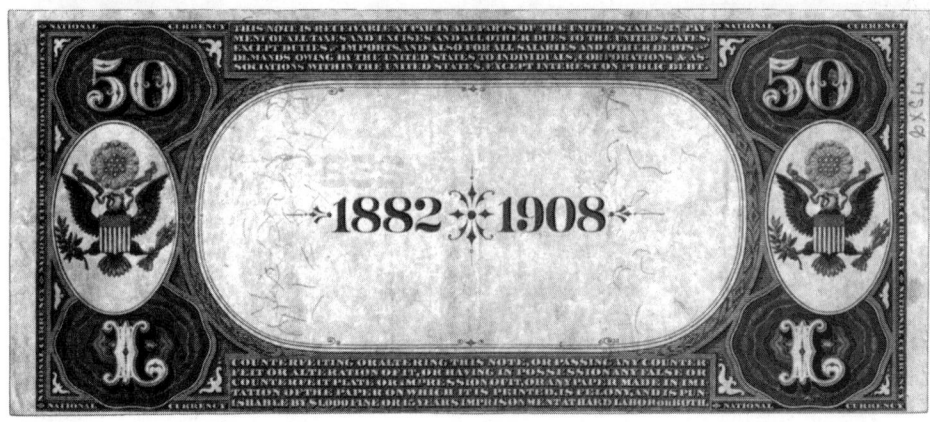

50 Dollar Notes

DESIGN NO. 116

(Notes 558-565)

At the left, Washington crossing the Delaware. At the right, Washington at prayer.

Reverse of Design No. 116.

Note illustrated from collection of the American Numismatic Association.

No.	Signatures		Very Good	Very Fine	Unc	No.	Signatures		Very Good	Very Fine	Unc
558.	Rosecrans	Huston	750.00	1,200.00	5,000.00	562.	Bruce	Roberts	800.00	1,350.00	5,250.00
559.	Rosecrans	Nebeker	750.00	1,200.00	5,000.00	563.	Lyons	Roberts	750.00	1,300.00	5,000.00
560.	Tillman	Morgan	750.00	1,200.00	5,000.00	564.	Vernon	Treat	900.00	1,300.00	5,500.00
561.	Tillman	Roberts	850.00	1,400.00	5,250.00	565.	Napier	McClung	950.00	1,550.00	6,000.00

These notes were issued from 1910 to 1922 in sheets of 50-50-50-100.

	State	No. of Banks	Fine		State	No. of Banks	Fine		State	No. of Banks	Fine
S-850.	Alabama	1	2,100.00	S-868.	Louisiana	Not Issued	- - - -	S-885.	North Dakota	1	1,850.00
S-851.	Arizona Terr.	1	Rare	S-869.	Maine	Not Issued	- - - -	S-886.	Ohio	21	950.00
S-852.	Arizona	Not Issued	- - - -	S-870.	Maryland	8	1,000.00	S-887.	Oklahoma	7	1,200.00
S-853.	Arkansas	1	Rare	S-871.	Massachusetts	11	950.00	S-888.	Oregon	Not Issued	- - - -
S-854.	California	11	1,000.00	S-872.	Michigan	2	1,100.00	S-889.	Pennsylvania	28	950.00
S-855.	Colorado	3	1,350.00	S-873.	Minnesota	5	1,000.00	S-890.	Rhode Island	Not Issued	- - - -
S-856.	Connecticut	1	Rare	S-874.	Mississippi	Not Issued	- - - -	S-891.	South Carolina	1	Rare
S-857.	Delaware	2	Rare	S-875.	Missouri	4	950.00	S-892.	South Dakota	Not Issued	- - - -
S-858.	Dist. of Columbia	1	3,000.00	S-876.	Montana	1	1,850.00	S-893.	Tennessee	2	1,600.00
S-859.	Florida	3	5,000.00	S-877.	Nebraska	4	1,100.00	S-894.	Texas	22	1,100.00
S-860.	Georgia	3	1,850.00	S-878.	Nevada	Not Issued	- - - -	S-895.	Utah	1	Rare
S-861.	Hawaii Terr.	1	Rare	S-879.	New Hampshire	1	Rare	S-896.	Vermont	2	2,500.00
S-862.	Idaho	1	Rare	S-880.	New Jersey	4	950.00	S-897.	Virginia	3	1,100.00
S-863.	Illinois	28	950.00	S-881.	New Mexico Terr.	1	5,200.00	S-898.	Washington	4	1,050.00
S-864.	Indiana	12	1,000.00	S-882.	New Mexico State	1	2,700.00	S-899.	West Virginia	1	Rare
S-865.	Iowa	17	1,000.00	S-883.	New York	15	850.00	S-900.	Wisconsin	Not Issued	- - - -
S-866.	Kansas	6	1,100.00	S-884.	North Carolina	3	1,000.00	S-901.	Wyoming	Not Issued	- - - -
S-867.	Kentucky	8	1,000.00								

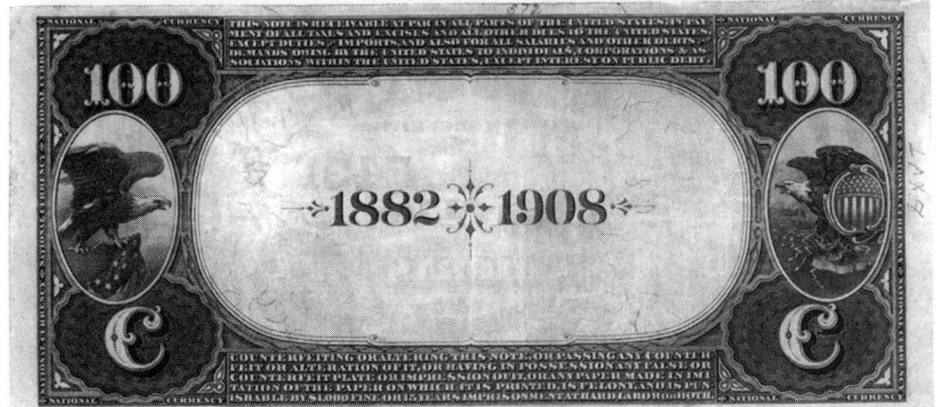

100 Dollar Notes

DESIGN NO. 117

(Notes 566-572-a)

At the left, Commodore Oliver H. Perry leaving the Lawrence, his flagship, during the battle of Lake Erie, September 10, 1813. At the right, Liberty seated by Fasces.

Reverse of Design No. 117.

Note illustrated from collection of the American Numismatic Association.

No.	Signatures		Very Good	Very Fine	Unc	No.	Signatures		Very Good	Very Fine	Unc
566.	Rosecrans	Huston	800.00	1,500.00	5,500.00	570.	Bruce	Roberts	850.00	1,600.00	6,000.00
567.	Rosecrans	Nebeker	850.00	1,600.00	6,000.00	571.	Lyons	Roberts	800.00	1,500.00	5,500.00
568.	Tillman	Morgan	850.00	1,600.00	6,000.00	572.	Vernon	Treat	850.00	1,750.00	6,500.00
569.	Tillman	Roberts	850.00	1,600.00	6,000.00	572-a.	Napier	McClung	1,100.00	2,200.00	8,000.00

These notes were issued from 1910 to 1922 in sheets of 50-50-50-100.

	State	No. of Banks	Fine		State	No. of Banks	Fine		State	No. of Banks	Fine
S-902.	Alabama	1	2,000.00	S-920.	Louisiana	Not Issued	- - - -	S-937.	North Dakota	1	2,000.00
S-903.	Arizona Terr.	1	Rare	S-921.	Maine	Not Issued	- - - -	S-938.	Ohio	21	1,000.00
S-904.	Arizona	Not Issued	- - - -	S-922.	Maryland	8	1,200.00	S-939.	Oklahoma	7	1,450.00
S-905.	Arkansas	1	Rare	S-923.	Massachusetts	11	1,000.00	S-940.	Oregon	Not Issued	- - - -
S-906.	California	11	1,350.00	S-924.	Michigan	2	1,300.00	S-941.	Pennsylvania	28	1,000.00
S-907.	Colorado	3	1,800.00	S-925.	Minnesota	5	1,200.00	S-942.	Rhode Island	Not Issued	- - - -
S-908.	Connecticut	1	Rare	S-926.	Mississippi	Not Issued	- - - -	S-943.	South Carolina	1	Rare
S-909.	Delaware	2	Rare	S-927.	Missouri	4	1,000.00	S-944.	South Dakota	Not Issued	- - - -
S-910.	Dist. of Columbia	1	3,000.00	S-928.	Montana	1	2,500.00	S-945.	Tennessee	2	1,550.00
S-911.	Florida	3	5,000.00	S-929.	Nebraska	4	1,350.00	S-946.	Texas	22	1,200.00
S-912.	Georgia	3	1,850.00	S-930.	Nevada	Not Issued	- - - -	S-947.	Utah	1	Rare
S-913.	Hawaii Terr.	1	Rare	S-931.	New Hampshire	1	Rare	S-948.	Vermont	2	2,500.00
S-914.	Idaho	1	Rare	S-932.	New Jersey	4	1,000.00	S-949.	Virginia	3	1,350.00
S-915.	Illinois	28	1,000.00	S-933.	New Mexico Terr.	1	5,000.00	S-950.	Washington	4	1,200.00
S-916.	Indiana	12	1,100.00	S-934.	New Mexico State	1	2,500.00	S-951.	West Virginia	1	Rare
S-917.	Iowa	17	1,000.00	S-935.	New York	11	1,000.00	S-952.	Wisconsin	Not Issued	- - - -
S-918.	Kansas	6	1,250.00	S-936.	North Carolina	3	1,100.00	S-953.	Wyoming	Not Issued	- - - -
S-919.	Kentucky	8	1,100.00								

Third Issue. Series of 1882 with Blue Seal and with denomination spelled out across Green Back.

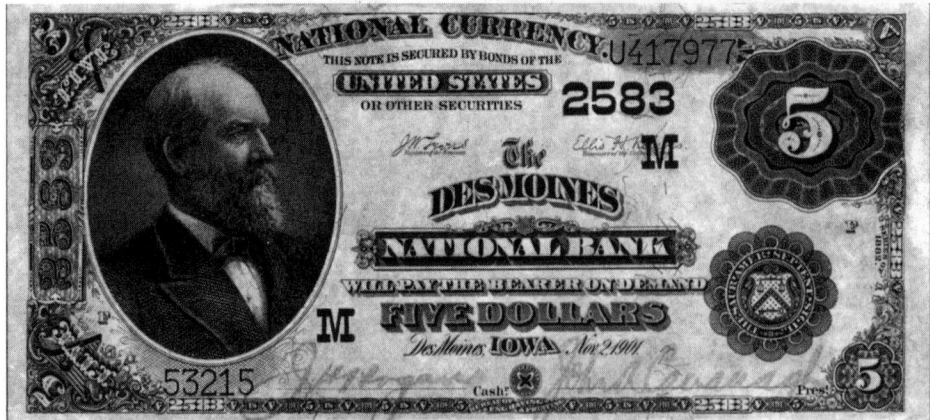

5 Dollar Notes

DESIGN NO. 118

(Notes 573-575-b)

Head of President James Garfield, assassinated seven months after he was elected to the Presidency in 1881.

Reverse of Design No. 118.

At the left, head of George Washington. At the right, the U.S. Capitol.

Note illustrated from collection of the American Numismatic Association.

No.	Signatures		Very Good	Very Fine	Unc	No.	Signatures		Very Good	Very Fine	Unc
573.	Tillman	Morgan	125.00	300.00	1,100.00	574-b.	Lyons	Treat	Unknown	—	—
573-a.	Tilman	Roberts	250.00	750.00	2,000.00	575.	Vernon	Treat	185.00	500.00	1,350.00
574.	Lyons	Roberts	125.00	300.00	1,100.00	575-a.	Napier	McClung	200.00	600.00	1,500.00
574-a.	Bruce	Roberts	200.00	700.00	1,750.00	575-b.	Teehee	Burke	Rare	—	—

These notes were issued from 1916 to 1922 in sheets of 5-5-5-5.

	State	No. of Banks	Fine		State	No. of Banks	Fine		State	No. of Banks	Fine
S-954.	Alabama	5	375.00	S-971.	Louisiana	Not Issued	- - - -	S-987.	North Dakota	3	800.00
S-955.	Arizona	Not Issued	- - - -	S-972.	Maine	2	850.00	S-988.	Ohio	27	175.00
S-956.	Arkansas	Not Issued	- - - -	S-973.	Maryland	9	225.00	S-989.	Oklahoma	21	400.00
S-957.	California	9	200.00	S-974.	Massachusetts	7	200.00	S-990.	Oregon	1	850.00
S-958.	Colorado	2	500.00	S-975.	Michigan	6	225.00	S-991.	Pennsylvania	46	175.00
S-959.	Connecticut	5	300.00	S-976.	Minnesota	19	175.00	S-992.	Rhode Island	Not Issued	- - - -
S-960.	Delaware	2	1,500.00	S-977.	Mississippi	1	1,500.00	S-993.	South Carolina	2	1,500.00
S-951.	Dist. of Columbia	1	500.00	S-978.	Missouri	4	325.00	S-994.	South Dakota	3	550.00
S-952.	Florida	3	1,250.00	S-979.	Montana	Not Issued	- - - -	S-995.	Tennessee	2	500.00
S-953.	Georgia	3	250.00	S-980.	Nebraska	4	325.00	S-996.	Texas	18	175.00
S-964.	Hawaii Terr.	1	600.00	S-981.	Nevada	Not Issued	- - - -	S-997.	Utah	3	850.00
S-965.	Idaho	2	1,000.00	S-982.	New Hampshire	6	400.00	S-998.	Vermont	3	900.00
S-966.	Illinois	23	200.00	S-983.	New Jersey	14	225.00	S-999.	Virginia	9	200.00
S-967.	Indiana	13	225.00	S-984.	New Mexico	4	800.00	S-1000.	Washington	2	500.00
S-968.	Iowa	21	225.00	S-985.	New York	48	200.00	S-1001.	West Virginia	6	275.00
S-969.	Kansas	5	250.00	S-986.	North Carolina	5	300.00	S-1002.	Wisconsin	11	200.00
S-970.	Kentucky	6	200.00					S-1003.	Wyoming	1	1,250.00

10 Dollar Notes

DESIGN NO. 119

(Notes 576-579-b)

At the left, Benjamin Franklin drawing electricity from the sky with a kite and a key. At the right, Liberty soaring on an eagle, clutching lightning in her hand.

Reverse of Design No. 119.

At the left, head of William P. Fessenden, Secretary of the Treasury in 1864. At the right, seated figure representing Mechanics.

Note illustrated from collection of the American Numismatic Association.

No.	Signatures		Very Good	Very Fine	Unc	No.	Signatures		Very Good	Very Fine	Unc
576.	Tillman	Morgan	160.00	420.00	1,500.00	578.	Vernon	Treat	225.00	600.00	1,700.00
576-a.	Tillman	Roberts	160.00	420.00	1,500.00	579.	Napier	McClung	200.00	525.00	1,600.00
576-b.	Bruce	Roberts	160.00	420.00	1,500.00	579-a.	Parker	Burke	Unknown	—	—
577.	Lyons	Roberts	150.00	400.00	1,400.00	579-b.	Teehee	Burke	Rare	—	—
577-a.	Lyons	Treat	Unknown	—	—						

These notes were issued from 1916 to 1922 in sheets of 10-10-10-10 and 10-10-10-20.

	State	No. of Banks	Fine		State	No. of Banks	Fine		State	No. of Banks	Fine
S-1004.	Alabama	8	325.00	S-1021.	Louisiana	1	1,250.00	S-1038.	Ohio	61	225.00
S-1005.	Arizona	2	Rare	S-1022.	Maine	4	700.00	S-1039.	Oklahoma	60	400.00
S-1006.	Arkansas	2	3,000.00	S-1023.	Maryland	16	250.00	S-1040.	Oregon	4	700.00
S-1007.	California	14	225.00	S-1024.	Massachusetts	9	250.00	S-1041.	Pennsylvania	123	225.00
S-1008.	Colorado	11	500.00	S-1025.	Michigan	11	250.00	S-1042.	Rhode Island	Not Issued	- - - -
S-1009.	Connecticut	6	300.00	S-1026.	Minnesota	36	250.00	S-1043.	South Carolina	2	1,500.00
S-1010.	Delaware	2	2,000.00	S-1027.	Mississippi	2	1,250.00	S-1044.	South Dakota	14	400.00
S-1011.	Dist. of Columbia	Not Issued	- - - -	S-1028.	Missouri	12	275.00	S-1045.	Tennessee	8	450.00
S-1012.	Florida	3	1,250.00	S-1029.	Montana	2	1,250.00	S-1046.	Texas	84	225.00
S-1013.	Georgia	7	225.00	S-1030.	Nebraska	20	275.00	S-1047.	Utah	3	850.00
S-1014.	Hawaii Terr.	1	600.00	S-1031.	Nevada	Not Issued	- - - -	S-1048.	Vermont	3	900.00
S-1015.	Idaho	2	1,750.00	S-1032.	New Hampshire	10	550.00	S-1049.	Virginia	17	250.00
S-1016.	Illinois	59	225.00	S-1033.	New Jersey	26	250.00	S-1050.	Washington	6	500.00
S-1017.	Indiana	30	250.00	S-1034.	New Mexico	6	900.00	S-1051.	West Virginia	16	275.00
S-1018.	Iowa	65	250.00	S-1035.	New York	64	225.00	S-1052.	Wisconsin	21	250.00
S-1019.	Kansas	19	275.00	S-1036.	North Carolina	12	300.00	S-1053.	Wyoming	4	1,250.00
S-1020.	Kentucky	16	250.00	S-1037.	North Dakota	20	800.00				

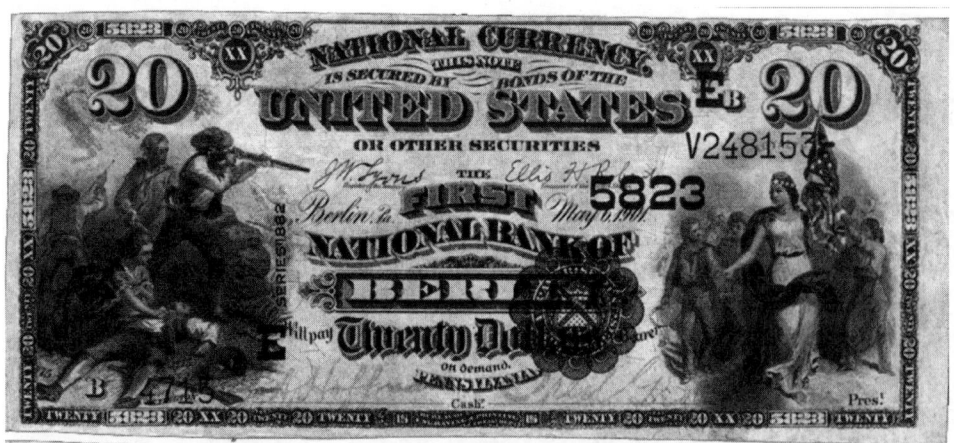

20 Dollar Notes

DESIGN NO. 120

(Notes 580-585)

At the left, the Battle of Lexington, April 19, 1775. At the right, Columbia leading procession.

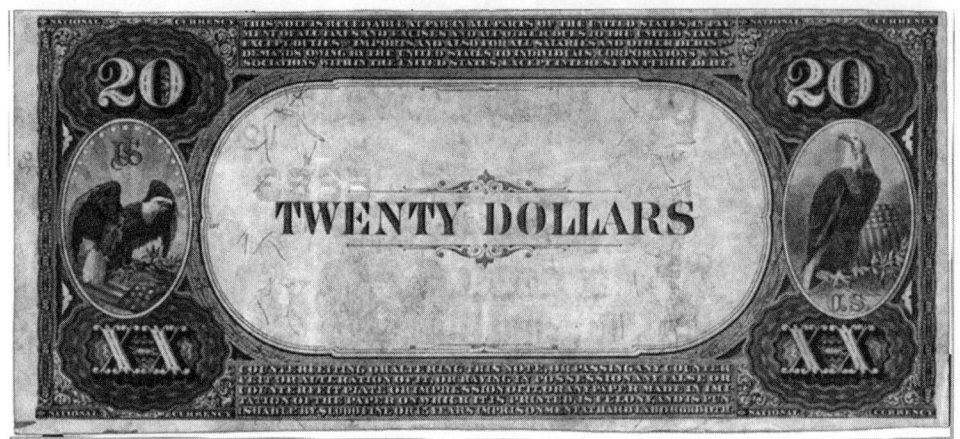

Reverse of Design No. 120.

Note illustrated from collection of the American Numismatic Association.

No	Signatures		Very Good	Very Fine	Unc	No.	Signatures		Very Good	Very Fine	Unc
580.	Tillman	Morgan	200.00	500.00	2,250.00	583.	Vernon	Treat	250.00	550.00	2,500.00
580-a.	Tillman	Roberts	Rare	—	—	584.	Napier	McClung	225.00	500.00	2,250.00
580-b.	Bruce	Roberts	Rare	—	—	584-a.	Parker	Burke	Rare	—	—
581.	Lyons	Roberts	175.00	425.00	2,000.00	585.	Teehee	Burke	250.00	500.00	2,500.00
582.	Lyons	Treat	250.00	500.00	2,500.00						

These notes were issued from 1916 to 1922 in sheets of 10-10-10-20.

State	No. of Banks	Fine	State	No. of Banks	Fine	State	No. of Banks	Fine
S-1054. Alabama	8	375.00	S-1071. Louisiana	1	1,500.00	S-1088. Ohio	61	225.00
S-1055. Arizona	2	Rare	S-1072. Maine	4	1,000.00	S-1089. Oklahoma	59	500.00
S-1056. Arkansas	2	3,500.00	S-1073. Maryland	15	275.00	S-1090. Oregon	4	800.00
S-1057. California	13	225.00	S-1074. Massachusetts	8	250.00	S-1091. Pennsylvania	123	175.00
S-1058. Colorado	11	600.00	S-1075. Michigan	11	250.00	S-1092. Rhode Island	Not Issued	- - - -
S-1059. Connecticut	6	325.00	S-1076. Minnesota	36	250.00	S-1093. South Carolina	2	3,000.00
S-1060. Delaware	2	2,500.00	S-1077. Mississippi	2	1,400.00	S-1094. South Dakota	14	550.00
S-1061. Dist. of Columbia	Not Issued	- - - -	S-1078. Missouri	12	275.00	S-1095. Tennessee	8	500.00
S-1062. Florida	2	1,500.00	S-1079. Montana	2	1,750.00	S-1096. Texas	83	175.00
S-1063. Georgia	7	300.00	S-1080. Nebraska	20	275.00	S-1097. Utah	3	1,000.00
S-1064. Hawaii Terr.	1	750.00	S-1081. Nevada	Not Issued	- - - -	S-1098. Vermont	3	1,250.00
S-1065. Idaho	2	2,250.00	S-1082. New Hampshire	10	750.00	S-1099. Virginia	17	600.00
S-1066. Illinois	58	225.00	S-1083. New Jersey	26	250.00	S-1100. Washington	6	600.00
S-1067. Indiana	30	250.00	S-1084. New Mexico	6	1,000.00	S-1101. West Virginia	16	250.00
S-1068. Iowa	63	250.00	S-1085. New York	64	225.00	S-1102. Wisconsin	21	250.00
S-1069. Kansas	19	275.00	S-1086. North Carolina	12	350.00	S-1103. Wyoming	4	1,500.00
S-1070. Kentucky	16	250.00	S-1087. North Dakota	20	900.00			

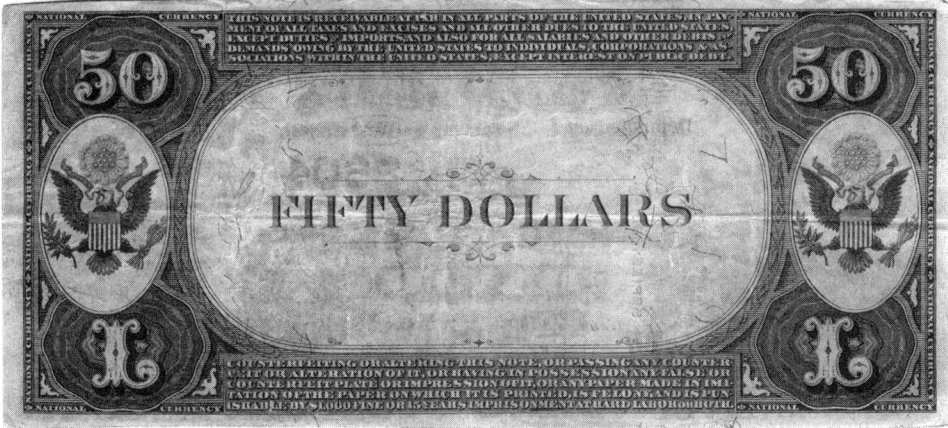

50 Dollar Notes

DESIGN NO. 121

(Note 586)

At the left, Washington crossing the Delaware. At the right, Washington at prayer.

Reverse of Design No. 121.

Note illustrated from collection of the Federal Reserve Bank of San Francisco.

No.	Signatures		
586.	Lyons	Roberts	Very Rare (4 known)

These notes were issued from 1919 to 1921 in sheets of 50-50-50-100.
(These notes were only issued in Louisiana and Ohio.)

	State	Very Fine
S-1117.	Louisiana	—
S-1134.	Ohio	—

100 Dollar Notes

DESIGN NO. 121-a.

(Note 586a)

At the left, Commodore Oliver H. Perry leaving the Lawrence, his flagship, during the battle of Lake Erie, September 10, 1813. At the right, Liberty seated by fasces.

Reverse of Design No. 121-a

This illustration by courtesy of the Federal Reserve Bank of Chicago.

No.	Signatures			
586-a.	Lyons	Roberts	Very Rare	(4 known)

These notes were issued from 1919 to 1921 in sheets of 50-50-50-100.

	State	Very Fine
S-1167.	Louisiana	—
S-1184.	Ohio	—

Notes of the Third Charter Period

April 12, 1902 to April 11, 1922

(Notes of Third Charter types were issued from 1902 to 1929)

Charter periods came to an official end in 1922. After that date, Congressional legislation gave all National Banks, both those in existence and those yet to be formed a permanent corporate status, so that it no longer became necessary for a bank to renew its charter.

The Congressional Act of April 12, 1902 created the Third Charter Period, the notes of which bear the designation, "Series of 1902."

The Act was passed to prolong the corporate life of those banks whose 20 year charters were due to expire beginning with the year 1902. The charters of such banks could thus be legally renewed and at the same time charters could be granted to National Banks organizing for the first time.

Large size notes of Third Charter types were issued from 1902 to 1929. In July, 1929, they were discontinued and were replaced by small size National Bank Notes of completely new designs.

When the Third Charter Period became law, new notes were issued to mark the transition, as had also been done at the commencement of the Second Charter Period. Three types of notes were likewise issued under the Third Charter Period and they are briefly described.

Red Seals. These notes, which bear a red seal were issued from 1902 to 1908, and like the brown backs would no doubt have continued until 1922 were it not for the changes made as a result of the Aldrich-Vreeland Act of 1908.

Of the three types of notes issued during the Third Charter Period, the red seals are by far the scarcest. They were issued by fewer banks and over fewer years than the other two types and are quite rare in comparison.

Blue Seals with Dates on Back. This type is analogous to the "Dates on back" issue of the Second Charter Period, but the changes made here were not as extreme, since the basic designs of the notes remained untouched. On the face, the color of the seal was now blue, rather than red; on the back, the dates "1902-1908" were added at the top in available white space. Notes of this type were issued from 1908 to 1915 and like the Second Charter Notes of these years, they are referred to as "Emergency Money." Likewise paralleling the Second Charter Notes, the 50 and 100 Dollar notes of this type kept being issued as late as 1926 for no explainable reason.

Blue Seals Only. These were issued from 1915 to 1929 and first appeared in 1915 upon expiration of the Aldrich-Vreeland Act. They differ from the type above mainly by the absence of the dates "1902-1908" from the back. The color of the seal remained blue. Notes of this type are the commonest and most plentiful of all National Bank Notes, more of these being in existence than of any other type. They are the last of the large size National Bank Notes and were discontinued in 1929 not because of any change in National Bank policy, but because of the introduction of the small size National Bank Notes.

The obligation on the Red Seal notes is the same as on the brown backs of the Second Charter Period, namely that the notes are secured by United States Bonds.

The obligation on the Blue Seal notes is the same as on the green backs of the Second Charter Period, wherein the notes are secured by United States Bonds "or other securities."

5 Dollar Notes

First Issue.
Series of 1902 with Red Seal

DESIGN NO. 122

(Notes 587-589)

Head of President Benjamin Harrison, 23rd President of the United States, 1889-1893.

Reverse of Design No. 122.

The Landing of the Pilgrims.

Note illustrated from collection of the American Numismatic Association.

No.	Signatures		Very Good	Very Fine	Unc
587.	Lyons	Roberts	120.00	200.00	900.00
588	Lyons	Treat	125.00	225.00	1,000.00
589.	Vernon	Treat	135.00	250.00	1,250.00

These notes were issued from 1902 to 1908 in sheets of 5-5-5-5.

	State	No. of Banks	Fine
S-1200.	Alabama	22	500.00
S-1200a.	Alaska	1	5,000.00
S-1201.	Arizona Terr.	1	4,000.00
S-1202.	Arkansas	21	1,500.00
S-1203.	California	62	160.00
S-1204.	Colorado	26	400.00
S-1205.	Connecticut	48	135.00
S-1206.	Delaware	4	1,500.00
S-1207.	Dist. of Columbia	3	600.00
S-1208.	Florida	21	1,250.00
S-1209.	Georgia	27	350.00
S-1210.	Hawaii Terr.	1	Rare
S-1211.	Idaho	15	2,000.00
S-1212.	Illinois	72	125.00
S-1213.	Indian Terr.	14	1,000.00
S-1214.	Indiana	65	135.00
S-1215.	Iowa	28	160.00
S-1216.	Kansas	35	185.00
S-1217.	Kentucky	24	210.00
S-1218.	Louisiana	9	185.00
S-1219.	Maine	31	210.00
S-1220.	Maryland	34	135.00
S-1221.	Massachusetts	127	125.00
S-1222.	Michigan	24	120.00
S-1223.	Minnesota	50	200.00
S-1224.	Mississippi	14	900.00
S-1225.	Missouri	34	125.00
S-1226.	Montana	8	1,750.00
S-1227.	Nebraska	28	210.00
S-1228.	Nevada	6	1,300.00
S-1229.	New Hampshire	29	185.00
S-1230.	New Jersey	59	125.00
S-1231.	New Mexico	4	2,000.00
S-1232.	New York	177	125.00
S-1233.	North Carolina	21	375.00
S-1234.	North Dakota	17	800.00
S-1235.	Ohio	77	125.00
S-1236.	Oklahoma Territory	81	1,000.00
S-1237.	Oklahoma State	7	1,200.00
S-1238.	Oregon	11	1,250.00
S-1239.	Pennsylvania	210	125.00
S-1240.	Puerto Rico	Not issued	- - - -
S-1241.	Rhode Island	16	185.00
S-1242.	South Carolina	9	900.00
S-1243.	South Dakota	8	900.00
S-1244.	Tennessee	23	350.00
S-1245.	Texas	56	500.00
S-1246.	Utah	2	2,250.00
S-1247.	Vermont	23	260.00
S-1248.	Virginia	31	260.00
S-1249.	Washington	12	650.00
S-1250.	West Virginia	23	185.00
S-1251.	Wisconsin	26	135.00
S-1252.	Wyoming	1	4,500.00

5 Dollar Notes

Second Issue.
Series of 1902 with Blue Seal and with "1902-1908" on back.

DESIGN NO. 122-a

(Notes 590-597a)

Head of President Benjamin Harrison.

Reverse of Design No. 122-a.

The Landing of the Pilgrims.

Note illustrated from collection of the American Numismatic Association.

No.	Signatures		Very Good	Very Fine	Unc	No.	Signatures		Very Good	Very Fine	Unc
590.	Lyons	Roberts	35.00	65.00	375.00	595.	Napier	Thompson	65.00	125.00	550.00
591.	Lyons	Treat	35.00	65.00	375.00	596.	Napier	Burke	40.00	70.00	400.00
592.	Vernon	Treat	35.00	65.00	375.00	597.	Parker	Burke	40.00	70.00	500.00
593.	Vernon	McClung	35.00	65.00	375.00	597-a.	Teehee	Burke	65.00	175.00	550.00
594.	Napier	McClung	38.00	70.00	400.00						

These notes were issued from 1908 to 1916 in sheets of 5-5-5-5.

	State	No. of Banks	Fine		State	No. of Banks	Fine		State	No. of Banks	Fine
S-1253.	Alabama	38	60.00	S-1271.	Kentucky	44	45.00	S-1289.	North Dakota	29	100.00
S-1254.	Alaska	1	Rare	S-1272.	Louisiana	13	45.00	S-1290.	Ohio	108	45.00
S-1255.	Arizona Territory	1	3,500.00	S-1273.	Maine	41	45.00	S-1291.	Oklahoma	50	55.00
S-1256.	Arizona State	3	450.00	S-1274.	Maryland	46	45.00	S-1292.	Oregon	25	50.00
S-1257.	Arkansas	34	90.00	S-1275.	Massachusetts	142	45.00	S-1293.	Pennsylvania	308	45.00
S-1258.	California	152	45.00	S-1276.	Michigan	45	45.00	S-1294.	Puerto Rico	Not Issued	- - - -
S-1259.	Colorado	43	50.00	S-1277.	Minnesota	76	45.00	S-1295.	Rhode Island	14	45.00
S-1260.	Connecticut	52	50.00	S-1278.	Mississippi	24	75.00	S-1296.	South Carolina	38	50.00
S-1261.	Delaware	7	225.00	S-1279.	Missouri	57	45.00	S-1297.	South Dakota	16	75.00
S-1262.	Dist. of Columbia	5	55.00	S-1280.	Montana	16	125.00	S-1298.	Tennessee	43	50.00
S-1263.	Florida	34	60.00	S-1281.	Nebraska	52	50.00	S-1299.	Texas	115	45.00
S-1264.	Georgia	47	50.00	S-1282.	Nevada	7	450.00	S-1300.	Utah	8	65.00
S-1265.	Hawaii Territory	1	Rare	S-1283.	New Hampshire	33	75.00	S-1301.	Vermont	28	55.00
S-1266.	Idaho	28	90.00	S-1284.	New Jersey	108	45.00	S-1302.	Virginia	62	50.00
S-1267.	Illinois	130	45.00	S-1285.	New Mexico Terr.	4	2,250.00	S-1303.	Washington	27	45.00
S-1268.	Indiana	104	45.00	S-1286.	New Mexico	4	150.00	S-1304.	West Virginia	53	45.00
S-1269.	Iowa	57	45.00	S-1287.	New York	232	45.00	S-1305.	Wisconsin	45	45.00
S-1270.	Kansas	51	45.00	S-1288.	North Carolina	48	55.00	S-1306.	Wyoming	6	150.00

5 Dollar Notes

Third Issue. Series of 1902 with Blue Seal and without "1902-1908" on back.

DESIGN NO. 122-b

(Notes 598-612)

Head of President Benjamin Harrison.

Reverse of Design No. 122-b.

The Landing of the Pilgrims.

Note illustrated from collection of the American Numismatic Association.

No.	Signatures		Very Good	Very Fine	Unc	No.	Signatures		Very Good	Very Fine	Unc
598.	Lyons	Roberts	35.00	57.50	300.00	606.	Teehee	Burke	35.00	57.50	300.00
599.	Lyons	Treat	35.00	57.50	300.00	607.	Elliott	Burke	35.00	57.50	300.00
600.	Vernon	Treat	35.00	57.50	300.00	608.	Elliott	White	35.00	57.50	300.00
601.	Vernon	McClung	35.00	57.50	300.00	609.	Speelman	White	35.00	57.50	300.00
602.	Napier	McClung	35.00	57.50	300.00	610.	Woods	White	37.50	70.00	300.00
603.	Napier	Thompson	40.00	100.00	475.00	611.	Woods	Tate	40.00	80.00	350.00
604.	Napier	Burke	35.00	57.50	300.00	612.	Jones	Woods	160.00	357.50	1,250.00
605.	Parker	Burke	35.00	57.50	300.00						

These notes were issued from 1916 to 1929 in sheets of 5-5-5-5.

	State	No. of Banks	Fine		State	No. of Banks	Fine		State	No. of Banks	Fine
S-1307.	Alabama	63	65.00	S-1324.	Kentucky	48	45.00	S-1341.	North Dakota	41	100.00
S-1308.	Alaska	1	9,000.00	S-1325.	Louisiana	14	50.00	S-1342.	Ohio	144	45.00
S-1309.	Arizona	8	900.00	S-1326.	Maine	41	55.00	S-1343.	Oklahoma	65	50.00
S-1310.	Arkansas	42	75.00	S-1327.	Maryland	48	45.00	S-1344.	Oregon	28	50.00
S-1311.	California	199	45.00	S-1328.	Massachusetts	139	45.00	S-1355.	Pennsylvania	371	45.00
S-1312.	Colorado	44	55.00	S-1329.	Michigan	67	45.00	S-1356.	Rhode Island	11	45.00
S-1313.	Connecticut	51	50.00	S-1330.	Minnesota	131	45.00	S-1357.	South Carolina	45	50.00
S-1314.	Delaware	6	200.00	S-1331.	Mississippi	26	75.00	S-1358.	South Dakota	26	75.00
S-1315.	Dist. of Columbia	4	50.00	S-1332.	Missouri	75	45.00	S-1359.	Tennessee	53	50.00
S-1316.	Florida	43	60.00	S-1333.	Montana	25	125.00	S-1360.	Texas	158	45.00
S-1317.	Georgia	57	50.00	S-1334.	Nebraska	40	50.00	S-1361.	Utah	11	65.00
S-1318.	Hawaii Territory	2	500.00	S-1335.	Nevada	6	700.00	S-1362.	Vermont	29	60.00
S-1319.	Idaho	33	90.00	S-1336.	New Hampshire	36	55.00	S-1363.	Virginia	88	50.00
S-1320.	Illinois	177	45.00	S-1337.	New Jersey	158	45.00	S-1364.	Washington	31	50.00
S-1321.	Indiana	116	45.00	S-1338.	New Mexico	9	150.00	S-1365.	West Virginia	63	45.00
S-1322.	Iowa	78	45.00	S-1339.	New York	340	45.00	S-1366.	Wisconsin	74	45.00
S-1323.	Kansas	65	45.00	S-1340.	North Carolina	55	55.00	S-1367.	Wyoming	7	150.00

10 Dollar Notes

First Issue. Series of 1902 with Red Seal.

DESIGN NO. 123

(Notes 613-615)

Head of President William McKinley, 25th President of the United States, who was shot at the Pan American Exposition in Buffalo and died September 14, 1901.

Reverse of Design No. 123.

Note illustrated from collection of the American Numismatic Association.

No.	Signatures		Very Good	Very Fine	Unc
613.	Lyons	Roberts	150.00	300.00	1,000.00
614.	Lyons	Treat	160.00	325.00	1,100.00
615.	Vernon	Treat	160.00	450.00	1,500.00

These notes were issued from 1902 to 1908 in sheets of 10-10-10-20 and rarely 10-10-10-10.

	State	No. of Banks	Fine		State	No. of Banks	Fine		State	No. of Banks	Fine
S-1358.	Alabama	59	450.00	S-1375.	Kentucky	88	275.00	S-1393.	Ohio	230	200.00
S-1358a.	Alaska	1	Rare	S-1376.	Louisiana	23	300.00	S-1394.	Oklahoma Terr.	75	2,500.00
S-1359.	Arizona Terr.	8	9,000.00	S-1377.	Maine	59	250.00	S-1395.	Oklahoma State	99	4,500.00
S-1360.	Arkansas	37	2,500.00	S-1378.	Maryland	58	225.00	S-1396.	Oregon	44	1,750.00
S-1361.	California	108	250.00	S-1379.	Massachusetts	163	200.00	S-1397.	Pennsylvania	485	200.00
S-1362.	Colorado	83	1,000.00	S-1380.	Michigan	56	225.00	S-1398.	Puerto Rico	1	Rare
S-1363.	Connecticut	69	220.00	S-1381.	Minnesota	189	275.00	S-1399.	Rhode Island	25	500.00
S-1364.	Delaware	18	2,500.00	S-1382.	Mississippi	25	1,750.00	S-1400.	South Carolina	21	4,000.00
S-1365.	Dist. of Columbia	6	500.00	S-1383.	Missouri	79	200.00	S-1401.	South Dakota	67	1,750.00
S-1366.	Florida	30	1,250.00	S-1384.	Montana	24	1,750.00	S-1402.	Tennessee	52	350.00
S-1367.	Georgia	69	325.00	S-1385.	Nebraska	143	250.00	S-1403.	Texas	323	900.00
S-1368.	Hawaii Territory	2	Rare	S-1386.	Nevada	8	7,500.00	S-1404.	Utah	9	6,000.00
S-1369.	Idaho	29	4,500.00	S-1387.	New Hampshire	35	250.00	S-1405.	Vermont	35	300.00
S-1370.	Illinois	232	200.00	S-1388.	New Jersey	114	200.00	S-1406.	Virginia	70	300.00
S-1371.	Indian Territory	114	2,500.00	S-1389.	New Mexico Terr.	31	5,000.00	S-1407.	Washington	41	650.00
S-1372.	Indiana	151	200.00	S-1390.	New York	313	200.00	S-1408.	West Virginia	68	225.00
S-1373.	Iowa	163	250.00	S-1391.	North Carolina	38	375.00	S-1409.	Wisconsin	69	225.00
S-1374.	Kansas	139	225.00	S-1392.	North Dakota	107	2,000.00	S-1410.	Wyoming	17	5,000.00

10 Dollar Notes

Second Issue. Series of 1902 with Blue Seal and with "1902-1908" on back.

DESIGN NO. 123-a

(Notes 616-623-a)

Head of President William McKinley.

Reverse of Design No. 123-a.

Note illustrated from collection of the American Numismatic Association.

No.	Signatures		Very Good	Very Fine	Unc	No.	Signatures		Very Good	Very Fine	Unc
616.	Lyons	Roberts	40.00	70.00	400.00	621.	Napier	Thompson	50.00	115.00	550.00
617.	Lyons	Treat	40.00	70.00	400.00	622.	Napier	Burke	50.00	80.00	425.00
618.	Vernon	Treat	40.00	70.00	400.00	623.	Parker	Burke	50.00	80.00	425.00
619.	Vernon	McClung	40.00	70.00	400.00	623-a.	Teehee	Burke	55.00	100.00	500.00
620.	Napier	McClung	44.00	90.00	425.00						

These notes were issued from 1908 to 1916 in sheets of 10-10-10-10 and 10-10-10-20.

	State	No. of Banks	Fine		State	No. of Banks	Fine		State	No. of Banks	Fine
S-1411.	Alabama	85	70.00	S-1429.	Kentucky	129	50.00	S-1447.	North Dakota	131	100.00
S-1412.	Alaska	1	Rare	S-1430.	Louisiana	28	50.00	S-1448.	Ohio	298	50.00
S-1413.	Arizona Territory	9	3,000.00	S-1431.	Maine	72	65.00	S-1449.	Oklahoma	311	50.00
S-1414.	Arizona State	11	300.00	S-1432.	Maryland	82	50.00	S-1450.	Oregon	78	50.00
S-1415.	Arkansas	60	100.00	S-1433.	Massachusetts	173	50.00	S-1451.	Pennsylvania	693	50.00
S-1416.	California	239	50.00	S-1434.	Michigan	94	50.00	S-1452.	Puerto Rico	1	20,000.00
S-1417.	Colorado	113	60.00	S-1435.	Minnesota	247	50.00	S-1453.	Rhode Island	23	50.00
S-1418.	Connecticut	74	50.00	S-1436.	Mississippi	42	90.00	S-1454.	South Carolina	63	55.00
S-1419.	Delaware	21	200.00	S-1437.	Missouri	125	50.00	S-1455.	South Dakota	85	70.00
S-1420.	Dist. of Columbia	12	55.00	S-1438.	Montana	57	125.00	S-1456.	Tennessee	107	55.00
S-1421.	Florida	52	60.00	S-1439.	Nebraska	209	50.00	S-1457.	Texas	460	50.00
S-1422.	Georgia	105	50.00	S-1440.	Nevada	12	500.00	S-1458.	Utah	20	70.00
S-1423.	Hawaii Territory	3	Rare	S-1441.	New Hampshire	46	85.00	S-1459.	Vermont	44	60.00
S-1424.	Idaho	54	125.00	S-1442.	New Jersey	176	50.00	S-1460.	Virginia	120	55.00
S-1425.	Illinois	363	50.00	S-1443.	New Mexico Territory	35	12250.00	S-1461.	Washington	77	50.00
S-1426.	Indiana	226	50.00	S-1444.	New Mexico State	33	150.00	S-1462.	West Virginia	104	50.00
S-1427.	Iowa	258	50.00	S-1445.	New York	416	50.00	S-1463.	Wisconsin	106	50.00
S-1428.	Kansas	183	50.00	S-1446.	North Carolina	70	60.00	S-1464.	Wyoming	30	150.00

10 Dollar Notes

Third Issue. Series of 1902 with Blue Seal and without "1902-1908" on back.
DESIGN NO. 123-b

(Notes 624-638)

Head of President William McKinley.

Reverse of Design No. 123-b.

Note illustrated from collection of the American Numismatic Association.

No.	Signatures		Very Good	Very Fine	Unc	No.	Signatures		Very Good	Very Fine	Unc
624.	Lyons	Roberts	37.50	60.00	300.00	632.	Teehee	Burke	37.50	60.00	300.00
625.	Lyons	Treat	37.50	60.00	300.00	633.	Elliott	Burke	37.50	60.00	300.00
626.	Vernon	Treat	37.50	60.00	300.00	634.	Elliott	White	37.50	60.00	300.00
627.	Vernon	McClung	37.50	60.00	300.00	635.	Speelman	White	37.50	60.00	300.00
628.	Napier	McClung	37.50	60.00	300.00	636.	Woods	White	37.50	60.00	300.00
629.	Napier	Thompson	80.00	150.00	550.00	637.	Woods	Tate	50.00	100.00	400.00
630.	Napier	Burke	37.50	60.00	300.00	638.	Jones	Woods	160.00	450.00	1,350.00
631.	Parker	Burke	37.50	60.00	300.00						

These notes were issued from 1916 to 1929 in sheets of 10-10-10-10 and 10-10-10-20.

	State	No. of Banks	Fine		State	No. of Banks	Fine		State	No. of Banks	Fine
S-1465.	Alabama	99	65.00	S-1482.	Kentucky	133	50.00	S-1499.	North Dakota	160	70.00
S-1466.	Alaska	2	6,000.00	S-1483.	Louisiana	33	50.00	S-1500.	Ohio	352	50.00
S-1467.	Arizona	19	500.00	S-1484.	Maine	69	60.00	S-1501.	Oklahoma	334	50.00
S-1468.	Arkansas	68	90.00	S-1485.	Maryland	87	50.00	S-1502.	Oregon	85	50.00
S-1469.	California	302	50.00	S-1486.	Massachusetts	154	50.00	S-1503.	Pennsylvania	865	50.00
S-1470.	Colorado	114	55.00	S-1487.	Michigan	116	50.00	S-1504.	Rhode Island	15	50.00
S-1471.	Connecticut	72	50.00	S-1488.	Minnesota	304	50.00	S-1505.	South Carolina	72	55.00
S-1472.	Delaware	20	175.00	S-1489.	Mississippi	35	90.00	S-1506.	South Dakota	110	70.00
S-1473.	Dist. of Columbia	13	50.00	S-1490.	Missouri	134	50.00	S-1507.	Tennessee	118	55.00
S-1474.	Florida	63	55.00	S-1491.	Montana	83	125.00	S-1508.	Texas	518	50.00
S-1475.	Georgia	111	50.00	S-1492.	Nebraska	183	50.00	S-1509.	Utah	25	75.00
S-1476.	Hawaii Territory	2	500.00	S-1493.	Nevada	9	600.00	S-1510.	Vermont	45	55.00
S-1477.	Idaho	62	110.00	S-1494.	New Hampshire	56	65.00	S-1511.	Virginia	163	50.00
S-1478.	Illinois	424	50.00	S-1495.	New Jersey	224	50.00	S-1512.	Washington	82	50.00
S-1479.	Indiana	247	50.00	S-1496.	New Mexico	38	25.00	S-1513.	West Virginia	125	50.00
S-1480.	Iowa	326	50.00	S-1497.	New York	521	50.00	S-1514.	Wisconsin	130	50.00
S-1481.	Kansas	207	50.00	S-1498.	North Carolina	84	50.00	S-1515.	Wyoming	41	150.00

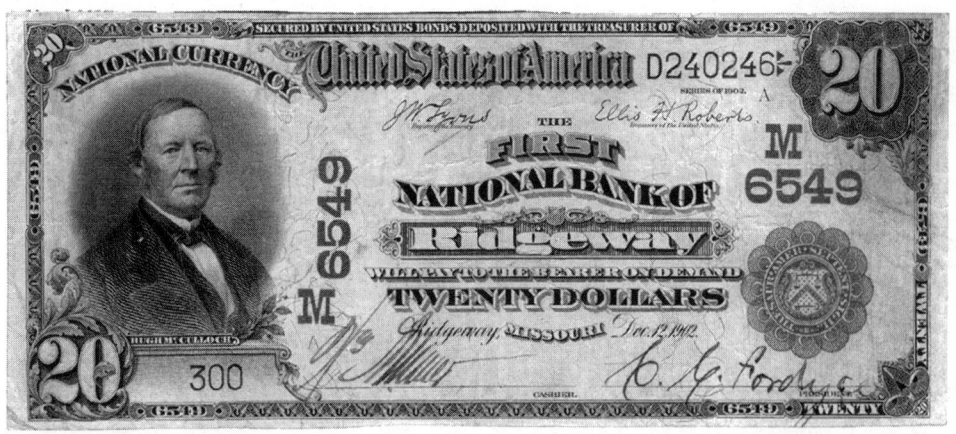

20 Dollar Notes

First Issue.
Series of 1902 with Red Seal.

DESIGN NO. 124
(Notes 639-641)

Head of Hugh McCulloch, Comptroller of the Currency from 1863-1865; Secretary of the Treasury from 1865-1869 and from 1884-1885.

Reverse of Design No. 124.

Note illustrated from collection of the Federal Reserve Bank of San Francisco.

No.	Signatures		Very Good	Very Fine	Unc
639.	Lyons	Roberts	225.00	400.00	1,100.00
640.	Lyons	Treat	250.00	450.00	1,200.00
641.	Vernon	Treat	275.00	550.00	1,600.00

These notes were issued from 1902 to 1908 in sheets of 10-10-10-20.

	State	No. of Banks	Fine		State	No. of Banks	Fine		State	No. of Banks	Fine
S-1516.	Alabama	57	900.00	S-1533.	Kentucky	85	305.00	S-1551.	Ohio	226	260.00
S-1516-a.	Alaska	1	Rare	S-1534.	Louisiana	17	375.00	S-1552.	Oklahoma Territory	74	2,500.00
S-1517.	Arizona Territory	8	7,500.00	S-1535.	Maine	59	450.00	S-1553.	Oklahoma State	96	4,500.00
S-1518.	Arkansas	34	4,000.00	S-1536.	Maryland	56	235.00	S-1554.	Oregon	44	1,750.00
S-1519.	California	106	300.00	S-1537.	Massachusetts	162	275.00	S-1555.	Pennsylvania	474	260.00
S-1520.	Colorado	80	1,250.00	S-1538.	Michigan	50	260.00	S-1556.	Puerto Rico	1	20,000.00
S-1521.	Connecticut	68	275.00	S-1539.	Minnesota	185	325.00	S-1557.	Rhode Island	25	500.00
S-1522.	Delaware	17	2,750.00	S-1540.	Mississippi	23	1,750.00	S-1558.	South Carolina	19	5,000.00
S-1523.	Dist. of Columbia	6	600.00	S-1541.	Missouri	69	260.00	S-1559.	South Dakota	62	2,000.00
S-1524.	Florida	26	2,500.00	S-1542.	Montana	24	1,750.00	S-1560.	Tennessee	43	500.00
S-1525.	Georgia	65	400.00	S-1543.	Nebraska	138	325.00	S-1561.	Texas	315	900.00
S-1526.	Hawaii Territory	2	Rare	S-1544.	Nevada	7	7,500.00	S-1562.	Utah	8	7,000.00
S-1527.	Idaho	27	5,500.00	S-1545.	New Hampshire	35	325.00	S-1563.	Vermont	35	350.00
S-1528.	Illinois	231	260.00	S-1546.	New Jersey	109	260.00	S-1564.	Virginia	63	350.00
S-1529.	Indian Territory	113	2,500.00	S-1547.	New Mexico Terr.	28	5,500.00	S-1565.	Washington	39	900.00
S-1530.	Indiana	143	260.00	S-1548.	New York	300	260.00	S-1566.	West Virginia	68	300.00
S-1531.	Iowa	159	325.00	S-1549.	North Carolina	28	500.00	S-1567.	Wisconsin	65	300.00
S-1532.	Kansas	135	300.00	S-1550.	North Dakota	105	2,000.00	S-1568.	Wyoming	15	6,000.00

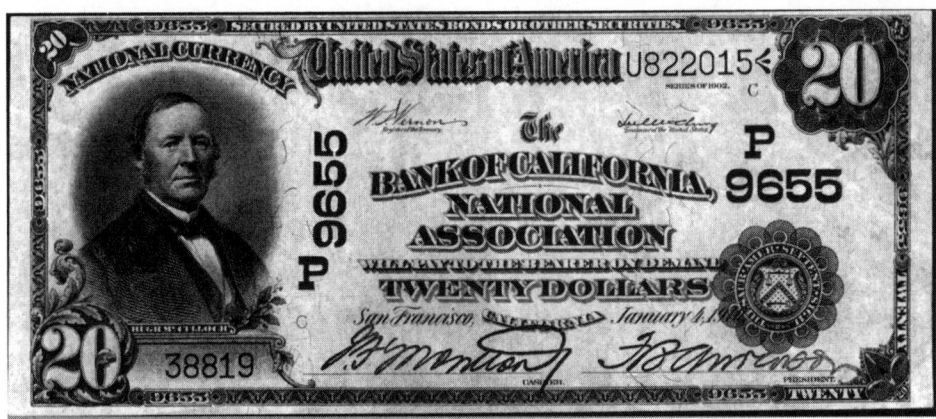

20 Dollar Notes

**Second Issue.
Series of 1902 with Blue Seal and with "1902-1908" on back.**

DESIGN NO. 124-a

(Notes 642-649a)

Head of Hugh McCulloch.

Reverse of Design No. 124-a.

Note illustrated from collection of the American Numismatic Association.

No.	Signatures		Very Good	Very Fine	Unc	No.	Signatures		Very Good	Very Fine	Unc
642.	Lyons	Roberts	55.00	85.00	400.00	647.	Napier	Thompson	85.00	125.00	600.00
643.	Lyons	Treat	55.00	85.00	400.00	648.	Napier	Burke	55.00	85.00	400.00
644.	Vernon	Treat	55.00	85.00	400.00	649.	Parker	Burke	55.00	85.00	400.00
645.	Vernon	McClung	55.00	85.00	400.00	649-a.	Teehee	Burke	80.00	175.00	650.00
646.	Napier	McClung	55.00	85.00	400.00						

These notes were issued from 1908 to 1916 in sheets of 10-10-10-20.

	State	No. of Banks	Fine		State	No. of Banks	Fine		State	No. of Banks	Fine
S-1569.	Alabama	77	85.00	S-1587.	Kentucky	124	65.00	S-1605.	North Dakota	117	150.00
S-1570.	Alaska	1	Rare	S-1588.	Louisiana	24	65.00	S-1606.	Ohio	286	65.00
S-1571.	Arizona Territory	9	3,000.00	S-1589.	Maine	71	75.00	S-1607.	Oklahoma	294	65.00
S-1572.	Arizona State	11	350.00	S-1590.	Maryland	81	65.00	S-1608.	Oregon	73	65.00
S-1573.	Arkansas	51	125.00	S-1591.	Massachusetts	167	65.00	S-1609.	Pennsylvania	689	65.00
S-1574.	California	235	65.00	S-1592.	Michigan	8	65.00	S-1610.	Puerto Rico	1	25,000.00
S-1575.	Colorado	107	70.00	S-1593.	Minnesota	232	65.00	S-1611.	Rhode Island	23	65.00
S-1576.	Connecticut	72	65.00	S-1594.	Mississippi	34	125.00	S-1612.	South Carolina	51	75.00
S-1577.	Delaware	20	240.00	S-1595.	Missouri	121	65.00	S-1613.	South Dakota	79	100.00
S-1578.	Dist. of Columbia	11	70.00	S-1596.	Montana	54	250.00	S-1614.	Tennessee	90	65.00
S-1579.	Florida	45	75.00	S-1597.	Nebraska	203	65.00	S-1615.	Texas	432	65.00
S-1580.	Georgia	84	65.00	S-1598.	Nevada	11	600.00	S-1616.	Utah	19	100.00
S-1581.	Hawaii Territory	3	Rare	S-1599.	New Hampshire	42	100.00	S-1617.	Vermont	42	85.00
S-1582.	Idaho	50	150.00	S-1600.	New Jersey	157	65.00	S-1618.	Virginia	120	70.00
S-1583.	Illinois	334	65.00	S-1601.	New Mexico Territory	31	2,250.00	S-1619.	Washington	73	65.00
S-1584.	Indiana	211	65.00	S-1602.	New Mexico State	30	200.00	S-1620.	West Virginia	97	65.00
S-1585.	Iowa	252	65.00	S-1603.	New York	383	65.00	S-1621.	Wisconsin	103	65.00
S-1586.	Kansas	176	65.00	S-1604.	North Carolina	51	75.00	S-1622.	Wyoming	29	300.00

20 Dollar Notes

**Third Issue.
Series of 1902 with Blue
Seal and without "1902-
1908" on back.**

DESIGN NO. 124-b

(Notes 650-663a)

Head of Hugh McCulloch.

Reverse of Design No. 124-b.

*Note illustrated from collection of the
American Numismatic Association.*

No.	Signatures		Very Good	Very Fine	Unc	No.	Signatures		Very Good	Very Fine	Unc
650.	Lyons	Roberts	50.00	80.00	350.00	658.	Teehee	Burke	55.00	80.00	350.00
651.	Lyons	Treat	50.00	80.00	350.00	659.	Elliott	Burke	55.00	80.00	350.00
652.	Vernon	Treat	50.00	80.00	350.00	660.	Elliott	White	55.00	80.00	350.00
653.	Vernon	McClung	50.00	80.00	350.00	661.	Speelman	White	55.00	80.00	350.00
654.	Napier	McClung	50.00	80.00	350.00	662.	Woods	White	125.00	250.00	650.00
665.	Napier	Thompson	80.00	150.00	500.00	663.	Woods	Tate	150.00	500.00	2,000.00
656.	Napier	Burke	55.00	85.00	400.00	663-a.	Jones	Woods	Rare	—	—
657.	Parker	Burke	55.00	85.00	400.00						

These notes were issued from 1916 to 1929 in sheets of 10-10-10-20.

	State	No. of Banks	Fine		State	No. of Banks	Fine		State	No. of Banks	Fine
S-1623.	Alabama	92	85.00	S-1640.	Kentucky	128	60.00	S-1657.	North Dakota	150	85.00
S-1624.	Alaska	2	7,000.00	S-1641.	Louisiana	28	60.00	S-1658.	Ohio	342	60.00
S-1625.	Arizona	19	900.00	S-1642.	Maine	66	75.00	S-1659.	Oklahoma	314	60.00
S-1626.	Arkansas	58	110.00	S-1643.	Maryland	87	60.00	S-1660.	Oregon	80	60.00
S-1627.	California	292	60.00	S-1644.	Massachusetts	135	60.00	S-1661.	Pennsylvania	827	60.00
S-1628.	Colorado	107	65.00	S-1645.	Michigan	106	60.00	S-1662.	Rhode Island	15	60.00
S-1629.	Connecticut	67	60.00	S-1646.	Minnesota	293	60.00	S-1663.	South Carolina	57	65.00
S-1630.	Delaware	18	200.00	S-1647.	Mississippi	28	120.00	S-1664.	South Dakota	102	85.00
S-1631.	Dist. of Columbia	13	60.00	S-1648.	Missouri	131	60.00	S-1665.	Tennessee	103	60.00
S-1632.	Florida	52	65.00	S-1649.	Montana	78	200.00	S-1666.	Texas	485	60.00
S-1633.	Georgia	98	60.00	S-1650.	Nebraska	179	60.00	S-1667.	Utah	24	90.00
S-1634.	Hawaii Territory	None Issued		S-1651.	Nevada	9	600.00	S-1668.	Vermont	39	70.00
S-1635.	Idaho	58	125.00	S-1652.	New Hampshire	50	95.00	S-1669.	Virginia	152	60.00
S-1636.	Illinois	396	60.00	S-1653.	New Jersey	200	60.00	S-1670.	Washington	79	60.00
S-1637.	Indiana	233	60.00	S-1654.	New Mexico	36	175.00	S-1671.	West Virginia	116	60.00
S-1638.	Iowa	315	60.00	S-1655.	New York	463	60.00	S-1672.	Wisconsin	119	60.00
S-1639.	Kansas	202	60.00	S-1656.	North Carolina	69	60.00	S-1673.	Wyoming	39	200.00

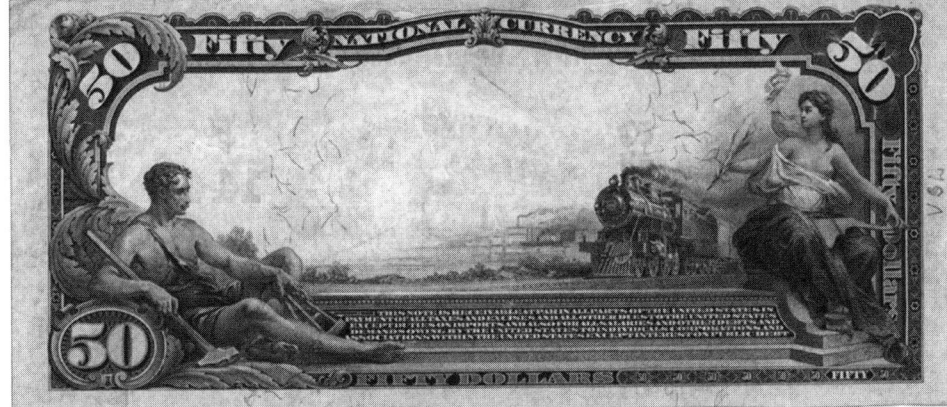

50 Dollar Notes

**First Issue.
Series of 1902 with Red Seal.**

DESIGN NO. 125

(Notes 664-666)

Head of John Sherman, Secretary of the Treasury from 1877-1881 and Secretary of State from 1897-1898

Reverse of Design No. 125.

"Mechanics and Navigation" engraved by G.F.C. Smillie after Ostrander Smith's design.

Note illustrated from collection of the American Numismatic Association.

No.	Signatures		Very Good	Very Fine	Unc
664.	Lyons	Roberts	1,500.00	3,000.00	20,000.00
665.	Lyons	Treat	1,500.00	3,000.00	20,000.00
666.	Vernon	Treat	1,500.00	3,000.00	20,000.00

These notes were issued from 1902 to 1908 in sheets of 50-100.

	State	No. of Banks	Fine
S-1674.	Alabama	1	Rare
S-1675.	Arizona Territory	Not Issued	- - - -
S-1676.	Arkansas	1	Rare
S-1677.	California	20	3,500.00
S-1678.	Colorado	3	7,500.00
S-1679.	Connecticut	8	6,000.00
S-1680.	Delaware	4	Rare
S-1681.	Dist. of Columbia	Not Issued	- - - -
S-1682.	Florida	2	Rare
S-1683.	Georgia	4	Rare
S-1684.	Hawaii Territory	Not Issued	- - - -
S-1685.	Idaho	3	Rare
S-1686.	Illinois	14	950.00
S-1687.	Indian Territory	1	9,000.00
S-1688.	Indiana	14	950.00
S-1689.	Iowa	8	1,000.00
S-1690.	Kansas	17	1,000.00

	State	No. of Banks	Fine
S-1691.	Kentucky	4	1,100.00
S-1692.	Louisiana	4	975.00
S-1693.	Maine	3	6,000.00
S-1694.	Maryland	9	7,000.00
S-1695.	Massachusetts	31	950.00
S-1696.	Michigan	2	Rare
S-1697.	Minnesota	5	4,500.00
S-1698.	Mississippi	3	Rare
S-1699.	Missouri	6	950.00
S-1700.	Montana	1	Rare
S-1701.	Nebraska	13	4,000.00
S-1702.	Nevada	3	25,000.00
S-1703.	New Hampshire	2	4,500.00
S-1704.	New Jersey	13	3,500.00
S-1705.	New Mexico Terr.	Not Issued	- - - -
S-1706.	New York	37	950.00
S-1707.	North Carolina	4	6,000.00
S-1708.	North Dakota	1	Rare

	State	No. of Banks	Fine
S-1709.	Ohio	22	950.00
S-1710.	Oklahoma Terr.	3	9,000.00
S-1711.	Oklahoma State	2	9,000.00
S-1712.	Oregon	5	2,500.00
S-1713.	Pennsylvania	70	950.00
S-1714.	Puerto Rico	1	15,000.00
S-1715.	Rhode Island	3	1,100.00
S-1716.	South Carolina	Not Issued	- - - -
S-1717.	South Dakota	4	9,000.00
S-1718.	Tennessee	7	4,500.00
S-1719.	Texas	31	4,500.00
S-1720.	Utah	Not Issued	- - - -
S-1721.	Vermont	4	Rare
S-1722.	Virginia	2	6,000.00
S-1723.	Washington	2	Rare
S-1724.	West Virginia	1	Rare
S-1725.	Wisconsin	8	3,500.00
S-1726.	Wyoming	Not Issued	- - - -

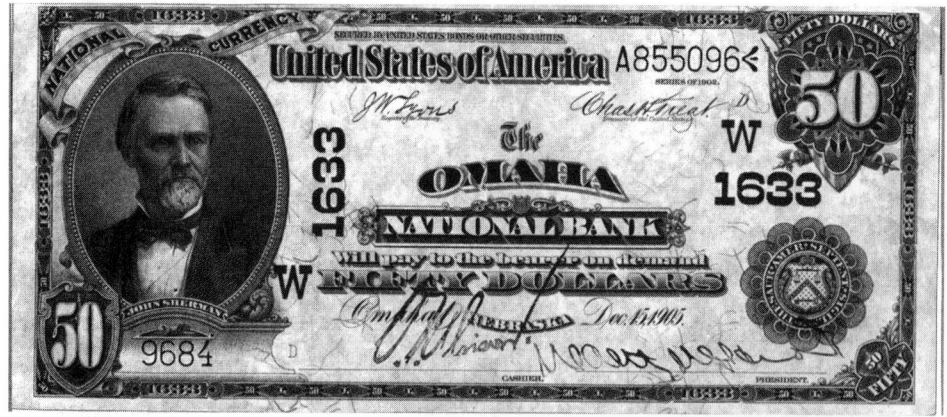

50 Dollar Notes

**Second Issue.
Series of 1902 with Blue Seal and with "1902-1908" on back.**

DESIGN NO. 125-a

(Notes 667-674-a)

Head of John Sherman.

Reverse of Design No. 125-a.

Note illustrated from collection of the American Numismatic Association.

No.	Signatures		Very Good	Very Fine	Unc	No.	Signatures		Very Good	Very Fine	Unc
667.	Lyons	Roberts	300.00	600.00	2,250.00	672.	Napier	Thompson	350.00	750.00	2,350.00
668.	Lyons	Treat	300.00	600.00	2,250.00	673.	Napier	Burke	300.00	600.00	2,250.00
669.	Vernon	Treat	300.00	600.00	2,250.00	674.	Parker	Burke	300.00	600.00	2,250.00
670.	Vernon	McClung	300.00	600.00	2,250.00	674-a.	Teehee	Burke	325.00	650.00	2,300.00
671.	Napier	McClung	300.00	600.00	2,250.00						

These notes were issued from 1908 to 1926 in sheets of 50-50-50-100 and rarely 50-100.

	State	No. of Banks	Fine		State	No. of Banks	Fine		State	No. of Banks	Fine
S-1727.	Alabama	2	5,000.00	S-1745.	Kentucky	14	425.00	S-1763.	North Dakota	2	3,500.00
S-1728.	Alaska	Not Issued	- - - -	S-1746.	Louisiana	4	450.00	S-1764.	Ohio	33	400.00
S-1729.	Arizona Territory	1	9,000.00	S-1747.	Maine	3	2,500.00	S-1765.	Oklahoma		800.00
S-1730.	Arizona State	Not Issued	- - - -	S-1748.	Maryland	17	400.00	S-1766.	Oregon	6	2,000.00
S-1731.	Arkansas	2	Rare	S-1749.	Massachusetts	32	400.00	S-1767.	Pennsylvania	75	400.00
S-1732.	California	33	400.00	S-1750.	Michigan	7	400.00	S-1768.	Puerto Rico	1	Rare
S-1733.	Colorado	8	500.00	S-1751.	Minnesota	5	1,200.00	S-1769.	Rhode Island	3	400.00
S-1734.	Connecticut	8	400.00	S-1752.	Mississippi	4	2,500.00	S-1770.	South Carolina	Not Issued	- - - -
S-1735.	Delaware	4	2,500.00	S-1753.	Missouri	11	400.00	S-1771.	South Dakota	7	1,200.00
S-1736.	Dist. of Columbia	Not Issued	- - - -	S-1754.	Montana	2	2,500.00	S-1772.	Tennessee	10	400.00
S-1737.	Florida	1	Rare	S-1755.	Nebraska	18	400.00	S-1773.	Texas	43	400.00
S-1738.	Georgia	4	3,500.00	S-1756.	Nevada	3	2,500.00	S-1774.	Utah	1	Rare
S-1739.	Hawaii Territory	Not Issued	- - - -	S-1757.	New Hampshire	2	1,500.00	S-1775.	Vermont	6	700.00
S-1740.	Idaho	5	650.00	S-1758.	New Jersey	16	400.00	S-1776.	Virginia	2	3,500.00
S-1741.	Illinois	33	400.00	S-1759.	New Mexico Terr.	Not Issued	- - - -	S-1777.	Washington	4	400.00
S-1742.	Indiana	24	400.00	S-1760.	New Mexico State	Not Issued	- - - -	S-1778.	West Virginia	Not Issued	- - - -
S-1743.	Iowa	18	500.00	S-1761.	New York	57	400.00	S-1779.	Wisconsin	10	450.00
S-1744.	Kansas	20	450.00	S-1762.	North Carolina	3	2,500.00	S-1780.	Wyoming	Not Issued	- - - -

50 Dollar Notes

Third Issue.
Series of 1902 with Blue Seal and without "1902-1908" on back.

DESIGN NO. 125-b

(Notes 675-685a)

Head of John Sherman.

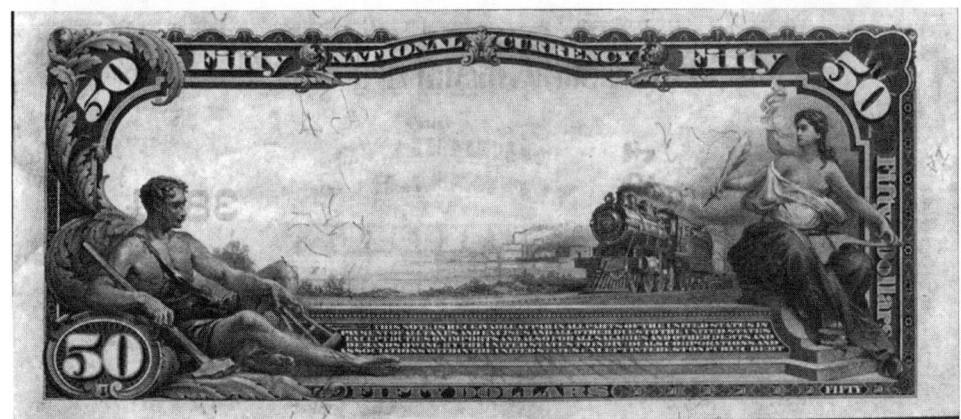

Reverse of Design No. 125-b.

Note illustrated from collection of the American Numismatic Association.

No.	Signatures		Very Good	Very Fine	Unc	No.	Signatures		Very Good	Very Fine	Unc
675.	Lyons	Roberts	250.00	500.00	1,950.00	681.	Parker	Burke	250.00	500.00	1,950.00
676.	Lyons	Treat	250.00	500.00	1,950.00	682.	Teehee	Burke	250.00	500.00	1,950.00
677.	Vernon	Treat	250.00	500.00	1,950.00	683.	Elliott	Burke	250.00	500.00	1,950.00
678.	Vernon	McClung	250.00	500.00	1,950.00	684.	Elhott	White	250.00	500.00	1,950.00
679.	Napier	McClung	250.00	500.00	1,950.00	685.	Speelman	White	250.00	500.00	1,950.00
679-a.	Napier	Thompson	350.00	600.00	2,200.00	685-a.	Woods	White	375.00	800.00	3,500.00
680.	Napier	Burke	250.00	500.00	1,950.00						

These notes were issued from 1916 to 1929 in sheets of 50-50-50-100.

State	No. of Banks	Fine	State	No. of Banks	Fine	State	No. of Banks	Fine
S-1781. Alabama	Not Issued	- - - -	S-1798. Kentucky	9	375.00	S-1815. North Dakota	1	3,500.00
S-1782. Alaska	Not Issued	- - - -	S-1799. Louisiana	3	350.00	S-1816. Ohio	33	350.00
S-1783. Arizona	Not Issued	- - - -	S-1780. Maine	Not Issued	- - - -	S-1817. Oklahoma	6	750.00
S-1784. Arkansas	Not Issued	- - - -	S-1801. Maryland	11	350.00	S-1818. Oregon	1	3,000.00
S-1785. California	16	350.00	S-1802. Massachusetts	9	450.00	S-1819. Pennsylvania	75	350.00
S-1786. Colorado	6	400.00	S-1803. Michigan	7	350.00	S-1820. Rhode Island	3	350.00
S-1787. Connecticut	3	550.00	S-1804. Minnesota	3	1,750.00	S-1821. South Carolina	Not Issued	- - - -
S-1788. Delaware	2	2,500.00	S-1805. Mississippi	2	2,500.00	S-1822. South Dakota	7	1,000.00
S-1789. Dist. of Columbia	1	900.00	S-1806. Missouri	5	350.00	S-1823. Tennessee	2	400.00
S-1790. Florida	3	3,500.00	S-1807. Montana	1	1,750.00	S-1824. Texas	38	350.00
S-1791. Georgia	Not issued	- - - -	S-1808. Nebraska	8	450.00	S-1825. Utah	Not Issued	- - - -
S-1792. Hawaii Territory	Not Issued	- - - -	S-1809. Nevada	2	2,500.00	S-1826. Vermont	5	900.00
S-1793. Idaho	2	650.00	S-1810. New Hampshire	3	1,250.00	S-1827. Virginia	Not Issued	- - - -
S-1794. Illinois	32	350.00	S-1811. New Jersey	9	350.00	S-1828. Washington	3	350.00
S-1795. Indiana	17	350.00	S-1812. New Mexico	Not Issued	- - - -	S-1829. West Virginia	1	Rare
S-1796. Iowa	13	450.00	S-1813. New York	17	350.00	S-1830. Wisconsin	5	350.00
S-1797. Kansas	15	400.00	S-1814. North Carolina	2	2,500.00	S-1831. Wyoming	Not Issued	- - - -

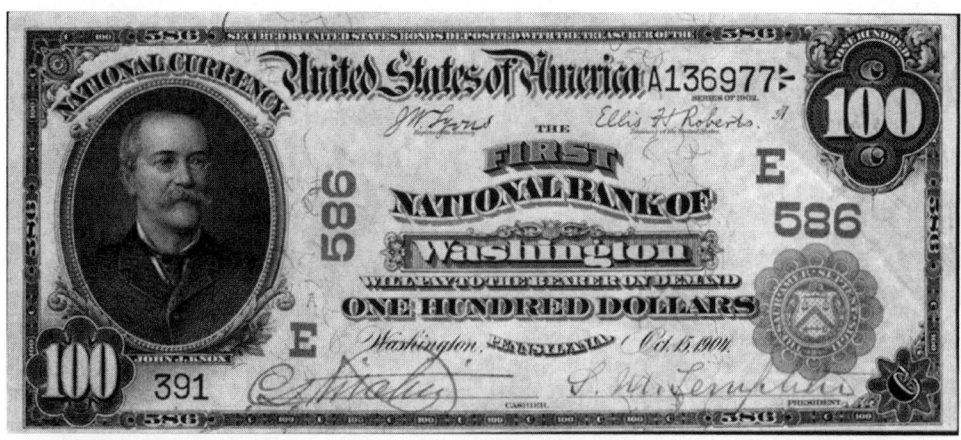

100 Dollar Notes

**First Issue.
Series of 1902 with
Red Seal.**

DESIGN NO. 126

(Notes 686-688)

*Head of John J. Knox, Comptroller of
Currency from 1872-1884.*

Reverse of Design No. 126.

*Note illustrated from collection of the
American Numismatic Association.*

No.	Signatures		Very Good	Very Fine	Unc
686.	Lyons	Roberts	1,750.00	4,500.00	25,000.00
687.	Lyons	Treat	1,750.00	4,500.00	25,000.00
688.	Vernon	Treat	1,750.00	4,500.00	25,000.00

These notes were issued from 1902 to 1908 in sheets of 50-100.

State	No. of Banks	Fine	State	No. of Banks	Fine	State	No. of Banks	Fine
S-1832. Alabama	1	Rare	S-1850. Louisiana	4	1,250.00	S-1868. Oklahoma Terr	3	7,000.00
S-1833. Arizona Territory	Not Issued	- - - -	S-1851. Maine	3	4,000.00	S-1869. Oklahoma State	2	8,000.00
S-1834. Arkansas	1	Rare	S-1852. Maryland	9	4,000.00	S-1870. Oregon	5	5,000.00
S-1835. California	20	3,500.00	S-1853. Massachusetts	2	1,200.00	S-1871. Pennsylvania	70	1,200.00
S-1836. Colorado	3	4,500.00	S-1854. Michigan	2	3,500.00	S-1872. Puerto Rico	1	75,000.00
S-1837. Connecticut	8	1,350.00	S-1855. Minnesota	5	4,500.00	S-1873. Rhode Island	3	1,200.00
S-1838. Delaware	4	Rare	S-1856. Mississippi	3	3,000.00	S-1874. South Carolina	Not Issued	- - - -
S-1839. Dist. of Columbia	Not Issued	- - - -	S-1857. Missouri	6	1,200.00	S-1875. South Dakota	4	7,500.00
S-1840. Florida	2	6,000.00	S-1858. Montana	1	Rare	S-1876. Tennessee	7	3,500.00
S-1841. Georgia	4	Rare	S-1859. Nebraska	13	1,250.00	S-1877. Texas	31	3,500.00
S-1842. Hawaii Territory	Not Issued	- - - -	S-1860. Nevada	3	10,000.00	S-1878. Utah	Not Issued	- - - -
S-1843. Idaho	3	9,000.00	S-1861. New Hampshire	2	4,000.00	S-1879. Vermont	4	4,000.00
S-1844. Illinois	14	1,200.00	S-1862. New Jersey	13	1,200.00	S-1880. Virginia	2	5,000.00
S-1845. Indian Territory	1	Rare	S-1863. New Mexico Terr.	Not Issued	- - - -	S-1881. Washington	2	5,000.00
S-1846. Indiana	14	1,200.00	S-1864. New York	37	1,200.00	S-1882. West Virginia	1	Rare
S-1847. Iowa	8	1,250.00	S-1865. North Carolina	4	6,000.00	S-1883. Wisconsin	8	1,250.00
S-1848. Kansas	17	1,250.00	S-1866. North Dakota	1	9,000.00	S-1884. Wyoming	Not Issued	- - - -
S-1849. Kentucky	4	1,400.00	S-1867. Ohio	22	1,200.00			

100 Dollar Notes

Second Issue.
Series of 1902 with Blue Seal and with "1902-1908" on back.

DESIGN NO. 126-a

(Notes 689-697)

Head of John J. Knox.

Reverse of Design No. 126-a.

Note illustrated from collection of the American Numismatic Association.

No.	Signatures		Very Good	Very Fine	Unc	No.	Signatures		Very Good	Very Fine	Unc
689.	Lyons	Roberts	350.00	650.00	2,700.00	694.	Napier	Thompson	425.00	750.00	3,000.00
690.	Lyons	Treat	350.00	650.00	2,700.00	695.	Napier	Burke	350.00	675.00	2,700.00
691.	Vernon	Treat	350.00	650.00	2,700.00	696.	Parker	Burke	350.00	675.00	2,700.00
692.	Vernon	McClung	350.00	650.00	2,700.00	697.	Teehee	Burke	375.00	600.00	2,900.00
693.	Napier	McClung	350.00	650.00	2,700.00						

These notes were issued from 1908 to 1926 in sheets of 50-50-50-100 and rarely 50-100.

	State	No. of Banks	Fine		State	No. of Banks	Fine		State	No. of Banks	Fine
S-1885.	Alabama	2	2,000.00	S-1903.	Kentucky	14	450.00	S-1921.	North Dakota	2	2,500.00
S-1886.	Alaska	Not Issued	- - - -	S-1904.	Louisiana	4	475.00	S-1922.	Ohio	33	425.00
S-1887.	Arizona Territory	1	10,000.00	S-1905.	Maine	3	700.00	S-1923.	Oklahoma	6	900.00
S-1888.	Arizona State	Not Issued	- - - -	S-1906.	Maryland	17	425.00	S-1924.	Oregon	6	425.00
S-1889.	Arkansas	2	Rare	S-1907.	Massachusetts	30	425.00	S-1925.	Pennsylvania	75	425.00
S-1890.	California	32	425.00	S-1908.	Michigan	7	900.00	S-1926.	Puerto Rico	1	Rare
S-1891.	Colorado	8	550.00	S-1909.	Minnesota	3	1,750.00	S-1927.	Rhode Island	3	425.00
S-1892.	Connecticut	8	425.00	S-1910.	Mississippi	4	850.00	S-1928.	South Carolina	Not Issued	- - - -
S-1893.	Delaware	4	4,000.00	S-1911.	Missouri	11	425.00	S-1929.	South Dakota	7	800.00
S-1894.	Dist. of Columbia	Not Issued	- - - -	S-1912.	Montana	2	2,500.00	S-1930.	Tennessee	10	425.00
S-1895.	Florida	1	Rare	S-1913.	Nebraska	18	425.00	S-1931.	Texas	41	425.00
S-1896.	Georgia	3	4,500.00	S-1914.	Nevada	3	4,000.00	S-1932.	Utah	1	2,500.00
S-1897.	Hawaii Territory	Not Issued	- - - -	S-1915.	New Hampshire	2	900.00	S-1933.	Vermont	6	700.00
S-1898.	Idaho	3	700.00	S-1916.	New Jersey	16	425.00	S-1934.	Virginia	2	700.00
S-1899.	Illinois	33	425.00	S-1917.	New Mexico Terr.	Not Issued	- - - -	S-1935.	Washington	3	425.00
S-1900.	Indiana	21	425.00	S-1918.	New Mexico State	Not Issued	- - - -	S-1936.	West Virginia	Not Issued	- - - -
S-1901.	Iowa	18	550.00	S-1919.	New York	57	425.00	S-1937.	Wisconsin	9	425.00
S-1902.	Kansas	19	500.0	S-1920.	North Carolina	3	2,500.00	S-1938.	Wyoming	Not Issued	- - - -

100 Dollar Notes

Third Issue.
Series of 1902 with Blue Seal and without "1902-1908" on back.

DESIGN NO. 126-b

(Notes 698-707a)

Head of John J. Knox.

Reverse of Design No. 126-b.

Note illustrated from collection of the American Numismatic Association.

No.	Signatures		Very Good	Very Fine	Unc	No.	Signatures		Very Good	Very Fine	Unc
698.	Lyons	Roberts	300.00	550.00	2,300.00	703.	Parker	Burke	300.00	575.00	2,400.00
699.	Lyons	Treat	300.00	550.00	2,300.00	704.	Teehee	Burke	300.00	550.00	2,300.00
700.	Vernon	Treat	300.00	550.00	2,300.00	705.	Elliott	Burke	300.00	550.00	2,300.00
701.	Vernon	McClung	300.00	550.00	2,300.00	706.	Elliott	White	300.00	550.00	2,300.00
702.	Napier	McClung	300.00	550.00	2,300.00	707.	Speelman	White	300.00	550.00	2,300.00
702-a.	Napier	Thompson	350.00	650.00	2,500.00	707-a.	Woods	White	Rare	—	—
702-b.	Napier	Burke	Unknown	—	—						

These notes were issued from 1916 to 1929 in sheets of 50-50-50-100.

State	No. of Banks	Fine	State	No. of Banks	Fine	State	No. of Banks	Fine
S-1939. Alabama	Not Issued	- - - -	S-1956. Kentucky	9	400.00	S-1973. North Dakota	1	1,250.00
S-1940. Alaska	Not Issued	- - - -	S-1957. Louisiana	3	375.00	S-1974. Ohio	24	375.00
S-1941. Arizona	Not Issued	- - - -	S-1958. Maine	Not Issued	- - - -	S-1975. Oklahoma	7	900.00
S-1942. Arkansas	Not Issued	- - - -	S-1959. Maryland	9	450.00	S-1976. Oregon	1	1,750.00
S-1943. California	16	375.00	S-1960. Massachusetts	8	375.00	S-1977. Pennsylvania	40	375.00
S-1944. Colorado	6	450.00	S-1961. Michigan	7	700.00	S-1978. Rhode Island	3	375.00
S-1945. Connecticut	3	850.00	S-1962. Minnesota	3	1,750.00	S-1979. South Carolina	Not Issued	- - - -
S-1946. Delaware	2	3,500.00	S-1963. Mississippi	2	850.00	S-1980. South Dakota	5	750.00
S-1947. Dist. of Columbia	1	375.00	S-1964. Missouri	5	375.00	S-1981. Tennessee	2	450.00
S-1948. Florida	3	2,500.00	S-1965. Montana	1	1,500.00	S-1982. Texas	38	375.00
S-1949. Georgia	Not issued	- - - -	S-1966. Nebraska	8	500.00	S-1983. Utah	Not Issued	- - - -
S-1950. Hawaii Territory	Not Issued	- - - -	S-1967. Nevada	2	4,000.00	S-1984. Vermont	5	750.00
S-1951. Idaho	2	750.00	S-1968. New Hampshire	3	850.00	S-1985. Virginia	Not Issued	- - - -
S-1952. Illinois	30	375.00	S-1969. New Jersey	8	375.00	S-1986. Washington	2	375.00
S-1953. Indiana	15	375.00	S-1970. New Mexico	Not Issued	- - - -	S-1987. West Virginia	1	2,000.00
S-1954. Iowa	12	375.00	S-1971. New York	17	375.00	S-1988. Wisconsin	5	375.00
S-1955. Kansas	14	500.00	S-1972. North Carolina	2	2,500.00	S-1989. Wyoming	Not Issued	- - - -

IX. FEDERAL RESERVE BANK NOTES

With the establishment of the Federal Reserve System, a new type of currency came into existence. The notes issued under this system are the Federal Reserve Bank Notes and the Federal Reserve Notes.

The Federal Reserve Bank Notes were also inscribed "National Currency"; the Federal Reserve Notes are not so inscribed and are currency of the system proper, and not of the individual banks in the system.

The obverse designs of these two issues are markedly different; the reverses are similar. See the illustrations.

There were two separate issues of the Federal Reserve Bank Notes, the series of 1915 and the series of 1918.

The first issue was authorized by the Federal Reserve Act of December 23, 1913 and consisted only of 5, 10 and 20 Dollar notes. These were not issued by all twelve banks in the system but only by the banks at Atlanta, Chicago, Kansas City, Dallas and San Francisco. The last named bank issued 5 Dollar notes only.

As mentioned above, these notes are inscribed "National Currency"and are similar in general to National Bank Notes. The obligation to pay the bearer on demand is made by the specific Federal Reserve Bank and not by the United States.

The obligation on the first issue of Federal Reserve Bank Notes is similar to that on the National Bank Notes of the First Charter Period, which see. There is a slight variance in the wording but not in the meaning.

The second issue of Federal Reserve Bank Notes were authorized by the Act of April 23, 1918 and all notes of this issue are series of 1918. The denominations consisted of 1, 2, 5, 10, 20 and 50 Dollar Notes and these notes were issued by all twelve banks. Each bank did not necessarily issue all the denominations. For example, the 50 Dollar Notes emanated only from the St. Louis Bank, the 20 Dollar Notes only from the Atlanta and St. Louis banks, etc. Please see the text for the full list.

Part of the obligation on this issue differs from that on the first issue, as follows, "Secured by United States bonds or United States Certificates of indebtedness or United States one year gold notes, deposited with the Treasurer of the United States of America. . ." The rest of the obligation is the same.

Although modern, the Federal Reserve Bank Notes are all quite scarce and are avidly collected. Most of the issue has long since been redeemed and according to Treasury Department records only a little more than 2 million dollars is still outstanding out of a total issue of nearly 762 million dollars.

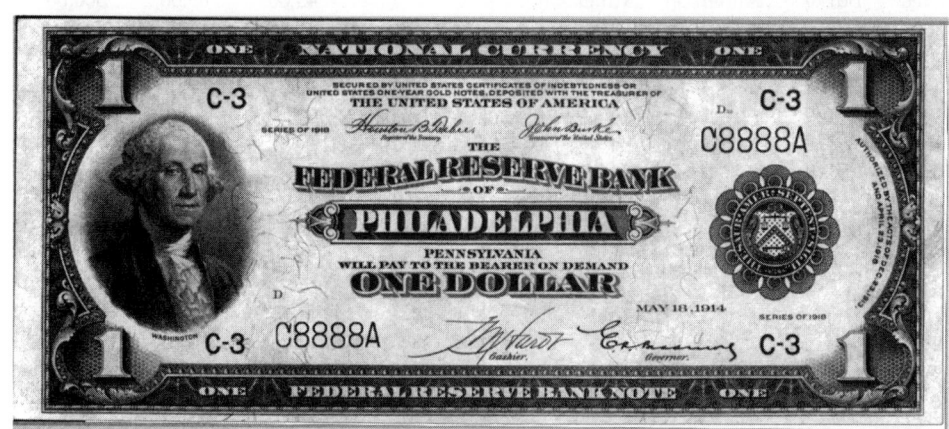

1 Dollar Notes

DESIGN NO. 127

(Notes 708-746)

Head of George Washington.

Reverse of Design No. 127.

Eagle holding American flag.

Note illustrated from collection of the American Numismatic Association.

No.	Issuing Bank	Series	Government Signatures		Bank Signatures		Very Good	Very Fine	Unc
708.	Boston	1918	Teehee	Burke	Bullen	Morss	45.00	65.00	300.00
709.	Boston	1918	Teehee	Burke	Willett	Morss	50.00	80.00	500.00
710.	Boston	1918	Elliott	Burke	Willett	Morss	45.00	65.00	300.00
711.	New York	1918	Teehee	Burke	Sailer	Strong	45.00	65.00	300.00
712.	New York	1918	Teehee	Burke	Hendricks	Strong	45.00	65.00	300.00
713.	New York	1918	Elliott	Burke	Hendricks	Strong	45.00	65.00	300.00
714.	Philadelphia	1918	Teehee	Burke	Hardt	Passmore	50.00	75.00	350.00
715.	Philadelphia	1918	Teehee	Burke	Dyer	Passmore	45.00	65.00	325.00

No.	Issuing Bank	Series	Government Signatures		Bank Signatures		Very Good	Very Fine	Unc
716.	Philadelphia	1918	Elliot	Burke	Dyer	Passmore	50.00	70.00	325.00
717.	Philadelphia	1918	Elliott	Burke	Dyer	Norris	45.00	65.00	300.00
718.	Cleveland	1918	Teehee	Burke	Baxter	Fancher	45.00	65.00	300.00
719.	Cleveland	1918	Teehee	Burke	Davis	Fancher	45.00	65.00	300.00
720.	Cleveland	1918	Elliott	Burke	Davis	Fancher	45.00	65.00	300.00
721.	Richmond	1918	Teehee	Burke	Keesee	Seay	50.00	70.00	300.00
722.	Richmond	1918	Elliott	Burke	Keesee	Seay	45.00	65.00	300.00
723.	Atlanta	1918	Teehee	Burke	Pike	McCord	45.00	65.00	300.00
724.	Atlanta	1918	Teehee	Burke	Bell	McCord	55.00	75.00	400.00
725.	Atlanta	1918	Teehee	Burke	Bell	Wellborn	45.00	65.00	300.00
726.	Atlanta	1918	Elliott	Burke	Bell	Wellborn	45.00	65.00	300.00
727.	Chicago	1918	Teehee	Burk	McCloud	McDougal	45.00	65.00	300.00
728.	Chicago	1918	Teehee	Burke	Cramer	McDougal	45.00	65.00	300.00
729.	Chicago	1918	Elliott	Burke	Cramer	McDougal	45.00	65.00	300.00
730.	St. Louis	1918	Teehee	Burke	Attebery	Wells	55.00	75.00	400.00
731.	St. Louis	1918	Teehee	Burke	Attebery	Biggs	55.00	75.00	400.00
732.	St. Louis	1918	Elliott	Burke	Attebery	Biggs	55.00	75.00	400.00
733.	St. Louis	1918	Elliott	Burke	White	Biggs	45.00	65.00	300.00
734.	Minneapolis	1918	Teehee	Burke	Cook	Wold	50.00	70.00	325.00
735.	Minneapolis	1918	Teehee	Burke	Cook	Young	100.00	650.00	3,500.00
736.	Minneapolis	1918	Elliott	Burke	Cook	Young	50.00	70.00	325.00
737.	Kansas City	1918	Teehee	Burke	Anderson	Miller	45.00	65.00	300.00
738.	Kansas City	1918	Elliott	Burke	Anderson	Miller	45.00	65.00	300.00
739.	Kansas City	1918	Elliot	Burke	Helm	Miller	45.00	65.00	300.00
740.	Dallas	1918	Teehee	Burke	Talley	Van Zandt	35.00	75.00	400.00
741.	Dallas	1918	Elliott	Burke	Talley	Van Zandt	60.00	175.00	1,250.00
742.	Dallas	1918	Elliott	Burke	Lawder	Van Zandt	35.00	75.00	400.00
743.	San Francisco	1918	Teehee	Burke	Clerk	Lynch	45.00	65.00	300.00
744.	San Francisco	1918	Teehee	Burke	Clerk	Calkins	45.00	65.00	300.00
745.	San Francisco	1918	Elliott	Burke	Clerk	Calkins	45.00	65.00	300.00
746.	San Francisco	1918	Elliott	Burke	Ambrose	Calkins	50.00	70.00	400.00

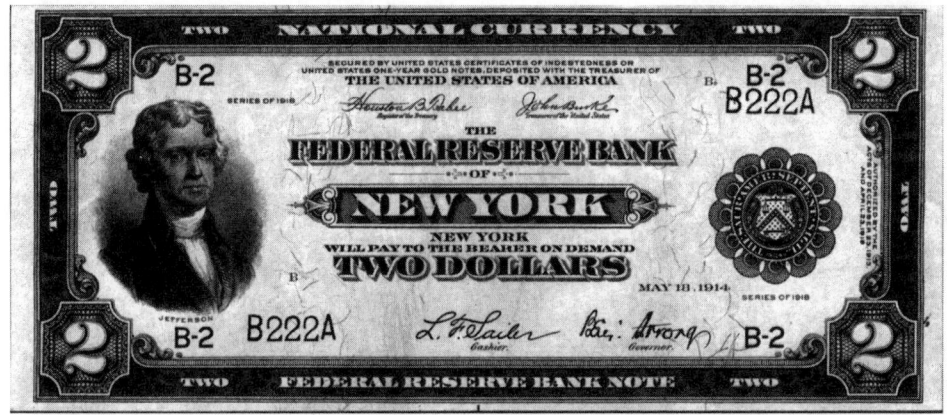

2 Dollar Notes

DESIGN NO. 128

(Notes 747-780)

Head of Thomas Jefferson, the third President of the United States, 1801-1805.

Reverse of Design No. 128.

A battleship of the period of 1914.

Note illustrated from collection of the American Numismatic Association.

No.	Issuing Bank	Series	Government Signatures		Bank Signatures		Very Good	Very Fine	Unc
747	Boston	1918	Teehee	Burke	Bullen	Morss	170.00	250.00	1,300.00
748.	Boston	1918	Teehee	Burke	Willett	Morss	175.00	275.00	1,300.00
749.	Boston	1918	Elliott	Burke	Willett	Morss	170.00	250.00	1,000.00
750.	New York	1918	Teehee	Burke	Sailer	Strong	170.00	250.00	1,000.00
751.	New York	1918	Teehee	Burke	Hendricks	Strong	170.00	250.00	1,000.00
752.	New York	1918	Elliott	Burke	Hendricks	Strong	170.00	250.00	1,000.00
753.	Philadelphia	1918	Teehee	Burke	Hardt	Passmore	170.00	270.00	1,050.00
754.	Philadelphia	1918	Teehee	Burke	Dyer	Passmore	170.00	250.00	1,050.00
755.	Philadelphia	1918	Elliott	Burke	Dyer	Passmore	170.00	270.00	1,050.00
756.	Philadelphia	1918	Elliott	Burke	Dyer	Norris	170.00	270.00	1,050.00
757.	Cleveland	1918	Teehee	Burke	Baxter	Fancher	170.00	270.00	1,050.00
758.	Cleveland	1918	Teehee	Burke	Davis	Fancher	170.00	270.00	1,050.00
759.	Cleveland	1918	Elliott	Burke	Davis	Fancher	170.00	250.00	1,000.00
760.	Richmond	1918	Teehee	Burke	Keesee	Seay	170.00	275.00	1,400.00
761.	Richmond	1918	Elliott	Burke	Keesee	Seay	170.00	270.00	1,050.00
762.	Atlanta	1918	Teehee	Burke	Pike	McCord	170.00	270.00	1,050.00
763.	Atlanta	1918	Teehee	Burke	Bell	McCord	200.00	200.00	1,450.00
764.	Atlanta	1918	Elliott	Burke	Bell	Wellborn	175.00	275.00	1,400.00
765.	Chicago	1918	Teehee	Burke	McCloud	McDougal	170.00	250.00	1,000.00
766.	Chicago	1918	Teehee	Burke	Cramer	McDougal	170.00	270.00	1,050.00
767.	Chicago	1918	Elliott	Burke	Cramer	McDougal	170.00	270.00	1,050.00
768.	St. Louis	1918	Teehee	Burke	Attebery	Wells	170.00	250.00	1,050.00
769.	St. Louis	1918	Teehee	Burke	Attebery	Biggs	170.00	250.00	1,050.00
770.	St. Louis	1918	Elliott	Burke	Attebery	Biggs	200.00	300.00	1,400.00
771.	St. Louis	1918	Elliott	Burke	White	Biggs	170.00	270.00	1,050.00
772.	Minneapolis	1918	Teehee	Burke	Cook	Wold	175.00	275.00	1,500.00
773.	Minneapolis	1918	Elliott	Burke	Cook	Young	170.00	270.00	1,100.00
774.	Kansas City	1918	Teehee	Burke	Anderson	Miller	170.00	250.00	1,100.00
775.	Kansas City	1918	Elliott	Burke	Helm	Miller	170.00	270.00	1,100.00
776.	Dallas	1918	Teehee	Burke	Talley	Van Zandt	170.00	250,00	1,100.00
777.	Dallas	1918	Elliott	Burke	Talley	Van Zandt	175.00	275.00	1,150.00
778.	San Francisco	1918	Teehee	Burke	Clerk	Lynch	170.00	250.00	1,100.00
779.	San Francisco	1918	Elliott	Burke	Clerk	Calkins	170.00	270.00	1,100.00
780.	San Francisco	1918	Elliott	Burke	Ambrose	Calkins	170.00	270.00	1,100.00

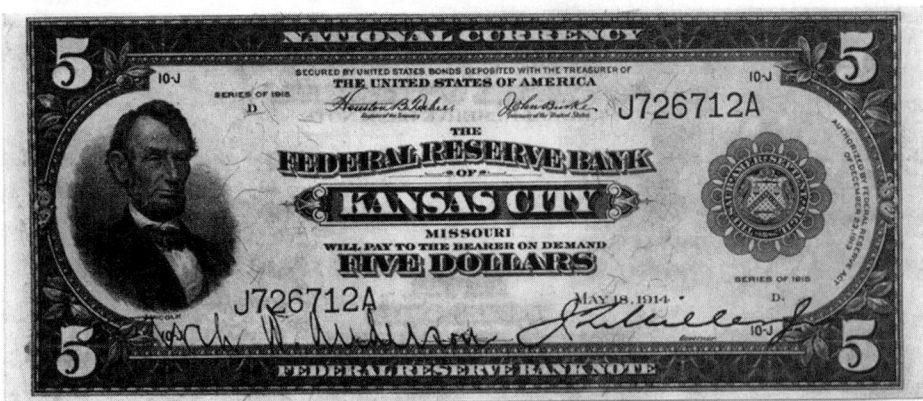

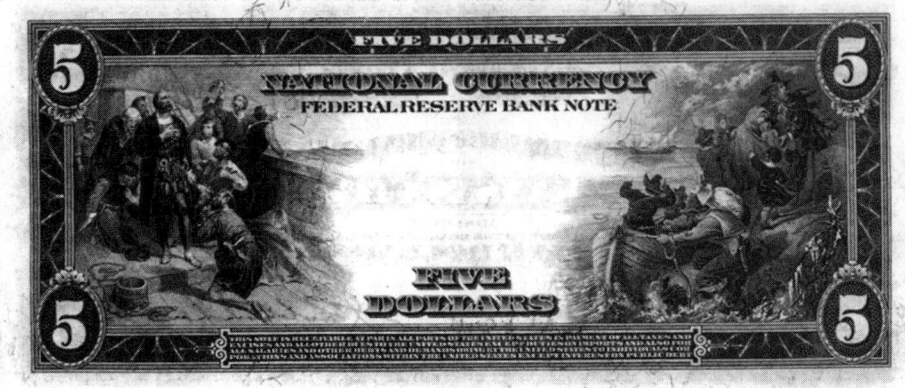

5 Dollar Notes

DESIGN NO. 129

(Notes 781-809-a)

Head of Abraham Lincoln.

Reverse of Design No. 129.

At the left, Columbus in sight of land. At the right, the landing of the Pilgrims.

Note illustrated from collection of the American Numismatic Association.

No.	Issuing Bank	Series	Government Signatures		Bank Signatures		Very Good	Very Fine	Unc
781.	Boston	1918	Teehee	Burke	Bullen	Morss	125.00	600.00	3,500.00
782.	New York	1918	Teehee	Burke	Hendricks	Strong	55.00	110.00	750.00
783.	Philadelphia	1918	Teehee	Burke	Hardt	Passmore	55.00	110.00	750.00
784.	Philadelphia	1918	Teehee	Burke	Dyer	Passmore	65.00	125.00	800.00
785.	Cleveland	1918	Teehee	Burke	Baxter	Fancher	50.00	100.00	725.00
786.	Cleveland	1918	Teehee	Burke	Davis	Fancher	70.00	140.00	800.00
787.	Cleveland	1918	Elliott	Burke	Davis	Fancher	70.00	140.00	800.00
788.	Atlanta	1915	Teehee	Burke	Bell	Wellborn	70.00	140.00	800.00
789.	Atlanta	1915	Teehee	Burke	Pike	McCord	80.00	150.00	825.00
790.	Atlanta	1918	Teehee	Burke	Pike	McCord	80.00	150.00	825.00
791.	Atlanta	1918	Teehee	Burke	Bell	Wellborn	80.00	150.00	825.00
792.	Atlanta	1918	Elliott	Burke	Bell	Wellborn	80.00	150.00	825.00
793.	Chicago	1915	Teehee	Burke	McLallen	McDougal	80.00	150.00	825.00
794.	Chicago	1918	Teehee	Burke	McCloud	McDougal	50.00	90.00	700.00
795.	Chicago	1918	Teehee	Burke	Cramer	McDougal	100.00	200.00	1,000.00
796.	St. Louis	1918	Teehee	Burke	Attebery	Wells	60.00	125.00	750.00
797.	St. Louis	1918	Teehee	Burke	Attebery	Biggs	45.00	85.00	675.00
798.	St. Louis	1918	Elliott	Burke	White	Biggs	45.00	85.00	675.00
799.	Minneapolis	1918	Teehee	Burke	Cook	Wold	70.00	125.00	800.00
800.	Kansas City	1915	Teehee	Burke	Anderson	Miller	45.00	85.00	675.00
801.	Kansas City	1915	Teehee	Burke	Cross	Miller	50.00	90.00	700.00
802.	Kansas City	1915	Teehee	Burke	Helm	Miller	50.00	90.00	700.00
803.	Kansas City	1918	Teehee	Burke	Anderson	Miller	45.00	85.00	675.00
804.	Kansas City	1918	Elliott	Burke	Helm	Miller	45.00	85.00	675.00
805.	Dallas	1915	Teehee	Burke	Hoopes	Van Zandt	50.00	90.00	700.00
806.	Dallas	1915	Teehee	Burke	Talley	Van Zandt	80.00	150.00	825.00
807.	Dallas	1918	Teehee	Burke	Talley	Van Zandt	80.00	150.00	825.00
808.	San Francisco	1915	Teehee	Burke	Clerk	Lynch	80.00	150.00	825.00
809.	San Francisco	1918	Teehee	Burke	Clerk	Lynch	80.00	150.00	825.00
809-a.	San Francisco	Similar, but with date May 18, 1914.							
		(All other San Francisco notes are with date May 20, 1914.)					200.00	500.00	3,000.00

No 5 Dollar Federal Reserve Bank notes were issued by the Richmond Bank.

10 Dollar Notes

DESIGN NO. 130

(Notes 810-821)

Head of Andrew Jackson.

Reverse of Design No. 130.

Farm and Factory scenes.

Note illustrated from collection of the American Numismatic Association.

No.	Issuing Bank	Series	Government Signatures		Bank Signatures		Very Good	Very Fine	Unc
810.	New York	1918	Teehee	Burke	Hendricks	Strong	285.00	550.00	2,400.00
811.	Atlanta	1915	Teehee	Burke	Bell	Wellborn	400.00	750.00	3,250.00
812.	Atlanta	1918	Elliott	Burke	Bell	Wellborn	300.00	575.00	2,500.00
813.	Chicago	1915	Teehee	Burke	McLallen	McDougal	285.00	550.00	2,400.00
814.	Chicago	1918	Teehee	Burke	McCloud	McDougal	300.00	675.00	3,250.00
815.	St. Louis	1918	Teehee	Burke	Attebery	Wells	325.00	700.00	2.500.00
816.	Kansas City	1915	Teehee	Burke	Anderson	Miller	225.00	450.00	2,000.00
817.	Kansas City	1915	Teehee	Burke	Cross	Miller	250.00	475.00	2,100.00
			Bank signatures plate engraved.						
817a.	Kansas City	1915	Teehee	Burke	Cross	Miller			
			Bank signatures hand stamped in red with Cross as "Acting" Secretary					Rare	—
818.	Kansas City	1915	Teehee	Burke	Helm	Miller	500.00	750.00	4,500.00
819.	Dallas	1915	Teehee	Burke	Hoopes	Van Zandt	300.00	575.00	2,550.00
820.	Dallas	1915	Teehee	Burke	Gilbert	Van Zandt	400.00	750.00	3,000.00
821.	Dallas	1915	Teehee	Burke	Talley	Van Zandt	350.00	750.00	2,900.00

No 10 Dollar Federal Reserve Bank Notes were issued by the banks at Boston, Philadelphia, Cleveland, Richmond, Minneapolis and San Francisco.

20 Dollar Notes

DESIGN NO. 131

(Notes 822-830)

Head of Grover Cleveland, 21st President of the United States, 1885-1889, and 1893-1897

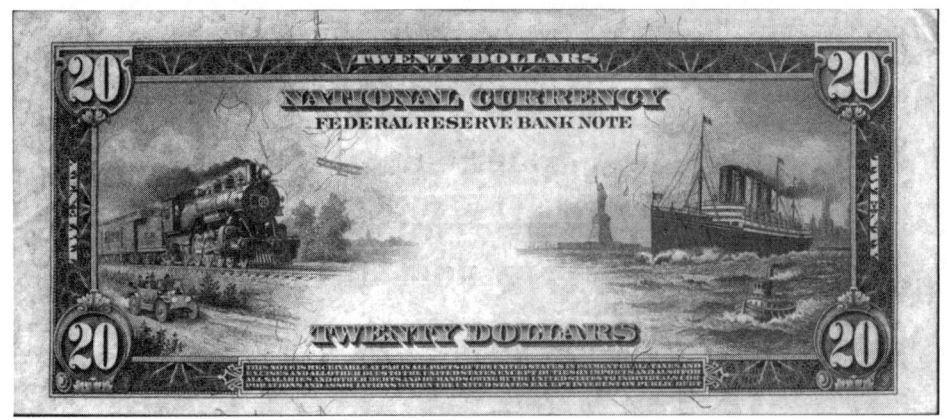

Reverse of Design No. 131.

The vignettes represent land, sea and air transportation.

Note illustrated from collection of the American Numismatic Association.

No.	Issuing Bank	Series	Government Signatures		Bank Signatures		Very Good	Very Fine	Unc
822.	Atlanta	1915	Teehee	Burke	Bell-Cashier	Wellborn	450.00	750.00	6,500.00
822-1.	Atlanta	Same but with Bell-Secretary.					600.00	975.00	8,000.00
822-a.	Atlanta	1915	Teehee	Burke	Pike	McCord	600.00	975.00	Rare
823.	Atlanta	1918	Elliott	Burke	Bell	Wellborn	375.00	650.00	5,500.00
824.	Chicago	1915	Teehee	Burke	McLallen	McDougal	385.00	650.00	5,500.00
825.	St. Louis	1918	Teehee	Burke	Attebery	Wells	375.00	650.00	5,500.00
826.	Kansas City	1915	Teehee	Burke	Anderson	Miller	375.00	650.00	5,500.00
827.	Kansas City	1915	Teehee	Burke	Cross	Miller	400.00	700.00	6,000.00
828.	Dallas	1915	Teehee	Burke	Hoopes	Van Zandt	385.00	650.00	5,500.00
829.	Dallas	1915	Teehee	Burke	Gilbert	Van Zandt	400.00	900.00	5,750.00
830.	Dallas	1915	Teehee	Burke	Talley	Van Zandt	550.00	1,000.00	6,500.00

No 20 Dollar Federal Reserve Bank Notes were issued by the banks at Boston, New York, Philadelphia, Cleveland, Richmond, Minneapolis and San Francisco.

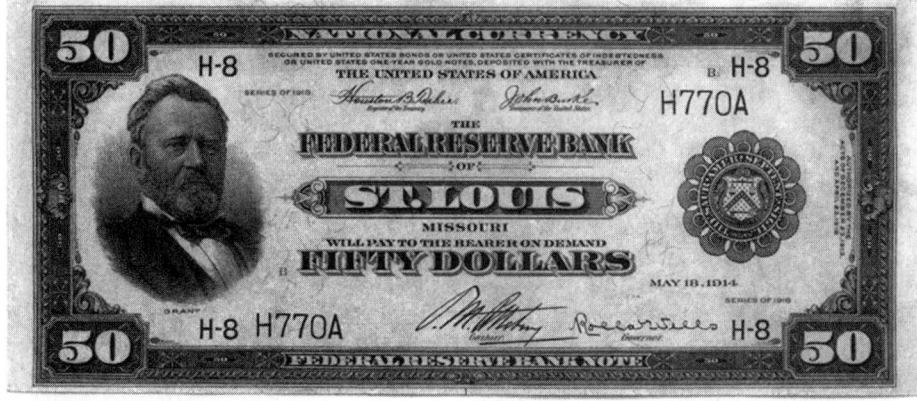

50 Dollar Note

DESIGN NO. 132

(Note 831)

Head of Ulysses S. Grant. This note is very rare as only 33 pieces are reported outstanding on U.S. Treasury books.

Reverse of Design No. 132.

Figure of Panama between two ships.

Note illustrated from collection of the American Numismatic Association.

No.	Issuing Bank	Series	Government Signatures		Bank Signatures		Very Good	Very Fine	Unc
831.	St. Louis	1918	Teehee	Burke	Attebery	Wells	1,650.00	6,000.00	16,500.00

This is the only bank that issued a 50 Dollar Federal Reserve Bank Note.

X. FEDERAL RESERVE NOTES

These were issued under the same Act which authorized the first issue of Federal Reserve Bank Notes, namely the Federal Reserve Act of December 23, 1913.

All denominations were issued from 5 to 10,000 Dollars. The notes from 5 to 100 Dollars are series of 1914, those from 500 to 10,000 Dollars are series of 1918.

The Federal Reserve Notes were issued by the United States to all twelve Federal Reserve Banks and through them to the member banks and the public. The notes were not issued by the banks themselves (as were the Federal Reserve Bank Notes) and the obligation to pay the bearer is borne by the government, and not by the banks.

Hence, these notes were not secured by United States bonds or other securities. (In practice, they were secured, but the nature of the security is not certified on the notes.)

The obligation on the Federal Reserve Notes is completely unlike that on the Federal Reserve Bank Notes, and is as follows, "The United States of America will pay to the bearer on demand ...... Dollars ... This note is receivable by all national and member banks and Federal Reserve Banks and for all taxes, customs and other public dues. It is redeemable in gold on demand at the Treasury Department of the United States in the city of Washington, District of Columbia or in gold or lawful money at any Federal Reserve Bank."

The reverses of all the following notes are similar to the reverses of the Federal Reserve Bank Notes, except that the words "National Currency" and "Bank" have been removed.

IMPORTANT NOTE: There were three separate issues of notes bearing the White-Mellon signatures and two issues bearing the Burke-McAdoo names. The first issue has a large letter and a numeral in the left bottom of the obverse (see Design No. 133 and 134). The second issue has a small letter and numeral in the same place (see Design No. 135). The third issue has again a large letter and numeral, but slightly higher and more to the left and in addition the seal on each side of the note has been moved closer to the center.

These issues are designated as a-b-c, or a-b, next to the city, depending on whether the note in question exists in all three issues. The lack of a letter alongside the city on White-Mellon or Burke-McAdoo signatures indicates that only the first or "a" issue exists.

The valuations for notes with the White-Mellon or Burke-McAdoo signatures are for the commonest, or first of the three issues of these signatures. The second issue would be valued about 25% more than the first issue and the third about 50% more than the first issue.

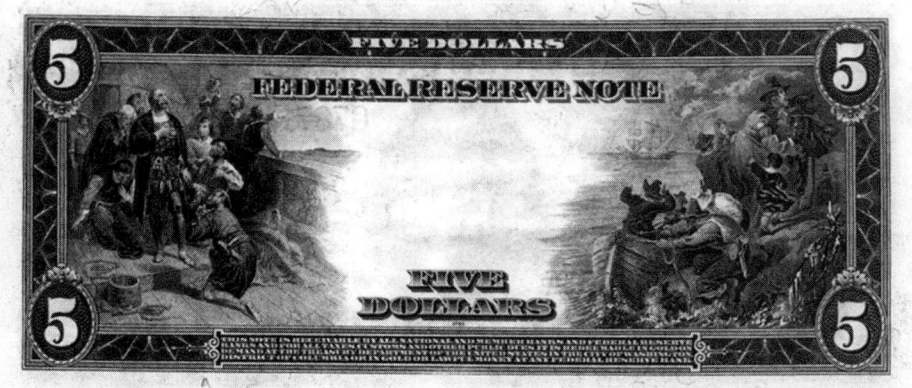

5 Dollar Notes

DESIGN NO. 133

(Notes 832-891)

Head of Abraham Lincoln.

The reverse is similar to Design No. 129.

Note illustrated from collection of the American Numismatic Association.

A. Series of 1914 With Red Seal and Signatures of Burke and McAdoo

No.	Issuing Bank	Very Good	Very Fine	Unc	No.	Issuing Bank	Very Good	Very Fine	Unc
832.	Boston a-b	140.00	275.00	1,800.00	838.	Chicago a-b	125.00	240.00	1,800.00
833.	New York a-b	125.00	240.00	1,800.00	839.	St. Louis a-b	125.00	275.00	1,800.00
834.	Philadelphia a-b	125.00	240.00	1,800.00	840.	Minneapolis a-b	175.00	375.00	2,000.00
835.	Cleveland a-b	125.00	240.00	1,800.00	841.	Kansas City a-b	140.00	275.00	1,800.00
836.	Richmond a-b	140.00	275.00	1,800.00	842.	Dallas a-b	175.00	325.00	2,000.00
837.	Atlanta a-b	140.00	275.00	1,800.00	843.	San Francisco a-b	120.00	275.00	1,800.00

B. Series of 1914 With Blue Seal

No.	Issuing Bank	Signatures		Very Fine	Unc	No.	Issuing Bank	Signatures		Very Fine	Unc
844.	Boston	Burke	McAdoo	55.00	240.00	868.	Chicago	Burke	McAdoo	50.00	195.00
845.	Boston	Burke	Glass	60.00	220.00	869.	Chicago	Burke	Glass	50.00	195.00
846.	Boston	Burke	Houston	55.00	220.00	870.	Chicago	Burke	Houston	50.00	195.00
847.	Boston a-b-c	White	Mellon	55.00	195.00	871.	Chicago a-b-c	White	Mellon	50.00	195.00
848.	New York	Burke	McAdoo	50.00	195.00	872.	St. Louis	Burke	McAdoo	55.00	195.00
849.	New York	Burke	Glass	50.50	110.00	873.	St. Louis	Burke	Glass	55.00	195.00
850.	New York	Burke	Houston	50.00	195.00	874.	St. Louis	Burke	Houston	55.00	195.00
851.	New York a-b-c	White	Mellon	50.00	195.00	875.	St. Louis a-b	White	Mellon	55.00	195.00
852.	Philadelphia	Burke	McAdoo	50.00	195.00	876.	Minneapolis	Burke	McAdoo	75.00	325.00
853.	Philadelphia	Burke	Glass	50.50	110.00	877.	Minneapolis	Burke	Glass	80.00	300.00
854.	Philadelphia	Burke	Houston	50.00	195.00	878.	Minneapolis	Burke	Houston	80.00	325.00
855.	Philadelphia a-b-c	White	Mellon	50.00	195.00	879.	Minneapolis a-b	White	Mellon	75.00	300.00
856.	Cleveland	Burke	McAdoo	50.50	110.00	880.	Kansas City	Burke	McAdoo	55.00	195.00
857.	Cleveland	Burke	Glass	50.00	110.00	881.	Kansas City	Burke	Glass	55.00	195.00
858.	Cleveland	Burke	Houston	50.00	195.00	882.	Kansas City	Burke	Houston	55.00	125.00
859.	Cleveland a-b-c	White	Mellon	50.00	195.00	883.	Kansas City a-b	White	Mellon	55.00	195.00
860.	Richmond	Burke	McAdoo	55.00	220.00	884.	Dallas	Burke	McAdoo	75.00	240.00
861.	Richmond	Burke	Glass	55.00	245.00	885.	Dallas	Burke	Glass	75.00	275.00
862.	Richmond	Burke	Houston	55.00	220.00	886.	Dallas	Burke	Houston	75.00	240.00
863.	Richmond a-b-c	White	Mellon	55.00	220.00	887.	Dallas a-b-c	White	Mellon	75.00	220.00
864.	Atlanta	Burke	McAdoo	60.00	220.00	888.	San Francisco	Burke	McAdoo	60.00	240.00
865.	Atlanta	Burke	Glass	55.00	250.00	889.	San Francisco	Burke	Glass	60.00	220.00
866.	Atlanta	Burke	Houston	55.00	220.00	890.	San Francisco	Burke	Houston	60.00	220.00
867.	Atlanta a-b	White	Mellon	55.00	200.00	891.	San Francisco a-b-c	White	Mellon	60.00	220.00

10 Dollar Notes

DESIGN NO. 134

(Notes 892-951)

Head of Andrew Jackson.

The reverse is similar to Design No. 130.

Note illustrated from collection of the American Numismatic Association.

A. Series of 1914 With Red Seal and Signatures of Burke and McAdoo

No.	Issuing Bank	Very Good	Very Fine	Unc	No.	Issuing Bank	Very Good	Very Fine	Unc
892.	Boston a-b	145.00	350.00	2,000.00	898.	Chicago a-b	125.00	275.00	2,000.00
893.	New York a-b	125.00	275.00	2,000.00	899.	St. Louis a-b	140.00	300.00	2,000.00
894.	Philadelphia a-b	125.00	275.00	2,000.00	900.	Minneapolis a-b	175.00	400.00	2,950.00
895.	Cleveland a-b	125.00	275.00	2,000.00	901.	Kansas City a-b	140.00	300.00	2,000.00
896.	Richmond a-b	140.00	300.00	2,000.00	902.	Dallas a-b	175.00	350.00	2,700.00
897.	Atlanta a-b	140.00	325.00	2,000.00	903.	San Francisco a-b	140.00	300.00	2,250.00

B. Series of 1914 With Blue Seal

No.	Issuing Bank	Signatures		Very Fine	Unc	No.	Issuing Bank		Signatures	Very Fine	Unc
904.	Boston	Burke	McAdoo	75.00	240.00	928.	Chicago	Burke	McAdoo	65.00	225.00
905.	Boston	Burke	Glass	75.00	240.00	929.	Chicago	Burke	Glass	65.00	225.00
906.	Boston	Burke	Houston	75.00	225.00	930.	Chicago	Burke	Houston	65.00	225.00
907.	Boston a-b	White	Mellon	75.00	225.00	931.	Chicago a-b-c	White	Mellon	65.00	225.00
908.	New York	Burke	McAdoo	65.00	225.00	932.	St. Louis	Burke	McAdoo	75.00	260.00
909.	New York	Burke	Glass	65.00	225.00	933.	St. Louis	Burke	Glass	75.00	260.00
910.	New York	Burke	Houston	65.00	225.00	934.	St. Louis	Burke	Houston	65.00	225.00
911.	New York a-b-c	White	Mellon	65.00	225.00	935.	St. Louis	White	Mellon	65.00	225.00
912.	Philadelphia	Burke	McAdoo	65.00	225.00	936.	Minneapolis	Burke	McAdoo	95.00	350.00
913.	Philadelphia	Burke	Glass	65.00	225.00	937.	Minneapolis	Burke	Glass	95.00	375.00
914.	Philadelphia	Burke	Houston	65.00	225.00	938.	Minneapolis	Burke	Houston	85.00	300.00
915.	Philadelphia a-c	White	Mellon	65.00	225.00	939.	Minneapolis	White	Mellon	85.00	300.00
916.	Cleveland	Burke	McAdoo	65.00	225.00	940.	Kansas City	Burke	McAdoo	75.00	250.00
917.	Cleveland	Burke	Glass	65.00	225.00	941.	Kansas City	Burke	Glass	75.00	250.00
918.	Cleveland	Burke	Houston	65.00	225.00	942.	Kansas City	Burke	Houston	65.00	225.00
919.	Cleveland a-b-c	White	Mellon	65.00	225.00	943.	Kansas City a-c	White	Mellon	65.00	225.00
920.	Richmond	Burke	McAdoo	85.00	240.00	944.	Dallas	Burke	McAdoo	85.00	325.00
921.	Richmond	Burke	Glass	85.00	240.00	945.	Dallas	Burke	Glass	85.00	325.00
922.	Richmond	Burke	Houston	75.00	240.00	946.	Dallas	Burke	Houston	75.00	295.00
923.	Richmond	White	Mellon	75.00	240.00	947.	Dallas	White	Mellon	75.00	295.00
924.	Atlanta	Burke	McAdoo	85.00	240.00	948.	San Francisco	Burke	McAdoo	65.00	250.00
925.	Atlanta	Burke	Glass	85.00	260.00	949.	San Francisco	Burke	Glass	75.00	250.00
926.	Atlanta	Burke	Houston	75.00	225.00	950.	San Francisco	Burke	Houston	65.50	225.00
927.	Atlanta a-b	White	Mellon	75.00	225.00	951.	San Francisco a-b-c	White	Mellon	65.00	225.00

20 Dollar Notes

DESIGN NO. 135

(Notes 952-1011)

Head of Grover Cleveland.

The reverse is similar to Design No. 131.

Note illustrated from collection of the American Numismatic Association.

A. Series of 1914 With Red Seal and Signatures of Burke and McAdoo

No.	Issuing Bank	Very Good	Very Fine	Unc	No.	Issuing Bank	Very Good	Very Fine	Unc
952.	Boston a-b	180.00	550.00	2,250.00	958.	Chicago a-b	160.00	500.00	2,500.00
953.	New York a-b	160.00	550.00	2,500.00	959.	St. Louis a-b	180.00	500.00	2,500.00
954.	Philadelphia a-b	160.00	550.00	2,500.00	960.	Minneapolis	240.00	750.00	2,750.00
955.	Cleveland a-b	160.00	550.00	2,500.00	961.	Kansas City a-b	180.00	550.00	2,500.00
956.	Richmond a-b	180.00	550.00	2,500.00	962.	Dallas	220.00	650.00	2,750.00
957.	Atlanta	180.00	550.00	2,500.00	963.	San Francisco a-b	200.00	600.00	2,500.00

B. Series of 1914 With Blue Seal

No.	Issuing Bank	Signatures		Very Fine	Unc	No.	Issuing Bank	Signatures		Very Fine	Unc
964.	Boston	Burke	McAdoo	95.00	300.00	979.	Cleveland a-b	White	Mellon	95.00	300.00
965.	Boston	Burke	Glass	110.00	350.00	980.	Richmond	Burke	McAdoo	110.00	320.00
966.	Boston	Burke	Houston	95.00	300.00	981.	Richmond	Burke	Glass	110.00	320.00
967.	Boston	White	Mellon	95.00	300.00	982.	Richmond	Burke	Houston	110.00	320.00
968.	New York	Burke	McAdoo	95.00	300.00	983.	Richmond a-b	White	Mellon	110.00	300.00
969.	New York	Burke	Glass	95.00	200.00	984.	Atlanta	Burke	McAdoo	110.00	320.00
970.	New York	Burke	Houston	95.00	300.00	985.	Atlanta	Burke	Glass	None	Printed
971.	New York a-b-c	White	Mellon	95.00	300.00	986.	Atlanta	Burke	Houston	110.00	320.00
972.	Philadelphia	Burke	McAdoo	95.00	300.00	987.	Atlanta a-b	White	Mellon	110.00	300.00
973.	Philadelphia	Burke	Glass	95.00	200.00	988.	Chicago	Burke	McAdoo	95.00	300.00
974.	Philadelphia	Burke	Houston	95.00	300.00	989.	Chicago	Burke	Glass	95.00	200.00
975.	Philadelphia	White	Mellon	95.00	300.00	990.	Chicago	Burke	Houston	95.00	300.00
976.	Cleveland	Burke	McAdoo	95.00	300.00	991.	Chicago a-b-c	White	Mellon	95.00	300.00
977.	Cleveland	Burke	Glass	95.00	200.00	992.	St. Louis	Burke	McAdoo	95.00	200.00
978.	Cleveland	Burke	Houston	95.00	300.00	993.	St. Louis	Burke	Glass	100.00	200.00

No.	Issuing Bank	Signatures		Very Fine	Unc	No.	Issuing Bank	Signatures		Very Fine	Unc
994.	St. Louis	Burke	Houston	100.00	300.00	1003.	Kansas City	White	Mellon	100.00	300.00
995.	St. Louis	White	Mellon	100.00	300.00	1004.	Dallas	Burke	McAdoo	110.00	350.00
996.	Minneapolis	Burke	McAdoo	125.00	375.00	1005.	Dallas	Burke	Glass	110.00	375.00
997.	Minneapolis	Burke	Glass	125.00	395.00	1006.	Dallas	Burke	Houston	110.00	350.00
998.	Minneapolis	Burke	Houston	125.00	375.00	1007.	Dallas	White	Mellon	110.00	325.00
999.	Minneapolis	White	Mellon	125.00	350.00	1008.	San Francisco	Burke	McAdoo	100.00	325.00
1000.	Kansas City	Burke	McAdoo	100.00	300.00	1009.	San Francisco	Burke	Glass	100.00	325.00
1001.	Kansas City	Burke	Glass	100.00	300.00	1010.	San Francisco	Burke	Houston	100.00	300.00
1002.	Kansas City	Burke	Houston	100.00	300.00	1011.	San Francisco a-b-c	White	Mellon	100.00	300.00

50 Dollar Notes

DESIGN NO. 136

(Notes 1012-1071)

Head of Ulysses S. Grant.

The reverse is similar to Design No. 132.

Note illustrated from collection of the American Numismatic Association.

A. Series of 1914 With Red Seal and Signatures of Burke and McAdoo

No.	Issuing Bank	Very Good	Very Fine	Unc	No.	Issuing Bank	Very Good	Very Fine	Unc
1012.	Boston a-b	650.00	1,250.00	5,500.00	1018.	Chicago a-b	650.00	1,250.00	5,500.00
1013.	New York a-b	650.00	1,250.00	5,500.00	1019.	St. Louis a-b	680.00	1,300.00	5,500.00
1014.	Philadelphia a-b	650.00	1,250.00	5,500.00	1020.	Minneapolis	775.00	1,450.00	5,500.00
1015.	Cleveland a-b	650.00	1,250.00	5,500.00	1021.	Kansas City a-b	680.00	1,250.00	5,500.00
1016.	Richmond a-b	680.00	1,250.00	5,500.00	1022.	Dallas	725.00	1,350.00	5,500.00
1017.	Atlanta	680.00	1,350.00	5,500.00	1023.	San Francisco a-b	680.00	1,250.00	5,500.00

B. Series of 1914 With Blue Seal

No.	Issuing Bank	Signatures		Very Fine	Unc	No.	Issuing Bank	Signatures		Very Fine	Unc
1024.	Boston	Burke	McAdoo	250.00	1,150.00	1038.	Cleveland	Burke	Houston	250.00	1,150.00
1025.	Boston	Burke	Glass	275.00	1,250.00	1039.	Cleveland a-b	White	Mellon	250.00	1,150.00
1026.	Boston	Burke	Houston	250.00	1,150.00	1040.	Richmond	Burke	McAdoo	275.00	1,250.00
1027.	Boston	White	Mellon	250.00	1,150.00	1041.	Richmond	Burke	Glass	300.00	1,250.00
1028.	New York	Burke	McAdoo	250.00	1,150.00	1042.	Richmond	Burke	Houston	250.00	1,150.00
1029.	New York	Burke	Glass	275.00	1,250.00	1043.	Richmond	White	Mellon	250.00	1,150.00
1030.	New York	Burke	Houston	250.00	1,150.00	1044.	Atlanta	Burke	McAdoo	250.00	1,150.00
1031.	New York a-b	White	Mellon	250.00	1,150.00	1045.	Atlanta	Burke	Glass	275.00	1,150.00
1032.	Philadelphia	Burke	McAdoo	250.00	1,150.00	1046.	Atlanta	Burke	Houston	275.00	1,250.00
1033.	Philadelphia	Burke	Glass	275.00	1,250.00	1047.	Atlanta	White	Mellon	250.00	1,150.00
1034.	Philadelphia	Burke	Houston	250.00	1,150.00	1048.	Chicago	Burke	McAdoo	250.00	1,150.00
1035.	Philadelphia	White	Mellon	250.00	1,150.00	1049.	Chicago	Burke	Glass	275.00	1,250.00
1036.	Cleveland	Burke	McAdoo	250.00	1,150.00	1050.	Chicago	Burke	Houston	250.00	1,150.00
1037.	Cleveland	Burke	Glass	275.00	1,250.00	1051.	Chicago	White	Mellon	250.00	1,150.00

No.	Issuing Bank	Signatures		Very Fine	Unc	No.	Issuing Bank	Signatures		Very Fine	Unc
1052.	St. Louis	Burke	McAdoo	275.00	1,250.00	1062.	Kansas City	Burke	Houston	None printed	
1053.	St. Louis	Burke	Glass	300.00	1,400.00	1063.	Kansas City	White	Mellon	300.00	1,150.00
1054.	St. Louis	Burke	Houston	275.00	1,250.00	1064.	Dallas	Burke	McAdoo	275.00	1,250.00
1055.	St. Louis	White	Mellon	275.00	1,250.00	1065.	Dallas	Burke	Glass	300.00	1,400.00
1056.	Minneapolis	Burke	McAdoo	275.00	1,250.00	1066.	Dallas	Burke	Houston	275.00	1,250.00
1057.	Minneapolis	Burke	Glass	None Printed		1067.	Dallas	White	Mellon	275.00	1,250.00
1058.	Minneapolis	Burke	Houston	275.00	1,250.00	1068.	San Francisco	Burke	McAdoo	275.00	1,250.00
1059.	Minneapolis	White	Mellon	275.00	1,250.00	1069.	San Francisco	Burke	Glass	None printed	
1060.	Kansas City	Burke	McAdoo	300.00	1,150.00	1070.	San Francisco	Burke	Houston	275.00	1,250.00
1061.	Kansas City	Burke	Glass	None printed		1071.	San Francisco	White	Mellon	275.00	1,250.00

100 Dollar Notes

DESIGN NO. 137

(Notes 1072-1131)

Head of Benjamin Franklin.

Reverse of Design No. 137.

Allegorical group of five figures.

Note illustrated from collection of the American Numismatic Association.

A. Series of 1914 With Red Seal and Signatures of Burke and McAdoo

No.	Issuing Bank	Very Good	Very Fine	Unc	No.	Issuing Bank	Very Good	Very Fine	Unc
1072.	Boston a-b	700.00	1,250.00	8,000.00	1078.	Chicago a-b	650.00	1,250.00	8,000.00
1073.	New York a-b	650.00	1,250.00	8,000.00	1079.	St. Louis a-b	650.00	1,250.00	8,000.00
1074.	Philadelphia a-b	650.00	1,250.00	8,000.00	1080.	Minneapolis	750.00	1,400.00	8,000.00
1075.	Cleveland a-b	650.00	1,250.00	8,000.00	1081.	Kansas City a-b	650.00	1,250.00	8,000.00
1076.	Richmond a-b	700.00	1,250.00	8,000.00	1082.	Dallas a-b	750.00	1,400.00	8,000.00
1077.	Atlanta a-b	700.00	1,400.00	8,000.00	1083.	San Francisco a-b	650.00	1,250.00	8,000.00

B. Series of 1914 With Blue Seal

No.	Issuing Bank	Signatures		Very Fine	Unc	No.	Issuing Bank	Signatures		Very Fine	Unc
1084.	Boston	Burke	McAdoo	450.00	2,000.00	1100.	Richmond	Burke	McAdoo	475.00	1,800.00
1085.	Boston	Burke	Glass	475.00	1,800.00	1101.	Richmond	Burke	Glass	475.00	2,000.00
1086.	Boston	Burke	Houston	None printed		1102.	Richmond	Burke	Houston	None printed	
1087.	Boston	White	Mellon	450.00	1,800.00	1103.	Richmond	White	Mellon	450.00	1,600.00
1088.	New York	Burke	McAdoo	450.00	1,500.00	1104.	Atlanta	Burke	McAdoo	450.00	1,500.00
1089.	New York	Burke	Glass	475.00	1,700.00	1105.	Atlanta	Burke	Glass	None printed	
1090.	New York	Burke	Houston	450.00	1,500.00	1106.	Atlanta	Burke	Houston	450.00	2,100.00
1091.	New York	White	Mellon	450.00	1,800.00	1107.	Atlanta	White	Mellon	450.00	2,100.00
1092.	Philadelphia	Burke	McAdoo	450.00	1,500.00	1108.	Chicago	Burke	McAdoo	450.00	1,600.00
1093.	Philadelphia	Burke	Glass	None printed		1109.	Chicago	Burke	Glass	None printed	
1094.	Philadelphia	Burke	Houston	None printed		1110.	Chicago	Burke	Houston	450.00	1,700.00
1095.	Philadelphia	White	Mellon	450.00	2,100.00	1111.	Chicago	White	Mellon	450.00	1,700.00
1096.	Cleveland	Burke	McAdoo	450.00	2,000.00	1112.	St. Louis	Burke	McAdoo	450.00	1,700.00
1097.	Cleveland	Burke	Glass	475.00	2,000.00	1113.	St. Louis	Burke	Glass	None printed	
1098.	Cleveland	Burke	Houston	450.00	1,800.00	1114.	St. Louis	Burke	Houston	None printed	
1099.	Cleveland	White	Mellon	450.00	2,000.00	1115.	St. Louis	White	Mellon	450.00	1,800.00

No.	Issuing Bank	Signatures		Very Fine	Unc	No.	Issuing Bank	Signatures		Very Fine	Unc
1116.	Minneapolis	Burke	McAdoo	450.00	2,000.00	1124.	Dallas	Burke	McAdoo	450.00	1,800.00
1117.	Minneapolis	Burke	Glass	None printed		1125.	Dallas	Burke	Glass	None printed	
1118.	Minneapolis	Burke	Houston	None printed		1126.	Dallas	Burke	Houston	None printed	
1119.	Minneapolis	White	Mellon	450.00	2,100.00	1127.	Dallas	White	Mellon	450.00	2,500.00
1120.	Kansas City	Burke	McAdoo	450.00	2,000.00	1128.	San Francisco	Burke	McAdoo	475.00	1,700.00
1121.	Kansas City	Burke.	Glass	None printed		1129.	San Francisco	Burke	Glass	None printed	
1122.	Kansas City	Burke	Houston	None printed		1130.	San Francisco	Burke	Houston	475.00	1,700.00
1123.	Kansas City	White	Mellon	450.00	2,100.00	1131.	San Francisco	White	Mellon	475.00	1,700.00

500 Dollar Notes

DESIGN NO. 138

(Notes 1132-1132-b)

Head of John Marshall. His portrait also appears on Design No. 93.

Reverse of Design No. 138.

De Soto discovering the Mississippi.

Note illustrated from collection of the American Numismatic Association.

Series of 1918
Different bank varieties are known.

No.	Signatures	Very Good	Very Fine	Unc
1132.	Burke-Glass	3,250.00	6,750.00	20,000.00
1132-a.	Burke-Houston	4,250.00	8,000.00	Rare
1132-b.	White-Mellon	3,950.00	7,250.00	Rare

1,000 Dollar Notes

DESIGN NO. 139

(Note 1133-1133-b)

Head of Alexander Hamilton.

Reverse of Design No. 139.

American eagle with flag.

Note illustrated from collection of the Federal Reserve Bank of San Francisco.

Series of 1918
Different bank varieties are known.

No.	Signatures	Very Good	Very Fine	Unc
1133.	Burke-Glass	3,500.00	7,500.00	24,000.00
1133a.	Burke-Houston	4,000.00	8,000.00	Rare
1133b.	White-Mellon	3,750.00	7,750.00	Rare

5,000 Dollar Notes

DESIGN NO. 140

(Note 1134)

Head of James Madison, fourth President of the United States, 1809-1817.

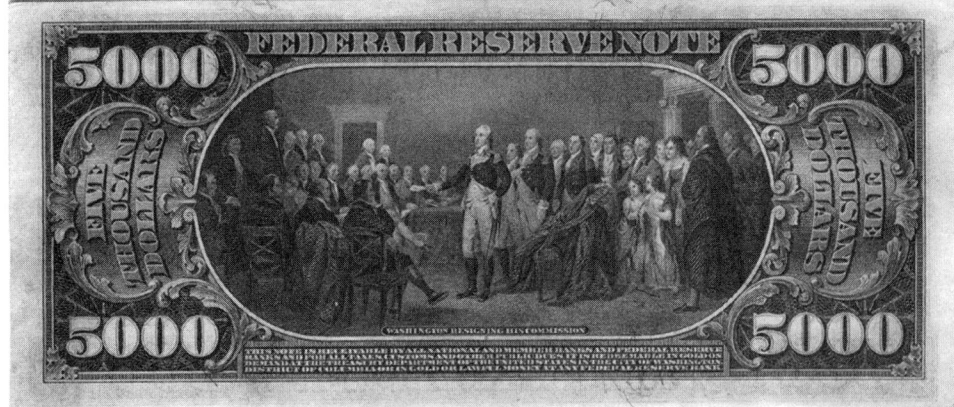

Reverse of Design No. 140.

George Washington resigning his Commission.

Note illustrated from collection of the Federal Reserve Bank of San Francisco.

1134.   5000 Dollar Note. Series of 1918. Different bank varieties were issued.

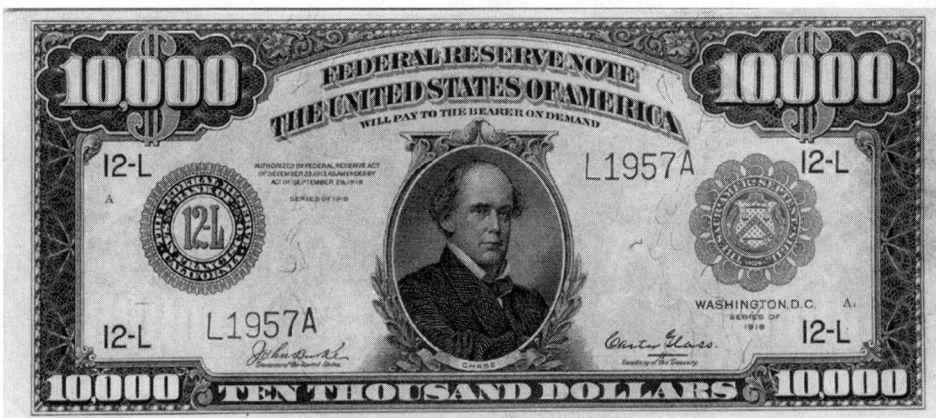

10,000 Dollar Notes

DESIGN NO. 141

(Note 1135)

Head of Salmon P. Chase.

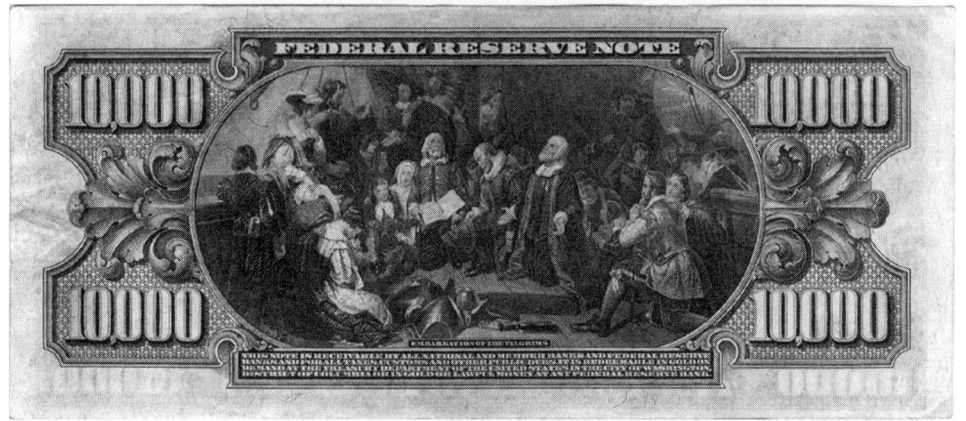

Reverse of Design No. 141.

The Embarkation of the Pilgrims.

Note illustrated from collection of the Federal Reserve Bank of San Francisco.

1135. 10,000 Dollar Note. Series of 1918. Different bank varieties were issued.

XI. THE NATIONAL GOLD BANK NOTES OF CALIFORNIA

These notes are the most romantic of all our currency issues. Their existence is directly traceable to the California Gold Rush of 1848 and they remain today as tangible mementos of the Winning of the West.

These notes are instinctively associated with gold. First, the paper on which they are printed is yellowish in imitation of gold and secondly, the reverses show a group of American gold coins of all denominations from 1 to 20 Dollars. See the illustration in the text.

As the population of California continued to grow, trade and commerce increased to such an extent that the California banks were soon handling enormous quantities of gold coin in their daily transactions. In those days in California, gold was the universal medium of exchange. The counting and handling of so much coin was burdensome and time consuming and was a barrier to the efficient operation of the banks.

Therefore, in order to facilitate these numerous gold transactions, Congress passed the Act of July 12, 1870, which authorized nine Gold Banks in California and one in Boston to issue and circulate currency redeemable in gold coin. This was indeed remarkable, since the Treasury Department had not yet resumed specie payments (which were not to come until 1879.) The denominations issued were 5, 10, 20, 50, 100 and 500 Dollars, but not all banks issued all denominations.

The vignettes on the obverse of these notes are the same as on the National Bank Notes of the First Charter Period.

The name of the Boston bank that was authorized to issue National Bank Notes was the Kidder National Gold Bank of Boston, Mass. It is believed that its entire issue of gold notes was recalled and destroyed before they were released to the public.

Only two specimen notes are known to exist, one of 50 Dollars and the other of 100 Dollars.

These banks were Gold Banks in addition to being National Banks, and so their operation came under the general provisions of the National Banking Act of 1863 and they were required to deposit the legal amount of United States Bonds with the Treasurer of the United States.

It must be remembered that the obligation of redeeming these notes in gold coin rested with the bank and not with the government.

These notes were readily accepted in California at par with gold, and they went through a long life of active and useful circulation. Indeed, so active was this circulation that very few notes have survived in their original new condition.

Any National Gold Bank Note in crisp new condition is practically unheard of and is an outstanding rarity. The general condition in which these notes are found is one of advanced circulation and notes in very fine or better condition are extremely rare. All these notes, regardless of their preservation, are very rare today and are greatly in demand by collectors.

The obligation on these National Gold Bank Notes is as follows. "This note is secured by bonds of the United States deposited with the U.S. Treasurer at Washington.... The (name of bank and city) will pay...... Dollars to bearer in gold coin on demand.... This note is receivable at par in all parts of the United States in payment of all taxes and excises and all other dues to the United States, except duties on imports, and also for all salaries and other debts and demands owing by the United States to individuals, corporations, and associations within the United States, except interest on public debt."

All the notes in this section have a red Treasury Seal and the signatures of Allison and Spinner except the following:
1153 and 1163 have the signatures of Bruce and Gilfillan
1147, 1150 and 1157 have the signatures of Scofield and Gilfillan

ALL NOTES IN THIS SECTION ARE VERY RARE IN A STATE OF PRESERVATION BETTER THAN VERY GOOD

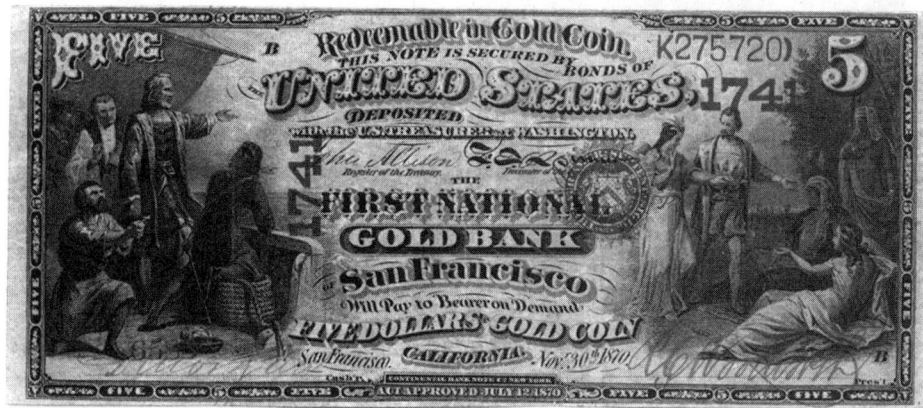

5 Dollar Notes

DESIGN NO. 142

(Notes 1136-1141)

Vignettes similar to Design No. 101, but the wording pertains to gold coin.

Reverse of Design No. 142.

A group of gold coins, showing the 1, 2 1/2, 3, 5, 10 and 20 Dollar pieces.

Note illustrated from collection of the American Numismatic Association.

No.	Date	Name of Bank	City	Fair	Very Good
1136.	1870	First National Gold Bank	San Francisco	550.00	950.00
1137.	1872	National Gold Bank and Trust Company	San Francisco	650.00	1,250.00
1138.	1872	National Gold Bank of D.O. Mills and Co.	Sacramento	600.00	1,050.00
1139.	1873	First National Gold Bank	Santa Barbara	800.00	1,550.00
1140.	1873	First National Gold Bank	Stockton	600.00	1,150.00
1141.	1874	Farmer's National Gold Bank	San Jose	600.00	1,500.00

10 Dollar Notes

DESIGN NO. 143
(Notes 1142-1151a)
Obverse: Vignettes similar to Design No. 102.
Reverse: Similar to Design No. 142.

No.	Date	Name of Bank	City	Fair	Very Good
1142.	1870	First National Gold Bank	San Francisco	825.00	1,750.00
1143.	1872	National Gold Bank and Trust Company	San Francisco	875.00	1,750.00
1144.	1872	National Gold Bank of D.O. Mills and Co.	Sacramento	850.00	1,800.00
1145.	1873	First National Gold Bank	Santa Barbara	850.00	1,800.00
1146.	1873	First National Gold Bank	Stockton	800.00	1,700.00
1147.	1875	Series. First National Gold Bank	Stockton	850.00	1,800.00
1148.	1874	Farmer's National Gold Bank	San Jose	750.00	1,800.00
1149.	1874	First National Gold Bank	Petaluma	750.00	1,850.00
1150.	1875	Series. First National Gold Bank	Petaluma	750.00	1,850.00
1151.	1875	First National Gold Bank	Oakland	850.00	1,800.00
1151a.	1875	Union National Gold Bank	Oakland	800.00	1,700.00

20 Dollar Notes

DESIGN NO. 144
(Notes 1152-1159b)
Obverse: Vignettes similar to Design No. 103.

Reverse: Similar to Design No. 142.

Note illustrated from collection of the American Numismatic Association..

No.	Date	Name of Bank	City	Fair	Very Good
1152.	1870	First National Gold Bank	San Francisco	1,650.00	5,000.00
1153.	1875	Series. First National Gold Bank	San Francisco	1,800.00	5,100.00
1154.	1872	National Gold Bank of D.O. Mills and Co.	Sacramento	1,650.00	5,000.00
1155.	1873	First National Gold Bank	Stockton	1,650.00	5,000.00
1155-a.	1875	First National Gold Bank	Stockton	Unique	—

No.	Date	Name of Bank	City	Fair	Very Good
1156.	1874	Farmer's National Gold Bank	San Jose	1,650.00	5,000.00
1157.	1875	Series. First National Gold Bank	Petaluma	Extremely Rare	—
1158.	1875	First National Gold Bank	Oakland	1,250.00	5,400.00
1159.	1875	Union National Gold Bank	Oakland	Extremely Rare	—
1159a.	1873	First National Gold Bank	Santa Barbara	Unique	
1159b.	1872	National Gold Bank and Trust Company	San Francisco	Unknown	—

50 Dollar Notes

DESIGN NO. 145
(Notes 1160-1161-f)
Obverse: Vignettes similar to Design No. 104.
Reverse: Similar to Design No. 142.

No.	Date	Name of Bank	City	Fair	Very Good
1160.	1870	First National Gold Bank	San Francisco	Extremely Rare	—
1160a.	1875	Series. First National Gold Bank	San Francisco	Unique	—
1161.	1874	Farmer's National Gold Bank	San Jose	Unique	—
1161a.	1872	National Gold Bank and Trust Company	San Francisco	Unknown	—
1161b.	1872	National Gold Bank of D.O. Mills and Co.	Sacramento	Unknown	—
1161c.	1873	First National Gold Bank	Stockton	Unknown	—
1161d.	1873	First National Gold Bank	Santa Barbara	Unknown	—
1161e.	1874	Series. First National Gold Bank	Petaluma	Unknown	—
1161f.	1873	Union National Gold Bank	Oakland	Unknown	—

100 Dollar Notes

DESIGN NO. 146
(Notes 1162-1166IV)
Obverse: Vignettes similar to Design No. 105.
Reverse: Similar to Design No. 142.

No.	Date	Name of Bank	City	Fair	Very Good
1162.	1870	First National Gold Bank	San Francisco	Rare	—
1163.	1875	Series. First National Gold Bank	San Francisco	Rare	—
1164.	1873	First National Gold Bank	Santa Barbara	Unique	—
1165.	1874	First National Gold Bank	Petaluma	Rare	—
1166.	1875	Union National Gold Bank	Oakland	Rare	—
1166I.	1872	National Gold Bank and Trust Company	San Francisco	Unknown	—
1166II.	1872	National Gold Bank of D.O. Mills and Co.	Sacramento	Unknown	—
1166III.	1873	First National Gold Bank	Stockton	Rare	—
1166IV.	1874	Farmer's National Gold Bank	San Jose	Unknown	—

500 Dollar Notes

DESIGN NO. 146-a
(Note 1166e)
Obverse: Vignettes similar to Design No. 106.
Reverse: Similar to Design No. 142.

1166a.   This denomination was issued by three banks—the two in San Francisco, and the one in Sacramento. No specimen of these notes is now known to exist, although four notes are still outstanding.

XII. GOLD CERTIFICATES

Gold Certificates are colorful and vivid and are among the most attractive of all currency issues. Their reverses are a brilliant golden orange, symbolic of the gold coin they represent.

Although there were nine emissions of gold certificates, only four of the issues were circulated to any extent, namely the fourth, seventh, eighth and ninth issues.

The first three issues appeared between 1865 and 1875. Some of the notes were printed on only one side. They. remained in general within the confines of banks and clearing houses and were used in settling gold balances.

The fifth and sixth issues were series of 1888 and 1900 and consisted of 5,000 and 10,000 Dollar notes only.

The fourth issue was the earliest for general circulation. The notes of this issue are series of 1882 and consist of all denominations from 20 to 10,000 Dollars. The 20, 50 and 100 Dollar notes are still occasionally seen.

The seventh issue consisted only of 10 and 20 Dollar notes of the series of 1905, 1906 and 1907. The 20 Dollar notes of 1905 are considered the most beautiful of all gold certificates because of their color. Their basic design is similar to that of other 20 Dollar notes, but the obverse center portion of the paper is gold tinted and part of the legends are printed in gold ink, and not the black and white of other issues. These notes also have a red seal and red serial numbers. Thus, the color combination formed by black and white and gold and red, makes a very pleasing impression.

The eighth issue consisted only of 1,000 Dollar Notes of the series of 1907.

The ninth and last issue of Gold Certificates forms the notes that are most frequently seen today. These notes are series of 1913 and 1922 and the issue consisted of all denominations from 10 to 1,000 Dollars. The series of 1913 appears only on 50 Dollar notes. See the text for a complete tabulation.

The obligation on gold certificates is as follows, "This certifies that there have been deposited in the Treasury of the United States of America...... Dollars in gold coin payable (or repayable, series 1882) to the bearer on demand."

In addition to the preceding, the notes of series 1922 bear the following, "This certificate is a legal tender in the amount thereof in payment of all debts and dues public and private. Acts of March 14, 1900, as amended and December 24, 1919.

THE REVERSES OF ALL GOLD CERTIFICATES ARE A BRILLIANT GOLDEN ORANGE COLOR.

Gold Certificates of the First Issue. Act of March 3, 1863.

DESIGN NO. 146-b

(Note 1166-b)

Eagle on draped shield. Countersigned and dated by hand These notes have one or more handwritten signatures.

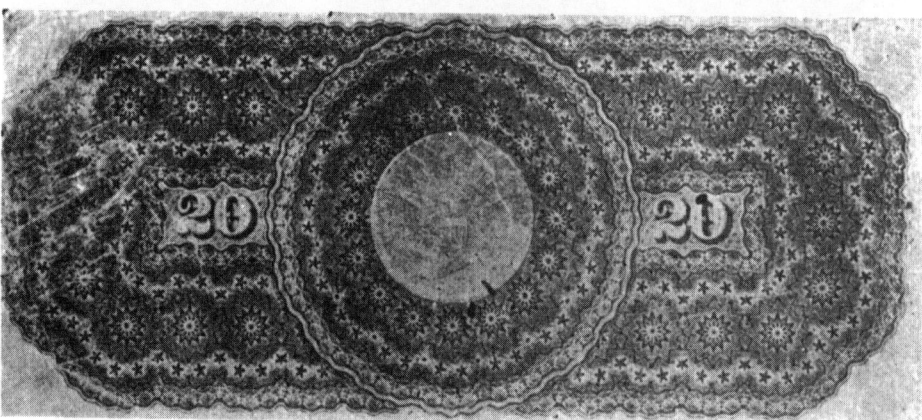

Reverse of Design No. 146-b.

1166-b.   20 Dollar Note.   Extremely Rare.

DESIGN NO. 146-c

(Note 1166-c)

Eagle on draped shield. Countersigned and dated by hand.

Reverse of Design No. 146-c.

1166-c.	100 Dollar Note.	Extremely Rare	
1166-d.	500 Dollar Note.	Unknown	**DESIGN NO. 146-d**
1166-e.	1,000 Dollar Note.	Unique	**DESIGN NO. 146-e**
1166-f.	5,000 Dollar Note.	Unique	**DESIGN NO. 146-f**
1166-g.	10,000 Dollar Note.	Unknown	**DESIGN NO. 146-g**

Gold Certificates of the Second Issue. Act of March 3, 1863.

Countersigned and dated in 1870 or 1871 by hand.

1166-h.	100 Dollar Note.	Head of Benton.	Unknown	**DESIGN NO. 146-h**
1166-I.	500 Dollar Note.	Head of Lincoln.	Unique	**DESIGN NO. 146-i**
1166-j.	1,000 Dollar Note.	Head of Hamilton.	Unique	**DESIGN NO. 146-j**
1166-k.	5,000 Dollar Note.	Head of Madison.	Unknown	**DESIGN NO. 146-k**
1166-1.	10,000 Dollar Note.	Head of Jackson.	Unknown	**DESIGN NO. 146-l**

Gold Certificates of the Third Issue. Act of March 3,1863.

Countersigned and dated by hand.

DESIGN NO. 146-m

(Note 1166-m)

Head of Thomas Hart Benton (1782-1858), who served in the United States Senate and House of Representatives for over 30 years.

This note is printed on only one side. The reverse is blank.

This illustration by courtesy of Mr. R.F Schermerhorn.

1166-m.	100 Dollar Note. Series of 1875.	Extremely Rare	
1166-n.	500 Dollar Note. Series of 1875. Head of Lincoln	Unknown	**DESIGN NO. 146-n**
1166-o.	1,000 Dollar Note. Series of 1875. Head of Hamilton.	Unknown	**DESIGN NO. 146-o**
1166-q.	10,000 Dollar Note. Series of 1875.	Unique	**DESIGN NO. 146-q**

Gold Certificates of the Fourth and Later Issues.

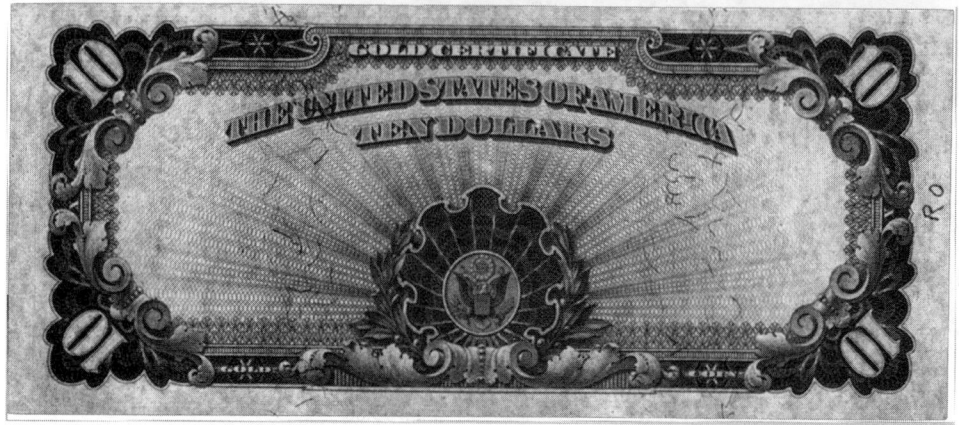

10 Dollar Notes

DESIGN NO. 147

(Notes 1167-1173-a)

Head of Michael Hillegas, the first Treasurer of the United States, 1775-1789.
(The obverse of the 1907 issue differs slightly from the 1922 issue. The reverses are similar.)

Reverse of Design No. 147

Note illustrated from collection of the American Numismatic Association.

No.	Series	Signatures		Seal	Very Good	Very Fine	Unc
1167.	1907	Vernon	Treat	Gold	65.00	125.00	1,500.00
1168.	1907	Vernon	McClung	Gold	65.00	125.00	1,400.00
1169.	1907	Napier	McClung	Gold Act of 1882	65.00	115.00	1,400.00
1169-a.	1907	Napier	McClung	Gold Act of 1907	65.00	115.00	1,400.00
1170.	1907	Napier	Thompson	Gold Act of 1882	100.00	200.00	3,000.00
1170-a.	1907	Napier	Thompson	Gold Act of 1907	100.00	200.00	3,000.00
1171.	1907	Parker	Burke	Gold	65.00	110.00	1,350.00
1172.	1907	Teehee	Burke	Gold	65.00	115.00	1,350.00
1173.	1922	Speelman	White	Gold	60.00	100.00	1,250.00
1173-a.	1922	Speelman	White	Gold, small serial nos.	80.00	125.00	1,750.00

A Countersigned Gold Certificate, Series of 1882

Illustrated to show the minor differences between the countersigned and normal issues of Series of 1882.
Notes 1175, 1189 and 1202 are countersigned.

This illustration by courtesy of Mr. Arthur M. Kagin.

20 Dollar Notes

DESIGN NO. 148

(Notes 1174-1178)

Head of President James A. Garfield, engraved by Charles Burt.

Reverse of Design No. 148.

Large eagle carrying a lightning bolt. This vignette, named "Ocean Telegraph," commemorated the completion of the Atlantic cable in 1858.

Note illustrated from collection of the American Numismatic Association.

No.	Series	Signatures		Seal	Very Good	Very Fine	Unc
1174.	1882	Bruce	Gilfillan	Brown	3,750.00	8,500.00	Rare
1175.	1882	Bruce	Gilfillan	Brown	4,750.00	12,500.00	Rare
	The above note with autographed countersignature by Thomas C. Acton, Ass't. Treasurer, and payable at New York.						
1175-a.	1882	Bruce	Gilfillan	Brown	4,000.00	8,000.00	Rare
	The above note with engraved countersignature by Thomas C. Acton, Ass't. Treasurer, and payable at New York.						
1176.	1882	Bruce	Wyman	Brown	1,300.00	2,800.00	Rare
1177.	1882	Rosecrans	Huston	Large Brown	1,400.00	3,000.00	Rare
1178.	1882	Lyons	Roberts	Small Red	225.00	1,100.00	7,500.00

DESIGN NO. 149

(Notes 1179-1187)

Head of George Washington (The obverses of the 1905, 1906 and 1922 issues all differ slightly in some respects. The reverses of all issues are similar.) Numbers 1179 and 1180 are the famous "Technicolor" notes, so called because of their coloring.

Reverse of Design No. 149.

Note illustrated from collection of the American Numismatic Association.

No.	Series	Signatures		Seal	Very Good	Very Fine	Unc
1179.	1905	Lyons	Roberts	Small Red	425.00	2,000.00	13,000.00
1180.	1905	Lyons	Treat	Small Red	400.00	1,500.00	12,000.00
1181.	1906	Vernon	Treat	Gold	95.00	200.00	2,500.00
1182.	1906	Vernon	McClung	Gold	95.00	200.00	2,500.00
1183.	1906	Napier	McClung	Gold	95.00	250.00	2,500.00
1184.	1906	Napier	Thompson	Gold	120.00	200.00	4,750.00
1185.	1906	Parker	Burke	Gold	95.00	200.00	2,100.00
1186.	1906	Teehee	Burke	Gold	95.00	200.00	2,100.00
1187.	1922	Speelman	White	Gold	95.00	200.00	2,000.00

50 Dollar Notes

DESIGN NO. 150

(Notes 1188-1197)

Head of Silas Wright, 1795-1847, famous contemporary figure in government. He was both a U.S. Senator (1833-1844) and Governor of New York (1845-1847). Wright's portrait was engraved by Charles Burt from a painting by Alonzo Chappell.

Reverse of Design No. 150.

Eagle on Draped Shield.

Note illustrated from collection of the American Numismatic Association.

No.	Series	Signatures		Seal	Very Good	Very Fine	Unc
1188.	1882	Bruce	Gilfillan	Brown	Rare	—	—
1189.	1882	Bruce	Gilfillan	Brown	Extremely Rare	—	—
				The above note with autographed countersignature by Thomas C. Acton, Ass't Treasurer, and payable at New York.			
1189-a.	1882	Bruce	Gilfillan	Brown	8,000.00	15,000.00	Rare
				The above note with engraved countersignature by Thomas C. Acton, Ass't Treasurer, and payable at New York.			
1190.	1882	Bruce	Wyman	Brown	Extremely Rare	—	—
1191.	1882	Rosecrans	Hyatt	Large Red	Extremely Rare	—	—
1192.	1882	Rosecrans	Huston	Large Brown	Extremely Rare	—	—

No.	Series	Signatures		Seal	Very Good	Very Fine	Unc
1192-a.	1882	Rosecrans	Huston	Small Red	Unique	—	—
1193.	1882	Lyons	Roberts	Small Red	575.00	1,250.00	7,000.00
1194.	1882	Lyons	Treat	Small Red	700.00	1,500.00	9,000.00
1195.	1882	Vernon	Treat	Small Red	600.00	1,300.00	8,000.00
1196.	1882	Vernon	McClung	Small Red	700.00	1,500.00	9.500.00
1197.	1882	Napier	McClung	Small Red	575.00	1,250.00	7,500.00

DESIGN NO. 151

(Notes 1198-1200-a)

Head of Ulysses S. Grant.

Reverse of Design No. 151.

Note illustrated from collection of the American Numismatic Association.

No.	Series	Signatures		Seal	Very Good	Very Fine	Unc
1198.	1913	Parker	Burke	Gold	350.00	700.00	5,000.00
1199.	1913	Teehee	Burke	Gold	375.00	750.00	5,500.00
1200.	1922	Speelman	White	Gold	350.00	650.00	4,500.00
1200-a.	1922	Speelman	White	Gold, small serial numbers	400.00	700.00	5,250.00

100 Dollar Notes

DESIGN NO. 152

(Notes 1201-1215)

Head of Thomas Hart Benton, who served in both the U.S. Senate, 1821-1851, and in the U.S. House of Representatives, 1853-1855. (The obverse of the 1882 issues differs in several minor respects from the 1922 issue. The reverses are similar.)

Reverse of Design No. 152.

Eagle on fasces.

Note illustrated from collection of the American Numismatic Association.

No.	Series	Signatures		Seal	Very Good	Very Fine	Unc
1201.	1882	Bruce	Gilfillan	Brown	Extremely Rare	—	—
1202.	1882	Bruce	Gilfillan	Brown	Extremely Rare	—	—
(The above note is countersigned by Thomas C. Acton, Ass't. Treasurer, and payable at New York.)							
1203.	1882	Bruce	Wyman	Brown	Extremely Rare	—	—
1204.	1882	Rosecrans	Hyatt	Large Red	Extremely Rare	—	—
1205.	1882	Rosecrans	Huston	Large Brown	Extremely Rare	—	—
1206.	1882	Lyons	Roberts	Small Red	425.00	900.00	9,000.00
1207.	1882	Lyons	Treat	Small Red	650.00	1,250.00	10,500.00
1208.	1882	Vernon	Treat	Small Red	650.00	11,250.00	9,750.00
1209.	1882	Vernon	McClung	Small Red	425.00	900.00	9,250.00
1210.	1882	Napier	McClung	Small Red	650.00	1,250.00	9,750.00
1211.	1882	Napier	Thompson	Small Red	450.00	1,000.00	9,250.00
1212.	1882	Napier	Burke	Small Red	450.00	1,000.00	7,000.00
1213.	1882	Parker	Burke	Small Red	450.00	900.00	7,000.00
1214.	1882	Teehee	Burke	Small Red	400.00	800.00	6,000.00
1215.	1922	Speelman	White	Small Red	375.00	700.00	5,500.00

500 Dollar Notes

DESIGN NO. 153

(Notes 1215-a-1217)

Head of Abraham Lincoln.

Reverse of Design No. 153.

Note illustrated from collection of the American Numismatic Association.

No.	Series	Signatures		Seal	Very Good	Very Fine	Unc
1215-a.	1882	Bruce	Gilfillan	Brown	Unique	—	—
1215-b.	1882	Bruce	Gilfillan	Brown	Unknown	—	—
(The above note is countersigned by Thomas C. Acton, Ass't. Treasurer, and payable at New York.)							

No.	Series	Signatures		Seal	Very Good	Very Fine	Unc
1215c.	1882	Bruce	Wyman	Brown	Unknown	—	—
1215d.	1882	Rosecrans	Hyatt	Large Red	Unique	—	—
1216.	1882	Lyons	Roberts	Small Red	3,500.00	9,000.00	Rare
1216a.	1882	Parker	Burke	Small Red	3,500.00	9,000.00	Rare
1216b.	1882	Teehee	Burke	Small Red	3,500.00	9,000.00	Rare
1217.	1922	Speelman	White	Small Red	3,000.00	8,000.00	Rare

1,000 Dollar Notes

DESIGN NO. 154

(Notes 1218-1218g)

Head of Alexander Hamilton.

Reverse of Design No. 154.

No.	Series	Signatures		Seal	
1218.	1882	Bruce	Gilfillan	Brown	Unknown
1218a.	1882	Bruce	Gilfillan	Brown	Extremely Rare
(The above note is countersigned by Thomas C. Acton, Ass't. Treasurer, and payable at New York.)					
1218b.	1882	Bruce	Wyman	Brown	Unique
1218c.	1882	Rosecrans	Hyatt	Large Red	Unique
1218d.	1882	Rosecrans	Huston	Large Brown	Extremely Rare
1218e.	1882	Rosecrans	Nebeker	Small Red	Extremely Rare
1218f.	1882	Lyons	Roberts	Small Red	Rare
1218g.	1882	Lyons	Treat	Small Red	Rare

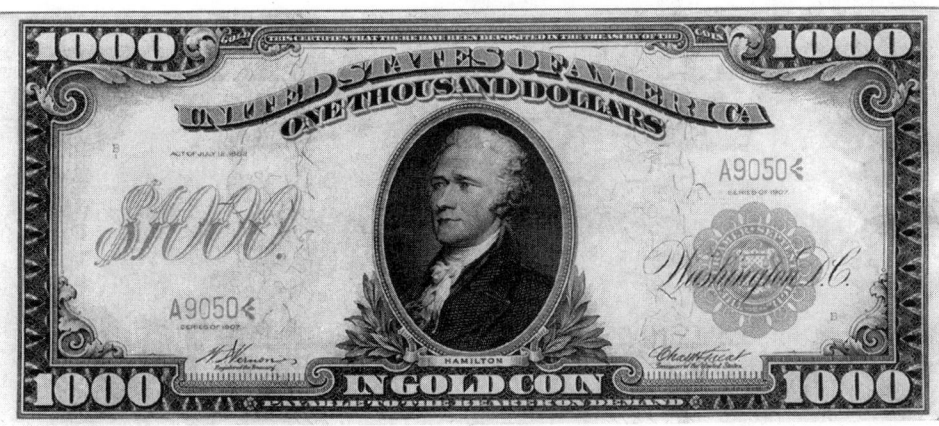

DESIGN NO. 154-a

(Notes 1219-1220)

Head of Alexander Hamilton.

Reverse of Design No. 154-a.

Note illustrated from collection of the Federal Reserve Bank of San Francisco.

No.	Series	Signatures		Seal	Very Good	Very Fine	Unc
1219.	1907	Vernon	Treat	Gold	Rare	—	—
1219-a.	1907	Vernon	McClung	Gold	Unknown	—	—
1219-b.	1907	Napier	McClung	Gold	Unique	—	—
1219-c.	1907	Napier	Burke	Gold	Extremely Rare	—	—
1219-d.	1907	Parker	Burke	Gold	5,500.00	17,500.00	—
1219-e.	1907	Teehee	Burke	Gold	5,000.00	15,000.00	Rare
1220.	1922	Speelman	White	Gold	4,000.00	15,000.00	Rare

5,000 Dollar Notes

DESIGN NO. 155

(Notes 1221-1222-b)

Head of James Madison.

Reverse of Design No. 155.

Note illustrated from collection of the Federal Reserve Bank of San Francisco.

No.	Series	Signatures		Seal	
1221.	1882	Bruce	Gilfillan	Brown	Unknown
1221-a.	1882	Bruce	Gilfillan	Brown	Unknown
(The above note is countersigned by Thomas C. Acton, Ass't. Treasurer, and payable at New York.)					
1221-b.	1882	Bruce	Wyman	Brown	Unknown
1221-c.	1882	Rosecrans	Hyatt	Large Red	Unknown
1221-d.	1882	Rosecrans	Nebeker	Small Red	Unknown
1221-e.	1882	Lyons	Roberts	Small Red	Unknown
1221-f.	1882	Vernon	Treat	Small Red	Unknown

No.	Series	Signatures		Seal	
1221g.	1882	Vemon	McClung	Small Red	Unknown
1221h.	1882	Napier	McClung	Small Red	Unknown
1221i.	1882	Parker	Burke	Small Red	Unknown
1221j.	1882	Teehee	Burke	Small Red	Extremely Rare (Two known)
1222.	1888	Rosecrans	Hyatt	Large Red	All Redeemed, None Outstanding
1222a.	1888	Rosecrans	Nebeker	Small Red	All Redeemed, None Outstanding
1222b.	1888	Lyons	Roberts	Small Red	All Redeemed, None Outstanding

10,000 Dollar Notes

DESIGN NO. 156

(Notes 1223-1225)

Head of Andrew Jackson.

Reverse of Design No. 156.

Note illustrated from collection of the Federal Reserve Bank of San Francisco.

No.	Series	Signatures		Seal	
1223.	1882	Bruce	Gilfillan	Brown	Unknown
1223a.	1882	Bruce	Gilfillan	Brown	Unknown
(The above note is countersigned by Thomas C. Acton, Ass't. Treasurer, and payable at New York.)					
1223b.	1882	Bruce	Wyman	Brown	Unknown
1223c.	1882	Rosecrans	Hyatt	Large Red	Unknown
1223d.	1882	Rosecrans	Nebeker	Small Red	Unknown
1223e.	1882	Lyons	Roberts	Small Red	Unknown
1223f.	1882	Vernon	Treat	Small Red	Unknown
1223g.	1882	Teehee	Burke	Small Red	Extremely Rare (Two known)
1224.	1888	Rosecrans	Hyatt	Large Red	All Redeemed, None Outstanding
1224a.	1888	Rosecrans	Nebeker	Small Red	All Redeemed, None Outstanding
1224b.	1888	Lyons	Roberts	Small Red	All Redeemed, None Outstanding
1225.	1900	All known notes are canceled.			

PART TWO
XIII. FRACTIONAL CURRENCY

The average person is surprised and somewhat incredulous when informed that there is such a thing as a genuine American 50 Cent bill, or even a 3 cent bill. With the great profusion of change in the pockets and purses of the last few generations, it does indeed seem strange to learn of valid United States paper money of 3, 5, 10, 15, 25 and 50 Cent denominations.

Yet it was not always so. During the early years of the Civil War, the banks suspended specie payments, which act had the effect of putting a premium on all coins. Under such conditions, coins of all denominations were jealously guarded and hoarded and soon had all but disappeared from circulation.

This was an intolerable situation since it became impossible for merchants to give small change to their customers. For a time, we reverted somewhat to the ancient barter system and one had to accept his change in the form of goods or produce which he did not necessarily want at that time.

The lives of millions of people were thus intimately affected and insistent demands were made on the Treasury Department to remedy this chaotic state of affairs.

Accordingly, on the recommendation of General Spinner who at that time was the Treasurer, Congress passed the Act of July 17, 1862 which authorized an issue of 5, 10, 25, and 50 Cent notes. These became known as Postage Currency, because they bore facsimiles of the then current 5 and 10 Cent postage stamps. This was the first of five issues produced by the government from 1862 to 1876. The later issues were called Fractional Currency, and were authorized by another act of Congress, that of March 3, 1863. In general, all issues of Postage and Fractional Currency were receivable for all United States Postage Stamps.

In the fourteen years that Fractional Currency was produced, nearly 369 million dollars of it was issued. Finally, Congress passed the Acts of January 14, 1875 and April 17, 1876 which authorized the redemption of Fractional Currency in actual silver coins. It is now estimated by the government that not quite 2 million dollars in all types of Fractional Currency is still outstanding.

First Issue. August 21, 1862 to May 27, 1863

This is the so-called Postage Currency. The issue consisted of 5, 10, 25 and 50 Cent notes. The face and backs of the notes were originally printed by the National Bank Note Company of New York. Later to increase security, the government had the backs printed by the American Bank Note Company of New York, who added the "ABN" monogram to the lower right corner of the back. Both companies produced both perforated and straight edge versions of the notes.

The eight notes of this issue are widely collected by stamp collectors in addition to being collected by numismatists.

The obligation on these is as follows, "Exchangeable for United States Notes by any Assistant Treasurer or designated U.S. Depositary in sums not less than five dollars. Receivable in payments of all dues to the U. States less than five Dollars."

Second Issue. October 10, 1863 to February 23, 1867

This issue consisted of 5, 10, 25, and 50 Cent notes. The obverses of all denominations have the bust of Washington in a bronze oval frame but each reverse is distinguished by a different color.

The obligation on this issue differs slightly, and is as follows,

"Exchangeable for United States Notes by the Assistant Treasurers and designated depositaries of the U.S. in sums not less than three dollars. Receivable in payment of all dues to the United States less than five dollars except customs."

Third Issue. December 5, 1864 to August 16, 1869

This issue consisted of 3, 5, 10, 25 and 50 Cent Notes. Each denomination is of a different design, as will be seen in the text.

The obligation on the Third Issue Notes is similar to that on the Second Issue.

Fourth Issue. July 14, 1869 to February 16, 1875

The notes of this issue consist on the 10, 15, 25 and 50 Cent denominations, each of a different design. With this issue, the Treasury Seal appears for the first time on the Fractional Currency.

The 15 cent notes appeared only in this issue and they are much scarcer than the other denominations. The obligation on the fourth issue is similar to that on the Second Issue.

Fifth Issue. February 26, 1874 to February 15, 1876

The notes of this issue consist only of 10, 25 and 50 cent denominations, each of a different design.

The obligation is similar to that of the Second Issue.

A Note on the Illustrations

The illustrations of Fractional Currency in this section are from the Robert T. Herdegen Collection of the Museum of the American Numismatic Association. Approximately 75% of the collection was from that of the legendary Col. E.H.R. Green. These notes were acquired by the creator of this book, Robert Friedberg, and in the late 1950's to early 1960's were sold to Mr. Herdegen by Peter Bartolomei at the J.L. Hudson department store in downtown Detroit. The price for the entire collection was a then-astronomical $6,000.

3 Cent Notes

The 3 Cent Notes are of the Third Issue of Fractional Currency.

DESIGN NO. 163

(Notes 1226-1227)

Head of George Washington.

No.	Variety	Very Good	Very Fine	Unc
1226.	With light background to portrait.	27.50	32.50	65.00
1227.	With dark background to portrait.	29.50	50.00	110.00

5 Cent Notes

First Issue

DESIGN NO. 164

(Notes 1232-1235)

Copy of a contemporary 5 cent postage stamp with head of Thomas Jefferson. Brown obverse, black reverse.

No.	Variety	Very Good	Very Fine	Unc
1228.	Perforated edges; with monogram of American Bank Note Co.. (ABCO) on reverse.	18.50	45.00	200.00
1229.	Perforated edges; without monogram.	22.50	80.00	275.00
1230.	Straight edges; with monogram.	15.00	18.00	65.00
1231.	Straight edges; without monogram.	22.50	55.00	210.00

Second Issue

DESIGN NO. 165

(Notes 1232-1235)

Head of George Washington in bronze oval frame. Brown reverse.

No.	Variety	Very Good	Very Fine	Unc
1232.	Without small surcharged figures on corners of reverse.	15.00	20.00	60.00
1233.	With surcharge "18-63" on corners of reverse.	15.00	20.00	60.00
1234.	With surcharge "18-63" and "S".	18.00	25.00	95.00
1235.	With surcharge "18-63" and "R-1". Fiber paper.	30.00	80.00	325.00

Third Issue

DESIGN NO. 166

(Notes 1236-1239)

Head of Spencer M. Clark, First Superintendent of the National Currency Bureau (now the Bureau of Engraving and Printing) under Abraham Lincoln.

No.	Variety	Very Good	Very Fine	Unc
1236.	Red reverse.	17.50	40.00	170.00
1237.	Red reverse; with design letter "a" at extreme left on obverse.	20.00	50.00	180.00
1238.	Green reverse.	14.50	25.00	95.00
1239.	Green reverse; with design letter "a" at extreme left on obverse.	16.00	27.50	110.00

10 Cent Notes

First Issue

DESIGN NO. 167

(Notes 1240-1243)

Copy of a contemporary 10 cent stamp with head of George Washington. Green obverse, black reverse.

No.	Variety	Very Good	Very Fine	Unc
1240.	Perforated edges; with monogram of American Bank Note Co. (ABCO) on reverse.	20.00	50.0	150.00
1241.	Perforated edges; without monogram.	22.50	70.00	200.00
1242.	Straight edges; with monogram.	12.50	20.00	60.00
1243.	Straight edges; without monogram.	17.50	70.00	260.00

Second Issue

DESIGN NO. 168

(Notes 1244-1249)

Head of George Washington in bronze oval frame. Green reverse.

No.	Variety	Very Good	Very Fine	Unc
1244.	Without small surcharged figures on corners of reverse.	11.50	20.00	70.00
1245.	With surcharge "18-63".	12.50	22.50	75.00
1246.	With surcharge "18-63" and "S".	15.00	30.00	100.00
1247.	With surcharge "18-63" and "I".	17.50	80.00	270.00
1248.	With surcharge "0-63".	375.00	1,000.00	2,500.00
1249.	With surcharge "18-63" and "T-1"; fiber paper.	18.50	125.00	325.00

Third Issue

DESIGN NO. 169

(Notes 1251-1256)

Head of George Washington.

No.	Variety	Very Good	Very Fine	Unc
1251.	Red reverse.	13.50	50.00	135.00
1252.	Red reverse with design numeral "1" on obverse.	15.00	70.00	175.00
1253.	Red reverse with autographed signatures of Colby and Spinner.	20.00	70.00	200.00
1254.	Red reverse with autographed signatures of Jeffries and Spinner	22.50	90.00	350.00
1255.	Green reverse.	13.50	30.00	65.00
1255a.	Green reverse with autographed signatures of Colby and Spinner	Extremely Rare	—	—
1256.	Green reverse with design numeral "1" on obverse.	13.50	30.00	80.00

Fourth Issue

DESIGN NO. 170

(Notes 1257-1261)

Bust of Liberty.

No.	Variety	Very Good	Very Fine	Unc
1257.	Large red seal; watermarked paper with pink silk fibers.	12.50	20.00	50.00
1258.	Large red seal; unwatermarked paper with pink silk fibers.	12.50	20.00	60.00
1259.	Large red seal; paper with violet silk fibers and blue right end on obverse.	12.50	20.00	65.00
1260.	The note previously listed does not exist.			
1261.	Smaller red seal; paper with violet silk fibers and blue right end on obverse.	12.50	20.00	65.00

 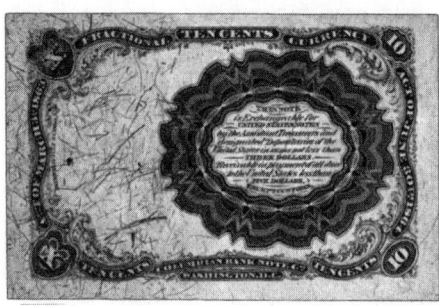

Fifth Issue

DESIGN NO. 171

(Notes 1264-1266)

Head of William M. Meredith, Secretary of the Treasury, 1849-1850.

No.	Variety	Very Good	Very Fine	Unc
1264.	Green seal.	12.00	25.00	70.00
1265.	Red seal with long, thin key.	10.50	15.00	35.00
1266.	Red seal with short, thick key.	10.50	15.00	35.00

15 Cent Notes

Fourth Issue

DESIGN NO. 172

(Notes 1267-1271)

Bust of Columbia.

No.	Variety	Very Good	Very Fine	Unc
1267.	Large red seal; watermarked paper with pink silk fibers.	42.50	60.00	160.00
1268.	Large red seal; unwatermarked paper with pink silk fibers.	52.00	125.00	350.00
1269.	Large red seal; paper with violet fibers and blue right end on obverse.	50.00	75.00	190.00
1270.	The note previously listed does not exist.			
1271.	Smaller red seal; paper with violet fibers and blue right end on obverse.	47.50	60.00	175.00

25 Cent Notes

First Issue

DESIGN NO. 174

(Notes 1279-1282)

Five 5 cents stamps of the type of Design No. 164. Brown obverse, black reverse.

No.	Variety	Very Good	Very Fine	Unc
1279.	Perforated edges; with monogram of American Bank Note Co. (ABCO) on reverse.	19.50	70.00	275.00
1280.	Perforated edges; without monogram.	22.50	85.00	350.00
1281.	Straight edges; with monogram.	12.50	25.00	100.00
1282.	Straight edges; without monogram.	25.00	95.00	390.00

Second Issue

DESIGN NO. 175

(Notes 1283-1290)

Head of George Washington in bronze oval frame. Purple reverse.

No.	Variety	Very Good	Very Fine	Unc
1283.	Without small surcharged figures on corners of reverse.	11.00	20.00	100.00
1284.	With surcharge "18-63".	14.00	40.00	160.00
1285.	With surcharge "18-63" and "A".	14.00	30.00	140.00
1286.	With surcharge "18-63" and "S".	14.00	30.00	135.00
1288.	With surcharge "18-63" and "2".	16.50	40.00	175.00
1289.	With surcharge "18-63" and "T-1"; fiber paper.	20.00	80.00	325.00
1290.	With surcharge "18-63" and "T-2"; fiber paper.	20.00	50.00	260.00

Third Issue

DESIGN NO. 176

(1291-1300)

Bust of William P. Fessenden, Secretary of the Treasury under President Lincoln.

No.	Variety	Very Good	Very Fine	Unc
1291.	Red reverse.	12.50	45.00	150.00
1292.	Red reverse with small design letter "a" on obverse.	15.00	50.00	175.00
1293.	The note listed in prior editions does not exist.			
1294.	Green reverse.	12.00	20.00	80.00
1295.	Green reverse with small design letter "a" on obverse.	10.00	40.00	95.00
1296.	Green reverse with large design letter "a" on obverse, 7 mm. to the lower right of the normal location.	750.00	1,500.00	3,500.00
1297.	Green reverse with surcharge "M-2-6-5"; fiber paper.	20.00	75.00	225.00
1298.	Same as above but with design letter "a" on obverse.	25.00	90.00	270.00
1299.	Green reverse with surcharge "M-2-6-5"; the two ornamental designs on obverse surcharged in heavy solid bronze, and not merely outlined as on previous issues; fiber paper.	175.00	700.00	1,500.00
1300.	Same as above but with design letter "a" on obverse.	400.00	1,500.00	4,000.00

Fourth Issue

DESIGN NO. 177

(Notes 1301-1307)

Bust of George Washington.

No.	Variety	Very Good	Very Fine	Unc
1301.	Large red seal; watermarked paper with pink silk fibers.	12.00	20.00	65.00
1302.	Large red seal; unwatermarked paper with pink silk fibers.	12.00	20.00	80.00
1303.	Large red seal; paper with violet fibers and blue right end on obverse.	13.00	25.00	95.00
1307.	Smaller red seal; paper with violet fibers and blue right end on obverse.	12.00	25.00	95.00

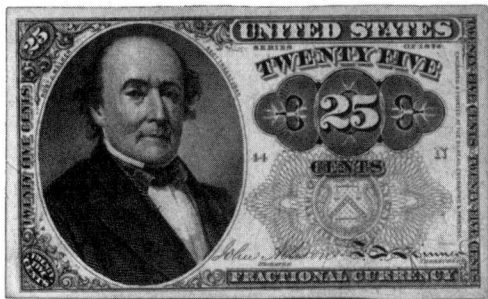 

Fifth Issue

DESIGN NO. 178

(Notes 1308-1309)

Bust of Robert J. Walker, Secretary of the Treasury 1845-1849.

No.	Variety	Very Good	Very Fine	Unc
1308.	With long, thin key in Treasury Seal (5 millimeters).	12.50	20.00	37.50
1309.	With short, thick key in Treasury Seal (4 millimeters).	12.50	20.00	37.50

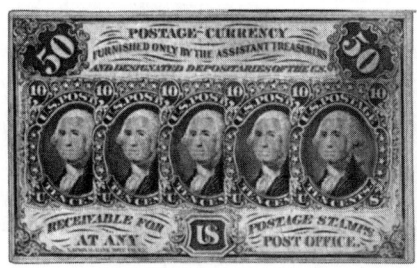 

50 Cent Notes

First Issue

DESIGN NO. 179

(Notes 1310-1313)

Five 10 cent stamps of the type of Design No. 167. Green obverse, black reverse.

No.	Variety	Very Good	Very Fine	Unc
1310.	Perforated edges; with monogram of American Bank Note Co. (ABCO) on reverse.	25.00	75.00	330.00
1310-a.	As above, except 14 perforations per 20 mm instead of 12 perforations	Rare	—	—
1311.	Perforated edges; without monogram.	32.50	90.00	425.00
1312.	Plain edges; with monogram.	17.00	40.00	160.00
1313.	Plain edges; without monogram.	35.00	135.00	500.00

Second Issue

DESIGN NO. 180

(Notes 1314-1322)

Head of George Washington in bronze oval frame. Red reverse.

No.	Variety	Very Good	Very Fine	Unc
1314.	Without small surcharged figures on corners of reverse.	Unknown	—	—
1316.	With surcharge "18-63".	15.00	75.00	275.00
1317.	With surcharge "18-63" and "A".	16.50	45.00	210.00
1318.	With surcharge "18-63" and "1".	16.50	45.00	210.00
1320.	With surcharge "18-63" and "0-1"; fiber paper.	20.00	80.00	335.00
1321.	With surcharge "18-63" and "R-2"; fiber paper.	22.50	95.00	475.00
1322.	With surcharge "18-63" and "T-1"; fiber paper.	25.00	65.00	290.00

Third Issue

DESIGN NO. 181

(Notes 1324-1338).

Head of General F.E. Spinner, Treasurer of the United States, 1861-1875.

181a. Red Reverse With Surcharge "A-2-6-5".

No.	Variety	Very Good	Very Fine	Unc
1324.	Without design figures on obverse.	35.00	75.00	260.00
1325.	Design figures "1" and "a" on obverse.	55.00	200.00	800.00
1326.	Design figure "1" only on obverse.	40.00	80.00	280.00
1327.	Design figure "a" only on obverse.	40.00	80.00	290.00
1328.	With autographed signatures of Colby and Spinner.	40.00	80.00	280.00
1329.	With autographed signatures of Allison and Spinner.	45.00	150.00	525.00
1330.	With autographed signatures of Allison and New.	750.00	2,000.00	3,900.00

181b. Green Reverse Without Surcharge.

No.	Variety	Very Good	Very Fine	Unc
1331.	Without design figures on obverse.	40.00	86.00	270.00
1332.	Design figures "1" and "a" on obverse.	45.00	100.00	375.00
1333.	Design figure "1" only on obverse.	40.00	90.00	275.00
1334.	Design figure "a" only on obverse.	42.50	90.00	275.00

181c. Green Reverse With Surcharge "A-2-6-5".

No.	Variety	Very Good	Very Fine	Unc
1335.	Without design figures oil obverse.	42.50	80.00	290.00
1336.	Design figures "1" and "a" on obverse.	250.00	1,200.00	2,700.00
1337.	Design figure "1" only on obverse.	42.50	95.00	390.00
1338.	Design figure "a" only on obverse.	42.50	110.00	410.00

DESIGN NO. 182

(Notes 1339-1342)

The obverse is similar to Design No. 181. The reverse is as shown.

No.	Variety	Very Good	Very Fine	Unc
1339.	Green reverse; without surcharges and design figures.	42.50	80.00	290.00
1340.	Green reverse; design figures and "a" on obverse.	75.00	175.00	625.00
1341.	Green reverse; design figure "1" only on obverse.	45.00	90.00	320.00
1342.	Green reverse; design figure "a" only on obverse.	45.00	95.00	360.00

 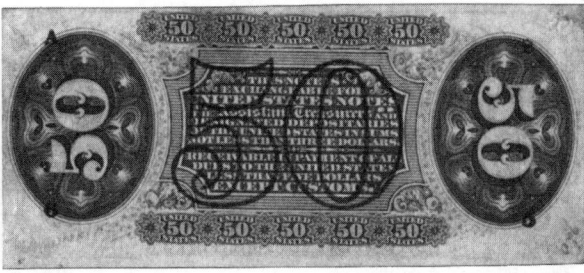

DESIGN NO. 183

(Notes 1343-1373-a)

Seated figure of Justice holding scales.

183a. Red Reverse Without Surcharge.

No.	Variety	Very Good	Very Fine	Unc
1343.	Without design figures on obverse.	45.00	85.00	380.00
1344.	With design figures "1" and "a" on obverse.	200.00	900.00	2,200.00
1345.	With design figure "1" only on obverse.	45.00	100.00	460.00
1346.	With design figure "a" only on obverse.	50.00	110.00	490.00

183b. Red Reverse With Surcharge "A-2-6-5".

No.	Variety	Very Good	Very Fine	Unc
1347.	Without design figures on obverse.	45.00	100.00	385.00
1348.	With design figures "1" and "a" on obverse.	200.00	1,000.00	2,750.00
1349.	With design figure "1" only on obverse.	45.00	125.00	550.00
1350.	With design figure "a" only on obverse.	50.00	150.00	580.00

183c. Red Reverse With Surcharge "S-2-6-4"; Printed Signatures.

No.	Variety	Very Good	Very Fine	Unc
1351.	Without design figures on obverse; fiber paper.	2,500.00	8,500.00	19,000.00
1352.	With design figures "1" and "a" on obverse; fiber paper.	Extremely Rare	—	—
1353.	With design figure "1" only on obverse; fiber paper	3,000.00	12,500.00	21,000.00
1354.	With design figure "a" only on obverse; fiber paper.	3,250.00	13,000.00	22,000.00

183d. Red Reverse; Autographed Signatures of Colby and Spinner.

No.	Variety	Very Good	Very Fine	Unc
1355.	Without surcharges and design figures.	50.00	110.00	380.00
1356.	With surcharge "A-2-6-5" on reverse.	35.00	125.00	425.00
1357.	With surcharge "S-2-6-4"; fiber paper.	65.00	275.00	950.00

183e. Green Reverse Without Surcharge.

No.	Variety	Very Good	Very Fine	Unc
1358.	Without design figures on obverse.	45.00	80.00	325.00
1359.	With design figures "1" and "a" on obverse.	200.00	900.00	2,250.00
1360.	With design figure "1" only on obverse.	45.00	95.00	340.00
1361.	With design figure "a" only on obverse.	45.00	110.00	360.00

183f. Green Reverse With Surcharge "A-2-6-5" Compactly Spaced.

No.	Variety	Very Good	Very Fine	Unc
1362.	Without design figures on obverse.	45.00	80.00	300.00
1363.	With design figures "1" and "a" on obverse.	75.00	250.00	725.00
1364.	With design figure "1" only on obverse.	27.50	95.00	325.00
1365.	With design figure "a" only on obverse.	30.50	110.00	350.00

183g. Green Reverse With Surcharge "A-2-6-5" Widely Spaced.

No.	Variety	Very Good	Very Fine	Unc
1366.	Without design figures on obverse.	45.00	125.00	300.00
1367.	With design figures "1" and "a" on obverse.	375.00	1,200.00	3,750.00
1368.	With design figure "1" only on obverse.	45.00	175.00	500.00
1369.	With design figure "a" only on obverse.	50.00	190.00	750.00

183h. Green Reverse With Surcharge "A-2-6-5"; Fiber Paper.

No.	Variety	Very Good	Very Fine	Unc
1370.	Without design figures on obverse.	50.00	125.00	600.00
1371.	With design figures "1" and "a" on obverse.	300.00	1,100.00	3,750.00
1372.	With design figure "1" only on obverse.	55.00	175.00	675.00
1373.	With design figure "a" only on obverse.	60.00	190.00	850.00
1373-a.	Green reverse with surcharge "S-2-6-4"; fiber paper; printed signatures; without design figure or letter.	3,500.00	8,500.00	19,000.00

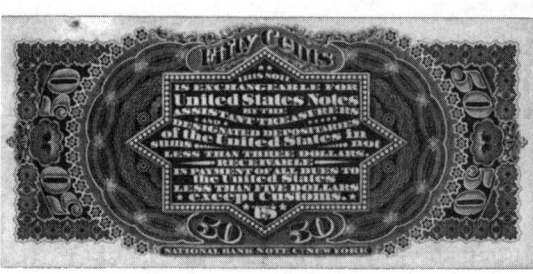

Fourth Issue

DESIGN NO. 184

(Notes 1374-1375)

Head of Abraham Lincoln.

No.	Variety	Very Good	Very Fine	Unc
1374.	Large seal; watermarked paper with pink silk fibers.	30.00	125.00	375.00
1375.	The note previously listed has been deleted.			

DESIGN NO. 185

(Note 1376)

Bust of Edwin M. Stanton, Secretary of War under President Lincoln.

No.	Variety	Very Good	Very Fine	Unc
1376.	Small red seal; paper with violet fibers and blue right end on obverse.	20.00	60.00	150.00

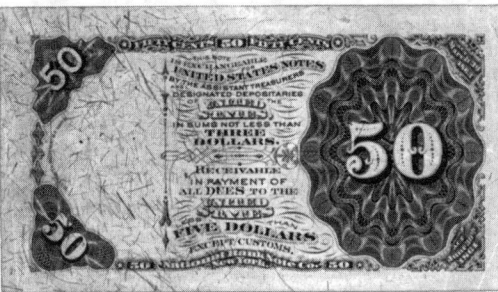

DESIGN NO. 186

(Note 1379)

Bust of Samuel Dexter, Secretary of both the War and Treasury Departments, 1800-1801.

No.	Variety	Very Good	Very Fine	Unc
1379.	Green seal; paper with light violet fibers and blue right end on obverse.	17.50	50.00	125.00

Fifth Issue

DESIGN NO. 187

(Notes 1380-1381)

Bust of William H. Crawford, Secretary of both the War and Treasury Departments, 1815-1825.

No.	Variety	Very Good	Very Fine	Unc
1380.	Red seal; paper on obverse a light pink color with silk fibers.	17.50	25.00	60.00
1381.	Red seal; white paper with silk fibers and blue right end on obverse.	17.50	25.00	60.00

FRACTIONAL CURRENCY SHIELDS

Fractional Currency Shields were made by the Treasury Department in Washington in 1866 and 1867. The outside dimensions of the shields are 20x25" and on the shield are mounted 39 specimens of fractional currency. Each note was printed on one side only, so that obverse and reverse appear as separate notes. As made, the shields are covered with glass and framed. The Treasury Department produced these for sale to banks so that they might detect counterfeit notes by comparison with the genuine notes on the shield. Complete and intact shields are now much in demand and are available only occasionally.

This illustration by courtesy of Mr. Theodore Kemm.

1382.	FRACTIONAL CURRENCY SHIELD. With gray background.	3,500.00
1383.	FRACTIONAL CURRENCY SHIELD. With pink background.	Very Rare
1383-a.	FRACTIONAL CURRENCY SHIELD. With green background.	Very Rare

INVERTED REVERSES. Some notes of the first three issues are known with inverted reverses, or inverted surcharges. Notes of the Second and Third Issues are known with surcharges partially or entirely missing. All such notes are very rare.

XIV. PROOFS AND SPECIMENS

These issues were not placed in circulation and all specimens are Proofs or Essays. The obverses and reverses of these notes were printed separately, with the back of each piece either being blank or having the word "SPECIMEN" printed in bronze, so that a complete note actually consists of two pieces. There are two varieties of each note and these are distinguished by a wide or narrow margin on all four sides.

Sometimes two or three reverses will share a common obverse, or vice versa. In these cases, one may collect one obverse note with its various reverses to form a type collection, or assemble a complete set of matching obverses and reverses. In the latter case, some obverses or reverses will be duplicated.

While most collectors prefer to assemble complete sets of Specimen notes, as a guide to type collectors we. have indicated in the listing below those cases where notes share a common obverse or reverse.

The illustrations of the notes listed below appear in the preceding pages of the book. For ease in referring to the illustrations, the Specimens below bear the same numbers as the regular issue notes, with the addition of the suffix letters "SP" to signify that the note is a Specimen.

Proofs and Specimens of Fourth and Fifth Issue notes are very rare. The prices quoted are for Specimens in new condition.

Proofs of the Following Notes Are Known:

3 Cent Notes

No.	Description	Narrow Margin	Wide Margin
1226-SP.	Obverse with light background to portrait.	95.00	Rare
1227-SP.	Obverse with dark background to portrait.	55.00	195.00
	Reverse of above 2 notes.	40.00	140.00

5 Cent Notes

No.	Description	Narrow Margin	Wide Margin
1231-SP.	Obverse with straight edges.	50.00	125.00
	Reverse of above note without monogram.	45.00	100.00
1232-SP.	Obverse.	50.00	125.00
	Reverse of above note without surcharge.	52.00	110.00
1236-SP.	Red Reverse.	45.00	160.00
1238-SP.	Green Reverse.	40.00	150.00
	Obverse of above 2 notes.	70.00	175.00

10 Cent Notes

No.	Description	Narrow Margin	Wide Margin
1243-SP.	Obverse with straight edges.	50.00	125.00
	Reverse of above note without monogram.	40.00	100.00
1244-SP.	Obverse.	60.00	125.00
	Reverse of above note without surcharge.	35.00	100.00
1251-SP.	Obverse with printed signatures of Colby and Spinner.	65.00	150.00
1253-SP.	Obverse with autographed signatures of Colby and Spinner.	85.00	175.00
1254-SP.	Obverse with autographed signatures of Jeffries and Spinner.	225.00	5,000.00
	Red Reverse of above 3 notes.	50.00	150.00
1255-SP.	Green Reverse.	45.00	135.00
	Obverse of above note (same obverse as 1251 -SP).	55.00	150.00

15 Cent Notes

 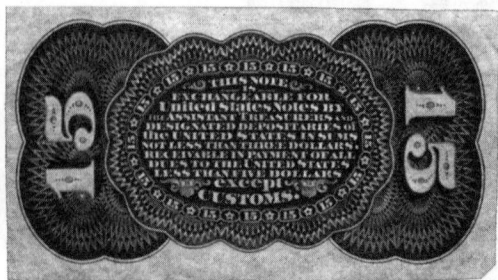

DESIGN NO. 173

(Notes 1272-SP - 1276-SP)

Heads of Union generals William T. Sherman and Ulysses S. Grant.

These notes exist only as specimens.

No.	Description	Narrow Margin	Wide Margin
1272-SP.	Obverse with printed signatures of Colby and Spinner.	125.00	300.00
	Green Reverse of above note.	95.00	175.00
1273-SP.	Obverse with autographed signatures of Colby and Spinner.	1,500.00	Unknown

No.	Description	Narrow Margin	Wide Margin
1274-SP.	Obverse with autographed signatures of Jeffries and Spinner.	175.00	250.00
1275-SP.	Obverse with autographed signatures of Allison and Spinner.	200.00	300.00
1276-SP.	Obverse without any signatures.	Rare	Unknown
	Red Reverse of above 4 notes.	95.00	175.00

25 Cent Notes

No.	Description	Narrow Margin	Wide Margin
1282-SP.	Obverse with straight edges.	55.00	150.00
	Reverse of above note without monogram.	45.00	125.00
1283-SP.	Obverse.	50.00	150.00
	Reverse of above note without surcharge.	40.00	140.00
1291-SP.	Red Reverse without surcharge.	40.00	125.00
1294-SP.	Green Reverse without surcharge.	50.00	130.00
	Obverse of above 2 notes.	65.00	135.00

50 Cent Notes

No.	Description	Narrow Margin	Wide Margin
1313-SP.	Obverse with plain edges.	85.00	145.00
	Reverse of above note without monogram.	75.00	120.00
1314-SP.	Obverse.	70.00	225.00
	Reverse of above note without surcharge.	60.00	160.00
1324-SP.	Obverse with printed signatures of Colby and Spinner.	90.00	275.00
1328-SP.	Obverse with autographed signatures of Colby and Spinner.	115.00	300.00
1329-SP.	Obverse with autographed signatures of Allison and Spinner.	3,000.00	Rare

No.	Description	Narrow Margin	Wide Margin
1330-a-SP.	Obverse. Same as Obverse of Design No. 181 but with autographed signatures of Jeffries and Spinner. THIS NOTE EXISTS ONLY AS A SPECIMEN.	150.00	5,000.00
	Red Reverse of above 4 notes without surcharge.	75.00	175.00
1331-SP.	Green Reverse without surcharge.	70.00	200.00
	Obverse of above note (same obverse as 1324-SP).	75.00	250.00
1339-SP.	Green Reverse without surcharge.	1,500.00	4,000.00
	Obverse of above note (same obverse as 1324-SP).	80.00	250.00
1343-SP.	Obverse with printed signatures of Colby and Spinner.	100.00	175.00
1355-SP.	Obverse with autographed signatures of Colby and Spinner.	125.00	250.00

No.	Description	Narrow Margin	Wide Margin
1357-a-SP.	Obverse. Same as Obverse of Design No. 183 but with autographed signatures of Jeffries and Spinner. THIS NOTE EXISTS ONLY AS A SPECIMEN.	225.00	5,000.00
	Red Reverse of above 3 notes without surcharge.	70.00	170.00
1358-SP.	Green Reverse without surcharge.	70.00	150.00
	Obverse of above note (same obverse as 1343-SP).	90.00	175.00

PART THREE. SMALL SIZE NOTES

After sixty-eight years, our large size currency felt the impact of modern times. It was discontinued and replaced with the smaller size notes we are now using. To the present generation, today's currency must doubtlessly seem to be the only kind we have ever had, since outside of numismatic circles large size notes are rarely seen or heard of today. In this instance, they are just as unfamiliar to the growing generation as are gold coins.

During the years of large size currency, the United States had reached the peak of its expansion. The rapid growth of industry, agriculture and population brought with it an ever increasing demand for the currency to accommodate this expansion.

By the 1920's, the Treasury Department was purchasing many tons of the high grade, specially prepared paper that was needed to print our currency. Since the number of notes produced annually had now reached astronomical figures compared to the past, it was soon realized that many millions of dollars could be saved if the currency was reduced in size.

This was ultimately decided upon, and on July 10, 1929, the first of the current, reduced size notes were placed in circulation.

In the following section, "star" notes are indicated by an asterisk (*) appearing after the catalog number.

(Our special thanks to Mr. Chuck O'Donnell for making available the results of his extensive research into the records at the Bureau of Engraving and Printing, enabling us to present accurate totals for the number of small size notes printed.)

The authors acknowledge with thanks the cooperation of Mr. David Sundman for providing the illustrations of the notes in Part Three.

XV. LEGAL TENDER NOTES

Only 1, 2, 5 and 100 Dollar notes have been issued. Of these, the 1, 2 and 5 Dollar notes are now obsolete and only the 100 Dollar notes are still current. The Act of May 3, 1878 decreed that the amount of United States Notes outstanding must be maintained at $346,681,016, and the requirement is being satisfied through circulation of the l00 dollar note.

Until the series of 1963, the obligation is as follows, "The United States of America will pay to the bearer on demand . . . . . . Dollars . . . . . This note is a legal tender at its face value for all debts public and private." With the 1963 series, the "will pay to the bearer on demand" clause was dropped from the obligation and the legal tender clause was changed to read, "This note is legal tender for all debts, public and private."

(Additional information on this series will be found in the introduction to large size Legal Tender Notes on page 14.)

All the following have a Red Seal.

1 Dollar Notes

All issues are with the head of George Washington.

DESIGN NO. 188.
(Note 1500)

Reverse of Design No. 188.

No.	Series	Signatures		No. Printed	Very Fine	Unc
1500.	1928	Woods	Woodin	1,872,012	45.00	300.00
1500*.	1928	Woods	Woodin	8,000	4,500.00	15,000.00

2 Dollar Notes

All issues are with the head of Thomas Jefferson.

DESIGN NO. 189.   (Note 1501-1508 Incl.)

Reverse of Design No. 189.
View of Monticello.

No.	Series	Signatures		No. Printed	Very Fine	Unc
1501.	1928	Tate	Mellon	55,889,424	15.00	42.50
1501*.	1928	Tate	Mellon		150.00	750.00
1502.	1928-A	Woods	Mellon	46,859,136	35.00	225.00
1502*.	1928-A	Woods	Mellon		1,250.00	6,000.00
1503.	1928-B	Woods	Mills	9,001,632	85.00	800.00
1503*.	1928-B	Woods	Mills		5,000.00	Rare
1504.	1928-C	Julian	Morgenthau	86,584,008	10.00	80.00
1504*.	1928-C	Julian	Morgenthau		175.00	1,100.00

No.	Series	Signatures		No. Printed	Very Fine	Unc
1505.	1928-D	Julian	Morgenthau	146,381,364	9.00	35.00
1505*.	1928-D	Julian	Morgenthau		50.00	275.00
1506.	1928-E	Julian	Vinson	5,261,016	10.00	60.00
1506*.	1928-E	Julian	Vinson		1,750.00	6,000.00
1507.	1928-F	Julian	Snyder	43,349,292	7.00	30.00
1507*.	1928-F	Julian	Snyder		60.00	275.00
1508.	1928-G	Clark	Snyder	52,208,000	7.00	30.00
1508*.	1928-G	Clark	Snyder		60.00	200.00

DESIGN NO. 190 (Notes 1509-1512 Incl.)

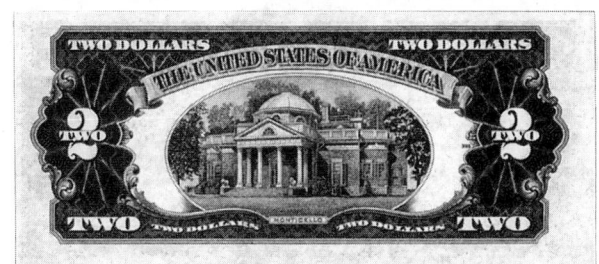

Reverse of Design No. 190.

No.	Series	Signatures		No. Printed	Very Fine	Unc
1509.	1953	Priest	Humphrey	45,360,000	4.00	12.00
1509*.	1953	Priest	Humphrey	2,160,000	9.00	30.00
1510.	1953-A	Priest	Anderson	18,000,000	4.00	10.00
1510*.	1953-A	Priest	Anderson	720,000	10.00	35.00

No.	Series	Signatures		No. Printed	Very Fine	Unc
1511.	1953-B	Smith	Dillon	10,800,000	4.00	11.00
1511*.	1953-B	Smith	Dillon	720,000	9.00	30.00
1512.	1953-C	Granahan	Dillon	5,760,000	4.00	10.00
1512*.	1953-C	Granahan	Dillon	360,000	10.00	45.00

DESIGN NO.191 (Notes 1513-1514)

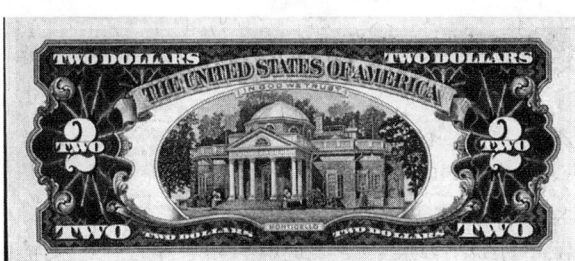

Reverse of Design No. 191.
With motto "In God We Trust."

No.	Series	Signatures		No. Printed	Very Fine	Unc
1513.	1963	Granahan	Dillon	15,360,000	3.00	10.00
1513*.	1963	Granahan	Dillon	640,000	5.00	20.00

No.	Series	Signatures		No. Printed	Very Fine	Unc
1514.	1963-A	Granahan	Fowler	3,200,000	3.00	11.00
1514*.	1963-A	Granahan	Fowler	640,000	5.00	22.00

5 Dollar Notes

All issues are with the head of Abraham Lincoln

DESIGN NO. 192 (Notes 1525-1531 Incl.)

Reverse of Design No. 192.
View of the Lincoln Memorial.

No.	Series	Signatures		No. Printed	Very Fine	Unc	No.	Series	Signatures		No. Printed	Very Fine	Unc
1525.	1928	Woods	Mellon	267,209,616	10.00	35.00	1528*.	1928-C	Julian	Morgenthau		100.00	750.00
1525*.	1928	Woods	Mellon		175.00	800.00	1529.	1928-D	Julian	Vinson	9,297,120	45.00	250.00
1526.	1928-A	Woods	Mills	58,194,600	15.00	65.00	1529*.	1928-D	Julian	Vinson		800.00	4,000.00
1526*.	1928-A	Woods	Mills		1,100.00	4,500.00	1530.	1928-E	Julian	Snyder	109,952,760	10.00	35.00
1527.	1928-B	Julian	Morgenthau	147,827,340	10.00	37.50	1530*.	1928-E	Julian	Snyder		65.00	525.00
1527*.	1928-B	Julian	Morgenthau		100.00	750.00	1531.	1928-F	Clark	Snyder	104,194,704	10.00	35.00
1528.	1928-C	Julian	Morgenthau	214,735,765	10.00	35.00	1531*.	1928-F	Clark	Snyder		35.00	300.00

DESIGN NO. 193 (Notes 1532-1535 Incl.)

Reverse of Design No. 193.

No.	Series	Signatures		No. Printed	Unc	No.	Series	Signatures		No. Printed	Unc
1532.	1953	Priest	Humphrey	120,880,000	20.00	1534.	1953-B	Smith	Dillon	44,640,000	20.00
1532*.	1953	Priest	Humphrey	5,760,000	80.00	1534*.	1953-B	Smith	Dillon	2,160,000	45.00
1533.	1953-A	Priest	Anderson	90,280,000	20.00	1535.	1953-C	Granahan	Dillon	8,640,000	20.00
1533*.	1953-A	Priest	Anderson	5,400,000	40.00	1535*.	1953-C	Granahan	Dillon	320,000	65.00

DESIGN NO. 194 (Note 1536)

Reverse of Design No. 194.
With motto "In God We Trust."

No.	Series	Signatures		No. Printed	Unc	No.	Series	Signatures		No. Printed	Unc
1536.	1963	Granahan	Dillon	63,360,000	20.00	1536*	1963	Granahan	Dillon	3,840,000	35.00

100 Dollar Notes
All issues are with the head of Benjamin Franklin.

DESIGN NO. 194-a (Notes 1550-1551 Incl.)

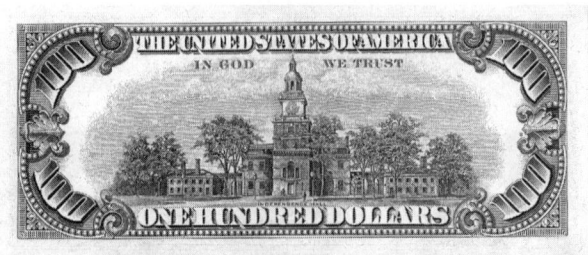

Reverse of Design No. 194-a.

No.	Series	Signatures		No. Printed	VF	Unc	No.	Series	Signatures		No. Printed	VF	Unc
1550.	1966	Granahan	Fowler	768,000		425.00	1551.	1966-A	Elston	Kennedy	512,000	225.00	1,250.00
1550*.	1966	Granahan	Fowler	128,000	375.00	1,000.00							

XVI. SILVER CERTIFICATES

Only 1, 5 and 10 Dollar notes were issued and all are now obsolete, abolished by the Act of June 4, 1963. During the tenure of Julian and Morgenthau, a different type of paper was used for part of the 1 Dollar notes series of 1935-A. An "R" and an "S" were used as control letters and were surcharged in red on the obverses of the notes. The obligation is as follows, "This certifies that there is on deposit in the Treasury of the United States of America...... Dollars in silver payable to the bearer on demand... This certificate is a legal tender for all debts public and private." The foregoing obligation varies somewhat among each series.

The differences can be seen by referring to the illustrations. On June 24, 1968, by Congressional Act, the Treasury halted the practice of redeeming silver certificates with silver bullion.

The motto "In God We Trust" appears on the reverse of 1 Dollar Notes beginning with the series 1935-G. The 1935-G series, however, appears both with and without the motto. (Additional information on this series will be found in the introduction to large size Silver Certificates on page 50.)

All the following have a Blue Seal.

1 Dollar Notes

All issues are with the head of George Washington.

DESIGN NO. 195. (Notes 1600-1605 Incl.)

Reverse of Design No. 195.

No.	Series		Signatures	No. Printed	Very Fine	Unc	No.	Series	Signatures		No. Printed	Very Fine	Unc
1600.	1928	Tate	Mellon	638,296,908	15.00	30.00	1603.	1928-C	Woods	Woodin	5,364,348	85.00	500.00
1600*.	1928	Tate	Mellon		30.00	350.00	1603*.	1928-C	Woods	Woodin		3,000.00	8,500.00
1601.	1928-A	Woods	Mellon	2,267,809,50	15.00	30.00	1604.	1928-D	Julian	Woodin	14,451,372	100.00	425.00
1601*.	1928-A	Woods	Mellon		40.00	275.00	1604*.	1928-D	Julian	Woodin		2,000.00	9,000.00
1602.	1928-B	Woods	Mills	674,597,808	15.00	35.00	1605.	1928-E	Julian	Morgenthau	3,519,324	325.00	1,750.00
1602*.	1928-B	Woods	Mills		60.00	550.00	1605*.	1928-E	Julian	Morgenthau		14,500.00	Rare

DESIGN NO. 196 (Note 1606)

Reverse of Design No. 196.

No.	Series	Signatures		No. Printed	Very Fine	Unc	No.	Series	Signatures		No. Printed	Very Fine	Unc
1606.	1934	Julian	Morgenthau	682,176,000	15.00	50.00	1606*.	1934	Julian	Morgenthau	7,680,000	75.00	650.00

DESIGN NO. 197 (Notes 1607-1616 Incl.)
(Also Note 2306)

The R & S surcharges in red ink appear only on notes 1609 and 1610.

Reverse of Design No. 197.

No.	Series	Signatures		No. Printed	Very Fine	Unc	No.	Series	Signatures		No. Printed	Very Fine	Unc
1607.	1935	Julian	Morgenthau	1,681,552,000	- - -	15.00	1608.	1935-A	Julian	Morgenthau	6,111,832,000	—	10.00
1607*.	1935	Julian	Morgenthau		35.00	275.00	1608*.	1935-A	Julian	Morgenthau		3.00	35.00

No.	Series	Signatures	No. Printed	Very Fine	Unc	No.	Series	Signatures	No. Printed	Very Fine	Unc
1609.	1935-A	Julian Morgenthau (R)	1,184,000	25.00	200.00	1613W*.	1935-D	Clark Snyder	4,656,968,000	3.00	20.00
1609*.	1935-A	Julian Morgenthau (R)	12,000	750.00	3,500.00	1613N.	1935-D	Clark Snyder		2.00	6.00
1610.	1935-A	Julian Morgenthau (S)	1,184,000	20.00	150.00	1613N*.	1935-D	Clark Snyder		3.00	18.00
1610*.	1935-A	Julian Morgenthau (S)	12,000	750.00	3,750.00	1614.	1935-E	Priest Humphrey	5,134,056,000	2.00	7.00
1611.	1935-B	Julian Vinson	806,612,000	2.00	8.00	1614*.	1935-E	Priest Humphrey		2.50	15.00
1611*.	1935-B	Julian Vinson		10.00	75.00	1615.	1935-F	Priest Anderson	1,173,360,000	2.00	7.00
1612.	1935-C	Julian Snyder	3,088,108,000	2.00	6.00	1615*.	1935-F	Priest Anderson	53,200,000	2.50	15.00
1612*.	1935-C	Julian Snyder		3.50	30.00	1616.	1935-G	Smith Dillon	194,600,000	2.00	8.00
1613W.	1935-D	Clark Snyder		2.00	6.00	1616*.	1935-G	Smith Dillon	8,640,000	2.50	12.00

(NOTE: The Series 1935-D notes were produced with reverses of two widths, with the wide variety 1/16 inch larger than the narrow one. Notes with the wide design have a 4 digit plate number of 5015 or less (see to the left of the Great Seal).

DESIGN NO. 198 (Notes 1617-1621 Incl.)

Reverse of Design No. 198, with motto "In God We Trust."

No.	Series	Signatures	No. Printed	Unc	No.	Series	Signatures	No. Printed	Unc
1617.	1935-G	Smith Dillon	31,320,000	19.50	1619*.	1957	Priest Anderson	307,640,000	10.00
1617*.	1935-G	Smith Dillon	1,080,000	60.00	1620.	1957-A	Smith Dillon	1,594,080,000	5.00
1618.	1935-H	Granahan Dillon	30,520,000	8.00	1620*.	1957-A	Smith Dillon	94,720,000	10.00
1618*.	1935-H	Granahan Dillon	1,436,000	17.00	1621.	1957-B	Granahan Dillon	718,400,000	5.00
1619.	1957	Priest Anderson	2,609,600,000	7.00	1621*.	1957-B	Granahan Dillon	49,280,000	10.00

5 Dollar Notes

All issues are with the head of Abraham Lincoln

DESIGN NO. 199 (Notes 1650-1654 Incl.)
(Also Note 2307)

Reverse of Design No. 199.
View of the Lincoln Memorial.

No.	Series	Signatures	No. Printed	Very Fine	Unc	No.	Series	Signatures	No. Printed	Very Fine	Unc
1650.	1934	Julian Morgenthau	393,088,368	7.00	25.00	1652*.	1934-B	Julian Vinson		35.00	500.00
1650*.	1934	Julian Morgenthau		25.00	200.00	1653.	1934-C	Julian Snyder	403,146,148	6.50	25.00
1651.	1934-A	Julian Morgenthau	656,265,948	6.50	20.00	1653*.	1934-C	Julian Snyder		25.00	150.00
1651*.	1934-A	Julian Morgenthau		25.00	150.00	1654.	1934-D	Clark Snyder	486,146,148	6.50	22.00
1652.	1934-B	Julian Vinson	59,128,500	10.00	30.00	1654*.	1934-D	Clark Snyder		17.50	90.00

DESIGN NO. 200 (Notes 1655-1658)

Reverse of Design No. 200.

No.	Series	Signatures		No. Printed	VF	Unc
1655.	1953	Priest	Humphrey	339,600,000		17.50
1655*.	1953	Priest	Humphrey	15,120,000	40.00	300.00
1656.	1953-A	Priest	Anderson	232,400,000		15.00
1656*.	1953-A	Priest	Anderson	12,960,000	75.00	500.00

No.	Series	Signatures		No. Printed		Unc
1657.	1953-B	Smith	Dillon	73,000,000†		15.00
1657*.	1953-B	Smith	Dillon	3,240,000	VF	1,000.00
						6,500.00
1658.	1953-C	Granahan	Dillon	Not released		——

†Only 14,196,000 notes were released.

10 Dollar Notes

All issues are with the head of Alexander Hamilton.

DESIGN NO. 201 (Note 1700 and 1700a.)

Reverse of Design No. 201.
View of the U.S. Treasury Building.

No.	Series	Signatures		No. Printed	Very Fine	Unc
1700.	1933	Julian	Woodin	216,000	7,000.00	12,500.00
1700*	1933	Julian	Woodin		Unique	—

No.	Series	Signatures		No. Printed	Very Fine	Unc
1700a.	1933-A	Julian	Morgenthau	336,000	Unknown	
				(not released)		

DESIGN NO. 202 (Notes 1701-1705 Incl.)
(Also Notes 2308-2309)

Reverse of Design No. 202.

No.	Series	Signatures		No. Printed	Very Fine	Unc
1701.	1934	Julian	Morgenthau	88,692,864	30.00	95.00
1701*.	1934	Julian	Morgenthau		85.00	425.00
1702.	1934-A	Julian	Morgenthau	42,346,428	25.00	125.00
1702*.	1934-A	Julian	Morgenthau		100.00	450.00
1703.	1934-B	Julian	Vinson	337,740	100.00	1,500.00

No.	Series	Signatures		No. Printed	Very Fine	Unc
1703*.	1934-B	Julian	Vinson		1,000.00	4,000.00
1704.	1934-C	Julian	Snyder	20,032,632	35.00	100.00
1704*.	1934-C	Julian	Snyder		60.00	185.00
1705.	1934-D	Clark	Snyder	11,801,112	35.00	115.00
1705*.	1934-D	Clark	Snyder		70.00	600.00

DESIGN NO. 203 (Notes 1706-1708 Incl.)

Reverse of Design No. 203.

No.	Series	Signatures		No. Printed	Unc
1706.	1953	Priest	Humphrey	10,440,000	100.00
1706*.	1953	Priest	Humphrey	576,000	250.00

No.	Series	Signatures		No. Printed	Unc
1707.	1953-A	Priest	Anderson	1,080,000	225.00
1707*.	1953-A	Priest	Anderson	144,000	275.00
1708.	1953-B	Smith	Dillon	720,000	125.00

XVII. NATIONAL BANK NOTES

These were issued from July, 1929 to May, 1935, after which date National Bank Notes ceased to be issued. This discontinuance was brought about by the Treasury recall of certain United States bonds, thus making them unavailable as security for further issues of National Bank Notes.

Only 5, 10, 20, 50 and 100 Dollar notes were issued and all are now obsolete. The obligation is as follows, "National Currency secured by United States bonds deposited with the Treasurer of the United States of America... The (name of bank and city) will pay to the bearer on demand...... Dollars ... Redeemable in lawful money of the United States at United States Treasury or at the bank of issue."

Charter Numbers. A complete list of the years of issue of the Charter Numbers of the National Banks will be found on page 75.

The Valuations. The listings that follow show in what states or territories the various types of National Bank Notes were issued. At the same time the valuations indicate the relative rarity of a given note issued in one state as against the same note issued in another state. The values given are for the most common specimens of each type.

Notes issued by banks in small towns are usually scarcer than those of banks in large cities, since they probably issued fewer notes. (More detailed information on this series will be found in the introduction to large size National Bank Notes on page 75.)

There are two distinct types for each denomination of National Bank Notes. On Type One, which was issued from July, 1929 to May, 1933, the charter number appears twice in heavy black numerals on the face of each note. On Type Two, which was issued from May, 1933 to 1935, the charter number appears four times, the two additional appearances being printed in brown ink alongside of the twice appearing serial number. The illustrations for Design No. 204 are for Type One and Type Two. Design Nos. 206 and 207 are Type One; Design Nos. 205 and 208 are Type Two.

All are series 1929 with the signatures of Jones and Woods and with a small brown seal. In addition, the notes bear two signatures of the issuing National Bank, those of its president and cashier, along with the signatures of the Register of the Treasury and the Treasurer of the United States.

5 Dollar Notes

All issues are with the head of Abraham Lincoln.

DESIGN NO. 204 (Note 1800-1)   TYPE 1

DESIGN NO. 204 -Note 1800-2)   TYPE 2

Reverse of Design No. 204.

No.	Type	Very Fine	Unc	No.	Type	Very Fine	Unc
1800-1.	Type 1	22.50	90.00	1800-2.	Type 2	27.50	100.00

These notes were issued from 1929 to 1935 in sheets of six notes.

	State	Ty. I	No. of Banks Fine	Ty. II	Fine		State	Ty. I	No. of Banks Fine	Ty. II	Fine		State	Ty. I	No. of Banks Fine	Ty. II	Fine
S-1990.	Alabama	60	25.00	51	30.00	S-2007.	Kentucky	44	20.00	42	25.00	S-2024.	North Dakota	32	25.00	20	30.00
S-1991.	Alaska	2	7,500.00	3	7,000.00	S-2008.	Louisiana	15	20.00	17	25.00	S-2025.	Ohio	123	20.00	113	25.00
S-1992.	Arizona	5	175.00	2	200.00	S-2009.	Maine	29	25.00	25	30.00	S-2026.	Oklahoma	48	25.00	54	30.00
S-1993.	Arkansas	40	60.00	28	75.00	S-2010.	Maryland	39	20.00	30	25.00	S-2027.	Oregon	32	20.00	22	25.00
S-1994.	California	100	20.00	85	25.00	S-2011.	Massachusetts	115	20.00	107	25.00	S-2028.	Pennsylvania	370	20.00	375	25.00
S-1995.	Colorado	33	20.00	27	25.00	S-2012.	Michigan	71	20.00	53	25.00	S-2029.	Rhode Island	7	20.00	10	25.00
S-1996.	Connecticut	40	20.00	35	25.00	S-2013.	Minnesota	106	20.00	90	25.00	S-2030.	South Carolina	27	25.00	14	30.00
S-1997.	Delaware	6	80.00	5	90.00	S-2014.	Mississippi	20	50.00	17	60.00	S-2031.	South Dakota	20	75.00	16	85.00
S-1998.	Dist. of Columbia	4	20.00	3	25.00	S-2015.	Missouri	59	20.00	45	25.00	S-2032.	Tennessee	53	20.00	34	25.00
S-1999.	Florida	39	25.00	40	30.00	S-2016.	Montana	14	70.00	15	75.00	S-2033.	Texas	159	20.00	175	25.00
S-2000.	Georgia	43	20.00	37	25.00	S-2017.	Nebraska	44	20.00	35	25.00	S-2034.	Utah	9	30.00	7	35.00
S-2001.	Hawaii	1	60.00	1	60.00	S-2018.	Nevada	7	175.00	4	200.00	S-2035.	Vermont	25	30.00	31	35.00
S-2002.	Idaho	15	70.00	11	75.00	S-2019.	New Hampshire	38	30.00	36	35.00	S-2036.	Virginia	75	20.00	67	25.00
S-2003.	Illinois	181	20.00	116	25.00	S-2020.	New Jersey	158	20.00	154	25.00	S-2037.	Washington	34	20.00	26	25.00
S-2004.	Indiana	108	20.00	68	25.00	S-2021.	New Mexico	7	45.00	7	50.00	S-2038.	West Virginia	68	20.00	55	25.00
S-2005.	Iowa	71	20.00	40	25.00	S-2022.	New York	301	20.00	278	25.00	S-2039.	Wisconsin	75	20.00	53	25.00
S-2006.	Kansas	74	20.00	67	25.00	S-2023.	North Carolina	37	25.00	33	30.00	S-2040.	Wyoming	4	175.00	5	200.00

10 Dollar Notes

All issues are with the head of Alexander Hamilton.

DESIGN NO. 205 (Notes 1801-1 - 1801-2)
TYPE 2

Reverse of Design No. 205.

No.	Type	Very Fine	Unc	No.	Type	Very Fine	Unc
1801-1.	Type 1	27.50	100.00	1801-2.	Type 2	30.00	110.00

No.	State	Ty. I	Fine	Ty. II	Fine	No.	State	Ty. I	Fine	Ty. II	Fine	No.	State	Ty. I	Fine	Ty. II	Fine
S-2041.	Alabama	89	25.00	65	30.00	S-2058.	Kentucky	120	20.00	92	25.00	S-2075.	North Dakota	104	25.00	49	30.00
S-2042.	Alaska	3	7,000.00	3	7,000.00	S-2059.	Louisiana	27	25.00	25	30.00	S-2076.	Ohio	276	20.00	232	25.00
S-2043.	Arizona	11	100.00	5	12500	S-2060.	Maine	50	30.00	37	35.00	S-2077.	Oklahoma	192	25.00	135	30.00
S-2044.	Arkansas	52	50.00	38	60.00	S-2061.	Maryland	72	20.00	54	25.00	S-2078.	Oregon	73	20.00	42	25.00
S-2045.	California	148	20.00	103	25.00	S-2062.	Massachusetts	121	20.00	104	25.00	S-2079.	Pennsylvania	782	20.00	692	25.00
S-2046.	Colorado	79	20.00	53	25.00	S-2063.	Michigan	124	20.00	77	25.00	S-2080.	Rhode Island	11	20.00	9	25.00
S-2047.	Connecticut	55	20.00	46	25.00	S-2064.	Minnesota	216	20.00	153	25.00	S-2081.	South Carolina	36	30.00	15	35.00
S-2048.	Delaware	16	65.00	12	75.00	S-2065.	Mississippi	28	55.00	20	85.00	S-2082.	South Dakota	62	60.00	39	70.00
S-2049.	Dist. of Columbia	10	20.00	6	25.00	S-2066.	Missouri	104	20.00	63	25.00	S-2083.	Tennessee	98	25.00	69	25.00
S-2050.	Florida	49	25.00	41	30.00	S-2067.	Montana	36	70.00	22	85.00	S-2084.	Texas	432	20.00	317	25.00
S-2051.	Georgia	68	25.00	53	30.00	S-2068.	Nebraska	136	20.00	92	25.00	S-2085.	Utah	17	35.00	12	40.00
S-2052.	Hawaii	1	70.00	1	75.00	S-2069.	Nevada	9	150.00	7	175.00	S-2086.	Vermont	42	30.00	42	35.00
S-2053.	Idaho	25	75.00	17	100.00	S-2070.	New Hampshire	54	35.00	15	40.00	S-2087.	Virginia	135	20.00	120	25.00
S-2054.	Illinois	373	20.00	219	25.00	S-2071.	New Jersey	204	20.00	182	25.00	S-2088.	Washington	73	20.00	46	25.00
S-2055.	Indiana	198	20.00	106	25.00	S-2072.	New Mexico	19	45.00	16	75.00	S-2089.	West Virginia	116	20.00	81	25.00
S-2056.	Iowa	219	20.00	83	25.00	S-2073.	New York	444	20.00	359	25.00	S-2090.	Wisconsin	127	20.00	83	25.00
S-2057.	Kansas	185	20.00	142	25.00	S-2074.	North Carolina	37	25.00	37	30.00	S-2091.	Wyoming	23	75.00	22	90.00

These notes were issued from 1929 to 1935 in sheets of six notes.

20 Dollar Notes

All issues are with the head of Andrew Jackson.

DESIGN NO. 206 (Notes 1802-1 - 1802-
TYPE 1

Reverse of Design No. 206. View of the White House.

No.	Type	Very Fine	Unc	No.	Type	Very Fine	Unc
1802-1.	Type 1	42.50	125.00	1802-2.	Type 2	45.00	130.00

These notes were issued from 1929 to 1935 in sheets of six notes.

No.	State	Ty. I	Fine	Ty. II	Fine	No.	State	Ty. I	Fine	Ty. II	Fine	No.	State	Ty. I	Fine	Ty. II	Fine
S-2092.	Alabama	74	30.00	50	35.00	S-2109.	Kentucky	113	30.00	85	35.00	S-2126.	North Dakota	97	35.00	45	40.00
S-2093.	Alaska	3	7,000.00	3	7,000.00	S-2110.	Louisiana	24	30.00	21	35.00	S-2127.	Ohio	275	30.00	219	35.00
S-2094.	Arizona	10	100.00	5	125.00	S-2111.	Maine	43	35.00	29	40.00	S-2128.	Oklahoma	178	35.00	134	40.00
S-2095.	Arkansas	44	60.00	30	80.00	S-2112.	Maryland	69	30.00	52	35.00	S-2129.	Oregon	68	30.00	38	35.00
S-2096.	California	136	30.00	88	35.00	S-2113.	Massachusetts	108	30.00	88	35.00	S-2130.	Pennsylvania	739	30.00	635	35.00
S-2097.	Colorado	72	30.00	48	35.00	S-2114.	Michigan	105	30.00	68	35.00	S-2131.	Rhode Island	11	30.00	9	35.00
S-2098.	Connecticut	46	30.00	35	35.00	S-2115.	Minnesota	205	30.00	141	35.00	S-2132.	South Carolina	28	40.00	11	45.00
S-2099.	Delaware	15	75.00	11	90.00	S-2116.	Mississippi	22	65.00	16	75.00	S-2133.	South Dakota	56	60.00	34	70.00
S-2100.	Dist. of Columbia	10	30.00	6	35.00	S-2117.	Missouri	98	30.00	54	35.00	S-2134.	Tennessee	81	30.00	58	30.00
S-2101.	Florida	41	35.00	31	40.00	S-2118.	Montana	32	70.00	19	80.00	S-2135.	Texas	413	30.00	291	35.00
S-2102.	Georgia	62	35.00	47	40.00	S-2119.	Nebraska	128	30.00	86	35.00	S-2136.	Utah	16	35.00	12	40.00
S-2103.	Hawaii	Not Issued		Not Issued		S-2120.	Nevada	10	150.00	6	175.00	S-2137.	Vermont	36	35.00	34	40.00
S-2104.	Idaho	22	70.00	13	95.00	S-2121.	New Hampshire	47	45.00	42	50.00	S-2138.	Virginia	125	35.00	100	40.00
S-2105.	Illinois	345	30.00	194	35.00	S-2122.	New Jersey	178	30.00	160	35.00	S-2139.	Washington	73	30.00	46	35.00
S-2106.	Indiana	182	30.00	87	35.00	S-2123.	New Mexico	19	50.00	15	75.00	S-2140.	West Virginia	116	30.00	81	35.00
S-2107.	Iowa	206	30.00	75	35.00	S-2124.	New York	390	30.00	329	35.00	S-2141.	Wisconsin	127	30.00	107	35.00
S-2108.	Kansas	178	30.00	127	35.00	S-2125.	North Carolina	45	35.00	30	40.00	S-2142.	Wyoming	22	85.00	21	125.00

50 Dollar Notes

All issues are with the head of Ulysses S. Grant.

DESIGN NO. 207 (Notes 1803-1 - 1803-2)
TYPE 1

Reverse of Design No. 2O7.
View of the U.S. Capitol.

No.	Type	Very Fine	Unc	No.	Type	Very Fine	Unc
1803-1.	Type 1	100.00	250.00	1803-2.	Type 2	110.00	275.00

These notes were issued from 1929 to 1935 in sheets of six notes.

State		Ty. I	Fine	Ty. II	Fine	State		Ty. I	Fine	Ty. II	Fine	State		Ty. I	Fine	Ty. II	Fine
S-2143.	Alabama	Not Issued		Not Issued		S-2160.	Kentucky	4	85.00	1	300.00	S-2178.	North Dakota	1	150.00	Not Issued	
S-2144.	Alaska	Not Issued		Not Issued		S-2162.	Louisiana	2	125.00	2	150.00	S-2179.	Ohio	16	85.00	1	100.00
S-2145.	Arizona	Not Issued		Not Issued		S-2163.	Maine	Not Issued		Not Issued		S-2180.	Oklahoma	7	85.00	3	150.00
S-2146.	Arkansas	Not Issued		1	Rare	S-2164.	Maryland	9	85.00	3	200.00	S-2181.	Oregon	3	350.00	Not Issued	
S-2147.	California	12	85.00	1	100.00	S-2165.	Massachusetts	7	85.00	Not Issued		S-2182.	Pennsylvania	31	85.00	4	100.00
S-2148.	Colorado	5	100.00	3	250.00	S-2166.	Michigan	7	85.00	2	125.00	S-2183.	Rhode Island	2	100.00	1	250.00
S-2149.	Connecticut	3	125.00	Not Issued		S-2167.	Minnesota	7	85.00	1	400.00	S-2184.	South Carolina	Not Issued		Not Issued	
S-2150.	Delaware	1	500.00	Not Issued		S-2168.	Mississippi	1	600.00	Not Issued		S-2185.	South Dakota	2	300.00	Not Issued	
S-2151.	Dist. of Columbia	Not Issued		Not Issued		S-2169.	Missouri	4	85.00	1	400.00	S-2186.	Tennessee	5	85.00	5	300.00
S-2152.	Florida	2	125.00	Not Issued		S-2170.	Montana	1	250.00	Not Issued		S-2187.	Texas	33	85.00	6	150.00
S-2153.	Georgia	Not Issued		Not Issued		S-2171.	Nebraska	6	85.00	1	250.00	S-2188.	Utah	1	400.00	Not Issued	
S-2154.	Hawaii	1	250.00	1	1,000.00	S-2172.	Nevada	1	250.00	Not Issued		S-2189.	Vermont	4	150.00	Not Issued	
S-2155.	Idaho	3	175.00	Not Issued		S-2173.	New Hampshire	2	100.00	Not Issued		S-2190.	Virginia	Not Issued		1	Rare
S-2156.	Illinois	30	85.00	4	100.00	S-2174.	New Jersey	10	85.00	2	300.00	S-2191.	Washington	3	85.00	Not Issued	
S-2157.	Indiana	13	85.00	2	100.00	S-2175.	New Mexico	Not Issued		Not Issued		S-2192.	West Virginia	1	Rare	Not Issued	
S-2158.	Iowa	12	85.00	Not Issued		S-2176.	New York	16	85.00	3	125.00	S-2193.	Wisconsin	6	85.00	1	Rare
S-2159.	Kansas	12	100.00	1	400.00	S-2177.	North Carolina	1	Rare	Not Issued		S-2194.	Wyoming	1	Rare	Not Issued	

100 Dollar Notes

All issues are with the head of Benjamin Franklin.

DESIGN NO. 208 (Notes 1804-1 - 1804-2)
TYPE 2

Reverse of Design No. 208.
View of Independence Hall.

No.	Type	Very Fine	Unc	No.	Type	Very Fine	Unc
1804-1.	Type 1	200.00	400.00	1804-2.	Type 2	225.00	1,000.00

These notes were issued from 1929 to 1935 in sheets of six notes.

State		Ty. I	Fine	Ty. II	Fine	State		Ty. I	Fine	Ty. II	Fine	State		Ty. I	Fine	Ty. II	Fine
S-2194.	.Alabama	Not Issued		Not Issued		S-2211.	Kentucky	4	140.00	1	300.00	S-2228.	North Dakota	1	250.00	Not Issued	
S-2195.	Alaska	Not Issued		Not Issued		S-2212.	Louisiana	2	175.00	1	200.00	S-2229.	Ohio	16	140.00	Not Issued	
S-2196.	Arizona	Not Issued		Not Issued		S-2213.	Maine	Not Issued		Not Issued		S-2230.	Oklahoma	6	140.00	Not Issued	
S-2197.	Arkansas	Not Issued		1	Rare	S-2214.	Maryland	10	140.00	3	250.00	S-2231.	Oregon	2	750.00	Not Issued	
S-2198.	California	12	140.00	1	175.00	S-2215.	Massachusetts	7	140.00	Not Issued		S-2232.	Pennsylvania	30	140.00	3	175.00
S-2199.	Colorado	6	200.00	2	400.00	S-2216.	Michigan	6	140.00	2	400.00	S-2233.	Rhode Island	2	175.00	1	300.00
S-2200.	Connecticut	3	175.00	Not Issued		S-2217.	Minnesota	7	140.00	Not Issued		S-2234.	South Carolina	Not Issued		Not Issued	
S-2201.	Delaware	1	500.00	Not Issued		S-2218.	Mississippi	1	800.00	Not Issued		S-2235.	South Dakota	2	1,000.00	Not Issued	
S-2202.	Dist. of Columbia	Not Issued		Not Issued		S-2219.	Missouri	4	140.00	Not Issued		S-2236.	Tennessee	5	140.00	Not Issued	
S-2203.	Florida	3	300.00	Not Issued		S-2220.	Montana	1	700.00	Not Issued		S-2237.	Texas	30	140.00	6	225.00
S-2204.	Georgia	Not Issued		Not Issued		S-2221.	Nebraska	5	140.00	Not Issued		S-2238.	Utah	Not Issued		Not Issued	
S-2205.	Hawaii	1	Rare	Not Issued		S-2222.	Nevada	1	300.00	Not Issued		S-2239.	Vermont	4	250.00	Not Issued	
S-2206.	Idaho	3	350.00	Not Issued		S-2223.	New Hampshire	2	200.00	Not Issued		S-2240.	Virginia	Not Issued		2	700.00
S-2207.	Illinois	28	140.00	2	175.00	S-2224.	New Jersey	9	140.00	2	400.00	S-2241.	Washington	2	140.00	Not Issued	
S-2208.	Indiana	12	140.00	1	175.00	S-2225.	New Mexico	Not Issued		Not Issued		S-2242.	West Virginia	1	Rare	Not Issued	
S-2209.	Iowa	12	140.00	Not Issued		S-2226.	New York	14	140.00	3	200.00	S-2243.	Wisconsin	6	140.00	1	Rare
S-2210.	Kansas	12	200.00	Not Issued		S-2227.	North Carolina	1	Rare	Not Issued		S-2244.	Wyoming	1	Rare	Not Issued	

XVIII. FEDERAL RESERVE BANK NOTES

Only 5, 10, 20, 50 and 100 Dollar notes were issued and all are now obsolete. The obligation is as follows, "National Currency secured by United States bonds deposited with the Treasurer of the United States of America or by like deposit of other securities... The (name of bank and city) will pay to the bearer .on demand...... Dollars... Redeemable in lawful money of the United States at United States Treasury or at the bank of issue." (Additional information on this series will be found in the introduction to large size Federal Reserve Bank Notes on page 119).

All are series of 1929 with signatures of Jones and Woods and with a brown seal that is larger than on the National Bank Notes preceding. In addition, the notes bear two signatures of the issuing Federal Reserve Bank, those of its Governor and Cashier, or of its Governor and Deputy Governor (N.Y.) or of its Governor and Ass't. Deputy Governor (Chicago) or of its Governor and Controller (St. Louis).

It is estimated that there are no more than about 300 star note of all denominations combined.

5 Dollar Notes

All issues are with the head of Abraham Lincoln.

DESIGN NO. 209 (Notes 1850-A - 1850-L Incl.)

Reverse of Design No. 209.

No.	Issuing Bank	No. Printed	Very Fine	Unc	No.	Issuing Bank	No. Printed	Very Fine	Unc
1850-A.	Boston	3,180,000	25.00	100.00	1850-H.	St. Louis	276,000	250.00	2,000.00
1850-B.	New York	2,100,000	20.00	90.00	1850-I.	Minneapolis	684,000	50.00	400.00
1850-C.	Philadelphia	3,096,000	25.00	90.00	1850-J.	Kansas City	2,460,000	25.00	100.00
1850-D.	Cleveland	4,236,000	20.00	90.00	1850-K.	Dallas	996,000	25.00	90.00
1850-F	Atlanta	1,884,000	20.00	250.00	1850-L.	San Francisco	360,000	1,750.00	Rare
1850-G.	Chicago	5,988,000	20.00	90.00	1850*.	Most Common Districts		400.00	1,250.00

10 Dollar Notes

All issues are with the head of Alexander Hamilton.

DESIGN NO. 210 (Notes 1860-A - 1860-L Incl.)

Reverse of Design No. 210.

No.	Issuing Bank	No. Printed	Very Fine	Unc	No.	Issuing Bank	No. Printed	Very Fine	Unc
1860-A.	Boston	1,680,000	35.00	95.00	1860-G.	Chicago	3,156,000	35.00	85.00
1860-B.	New York	5,556,000	35.00	85.00	1860-H.	St. Louis	1,584,000	35.00	85.00
1860-C.	Philadelphia	1,416,000	35.00	85.00	1860-I.	Minneapolis	558,000	40.00	85.00
1860-D	Cleveland	2,412,000	35.00	85.00	1860-J.	Kansas City	1,284,000	35.00	85.00
1860-E	Richmond	1,356,000	35.00	90.00	1860-K.	Dallas	504,000	175.00	750.00
1860-F.	Atlanta	1,056,000	40.00	90.00	1860-L.	San Francisco	1,080,000	35.00	100.00
					1860*.	Most Common Districts		500.00	1,500.00

20 Dollar Notes

All issues are with the head of Andrew Jackson.

DESIGN NO. 211 (Notes 1870-A - 1870-L Incl.)

Reverse of Design No. 211.

No.	Issuing Bank	No. Printed	Very Fine	Unc	No.	Isssuing Bank	No. Printed	Very Fine	Unc
1870-A.	Boston	972,000	50.00	150.00	1870-G.	Chicago	2,028,000	40.00	125.00
1870-B.	New York	2,568,000	40.00	125.00	1870-H.	St. Louis	444,000	40.00	125.00
1870-C.	Philadelphia	1,008,000	40.00	125.00	1870-I.	Minneapolis	864,000	40.00	125.00
1870-D.	Cleveland	1,020,000	50.00	150.00	1870-J.	Kansas City	612,000	100.00	200.00
1870-E.	Richmond	1,632,000	80.00	250.00	1870-K.	Dallas	468,000	115.00	350.00
1870-F.	Atlanta	960,000	100.00	300.00	1870-L.	San Francisco	888,000	100.00	300.00
					1870*.	Most Common Districts VF 500.00			1,500.00

50 Dollar Notes

All issues are with the head of Ulysses S. Grant.

DESIGN NO. 212 (Notes 1880-B - 1880-L Incl.)

Reverse of Design No. 212.

No.	Issuing Bank	No. Printed	Unc	No.	Issuing Bank	No. Printed	Unc
1880-B.	New York	636,000	225.00	1880-J.	Kansas City	276,000	225.00
1880-D.	Cleveland	684,000	225.00	1880-K.	Dallas	168,000	400.00
1880-G.	Chicago	300,000	225.00	1880-L.	San Francisco	576,000	350.00
1880-I.	Minneapolis	132,000	225.00	1880*.	Most Common Districts VF 300.00		1,500.00

100 Dollar Notes

All issues are with the head of Benjamin Franklin.

DESIGN NO. 213 (Notes 1890-B - 1890-K Incl.)

Reverse of Design No. 213.

No.	Issuing Bank	No. Printed	Unc	No.	Issuing Bank	No. Printed	Unc
1890-B.	New York	480,000	300.00	1890-I.	Minneapolis	144,000	350.00
1890-D.	Cleveland	276,000	300.00	1890-J.	Kansas City	96,000	800.00
1890-E.	Richmond	142,000	350.00	1890-K.	Dallas	36,000	700.00
1890-G.	Chicago	384,000	300.00	1890*.	Most Common Districts VF 400.00		2,000.00

XIX. FEDERAL RESERVE NOTES

Federal Reserve Notes form the largest issues of our contemporary currency and are the mainstay of our present currency system. All denominations from 1 to 10,000 Dollars have been issued but only the 1, 5, 10, 20, 50 and 100 Dollar notes are still current. Notes of 500 Dollars and higher are no longer being printed. The notes of all issues of the 1928 series were redeemable in gold and the obligation on these notes is as follows, "The United States of America will pay to the bearer on demand...... Dollars ... Redeemable in gold on demand at the United States Treasury, or in gold or lawful money at any Federal Reserve Bank."

After passage of the Gold Reserve Act of 1933, paper money no longer became redeemable in gold. The obligation on succeeding issues of Federal Reserve Notes was therefore altered, and beginning with the series of 1934, that portion pertaining to gold convertibility was amended to read as follows, "This note is legal tender for all debts, public and private, and is redeemable in lawful money at the United States Treasury, or at any Federal Reserve Bank."

Beginning with the series of 1963, the inscriptions "Will pay to the bearer on demand" and "Is redeemable in lawful money at the United States Treasury, or at any Federal Reserve Bank" were dropped. The obligation now reads as follows, "This note is legal tender for all debts, public and private."

(Additional information on this series will be found in the introduction to large size Federal Reserve Notes on page 125.)

All the following have a Green Seal.

1 Dollar Notes

All issues are with the head of George Washington.

DESIGN NO. 214 (Notes 1900-A - 1925-L Incl.)

Reverse of Design No. 214.

1. Series of 1963.
Signatures of Granahan and Dillon.

No.	Issuing Bank	No. Printed	Unc	No.	Issuing Bank	No. Printed	Unc	No.	Issuing Bank	No. Printed	Unc
1900-A.	Boston	87,680,000	4.00	1900-E*.	Richmond	12,160,000	5.00	1900-J.	Kansas City	88,960,000	4.00
1900-A*.	Boston	6,400,000	5.00	1900-F.	Atlanta	221,120,000	4.00	1900-J*.	Kansas City	8,960,000	5.00
1900-B.	New York	219,200,000	4.00	1900-F*.	Atlanta	19,200,000	4.00	1900-K.	Dallas	85,760,000	4.00
1900-B*.	New York	15,360,000	4.50	1900-G.	Chicago	279,360,000	4.00	1900-K*.	Dallas	8,960,000	5.00
1900-C.	Philadelphia	123,680,000	4.00	1900-G*.	Chicago	19,840,000	5.00	1900-L.	San Francisco	199,999,999	4.00
1900-C*.	Philadelphia	10,880,000	5.00	1900-H.	St. Louis	99,840,000	4.00	1900-L*.	San Francisco	14,720,000	7.50
1900-D.	Cleveland	108,320,000	4.00	1900-H*.	St. Louis	9,600,000	5.00	1900.	Set of 12 districts		27.50
1900-D.	Cleveland	8,320,000	5.00	1900-I.	Minneapolis	44,800,000	4.00	1900*.	Set of 12 districts		40.00
1900-E.	Richmond	159,520,000	4.00	1900-I*.	Minneapolis	5,120,000	5.00				

2. Series of 1963-A.
Signatures of Granahan and Fowler.

No.	Issuing Bank	No. Printed	Unc	No.	Issuing Bank	No. Printed	Unc	No.	Issuing Bank	No. Printed	Unc
1901-A.	Boston	319,840,000	3.50	1901-E*.	Richmond	41,600,000	4.50	1901-J.	Kansas City	219,200,000	4.00
1901-A*.	Boston	19,840,000	4.50	1901-F.	Atlanta	636,480,000	4.00	1901-J*.	Kansas City	14,720,000	4.50
1901-B.	New York	657,600,000	3.25	1901-F*.	Atlanta	40,960,000	4.50	1901-K.	Dallas	288,960,000	4.00
1901-B*.	New York	47,680,000	3.50	1901-G.	Chicago	784,480,000	4.00	1901-K*.	Dallas	19,184,000	4.50
1901-C.	Philadelphia	375,520,000	3.25	1901-G*.	Chicago	52,640,000	4.50	1901-L.	San Francisco	576,800,000	4.00
1901-C*.	Philadelphia	26,240,000	4.50	1901-H.	St. Louis	264,000,000	4.00	1901-L*.	San Francisco	43,040,000	4.50
1901-D.	Cleveland	337,120,000	3.25	1901-H*.	St. Louis	17,920,000	4.50	1901.	Set of 12 districts		45.00
1901-D*.	Cleveland	21,120,000	4.50	1901-I.	Minneapolis	112,160,000	4.00	1901*.	Set of 12 districts		50.00
1901-E.	Richmond	532,000,000	3.25	1901-I*.	Minneapolis	7,040,000	4.50				

3. Series of 1963-B.
Signatures of Granahan and Barr.

No.	Issuing Bank	No. Printed	Unc	No.	Issuing Bank	No. Printed	Unc	No.	Issuing Bank	No. Printed	Unc
1902-B.	New York	123,040,000	4.50	1902-G.	Chicago	91,040,000	4.50	1902-L.	San Francisco	106,400,000	4.50
1902-B*.	New York	3,680,000	5.50	1902-G*.	Chicago	2,400,000	5.50	1902-L*.	San Francisco	3,040,000	5.50
1902-E.	Richmond	93,600,000	4.50	1902-J.	Kansas City	44,800,000	4.50	1902.	Set of 5 districts		22.50
1902-E*.	Richmond	3,200,000	7.00	1902-J*.	Kansas City	None printed	-	1902*.	Set of 4 districts		22.50

4. Series of 1969.
Signatures of Elston and Kennedy. With new Treasury seal.

No.	Issuing Bank	No. Printed	Unc	No.	Issuing Bank	No. Printed	Unc	No.	Issuing Bank	No. Printed	Unc
1903-A.	Boston	99,200,000	3.00	1903-E*.	Richmond	10,880,000	3.50	1903-J.	Kansas City	95,360,000	3.00
1903-A*.	Boston	5,120,000	3.50	1903-F.	Atlanta	185,120,000	3.00	1903-J*.	Kansas City	5,760,000	3.50
1903-B.	New York	269,120,000	3.00	1903-F*.	Atlanta	7,680,000	3.50	1903-K.	Dallas	113,440,000	3.00
1903-B*.	New York	14,080,000	3.50	1903-G.	Chicago	359,520,000	3.00	1903-K*.	Dallas	5,120,000	3.50
1903-C.	Philadelphia	68,480,000	3.00	1903-G*.	Chicago	12,160,000	3.50	1903-L.	San Francisco	226,240,000	3.00
1903-C*.	Philadelphia	3,776,000	3.50	1903-H.	St. Louis	74,880,000	3.00	1903-L*.	San Francisco	9,600,000	3.50
1903-D.	Cleveland	120,480,000	3.00	1903-H*.	St. Louis	3,840,000	3.50	1903.	Set of 12 districts		36.00
1903-D*.	Cleveland	5,760,000	3.50	1903-I.	Minneapolis	48,000,000	3.00	1903*.	Set of 12 districts		42.00
1903-E.	Richmond	250,560,000	3.00	1903-I*.	Minneapolis	1,920,000	3.50				

5. Series of 1969-A.
Signatures of Kabis and Kennedy.

No.	Issuing Bank	No. Printed	Unc
1904-A.	Boston	40,480,000	3.00
1904-A*.	Boston	1,120,000	3.50
1904-B.	New York	122,400,000	3.50
1904-B*.	New York	6,240,000	3.50
1904-C.	Philadelphia	44,960,000	3.00
1904-C*.	Philadelphia	1,760,000	3.50
1904-D.	Cleveland	30,080,000	3.00
1904-D*.	Cleveland	1,280,000	3.50
1904-E	Richmond	66,080,000	3.00
1904-E*.	Richmond	3,200,000	3.50
1904-F.	Atlanta	70,560,000	3.00
1904-F*.	Atlanta	2,400,000	3.50
1904-G.	Chicago	75,680,000	3.00
1904-G*.	Chicago	4,480,000	3.50
1904-H.	St. Louis	41,420,000	3.00
1904-H*.	St. Louis	1,280,000	3.50
1904-I.	Minneapolis	21,760,000	3.00
1904-I*.	Minneapolis	640,000	7.00
1904-J.	Kansas City	40,480,000	3.50
1904-J*.	Kansas City	1,120,000	5.00
1904-K.	Dallas	27,520,000	3.00
1904-K*.	Dallas	None Printed	—
1904-L	San Francisco	51,840,000	3.00
1904-L*.	San Francisco	3,840,000	3.50
1904.	Set of 12 districts		27.00
1904*.	Set of 11 districts		31.50

6. Series of 1969-B.
Signatures of Kabis and Connally.

No.	Issuing Bank	No. Printed	Unc
1905-A.	Boston	94,720,000	3.00
1905-A*.	Boston	1,920,000	3.50
1905-B.	New York	329,440,000	3.00
1905-B*.	New York	7,040,000	3.50
1905-C.	Philadelphia	133,280,000	3.00
1905-C*.	Philadelphia	3,200,000	4.00
1905-D.	Cleveland	91,520,000	3.00
1905-D*.	Cleveland	4,480,000	3.50
1905-E.	Richmond	180,000,000	3.00
1905-E*.	Richmond	3,840,000	3.50
1905-F.	Atlanta	200,000,000	3.00
1905-F*.	Atlanta	3,840,000	3.50
1905-G.	Chicago	204,480,000	3.00
1905-G*.	Chicago	4,480,000	3.50
1905-H.	St. Louis	59,520,000	3.00
1905-H*.	St. Louis	1,920,000	3.50
1905-I.	Minneapolis	33,920,000	3.00
1905-I*.	Minneapolis	640,000	5.00
1905-J.	Kansas City	67,200,000	3.00
1905-J*.	Kansas City	2,560,000	3.50
1905-K.	Dallas	116,640,000	3.00
1905-K*.	Dallas	5,120,000	3.50
1905-L	San Francisco	208,960,000	3.00
1905-L*.	San Francisco	5,760,000	3.50
1905.	Set of 12 districts		26.00
1905*.	Set of 12 districts		31.25

7. Series of 1969-C.
Signatures of Banuelos and Connally.

No.	Issuing Bank	No. Printed	Unc
1906-B.	New York	49,920,000	2.75
1906-B*.	New York	None Printed	-
1906-D.	Cleveland	15,520,000	3.00
1906-D*.	Cleveland	480,000	5.00
1906-E.	Richmond	61,600,000	2.75
1906-E*.	Richmond	480,000	5.00
1906-F.	Atlanta	60,960,000	2.75
1906-F*.	Atlanta	3,680,000	4.00
1906-G.	Chicago	137,120,000	2.75
1906-G*.	Chicago	1,748,000	4.00
1906-H.	St. Louis	23,680,000	2.75
1906-H*.	St. Louis	640,000	5.00
1906-I.	Minneapolis	25,600,000	2.75
1906-I*.	Minneapolis	640,000	5.00
1906-J.	Kansas City	38,560,000	2.75
1906-J*.	Kansas City	1,120,000	4.50
1906-K.	Dallas	29,440,000	2.75
1906-K*.	Dallas	640,000	5.00
1906-L	San Francisco	101,280,000	2.75
1906-L*.	San Francisco	2,400,000	30.00
1906.	Set of 10 districts		23.00
1906*.	Set of 9 districts		70.00

8. Series of 1969-D.

No.	Issuing Bank	No. Printed	Unc
1907-A.	Boston	187,040,000	2.75
1907-A*.	Boston	1,120,000	3.50
1907-B.	New York	468,480,000	2.75
1907-B*.	New York	4,480,000	3.50
1907-C.	Philadelphia	218,560,000	2.75
1907-C*.	Philadelphia	4,320,000	3.50
1907-D.	Cleveland	161,440,000	2.75
1907-D*.	Cleveland	2,400,000	3.50
1907-E.	Richmond	374,240,000	2.75
1907-E*.	Richmond	8,480,000	3.50
1907-F.	Atlanta	377,440,000	2.75
1907-F*.	Atlanta	5,280,000	3.50
1907-G.	Chicago	378,080,000	2.75
1907-G*.	Chicago	5,270,000	3.50
1907-H.	St. Louis	168,480,000	2.75
1907-H*.	St. Louis	1,760,000	3.50
1907-I.	Minneapolis	83,200,000	2.75
1907-I*.	Minneapolis	None Printed	-
1907-J.	Kansas City	185,760,000	2.75
1907-J*.	Kansas City	3,040,000	3.50
1907-K.	Dallas	158,240,000	2.75
1907-K*.	Dallas	6,240,000	3.50
1907-L.	San Francisco	400,640,000	2.75
1907-L*.	San Francisco	6,400,000	3.50
1907.	Set of 12 districts		27.00
1907*.	Set of 11 districts		36.25

9. Series of 1974.
Signatures of Banuelos and Shultz.

No.	Issuing Bank	No. Printed	Unc
1908-A.	Boston	269,760,000	2.50
1908-A*.	Boston	2,400,000	3.50
1908-B.	New York	740,320,000	2.50
1908-B*.	New York	8,800,000	3.50
1908-C.	Philadelphia	308,800,000	2.50
1908-C*.	Philadelphia	1,600,000	3.50
1908-D.	Cleveland	240,960,000	2.50
1908-D*.	Cleveland	960,000	4.50
1908-E.	Richmond	644,000,000	2.50
1908-E*.	Richmond	4,960,000	3.50
1908-F.	Atlanta	599,680,000	2.50
1908-F*.	Atlanta	5,632,000	3.50
1908-G.	Chicago	473,600,000	2.50
1908-G*.	Chicago	4,992,000	3.50
1908-H.	St. Louis	291,520,000	2.50
1908-H*.	St. Louis	2,880,000	3.50
1908-I.	Minneapolis	144,160,000	2.50
1908-I*.	Minneapolis	480,000	3.50
1908-J.	Kansas City	223,520,000	2.50
1908-J*.	Kansas City	2,144,000	3.50
1908-K.	Dallas	330,560,000	2.50
1908-K*.	Dallas	1,216,000	3.50
1908-L	San Francisco	736,960,000	2.50
1908-L*.	San Francisco	3,520,000	3.50
1908.	Set of 12 districts		24.00
1908*.	Set of 12 districts		43.00

10. Series of 1977.
Signatures of Neff and Simon.

No.	Issuing Bank	No. Printed	Unc
1909-A.	Boston	188,160,000	2.00
1909-A*.	Boston	3,072,000	3.50
1909-B.	New York	635,520,000	2.00
1909-B*.	New York	10,112,000	3.50
1909-C.	Philadelphia	216,960,000	2.00
1909-C*.	Philadelphia	4,480,000	3.50
1909-D.	Cleveland	213,120,000	2.00
1909-D*.	Cleveland	3,328,000	3.50
1909-E.	Richmond	418,560,000	2.00
1909-E*.	Richmond	6,400,000	3.50
1909-F.	Atlanta	565,120,000	2.00
1909-F*.	Atlanta	8,960,000	3.50
1909-G.	Chicago	615,680,000	2.00
1909-G*.	Chicago	9,472,000	3.50
1909-H.	St. Louis	199,680,000	2.00
1909-H*.	St. Louis	2,048,000	3.50
1909-I.	Minneapolis	115,200,000	2.00
1909-I*.	Minneapolis	2,944,000	3.50
1909-J.	Kansas City	223,360,000	2.00
1909-J*.	Kansas City	3,840,000	3.50
1909-K.	Dallas	289,280,000	2.00
1909-K*.	Dallas	4,608,000	3.50
1909-L.	San Francisco	516,480,000	2.00
1909-L*.	San Francisco	8,320,000	3.50
1909.	Set of 12 districts		24.00
1909*.	Set of 12 districts		43.00

11. Series of 1977-A.
Signatures of Morton and Miller.

No.	Issuing Bank	No. Printed	Unc	No.	Issuing Bank	No. Printed	Unc	No.	Issuing Bank	No. Printed	Unc
1910-A.	Boston	204,800,000	2.50	1910-E*.	Richmond	6,400,000	3.75	1910-J.	Kansas City	266,880,000	2.50
1910-A*.	Boston	2,432,000	3.75	1910-F.	Atlanta	396,160,000	2.50	1910-J*.	Kansas City	4,864,000	3.75
1910-B.	New York	592,000,000	2.50	1910-F*.	Atlanta	5,376,000	3.75	1910-K.	Dallas	313,600,000	2.50
1910-B*.	New York	9,472,000	3.75	1910-G.	Chicago	250,680,000	2.50	1910-K*.	Dallas	6,016,000	3.75
1910-C.	Philadelphia	196,480,000	2.50	1910-G*.	Chicago	2,560,000	3.75	1910-L.	San Francisco	432,280,000	2.50
1910-C*.	Philadelphia	2,688,000	3.75	1910-H.	St. Louis	103,680,000	2.50	1910-L*.	San Francisco	5,888,000	3.75
1910-D.	Cleveland	174,720,000	2.50	1910-H*.	St. Louis	1,664,000	3.75	1910.	Set of 12 districts		30.00
1910-D*.	Cleveland	2,560,000	3.75	1910-I.	Minneapolis	38,400,000	2.50	1910*.	Set of 12 districts		44.00
1910-E.	Richmond	377,600,000	2.50	1910-I*.	Minneapolis	384,000	3.75				

12. Series of 1981.
Signatures of Buchanan and Regan.

No.	Issuing Bank	No. Printed	Unc	No.	Issuing Bank	No. Printed	Unc	No.	Issuing Bank	No. Printed	Unc
1911-A.	Boston	308,480,000	2.50	1911-E*.	Richmond	3,840,000	3.50	1911-J.	Kansas City	302,080,000	2.50
1911-A*.	Boston	3,200,000	3.50	1911-F.	Atlanta	741,760,000	2.50	1911-J*.	Kansas City	3,216,000	3.50
1911-B.	New York	963,840,000	2.50	1911-F*.	Atlanta	3,200,000	3.50	1911-K.	Dallas	385,920,000	2.50
1911-B*.	New York	11,776,000	3.25	1911-G.	Chicago	629,760,000	2.50	1911-K*.	Dallas	1,920,000	4.00
1911-C.	Philadelphia	359,680,000	2.50	1911-G*.	Chicago	5,184,000	3.25	1911-L.	San Francisco	677,760,000	2.50
1911-C*.	Philadelphia	1,536,000	3.25	1911-H.	St. Louis	163,840,000	2.50	1911-L*.	San Francisco	4,992,000	3.50
1911-D.	Cleveland	295,680,000	2.50	1911-H*.	St. Louis	1,056,000	4.00	1911.	Set of 12 districts		29.00
1911-D*.	Cleveland	1,792,000	4.50	1911-I.	Minneapolis	105,600,000	2.50	1911*.	Set of 12 districts		45.00
1911-E.	Richmond	603,520,000	2.50	1911-I*.	Minneapolis	1,152,000	4.00				

13. Series of 1981-A.
Signatures of Ortega and Regan.

No.	Issuing Bank	No. Printed	Unc	No.	Issuing Bank	No. Printed	Unc	No.	Issuing Bank	No. Printed	Unc
1912-A.	Boston	204,800,000	3.50	1912-E*.	Richmond	6,400,000	4.50	1912-J.	Kansas City	176,000,000	3.50
1912-A*.	Boston	none printed	—	1912-F.	Atlanta	483,200,000	3.50	1912-J*.	Kansas City	none printed	—
1912-B.	New York	537,600,000	3.50	1912-F*.	Atlanta	none printed	—	1912-K.	Dallas	188,800,000	3.50
1912-B*.	New York	9,216,000	4.50	1912-G.	Chicago	482,000,000	3.50	1912-K*.	Dallas	3,200,000	40.00
1912-C.	Philadelphia	99,200,000	3.50	1912-G*.	Chicago	3,200,000	4.00	1912-L.	San Francisco	659,000,000	3.50
1912-C*.	Philadelphia	none printed	—	1912-H.	St. Louis	182,400,000	3.50	1912-L*.	San Francisco	3,200,000	4.50
1912-D.	Cleveland	188,800,000	3.50	1912-H*.	St. Louis	none printed	—	1912.	Set of 12 districts		42.00
1912-D*.	Cleveland	none printed	—	1912-I.	Minneapolis	122,400,000	3.50	1912*.	Set of 5 districts		65.00
1912-E.	Richmond	441,600,000	3.50	1912-I*.	Minneapolis	none printed	—				

14. Series of 1985.
Signatures of Ortega and Baker

No.	Issuing Bank	No. Printed	Unc	No.	Issuing Bank	No. Printed	Unc	No.	Issuing Bank	No. Printed	Unc
1913-A.	Boston	553,600,000	2.00	1913-E*.	Richmond	6,400,000	3.50	1913-J.	Kansas City	390,400,000	2.00
1913-A*.	Boston	none printed	—	1913-F.	Atlanta	1,414,400,000	2.00	1913-J*.	Kansas City	none printed	—
1913-B.	New York	1,795,200,000	2.00	1913-F*.	Atlanta	none printed	—	1913-K.	Dallas	697,600,000	2.00
1913-B*.	New York	none printed	—	1913-G.	Chicago	1,190,400,000	2.00	1913-K*.	Dallas	3,200,000	3.50
1913-C.	Philadelphia	422,400,000	2.00	1913-G*.	Chicago	5,120,000	3.50	1913-L.	San Francisco	1,881,600,000	2.00
1913-C*.	Philadelphia	none printed	—	1913-H.	St. Louis	400,000,000	2.00	19L3-L*.	San Francisco	9,600,000	3.50
1913-D.	Cleveland	636,800,000	2.00	1913-H*.	St. Louis	640,000	75.00	1913.	Set of 12 districts		24.00
1913-D*.	Cleveland	none printed	—	1913-I.	Minneapolis	246,400,000	2.00	1913*.	Set of 6 districts		90.00
1913-E	Richmond	1,190,400,000	2.00	1913-I*.	Minneapolis	3,200,000	3.50				

15. Series of 1988.
Signatures of Ortega and Brady.

No.	Issuing Bank	No. Printed	Unc	No.	Issuing Bank	No. Printed	Unc	No.	Issuing Bank	No. Printed	Unc
1914-A.	Boston	214,400,000	2.00	1914-E*.	Richmond	2,688,000	3.50	1914-J.	Kansas City	390,400,000	2.00
1914-A*.	Boston	3,200,000	3.50	1914-F.	Atlanta	390,400,000	2.00	1914-J*.	Kansas City	3,200,000	3.50
1914-B.	New York	921,600,000	2.00	1914-F*.	Atlanta	3,840,000	175.00	1914-K.	Dallas	80,000,000	2.00
1914-B*.	New York	2,560,000	3.50	1914-G.	Chicago	416,400,000	2.00	1914-K*.	Dallas	1,248,000	3.50
1914-C.	Philadelphia	96,000,000	2.00	1914-G*.	Chicago	none printed	—	1914-L.	San Francisco	585,600,000	2.00
1914-C*.	Philadelphia	none printed	—	1914-H.	St. Louis	396,800,000	2.00	1914-L*.	San Francisco	3,200,000	3.50
1914-D.	Cleveland	195,200,000	2.00	1914-H*.	St. Louis	none printed	—	1914.	Set of 12 districts		24.00
1914-D*.	Cleveland	none printed	—	1914-I.	Minneapolis	246,400,000	2.00	1914*.	Set of 7 districts		200.00
1914-E	Richmond	728,800,000	2.00	1914-I*.	Minneapolis	none printed					

16. Series of 1988-A.
Signatures of Villalpando and Brady. Printed in Washington, DC, on sheet-fed presses.

No.	Issuing Bank	No. Printed	Unc	No.	Issuing Bank	No. Printed	Unc	No.	Issuing Bank	No. Printed	Unc
1915-A.	Boston	582,400,000	2.00	1915-E.	Richmond	1,593,600,000	2.00	1915-I.	Minneapolis	76,800,000	2.00
1915-A*.	Boston	None printed	—	1915-E*.	Richmond	10,880,000	3.50	1915-I*.	Minneapolis	5,760,000	3.50
1915-B.	New York	2,161,344,000	2.00	1915-F.	Atlanta	1,747,200,000	2.00	1915-J.	Kansas City	96,000,000	2.00
1915-B*.	New York	12,800,000	3.50	1915-F*.	Atlanta	12,800,000	3.50	1915-J*.	Kansas City	none printed	—
1915-C.	Philadelphia	472,320,000	2.00	1915-G.	Chicago	1,728,000,000	2.00	1915-K.	Dallas	211,200,000	2.00
1915-C*.	Philadelphia	None printed	—	1915-G*.	Chicago	19,200,000	3.50	1915-K*.	Dallas	none printed	—
1915-D.	Cleveland	454,400,00	2.00	1915-H.	St. Louis	410,400,000	2.00	1915-L.	San Francisco	280,600,000	2.00
1915-D*.	Cleveland	6,400,000	3.50	1915-H*.	St. Louis	3,200,000	3.50	1915-L*.	San Francisco	none printed	—

17. Series of 1988-A.
Signatures of Villalpando and Brady. Printed at the Western Facility, (Fort Worth, Texas) on sheet-fed presses.

Notes printed at the Fort Worth facility may be identified by a small "FW" on the right front side next to the plate check letter-number.

No.	Issuing Bank	No. Printed	Unc	No.	Issuing Bank	No. Printed	Unc	No.	Issuing Bank	No. Printed	Unc
1916-F.	Atlanta	533,000,000	2.00	1916-I.	Minneapolis	844,800,000	2.00	1916-K.	Dallas	761,000,000	2.00
1916-F*.	Atlanta	none printed	- - - -	1916-I*.	Minneapolis	7,680,000	3.00	1916-K*.	Dallas	3,200,000	3.00
1916-G.	Chicago	748,800,000	2.00	1916-J.	Kansas City	300,800,000	2.00	1916-L.	San Francisco	2,009,600,000	2.00
1916-G*.	Chicago	6,400,000	3.00	1916-J*.	Kansas City	none printed	- - - -	1916-L*.	San Francisco	19,200,000	3.00
1916-H.	St. Louis	326,400,000	2.00								
1916-H*.	St. Louis	none printed	- - - -								

18. Series of 1988-A.
Signatures of Villalpando and Brady. Printed in Washington, D.C. on a web-fed press.

Notes printed by this method may be identified by the absence of the check letter-number on the face and the placement of a check number only (no letter on the back, to the right of "In God We Trust").

No.	Issuing Bank	No. Printed	Unc	No.	Issuing Bank	No. Printed	Unc	No.	Issuing Bank	No. Printed	Unc
1917-A.	Boston	64,000,000	45.00	1917-C*.	Philadelphia	none printed	- - - -	1917-F*.	Atlanta	640,000	1,250.00
	Blocks AE, AF, AG			1917-E.	Richmond	38,400,000	45.00	1917-G.	Chicago	19,200,000	175.00
1917-A*.	Boston	none printed	- - - -		Blocks EI, EK				Blocks GP, GQ		
1917-B.	New York	1,920,000	2,000.00	1917-E*.	Richmond	none printed	- - - -	1917-G*.	Chicago	none printed	- - - -
	Block BL			1917-F.	Atlanta	89,600,000	45.00				
1917-B*.	New York	none printed	- - - -		Blocks FU, FV						
1917-C.	Philadelphia	12,800,000	45.00		Blocks FM, FN		200.00				
	Block CA				Block FL		250.00				

19. Series of 1993.
Signatures of Withrow and Bentsen. Printed in Washington D.C.

No.	Issuing Bank	No. Printed	Unc	No.	Issuing Bank	No. Printed	Unc	No.	Issuing Bank	No. Printed	Unc
1918-A.	Boston	140,800,000	2.00	1918-D.	Cleveland	108,800,000	2.00	1918-G.	Chicago	96,000,000	2.00
1918-A*.	Boston	none printed	- - - -	1918-D*.	Cleveland	none printed	- - - -	1918-G*.	Chicago	none printed	- - - -
1918-B.	New York	716,800,000	2.00	1918-E.	Richmond	524,800,000	2.00	1905-H	St. Louis	76,800,000	2.00
1918-B*.	New York	2,240,000	3.25	1918-E*.	Richmond	none printed	- - - -	1918-H*.	St. Louis	none printed	- - - -
1918-C.	Philadelphia	70,400,000	2.00	1918-F.	Atlanta	787,200,000	2.00	1918-L.	San Francisco	128,000,000	2.00
1918-C*.	Philadelphia	640,000	100.00	1918-F*.	Atlanta	16,000,000	3.25	1918-L*.	San Francisco	none printed	- - - -

20. Series of 1993.
Signatures of Withrow and Bentsen. Printed at the Western Facility (Fort Worth, Texas).

No.	Issuing Bank	No. Printed	Unc	No.	Issuing Bank	No. Printed	Unc	No.	Issuing Bank	No. Printed	Unc
11919-G.	Chicago	646,400,000	2.00	1919-I.	Minneapolis	25,600,000	30.00	1919-L.	San Francisco	1,171,200,000	2.00
1919-G*.	Chicago	8,960,000	3.50	1919-I*.	Minneapolis	none printed	- - - -	1919-L*.	San Francisco	none printed	- - - -
1919-H.	St. Louis	121,600,000	2.00	1919-K.	Dallas	620,800,000	2.00				
1919-H*.	St. Louis	none printed	- - - -	1919-K*.	Dallas	19,200,000	3.50				

21. Series of 1993.
Signatures of Withrow and Bentsen. Printed in Washington D.C. on a web-fed press.

No.	Issuing Bank	No. Printed	Unc	No.	Issuing Bank	No. Printed	Unc
1920-B.	New York	12,800,000	15.00	1920-C.	Philadelphia	12,800,000	15.00
	Block BH				Block CA		
1920-B*.	New York	none printed	- - - -	1920-C*.	Philadelphia	none printed	- - - -

22. Series of 1995.
Signatures of Withrow and Rubin. Printed in Washington D.C.

No.	Issuing Bank	No. Printed	Unc	No.	Issuing Bank	No. Printed	Unc	No.	Issuing Bank	No. Printed	Unc
1921-A.	Boston	1,134,745,600	Current	1921-D.	Cleveland	1,452,800,000	Current	1921-H.	St. Louis	76,800,000	Current
1921-A*.	Boston	12,160,000	Current	1921-D*.	Cleveland		Current	1921-H*.	St. Louis	none printed	
1921-B.	New York	2,062,080,000	Current	1921-E.	Richmond	1,831,400,000	Current	1921-J	Kansas City	83,200,000	Current
1921-B*.	New York	9,600,000	Current	1921-E*.	Richmond	7,040,000	Current	1921-J*.	Kansas City	none printed	- - - -
1921-C.	Philadelphia	428,800,000	Current	1921-F.	Atlanta	1,279,360,000	Current	1922-L.	San Francisco	44,800,000	Current
1921-C*.	Philadelphia	9,600,000	Current	1921-F*.	Atlanta	19,840,000	Current	1922-L*.	San Francisco	none printed	- - - -

23. Series of 1995.
Signatures of Withrow and Rubin. Printed at the Western Facility (Fort Worth, Texas).

No.	Issuing Bank	No. Printed	Unc	No.	Issuing Bank	No. Printed	Unc	No.	Issuing Bank	No. Printed	Unc
1922-C.	Philadelphia	76,800,000	Current	1922-G.	Chicago	1,459,200,000	Current	1922-J.	Kansas City	262,400,000	Current
1922-C*.	Philadelphia	3,200,000	Current	1922-G*.	Chicago	10,240,000	Current-	1922-J*.	Kansas City	6,400,000	Current
1922-D.	Cleveland	134,400,000	Current	1922-H.	St. Louis	921,600,000	Current	1922-K.	Dallas	1,273,600,000	Current
1922-D*.	Cleveland	none printed	- - - -	1922-H*.	St. Louis	none printed	- - - -	1922-K*.	Dallas	none printed	- - - -
1922-F.	Atlanta	452,480,000	Current	1922-I.	Minneapolis	1,310,720,000	Current	1922-L.	San Francisco	2,252,800,000	Current
1922-F*.	Atlanta	3,584,000	Current	1922-I*.	Minneapolis	14,080,000	Current-	1922-L*.	San Francisco	3,200,000	- - - -

24. Series of 1995.
Signatures of Withrow and Rubin. Printed in Washington D.C. on a web-fed press.

No.	Issuing Bank	No. Printed	Unc	No.	Issuing Bank	No. Printed	Unc	No.	Issuing Bank	No. Printed	Unc
1923-A.	Boston Blocks AC, AD	18,560,000	15.00	1923-D.	Cleveland Block DC	6,400,000	15.00	1923-F.	Atlanta Block FD	12,800,000	15.00
1923-B.	New York Block BH	12,800,000	15.00								

25. Series of 1999
Signatures of Withrow and Summers. Printed in Washington D.C.

No.	Issuing Bank	Unc	No.	Issuing Bank	Unc	No.	Issuing Bank	Unc
1924-A.	Boston	Current	1924-E.	Richmond	Current	1924-I.	Minneapolis	- - - -
1924-A*.	Boston	Current	1924-E*.	Richmond	- - - -	1924-I*.	Minneapolis	- - - -
1924-B.	New York	Current	1924-F.	Atlanta	Current	1924-J.	Kansas City	- - - -
1924-B*.	New York	Current	1924-F*.	Atlanta	- - - -	1924-J*.	Kansas City	- - - -
1924-C.	Philadelphia	Current	1924-G.	Chicago	- - - -	1924-K.	Dallas	- - - -
1924-C*.	Philadelphia	Current	1924-G*.	Chicago	- - - -	1924-K*.	Dallas	- - - -
1924-D.	Cleveland	Current	1924-H.	St. Louis	- - - -	1924-L.	San Francisco	- - - -
1924-D*.	Cleveland	- - - -	1924-H*.	St. Louis	- - - -	1924-L*.	San Francisco	- - - -

25. Series of 1999
Signatures of Withrow and Summers. Printed at the Western Facility (Fort Worth, Texas).

No.	Issuing Bank	Unc	No.	Issuing Bank	Unc	No.	Issuing Bank	Unc
1925-A.	Boston		1925-E.	Richmond	- - - -	1925-I.	Minneapolis	- - - -
1925-A*.	Boston	- - - -	1925-E*.	Richmond	- - - -	1925-I*.	Minneapolis	- - - -
1925-B.	New York		1925-F.	Atlanta	Current	1925-J.	Kansas City	Current
1925-B*.	New York	- - - -	1925-F*.	Atlanta	- - - -	1925-J*.	Kansas City	- - - -
1925-C.	Philadelphia	- - - -	1925-G.	Chicago	Current	1925-K.	Dallas	Current
1925-C*.	Philadelphia	- - - -	1925-G*.	Chicago	- - - -	1925-K*.	Dallas	- - - -
1925-D.	Cleveland		1925-H.	St. Louis	- - - -	1925-L.	San Francisco	Current
1925-D*.	Cleveland	- - - -	1925-H*.	St. Louis	- - - -	1925-L*.	San Francisco	Current

2 Dollar Notes

All issues are with the head of Thomas Jefferson.

DESIGN NO. 214-a.
(Notes 1935-A - 1936-F Incl.)

Reverse of Design No. 214-a. Shortened version of John Trumbull's famous painting, "The Signing of the Declaration of Independence."

1. Series of 1976.
Signatures of Neff and Simon.

No.	Issuing Bank	No. Printed	Unc	No.	Issuing Bank	No. Printed	Unc	No.	Issuing Bank	No. Printed	Unc
1935-A.	Boston	29,440,000	4.50	1935-E.	Richmond	56,960,000	4.50	1935-I.	Minneapolis	23,680,000	4.50
1935-A*.	Boston	1,280,000	10.00	1935-E*.	Richmond	640,000	20.00	1935-I*.	Minneapolis	640,000	12.00
1935-B.	New York	67,200,000	7.50	1935-F.	Atlanta	60,800,000	4.50	1935-J.	Kansas City	24,960,000	4.50
1935-B*.	New York	2,560,000	10.00	1935-F*.	Atlanta	1,280,000	10.00	1935-J*.	Kansas City	640,000	12.00
1935-C.	Philadelphia	33,280,000	4.50	1935-G.	Chicago	84,480,000	4.50	1935-K.	Dallas	41,600,000	4.50
1935-C*.	Philadelphia	1,280,000	10.00	1935-G*.	Chicago	1,280,000	10.00	1935-K*.	Dallas	1,280,000	10.00
1935-D.	Cleveland	31,360,000	4.50	1935-H.	St. Louis	39,040,000	4.50	1935-L.	San Francisco	82,560,000	4.50
1935-D*.	Cleveland	1,280,000	10.00	1935-H*.	St. Louis	1,280,000	10.00	1935-L*.	San Francisco	1,920,000	20.00

Complete set of 12 Districts:
Regular 57.50 Stars-150.00

2. Series of 1995.
Signatures of Withrow and Rubin.

1936-F.	Atlanta	153,600,000	Current
1936-F.*	Atlanta	640,000	Current

5 Dollar Notes

All issues are with the head of Abraham Lincoln.

DESIGN NO. 215
(Notes 1950-A - 1951-L Incl.)

Reverse of Design No. 215.
View of the Lincoln Memorial.

1. Series of 1928.
Signatures of Tate and Mellon.

No.	Issuing Bank	No. Printed	Unc	No.	Issuing Bank	No. Printed	Unc	No.	Issuing Bank	No. Printed	Unc
1950-A.	Boston	8,025,300	65.00	1950-F.	Atlanta	10,964,400	65.00	1950-K.	Dallas	8,137,824	65.00
1950-B.	New York	14,701,884	65.00	1950-G.	Chicago	12,320,052	65.00	1950-L.	San Francisco	9,792,000	80.00
1950-C.	Philadelphia	11,819,712	65.00	1950-H.	St. Louis	4,675,200	65.00	1950*.	Most Common Districts		
1950-D.	Cleveland	9,049,500	65.00	1950-I.	Minneapolis	4,284,300	80.00		VF 110.00 Unc 450.00		
1950-E.	Richmond	6,027,600	65.00	1950-J.	Kansas City	4,480,800	65.00				

2. Series of 1928-A.
Signatures of Woods and Mellon.

No.	Issuing Bank	No. Printed	Unc	No.	Issuing Bank	No. Printed	Unc	No.	Issuing Bank	No. Printed	Unc
1951-A.	Boston	9,404,352	42.50	1951-F.	Atlanta	3,537,600	45.00	1951-K	Dallas	2,564,400	80.00
1951-B.	New York	42,878,196	43.00	1951-G.	Chicago	37,882,176	40.00	1951-L	San Francisco	6,565,500	60.00
1951-C.	Philadelphia	10,806,012	40.00	1951-H.	St. Louis	2,731,824	57.50	1951*.	Most Common Districts		
1951-D.	Cleveland	6,822,000	40.00	1951-I.	Minneapolis	652,800	150.00		VF 125.00 Unc 550.00		
1951-E.	Richmond	2,409,900	60.00	1951-J.	Kansas City	3,572,400	55.00				

DESIGN NO. 216
(Notes 1952-A - 1960-L Incl.)

Reverse of Design No. 216.

3. Series of 1928-B.
Signatures of Woods and Mellon.

No.	Issuing Bank	No. Printed	Unc	No.	Issuing Bank	No. Printed	Unc	No.	Issuing Bank	No. Printed	Unc
1952-A.	Boston	28,430,724	40.00	1952-E.	Richmond	15,151,932	45.00	1952-I.	Minneapolis	6,954,060	55.00
1952-B.	New York	51,157,536	40.00	1952-F.	Atlanta	13,386,420	45.00	1952-J.	Kansas City	10,677,636	45.00
1952-C.	Philadelphia	25,698,396	40.00	1952-G.	Chicago	17,157,036	40.00	1952-K.	Dallas	4,334,400	45.00
1952-D.	Cleveland	24,874,272	40.00	1952-H.	St. Louis	20,251,716	42.50	1952-L.	San Francisco	28,840,000	40.00
								1952*.	Most Common Districts		
									VF100.00	Unc 375.00	

4. Series of 1928-C.
Signatures of Woods and Mills.

No.	Issuing Bank	No. Printed	Unc	No.	Issuing Bank	No. Printed	Unc	No.			Unc
1953-D.	Cleveland	3,293,640	Unknown	1953-L.	San Francisco	266,304	Unknown	1953*.			Unknown
1953-F.	Atlanta	2,056,200	1,250.00								

5. Series of 1928-D.
Signatures of Woods and Woodin.

No.	Issuing Bank	No. Printed	VF	Unc	No.			Unc
1954-F.	Atlanta	1,281,600	VF 600.00	1,500.00	1954-F*.			Unknown

6. Series of 1934.
Signatures of Julian and Morgenthau.
The number printed is the combined total for both light and dark seal notes.
A. Notes with a vivid light green seal.

No.	Issuing Bank	No. Printed	Unc	No.	Issuing Bank	No. Printed	Unc	No.	Issuing Bank	No. Printed	Unc
1955-A.	Boston	30,510,036	40.00	1955-F.	Atlanta	50,548,608	37.50	1955-K.	Dallas	33,332,208	42.50
1955-B.	New York	47,888,760	37.50	1955-G.	Chicago	31,299,156	40.00	1955-L.	San Francisco	39,324,168	40.00
1955-C.	Philadelphia	47,327,760	37.50	1955-H.	St. Louis	48,737,280	37.50	1955*.	Most Common Districts		200.00
1955-D.	Cleveland	62,273,508	34.50	1955-I.	Minneapoli	16,795,392	45.00				
1955-E.	Richmond	62,128,452	34.50	1955-J.	Kansas City	31,854,432	42.50				

B. Notes with a darker and duller blue-green seal.

No.	Issuing Bank		Unc	No.	Issuing Bank		Unc	No.	Issuing Bank		Unc
1956-A.	Boston		37.50	1956-F.	Atlanta		35.00	1956-K.	Dallas		40.00
1956-B.	New York		35.00	1956-G.	Chicago		37.50	1956-L.	San Francisco		37.50
1956-C.	Philadelphia		35.00	1956-H.	St. Louis		35.00	1956*.	Most Common Districts		150.00
1956-D.	Cleveland		32.00	1956-I.	Minneapolis		42.50				
1956-E.	Richmond		32.00	1956-J.	Kansas City		40.00				

7. Series of 1934-A.
Signatures of Julian and Morgenthau.

No.	Issuing Bank	No. Printed	Unc	No.	Issuing Bank	No. Printed	Unc	No.	Issuing Bank	No. Printed	Unc
1957-A.	Boston	23,231,568	30.00	1957-E.	Richmond	6,555,168	32.00	1957-L.	San Francisco	72,118,452	30.00
1957-B.	New York	143,199,336	30.00	1957-F.	Atlanta	22,811,916	30.00	1957*.	Most Common Districts		125.00
1957-C.	Philadelphia	30,691,632	30.00	1957-G.	Chicago	88,376,376	30.00				
1957-D.	Cleveland	1,610,676	35.00	1957-H.	St. Louis	7,843,452	32.50				

8. Series of 1934-B.
Signatures of Julian and Vinson.

No.	Issuing Bank	No. Printed	Unc	No.	Issuing Bank	No. Printed	Unc	No.	Issuing Bank	No. Printed	Unc
1958-A.	Boston	3,457,800	42.50	1958-E.	Richmond	5,902,848	37.50	1958-I.	Minneapolis	2,482,500	50.00
1958-B.	New York	14,099,580	37.50	1958-F.	Atlanta	4,314,048	42.50	1958-J.	Kansas City	73,800	70.00
1958-C.	Philadelphia	8,306,820	37.50	1958-G.	Chicago	9,070,932	37.50	1958-L.	San Francisco	9,910,296	47.50
1958-D.	Cleveland	11,348,184	37.50	1958-H.	St. Louis	4,307,712	47.50	1958*.	Most Common Districts		225.00

9. Series of 1934-C.
Signatures of Julian and Snyder.

No.	Issuing Bank	No. Printed	Unc	No.	Issuing Bank	No. Printed	Unc	No.	Issuing Bank	No. Printed	Unc
1959-A.	Boston	14,463,600	35.00	1959-F.	Atlanta	23,572,968	30.00	1959-K.	Dallas	5,107,800	45.00
1959-B.	New York	74,383,248	30.00	1959-G.	Chicago	60,598,812	30.00	1959-L.	San Francisco	9,451,944	30.00
1959-C.	Philadelphia	22,879,212	30.00	1959-H.	St. Louis	20,393,340	40.00	1959*.	Most Common Districts		300.00
1959-D.	Cleveland	19,898,256	30.00	1959-I.	Minneapolis	5,089,200	42.50				
1959-E.	Richmond	23,800,524	30.00	1959-J.	Kansas City	8,313,504	40.00				

10. Series of 1934-D.
Signatures of Clark and Snyder.

No.	Issuing Bank	No. Printed	Unc	No.	Issuing Bank	No. Printed	Unc	No.	Issuing Bank	No. Printed	Unc
1960-A	Boston	12,660,552	35.00	1960-F.	Atlanta	9,599,352	35.00	1960-K.	Dallas	4,139,016	40.00
1960-B.	New York	50,976,576	32.50	1960-G.	Chicago	36,601,680	35.00	1960-L.	San Francisco	11,704,200	37.50
1960-C.	Philadelphia	12,106,740	35.00	1960-H.	St. Louis	8,093,412	37.50	1960*.	Most Common Districts		150.00
1960-D.	Cleveland	8,969,052	35.00	1960-1.	Minneapolis	3,594,900	40.00				
1960-E.	Richmond	13,333,032	35.00	1960-J.	Kansas City	6,538,740	37.50				

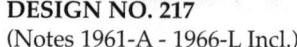

DESIGN NO. 217
(Notes 1961-A - 1966-L Incl.)

The reverse is similar to Design No. 215.

11. Series of 1950.
Signatures of Clark and Snyder.

No.	Issuing Bank	No. Printed	Unc	No.	Issuing Bank	No. Printed	Unc	No.	Issuing Bank	No. Printed	Unc
1961-A.	Boston	30,672,000	32.50	1961-E.	Richmond	47,088,000	32.50	1961-I.	Minneapolis	11,796,000	32.50
1961-A*.	Boston	408,000	225.00	1961-E*.	Richmond	684,000	200.00	1961-I*.	Minneapolis	144,000	250.00
1961-B.	New York	106,768,000	32.50	1961-F.	Atlanta	52,416,000	32.50	1961-J.	Kansas City	25,428,000	32.50
1961-B*.	New York	1,464,000	132.50	1961-F*.	Atlanta	696,000	200.00	1961-J*.	Kansas City	360,000	200.00
1961-C.	Philadelphia	44,784,000	32.50	1961-G.	Chicago	85,104,000	32.50	1961-K.	Dallas	22,848,000	32.50
1961-C*.	Philadelphia	600,000	175.00	1961-G*.	Chicago	1,176,000	132.50	1961-K*.	Dallas	372,000	200.00
1961-D.	Cleveland	54,000,000	32.50	1961-H.	St. Louis	36,864,000	35.00	1961-L.	San Francisco	55,008,000	32.50
1961-D*.	Cleveland	744,000	175.00	1961-H*.	St. Louis	552,000	200.00	1961-L*.	San Francisco	744,000	200.00

12. Series of 1950-A.
Signatures of Priest and Humphrey.

No.	Issuing Bank	No. Printed	Unc	No.	Issuing Bank	No. Printed	Unc	No.	Issuing Bank	No. Printed	Unc
1962-A.	Boston	53,568,000	17.50	1962-E.	Richmond	76,672,000	17.50	1962-I.	Minneapolis	11,232,000	22.50
1962-A*.	Boston	2,808,000	50.00	1962-E*.	Richmond	5,400,000	30.00	1962-I *.	Minneapolis	864,000	50.00
1962-B.	New York	186,472,000	17.50	1962-F.	Atlanta	86,464,000	17.50	1962-J.	Kansas City	29,952,000	20.00
1962-B*.	New York	9,216,000	30.00	1962-F*.	Atlanta	5,040,000	30.00	1962-J*.	Kansas City	1,088,000	55.00
1962-C.	Philadelphia	69,616,000	17.50	1962-G.	Chicago	129,296,000	17.50	1962-K.	Dallas	24,984,000	20.00
1962-C*.	Philadelphia	4,320,000	30.00	1962-G*.	Chicago	6,264,000	30.00	1962-K*.	Dallas	1,368,000	55.00
1962-D.	Cleveland	45,360,000	17.50	1962-H.	St. Louis	54,936,000	17.50	1962-L.	San Francisco	90,712,000	17.50
1962-D*.	Cleveland	2,376,000	50.00	1962-H*.	St. Louis	3,384,000	40.00	1962-L*.	San Francisco	744,000	30.00

13. Series of 1950-B.
Signatures of Priest and Anderson.

No.	Issuing Bank	No. Printed	Unc	No.	Issuing Bank	No. Printed	Unc	No.	Issuing Bank	No. Printed	Unc
1963-A.	Boston	30,880,000	15.00	1963-E.	Richmond	52,920,000	14.00	1963-I.	Minneapolis	20,880,000	20.00
1963-A*.	Boston	2,520,000	40.00	1963-E*.	Richmond	2,080,000	40.00	1963-I*.	Minneapolis	792,000	50.00
1963-B.	New York	85,960,000	14.00	1963-F.	Atlanta	80,560,000	14.00	1963-J.	Kansas City	32,400,000	15.00
1963-B*.	New York	4,680,060	20.00	1963-F*.	Atlanta	3,960,000	150.00	1963-J*.	Kansas City	2,520,000	40.00
1963-C.	Philadelphia	43,560,000	14.00	1963-G.	Chicago	104,320,000	14.00	1963-K.	Dallas	52,120,000	14.00
1963-C*.	Philadelphia	2,880,000	40.00	1963-G*.	Chicago	6,120,000	20.00	1963-K*.	Dallas	3,240,000	30.00
1963-D.	Cleveland	38,800,000	14.00	1963-H.	St. Louis	25,840,000	17.50	1963-L.	San Francisco	56,080,000	14.00
1963.D*.	Cleveland	2,880,000	40.00	1963-H*.	St. Louis	1,440,000	50.00	1963-L*.	San Francisco	3,600,000	150.00

14. Series of 1950-C.
Signatures of Smith and Dillon.

No.	Issuing Bank	No. Printed	Unc	No.	Issuing Bank	No. Printed	Unc	No.	Issuing Bank	No. Printed	Unc
1964-A.	Boston	20,880,000	16.00	1964-E.	Richmond	33,480,000	15.00	1964-I.	Minneapolis	12,960,000	17.50
1964-A*.	Boston	720,000	50.00	1964-E*.	Richmond	2,160,000	35.00	1964-I*.	Minneapolis	720,000	50.00
1964-B.	New York	47,440,000	15.00	1964-F.	Atlanta	54,360,000	15.00	1964-J.	Kansas City	24,760,000	16.00
1964-B*.	New York	2,880,000	30.00	1964-F*.	Atlanta	3,240,000	30.00	1964-J*.	Kansas City	1,800,000	35.00
1964-C.	Philadelphia	29,520,000	15.00	1964-G.	Chicago	56,880,000	15.00	1964-K.	Dallas	3,960,000	30.00
1964-C*.	Philadelphia	1,800,000	35.00	1964-G*.	Chicago	3,240,000	27.50	1964-K*.	Dallas	360,000	75.00
1964-D.	Cleveland	33,840,000	15.00	1964-H.	St. Louis	22,680,000	16.00	1964-L.	San Francisco	25,920,000	15.00
1964-D*.	Cleveland	1,800,000	35.00	1964-H*.	St. Louis	720,000	50.00	1964-L*.	San Francisco	1,440,000	35.00

15. Series of 1950-D.
Signatures of Granahan and Dillon.

No.	Issuing Bank	No. Printed	Unc	No.	Issuing Bank	No. Printed	Unc	No.	Issuing Bank	No. Printed	Unc
1965-A.	Boston	25,200,000	15.00	1965-E.	Richmond	42,490,000	15.00	1965-I.	Minneapolis	7,920,000	17.50
1965-A*.	Boston	1,080,000	32.50	1965-E*.	Richmond	1,080,000	32.50	1965-I*.	Minneapolis	360,000	100.00
1965-B.	New York	102,160,000	14.00	1965-F.	Atlanta	35,200,000	15.00	1966-J.	Kansas City	11,160,000	16.00
1965-B*.	New York	5,040,000	20.00	1965-F*.	Atlanta	1,800,000	32.50	1965-J*.	Kansas City	720,000	50.00
1965-C.	Philadelphia	21,520,000	15.00	1965-G.	Chicago	67,240,000	15.00	1965-K.	Dallas	7,200,000	17.50
1966-C*.	Philadelphia	1,080,000	32.50	1965-G*.	Chicago	3,600,000	27.50	1965-K*.	Dallas	360,000	60.00
1965-D.	Cleveland	23,400,000	15.00	1965-H.	St. Louis	20,160,000	16.00	1965-L.	San Francisco	53,280,000	15.00
1965-D*.	Cleveland	1,080,000	32.50	1965-H*.	St. Louis	720,000	35.00	1965-L*.	San Francisco	3,600,000	30.00

16. Series of 1950-E.
Signatures of Granahan and Fowler.

No.	Issuing Bank	No. Printed	Unc	No.	Issuing Bank	No. Printed	Unc	No.	Issuing Bank	No. Printed	Unc
1966-B.	New York	82,000,000	25.00	1966-G.	Chicago	14,760,000	25.00	1966-L.	San Francisco	24,400,000	25.00
1966-B*.	New York	6,678,000	40.00	1966-G*.	Chicago	1,080,000	60.00	1966-L*.	San Francisco	1,800,000	60.00

DESIGN NO. 217-A
(Notes 1967-A - 1985-L Incl.)

Reverse of Design No. 217-A.
With motto "In God We Trust."

17. Series of 1963.
Signatures of Granahan and Dillon.

No.	Issuing Bank	No. Printed	Unc	No.	Issuing Bank	No. Printed	Unc	No.	Issuing Bank	No. Printed	Unc
1967-A.	Boston	4,480,000	16.00	1967-D*.	Cleveland	1,920,000	22.50	1967-J.	Kansas City	1,920,000	15.00
1967-A*.	Boston	640,000	22.50	1967-F.	Atlanta	17,920,000	15.00	1967-J*.	Kansas City	640,000	22.50
1967-B.	New York	12,160,000	15.00	1967-F*.	Atlanta	2,560,000	22.50	1967-K.	Dallas	5,760,000	15.00
1967-B*.	New York	1,280,000	22.50	1967-G.	Chicago	22,400,000	15.00	1967-K*.	Dallas	1,920,000	22.50
1997-C.	Philadelphia	8,320,000	15.00	1997-G*.	Chicago	3,200,000	22.50	1967-L.	San Francisco	18,560,000	15.00
1967-C*.	Philadelphia	1,920,000	22.50	1967-H.	St. Louis	14,080,000	15.00	1967-L*.	San Francisco	1,920,000	22.50
1967-D.	Cleveland	10,240,000	15.00	1967-H*.	St. Louis	1,920,000	22.50				

18. Series of 1963-A.
Signatures of Granahan and Fowler.

No.	Issuing Bank	No. Printed	Unc	No.	Issuing Bank	No. Printed	Unc	No.	Issuing Bank	No. Printed	Unc
1968-A.	Boston	77,440,000	12.50	1968-E.	Richmond	118,560,000	12.50	1968-I.	Minneapolis	32,640,000	12.50
1968-A*.	Boston	5,760,000	20.00	1968-E*.	Richmond	10,880,000	20.00	1968-I*.	Minneapolis	3,200,000	20.00
1968-B.	New York	98,080,000	12.50	1968-F.	Atlanta	117,920,000	12.50	1968-J.	Kansas City	55,040,000	12.50
1968-B*.	New York	7,680,000	20.00	1968-F*.	Atlanta	9,600,000	20.00	1968-J*.	Kansas City	5,760,000	20.00
1968-C.	Philadelphia	106,400,000	12.50	1968-G.	Chicago	213,440,000	12.50	1968-K.	Dallas	64,000,000	12.50
1968-C*.	Philadelphia	10,240,000	20.00	1968-G*.	Chicago	16,640,000	20.00	1968-K*.	Dallas	3,840,000	20.00
1968-D.	Cleveland	83,840,000	12.50	1968-H.	St. Louis	56,960,000	12.50	1968-L.	San Francisco	128,900,000	12.50
1968-D*.	Cleveland	7,040,000	20.00	1968-H*.	St. Louis	5,120,000	20.00	1968-L*.	San Francisco	12,153,000	20.00

19. Series of 1969.
Signatures of Elston and Kennedy. With new Treasury seal.

No.	Issuing Bank	No. Printed	Unc	No.	Issuing Bank	No. Printed	Unc	No.	Issuing Bank	No. Printed	Unc
1969-A.	Boston	51,200,000	11.00	1969-E.	Richmond	84,480,000	11.00	1969-I.	Minneapolis	16,640,000	11.00
1969-A*.	Boston	1,920,000	25.00	1969-E*.	Richmond	3,200,000	25.00	1969-I*.	Minneapolis	640,000	25.00
1969-B.	New York	198,560,000	11.00	1969-F.	Atlanta	84,480,000	11.00	1969-J.	Kansas City	48,640,000	11.00
1969-B*.	New York	8,960,000	25.00	1969-F*.	Atlanta	3,840,000	25.00	1969-J*.	Kansas City	3,192,000	25.00
1969-C.	Philadelphia	69,120,000	11.00	1969-G.	Chicago	125,600,000	11.00	1969-K.	Dallas	39,680,000	11.00
1969-C*.	Philadelphia	2,560,000	25.00	1969-G*.	Chicago	5,120,000	25.00	1969-K*.	Dallas	1,920,000	25.00
1969-D.	Cleveland	56,320,000	11.00	1969-H.	St. Louis	27,520,000	11.00	1969-L.	San Francisco	103,840,000	11.00
1969-D*.	Cleveland	2,560,000	25.00	1969-H*.	St. Louis	1,280,000	25.00	1969-L*.	San Francisco	4,480,000	25.00

20. Series of 1969-A.
Signatures of Kabis and Connally.

No.	Issuing Bank	No. Printed	Unc	No.	Issuing Bank	No. Printed	Unc	No.	Issuing Bank	No. Printed	Unc
1970-A.	Boston	23,040,000	15.00	1970-E.	Richmond	37,920,000	15.00	1970-I.	Minneapolis	8,960,000	15.00
1970-A*.	Boston	1,280,000	30.00	1970-E*.	Richmond	1,120,000	30.00	1970-I*.	Minneapolis	none printed	—
1970-B.	New York	62,240,000	15.00	1970-F.	Atlanta	25,120,000	15.00	1970-J.	Kansas City	17,920,000	15.00
1970-B*.	New York	1,760,000	30.00	1970-F*.	Atlanta	480,000	15.00	1970-J*.	Kansas City	640,000	30.00
1970-C.	Philadelphia	41,160,000	15.00	1970-G.	Chicago	60,800,000	15.00	1970-K.	Dallas	21,120,000	15.00
1970-C*.	Philadelphia	1,920,000	30.00	1970-G*.	Chicago	1,920,000	30.00	1970-K*.	Dallas	640,000	30.00
1970-D.	Cleveland	21,120,000	15.00	1970-H.	St. Louis	15,360,000	15.00	1970-L.	San Francisco	44,800,000	15.00
1970-D*.	Cleveland	640,000	30.00	1970-H*.	St. Louis	640,000	30.00	1970-L*.	San Francisco	1,920,000	30.00

21. Series of 1969-B.
Signatures of Banuelos and Connally.

No.	Issuing Bank	No. Printed	Unc	No.	Issuing Bank	No. Printed	Unc	No.	Issuing Bank	No. Printed	Unc
1971-A.	Boston	5,760,000	17.50	1971-E.	Richmond	15,360,000	17.50	1971-I.	Minneapolis	8,320,000	17.50
1971-A*.	Boston	none printed	—	1971-E*.	Richmond	640,000	60.00	1971-I*.	Minneapolis	none printed	—
1971-B.	New York	34,560,000	17.50	1971-F.	Atlanta	18,560,000	17.50	1971-J.	Kansas City	8,320,000	17.50
1971-B*.	New York	634,000	60.00	1971-F*.	Atlanta	640,000	60.00	1971-J*.	Kansas City	640,000	60.00
1971-C.	Philadelphia	5,120,000	17.50	1971-G.	Chicago	27,040,000	17.50	1971-K.	Dallas	12,160,000	17.50
1971-C*.	Philadelphia	none printed	—	1971-G*.	Chicago	480,000	60.00	1971-K*.	Dallas	none printed	—
1971-D.	Cleveland	12,160,000	17.50	1971-H.	St. Louis	5,120,000	17.50	1971-L.	San Francisco	23,160,000	17.50
1971-D*.	Cleveland	none printed	—	1971-H*.	St. Louis	none printed	—	1971-L*.	San Francisco	640,000	60.00

22. Series of 1969-C.
Signatures of Banuelos and Shultz.

No.	Issuing Bank	No. Printed	Unc	No.	Issuing Bank	No. Printed	Unc	No.	Issuing Bank	No. Printed	Unc
1972-A.	Boston	50,720,000	11.00	1972-E.	Richmond	73,760,000	11.00	1972-I.	Minneapolis	14,080,000	11.00
1972-A*.	Boston	1,920,000	25.00	1972-E*.	Richmond	640,000	25.00	1972-I*.	Minneapolis	none printed	—
1972-B.	New York	120,000,000	11.00	1972-F.	Atlanta	81,440,000	11.00	1972-J.	Kansas City	41,120,000	11.00
1972-B*.	New York	2,400,000	25.00	1972-F*.	Atlanta	3,200,000	25.00	1972-J*.	Kansas City	1,920,000	25.00
1972-C.	Philadelphia	53,760,000	11.00	1972-G.	Chicago	54,400,000	11.00	1972-K.	Dallas	41,120,000	11.00
1972-C*.	Philadelphia	1,280,000	25.00	1972-G*.	Chicago	none printed	—	1972-K*.	Dallas	1,920,000	25.00
1972-D.	Cleveland	43,680,000	11.00	1972-H.	St. Louis	37,760,000	11.00	1972-L.	San Francisco	80,800,000	11.00
1972-D*.	Cleveland	1,120,000	25.00	1972-H*.	St. Louis	1,280,000	25.00	1972-L*.	San Francisco	3,680,000	25.00

23. Series of 1974.
Signatures of Neff and Simon.

No.	Issuing Bank	No. Printed	Unc
1973-A.	Boston	58,240,000	10.00
1973-A*.	Boston	1,408,000	22.50
1973-B.	New York	153,120,000	10.00
1973-B*.	New York	2,656,000	20.00
1973-C.	Philadelphia	53,920,000	10.00
1973-C*.	Philadelphia	3,040,000	20.00
1973-D.	Cleveland	78,080,000	10.00
1973-D*.	Cleveland	1,920,000	20.00
1973-E.	Richmond	135,200,000	10.00
1973-E*.	Richmond	1,760,000	20.00
1973-F.	Atlanta	127,520,000	10.00
1973-F*.	Atlanta	3,040,000	20.00
1973-G.	Chicago	95,520,000	10.00
1973-G*.	Chicago	1,760,000	20.00
1973-H.	St. Louis	64,800,000	10.00
1973-H*.	St. Louis	1,760,000	20.00
1973-I.	Minneapolis	41,600,000	10.00
1973-I*.	Minneapolis	2,560,000	20.00
1973-J.	Kansas City	42,240,000	10.00
1973-J*.	Kansas City	2,176,000	20.00
1973-K.	Dallas	57,600,000	10.00
1973-K*.	Dallas	1,408,000	20.00
1973-L.	San Francisco	139,680,000	10.00
1973-L*.	San Francisco	5,088,000	20.00

24. Series of 1977.
Signatures of Morton and Blumenthal.

No.	Issuing Bank	No. Printed	Unc
1974-A.	Boston	60,800,000	10.00
1974-A*.	Boston	1,664,000	20.00
1974-B.	New York	183,040,000	10.00
1974-B*.	New York	3,072,000	20.00
1974-C.	Philadelphia	78,720,000	10.00
1974-C*.	Philadelphia	1,280,000	20.00
1974-D.	Cleveland	72,960,000	10.00
1974-D*.	Cleveland	1,152,000	20.00
1974-E.	Richmond	110,720,000	10.00
1974-E*.	Richmond	2,816,000	20.00
1974-F.	Atlanta	127,360,000	10.00
1974-F*.	Atlanta	1,920,000	20.00
1974-G.	Chicago	177,920,000	10.00
1974-G*.	Chicago	2,816,000	20.00
1974-H.	St. Louis	46,080,000	10.00
1974-H*.	St. Louis	128,000	20.00
1974-I.	Minneapolis	21,760,000	10.00
1974-I*.	Minneapolis	none printed	—
1974-J.	Kansas City	78,080,000	10.00
1974-J*.	Kansas City	1,408,000	20.00
1974-K.	Dallas	60,800,000	10.00
1974-K*.	Dallas	2,408,000	20.00
1974-L.	San Francisco	135,040,000	10.00
1974-L*.	San Francisco	2,432,000	20.00

25. Series of 1977-A.
Signatures of Morton and Miller.

No.	Issuing Bank	No. Printed	Unc
1975-A.	Boston	48,000,000	10.00
1975-A*.	Boston	512,000	20.00
1975-B.	New York	113,920,000	10.00
1975-B*.	New York	2,304,000	20.00
1975-C.	Philadelphia	55,680,000	10.00
1975-C*.	Philadelphia	640,000	20.00
1975-D.	Cleveland	58,880,000	10.00
1975-D*.	Cleveland	1,280,000	20.00
1975-E.	Richmond	77,440,000	10.00
1975-E*.	Richmond	768,000	20.00
1975-F.	Atlanta	76,160,000	10.00
1975-F*.	Atlanta	1,152,000	20.00
1975-G.	Chicago	80,640,000	10.00
1975-G*.	Chicago	1,408,000	20.00
1975-H.	St. Louis	42,240,000	10.00
1975-H*.	St. Louis	640,000	20.00
1975-I.	Minneapolis	10,240,000	10.00
1975-I*.	Minneapolis	256,000	20.00
1975-J.	Kansas City	52,480,000	10.00
1975-J*.	Kansas City	1,024,000	20.00
1975-K.	Dallas	76,160,000	10.00
1975-K*.	Dallas	1,408,000	20.00
1975-L	San Francisco	106,880,000	10.00
1975-L*.	San Francisco	1,152,000	20.00

26. Series of 1981.
Signatures of Buchanan and Regan.

No.	Issuing Bank	No. Printed	Unc
1976-A.	Boston	109,000,000	10.00
1976-B.	New York	250,880,000	10.00
1976-B*.	New York	4,464,000	15.00
1976-C.	Philadelphia	112,640,000	10.00
1976-C*.	Philadefphia	640,000	20.00
1976-D.	Cleveland	122,240,000	10.00
1976-D*.	Cleveland	1,268,000	18.00
1976-E.	Richmond	234,880,000	10.00
1976-E*.	Richmond	640,000	20.00
1976-F.	Atlanta	234,880,000	10.00
1976-F*.	Atlanta	1,644,000	18.00
1976-G.	Chicago	241,280,000	10.00
1976-G*.	Chicago	768,000	18.00
1976-H.	St. Louis	199,680,000	10.00
1976-H*.	St. Louis	628,000	20.00
1976-I.	Minneapolis	109,440,000	10.00
1976-I*.	Minneapolis	640,000	20.00
1976-J.	Kansas City	125,440,000	10.00
1976-J*.	Kansas City	960,000	18.00
1976-K.	Dallas	138,240,000	10.00
1976-K*.	Dalas	640,000	20.00
1976-L	San Francisco	263,680,000	10.00
1976-L*.	San Francisco	2;560,000	20.00

27. Series of 1981-A.
Signatures of Ortega and Regan.

No.	Issuing Bank	No. Printed	Unc
1977-A.	Boston	192,000,000	10.00
1977-B.	New York	448,000,000	10.00
1977-B*.	New York	3,200,000	17.50
1977-C.	Philadelphia	169,600,000	10.00
1977-D.	Cleveland	214,400,000	17.50
1977-E.	Richmond	332,800,000	10.00
1977-E*.	Richmond	3,200,000	17.50
1977-F.	Atlanta	352,000,000	10.00
1977-G.	Chicago	345,600,000	10.00
1977-H.	St. Louis	128,000,000	10.00
1977-I.	Minneapolis	73,800,000	10.00
1977-J.	Kansas City	134,400,000	10.00
1977-K.	Dallas	176,000,000	10.00
1977-L	San Francisco	438,400,000	10.00
1977-L*.	San Francisco	3,200,000	17.50

28. Series of 1985.
Signatures of Ortega and Baker.

No.	Issuing Bank	No. Printed	Unc
1978-A.	Boston	192,000,000	9.50
1978-B.	New York	451,200,000	9.50
1978-B*.	New York	3,200,000	17.50
1978-C.	Philadelphia	170,400,000	9.50
1978-C*.	Philadelphia	6,400,000	17.50
1978-D.	Cleveland	216,000,000	9.50
1978-E.	Richmond	335,200,000	9.50
1978-E*.	Richmond	3,200,000	17.50
1978-F.	Atlanta	354,400,000	9.50
1978-F*.	Atlanta	6,400,000	17.50
1978-G.	Chicago	348,000,000	9.50
1978-G*.	Chicago	6,400,000	17.50
1978-H.	St. Louis	128,000,000	9.50
1978-I.	Minneapolis	173,600,000	9.50
1978-J.	Kansas City	135,200,000	9.50
1978-K.	Dallas	176,800,000	9.50
1978-K*.	Dallas	3,200,000	17.50
1978-L	San Francisco	460,800,000	9.50
1978-L*.	San Francisco	3,200,000	17.50

29. Series of 1988.
Signatures of Ortega and Brady.

No.	Issuing Bank	No. Printed	Unc
1979-A.	Boston	86,400,000	9.50
1979-A*.	Boston	768,000	17.50
1979-B.	New York	185,600,000	9.50
1979-B*.	New York	3,200,000	17.50
1979-C.	Philadelphia	54,400,000	9.50
1979-D.	Cleveland	111,200,000	9.50
1979-E.	Richmond	131,200,000	9.50
1979-E*.	Richmond	none printed	—
1979-F.	Atlanta	137,200,000	9.50
1979-F*.	Atlanta	6,400,000	17.50
1979-G.	Chicago	134,400,000	9.50
1979-H.	St. Louis	51,200,000	9.50
1979-I.	Minneapolis	9,600,000	9.50
1979-J.	Kansas City	44,800,000	9.50
1979-K.	Dallas	54,500,000	9.50
1979-L.	San Francisco	70,400,000	9.50

30. Series of 1988-A.
Signatures of Villalpando and Brady. Printed in Washington, D.C.

No.	Issuing Bank	No. Printed	Unc
1980-A.	Boston	140,800,000	9.50
1980-A*.	Boston	3,200,000	20.00
1980-B.	New York	640,000,000	9.50
1980-B*.	New York	4,608,000	20.00
1980-C.	Philadelphia	70,400,000	9.50
1980-D.	Cleveland	166,000,000	9.50
1980-D*.	Cleveland	4,864,000	20.00
1980-E.	Richmond	486,400,000	9.50
1980-E*.	Richmond	3,020,000	20.00
1980-F.	Atlanta	192,000,000	9.50
1980-F*.	Atlanta	2,640,000	20.00
1980-G.	Chicago	633,600,000	9.50
1980-H.	St. Louis	185,600,000	9.50
1980-H*.	St. Louis	1,280,000	20.00
1980-I.	Minneapolis	73,600,000	9.50
1980-I*.	Minneapolis	3,200,000	20.00
1980-J.	Kansas City	115,200,000	9.50
1980-K.	Dallas	128,000,000	9.50
1980-L	San Francisco	492,800,000	9.50

31. Series of 1988-A.
Signatures of Villalpando and Brady. Printed at the Western Facility (Fort Worth).
Notes printed in Ft. Worth may be identified by a small "FW" on the right front side next to the plate check letter-number. (See page 172.)

1981-C.	Philadelphia	25,600,000	9.50	1981-G.	Chicago	76,800,000	9.50	1981-J.	Kansas City	25,600,000	9.50
1981-C*.	Philadelphia	none printed	—	1981-G*.	Chicago	1,280,000	20.00	1981-J*.	Kansas City	none printed	—
1981-F.	Atlanta	282,400,000	9.50								
1981-F*.	Atlanta	640,000	20.00								

32. Series of 1993.
Signatures of Withrow and Bentsen. Printed in Washington D.C.

1982-A.	Boston	38,400,000	Current	1982-E.	Richmond	76,800,000	Current	1982-H.	St. Louis	64,000,000	Current
1982-B.	New York	102,400,000	Current	1982-E*.	Richmond	1,920,000	Current	1982-K.	Dallas	51,200,000	Current
1982-B*.	New York	2,816,000	Current	1982-F.	Atlanta	70,400,000	Current				
1982-C.	Philadelphia	38,400,000	Current								

33. Series of 1993.
Signatures of Withrow and Bentsen. Printed at the Western Facility (Fort Worth).

1983-G.	Chicago	128,000,000	Current	1983-I*.	Minneapolis	none printed	—	1983-L	San Francisco	185,600,000	Current
1983-G*.	Chicago	1,280,000	Current	1983-J.	Kansas City	32,000,000	Current	1983-L*.	San Francisco	2,560,000	Current
1983-H.	St. Louis	128,000,000	Current	1983-J*.	Kansas City	none printed	—				
1983-H*.	St. Louis	2,560,000	Current	1983-K.	Dallas	57,600,000	Current				
1983-I.	Minneapolis	6,400,000	Current	1983-K*.	Dallas	none printed	—				

34. Series of 1995.
Signatures of Withrow and Rubin. Printed in Washington D.C.

1984-A.	Boston	160,000,000	Current	1984-E.	Richmond	300,800,000	Current	1984-I.	Minneapolis		
1984-A*.	Boston	640,000	Current	1984-E*.	Richmond		—	1984-I*.	Minneapolis		
1984-B.	New York	390,040,444	Current	1984-F.	Atlanta	179,200,000	Current	1984-J.	Kansas City		
1984-B*.	New York	3,840,000	Current	1984-F*.	Atlanta		—	1984-J*.	Kansas City		
1984-C.	Philadelphia	128,000,000	Current	1984-G.	Chicago			1984-K.	Dallas		
1984-C*.	Philadelphia		—	1984-G*.	Chicago			1984-K*.	Dallas		
1984-D.	Cleveland	89,600,000	Current	1984-H.	St. Louis			1984-L	San Francisco		
1984-D*.	Cleveland		—	1984-H*.	St. Louis			1984-L*.	San Francisco		

35. Series of 1995.
Signatures of Withrow and Rubin. Printed at the Western Facility (Fort Worth).

1985-A.	Boston	57,600,000	Current	1985-E.	Richmond	108,000,000	Current	1985-I.	Minneapolis	64,000,000	Current
1985-A*.	Boston	none printed	—	1985-E*.	Richmond			1985-I*.	Minneapolis		
1985-B.	New York	76,800,000	Current	1985-F.	Atlanta	448,000,000	Current	1985-J.	Kansas City	160,000,000	Current
1985-B*.	New York	none printed	—	1985-F*.	Atlanta	70,400,000	Current	1985-J*.	Kansas City		
1985-C.	Philadelphia	none printed	—	1985-G.	Chicago	524,800,000	Current	1985-K.	Dallas	204,800,000	Current
1985-C*.	Philadelphia	none printed	—	1985-G*.	Chicago	9,600,000	Current	1985-K*.	Dallas		
1985-D.	Cleveland	64,000,000	Current	1985-H.	St. Louis	204,800,000	Current	1985-L	San Francisco	706,800,000	Current
1985-D*.	Cleveland	3,200,000	Current	1985-H*.	St. Louis			1985-L*.	San Francisco		

DESIGN NO. 217-B
(Notes 1986-A - 1987-L Incl.)

Reverse of Design No. 217-B.

36. Series of 1999.
Signatures of Withrow and Summers. Printed in Washington D.C.

1986-A.	Boston	—	1986-E.	Richmond	—	1986-I.	Minneapolis	—		
1986-A*.	Boston	—	1986-E*.	Richmond	—	1986-I*.	Minneapolis	—		
1986-B.	New York	Current	1986-F.	Atlanta	—	1986-J.	Kansas City	—		
1986-B*.	New York	Current	1986-F*.	Atlanta	—	1986-J*.	Kansas City	—		
1986-C.	Philadelphia	—	1986-G.	Chicago	—	1986-K.	Dallas	—		
1986-C*.	Philadelphia	—	1986-G*.	Chicago	—	1986-K*.	Dallas	—		
1986-D.	Cleveland	—	1986-H.	St. Louis	—	1986-L	San Francisco	—		
1986-D*.	Cleveland	—	1986-H*.	St. Louis	—	1986-L*.	San Francisco	—		

37. Series of 1999.
Signatures of Withrow and Summers. Printed at the Western Facility (Fort Worth).

1987-A.	Boston	—	1987-E.	Richmond	—	1987-I.	Minneapolis	—		
1987-A*.	Boston	—	1987-E*.	Richmond	—	1987-I*.	Minneapolis	—		
1987-B.	New York	Current	1987-F.	Atlanta	—	1987-J.	Kansas City	—		
1987-B*.	New York	Current	1987-F*.	Atlanta	—	1987-J*.	Kansas City	—		
1987-C.	Philadelphia	—	1987-G.	Chicago	—	1987-K.	Dallas	—		
1987-C*.	Philadelphia	—	1987-G*.	Chicago	—	1987-K*.	Dallas	—		
1987-D.	Cleveland	—	1987-H.	St. Louis	—	1987-L	San Francisco	—		
1987-D*.	Cleveland	—	1987-H*.	St. Louis	—	1987-L*.	San Francisco	—		

10 Dollar Notes

All issues are with the head of Alexander Hamilton

DESIGN NO. 218
(Notes 2000-A - 2001-L Incl.)

Reverse of Design No. 218.
View of the U.S. Treasury Building.

1. Series of 1928.
Signatures of Tate and Mellon.

No.	Issuing Bank	No. Printed	Unc	No.	Issuing Bank	No. Printed	Unc	No.	Issuing Bank	No. Printed	Unc
2000-A.	Boston	9,804,552	130.00	2000-F.	Atlanta	6,807,720	130.00	2000-K.	Dallas	4,855,500	140.00
2000-B.	New York	11,295,796	120.00	2000-G.	Chicago	8,130,000	120.00	2000-L.	San Francisco	7,086,900	120.00
2000-C.	Philadelphia	8,114,412	120.00	2000-H.	St. Louis	4,124,100	140.00	2000*.	Most Common Districts		
2000-D.	Cleveland	7,570,8120	120.00	2000-I.	Minneapolis	3,874,440	140.00		VF 100.00 Unc 700.00		
2000-E.	Richmond	4,534,800	130.00	2000-J.	Kansas City	3,620,400	140.00				

2. Series of 1928-A.
Signatures of Woods and Mellon.

No.	Issuing Bank	No. Printed	Unc	No.	Issuing Bank	No. Printed	Unc	No.	Issuing Bank	No. Printed	Unc
2001-A.	Boston	2,893,440	180.00	2001-F.	Atlanta	3,033,480	180.00	2001-K.	Dallas	961,800	250.00
2001-B.	New York	18,631,056	160.00	2001-G.	Chicago	8,715,000	160.00	2001-L.	San Francisco	2,547,900	200.00
2001-C.	Philadelphia	2,710,680	180.00	2001-H.	St. Louis	531,600	250.00	2001*	Most Common Districts		
2001-D.	Cleveland	5,610,000	175.00	2001-I.	Minneapolis	102,600	350.00		VF 200.00 Unc 900.00		
2001-E.	Richmond	552,300	250.00	2001-J.	Kansas City	410,400	250.00				

DESIGN NO. 219
(Notes 2002-A - 2009-L Incl.)

Reverse of Design No. 219.

3. Series of 1928-B.
Signatures of Woods and Mellon.
Exists with both light and dark green seals.

No.	Issuing Bank	No. Printed	Unc	No.	Issuing Bank	No. Printed	Unc	No.	Issuing Bank	No. Printed	Unc
2002-A.	Boston	33,218,088	80.00	2002-F.	Atlanta	5,246,700	70.00	2002-K.	Dallas	3,396,096	80.00
2002-B.	New York	44,808,308	70.00	2002-G.	Chicago	38,035,000	70.00	2002-L.	San Francisco	22,695,300	70.00
2002-C.	Philadelphia	22,689,216	70.00	2002-H.	St. Louis	10,814,664	70.00	2002*.	Most Common Districts		
2002-D.	Cleveland	17,418,024	70.00	2002-I.	Minneapolis	5,294,460	80.00		VF 100.00 Unc 400.00		
2002-E.	Richmond	12,714,504	70.00	2002-J.	Kansas City	7,748,040	80.00				

4. Series of 1928-C.
Signatures of Woods and Mills.

No.	Issuing Bank	No. Printed	Unc	No.	Issuing Bank	No. Printed	Unc	No.	Issuing Bank	No. Printed	Unc
2003-B.	New York	2,902,678	185.00	2003-E.	Richmond	304,800	Rare	2003-G.	Chicago	2,423,400	150.00
2003-D.	Cleveland	4,230,428	425.00	2003-F.	Atlanta	688,380	Unknown	2003*.			Very Rare

5. Series of 1934.
Signatures of Julian and Morgenthau.
A. Notes with a vivid, light green seal.
The number of notes printed is the combined total for both light and dark seal notes.

No.	Issuing Bank	No. Printed	Unc	No.	Issuing Bank	No. Printed	Unc	No.	Issuing Bank	No. Printed	Unc
2004-A.	Boston	46,276,152	32.50	2004-F.	Atlanta	20,656,872	42.50	2004-K.	Dallas	21,403,488	40.00
2004-B.	New York	117,298,008	32.50	2004-G.	Chicago	69,962,064	30.00	2004-L.	San Francisco	37,402,308	32.50
2004-C.	Philadelphia	34,770,768	35.00	2004-H.	St. Louis	22,593,204	42.50	2004*.	Most Common Districts		Unc 300.00
2004-D.	Cleveland	28,764,108	40.00	2004-I.	Minneapolis	16,840,980	45.00				
2004-E.	Richmond	16,437,252	40.00	2004-J.	Kansas City	22,627,824	45.00				

B. Notes with a darker and duller blue-green seal.

No.	Issuing Bank	Unc	No.	Issuing Bank	Unc	No.	Issuing Bank	Unc
2005-A.	Boston	30.00	2005-F.	Atlanta	40.00	2005-K.	Dallas	35.00
2005-B.	New York	30.00	2005-G.	Chicago	30.00	2005-L.	San Francisco	30.00
2005-C.	Philadelphia	32.50	2005-H.	St. Louis	30.00	2005*.	Most Common Districts	Unc 300.00
2005-D.	Cleveland	32.50	2005-I.	Minneapolis	40.00			
2005-E.	Richmond	32.50	2005-J.	Kansas City	35.00			

6. Series of 1934-A.
Signatures of Julian and Morgenthau.

No.	Issuing Bank	No. Printed	Unc	No.	Issuing Bank	No. Printed	Unc	No.	Issuing Bank	No. Printed	Unc
2006-A.	Boston	104,540,088	25.00	2006-F.	Atlanta	85,478,160	32.50	2006-K.	Dallas	28,263,156	32.50
2006-B.	New York	281,940,996	25.00	2006-G.	Chicago	177,285,960	25.00	2006-L.	San Francisco	125,537,592	30.00
2006-C.	Philadelphia	95,338,032	25.00	2006-H.	St. Louis	50,694,312	45.00	2006*.	Most Common Districts	Unc	200.00
2006-D.	Cleveland	93,332,004	30.00	2006-I.	Minneapolis	16,340,016	40.00				
2006-E.	Richmond	101,037,912	32.50	2006-J.	Kansas City	31,069,978	30.00				

7. Series of 1934-B.
Signatures of Julian and Vinson.

No.	Issuing Bank	No. Printed	Unc	No.	Issuing Bank	No. Printed	Unc	No.	Issuing Bank	No. Printed	Unc
2007-A.	Boston	3,999,600	35.00	2007-F.	Atlanta	6,746,076	35.00	2007-K.	Dallas	3,085,200	37.50
2007-B.	New York	34,815,948	27.50	2007-G.	Chicago	18,130,836	30.00	2007-L.	San Francisco	9,076,800	30.00
2007-C.	Philadelphia	10,339,020	30.00	2007-H.	St. Louis	6,849,348	37.50	2007*.	Most Common Districts	Unc	200.00
2007-D.	Cleveland	1,394,700	35.00	2007-I.	Minneapolis	2,254,800	40.00				
2007-E.	Richmond	4,018,272	35.00	2007-J.	Kansas City	3,835,764	40.00				

8. Series of 1934-C.
Signatures of Julian and Snyder.

No.	Issuing Bank	No. Printed	Unc	No.	Issuing Bank	No. Printed	Unc	No.	Issuing Bank	No. Printed	Unc
2008-A.	Boston	42,431,404	25.00	2008-F.	Atlanta	44,838,264	27.50	2008-K.	Dallas	25,642,620	30.00
2008-B.	New York	115,675,644	22.50	2008-G.	Chicago	105,875,412	22.50	2008-L.	San Francisco	49,164,480	25.00
2008-C.	Philadelphia	46,874,760	25.00	2008-H.	St. Louis	36,541,404	30.00	2008*.	Most Common Districts	Unc	200.00
2008-D.	Cleveland	332,400	32.50	2008-I.	Minneapolis	11,944,848	40.00				
2008-E.	Richmond	37,422,600	27.50	2008-J.	Kansas City	20,874,072	30.00				

9. Series of 1934-D.
Signatures of Clark and Snyder.

No.	Issuing Bank	No. Printed	Unc	No.	Issuing Bank	No. Printed	Unc	No.	Issuing Bank	No. Printed	Unc
2009-A.	Boston	19,917,900	27.50	2009-F.	Atlanta	17,064,816	27.50	2009-K.	Dallas	7,178,196	35.00
2009-B.	New York	64,067,904	22.50	2009-G.	Chicago	55,943,844	22.50	2009-L.	San Francisco	23,956,584	22.50
2009-C.	Philadelphia	18,432,000	25.00	2009-H.	St. Louis	15,828,048	30.00	2009*.	Most Common Districts	Unc	200.00
2009-D.	Cleveland	20,291,316	25.00	2009-I.	Minneapolis	5,237,220	40.00				
2009-E.	Richmond	18,090,312	27.50	2009-J.	Kansas City	7,992,000	35.00				

DESIGN NO. 220.
(Notes 2010-A - 2015-L Incl.)

Reverse of Design No. 220.

10. Series of 1950.
Signatures of Clark and Snyder.

No.	Issuing Bank	No. Printed	Unc	No.	Issuing Bank	No. Printed	Unc	No.	Issuing Bank	No. Printed	Unc
2010-A.	Boston	70,992,000	55.00	2010-E.	Richmond	61,776,000	55.00	2010-I.	Minneapolis	18,864,000	65.00
2010-A*.	Boston	1,008,000	175.00	2010-E*.	Richmond	876,000	175.00	2010-I*.	Minneapolis	552,000	250.00
2010-B.	New York	218,576,000	45.00	2010-F.	Atlanta	63,792,000	50.00	2010-J.	Kansas City	36,332,000	60.00
2010-B*.	New York	2,586,000	165.00	2010-F*.	Atlanta	864,000	175.00	2010-J*.	Kansas City	456,000	200.00
2010-C.	Philadelphia	76,320,000	50.00	2010-G.	Chicago	161,056,000	45.00	2010-K.	Dallas	33,264,000	60.00
2010-C*.	Philadelphia	1,008,000	175.00	2010-G*.	Chicago	2,088,000	90.00	2010-K*.	Dallas	480,000	200.00
2010-D.	Cleveland	76,032,000	50.00	2010-H.	St. Louis	47,808,000	60.00	2010-L.	San Francisco	76,896,000	50.00
2010-D*.	Cleveland	1,008,000	175.00	2010-H*.	St. Louis	648,000	200.00	2010-L*.	San Francisco	1,152,000	175.00

11. Series of 1950-A.
Signatures of Priest and Humphrey.

No.	Issuing Bank	No. Printed	Unc	No.	Issuing Bank	No. Printed	Unc	No.	Issuing Bank	No. Printed	Unc
2011-A.	Boston	104,248,000	40.00	2011-E.	Richmond	82,144,000	40.00	2011-I.	Minneapolis	8,136,000	60.00
2011-A*.	Boston	5,112,000	130.00	2011-E*.	Richmond	4,392,000	130.00	2011-I*.	Minneapolis	432,000	175.00
2011-B.	New York	356,664,000	40.00	2011-F.	Atlanta	73,288,000	40.00	2011-J.	Kansas City	25,488,000	55.00
2011-B*.	New York	16,992,000	95.00	2011-F*.	Atlanta	3,816,000	130.00	2011-J*.	Kansas City	2,304,000	140.00
2011-C.	Philadelphia	71,920,000	40.00	2011-G.	Chicago	235,064,000	40.00	2011-K.	Dallas	21,816,000	55.00
2011-C*.	Philadelphia	3,672,000	130.00	2011-G*.	Chicago	11,160,000	90.00	2011-K*.	Dallas	1,584,000	150.00
2011-D.	Cleveland	75,088,000	40.00	2011-H.	St. Louis	46,512,000	60.00	2011-L.	San Francisco	101,584,000	40.00
2011-D*.	Cleveland	3,672,000	130.00	2011-H*.	St. Louis	2,880,000	140.00	2011-L*.	San Francisco	6,408,000	90.00

12. Series of 1950-B.
Signatures of Priest and Anderson.

No.	Issuing Bank	No. Printed	Unc	No.	Issuing Bank	No. Printed	Unc	No.	Issuing Bank	No. Printed	Unc
2012-A.	Boston	49,240,000	35.00	2012-E.	Richmond	51,120,000	35.00	2012-I.	Minneapolis	13,320,000	47.50
2012-A*.	Boston	2,880,000	65.00	2012-E*.	Richmond	2,880,000	65.00	2012-I*.	Minneapolis	720,000	65.00
2012-B.	New York	170,840,000	32.50	2012-F.	Atlanta	66,520,000	35.00	2012-J.	Kansas City	33,480,000	35.00
2012-B*.	New York	8,280,000	65.00	2012-F*.	Atlanta	2,880,000	65.00	2012-J*.	Kansas City	2,520,000	65.00
2012-C.	Philadelphia	66,880,000	35.00	2012-G.	Chicago	165,080,000	32.50	2012-K.	Dallas	26,280,000	35.00
2012-C*.	Philadelphia	3,240,000	60.00	2012-G*.	Chicago	6,480,000	55.00	2012-K*.	Dallas	1,440,000	70.00
2012-D.	Cleveland	55,360,000	35.00	2012-H.	St. Louis	33,040,000	35.00	2012-L.	San Francisco	55,000,000	35.00
2012-D*.	Cleveland	2,880,000	65.00	2012-H*.	St. Louis	1,800,000	70.00	2012-L*.	San Francisco	2,880,000	65.00

13. Series of 1950-C.
Signatures of Smith and Dillon.

No.	Issuing Bank	No. Printed	Unc	No.	Issuing Bank	No. Printed	Unc	No.	Issuing Bank	No. Printed	Unc
2013-A.	Boston	51,120,000	40.00	2013-E.	Richmond	45,640,000	40.00	2013-I.	Minneapolis	9,000,000	25.00
2013-A*.	Boston	2,160,000	50.00	2013-E*.	Richmond	1,800,000	50.00	2013-I*.	Minneapolis	720,000	55.00
2013-B.	New York	126,520,000	37.50	2013-F.	Atlanta	38,880,000	40.00	2013-J.	Kansas City	23,320,000	40.00
2013-B*.	New York	6,840,000	40.00	2013-F*.	Atlanta	2,880,000	55.00	2013-J*.	Kansas City	800,000	55.00
2013-C.	Philadelphia	25,200,000	40.00	2013-G.	Chicago	69,400,000	40.00	2013-K.	Dallas	17,640,000	40.00
2013-C*.	Philadelphia	720,000	55.00	2013-G*.	Chicago	3,600,000	40.00	2013-K*.	Dallas	720,000	55.00
2013-D.	Cleveland	33,120,000	40.00	2013-H.	St. Louis	23,040,000	40.00	2013-L.	San Francisco	35,640,000	40.00
2013-D*.	Cleveland	1,800,000	50.00	2013-H*.	St. Louis	1,080,000	50.00	2013-L*.	San Francisco	1,800,000	50.00

14. Series of 1950-D.
Signatures of Granahan and Dillon.

No.	Issuing Bank	No. Printed	Unc	No.	Issuing Bank	No. Printed	Unc	No.	Issuing Bank	No. Printed	Unc
2014-A.	Boston	38,800,000	40.00	2014-E.	Richmond	33,840,000	40.00	2014-J.	Kansas City	15,480,000	40.00
2014-A*.	Boston	1,800,000	45.00	2014-E*.	Richmond	720,000	50.00	2014-J*.	Kansas City	1,080,000	45.00
2014-B.	New York	150,320,000	37.50	2014-F.	Atlanta	36,000,000	40.00	2014-K.	Dallas	18,280,000	40.00
2014-B*.	New York	6,840,000	40.00	2014-F*.	Atlanta	1,440,000	45.00	2014-K*.	Dallas	800,000	50.00
2014-C.	Philadelphia	19,080,000	40.00	2014-G.	Chicago	115,480,000	37.50	2014-L.	San Francisco	62,560,000	40.00
2014-C*.	Philadelphia	1,080,000	45.00	2014-G*.	Chicago	5,040,000	40.00	2014-L*.	San Francisco	3,600,000	42.50
2014-D.	Cleveland	24,120,000	40.00	2014-H.	St. Louis	10,440,000	42.50				
2014-D*.	Cleveland	360,000	50.00	2014-H*.	St. Louis	720,000	50.00				

15. Series of 1950-E.
Signatures of Granahan and Fowler.

No.	Issuing Bank	No. Printed	Unc	No.	Issuing Bank	No. Printed	Unc	No.	Issuing Bank	No. Printed	Unc
2015-B.	New York	12,600,000	50.00	2015-G.	Chicago	65,080,000	50.00	2015-L.	San Francisco	17,280,000	50.00
2015-B*.	New York	2,621,000	125.00	2015-G*.	Chicago	4,320,000	125.00	2015-L*.	San Francisco	720,000	150.00

DESIGN NO. 221
(Notes 2016-A - 2033-L Incl.)

Reverse of Design No. 221.
With motto "In God We Trust."

16. Series of 1963.
Signatures of Granahan and Dillon.

No.	Issuing Bank	No. Printed	Unc	No.	Issuing Bank	No. Printed	Unc	No.	Issuing Bank	No. Printed	Unc
2016-A.	Boston	5,760,000	24.00	2016-E.	Richmond	4,480,000	24.00	2016-J.	Kansas City	3,840,000	27.50
2016-A*.	Boston	640,000	37.50	2016-E*.	Richmond	640,000	37.50	2016-J*.	Kansas City	640,000	37.50
2016-B.	New York	24,960,000	21.00	2016-F.	Atlanta	10,880,000	21.00	2016-K.	Dallas	5,120,000	25.00
2016-B*.	New York	1,920,000	30.00	2016-F*.	Atlanta	1,280,000	32.50	2016-K*.	Dallas	640,000	37.50
2016-C.	Philadelphia	6,400,000	21.00	2016-G.	Chicago	35,200,000	21.00	2016-L.	San Francisco	14,080,000	25.00
2016-C*.	Philadelphia	1,280,000	32.50	2016-G*.	Chicago	2,560,000	30.00	2016-L*.	San Francisco	1,280,000	32.50
2016-D.	Cleveland	7,040,000	21.00	2016-H.	St. Louis	13,440,000	24.00				
2016-D*.	Cleveland	640,000	37.50	2016-H*.	St. Louis	1,280,000	32.50				

17. Series of 1963-A.
Signatures of Granahan and Fowler.

No.	Issuing Bank	No. Printed	Unc	No.	Issuing Bank	No. Printed	Unc	No.	Issuing Bank	No. Printed	Unc
2017-A.	Boston	131,360,000	20.00	2017-E.	Richmond	114,720,000	20.00	2017-I.	Minneapolis	16,640,000	21.00
2017-A*.	Boston	6,400,000	32.50	2017-E*.	Richmond	5,120,000	32.50	2017-I*.	Minneapolis	640,000	35.00
2017-B.	New York	199,360,000	20.00	2017-F.	Atlanta	80,000,000	20.00	2017-J.	Kansas City	31,360,000	20.00
2017-B*.	New York	9,600,000	25.00	2017-F*.	Atlanta	3,840,000	32.50	2017-J*.	Kansas City	1,920,000	35.00
2017-C.	Philadelphia	100,000,000	20.00	2017-G.	Chicago	195,520,000	20.00	2017-K.	Dallas	51,200,000	20.00
2017-C*.	Philadelphia	4,480,000	32.50	2017-G*.	Chicago	9,600,000	25.00	2017-K*.	Dallas	1,920,000	35.00
2017-D.	Cleveland	72,960,000	20.00	2017-H.	St. Louis	43,520,000	20.00	2017-L.	San Francisco	87,200,000	20.00
2017-D*.	Cleveland	3,840,000	32.50	2017-H*.	St. Louis	1,920,000	35.00	2017-L*.	San Francisco	5,120,000	32.50

18. Series of 1969.
Signatures of Elston and Kennedy. With new Treasury seal.

No.	Issuing Bank	No. Printed	Unc	No.	Issuing Bank	No. Printed	Unc	No.	Issuing Bank	No. Printed	Unc
2018-A.	Boston	71,880,000	20.00	2018-E.	Richmond	56,960,000	20.00	2018-I.	Minneapolis	12,800,000	20.00
2018-A*.	Boston	2,560,000	30.00	2018-E*.	Richmond	2,560,000	30.00	2018-I*.	Minneapolis	1,280,000	30.00
2018-B.	New York	247,360,000	20.00	2018-F.	Atlanta	53,760,000	20.00	2018-J.	Kansas City	31,360,000	20.00
2018-B*.	New York	10,240,000	30.00	2018-F*.	Atlanta	2,560,000	30.00	2018-J*.	Kansas City	1,280,000	30.00
2018-C.	Philadelphia	56,960,000	20.00	2018-G.	Chicago	142,240,000	20.00	2018-K.	Dallas	30,080,000	20.00
2018-C*.	Philadelphia	2,560,000	30.00	2018-G*.	Chicago	6,400,000	30.00	2018-K*.	Dallas	1,280,000	30.00
2018-D.	Cleveland	57,600,000	20.00	2018-H.	St. Louis	22,400,000	20.00	2018-L.	San Francisco	56,320,000	20.00
2018-D*.	Cleveland	2,560,000	30.00	2018-H*.	St. Louis	640,000	35.00	2018-L*.	San Francisco	3,185,000	30.00

19. Series of 1969-A.
Signatures of Kabis and Connally.

No.	Issuing Bank	No. Printed	Unc	No.	Issuing Bank	No. Printed	Unc	No.	Issuing Bank	No. Printed	Unc
2019-A.	Boston	41,120,000	20.00	2019-E.	Richmond	25,600,000	20.00	2019-I.	Minneapolis	8,320,000	20.00
2019-A*.	Boston	1,920,000	25.00	2019-E*.	Richmond	640,000	30.00	2019-I*.	Minneapolis	none printed	—
2019-B.	New York	111,840,000	20.00	2019-F.	Atlanta	13,440,000	20.00	2019-J.	Kansas City	10,880,000	20.00
2019-B*.	New York	3,840,000	25.00	2019-F*.	Atlanta	640,000	30.00	2019-J*.	Kansas City	none printed	—
2019-C.	Philadelphia	24,320,000	20.00	2019-G.	Chicago	80,160,000	20.00	2019-K.	Dallas	20,480,000	20.00
2019-C*.	Philadelphia	1,920,000	25.00	2019-G*.	Chicago	3,560,000	25.00	2019-K*.	Dallas	640,000	30.00
2019-D.	Cleveland	23,680,000	20.00	2019-H.	St. Louis	15,360,000	20.00	2019-L.	San Francisco	23,840,000	20.00
2019-D*.	Cleveland	1,276,000	25.00	2019-H*.	St. Louis	640,000	30.00	2019-L*.	San Francisco	640,000	30.00

20. Series of 1969-B.
Signatures of Banuelos and Connally.

No.	Issuing Bank	No. Printed	Unc	No.	Issuing Bank	No. Printed	Unc	No.	Issuing Bank	No. Printed	Unc
2020-A.	Boston	16,640,000	20.00	2020-E.	Richmond	12,160,000	20.00	2020-I.	Minneapolis	3,200,000	20.00
2020-A*.	Boston	none printed	—	2020-E*.	Richmond	640,000	30.00	2020-I*.	Minneapolis	none printed	—
2020-B.	New York	60,320,000	20.00	2020-F.	Atlanta	13,440,000	20.00	2020-J.	Kansas City	5,120,000	20.00
2020-B*.	New York	1,920,000	30.00	2020-F*.	Atlanta	640,000	30.00	2020-J*.	Kansas City	640,000	30.00
2020-C.	Philadelphia	16,000,000	20.00	2020-G.	Chicago	32,640,000	20.00	2020-K.	Dallas	5,760,000	20.00
2020-C*.	Philadelphia	none printed	—	2020-G*.	Chicago	1,268,000	30.00	2020-K*.	Dallas	none printed	—
2020-D.	Cleveland	12,800,000	20.00	2020-H.	St. Louis	8,960,000	20.00	2020-L.	San Francisco	23,840,000	20.00
2020-D*.	Cleveland	none printed	—	2020-H*.	St. Louis	1,280,000	30.00	2020-L*.	San Francisco	640,000	30.00

21. Series of 1969-C.
Signatures of Banuelos and Schultz.

No.	Issuing Bank	No. Printed	Unc	No.	Issuing Bank	No. Printed	Unc	No.	Issuing Bank	No. Printed	Unc
2021-A.	Boston	44,800,000	20.00	2021-E.	Richmond	45,600,000	20.00	2021-I.	Minneapolis	11,520,000	20.00
2021-A*.	Boston	640,000	30.00	2021-E*.	Richmond	1,120,000	30.00	2021-I*.	Minneapolis	640,000	30.00
2021-B.	New York	203,200,000	20.00	2021-F.	Atlanta	46,240,000	20.00	2021-J.	Kansas City	23,040,000	20.00
2021-B*.	New York	7,040,000	30.00	2021-F*.	Atlanta	1,920,000	30.00	2021-J*.	Kansas City	640,000	30.00
2021-C.	Philadelphia	69,920,000	20.00	2021-G.	Chicago	55,200,000	20.00	2021-K.	Dallas	24,960,000	20.00
2021-C*.	Philadelphia	1,280,000	30.00	2021-G*.	Chicago	880,000	30.00	2021-K*.	Dallas	640,000	30.00
2021-D.	Cleveland	46,880,000	20.00	2021-H.	St. Louis	29,800,000	20.00	2021-L.	San Francisco	56,960,000	20.00
2021-D*.	Cleveland	2,400,000	30.00	2021-H*.	St. Louis	1,280,000	30.00	2021-L*.	San Francisco	640,000	30.00

22. Series of 1974.
Signatures of Neff and Simon.

No.	Issuing Bank	No. Printed	Unc	No.	Issuing Bank	No. Printed	Unc	No.	Issuing Bank	No. Printed	Unc
2022-A.	Boston	104,480,000	20.00	2022-E.	Richmond	105,760,000	20.00	2022-I.	Minneapolis	27,520,000	20.00
2022-A*.	Boston	1,888,000	30.00	2022-E*.	Richmond	3,040,000	30.00	2022-I*.	Minneapolis	1,024,000	30.00
2022-B.	New York	239,040,000	20.00	2022-F.	Atlanta	75,520,000	20.00	2022-J.	Kansas City	24,320,000	20.00
2022-B*.	New York	4,192,000	30.00	2022-F*.	Atlanta	3,200,000	30.00	2022-J*.	Kansas City	640,000	35.00
2022-C.	Philadelphia	69,280,000	20.00	2022-G.	Chicago	104,320,000	20.00	2022-K.	Dallas	39,840,000	20.00
2022-C*.	Philadelphia	2,400,000	30.00	2022-G*.	Chicago	4,352,000	30.00	2022-K*.	Dallas	1,760,000	30.00
2022-D.	Cleveland	82,080,000	20.00	2022-H.	St. Louis	46,240,000	20.00	2022-L.	San Francisco	70,560,000	20.00
2022-D*.	Cleveland	1,760,000	30.00	2022-H*.	St. Louis	1,120,000	30.00	2022-L*.	San Francisco	1,760,000	30.00

23. Series of 1977.
Signatures of Morton and Blumenthal.

No.	Issuing Bank	No. Printed	Unc	No.	Issuing Bank	No. Printed	Unc	No.	Issuing Bank	No. Printed	Unc
2023-A.	Boston	96,640,000	20.00	2023-E.	Richmond	71,040,000	20.00	2023-I.	Minneapolis	10,240,000	20.00
2023-A*.	Boston	2,688,000	35.00	2023-E*.	Richmond	1,920,000	35.00	2023-I*.	Minneapolis	256,000	45.00
2023-B.	New York	277,120,000	20.00	2023-F.	Atlanta	88,960,000	20.00	2023-J.	Kansas City	50,560,000	20.00
2023-B*.	New York	7,168,000	32.50	2023-F*.	Atlanta	1,536,000	35.00	2023-J*.	Kansas City	896,000	40.00
2023-C.	Philadelphia	83,200,000	20.00	2023-G.	Chicago	174,720,000	20.00	2023-K.	Dallas	53,760,000	20.00
2023-C*.	Philadelphia	896,000	40.00	2023-G*.	Chicago	3,968,000	35.00	2023-K*.	Dallas	640,000	45.00
2023-D.	Cleveland	83,200,000	20.00	2023-H.	St. Louis	46,720,000	20.00	2023-L.	San Francisco	73,600,000	20.00
2023-D*.	Cleveland	768,000	400.0	2023-H*.	St. Louis	896,000	400.0	2023-L*.	San Francisco	1,792,000	35.00

24. Series of 1977-A.
Signatures of Morton and Miller.

No.	Issuing Bank	No. Printed	Unc	No.	Issuing Bank	No. Printed	Unc	No.	Issuing Bank	No. Printed	Unc
2024-A.	Boston	83,840,000	20.00	2024-E.	Richmond	104,320,000	20.00	2024-I.	Minneapolis	7,680,000	20.00
2024-A*.	Boston	1,664,000	35.00	2024-E*.	Richmond	3,072,000	30.00	2024-I*.	Minneapolis	128,000	50.00
2024-B.	New York	259,280,000	20.00	2024-F.	Atlanta	33,920,000	20.00	2024-J.	Kansas City	40,320,000	20.00
2024-B*.	New York	5,248,000	30.00	2024-F*.	Atlanta	640,000	40.00	2024-J*.	Kansas City	2,136,000	35.00
2024-C.	Philadelphia	96,000,000	20.00	2024-G.	Chicago	108,160,000	20.00	2024-K.	Dallas	60,160,000	20.00
2024-C*.	Philadelphia	2,048,000	32.50	2024-G*.	Chicago	3,200,000	30.00	2024-K*.	Dallas	4,224,000	32.50
2024-D.	Cleveland	44,800,000	20.00	2024-H.	St. Louis	27,520,000	20.00	2024-L.	San Francisco	59,520,000	20.00
2024-D*.	Cleveland	2,048,000	32.50	2024-H*.	St. Louis	640,000	40.00	2024-L*.	San Francisco	2,048,000	35.00

25. Series of 1981.
Signatures of Buchanan and Regan.

No.	Issuing Bank	No. Printed	Unc	No.	Issuing Bank	No. Printed	Unc	No.	Issuing Bank	No. Printed	Unc
2025-A.	Boston	172,160,000	20.00	2025-E.	Richmond	131,840,000	20.00	2025-I.	Minneapolis	23,680,000	30.00
2025-A*.	Boston	1,280,000	35.00	2025-E*.	Richmond	2,576,000	32.50	2025-I*.	Minneapolis	256,000	50.00
2025-B.	New York	434,560,000	20.00	2025-F.	Atlanta	131,840,000	20.00	2025-J.	Kansas City	53,120,000	20.00
2025-B*.	New York	1,920,000	30.00	2025-F*.	Atlanta	1,908,000	32.50	2025-J*.	Kansas City	none printed	—
2025-C.	Philadelphia	131,840,000	20.00	2025-G.	Chicago	254,080,000	20.00	2025-K.	Dallas	50,560,000	20.00
2025-C*.	Philadelphia	632,000	45.00	2025-G*.	Chicago	1,280,000	32.50	2025-K*.	Dallas	none printed	—
2025-D.	Cleveland	122,240,000	20.00	2025-H.	St. Louis	55,280,000	13.50	2025-L.	San Francisco	144,000,000	20.00
2025-D*.	Cleveland	1,268,000	35.00	2025-H*.	St. Louis	none printed	—	2025-L*.	San Francisco	1,280,000	35.00

26. Series of 1981-A.
Signatures of Ortega and Regan.

No.	Issuing Bank	No. Printed	Unc	No.	Issuing Bank	No. Printed	Unc	No.	Issuing Bank	No. Printed	Unc
2026-A.	Boston	112,000,000	20.00	2026-E.	Richmond	92,800,000	20.00	2026-I.	Minneapolis	19,200,000	20.00
2026-A*.	Boston	none printed	—	2026-E*.	Richmond	3,200,000	35.00	2026-I*.	Minneapolis	none printed	—
2026-B.	New York	259,000,000	20.00	2026-F.	Atlanta	83,200,000	20.00	2026-J.	Kansas City	48,000,000	20.00
2026-B*.	New York	3,200,000	35.00	2026-F*.	Atlanta	4,736,000	35.00	2026-J*.	Kansas City	none printed	—
2026-C.	Philadelphia	48,000,000	20.00	2026-G.	Chicago	183,600,000	20.00	2026-K.	Dallas	48,000,000	20.00
2026-C*.	Philadelphia	none printed	—	2026-G*.	Chicago	none printed	—	2026-K*.	Dallas	none printed	—
2026-D.	Cleveland	80,000,000	20.00	2026-H.	St. Louis	25,600,000	20.00	2026-L.	San Francisco	115,200,000	20.00
2026-D*.	Cleveland	none printed	—	2026-H*.	St. Louis	none printed	—	2026-L*.	San Francisco	none printed	—

27. Series of 1985.
Signatures of Ortega and Baker.

No.	Issuing Bank	No. Printed	Unc	No.	Issuing Bank	No. Printed	Unc	No.	Issuing Bank	No. Printed	Unc
2027-A.	Boston	380,800,000	17.50	2027-E.	Richmond	211,200,000	17.50	2027-I.	Minneapolis	64,000,000	17.50
2027-A*.	Boston	7,296,000	30.00	2027-E*.	Richmond	none printed	30.00	2027-I*.	Minneapolis	none printed	30.00
2027-B.	New York	1,027,200,000	17.50	2027-F.	Atlanta	297,600,000	17.50	2027-J.	Kansas City	86,400,000	17.50
2027-B*.	New York	3,200,000	30.00	2027-F*.	Atlanta	3,200,000	30.00	2027-J*.	Kansas City	none printed	30.00
2027-C.	Philadelphia	163,200,000	17.50	2027-G.	Chicago	358,400,000	17.50	2027-K.	Dallas	115,200,000	17.50
2027-C*.	Philadelphia	none printed	30.00	2027-G*.	Chicago	none printed	30.00	2027-K*.	Dallas	3,136,000	30.00
2027-D.	Cleveland	304,000,000	17.50	2027-H.	St. Louis	131,200,000	17.50	2027-L.	San Francisco	300,800,000	17.50
2027-D*.	Cleveland	3,200,000	30.00	2027-H*.	St. Louis	3,200,000	30.00	2027-L*.	San Francisco	3,200,000	30.00

28. Series of 1988
None printed
29. Series of 1988-A.
Signatures of Villalpando and Brady.

No.	Issuing Bank	No. Printed	Unc	No.	Issuing Bank	No. Printed	Unc	No.	Issuing Bank	No. Printed	Unc
2029-A.	Boston	198,400,000	17.50	2029-E.	Richmond	105,600,000	17.50	2029-I.	Minneapolis	19,200,000	17.50
2029-A*.	Boston	6,400,000	27.50	2029-E*.	Richmond	none printed	—	2029-I*.	Minneapolis	none printed	—
2029-B.	New York	339,200,000	17.50	2029-F.	Atlanta	236,800,000	17.50	2029-J.	Kansas City	51,200,000	27.50
2029-B*.	New York	3,200,000	27.50	2029-F*.	Atlanta	none printed	—	2029-J*.	Kansas City	none printed	—
2029-C.	Philadelphia	57,600,000	17.50	2029-G.	Chicago	236,800,000	17.50	2029-K.	Dallas	115,200,000	17.50
2029-C*.	Philadelphia	none printed	—	2029-G*.	Chicago	none printed	—	2029-K*.	Dallas	none printed	—
2029-D.	Cleveland	128,000,000	17.50	2029-H.	St. Louis	70,400,000	17.50	2029-L.	San Francisco	217,600,000	17.50
2029-D*.	Cleveland	3,200,000	27.50	2029-H*.	St. Louis	none printed	—	2029-L*.	San Francisco	3,200,000	27.50

30. Series of 1990.
Signatures of Villalpando and Brady. Printed in Washington D.C.
(No notes printed in Ft. Worth.)
Security thread & micro size printing introduced.

No.	Issuing Bank	No. Printed	Unc	No.	Issuing Bank	No. Printed	Unc	No.	Issuing Bank	No. Printed	Unc
2030-A.	Boston	128,000,000	15.00	2030-E.	Richmond	105,600,000	15.00	2030-I.	Minneapolis	12,800,000	15.00
2030-A*.	Boston	None printed	—	2030-E*.	Richmond	none printed	—	2030-I*.	Minneapolis	none printed	—
2030-B.	New York	742,400,000	15.00	2030-F.	Atlanta	160,000,000	15.00	2030-J.	Kansas City	70,400,000	15.00
2030-B*.	New York	16,874,000	25.00	2030-F*.	Atlanta	none printed	—	2030-J*.	Kansas City	none printed	—
2030-C.	Philadelphia	19,200,000	15.00	2030-G.	Chicago	307,200,000	15.00	2030-K.	Dallas	57,600,000	15.00
2030-C*.	Philadelphia	2,560,000	25.00	2030-G*.	Chicago	2,560,000	25.00	2030-K*.	Dallas	none printed	—
2030-D.	Cleveland	89,600,000	15.00	2030-H.	St. Louis	70,400,000	15.00	2030-L.	San Francisco	83,200,000	15.00
2030-D*.	Cleveland	none printed	—	2030-H*.	St. Louis	1,920,000	25.00	2030-L*.	San Francisco	none printed	—

31. Series of 1993.
Signatures of Withrow and Bentsen. Printed in Washington D.C.
(No notes printed in Ft. Worth.)

No.	Issuing Bank	No. Printed	Unc	No.	Issuing Bank	No. Printed	Unc	No.	Issuing Bank	No. Printed	Unc
2031-A.	Boston	147,200,000	15.00	2031-E.	Richmond	none printed	—	2031-I.	Minneapolis	none printed	—
2031-A*.	Boston	none printed	—	2031-E*.	Richmond	none printed	—	2031-I*.	Minneapolis	none printed	—
2031-B.	New York	480,000,000	15.00	2031-F.	Atlanta	121,600,000	15.00	2031-J.	Kansas City	19,200,000	15.00
2031-B*.	New York	5,120,000	25.00	2031-F*.	Atlanta	none printed	—	2031-J*.	Kansas City	none printed	—
2031-C.	Philadelphia	83,200,000	15.00	2031-G.	Chicago	128,000,000	15.00	2031-K.	Dallas	none printed	—
2031-C*.	Philadelphia	1,920,000	25.00	2031-G*.	Chicago	2,176,000	25,00	2031-K*.	Dallas	none printed	—
2031-D.	Cleveland	115,200,000	15.00	2031-H.	St. Louis	89,600,000	15.00	2031-L.	San Francisco	192,000,000	15.00
2031-D*.	Cleveland	none printed	—	2031-H*.	St. Louis	none printed	—	2031-L*.	San Francisco	none printed	—

32. Series of 1995.
Signatures of Withrow and Rubin. Printed in Washington, D.C.

No.	Issuing Bank	No. Printed	Unc	No.	Issuing Bank	No. Printed	Unc	No.	Issuing Bank	No. Printed	Unc
2032-A.	Boston	192,000,000	Current	2032-E.	Richmond	153,600,000	Current	2032-I.	Minneapolis		—
2032-A*.	Boston		—	2032-E*.	Richmond		—	2032-I*.	Minneapolis		—
2032-B.	New York	358,400,000	Current	2032-F.	Atlanta	70,400,000	Current	2032-J.	Kansas City		—
2032-B*.	New York		—	2032-F*.	Atlanta	640,000	Current	2032-J*.	Kansas City		—
2032-C.	Philadelphia	57,600,000	Current	2032-G.	Chicago		—	2032-K.	Dallas		—
2032-C*.	Philadelphia		—	2032-G*.	Chicago		—	2032-K*.	Dallas		—
2032-D.	Cleveland	108,000,000	Current	2032-H.	St. Louis		—	2032-L.	San Francisco		—
2032-D*.	Cleveland		—	2032-H*.	St. Louis		—	2032-L*.	San Francisco		—

33. Series of 1995.
Signature of Withrow and Rubin. Printed at the Western Facility (Ft. Worth).

2033-A.	Boston		—	2033-E.	Richmond	134,400,000	Current	2033-I.	Minneapolis	70,400,000	Current
2033-A*.	Boston			2033-E*.	Richmond	1,280,000	Current	2033-I*.	Minneapolis		—
2033-B.	New York	76,800,000	Current	2033-F.	Atlanta	377,600,000	Current	2033-J.	Kansas City	147,200,000	Current
2033-B*.	New York		—	2033-F*.	Atlanta	320,000	Current	2033-J*.	Kansas City		—
2033-C.	Philadelphia	89,600,000	Current	2033-G.	Chicago	448,000,000	Current	2033-K.	Dallas	166,400,000	Current
2033-C*.	Philadelphia		—	2033-G*.	Chicago	3,200,000	Current	2033-K*.	Dallas		—
2033-D.	Cleveland	70,400,000	Current	2033-H.	St. Louis	153,600,000	Current	2033-L.	San Francisco	275,200,000	Current
2033-D*.	Cleveland	1,920,00	Current	2033-H*.	St. Louis	6,400,000	Current	2033-L*.	San Francisco	3,200,000	Current

DESIGN NO. 221-a.
(Notes 2083-A-   )
Larger, off-center portrait of Alexander Hamilton.
Color-shifting (black/green) ink used in numeral at bottom right.

Reverse of Design No. 221-a
Frontal view of the Treasury Department.
Printed with microsize printing and a security thread on watermarked paper.

34. Series of 1999.
Signatures of Withrow and Summers. Printed in Washington, D.C

2034-A.	Boston		2034-E.	Richmond		2034-I.	Minneapolis	
2034-A*.	Boston		2034-E*.	Richmond		2034-I*.	Minneapolis	
2034-B.	New York	Current	2034-F.	Atlanta		2034-J.	Kansas City	
2034-B*.	New York	Current	2034-F*.	Atlanta		2034-J*.	Kansas City	
2034-C.	Philadelphia		2034-G.	Chicago		2034-K.	Dallas	
2034-C*.	Philadelphia		2034-G*.	Chicago		2034-K*.	Dallas	
2034-D.	Cleveland		2034-H.	St. Louis		2034-L.	San Francisco	
2034-D*.	Cleveland		2034-H*.	St. Louis		2034-L*.	San Francisco	

35. Series of 1999.
Signature of Withrow and Summers. Printed at the Western Facility (Ft. Worth).

2035-A.	Boston		2035-E.	Richmond		2035-I.	Minneapolis	
2035-A*.	Boston		2035-E*.	Richmond		2035-I*.	Minneapolis	
2035-B.	New York	Current	2035-F.	Atlanta		2035-J.	Kansas City	
2035-B*.	New York	Current	2035-F*.	Atlanta		2035-J*.	Kansas City	
2035-C.	Philadelphia		2035-G.	Chicago		2035-K.	Dallas	
2035-C*.	Philadelphia		2035-G*.	Chicago		2035-K*.	Dallas	
2035-D.	Cleveland		2035-H.	St. Louis		2035-L.	San Francisco	
2035-D*.	Cleveland		2035-H*.	St. Louis		2035-L*.	San Francisco	

20 Dollar Notes

All issues are with the head of Andrew Jackson.

DESIGN NO. 222
(Notes 2050-A - 2051-K Incl.)

Reverse of Design No. 222
View of the White House.

1. Series of 1928.
Signatures of Tate and Mellon.

No.	Issuing Bank	No. Printed	Unc	No.	Issuing Bank	No. Printed	Unc	No.	Issuing Bank	No. Printed	Unc
2050-A.	Boston	3,790,880	110.00	2050-F.	Atlanta	3,842,388	125.00	2050-K.	Dallas	1,568,500	85.00
2050-B.	New York	12,797,200	90.00	2050-G.	Chicago	10,891,740	90.00	2050-L.	San Francisco	8,404,800	90.00
2050-C.	Philadelphia	3,797,200	100.00	2050-H.	St. Louis	2,523,300	125.00	2050*.	Most Common Districts		
2050-D.	Cleveland	10,626,900	100.00	2050-I.	Minneapolis	2,633,100	125.00		VF 145.00 Unc 700.00		
2050-E.	Richmond	4,119,600	125.00	2050-J.	Kansas City	2,584,500	90.00				

2. Series of 1928-A.
Signatures of Woods and Mellon.

No.	Issuing Bank	No. Printed	Unc	No.	Issuing Bank	No. Printed	Unc	No.	Issuing Bank	No. Printed	Unc
2051-A.	Boston	1,293,900	90.00	2051-E.	Richmond	1,534,500	95.00	2051-J.	Kansas City	113,900	120.00
2051-B.	New York	1,055,800	85.00	2051-F.	Atlanta	1,442,400	95.00	2051-K.	Dallas	1,032,000	95.00
2051-C.	Philadelphia	1,717,200	80.00	2061-G.	Chicago	822,000	80.00	2051*.	Most Common Districts		
2051-D.	Cleveland	625,200	95.00	2061-H.	St. Louis	573,300	95.00		VF 800.00	Unc Rare	

DESIGN NO. 223
(Notes 2052-A - 2056-L Incl.)

Reverse of Design No. 223

3. Series of 1928-B.
Signatures of Woods and Mellon.
This series comes with both light and dark green seals.

No.	Issuing Bank	No. Printed	Unc	No.	Issuing Bank	No. Printed	Unc	No.	Issuing Bank	No. Printed	Unc
2052-A.	Boston	7,749,636	82.50	2052-F.	Atlanta	2,390,240	80.00	2052-K.	Dallas	2,406,060	80.00
2052-B.	New York	19,448,436	80.00	2052-G.	Chicago	17,220,276	80.00	2052-L.	San Francisco	9,689,124	82.50
2052-C.	Philadelphia	8,095,548	82.50	2052-H.	St. Louis	3,834,600	80.00	2052*.	Most Common Districts		
2052-D.	Cleveland	11,684,196	80.00	2052-I.	Minneapolis	3,298,920	80.00		VF 175.00 Unc 600.00		
2052-E.	Richmond	4,413,900	90.00	2052-J.	Kansas City	4,941,252	92.50				

4. Series of 1928-C.
Signatures of Woods and Mills.

No.	Issuing Bank	No. Printed	Unc	No.	Issuing Bank	No. Printed	Unc	No.	Issuing Bank	No. Printed	Unc
2053-G.	Chicago	3,363,300 VF 250.00	550.00	2053-L.	San Francisco	1,420,200 VF 300.00	650.00	2053*.		Unknown	

5. Series of 1934.
Signatures of Julian and Morgenthau.
As on the 5 and 10 Dollar notes, there are two distinct shades of green seals in this series, the light, vivid green and the darker, duller blue green. On the 20 Dollar notes, however, the values are about the same.

No.	Issuing Bank	No. Printed	Unc	No.	Issuing Bank	No. Printed	Unc	No.	Issuing Bank	No. Printed	Unc
2054-A.	Boston	37,673,068	57.50	2054-F.	Atlanta	41,547,660	55.00	2054-K.	Dallas	20,852,160	60.00
2054-B.	New York	27,573,264	55.00	2054-G.	Chicago	20,777,832	55.00	2054-L.	San Francisco	32,203,956	55.00
2054-C.	Philadelphia	53,209,968	55.00	2054-H.	St. Louis	27,174,552	65.00	2054*.	Most Common Districts		Unc 375.00
2054-D.	Cleveland	48,301,416	55.00	2054-I.	Minneapoli	16,795,116	65.00				
2054-E.	Richmond	36,259,224	55.00	2054-J.	Kansas City	28,865,304	60.00				

6. Series of 1934-A.
Signatures of Julian and Morganthau.

No.	Issuing Bank	No. Printed	Unc	No.	Issuing Bank	No. Printed	Unc	No.	Issuing Bank	No. Printed	Unc
2055-A.	Boston	3,302,416	65.00	2055-F.	Atlanta	6,756,816	62.50	2055-K.	Dallas	2,531,700	62.50
2055-B.	New York	102,555,538	62.50	2055-G.	Chicago	91,141,452	60.00	2055-L.	San Francisco	94,454,112	60.00
2055-C.	Philadelphia	3,371,316	60.00	2055-H.	St. Louis	3,701,568	70.00	2055*.	Most Common Districts		Unc 225.00
2055-D.	Cleveland	23,475,108	62.50	2055-I.	Minneapolis	1,162,500	75.00				
2055-E.	Richmond	46,816,224	62.50	2055-J.	Kansas City	3,221,184	65.00				

7. Series of 1934-B.
Signatures of Julian and Vinson.

No.	Issuing Bank	No. Printed	Unc	No.	Issuing Bank	No. Printed	Unc	No.	Issuing Bank	No. Printed	Unc
2056-A.	Boston	3,904,800	60.00	2056-E.	Richmond	9,451,632	60.00	2056-I.	Minneapolis	2,304,800	65.00
2056-B.	New York	14,876,436	57.50	2056-F.	Atlanta	6,887,640	57.50	2056-J.	Kansas City	3,524,244	65.00
2056-C.	Philadelphia	3,271,452	60.00	2056-G.	Chicago	9,084,600	57.50	2056-K.	Dallas	2,807,388	65.00
2056-D.	Cleveland	2,814,600	60.00	2056-H.	St. Louis	5,817,300	60.00	2056-L.	San Francisco	5,289,540	57.50
								2056*.	Most Common Districts		250.00

DESIGN NO. 224 (Notes 2057-A-L-2058-L Incl.)
The reverse is as shown, with view of remodeled White House.
The obverse is similar to Design No. 223.

8. Series of 1934-C.
Signatures of Julian and Snyder.
This series exists with two different reverses: Design No. 206 and Design No. 224.

No.	Issuing Bank	No. Printed	Unc	No.	Issuing Bank	No. Printed	Unc	No.	Issuing Bank	No. Printed	Unc
2057-A.	Boston	7,397,352	52.50	2057-F.	Atlanta	18,858,876	50.00	2057-K.	Dallas	10,205,364	52.50
2057-B.	New York	18,668,148	50.00	2057-G.	Chicago	26,031,660	50.00	2057-L.	San Francisco	20,580,000	50.00
2057-C.	Philadelphia	11,590,752	50.00	2057-H.	St. Louis	13,276,984	50.00	2057*.	Most Common Districts		
2057-D.	Cleveland	17,912,424	50.00	2057-I.	Minneapolis	3,490,200	60.00		1st Reverse		250.00
2057-E.	Richmond	22,526,568	50.00	2057-J.	Kansas City	9,675,468	52.50		2nd Reverse		225.00

9. Series of 1934-D.
Signatures of Clark and Snyder.

No.	Issuing Bank	No. Printed	Unc	No.	Issuing Bank	No. Printed	Unc	No.	Issuing Bank	No. Printed	Unc
2058-A.	Boston	4,520,000	50.00	2058-F.	Atlanta	7,495,440	52.50	2058-K.	Dallas	3,707,364	52.50
2058-B.	New York	27,894,260	50.00	2058-G.	Chicago	15,187,596	50.00	2058-L.	San Francisco	12,015,228	50.00
2058-C.	Philadelphia	6,022,428	52.50	2058-H.	St. Louis	5,923,248	52.50	2058*.	Most Common Districts		150.00
2058-D.	Cleveland	8,981,688	50.00	2058-I.	Minneapolis	2,422,416	57.50				
2058-E.	Richmond	14,055,984	52.50	2058-J.	Kansas City	4,211,904	52.50				

DESIGN NO. 225

(Notes 2059-A - 2064-L Incl.)

The obverse is as shown.
The reverse is similar to Design No. 224.

10. Series of 1950.
Signatures of Clark and Snyder.

No.	Issuing Bank	No. Printed	Unc	No.	Issuing Bank	No. Printed	Unc	No.	Issuing Bank	No. Printed	Unc
2059-A.	Boston	23,184,000	57.50	2059-F.	Atlanta	39,312,000	57.50	2059-K.	Dallas	22,656,000	57.50
2059-B.	New York	80,064,000	55.00	2059-G.	Chicago	70,464,000	57.50	2059-L.	San Francisco	70,272,000	55.00
2059-C.	Philadelphia	29,520,000	57.50	2059-H.	St. Louis	27,352,000	57.50	2059*.	Most Common Districts		250.00
2059-D.	Cleveland	51,120,000	55.00	2059-I.	Minneapolis	9,216,000	62.50				
2059-E.	Richmond	67,536,000	57.50	2059-J.	Kansas City	22,752,000	57.50				

11. Series of 1950-A.
Signatures of Priest and Humphrey.

No.	Issuing Bank	No. Printed	Unc	No.	Issuing Bank	No. Printed	Unc	No.	Issuing Bank	No. Printed	Unc
2059-A.	Boston	19,656,000	52.50	2059-F.	Atlanta	27,648,000	52.50	2059-K.	Dallas	10,728,000	52.50
2059-B.	New York	82,568,000	50.00	2059-G.	Chicago	73,720,000	52.50	2059-L.	San Francisco	85,528,000	50.00
2059-C.	Philadelphia	16,560,000	52.50	2059-H.	St. Louis	22,680,000	52.50	2059*.	Most Common Districts		175.00
2059-D.	Cleveland	50,320,000	50.00	2059-I.	Minneapolis	5,544,000	52.50				
2059-E.	Richmond	69,544,000	52.50	2059-J.	Kansas City	22,968,000	52.50				

12. Series of 1950-B.
Signatures of Priest and Anderson.

No.	Issuing Bank	No. Printed	Unc	No.	Issuing Bank	No. Printed	Unc	No.	Issuing Bank	No. Printed	Unc
2061-A.	Boston	5,040,000	52.50	2061-F.	Atlanta	40,240,000	45.00	2061-K.	Dallas	11,880,000	52.50
2061-B.	New York	49,960,000	45.00	2061-G.	Chicago	80,560,000	45.00	2061-L.	San Francisco	51,040,000	45.00
2061-C.	Philadelphia	7,920,000	52.50	2061-H.	St. Louis	19,440,000	47.50	2061*.	Most Common Districts		Unc 150.00
2061-D.	Cleveland	38,160,000	45.00	2061-I.	Minneapolis	12,240,000	52.50				
2061-E.	Richmond	42,120,000	45.00	2061-J.	Kansas City	28,440,000	47.50				

13. Series of 1950-C.
Signatures of Smith and Dillon.

No.	Issuing Bank	No. Printed	Unc	No.	Issuing Bank	No. Printed	Unc	No.	Issuing Bank	No. Printed	Unc
2062-A	Boston	7,200,000	52.50	2062-F.	Atlanta	19,080,000	52.50	2062-K.	Dallas	9,000,000	57.50
2062-B.	New York	43,200,000	50.00	2062-G.	Chicago	29,160,000	50.00	2062-L.	San Francisco	45,360,000	50.00
2062-C.	Philadelphia	7,560,000	52.50	2062-H.	St. Louis	12,960,000	52.50	2062*.	Most Common Districts		125.00
2062-D.	Cleveland	28,440,000	50.00	2062-I.	Minneapolis	6,480,000	57.50				
2062-E.	Richmond	37,000,000	50.00	2062-J.	Kansas City	18,360,000	55.00				

14. Series of 1950-D.
Signatures of Granahan and Dillon.

No.	Issuing Bank	No. Printed	Unc	No.	Issuing Bank	No. Printed	Unc	No.	Issuing Bank	No. Printed	Unc
2063-A.	Boston	9,320,000	52.50	2063-E.	Richmond	30,240,000	50.00	2063-I.	Minneapolis	3,240,000	57.50
2063-B.	New York	64,280,000	50.00	2063-F.	Atlanta	22,680,000	50.00	2063-J.	Kansas City	8,200,000	52.50
2063-C.	Philadelphia	5,400,000	55.00	2063-G.	Chicago	67,960,000	50.00	2063-K.	Dallas	6,480,000	52.50
2063-D.	Cleveland	23,760,000	50.00	2063-H.	St. Louis	6,120,000	55.00	2063-L.	San Francisco	69,400,000	50.00
								2063*.	Most Common Districts	Unc	150.00

15. Series of 1950-E.
Signatures of Granahan and Fowler.

No.	Issuing Bank	No. Printed	Unc	No.	Issuing Bank	No. Printed	Unc	No.	Issuing Bank	No. Printed	Unc
2064-B.	New York	8,640,000	75.00	2064-G.	Chicago	9,360,000	75.00	2064-L.	San Francisco	8,640,000	75.00
2064-B*	New York		275.00	2064-G*.	Chicago		275.00	2064-L*.	San Francisco		275.00

DESIGN NO. 225-a.
(Notes 2065-A - 2082-L Incl.)

Reverse of Design No. 225-a.
With motto "In God We Trust."

16. Series of 1963.
Signatures of Granahan and Dillon.

No.	Issuing Bank	No. Printed	Unc	No.	Issuing Bank	No. Printed	Unc	No.	Issuing Bank	No. Printed	Unc
2065-A.	Boston	2,560,000	45.00	2065-F.	Atlanta	10,240,000	42.50	2065-K.	Dallas	2,560,000	57.50
2065-B.	New York	16,640,000	42.50	2065-G.	Chicago	2,560,000	45.00	2065-L.	San Francisco	7,040,000	42.50
2065-D.	Cleveland	7,680,000	42.50	2065-H.	St. Louis	3,200,000	45.00	2065*.	Most Common Districts		75.00
2065-E.	Richmond	4,480,000	45.00	2065-J.	Kansas City	3,840,000	45.00				

17. Series of 1963-A.
Signatures of Granahan and Fowler.

No.	Issuing Bank	No. Printed	Unc	No.	Issuing Bank	No. Printed	Unc	No.	Issuing Bank	No. Printed	Unc
2066-A.	Boston	23,680,000	30.00	2066-E.	Richmond	128,800,000	40.00	2066-I.	Minneapolis	10,240,000	40.00
2066-A*.	Boston	1,280,000	45.00	2066-E*.	Richmond	5,760,000	50.00	2066-I*.	Minneapolis	640,000	60.00
2066-B.	New York	93,600,000	40.00	2066-F.	Atlanta	42,880,000	40.00	2066-J.	Kansas City	37,120,000	40.00
2066-B*.	New York	3,840,000	50.00	2066-F*.	Atlanta	1,920,000	55.00	2066-J*.	Kansas City	1,920,000	50.00
2066-C.	Philadelphia	17,920,000	40.00	2066-G.	Chicago	156,320,000	40.00	2066-K.	Dallas	38,400,000	40.00
2066-C*.	Philadelphia	640,000	60.00	2066-G*.	Chicago	7,040,000	50.00	2066-K*.	Dallas	1,280,000	50.00
2066-D.	Cleveland	68,480,000	40.00	2066-H.	St. Louis	34,560,000	40.00	2066-L.	San Francisco	169,120,000	40.00
2066-D*.	Cleveland	2,560,000	50.00	2066-H*.	St. Louis	1,920,000	50.00	2066-L*.	San Francisco	8,320,000	50.00

18. Series of 1969.
Signatures of Elston and Kennedy. With new Treasury seal.

No.	Issuing Bank	No. Printed	Unc	No.	Issuing Bank	No. Printed	Unc	No.	Issuing Bank	No. Printed	Unc
2067-A.	Boston	19,200,000	32.50	2067-E.	Richmond	66,560,000	32.50	2067-I.	Minneapolis	12,160,000	32.50
2067-A*.	Boston	1,280,000	45.00	2067-E*.	Richmond	2,560,000	45.00	2067-I*.	Minneapolis	640,000	50.00
2067-B.	New York	106,400,000	32.50	2067-F.	Atlanta	36,480,000	32.50	2067-J.	Kansas City	39,040,000	32.50
2067-B*.	New York	5,106,000	45.00	2067-F*.	Atlanta	1,280,000	45.00	2067-J*.	Kansas City	1,280,000	45.00
2067-C.	Philadelphia	10,880,000	32.50	2067-G.	Chicago	107,680,000	32.50	2067-K.	Dallas	25,600,000	32.50
2067-C*.	Philadelphia	1,280,000	45.00	2067-G*.	Chicago	3,200,000	45.00	2067-K*.	Dallas	640,000	50.00
2067-D.	Cleveland	60,160,000	32.50	2067-H.	St. Louis	19,200,000	32.50	2067-L.	San Francisco	103,840,000	32.50
2067-D*.	Cleveland	2,560,000	45.00	2067-H*.	St. Louis	640,000	50.00	2067-L*.	San Francisco	5,120,000	45.00

19. Series of 1969-A.
Signatures of Kabis and Connally.

No.	Issuing Bank	No. Printed	Unc	No.	Issuing Bank	No. Printed	Unc	No.	Issuing Bank	No. Printed	Unc
2068-A.	Boston	13,440,000	42.50	2068-E.	Richmond	42,400,000	42.50	2068-I.	Minneapolis	7,040,000	42.50
2068-A*.	Boston	none printed	—	2068-E*.	Richmond	1,920,000	55.00	2068-I*.	Minneapolis	none printed	—
2068-B.	New York	69,760,000	42.50	2068-F.	Atlanta	13,440,000	42.50	2068-J.	Kansas City	16,040,000	42.50
2068-B*.	New York	2,460,000	50.00	2068-F*.	Atlanta	none printed	—	2068-J*.	Kansas City	none printed	—
2068-C.	Philadelphia	13,440,000	42.50	2068-G.	Chicago	81,840,000	42.50	2068-K.	Dallas	14,720,000	42.50
2068-C*.	Philadelphia	none printed	—	2068-G.	Chicago	1,920,000	50.00	2068-K*.	Dallas	640,000	55.00
2068-D.	Cleveland	29,440,000	42.50	2068-H.	St. Louis	14,080,000	42.50	2068-L.	San Francisco	50,560,000	42.50
2068-D*.	Cleveland	640,000	55.00	2068-H*.	St. Louis	640,000	55.00	2068-L*.	San Francisco	1,280,000	55.00

20. Series of 1969-B.
Signatures of Banuelos and Connally.

No.	Issuing Bank	No. Printed	Unc	No.	Issuing Bank	No. Printed	Unc	No.	Issuing Bank	No. Printed	Unc
2069-B.	New York	39,200,000	37.50	2069-F*.	Atlanta	640,000	57.50	2069-J.	Kansas City	3,840,000	37.50
2069-B*.	New York	480,000	57.50	2069-G.	Chicago	14,240,000	37.50	2069-J*.	Kansas City	640,000	57.50
2069-D.	Cleveland	6,400,000	37.50	2069-G*.	Chicago	1,112,000	57.50	2069-K.	Dallas	12,160,000	37.50
2069-D*.	Cleveland	none printed	—	2069-H.	St. Louis	5,120,000	37.50	2069-K*.	Dallas	none printed	—
2069-E.	Richmond	27,520,000	37.50	2069-H*.	St. Louis	none printed	—	2069-L.	San Francisco	26,000,000	37.50
2069-E*.	Richmond	none printed	—	2069-I.	Minneapolis	2,560,000	37.50	2069-L*.	San Francisco	640,000	57.50
2069-F.	Atlanta	14,080,000	37.50	2069-I*.	Minneapolis	none printed	—				

21. Series of 1969-C.
Signatures of Banuelos and Shultz.

No.	Issuing Bank	No. Printed	Unc	No.	Issuing Bank	No. Printed	Unc	No.	Issuing Bank	No. Printed	Unc
2070-A.	Boston	17,280,000	37.50	2070-E.	Richmond	80,160,000	37.50	2070-I.	Minneapolis	14,080,000	37.50
2070-A*.	Boston	640,000	47.50	2070-E*.	Richmond	1,920,000	47.50	2070-I*.	Minneapolis	640,000	47.50
2070-B.	New York	135,200,000	37.50	2070-F.	Atlanta	35,840,000	37.50	2070-J.	Kansas City	32,000,000	37.50
2070-B*.	New York	1,640,000	47.50	2070-F*.	Atlanta	640,000	47.50	2070-J*.	Kansas City	640,000	47.50
2070-C.	Philadelphia	40,960,000	37.50	2070-G.	Chicago	78,720,000	37.50	2070-K.	Dallas	31,360,000	37.50
2070-C*.	Philadelphia	640,000	47.50	2070-G*.	Chicago	640,000	47.50	2070-K*.	Dallas	1,920,000	47.50
2070-D.	Cleveland	57,760,000	37.50	2070-H.	St. Louis	33,920,000	37.50	2070-L.	San Francisco	82,080,000	37.50
2070-D*.	Cleveland	480,000	47.50	2070-H*.	St. Louis	640,000	47.50	2070-L*.	San Francisco	1,120,000	47.50

22. Series of 1974.
Signatures of Neff and Simon.

No.	Issuing Bank	No. Printed	Unc	No.	Issuing Bank	No. Printed	Unc	No.	Issuing Bank	No. Printed	Unc
2071-A.	Boston	56,960,000	32.50	2071-E.	Richmond	149,920,000	32.50	2071-I.	Minneapolis	39,040,000	32.50
2071-A*.	Boston	768,000	42.50	2071-E*.	Richmond	3,040,000	42.50	2071-I*.	Minneapolis	1,280,000	42.50
2071-B.	New York	296,640,000	32.50	2071-F.	Atlanta	53,280,000	32.50	2071-J.	Kansas City	74,400,000	32.50
2071-B*.	New York	7,616,000	42.50	2071-F*.	Atlanta	480,000	30.00	2071-J*.	Kansas City	736,000	42.50
2071-C.	Philadelphia	59,680,000	32.50	2071-G.	Chicago	249,920,000	32.50	2071-K.	Dallas	68,640,000	32.50
2071-C*.	Philadelphia	1,760,000	42.50	2071-G*.	Chicago	4,608,000	42.50	2071-K*.	Dallas	608,000	30.00
2071-D.	Cleveland	148,000,000	32.50	2071-H.	St. Louis	73,120,000	32.50	2071-L.	San Francisco	128,800,000	32.50
2071-D*.	Cleveland	3,296,000	42.50	2071-H*.	St. Louis	1,120,000	42.50	2071-L*.	San Francisco	4,320,000	42.50

23. Series of 1977
Signatures of Morton and Blumenthal.

No.	Issuing Bank	No. Printed	Unc	No.	Issuing Bank	No. Printed	Unc	No.	Issuing Bank	No. Printed	Unc
2072-A.	Boston	94,720,000	32.50	2072-E.	Richmond	257,280,000	32.50	2072-I.	Minneapolis	15,360,000	32.50
2072-A*.	Boston	2,688,000	42.50	2072-E*.	Richmond	6,272,000	42.50	2072-I*.	Minneapolis	512,000	50.00
2072-B.	Ncw York	569,600,000	32.50	2072-F.	Atlanta	70,400,000	32.50	2072-J.	Kansas City	148,480,000	32.50
2072-B*.	New York	12,416,000	42.50	2072-F*.	Atlanta	2,698,000	42.50	2072-J*.	Kansas City	4,864,000	42.50
2072-C.	Philadelphia	117,760,000	32.50	2072-G	Chicago	358,400,000	32.50	2072-K.	Dallas	163,840,000	32.50
2072-C*.	Philadelphia	2,176,000	42.50	2072-G*.	Chicago	7,552,000	42.50	2072-K*.	Dallas	6,656,000	42.50
2072-D.	Cleveland	189,440,000	32.50	2072-H.	St. Louis	98,560,000	32.50	2072-L	San Francisco	263,680,000	32.50
2072-D*.	Cleveland	5,632,000	42.50	2072-H*.	St. Louis	1,792,000	42.50	2072-L*.	San Francisco	6,528,000	42.50

24. Series of 1981
Signatures of Buchanan and Regan.

No.	Issuing Bank	No. Printed	Unc	No.	Issuing Bank	No. Printed	Unc	No.	Issuing Bank	No. Printed	Unc
2073-A.	Boston	191,360,000	32.50	2073-E	Richmond	296,320,000	32.50	2073-I.	Minneapolis	23,040,000	32.50
2073-A*.	Boston	1,024,000	42.50	2073-E*.	Richmond	1,280,000	42.50	2073-I*.	Minneapolis	256,000	47.50
2073-B.	New York	559,360,000	32.50	2073-F.	Atlanta	93,440,000	32.50	2073-J.	Kansas City	147,840,000	32.50
2073-B*.	New York	5,312,000	42.50	2073-F*.	Atlanta	3,200,000	42.50	2073-J*.	Kansas City	1,280,000	42.50
2073-C.	Philadelphia	146,560,000	32.50	2073-G.	Chicago	361,600,000	32.50	2073-K.	Dallas	95,360,000	32.50
2073-C*.	Philadelphia	1,280,000	42.50	2073-G*.	Chicago	2,688,000	42.50	2073-K*.	Dallas	896,000	42.50
2073-D.	Cleveland	146,560,000	32.50	2073-H.	St. Louis	76,160,000	32.50	2073-L.	San Francisco	404,480,000	32.50
2073-D*.	Cleveland	1,280,000	42.50	2073-H*.	St. Louis	1,536,000	42.50	2073-L*.	San Francisco	1,424,000	42.50

25. Series of 1981-A.
Signatures of Ortega and Regan.

No.	Issuing Bank	No. Printed	Unc	No.	Issuing Bank	No. Printed	Unc	No.	Issuing Bank	No. Printed	Unc
2074-A.	Boston	156,800,000	32.50	2074-E.	Richmond	214,400,000	32.50	2074-I.	Minneapolis	19,200,000	32.50
2074-A*.	Boston	none printed	—	2074-E*.	Richmond	none printed	—	2074-I*.	Minneapolis	none printed	—
2074-B.	New York	352,000,000	32.50	2074-F.	Atlanta	140,800,000	32.50	2074-J.	Kansas City	86,400,000	32.50
2074-B*.	New York	none printed	—	2074-F*.	Atlanta	3,200,000	42.50	2074-J*.	Kansas City	none printed	—
2074-C.	Philadelphia	57,600,000	32.50	2074-G.	Chicago	211,200,000	32.50	2074-K.	Dallas	99,200,000	32.50
2074-C*.	Philadelphia	3,840,000	42.50	2074-G*.	Chicago	none printed	—	2074-K*.	Dallas	none printed	—
2074-D.	Cleveland	160,000,000	32.50	2074-H.	St. Louis	73,600,000	32.50	2074-L	San Francisco	457,600,000	32.50
2074-D*.	Cleveland	3,840,000	42.50	2074-H*.	St. Louis	none printed	—	2074-L*.	San Francisco	6,400,000	42.50

26. Series of 1985
Signatures of Ortega and Baker.

No.	Issuing Bank	No. Printed	Unc	No.	Issuing Bank	No. Printed	Unc	No.	Issuing Bank	No. Printed	Unc
2075-A.	Boston	416,000,000	32.50	2075-E.	Richmond	864,000,000	32.50	2075-I.	Minneapolis	112,000,000	32.50
2075-A*.	Boston	3,200,000	42.50	2075-E*.	Richmond	6,400,000	42.50	2075-I*.	Minneapolis	none printed	—
2075-B.	New York	1,728,000,000	32.50	2073-F.	Atlanta	313,600,000	32.50	2075-J.	Kansas City	204,800,000	32.50
2075-B*.	New York	5,760,000	42.50	2075-F*.	Atlanta	none printed	—	2075-J*	Kansas City	3,200,000	42.50
2075-C.	Philadelphia	224,000,000	32.50	2075-G.	Chicago	729,600,000	32.50	2075-K.	Dallas	192,000,000	32.50
2075-C*.	Philadelphia	6,400,000	42.50	2075-G*.	Chicago	5,760,000	42.50	2075-K*.	Dallas	3,200,000	42.50
2075-D.	Cleveland	585,600,000	32.50	2073-H.	St. Louis	203,400,000	32.50	2075-L	San Francisco	1,129,600,000	32.50
2075-D*.	Cleveland	6,400,000	42.50	2075-H*.	St. Louis	none printed	—	2075-L*.	San Francisco	3,200,000	42.50

27. Series of 1988.
None printed
28. Series of 1988-A.
Signatures of Villalpando and Brady.

No.	Issuing Bank	No. Printed	Unc	No.	Issuing Bank	No. Printed	Unc	No.	Issuing Bank	No. Printed	Unc
2076-A.	Boston	313,600,000	32.50	2076-E.	Richmond	281,600,000	32.50	2076-I.	Minneapolis	25,600,000	32.50
2076-A*.	Boston	none printed	—	2076-E*.	Richmond	none printed	—	2076-I*.	Minneapolis	none printed	—
2076-B.	New York	979,200,000	32.50	2076-F.	Atlanta	288,000,000	32.50	2076-J.	Kansas City	137,200,000	32.50
2076-B*.	New York	6,560,000	42.50	2076-F*.	Atlanta	3,200,000	42.50	2076-J*.	Kansas City	none printed	—
2076-C.	Philadelphia	96,000,000	32.50	2076-G.	Chicago	563,200,000	32.50	2076-K.	Dallas	51,200,000	32.50
2076-C*.	Philadelphia	3,200,000	42.50	2076-G*.	Chicago	3,200,000	42.50	2076-K*.	Dallas	3,200,000	42.50
2076-D.	Cleveland	307,200,000	32.50	2076-H.	St. Louis	108,800,000	32.50	2076-L.	San Francisco	729,600,000	32.50
2076-D*.	Cleveland	none printed	—	2076-H*.	St. Louis	none printed	—	2076-L*.	San Francisco	none printed	—

29. Series of 1990.
Signatures of Villalpando and Brady. With security thread and microsize printing.
Printed in Washington, D.C.

No.	Issuing Bank	No. Printed	Unc	No.	Issuing Bank	No. Printed	Unc	No.	Issuing Bank	No. Printed	Unc
2077-A.	Boston	345,600,000	32.50	2077-E.	Richmond	307,200,000	32.50	2077-I.	Minneapolis	38,400,000	32.50
2077-A*.	Boston	3,200,000	42.50	2077-E*.	Richmond	3,200,000	42.50	2077-I*.	Minneapolis	none printed	—
2077-B.	New York	1,446,400,000	32.50	2077-F.	Atlanta	460,800,000	32.50	2077-J.	Kansas City	83,200,000	32.50
2077-B*.	New York	16,640,000	42.50	2077-F*.	Atlanta	1,280,000	42.50	2077-J*.	Kansas City	none printed	—
2077-C.	Philadelphia	96,000,000	32.50	2077-G.	Chicago	652,800,000	32.50	2077-K.	Dallas	25,600,000	32.50
2077-C*.	Philadelphia	none printed	—	2077-G*.	Chicago	2,560,000	42.50	2077-K*.	Dallas	none printed	—
2077-D.	Cleveland	281,600,000	32.50	2077-H.	St. Louis	172,800,000	32.50	2077-L.	San Francisco	416,000,000	32.50
2077-D*.	Cleveland	3,200,000	42.50	2077-H*.	St. Louis	3,200,000	37.50	2077-L*.	San Francisco	none printed	—

30. Series of 1990.
Signatures of Villalpando and Brady. With security thread and microsize printing.
Printed at the Western Facility (Fort Worth).
Notes printed in Ft. Worth may be identified by a small "FW" on the right front side next to the plate check letter-number.

No.	Issuing Bank	No. Printed	Unc	No.	Issuing Bank	No. Printed	Unc	No.	Issuing Bank	No. Printed	Unc
2078-F.	Atlanta	none printed	—	2078-G.	Chicago	none printed	—	2078-I.	Minneapolis	32,000,000	32.50
2078-F*.	Atlanta	1,280,000	45.00	2078-G*.	Chicago	13,400,000	45.00	2078-I*.	Minneapolis	5,120,000	45.00

31. Series of 1993.
Signatures of Withrow and Bentsen. Printed in Washington, D.C.

No.	Issuing Bank	No. Printed	Unc	No.	Issuing Bank	No. Printed	Unc	No.	Issuing Bank	No. Printed	Unc
2079-A.	Boston	288,000,000	Current	2079-E.	Richmond	656,000,000	Current	2079-I.	Minneapolis	none printed	—
2079-A*.	Boston	2,560,000	Current	2079-E*.	Richmond	8,960,000	Current	2079-I*.	Minneapolis	none printed	—
2079-B.	New York	640,000,000	Current	2079-F.	Atlanta	300,800,000	Current	2079-J.	Kansas City	none printed	—
2079-B*.	New York	4,920,000	Current	2079-F*.	Atlanta	none printed	—	2079-J*.	Kansas City	none printed	—
2079-C.	Philadelphia	147,200,000	Current	2079-G.	Chicago	none printed	—	2079-K.	Dallas	32,000,000	Current
2079-C*.	Philadelphia	none printed	—	2079-G*.	Chicago	none printed	—	2079-K*.	Dallas	none printed	—
2079-D.	Cleveland	329,600,000	Current	2079-H.	St. Louis	19,200,000	Current	2079-L.	San Francisco	none printed	—
2079-D*.	Cleveland	1,920,000	Current	2079-H*.	St. Louis	none printed	—	2079-L*.	San Francisco	none printed	—

32. Series of 1993.
Signatures of Withrow and Bentsen. Printed at the Western Facility (Fort Worth).

No.	Issuing Bank	No. Printed	Unc	No.	Issuing Bank	No. Printed	Unc
2080-F.	Atlanta	51,200,000	Current	2080-H*.	St. Louis	none printed	—
2080-F*.	Atlanta	3,200,000	—	2080-J.	Kansas City	102,400,000	Current
2080-G.	Chicago	390,400,000	Current	2080-J*.	Kansas City	none printed	—
2080-G*.	Chicago	none printed	—	2080-L.	San Francisco	806,400,000	Current
2080-H.	St. Louis	166,400,000	Current	2080-L*.	San Francisco	6,528,00,000	Current

33. Series of 1995.
Signatures of Withrow and Rubin. Printed in Washington, D.C.

No.	Issuing Bank	No. Printed	Unc	No.	Issuing Bank	No. Printed	Unc	No.	Issuing Bank	No. Printed	Unc
2081-A.	Boston	none printed	—	2081-E.	Richmond	166,400,000	Current	2081-I.	Minneapolis		—
2081-A*.	Boston	none printed	—	2081-E*.	Richmond		—	2081-I*.	Minneapolis		—
2081-B.	New York	403,200,000	Current	2081-F.	Atlanta		—	2081-J.	Kansas City		—
2081-B*.	New York	5,760,000	Current	2081-F*.	Atlanta		—	2081-J*.	Kansas City		—
2081-C.	Philadelphia	70,400,000	Current	2081-G.	Chicago		—	2081-K.	Dallas		—
2081-C*.	Philadelphia	none printed	—	2081-G*.	Chicago		—	2081-K*.	Dallas		—
2081-D.	Cleveland	140,800,000	Current	2081-H.	St. Louis		—	2081-L.	San Francisco		—
2081-D*.	Cleveland	640,000	Current	2081-H*.	St. Louis		—	2081-L*.	San Francisco		—

34. Series of 1995.
Signatures of Withrow and Rubin. Printed at the Western Facility (Fort Worth).

No.	Issuing Bank	No. Printed	Unc	No.	Issuing Bank	No. Printed	Unc	No.	Issuing Bank	No. Printed	Unc
2082-A.	Boston	none printed	—	2082-E.	Richmond	none printed	—	2082-I.	Minneapolis	44,800,000	Current
2082-A*.	Boston	none printed	—	2082-E*.	Richmond	none printed	—	2082-I*.	Minneapolis	none printed	—
2082-B.	New York	none printed	—	2082-F.	Atlanta	307,200,000	Current	2082-J.	Kansas City	230,400,000	Current
2082-B*.	New York	none printed	—	2082-F*.	Atlanta	none printed	—	2082-J*.	Kansas City	none printed	—
2082-C.	Philadelphia	none printed	—	2082-G.	Chicago	492,800,000	Current	2082-K.	Dallas	249,600,000	Current
2082-C*.	Philadelphia	none printed	—	2082-G*.	Chicago	none printed	—	2082-K*.	Dallas	none printed	—
2082-D.	Cleveland	none printed	—	2082-H.	St. Louis	140,800,000	Current	2082-L.	San Francisco	556,800,000	Current
2082-D*.	Cleveland	none printed	—	2082-H*.	St. Louis	none printed	—	2082-L*.	San Francisco	none printed	—

DESIGN NO. 225-b.

(Notes 2083-A -   )

Larger and younger portrait of Andrew Jackson positioned off-center. Color-shifting (black/green) ink used in numeral at lower right.

Reverse of Design No. 225-b.
View of north portico of the White House.
Printed with microsize printing and security thread on watermarked paper.

35. Series of 1996.
Signatures of Withrow and Rubin. Printed in Washington, D.C.

2083-A.	Boston		—	2083-E.	Richmond	—	2083-I.	Minneapolis	—
2083-A*.	Boston		—	2083-E*.	Richmond	—	2083-I*.	Minneapolis	—
2083-B.	New York	2,649,600,000	Current	2083-F.	Atlanta	—	2083-J.	Kansas City	—
2083-B*.	New York	32,000,000	Current	2083-F*.	Atlanta	—	2083-J*.	Kansas City	—
2083-C.	Philadelphia		—	2083-G.	Chicago	—	2083-K.	Dallas	—
2083-C*.	Philadelphia		—	2083-G*.	Chicago	—	2083-K*.	Dallas	—
2083-D.	Cleveland		—	2083-H.	St. Louis	—	2083-L.	San Francisco	—
2083-D*.	Cleveland		—	2083-H*.	St. Louis	—	2083-L*.	San Francisco	—

36. Series of 1996.
Signatures of Withrow and Rubin. Printed at the Western Facility (Fort Worth).

2084-A.	Boston		—	2084-E.	Richmond	—	2084-I.	Minneapolis	—
2084-A*.	Boston		—	2084-E*.	Richmond	—	2084-I*.	Minneapolis	—
2084-B.	New York	3,980,800,000	Current	2084-F.	Atlanta	—	2084-J.	Kansas City	—
2084-B*.	New York	29,460,000	Current	2084-F*.	Atlanta	—	2084-J*.	Kansas City	—
2084-C.	Philadelphia		—	2084-G.	Chicago	—	2084-K.	Dallas	—
2084-C*.	Philadelphia		—	2084-G*.	Chicago	—	2084-K*.	Dallas	—
2084-D.	Cleveland		—	2084-H.	St. Louis	—	2084-L.	San Francisco	—
2084-D*.	Cleveland		—	2084-H*.	St. Louis	—	2084-L*.	San Francisco	—

37. Series of 1999
Signatures of Withrow and Summers. Printed in Washington, D.C.

2085-A.	Boston		—	2085-E.	Richmond	—	2085-I.	Minneapolis	—
2085-A*.	Boston		—	2085-E*.	Richmond	—	2085-I*.	Minneapolis	—
2085-B.	New York		Current	2085-F.	Atlanta	—	2085-J.	Kansas City	—
2085-B*.	New York		Current	2085-F*.	Atlanta	—	2085-J*.	Kansas City	—
2085-C.	Philadelphia		—	2085-G.	Chicago	—	2085-K.	Dallas	—
2085-C*.	Philadelphia		—	2085-G*.	Chicago	—	2085-K*.	Dallas	—
2085-D.	Cleveland		—	2085-H.	St. Louis	—	2085-L.	San Francisco	—
2085-D*.	Cleveland		—	2085-H*.	St. Louis	—	2085-L*.	San Francisco	—

38. Series of 1999.
Signatures of Withrow and Summers. Printed at the Western Facility (Fort Worth).

2086-A.	Boston		—	2086-E.	Richmond	—	2086-I.	Minneapolis	—
2086-A*.	Boston		—	2086-E*.	Richmond	—	2086-I*.	Minneapolis	—
2086-B.	New York		Current	2086-F.	Atlanta	—	2086-J.	Kansas City	—
2086-B*.	New York		Current	2086-F*.	Atlanta	—	2086-J*.	Kansas City	—
2086-C.	Philadelphia		—	2086-G.	Chicago	—	2086-K.	Dallas	—
2086-C*.	Philadelphia		—	2086-G*.	Chicago	—	2086-K*.	Dallas	—
2086-D.	Cleveland		—	2086-H.	St. Louis	—	2086-L.	San Francisco	—
2086-D*.	Cleveland		—	2086-H*.	St. Louis	—	2086-L*.	San Francisco	—

50 Dollar Notes

All issues are with the head of Ulysses S. Grant.

DESIGN NO. 226
(Notes 2100-A - 2101-L Incl.)

Reverse of Design No. 226.
View of the U.S. Capitol.

1. Series of 1928.
Signatures of Woods and Mellon.

No.	Issuing Bank	No. Printed	Unc	No.	Issuing Bank	No. Printed	Unc	No.	Issuing Bank	No. Printed	Unc
2100-A.	Boston	265,200	325.00	2100-F.	Atlanta	538,800	225.00	2100-J.	Kansas City	252,600	250.00
2100-B.	New York	1,351,800	200.00	2100-G.	Chicago	1,348,620	200.00	2100-K.	Dallas	109,920	325.00
2100-C.	Philadelphia	997,056	200.00	2100-H.	St. Louis	627,300	225.00	2100-L.	San Francisco	447,600	225.00
2100-D.	Cleveland	1,161,900	200.00	2100-I.	Minneapolis	106,200	325.00	2100*.	Most Common Districts		
2100-E.	Richmond	539,400	225.00						VF 250.00 Unc 850.00		

2. Series of 1928-A.
Signatures of Woods and Mellon.

No.	Issuing Bank	No. Printed	Unc	No.	Issuing Bank	No. Printed	Unc	No.	Issuing Bank	No. Printed	Unc
2101-A.	Boston	1,834,989	175.00	2101-F.	Atlanta	338,400	275.00	2101-K.	Dallas	701,496	200.00
2101-B.	New York	3,392,328	155.00	2101-G.	Chicago	5,263,956	175.00	2101-L.	San Francisco	1,522,620	175.00
2101-C.	Philadelphia	3,078,944	175.00	2101-H.	St. Louis	880,500	200.00	2101*.	Most Common Districts		2,000.00
2101-D.	Cleveland	2,453,364	175.00	2101-I.	Minneapolis	780,240	200.00				
2101-E.	Richmond	1,516,500	175.00	2101-J.	Kansas City	791,604	200.00				

DESIGN NO. 227

(Notes 2102-A - 2106-K Incl.)

The obverse is as shown.
The reverse is similar to Design No. 226.

3. Series of 1934.
Signatures of Julian and Morgenthau.
The two shades of green seals also exist in this series.

No.	Issuing Bank	No. Printed	Unc	No.	Issuing Bank	No. Printed	Unc	No.	Issuing Bank	No. Printed	Unc
2102-A.	Boston	2,729,400	200.00	2102-F.	Atlanta	3,069,348	200.00	2102-K.	Dallas	1,194,876	200.00
2102-B.	New York	17,894,676	200.00	2102-G.	Chicago	8,675,940	200.00	2102-L.	San Francisco	8,101,200	200.00
2102-C.	Philadelphia	5,833,200	200.00	2102-H.	St. Louis	1,497,144	225.00	2102*.	Most Common Districts		
2102-D.	Cleveland	8,817,720	200.00	2102-I.	Minneapolis	539,700	250.00		Light seal		500.00
2102-E.	Richmond	4,826,628	200.00	2102-J.	Kansas City	1,133,520	200.00		Dark seal		450.00

4. Series of 1934-A.
Signatures of Julian and Morgenthau.

No.	Issuing Bank	No. Printed	Unc	No.	Issuing Bank	No. Printed	Unc	No.	Issuing Bank	No. Printed	Unc
2103-A.	Boston	406,200	185.00	2103-F.	Atlanta	416,100	200.00	2103-J.	Kansas City	189,300	200.00
2103-B.	New York	4,710,648	175.00	2103-G.	Chicago	1,014,600	175.00	2103-K.	Dallas	266,700	160.00
2103-D.	Cleveland	864,168	180.00	2103-H.	St. Louis	361,944	200.00	2103-L.	San Francisco	162,000	180.00
2103-E.	Richmond	2,235,372	175.00	2103-I.	Minneapolis	93,300	225.00	2103*.	Most Common Districts		600.00

5. Series of 1934-B.
Signatures of Julian and Vinson.

No.	Issuing Bank	No. Printed	Unc	No.	Issuing Bank	No. Printed	Unc	No.	Issuing Bank	No. Printed	Unc
2104-C.	Philadelphia	509,100	125.00	2104-G.	Chicago	306,000	150.00	2104-K.	Dallas	120,108	150.00
2104-D.	Cleveland	359,100	135.00	2104-H.	St. Louis	306,000	125.00	2104-L.	San Francisco	441,000	125.00
2104-E.	Richmond	596,700	125.00	2104-I.	Minneapolis	120,000	150.00	2104*.	Most Common Districts VF		2,500.00
2104-F.	Atlanta	416,720	125.00	2104-J.	Kansas City	221,340	140.00				

6. Series of 1934-C.
Signatures of Julian and Snyder.

No.	Issuing Bank	No. Printed	Unc	No.	Issuing Bank	No. Printed	Unc	No.	Issuing Bank	No. Printed	Unc
2105-A.	Boston	117,600	120.00	2105-E.	Richmond	1,821,960	100.00	2105-I.	Minneapolis	118,800	120.00
2105-B.	Neyv York	1,556,400	120.00	2105-F.	Atlanta	107,640	120.00	2105-J.	Kansas City	303,600	110.00
2105-C.	Philadelphia	107,283	120.00	2105-G.	Chicago	294,432	110.00	2105-K.	Dallas	429,900	100.00
2105-D.	Cleveland	374,400	100.00	2105-H.	St. Louis	535,200	100.00	2105*.	Most Common Districts		2,000.00

7. Series of 1934-D.
Signatures of Clark and Snyder.

No.	Issuing Bank	No. Printed	Unc	No.	Issuing Bank	No. Printed	Unc	No.	Issuing Bank	No. Printed	Unc
2106-A.	Boston	279,600	230.00	2106-E.	Richmond	156,000	245.00	2106-I	Minneapolis		Rare
2106-B.	New York	898,776	200.00	2106-F.	Atlanta	216,000	235.00	2106-K.	Dallas	103,200	250.00
2106-C.	Philadelphia	699,000	215.00	2106-G.	Chicago	494,016	220.00	2106*.	Most Common Districts	EF	3,000.00

DESIGN NO. 228

(Notes 2107-A - 2112-L Incl.)

The obverse is as shown.
The reverse is similar to Design No. 226.

8. Series of 1950.
Signatures of Clark and Snyder.

No.	Issuing Bank	No. Printed	Unc	No.	Issuing Bank	No. Printed	Unc	No.	Issuing Bank	No. Printed	Unc
2107-A.	Boston	1,248,000	135.00	2107-F.	Atlanta	1,812,000	130.00	2107-K.	Dallas	1,100,000	130.00
2107-B.	New York	10,236,000	120.00	2107-G.	Chicago	4,212,000	125.00	2107-L.	San Francisco	3,996,000	125.00
2107-C.	Philadelphia	2,352,000	130.00	2l07-H.	St. Louis	892,000	135.00	2107*.	Most Common Districts		400.00
2107-D.	Cleveland	6,180,000	125.00	2107-I.	Minneapolis	384,000	145.00				
2107-E.	Richmond	5,064,000	125.00	2107-J.	Kansas City	696,000	135.00				

9. Series of 1950-A.
Signatures of Priest and Humphrey.

No.	Issuing Bank	No. Printed	Unc	No.	Issuing Bank	No. Printed	Unc	No.	Issuing Bank	No. Printed	Unc
2108-A.	Boston	720,000	135.00	2108-E.	Richmond	2,016,000	130.00	2108-J.	Kansas City	144,000	125.00
2108-B.	New York	6,495,000	135.00	2108-F.	Atlanta	288,000	125.00	2108-K.	Dallas	864,000	135.00
2108-C.	Philadelphia	1,728,000	130.00	2108-G.	Chicago	2,016,000	130.00	2108-L.	San Francisco	576,000	135.00
2108-D.	Cleveland	1,872,000	120.00	2108-H.	St. Louis	576,000	135.00	2108*.	Most Common Districts		400.00

10. Series of 1950-B.
Signatures of Priest and Anderson.

No.	Issuing Bank	No. Printed	Unc	No.	Issuing Bank	No. Printed	Unc	No.	Issuing Bank	No. Printed	Unc
2109-A.	Boston	864,000	125.00	2109-E.	Richmond	1,584,000	125.00	2109-K.	Dallas	1,008,000	125.00
2109-B.	New York	8,352,000	115.00	2109-G.	Chicago	4,320,000	115.00	2109-L.	San Francisco	1,872,000	125.00
2109-C.	Philadelphia	2,592,000	125.00	2109-H.	St. Louis	576,000	125.00	2109*.	Most Common Districts		350.00
2109-D.	Cleveland	1,728,000	125.00	2109-J.	Kansas City	1,008,000	125.00				

11. Series of 1950-C.
Signatures of Smith and Dillon.

No.	Issuing Bank	No. Printed	Unc	No.	Issuing Bank	No. Printed	Unc	No.	Issuing Bank	No. Printed	Unc
2110-A.	Boston	720,000	130.00	2110-E.	Richmond	1,296,000	125.00	2110-J.	Kansas City	432,000	125.00
2110-B.	New York	5,328,000	115.00	2110-G.	Chicago	1,728,000	125.00	2110-K.	Dallas	720,000	125.00
2110-C.	Philadelphia	1,296,000	125.00	2110-H.	St. Louis	576,000	130.00	2110-L.	San Francisco	1,152,000	125.00
2110-D.	Cleveland	1,296,000	125.00	2110-I.	Minneapolis	144,000	125.00	2110*.	Most Common Districts		400.00

12. Series of 1950-D.
Signatures of Granahan and Dillon.

No.	Issuing Bank	No. Printed	Unc	No.	Issuing Bank	No. Printed	Unc	No.	Issuing Bank	No. Printed	Unc
2111-A.	Boston	1,728,000	125.00	2111-F.	Atlanta	576,000	135.00	2111-K.	Dallas	1,296,000	125.00
2111-B.	New York	7,200,000	115.00	2111-G.	Chicago	4,176,000	115.00	2111-L.	San Francisco	2,160,000	125.00
2111-C.	Philadelphia	2,736,000	125.00	2111-H.	St. Louis	1,440,000	125.00	2111*.	Most Common Districts		450.00
2111-D.	Cleveland	2,8125,000	125.00	2111-I.	Minneapolis	288,000	125.00				
2111-E.	Richmond	2,616,000	125.00	2111-J.	Kansas City	720,000	135.00				

13. Series of 1950-E.
Signatures of Granahan and Fowler.

No.	Issuing Bank	No. Printed	Unc	No.	Issuing Bank	No. Printed	Unc	No.	Issuing Bank	No. Printed	Unc
2112-B.	New York	3,024,000	175.00	2112-L.	San Francisco	1,296,000	175.00	2112*.	Most Common Districts		400.00
2112-G.	Chicago	1,008,000	175.00								

DESIGN NO. 228-a.
(Notes 2113-A - 2125-L Incl.)

Reverse of Design No. 228-a.
With motto "In God We Trust."

14. Series of 1963-A.
Signatures of Granahan and Fowler.

No.	Issuing Bank	No. Printed	Unc	No.	Issuing Bank	No. Printed	Unc	No.	Issuing Bank	No. Printed	Unc
2113-A.	Boston	1,536,000	110.00	2113-E.	Richmond	3,072,000	110.00	2113-I.	Minneapolis	512,000	110.00
2113-A*.	Boston	320,000	185.00	2113-E*.	Richmond	704,000	185.00	2113-I*.	Minneapolis	128,000	100.00
2113-B.	New York	11,008,000	100.00	2113-F.	Atlanta	768,000	110.00	2113-J.	Kansas City	512,000	110.00
2113-B*.	New York	1,408,000	185.00	2113-F*.	Atlanta	384,000	185.00	2113-J*.	Kansas City	64,000	200.00
2113-C.	Philadelphia	3,328,000	110.00	2113-G.	Chicago	6,912,000	100.00	2113-K.	Dallas	1,536,000	110.00
2113-C*.	Philadelphia	704,000	185.00	2113-G*.	Chicago	768,000	185.00	2113-K*.	Dallas	128,000	200.00
2113-D.	Cleveland	3,584,000	110.00	2113-H.	St. Louis	512,000	120.00	2113-L.	San Francisco	4,352,000	110.00
2113-D*.	Cleveland	256,000	185.00	2113-H*.	St. Louis	128,000	200.00	2113-L*.	San Francisco	704,000	185.00

15. Series of 1969.
Signatures of Elston and Kennedy. With new Treasury seal.

No.	Issuing Bank	No. Printed	Unc	No.	Issuing Bank	No. Printed	Unc	No.	Issuing Bank	No. Printed	Unc
2114-A.	Boston	2,048,000	100.00	2114-E.	Richmond	2,560,000	100.00	2114-I.	Minneapolis	512,000	100.00
2114-A*.	Boston	none printed	—	2114-E*.	Richmond	64,000	175.00	2114-I*.	Minneapolis	none printed	—
2114-B.	New York	12,032,000	100.00	2114-F.	Atlanta	256,000	100.00	2114-J.	Kansas City	1,280,000	100.00
2114-B*.	New York	384,000	175.00	2114-F*.	Atlanta	none printed	—	2114-J*.	Kansas City	64,000	175.00
2114-C.	Philadelphia	3,584,000	100.00	2114-G.	Chicago	9,728,000	100.00	2114-K.	Dallas	1,536,000	100.00
2114-C*.	Philadelphia	128,000	165.00	2114-G*.	Chicago	256,000	165.00	2114-K*.	Dallas	64,000	175.00
2114-D.	Cleveland	3,584,000	100.00	2114-H.	St. Louis	256,000	100.00	2114-L.	San Francisco	6,912,000	100.00
2114-D*.	Cleveland	192,000	165.00	2114-H*.	St. Louis	none printed	—	2114-L*.	San Francisco	256,000	175.00

16. Series of 1969-A.
Signatures of Kabis and Connally.

No.	Issuing Bank	No. Printed	Unc	No.	Issuing Bank	No. Printed	Unc	No.	Issuing Bank	No. Printed	Unc
2115-A.	Boston	1,536,000	100.00	2115-E.	Richmond	2,304,000	100.00	2115-I.	Minneapolis	512,000	100.00
2115-A*.	Boston	128,000	125.00	2115-E*.	Richmond	64,000	125.00	2115-I*.	Minneapolis	none printed	—
2115-B.	New York	9,728,000	100.00	2115-F.	Atlanta	256,000	100.00	2115-J.	Kansas City	256,000	100.00
2115-B*.	New York	704,000	125.00	2115-F*.	Atlanta	64,000	125.00	2115-J*.	Kansas City	none printed	—
2115-C.	Philadelphia	2,560,000	100.00	2115-G.	Chicago	3,584,000	100.00	2115-K.	Dallas	1,024,000	100.00
2115-C*.	Philadelphia	none printed	—	2115-G*.	Chicago	192,000	125.00	2115-K*.	Dallas	64,000	125.00
2115-D.	Cleveland	2,816,000	100.00	2115-H.	St. Louis	256,000	100.00	2115-L	San Francisco	5,120,000	100.00
2115-D*.	Cleveland	none printed	—	2115-H*.	St. Louis	none printed	—	2115-L*.	San Francisco	256,000	125.00

17. Series of 1969-B.
Signatures of Banuelos and Connally.

No.	Issuing Bank	No. Printed	Unc	No.	Issuing Bank	No. Printed	Unc	No.	Issuing Bank	No. Printed	Unc
2116-A.	Boston	1,024,000	95.00	2116-F.	Atlanta	512,000	95.00	2116-K*.	Dallas	128,000	Rare
2116-B.	New York	2,560,000	95.00	2116-G.	Chicago	1,024,000	95.00				
2116-E.	Richmond	1,536,000	95.00	2116-K.	Dallas	1,024,000	95.00				

18. Series of 1969-C.
Signatures of Banuelos and Schultz.

No.	Issuing Bank	No. Printed	Unc	No.	Issuing Bank	No. Printed	Unc	No.	Issuing Bank	No. Printed	Unc
2117-A.	Boston	1,792,000	90.00	2117-E.	Richmond	2,304,000	90.00	2117-I.	Minneapolis	256,000	90.00
2117-A*.	Boston	64,000	125.00	2117-E*.	Richmond	64,000	125.00	2117-I*.	Minneapolis	64,000	125.00
2117-B.	New York	7,040,000	90.00	2117-F.	Atlanta	256,000	90.00	2117-J.	Kansas City	1,280,000	90.00
2117-B*.	New York	192,000	125.00	2117-F*.	Atlanta	64,000	125.00	2117-J*.	Kansas City	128,000	125.00
2117-C.	Philadelphia	3,584,000	90.00	2117-G.	Chicago	6,784,000	90.00	2117-K.	Dallas	3,456,000	90.00
2117-C*.	Philadelphia	256,000	125.00	2117-G*.	Chicaio	576,000	125.00	2117-K*.	Dallas	64,000	125.00
2117-D.	Cleveland	5,120,000	90.00	2117-H.	St. Louis	2,688,000	90.00	2117-L	San Francisco	4,608,000	90.00
2117-D*.	Cleveland	192,000	125.00	2117-H*.	St. Louis	64,000	125.00	2117-L*.	San Francisco	256,000	125.00

19. Series of 1974.
Signatures of Neff and Simon.

No.	Issuing Bank	No. Printed	Unc	No.	Issuing Bank	No. Printed	Unc	No.	Issuing Bank	No. Printed	Unc
2118-A.	Boston	3,840,000	100.00	2118-E.	Richmond	14,080,000	100.00	2118-I.	Minneapolis	3,200,000	100.00
2118-A*.	Boston	256,000	165.00	2118-E*.	Richmond	576,000	165.00	2118-I*.	Minneapolis	192,000	165.00
2118-B.	New York	38,400,000	100.00	2118-F.	Atlanta	1,280,000	100.00	2118-J.	Kansas City	4,480,000	100.00
2118-B*.	New York	768,000	165.00	2118-F*.	Atlanta	640,000	165.00	2119-J*.	Kansas City	192,000	165.00
2118-C.	Philadelphia	7,040,000	100.00	2118-G.	Chicago	30,720,000	100.00	2118-K.	Dallas	8,320,000	100.00
2118-C*.	Philadelphia	192,000	165.00	2119-G*.	Chicago	1,536,000	165.00	2118-K*.	Dallas	128,000	165.00
2118-D.	Cleveland	21,200,000	100.00	2118-H.	St. Louis	1,920,000	100.00	2119-L	San Francisco	7,378,000	100.00
2118-D*.	Cleveland	640,000	165.00	2118-H*.	St. Louis	128,000	165.00	2119-L*.	San Francisco	64,000	175.00

20. Series of 1977.
Signatures of Morton and Blumenthal.

No.	Issuing Bank	No. Printed	Unc	No.	Issuing Bank	No. Printed	Unc	No.	Issuing Bank	No. Printed	Unc
2119-A.	Boston	16,400,000	100.00	2119-E.	Richmond	19,200,000	100.00	2119-I.	Minneapolis	3,840,000	100.00
2119-A*.	Boston	1,088,000	125.00	2119-E*.	Richmond	896,000	125.00	2119-I*.	Minneapolis	128,000	125.00
2119-B.	New York	49,920,000	100.00	2119-F.	Atlanta	2,560.00,000	100.00	2119-J.	Kansas City	7,680,000	100.00
2119-B*.	New York	2,112,000	125.00	2119-F*.	Atlanta	128,000	150.00	2119-J*.	Kansas City	256,000	125.00
2119-C.	Philadelphia	5,120,000	100.00	2119-G.	Chicago	47,360,000	100.00	2119-K.	Dallas	14,080,000	100.00
2119-C*.	Philadelphia	128,000	125.00	2119-G*.	Chicago	2,304,000	125.00	2119-K*.	Dallas	576,000	125.00
2119-D.	Cleveland	23,040,000	100.00	2119-H.	St. Louis	3,840,000	100.00	2119-L	San Francisco	19,200,000	100.00
2119-D*.	Cleveland	1,024,000	125.00	2119-H*.	St. Louis	512,000	150.00	2119-L*.	San Francisco	768,000	125.00

21. Series of 1981.
Signatures of Buchanan and Regan.

No.	Issuing Bank	No. Printed	Unc.	No.	Issuing Bank	No. Printed	Unc.	No.	Issuing Bank	No. Printed	Unc.
2120-A.	Boston	18,560,000	95.00	2120-E.	Richmond	25,600,000	95.00	2120-I.	Minneapolis	5,760,000	95.00
2120-A*.	Boston	none printed	—	2120-E*.	Richmond	none printed	—	2120-I*.	Minneapolis	128,000	125.00
2120-B.	New York	78,080,000	95.00	2120-F.	Atlanta	4,480,000	95.00	2120-J.	Kansas City	18,560,000	95.00
2120-B*.	New York	768,000	125.00	2120-F*.	Atlanta	768,000	125.00	2120-J*.	Kansas City	128,000	125.00
2120-C.	Philadelphia	1,280,000	95.00	2120-G.	Chicago	67,200,000	95.00	2120-K.	Dallas	19,840,000	95.00
2120-C*.	Philadelphia	none printed	—	2120-G*.	Chicago	128,000	125.00	2120-K*.	Dallas	none printed	—
2120-D.	Cleveland	28,160,000	95.00	2120-H.	St. Louis	4,480,000	95.00	2120-L.	San Francisco	35,200,000	95.00
2120-D*.	Cleveland	256,000	125.00	2120-H*.	St. Louis	none printed	—	2120-L*.	San Francisco	256,000	125.00

22. Series of 1981-A.
Signatures of Ortega and Regan.

No.	Issuing Bank	No. Printed	Unc.	No.	Issuing Bank	No. Printed	Unc.	No.	Issuing Bank	No. Printed	Unc.
2121-A.	Boston	9,600,000	95.00	2121-E.	Richmond	12,800,000	95.00	2121-I.	Minneapolis	3,200,000	95.00
2121-A*.	Boston	none printed	—	2121-E*.	Richmond	704,000	125.00	2121-I*.	Minneapolis	none printed	—
2121-B.	New York	28,800,000	95.00	2121-F.	Atlanta	3,200,000	95.00	2121-J.	Kansas City	6,400,000	95.00
2121-B*.	New York	3,200,000	125.00	2121-F*.	Atlanta	none printed	—	2121-J*.	Kansas City	none printed	—
2121-C.	Philadelphia	none printed	—	2121-G.	Chicago	28,800,000	95.00	2121-K.	Dallas	6,400,000	95.00
2121-C*.	Philadelphia	none printed	—	2121-G*.	Chicago	none printed	—	2121-K*.	Dallas	none printed	—
2121-D.	Cleveland	12,800,000	95.00	2121-H.	St. Louis	3,200,000	95.00	2121-L.	San Francisco	22,400,000	95.00
2121-D*.	Cleveland	none printed	—	2121-H*.	St. Louis	none printed	—	2121-L*.	San Francisco	640,000	125.00

23. Series of 1985
Signatures of Ortega and Baker.

No.	Issuing Bank	No. Printed	Unc.	No.	Issuing Bank	No. Printed	Unc.	No.	Issuing Bank	No. Printed	Unc.
2122-A.	Boston	51,200,000	90.00	2122-E.	Richmond	54,400,000	90.00	2122-I.	Minneapolis	12,800,000	90.00
2122-A*.	Boston	64,000	125.00	2122-E*.	Richmond	none printed	—	2122-I*.	Minneapolis	none printed	—
2122-B.	New York	182,400,000	90.00	2122-F.	Atlanta	9,600,000	90.00	2122-J.	Kansas City	9,600,000	90.00
2122-B*.	New York	1,408,000	125.00	2122-F*.	Atlanta	none printed	—	2122-J*.	Kansas City	none printed	—
2122-C.	Philadelphia	3,200,000	90.00	2122-G.	Chicago	112,000,000	125.00	2122-K.	Dallas	25,600,000	90.00
2122-C*.	Philadelphia	none printed	—	2122-G*.	Chicago	1,280,000	125.00	2122-K*.	Dallas	none printed	—
2122-D.	Cleveland	57,600,000	90.00	2122-H.	St. Louis	6,400,000	90.00	2122-L	San Francisco	57,600,000	90.00
2122-D*.	Cleveland	64,000	150.00	2122-H*.	St. Louis	none printed	—	2122-L*.	San Francisco	none printed	—

24. Series of 1988
Signatures of Ortega and Brady.

No.	Issuing Bank	No. Printed	Unc.	No.	Issuing Bank	No. Printed	Unc.	No.	Issuing Bank	No. Printed	Unc.
2123-A.	Boston	9,600,000	85.00	2123-E.	Richmond	12,800,000	85.00	2123-I.	Minneapolis	none printed	—
2123-A*.	Boston	none printed	—	2123-E*.	Richmond	none printed	—	2123-I*.	Minneapolis	none printed	—
2123-B.	New York	214,400,000	85.00	2123-F.	Atlanta	none printed	—	2123-J.	Kansas City	6,400,000	85.00
2123-B*.	New York	1,408,000	125.00	2123-F*.	Atlanta	none printed	—	2123-J*.	Kansas City	none printed	—
2123-C.	Philadelphia	none printed	—	2123-G.	Chicago	80,000,000	85.00	2123-K.	Dallas	none printed	—
2123-C*.	Philadelphia	none printed	—	2123-G*.	Chicago	none printed	—	2123-K*.	Dallas	none printed	—
2123-D.	Cleveland	32,000,000	85.00	2123-H.	St. Louis	none printed	—	2123-L.	San Francisco	12,800,000	85.00
2123-D*.	Cleveland	none printed	—	2123-H*.	St. Louis	none printed	—	2123-L*.	San Francisco	none printed	—

25. Series of 1988-A.
None printed

26. Series of 1990.
Signatures of Villalpando and Brady.

No.	Issuing Bank	No. Printed	Unc.	No.	Issuing Bank	No. Printed	Unc.	No.	Issuing Bank	No. Printed	Unc.
2124-A.	Boston	28,800,000	85.00	2124-E.	Richmond	76,800,000	85.00	2124-I.	Minneapolis	22,400,000	85.00
2124-A*.	Boston	None printed	—	2124-E*.	Richmond	None printed	—	2124-I*.	Minneapolis	none printed	—
2124-B.	New York	232,000,000	85.00	2124-F.	Atlanta	None printed	—	2124-J.	Kansas City	35,200,000	85.00
2124-B*.	New York	3,116,000	125.00	2124-F*.	Atlanta	None printed	—	2124-J*.	Kansas City	640,000	125.00
2124-C.	Philadelphia	41,600,000	85.00	2124-G.	Chicago	108,800,000	85.00	2124-K.	Dallas	16,000,000	85.00
2124-C*.	Philadelphia	1,280,000	125.00	2124-G*.	Chicago	1,032,000	125.00	2124-K*.	Dallas	none printed	—
2124-D.	Clcvelalid	92,800,000	85.00	2124-H.	St. Louis	16,000,000	85.00	2124-L	San Francisco	119,200,000	85.00
2124-D*.	Cleveland	None printed	—	2124-H*.	St. Louis	None printed	—	2124-L*.	San Francisco	none printed	—

27. Series of 1993.
Signatures of Withrow and Bentsen.

No.	Issuing Bank	No. Printed	Unc.	No.	Issuing Bank	No. Printed	Unc.	No.	Issuing Bank	No. Printed	Unc.
2125-A.	Boston	41,600,000	Current	2125-E.	Richmond	35,200,000	Current	2125-I.	Minneapolis	none printed	—
2125-A*.	Boston	none printed	—	2125-E*.	Richmond	none printed	—	2125-I*.	Minneapolis	none printed	—
2125-B.	New York	544,000,000	Current	2125-F.	Atlanta	none printed	—	2125-J.	Kansas City	12,800,000	Current
2125-B*.	New York	4,224,000	Current	2125-F*.	Atlanta	none printed	—	2125-J*.	Kansas City	none printed	—
2125-C.	Philadelphia	none printed	—	2125-G.	Chicago	144,000,000	Current	2125-K.	Dallas	9,600,000	Current
2125-C*.	Philadelphia	none printed	—	2125-G*.	Chicago	1,280,000	Current	2125-K*.	Dallas	none printed	—
2125-D.	Clcvelalid	60,800,000	Current	2125-H.	St. Louis	3,200,000	Current	2125-L	San Francisco	none printed	—
2125-D*.	Cleveland	1,280,000	Current	2125-H*.	St. Louis	none printed	—	2125-L*.	San Francisco	none printed	—

DESIGN NO. 228-b.

(Notes 2126-A -   )

Bust of Ulysses S. Grant

Larger portrait, positioned off-center. Color-shifting (black/green) ink used in numeral at lower right.
Printed with microsize printing and security thread on watermarked paper.

Reverse of Design No. 228-b.
View of the U.S. Capitol.

28. Series of 1996.
Signatures of Withrow and Rubin. Printed in Washington, D.C.

2126-A.	Boston		—	2126-E.	Richmond	—	2126-I.	Minneapolis		—
2126-A*.	Boston		—	2126-E*.	Richmond	—	2126-I*.	Minneapolis		—
2126-B.	New York	1,689,280,000	Current	2126-F.	Atlanta	—	2126-J.	Kansas City		—
2126-B*.	New York	33,280,000	Current	2126-F*.	Atlanta	—	2126-J*.	Kansas City		—
2126-C.	Philadelphia			2126-G.	Chicago	—	2126-K.	Dallas		—
2126-C*.	Philadelphia		—	2126-G*.	Chicago	—	2126-K*.	Dallas		—
2126-D.	Clcvelalid		—	2126-H.	St. Louis	—	2126-L	San Francisco		—
2126-D*.	Cleveland		—	2126-H*.	St. Louis	—	2126-L*.	San Francisco		—

100 Dollar Notes

All issues are with the head of Benjamin Franklin.

DESIGN NO. 229
(Notes 2150-A - 2150-L Incl.)

Reverse of Design No. 229.
View of Independence Hall.

1. Series of 1928.
Signatures of Woods and Mellon.

No.	Issuing Bank	No. Printed	Unc	No.	Issuing Bank	No. Printed	Unc	No.	Issuing Bank	No. Printed	Unc
2150-A.	Boston	376,000	350.00	2150-F.	Atlanta	357,000	325.00	2150-K.	Dallas	80,140	375.00
2150-B.	New York	755,400	300.00	2150-G.	Chicago	783,300	200.00	2150-L.	San Francisco	486,000	300.00
2150-C.	Philadelphia	389,100	300.00	2150-H.	St. Louis	187,200	310.00	2150*.	Most Comon Districts		
2150-D.	Cleveland	542,400	300.00	2150-I.	Minneapolis	102,000	340.00		VF 250.00	Unc 950.00	
2150-E.	Richmond	364,416	325.00	2150-J.	Kansas City	234,612	310.00				

DESIGN NO. 230

(Notes 2151-A - 2156-K Incl.)

The obverse is as shown.
The reverse is similar to Design No. 229.

2. Series of 1928-A.
Signatures of Woods and Mellon.

No.	Issuing Bank	No. Printed	Unc	No.	Issuing Bank	No. Printed	Unc	No.	Issuing Bank	No. Printed	Unc
2151-A.	Boston	980,400	300.00	2151-F.	Atlanta	371,400	315.00	2151-K.	Dallas	594,456	310.00
2151-B.	New York	2,938,176	280.00	2151-G.	Chicago	4,010,424	280.00	2151-L.	San Francisco	1,228,032	295.00
2151-C.	Philadelphia	1,496,844	295.00	2151-H.	St. Louis	749,544	310.00	2151*.	St. Louis	24,000	
2151-D.	Cleveland	992,436	295.00	2151-I.	Minneapolis	503,040	315.00		VF 1,500.00	Unc Rare	
2151-E.	Richmond	621,364	310.00	2151-J.	Kansas City	681,804	310.00				

3. Series of 1934.
Signatures of Julian and Morgenthau.
The two shades of green seals also exist in this series.

No.	Issuing Bank	No. Printed	Unc	No.	Issuing Bank	No. Printed	Unc	No.	Issuing Bank	No. Printed	Unc
2152-A.	Boston	3,710,000	225.00	2152-F.	Atlanta	3,264,420	225.00	2152-K.	Dallas	1,506,516	235.00
2152-B.	New York	3,086,000	225.00	2152-G.	Chicago	7,075,000	220.00	2152-L.	San Francisco	6,521,940	220.00
2152-C.	Philadelphia	2,776,800	225.00	2152-H.	St. Louis	2,106,192	225.00	2152*.	Most Common Districts Light seal		600.00
2152-D.	Cleveland	3,447,108	225.00	2152-I.	Minneapolis	852,600	220.00			Dark seal	2650.00
2152-E.	Richmond	4,317,600	225.00	2152-J.	Kansas City	1,932,900	210.00				

4. Series of 1934-A.
Signatures of Julian and Morgenthau.

No.	Issuing Bank	No. Printed	Unc	No.	Issuing Bank	No. Printed	Unc	No.	Issuing Bank	No. Printed	Unc
2153-A.	Boston	102,000	225.00	2153-F.	Atlanta	589,886	200.00	2153-K.	Dallas	226,164	215.00
2153-B.	New York	15,278,892	185.00	2153-G.	Chicago	3,328,800	190.00	2153-L.	San Francisco	1,130,400	190.00
2153-C.	Philadelphia	588,000	200.00	2153-H.	St. Louis	434,208	200.00	2153*.	Most Common Districts		Unc 600.00
2153-D.	Cleveland	645,300	200.00	2153-I.	Minneapolis	153,000	225.00				
2153-E.	Richmond	770,000	200.00	2153-J.	Kansas City	455,000	200.00				

5. Series of 1934-B.
Signatures of Julian and Vinson.

No.	Issuing Bank	No. Printed	Unc	No.	Issuing Bank	No. Printed	Unc	No.	Issuing Bank	No. Printed	Unc
2154-A.	Boston	41,400	260.00	2154-F.	Atlanta	645,000	205.00	2154-J.	Kansas City	364,500	220.00
2154-C.	Philadelphia	39,600	260.00	2154-G.	Chicago	396,000	210.00	2154-K.	Dallas	392,700	210.00
2154-D.	Cleveland	61,200	260.00	2154-H.	St. Louis	676,200	205.00	2154*.	Most Common Districts	VF 1,250.00	
2154-E.	Richmond	977,400	200.00	2154-I.	Minneapolis	377,000	210.00			Unc 3,250.00	

6. Series of 1934-C.
Signatures of Julian and Snyder.

No.	Issuing Bank	No. Printed	Unc	No.	Issuing Bank	No. Printed	Unc	No.	Issuing Bank	No. Printed	Unc
2155-A.	Boston	13,800	275.00	2155-F.	Atlanta	493,900	200.00	2155-J.	Kansas City	401,100	200.00
2155-B.	New York	1,556,400	195.00	2155-G.	Chicago	612,000	200.00	2155-K.	Dallas	280,700	210.00
2155-C.	Philadelphia	13,200	275.00	2155-H.	St. Louis	957,000	200.00	2155-L.	San Francisco	432,600	200.00
2155-D.	Cleveland	1,473,200	195.00	2155-I.	Minneapolis	392,904	200.00	2155*.	Atlanta	EF	2,250.00

7. Series of 1934-D.
Signatures of Clark and Snyder.

No.	Issuing Bank	No. Printed	Unc	No.	Issuing Bank	No. Printed	Unc	No.	Issuing Bank	No. Printed	Unc
2156-B.	New York	156	Rare	2156-F.	Atlanta	260,400	450.00	2156-H.	St. Louis	166,800	400.00
2156-C.	Philadelphia	308,400	400.00	2156-G.	Chicago	78,000	450.00	2156-K.	Dallas	66,000	450.00

DESIGN NO. 231.

(Notes 2157-A - 2162-L Incl.)

The obverse is as shown.
The reverse is similar to Design No. 229.

8. Series of 1950.
Signatures of Clark and Snyder.

No.	Issuing Bank	No. Printed	Unc	No.	Issuing Bank	No. Printed	Unc	No.	Issuing Bank	No. Printed	Unc
2157-A.	Boston	768,000	265.00	2157-F.	Atlanta	1,824,000	255.00	2157-K.	Dallas	1,216,000	255.00
2157-B.	New York	3,908,000	250.00	2157-G.	Chicago	4,428,000	350.00	2157-L.	San Francisco	2,524,000	250.00
2157-C.	Philadelphia	1,332,000	255.00	2157-H.	St. Louis	1,284,000	255.00	2157*.	Most Common Districts	Unc	700.00
2157-D.	Cleveland	1,632,000	255.00	2157-I.	Minneapolis	564,000	275.00				
2157-E.	Richmond	4,076,000	250.00	2157-J.	Kansas City	864,000	265.00				

9. Series of 1950-A.
Signatures of Priest and Humphrey.

No.	Issuing Bank	No. Printed	Unc	No.	Issuing Bank	No. Printed	Unc	No.	Issuing Bank	No. Printed	Unc
2158-A.	Boston	1,008,000	175.00	2158-F.	Atlanta	288,000	190.00	2158-K.	Dallas	432,000	180.00
2158-B.	New York	2,880,000	170.00	2158-G.	Chicago	864,000	175.00	2158-L.	San Francisco	720,000	180.00
2158-C.	Philadelphia	576,000	180.00	2158-H.	St. Louis	432,000	180.00	2158*.	Most Common Districts	Unc	600.00
2158-D.	Cleveland	288,000	190.00	2158-I.	Minneapolis	144,000	200.00				
2158-E.	Richmond	2,160,000	170.00	2158-J.	Kansas City	288,000	190.00				

10. Series of 1950-B.
Signatures of Priest and Anderson.

No.	Issuing Bank	No. Printed	Unc	No.	Issuing Bank	No. Printed	Unc	No.	Issuing Bank	No. Printed	Unc
2159-A.	Boston	720,000	245.00	2159-F.	Atlanta	576,000	245.00	2159-K.	Dallas	1,728,000	235.00
2159-B.	New York	6,636,000	235.00	2159-G.	Chicago	2,592,000	235.00	2159-L.	San Francisco	2,880,000	235.00
2159-C.	Philadelphia	720,000	245.00	2159-H.	St. Louis	1,152,000	235.00	2159*.	Most Common Districts	Unc	600.00
2159-D.	Cleveland	432,000	245.00	2159-I.	Minneapolis	288,000	260.00				
2159-E.	Richmond	1,008,000	235.00	2159-J.	Kansas City	720,000	245.00				

11. Series of 1950-C.
Signatures of Smith and Dillon.

No.	Issuing Bank	No. Printed	Unc	No.	Issuing Bank	No. Printed	Unc	No.	Issuing Bank	No. Printed	Unc
2160-A.	Boston	864,000	240.00	2160-F.	Atlanta	1,296,000	235.00	2160-K.	Dallas	720,000	240.00
2160-B.	New York	2,448,000	235.00	2160-G.	Chicago	1,584,000	235.00	2160-L.	San Francisco	2,160,000	235.00
2160-C.	Philadelphia	576,000	240.00	2160-H.	St. Louis	720,000	240.00	2160*.	Most Common Districts	Unc	700.00
2160-D.	Cleveland	576,000	240.00	2160-I.	Minneapolis	288,000	260.00				
2160-E.	Richmond	1,440,000	235.00	2160-J.	Kansas City	432,000	250.00				

12. Series of 1950-D.
Signatures of Granahan and Dillon.

No.	Issuing Bank	No. Printed	Unc	No.	Issuing Bank	No. Printed	Unc	No.	Issuing Bank	No. Printed	Unc
2161-A.	Boston	1,872,000	235.00	2161-F.	Atlanta	1,872,000	235.00	2161-K.	Dallas	1,728,000	235.00
2161-B.	New York	7,632,000	230.00	2161-G.	Chicago	4,608,000	230.00	2161-L.	San Francisco	3,312,000	230.00
2161-C.	Philadelphia	1,872,000	235.00	2161-H.	St. Louis	1,440,000	235.00	2161*.	Most Common Districts	Unc	600.00
2161-D.	Cleveland	1,584,000	235.00	2161-I.	Minneapolis	432,000	245.00				
2161-E.	Richmond	2,880,000	235.00	2161-J.	Kansas City	864,000	240.00				

13. Series of 1950-E.
Signatures of Granahan and Fowler.

No.	Issuing Bank	No. Printed	Unc	No.	Issuing Bank	No. Printed	Unc	No.	Issuing Bank	No. Printed	Unc
2162-B.	New York	3,024,000	500.00	2162-L.	San Francisco	2,736,000	750.00	2162*.	Most Common Districts	Unc	1,500.00
2162-G.	Chicago	576,000	750.00								

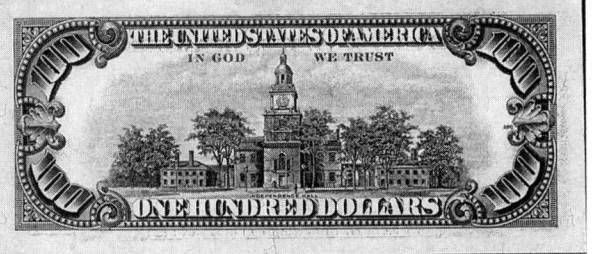

DESIGN NO. 231-a
(Notes 2163-A - 2167-L Incl.)

Reverse of Design No. 231-a.
With motto "In God We Trust."

14. Series of 1963-A.
Signatures of Granahan and Fowler.

No.	Issuing Bank	No. Printed	Unc	No.	Issuing Bank	No. Printed	Unc	No.	Issuing Bank	No. Printed	Unc
2163-A.	Boston	1,536,000	200.00	2163-E.	Richmond	2,816,000	200.00	2163-I.	Minneapolis	512,000	200.00
2163-A*.	Boston	128,000	260.00	2163-E*.	Richmond	192,000	255.00	2163-I*.	Minneapolis	128,000	260.00
2163-B.	New York	12,544,000	185.00	2163-F.	Atlanta	1,280,000	200.00	2163-J.	Kansas City	1,024,000	200.00
2163-B*.	New York	1,536,000	245.00	2163-F*.	Atlanta	128,000	260.00	2163-J*.	Kansas City	128,000	260.00
2163-C.	Philadelphia	1,792,000	200.00	2163-G.	Chicago	4,352,000	200.00	2163-K.	Dallas	1,536,000	200.00
2163-C*.	Philadelphia	192,000	255.00	2163-G*.	Chicago	512,000	255.00	2163-K*.	Dallas	192,000	255.00
2163-D.	Cleveland	2,304,000	200.00	2163-H.	St. Louis	1,536,000	200.00	2163-L.	San Francisco	6,400,000	200.00
2163-D*.	Cleveland	192,000	255.00	2163-H*.	St. Louis	256,000	255.00	2163-L*.	San Francisco	832,000	325.00

15. Series of 1969.
Signatures of Elston and Kennedy. With new Treasury seal.

No.	Issuing Bank	No. Printed	Unc	No.	Issuing Bank	No. Printed	Unc	No.	Issuing Bank	No. Printed	Unc
2164-A.	Boston	2,048,000	180.00	2164-E.	Richmond	2,560,000	180.00	2164-I.	Minneapolis	512,000	185.00
2164-A*.	Boston	128,000	240.00	2164-E*.	Richmond	192,000	240.00	2164-I*.	Minneapolis	64,000	250.00
2164-B.	New York	11,520,000	175.00	2164-F.	Atlanta	2,304,000	180.00	2164-J.	Kansas City	1,792,000	180.00
2164-B*.	New York	128,000	240.00	2164-F*.	Atlanta	128,000	240.00	2164-J*.	Kansas City	384,000	240.00
2164-C.	Philadelphia	2,560,000	180.00	2164-G.	Chicago	5,888,000	180.00	2164-K.	Dallas	2,048,000	180.00
2164-C*.	Philadelphia	128,000	240.00	2164-G*.	Chicago	256,000	240.00	2164-K*.	Dallas	128,000	250.00
2164-D.	Cleveland	768,000	180.00	2164-H.	St. Louis	1,280,000	180.00	2164-L.	San Francisco	7,168,000	175.00
2164-D*.	Cleveland	64,000	250.00	2164-H*.	St. Louis	64,000	250.00	2164-L*.	San Francisco	320,000	240.00

16. Series of 1969-A.
Signatures of Kabis and Connally.

No.	Issuing Bank	No. Printed	Unc	No.	Issuing Bank	No. Printed	Unc	No.	Issuing Bank	No. Printed	Unc
2165-A.	Boston	1,280,000	175.00	2165-E.	Richmond	2,304,000	175.00	2165-I.	Minneapolis	1,024,000	175.00
2165-A*.	Boston	320,000	285.00	2165-E*.	Richmond	192,000	285.00	2165-I*.	Minneapolis	none printed	—
2165-B.	New York	11,264,000	175.00	2165-F.	Atlanta	2,304,000	175.00	2165-J.	Kansas City	512,000	175.00
2165-B*.	New York	640,000	230.00	2165-F*.	Atlanta	64,000	285.00	2165-J*.	Kansas City	none printed	—
2165-C.	Philadelphia	2,048,000	175.00	2165-G.	Chicago	5,376,000	175.00	2165-K.	Dallas	3,328,000	175.00
2165-C*.	Philadelphia	448,000	230.00	2165-G*.	Chicago	320,000	285.00	2165-K*.	Dallas	128,000	285.00
2165-D.	Cleveland	1,280,000	175.00	2165-H.	St. Louis	1,024,000	175.00	2165-L	San Francisco	4,352,000	175.00
2165-D*.	Cleveland	192,000	285.00	2165-H*.	St. Louis	64,000	285.00	2165-L*.	San Francisco	640,000	285.00

17. Series of 1969-B.
None printed.

18. Series of 1969-C.
Signatures of Banuelos and Shultz.

No.	Issuing Bank	No. Printed	Unc	No.	Issuing Bank	No. Printed	Unc	No.	Issuing Bank	No. Printed	Unc
2166-A.	Boston	2,048,000	165.00	2166-E.	Richmond	7,296,000	165.00	2166-I.	Minneapolis	512,000	165.00
2166-A*.	Boston	64,000	245.00	2166-E*.	Richmond	128,000	245.00	2166-I*.	Minneapolis	64,000	245.00
2166-B.	New York	15,616,000	165.00	2166-F.	Atlanta	2,432,000	165.00	2166-J.	Kansas City	4,736,000	165.00
2166-B*.	New York	256,000	245.00	2166-F*.	Atlanta	64,000	245.00	2166-J*.	Kansas City	192,000	245.00
2166-C.	Philadelphia	2,816,000	165.00	2166-G.	Chicago	6,016,000	165.00	2166-K.	Dallas	2,944,000	165.00
2166-C*.	Philadelphia	64,000	245.00	2166-G*.	Chicago	320,000	245.00	2166-K*.	Dallas	64,000	245.00
2166-D.	Cleveland	3,456,000	165.00	2166-H.	St. Louis	5,376,000	165.00	2166-L	San Francisco	10,240,000	165.00
2166-D*.	Cleveland	64,000	245.00	2166-H*.	St. Louis	64,000	245.00	2166-L*.	San Francisco	512,000	245.00

19. Series of 1974.
Signatures of Neff and Simon.

No.	Issuing Bank	No. Printed	Unc	No.	Issuing Bank	No. Printed	Unc	No.	Issuing Bank	No. Printed	Unc
2167-A.	Boston	11,520,000	160.00	2167-E.	Richmond	11,520,000	160.00	2167-I.	Minneapolis	4,480,000	160.00
2167-A*.	Boston	320,000	200.00	2167-E*.	Richmond	256,000	200.00	2167-I*.	Minneapolis	256,000	200.00
2167-B.	New York	62,720,000	160.00	2167-F.	Atlanta	4,480,000	160.00	2167-J.	Kansas City	5,760,000	160.00
2167-B*.	New York	1,728,000	200.00	2167-F*.	Atlanta	128,000	200.00	2167-J*.	Kansas City	448,000	200.00
2167-C.	Philadelphia	7,680,000	160.00	2167-G.	Chicago	26,880,000	160.00	2167-K.	Dallas	10,240,000	160.00
2167-C*.	Philadelphia	192,000	200.00	2167-G*.	Chicago	1,216,000	200.00	2167-K*.	Dallas	192,000	200.00
2167-D.	Cleveland	8,320,000	160.00	2167-H.	St. Louis	5,760,000	160.00	2167-L.	San Francisco	29,440,000	160.00
2167-D*.	Cleveland	256,000	200.00	2167-H*.	St. Louis	192,000	200.00	2167-L*.	San Francisco	896,000	200.00

20. Series of 1977.
Signatures of Morton and Blumenthal.

No.	Issuing Bank	No. Printed	Unc	No.	Issuing Bank	No. Printed	Unc	No.	Issuing Bank	No. Printed	Unc
2168-A.	Boston	19,200,000	160.00	2168-E.	Richmond	24,320,000	160.00	2168-I.	Minneapolis	5,195,000	160.00
2168-A*.	Boston	320,000	200.00	2168-E*.	Richmond	384,000	125.00	2168-I*.	Minneapolis	192,000	210.00
2168-B.	New York	166,400,000	160.00	2168-F.	Atlanta	3,840,000	160.00	2168-J.	Kansas City	38,400,000	160.00
2168-B*.	New York	1,664,000	195.00	2168-F*.	Atlanta	64,000	215.00	2168-J*.	Kansas City	640,000	125.00
2168-C.	Philadelphia	5,195,000	160.00	2168-G.	Chicago	39,680,000	160.00	2168-K.	Dallas	38,400,000	160.00
2168-C.	Philadelphia	128,000	215.00	2168-G*.	Chicago	960,000	195.00	2168-K*.	Dallas	640,000	125.00
2168-D.	Cleveland	16,640,000	160.00	2168-H.	St. Louis	15,360,000	160.00	2168-L.	San Francisco	39,680,000	160.00
2168-D*.	Cleveland	192,000	215.00	2168-H*.	St. Louis	448,000	195.00	2168-L*.	San Francisco	576,000	195.00

21. Series of 1981
Signatures of Buchanan and Regan.

No.	Issuing Bank	No. Printed	Unc	No.	Issuing Bank	No. Printed	Unc	No.	Issuing Bank	No. Printed	Unc
2169-A.	Boston	8,960,000	200.00	2169-E.	Richmond	23,680,000	175.00	2169-I.	Minneapolis	3,200,000	225.00
2169-A*.	Boston	none printed	—	2169-E*.	Richmond	640,000	375.00	2169-I*.	Minneapolis	none printed	—
2169-B.	New York	105,600,000	175.00	2169-F.	Atlanta	6,400,000	200.00	2169-J.	Kansas City	23,680,000	200.00
2169-B*.	New York	none printed	—	2169-F*.	Atlant	none printed	—	2169-J*.	Kansas City	none printed	—
2169-C.	Philadelphia	12,800,000	200.00	2169-G.	Chicago	33,280,000	175.00	2169-K.	Dallas	23,680,000	200.00
2169-C*.	Philadelphia	none printed	—	2169-G*.	Chicago	none printed	—	2169-K*.	Dallas	none printed	—
2169-D.	Cleveland	5,760,000	200.00	2169-H.	St. Louis	5,760,000	200.00	2169-L.	San Francisco	24,960,000	200.00
2169-D*.	Cleveland	none printed	—	2169-H*.	St. Louis	none printed	—	2169-L*.	San Francisco	none printed	—

22. Series of 1981-A.
Signatures of Ortega and Regan.

No.	Issuing Bank	No. Printed	Unc	No.	Issuing Bank	No. Printed	Unc	No.	Issuing Bank	No. Printed	Unc
2170-A.	Boston	16,000,000	175.00	2170-E.	Richmond	12,800,000	175.00	2170-I.	Minneapolis	3,200,000	175.00
2170-A*.	Boston	none printed	—	2170-E*.	Richmond	none printed	—	2170-I*.	Minneapolis	none printed	—
2170-B.	New York	64,000,000	175.00	2170-F.	Atlanta	12,800,000	175.00	2170-J.	Kansas City	none printed	—
2170-B*.	New York	none printed	—	2170-F*.	Atlanta	none printed	—	2170-J*.	Kansas City	none printed	—
2170-C.	Philadelphia	3,200,000	175.00	2170-G.	Chicago	22,400,000	175.00	2170-K.	Dallas	3,200,000	175.00
2170-C*.	Philadelphia	none printed	—	2170-G*.	Chicago	none printed	—	2170-K*.	Dallas	none printed	—
2170-D.	Cleveland	6,400,000	175.00	2170-H.	St. Louis	12,800,000	175.00	2170-L.	San Francisco	19,200,000	175.00
2170-D*.	Cleveland	none printed	—	2170-H*.	St. Louis	none printed	—	2170-L*.	San Francisco	640,000	300.00

23. Series of 1985
Signatures of Ortega and Baker.

No.	Issuing Bank	No. Printed	Unc	No.	Issuing Bank	No. Printed	Unc	No.	Issuing Bank	No. Printed	Unc
2171-A.	Boston	32,000,000	175.00	2171-E.	Richmond	54,400,000	175.00	2171-I.	Minneapolis	12,800,000	175.00
2171-A*.	Boston	none printed	—	2171-E*.	Richmond	none printed	—	2171-I*.	Minneapolis	none printed	—
2171-B.	New York	259,200,000	175.00	2171-F.	Atlanta	16,000,000	175.00	2171-J.	Kansas City	12,800,000	175.00
2171-B*.	New York	none printed	---	2171-F*.	Atlanta	none printed	—	2171-J*.	Kansas City	1,280,000	250.00
2171-C.	Philadelphia	19,200,000	175.00	2171-G.	Chicago	64,000,000	175.00	2171-K.	Dallas	48,000,000	175.00
2171-C*.	Philadelphia	none printed	—	2171-G*.	Chicago	none printed	—	2171-K*.	Dallas	3,200,000	250.00
2171-D.	Cleveland	28,800,000	175.00	2171-H.	St. Louis	12,800,000	175.00	2171-L	San Francisco	38,400,000	175.00
2171-D*.	Cleveland	1,280,000	250.00	2171-H*.	St. Louis	none printed	—	2171-L*.	San Francisco	none printed	—

24. Series of 1988
Signatures of Ortega and Brady.

No.	Issuing Bank	No. Printed	Unc	No.	Issuing Bank	No. Printed	Unc	No.	Issuing Bank	No. Printed	Unc
2172-A.	Boston	9,600,000	175.00	2172-E.	Richmond	19,200,000	175.00	2172-I.	Minneapolis	none printed	—
2172-A*.	Boston	none printed	—	2172-E*.	Richmond	none printed	—	2172-I*.	Minneapolis	none printed	—
2172-B.	New York	448,000,000	175.00	2172-F.	Atlanta	none printed	—	2172-J.	Kansas City	9,600,000	175.00
2172-B*.	New York	4,480,000	225.00	2172-F*.	Atlanta	none printed	—	2172-J*.	Kansas City	none printed	—
2172-C	Philadelphia	9,600,000	175.00	2172-G.	Chicago	51,200,000	175.00	2172-K.	Dallas	none printed	—
2172-C*.	Philadelphia	none printed	—	2172-G*.	Chicago	none printed	—	2172-K*	Dallas	none printed	—
2172-D.	Cleveland	35,200,000	175.00	2172-H.	St. Louis	9,600,000	175.00	2172-L.	San Francisco	10,200,000	175.00
2172-D*.	Cleveland	none printed	—	2172-H*.	St. Louis	none printed	—	2172-L*.	San Francisco	none printed	—

25. Series of 1988-A.
None Printed
26. Series of 1990.
Signatures of Villalpando and Brady.

No.	Issuing Bank	No. Printed	Unc	No.	Issuing Bank	No. Printed	Unc	No.	Issuing Bank	No. Printed	Unc
2173-A.	Boston	76,800,000	150.00	2173-E.	Richmond	108,800,000	150.00	2173-I.	Minneapolis	48,000,000	150.00
2173-A*.	Boston	none printed	—	2173-E*.	Richmond	none printed	—	2173-I*.	Minneapolis	none printed	—
2173-B.	New York	595,200,000	150.00	2173-F.	Atlanta	64,000,000	150.00	2173-J.	Kansas City	76,800,000	150.00
2173-B*.	New York	1,880,000	175.00	2173-F*.	Atlanta	none printed	—	2173-J*.	Kansas City	3,200,000	175.00
2173-C.	Philadelphia	112,000,000	150.00	2173-G.	Chicago	134,400,000	150.00	2173-K.	Dallas	165,400,000	150.00
2173-C*.	Philadelphia	1,280,000	175.00	2173-G*.	Chicago	640,000	175.00	2173-K*.	Dallas	1,920,000	175.00
2173-D.	Cleveland	115,200,000	150.00	2173-H.	St. Louis	121,600,000	150.00	2173-L	San Francisco	147,200,000	150.00
2173-D*.	Cleveland	none printed	—	2173-H*.	St. Louis	none printed	—	2173-L*.	San Francisco	3,200,000	175.00

27. Series of 1993.
Signatures of Withrow and Bentsen.

No.	Issuing Bank	No. Printed	Unc	No.	Issuing Bank	No. Printed	Unc	No.	Issuing Bank	No. Printed	Unc
2174-A.	Boston	83,200,000	125.00	2174-E.	Richmond	64,000,000	125.00	2174-I.	Minneapolis	9,600,000	125.00
2174-A*.	Boston	none printed	—	2174-E*.	Richmond	none printed	—	2174-I*.	Minneapolis	none printed	—
2174-B.	New York	288,,000,000	125.00	2174-F.	Atlanta	150,400,000	125.00	2174-J.	Kansas City	9,600,000	125.00
2174-B*.	New York	2,560,000	140.00	2174-F*.	Atlanta	none printed	—	2174-J*.	Kansas City	none printed	—
2174-C.	Philadelphia	41,600,000	125.00	2174-G.	Chicago	44,800,000	125.00	2174-K.	Dallas	51,200,000	125.00
2174-C*.	Philadelphia	1,280,000	140.00	2174-G*.	Chicago	none printed	—	2174-K*.	Dallas	none printed	—
2174-D.	Cleveland	9,600,000	125.00	2174-H.	St. Louis	16,000,000	—	2174-L	San Francisco	19,200,000	125.00
2174-D*.	Cleveland	1,024,000	140.00	2174-H*.	St. Louis	640,000	140.00	2174-L*.	San Francisco	none printed	—

Design No. 231-b.
(Notes 2175-A -)
Larger portrait of Benjamin Franklin positioned off-center.
Color-shifting (black/green) ink used in numeral at lower right.
Printed with microsize printing and security thread on watermarked paper.

Reverse of Design No. 231-b.
View of Independence Hall in Philadelphia.

28. Series of 1996.
Signatures of Withrow and Rubin. Printed in Washington, D.C.

2175-A.	Boston		—	2175-E.	Richmond	—	2175-I.	Minneapolis	—
2175-A*.	Boston		—	2175-E*.	Richmond	—	2175-I*.	Minneapolis	—
2175-B.	New York	4,063,200,000	Current	2175-F.	Atlanta	—	2175-J.	Kansas City	—
2175-B*.	New York	34,080,000	Current	2175-F*.	Atlanta	—	2175-J*.	Kansas City	—
2175-C.	Philadelphia		—	2175-G.	Chicago	—	2175-K.	Dallas	—
2175-C*.	Philadelphia		—	2175-G*.	Chicago	—	2175-K*.	Dallas	—
2175-D.	Cleveland		—	2175-H.	St. Louis	—	2175-L	San Francisco	—
2175-D*.	Cleveland		—	2175-H*.	St. Louis	—	2175-L*.	San Francisco	—

HIGH DENOMINATION NOTES

Valuations have not been placed on any of the following 5,000 and 10,000 Dollar notes. Because of their high face value, they are beyond the reach of the ordinary collector and the market for them is limited. (See under "High Denomination Notes," page 8.)

500 Dollar Notes

All issues are with the head of William McKinley.

DESIGN NO. 232. (a and b)
Federal Reserve Note and Gold Certificate.
(Notes 2200-2204) (Also Note 2407)

Reverse of Design No. 232.

1. Series of 1928.
Signatures of Woods and Mellon.

No.	Issuing Bank	No. Printed	VF	UNC	No.	Issuing Bank	No. Printed	VF	UNC	No.	Issuing Bank	No. Printed	VF	UNC
2200-A.	Boston	69,120	850.00	1,750.00	2200-E.	Richmond	84,720	850.00	1,750.00	2200-I.	Minneapolis	34,680	850.00	1,750.00
2200-B.	New York	299,400	850.00	1,750.00	2200-F.	Atlanta	69,360	850.00	1,750.00	2200-J.	Kansas City	510,720	850.00	1,750.00
2200-C.	Philadephia	135,120	850.00	1,750.00	2200-G.	Chicago	573,600	850.00	1,750.00	2200-K.	Dallas	70,560	850.00	1,750.00
2200-D.	Cleveland	166,440	850.00	1,750.00	2200-H.	St. Louis	66,180	850.00	1,750.00	2200-L.	San Francisco	64,080	850.00	1,750.00
										2200*			2,000.00	

2. Series of 1934.
Signatures of Julian and Morgenthau.

No.	Issuing Bank	No. Printed	VF	UNC	No.	Issuing Bank	No. Printed	VF	UNC	No.	Issuing Bank	No. Printed	VF	UNC
2201-A.	Boston	56,628	850.00	1,750.00	2201-F.	Atlanta	46,200	850.00	1,750.00	2201-K.	Dallas	31,200	850.00	1,750.00
2201-B.	New York	288,000	850.00	1,750.00	2201-G.	Chicago	212,400	850.00	1,750.00	2201-L.	San Francisco	83,400	850.00	1,750.00
2201-C.	Philadelphia	31,200	850.00	1,750.00	2201-H.	St. Louis	24,000	850.00	1,750.00	2201*			2,000.00	
2201-D.	Cleveland	39,000	850.00	1,750.00	2201-I.	Minneapolis	24,000	850.00	1,750.00					
2201-E.	Richmond	40,800	850.00	1,750.00	2201-J.	Kansas City	40,800	850.00	1,750.00					

3. Series of 1934-A.
Signatures of Julian and Morgenthau.

No.	Issuing Bank	No. Printed	VF	UNC	No.	Issuing Bank	No. Printed	VF	UNC	No.	Issuing Bank	No. Printed	VF	UNC
2202-B.	New York	276,000	850.00	1,750.00	2202-F.	Atlanta	incl. above	850.00	1,750.00	2202-J.	Kansas City	55,200	850.00	1,750.00
2202-C.	Philadelphia	45,300	850.00	1,750.00	2202-G.	Chicago	214,800	850.00	1,750.00	2202-K.	Dallas	34,800	850.00	1,750.00
2202-D.	Cleveland	28,800	850.00	1,750.00	2202-H.	St. Louis	57,600	850.00	1,750.00	2202-L.	San Francisco	93,000	850.00	1,750.00
2202-E.	Richmond	36,000	850.00	1,750.00	2202-I.	Minneapolis	14,400	850.00	1,750.00	2202*			2,000.00	

4. Series of 1934-B.
Signatures of Julian and Vinson.
Bureau of Engraving and Printing records indicate the existence of these notes although none have been seen.

2203-F. Atlanta   2,472

5. Series of 1934-C.
Signatures of Julian and Snyder.
Bureau of Engraving and Printing records indicate the existence of these notes although none have been seen.

2204-A. Boston   1,440 | 2204-B. New York   204

1,000 Dollar Notes

All issues are with the head of Grover Cleveland.

DESIGN NO. 233. (a and b)
Federal Reserve Note and Gold Certificate.
(Notes 2210-2213 Incl.) (Also Note 2408)

Reverse of Design No. 233.

1. Series of 1928.
Signatures of Woods and Mellon.

No.	Issuing Bank	No. Printed	VF	UNC	No.	Issuing Bank	No. Printed	VF	UNC	No.	Issuing Bank	No. Printed	VF	UNC
2210-A.	Boston	58,320	1,600.00	2,850.00	2210-E.	Richmond	66,840	1,600.00	2,850.00	2210-I.	Minneapolis	26,640	1,600.00	2,850.00
2210-B.	New York	139,200	1,600.00	2,850.00	2210-F.	Atlanta	47,400	1,600.00	2,850.00	2210-J.	Kansas City	62,172	1,600.00	2,850.00
2210-C.	Philadelphia	96,708	1,600.00	2,850.00	2210-G.	Chicago	355,800	1,600.00	2,850.00	2210-K.	Dallas	42,960	1,600.00	2,850.00
2210-D.	Cleveland	79,680	1,600.00	2,850.00	2210-H.	St. Louis	60,000	1,600.00	2,850.00	2210-L.	San Francisco	67,920	1,600.00	2,850.00
										2210*			4,000.00	

2. Series of 1934.
Signatures of Julian and Morgenthau.

No.	Issuing Bank	No. Printed	VF	UNC	No.	Issuing Bank	No. Printed	VF	UNC	No.	Issuing Bank	No. Printed	VF	UNC
2211-A.	Boston	46,200	1,600.00	2,850.00	2211-F.	Atlanta	67,800	1,600.00	2,850.00	2211-K.	Dallas	46,800	1,600.00	2,850.00
2211-B.	New York	332,784	1,600.00	2,850.00	2211-G.	Chicago	167,040	1,600.00	2,850.00	2211-L.	San Francisco	90,600	1,600.00	2,850.00
2211-C.	Philadelphia	33,000	1,600.00	2,850.00	2211-H.	St. Louis	22,440	1,600.00	2,850.00	2211*			4,000.00	
2211-D.	Cleveland	35,400	1,600.00	2,850.00	2211-I.	Minneapolis	12,000	1,600.00	2,850.00					
2211-E.	Richmond	19,560	1,600.00	2,850.00	2211-J.	Kansas City	51,840	1,600.00	2,850.00					

3. Series of 1934-A.
Signatures of Julian and Morgenthau.

No.	Issuing Bank	No. Printed	VF	UNC	No.	Issuing Bank	No. Printed	VF	UNC	No.	Issuing Bank	No. Printed	VF	UNC
2212-A.	Boston	30,000	1,600.00	2,850.00	2212-E.	Richmond	16,800	1,600.00	2,850.00	2212-I.	Minneapolis	4,800	1,600.00	2,850.00
2212-B.	New York	174,348	1,600.00	2,850.00	2212-F.	Atlanta	80,964	1,600.00	2,850.00	2212-J.	Kansas City	21,600	1,600.00	2,850.00
2212-C.	Philadelphia	78,000	1,600.00	2,850.00	2212-G.	Chicago	134,400	1,600.00	2,850.00	2212-L.	San Francisco	36,600	1,600.00	2,850.00
2212-D.	Cleveland	28,800	1,600.00	2,850.00	2212-H.	St. Louis	39,600	1,600.00	2,850.00	2212*			4,000.00	

4. Series of 1934-C.
Signatures of Julian and Snyder.

Bureau of Engraving and Printing records indicate the existence of these notes although none have been seen.

2213-A.	Boston	1,200		2213-B.	New York	168

5,000 Dollar Notes

All issues are with the head of James Madison.

DESIGN NO. 234. (a and b)
Federal Reserve Note and Gold Certificate.
(Notes 2220-2223) (Also Note 2410)

Reverse of Design No. 234.

1. Series of 1928.
Signatures of Woods and Mellon.

No.	Issuing Bank	No. Printed	No.	Issuing Bank	No. Printed	No.	Issuing Bank	No. Printed
2220-A.	Boston	1,320	2220-E.	Richmond	3,984	2220-J.	Kansas City	720
2220-B.	New York	2,640	2220-F.	Atlanta	1,440	2220-K.	Dallas	360
2220-D.	Cleveland	3,000	2220-G.	Chicago	3,480	2220-L.	San Francisco	1,300

2. Series of 1934.
Signatures of Julian and Morgenthau.

No.	Issuing Bank	No. Printed	No.	Issuing Bank	No. Printed	No.	Issuing Bank	No. Printed
2221-A.	Boston	9,480	2221-E.	Richmond	2,400	2221-J.	Kansas City	2,400
2221-B.	New York	11,520	2221-F.	Atlanta	3,600	2221-K.	Dallas	2,400
2221-C.	Philadelphia	3,000	2221-G.	Chicago	6,600	2221-L.	San Francisco	6,000
2221-D.	Cleveland	1,680	2221-H.	St. Louis	2,400			

3. Series of 1934-A.
Signatures of Julian and Morgenthau.

No.	Issuing Bank	No. Printed
2222-H.	St. Louis %	1,440

4. Series of 1934-B.
Signatures of Julian and Vinson.

No.	Issuing Bank	No. Printed	No.	Issuing Bank	No. Printed
2223-A.	Boston %	1,200	2223-B.	New York %	12

% Bureau of Engraving and Printing records indicate the existence of these notes although none have been seen.

10,000 Dollar Notes

All issues are with the head of Salmon P. Chase.

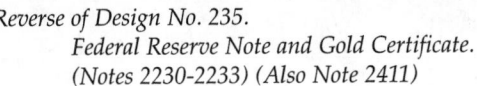

DESIGN NO. 235. (a and b)

Reverse of Design No. 235.
Federal Reserve Note and Gold Certificate.
(Notes 2230-2233) (Also Note 2411)

1. Series of 1928.
Signatures of Woods and Mellon.

No.	Issuing Bank	No. Printed	No.	Issuing Bank	No. Printed	No.	Issuing Bank	No. Printed
2230-A.	Boston	1,320	2230-F.	Atlanta	1,440	2230-J.	Kansas City	480
2230-B.	New York	4,680	2230-G.	Chicago	1,800	2230-K.	Dallas	360
2230-D.	Cleveland	960	2230-H.	St. Louis	480	2230-L.	San Francisco	1,824
2230-E.	Richmond	3,024	2230-I.	Minneapolis	480			

2. Series of 1934.
Signatures of Julian and Morgenthau.

No.	Issuing Bank	No. Printed	No.	Issuing Bank	No. Printed	No.	Issuing Bank	No. Printed
2231-A.	Boston	9,720	2231-E.	Richmond	1,200	2231-J.	Kansas City	1,200
2231-B.	New York	11,520	2231-F.	Atlanta	2,400	2231-K.	Dallas	1,200
2231-C.	Philadelphia	6,000	2231-G.	Chicago	3,840	2231-L.	San Francisco	3,600
2231-D.	Cleveland	1,480	2231-H.	St. Louis	2,040			

3. Series of 1934-A.
Signatures of Julian and Morgenthau.

2232-G.	Chicago	1,560

4. Series of 1934-B.
Signatures of Julian and Vinson.

2233-B.	New York	24

XX. EMERGENCY NOTES
ISSUED DURING WORLD WAR II
1. Notes Issued for Hawaii After the Attack on Pearl Harbor.

1 Dollar Notes

Silver Certificate Surcharged "Hawaii" on both sides, with Signatures of Julian and Morgenthau
and with a Brown Seal (not Blue).

DESIGN NO. 236
(Note 2300)

Reverse of Design No. 236.

No.	Denomination	Series	No. Printed	Very Fine	Unc	No.	Denomination	Series	No. Printed	Very Fine	Unc
2300.	1 Dollar	1935-A	35,052,000	25.00	85.00	2300*.	1 Dollar	1935-A		200.00	1,000.00

5 Dollar Notes

Federal Reserve Notes of San Francisco with same surcharge, seal and signatures.

DESIGN NO. 237
(Notes 2301, 2302)

Reverse of Design No. 237.

No.	Denomination	Series	No. Printed	Very Fine	Unc	No.	Denomination	Series	No. Printed	Very Fine	Unc
2301.	5 Dollars	1934	9,416,000	50.00	225.00	2302.	5 Dollars	1934-A	incl. above	50.00	250.00
2301*.	5 Dollars	1934		1,250.00	4,000.00	2302*.	5 Dollars	1934-A		6,000.00	Rare

10 Dollar Notes

Federal Reserve Notes of San Francisco with same surcharge, seal and signatures.

DESIGN NO. 238
(Note 2303)

Reverse of Design No. 238.

No.	Denomination	Series	No. Printed	Very Fine	Unc	No.	Denomination	Series	No. Printed	Very Fine	Unc
2303.	10 Dollars	1934-A	10,424,000	75.00	375.00	2303*.	10 Dollars	1934-A		3,000.00	8,000.00

20 Dollar Notes

Federal Reserve Notes of San Francisco with same surcharge, seal and signatures.

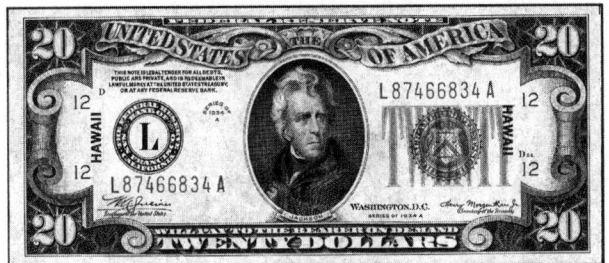

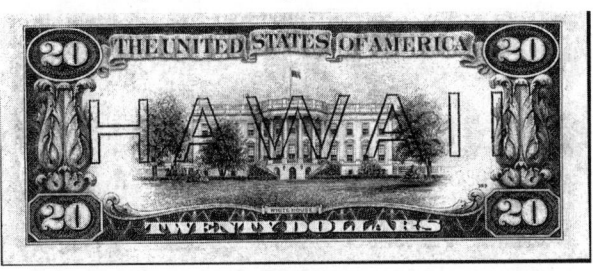

DESIGN NO. 239
(Notes 2304, 2305)

Reverse of Design No. 239.

No.	Denomination	Series	No. Printed	Very Fine	Unc	No.	Denomination	Series	No. Printed	Very Fine	Unc
2304.	20 Dollars	1934	11,24 6,000	200.00	1,100.00	2305.	20 Dollars	1934-A	incl. above	60.00	550.00
2304*.	20 Dollars	1934		900.00	10,000.00	2305*.	20 Dollars	1934-A		600.00	7,500.00

2. Notes Issued for Use With the Armed Forces in Europe and North Africa.

These notes are Silver Certificates with signatures of Julian and Morgenthau and with a yellow seal (not blue).

No.	Denomination	Series	Design No.	No. Printed	Very Fine	Unc
2306.	1 Dollar	1935-A	197	26,916,000	27.50	100.00
2306*.	1 Dollar	1935-A	197		200.00	1,400.00
2307.	5 Dollars	1934-A	199	16,710,000	70.00	175.00
2307*.	5 Dollars	1934-A	199		175.00	750.00
2308.	10 Dollars	1934	202		2,000.00	12,000.00
2308*.	10 Dollars	1934	202		Unique	—
2309.	10 Dollars	1934-A	202	21,860,000*	40.00	150.00
2309*.	10 Dollars	1934-A	202		125.00	500.00

No. Printed is combined total of No. 2308-2309.

XXI. GOLD CERTIFICATES

All are now obsolete. The issue was short lived as the Gold Reserve Act of 1933 required the surrender of all gold certificates, both large and small size. On April 24, 1964, Secretary of the Treasury C. Douglas Dillon removed all restrictions on the acquisition or holding of gold certificates and it is now legal to collect them. Unlike the large notes, the reverses of these gold certificates were printed in green. Small size gold certificates are considered much scarcer than the old large size notes. The obligation is as follows, "This certifies that there have been deposited in the Treasury of the United States of America ...... Dollars in gold coin payable to the bearer on demand... This certificate is a legal tender in the amount thereof in payment of all debts and dues public and private." (Additional information on this series will be found in the introduction to large size Gold Certificates on page 136.)

All the following have a Gold Seal.

10 Dollar Notes

DESIGN NO. 240
(Notes 2400, 2401)

Reverse of Design No. 240.

No.	Denomination	Series	Signatures		No. Printed	Very Fine	Unc
2400.	10 Dollars	1928	Woods	Mellon	130,812,000	85.00	400.00
2400*.	10 Dollars	1928	Woods	Mellon		300.00	2,000.00
2401.	10 Dollars	1928-A	Woods	Mellon	2,544,000	Not Issued	—

20 Dollar Notes

DESIGN NO. 241
(Notes 2402, 2403)

Reverse of Design No. 241.

2402.	20 Dollars	1928	Woods	Mellon	66,204,000	80.00	375.00
2402*.	20 Dollars	1928	Woods	Mellon		400.00	2,500.00
2403.	20 Dollars	1928-A	Woods	Mills	1,500,000	Not Issued	—

50 Dollar Notes

DESIGN NO. 242.
(Note 2404)

Reverse of Design No. 242.

2404.	50 Dollars	1928	Woods	Mellon	5,520,000	200.00	800.00
2404*.	50 Dollars	1928	Woods	Mellon		2,000.00	9,000.00

100 Dollar Notes

DESIGN NO. 243
(Notes 2405, 2406)

Reverse of Design No. 243.

No.	Denomination	Series	Signatures	No. Printed	Very Fine	Unc
2405.	100 Dollars	1928	Woods Mellon	3,240,000	350.00	1,750.00
2405*.	100 Dollars	1928	Woods Mellon		2,000.00	11,000.00
2406.	100 Dollars	1934	Julian Morgenthau	120,000	Not Issued	—

The Following High Denominations Were Also Issued.
The designs are the same as the Federal Reserve Notes indicated except that the obligation and seal are different.

DESIGN NO. 232
(Note 2407)

Reverse of Design No. 232.
This illustration by courtesy of Mr. Dick Erett.

No.	Denomination	Series	Signatures	No. Printed	Very Fine	Unc
2407.	500 Dollars	1928	Woods Mellon	420,000	3,000.00	8,000.00

DESIGN NO. 233
(Notes 2408, 2409)

Reverse of Design No. 233.
This illustration by courtesy of Mr. Dick Erett.

No.	Denomination	Series	Signatures	No.Printed	Very Fine	Unc
2408.	1,000 Dollars	1928	Woods Mellon	288,00	3,500.00	12,500.00
2409.	1,000 Dollars	1934	Julian Morgenthau	84,000	Rare	—

No.	Denomination	Series	Signatures	Design No.	No.Printed	Unc
2410.	5,000 Dollars	1928	Woods Mellon	234	24,000	Rare
2411.	10,000 Dollars	1928	Woods Mellon	235	48,000	Rare
2412.	10,000 Dollars	1934	Julian Morgenthau	235	36,000	—
2413.	100,000 Dollars	1934	Julian Morgenthau		42,000	—

The above notes (Series 1934) have bright orange reverses. They were issued exclusively for transactions within the U.S. Treasury and the Federal Reserve System and were never released to commercial banks or to the public. Possession may be considered illegal.

PART FOUR
XXII. ENCASED POSTAGE STAMPS

Although not strictly paper money, Encased Postage Stamps have been included in this volume because they are essentially government printed paper that was actually used as money.

Encased Postage Stamps had their beginnings under the same circumstances that produced Fractional Currency—namely, the absence of circulating coin during the years of the Civil War.

A Mr. J. Gault was responsible for the issuance of Encased Postage Stamps, which were his own invention for alleviating the shortage of coins. He patented his Encased Postage Stamp in 1862, and subsequently issued them in denominations of 1, 2, 3, 5, 10, 12, 24, 30 and 90 Cents. They were at once popular and welcome, as anything would have been in those years that enabled one to make small change.

Since postage stamps were already being widely used in lieu of coins, a way had to be found to prolong their life. After only a very short time of going from hand to hand, stamps quickly became worthless as postage and unacceptable as money. Accordingly, Mr. Gault devised a round, brassy metal frame in which a stamp could be encased, so that it would not be subject to dirt, wear or tear. A layer of clear transparent mica covered the face of the frame, so that the stamp could be seen without being touched. The back of the frame was solid metal. Many merchants used the back of Encased

Postage Stamps as an advertising medium and embossed messages on them. The illustration in the text will show the general appearance of an Encased Postage Stamp. The text proper lists all of the merchants whose names and products appear on the backs.

The denominations of Encased Postage Stamps were necessarily limited by the then current issues of the Post Office. The stamp issues of 1861 were used for this purpose, and this accounts for such unusual denominations as 12, 24, 30 and 90 Cents, which are completely foreign to our coinage system. At least, Encased Postage Stamps gave the public the familiar roundness of coins.

Like the first issues of Fractional Currency (Postage Currency) Encased Postage Stamps are collected by both coin and stamp collectors. As will be seen in the text, there are many rare and valuable items in existence, and the search for these is no less intense than for rare large notes.

The illustrations above are typical of all examples. They are all of the same size and differ only in the denomination on the obverse and in the advertisement on the reverse.

The prices quoted are for specimens in Very Fine condition, light circulation wear on the case, and with all the mica clear and unbroken. All encased postage is very rare in new condition.

1 CENT STAMPS

No.	Issued By	Value	No.	Issued by	Value
EP-1.	Aerated Bread Co., New York	1,750.00	EP-17.	Gault, J., Ribbed frame	700.00
EP-2.	Ayer's Cathartic Pills	300.00	EP-17a.	Hopkins, L.C. & Co., Cincinnati	1,500.00
EP-3.	"Take Ayer's Pills"	275.00	EP-18.	Hunt & Nash, Irving House, N.Y	600.00
EP4.	Ayer's Sarsaparilla Small "Ayer's"	500.00	EP-19.	Kirkpatrick & Gault, N.Y	350.00
EP4a.	As above but medium "Ayer's"	275.00	EP-20.	Lord and Taylor, N.Y	750.00
EP-5.	Bailey & Co., Philadelphia	700.00	EP-21.	Mendum's Family Wine Emporium, N.Y.	550.00
EP-6.	Bates, Joseph L., Boston "Fancy Goods"	300.00	EP-22.	Miles, B.F. John W., Chicago	3,000.00
EP-6a.	As above but "Fancygoods" in one word	275.00	EP-23.	Norris, John W., Chicago	2,500.00
EP-7.	Brown's Bronchial Troches	675.00	EP-24.	North American Life Insurance Co., N.Y. Straight inscr.	325.00
EP-8.	Buhl, F. & Co., Detroit	750.00	EP-24a.	As above but curved inscr.	550.00
EP-9.	Bumett's Cocoaine Kalliston	400.00	EP-24b.	Pearce, Tolle & Holton, Cincinnati	2,000.00
EP-10.	Burnett's Cooking Extracts	300.00	EP-25.	Schapker & Bussing, Evansville, Ind	650.00
EP-11.	Claflin, A.M., Hopkinton, R.I.	7,500.00	EP-26.	Shillito, John & Co., Cincinnati	700.00
EP-12.	Dougan, New York	1,750.00	EP-27.	Steinfeld, S., N.Y.	2,000.00
EP-13.	Drake's Plantation Bitters	250.00	EP-28.	Taylor N.G. & Co., Philadelphia	2,250.00
EP-13a.	Ellis, McAlpin & Co., Cincinnati	1,200.00	EP-29.	Weir & Larminie, Montreal, Canada	1,750.00
EP-14.	Evans, G.G	700.00	EP-30.	White the Hatter, N.Y.	1,500.00
EP-15.	Gage Brothers & Drake, Chicago	500.00			
EP-16.	Gault, J., Plain frame	900.00			

2 CENT STAMPS

EP-31	Gault, J., Very Rare, not a regular issue	9,000.00

3 CENT STAMPS

No.	Issued By	Value	No.	Issued by	Value
EP-32.	Ayer's Cathartic Pills	200.00	EP-37.	Bates, Joseph L., Boston "Fancy Goods"	475.00
EP-32a.	As above but with longer arrows	225.00	EP-37a.	Same, "Fancygoods" in one word	450.00
EP-33.	"Take Ayer's Pills"	185.00	EP-38.	Brown's Bronchial Troches	325.00
EP-34.	Ayer's Sarsaparilla, Plain frame	450.00	EP-38a.	Buhl, F. & Co., Detroit	850.00
EP-34a.	As above but medium "Ayer's" (EP-34 is small)	250.00	EP-39.	Bumett's Cocoaine Kalliston	300.00
EP-34b.	As above but large "Ayer's"	400.00	EP-40.	Bumett's Cooking Extracts	300.00
EP-35.	Ayer's Sarsaparilla, Ribbed frame	650.00	EP-40a.	Claflin, A.M., Hopkinton, R.I.	4,500.00
EP-36.	Bailey & Co., Philadelphia	650.00	EP-41.	Dougan, N.Y.	1,750.00

3 CENT STAMPS

No.	Issued By	Value	No.	Issued By	Value
EP-42.	Drake's Plantation Bitters	200.00	EP-52.	Mendum's Family Wine Emporium, N.Y.	800.00
EP-43.	Ellis, McAlpin & Co., Cincinnati	1,300.00	EP-52a.	Norris, John W., Chicago	1,150.00
EP-44.	Evans, G.G.	750.00	EP-53.	North American Life Insurance Co., N.Y.	475.00
EP-45.	Gage Brothers & Drake, Chicago	500.00	EP-53a.	As above, but curved inscr.	525.00
EP-46.	Gault, J., Plain frame	200.00	EP-54.	Pearce, Tolle & Holton, Cincinnati	1,850.00
EP-47.	Gault, J., Ribbed frame	650.00	EP-55.	Schapker & Bussing, Evansville, Ind.	650.00
EP-48.	Hopkins, L.C. & Co., Cincinnati	900.00	EP-56.	Shillito, John & Co., Cincinnati	475.00
EP-49.	Hunt & Nash, Irving House, N.Y.	900.00	EP-57.	Taylor, N.G. & Co., Philadelphia	1,250.00
EP-49a.	Same, but with ribbed frame	1,000.00	EP-58.	Weir & Larminie, Montreal, Canada	1,500.00
EP-50.	Kirkpatrick & Gault, N.Y.	525.00	EP-59.	White the Hatter, N.Y.	1,500.00
EP-51.	Lord & Taylor, N.Y.	850.00			

5 CENT STAMPS

No.	Issued By	Value	No.	Issued By	Value
EP-60.	Ayer's Cathartic Pills	275.00	EP-80.	Hopkins, L.C. & Co., Cincinnati	1,250.00
EP-60a.	As above but with longer arrows	275.00	EP-81.	Hunt & Nash, Irving House, N.Y., Plain frame	800.00
EP-61.	"Take Ayer's Pills", Plain frame	275.00			
EP-62.	"Take Ayer's Pills", Ribbed frame	975.00	EP-82.	Hunt & Nash, Irving House, N.Y., Ribbed frame	450.00
EP-63.	Ayer's Sarsaparilla, Medium "Ayer's"	275.00			
EP-63a.	Ayer's Sarsaparilla, large "Ayer's"	600.00	EP-83.	Kirkpatrick & Gault, N.Y	325.00
EP-64.	Bailey & Co., Philadelphia	950.00	EP-84.	Lord & Taylor, N.Y	850.00
EP-65.	Bates, Joseph L., Boston, Plain frame	650.00	EP-85.	Mendum's Family Wine Emporium, N.Y.	750.00
EP-66.	Bates, Joseph L., Boston, Ribbed frame	800.00	EP-86.	Miles, B.F., Peoria	3,250.00
EP-66a.	Same, "Fancygoods" in one word, Plain	800.00	EP-87.	Norris, John W., Chicago	1,500.00
EP-67.	Brown's Bronchial Troches	350.00	EP-88.	North American Life Insurance Co., N.Y., Plain frame, straight inscr.	600.00
EP-68.	Buhl, F. & Co., Detroit	850.00			
EP-69.	Burnett's Cocoaine Kalliston	450.00	EP-88a.	North American Life Ins. Co., N.Y., Ribbed frame	950.00
EP-70.	Burnett's Cooking Extracts	350.00			
EP-71.	Claflin, A.M., Hopkinton, R.I.	5,500.00	EP-89.	Pearce, Tolle & Holton, Cincinnati	2,000.00
EP-72.	Cook, H.A., Evansville, Ind.	800.00	EP-90.	Sands Ale	2,500.00
EP-73.	Dougan, N.Y.	1,750.00	EP-91.	Schapker & Bussing, Evansville, Ind.	800.00
EP-74.	Drake's Plantation Bitters, Plain frame	300.00	EP-92.	Shillito, John & Co., Cincinnati	500.00
EP-75.	Drake's Plantation Bitters, Ribbed frame	950.00	EP-93.	Steinfeld, S., N.Y.	1,750.00
EP-76.	Ellis, McAlpin & Co., Cincinnati	2,000.00	EP-93a.	Taylor, N.G. & Co., Philadelphia	1,450.00
EP-76a.	Evans, G.G.	950.00	EP-94.	Weir & Larminie, Montreal, Canada	1,400.00
EP-77.	Gage Brothers & Drake, Chicago	400.00	EP-95.	White the Hatter, N.Y.	1,500.00
EP-78.	Gault, J., Plain frame	375.00			
EP-79.	Gault, J., Ribbed frame	450.00			

9 CENT STRIPS

EP-95a.	Three 3¢ stamps in a brass, rectangular frame, sometimes referred to as having a Feuchtwanger back. Of doubtful origin	275.00

10 CENT STAMPS

No.	Issued By	Value	No.	Issued By	Value
EP-96.	Ayer's Cathartic Pills. Short arrows	500.00	EP-111.	Drake's Plantation Bitters, Ribbed frame	875.00
EP-96a.	As above, but long arrows	475.00	EP-112.	Ellis, McAlpin & Co., Cincinnati	1,250.00
EP-97.	"Take Ayer's Pills"	475.00	EP-113.	Evans, G.G.	1,200.00
EP-98.	Ayer's Sarsaparilla, Plain frame	550.00	EP-114.	Gage Brothers & Drake, Chicago, Plain frame	425.00
EP-98a.	As above, but medium "Ayer's" (EP-98 is small)	500.00	EP-115.	Gage Brother & Drake, Chicago, Ribbed frame	1,200.00
EP-98b.	As above, but large "Ayer's"	4550.00	EP-116.	Gault, J., Plain frame	325.00
EP-99.	Ayer's Sarsaparilla, Ribbed frame	750.00	EP-117.	Gault, J., Ribbed frame	525.00
EP-100.	Bailey & Co., Philadelphia	950.00	EP-117a.	Hopkins, L.C. & Co., Cincinnati	1,500.00
EP-101.	Bates, Joseph L., Boston, Plain frame	550.00	EP-118.	Hunt & Nash, Irving House, N.Y., Plain frame	475.00
EP-102.	Bates, Joseph L., Boston, Ribbed frame	850.00	EP-119.	Hunt & Nash, Irving House, N.Y., Ribbed frame	650.00
EP-102a.	Same, "Fancygoods" in one word. Plain.	600.00	EP-120.	Kirkpatrick & Gault, N.Y.	375.00
EP-103.	Brown's Bronchial Troches	500.00	EP-121.	Lord & Taylor, N.Y.	900.00
EP-104.	Buhl, F. & Co., Detroit	950.00	EP-122.	Mendum's Family Wine Emporium, N.Y., Plain frame	600.00
EP-105.	Burnett's Cocoaine Kalliston	450.00			
EP-106.	Burnett's Cooking Extracts, Plain frame	400.00	EP-123.	Mendum's Family Wine Emporium, N.Y., Ribbed frame	1,750.00
EP-107.	Burnett's Cooking Extracts, Ribbed frame	950.00			
EP-108.	Cook, H.A., Evansville, Ind	900.00	EP-124.	Norris, John W., Chicago	2,000.00
EP-108a.	Claflin, A.M., Hopkinton, R.I.	5,250.00	EP-125.	North American Life Insurance Co., N.Y., Plain frame, straight inscr.	600.00
EP-109.	Dougan, N.Y.	1,850.00			
EP-110.	Drake's Plantation Bitters, Plain frame	350.00	EP-125a.	As above, but curved inscr.	650.00

10 CENT STAMPS

No.	Issued By	Value	No.	Issued By	Value
EP-126.	North American Life Insurance Co., N.Y., Ribbed frame, curved inscr.	1,500.00	EP-130.	Shillito, John & Co., Cincinnati	800.00
EP-127.	Pearce, Tolle & Holton, Cincinnati	2,250.00	EP-131.	Steinfeld, S., N.Y.	1,750.00
EP-128.	Sands Ale	2,500.00	EP-132.	Taylor, N. & Co., Philadelphia	1,750.00
EP-129.	Schapker & Bussing, Evansville, Ind.	700.00	EP-133	Weir & Larminie, Montreal, Canada	1,500.00
			EP-134.	White the Hatter, N.Y.	1,500.00

12 CENT STAMPS

No.	Issued By	Value	No.	Issued By	Value
EP-135.	Ayer's Cathartic Pills	850.00	EP-149.	Gault, J., Ribbed frame	1,450.00
EP-136.	"Take Ayer's Pills"	1,000.00	EP-150.	Hunt & Nash, Irving House, N.Y., Plain frame	1,000.00
EP-137.	Ayer's Sarsaparilla, Medium "Ayer's"	900.00	EP-151.	Hunt & Nash, Irving House, N.Y., Ribbed frame	1,450.00
EP-137a.	As above, but small "Ayer's"	1,500.00	EP-152.	Kirkpatrick & Gault, N.Y.	700.00
EP-138.	Bailey & Co., Philadelphia	1,750.00	EP-153.	Lord & Taylor, N.Y.	1,750.00
EP-139.	Bates, Joseph L., Boston	1,000.00	EP-154.	Mendum's Family Wine Emporium, N.Y.	1,250.00
EP-140.	Brown's Bronchial Troches	1,000.00	EP-155.	North American Life Insurance Co., N.Y.	1,500.00
EP-141.	Buhl, F. & Co., Detroit	1,450.00	EP-156.	Pearce, Tolle & Holton, Cincinnati	3,000.00
EP-142.	Burnett's Cocoaine Kalliston	1,250.00	EP-156a.	Sands Ale	3,500.00
EP-143.	Bumett's Cooking Extracts	1,250.00	EP-157.	Schapker & Bussing, Evansville, Ind.	1,750.00
EP-144.	Claflin, A.M., Hopkinton, R.I.	6,500.00	EP-158.	Shillito, John & Co., Cincinnati	2,000.00
EP-145.	Drake's Plantation Bitters	800.00	EP-159.	Steinfeld, S., N.Y.	2,750.00
EP-146.	Ellis, McAlpin & Co., Cincinnati	2,500.00	EP-159a.	Taylor, N.G. & Co., Philadelphia	3,500.00
EP-147	Gage Brothers & Drake, Chicago	1,350.00			
EP-148.	Gault, J., Plain frame	900.00			

24 CENT STAMPS

No.	Issued By	Value	No.	Issued By	Value
EP-159b.	Ayer's Cathartic Pills	2,000.00	EP-167.	Gault, J., Plain frame	1,500.00
EP-160.	Ayer's Sarsaparilla	2,000.00	EP-168.	Gault, J., Ribbed frame	2,250.00
EP-160a.	Bates, Joseph L., Boston	Unique	EP-169.	Hunt & Nash, Irving House, N.Y., Plain frame	1,750.00
EP-161.	Brown's Bronchial Troches	2,500.00	EP-170.	Hunt & Nash, Irving House, N.Y., Ribbed frame	2,250.00
EP-162.	Buhl, F. & Co., Detroit	2,500.00	EP-171.	Kirkpatrick & Gault, N.Y.	1,500.00
EP-163.	Burnett's Cocoaine Kalliston	2,250.00	EP-172.	Lord & Taylor, N.Y.	2,300.00
EP-164.	Burnett's Cooking Extracts	1,950.00	EP-172a.	Pearce, Tolle & Holton, Cincinnati	2,750.00
EP-165.	Drake's Plantation Bitters	2,000.00			
EP-166.	Ellis, McAlpin & Co., Cincinnati	1,900.00			

30 CENT STAMPS

No.	Issued By	Value	No.	Issued By	Value
EP-172b.	Ayer's Cathartic Pills	2,750.00	EP-178.	Gault, J., Plain frame	2,250.00
EP-173.	Ayer's Sarsaparilla	2,750.00	EP-179.	Gault, J., Ribbed frame	3,600.00
EP-174.	Brown's Bronchial Troches	3,500.00	EP-180.	Hunt & Nash, Irving House, N.Y.	3,350.00
EP-175.	Burnett's Cocoaine Kalliston	3,000.00	EP-181.	Kirkpatrick & Gault, N.Y.	2,500.00
EP-176.	Burnett's Cooking Extracts	3,000.00	EP-182.	Lord & Taylor, N.Y.	2,950.00
EP-177.	Drake's Plantation Bitters	3,250.00	EP-183.	Sands Ale	3,850.00

90 CENT STAMPS

No.	Issued By	Value	No.	Issued By	Value
EP-183a.	"Take Ayer's Pills"	5,250.00	EP-185.	Drake's Plantation Bitters	8,000.00
EP-183b.	Ayer's Sarsaparilla	5,000.00	EP-186.	Gault, J.	6,250.00
EP-184.	Burnett's Cocoaine Kalliston	8,250.00	EP-187.	Kirkpatrick & Gault, N.Y.	5,750.00
EP-184a.	Burnett's Cooking Extracts	Unique	EP-188.	Lord & Taylor, N.Y.	5,500.00

According to Arnold Perl, well-known authority on encased postage, a number of other, unlisted specimens have been seen bearing stamps other than the conventional ones. Several bear the 1851 1 cent stamp, envelope stamps, etc. Research indicates these to be trial pieces or specimens—never released for general issuance by Gault. They are unquestionably authentic and a part, at least, of the history of encased U.S. postage stamps.

PART FIVE
COLONIAL AND CONTINENTAL CURRENCY
XXIII. ISSUES OF THE CONTINENTAL CONGRESS
(CONTINENTAL CURRENCY)

The notes listed are representative of the types of this currency; there are actually hundreds of different varieties. Any notes signed by signers of the Declaration of Independence, the Constitution or the Articles of Confederation command an additional 50-100% above the prices listed. Unless otherwise indicated, the illustrations in this section are from the collection of the Federal Reserve Bank of San Francisco. (Notes marked with as asterisk (*) are illustrated.

		VG	VF	UNC
May 10, 1775				
CC-1	$1	40.00	85.00	200.00
CC-2	$2	30.00	65.00	180.00
CC-3	$3	30.00	65.00	180.00
CC-4	$4	30.00	65.00	180.00
CC-5	$5	30.00	65.00	180.00
CC-6	$6	30.00	65.00	180.00
CC-7	$7	30.00	65.00	180.00
CC-8	$8	30.00	65.00	180.00
CC-9	$20	400.00	900.00	2200.00
CC-10	$30	45.00	100.00	250.00
November 29, 1775				
CC-11	$1	25.00	50.00	140.00
CC-12	$2	25.00	50.00	140.00
CC-13	$3	25.00	50.00	140.00
CC-14	$4	25.00	50.00	140.00
CC-15	$5	25.00	50.00	140.00
CC-16	$6	25.00	50.00	140.00
CC-17	$7	25.00	50.00	140.00
CC-18	$8	25.00	50.00	140.00
February 17, 1776				
CC-19	$1/6	35.00	65.00	400.00
CC-20*	$1/3	35.00	65.00	400.00
CC-21	$1/2	35.00	65.00	400.00
CC-22	$2/3	35.00	65.00	400.00
CC-23	$1	22.00	45.00	180.00
CC-24	$2	22.00	45.00	180.00
CC-25	$3	22.00	45.00	180.00
CC-26	$4	22.00	45.00	180.00
CC-27	$5	25.00	50.00	200.00
CC-28	$6	25.00	50.00	200.00
CC-29	$7	25.00	50.00	200.00
CC-30	$8	25.00	50.00	200.00
May 9, 1776				
CC-31	$1	22.00	45.00	140.00
CC-32	$2	22.00	45.00	140.00
CC-33	$3	22.00	45.00	140.00
CC-34	$4	22.00	45.00	140.00
CC-35	$5	22.00	45.00	140.00
CC-36	$6	22.00	45.00	140.00
CC-37	$7	22.00	45.00	140.00
CC-38	$8	22.00	45.00	140.00
July 22, 1776				
CC-39	$2	25.00	55.00	200.00
CC-40	$3	27.00	55.00	200.00
CC-41	$4	27.00	55.00	200.00
CC-42	$5	27.00	55.00	200.00
CC-43	$6	27.00	55.00	200.00
CC-44	$7	27.00	55.00	200.00
CC-45	$8	27.00	55.00	200.00
CC-46	$30	27.00	55.00	200.00
November 2, 1776				
CC-47	$2	27.00	55.00	170.00
CC-48	$3	27.00	55.00	170.00

		VG	VF	UNC
CC-49	$4	27.00	55.00	170.00
CC-50	$5	27.00	55.00	170.00
CC-51	$6	27.00	55.00	170.00
CC-52	$7	27.00	55.00	170.00
CC-53	$8	27.00	55.00	170.00
CC-54	$30	27.00	55.00	170.00
February 26, 1777				
CC-55	$2	35.00	65.00	200.00
CC-56	$3	35.00	65.00	200.00
CC-57	$4	35.00	65.00	200.00
CC-58	$5	35.00	65.00	200.00
CC-59	$6	35.00	65.00	200.00
CC-60	$7	35.00	65.00	200.00
CC-61	$8	35.00	65.00	200.00
CC-62	$30	35.00	65.00	200.00
May 20, 1777				
CC-63	$2	45.00	140.00	400.00
CC-64	$3	45.00	140.00	400.00
CC-65	$4	45.00	140.00	400.00
CC-66	$5	45.00	140.00	400.00
CC-67	$6	45.00	140.00	400.00
CC-68	$7	45.00	140.00	400.00
CC-69	$8	45.00	140.00	400.00
CC-70	$30	45.00	140.00	400.00
April 11, 1778				
CC-71	$4	220.00	450.00	1200.00
CC-72	$5	220.00	450.00	1200.00
CC-73	$6	220.00	450.00	1200.00
CC-74	$7	220.00	450.00	1200.00
CC-75	$8	200.00	400.00	1000.00
CC-76	$20	200.00	400.00	1000.00
CC-77	$30	200.00	400.00	1000.00
CC-78	$40	200.00	400.00	1000.00
September 26, 1778				
CC-79	$5	27.00	60.00	160.00
CC-80	$7	27.00	60.00	160.00
CC-81	$8	27.00	60.00	160.00
CC-82	$20	27.00	60.00	160.00
CC-83	$30	25.00	55.00	150.00
CC-84	$40	25.00	55.00	150.00
CC-85	$50	25.00	55.00	150.00
CC-86	$60	25.00	55.00	150.00
January 14, 1779				
CC-87	$1	35.00	60.00	190.00
CC-88	$2	35.00	60.00	190.00
CC-89	$3	35.00	60.00	190.00
CC-90	$4	35.00	60.00	190.00
CC-91	$5	35.00	60.00	190.00
CC-92	$20	35.00	60.00	190.00
CC-93	$30	30.00	50.00	180.00
CC-94	$35	30.00	50.00	180.00
CC-95	$40	30.00	50.00	180.00
CC-96	$45	30.00	50.00	180.00
CC-97	$50	30.00	50.00	180.00
CC-98	$55	30.00	50.00	180.00

		VG	VF	UNC
CC-99	$60	30.00	50.00	180.00
CC-100	$65	30.00	50.00	180.00
CC-101	$70	40.00	80.00	210.00
CC-102	$80	50.00	100.00	250.00

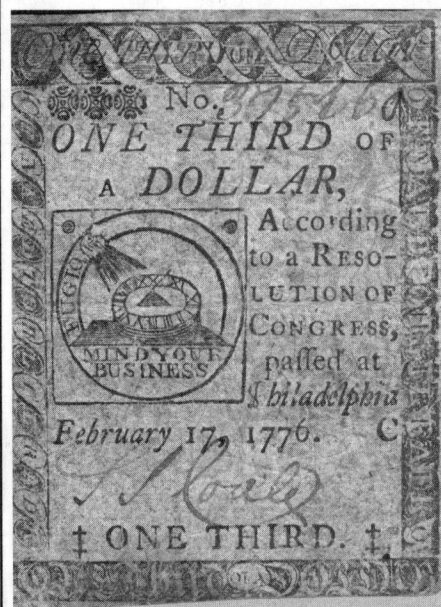

Above illustrations reduced in size.

XXIV. ISSUES OF THE STATES (COLONIAL CURRENCY)
CONNECTICUT

ALL OF THE ISSUES FROM CT-1 TO CT-104 ARE VERY RARE

July 12, 1709

There are four variations of this issue as follows:
a. The regular issues of July 12, 1709.
b. Identical except for a large AR monogram on the face.
c. Identical except redated "May 1713" below 1709"
d. Identical to type "c" except flowers replace the scroll on back

CT-1a	2s	CT-5a	10s	
CT-1b	2s	CT-5b	10s	
CT-1c	2s	CT-5c	10s	
CT-1d	2s	CT-5d	10s	
CT-2a	2s/6d	CT-6a	20s	
CT-2b	2s/6d	CT-6b	20s	
CT-2c	2s/6d	CT-6c	20s	
CT-2d	2s/6d	CT-6d	20s	
CT-3a	3s	CT-7a	40s	
CT-3b	3s	CT-7b	40s	
CT-3c	3s	CT-7c	40s	
CT-3d	3s	CT-7d	40s	
CT-4a	5s	CT-8a	£5	
CT-4b	5s	CT-8b	£5	
CT-4c	5s	CT-8c	£5	
CT-4d	5s	CT-8d	£5	

December 1, 1724

CT-9	10s	CT-11	40s
CT-10	20s	CT-12	£5

November 7, 1727

CT-13	2s	CT-17	10s
CT-14	2s/6d	CT-18	20s
CT-15	3s	CT-19	40s
CT-16	5s	CT-20	£5

October, 1728

CT-21	10s	CT-23	40s
CT-22	20s	CT-24	£5

May, 1729

CT-25	2s	CT-29	10s
CT-26	2s/6d	CT-30	20s
CT-27	3s	CT-31	40s
CT-28	5s	CT-32	£5

August, 1732

CT-33	2s	CT-37	10s
CT-34	2s/6d	CT-38	20s
CT-35	3s	CT-39	40s
CT-36	5s	CT-40	£5

July 10, 1733

There are five variations of this issue as follows:
a. The original issue of July 10, 1733
b. Redated 1735
c. Redated May 1740
d. Redated May 1740 and July 8, 740 on reverse
e. Redated May 8, 1746

CT-41a	2s	CT-45c	10s
CT-41b	2s	CT-45d	10s
CT-41c	2s	CT-46a	20s
CT-42a	2s/6d	CT-46b	20s
CT-42b	2s/6d	CT-46c	20s
CT-42e	2s/6d	CT-46d	20s
CT-43a	3s	CT-47a	40s
CT-43b	3s	CT-47b	40s
CT-43e	3s	CT-47c	40s
CT-44a	5s	CT-47d	40s
CT-44b	Ss	CT-48a	£5
CT-44e	5s	CT-48b	£5
CT-45a	10s	CT-48c	£5
CT-45b	10s	CT-48d	£5

May 8, 1740

There are five variations of this issue as follows:
a. The original issue of May 8, 1740
b. Redated May 10, 1744
c. Redated October 11, 1744
d. Redated March 14, 1744 (1745 on reverse)
e. Redated May 8, 1746

CT-49a	1s	CT-53a	12s
CT-49b	1s	CT-53b	12s
CT-49c	1s	CT-53c	12s
CT-49d	1s	CT-53d	12s
CT-49e	1s	CT-53e	12s
CT-50a	2s	CT-54a	20s
CT-50b	2s	CT-54b	20s
CT-50c	2s	CT-54c	20s
CT-50d	2s	CT-54d	20s
CT-50e	2s	CT-54e	20s
CT-51a	4s	CT-55a	40s
CT-51b	4s	CT-55b	40s
CT-51c	4s	CT-55c	40s
CT-51d	4s	CT-55d	40s
CT-51e	4s	CT-55e	40s
CT-52a	7s	CT-56a	£3
CT-52b	7s	CT-56b	£3
CT-52c	7s	CT-56c	£3
CT-52d	7s	CT-56d	£3
CT-52e	7s	CT-56e	£3

January 8, 1755

CT-57	9d	Very Rare
CT-58	1s	Very Rare
CT-59	2s/6d	Very Rare
CT-60	5s	Very Rare
CT-61	10s	Very Rare
CT-62	20s	Very Rare
CT-63	30s	Very Rare
CT-64	40s	Very Rare

March 13, 1755

CT-65	9d	Very Rare
CT-66	1s	Very Rare
CT-67	2s/6d	Very Rare
CT-68	5s	Very Rare
CT-69	10s	Very Rare
CT-70	20s	Very Rare
CT-71	30s	Very Rare
CT-72	40s	Very Rare

August 27, 1755

CT-73	9d	Very Rare
CT-74	1s	Very Rare
CT-75	2s/6d	Very Rare
CT-76	5s	Very Rare
CT-77	10s	Very Rare
CT-78	20s	Very Rare
CT-79	30s	Very Rare
CT-80	40s	Very Rare

October 9, 1755

CT-81	9d	Very Rare
CT-82	1s	Very Rare
CT-83	2s/6d	Very Rare
CT-84	5s	Very Rare
CT-85	10s	Very Rare
CT-86	20s	Very Rare
CT-87	30s	Very Rare
CT-88	40s	Very Rare

March 8, 1758

CT-89	9d	Very Rare
CT-90	1s	Very Rare
CT-91	2s/6d	Very Rare
CT-92	5s	Very Rare
CT-93	10	Very Rare
CT-94	20	Very Rare
CT-95	30s	Very Rare
CT-96	40s	Very Rare

February 7, 1759

CT-97	9d	Very Rare
CT-98	1s	Very Rare
CT-99	2s/6d	Very Rare
CT-100	5s	Very Rare
CT-101	10s	Very Rare
CT-102	20s	Very Rare
CT-103	30s	Very Rare
CT-104	40s	Very Rare

March 8, 1759

		VG	VF	UNC
CT-105	9d	1500.00	2000.00	Rare
CT-106	1s	1500.00	2000.00	Rare
CT-107	2s/6d	1500.00	2000.00	Rare
CT-108	5s	1500.00	2000.00	Rare
CT-109	10s	1500.00	2000.00	Rare
CT-110	20s	1500.00	2000.00	Rare
CT-111	30s	1500.00	2000.00	Rare
CT-112	40s	1500.00	2000.00	Rare

May 10, 1759

		VG	VF	UNC
CT-113	9d	1500.00	2000.00	Rare
CT-114	1s	1500.00	2000.00	Rare
CT-115	2s/6d	1500.00	2000.00	Rare
CT-116	5s	1500.00	2000.00	Rare
CT-117	10s	1500.00	2000.00	Rare
CT-118	20s	1500.00	2000.00	Rare
CT-119	30s	1500.00	2000.00	Rare
CT-120	40s	1500.00	2000.00	Rare

March 13, 1760

		VG	VF	UNC
CT-121	9d	1500.00	2000.00	Rare
CT-122	1s	1500.00	2000.00	Rare
CT-123	2s/6d	1500.00	2000.00	Rare
CT-124	5s	1500.00	2000.00	Rare
CT-125	10s	1500.00	2000.00	Rare
CT-126	20s	1500.00	2000.00	Rare
CT-127	30s	1500.00	2000.00	Rare
CT-128	40s	1500.00	2000.00	Rare

March 26, 1761

		VF
CT-129	9d	Very Rare
CT-130	1s	Very Rare
CT-131	2s/6d	Very Rare
CT-132	5s	Very Rare
CT-133	10s	Very Rare
CT-134	20s	Very Rare
CT-135	30s	Very Rare
CT-136	40s	Very Rare

NOTE: ALL VALUATIONS FROM CT-137 FORWARD ARE FOR CANCELED NOTES. UNCANCELED SPECIMENS ARE WORTH TWICE THE LISTED PRICES.

March 4, 1762

		VF
CT-137	9d	Very Rare
CT-138	1s	Very Rare
CT-139	2s/6d	Very Rare
CT-140	5S	Very Rare
CT-141	10s	Very Rare
CT-142	20s	Very Rare
CT-143	30s	Very Rare
CT-144	40s	Very Rare

May 12, 1763

		VG	VF	UNC
CT-145	5s	1500.00	2500.00	3500.00
CT-146	10s	1500.00	2500.00	3500.00
CT-147	20s	1500.00	2500.00	3500.00
CT-148	30s	1500.00	2500.00	3500.00
CT-149	40s	1500.00	2500.00	3500.00

March 8, 1764

		VG	VF	UNC
CT-150	9d		Very Rare	
CT-151	1s		Very Rare	
CT-152	1s/6d		Very Rare	
CT-153	2s/6d		Very Rare	
CT-154	5s		Very Rare	
CT-155	10s	1000.00	1750.00	Rare

		VG	VF	UNC
CT-156	20s	1000.00	1750.00	Rare
CT-157	30s	1000.00	1750.00	Rare
CT-158	40s	1000.00	1750.00	Rare

May 10, 1770

		VG	VF	UNC
CT-159	2s/6d	100.00	250.00	Rare
CT-160	5s	100.00	250.00	Rare
CT-161	10s		Very Rare	
CT-162	20s		Very Rare	
CT-163	40s		Very Rare	

October 10, 1771

		VG	VF	UNC
CT-164	2s/6d	80.00	125.00	Rare
CT-165	5s	80.00	125.00	Rare
CT-166	10s	80.00	125.00	Rare
CT-167	20s	80.00	125.00	Rare
CT-168	40s	80.00	125.00	Rare

June 1, 1773

		VG	VF	UNC
CT-169	2s/6d	65.00	100.00	Rare
CT-170	5s	65.00	100.00	Rare
CT-171	10s	65.00	100.00	Rare
CT-172	20s	65.00	100.00	Rare
CT-173	40s	65.00	100.00	Rare

January 2, 1775

		VG	VF	UNC
CT-174	2s/6d	55.00	80.00	325.00
CT-175	5s	55.00	80.00	325.00
CT-176	10s	55.00	80.00	325.00
CT-177	20s	55.00	80.00	325.00
CT-178	40s	55.00	80.00	325.00

May 10, 1775

		VG	VF	UNC
CT-179	2s/6d	27.00	40.00	165.00
CT-180	10s	27.00	40.00	165.00
CT-181	20s	27.00	40.00	165.00
CT-182*	40s	27.00	40.00	165.00

June 1, 1775

		VG	VF	UNC
CT-183	2s/6d	22.00	35.00	150.00
CT-184	6s	22.00	35.00	150.00
CT-185	10s	20.00	35.00	150.00
CT-186	20s	22.00	35.00	150.00
CT-187	40s	22.00	35.00	150.00

July 1, 1775

		VG	VF	UNC
CT-188	2s	22.00	35.00	150.00
CT-189	2s/6d	22.00	35.00	150.00
CT-190	6s	22.00	35.00	150.00
CT-191	10s	22.00	35.00	150.00
CT-192	20s	22.00	35.00	150.00
CT-193	40s	22.00	35.00	150.00

June 7, 1776

CT-194	1s	35.00	55.00	150.00
CT-195	1s/3d	35.00	55.00	150.00
CT-196	2s	35.00	55.00	150.00
CT-197	2s/6d	35.00	55.00	150.00
CT-198	3s	35.00	55.00	150.00
CT-199	5s	35.00	55.00	150.00
CT-200	6s	35.00	55.00	150.00
CT-201	10s	35.00	55.00	150.00
CT-202	15s	35.00	55.00	150.00
CT-203	£1	35.00	55.00	150.00
CT-204	£2	35.00	55.00	150.00

June 19, 1776

CT-205	6d	15.00	25.00	90.00
CT-206	9d	15.00	25.00	90.00

		VG	VF	UNC
CT-207	1s	15.00	25.00	90.00
CT-208	1s/3d	15.00	25.00	90.00
CT-209	1s/6d	15.00	25.00	90.00
CT-210	2s	15.00	25.00	90.00
CT-211	2s/6d	15.00	25.00	90.00
CT-212	5s	15.00	25.00	90.00
CT-213	40s	15.00	25.00	90.00

October 11, 1777

CT-214	2d	20.00	30.00	80.00
CT-215	3d	20.00	30.00	80.00
CT-216*	4d	20.00	30.00	80.00
CT-217	5d	20.00	30.00	80.00
CT-218	7d	20.00	30.00	80.00

The above issue normally appears on blue paper; however, there are notes on white paper which are worth 50% above the listed prices.

March 1, 1780

CT-219	9d	18.00	25.00	50.00
CT-220	1s/3d	18.00	25.00	50.00
CT-221	2s/6d	18.00	25.00	50.00
CT-222	5s	18.00	25.00	50.00
CT-223	10s	18.00	25.00	50.00
CT-224	20s	18.00	25.00	50.00
CT-225	40s	18.00	25.00	50.00

June 1, 1780

CT-226	9d	20.00	30.00	60.00
CT-227	1s/3d	20.00	30.00	60.00
CT-228	2s/6d	20.00	30.00	60.00
CT-229	5s	20.00	30.00	60.00
CT-230	10s	20.00	30.00	60.00
CT-231	20s	20.00	30.00	60.00
CT-232	40s	20.00	30.00	60.00

July 1, 1780

CT-233	9d	18.00	25.00	50.00
CT-234	1s	18.00	25.00	50.00
CT-235	1s/3d	18.00	25.00	50.00
CT-236	2s/6d	18.00	25.00	50.00
CT-237	5s	18.00	25.00	50.00
CT-238	10s	18.00	25.00	50.00
CT-238	20s	18.00	25.00	50.00
CT-240	40s	18.00	25.00	50.00

DELAWARE

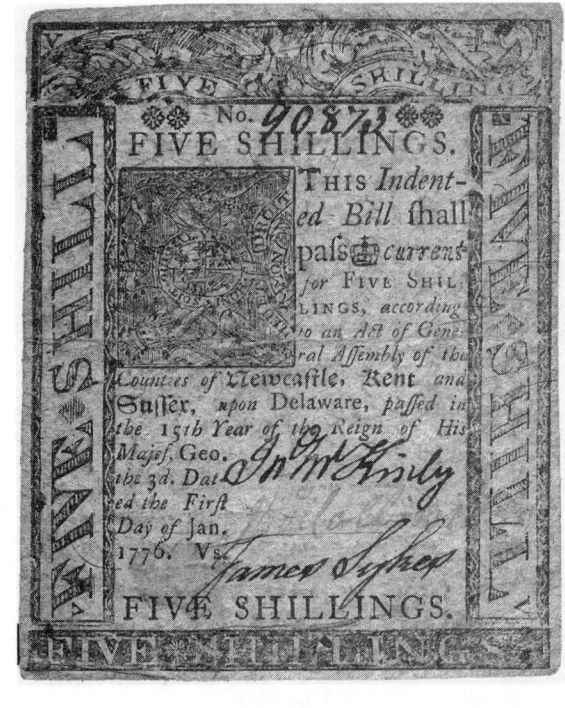

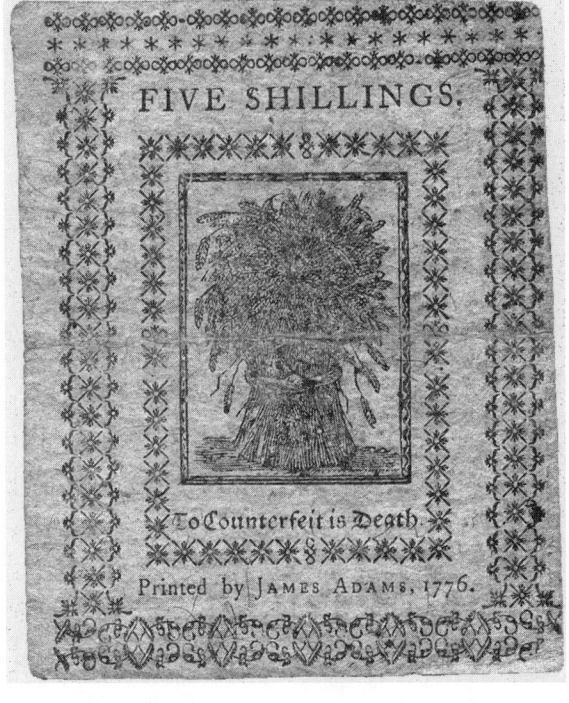

ALL ISSUES UNTIL THAT OF FEBRUARY 28, 1776 ARE VERY RARE.

1729

DE-1	1s	DE-5	5s
DE-2	18d	DE-6	10s
DE-3	2s	DE-7	15s
DE4	2s/6d	DE-8	20s

March 1, 1734

DE-9	1s	DE-13	5s
DE-10	18d	DE-14	10s
DE-11	2s	DE-15	15s
DE-12	2s/6d	DE-16	20s

December 1, 1739

DE-17	1s	DE-20	2s/6d
DE-18	18d	DE-21	5s
DE-19	2s	DE-22	10s

February 28, 1746

		VG	VF	UNC
DE-23	1s	Rare	Very Rare	
DE-24	18d	Rare	Rare	Very Rare
DE-25	2s	Rare	Rare	Very Rare
DE-26	2s/6d	Rare	Rare	Very Rare
DE-27	5s	125.00	Rare	Very Rare
DE-28	10s	125.00	Rare	Very Rare
DE-29	15s	125.00	Rare	Very Rare
DE-30	20s	125.00	Rare	Very Rare

January 1, 1753

DE-31	1s	Very Rare
DE-32	18d	Very Rare
DE-33	2s	Very Rare
DE-34	2s/6d	Very Rare
DE-35	5s	Very Rare
DE-36	10s	Very Rare

May 1, 1756

DE-37	1s	Very Rare
DE-38	18d	Very Rare
DE-39	2s	Very Rare
DE-40	2s/6d	Very Rare

		VG	VF	UNC
DE-41	5s	150.00	Very Rare	
DE-42	10s	150.00	Very Rare	
DE-43	15s	150.00	Very Rare	
DE-44	20s	150.00	Very Rare	

March 1, 1758

DE-45	1s	Very Rare
DE46	18d	Very Rare
DE-47	2s	Very Rare
DE-48	2s/6d	Very Rare
DE-49	5s	140.00	Very Rare
DE-50	10s	140.00	Very Rare
DE-51	15s	140.00	Very Rare
DE-52	20s	140.00	Very Rare

May 1, 1758

DE-53	1s	Very Rare
DE-54	18d	Very Rare
DE-55	2s	Very Rare
DE-56	2s/6d	Very Rare
DE-57	5s	200.00	Very Rare
DE-58	10s	200.00	Very Rare
DE-59	15s	200.00	Very Rare
DE-60	20s	200.00	Very Rare

June 1, 1759

DE-61	1s		Very Rare	
DE-62	18d		Very Rare	
DE-63	2s		Very Rare	
DE-64	2s/6d		Very Rare	
DE-65	5s	225.00	400.00	Rare

		VG	VF	UNC
DE-66	10s	225.00	400.00	Rare
DE-67	15s	225.00	350.00	Rare
DE-68	20s	225.00	350.00	Rare

May 31, 1760

DE-69	20s	150.00	450.00	Rare
DE-70	30s	150.00	450.00	Rare
DE-71	40s	150.00	450.00	Rare
DE-72	50s	150.00	450.00	Rare

January 1, 1776

DE-73	1s	28.00	55.00	125.00
DE-74	18d	28.00	55.00	125.00
DE-75	2s/6d	28.00	55.00	125.00
DE-76	4s	28.00	55.00	125.00
DE-77*	5s	28.00	55.00	125.00
DE-78	6s	28.00	55.00	125.00
DE-79	10s	28.00	55.00	125.00
DE-80	20s	28.00	55.00	125.00

May 1, 1777

DE-81	3d	55.00	100.00	270.00
DE-82	4d	55.00	100.00	270.00
DE-83	6d	55.00	100.00	270.00
DE-84	9d	55.00	100.00	270.00
DE-85	1s	40.00	70.00	185.00
DE-86	18d	40.00	70.00	185.00
DE-87	2s/6d	40.00	70.00	185.00
DE-88	4s	40.00	70.00	185.00
DE-89	5s	40.00	70.00	185.00
DE-90	6s	40.00	70.00	185.00
DE-91	10s	40.00	70.00	185.00
DE-92	20s	40.00	70.00	185.00

GEORGIA

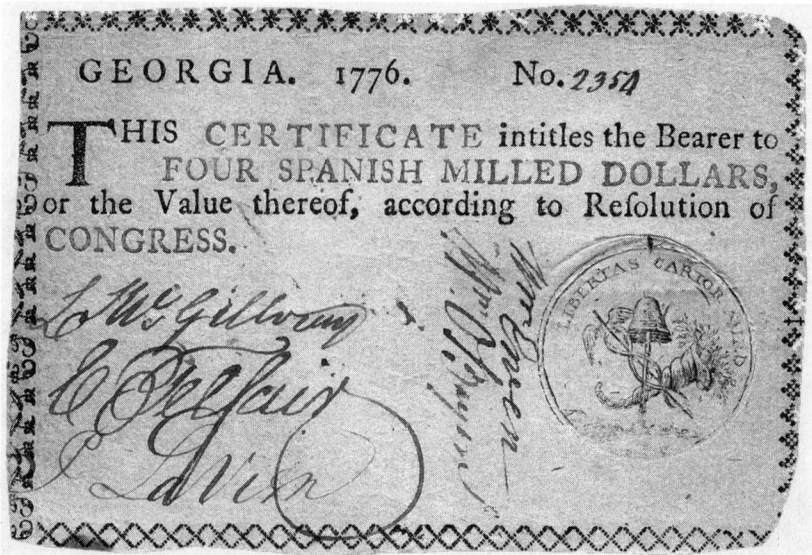

ALL ISSUES FROM GA-1 TO GA-39 ARE EXTREMELY RARE

Issues of 1735-1745 (Oglethorpe)

GA-1	1s	GA-3	5s
GA-2	4s	GA-4	£1

Issues of 1735-50 (Sola)

GA-5	£1	GA-8	£10
GA-6	£2	GA-9	£20
GA-7	£5		

1755

GA-11	3d	GA-20	3s
GA-12	4d	GA-21	3s/6d
GA-13	6d	GA-22	4s
GA-14	9d	GA-23	5s
GA-15	1s	GA-24	10s
GA-16	1s/3d	GA-25	20s
GA-17	1s/6d		
GA-18	2s		
GA-19	2s/6d		

May 1, 1760

GA-26	£1

1762

GA-27	2d	GA-33	1s/3d
GA-28	3d	GA-34	1s/6d
GA-29	4d	GA-35	2s
GA-30	6d	GA-36	2s/6d
GA-31	9d	GA-37	3s
GA-32	1s	GA-38	3s/6d

		VG	VF
GA-39	4s		
GA-40	5s	1500.00	Very Rare
GA-41	10s	1500.00	Very Rare
GA-42	20s	1500.00	Very Rare
GA-42a	Horse	1500.00	Very Rare

March 25, 1762

GA-43	£1	Very Rare

July 8, 1765

GA-44	£1	Very Rare

1766-1767
(Savannah Courthouse, written dates)

GA-45	£1	Very Rare

		VG	VF	UNC
1768-1770				
(Tax Certificates)				
GA-46	£5		Very Rare	
1769				
(Lighthouse, written dates)				
GA-47	£1	900.00	Rare	Rare
Issue of 1773				
GA-48	20s	700.00	Rare	Rare
1774 (December 31, 1777)				
GA-49	1s		Extremely Rare	
GA-50	2s		Extremely Rare	
GA-51	2s/6d		Extremely Rare	
GA-52	5s		Extremely Rare	
GA-53	10s	800.00	Rare	Rare
1775				
GA-54	1s/6d		Extremely Rare	
GA-55	2s/6d		Extremely Rare	
GA-56	5s		Extremely Rare	
GA-57	10s		Extremely Rare	
GA-58	20s		Extremely Rare	
GA-59	60s		Extremely Rare	
GA-60	£5		Extremely Rare	
1776				
(Many different border varieties exist)				
GA-61	3d	180.00	300.00	Rare
GA-62	6d	200.00	325.00	Rare
GA-63	1s	225.00	350.00	Rare
GA-64	1/6d	240.00	375.00	Rare
GA-65	2s/6d	260.00	400.00	Rare
GA-65a	2s/6d	260.00	400.00	Rare
GA-66	5s	275.00	425.00	Rare
GA-66a	5s	550.00	600.00	Rare
GA-67	10s	300.00	450.00	Rare
GA-68	£1	325.00	500.00	Rare
1776 (Fractional Dollar Denominations)				
(Many different border varieties exist).				
GA-69	$1/4	270.00	450.00	Rare
GA-70	$1/2	300.00	475.00	Rare

1776 (Dollar Denominations)
There are different color vignettes in this issue; they are:
- a) blue   b) maroon
- c) orange ` d) green
- e) blue-green

		VG	VF	UNC
GA-71a	$1	160.00	300.00	Rare
GA-71c	$1	200.00	375.00	Rare
GA-71d	$1	160.00	300.00	Rare

		VG	VF	UNC
GA-71e	$1	250.00	450.00	Rare
Jugs				
GA-72a	$2	175.00	300.00	Rare
GA-72b	$2	200.00	325.00	Rare
GA-72c	$2	125.00	325.00	Rare
GA-72d	$2	200.00	375.00	Rare
Caduceus				
GA-73a	$2	165.00	325.00	Rare
Jugs				
GA-74a	$4	200.00	375.00	Rare
Caduceus				
GA-75a	$4	160.00	325.00	Rare
GA-75b	$4	200.00	375.00	Rare
GA-75c	$4	180.00	350.00	Rare
GA-75e	$4		Very Rare	
GA-76a	$10	200.00	375.00	Rare
GA-76b	$10	250.00	450.00	Rare
GA-76c	$10	225.00	400.00	Rare
GA-77a	$20	200.00	325.00	Rare
GA-77b	$20	225.00	400.00	Rare
GA-77c	$20	300.00	500.00	Rare
1776 (Payable in gold or silver)				
GA-78	$2	300.00	600.00	Rare
1776 (undated issue)				
GA-79	$3	350.00	700.00	Rare
GA-80*	$4	300.00	600.00	Rare
GA-81	$5	300.00	600.00	Rare
GA-82	$8	300.00	600.00	Rare
GA-83	$10	300.00	750.00	Rare
1777				
GA-84	$2	300.00	600.00	Rare
GA-85	$3	180.00	350. 00	Rare
GA-86	$4	400.00	800.00	Rare
GA-87	$5	180.00	350.00	Rare
GA-88	$7	300.00	600.00	Rare
GA-89	$9	300.00	600.00	Rare
GA-90	$11	250.00	500.00	Rare
GA-91	$13	250.00	500.00	Rare
GA-92	$15	300.00	600.00	Rare
GA-93	$17	300.00	600.00	Rare

June 8, 1777
(The fractional denominations also have the value in shillings/pence)
There are 2 varieties in this issue:
- a) red "n" in "in"
- b) black

		VG	VF	UNC
GA-94	$1/10	250.00	500.00	Rare
GA-95	$1/5	250.00	500.00	Rare
GA-96	$1/4	180.00	280.00	Rare
GA-97	$	180.00	280.00	Rare
GA-98	$2/5	180.00	280.00	Rare
GA-99	$1/2	180.00	280.00	Rare

		VG	VF	UNC
GA-100	$	180.00	280.00	Rare
GA-101	$3/4	180.00	280.00	Rare
GA-102	$4/5	150.00	225.00	Rare
GA-103a	$1	180.00	350.00	Rare
GA-103b	$1	250.00	500.00	Rare
GA-104a	$2	180.00	350.00	Rare
GA-104b	$2	250.00	500.00	Rare
GA-105a	$3	180.00	350.00	Rare
GA-105b	$3	250.00	500.00	Rare
GA-106a	$4	180.00	350.00	Rare
GA-106b	$4	250.00	500.00	Rare
GA-107a	$5	250.00	500.00	Rare
GA-107b	$5	375.00	750.00	Rare
GA-108a	$6	180.00	350.00	Rare
GA-108b	$6	200.00	500.00	Rare
GA-109a	$7	180.00	350.00	Rare
GA-109b	$7	250.00	500.00	Rare
GA-110a	$8	180.00	350.00	Rare
GA-110b	$8	250.00	500.00	Rare

September 10, 1777
(There are many border varieties on the fractional denominations)

		VG	VF	UNC
GA-111	$1/5	230.00	425.00	Rare
GA-112	$1/2	270.00	480.00	Rare
GA-113	$4/5	180.00	280.00	Rare
GA-114	$1	180.00	300.90	Rare
GA-115	$2	180.00	300.00	Rare
GA-116	$3	180.00	300.00	Rare
GA-117	$4	180.00	300.00	Rare
GA-118	$5	250.00	420.00	Rare
GA-119	$6	180.00	300.00	Rare
GA-120	$7	200.00	300.00	Rare
GA-121	$8	250.00	400.00	Rare

1778 (Numerous border varietes)

		VG	VF	UNC
GA-122	$20	250.00	500.00	1500.00
GA-123	$30	250.00	500.00	1500.00
GA-124	$40	300.00	600.00	1800.00

January 9, 1782 (written denominations)
Prices are for forged or falsely filled in text and signatures items; no genuine specimens are known.

		VG	VF	UNC
GA-125		600.00	900.00	Rare

October 16, 1786

		VG	VF	UNC
GA-126	6d	350.00	500.00	Rare
GA-127	1s	300.00	400.00	Rare
GA-128	2s/6d	250.00	350.00	1100.00
GA-129	5s	200.00	350.00	1000.00
GA-130	10s	200.00	350.00	1000.00
GA-131	20s	200.00	350.00	1000.00

MARYLAND

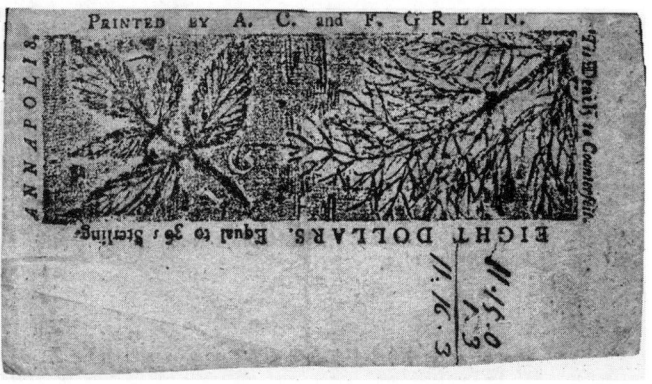

Illustration of this note is 3/4 actual size

ALL ISSUES UNTIL THAT OF JULY 14, 1756 ARE VERY RARE.

PRICES QUOTED FOR UNISSUED REMAINDER NOTES (MD1-7) ONLY.

1733

		VG	VF	UNC
MD-1	1s	—	150.00	300.00
MD-2	1s/6d	—	150.00	300.00
MD-3	2s/6d	—	150.00	300.00
MD4	5s	—	150.00	300.00
MD-5	10s	—	150.00	300.00
MD-6	15s	—	150.00	300.00
MD-7	20s	—	150.00	300.00

June 2, 1740

MD-8	1s
MD-9	1s/6d
MD-11	5s
MD-10	2s/6d
MD-12	10s
MD-13	15s
MD-14	20s

October 1, 1748

MD-15	1s
MD-16	1s/6d
MD-17	2s/6d
MD-18	5s
MD-19	10s
MD-20	15s
MD-21	20s

April 6, 1751

MD-22	1s
MD-23	1s/6d
MD-24	2s/6d
MD-25	5s
MD-26	10s
MD-27	15s
MD-28	20s

July 14, 1756

MD-29	6d
MD-30	1s
MD-31	1s/6d
MD-32	2s
MD-33	2s/6d
MD-34	5s
MD-35	10s
MD-36	15s
MD-37	20s

January 1, 1767

		VG	VF	UNC
MD-38	$1/9	45.00	85.00	Rare
MD-39	$1/6	45.00	85.00	Rare
MD-40	$2/9	45.00	85.00	Rare
MD-41	$1/3	45.00	80.00	Rare
MD-42	$1/2	40.00	80.00	Rare
MD-43	$2/3	40.00	80.00	Rare
MD-44	$1	40.00	80.00	Rare

		VG	VF	UNC
MD-45	$2	40.00	75.00	Rare
MD-46	$4	35.00	75.00	Rare
MD-47	$6	35.00	75.00	Rare
MD-48	$8	35.00	75.00	Rare

March 1, 1770

		VG	VF	UNC
MD-49	$1/9	40.00	75.00	400.00
MD-50	$1/6	40.00	75.00	400.00
MD-51	$2/9	40.00	75.00	350.00
MD-52	$1/3	40.00	75.00	350.00
MD-53	$1/2	35.00	70.00	300.00
MD-54	$2/3	35.00	70.00	300.00
MD-55	$1	35.00	70.00	300.00
MD-56	$2	35.00	65.00	250.00
MD-57	$4	30.00	65.00	250.00
MD-58	$6	30.00	65.00	250.00
MD-59	$8	30.00	65.00	250.00

April 10, 1774

		VG	VF	UNC
MD-60	$1/9	35.00	65.00	350.00
MD-61	$1/6	35.00	65.00	350.00
MD-62	$2/9	35.00	65.00	300.00
MD-63	$1/3	35.00	65.00	300.00
MD-64	$1/2	30.00	60.00	250.00
MD-65	$2/3	30.00	60.00	250.00
MD-66	$1	30.00	60.00	250.00
MD-67	$2	30.00	60.00	200.00
MD-68	$4	25.00	50.00	200.00
MD-69	$6	25.00	50.00	200.00
MD-70*	$8	25.00	50.00	200.00

July 26, 1775

		VG	VF
MD-71	$2/3	350.00	Rare
MD-72	$1	350.00	Rare
MD-73	$1	350.00	Rare
MD-74	$1	350.00	Rare
MD-75	$2	350.00	Rare
MD-76	$4	350.00	Rare
MD-77	$8	350.00	Rare
MD-78	$16	350.00	Rare

December 7, 1775

		VG	VF	UNC
MD-79	$1/9	35.00	70.00	Rare
MD-80	$1/6	35.00	70.00	Rare
MD-81	$1/3	35.00	70.00	Rare
MD-82	$1/2	35.00	70.00	Rare
MD-83	$2/3	30.00	65.00	Rare
MD-84	$1	30.00	65.00	Rare
MD-85	$1	30.00	65.00	Rare
MD-86	$2	30.00	65.00	Rare
MD-87	$2	25.00	60.00	Rare
MD-88	$4	25.00	60.00	Rare
MD-89	$6	25.00	60.00	Rare
MD-90	$8	25.00	60.00	Rare

August 14, 1776

		VG	VF	UNC
MD-91	$1/9	35.00	65.00	Rare
MD-92	$1/6	35.00	65.00	Rare
MD-93	$1/3	35.00	65.00	Rare

		VG	VF	UNC
MD-94	$1/2	30.00	65.00	Rare
MD-95	$2/3	30.00	65.00	Rare
MD-96	$1	30.00	65.00	Rare
MD-97	$1	30.00	65.00	Rare
MD-98	$2	30.00	65.00	Rare
MD-99	$2	25.00	60.00	Rare
MD-100	$4	25.00	60.00	Rare
MD-101	$6	25.00	60.00	Rare
MD-102	$8	25.00	60.00	Rare

June 8, 1780

		VG	VF
MD-103	$1/9	Rare	Very Rare
MD-104	$1/6	Rare	Very Rare
MD-105	$1/3	Rare	Very Rare
MD-106	$1/2	Rare	Very Rare
MD-107	$2/3	Rare	Very Rare
MD-108	$1	Rare	Very Rare
MD-109	$1	Rare	Very Rare
MD-110	$2	Rare	Very Rare
MD-111	$2	250.00	Very Rare
MD-112	$4	250.00	Very Rare
MD-113	$6	250.00	Very Rare
MD-114	$8	250.00	Very Rare

June 28, 1780

		VG	VF	UNC
MD-115	$1	200.00	300.00	600.00
MD-116	$2	200.00	300.00	600.00
MD-117	$3	200.00	300.00	600.00
MD-118	$4	200.00	300.00	600.00
MD-119	$5	150.00	250.00	500.00
MD-120	$7	150.00	250.00	500.00
MD-121	$8	150.00	250.00	500.00
MD-122	$20	150.00	250.00	500.00

October 17, 1780

		VF
MD-123	$1/15	Very Rare
MD-124	$1/10	Very Rare
MD-125	$1/6	Very Rare
MD-126	$1/5	Very Rare

May 10, 1781

		VG	VF	UNC
MD-127	1s	400.00	800.00	Very Rare
MD-128	1s/6d	400.00	800.00	Very Rare
MD-129	2s/6d	400.00	800.00	Very Rare
MD-130	5s	400.00	800.00	Very Rare
MD-131	7s/6d			Very Rare
MD-132	15s			Very Rare
MD-133	30s			Very Rare
MD-134	£3			Very Rare

August 8, 1781

		VF
MD-135	3d	Extremely Rare
MD-136	4d	Extremely Rare
MD-137	6d	Extremely Rare
MD-138	9d	Extremely Rare

MASSACHUSETTS

ALL ISSUES UNTIL THAT OF MAY 25, 1775 ARE VERY RARE.

December 10,1690

MA-1	5s
MA-2	10s
MA-3	20s
MA-4	£5

February 3, 1690

MA-5	2s	MA-7	£3
MA-6	2s/6d	MA-8	£10

November 21, 1702

MA-9	2s	MA-13	20s
MA-10	2s/6d	MA-14	40s
MA-11	5s	MA-15	£3
MA-12	10s	MA-16	£5

November 21, 1708

MA-17	2s	MA-22	10s
MA-18	2s/6d	MA-23	20s
MA-19	3s	MA-24	40s
MA-20	3s/6d	MA-25	£3
MA-21	5s	MA-26	£5

May 31, 1710

MA-27	2s	MA-33	10s
MA-28	2s/6d	MA-34	20s
MA-29	3s	MA-35	40s
MA-30	3s/6d	MA-36	50s
MA-31	4s	MA-37	£3
MA-32	5s	MA-38	£5

May 31, 1710 with 1711 date

MA-39	4s	MA-43	40s
MA-40	5s	MA-44	50s
MA-41	10s	MA-45	£3
MA-42	20s	MA-46	£5

October 14, 1713

MA-47	1s	MA-51	3s
MA-48	1s/6d	MA-52	5s
MA-49	2s	MA-53	10s
MA-50	2s/6d	MA-54	10s
		MA-55	20s

October 14, 1713

There are 18 variations of this issue as the same plates were reused and redated as follows:

a. Redated 1714	j. Redated 1725
b. Redated 1716	k. 2nd issue (dagger)
c. 2nd issue (star)	l. Redated 1727
d. Redated 1718	m. Redated 1728
e. Redated 1719	n. Redated 1731
f. Redated 1721	o. Redated 1733
g. Redated 1722	p. Redated 1735
h. Redated 1723	q. Redated 1736
i. Redated 1724	r. Redated 1740

MA-56a-r	12d	MA-60a-r	3s
MA-57a-r	1s/6d	MA-61a-r	5s
MA-58a-r	24d	MA-62a-r	10s
MA-59a-r	2s/6d	MA-63a-r	20s

May 26, 1714

MA-64	30s	MA-65	40s
MA-65	60s	MA-66	100s

May 26, 1714

There are 15 variations of this issue as follows:

a. Redated 1716	h. Redated 1725
b. 2nd issue (star)	i. 2nd issue (dagger)
c. Redated 1718	j. Redated 1727
d. Redated 1721	k. Redated 1733
e. Redated 1722	l. Redated 1735
f. Redated 1723	m. Redated 1736
g. Redated 1724	n. Redated 1740

MA-67a-n	30s	MA-69a-n	60s
MA-68a-n	40s	MA-70a-n	100s

June, 1722

MA-71	1d
MA-72	2d
MA-73	3d

February 4, 1736

There are two variations of this issue as follows:
a. Original issue   b. Redated 1737

MA-74	10d	MA-78	10s
MA-75	1s/8d	MA-79	20s
MA-76	3s/4d	MA-80	30s
MA-77	6s/8d	MA-81	40s

1737

MA-82	1d	MA-85	4d
MA-83	2d	MA-86	5d
MA-84	3d	MA-87	6d

January 15, 1741

MA-88	2d	MA-95	4s
MA-89	4d	MA-96	5s
MA-90	6d	MA-97	10s
MA-91	8d	MA-98	15s
MA-92	1s	MA-99	20s
MA-93	2s	MA-100	30s
MA-94	3s	MA-101	40s

January 15, 1741 with 1742 date

(Note: The 3d, 9d, 15d and 2s/6d notes below were made from changed plates.)

MA-102	2d	MA-111	2s/6d
MA-103	3d	MA-112	3s
MA-104	4d	MA-113	4s
MA-105	6d	MA-114	5s
MA-106	8d	MA-115	10s
MA-107	9d	MA-116	15s
MA-108	1s	MA-117	20s
MA-109	15d	MA-118	30s
MA-110	2s	MA-119	40s

June 20, 1744

MA-120	2d	MA-127	2s/6d
MA-121	3d	MA-128	5s
MA-122	4d	MA-129	10s
MA-123	6d	MA-130	15s
MA-124	9d	MA-131	20s
MA-125	1s	MA-132	30s
MA-126	15d	MA-133	40s

1750

(These notes also bear the denomination in pence.)

MA-134	$1/72	MA-137	$1/12
MA-135	$1/24	MA-138	$1/8
MA-136	$1/16	MA-139	$1/4

May 25, 1775

(Notes of this issue with a hole cancel are worth 1/3 less.)

		VG	VF	UNC
MA-140	6s	1250.00	3500.00	Very Rare
MA-141	9s	1250.00	3500.00	Very Rare
MA-142	10s	1250.00	3500.00	Very Rare
MA-143	12s	1250.00	3500.00	Very Rare
MA-144	14s	1250.00	3500.00	Very Rare
MA-145	15s	1250.00	3500.00	Very Rare
MA-146	16s	1250.00	3500.00	Very Rare
MA-147	18s	1250.00	3500.00	Very Rare
MA-148	20s	1250.00	3500.00	Very Rare

July 8, 1775

MA-149	6s	Very Rare
MA-150	9s	Very Rare
MA-151	10s	Very Rare
MA-152	12s	Very Rare
MA-153	14s	Very Rare
MA-154	15s	Very Rare
MA-155	16s	Very Rare
MA-156	18s	Very Rare
MA-157	20s	Very Rare

August 18, 1775

		VG	VF	UNC
MA-158	1s	1000.00	Rare	Very Rare
MA-159	2s	1000.00	Rare	Very Rare
MA-160	2s/6d	1000.00	Rare	Very Rare
MA-161	4s	1000.00	Rare	Very Rare
MA-162	5s	1000.00	Rare	Very Rare
MA-163	6s	1000.00	Rare	Very Rare
MA-164	7s/6d	1000.00	Rare	Very Rare
MA-165	8s	1000.00	Rare	Very Rare

		VG	VF	UNC
MA-166	10s	1000.00	Rare	Very Rare
MA-167	11s	1000.00	Rare	Very Rare
MA-168	12s	1000.00	Rare	Very Rare
MA-169	17s	1000.00	Rare	Very Rare
MA-170	20s	1000.00	Rare	Very Rare
MA-171	24s	1000.00	Rare	Very Rare
MA-172	30s	1000.00	Rare	Very Rare
MA-173	40s	1000.00	Rare	Very Rare

December 7, 1775

		VG	VF	UNC
MA-174	8d	1250.00	Rare	Very Rare
MA-175	1s/4d	1250.00	Rare	Very Rare
MA-176	1s/6d	1250.00	Rare	Very Rare
MA-177	2s/8d	1250.00	Rare	Very Rare
MA-178	3s	1250.00	Rare	Very Rare
MA-179	3s/4d	1250.00	Rare	Very Rare
MA-180	4s/6d	1250.00	Rare	Very Rare
MA-181	7s	1250.00	Rare	Very Rare
MA-182	10s	1250.00	Rare	Very Rare
MA-183	14s	1250.00	Rare	Very Rare
MA-184	16s	1250.00	Rare	Very Rare
MA-185	22s	1250.00	Rare	Very Rare
MA-186	28s	1250.00	Rare	Very Rare
MA-187	36s	1250.00	Rare	Very Rare
MA-188	42s	1250.00	Rare	Very Rare
MA-189	48s	1250.00	Rare	Very Rare

June 18, 1776

		VG	VF	UNC
MA-190	3d	180.00	325.00	Rare
MA-191	4d	180.00	325.00	Rare
MA-192	5d	180.00	325.00	Rare
MA-193	6d	180.00	325.00	Rare
MA-194	9d	180.00	325.00	Rare
MA-195	10d	180.00	325.00	Rare
MA-196	1s	180.00	325.00	Rare
MA-197	1s/3d	180.00	325.00	Rare
MA-198	1s/8d	180.00	325.00	Rare
MA-199	2s/4d	180.00	325.00	Rare
MA-200	2s/6d	180.00	325.00	Rare
MA-201	3s/6d	180.00	325.00	Rare
MA-202	4s	180.00	325.00	Rare
MA-203	4s/6d	180.00	325.00	Rare
MA-204	5s	180.00	325.00	Rare
MA-205	5s/4d	180.00	325.00	Rare
MA-206	6s	300.00	550.00	Rare
MA-207	12s	300.00	550.00	Rare
MA-208	18s	300.00	550.00	Rare
MA-209	24s	300.00	550.00	Rare
MA-210	30s	300.00	550.00	Rare
MA-211	36s	300.00	550.00	Rare
MA-212	42s	300.00	550.00	Rare
MA-213	48s	300.00	550.00	Rare

September 17, 1776

MA-214	10s	Very Rare
MA-215	14s	Very Rare
MA-216	16s	Very Rare
MA-217	22s	Very Rare
MA-218	28s	Very Rare
MA-219	36s	Very Rare
MA-220	42s	Very Rare
MA-221	48s	Very Rare

October 18, 1776

		VG	VF	UNC
MA-222	2d	150.00	300.00	1000.00
MA-223	3d	150.00	300.00	1000.00
MA-224	4d	150.00	300.00	1000.00
MA-225	6d	150.00	300.00	1000.00
MA-226	8d	150.00	300.00	1000.00
MA-227	9d	150.00	300.00	1000.00
MA-228*	1s	150.00	300.00	1000.00
MA-229	1s/6d	150.00	300.00	1000.00
MA-230	2s	150.00	300.00	1000.00
MA-231	3s	150.00	300.00	1000.00
MA-232	4s	150.00	300.00	1000.00
MA-233	4s/6d	150.00	300.00	1000.00
MA-234	6s		Very Rare	
MA-235	12s		Very Rare	
NU-236	18s		Very Rare	
MA-237	24s		Very Rare	
MA-238	30s		Very Rare	
MA-239	36s		Very Rare	
MA-240	42s		Very Rare	
MA-241	48s		Very Rare	

MA-242	54s		Very Rare
MA-243	60s		Very Rare
MA-244	66s		Very Rare
MA-245	72s		Very Rare

November 17, 1776

MA-246	10s		Very Rare
MA-247	14s		Very Rare
MA-248	16s		Very Rare
MA-249	22s		Very Rare
MA-250	28s		Very Rare
MA-251	36s		Very Rare
MA-252	42s		Very Rare
MA-253	48s		Very Rare

		VG	VF	UNC
October 16, 1778				
MA-254	2d	125.00	250.00	700.00
MA-255	3d	125.00	250.00	700.00
MA-256	4d	125.00	250.00	700.00
MA-257	6d	125.00	250.00	700.00
MA-258	8d	125.00	250.00	700.00
MA-259	9d	125.00	250.00	700.00
MA-260	12d	125.00	250.00	700.00
MA-261	1s/6d	125.00	250.00	700.00
MA-262	2s	125.00	250.00	700.00
MA-263	3s	125.00	250.00	700.00
MA-264	4s	125.00	250.00	700.00
MA-265	4s/6d	125.00	250.00	700.00

		VG	VF	UNC
December 1, 1779				
MA-266	1s	150.00	300.00	Rare
MA-267	1s/6d	150.00	300.00	Rare

		VG	VF	UNC
MA-268	2s	150.00	300.00	Rare
MA-269	2s/6d	150.00	300.00	Rare
MA-270	3s	150.00	300.00	Rare
MA-271	3s/6d	150.00	300.00	Rare
MA-272	4s	150.00	300.00	Rare
MA-273	4s/6d	150.00	300.00	Rare
MA-274	4s/8d	150.00	300.00	Rare
MA-275	5s	150.00	300.00	Rare
MA-276	5s/4d	150.00	300.00	Rare
MA-277	5s/6d	150.00	300.00	Rare

May 5, 1780

(Prices below are for cancelled notes. Uncancelled specimens are worth approximately 50% more.)

MA-278	$1	15.00	22.00	50.00
MA-279	$2	15.00	22.00	50.00
MA-280	$3	15.00	22.00	50.00
MA-281	$4	15.00	22.00	50.00
MA-282	$5	15.00	22.00	50.00
MA-283	$7	15.00	22.00	50.00
MA-284	$8	15.00	22.00	50.00
MA-285	$20	15.00	22.00	50.00

1781 (Dates written by hand)

MA-286	$4		Extremely Rare
MA-287	$6		Extremely Rare
MA-288	$8		Extremely Rare
MA-289	$16		Extremely Rare

NEW HAMPSHIRE

ALL ISSUES THROUGH THAT OF
JANUARY 1, 1763 ARE VERY RARE

1709

| NH-1 | 15s |
| NH-2 | 50s |

May 20, 1717

NH-3	1s	NH-7	25s
NH4	1s/6d	NH-8	30s
NH-5	4s/6d	NH-9	£3s/10s
NH-6	15s	NH-10	£4

May 20, 1717 Redated 1714

| NH-7 | 1s | NH-9 | 4s/6d |
| NH-8 | 1s/6d | NH-10 | 25s |

May 20, 1717 Redated 1717

| NH-11 | 1s | NH-13 | 4s/6d |
| NH-12 | 1s/6d | NH-14 | 25s |

May 20, 1717 Redated 1722

NH-15	1s	NH-19	25s
NH-16	1s/6d	NH-20	30s
NH-17	4s/6d	NH-21	£3/10s
NH-18	15s	NH-22	£4

May 20, 1717 Redated 1724-27

These were redated as follows:
a. Redated 1724
b. Redated 1725
c. Redated 1726
d. Redated 1727

NH-23a-d	1s	NH-27a-d	25s
NH-24a-d	1s/6d	NH-2ga-d	30s
NH-25a-d	4s/6d	NH-29a-d	3/10s
NH-26a-d	15s	NH-30a-d	£4

May 20, 1717 Redated 1729

NH-31	1s	NH-35	25s
NH-32	1s/6d	NH-36	30s
NH-33	4s/6d	NH-37	£3/10s
NH-34	15s	NH-38	£4

April 1, 1737

NH-39	2s	NH43	20s
NH-40	3s	NH-44	40s
NH-41	5s	NH-45	60s
NH42	10s	NH-46	100s

April 1, 1737 Redated August 7, 1740

| NH-47 | 20s | NH49 | 60s |
| NH-48 | 40s | NH-50 | 100s |

April 3, 1742

NH-51	6d	NH-55	7s/6d
NH-52	1s	NH-56	10s
NH-53	2s/6d	NH-57	20s
NH-54	6s	NH-58	40s

April 3, 1742 Redated 1743

NH-59	6d	NH-63	7s/6d
NH-60	1s	NH-64	10s
NH-61	2s/6d	NH-65	20s
NH-62	6s	NH-66	40s

April 3, 1742, Redated February 1744

NH-67	6d		NH-71	7s/6d
NH-68	1s		NH-72	10s
NH-69	2s/6d		NH-73	20s
NH-70	6s		NH-74	40s

April 3, 1755

NH-75	6d		NH-80	7s/6d
NH-76	1s		NH-81	10s
NH-77	3s		NH-82	15s
NH-78	3s/9d		NH-83	30s
NH-79	5s		NH-84	£3

April 3, 1755 Redated January 1, 1756

NH-85	10s		NH-87	30s
NH-86	15s		NH-88	£3

April 3, 1755 Redated June 1, 1756

NH-89	6d		NH-94	7s/6d
NH-90	1s		NH-95	10s
NH-91	3s		NH-96	15s
NH-92	3s/9d		NH-97	30s
NH-93	5s		NH-98	£3

1759

NH-99	6d		NH-101	2s/6d
NH-100	1s		NH-102	10s

March 1,1760

NH-103	6d		NH-105	2s/6d
NH-104	1s		NH-106	10s

January 1, 1761

NH-107	6d		NH-109	2s/6d
NH-108	1s		NH-110	10s

May 1, 1761

NH-111	6d		NH-113	2s/6d
NH-112	1s		NH-114	10s

January 1, 1762

NH-115	6d		NH-117	2s/6d
NH-116	1s		NH-118	10s

July 1, 1762

NH-119	6d		NH-121	2s/6d
NH-120	1s		NH-122	10s

January 1, 1763

NH-123	6d		NH-125	2s/6d
NH-124	1s		NH-126	10s

June 20, 1775

		VG	VF	UNC
NH-1-27	1s	1000.00	Rare	Very Rare
NH-128	6s	1000.00	Rare	Very Rare
NH-1-29	20s	1000.00	Rare	Very Rare
NH-130	40s	1000.00	Rare	Very Rare

July 25, 1775

NH-131	6d	350.00	Rare	Very Rare
NH-132	9d	350.00	Rare	Very Rare
NH-133	1s/6d	350.00	Rare	Very Rare
NH-134	1s/9d	350.00	Rare	Very Rare
NH-135	2s/6d	350.00	Rare	Very Rare
NH-136	3s	350.00	Rare	Very Rare
NH-137	5s	300.00	600.00	Rare
NH-138	10s	300.00	600.00	Rare
NH-139	15s	300.00	600.00	Rare
NH-140	30s	300.00	600.00	Rare
NH-141	£3	300.00	600.00	Rare

November 3, 1775

NH-142	6d	325.00	600.00	Very Rare
NH-143	9d	325.00	600.00	Very Rare
NH-144	1s/6d	325.00	600.00	Very Rare
NH-145	1s/9d	325.00	600.00	Very Rare
NH-146	2s/6d	325.00	600.00	Very Rare
NH-147	3s	325.00	600.00	Very Rare
NH-148	5s	250.00	450.00	Rare
NH-149	10s	250.00	450.00	Rare
NH-150	15s	250.00	450.00	Rare
NH-151	30s	185.00	350.00	600.00
NH-152	40s	185.00	350.00	600.00

January 26, 1776

NH-153	$1	Very Rare
NH-154	$2	Very Rare
NH-155	$3	Very Rare
NH-156	$4	Very Rare
NH-157	$5	Very Rare
NH-158	$6	Very Rare

June 28, 1776

		VG	VF	UNC
NH-159	3d	500.00	Rare	Very Rare
NH-160	4d	500.00	Rare	Very Rare
NH-161	5d	500.00	Rare	Very Rare
NH-162	7d	500.00	Rare	Very Rare
NH-163	8d	500.00	Rare	Very Rare
NH-164	10d	500.00	Rare	Very Rare
NH-165	1s	500.00	Rare	Very Rare
NH-166	15d	500.00	Rare	Very Rare
NH-167	2s	500.00	Rare	Very Rare
NH-168	4s	500.00	Rare	Very Rare

July 3, 1776

NH-169	$1	Very Rare
NH-170	$2	Very Rare
NH-171	$3	Very Rare
NH-172	$4	Very Rare
NH-175	$5	Very Rare
NH-176	$6	Very Rare

1777 (Date Written by Hand)

NH-177	£5	Rare
NH-178	£10	Rare

April 29, 1780
(Two prices are given for each note of this issue. The first is for cancelled specimens, the second for uncancelled.)

NH-179	$1	125.00	300.00	600.00
Uncancelled		300.00	750.00	Rare
NH-180	$2	125.00	300.00	600.00
Uncancelled		300.00	750.00	Rare
NH-181	$4	125.00	300.00	600.00
Uncancelled		300.00	750.00	Rare
NH-182	$5	125.00	300.00	600.00
Uncancelled		300.00	750.00	Rare
NH-183	$7	125.00	300.00	600.00
Uncancelled		300.00	750.00	Rare
NH-184	$8	125.00	300.00	600.00
Uncancelled		300.00	750.00	Rare
NH-185	$20	125.00	300.00	600.00
Uncancelled		300,00	750.00	Rare

NEW JERSEY

ALL ISSUES THROUGH THAT OF JUNE 22,1756 ARE VERY RARE.

NOTES SIGNED BY JOHN HART (a signer of the Declaration of Independence) COMMAND A PREMIUM OF 100% OF THE BELOW PRICES.

July 1, 1709

NJ-1	5s		NJ4	40s
NJ-2	10s		NJ-5	£5
NJ-3	20s			

July 14, 1711

NJ-6	2s/6d		NJ-9	20s
NJ-7	5s		NJ-10	40s
NJ-8	10s		NJ-11	£5

January 24, 1716

NJ-12	2s		NJ-17	16s
NJ-13	4s		NJ-18	20s
NJ-14	5s		NJ-19	30s
NJ-15	8s		NJ-20	40s
NJ-16	10s			

March 25, 1724

NJ-21	1s		NJ-25	12s
NJ-22	1s/6d		NJ-26	15s
NJ-23	3s		NJ-27	30s
NJ-24	6s		NJ-28	£3

March 25, 1728

NJ-29	1s		NJ-34	15s
NJ.30	1s/6d		NJ-35	30s
NJ-31	3s		NJ-36	£3
NJ-32	6s		NJ-37	£6
NJ-33	12s			

March 25, 1733

NJ-38	1s		NJ-43	15s
NJ-39	1s/6d		NJ-44	30s
NJ-40	3s		NJ-45	£3
NJ-41	6s		NJ-46	£6
NJ-42	12s			

March 25, 1737

NJ47	1s		NJ-52	15s
NJ-48	1s/6d		NJ-53	30s
NJ49	3s		NJ-54	£3
NJ-50	6s		NJ-55	£6
NJ-51	12s			

July 2, 1746

NJ-56	1s	Rare
NJ-57	1s/6d	Rare
NJ-58	3s	Rare
NJ-59	6s	Rare
NJ-60	12s	Rare
NJ-61	15s	Rare
NJ-62	30s	Rare
NJ-63	£3	Rare
NJ-64	£6	Rare

May 15, 1755

NJ-65	1s	Rare
NJ-66	1s/6d	Rare
NJ-67	3s	Rare
NJ-68	6s	Rare
NJ-69	12s	Rare
NJ-70	15s	Rare
NJ-71	30s	Rare
NJ-72	£3	Rare

NJ-73	£6	Rare

September 8, 1755

NJ-74	1s	Rare
NJ-75	1s/6d	Rare
NJ-76	3s	Rare
NJ-77	6s	Rare
NJ-78	12s	Rare
NJ-79	15s	Rare
NJ-80	30s	Rare
NJ-81	£3	Rare
NJ-82	£6	Rare

January 26, 1756

NJ-83	1s	Rare
NJ-84	18d	Rare
NJ-85	3s	Rare
NJ-86	6s	Rare
NJ-87	12s	Rare
NJ-88	15s	Rare
NJ-89	30s	Rare
NJ-90	£3	Rare
NJ-91	£6	Rare

June 22, 1756

		VG	VF	UNC
NJ-92	1s	40.00	85.00	170.00
NJ-93	18d	40.00	85.00	170.00
NJ-94	3s	40.00	85.00	170.00
NJ-95	6s	75.00	150.00	300.00
NJ-96	12s	75.00	150.00	300.00
NJ-97	15s	75.00	150.00	300.00
NJ-98	30s	125.00	400.00	950.00
NJ-99	£3	125.00	400.00	Rare
NJ-100	£6	150.00	Rare	Very Rare

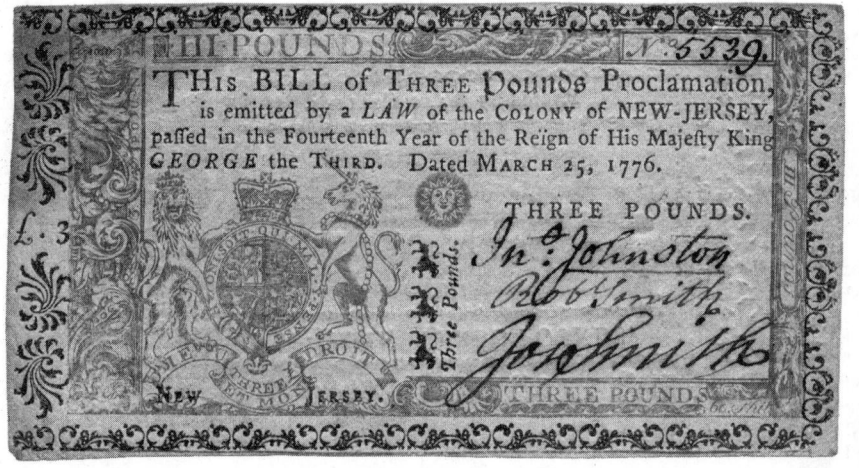

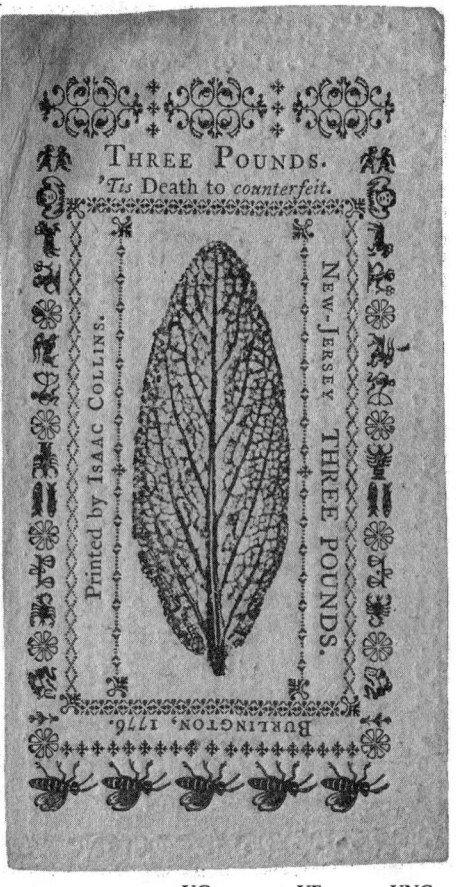

		VG	VF	UNC
April 12, 1757				
NJ-101	15s	85.00	Rare	Very Rare
NJ-102	30s	85.00	Rare	Very Rare
NJ-103	£3	175.00	Rare	Very Rare
NJ-104	£6	200.00	550.00	Rare
June 14, 1757				
NJ-105	15s	125.00	Very Rare	
NJ-106	30s	100.00	Very Rare	
NJ-107	£3	140.00	Very Rare	
NJ-108	£6	200.00	Very Rare	
November 20, 1757				
NJ-109	6s	60.00	Rare	Very Rare
NJ-110	15s	50.00	Rare	Very Rare
NJ-111	30s	40.00	Rare	Very Rare
NJ-112	£3	50.00	Rare	Very Rare
NJ-113	£6	150.00	Rare	Very Rare
May 1, 1758				
NJ-114	6s	35.00	Rare	Very Rare
NJ-115	15s	30.00	Rare	Very Rare
NJ-116	30s	25.00	Rare	Very Rare
NJ-117	£3	35.00	Rare	Very Rare
NJ-118	£6	75.00	750.00	1450.00
October 20, 1758				
NJ-119	1s	60.00	Rare	Very Rare
NJ-120	18d	70.00	Rare	Very Rare
NJ-121	3s	75.00	Rare	Very Rare
NJ-122	6s	90.00	Rare	Very Rare
NJ-123	12s	90.00	Rare	Very Rare
NJ-124	15s	110.00	Rare	Very Rare
NJ-12S	30s	150.00	Rare	Very Rare
NJ-126	£3	210.00	Rare	Very Rare
NJ-127	£6	300.00	Rare	Very Rare
April 10, 1759				
NJ-128	6s	47.50	Rare	Very Rare
NJ-129	15s	42.50	Rare	Very Rare
NJ-130	30s	35.00	Rare	Very Rare
NJ-131	£3	50.00	Rare	Very Rare
NJ-132	£6	80.00	500.00	1100.00
April 12, 1760				
NJ-133	1s	40.00	Rare	Very Rare
NJ-134	18d	45.00	Rare	Very Rare
NJ-135	3s	50.00	Rare	Very Rare
NJ-136	6s	60.00	Rare	Very Rare
NJ-137	12s	70.00	Rare	Very Rare
NJ-138	15s	90.00	Rare	Very Rare
NJ-139	30s	60.00	Rare	Very Rare
NJ-140	£3	75.00	Rare	Very Rare
NJ-141	£6	90.00	Rare	Very Rare
April 23, 1761				
NJ-142	12s	115.00	Rare	Very Rare
NJ-143	15s	70.00	Rare	Very Rare
NJ-144	30s	60.00	Rare	Very Rare
NJ-145	£3	80.00	Rare	Very Rare
NJ-146	£6	140.00	Rare	Very Rare

		VG	VF	UNC
April 8, 1762				
NJ-147	12s	125.00	Rare	Very Rare
NJ-148	15s	90.00	Rare	Very Rare
NJ-149	30s	65.00	Rare	Very Rare
NJ-150	£3	85.00	Rare	Very Rare
NJ-151	£6	150.00	350.00	750.00
December 31, 1763				
NJ-152	1s	35.00	50.00	120.00
NJ-153	18d	40.00	60.00	125.00
NJ-154	3s	45.00	65.00	130.00
NJ-155	6s	50.00	70.00	135.00
NJ-156	12s	50.00	75.00	135.00
NJ-157	15s	60.00	85.00	140.00
NJ-158	30s	90.00	170.00	Rare
NJ-159	£3	125.00	200.00	Rare
NJ-160	£6	200.00	400.00	1650.00
April 16, 1764				
NJ-161	1s	Rare		
NJ-162	18d	Rare		
NJ-163	3s	Rare		
NJ-164	6s	Rare		
NJ-165	12s	105.00	Rare	Very Rare
NJ-166	15s	55.00	Rare	Very Rare
NJ-167	30s	65.00	Rare	Very Rare
NJ-168	£3	70.00	Rare	Very Rare
NJ-169	£6	200.00	400.00	1650.00
February 20, 1776				
NJ-170	6s	45.00	115.00	Rare
NJ-172	15s	40.00	100.00	Rare
NJ-173	30s	32.00	80.00	Rare
NJ-174	£3	35.00	85.00	Rare
March 25, 1776				
NJ-175	1s	20.00	35.00	80.00
NJ-176	18d	25.00	40.00	90.00
NJ-177	3s	20.00	45.00	105.00
NJ-178	6s	35.00	50.00	110.00
NJ-179	12s	35.00	50.00	120.00
NJ-180	15s	40.00	60.00	150.00
NJ-181	30s	50.00	80.00	200.00
NJ-182*	£3	75.00	125.00	300.00
NJ-183	£6	125.00	225.00	450.00
June 9, 1780				
NJ-184	$1	65.00	125.00	Rare
NJ-185	$2	65.00	125.00	Rare
NJ-186	$3	65.00	125.00	Rare
NJ-187	$4	65.00	125.00	Rare
NJ-188	$5	65.00	125.00	Rare
NJ-189	$7	65.00	125.00	Rare
NJ-190	$8	65.00	125.00	Rare
NJ-191	$20	65.00	125.00	Rare
January 9, 1781				
NJ-192	6d	100.00	200.00	350.00
NJ-193	9d	100.00	200.00	350.00
NJ-194	15	100.00	200.00	350.00
NJ-195	1s/6d	100.00	200.00	350.00
NJ-196	2s/6d	100.00	200.00	350.00

		VG	VF	UNC
NJ-197	3s/6d	100.00	200.00	350.00
NJ-198	3s/9d	100.00	200.00	350.00
NJ-199	4s	100.00	200.00	350.00
NJ-200	5s	100.00	200.00	350.00
NJ-201	7s/6d	100.00	200.00	350.00
December 20, 1783				
NJ-202	2s/6d		Very Rare	
NJ-203	3s/9d	1250.00		Extremely Rare
NJ-204	5s			Extremely Rare
NJ-205	7s/6d			Extremely Rare
NJ-206	12s			Extremely Rare
NJ-207	15s			Extremely Rare
NJ-208	30s			Extremely Rare
NJ-209	£3			Extremely Rare
NJ-210	£6			Extremely Rare
May 17, 1786				
NJ-211	1s	350.00	Very Rare	
NJ-212	3s	450.00	Very Rare	
NJ-213	6s	550.00	Very Rare	
NJ-214	12s	750.00	Very Rare	
NJ-215	15s	900.00	1600.00	Very Rare
NJ-216	30s	1400.00	Very Rare	
NJ-217	£3	2000.00	Very Rare	
NJ-218	£6	2500.00	Very Rare	

NEW YORK

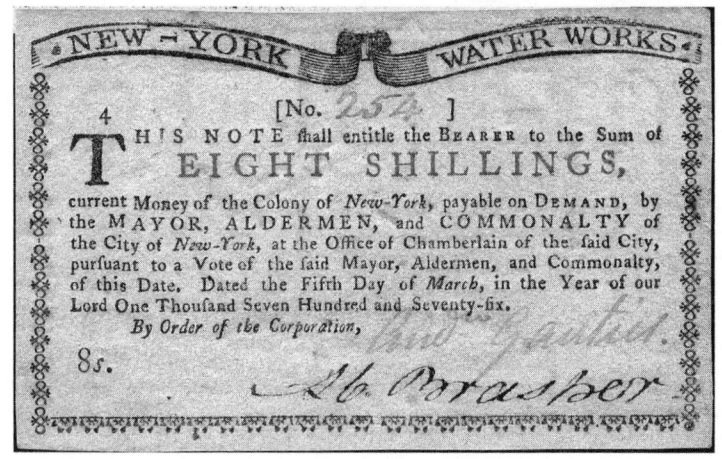

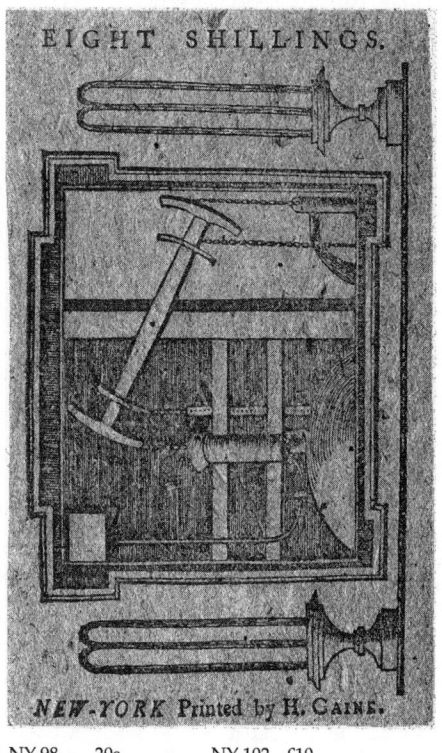

	VG	VF	UNC
May 31, 1709			
NY-1	5s	2500.00	6000.00	Very Rare
NY-2	10s	2500.00	6000.00	Very Rare
NY-3	20s		Very Rare	
NY4	40s		Very Rare	
NY-5	£5		Very Rare	

November 1, 1709

NY-6	25s	2500.00	6000.00	Very Rare
NY-7	50s	2500.00	6000.00	Very Rare
NY-8	£5		Very Rare	

ALL ISSUES FROM HERE THROUGH THAT OF
APRIL 20,1756 ARE VERY RARE

November 1, 1709 (Lyon Dollars)

NY-9	2 Ounces, 15 Pennyweights or 4 Lyon Dollars
NY-10	5 Ounces, 10 Pennyweights or 8 Lyon Dollars
NY-11	11 Ounces or 16 Lyon Dollars
NY-12	13 Ounces, 15 Pennyweights or 20 Lyon Dollars

July 20, 1711

(These notes also bear the value in shillings, with 1 ounce = 8 shillings.)

NY-12	1/4 Ounce	NY-16	2fi Ounce
NY-13	1/2 Ounce	NY-17	5 Ounces
NY-14	1 Ounce	NY-18	10 Ounces
NY-15	2 Ounces	NY-19	20 Ounces

July 1, 1714

(Value also given in pounds and shillings.)

NY-20	7 Pennyweights, 12 Grains
NY-21	15 Pennyweights
NY-22	1 Ounce, 10 Pennyweights
NY-23	1 Ounce, 17 Pennyweights, 12 Grains
NY-24	3 Ounces, 2 Pennyweights, 12 Grains
NY-25	3 Ounces, 15 Pennyweights
NY-26	6 Ounces, 15 Pennyweights
NY-27	7 Ounces, 10 Pennyweights
NY-28	12 Ounces, 10 Pennyweights
NY-29	15 Ounces
NY-30	18 Ounces, 15 Pennyweights
NY-31	25 Ounces

July 5, 1715

NY-32	12 Pennyweights, 12 Grains
NY-33	1 Ounce, 5 Pennyweights
NY-34	2 Ounces, 10 Pennyweights
NY-35	5 Ounces
NY-36	10 Ounces
NY-37	12 Ounces, 10 Pennyweights
NY-38	25 Ounces

November 28, 1717

NY-39	5 Pennyweights
NY40	10 Pennyweights
NY-41	15 Pennyweights
NY-42	1 Ounce
NY-43	1 Ounce, 5 Pennyweights
NY-44	1 Ounce, 10 Pennyweights
NY-45	2 Ounces
NY-46	2 Ounces, 10 Pennyweights
NY-47	5 Ounces
NY-48	7 Ounces, 10 Pennyweights
NY-49	10 Ounces

November 10, 1720

NY-50	2 Pennyweights, 12 Grains
NY-51	3 Pennyweights, 18 Grains
NY-52	6 Pennyweights, 6 Grains
NY-53	7 Pennyweights, 12 Grains
NY-54	8 Pennyweights, 18 Grains

July 2, 1723

NY-55	8 Ounces, 15 Pennyweights
NY-56	11 Ounces, 5 Pennyweights

July 10, 1724

NY-57	1s/3d	NY-61	£1/12s
NY-58	3s/9d	NY-62	£3/4s
NY-59	7s/6d	NY-63	£3/12s
NY-60	14s		

July 22, 1724

NY-64	1s	NY-69	3s/6d
NY-65	1s/6d	NY-70	4s
NY-66	2s	NY-71	6s
NY-67	2s/6d	NY-72	8s/6d
NY-68	3s	NY-73	12s

November 16, 1726

NY-74	1s	NY-80	3s/6d
NY-75	1s/3d	NY-81	4s
NY-76	1s/6d	NY-82	6s
NY-77	2s	NY-83	8s
NY-78	2s/6d	NY-84	12s
NY-79	3s		

October 20, 1730

NY-85	2s/6d	NY-87	10s
NY-86	5s	NY-88	20s

November 15, 1734

NY-89	5s	NY-93	£3
NY-90	10s	NY-94	£5
NY-91	20s	NY-95	£10
NY-92	£2		

December 10, 1737

NY-96	5s	NY-100		£3
NY-97	10s	NY-101	£5
NY-98	20s	NY-102	£10
NY-99	£2		

October 20, 1739

NY-103	5s	NY-107	£3
NY-104	10s	NY-108	£5
NY-105	20s	NY-109	£10
NY-106	£2		

May 10, 1746

NY-110	£2	NY-112	£5
NY-111	£3	NY-113	£10

July 21, 1746

NY-114	10s	NY-117	£3
NY-115	20s	NY-118	£5
NY-116	£2	NY-119	£10

November 2, 1747

NY-120	20s	NY-123	£5
NY-121	£2	NY-124	£10
NY-122	£3		

March 25, 1755

NY-125	10s	NY-128	£3
NY-126	20s	NY-129	£5
NY-127	£2	NY-130	£10

May 12, 1755

NY-131	5s	NY-135	£3
NY-132	10s	NY-136	£4
NY-133	20s	NY-137	£5
NY-134	£2	NY-138	£10

September 15, 1755

NY-139	5s	NY-143	£3
NY-140	10s	NY-144	£4
NY-141	20s	NY-145	£5
NY-142	£2	NY-146	£10

February 16, 1756

NY-147	£10

		VG	VF	UNC
April 20, 1756				
NY-148	20s	140.00	Rare	Very Rare
NY-149	£2	200.00	Rare	Very Rare
NY-150	£3	140.00	Rare	Very Rare
NY-151	£5	100.00	Rare	Very Rare
NY-152	£10	135.00	Rare	Very Rare

New York

April 15, 1758

		VG	VF	UNC
NY-153	£5	105.00	325.00	Rare
NY-154	£10	75.00	225.00	Rare

April 2, 1759

		VG	VF	UNC
NY-155	£2	65.00	Rare	Very Rare
NY-156	£5	85.00	Rare	Very Rare
NY-157	£10	75.00	Rare	Very Rare

April 21, 1760

		VG	VF	UNC
NY-158	£2	85.00	150.00	Rare
NY-159	£5	95.00	175.00	Rare
NY-160	£10	95.00	175.00	Rare

February 16, 1771

		VG	VF	UNC
NY-161	5s	40.00	100.00	Rare
NY-162	10s	40.00	100.00	Rare
NY-163	£1	45.00	115.00	Rare
NY-164	£2	45.00	115.00	Rare
NY-165	£3	45.00	115.00	Rare
NY-166	£5	45.00	115.00	Rare
NY-167	£10	45.00	115.00	Rare

August 25, 1774 (Water Works)

		VG	VF	UNC
NY-168	1s	40.00	75.00	175.00
NY-169	2s	40.00	75.00	175.00
NY-170	4s	40.00	75.00	175.00
NY-171	8s	40.00	75.00	175.00

August 2, 1775 (Water Works)

		VG	VF	UNC
NY-172	1s		Unique	
NY-173	2s	40.00	75.00	175.00
NY-174	4s	40.00	75.00	175.00
NY-175	8s	40.00	75.00	175.00

September 2, 1775

		VG	VF	UNC
NY-176	$1/2	50.00	120.00	350.00
NY-177	$1	45.00	100.00	300.00
NY-178	$2	50.00	120.00	350.00
NY-179	$3	50.00	120.00	350.00
NY-180	$5	50.00	120.00	350.00
NY-181	$10	50.00	120.00	350.00

January 6, 1776 (Water Works)

		VG	VF	UNC
NY-182	2s	65.00	105.00	240.00
NY-183	4s	65.00	105.00	240.00
NY-184	8s	50.00	85.00	200.00

March 5, 1776

		VG	VF	UNC
NY-185	$1/8	35.00	100.00	300.00
NY-186	$1/6	35.00	100.00	300.00
NY-187	$1/4	35.00	100.00	300.00
NY-188	$	35.00	100.00	300.00
NY-189	$1/2	35.00	100.00	300.00
NY-190	$	35.00	100.00	300.00
NY-191	$1	35.00	100.00	300.00
NY-192	$2	55.00	150.00	500.00
NY-193	$3	55.00	150.00	500.00
NY-194	$5	55.00	150.00	500.00
NY-195	$10	55.00	150.00	500.00

March 5,1776 (Water Works)

		VG	VF	UNC
NY-196	4s	45.00	75.00	180.00
NY-197*	8s	45.00	75.00	180.00

August 13, 1776

		VG	VF	UNC
NY-198	$1/16	30.00	70.00	200.00
NY-199	$	30.00	70.00	200.00
NY-200	$1/4	30.00	70.00	200.00
NY-201	$1/2	30.00	70.00	200.00
NY-202	$2	40.00	80.00	250.00
NY-203	$3	40.00	80.00	250.00
NY-204	$5	40.00	80.00	250.00
NY-205	$10	40.00	80.00	250.00

June 15, 1780

		VG	VF	UNC
NY-206	$1	300.00	Rare	Very Rare
NY-207	$2	300.00	Rare	Very Rare
NY-208	$3	300.00	Rare	Very Rare
NY-209	$4	300.00	Rare	Very Rare
NY-210	$5	300.00	Rare	Very Rare
NY-211	$7	300.00	Rare	Very Rare
NY-212	$8	300.00	Rare	Very Rare
NY-213	$20	300.00	Rare	Very Rare

March 27, 1781

		VG	VF	UNC
NY-214	$1		Very Rare	
NY-215	$2		Very Rare	
NY-216	$3		Very Rare	
NY-217	$4		Very Rare	
NY-218	$5		Very Rare	
NY-219	$7		Very Rare	
NY-220	$8		Very Rare	
NY-221	$20		Very Rare	

April 18, 1786

		VG	VF	UNC
NY-222	5s		Very Rare	
NY-223	10s		Very Rare	
NY-224	£1		Very Rare	
NY-225	£2		Very Rare	
NY-226	£3		Very Rare	
NY-227	£4		Very Rare	
NY-228	£5		Very Rare	
NY-229	£10		Very Rare	

February 8, 1788

		VG	VF	UNC
NY-230	5s		Very Rare	
NY-231	10s		Very Rare	
NY-232	£1		Very Rare	
NY-233	£2		Very Rare	
NY-234	£3		Very Rare	
NY-235	£4		Very Rare	
NY-236	£5		Very Rare	
NY-237	£10		Very Rare	

NORTH CAROLINA

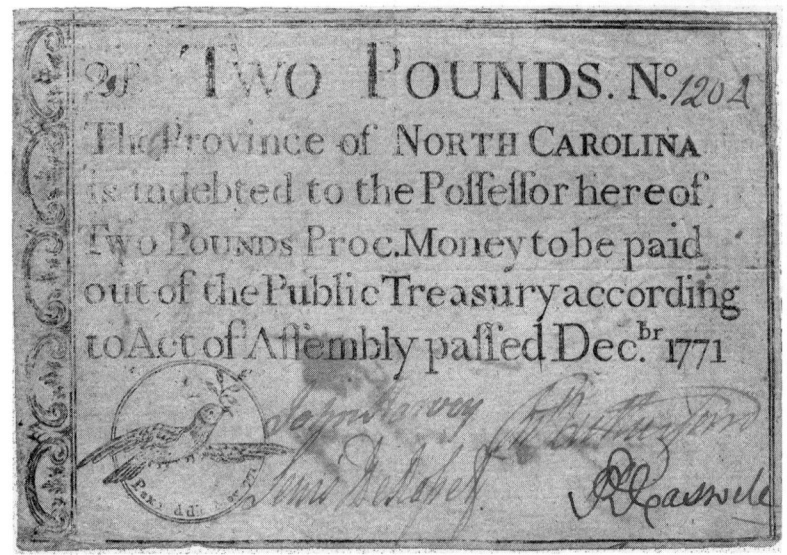

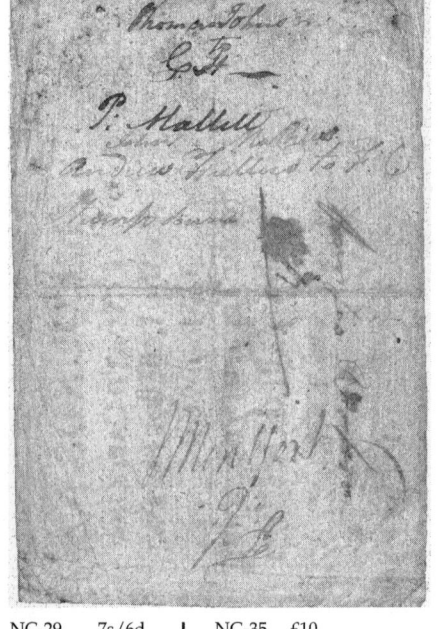

Photo of reverse side reduced.

ALL ISSUES THROUGH THAT OF
1735 ARE VERY RARE

1712-1713

NC-1	£3	NC-3	£10
NC-2	£5	NC4	£20

1715

NC-5	2s/6d	NC-10	£3
NC-6	5s	NC-11	£5
NC-7	8s	NC-12	£10
NC-8	10s	NC-13	£15
NC-9	20s	NC-14	£20

October 19, 1722

NC-15	12d	NC-20	10s
NC-16	2s	NC-21	20s
NC-17	2s/6d	NC-22	40s
NC-18	5s	NC-23	£3
NC-19	7s/6d	NC-24	£5

November 27, 1729

NC-25	12d	NC-31	20s
NC-26	2s	NC-32	40s
NC-27	2s/6d	NC-33	£3
NC-28	5s	NC-34	£5
NC-29	7s/6d	NC-35	£10
NC-30	10s		

1734

NC-36	1s	NC-41	40s
NC-37	2s/6d	NC-42	£3
NC-38	5s	NC-43	£5
NC-39	10s	NC-44	£10
NC-40	20s		

1735

NC-45	1s		NC-50	40s
NC-46	2s/6d		NC-51	£3
NC-47	5s		NC-52	£5
NC-48	10s		NC-53	£10
NC-49	20s			

April 4, 1748

		VG	VF
NC-54	4d	175.00	Very Rare
NC-55	8d	175.00	Very Rare
NC-56	1s	175.00	Very Rare
NC-57	1s/6d	175.00	Very Rare
NC-58	2s	175.00	Very Rare
NC-59	2s/6d	175.00	Very Rare
NC-60	3s	175.00	Very Rare
NC-61	5s	175.00	Very Rare
NC-62	6s	175.00	Very Rare
NC-63	7s/6d	175.00	Very Rare
NC-64	9s	175.00	Very Rare
NC-65	10s	175.00	Very Rare
NC-66	15s	175.00	Very Rare
NC-67	20s	175.00	Very Rare
NC-68	30s	175.00	Very Rare
NC-69	40s	175.00	Very Rare
NC-70	£3	175.00	Very Rare

March 9, 1754

(NC-71 through NC-74 exist with two different designs on the face of each issue.)

NC-71	4d	150.00	Rare	Very Rare
NC-72	8d	150.00	Rare	Very Rare
NC-73	1s	150.00	Rare	Very Rare
NC-74	2s/8d	150.00	Rare	Very Rare
NC-75	4s	150.00	Rare	Very Rare
NC-76	5s	150.00	Rare	Very Rare
NC-77	10s	150.00	Rare	Very Rare
NC-78	15s	125.00	400.00	Very Rare
NC-79	20s	125.00	400.00	Very Rare
NC-80	26s/8d	125.00	400.00	Very Rare
NC-81	30s	125.00	400.00	Very Rare
NC-82	40s	125.00	450.00	Very Rare

1756-1757 (written dates)

NC-83	£5	Very Rare
NC-84	£10	Very Rare
NC-85	£20	Very Rare
NC-86	£50	Very Rare

May 28, 1757

NC-87	10s	Very Rare
NC-88	20s	Very Rare
NC-89	40s	Very Rare
NC-90	£5	Very Rare

November 21, 1757

NC-91	10s	Very Rare
NC-92	20s	Very Rare
NC-93	40s	Very Rare
NC-94	£5	Very Rare

May 4, 1758

NC-95	10s	Very Rare
NC-96	20s	Very Rare
NC-97	40s	Very Rare

December 22, 1758

NC-98	10s	Very Rare
NC-99	20s	Very Rare
NC-100	40s	Very Rare

July 14, 1760

NC-101	4d	Very Rare
NC-102	6d	Very Rare
NC-103	8d	Very Rare
NC-104	1s	Very Rare
NC-105	2s	Very Rare

		VG	VF	UNC
NC-106	2s/8d		Very Rare	
NC-107	5s	125.00	150.00	Rare
NC-108	10s	110.00	220.00	Rare
NC-109	20s	120.00	240.00	Rare
NC-110	30s	150.00	300.00	Rare
NC-111	40s	150.00	300.00	Rare
NC-112	£3	150.00	300.00	Rare

April 23, 1761

		VG	VF	UNC
NC-113	4d	150.00	Very Rare	
NC-114	6d	150.00	Very Rare	
NC-115	8d	150.00	Very Rare	
NC-116	1s	150.00	Very Rare	
NC-117	2s	150.00	Very Rare	
NC-118	2s/6d	150.00	Very Rare	
NC-119	3s	180.00	350.00	Rare
NC-120	4s	180.00	350.00	Rare
NC-1-21	5s	180.00	350.00	Rare
NC-122	10s	180.00	350.00	Rare
NC-123	15s	180.00	350.00	Rare
NC-124	20s	180.00	350.00	Rare
NC-125	30s	300.00	500.00	Rare
NC-126	40s	300.00	500.00	Rare
NC-127	£3	300.00	500.00	Rare

December, 1768

		VG	VF	UNC
NC-128	2s/6d	75.00	400.00	Rare
NC-129	5s	80.00	250.00	Rare
NC-130	10s	80.00	250.00	Rare
NC-131	20s	80.00	250.00	Rare
NC-132	40s	80.00	250.00	Rare
NC-133	£3	100.00	350.00	Rare
NC-134	£5	100.00	350.00	Rare

December, 1771

There are 2 varieties of NC-136

		VG	VF	UNC
NC-135	1s	65.00	120.00	350.00
NC-136	2s/6d	70.00	135.00	375.00
NC-137	5s	65.00	120.00	350.00
NC-138	10s	80.00	170.00	450.00
NC-139	£1	80.00	170.00	500.00
NC-140	30s	130.00	270.00	550.00
NC-141*	£2	100.00	240.00	700.00
NC-142	£3	90.00	200.00	600.00
NC-143	£5	135.00	300.00	725.00

August 21, 1775

		VG	VF	UNC
NC-144	$1/4	150.00	325.00	800.00
NC-145	$1/2		Very Rare	
NC-146	$1		Very Rare	
NC-147	$2		Very Rare	
NC-148	$3		Very Rare	
NC-149	$4		Very Rare	
NC-150	$5		Very Rare	
NC-151	$8		Very Rare	
NC-152	$10		Very Rare	

April 2, 1776

(NC-153 through NC-157 exist in 6-8 distinct varieties; the others in 1 or 2 varieties.)

		VG	VF	UNC
NC-153	$1/16	160.00	240.00	475.00
NC-154	$	160.00	240.00	475.00
NC-155	$1/4	160.00	240.00	475.00
NC-156	$1/2	160.00	240.00	475.00
NC-157	$1	190.00	275.00	550.00
NC-158	$2	190.00	275.00	550.00
NC-159	$21/2	190.00	275.00	550.00
NC-160	$3	190.00	275.00	550.00
NC-161	$4	190.00	275.00	550.00
NC-162	$5	190.00	27500	550.00
NC-163	$6	190.00	275.00	550.00
NC-164	$71/2	190.00	275.00	550.00
NC-165	$8	190.00	275.00	550.00

		VG	VF	UNC
NC-166	$10	190.00	275.00	550.00
NC-167	$121/2	240.00	400.00	900.00
NC-168	$15	220.00	325.00	800.00
NC-169	$20	220.00	400.00	800.00

August 8, 1778

(There are varieties of NC-173, 176 and 177)

		VG	VF	UNC
NC-170	$	50.00	120.00	350.00
NC-171	$1/4	45.00	115.00	330.00
NC-172	$1/2	40.00	110.00	320.00
NC-173	$1	40.00	100.00	320.00
NC-174	$2	40.00	100.00	320.00
NC-175	$4	50.00	120.00	350.00
NC-176	$5	45.00	110.00	330.00
NC-177	$10	45.00	110.00	330.00
NC-178	$20	50.00	120.00	350.00
NC-179	$25	60.00	130.00	375.00
NC-180	$40	85.00	150.00	450.00
NC-181	$50	75.00	145.00	425.00
NC-182	$100	100.00	175.00	475.00

May 15, 1779

(There are varieties of NC-183, 184 and 186)

		VG	VF	UNC
NC-183	$5	50.00	100.00	Rare
NC-184	$10	50.00	100.00	Rare
NC-185	$20	50.00	100.00	Rare
NC-186	$25	65.00	125.00	Rare
NC-187	$50	100.00	205.00	Rare
NC-188	$100	110.00	225.00	Rare
NC-189	$250	125.00	250.00	Rare

1780

(This issue is identical to No. NC-187, with the addition of "1780" on the reverse. Three varieties exist.)

NC-190	$50		Very Rare	

May 10, 1780

(Many varieties exist.)

		VG	VF	UNC
NC-191	$25	50.00	115.00	Rare
NC-192	$50	60.00	140.00	Rare
NC-193	$100	70.00	160.00	Rare
NC-194	$200	100.00	240.00	Rare
NC-195	$250	85.00	200.00	Rare
NC-196	$300	100.00	250.00	Rare
NC-197	$400	100.00	250.00	Rare
NC-198	$500	70.00	225.00	Rare
NC-199	$600	125.00	350.00	Rare

May 17, 1783

		VG	VF	UNC
NC-201	6d	Rare		
NC-202	1s	Rare		
NC-203	2s	Rare		
NC-204	5s	250.00	Rare	
NC-205	10s	250.00	Rare	
NC-206	20s	250.00	Rare	
NC-207	40s	250.00	Rare	

December 29, 1785

		VG	VF	UNC
NC-208	6d	Rare		
NC-209	1s	Rare		
NC-210	2s	Rare		
NC-211	2s/6d	Rare		
NC-21-2	5s	250.00	Rare	
NC-213	10s	250.00	Rare	
NC-214	20s	250.00	Rare	
NC-215	40s	220.00	Rare	

PENNSYLVANIA

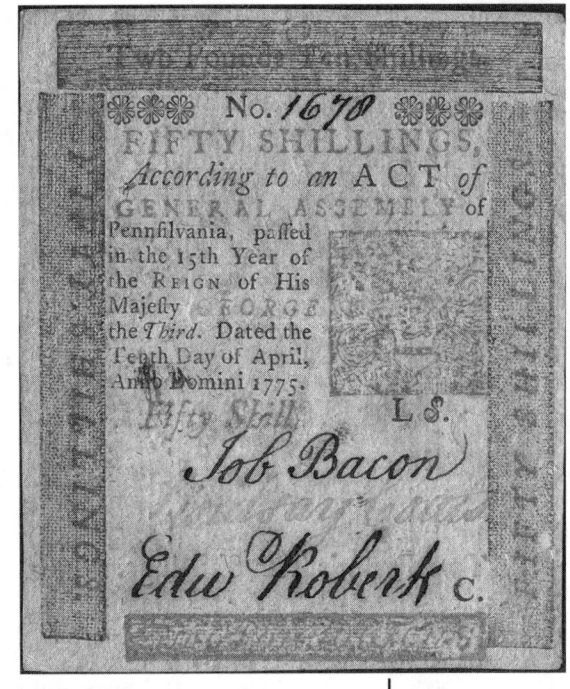

ALL ISSUES THROUGH THAT OF MAY 16, 1749
ARE VERY RARE

April 2, 1723

PA-1	1s	PA-5	10s
PA-2	2s	PA-6	15s
PA-3	2s/6d	PA-7	20s
PA-4	5s		

January 17, 1723

PA-8	1s	PA-12	5s
PA-9	1s/6d	PA-13	10s
PA-10	2s	PA-14	15s
PA-11	2s/6d	PA-15	20s

March 25, 1726

PA-16	1s	PA-19	2s/6d
PA-17	1s/6d	PA-20	5s
PA-18	2s	PA-21	10s

September 15, 1729

PA-22	1s	PA-26	5s
PA-23	1s/6d	PA-27	10s
PA-24	2s	PA-28	15s
PA-25	2s/6d	PA-29	20s

April 10, 1731

PA-30	1s	PA-34	5s
PA-31	1s/6d	PA-35	10s
PA-32	2s	PA-36	15s
PA-33	2s/6d	PA-37	20s

August 10, 1739

PA-38	1s	PA-42	5s
PA-39	18d	PA-43	10s
PA-40	25	PA-44	15s
PA-41	2s/6d	PA-45	20s

August 1, 1744

PA-46	1s	PA-49	2s/6d
PA-47	18d	PA-50	5s
PA-48	2s		

August 1, 1746

PA-51	4d	PA-53	9d
PA-52	6d	PA-54	20s

May 16, 1749

PA-55	3d	PA-57	6d
PA-56	4d	PA-58	9d

October 1, 1755

PA-59	3d	Very Rare	
PA-60	4d	Very Rare	
PA-61	6d	Very Rare	
PA-62	9d	Very Rare	
PA-63	1s	Very Rare	
PA-64	18d	Very Rare	
PA-65	2s	Very Rare	
PA-66	2s/6d	Very Rare	
PA-67	5s	400.00	Rare Very Rare
PA-68	10s	350.00	Rare Very Rare

January 1, 1756

		VG	VF	UNC
PA-69	1s	190.00	Rare	Very Rare
PA-70	18d	190.00	Rare	Very Rare
PA-71	2s	190.00	Rare	Very Rare
PA-72	2s/6d	190.00	Rare	Very Rare
PA-73	5s	190.00	Rare	Very Rare
PA-74	10s	225.00	Rare	Very Rare
PA-75	15s	225.00	Rare	Very Rare
PA-76	20s	225.00	Rare	Very Rare

October 1, 1756

PA-77	5s	160.00	Rare	Very Rare
PA-78	10s	160.00	Rare	Very Rare
PA-79	15s	160.00	Rare	Very Rare
PA-80	20s	160.00	Rare	Very Rare

March 10, 1757

PA-81	5s	145.00	Rare	Very Rare
PA-82	10s	145.00	Rare	Very Rare
PA-83	15s	145.00	Rare	Very Rare
PA-84	20s	145.00	Rare	Very Rare

July 1, 1757

PA-85	5s	125.00	Rare	Very Rare
PA-86	10s	125.00	Rare	Very Rare
PA-87	15s	125.00	Rare	Very Rare
PA-88	20s	125.00	Rare	Very Rare

May 20, 1758

PA-89	1s		Very Rare	
PA-90	18d		Very Rare	
PA-91	2s		Very Rare	
PA-92	2s/6d		Very Rare	
PA-93	5s	140.00	Rare	Very Rare
PA-94	10s	140.00	Rare	Very Rare
PA-95	15s	140.00	Rare	Very Rare
PA-96	20s	140.00	Rare	Very Rare

		VG	VF	UNC
April 25, 1759				
PA-97	5s	135.00	325.00	Very Rare
PA-98	10s	135.00	325.00	Very Rare
PA-99	15s	110.00	250.00	Rare
PA-100	20s	110.00	250.00	Rare
PA-101	50s	110.00	250.00	Rare
PA-102	£5	110.00	250.00	Rare

June 21, 1759

PA-103	50s		Very Rare	
PA-104	£5		Very Rare	

May 1, 1760

PA-105	3d		Very Rare	
PA-106	4d		Very Rare	
PA-107	6d		Very Rare	
PA-108	9d		Very Rare	
PA-109	5s	150.00	320.00	Very Rare
PA-110	10s	150.00	320.00	Very Rare
PA-111	15s	150.00	275.00	Very Rare
PA-112	20s	105.00	240.00	Very Rare
PA-113	50s	105.00	240.00	Very Rare
PA-114	£5	105.00	240.00	Very Rare

June 18, 1764

PA-115	3d	110.00	220.00	700.00
PA-116	4d	145.00	260.00	850.00
PA-117	6d	145.00	260.00	850.00
PA-118	9d	145.00	260.00	850.00
PA-119	1s	105.00	200.00	Rare
PA-120	1s/6d	105.00	200.00	Rare
PA-121	2s	105.00	200.00	Rare
PA-122	2s/6d	105.00	200.00	Rare
PA-123	5s	105.00	200.00	Rare
PA-124	10s	105.00	200.00	Rare
PA-125	15s	105.00	200.00	Rare
PA-126	20s	105.00	200.00	Rare

June 15, 1767

PA-127	40s		Very Rare	
PA-128	£4		Very Rare	
PA-129	£6		Very Rare	

March 1, 1769

PA-130	8s	190.00	Rare	Very Rare
PA-131	12s	190.00	Rare	Very Rare
PA-132	£1/10s	150.00	Rare	Very Rare
PA-133	£3	150.00	Rare	Very Rare

March 10, 1769

		VG	VF	UNC
PA-134	3d	115.00	450.00	Very Rare
PA-135	4d	115.00	450.00	Very Rare
PA-136	6d	115.00	450.00	Very Rare
PA-137	9d	115.00	450.00	Very Rare
PA-138	1s	75.00	300.00	Rare
PA-139	18d	75.00	300.00	Rare
PA-140	2s	75.00	300.00	Rare
PA-141	2s/6d	75.00	300.00	Rare
PA-142	5s	75.00	300.00	Rare
PA-143	10s	75.00	300.00	Rare
PA-144	15s	75.00	300.00	Rare
PA-145	20s	75.00	300.00	Rare

March 20, 1771

Notes signed by Francis Hopkinson (a signer of the Declaration of Independence) are worth three times the quoted prices

		VG	VF	UNC
PA-146	5s	35.00	100.00	300.00
PA-147	10s	35.00	100.00	300.00
PA-148	15s	35.00	100.00	300.00
PA-149	20s	35.00	100.00	300.00

April 3, 1772

Notes signed by John Morton (a signer of the Declaration of Independence) are worth two to three times the quoted prices.

		VG	VF	UNC
PA-150	3d	30.00	80.00	Rare
PA-151	4d	30.00	80.00	Rare
PA-152	6d	30.00	80.00	Rare
PA-153	9d	30.00	80.00	Rare
PA-154	1s	25.00	60.00	125.00
PA-155	18d	25.00	60.00	125.00
PA-156	2s	25.00	60.00	125.00
PA-157	2s/6d	25.00	60.00	125.00
PA-158	40s	50.00	150.00	Rare

March 20, 1773

		VG	VF	UNC
PA-159	4s	30.00	55.00	200.00
PA-160	6s	30.00	55.00	200.00
PA-161	14s	30.00	55.00	200.00
PA-162	16s	30.00	55.00	200.00

October 1, 1773

		VG	VF	UNC
PA-163	18d	20.00	40.00	100.00
PA-164	2s	20.00	40.00	100.00
PA-165	2s/6d	20.00	40.00	100.00
PA-166	5s	20.00	40.00	100.00
PA-167	10s	20.00	40.00	100.00
PA-168	15s	20.00	40.00	100.00
PA-169	20s	20.00	40.00	100.00
PA-170	50s	20.00	40.00	100.00

March 25, 1775

		VG	VF	UNC
PA-171	4s	30.00	70.00	300.00
PA-172	6s	30.00	70.00	300.00
PA-173	14s	30.00	70.00	300.00
PA-174	16s	30.00	70.00	300.00

April 10, 1775

		VG	VF	UNC
PA-175*	50s	35.00	90.00	300.00
PA-176	£5	35.00	90.00	300.00

July 20, 1775

		VG	VF	UNC
PA-177	10s	25.00	55.00	150.00
PA-178	20s	25.00	55.00	150.00
PA-179	30s	25.00	55.00	150.00
PA-180	40s	25.00	55.00	150.00

October 25, 1775

		VG	VF	UNC
PA-181	3d	15.00	30.00	100.00
PA-182	4d	15.00	30.00	100.00
PA-183	6d	15.00	30.00	100.00
PA-184	9d	15.00	30.00	100.00
PA-185	1s	15.00	30.00	100.00
PA-186	18d	15.00	30.00	100.00
PA-187	2s	15.00	30.00	100.00
PA-188	2s/6d	15.00	30.00	100.00
PA-189	5s	18.00	35.00	120.00
PA-190	10s	18.00	35.00	120.00
PA-191	15s	18.00	35.00	120.00
PA-192	20s	18.00	35.00	120.00

December 8, 1775

		VG	VF	UNC
PA-193	10s	15.00	30.00	90.00
PA-194	20s	15.00	30.00	90.00
PA-195	30s	15.00	30.00	90.00
PA-196	40s	15.00	30.00	90.00

April 25, 1776

		VG	VF	UNC
PA-197	3d	12.00	28.00	70.00
PA-198	4d	12.00	28.00	70.00
PA-199	6d	12.00	28.00	70.00
PA-200	9d	12.00	28.00	70.00
PA-201	1s	15.00	30.00	80.00
PA-202	18d	15.00	30.00	80.00
PA-203	2s	15.00	30.00	80.00
PA-204	2s/6d	15.00	30.00	80.00
PA-205	10s	18.00	45.00	100.00
PA-206	20s	18.00	45.00	100.00
PA-207	30s	18.00	45.00	100.00
PA-208	40s	18.00	45.00	100.00

April 10, 1777

There are two different issues of this date; they are a) printed in black and b) printed in red and black.

		VG	VF	UNC
PA-209	3d	12.00	30.00	100.00
PA-210	4d	12.00	30.00	100.00
PA-211	6d	12.00	30.00	100.00
PA-212	9d	12.00	30.00	100.00
PA-213a	1s	15.00	35.00	90.00
PA-213b	1s	18.00	40.00	100.00
PA-214a	1s/6d	15.00	35.00	90.00
PA-214b	1/6d	18.00	40.00	100.00
PA-215a	2s	15.00	35.00	90.00
PA-215b	2s	18.00	40.00	100.00
PA-216a	3s	15.00	35.00	90.00
PA-216b	3s	18.00	40.00	100.00
PA-217a	4s	15.00	35.00	90.00
PA-217b	4s	18.00	40.00	100.00
PA-218a	6s	15.00	35.00	90.00
PA-218b	6s	18.00	40.00	100.00
PA-219a	8s	15.00	35.00	90.00
PA-219b	8s	18.00	40.00	100.00
PA-220a	12s	15.00	35.00	90.00
PA-220b	12s	18.00	40.00	100.00
PA-221a	16s	15.00	35.00	90.00
PA-221b	16s	18.00	40.00	100.00
PA-222a	20s	15.00	35.00	90.00
PA-222b	20s	18.00	40.00	100.00
PA-223a	40s	20.00	50.00	110.00
PA-223b	40s	25.00	55.00	125.00
PA-224a	£4	20.00	50.00	110.00
PA-224b	£4	25.00	55.00	125.00

April 29, 1780

		VG	VF	UNC
PA-225	5s		Very Rare	
PA-226	10s		Very Rare	
PA-227	15s		Very Rare	
PA-228	20s		Very Rare	
PA-229	30s		Very Rare	
PA-230	40s		Very Rare	
PA-231	50s		Very Rare	
PA-232	60s		Very Rare	

June 1, 1780

		VG	VF	UNC
PA-233	$1	250.00	600.00	Rare
PA-234	$2	250.00	600.00	Rare
PA-235	$3	250.00	600.00	Rare
PA-236	$4	250.00	600.00	Rare
PA-237	$5	250.00	600.00	Rare
PA-238	$7	250.00	600.00	Rare
PA-239	$8	250.00	600.00	Rare
PA-240	$20	250.00	600.00	Rare

April 20, 1781

		VG	VF	UNC
PA-241	3d	50.00	150.00	300.00
PA-242	6d	50.00	150.00	300.00
PA-243	9d	50.00	150.00	300.00
PA-244	1s	75.00	200.00	350.00
PA-245	1s/6d	85.00	235.00	400.00
PA-246	2s	85.00	235.00	400.00
PA-247	2s/6d	85.00	235.00	400.00
PA-248	5s	85.00	235.00	400.00
PA-249	10s	95.00	260.00	450.00
PA-250	15s	95.00	260.00	450.00
PA-251	20s	95.00	260.00	450.00
PA-252	30s	95.00	260.00	450.00
PA-253	40s	95.00	260.00	450.00
PA-254	50s	95.00	260.00	450.00
PA-255	60s	150.00	350.00	600.00
PA-256	£5	200.00	450.00	750.00

March 21, 1783

		VG	VF	UNC
PA-257	$1/4		Extremely Rare	
PA-258	$1		Extremely Rare	
PA-259	$2		Extremely Rare	
PA-260	$3		Extremely Rare	

March 16, 1785

(Note: This issue also bears denominations in dollars.)

		VG	VF	UNC
PA-261	$6		Extremely Rare	
PA-262	$12		Extremely Rare	
PA-263	$15		Extremely Rare	
PA-264	$20		Extremely Rare	
PA-265	3d	75.00	125.00	500.00
PA-266	9d	75.00	125.00	500.00
PA-267	1s/6d	75.00	125.00	500.00
PA-268	2s/6d	75.00	125.00	500.00
PA-269	5s	85.00	150.00	Rare
PA-270	10s	85.00	150.00	Rare
PA-271	15s	85.00	150.00	Rare
PA-272	20s	85.00	150.00	Rare

RHODE ISLAND

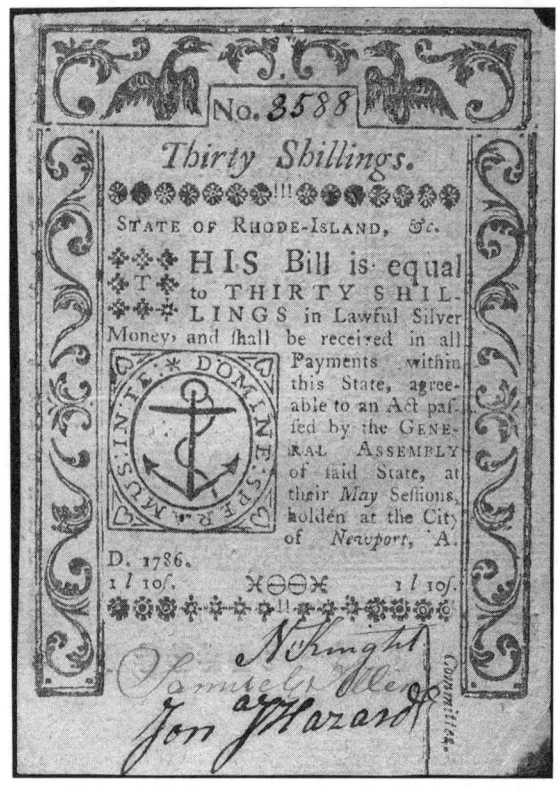

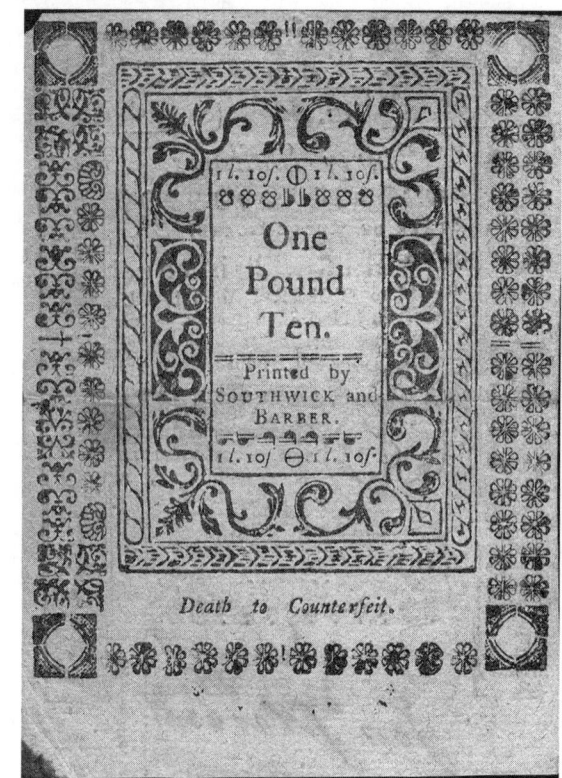

ALL ISSUES THROUGH THAT OF FEBRUARY 28, 1767 ARE VERY RARE

August 16, 1710

RI-1	2s	RI-5	20s
RI-2	2s/6d	RI-6	40s
RI-3	5s	RI-7	£3
RI-4	10s	RI-8	£5

July 5, 1715

In addition to the original issue, these notes were redated as follows:

a) Original issue   e) Redated 1728
b) Redated 1721   f) Redated 1731
c) Redated 1724   g) Redated 1733
d) Redated 1726   h) Redated 1737

RI-9a	12d	RI-12g	4s/6d
RI-9b	12d	RI-12h	4s/6d
RI-9c	12d	RI-13a	5s
RI-9d	12d	RI-13b	5s
RI-9e	12d	RI-13d	5s
RI-9f	12d	RI-14a	10s
RI-9g	12d	RI-14b	10s
RI-9h	12d	RI-14c	10s
RI-10a	2s/6d	RI-15a	20s
RI-10b	2s/6d	RI-15b	20s
RI-10c	2s/6d	RI-15c	20s
RI-10d	2s/6d	RI-16a	40s
RI-10e	2s/6d	RI-16b	40s
RI-10f	2s/6d	RI-16c	40s
RI-10g	2s/6d	RI-17a	£3
RI-10h	2s/6d	RI-17b	£3
RI-11a	3s	RI-17c	£3
RI-11b	3s	RI-18a	£5
RI-11c	3s	RI-18b	£5
RI-11d	3s	RI-18c	£5
RI-11e	3s		
RI-11f	3s		
RI-11g	3s		
RI-11h	3s		
RI-12a	4s/6d		
RI-12b	4s/6d		
RI-12c	4s/6d		
RI-12d	4s/6d		
RI-12e	4s/6d		
RI-12f	4s/6d		

June 14, 1726

In addition to the original issue, these notes were redated as follows:

a) Original issue
b) Redated 1728
c) Redated 1731
d) Redated 1733

RI-19a	5s	RI-22a	40s
RI-19b	5s	RI-22b	40s
RI-19c	5s	RI-22c	40s
RI-19d	5s	RI-22d	40s
RI-20a	10s	RI-23a	£3
RI-20b	10s	RI-23b	£3
RI-20c	10s	RI-23c	£3
RI-20d	10s	RI-23d	£3
RI-21a	20s	RI-24a	£5
RI-21b	20s	RI-24b	£5
RI-21c	20s	RI-24c	£5
RI-21d	20s	RI-24d	£5

August 15, 1737

This issue was redated as follows:

a) Original issue
b) Redated 1738

RI-25a	£1	RI-27a	£3
RI-25b	£1	RI-27b	£3
RI-26a	£2	RI-28a	£5
RI-26b	£2	RI-28b	£5

August 22, 1738

RI-29	1s	RI-32	5s
RI-30	2s/6d	RI-33	7s/6d
RI-31	3s	RI-34	10s

December 2, 1740

RI-35	6d	RI-39	5s
RI-36	1s	RI-40	10s
RI-37	1s/6d	RI-41	20s
RI-38	2s/6d	RI-42	40s

February 2, 1741

RI-43	6	RI-47	5s
RI-44	1s	RI-48	10s
RI-45	1s/6d	RI-49	20s
RI-46	2s/6d	RI-50	40s

February 14, 1743

In addition to the original issue, these notes were redated as follows: a) Original issue   d) Redated 1746

b) Redated 1744   e) Redated 1746-7
c) Redated 1745   f) Redated 1747

RI-51a	4d	RI-56a	10s
RI-51d	4d	RI-56b	10s
RI-5le	4d	RI-56c	10s
RI-51f	4d	RI-56d	10s
RI-52a	6d	RI-56e	10s
RI-52d	6d	RI-56f	10s
RI-52e	6d	RI-57a	20s
RI-52f	6d	RI-57b	20s
RI-53a	1s	RI-57c	20s
RI-53d	1s	RI-57d	20s
RI-53e	1s	RI-57e	20s
RI-53f	1s	RI-57f	20s
RI-54a	2s/6d	RI-58a	40s
RI-54d	2s/6d	RI-58b	40s
RI-54e	2s/6d	RI-58c	40s
RI-54f	2s/6	RI-58d	40s
RI-55a	5s	RI-58e	40s
RI-55b	5s	RI-58f	40s
RI-55c	5s		
RI-55d	5s		
RI-55e	5s		
RI-55f	5s		

March 18, 1750

All but one note of this issue also exists redated 1755.

a) Original issue
b) Redated 1755

RI-59a	15 Grains
RI-59b	15 Grains
RI-60a	1 Pennyweight 13 1/2 Grains
RI-60b	1 Pennyweight 13 1/2 Grains
RI-61a	2 Pennyweight 12 Grains
RI-61b	2 Pennyweight 12 Grains
RI-62a	6 Pennyweight 6 Grains
RI-62b	6 Pennyweight 6 Grains
RI-63a	12 Pennyweight 12 Grains
RI-63b	12 Pennyweight 12 Grains
RI-64a	1 Ounce 5 Pennyweight
RI-64b	1 Ounce 5 Pennyweight
RI-65a	2 Ounces 10 Pennyweight
RI-65b	2 Ounces 10 Pennyweight

RI-66a 5 Ounces
RI-66b 5 Ounces

February 27, 1756

RI-67	6d		RI-72	5s
RI-68	9d		RI-73	10s
RI-69	1s		RI-74	20s
RI-70	2s		RI-75	25s
RI-71	3s			

August, 1756

RI-76	6d		RI-81	5s
RI-77	9d		RI-82	10s
RI-78	1s		RI-83	20s
RI-79	2s		RI-84	25s
RI-80	3s			

May 8, 1758

RI-85	6d		RI-89	10s
RI-86	1s		RI-90	20s
RI-87	2s		RI-91	30s
RI-88	5s			

December 23, 1758

RI-92	6d		RI-96	10s
RI-93	1s		RI-97	20s
RI-94	2s		RI-98	30s
RI-95	5s			

March 15, 1759

RI-99	6d		RI-103	10s
RI-100	1s		RI-104	20s
RI-101	2s		RI-105	30s
RI-102	5s			

April 4, 1759

RI-106	6d		RI-110	10s
RI-107	1s		RI-111	20s
RI-108	2s		RI-112	30s
RI-109	5s			

June 23, 1759

RI-113	6d		RI-117	10s
RI-114	1s		RI-118	20s
RI-115	2s		RI-119	30s
RI-116	5s			

March 10, 1760

RI-120	6d		RI-124	5s
RI-121	9d		RI-125	10s
RI-122	1s		RI-126	20s
RI-123	2s		RI-127	30s

May 12, 1760

RI-128	5s		RI-130	20s
RI-129	10s		RI-131	30s

March 20, 1762

RI-132	3d		RI-137	5s
RI-133	6d		RI-138	10s
RI-134	9d		RI-139	20s
RI-135	1s		RI-140	30s
RI-136	2s			

April 10, 1762

RI-141	5s		RI-143	20s
RI-142	10s		RI-144	30s

May 8, 1762

RI-145	5s		RI-147	20s
RI-146	10s		RI-148	30s

November 1, 1762

RI-149	3d		RI-154	3s
RI-150	6d		RI-155	4s
RI-151	9d		RI-156	5s
RI-152	1s		RI-157	10s
RI-153	2s		RI-158	20s

March 1, 1766

RI-159	3d		RI-163	2s
RI-160	6d		RI-164	3s
RI-161	9d		RI-165	5s
RI-162	1s			

February 28, 1767

		VG	VF	UNC
RI-166	4d	1000.00	2100.00	Unknown
RI-167	8d		Extremely Rare	
RI-168	1s		Extremely Rare	
RI-169	2s		Extremely Rare	
RI-170	3s		Extremely Rare	
RI-171	4s		Extremely Rare	
RI-172	6s		Extremely Rare	
RI-173	10s		Extremely Rare	
RI-174	20s		Extremely Rare	

May 3, 1775

RI-175	6d	150.00	Very Rare
RI-176	9d	150.00	Very Rare
RI-177	1s	150.00	Very Rare
RI-178	2s	150.00	Very Rare
RI-179	3s	200.00	Very Rare
RI-180	4s	200.00	Very Rare
RI-181	5s	200.00	Very Rare
RI-182	10s	200.00	Very Rare
RI-183	20s	200.00	Very Rare
RI-184	30s	200.00	Very Rare
RI-185	40s	300.00	Very Rare

June 16, 1775

RI-186	6d	210.00	Very Rare
RI-187	9d	210.00	Very Rare
RI-188	1s	210.00	Very Rare
RI-189	2s	210.00	Very Rare
RI-190	3s	300.00	Very Rare
RI-191	4s	300.00	Very Rare
RI-192	5s	300.00	Very Rare
RI-193	10s	300.00	Very Rare
RI-194	20s	300.00	Very Rare
RI-195	30s	300.00	Very Rare
RI-196	40s	425.00	Very Rare

June 29, 1775

RI-197	6d	210.00	Very Rare
RI-198	9d	210.00	Very Rare
RI-199	1s	210.00	Very Rare
RI-200	2s	210.00	Very Rare
RI-201	3s	300.00	Very Rare
RI-202	4s	300.00	Very Rare
RI-203	5s	300.00	Very Rare
RI-204	10s	300.00	Very Rare
RI-205	20s	300.00	Very Rare
RI-206	30s	300.00	Very Rare
RI-207	40s	425.00	Very Rare

November 6, 1775

RI-208	6d	110.00	300.00
RI-209	9d	110.00	300.00
RI-210	1s	110.00	300.00
RI-211	2s	120.00	350.00
RI-212	3s	140.00	400.00
RI-213	5s	160.00	Very Rare
RI-214	10s	180.00	Very Rare
RI-215	20s	200.00	Very Rare
RI-216	30s	225.00	Very Rare
RI-217	40s	250.00	Very Rare

January 15, 1776

RI-218	6d	135.00	300.00
RI-219	9d	135.00	300.00
RI-220	1s	135.00	300.00
RI-221	2s	140.00	325.00
RI-222	3s	135.00	300.00
RI-223	4s	135.00	300.00
RI-224	5s	135.00	300.00
RI-225	10s	135.00	300.00
RI-226	20s	135.00	300.00
RI-227	30s	135.00	Very Rare
RI-228	40s	150.00	Very Rare
RI-229	60s	125.00	Very Rare

March 18, 1776

RI-230	9d	200.00	360. 00	Rare
RI-231	1s	200.00	360.00	Rare
RI-232	2s	200.00	360.00	Rare
RI-233	3s	200.00	360.00	Rare
RI-234	4s	200.00	360.00	Rare
RI-235	5s	200.00	360.00	Rare

		VG	VF	UNC
RI-236	10s	200.00	360.00	Rare
RI-237	20s	200.00	360.00	Rare
RI-238	30s	200.00	360.00	Rare
RI-239	40s	200.00	360.00	Rare
RI-240	60s	200.00	360.00	Rare

September 5, 1776

		VG	VF	UNC
RI-241	$1/16	200.00	Very Rare	
RI-242	$	200.00	Very Rare	
RI-243	$1/4	200.00	Very Rare	
RI-244	$1/2	200.00	Very Rare	
RI-245	$1	250.00	Very Rare	
RI-246	$2	Rare		
RI-247	$3	Rare		
RI-248	$4	Rare		
RI-249	$5	Rare		
RI-250	$6	Rare		
RI-251	$7	Rare		
RI-252	$8	Rare		
RI-253	$10	Rare		
RI-254	$20	Rare		
RI-255	$30	Rare		

1777 (handwritten dates)

RI-256	$5	Extremely Rare
RI-257	$6	Extremely Rare
RI-258	$7	Extremely Rare
RI-259	$8	Extremely Rare
RI-260	$10	Extremely Rare
RI-261	$20	Extremely Rare
RI-262	$30	Extremely Rare
RI-263hd	Handwritten denominations	
		Extremely Rare

May 22, 1777

		VG	VF	UNC
RI-264	$1/36	100.00	300.00	850.00
RI-265	$1/24	100.00	300.00	850.00
RI-266	$1/18	100.00	300.00	850.00
RI-267	$1/12	100.00	300.00	850.00
RI-268	$1/9	100.00	300.00	850.00
RI-269	$1/8	100.00	300.00	Very Rare
RI-270	$1/6	100.00	300.00	Very Rare
RI-271	$1/4	100.00	360.00	Very Rare
RI-272	$	100.00	420.00	Very Rare

1778-1779. Handwritten dates.

RI-273	£10	Very Rare

June, 1780

		VF
RI-274	$1	Very Rare
RI-275	$2	Very Rare
RI-276	$3	Very Rare
RI-277	$4	Very Rare
RI-278	$5	Very Rare
RI-279	$7	Very Rare
RI-280	$8	Very Rare
RI-281	$20	Very Rare

July 2, 1780

		VG	VF	UNC
RI-282	$1	15.00	35.00	85.00
RI-283	$2	15.00	35.00	85.00
RI-284	$3	15.00	35.00	85.00
RI-285	$4	15.00	35.00	85.00
RI-286	$5	15.00	35.00	85.00
RI-287	$7	15.00	35.00	85.00
RI-288	$8	15.00	35.00	85.00
RI-289	$20	15.00	35.00	85.00

May, 1786

		VG	VF	UNC
RI-290	6d	20.00	40.00	75.00
RI-291	9d	20.00	40.00	75.00
RI-292	1s	20.00	40.00	75.00
RI-293	2s/6d	20.00	40.00	75.00
RI-294	3s	20.00	40.00	75.00
RI-295	5s	20.00	40.00	75.00
RI-296	6s	20.00	40.00	75.00
RI-297	10s	20.00	40.00	75.00
RI-298	20s	20.00	40.00	75.00
RI-299*	30s	20.00	40.00	75.00
RI-300	40s	20.00	40.00	75.00
RI-301	£3	30.00	65.00	100.00

SOUTH CAROLINA

ALL ISSUES THROUGH THAT OF 1, 1775 ARE VERY RARE.

May 8, 1703
SC-1   50s
SC-2   £20

July 5, 1707
SC-3   20s   SC-6   £6
SC-4   40s   SC-7   £10
SC-5   £4   SC-8   £20

February 14, 1707
SC-9   20s

April 24, 1708
SC-10   20s   SC-11   40s

March 1, 1710
SC-12   5s   SC-13   10s

Issue of November 10, 1711
SC-14

June 7, 1712
SC-15   5s   SC-16   20

August 27, 1715
SC-17   £4

March 24, 1715
SC-18   Unknown

June 30, 1716
SC-19   £5   SC-20   £20

August 4, 1716
SC-20   Unknown

February 20, 1718
SC-21   Unknown

June 18, 1720
SC-22   Unknown

December 10, 1720
(Note: This issue, while legal tender at 30 shillings, was payable to bearer in rice.)
SC-23   1 Hundredweight

1723
SC-24   5s   SC-27   10s
SC-25   6s/3d   SC-28   £1
SC-26   7s/6d   SC-29   £2

1731
SC-30   4s/6d   SC-36   £4
SC-31   5s   SC-37   £6/5s

SC-32   7s/6d   SC-38   £10
SC-33   20s   SC-39   £12/10s
SC-34   £2   SC-40   £15
SC-35   £3   SC-41   £20

August 20, 1731
SC-42   £5   SC-45   £25
SC-43   £6/5s   SC-46   £50
SC-44   £12/10s

March 5, 1736
SC-47   £6   SC-48   £12

April 5, 1740
SC-49   £4   SC-50   £8

September 19, 1740
SC-51   £4   SC-52   £8

June 30, 1748
SC-53   2s/6d   SC-58   £1
SC-54   5s   SC-59   £2
SC-55   6s/3d   SC-60   £5
SC-56   7s/6d   SC-61   £10
SC-57   10s   SC-62   £20

1750-1769. Dates handwritten.
SC-63   £5   SC-66   £30
SC-64   £10   SC-67   £50
SC-65   £20

May 16, 1752
SC-68   5s   SC-71   £2
SC-69   6s/3d   SC-72   £5
SC-70   £1   SC-73   £10

July 6, 1757
SC-74   £10   SC-75   £20

1760
SC-76   £20
SC-77   £25
SC-78   £50

July 25, 1761
SC-79   2s/6d   SC-82   10s
SC-80   5s   SC-83   £1
SC-81   7s/6d

May 29, 1762
SC-84   £2

1767. Dates handwritten
SC-85   £20

January 1, 1770
SC-86   2s/6d   SC-91   £1
SC-87   5s   SC-92   £2
SC-88   6s/3d   SC-93   £5

SC-89   7s/6d   SC-94   £10
SC-90   10s   SC-95   £20

April 7, 1770
SC-96   £10

April 10, 1774
SC-97   £100

June 1, 1775

	VG	VF	UNC
SC-98 £5	100.00	200.00	Very Rare
SC-99 £10	90.00	200.00	Very Rare
SC-100 £20	100.00	225.00	Very Rare
SC-101 £50	135.00	250.00	Very Rare

June 10, 1775

SC-102 £10			Very Rare

November 15, 1775

	VG	VF	UNC
SC-103 2s/6d	150.00	450.00	Very Rare
SC-104 5s	150.00	450.00	Very Rare
SC-105 7s/6d	150.00	450.00	Very Rare
SC-106 10s	150.00	450.00	Very Rare
SC-107 15s	150.00	450.00	Very Rare
SC-108 20s	150.00	450.00	Very Rare
SC-109 30s	150.00	450.00	Very Rare
SC-110 £2	150.00	450.00	Very Rare
SC-111 £2/10s	150.00	450.00	Very Rare
SC-112 £3	150.00	450.00	Very Rare

March 6, 1776

	VG	VF	UNC
SC-113 1s/3d	250.00	600.00	Unknown
SC-114 2s/6d	250.00	600.00	Unknown
SC-115 3s/9d	250.00	600.00	Unknown
SC-116 5s	250.00	600.00	Unknown
SC-117 6s/3d	250.00	600.00	Unknown
SC-118 12s/6d	250.00	600.00	Unknown
SC-119 17s/6d	250.00	600.00	Unknown
SC-120 £1/10s	250.00	600.00	Unknown
SC-121 £1/15s	250.00	600.00	Unknown
SC-122 £2	250.00	600.00	Unknown
SC-123 £2/5s	250.00	600.00	Unknown
SC-124 £3	250.00	600.00	Unknown
SC-125 £15	150.00	300.00	Unknown
SC-126 £25	150.00	300.00	Unknown
SC-127 £50	150.00	300.00	Unknown
SC-128 £100	150.00	300.00	Unknown

October 19, 1776
(Note: These notes also bear the denomination in English currency.)

	VG	VF	UNC
SC-129 $1	100.00	200.00	Very Rare
SC-130 $2	100.00	200.00	Very Rare
SC-131 $4	100.00	200.00	Very Rare
SC-132 $6	100.00	200.00	Very Rare
SC-133 $8	100.00	200.00	Very Rare
SC-134 $10	100.00	200.00	Very Rare

December 23, 1776, 1777 on back
(Note: These notes also bear the denominaton in English currency.)
SC-136b & SC138b were erroneously dated "December 23, 1777."

	VG	VF	UNC
SC-135 $1	85.00	140.00	400.00
SC-136a $2	90.00	150.00	450.00
SC-136b $2	200.00	400.00	700.00
SC-137 $3	90.00	150.00	400.00
SC-138a $4	90.00	150.00	400.00
SC-138b $4	200.00	400.00	700.00
SC-139 $5	120.00	180.00	450.00
SC-140 $6	90.00	150.00	400.00
SC-141 $8	90.00	150.00	400.00
SC-142 $20	150.00	210.00	500.00

February 14, 1777
(Note: Denomination also appears in English currency.)

	VG	VF	UNC
SC-143 $20	60.00	200.00	Rare
SC-144 $30	60.00	200.00	Rare

	VG	VF	UNC
April 10, 1778			
SC-145	2s/6d	75.00	135.00	300.00
SC-146	3s/9d	75.00	135.00	300.00
SC-147	5s	75.00	135.00	300.00
SC-148	7s/6d	95.00	150.00	350.00
SC-149	10s	75.00	135.00	300.00
SC-150	15s	90.00	150.00	350.00
SC-151	20s	90.00	150.00	350.00
SC-152	30s	90.00	150.00	350.00

February 8, 1779

(Note: Denomination also appears in English currency.)

		VG	VF	
SC-153	$40	150.00	300.00	Rare
SC-154	$50	100.00	200.00	Rare
SC-155	$60	150.00	300.00	Rare
SC-156	$70	100.00	200.00	Rare
SC-157	$80	150.00	350.00	Rare
SC-158	$90	100.00	200.00	Rare
SC-159	$100	160.00	325.00	Rare

1786

SC-160	2s/6d	Very Rare
SC-161	5s	Very Rare
SC-162	10s	Very Rare
SC-163	£1	Very Rare
SC-164	£1/10s	Very Rare
SC-165	£3	Very Rare
SC-166	£5	Very Rare
SC-167	£10	Very Rare
SC-168	£20	Very Rare

May 1, 1786

SC-169	£1	Very Rare
SC-170	£2	Very Rare
SC-171	£3	Very Rare
SC-172	£10	Very Rare

1787

SC-173	2s/6d	Very Rare
SC-174	5s	Very Rare

SC-175	10s	Very Rare
SC-176	£1	Very Rare
SC-177	£3	Very Rare
SC-178	£5	Very Rare
SC-179	£6	Very Rare
SC-180	£10	Very Rare
SC-181	£20	Very Rare

1798

SC-182	1s	Very Rare
SC-183	1s/6d	Very Rare
SC-184	5s	Very Rare
SC-185	10s	Very Rare
SC-186	£1	Very Rare
SC-187	£2	Very Rare
SC-188	£3	Very Rare
SC-189	£5	Very Rare
SC-190	£6	Very Rare
SC-191	£10	Very Rare
SC-192	£20	Very Rare

VERMONT

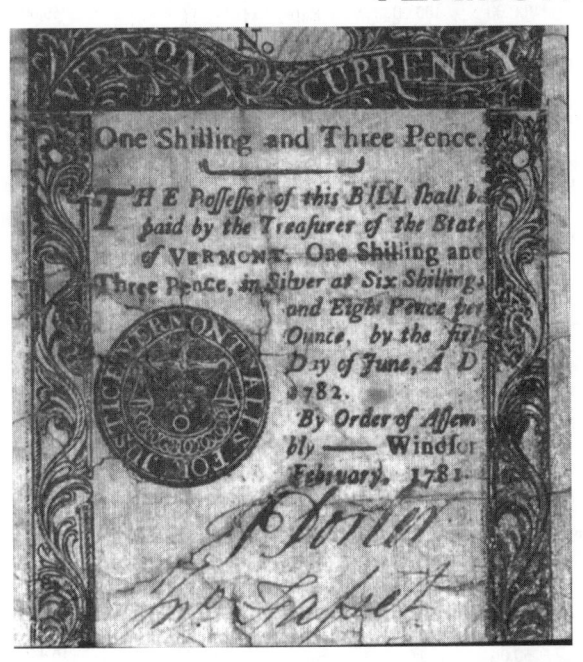

All Vermont notes are cancelled.

February, 1781

		VG	VF	UNC
VT-1	1s	3500.00	7000.00	Unknown
VT-2*	1s/3d	3500.00	7000.00	Unknown
VT-3	2s/6d	3500.00	7000.00	Unknown
VT-4	5s	3500.00	7000.00	Unknown
VT-5	10s	3500.00	7000.00	Unknown
VT-6	20s	3750.00	7500.00	Unknown
VT-7	40s	4000.00	8000.00	Unknown
VT-8	£3	4500.00	9000.00	Unknown

Illustration courtesy of Stacks'.

VIRGINIA

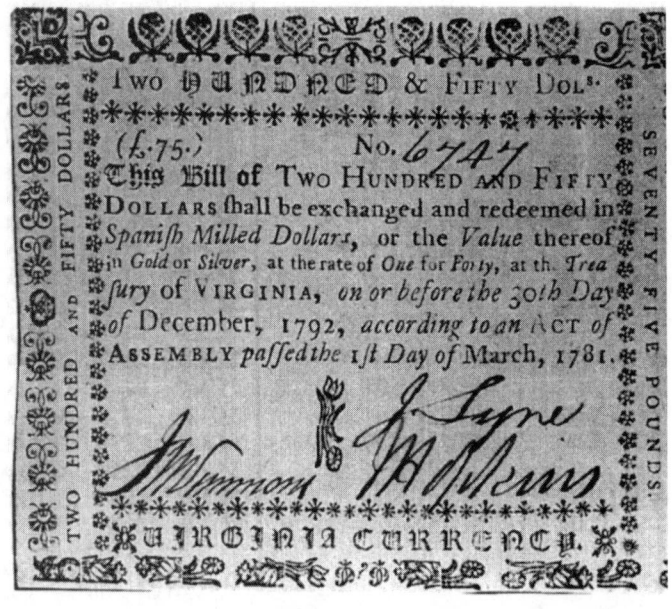

ALL ISSUES THROUGH THAT OF JULY 11, 1771
ARE VERY RARE.

June, 1755

VA-1	Unknown

December 11, 1755

VA-2	10s	VA-3	£5

March, 1756

VA-4	Unknown

Issue of June 8, 1757

VA-5	1s	VA-10	20s
VA-6	1s/3d	VA-11	£2
VA-7	2s/6d	VA-12	£3
VA-8	5s	VA-13	£5
VA-9	10s	VA-14	£10

October 12, 1758

VA-15	1s	VA-20	20s
VA-16	1s/3d	VA-21	£2
VA-17	2s/6	VA-22	£3
VA-18	5s	VA-23	£5
VA-19	10s		

April 5, 1759

VA-24	1s	VA-29	20s
VA-25	1s/3d	VA-30	£2
VA-26	2s/6d	VA-31	£3
VA-27	5s	VA-32	£5
VA-28	10s		

November 21, 1759

VA-33	£3	VA-34	£5

March 11, 1760

VA-35	2s/6d	VA-38	£3
VA-36	5s	VA-39	£5
VA-37	£2		

May 24, 1760

VA-40	1s	VA-45	20s
VA-41	1/3d	VA-46	£2
VA-42	2s/6d	VA-47	£3
VA-43	5s	VA-48	£5
VA-44	10s		

April 7, 1762

VA-49	2s/6d	VA-53	£2
VA-50	5s	VA-54	£3
VA-51	10s	VA-55	£5
VA-52	20s		

November 7, 1769

VA-56	20s	VA-58	£5
VA-57	£2		

July 11, 1771

VA-59	£2	VA-61	£5
VA-60	£3		

April 1, 1773

		VG	VF	UNC
VA-62	20s	400.00	700.00	Unknown
VA-63	£3	400.00	700.00	Unknown
VA-64	£5	400.00	700.00	Unknown
VA-65	£8	450.00	750.00	Unknown
VA-66	£12	500.00	800.00	Unknown

March 4, 1773

		VG	VF	UNC
VA-67	20s	600.00	900.00	Unknown
VA-68	£2	600.00	900.00	Unknown
VA-69	£3	600.00	900.00	Unknown
VA-70	£5	600.00	900.00	Unknown

July 17, 1775

There were two different sizes of the same denominations in this series. They are denoted as a) small b)
large.

		VG	VF	UNC
VA-71	1s/3d	50.00	110.00	Very Rare
VA-72	2s/6d	50.00	110.00	Very Rare
VA-73	5s	50.00	110.00	Very Rare
VA-74	7s/6d	50.00	110.00	Very Rare
VA-75	10s	50.00	110.00	Very Rare
VA-76	12s/6d	75.00	150.00	Very Rare
VA-77a	20s	75.00	150.00	Very Rare
VA-77b	20s	350.00	550.00	Unknown
VA-78a	£2	75.00	150.00	Very Rare
VA-78b	£2	350.00	550.00	Unknown
VA-79a	£3	75.00	150.00	Very Rare
VA-79b	£3	350.00	550.00	Unknown
VA-80b	£5	350.00	550.00	Unknown

September 1, 1775

		VG	VF	UNC
VA-81	10s		Unknown	
VA-82	20s	200.00	400.00	Very Rare
VA-93	£4	200.00	400.00	Very Rare
VA-84	£5	200.00	400.00	Very Rare
VA-85	£8	200.00	400.00	Very Rare
VA-86	£10	200.00	400.00	Very Rare
VA-87	£12	200.00	400.00	Very Rare

May 6, 1776

		VG	VF	UNC
VA-88	$1/6	40.00	100.00	Rare
VA-89	1s/3d	55.00	90.00	Rare
VA-90	$	40.00	100.00	Rare
VA-91	2s/6d	55.00	90.00	Rare
VA-92	5s	55.00	100.00	Rare
VA-93	7s/6d	55.00	100.00	Rare
VA-94	10s	55.00	100.00	Rare
VA-95	12s/6d	55.00	100.00	Rare
VA-96	20s	75.00	120.00	Rare
VA-97	$4	40.00	90.00	Rare
VA-98	$5	40.00	90.00	Rare
VA-99	£2	75.00	120.00	Rare
VA-100	£3	75.00	120.00	Rare
VA-101	£4	75.00	120.00	Rare

October 7, 1776

		VG	VF	UNC
VA-102	$1/6	50.00	120.00	Rare
VA-103	$	50.00	120.00	Rare
VA-104	$	50.00	120.00	Rare
VA-105	$1	50.00	120.00	Rare
VA-106	$4	50.00	120.00	Rare
VA-107	$5	50.00	120.00	Rare
VA-108	$6	50.00	120.00	Rare
VA-109	$8	50.00	120.00	Rare
VA-110	$10	50.00	120.00	Rare
VA-111	$15	50.00	120.00	Rare

May 5, 1777

		VG	VF	UNC
VA-112	$1/6	40.00	90.00	Rare
VA-113	$1/3	40.00	90.00	Rare
VA-114	$2/3	40.00	90.00	Rare
VA-115	$1	40.00	90.00	Rare
VA-116	$4	40.00	90.00	Rare
VA-117	$5	40.00	90.00	Rare
VA-118	$6	40.00	90.00	Rare
VA-119	$8	40.00	90.00	Rare
VA-120	$10	40.00	90.00	Rare
VA-121	$15	40.00	90.00	Rare

October 20, 1777

		VG	VF	UNC
VA-122	$1/6	35.00	80.00	350.00
VA-123	$1/3	35.00	80.00	350.00
VA-124	$2/3	35.00	80.00	350.00
VA-125	$1	35.00	80.00	350.00
VA-126	$4	35.00	80.00	350.00
VA-127	$5	35.00	80.00	350.00
VA-128	$6	35.00	80.00	350.00
VA-129	$8	35.00	80.00	350.00
VA-130	$10	35.00	80.00	350.00

		VG	VF	UNC
VA-131	$15	35.00	80.00	350.00

May 4, 1778 (Dates Handwritten)

		VG	VF	UNC
VA-132	$1/6	40.00	90.00	Rare
VA-133	$1/3	40.00	90.00	Rare
VA-134	$2/3	40.00	90.00	Rare
VA-135	$1	40.00	90.00	Rare
VA-136	$4	40.00	90.00	Rare
VA-137	$5	40.00	90.00	Rare
VA-138	$6	40.00	90.00	Rare
VA-139	$8	40.00	90.00	Rare

May 4, 1778 (Dates Printed)

Two varieties exist of each of these notes, as follows:
  a) Thin paper   b) Thick paper

		VG	VF	UNC
VA-140a	$1/6	35.00	80.00	Rare
VA-140b	$1/6	40.00	80.00	Rare
VA-141a	$1/4	35.00	80.00	Rare
VA-141b	$1/4	40.00	90.00	Rare
VA-142a	$	35.00	80.00	Rare
VA-142b	$	40.00	90.00	Rare
VA-143a	$	35.00	80.00	Rare
VA-143b	$	40.00	90.00	Rare
VA-144a	$1	35.00	85.00	Rare
VA-144b	$1	40.00	90.00	Rare
VA-145a*	$3	35.00	85.00	Rare
VA-145b	$3	40.00	90.00	Rare
VA-146a	$4	35.00	85.00	Rare
VA-146b	$4	40.00	90.00	Rare
VA-147a	$5	35.00	85.00	Rare
VA-147b	$5	40.00	90.00	Rare
VA-148a	$6	35.00	80.00	Rare
VA-148b	$6	40.00	90.00	Rare
VA-149a	$7	35.00	80.00	Rare
VA-149b	$7	40.00	90.00	Rare
VA-150a	$10	35.00	80.00	Rare
VA-150b	$10	40.00	90.00	Rare
VA-151a	$15	35.00	80.00	Rare
VA-151b	$15	40.00	90.00	Rare

October 5, 1778

		VG	VF	UNC
VA-152	$1/6	60.00	100.00	Rare
VA-153	$1/4	60.00	100.00	Rare
VA-154	$1/3	60.00	100.00	Rare
VA-155	$2/3	60.00	100.00	Rare
VA-156	$1	60.00	100.00	Rare
VA-157	$3	60.00	100.00	Rare
VA-158	$5	60.00	100.00	Rare
VA-159	$7	60.00	100.00	Rare
VA-160	$10	60.00	100.00	Rare
VA-161	$15	60.00	100.00	Rare
VA-162	$50	180.00	350.00	Rare
VA-163	$100	180.00	350.00	Rare

May 3, 1779

		VG	VF	UNC
VA-164	$3	75.00	125.00	Rare
VA-165	$5	75.00	125.00	Rare
VA-166	$7	75.00	125.00	Rare
VA-167	$10	75.00	125.00	Rare
VA-168	$15	75.00	125.00	Rare
VA-169	$50	125.00	300.00	Rare
VA-170	$100	125.00	300.00	Rare

Note: the value on the following issues are also given
in English Currency.

May 1, 1780

		VG	VF	UNC
VA-171	$1	125.00	225.00	Rare
VA-172	$2	125.00	225.00	Rare
VA-173	$3	125.00	225.00	Rare
VA-174	$4	125.00	225.00	Rare
VA-175	$5	125.00	225.00	Rare
VA-176	$7	125-00	225.00	Rare
VA-177	$8	125.00	225.00	Rare
VA-178	$20	125.00	225.00	Rare

July 14, 1780

		VG	VF	UNC
VA-179	$3	50.00	130.00	300.00
VA-180	$6	50.00	130.00	300.00
VA-181	$10	50.00	130.00	300.00
VA-182	$13	50.00	130.00	300.00
VA-183	$15	50.00	130.00	300.00
VA-184	$20	50.00	130.00	300.00
VA-185	$35	50.00	130.00	300.00
VA-186	$45	50.00	130.00	300.00
VA-187	$55	50.00	130.00	300.00
VA-188	$60	50.00	130.00	300.00
VA-189	$80	50.00	130.00	300.00
VA-190	$100	50.00	130.00	300.00

October 16, 1780

		VG	VF	UNC
VA-191	$50	40.00	100.00	300.00
VA-192	$100	40.00	100.00	300.00
VA-193	$200	40.00	100.00	300.00
VA-194	$300	40.00	100.00	300.00
VA-195	$400	40.00	100.00	300.00
VA-196	$500	40.00	100.00	300.00

October 16, 1780 ("For Clothing the Army")

		VG	VF	UNC
VA-197	$100	300.00	850.00	Unknown
VA-198	$200	300.00	850.00	Unknown
VA-199	$300	300.00	850.00	Unknown
VA-200	$400	300.00	850.00	Unknown
VA-201	$500	300.00	850.00	Unknown
VA-202	$1000	300.00	850.00	Unknown

March 1, 1781

Two varieties exist of each of these notes as follows:
a) Thin paper   b) Thick paper

		VG	VF	UNC
VA-203	$20	50.00	120.00	425.00
VA-204	$50	50.00	120.00	425.00
VA-205	$80	50.00	120.00	425.00
VA-206	$150	50.00	120.00	425.00
VA-207*	$250	50.00	120.00	425.00
VA-208	$500	50.00	120.00	425.00
VA-209	$1000	50.00	120.00	425.00

May 7, 1781

		VG	VF	UNC
VA-210	$10	80.00	160.00	400.00
VA-211	$15	80.00	160.00	400.00
VA-212	$25	80 00	160.00	400.00
VA-213	$30	80.00	160.00	400.00
VA-214	$35	80.00	160.00	400.00
VA-215	$40	80.00	160.00	400.00
VA-216	$50	80.00	160.00	400.00
VA-217	$70	80.00	160.00	400.00
VA-218	$75	75.00	150.00	400.00
VA-219	$100	75.00	150.00	400.00
VA-220	$200	75.00	150.00	400.00
VA-221	$500	75.00	150.00	400.00
VA-222	$1000	75.00	150.00	400.00
VA-223	$1200	90.00	200.00	500.00
VA-224	$1500	110.00	275.00	600.00
VA-225	$2000	140.00	325.00	700.00

PART SIX
XXV. THE TREASURY NOTES OF THE WAR OF 1812

It is argued that the first circulating currency issued by the United States did not appear in 1861 as commonly believed, but in 1815 – forty-six years earlier than the first Demand Notes. These treasury notes were issued following the outbreak of war with Great Britèan in June of 1812. With the demise of the First Bank of the United States and no provision for internal revenue taxes, only loans and these innovative notes which bore interest at 1fi cents a day per $100 (except for the "Small Notes" of 1815) were left to provide revenue to prosecute the war.

A total of five issues between 1812 and 1815 totalling $36 million in denominations of $3 to $1,000 were emitted. The notes proved to be extremely successful and were fully subscribed and accepted by banks and merchants.

First Treasury Notes Issue

Originally suggested in 1810 by then Secretary of Treasury Albert Gallatin, Treasury Notes as a resource for raising government revenue were first authorized by Congress on June 30, 1812. A total of $15,000,000 in denominations of $100 and $1,000 were authorized and by December 1812 were fully subscribed by the banks . They bore interest at 5.4% or 1fi cents a day per $100.

Subsequent issues followed a pattern in which Congress first attempted to raise funds by floating long-term loans and then making up the difference with the issue of Treasury Notes. Congress therefore authorized a second issue of $5,000,000 in Treasury Notes on February 25, 1813.

The third issue on March 4, 1814 authorized another $10,000,000 of Treasury Notes. Unlike the first two issues that only authorized $100 and $1,000 notes, this issue and the next included $20 notes.

The fourth Treasury Note issue on December 26, 1814, authorized an additional $10,500,000 of Treasury Notes, but for the first time not all were fully subscribed ($8,318,400). Only $100 and $20 notes are believed to have been printed.

Issuance of Small Size Treasury Notes

With new loans and fiscal revenues far from adequate, a new monetary expedient was necessary. Specifically, the Chairman of the House Ways and Means Committee argued for a circulating currency of small denominations payable to bearer, transferable by delivery and receivable in all payments for public lands and taxes.

On February 24, 1815, Congress authorized 25,000,000 of these "Small" Treasury Notes. A few days later, the war ended and only $4,969,400 of $100 notes bearing interest at 5.4% and $3,392.994 of "Small" $3, $5, $10, $20 and $50 denominations were actually issued (although a total of $9,070,386 worth were reissued). The latter bore no interest by circulating as money.

All Treasury Notes were made by Murray, Draper, Fairman, and Co. and are one-sided. The first two issues were signed by Timothy Matlock and Charles Biddle while the latter three were signed by Earnest Fox and Samuel Clarke. The last issue was alternately signed by F. W. McGeary and C. A. Colville. Some were countersigned by William White (first two issues), T. D. T. Tucker (last two issues) or Joseph Nourse (the Register on the last issue only).

The "Small Treasury Notes" of $3 - $50 were used to purchase goods and services by individuals, pay customs duties by merchants, and acted as cash reserves for banks, thus preventing them from being discounted. As a result, they became the first circulating currency issued by the United States.

All these series are extremely rare in any form, and nearly all of the few known are specimens, proofs, or remainders, with most cancelled in some way. Fully signed, dated, numbered, and uncancelled notes are virtually non-existent.

Thanks to Donald H. Kagin for his contribution in the preparation of this section.

A.   Act of June 30, 1812

1-year notes of this issue bore interest at 5.4%. 100 notes outstanding.

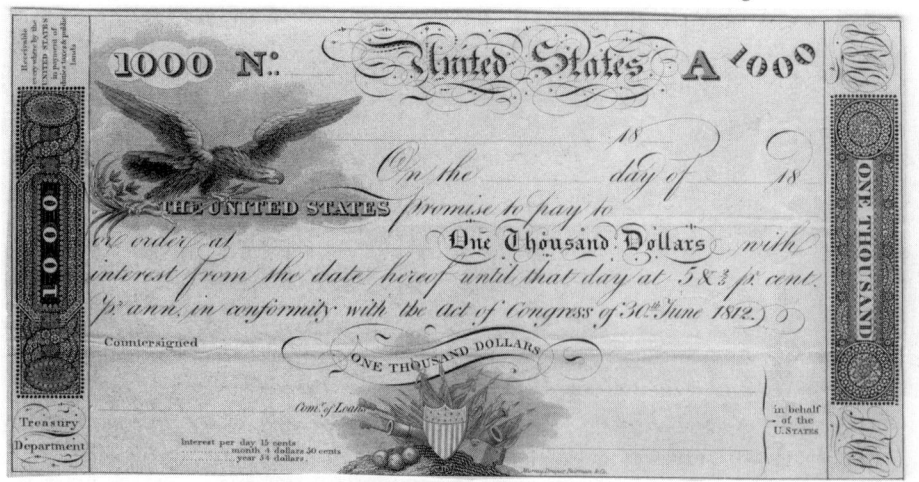

Spread Eagle facing right at upper left. Shield and cannon at lower center.

	VF	Unc
TN-1. 1,000 Dollar note. Unsigned Remainder. Two Known. (2,000 issued)	20,000.00	30,000.00

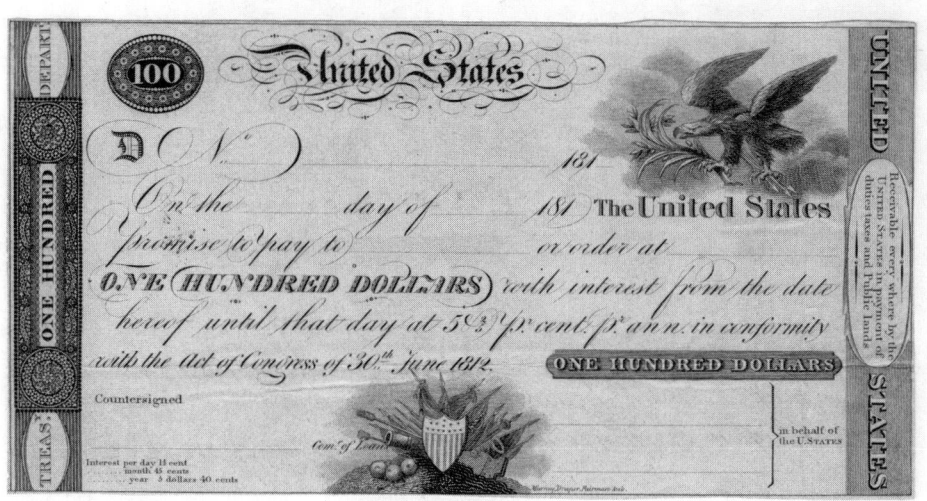

Eagle on branch at upper right.
Shield and cannon at lower center.

			VF	Unc
TN-2.	100 Dollar note. Unsigned Remainder.	Two Known. (15,000 issued)	15,000.00	25,000.00

B. Act of February 25, 1813
1-year notes of this issue bore interest at 5.4%. 900 notes outstanding.

TN-3.	1000 Dollar note. (4000 issued).	No notes known.		
TN-4.	100 Dollar notes (5000 issued).	No notes known.		

C. Act of March 4, 1814
1-year notes bore interest at 5.4%. 43,160 outstanding.

TN-5.	1000 Dollarnote. (6000 issued, est.).	No notes known.		
TN-6.	100 Dollar note. Signed by Earnest Fox & Samuel Clarke. Signed Remainder dated 1/15/15.	Two known. (24,000 issued, est.)	10,000.00	15,000.00
TN-7.	20 Dollar note.	No notes known. (8000 issued, est.).		

D. Act of December 26, 1814
1-year notes bore interest at 5.4%.   41,030 outstanding.

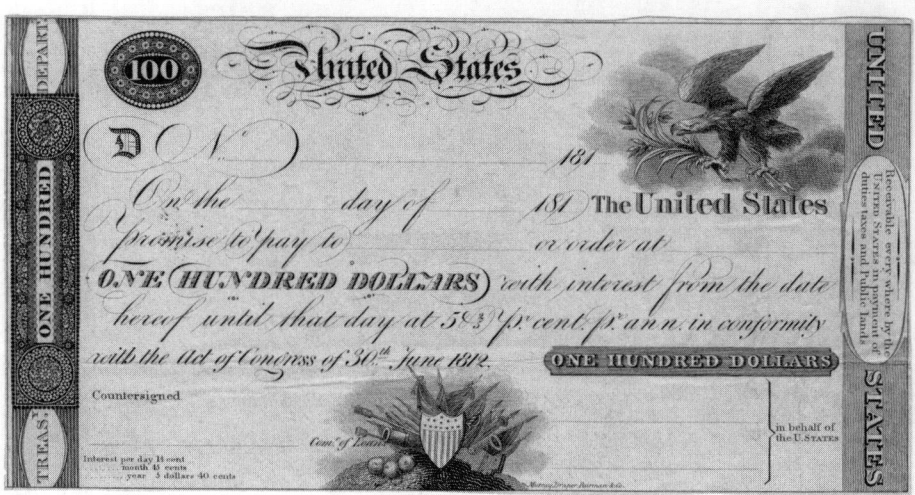

Eagle on branch at upper right corner.
Shield and cannon below center. Signed
by Earnest Fox and Samuel Clarke.

TN-8.	100 Dollar note. Unsigned but dated 2/11/15. One known.		15,000.00	25,000.00
TN-8a.	100 Dollar note. Signed undated Remainder (most cancelled). Four known.		12,500.00	17,500.00

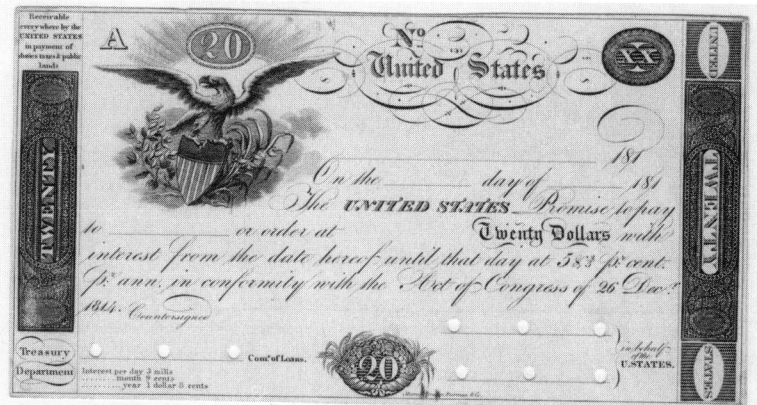

Spread Eagle on Shield at upper left. "20" surrounded by cornucopia in lower center.

TN-9. 20 Dollar note. Unsigned. One known. (Two proofs known.)
TN-9a. Signed Remainder. Very rare

E. Act of February 24, 1815
$100 notes bore interest at 5.4%. Unknown outstanding for $100; $2,061 for "Small Notes."

Eagle on branch at upper right. Shield at lower center.

TN-10. 100 Dollar note. Unsigned Remainder. Three known. (49,694 issued)
TN-10a. 100 Dollar note. Signed. Unconfirmed.

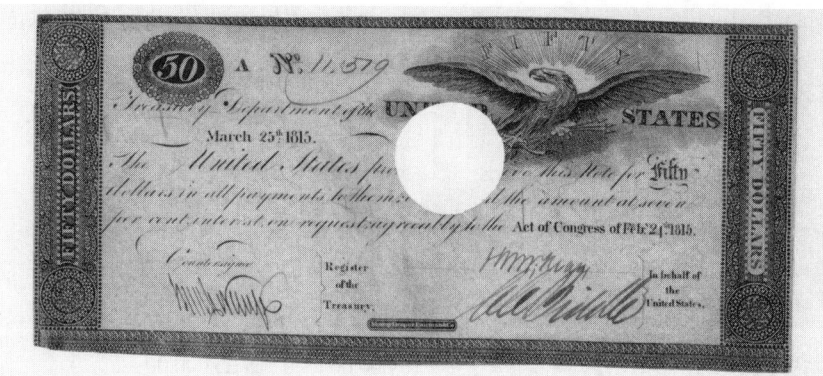

Spread Eagle on branch at upper right. Signed by F. W. McGeary and C. A. Colville. Countersigned by Joseph Nourse.

TN-11. 50 Dollar note. Signed. All known specimens are cancelled. Rare
TN-11a. 50 Dollar note. Unsigned Remainder. Unconfirmed.

Spread Eagle at upper left.
TN-12. 20 Dollar note. Unsigned Remainder. Very Rare
TN-12a. 20 Dollar note. Signed Remainder. Unconfirmed.

Spread Eagle with shield at upper left.
Text at right. Signed by F. W. McGeary and C. A. Colville.

TN-13. 10 Dollar note. Unsigned Remainder.   Unconfirmed.

TN-13a. 10 Dollar note. Signed Remainder.   Extremely rare.

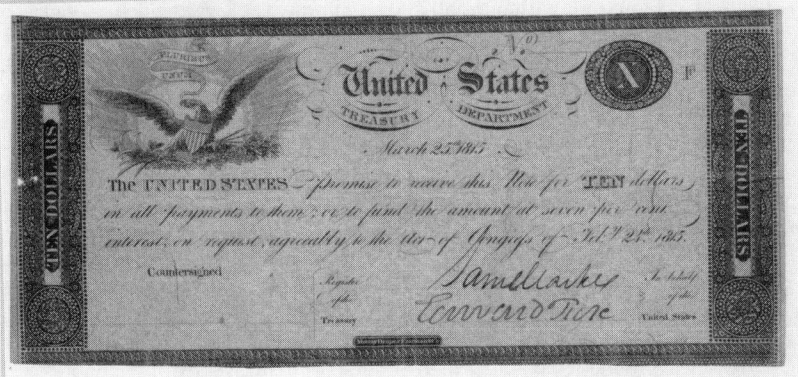

Similar to above. No text on right.
Signed by Samuel Clarke and Earnest Fox.

TN-14. 10 Dollar note. Unsigned Remainder.   Extremely rare

TN-14a. 10 Dollar note. Signed Remainder.

Spread Eagle with shield at upper right.

			VF	UNC
TN-15.	5 Dollar note. Unsigned Remainder.	(1 Proof known).	5,000.00	7,500.00
TN-15a.	5 Dollar note. Signed Remainder.		10,000.00	15,000.00

Shield with motto in upper center.

TN-16. 3 Dollar note. Unsigned Remainder.   Rare

TN-16a. Signed Remainder.   Very Rare

PART SEVEN
XXVI. ISSUES OF THE CONFEDERATE STATES OF AMERICA

The necessity for a United States paper currency originated as a result of the dire need for money to finance the Civil War. Concurrently, a new aspiring nation, the Confederate States of America, similarly needed to institute a monetary system of its own.

Precipitated by Abraham Lincoln's election as President in 1860, after more than 40 years of bickering between the Northern and Southern sections of the country, eleven slave-holding states (Alabama, Arkansas, Florida, Georgia, Louisiana, Mississippi, North Carolina, South Carolina, Tennessee, Texas and Virginia) broke away from the Union and set up a government of their own.

One result of secession was the immediate hoarding of United States coins, requiring the printing of a paper currency. The first issue of Confederate notes, in March, 1861, bore interest, and had a total circulation of $1,000,000.

Christopher Memminger, the Treasurer, instituted a monetary plan for the new republic, geared for a young nation at peace.

However, within months, the nation was at war, which accelerated after the first battle of Manassas in July, 1861. Eventually, the Confederacy was blockaded and cut off from most of the world, making foreign trade almost impossible. To finance the war, the Confederacy made subsequent monetary issues, through 1864. The result was rampant inflation. At Lee's surrender at Appomattox, the currency was worthless.

There were 72 major different issues from 1861–1864. There are numerous varieties within these issues, which are not listed below, but which may be found in *Confederate and Southern States Currency* by Grover C. Criswell, Jr. The order and numbering below follows the type listings found therein.

Special thanks to Douglas Ball and Stephen Goldsmith of R.M. Smythe & Co., Inc., New York for providing many of the photos and for their cooperation in the preparation of this section. Updated pricing for this edition courtesy of Hugh Shull and Bruce R. Hagen.

1861 ISSUES - MONTGOMERY, ALABAMA
Act of March 9, 1861

1,000 Dollar Note

Statesman John C. Calhoun (1782-1850) of S. Carolina at left; Andrew Jackson, President of the United States from 1829-1837 at right. Green & black. Blank reverse.

No.	Very Good	Very Fine	Extra Fine	Uncirculated
CS-1.	18,000.00	25,000.00	37,500.00	—

100 Dollar Note

A railroad vignette, Minerva standing at left. Blank reverse.

No.	Very Good	Very Fine	Extra Fine	Unc
CS- 3.	8,000.00	13,500.00	20,000.00	30,000.00

50 Dollar Note

Three slaves working in cotton field. Blank reverse.

CS-4.	8,000.00	13,500.00	20,000.00	30,000.00

500 Dollar Note

Cattle crossing brook. Train on bridge in background. Blank reverse.

CS-2.	18,000.00	25,0000.00	37,500.00	—

1861 ISSUES - RICHMOND, VIRGINIA

Act of March 9, 1861 as amended August 3, 1861
100 Dollar Note

A railroad vignette. Justice standing to left, Minerva to right. Blank reverse.

No.	Very Good	Very Fine	Extra Fine	Uncirculated
CS-5.	750.00	1,250.00	1,800.00	3,250.00

50 Dollar Note

Pallas and Ceres seated on cotton bale. Justice holding scales at left. Bust of George Washington at right. Blank reverse.

CS-6.	800.00	1,350.00	2,000.00	3,500.00

Act of August 19, 1861
100 Dollar Note

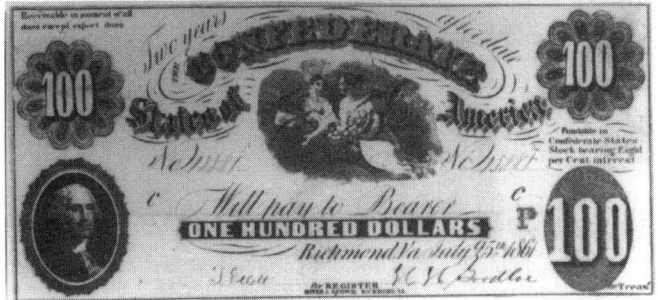

Ceres and Prosperina. George Washington at left. Blank reverse.

CS-7.	650.00	1,000.00	1,600.00	2,500.00

50 Dollar Note

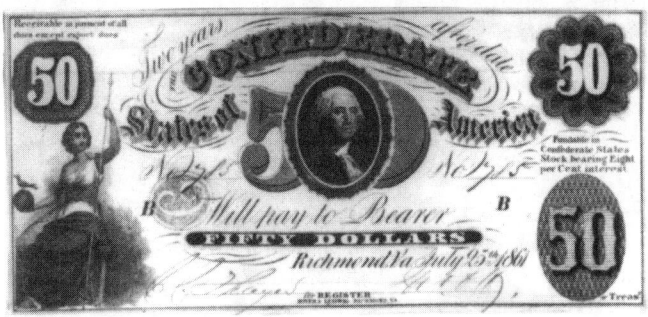

George Washington at center. Vignette of Tellus, the earth goddess, seated at left. Blank reverse.

No.	Very Good	Very Fine	Extra Fine	Uncirculated
CS-8.	125.00	200.00	250.00	375.00

20 Dollar Note

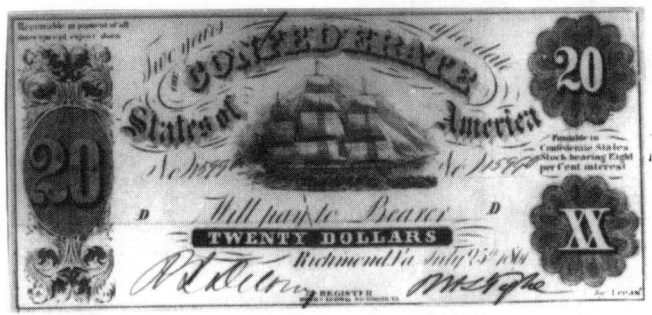

Three-masted sailing ship. Blank reverse.

CS-9.	90.00	175.00	250.00	475.00

10 Dollar Note

Liberty seated, leaning on Confederate shield. Eagle at rear. Blank reverse.

CS-10.	200.00	75.00	Very Rare	—

5 Dollar Notes

Seated Liberty and eagle behind numeral "5." Sailor leaning on capstan at left. Blank reverse.

No.	Very Good	Very Fine	Extra Fine	Uncirculated
CS-11.	2,000.00	Rare	Very Rare	——

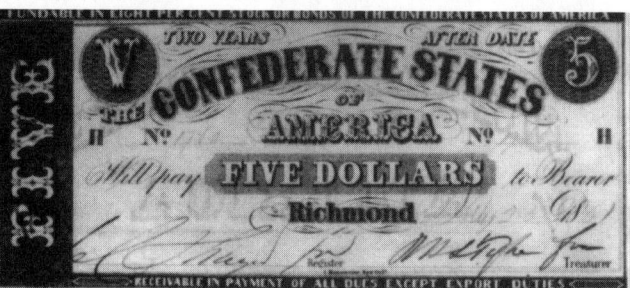

The legend "Confederate States of America" and value.

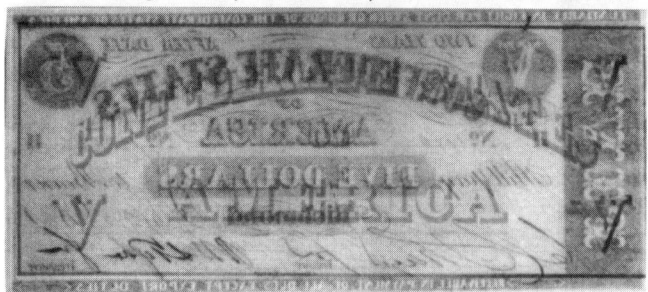

"Confederate States of America" in blue on blue reverse.

CS-12.	1,000.00	3,500.00	Rare	Very Rare

100 Dollar Note
Dated September 2, 1861

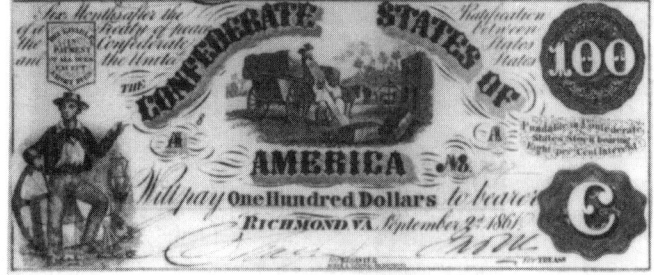

Slaves loading cotton bales onto wagon. Sailor standing at left. Blank reverse.

CS-13.	75.00	125.00	175.00	275.00

50 Dollar Notes

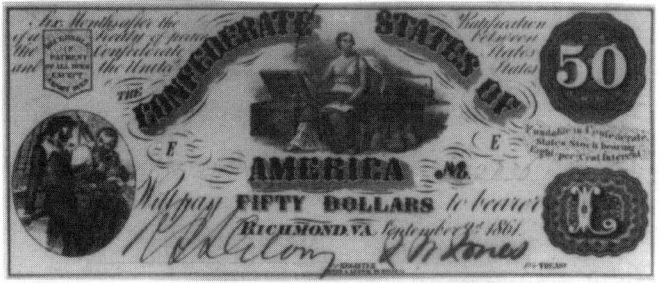

Moneta at center seated among treasure chests. Two sailors in oval at left. Blank reverse.

No.	Very Good	Very Fine	Extra Fine	Uncirculated
CS-14.	60.00	100.00	150.00	250.00

A railroad train under steam. Hope with anchor at left; Justice at right. Blank reverse.

CS-15.	2,500.00	5,000.00	Extremely Rare	Unknown

Bust of President Jefferson Davis at center. Blank reverse.

CS-16.	125.00	275.00	600.00	1,500.00

20 Dollar Notes

Ceres seated at center between allegories of Commerce and Navigation. Liberty standing at left. Blank reverse.

CS-17.	475.00	1,100.00	1,750.00	2,750.00

10 Dollar Notes

Three-masted sailing ship. At left, sailor leaning on capstan. Blank reverse.

No.	Very Good	Very Fine	Extra Fine	Uncirculated
CS-18.	35.00	50.00	85.00	125.00

Three Native Americans in center. Thetis at left, Female holding Roman numeral "X" at right. Blank reverse.

No.	Very Good	Very Fine	Extra Fine	Uncirculated
CS-22.	450.00	1,000.00	2,000.00	Very Rare

Navigation seated at center. Minerva seated at left. Blacksmith standing at right. Blank reverse.

CS-19.	1,500.00	4,000.00	Very Rare	——

Two horses pulling wagon of cotton. Bust of John E. Ward in oval at left. Worker harvesting sugar cane at right. Blank reverse.

CS-23.	850.00	1,750.00	3,250.00	Rare

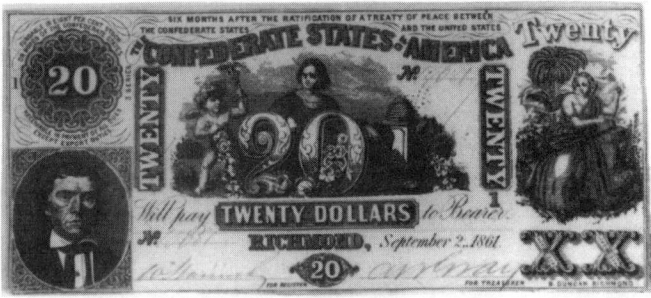

Industry seated at center behind numeral "20" and between Cupid and bee-hive. Bust of Vice President Alexander Hamilton Stephens in oval at left. Blank reverse.

CS-20.	45.00	75.00	110.00	175.00

Bust of Secretary of State Robert Mercer Taliaferro Hunter at left; At right, the Rev. Dr. Alfred L. Elwyn, an abolitionist from Philadelphia, as child. His identity was unknown when the portrait was selected. Blank reverse.

CS-24.	150.00	300.00	800.00	1,250.00

Bust of Vice President Alexander Stephens in oval frame at center. Blank reverse.

CS-21.	250.00	500.00	1,000.00	2,000.00

Hope standing with anchor. Secretary of State Robert M. Taliaferro Hunter at left. Secretary of the Treasury Christopher Gustavus Memminger at right. Blank reverse.

CS-25.	100.00	200.00	450.00	850.00

Hope with anchor standing between two Roman numeral "X." R.M.T. Hunter at left; C.G. Memminger at right. The Roman numeral is printed in three varieties: 1) a fine chain mail pattern, 2) solid red, or 3) in a coarse, lace pattern. Blank reverse.

No.	Very Good	Very Fine	Extra Fine	Uncirculated
CS-26.	75.00	200.00	400.00	750.00

Liberty seated at left with eagle behind shield. Blank reverse.

CS-27.	7,000.00	12,500.00	—	—

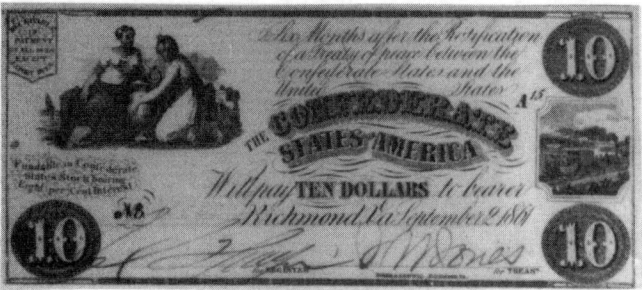

Ceres and Commerce in upper left with urn between them. Blank reverse.

CS-28.	50.00	150.00	325.00	675.00

A slave picking cotton at center. Blank reverse.

CS-29.	225.00	675.00	1,750.00	Very Rare

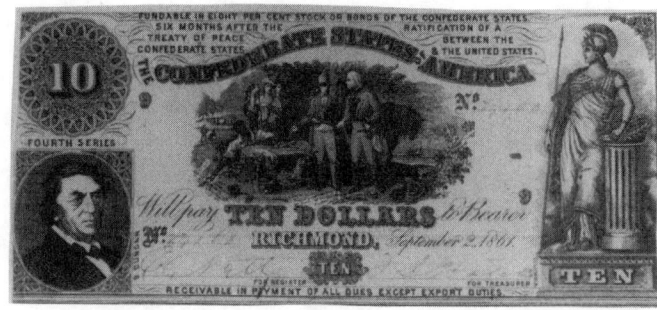

Vignette of General Francis Marion and an aide standing before a table with sweet potatoes. Slave kneeling behind. Bust of R.M.T. Hunter at left, Minerva standing at right. Blank reverse.

No.	Very Good	Very Fine	Extra Fine	Uncirculated
CS-30.	45.00	90.00	225.00	475.00

5 Dollar Notes

Allegorical vignette of Agriculture, Commerce, Industry, Justice and Liberty seated behind numeral "5" at center. Navigation standing at left. At right, statue from the Massachusetts State House of George Washington standing . Blank reverse.

CS-31	275.00	1,000.00	1,500.00	Very Rare

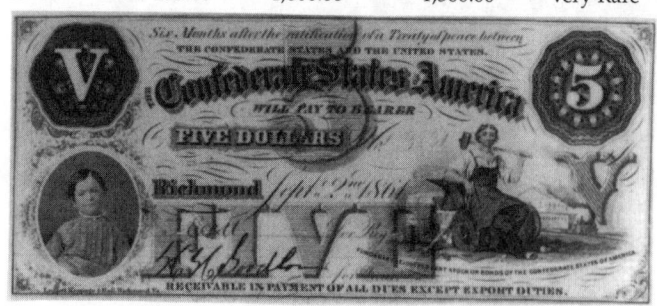

At right, laborer sitting with hammer on shoulder; railroad train in rear. At left, young boy in oval frame. Blank reverse.

CS-32.	950.00	1,750.00	3,750.00	Very Rare

Bust of C. G. Memminger at center. Minerva standing at right with arm on column capped with numeral "5." Blank reverse. Black and white.

CS-33	200.00	400.00	650.00	2,000.00

Bust of C. G. Memminger at center. Minerva standing at right with arm on column capped with numeral "5." Blank reverse.

No.	Very Good	Very Fine	Extra Fine	Uncirculated
CS-34.	125.00	275.00	375.00	750.00

At left, field hands loading cotton. Native American princess at right. Blank reverse.

CS-35.	14,000.00	27,500.00	——	——

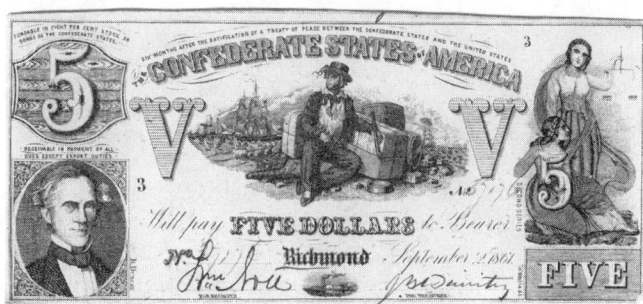

Ceres holding caduceus seated on bale of cotton. At left, sailor leaning on capstan. Blank reverse.

CS-36.	40.00	75.00	135.00	250.00

A sailor at center seated with bales of cotton. Bust of C.G. Memminger at left, Ceres seated and Justice standing at right. Blank reverse.

CS-37.	75.00	175.00	400.00	700.00

2 Dollar Note

Allegory of the South slaying the Union. Attorney General (1861), Secretary of War (1862), and then Secretary of State Judah P. Benjamin at left. Blank reverse.

No.	Very Good	Very Fine	Extra Fine	Uncirculated
CS-38.	550.00	Very Rare	—	—

1862 ISSUES

Act of April 17, 1862

100 Dollar Notes

A railroad vignette. White steam rises straight from stack of locomotive. Milkmaid standing at left. Blank reverse.

CS-39.	45.00	55.00	75.00	125.00

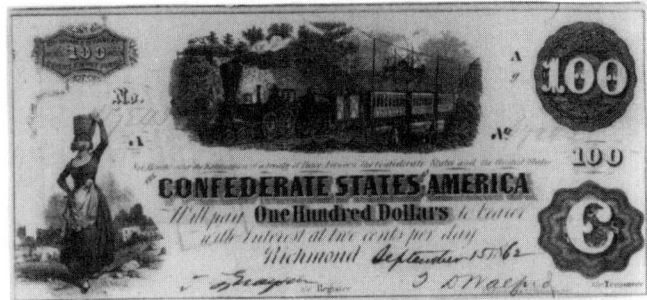

As above, but white steam is not visible emerging from stack. Blank reverse.

CS- 40.	45.00	55.00	75.00	125.00

Slaves working in cotton field. At left, bust of American statesman John C. Calhoun of South Carolina (1782-1850). Columbia standing at right. Blank reverse.

No.	Very Good	Very Fine	Extra Fine	Uncirculated
CS-41.	50.00	75.00	90.00	115.00

Act of April 18, 1862

2 Dollar Notes

Allegory of the South slaying the Union. Attorney General (1861), Secretary of War (1862), and then Secretary of State Judah P. Benjamin at left. Blank reverse.

CS-42.	45.00	75.00	150.00	250.00

Identical to CS-42, with the denomination overprinted in green ink. Blank reverse.

CS-43.	60.00	475.00	Rare	Very Rare

1 Dollar Notes

In center, vignette of three-masted steamship at sea. Liberty standing at left; Bust of Lucy Holcombe Pickens in oval frame at right. Blank reverse.

No.	Very Good	Very Fine	Extra Fine	Uncirculated
CS-44.	45.00	110.00	150.00	250.00

Identical to CS-44, with the denomination overprinted in green ink. Blank reverse.

CS-45.	60.00	375.00	550.00	1,350.00

10 Dollar Note

Ceres seated, leaning on bales of cotton; ships in background. Bust of Secretary of State Robert M.T. Hunter at right. Blank reverse.

S 46.	65.00	150.00	250.00	475.00

20 Dollar Note

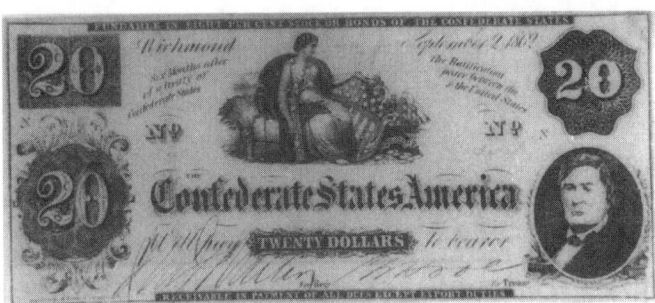

Liberty seated on cotton bale; shield to her left. Secretary of State R.M.T. Hunter in oval frame at right. Blank reverse. "Fantasy" counterfeit.

No.	Very Good	Very Fine	Extra Fine	Uncirculated
CS-47.	2,750.00	4,000.00	5,500.00	—

10 Dollar Notes

Ceres seated with elbow on sheaves of wheat. R.M.T. Hunter at right. Blank reverse. "Fantasy" counterfeit.

CS-48.	3,750.00	5,500.00	7,000.00	—

Notes dated December 2, 1862

100 Dollar Note

Bust of Lucy Holcombe Pickens facing right. Vignette of two Confederate soldiers at left; at right bust of George Wythe Randolph, Secretary of War in 1862.

Elaborate green reverse.

No.	Very Good	Very Fine	Extra Fine	Uncirculated
CS-49.	225.00	325.00	450.00	800.00

50 Dollar Note

Bust of President Jefferson Davis at center.

Ornate green reverse.

CS-50.	200.00	450.00	650.00	1,400.00

20 Dollar Note

Vignette of the state capitol building in Nashville, Tennessee. Bust of Vice President Alexander H. Stephens in oval at right.

Ornate blue reverse.

CS-51	75.00	150.00	275.00	500.00

10 Dollar Note

State capitol building in Columbia, S.C. Bust of Secretary of State R.M.T. Hunter at right.

Ten of the Roman numeral "X" on an ornate blue reverse.

No.	Very Good	Very Fine	Extra Fine	Uncirculated
CS-52.	30.00	45.00	80.00	125.00

5 Dollar Note

State capitol building in Richmond, Virginia. Bust of Secretary of the Treasury C.G. Memminger in oval frame at right.

Five of the number "5" over a Roman numeral "V" on an ornate blue reverse.

CS-53.	30.00	45.00	80.00	125.00

2 Dollar Note

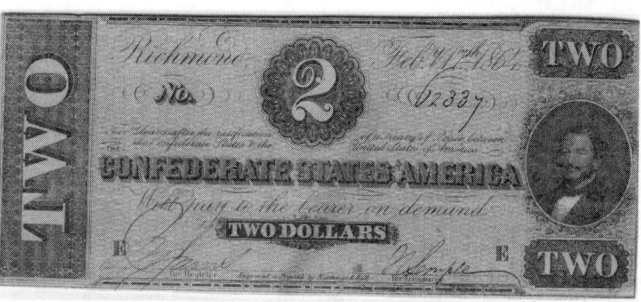

Large numeral "2" in center. Bust of Attorney General (1861), Secretary of War (1862), and then Secretary of State Judah P. Benjamin in oval frame at right. Blank reverse.

No.	Very Good	Very Fine	Extra Fine	Uncirculated
CS-54.	60.00	100.00	140.00	200.00

1 Dollar Note

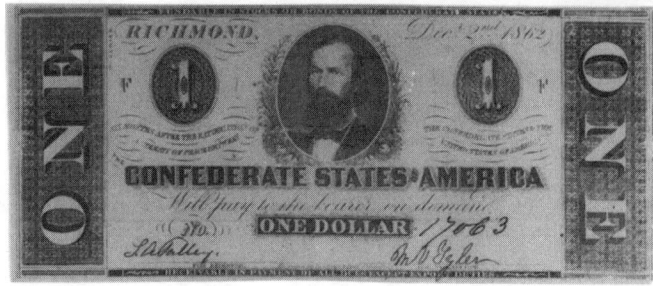

Bust of U.S. and then Confederate Senator Clement Claiborne Clay of Alabama in center. Blank reverse.

CS-55.	65.00	125.00	175.00	300.00

Notes dated April 6, 1863

100 Dollar Note

Bust of Lucy Holcombe Pickens facing right. Vignette of two Confederate soldiers at left; at right bust of George Wythe Randolph, Secretary of War in 1862.

Green reverse.

CS-56.	100.00	175.00	225.00	325.00

50 Dollar Note

Bust of President Jefferson Davis at center.

Ornate green reverse.

No.	Very Good	Very Fine	Extra Fine	Uncirculated
CS- 57.	75.00	12500	175.00	325.00

20 Dollar Note

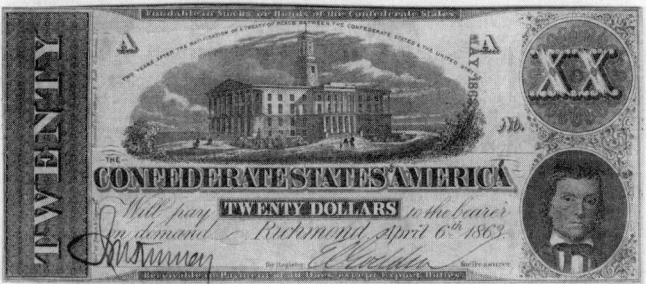

Vignette of the state capitol building in Nashville, Tennessee. Bust of Vice President Alexander H. Stephens in oval at right.

Roman numeral "XX" in center of ornate blue reverse.

CS-58.	35.00	60.00	90.00	200.00

10 Dollar Note

State capitol building in Columbia, S.C.
Bust of Secretary of State R.M.T. Hunter at right.

Ten Roman numeral "X" on blue reverse.

No.	Very Good	Very Fine	Extra Fine	Uncirculated
CS-59.	30.00	45.00	65.00	125.00

5 Dollar Note

State capitol building in Richmond, Virginia. Bust of Secretary of the Treasury C.G. Memminger in oval frame at right.

Five of the number "5" over a Roman numeral "V"
on an ornate blue reverse.

CS-60.	30.00	45.00	70.00	125.00

2 Dollar Note

Large numeral "2" in center. Bust of Attorney General (1861), Secretary of War (1862), and then Secretary of State Judah P. Benjamin in oval frame at right. Blank reverse.

No.	Very Good	Very Fine	Extra Fine	Uncirculated
CS-61.	75.00	150.00	250.00	400.00

1 Dollar Note

Bust of U.S. and then Confederate Senator Clement Claiborne Clay of

Alabama in center. Blank reverse.

CS-62.	45.00	80.00	100.00	150.00

50 Cent Note

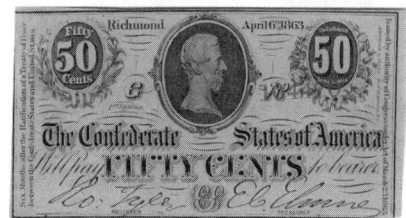

Bust of Jefferson Davis at center in ornate oval frame. Blank reverse.

CS-63.	20.00	30.00	40.00	60.00

Notes dated February 17, 1864

500 Dollar Note

At left, George Washington on horseback, Confederate flag above. Bust of Stonewall Jackson at right. Blank reverse.

No.	Very Good	Very Fine	Extra Fine	Uncirculated
CS-64.	250.00	325.00	450.00	650.00

100 Dollar Note

Bust of Lucy Holcombe Pickens facing right. Vignette of two Confederate soldiers at left; at right bust of George Wythe Randolph, Secretary of War in 1862.

Denomination in large letters on elaborate blue reverse.

CS-65.	45.00	65.00	85.00	125.00

50 Dollar Note

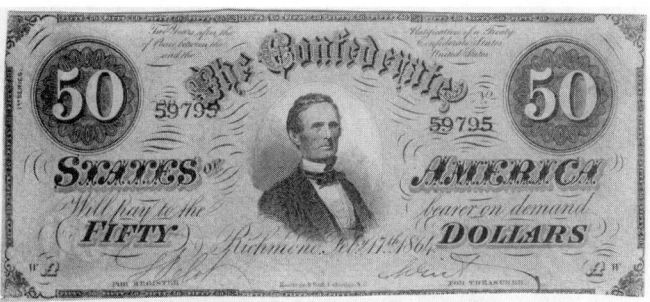

Bust of President Jefferson Davis at center.

Denomination in large letters on elaborate blue reverse.

No.	Very Good	Very Fine	Extra Fine	Uncirculated
CS-66.	40.00	55.00	80.00	110.00

20 Dollar Note

Vignette of the state capitol building in Nashville, Tennessee. Bust of Vice President Alexander H. Stephens in oval at right.

Denomination in large letters on elaborate blue reverse.

CS-67.	25.00	35.00	45.00	65.00

10 Dollar Note

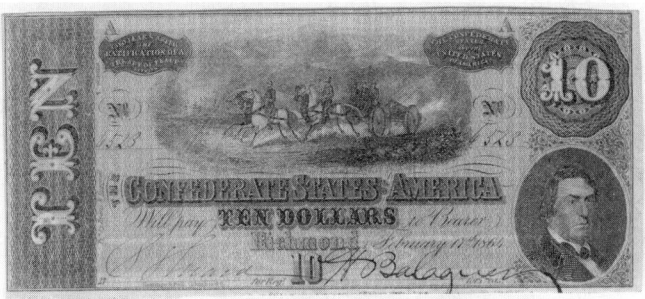

Battlefield scene of horses pulling cannon. Bust of Secretary of State R.M.T. Hunter at right.

Denomination on elaborate blue reverse.

No.	Very Good	Very Fine	Extra Fine	Uncirculated
CS-68.	20.00	25.00	30.00	45.00

5 Dollar Note

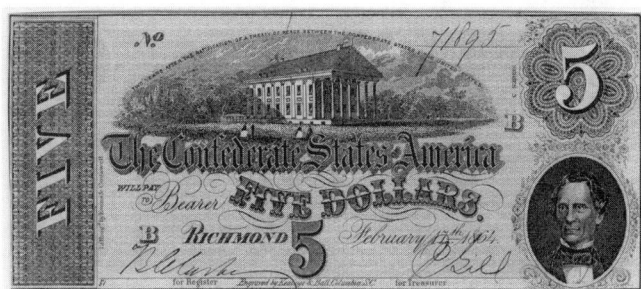

State capitol building in Richmond, Virginia. Bust of Secretary of the Treasury C.G. Memminger in oval frame at right.

Denonimation on elaborate blue reverse.

CS-69.	20.00	25.00	30.00	45.00

2 Dollar Note

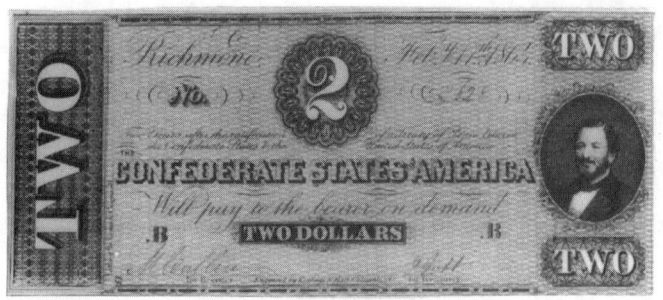

Large numeral "2" in center. Bust of Attorney General (1861), Secretary of
War (1862), and then Secretary of State Judah P. Benjamin
in oval frame at right. Blank reverse.

No.	Very Good	Very Fine	Extra Fine	Uncirculated
CS-70.	40.00	60.00	75.00	120.00

1 Dollar Note

Bust of U.S. and then Confederate Senator Clement Claiborne Clay of
Alabama in center. Blank reverse.

CS-71.	50.00	85.00	110.00	175.00

50 Cent Note

Bust of President Jefferson Davis at center in ornate oval frame.
Blank reverse.

CS-72.	20.00	25.00	30.00	45.00

XXVII. LIST OF NATIONAL BANKS

The following list was compiled from official records of the Treasury Department, mainly from the National Bank Redemption Agency and the Comptroller of the Currency.

The banks are arranged by state, and numerically by charter numbers within each state. Numismatically, this arrangement was deemed best since it forms a chronological history of banking in each state, from which it is possible to infer important numismatic information, such as the types of notes possible to have been issued in each state, the relative frequency of such notes, etc.

A further breakdown of the banks could have been made by listing them under their cities arranged alphabetically within their states, such as exists in most government records for purely fiscal purposes. Such a listing would have destroyed the chronology of bank formation in each state and would have served no useful numismatic purpose. Those who wish to make their own city-list of banks can easily extract the information required from the state-list below.

In consulting or using this list of banks, the following points might be helpful:

1. The name of the bank as listed here was its name at the time it was given its charter. Subsequent mergers, liquidations or other events caused many banks to change or alter their names. That is why certain bank notes exist bearing the same charter numbers but differently named banks.

2. Not all banks issued circulating notes. Many did not; others had notes printed but did not issue them. These were later canceled and destroyed at the Treasury Department. In some cases, banks failed shortly after organization. In other cases, the entire issue of a bank's notes may subsequently have been redeemed. In the interest of completeness, all 14,348 banks have been listed that were char-tered during the note issuing period, 1863-1935. New national banks continued to be chartered after this period, but they are not listed here.

3. It will be both practical and instructive to use this list in conjunction with the list entitled "Years of Issue of Charter Numbers" on page 76.

4. An analysis of the charter numbers will reveal more graphically than any words can, the pattern of expansion, growth and prosperity of this country. For example, note that the earlier charter numbers are concentrated in the populous, long-established eastern part of the country; later charter numbers in the southern and western areas. The establishment of new frontiers, new cities and towns, and new industrial, mining and agricultural centers brought with it the formation of thousands of new national banks.

5. It goes without saying that a note from a bank situated in a city or town of small population would be of greater numismatic and historical interest than a similar type note issued by a large bank in a metropolis. Many of these small banks had a capital of only $25,000.00 and their note issues were correspondingly small. There is no doubt that there are many unique national bank notes presently in the hands of collectors—unique in the sense that the specific note is the only surviving example of the notes of that type issued by the specific national bank named thereon. Only time, further research and the exchange of information will reveal which notes are truly unique.

6. Almost every aspect of American life is touched upon in the varied names of the national banks. These names are interesting enough to be read almost as literature. Similarly, a study of the list of the cities themselves is a revelation of local geography.

Charter Number	City	Name of Bank
ALABAMA		
1537.	Selma.	First N.B.
1560.	Huntsville.	N.B. of Huntsville.
1595.	Mobile.	First N.B.
1736.	Selma.	City N.B.
1814.	Montgomery	First N.B.
1817.	Mobile.	Alabama N.B.
1822.	Gainesville.	Gainesville N.B.
1853.	Tuskaloosa.	First N.B.
2029.	Montgomery.	Merchants and Planters' N.B.
2065.	Birmingham.	N.B. of Birmingham.
2309.	Eufaula.	Eufaula N.B.
3041.	Anniston.	First N.B.
3185.	Birmingham.	First N.B.
3442.	Birmingham.	Berney N.B.
3452.	Opelika.	First N.B.
3587.	Birmingham.	Alabama N.B.
3617.	Sheffield.	First N.B.
3622.	Eufaula.	East Alabama N.B.
3663.	Gadsden.	First N.B.
3678.	Tuscaloosa.	Merchants' N.B.
3679.	Birmingham.	Birmingham N.B.
3699.	Decatur.	First N.B.
3734.	Birmingham.	American N.B.
3899.	Talladega.	First N.B.
3931.	Eutaw.	First N.B.
3981.	Florence.	First N.B.
3993.	Birmingham.	City N.B.
4064.	Fort Payne.	First N.B.
4067.	Huntsville.	First N.B.
4135.	Florence.	Florence N.B.
4180.	Montgomery.	Merchants and Planters'-Farley N.B.
4220.	Bessemer.	First N.B.
4250.	Anniston.	Anniston N.B.
4319.	Jacksonville.	First N.B.
4394.	Demopolis.	First N.B.
4591.	Bridgeport.	First N.B.
4689.	Huntsville.	Farmers and Merchants' N.B.
4838.	Talladega.	Isbell N.B.
5024.	Eufaula.	Commercial N.B.
5219.	Mobile.	City N.B.
5249.	Dothan.	First N.B.
5572.	Greenville.	First N.B.
5593.	Troy.	First N.B.
5664.	Thomasville.	First N.B.
5693.	Greensboro.	First N.B.
5714.	Geneva.	First N.B.
5877.	Montgomery.	Fourth N.B.
5909.	Dothan.	Dothan N.B.
5962.	Ensley.	First N.B.
5970.	Andalusia.	First N.B.
5983.	Jackson.	First N.B.
5987.	Abbeville.	First N.B.
6021.	Anniston.	City N.B.
6146.	Athens.	First N.B.
6173.	Tuscaloosa.	City N.B.
6319.	Enterprise.	First N.B.
6380.	Albany.	Morgan County N.B.
6759.	Sheffield.	Sheffield N.B.
6835.	Citronelle.	First N.B.
6897.	Elba.	First N.B.
6961.	Bessemer.	First N.B.
7020.	Birmingham.	Traders N.B.
7044.	Troy.	Farmers and Merchants' N.B.
7062.	Mobile.	Bank of Mobil N.B. Assn.
7073.	Oxford.	First N.B.
7084.	Selma.	Selma N.B.
7097.	Cullman.	First N.B.
7141.	Montgomery	American N.B.
7148.	Linden.	First N.B.
7371.	Thomasville.	Citizens N.B.
7417.	Alexander City	First N.B.
7424.	Headland.	First N.B.
7429.	Brundidge.	First N.B.
7451.	Sylacauga.	First N.B.
7464.	Piedmont.	First N.B.
7467.	Union Springs.	First N.B.
7484.	Sylacauga.	Merchants and Planters' N.B.
7516.	Lineville.	First N.B.
7551.	Lineville.	Lineville N.B.
7558.	Talladega.	Talladega N.B.
7568.	Wetumpka.	First N.B.
7592.	Hartford.	First N.B.
7629.	Ozark.	First N.B.
7687.	Evergreen.	First N.B.
7746.	Jasper.	First N.B.
7871.	Slocomb.	First N.B.
7932.	Dothan.	Houston N.B.
7938.	Dothan.	Third N.B.
7940.	Slocomb.	Slocomb N.B.
7951.	Attalla.	First N.B.
7975.	Hayneville.	First N.B.
7985.	Opp.	First N.B.
7991.	Brantley.	First N.B.
7992.	Luverne.	First N.B.
8028.	Samson.	First N.B.
8067.	Hartselle.	First N.B.
8095.	Columbia.	First N.B.
8217.	Camden.	Camden N.B.
8284.	Montgomery.	Exchange N.B.
8458.	Midland City.	First N.B.
8460.	Montgomery.	Capital N.B.
8560.	Gadsden.	Gadsden N.B.
8765.	Huntsville.	Henderson N.B.
8856.	Lineville.	Citizens N.B.
8910.	Florala.	First N.B.
8963.	Scottsboro.	First N.B.
9055.	Prattville.	First N.B.
9506.	Pell City.	First N.B.
9550.	Opelika.	Farmers N.B.
9580.	Ashland.	First N.B.
9614.	Cullman.	Leeth N.B.
9681.	Dozier.	First N.B.
9855.	Stevenson.	First N.B.
9925.	Oxford.	Oxford N.B.
9927.	Newville.	First N.B.
10035.	Demopolis.	Commercial N.B.
10066.	Childersburg.	First N.B.
10102.	Ashford.	First N.B.
10131.	Lincoln.	First N.B.
10307.	Geneva.	Farmers' N.B.
10336.	Decatur.	City N.B.
10377.	Fayette.	First N.B.
10421.	Enterprise.	Farmers and Merchants' N.B.
10423.	Albany.	Central N.B.
10441.	Boaz.	First N.B.
10457.	New Brockton.	First N.B.
10654.	Seale.	First N.B.
10697.	Atmore.	First N.B.
10732.	Mobile.	Nat. City Bank.
10766.	Tallassee.	First N.B.
10799.	La Pine.	First N.B.
10879.	Sylacauga.	City N.B.
10959.	Abbeville.	Henry N.B.
10990.	Guntersville.	First N.B.
11168.	Bridgeport.	American N.B.
11233.	Reform.	First N.B.
11259.	Coffee Springs.	First N.B.
11281.	Tuscumbia.	First N.B.
11337.	Collinsville.	First N.B.
11445.	Headland.	Farmers and Merchants' N.B.
11451.	Fort Payne.	First N.B.
11515.	Clanton.	First N.B.
11613.	Haleyville.	First N.B.
11635.	Opelika.	N.B. of Opelika.
11753.	Anniston.	Commercial N.B.
11766.	Fairfield.	First N.B.
11819.	Albertville.	First N.B.
11820.	Albertville.	Albertville N.B.
11846.	Russellville.	First N.B.
11870.	Boaz.	N.B.of Boaz.
11905.	Bessemer.	City N.B.
11955.	Andalusia.	Andalusia N.B.
12006.	Oneonta.	First N.B.
12455.	Auburn.	First N.B.
12642.	Monroeville.	First N.B.
12906.	Birmingham.	Ensley.Ensley N.B.
12960.	Goodwater.	First N.B.
12962.	Union Springs.	American N.B.
12993.	Montgomery.	Alabama N.B.
13097.	Mobile.	Merchants N.B.
13128.	Hartford.	Hartford N.B.
13195.	Mobile.	Mobile N.B.
13358.	Birmingham.	Woodlawn-American N.B.
13359.	Leeds.	Leeds-American N.B.
13412.	Gadsden.	American N.B.
13414.	Mobile.	American N.B. and Trust Co.
13728.	Gadsden.	First N.B.
13752.	Headland.	Headland N.B.
13789.	Bessemer.	First N.B.
14160.	Tuscumbia.	First N.B.

ALASKA

Charter Number	City	Name of Bank
5117.	Juneau.	First N.B.
7718.	Fairbanks.	First N.B.
10705.	Seward.	Harriman N.B.
12072.	Anchorage.	First N.B.
12578.	Ketchikan.	First. N.B.

ARIZONA

Charter Number	City	Name of Bank
2639.	Tucson.	First N.B.
3054.	Phoenix.	First N.B.
3122.	Prescott.	First N.B.
3728.	Phoenix.	N.B. of Arizona.
4287.	Tucson.	Consolidated N.B.
4440.	Tucson.	Arizona N.B.
4729.	Phoenix.	Phoenix N.B.
4851.	Prescott.	Prescott N.B.
5720.	Tempe.	Tempe N.B.
5821.	Clifton.	First N.B.
6439.	Tombstone.	First N.B.
6579.	Globe.	First N.B.
6591.	Nogales.	First N.B.
6633.	Douglas.	First N.B.
7182.	Bisbee.	First N.B.
7591.	Yuma.	First N.B.
8193.	Globe.	Globe N.B.
9608.	Yuma.	Yuma N.B.
10998.	Florence.	First N.B.
11012.	Nogales.	Nogales N.B.
11120.	Flagstaff.	First N.B.
11130.	Mesa.	First N.B.
11139.	Glendale.	First N.B.
11159.	Tucson.	Tucson N.B.
11395.	Chandler.	First N.B.
11559.	Phoenix.	Commercial N.B.
11663.	Casa Grande.	First N.B.
12198.	Holbrook.	First N.B.
12581.	Winslow.	First N.B.
13262.	Prescott.	First N.B.
14324.	Phoenix.	Valley N.B.

ARKANSAS

Charter Number	City	Name of Bank
1631.	Fort Smith.	First N.B.
1648.	Little Rock.	First N.B.
1950.	Fort Smith.	First N.B.
2776.	Pine Bluff.	First N.B.
2832.	Hot Springs.	Arkansas N.B.
2887.	Hot Springs.	Hot Springs N.B.
3300.	Little Rock.	Exchange N.B.
3318.	Little Rock.	American N.B.
3634.	Fort Smith.	American N.B.
3662.	Helena.	First N.B.
4066.	Camden.	Camden N.B.
4401.	Texarkana.	Gate City N.B.
4582.	Russellville.	First N.B.
4995.	Fort Smith.	Fort Smith N.B.
5849.	Waldron.	First N.B.
5890.	Harrison.	First N.B.
5929.	De Queen.	First N.B.
6680.	Pine Bluff.	Simmons N.B.
6706.	Perry.	First N.B.
6758.	Newport.	First N.B.
6786.	Greenwood.	First N.B.
6846.	Paragould.	First N.B.
6902.	Little Rock.	State N.B.
7046.	El Dorado.	First N.B.
7138.	Texarkana.	State N.B.
7163.	Mena.	First N.B.
7240.	Fort Smith.	Merchants' N.B.
7311.	Corning.	First N.B.
7323.	El Dorado.	Citizens' N.B.
7346.	Fayetteville.	First N.B.
7361.	Van Buren.	First N.B.
7523.	Bentonville.	First N.B.
7531.	Hot Springs.	Citizens' N.B.
7556.	Batesville.	First N.B.
7634.	Malvern.	First N.B.
7789.	Rogers.	First N.B.
7829.	Mena.	N.B. of Mena.
7952.	Fayetteville.	N.B. of Fayetteville.
8030.	Prairie Grove.	First N.B.
8086.	Jonesboro.	First N.B.
8135.	Bentonville.	Benton County N.B.
8237.	Gravette.	First N.B.
8495.	Eureka Springs.	First N.B.
8594.	Hope.	Hope N.B.
8763.	Springdale.	First N.B.
8786.	Fayetteville.	Arkansas N.B.
8864.	Batesville.	N.B. of Batesville.
8952.	Huntsville.	First N.B.
9022.	Newark.	First N.B.
9037.	Little Rock.	England N.B.
9324.	Earle.	First N.B.
9332.	Walnut Ridge.	First N.B.
9354.	Lewisville.	First N.B.
9494.	Benton.	First N.B.
9501.	Fordyce.	First N.B.
9633.	Clarksville.	First N.B.
9871.	Siloam Springs.	First N.B.
10004.	Paragould.	N.B. of Commerce.
10060.	Huttig.	First N.B.
10087.	Arkdelphia.	Citizens' N.B.
10138.	Leslie.	First N.B.
10178.	De Witt.	First N.B.
10406.	Berryville.	First N.B.
10422.	Green Forest.	First N.B.
10434.	Morrilton.	First N.B.
10439.	Judsonia.	First N.B.
10447.	Horatio.	First N.B.
10459.	Stuttgart.	First N.B.
10484.	Tuckerman.	First N.B.
10486.	Ashdown.	First N.B.
10550.	Forrest City.	First N.B.
10579.	Hope.	Citizens N.B.
10609.	Fort Smith.	City N.B.
10723.	Cotton Plant.	First N.B.
10750.	Rogers.	American N.B.
10768.	Pine Bluff.	N.B. of Arkansas.
10794.	Marshall.	First N.B.
10795.	Marshall.	Arkansas N.B.
10801.	Harrison.	People's N.B.
10807.	Wynne.	First N.B.
10853.	Rector.	First N.B.
10854.	Marianna.	Lee County N.B.
10867.	Newport.	Farmers' N.B.
10983.	Greenwood.	First N.B.
11046.	Junction City.	First N.B.
11113.	Mineral Springs.	First N.B.
11116.	Monette.	First N.B.
11122.	Marked Tree.	First N.B.
11180.	Heber Springs.	First N.B.
11195.	Mansfield.	First N.B.
11196.	Mansfield.	N.B. of Mansfield.
11214.	Belmont.	Army N.B.
11221.	Des Arc.	First N.B.
11225.	Benton.	Farmers and Merchants' N.B.
11234.	Helena.	Interstate N.B.
11262.	Lake Village.	First N.B.
11276.	Dardanelle.	First N.B.
11312.	Black Rock.	First N.B.
11322.	Lepanto.	First N.B.
11367.	Heber Springs.	Arkansas N.B.
11542.	Hughes.	Planters' N.B.
11580.	Clarksville.	Farmere N.B.
11592.	Paris.	First N.B.
11645.	Pocahontas.	First N.B.
11651.	Blytheville.	First N.B.
11748.	Hartford.	First N.B.
11825.	Lincoln.	First N.B.
11830.	Hartford.	Farmers and Miners' N.B.
12083.	Walnut Ridge.	Planters' N.B.
12156.	Stuttgart.	People's N.B.
12219.	Cotton Plant.	Farmers' N.B.
12238.	Lamar.	First N.B.
12291.	Harrison.	Citizens' N.B.
12296.	Holly Grove.	First N.B.
12340.	Gentry.	First N.B.
12429.	El Dorado.	N.B. of Commerce.
12447.	North Little Rock.	First N.B.
12533.	Hope.	First N.B.
12813.	Eudora.	First N.B.
12914.	Tuckerman.	First N.B.
12985.	Ozark.	First N.B.
13155.	Paragould.	New First N.B.
13210.	Gurdon.	First N.B.
13274.	Siloam Springs.	First N.B.
13280.	McGehee.	First N.B.
13506.	Siloam Springs.	Hutchings First N.B.
13520.	Helena.	Phillips N.B.
13534.	Ashdown.	First N.B.
13543.	Green Forest.	First N.B.
13632.	Lake Village.	First N.B.
13637.	Forrest City.	N.B. of Eastern Arkansas.
13693.	Mena.	Planters N.B.
13719.	Conway.	First N.B.
13949.	Little Rock.	Peoples N.B.
13958.	Little Rock.	Union N.B.
14000.	Little Rock.	Commercial N.B.
14056.	Pine Bluff.	N.B. of Commerce.
14096.	Camden.	Citizens N.B.
14097.	Marianna.	First N.B.
14209.	Paris.	First N.B.
14238.	Malvern.	Malvern N.B.

CALIFORNIA

Charter Number	City	Name of Bank
1741.	San Francisco.	First Nat. Gold Bank
1994.	San Francisco.	Nat. Gold Bank and Trust Co.
2014.	Sacramento.	Nat. Gold Bank of D.O. Mills and C.O.
2077.	Stockton.	First Nat. Gold Bank
2104.	Santa Barbara.	First Nat. Gold Bank
2158.	San Jose.	Farmers' Nat.Gold Bank
2193.	Petaluma.	First Nat. Gold Bank
2248.	Oakland.	First Nat. Gold Bank
2266.	Oakland.	Union Nat. Gold.
2412.	Stockton.	First N.B.
2431.	Alameda.	First N.B.
2456.	Santa Barbara.	County N.B. and Trust Co.
2491.	Los Angeles.	First N.B.
2794.	Stockton.	Stockton N.B.
2938.	Los Angeles.	Los Angeles N.B.
3050.	San Diego.	First N.B.
3056.	San Diego.	Consolidated N.B.
3136.	Modesto.	First N.B.
3321.	Fresno.	First N.B.
3348.	Riverside.	First N.B.
3499.	Pasadena.	First N.B.
3518.	Pomona.	First N.B.
3520.	Santa Ana.	First N.B.
3527.	San Bernardino.	First N.B.
3538.	Los Angeles.	Merchants N.B.
3555.	San Francisco.	Crocker N.B.
3558.	Santa Rosa.	Santa Rosa N.B.
3568.	Pasadena.	Pasadena N.B.
3573.	Colton.	First N.B.
3592.	San Francisco.	California N.B.
3648.	Grass Valley.	First N.B.
3715.	San Jose.	Garden City N.B.
3733.	Merced.	First N.B.
3743.	Monrovia.	First N.B.
3757.	Saint Helena.	First N.B.
3780.	San Diego.	San Diego N.B.
3818.	San Bernardino.	San Bernardino N.B.
3826.	San Luis Obispo.	First N.B.
3828.	San Diego.	California N.B.
3845.	Santa Monica.	First N.B.
3870.	Fresno.	Fresno N.B.
3892.	Redlands.	First N.B.
4096.	Los Angeles.	N.B. of California.
4120.	Santa Paula.	First N.B.
4663.	Pomona.	American N.B.
4757.	Riverside.	Riverside N.B.
4873.	Needles.	Needles N.B.
4886.	San Diego.	Merchants' N.B.
5074.	Salinas.	First N.B.
5096.	San Francisco.	San Francisco N.B.
5105.	San Francisco.	Wells-Fargo Nevada N.B.
5162.	Fresno.	Farmers N.B.
5380.	Berkeley.	First N.B.
5395.	Selma.	First N.B.
5456.	Long Beach.	First N.B.
5588.	Whittier.	First N.B.
5654.	Fullerton.	First N.B.
5688.	San Francisco.	Western N.B.
5830.	Covina.	First N.B.
5863.	Hanford.	First N.B.
5927.	Los Angeles.	Citizens' N.B.
5986.	Eureka.	First N.B.
5993.	Los Angeles.	Southwestern N.B.
6027.	Imperial.	First N.B.
6044.	Bakersfield.	First N.B.
6268.	Ontario.	First N.B.
6426.	San Francisco.	American N.B.
6481.	Anaheim.	First N.B.
6545.	Los Angeles.	American N.B.
6592.	San Francisco.	Germania N.B.
6617.	Los Angeles.	Farmers and Merchants' N.B.
6730.	Long Beach.	N.B. of LoN.B.ach.
6749.	Long Beach.	American N.B.
6808.	Porterville.	First N.B.
6833.	Riverside.	Orange Growers N.B.
6864.	Los Angeles.	Commercial N.B.
6869.	San Diego.	N.B. of Commerce.
6873.	Hanford.	Hanford N.B.
6904.	Petaluma.	Petaluma N.B.
6919.	Oroville.	First N.B.
6945.	Santa Monica.	Merchants N.B.
6993.	El Monte.	First N.B.
7057.	San Pedro.	First N.B.
7058.	Monterey.	First N.B.
7063.	Visalia.	First N.B.
7069.	Palo Alto.	First N.B.
7152.	Cucamonga.	First N.B.
7176.	Napa.	First N.B.
7202.	Sonora.	First N.B.
7210.	Ventura.	First N.B.
7219.	Alturas.	First N.B.
7259.	Redlands.	Redlands N.B.
7279.	Redwood City.	First N.B. of San Mateo Co.
7336.	Madera.	First N.B.
7388.	Calistoga.	First N.B.
7390.	Fowler.	First N.B.
7418.	San Diego.	American N.B.
7480.	Santa Maria.	First N.B.
7502.	Oakdale.	First N.B.
7543.	Hollywood.	First N.B.
7632.	Los Angeles.	United States N.B.
7658.	Hanford.	Farmers and Merchants.N.B.
7690.	Ocean Park.	First N.B.
7691.	San Francisco.	United States N.B.
7705.	Monrovia.	N.B. of Monrovia.
7713.	San Francisco.	Citizens N.B.
7719.	Lodi.	First N.B.
7738.	Turlock.	First N.B.
7776.	Sacramento.	Fort Sutter N.B.
7779.	Lemoore.	First N.B.
7801.	Escondido.	First N.B.
7803.	Hollywood.	Hollywood N.B.
7849.	Berkeley.	Berkeley N.B.
7867.	Corona.	First N.B.
7869.	Huntington Beach	First N.B.
7877.	San Luis Obispo.	Union N.B.
7894.	San Francisco.	N.B. of the Pacific.
7895.	Redondo.	Farmers and Merchants' N.B.
7965.	Lindsay.	First N.B.
7980.	Santa Ana.	Farmers and Merchants' N.B.
7987.	Glendale.	First N.B.
7997.	San Jacinto.	First N.B.
7999.	Whittier.	Whittier N.B.
8002.	Livermore.	First N.B.
8040.	Escondido.	Escondido N.B.
8063.	Artesia.	First N.B.
8065.	Azusa.	First N.B.
8069.	Oceanside.	First N.B.
8073.	Redlands.	Citizens N.B.
8074.	Azusa.	United States N.B.
8085.	Compton.	First N.B.
8117.	Los Angeles.	N.B. of Commerce.
8143.	Redondo, Redondo Beach.	First N.B.
8181.	Orange.	First N.B.
8222.	Covina.	Covina N.B.
8266.	Upland.	First N.B.
8377.	Riverside.	N.B. of Riverside.
8403.	Santa Cruz.	First N.B.
8409.	Kingsburg.	First N.B.
8436.	Corona.	Corona N.B.
8487.	San Francisco.	Merchants' N.B.
8490.	Alhambra.	First N.B.
8504.	Sacramento.	California N.B.

Charter Number	City	Name of Bank
8510.	Long Beach.	Exchange N.B.
8544.	South Pasadena.	First N.B.
8549.	Hermon.	Highland N.B.
8608.	Colton.	Colton N.B.
8618.	San Bernardino.	Farmers Exchange N.B.
8626.	Tulare.	First N.B.
8652.	Glendora.	First N.B.
8692.	Martinez.	First N.B. of Contra Costa Co.
8707.	Sierra Madre.	First N.B.
8718.	Fresno.	Union N.B.
8768.	Rialto.	First N.B.
8798.	Chico.	First N.B.
8827.	Los Angeles.	Security N.B.
8857.	Reedley.	First N.B.
8870.	Long Beach.	City N.B.
8907.	Riverside.	Citizens' N.B.
9093.	Inglewood.	First N.B.
9121.	Pasadena.	Union N.B.
9141.	San Francisco.	Seaboard N.B.
9156.	Dinuba.	United States N.B.
9158.	Dinuba.	First N.B.
9167.	Orosi.	First N.B.
9173.	Visalia.	N.B. of Visalia.
9174.	San Francisco.	Anglo and London Paris N.B.
9195.	Delano.	First N.B.
9220.	Alameda.	Alameda N.B.
9227.	Auburn, E. Auburn.	First N.B.
9234.	Kerman.	First N.B.
9294.	Chico.	Butte County N.B.
9308.	Sanger.	First N.B.
9323.	Coalinga.	First N.B.
9349.	El Centro.	El Centro N.B.
9350.	El Centro.	First N.B.
9366.	Pasadena.	Crown City N.B.
9370.	Exeter.	First N.B.
9378.	Hollister.	First N.B.
9410.	Emeryville.	First N.B.
9424.	San Mateo.	N.B. of San Mateo.
9437.	Merced.	First N.B.
9459.	Banning.	First N.B.
9467.	Claremont.	First N.B.
9479.	McCloud.	McCloud N.B.
9481.	Oxnard.	First N.B.
9483.	San Diego.	Marine N.B.
9493.	Woodland.	First N.B.
9502.	Oakland.	Central N.B.
9512.	National City.	People's N.B.
9515.	Wilmington.	First N.B.
9538.	Fullerton.	Farmers and Merchants N.B.
9546.	Corcoran.	First N.B.
9551.	Calistoga.	Calistoga N.B.
9570.	Upland.	Commercial N.B.
9573.	Vallejo.	First N.B.
9575.	San Fernando.	First N.B.
9599.	La Verne.	First N.B.
9621.	Watsonville.	Pajaro Valley N.B.
9626.	Fort Bragg.	First N.B.
9648.	Sebastopol.	First N.B.
9655.	San Francisco.	Bank of California Nat. Assn.
9673.	Brawley.	First N.B.
9683.	San Francisco.	Mercantile N.B.
9685.	Ventura.	N.B. of Ventura.
9686.	Calexico.	First N.B.
9688.	Reedley.	Reedley N.B.
9705.	Calexico.	Calexico N.B.
9710.	Lindsay.	Lindsay N.B.
9713.	Willows.	First N.B.
9735.	Richmond.	First N.B.
9745.	Santa Cruz.	Santa Cruz Co. N.B.
9760.	Newman.	First N.B.
9763.	Prairie City.	First N.B.
9765.	Crows Landing.	First N.B.
9770.	Holtville.	First N.B.
9787.	Scotia.	First N.B.
9795.	Vacaville.	First N.B.
9800.	San Leandro.	First N.B.
9818.	Laton.	First N.B.
9844.	Paso Robles.	First N.B.
9873.	Weed.	First N.B.
9878.	Orange.	N.B. of Orange.
9882.	San Francisco.	Merchants N.B.
9889.	Terra Bella.	First N.B.
9892.	Antioch.	First N.B.
9894.	Puente.	First N.B.
9897.	Pleasanton.	First N.B.
9904.	Santa Ana.	California N.B.
9914.	Livermore.	Farmers and Merchants' N.B.
9918.	Petaluma.	Sonoma County N.B.
9919.	Hynes.	First N.B.
9933.	Los Banos.	First N.B.
9935.	Ontario.	Ontario N.B.
9945.	Concord.	First N.B.
9957.	Maricopa.	First N.B.
9966.	Alhambra.	Alhambra N.B.
10018.	Hayward.	First N.B.
10068.	San Dimas.	First N.B.
10070.	Redding.	Redding N.B.
10072.	Colusa.	First N.B.
10082.	Pasadena.	N.B. of Pasadena.
10088.	Taft.	First N.B.
10091.	Los Gatos.	First N.B.
10092.	Placentia.	Placentia N.B.
10099.	Burbank.	First N.B.
10100.	Redding.	Northern California N.B.
10107.	Sacramento.	Capital N.B.
10114.	Red Bluff.	Red Bluff N.B.
10120.	Dixon.	First N.B.
10124.	Parlier.	First N.B.
10133.	Winters.	First N.B.
10134.	Tustin.	First N.B.
10149.	Suisun.	First N.B.
10150.	Alameda.	Citizens N.B.
10166.	Gilroy.	First N.B.
10167.	Pasadena.	Security N.B.
10168.	Van Nuys.	First N.B.
10177.	San Rafael.	Marin County N.B.
10184.	Healdsburg.	First N.B.
10197.	Madera.	Commercial N.B.
10200.	Riverdale.	First N.B.
10201.	Tulare.	N.B. of Tulare.
10204.	Healdsburg.	Healdsburg N.B.
10208.	Claremont.	Claremont N.B.
10213.	Clovis.	First N.B.
10228.	Anaheim.	Anaheim N.B.
10233.	Venice.	First N.B.
10259.	Sonoma.	First N.B.
10271.	Chino.	First N.B.
10273.	San Fernando.	San Fernando N.B.
10281.	Walnut Creek.	First N.B.
10282.	Oroville.	Rideout, Smith N.B.
10284.	Jamestown.	Union N.B.
10292.	Coachella.	First N.B.
10293.	Selma.	Selma N.B.
10299.	Yuba City.	First N.B.
10301.	Ducor.	First N.B.
10309.	Woodlake.	First N.B.
10312.	Fowler.	Fowler N.B.
10324.	Mountain View.	First N.B.
10328.	Orosi.	N.B. of Orosi.
10352.	Merced.	Farmers and Merchants' N.B.
10357.	Bakersfield.	N.B. of Bakersfield.
10362.	Jamestown.	Jamestown N.B.
10364.	Hardwick.	First N.B.
10372.	Arcata.	First N.B.
10378.	Orland.	First N.B.
10387.	McFarland.	First N.B.
10391.	San Diego.	United States N.B.
10396.	Torrance.	First N.B.
10412.	Glendale.	Glendale N.B.
10427.	Riverbank.	First N.B.
10435.	San Diego.	Union N.B.
10453.	Gardena.	First N.B.
10461.	Sonora.	Sonora N.B.
10462.	Seeley.	First N.B.
10490.	Exeter.	Citrus N.B.
10503.	Heber.	First N.B.
10528.	Eureka.	Humboldt N.B.
10556.	Temecula.	First N.B.
10571.	Santa Cruz.	Farmers and Merchants' N.B.
10584.	Coalinga.	N.B. of Coaling.
10656.	Los Angeles.	Continental N.B.
10685.	Baldwin Park.	First N.B.
10687.	Calipatria.	First N.B.
10702.	Newport Beach.	First N.B.
10719.	Rio Vista.	First N.B.
10731.	Yreka.	First N.B.
10764.	Hemet.	First N.B.
10817.	Stockton.	San Joaquin Valley N.B.
10843.	Barstow.	First N.B.
10878.	Woodland.	Bank of Woodland Nat. Assn.
10891.	Olive.	First N.B.
10894.	Lamanda Park.	First N.B.
10897.	Lompoc.	First N.B.
10905.	Yorba Linda.	First N.B.
10931.	San Bernardino.	American N.B.
10944.	Blythe.	First N.B.
10972.	King City.	First N.B.
10977.	Ukiah.	First N.B.
10978.	Chowchilla.	First N.B.
10984.	Fairfield.	First N.B.
10988.	Modesto.	California N.B.
10999.	Bishop.	First N.B.
11005.	Victorville.	First N.B.
11025.	Sherman.	First N.B.
11041.	Del Rey.	First N.B.
11123.	Marysville.	First N.B.
11124.	Turlock.	First N.B.
11126.	Lodi.	Lodi N.B.
11151.	Chowchilla.	Chowchilla N.B.
11161.	Sebastopol.	Sebastopol N.B.
11164.	Gridley.	First N.B.
11201.	Rodeo.	First N.B.
11206.	Vallejo.	Vallejo Comme N.B.
11240.	Calipatria.	Farmers and Merchants' N.B.
11241.	Cutler.	First N.B.
11250.	Arcadia.	First N.B.
11251.	Garden Grove.	First N.B.
11273.	Montebello.	First N.B.
11282.	Cloverdale.	First N.B.
11296.	San Juan, San Juan Bautista.	First N.B.
11303.	Puente.	Puente N.B.
11326.	Crockett.	First N.B.
11327.	Bakersfield.	First N.B.
11330.	Caruthers.	First N.B.
11359.	Pittsburg.	First N.B.
11362.	Vernon.	First N.B.
11371.	Pixley.	First N.B.
11421.	Bell.	First N.B.
11421.	Pasadena.	N.B. and Trust.
11433.	Tranquility.	First N.B.
11461.	Beverly Hills.	First N.B.
11473.	Fresno.	Growers' N.B.
11484.	San Joaquin.	First N.B.
11495.	Berkeley.	College N.B.
11497.	Half Moon Bay.	Security N.B. of San Mateo
Co.		
11520.	Pescadero.	First N.B.
11522.	Los Altos.	First N.B.
11528.	Blythe.	Farmers and Merchants' N.B.
11532.	Mountain View.	Farmers and Merchants' N.B.
11534.	Shafter.	First N.B.
11560.	Watsonville.	Fruit Growers' N.B.
11561.	Bay Point.	First N.B.
11566.	Willits.	First N.B.
11572.	Campbell.	Growers' N.B.
11587.	Huntington Park.	First N.B.
11601.	Salida.	First N.B.
11616.	Orange Cove.	First N.B.
11678.	Geyersville.	First N.B.
11684.	Suisun City.	Bank of Suisun Nat. Assn.
11699.	Niland.	First N.B.
11701.	Downey.	First N.B.
11720.	Manteca.	First N.B.
11729.	Los Angeles.	American Marine N.B.
11732.	Culver City.	First N.B.
11743.	Centerville.	First N.B.
11752.	Hayward.	Farmers and Merchants' N.B.
11756.	Lompoc.	Farmers and Merchants' N.B.
11769.	Biola, Kerman.	First N.B.
11787.	Indio.	First N.B.
11806.	Earlimart.	First N.B.
11823.	Anaheim.	Golden State N.B.
11827.	La Habra.	First N.B.
11840.	Westwood.	Westwood N.B.
11850.	El Segundo.	First N.B.
11853.	Modesto.	American N.B.
11867.	Rialto.	Citizens' N.B.
11869.	Santa Ana.	American N.B.
11873.	Long Beach.	California N.B.
11875.	Sacramento.	Merchants' N.B.
11880.	Crescent Heights.	Crescent Heights N.B.
11918.	Ripon.	First N.B.
11922.	Elsinore.	First N.B.
11925.	Huntington Park.	N.B. of Huntington Park.
11926.	Pasadena.	Central N.B.
11942.	Alameda.	Commercial N.B.
11961.	Roseville.	Roseville N.B.
11962.	Brea.	First N.B.
11991.	Lankershim.	First N.B.
11992.	Roseville.	Railroad N.B.
12056.	Placerville.	Placerville N.B.
12061.	Monterey.	First N.B.
12112.	Lodi.	Citizens' N.B.
12127.	Lemoore.	N.B. of Lemoore.
12160.	Dinuba.	N.B. of Dinuba.
12172.	Paso Robles.	First N.B.
12201.	Santa Rosa.	First N.B.
12209.	Hermosa Beach.	First N.B.
12210.	Watts.	First N.B.
12226.	Sawtelle.	United States N.B.
12253.	East San Gabriel.	First N.B.
12271.	Hermosa Beach.	N.B. of Hermosa Beach.
12306.	Hayward.	First N.B.
12316.	Redlands.	First N.B.
12320.	Berkeley.	First N.B.
12328.	Bellflower.	First N.B.
12341.	Richmond.	First N.B.
12345.	Huntington Beach.	First N.B.
12360.	Sonoma.	Valley N.B.
12364.	South San Francisco.	Citizens' N.B.
12385.	Pasadena.	Pasadena N.B.
12410.	Los Angeles.	Nat. City Bank
12433.	Grass Valley.	First N.B.
12435.	Burbank.	First N.B.
12453.	Sausalito.	First N.B.
12454.	Los Angeles.	Pacific N.B.
12511.	Martinez.	N.B. of Martinez.
12545.	Los Angeles.	Seaboard N.B.
12572.	Walnut Park.	Walnut Park N.B.
12577.	Los Angeles.	Wilshire N.B.
12579.	San Francisco.	Pacific N.B.
12584.	Kerman.	First N.B.
12624.	Florence District, Los Angeles.	Florence N.B.
12640.	San Rafael.	First N.B.
12647.	Beverly Hills.	Beverly N.B.
12665.	Oakland.	New First N.B.
12673.	Graham. Los Angeles.	Graham N.B.
12678.	Visalia.	New First N.B.
12693.	Claremont.	Citizens' N.B.
12735.	Pasadena.	N.B. of Commerce.
12754.	Bellflower.	Commercial N.B.
12755.	Los Angeles.	People's N.B.
12764.	Fullerton.	New First N.B.
12766.	Temple.	Temple N.B.
12787.	Santa Monica.	American N.B.
12797.	South Pasadena.	First N.B.
12802.	San Leandro.	San Leandro N.B.
12804.	Los Angeles.	N.B. of Hollywood.
12807.	South Gate.	South Gate N.B.
12819.	Long Beach.	Seaside N.B.
12833.	Atascadero.	First N.B.
12852.	South Pasadena.	South Pasadena N.B.
12856.	Santa Paula.	New First N.B.
12893.	Alameda.	Encinal N.B.
12904.	Compton.	Compton N.B.
12909.	Beverly Hills.	Liberty N.B.
12910.	Altadena.	Altadena N.B.
12913.	Santa Maria.	Commercial N.B.
12929.	Dinuba.	Dinuba N.B.
12937.	Oakland.	East Bay N.B.
12976.	Fontana.	First N.B.
12986.	Los Angeles.	Hellman Commercial Trust &

Charter Number	City	Name of Bank
		Savings Bank
12988.	Huntington Park.	City N.B.
12996.	Ventura.	Union N.B.
13001.	Brea.	Oilfields N.B.
13007.	Verdugo City.	First N.B.
13010.	Berkeley.	Commercial N.B.
13016.	San Francisco.	Brotherhood N.B.
13028.	Merced.	First N.B.
13029.	Escondido.	First N.B.
13044.	San Francisco.	Bank of America Nat. Trust
13049.	Carlsbad.	First N.B.
13054.	Calexico.	First Central N.B.
13069.	Burbank.	Magnolia Park N.B.
13071.	Glendale.	American N.B.
13079.	Fallbrook.	First N.B.
13092.	Ontario.	Citizens N.B.
13094.	Beverly Hills.	California N.B.
13135.	Lynwood.	N.B. of Lynwood.
13178.	Vista.	First N.B.
13179.	Pico.	N.B. of Pico.
13187.	Los Angeles.	N.B. for Savings.
13200.	Los Angeles.	Commercial N.B.
13208.	San Diego.	La Jolla N.B.
13212.	Palo Alto.	Palo Alto N.B.
13217.	San Leandro.	First N.B.
13312.	Winter.	Winter N.B.
13332.	Loma Linda.	First N.B.
13335.	Arcadia.	Arcadia N.B.
13338.	San Jose.	San Jose N.B.
13340.	Yreka.	First N.B.
13348.	Beverly Hills.	Beverly Hills N.B. & Trust Co.
13356.	Colton.	Citizens N.B.
13368.	Vallejo.	Mechanics & Merchants N.B.
13375.	Pacific Grove.	First N.B.
13380.	Salinas.	Salinas N.B.
13418.	Turlock.	First N.B.
13465.	Orosi.	First N.B.
13510.	Hollister.	Hollister N.B.
13711.	Chico.	First N.B.
13787.	Fort Bragg.	Coast N.B.
13877.	Brea.	Oilfields N.B.
14045.	Santa Ana.	First N.B.
14202.	Torrance.	Torrance N.B.
14230.	Corcoran.	First N.B.
14298.	Glendale.	First N.B.
14307.	Madera.	First N.B.
14317.	Coachella.	First N.B.
	COLORADO	
1016.	Denver.	First N.B.
1651.	Denver.	Colorado N.B.
1652.	Central City.	Rocky Mountain N.B.
1833.	Pueblo.	First N.B.
1955.	Denver.	City N.B.
1991.	Georgetown.	First N.B.
2129.	Central City.	First N.B.
2134.	Pueblo.	People's N.B.
2140.	Golden.	First N.B.
2179.	Colorado Springs.	First N.B.
2199.	Georgetown.	Miners' N.B.
2300.	Trinidad.	First N.B.
2310.	Pueblo.	Stockgrowers' N.B.
2351.	Denver.	German N.B.
2352.	Boulder.	First N.B.
2354.	Lake City.	First N.B.
2355.	Boulder.	Nat. State Bank.
2394.	Georgetown.	Merchants' N.B.
2420.	Leadville.	First N.B.
2523.	Denver.	Merchants' N.B.
2541.	Pueblo.	Central N.B.
2546.	Pueblo.	Western N.B.
2622.	Fort Collins.	First N.B.
2637.	Durango.	First N.B.
2686.	Gunnison.	First N.B.
2694.	Denver.	State N.B.
2930.	Silverton.	First N.B.
2962.	Idaho Springs.	First N.B.
2975.	Gunnison.	Iron N.B.
3114.	Alamosa.	First N.B.
3178.	Greeley.	First N.B.
3246.	Boulder.	Boulder N.B.
3269.	Denver.	Denver N.B.
3354.	Longmont.	First N.B.
3450.	Trinidad.	Trinidad N.B.
3485.	Aspen.	First N.B.
3661.	Glenwood Springs.	First N.B.
3722.	Glenwood Springs.	Glenwood N.B.
3746.	Leadville.	Carbonate N.B.
3749.	Lamar.	First N.B.
3860.	Grand Junction.	First N.B.
3879.	Canon City.	First N.B.
3913.	Colorado Springs.	Exchange N.B.
3949.	Leadville.	American N.B.
4007.	Montrose.	First N.B.
4084.	Denver.	People's N.B.
4108.	Pueblo.	Mercantile N.B.
4109.	Ouray.	First N.B.
4113.	Denver.	Commercial N.B.
4126.	Durango.	Durango N.B.
4159.	Denver.	American N.B.
4172.	Salida.	First N.B.
4264.	Del Norte.	First N.B.
4334.	Rico.	First N.B.
4358.	Denver.	N.B. of Commerce.
4382.	Denver.	Union N.B.
4417.	Telluride.	First N.B.
4437.	Greeley.	Greeley N.B.
4498.	Pueblo.	Pueblo N.B.
4507.	La Junta.	First N.B.
4653.	Longmont.	Farmers' N.B.
4716.	Creede.	First N.B.
4733.	Aspen.	Aspen N.B.
4776.	Durango.	Smelter N.B.
4845.	Cripple Creek.	First N.B.
5283.	Colorado Springs.	El Paso N.B.
5381.	Florence.	First N.B.
5467.	Delta.	First N.B.
5503.	Fort Collins.	Fort Collins N.B.
5586.	Victor.	First N.B.
5624.	Sterling.	First N.B.
5976.	Hotchkiss.	First N.B.
5989.	Idaho Springs.	Merchants and Miners' N.B.
6030.	Las Animas.	First N.B.
6057.	Eaton.	First N.B.
6137.	Grand Junction.	Grand Valley N.B.
6178.	Rifle.	First N.B.
6238.	Colorado Springs.	City N.B.
6355.	Denver.	Capitol N.B.
6437.	Brush.	First N.B.
6454.	Steamboat Springs.	First N.B.
6472.	Sugar City.	Citizens' N.B.
6497.	Golden.	Rubey N.B.
6556.	Castle Rock.	First N.B. of Douglas County.
6671.	Paonia.	First N.B.
6772.	Fountain.	First N.B.
6957.	Glenwood Springs.	Citizens' N.B.
7004.	Fort Morgan.	First N.B.
7022.	Walsenburg.	First N.B.
7082.	Rocky Ford.	First N.B.
7228.	Monte Vista.	First N.B.
7288.	Montrose.	Montrose N.B.
7408.	Denver.	United States N.B.
7435.	Meeker.	First N.B.
7501.	Arvada.	First N.B.
7533.	Littleton.	First N.B.
7577.	Brighton.	First N.B.
7604.	Greeley.	Union N.B.
7637.	Fowler.	First N.B.
7648.	Loveland.	First N.B.
7704.	Holly.	First N.B.
7766.	Grand Junction.	Mesa County N.B.
7784.	Silverton.	Silverton N.B.
7793.	Wellington.	First N.B.
7809.	Granada.	First N.B.
7832.	Fort Morgan.	Morgan County N.B.
7837.	Fort Collins.	Poudre Valley N.B.
7839.	Longmont.	Longmont N.B.
7888.	Salida.	Commercial N.B.
7904.	Alarnosa.	American N.B.
7973.	Sterling.	Logan County N.B.
7995.	Berthoud.	Berthoud N.B.
8004.	Palisades.	Palisades N.B.
8033.	Berthoud.	First N.B.
8088.	Ault.	First N.B.
8116.	Loveland.	Loveland N.B.
8167.	Ault.	Farmers' N.B.
8205.	Julesburg.	First N.B.
8271.	Elizabeth.	First N.B.
8296.	Windsor.	First N.B.
8412.	Eads.	First N.B.
8433.	Canon City.	Fremont County N.B.
8489.	Hugo.	First N.B.
8520.	Brush.	Stockmen's N.B.
8541.	Alamosa.	Alarnosa N.B.
8548.	Akron.	First N.B.
8572.	Colorado Springs.	Colorado Springs N.B.
8636.	Johnstown.	First N.B.
8658.	Eaton.	Eaton N.B.
8675.	Delta.	Delta N.B.
8695.	Ordway.	First N.B.
8735.	Buena Vista.	First N.B.
8752.	Wray.	First N.B.
8755.	Platteville.	First N.B.
8774.	Denver.	Central N.B.
8815.	Aspen.	People's N.B.
8840.	Fruita.	First N.B.
8909.	Lafayette.	First N.B.
8951.	Salida.	Merchants' N.B.
8967.	Cortez.	First N.B.
9009.	Carbondale.	First N.B.
9013.	Eagle.	First N.B. of Eagle.
9036.	Lamar.	Lamar N.B.
9045.	Sedgwick.	First N.B.
9100.	Cortez.	Montezuma Valley N.B.
9117.	Rocky Ford.	Rocky Ford N.B.
9120.	Windsor.	Farmers' N.B.
9278.	Holyoke.	First N.B.
9451.	Platteville.	Platteville N.B.
9454.	Sterling.	Farmers' N.B.
9603.	Julesburg.	Citizens' N.B.
9674.	Mancos.	First N.B.
9676.	Wray.	N.B. of Wray.
9697.	Gill.	First N.B.
9719.	Olathe.	First N.B.
9743.	Center.	First N.B.
9797.	Durango.	Bums N.B.
9840.	La Jara.	First N.B.
9875.	Clifton.	First N.B.
9887.	Denver.	Hamilton N.B.
9907.	Englewood.	First N.B.
9997.	Saguache.	First N.B.
10038.	Greeley.	City N.B.
10064.	Denver.	Federal N.B.
10093.	Yuma.	First N.B.
10272.	Cedaredge.	First N.B.
10558.	Craig.	First N.B.
10560.	Craig.	Craig N.B.
10730.	Hayden.	First N.B.
10770.	Dolores.	First N.B.
10786.	Hugo.	Hugo N.B.
10852.	Otis.	First N.B.
10901.	Akron.	Citizens' N.B.
11099.	Haxtun.	First N.B.
11117.	Boulder.	Citizens' N.B.
11197.	Stratton.	First N.B.
11248.	Walden.	First N.B.
11253.	Longmont.	American N.B.
11321.	Mead.	First N.B.
11354.	Simla.	First N.B.
11455.	Burlington.	First N.B.
11504.	Limon.	First N.B.
11523.	Peetz.	First N.B.
11530.	Keenesburg.	First N.B.
11540.	Denver.	Stock Yards N.B.
11564.	Denver.	Drovers' N.B.
11571.	Fleming.	First N.B.
11574.	Deer Trail.	First N.B.
11619.	Limon.	Limon N.B.
11623.	Denver.	Globe N.B.
11640.	Strasburg.	First N.B.
11660.	Springfield.	First N.B.
11681.	Elbert.	First N.B.
11682.	Aurora.	First N.B.
11871.	Pagosa Springs.	First N.B.
11872.	Flagler.	First N.B.
11949.	Littleton.	Littleton N.B.
11972.	Sterling.	Sterling N.B.
12250.	Denver.	Broadway N.B.
12431.	Florence.	Security N.B.
12517.	Denver.	American N.B.
12531.	La Veta.	First N.B.
12716.	Genoa.	First N.B.
12974.	Denver.	South Broadway N.B.
13098.	Denver.	West Side N.B.
13536.	Rifle.	Rifle N.B.
13624.	Loveland.	First N.B.
13902.	Grand Junction.	First N.B.
13928.	Greeley.	Greeley.N.B.
14021.	Boulder.	First N.B.
14146.	Fort Collins.	First N.B.
14148.	Trinidad.	Trinidad N.B.
14213.	Eads.	First N.B.
14222.	Trinidad.	First N.B.
14248.	Denver.	Union N.B.
14254.	Lamar.	Lamar N.B.
	CONNECTICUT	
2.	New Haven.	First N.B.
4.	Stamford.	First-Stamford N.B.
65.	Norwich.	First N.B.
121.	Hartford.	First N.B.
186.	Rockville.	First N.B.
196.	New London.	First N.B.
224.	Norwich.	Second N.B.
227.	New Haven.	Second N.B.
250.	Meriden.	First N.B.
251.	Mystic Bridge.	First N.B.
335.	Greenport.	First N.B.
361.	Hartford.	Nat. Exchange Bank
394.	Westport.	First N.B.
397.	Middletown.	First N.B.
448.	Putnam.	First N.B.
450.	Killingly, Danielson.	First N.B.
458.	Norwich.	First N.B.
486.	Hartford.	Charter Oak N.B.
497.	Suffield.	First N.B.
502.	South Norwalk.	First N.B.
509.	Rockville.	Rockville N.B.
645.	Mystic.	Mystic River N.B.
657.	Norwich.	Thames N.B.
660.	Southport.	Southport N.B.
666.	New London.	N.B. of Commerce.
670.	Hartford.	Phoenix N.B.
686.	Stafford Springs.	Stafford N.B.
709.	Litchfield.	First N.B.
720.	Meriden.	Home N.B.
735.	Stonington.	First N.B.
754.	Norwalk.	Fairfield County N.B.
756.	Hartford.	Aetna N.B.
780.	Waterbury.	Waterbury N.B.
791.	Waterbury.	Citizene N.B.
796.	New Haven.	Yale N.B.
845.	Middletown.	Middlesex County N.B.
910.	Bridgeport.	Bridgeport N.B.
919.	Pawcatuck.	Pawcatuck N.B.
921.	Bridgeport.	City N.B.
927.	Bridgeport.	Connecticut N.B.
928.	Bridgeport.	Pequonnock N.B.
942.	Norwalk.	N.B. of Norwalk.
943.	Danbury.	Danbury N.B.
978.	New London.	Nat. Whaling Bank.
1013.	Portland.	First N.B.
1037.	New London.	New London City N.B.
1038.	Stamford.	Stamford N.B.
1084.	Essex.	Saybrook N.B.
1093.	Ansonia.	Ansonia N.B.
1098.	Derby.	Birmingham N.B.
1128.	New Haven.	Merchants' N.B.
1132.	Danbury.	City N.B.
1139.	Deep River.	Deep River N.B.
1141.	Bethel.	First N.B.
1165.	Hartford.	American N.B.
1175.	New London.	Nat. Union Bank.
1184.	New Britain.	New Britain N.B.
1187.	Norwich.	Uncas N.B.
1193.	New Milford.	First N.B.
1202.	New Haven.	Nat. Tradesmen's Bank
1214.	Falls Village.	Nat. Iron Bank.

Charter Number	City	Name of Bank
1216.	Middletown.	Middletown N.B.
1243.	New Haven.	New Haven Bank Nat. Bkg. Assn.
1245.	New Haven.	New Haven County N.B.
1249.	New Canaan.	First N.B.
1268.	Mystic.	Mystic N.B.
1300.	Hartford.	Mercantile N.B.
1314.	Clinton.	Clinton N.B.
1321.	Hartford.	Farmers and Mechanics' N.B.
1338.	Hartford.	Hartford and Aetna N.B.
1340.	Middletown.	Central N.B.
1358.	Norwich.	Norwich N.B.
1360.	Danielson.	Windham County N.B.
1377.	Hartford.	City N.B.
1379.	Norwich.	Shetucket N.B.
1382.	Meriden.	Meriden N.B.
1385.	Tolland.	Tolland County N.B.
1477.	Putnam.	Thompson N.B.
1478.	Jewett City.	Jewett City N.B.
1480.	East Haddam.	N.B. of New England.
1481.	Norwich.	Merchants' N.B.
1494.	Winsted.	Hurlbut N.B.
1614.	Willimantic.	Windham N.B.
2250.	Bristol.	Bristol N.B.
2342.	Norwalk.	Central N.B.
2388.	Willimantic.	First N.B.
2414.	Winsted.	First N.B.
2419.	Winsted.	Winsted N.B.
2494.	Waterbury.	Manufacturers' N.B.
2599.	Wallingford.	First N.B.
2643.	South Norwalk.	City N.B.
2682.	New Haven.	First N.B.
2814.	Southington.	Southington N.B.
3020.	Naugatuck.	Naugatuck N.B.
3668.	New Britain.	Mechanics' N.B.
3768.	Waterbury.	Fourth N.B.
3914.	Stafford.	Springs First N.B.
3964.	Thomaston.	Thomaston N.B.
5231.	Torrington.	Brooks N.B.
5235.	Torrington.	Torrington N.B.
5309.	Ridgefield.	First N.B. and Trust Co.
5358.	Guilford.	Guilford N.B.
5499.	Seymour.	Valley N.B.
7812.	East Haddam.	N.B. of New England.
8243.	Greenwich.	Greenwich N.B.
8511.	Canaan.	Canaan N.B.
8936.	Essex.	Essex N.B.
9313.	Plainville.	First N.B.
10145.	Plainfield.	First N.B.
10289.	Bethel.	Bethel N.B.
10796.	Hartford.	Colonial N.B.
12400.	Stamford.	People's N.B.
12594.	Putnam.	Citizens' N.B.
12637.	Plantsville.	Plantsville N.B.
12846.	New Britain.	City N.B.
12973.	East Port Chester.	Byrarn N.B.
13038.	Hartford.	Capitol N.B.
13042.	Greenwich.	First N.B.
13245.	Sharon.	Sharon N.B.
13704.	New Haven.	Tradesmens N.B.

DELAWARE

Charter Number	City	Name of Bank
473.	Wilmington.	First N.B.
795.	Seaford.	First N.B.
997.	Newport.	Newport N.B.
1181.	Middletown.	Citizens' N.B.
1190.	Wilmington.	N.B. of Wilmington and Brandywine.
1281.	Odessa.	New Castle County N.B.
1332.	Delaware City.	Delaware City N.B.
1390.	Wilmington.	Union N.B.
1420.	Wilmington.	N.B. of Delaware.
1536.	Newark.	N.B. of Newark.
1567.	Dover.	First N.B.
2336.	Smyrna.	Fruit Growers' N.B.
2340.	Milford.	First N.B.
2381.	Smyrna.	N.B. of Smyrna.
3019.	Middletown.	People's N.B.
3395.	Wilmington.	Central N.B.
3693.	Seaford.	Sussex N.B.
3883.	Harrington.	First N.B.
5148.	Lewes.	Lewes N.B.
5421.	Frederica.	First N.B.
5930.	Georgetown.	First N.B.
6718.	Selbyville.	Selbyville N.B.
6726.	Laurel.	People's N.B.
7211.	Delmar.	First N.B.
8918.	Frankford.	First N.B.
8972.	Dagsboro.	First N.B.
9132.	Felton.	First N.B.
9428.	Wyoming.	First N.B.
12882.	Milton.	First N.B.
13278.	Georgetown.	First N.B.

DISTRICT OF COLUMBIA

Charter Number	City	Name of Bank
26.	Washington.	First N.B.
526.	Washington.	N.B. of the Metropolis.
627.	Washington.	Merchants' N.B.
682.	Georgetown.	N.B. of Commerce.
975.	Washington.	N.B. of the Republic.
1069.	Washington.	Nat. Metropolitan Bank
1893.	Washington.	Citizens' N.B.
1928.	Georgetown.	Farmers and Mechanics' N.B.
2038.	Washington.	Second N.B.
2358.	Washington.	German American N.B.
2382.	Washington.	Central N.B.
3425.	Washington.	N.B. of Washington.
3625.	Washington.	Columbia N.B.
4107.	Washington.	Nat. Capital Bank.
4195.	Washington.	West End N.B.
4244.	Washington.	Traders' N.B.
4247.	Washington.	Lincoln N.B.
4522.	Washington.	Ohio N.B.
5046.	Washington.	Riggs N.B.
6716.	Washington.	American N.B.
7446.	Washington.	Commercial N.B.
7936.	Washington.	Nat. City Bank.
9545.	Washington.	District N.B.
10316.	Washington.	Federal N.B.
10504.	Washington.	Franklin N.B.
10825.	Washington.	Dupont N.B.
11633.	Washington.	Liberty N.B.
12139.	Washington.	Standard N.B.
12194.	Washington.	Hamilton N.B.
12721.	Washington.	Northwest N.B.
13782.	Washington.	Hamilton N.B.

FLORIDA

Charter Number	City	Name of Bank
2174.	Jacksonville.	First N.B. of Florida.
2194.	Jacksonville.	Ambler N.B.
2490.	Pensacola.	First N.B.
3223.	Palatka.	First N.B.
3266.	Palatka.	Palatka N.B.
3327.	Jacksonville.	N.B. of the State of Florida.
3462.	Saint Augustine.	First N.B.
3469.	Orlando.	First N.B.
3470.	Ocala.	First N.B.
3497.	Tampa.	First N.B.
3798.	Sanford.	First N.B.
3802.	Orlando.	Citizens' N.B.
3815.	Ocala.	Merchants' N.B.
3869.	Jacksonville.	N.B. of Jacksonville.
3894.	Gainesville.	First N.B.
4132.	Tallahassee.	First N.B.
4332.	Jacksonville.	Merchants' N.B.
4478.	Tampa.	Gulf N.B.
4539.	Tampa.	Tampa N.B.
4558.	Fernandina.	First N.B.
4627.	Bartow.	Polk County N.B.
4672.	Key West.	First N.B.
4813.	Palatka.	Putnam N.B.
4837.	Pensacola.	Citizens' N.B.
4949.	Tampa.	Exchange N.B.
5534.	Arcadia.	First N.B.
5603.	Pensacola.	American N.B.
6055.	Live Oak.	First N.B.
6110.	Marianna.	First N.B.
6274.	Apalachicola.	First N.B.
6370.	Miami.	First N.B.
6774.	Miami.	Fort Dallas N.B.
6825.	Ocala.	Central N.B.
6888.	Jacksonville.	Atlantic N.B.
7034.	Milton.	First N.B.
7153.	Tampa.	American N.B.
7190.	Madison.	First N.B.
7253.	Quincy.	First N.B.
7404.	De Funiak Springs.	First N.B.
7423.	Graceville.	First N.B.
7540.	Lake City.	First N.B.
7730.	Saint Petersburg.	First N.B.
7757.	Jasper.	First N.B.
7778.	Chipley.	First N.B.
7796.	Saint Petersburg.	Central N.B.
7865.	Perry.	First N.B.
7942.	Key West.	Island City N.B.
8321.	Jacksonville.	Florida N.B.
8728.	Arcadia.	De Soto N.B.
8802.	Gainesville.	Gainesville N.B.
8980.	Alachua.	First N.B.
9007.	Pensacola.	Citizens and People's N.B.
9035.	Fort Myers.	First N.B.
9049.	Jacksonville.	Barnett N.B.
9628.	Jacksonville.	Fourth N.B.
9657.	De Land.	First N.B.
9707.	Saint Cloud.	First N.B.
9811.	Lakeland.	First N.B.
9891.	Brooksville.	First N.B.
9926.	Ocala.	Ocala N.B.
10024.	Fernandina.	Citizens' N.B.
10069.	Orlando.	First N.B.
10136.	Jacksonville.	Heard N.B.
10236.	Plant City.	First N.B.
10245.	Bradentown.	First N.B.
10310.	Gainesville.	Florida N.B.
10346.	Panama City.	First N.B.
10379.	Winter Haven.	Snell N.B.
10386.	Fort Meade.	First N.B.
10414.	Sarasota.	First N.B.
10512.	Punta Gorda.	First N.B.
10535.	Pensacola.	N.B. of Commerce.
10545.	Daytona.	First N.B.
10578.	Ocala.	Munroe and Chanbliss N.B.
10691.	Wauchula.	Carlton N.B.
10826.	Avon Park.	First N.B.
10958.	Tampa.	Nat. City Bank.
11038.	Leesburg.	First N.B.
11073.	West Palm Beach.	First N.B.
11156.	Vero.	First N.B.
11389.	Winter Garden.	First N.B.
11420.	Saint Augustine.	Saint Augustine N.B.
11703.	Lake Hamilton.	First N.B.
11716.	Lake Worth.	First N.B.
11921.	Clermont.	First N.B.
12011.	Miami.	Miami N.B.
12020.	Fort Lauderdale.	First N.B.
12047.	Miami Beach.	Miami Beach First N.B.
12057.	West Palm Beach.	American N.B.
12090.	Sebring.	First N.B.
12100.	Winter Haven.	N.B. of Winter Haven.
12274.	Tarpon Springs.	First N.B.
12275.	Palm Beach.	First N.B.
12546.	Seabreeze.	First N.B.
12600.	Palm Beach.	Palm Beach N.B.
12623.	Saint Petersburg.	Alexander N.B.
12751.	Sarasota.	American N.B.
12841.	Boynton.	First N.B.
12842.	Tampa.	N.B. of Commerce.
12868.	Miami.	City N.B.
12871.	Kissimmee.	First N.B.
12880.	Bradenton.	American N.B.
12887.	Miami.	Third N.B.
12905.	Clearwater.	First N.B.
12930.	West Palm Beach.	N.B. of West Palm Beach.
12983.	Auburndale.	First N.B.
13008.	Coral Gables.	Coral Gables First N.B.
13090.	Palm Beach.	First N.B.
13102.	Mount Dora.	First N.B.
13157.	Sanford.	Sanford Atlantic N.B.
13159.	Miami.	City N.B.
13214.	Palatka.	Palatka Atlantic N.B.
13300.	West Palm Beach.	West Palm Beach Atlantic N.B.
13309.	Bartow.	Polk County N.B.
13320.	Brooksville.	First N.B.
13352.	Sarasota.	Palmer N.B. and Trust Co.
13370.	Lakeland.	Florida N.B.
13383.	Winter Haven.	American N.B.
13388.	Deland.	Barnett N.B.
13389.	Bartow.	Florida N.B.
13390.	Cocoa.	Barnett N.B.
13421.	Avon Park.	Barnett N.B.
13437.	Winter Haven.	Snell N.B.
13498.	St. Petersburg.	Florida N.B.
13570.	Miami.	Florida N.B. and Trust Co.
13641.	Homestead.	First N.B.
13828.	Miami Beach.	Mercantile N.B.
13961.	Tarpon Springs.	First N.B.
13968.	Milton.	First N.B.
14003.	Orlando.	First N.B.
14195.	Fort Myers.	First N.B.
14338.	Panama City.	Bay N.B.

GEORGIA

Charter Number	City	Name of Bank
1255.	Savannah.	Savannah N.B.
1559.	Atlanta.	Atlanta N.B.
1586.	Savannah.	City N.B.
1605.	Atlanta.	Georgia N.B.
1613.	Augusta.	N.B. of Augusta.
1617.	Macon.	First N.B.
1630.	Columbus.	Chattahoochee N.B.
1639.	Athens.	N.B. of Athens.
1640.	Savannah.	Merchants' N.B.
1703.	Augusta.	Merchants and Planters' N.B.
1860.	Augusta.	Nat. Exchange Bank
1861.	Newnan.	First N.B.
2009.	Americus.	First N.B.
2064.	Atlanta.	State N.B.
2075.	Griffin.	City N.B.
2338.	Columbus.	First N.B.
2368.	Rome.	First N.B.
2424.	Atlanta.	Gate City N.B.
2839.	Americus.	People's N.B.
3093.	La Grange.	First N.B.
3116.	Brunswick.	First N.B.
3382.	Newnan.	Newnan N.B.
3406.	Savannah.	N.B. of Savannah.
3670.	Rome.	Merchants' N.B.
3740.	Macon.	Merchants' N.B.
3753.	Brunswick.	Oglethorpe N.B.
3767.	Thomasville.	First N.B.
3830.	Marietta.	First N.B.
3872.	Albany.	Citizens' First N.B.
3907.	Dalton.	First N.B.
3937.	Columbus.	Third N.B.
3983.	Gainesville.	First N.B.
4012.	Cartersville.	First N.B.
4075.	Cedartown.	First N.B.
4115.	Dawson.	Dawson N.B.
4369.	Rome.	Rome N.B.
4429.	Valdosta.	First N.B.
4547.	Macon.	American N.B.
4554.	Cordele.	First N.B.
4691.	Columbus.	Fourth N.B.
4944.	Brunswick.	N.B. of Brunswick.
4963.	Waycross.	First N.B.
5030.	Atlanta.	Third N.B.
5045.	Atlanta.	Fourth N.B.
5264.	Carrollton.	First N.B.
5318.	Atlanta.	Lowry N.B.
5490.	Atlanta.	Capital City N.B.
5512.	Albany.	Albany N.B.
5644.	Forsyth.	First N.B.
5709.	Jackson.	First N.B.
5975.	Cordele.	Cordele N.B.
6002.	Fort Gaines.	First N.B.
6004.	Bainbridge.	First N.B.
6047.	Newnan.	Coweta N.B.
6079.	Blue Ridge.	North Georgia N.B.
6082.	Fitzgerald.	First N.B.
6180.	Sylvester.	First N.B.
6207.	Louisville.	First N.B.
6243.	Barnesville.	First N.B.
6336.	Albany.	Third N.B.
6374.	Dublin.	First N.B.
6496.	Dawson.	City N.B.
6498.	Colquitt.	First N.B.
6525.	Athens.	Georgia N.B.

Charter Number	City	Name of Bank
6542.	Tifton.	First N.B.
6576.	Montezuma.	First N.B.
6687.	Toccoa.	First N.B.
6967.	Greensboro.	Greensboro N.B.
7018.	Blakely.	First N.B.
7067.	Sparta.	First. N.B.
7220.	Tallapoosa.	First N.B.
7247.	La Fayette.	First N.B.
7300.	Madison.	First N.B.
7330.	Union Point.	N.B. of Union Point.
7431.	Commerce.	First N.B.
7459.	Fort Valley.	First N.B.
7468.	Statesboro.	First N.B.
7549.	Calhoun.	Calhoun N.B.
7565.	Moultrie.	First N.B.
7567.	Cochran.	First N.B.
7580.	Hawkinsville.	First N.B.
7616.	Gainesville.	Gainesville N.B.
7762.	La Grange.	La Grange N.B.
7777.	Albany.	Citizens' N.B.
7899.	Waynesboro.	First N.B.
7934.	Sandersville.	First N.B.
7963.	Buena Vista.	First N.B.
7969.	McDonough.	First N.B.
7979.	Lyons.	First N.B.
7986.	Maysville.	Atkins N.B.
7994.	Quitman.	First N.B.
8023.	Wrightsville.	First N.B.
8046.	West Point.	First N.B.
8128.	Dublin.	City N.B.
8250.	Fitzgerald.	Exchange N.B.
8305.	Americus.	Americus N.B.
8314.	Arlington.	First N.B.
8350.	Tifton.	N.B. of Tifton.
8365.	Macon.	Fourth N.B.
8417.	Shellman.	First N.B.
8452.	Greensboro.	Copelan N.B.
8470.	Lavonia.	First N.B.
8477.	Newnan.	Manufacturers' N.B.
8527.	Senoia.	First N.B.
8580.	Ocilla.	First N.B.
8628.	Rockmart.	Citizens' N.B.
8680.	Pembroke.	Pembroke N.B.
8848.	Washington.	N.B. of Wilkes.
8894.	Washington.	Citizens' N.B.
8945.	Covington.	First N.B.
8966.	Fitzgerald.	Ben Hill N.B.
8990.	Macon.	Citizens' N.B.
9039.	Jefferson.	First N.B.
9051.	Winder.	First N.B.
9074.	Cordele.	American N.B.
9088.	Millen.	First N.B.
9105.	Atlanta.	American N.B.
9106.	Nashville.	First N.B.
9186.	Jackson.	Jackson N.B.
9212.	Macon.	Commercial N.B.
9252.	Elberton.	First N.B.
9254.	Colquitt.	Colquitt N.B.
9302.	Thomson.	First N.B.
9329.	Monticello.	Farmers' N.B.
9346.	Monticello.	First N.B.
9593.	Eastman.	First N.B.
9607.	Byromville.	Byrom N.B.
9613.	Cornelia.	First N.B.
9615.	Reynolds.	First N.B.
9617.	Atlanta.	Fulton N.B.
9618.	Vienna.	First N.B.
9636.	Rome.	Cherokee N.B.
9641.	Sandersville.	Cohen N.B.
9672.	Milledgeville.	First N.B.
9729.	Albany.	Georgia N.B.
9777.	Adel.	First N.B.
9870.	Pelham.	First N.B.
9879.	Vidalia.	First N.B.
10089.	Hampton.	First N.B.
10270.	Macon.	Macon N.B.
10279.	Cuthbert.	First N.B.
10302.	Rome.	Nat. City Bank.
10303.	Rome.	Exchange N.B.
10333.	Claxton.	First N.B.
10756.	East Point.	First N.B.
10805.	Winder.	Winder N.B.
10829.	Sylvania.	N.B. of Sylvania.
10900.	Rockmart.	Farmers and Merchants' N.B.
10945.	Macon.	Bibb N.B.
11255.	Conyers.	First N.B.
11290.	Quitman.	People's N.B.
11597.	Griffin.	Second N.B.
11695.	Hartwell.	First N.B.
11833.	Cedartown.	Liberty N.B.
11936.	Lawrenceville.	First N.B.
11939.	Montezuma.	Citizens' N.B.
12030.	Savannah.	Mercantile N.B.
12105.	Dallas.	First N.B.
12232.	Marietta.	Citizens' N.B.
12249.	Atlanta.	Ninth N.B.
12254.	Lumpkin.	N.B. of Lumpkin.
12317.	Sparta.	Hancock N.B.
12404.	Barnesville.	Citizens' N.B.
12492.	Atlanta.	City N.B.
12635.	Cartersville.	Cartersville N.B.
12863.	Albany.	New Georgia N.B.
13068.	Savannah.	Citizens' and Southern N.B.
13161.	Moultrie.	Moultrie N.B.
13223.	Albany.	City N.B.
13227.	Douglasville.	First N.B.
13469.	Marietta.	Citizens' N.B.
13472.	Savannah.	Liberty N.B. and Trust Co.
13550.	Fitzgerald.	N.B. of Fitzgerald.
13725.	Sandersville.	Geo. D. Warthen N.B.
13897.	Jackson.	Jackson N.B.
14046.	Monroe.	N.B. of Monroe.
14061.	Elberton.	First N.B.
14193.	Waycross.	First N.B.
14243.	Claxton.	Claxton N.B.
14255.	Quitman.	Citizens' N.B.
14257.	Cordele.	First N.B.

HAWAII

Charter Number	City	Name of Bank
5550.	Honolulu.	First N.B. of Hawaii.
5994.	Wailuku.	First N.B.
8101.	Lahaina.	Lahaina N.B.
8207.	Kahului.	Baldwin N.B.
10451.	Paia.	First N.B.
11050.	Honolulu.	Army N.B. of Schofield Barracks.

IDAHO

Charter Number	City	Name of Bank
1668.	Boise.	First N.B. of Idaho.
2972.	Lewiston.	First N.B.
3023.	Lewiston.	Lewiston N.B.
3142.	Ketchum.	First N.B.
3408.	Moscow.	First N.B.
3471.	Boise.	Boise City N.B.
3895.	Hailey.	First N.B.
4023.	Pocatello.	First N.B.
4584.	Moscow.	Moscow N.B.
4690.	Caldwell.	First N.B.
4773.	Wallace.	First N.B.
4790.	Kendrick.	First N.B.
4808.	Genesee.	First N.B.
4827.	Pocatello.	Idaho N.B.
5600.	Lewiston.	Idaho N.B.
5764.	Saint Anthony.	First N.B.
5820.	Idaho Falls.	First N.B.
5906.	Payette.	First N.B.
6145.	Emmett.	First N.B.
6347.	Pocatello.	Bannock N.B.
6521.	Mountainhome.	First N.B.
6577.	Shoshone.	First N.B.
6697.	Nezperce.	First N.B.
6754.	Weiser.	First N.B.
6793.	Coeur d'Alene.	First N.B.
6927.	Grangeville.	First N.B.
6982.	Idaho Falls.	American N.B.
7120.	Coeur d'Alene.	First-Exchange N.B.
7133.	Rexburg.	First N.B.
7230.	Saint Anthony.	Commercial N.B.
7381.	Montpelier.	First N.B.
7419.	Blackfoot.	First N.B.
7526.	Preston.	First N.B.
7608.	Twin Falls.	First N.B.
7923.	Cottonwood.	First N.B.
8075.	Payette.	Payette N.B.
8080.	Salmon.	First N.B.
8139.	Weiser.	Weiser N.B.
8225.	Caldwell.	Western N.B.
8341.	Sandpoint.	First N.B.
8346.	Boise.	Idaho N.B.
8370.	Nampa.	First N.B.
8822.	Malad City.	First N.B.
8869.	American Falls.	First N.B.
8906.	Mullan.	First N.B.
9134.	Wallace.	Wallace N.B.
9145.	Hailey.	Hailey N.B.
9263.	Sandpoint.	Bonner County N.B.
9272.	Shoshone.	Lincoln County N.B.
9333.	Caldwell.	American N.B.
9371.	Gooding.	First N.B.
9432.	Salmon.	Citizens' N.B.
9477.	Challis.	First N.B.
9491.	Wendell.	First N.B.
9566.	Kellogg.	First N.B.
9680.	Jerome.	First N.B.
10083.	Boise.	Pacific N.B.
10162.	Fairfield.	First N.B.
10212.	Lewiston.	Empire N.B.
10221.	Meridian.	First N.B.
10269.	Ashton.	First N.B.
10278.	Driggs.	First N.B.
10294.	Hagerman.	First N.B.
10341.	Burley.	First N.B.
10429.	Rupert.	First N.B.
10517.	Rupert.	Rupert N.B.
10693.	Nampa.	Citizens' N.B.
10727.	Bonners Ferry.	First N.B.
10751.	Boise.	Overland N.B.
10771.	Saint Maries.	First N.B.
10909.	Wilder.	First N.B.
10916.	Nampa.	Farmers and Merchants' N.B.
10920.	Ririe.	First N.B.
10969.	Kimberly.	First N.B.
10975.	Newdale.	First N.B.
11053.	Halley.	Blaine County N.B.
11065.	Buhl.	First N.B.
11076.	Buhl.	Farmers' N.B.
11100.	Filer.	First N.B.
11135.	Jerome.	Jerome N.B.
11179.	Grace.	First N.B.
11183.	Bancroft.	First N.B.
11198.	Firth.	First N.B.
11274.	Twin Falls.	Twin Falls N.B.
11278.	Idaho Falls.	Idaho Falls N.B.
11385.	Rigby.	First N.B.
11434.	Shelley.	First N.B.
11438.	Burley.	Burley N.B.
11458.	Rigby.	Jefferson County N.B.
11471.	Driggs.	Teton N.B.
11496.	Parma.	First N.B.
11508.	Dubois.	First N.B.
11556.	Parma.	Parma N.B.
11578.	Jerome.	City N.B.
11600.	Roberts.	First N.B.
11609.	Nampa.	Stockmen's N.B.
11636.	Mackay.	First N.B.
11721.	Pocatello.	N.B. of Idaho.
11736.	Minidoka.	First N.B.
11745.	Lewiston.	American N.B.
11794.	Arco.	First N.B.
11821.	Nampa.	Nampa N.B.
11884.	Fairfield.	Securitv N.B.
12256.	Burley.	Cassia N.B.
12432.	Wendell.	Wendell N.B.
12832.	Hailey.	First N.B.
13267.	Driggs.	First N.B.
13288.	Coeur d'Alene.	First N.B.
13819.	Lewiston.	Lewiston N.B.

ILLINOIS

Charter Number	City	Name of Bank
8.	Chicago.	First N.B.
33.	Cairo.	First N.B.
38.	Aurora.	First N.B.
85.	Monmouth.	First N.B.
108.	Rock Island.	First N.B.
113.	Danville.	First N.B.
114.	La Salle.	First N.B.
160.	Moline.	First N.B.
176.	Peoria.	First N.B.
177.	Wilmington.	First N.B.
205.	Springfield.	First N.B.
207.	Peoria.	Second N.B.
225.	Chicago.	Second N.B.
236.	Chicago.	Third N.B.
241.	Galesburg.	First N.B.
276.	Chicago.	Fourth N.B.
319.	Freeport.	First N.B.
320.	Chicago.	Fifth N.B.
339.	Batavia.	First N.B.
347.	Lacon.	First N.B.
372.	Woodstock.	First N.B.
385.	Freeport.	Second N.B.
409.	Mount Carrol I.	First N.B.
415.	Canton.	First N.B.
424.	Quincy.	First N.B.
429.	Rockford.	First N.B.
441.	Peru.	First N.B.
466.	Chicago.	Mechanics' N.B.
477.	Decatur.	First N.B.
479.	Rockford.	Third N.B.
482.	Rockford.	Second N.B.
491.	Galesburg.	Second N.B.
495.	Warsaw.	First N.B.
508.	Chicago.	Northwestern N.B.
511.	Jacksonville.	First N.B.
512.	Joliet.	First N.B.
531.	Morris.	Grundy County N.B.
534.	Geneseo.	First N.B.
642.	Chicago.	Merchants' N.B.
698.	Chicago.	Union N.B.
703.	Quincy.	Merchants and Farmers' N.B.
713.	Chicago.	Commercial N.B.
724.	Chicago.	Manufacturers' N.B.
759.	Knoxville.	First N.B.
763.	Charleston.	First N.B.
785.	Cairo.	City N.B.
818.	Chicago.	City N.B.
819.	Bloomington.	First N.B.
827.	Galva.	First N.B.
831.	Galena.	N.B. of Galena.
849.	Warren.	Farmers' N.B.
883.	Rockford.	Winnebago N.B.
902.	Dixon.	Lee County N.B.
903.	Princeton.	First N.B.
913.	Champaign.	First N.B.
915.	Shawneetown.	First N.B.
945.	Waukegan.	First N.B.
966.	Chicago.	Traders' N.B.
967.	Macomb.	First N.B.
979.	Galena.	Merchants' N.B.
1001.	Centralia.	First N.B.
1024.	Mattoon.	First N.B.
1033.	Morrison.	First N.B.
1042.	Pittsfield.	First N.B.
1097.	Belvidere.	First N.B.
1117.	Peoria.	Mechanics' N.B.
1154.	Ottawa.	First N.B.
1167.	Carthage.	Hancock County N.B.
1177.	Mendota.	First N.B.
1365.	Elgin.	First N.B.
1428.	Alton.	Alton N.B.
1445.	Alton.	First N.B.
1453.	Rushville.	First N.B.
1465.	Ottawa.	Nat. City Bank.
1471.	Virginia.	Farmers' N.B.
1482.	Henry.	First N.B.
1484.	Winchester.	First N.B.
1517.	Vandalia.	N.B. of Vandalia.
1555.	Paris.	First N.B.
1637.	Pekin.	First N.B.
1641.	Olney.	First N.B.
1662.	Springfield.	Ridgely N.B.
1678.	Chicago.	Union Stock Yard. N.B.
1693.	Chicago.	N.B. of Commerce.
1706.	Monmouth.	Monmouth N.B.
1709.	Chicago.	Corn Exchange N.B.
1715.	Salem.	Salem N.B.
1717.	Sterling.	First N.B.
1719.	Jacksonville.	Jacksonville N.B.
1721.	Watseka.	First N.B.
1723.	Tuscola.	First N.B.

Charter Number	City	Name of Bank
1733.	Springfield.	State N.B.
1734.	Chicago.	German N.B.
1755.	Lanark.	First N.B.
1773.	Morris.	First N.B.
1775.	Shawneetown.	Gallatin N.B.
1779.	Vandalia.	Farmers and Merchants' N.B.
1785.	Kewanee.	First N.B.
1791.	Bushnell.	Farmers' N.B.
1792.	Aurora.	Union N.B.
1793.	Kankakee.	First N.B.
1805.	Keithsburg.	Farmers' N.B.
1806.	Polo.	Exchange N.B.
1808.	Lewiston.	First N.B.
1816.	Rockford.	Rockford N.B.
1821.	Winchester.	People's N.B.
1837.	Pontiac.	Livingston County N.B.
1841.	Greenville.	First N.B.
1845.	Chicago.	Cook County N.B.
1850.	Mason City.	First N.B.
1851.	Charleston.	Second N.B.
1852.	Marseilles.	First N.B.
1867.	Chicago.	N.B. of Illinois.
1870.	Marengo.	First N.B.
1872.	Macomb.	Union N.B.
1876.	Paxton.	First N.B.
1881.	Dixon.	Dixon N.B.
1882.	Joliet.	Will County N.B.
1889.	Rock Island.	Rock Island N.B.
1896.	Sycamore.	Sycamore N.B.
1907.	Rochelle.	Rochelle N.B.
1909.	Aurora.	Second N.B.
1922.	Rochelle.	First N.B.
1926.	Clinton.	De Witt County N.B.
1934.	Nokomis.	Nokomis N.B.
1941.	Moline.	Moline N.B.
1961.	Flora.	First N.B.
1964.	Wilmington.	Commercial N.B.
1968.	Prophetstown.	First N.B.
1969.	Oregon.	First N.B.
1978.	Chicago.	Scandinavian N.B.
1987.	Fairbury.	First N.B.
1996.	Mount Vernon.	Mount Vernon N.B.
2011.	Kansas.	First N.B.
2016.	Elgin.	Home N.B.
2021.	Saint Charles.	Kane County N.B.
2042.	Carlinville.	First N.B.
2047.	Chicago.	Central N.B.
2048.	Chicago.	Home N.B.
2100.	Paris.	Edgar County N.B.
2116.	Griggsville.	Griggsville N.B.
2124.	Decatur.	Decatur N.B.
2126.	Lincoln.	First N.B.
2128.	Shelbyville.	First N.B.
2141.	Pontiac.	N.B. of Pontiac.
2147.	Mattoon.	Mattoon N.B.
2154.	Belleville.	First N.B.
2155.	Rock Island.	People's N.B.
2156.	Farmer City.	First N.B.
2165.	Princeton.	Farmers' N.B.
2170.	Streator.	First N.B.
2176.	Streator.	Union N.B.
2204.	Arcola.	First N.B.
2205.	Monmouth.	Second N.B.
2212.	Oakland.	Oakland N.B.
2242.	Havana.	Havana N.B.
2254.	Prairie City.	First N.B.
2283.	Atlanta.	First N.B.
2287.	Pekin.	Farmers' N.B.
2313.	Kirkwood.	First N.B.
2328.	Jerseyville.	First N.B.
2330.	Virginia.	Centennial N.B.
2332.	Genesco.	Farmers' N.B.
2386.	Bloomington.	Nat. State Bank.
2390.	Carrollton.	Greene County N.B.
2402.	Mount Sterling.	First N.B.
2413.	Princeton.	Citizens' N.B.
2450.	Chicago.	Hide and Leather N.B.
2501.	Kewanee.	Union N.B.
2503.	La Salle.	La Salle N.B.
2519.	Quincy.	Ricker N.B.
2540.	Cambridge.	First N.B.
2572.	Cambridge.	Farmers' N.B.
2584.	Danville.	Second N.B.
2601.	Chicago.	Chicago N.B.
2629.	Olney.	Olney N.B.
2670.	Chicago.	First N.B.
2675.	Woodstock.	First N.B.
2676.	Bloomington.	Third N.B.
2681.	Streator.	Streator N.B.
2684.	Walnut.	First N.B.
2688.	Springfield.	Farmers' N.B.
2702.	De Kalb.	First N.B.
2709.	Sterling.	Sterling N.B.
2751.	Monmouth.	First N.B.
2789.	Hillsboro.	Hillsboro N.B.
2793.	Galva.	Galva First N.B.
2804.	La Salle.	City N.B.
2808.	Hoopeston.	First N.B.
2815.	Wyoming.	First N.B.
2824.	Lexington.	First N.B.
2826.	Chicago.	N.B. of America.
2829.	Champaign.	Champaign N.B.
2858.	Lake.	Drovers' N.B. of Union Stock Yards
2875.	Freeport.	First N.B.
2878.	Peoria.	Peoria N.B.
2894.	Chicago.	Continental and Commercial N.B.
2915.	Urbana.	First N.B.
2945.	Aurora.	Aurora N.B.
2951.	Peru.	Peru N.B.
2965.	Homer.	First N.B.
2997.	El Paso.	First N.B.
3003.	Biggsville.	First N.B.
3036;	Chicago.	Corn Exchange N.B.
3043.	Petersburg.	First N.B.
3070.	Peoria.	German American N.B.
3102.	Chicago.	Calumet N.B.
3138.	Galesburg.	Galesburg N.B.
3156.	Metropolis.	First N.B.
3179.	Chicago.	Metropolitan N.B.
3190.	Belvidere.	Second N.B.
3214.	Peoria.	Central N.B.
3254.	Peoria.	Merchants' and Illinois N.B.
3278.	Chicago.	Union N.B.
3279.	Galena.	Galena N.B.
3287.	Knoxville.	Farmers' N.B.
3294.	Dixon.	City N.B.
3296.	Peoria.	Commercial N.B.
3303.	Centralia.	Old N.B.
3323.	Earlville.	First N.B.
3369.	Lincoln.	Lincoln N.B.
3376.	Paris.	First N.B.
3377.	Abingdon.	First N.B.
3407.	Farmer City.	John Weedmian N.B.
3465.	Spring Valley.	Spring Valley N.B.
3500.	Chicago.	American Exchange N.B.
3502.	Chicago.	Park N.B.
3503.	Chicago.	Atlas N.B.
3548.	Springfield.	Illinois N.B.
3579.	Taylorville.	First N.B.
3593.	Canton.	Canton N.B.
3613.	Lincoln.	American N.B.
3620.	Wenona.	First N.B.
3640.	Beardstown.	First N.B.
3647.	Chicago.	Lincoln N.B.
3677.	Chicago.	Columbia N.B.
3698.	Chicago.	Fort Dearborn N.B.
3711.	Atlanta.	Atlanta N.B.
3735.	Cairo.	Alexander County N.B.
3752.	Quincy.	Quincy N.B.
3770.	Pekin.	American N.B.
3781.	Delavan.	Tazewell County N.B.
3839.	Mount Pulaski.	First N.B.
3847.	Chicago.	Nat. Live Stock Bank.
3854.	Aurora.	Merchants' N.B.
3882.	Chicago.	Prairie State N.B.
3916.	Chicago.	Washington Park N.B.
3952.	Rockford.	Manufacturers' N.B.
3962.	Litchfield.	First N.B.
4003.	Harrisburg.	First N.B.
4019.	Murphysboro.	First N.B.
4038.	Pana.	First N.B.
4073.	Englewood.	First N.B.
4187.	Chester.	First N.B.
4233.	Effingham.	First N.B.
4299.	Carlinville.	Carlinville N.B.
4313.	Monmouth.	People's N.B.
4325.	Rockford.	Forest City N.B.
4328.	East Saint Louis.	First N.B.
4342.	Kankakee.	City N.B.
4400.	Monmouth.	N.B. of Monmouth.
4433.	Vienna.	First N.B.
4449.	Anna.	First N.B.
4469.	Aurora.	American N.B.
4476.	Streator.	City N.B.
4480.	Mount Carmel.	First N.B.
4489.	Chicago.	Globe N.B.
4502.	Marion.	First N.B.
4520.	Joliet.	Joliet N.B.
4551.	Naperville.	First N.B.
4576.	Decatur.	Citizens' N.B.
4596.	Aurora.	Old Second N.B.
4605.	Chicago.	N.B. of the Republic.
4646.	Batavia.	First N.B.
4666.	Chicago.	Chemical N.B.
4709.	Bushnell.	First N.B.
4731.	Danville.	Palmer N.B.
4735.	Elgin.	Elgin N.B.
4737.	Du Quoin.	First N.B.
4759.	Marshall.	Dulaney N.B.
4767.	Evanston.	Evanston N.B.
4787.	Chicago.	Bankers' N.B.
4804.	Murphysboro.	City N.B.
4826.	Monticello.	First N.B.
4829.	Bement.	First N.B.
4854.	Kewanee.	Kewanee N.B.
4871.	Toluca.	First N.B.
4904.	Carbondale.	First N.B.
4920.	Decatur.	N.B. of Decatur.
4930.	Normal.	First N.B.
4934.	Carmi.	First N.B.
4941.	Lewiston.	Lewiston N.B.
4952.	Jerseyville.	N.B. of Jerseyville.
4958.	Farmer City.	Old First N.B.
4967.	Alexis.	First N.B.
4994.	Vandalia.	First N.B.
4999.	Grayville.	First N.B.
5009.	Fairfield.	First N.B.
5049.	Robinson.	First N.B.
5057.	Mount Vernon.	Ham N.B.
5062.	Edwardsville.	First N.B.
5070.	East Saint Louis.	Southern Illinois N.B.
5086.	Mendota.	Mendota N.B.
5089.	Decatur.	Millikin N.B.
5106.	Chicago.	Corn Exchange N.B.
5111.	Chicago.	American N.B.
5119.	Bloomington.	State N.B.
5124.	Grant Park.	Grant Park N.B.
5149.	Milford.	First N.B.
5153.	Harrisburg.	City N.B.
5188.	Alton.	Citizens' N.B.
5193.	Rantoul.	First N.B.
5223.	Amboy.	First N.B.
5233.	Arthur.	First N.B.
5254.	Metropolis.	Nat. State Bank.
5273.	Toledo.	First N.B.
5279.	Evanston.	First N.B.
5285.	Georgetown.	First N.B.
5291.	Stonington.	First N.B.
5303.	Herrin.	First N.B.
5304.	Ogden.	First N.B.
5313.	Ridge Farm.	First N.B.
5316.	Assumption.	First N.B.
5322.	Piper City.	First N.B.
5357.	Carmi.	N.B. of Carmi.
5361.	Peoria.	Illinois N.B.
5385.	Lawrenceville.	First N.B.
5398.	Rossville.	First N.B.
5410.	Taylorville.	Farmers' N.B.
5426.	Neoga.	Cumberland County N.B.
5433.	Granite City.	First N.B.
5470.	Saint Anne.	First N.B.
5494.	Lovington.	First N.B.
5510.	El Paso.	Woodford County N.B.
5519.	Chatsworth.	Commercial N.B.
5525.	Anna.	Anna N.B.
5538.	Hindsboro.	First N.B.
5548.	Carlyle.	First N.B.
5584.	Chillicothe.	First N.B.
5609.	Dallas City.	First N.B.
5619.	Chadwick.	First N.B.
5630.	Cobden.	First N.B.
5638.	Dundee.	First N.B.
5689.	Mount Vernon.	Third N.B.
5699.	De Land.	First N.B.
5763.	Jacksonville.	Ayers N.B.
5771.	Barry.	First N.B.
5782.	Mount Carmel.	American N.B.
5812.	Danville.	Danville N.B.
5813.	Stronghurst.	First N.B.
5815.	Malta.	First N.B.
5856.	Gilman.	First N.B.
5869.	Newton.	First N.B.
5876.	Chicago Heights.	First N.B.
5883.	Roseville.	First N.B.
6007.	Secor.	First N.B.
6025.	Pinckneyville.	First N.B.
6026.	Casey.	First N.B.
6065.	Little York.	First N.B.
6086.	Oquawka.	First N.B.
6089.	Albany.	First N.B.
6096.	Mansfield.	First N.B.
6116.	Waverly.	First N.B.
6125.	Collinsville.	First N.B.
6133.	Ivesdale.	First N.B.
6136.	Benton.	First N.B.
6143.	Kindmundy.	First N.B.
6191.	Greenup.	First N.B.
6192.	Garrett.	First N.B.
6211.	Philo.	First N.B.
6219.	Saint Charles.	Saint Charles N.B.
6228.	Pawpaw.	First N.B.
6239.	Yorkville.	Yorkville N.B.
6290.	Chicago.	N.B. of North America.
6318.	Clifton.	First N.B.
6359.	Atwood.	First N.B.
6375.	Prophetstown.	Farmers' N.B.
6421.	Tremont.	First N.B.
6423.	Joliet.	Citizens' N.B.
6451.	Paris.	Citizens' N.B.
6460.	Grayville.	Farmers' N.B.
6514.	Libertyville.	First N.B.
6524.	Nashville.	First N.B.
6535.	Chicago.	Drovers' N.B.
6543.	Steward.	First N.B.
6564.	Granite City.	Granite City N.B.
6586.	Le Roy.	First N.B.
6598.	Crescent City.	First N.B.
6609.	Fairfield.	Fairfield N.B.
6629.	Wyoming.	N.B. of Wyoming.
6649.	McLeansboro.	First N.B.
6653.	Highland.	First N.B.
6670.	Libertyville.	Lake County N.B.
6684.	Grand Ridge.	First N.B.
6691.	Marissa.	First N.B.
6713.	Brookport.	Brookport N.B.
6721.	Martinsville.	First N.B.
6723.	Chicago.	Hamilton N.B.
6724.	East Peoria.	First N.B.
6734.	Pana.	Pana N.B.
6740.	Danvers.	First N.B.
6745.	Morrisonville.	First N.B.
6751.	Augusta.	First N.B.
6811.	Woodstock.	American N.B.
6815.	Cairo.	Cairo N.B.
6824.	Potomac.	Potomac N.B.
6861.	Findlay.	First N.B.
6907.	Sumner.	First N.B.
6910.	Raymond.	First N.B.
6924.	O'Fallon.	First N.B.
6951.	Erie.	First N.B.
6978.	Equality.	First N.B.
6998.	Rock Falls.	First N.B.
7015.	Sparta.	First N.B.
7031.	Compton.	First N.B.
7049.	Henry.	Henry N.B.

Charter Number	City	Name of Bank
7077.	White Hall.	White Hall N.B.
7079.	Momence.	First N.B.
7088.	Villa Grove.	First N.B.
7111.	Chrisman.	First N.B.
7121.	White Hall.	First N.B.
7145.	Aledo.	First N.B.
7151.	Strawn.	Farmers' N.B.
7168.	Humboldt.	First N.B.
7236.	Elgin.	Union N.B.
7276.	Catlin.	First N.B.
7339.	Windsor.	First N.B.
7350.	Mount Olive.	First N.B.
7358.	Chicago.	Prairie N.B.
7365.	Georgetown.	Georgetown N.B.
7379.	Mulberry Grove.	First N.B.
7385.	Golconda.	First N.B.
7396.	Shelbyville.	Citizens' N.B.
7440.	Pawnee.	N.B. of Pawnee.
7443.	Mound City.	First N.B.
7458.	Johnston City.	First N.B.
7500.	Westville.	First N.B.
7538.	Witt.	First N.B.
7539.	Eldorado.	First N.B.
7547.	Nokomis.	Farmers' N.B.
7555.	Earlville.	Earlville N.B.
7575.	Newman.	Newman N.B.
7579.	Coffeen.	Coffeen N.B.
7598.	Carbondale.	Carbondale N.B.
7606.	Goreville.	First N.B.
7627.	Percy.	First N.B.
7660.	Triumph.	First N.B.
7673.	West Frankfort.	First N.B.
7680.	Forrest.	First N.B.
7692.	Sullivan.	First N.B.
7712.	Grand Tower.	First N.B.
7717.	Columbia.	First N.B.
7726.	Beecher.	First N.B.
7728.	Berild.	N.B. of Benld.
7739.	Moweaqua.	First N.B.
7750.	Dahigren.	First N.B.
7752.	Shawneetown.	N.B. of Shawneetown.
7791.	Middletown.	First N.B.
7841.	Neoga.	Neoga N.B.
7864.	Leland.	First N.B.
7889.	Carterville.	First N.B.
7903.	Gillespie.	Gillespie N.B.
7926.	Chicago.	Federal N.B.
7948.	Enfield.	First N.B.
7954.	Metcalf.	First N.B.
7971.	Norris City.	First N.B.
8006.	Hillsboro.	People's N.B.
8015.	Carrier Mills.	First N.B.
8043.	Casey.	Casey N.B.
8044.	Dwight.	First N.B.
8053.	New Haven.	First N.B.
8115.	Greenup.	Greenup N.B.
8121.	Chicago.	Monroe N.B.
8155.	Thomasboro.	First N.B.
8163.	Morris.	Farmers and Merchants' N.B.
8174.	Gibson, Gibson City.	First N.B.
8180.	Ullin.	First N.B.
8212.	Findlay.	Findlay N.B.
8216.	Westfield.	First N.B.
8221.	Nashville.	Farmers and Merchants' N.B.
8224.	Lerna.	First N.B.
8234.	Benton.	Coal Belt N.B.
8256.	Oakford.	First N.B.
8260.	Christopher.	First N.B.
8289.	Ransom.	First N.B.
8293.	Allendale.	First N.B.
8347.	Bridgeport.	First N.B.
8374.	Sidell.	First N.B.
8425.	Millstadt.	First N.B.
8429.	Albion.	First N.B.
8457.	Madison.	First N.B.
8468.	La Harpe.	First N.B.
8473.	Greenfield.	First N.B.
8482.	Maquon.	First N.B.
8485.	Colchester.	N.B. of Colchester.
8532.	Chicago.	Nat. City Bank.
8540.	Savanna.	First N.B.
8605.	Hegewisch, Chicago.	Inter State N.B.
8607.	Oblong.	First N.B.
8629.	Tamaroa.	First N.B.
8630.	Ridge Farm.	City N.B.
8637.	Roodhouse.	First N.B.
8647.	Irving.	Irving N.B.
8648.	Manlius.	First N.B.
8667.	Harvey.	First N.B.
8670.	Herrin.	City N.B.
8679.	Dolton.	First N.B.
8684.	Cullom.	First N.B.
8696.	Oblong.	Oil Belt N.B.
8713.	Manhattan.	First N.B.
8732.	Mackinaw.	First N.B.
8733.	Altamont.	First N.B.
8740.	Geneva.	First N.B.
8745.	Metropolis.	City N.B.
8758.	Sesser.	First N.B.
8801.	Crossville.	First N.B.
8842.	Chicago.	Nat. Produce Bank
8846.	Saint Francisville.	People's N.B.
8892.	Palestine.	First N.B.
8898.	Nauvoo.	First N.B.
8908.	Blandinsville.	First N.B.
8932.	East Saint Louis.	City N.B.
8933.	Lockport.	First N.B.
8937.	Lake Forest.	First N.B.
9010.	Chicago.	Live Stock Exchange N.B.
9025.	Albion.	Albion N.B.
9096.	Warren.	First N.B.
9118.	National Stock Yards.	National Stock Yards N.B.
9169.	Macomb.	Macomb N.B.
9183.	Arenzville.	First N.B.
9208.	Minooka.	Farmers' First N.B.
9230.	Tampico.	First N.B.
9277.	Wyanet.	First N.B.
9293.	Kansas.	Farmers' N.B.
9325.	Tremont.	Tremont N.B.
9338.	West Salem.	First N.B.
9368.	Wheaton.	First N.B.
9388.	Saint Elmo.	First N.B.
9397.	Brighton.	First N.B.
9398.	Hopedale.	Hopedale N.B.
9406.	Gardner.	First N.B.
9408.	McLeansboro.	People's N.B.
9425.	Hoopeston.	Hoopeston N.B.
9435.	Shawneetown.	City N.B.
9438.	Stewardson.	First N.B.
9439.	Ridgway.	First N.B.
9500.	Batavia.	Batavia N.B.
9525.	Odin.	First N.B.
9527.	Noble.	First N.B.
9530.	Blue Mound.	First N.B.
9572.	Sycamore.	Citizens' N.B.
9582.	Dieterich.	First N.B.
9601.	Minonk.	First N.B.
9624.	Odell.	Farmers' N.B.
9649.	Aledo.	Farmers' N.B.
9700.	Cowden.	First N.B.
9725.	Downers Grove.	First N.B.
9734.	Greenville.	Bradford N.B.
9736.	Mascoutah.	First N.B.
9750.	Chicago.	La Salle Street N.B.
9786.	Sandoval.	First N.B.
9788.	Pekin.	Herget N.B.
9823.	Rockford.	Swedish-American N.B.
9836.	Elmhurst.	First N.B.
9877.	Rossville.	Farmers' N.B.
9883.	Hamilton.	First N.B.
9893.	Breese.	First N.B.
9895.	Ramsey.	Ramsey N.B.
9896.	Saint Peter.	First N.B.
9922.	Mount Auburn.	First N.B.
9929.	Warsaw.	Farmers' N.B.
10045.	Mattoon.	N.B. of Mattoon.
10048.	Mount Prospect.	Mount Prospect N.B.
10057.	Farmersville.	First N.B.
10079.	Litchfield.	Litchfield N.B.
10086.	Dongola.	First N.B.
10108.	Chicago.	Jefferson Park N.B.
10125.	Trenton.	First N.B.
10132.	Coal City.	First N.B.
10144.	Mattoon.	State N.B.
10173.	Staunton.	First N.B.
10179.	Irving Park, Chicago.	Irving Park N.B.
10180.	Waterloo.	First N.B.
10186.	Mazon.	First N.B.
10215.	Ravenswood, Chicago.	Ravenswood N.B.
10237.	Chicago.	Bowmanville N.B.
10257.	Annapolis.	First N.B.
10264.	Witt.	Witt N.B.
10291.	Omaha.	First N.B.
10296.	Divernon.	First N.B.
10305.	Rogers Park, Chicago.	Rogers Park N.B.
10318.	Allendale.	Farmers' N.B.
10319.	Des Plaines.	First N.B.
10337.	Chicago.	Austin N.B.
10355.	Waukegan.	Waukegan N.B.
10365.	Vermillion.	First N.B.
10397.	Brownstown.	First N.B.
10399.	Fast Saint Louis.	Drovers' N.B.
10445.	Mounds.	First N.B.
10458.	Granville.	First N.B.
10460.	Wayne City.	First N.B.
10492.	Nebo.	First N.B.
10505.	Sorento.	Sorento N.B.
10514.	La Rose.	La Rose N.B.
10516.	Bunker Hill.	First N.B.
10567.	Caledonia.	Caledonia N.B.
10572.	Beason.	First N.B.
10582.	Marine.	First N.B.
10591.	Eureka.	First N.B.
10641.	Westervelt.	Farmers' N.B.
10669.	Worden.	First N.B.
10690.	Gorham.	First N.B.
10716.	Woodhull.	First N.B.
10752.	Oneida.	First N.B.
10760.	Sheridan.	First N.B.
10763.	Chicago.	Atlas Exchange N.B.
10777.	Staunton.	Staunton N.B.
10828.	Wilmette.	First N.B.
10911.	Willisdale.	First N.B.
11009.	Chicago.	West Side N.B.
11039.	Edwardsville.	Edwardsville N.B.
11088.	New Bedford.	Farmers' N.B.
11092.	Chicago.	Mutual N.B.
11108.	Hume.	First N.B.
11118.	Minonk.	Minonk N.B.
11144.	Cuba.	First N.B.
11170.	Hinckley.	First N.B.
11208.	Gridley.	First N.B.
11283.	Barrington.	First N.B.
11299.	Foosland.	First N.B.
11308.	Hinsdale.	First N.B.
11331.	Altona.	First N.B.
11333.	Toluca.	Citizens' N.B.
11358.	Charleston.	Nat. Trust Bank.
11422.	Lemont.	First N.B.
11443.	Fairmount.	Firs t N.B.
11478.	Belleville.	Saint Clair N.B.
11507.	Oak Park.	First N.B.
11509.	Flora.	Flora N.B.
11516.	Waltonville.	First N.B.
11596.	East Saint Louis.	First N.B.
11602.	Hampshire.	First N.B.
11610.	Woodstock.	Woodstock N.B.
11662.	Cicero.	First N.B.
11675.	Waddams Grove.	First N.B.
11679.	Rockford.	Commercial N.B.
11715.	Lemont.	Lemont N.B.
11731.	Rockford.	Security N.B.
11737.	Chicago.	Albany Park N.B.
11754.	Okawville.	First N.B.
11779.	Viola.	Farmers' N.B.
11780.	Okawville.	Old Exchange N.B.
11845.	Livingston.	First N.B.
11876.	Wood River.	First N.B.
11882.	Homer.	First N.B.
11886.	Maroa.	First N.B.
11895.	Braidwood.	First N.B.
11904.	Centralia.	Centralia N.B.
11923.	Centralia.	City N.B.
11934.	Palatine.	First N.B.
11952.	Grant Park.	First N.B.
11980.	Chicago.	N.B. of Woodlawn.
11999.	Chicago.	Kenwood N.B.
12000.	Coulterville.	First N.B.
12001.	Chicago.	Alliance N.B.
12004.	Chicago.	West Englewood N.B.
12096.	Xenia.	First N.B.
12097.	Zeigler.	First N.B.
12178.	East Saint Louis.	Security N.B.
12227.	Chicago.	Douglass N.B.
12285.	Chicago.	Portage Park N.B.
12314.	Gillespie.	American N.B.
12323.	Chicago.	Broadway N.B.
12366.	Lebanon.	First N.B.
12373.	Jonesboro.	First N.B.
12386.	Riverside.	First N.B.
12391.	Chicago.	Jackson Park N.B.
12403.	Chicago.	Foreman N.B.
12426.	Berwyn.	First N.B.
12479.	Valier.	First N.B.
12480.	Chicago.	Ogden N.B.
12493.	Chicago.	Stock Yards N.B.
12525.	Woodhull.	First N.B.
12528.	Wood River.	Wood River N.B.
12596.	Carbondale.	First N.B.
12605.	Chicago.	Roseland N.B.
12615.	Chicago.	Guardian N.B.
12630.	Wilsonville.	First N.B.
12653.	La Grange.	First N.B.
12658.	Plymouth.	First N.B.
12779.	Blue Island.	First N.B.
12870.	Antioch.	First N.B.
12873.	Chicago.	Lawrence Avenue N.B.
12926.	Roseville.	Farmers and Merchants' N.B.
12945.	Chicago.	Halsted Exchange N.B.
12991.	National City.	National Stock Yards N.B.
13036.	Chicago.	Midland N.B.
13119.	Chicago.	Addison N.B.
13144.	Witt.	N.B. of Witt.
13146.	Chicago.	National Builders Bank
13213.	Mount Sterling.	First N.B.
13216.	Chicago.	Straus N.B. and Trust Co.
13218.	Niles Center.	N.B. of Niles Center.
13226.	Stewardson.	Stewardson N.B.
13235.	Chicago.	Hyde Park N.B.
13236.	Belleville.	Belleville N.B.
13253.	Chicago.	Ashland-69th N.B.
13258.	Downers Grove.	Security N.B.
13311.	Chicago.	Peoples N.B. and Trust Co.
13372.	Chicago.	Standard N.B.
13373.	Chicago Heights.	Citizens' N.B.
13382.	Chicago.	Terminal N.B.
13448.	Georgetown.	First N.B.
13449.	Albion.	N.B. of Albion.
13451.	Dahlgren.	Farmers N.B.
13452.	Mount Olive.	First N.B.
13464.	Alton.	First N.B. and Trust Co.
13478.	Pana.	First N.B.
13497.	Polo.	First N.B.
13499.	Bloomington.	First N.B. and Trust Co.
13525.	Smithton.	First N.B.
13565.	Aurora.	First N.B.
13577.	Peru.	State-National Bank.
13579.	Ttemont.	First N.B.
13597.	Blandinsville.	First N.B.
13605.	Robinson.	Second N.B.
13611.	Mendota.	N.B. of Mendota.
13625.	Altona.	Altona N.B.
13630.	Champaigne.	First N.B.
13631.	El Paso.	El Paso N.B.
13638.	Chicago.	City N.B. & Trust Co.
13639.	Chicago.	Continental Illinois N.B. & Trust Co.
13650.	Witt.	Security N.B.
13652.	Rockford.	Illinois N.B. & Trust.
13659.	Chicago.	Terminus N.B.
13660.	Moline.	Moline N.B.
13666.	Stockton.	First N.B.
13672.	Chicago.	National Boulevard Bank.
13673.	Casey.	First N.B.

Charter Number	City	Name of Bank
13674.	Chicago.	Live Stock N.B.
13682.	Toledo.	First N.B.
13684.	Chicago.	Mid-City N.B.
13691.	Chicago.	National Security Bank
13695.	Freeport.	First N.B.
13696.	New Douglas.	Prange N.B.
13705.	Joliet.	First N.B.
13709.	Evanston.	First N.B. & Trust Co.
13714.	Galena.	First N.B.
13718.	Libertyville.	First Lake County N.B.
13735.	Marissa.	First N.B.
13744.	Hoopeston.	City N.B.
13795.	Mascoutah.	First N.B.
13804.	Cairo.	Security N.B.
13805.	Columbia.	First N.B.
13809.	Paxton.	First N.B.
13838.	Canton.	N.B. of Canton.
13856.	Dixon.	City N.B.
13864.	Mount Vernon.	First N.B.
13865.	Monticello.	N.B. of Monticello.
13872.	Sycamore.	N.B. & Trust Co.
13886.	Savanna.	N.B. of Savanna.
13892.	Neoga.	Cumberland County N.B.
13903.	Peru.	First N.B.
13941.	La Grange.	La Grange N.B.
13963.	Sterling.	N.B. of Sterling.
13966.	Carlinville.	Farmers & Merchants N.B.
13975.	Pinckneyville.	First N.B.
13993.	Altamont.	First N.B.
14008.	De Kalb.	First N.B.
14010.	East Peoria.	First N.B.
14024.	Charleston.	Charleston N.B.
14035.	Grandville.	Grandville N.B.
14074.	Newton.	First N.B.
14110.	Chicago.	District N.B.
14115.	Naperville.	Naperville N.B.
14118.	Lincoln.	First N.B.
14127.	East St. Louis.	First N.B.
14134.	Carthage.	First N.B.
14137.	Woodstock.	First N.B.
14140.	Winchester.	Neat Condit & Grout N.B.
14159.	Galva.	First N.B.
14161.	Aurora.	Aurora N.B.
14173.	Golconda.	First N.B.
14178.	Bloomington.	N.B. of Bloomington.
14217.	Olney.	First N.B.
14221.	Rochelle.	N.B. of Rochelle.
14235.	Madison.	First N.B.
14237.	Cambridge.	Peoples N.B.
14244.	Amboy.	First N.B.
14245.	Chicago.	Milwaukee Avenue N.B.
14246.	Chicago.	Liberty N.B.
14247.	Mount Carroll.	Mount Carroll N.B.
14260.	Pontiac.	Pontiac N.B.
14265.	Shawneetown.	First N.B.
14268.	Carlyle.	First N.B.
14285.	Mount Olive.	Mount Olive N.B.
14297.	Lanark.	N.B. of Lanark.
14310.	Staunton.	First N.B.
14313.	Chicago.	Merchants N.B.
14319.	Dalton.	First N.B.
14327.	Chicago.	South East N.B.
14331.	Aledo.	N.B. of Aledo.
14332.	Wyoming.	First N.B.
14342.	Polo.	Polo N.B.
14343.	Chicago.	Chicago Heights N.B.
14346.	Oregon.	Ogle County N.B.
14347.	Carrollton.	Greene County N.B.
14348.	Roodhouse.	Roodhouse N.B.
	INDIANA	
11.	Fort Wayne.	First N.B.
17.	Richmond.	First N.B.
23.	La Fayette.	First N.B.
28.	Evansville.	First N.B.
37.	Centerville.	First N.B.
41.	Kendallville.	First N.B.
44.	Anderson.	First N.B.
47.	Terre Haute.	First N.B.
50.	Franklin.	First N.B.
55.	Indianapolis.	First N.B.
58.	Bluffton.	First N.B.
63.	Rockville.	First N.B.
70.	Cambridge City.	First N.B.
78.	Franklin.	Second N.B.
82.	Lawrenceburg.	First N.B.
88.	Warsaw.	First N.B.
105.	Valparaiso.	First N.B.
111.	Madison.	First N.B.
126.	South Bend.	First N.B.
129.	Wabash.	First N.B.
145.	Huntington.	First N.B.
146.	Goshen.	First N.B.
152.	Danville.	First N.B.
206.	Elkhart.	First N.B.
219.	Greencastle.	First N.B.
346.	Vevay.	First N.B.
356.	Greensburg.	First N.B.
363.	Peru.	First N.B.
366.	Mount Vernon.	First N.B.
377.	Laporte.	First N.B.
417.	La Fayette.	Second N.B.
571.	Crawfordsville.	First N.B.
577.	Attica.	First N.B.
581.	Indianapolis.	Indianapolis N.B.
617.	Indianapolis.	Citizens' N.B.
699.	Aurora.	First N.B.
701.	New Albany.	First N.B.
730.	Evansville.	Evansville N.B.

Charter Number	City	Name of Bank
775.	New Albany.	New Albany N.B.
783.	Indianapolis.	Fourth N.B.
793.	Muncie.	Muncie N.B.
794.	Martinsville.	First N.B.
804.	New Castle.	First N.B.
815.	Union City.	First N.B.
865.	Fort Wayne.	Fort Wayne N.B.
869.	Indianapolis.	Merchants' N.B.
872.	Knightstown.	First N.B.
882.	La Fayette.	Union N.B.
889.	Winchester.	First N.B.
894.	Kokomo.	First N.B.
930.	La Fayette.	Nat. State Bank.
956.	Jeffersonville.	First N.B.
965.	New Albany.	Merchants' N.B.
984.	Indianapolis.	Indiana N.B.
989.	Evansville.	Merchants' N.B.
1031.	Logansport.	Logansport N.B.
1032.	Seymour.	First N.B.
1034.	Connersville.	First N.B.
1046.	Thomtown.	First N.B.
1066.	Columbus.	First N.B.
1100.	Fort Wayne.	Merchants' N.B.
1102.	Richmond.	Richmond N.B.
1103.	Terre Haute.	Nat. State Bank.
1234.	Lima.	Nat. State Bank.
1263.	Shelbyville.	First N.B.
1418.	Lawrenceburg.	Lawrenceburg N.B.
1454.	Vincennes.	Vincennes N.B.
1456.	Rushville.	Rushville N.B.
1457.	Madison.	Nat. Branch Bank.
1466.	Jeffersonville.	Citizens' N.B.
1619.	Brookville.	Brookville N.B.
1739.	South Bend.	South Bend N.B.
1772.	Evansville.	German N.B.
1854.	Frankfort.	First N.B.
1869.	Rushville.	Rush County N.B.
1873.	Vincennes.	First N.B.
1878.	Indianapolis.	Meridian N.B.
1879.	Peru.	Citizens' N.B.
1888.	Bloomington.	First N.B.
1890.	Greensburg.	Citizens' N.B.
1892.	Bedford.	Bedford N.B.
1897.	Newport.	First N.B.
1925.	Liberty.	First N.B.
1932.	Sullivan.	First N.B.
1949.	Delphi.	First N.B.
1952.	Rochester.	First N.B.
1959.	Rising Sun.	N.B. of Rising Sun.
1967.	La Fayette.	Indiana N.B.
1988.	Richmond.	Second N.B.
2007.	Liberty.	Union County N.B.
2043.	Washington.	Washington N.B.
2057.	Lebanon.	First N.B.
2066.	Princeton.	Gibson County N.B.
2067.	Goshen.	City N.B.
2090.	Richmond.	Richmond N.B.
2101.	Michigan City.	First N.B.
2119.	Plymouth.	First N.B. of Marsh County.
2166.	New Albany.	Second N.B.
2173.	Salem.	N.B. of Salem.
2178.	Spencer.	First N.B.
2180.	Princeton.	People's N.B.
2183.	Crown Point.	First N.B.
2184.	LaGrange.	First N.B.
2188.	Evansville.	Citizens' N.B.
2201.	Tell City.	First N.B.
2202.	New Castle.	Bundy N.B.
2207.	Boonville.	Boonville N.B.
2208.	Monticello.	First N.B.
2213.	La Fayette.	La Fayette N.B.
2234.	Muncie.	Merchants' N.B.
2238.	Auburn.	First N.B.
2346.	Anderson.	Madison County N.B.
2361.	Rockville.	N.B. of Rockville.
2369.	Sullivan.	Farmers' N.B.
2375.	Kokomo.	Howard N.B.
2403.	Valparaiso.	Farmers' N.B.
2439.	Fort Wayne.	Hamilton N.B.
2502.	Elkhart.	Elkhart N.B.
2508.	Huntington.	First N.B.
2533.	Crawfordsville.	Citizens' N.B.
2556.	Indianapolis.	First N.B.
2596.	Logansport.	State N.B.
2612.	Lawrenceburg.	People's N.B.
2660.	Lebanon.	Lebanon N.B.
2680.	Richmond.	First N.B.
2687.	Kendallville.	First N.B.
2692.	Evansville.	First N.B.
2696.	Centreville.	First N.B.
2701.	Fort Wayne.	First N.B.
2704.	Valparaiso.	First N.B. of Porter County.
2717.	La Fayette.	First N.B.
2734.	Cambridge City.	First N.B.
2742.	Terre Haute.	First N.B.
2747.	Michigan City.	First N.B.
2769.	Franklin.	N.B. of Franklin.
2844.	Greensburg.	Third N.B.
2889.	Lawrenceburg.	City N.B.
2896.	Green Castle.	Central N.B.
2903.	North Manchester.	First N.B.
2963.	Aurora.	Aurora N.B.
3013.	Bedford.	Indiana N.B.
3028.	Decatur.	First N.B.
3084.	Logansport.	First N.B.
3280.	La Fayette.	Fowler N.B.
3281.	Evansville.	Old N.B.
3285.	Fort Wayne.	Old N.B.
3338.	Franklin.	Franklin N.B.

Charter Number	City	Name of Bank
3413.	Richmond.	Union N.B.
3474.	North Manchester.	Lawrence N.B.
3478.	Hammond.	First N.B.
3583.	Brazil.	First N.B.
3755.	Attica.	Central N.B.
3842.	Washington.	People's N.B.
3864.	Vincennes.	American N.B.
3929.	Terre Haute.	Vigo County N.B.
3935.	Wabash.	Wabash N.B.
3967.	Franklin.	Citizens' N.B.
4121.	Kokomo.	Citizens' N.B.
4158.	Indianapolis.	Capital N.B.
4189,	Marion.	First N.B.
4281.	Lawrenceburg.	Citizens' N.B.
4468.	La Fayette.	Merchants' N.B.
4652.	Seymour.	Seymour N.B.
4656.	La Fayette.	Perrin N.B.
4674.	Muncie.	Farmers' N.B.
4675.	Elwood.	First N.B.
4678.	North Vernon.	First N.B.
4685.	Anderson.	Nat. Exchange Bank.
4688.	Vernon.	First N.B.
4725.	Fort Wayne.	White N.B.
4764.	South Bend.	Citizens' N.B.
4800.	Shelbyville.	Farmers' N.B.
4801.	Mulberry.	Farmers' N.B.
4809.	Muncie.	Delaware County N.B.
4825.	Gas City.	First N.B.
4835.	Alexandria.	Alexandria N.B.
4841.	Elkhart.	Indiana N.B.
4852.	Muncie.	Merchants' N.B.
4882.	Noblesville.	First N.B.
4888.	Dunkirk.	First N.B.
4901.	Vincennes.	Second N.B.
4964.	Martinsville.	Citizens' N.B.
4972.	La Grange.	N.B. of La Grange.
5067.	Rockville.	Rockville N.B.
5076.	Logansport.	City N.B.
5094.	Union City.	Commercial N.B.
5116.	Indianapolis.	Fletcher N.B.
5167.	Mishawaka.	First N.B.
5173.	Bedford.	Citizens' N.B.
5187.	Bedford.	Bedford N.B.
5267.	Brazil.	Riddell N.B.
5278.	Montpelier.	First N.B.
5296.	Sheridan.	First N.B.
5300.	Petersburg.	First N.B.
5369.	Lowell.	First N.B.
5392.	Sullivan.	N.B. of Sullivan.
5430.	Fowler.	First N.B.
5432.	Owensville.	First N.B.
5435.	Greensburg.	Greensburg N.B.
5476.	Boswell.	First N.B.
5524.	Russiaville.	First N.B.
5526.	Lewisville.	First N.B.
5558.	Orleans.	N.B. of Orleans.
5629.	Brookville.	Franklin County N.B.
5639.	New Carlisle.	First N.B.
5672.	Indianapolis.	American N.B.
5726.	Hope.	Citizens' N.B.
5734.	Montgomery.	First N.B.
5756.	Tell City.	Tell City N.B.
5842.	Thorntown.	Home N.B.
5845.	Indianapolis.	Columbia N.B.
5889.	La Fayette.	Nat. Fowler Bank.
5919.	Knox.	First N.B.
5931.	Lowell.	First N.B.
5940.	La Fayette.	City N.B.
5997.	Dana.	First N.B.
5998.	Matthews.	First N.B.
6070.	Sheridan.	Farmers' N.B.
6172.	Monticello.	Monticello N.B.
6194.	Rockport.	First N.B.
6200.	Evansville.	City N.B.
6215.	Valparaiso.	Valparaiso N.B.
6217.	Frankfort.	American N.B.
6251.	Tipton.	First N.B.
6261.	Kokomo.	Kokomo N.B.
6265.	Connersville.	Fayette N.B.
6309.	Wabash.	Farmers and Merchants' N.B.
6334.	South Bend.	Merchants' N.B.
6354.	Monrovia.	First N.B.
6388.	West Baden.	West Baden N.B.
6433.	Mitchell.	First N.B.
6480.	Clinton.	First N.B.
6504.	Farmland.	First N.B.
6509.	Auburn.	City N.B.
6513.	Indianapolis.	Union N.B.
6526.	Whiting.	First N.B.
6625.	Corydon.	First N.B.
6651.	Rensselaer.	First N.B.
6699.	New Harmony.	First N.B.
6765.	Lowell.	Lowell N.B.
6876.	Mooresville.	First N.B.
6882.	Dillsboro.	First N.B.
6905.	Edinburg.	Farmers' N.B.
6909.	Dyer.	First N.B.
6952.	Charlestown.	First N.B.
6959.	Hartford City.	First N.B.
6986.	Delphi.	Citizens' N.B.
7011.	Plainfield.	First N.B.
7023.	Angola.	First N.B.
7036.	Poseyville.	First N.B.
7124.	Greens Fork.	First N.B.
7132.	Columbia City.	First N.B.
7155.	Bicknell.	First N.B.
7175.	Columbia City.	Columbia City N.B.
7180.	Portland.	First N.B.
7241.	Loogootee.	First N.B.

Charter Number	City	Name of Bank
7260.	Odon.	First N.B.
7342.	Jasonville.	First N.B.
7354.	Hartsville.	First N.B.
7374.	Rushville.	People's N.B.
7375.	Tell City.	Citizens' N.B.
7411.	Linton.	First N.B.
7415.	La Fayette.	American N.B.
7437.	Freeland Park.	First N.B.
7454.	Muncie.	People's N.B.
7463.	Montezuma.	First N.B.
7478.	Evansville.	Old State N.B.
7491.	Trafalgar.	Farmers' N.B.
7496.	Tipton.	Citizens' N.B.
7513.	Shelburn.	First N.B.
7562.	Terre Haute.	Terre Haute N.B.
7601.	East Chicago.	First N.B.
7652.	Morgantown.	First N.B.
7655.	Rochester.	First N.B.
7725.	Fort Wayne.	Lincoln N.B.
7758.	Marion.	Marion N.B.
7760.	Corydon.	Corydon N.B.
7761.	Winamac.	First N.B.
7773.	Crawfordsville.	Elston N.B.
7786.	Mount Vernon.	Mount Vernon N.B.
7802.	Flora.	First N.B.
7805.	Brookville.	Nat. Brookville Bank.
7824.	Batesville.	First N.B.
7830.	Ferdinand.	Ferdinand N.B.
7863.	Goodland.	First N.B.
7902.	Hagerstown.	First N.B.
7909.	Lawrenceburg.	Dearborn N.B.
7922.	Terre Haute.	McKeen N.B.
7930.	Warren.	First N.B.
7946.	Shelbyville.	Shelby N.B.
8014.	Flora.	Bright N.B.
8060.	Remington.	First N.B.
8149.	Poseyville.	Bozeman-Waters N.B.
8154.	Amo.	First N.B.
8166.	Princeton.	American N.B.
8192.	Kewanna.	First N.B.
8199.	Hammond.	Citizens' N.B.
8337.	Fairland.	Fairland N.B.
8351.	Ridgeville.	First N.B.
8368.	Mentone.	First N.B.
8408.	New Point.	First N.B.
8415.	Bloomington.	Bloomington N.B.
8422.	Greenwood.	First N.B.
8426.	Gary.	First N.B.
8447.	Coatesville.	First N.B.
8461.	Greenwood.	Citizens' N.B.
8492.	Evansville.	Mercantile N.B.
8537.	Medaryville.	First N.B.
8620.	Brazil.	Citizens' N.B.
8625.	Williamsburg.	First N.B.
8650.	Milltown.	First N.B.
8700.	Mays.	First N.B.
8747.	Winamac.	Citizens' N.B.
8785.	Nappanee.	First N.B.
8804.	Dublin.	First N.B.
8805.	Carlisle.	First N.B.
8820.	Swayzee.	First N.B.
8832.	Evansville.	Bankers N.B.
8835.	Birdseye.	Birdseye N.B.
8868.	Lynnville.	Lynnville N.B.
8871.	Cambridge City.	Wayne N.B.
8878.	Sunman.	Farmers' N.B.
8912.	Albion.	Albion N.B.
8927.	Wadesville.	Farmers' N.B.
8929.	Huntingburg.	First N.B.
8956.	Tennyson.	Tennyson N.B.
9006.	Rosedale.	Rosedale N.B.
9073.	Fort Branch.	First N.B.
9077.	Fort Branch.	Farmers and Merchants' N.B.
9090.	Holland.	Holland N.B.
9115.	Kirklin.	First N.B.
9122.	North Vernon.	North Vernon N.B.
9143.	Brownstown.	First N.B.
9152.	Knightstown.	Citizens' N.B.
9159.	Winslow.	First N.B.
9175.	Westport.	First N.B.
9189.	Cayuga.	First N.B.
9209.	Shirley.	First N.B.
9250.	Center Point.	First N.B.
9266.	Boonville.	Farmers and Merchants' N.B.
9279.	Wilkinson.	Farmers' N.B.
9286.	Butler.	First N.B.
9299.	Fortville.	First N.B.
9352.	Patoka.	Patoka N.B.
9381.	Michigan City.	Merchants' N.B.
9401.	Cannelton.	First N.B.
9463.	Princeton.	Farmers' N.B.
9488.	Arcadia.	First N.B.
9492.	Whiteland.	Whiteland N.B.
9510.	Ambia.	First N.B.
9537.	Indianapolis.	Continental N.B.
9540.	Clay City.	First N.B.
9562.	Oakland City.	First N.B.
9670.	Rodkey.	Farmers and Merchants' N.B.
9682.	Cannelton.	Cannelton N.B.
9715.	Spencer.	Spencer N.B.
9726.	Argos.	First N.B.
9756.	Noblesville.	American N.B.
9784.	Monterey.	First N.B.
9829.	Indianapolis.	Fletcher American N.B.
9852.	New Castle.	Farmers' N.B.
9860.	Covington.	First N.B.
10121.	Indianapolis.	Nat. City Bank.
10171.	East Chicago, Indiana Harbor.	Indiana Harbor N.B.
10234.	Mulberry.	Citizens' N.B.

Charter Number	City	Name of Bank
10290.	Anderson.	People's State N.B.
10409.	Greencastle.	Citizens' N.B.
10419.	Fishers.	Fishers N.B.
10465.	Cloverdale.	First N.B.
10551.	Princeton.	People's American N.B.
10613.	Boonville.	City N.B.
10616.	Kewanna.	American N.B.
10671.	Indianapolis.	Commercial N.B.
10718.	Fremont.	First N.B.
10720.	Cicero.	Citizens' N.B.
10989.	Winchester.	Citizens' N.B.
11035.	Farmersburg.	First N.B.
11043.	Wakarusa.	First N.B.
11044.	Veedersburg.	First N.B.
11094.	Gary.	N.B. of America.
11148.	La Fayette.	First-Merchants' N.B.
11355.	Remington.	Farmers' N.B.
11424.	Cedar Grove.	Cedar Grove N.B.
11427.	Roanoke.	First N.B.
11470.	Rensselaer.	Farmers and Merchants' N.B.
11671.	Converse.	First N.B.
11782.	Milroy.	First N.B.
12028.	Spurgeon.	First N.B.
12058.	East Chicago, Indiana Harbor	United States N.B. of Indiana Harbor.
12132.	Evansville.	Nat. City Bank.
12420.	Rushville.	American N.B.
12444.	Evansville.	Old N.B.
12466.	Mount.	Old First N.B. Vernon.
12532.	Kendallville.	Citizens' N.B.
12780.	Mount Vernon	Mount Vernon N.B. and Trust Co.
12866.	Farmland.	New First N.B.
12952.	Monticello.	N.B. of Monticello.
13050.	Sheridan.	Sheridan N.B.
13082.	Covington.	N.B. of Covington.
13224.	Terre Haute.	Citizens' N.B. &Trust Co.
13305.	Bluffton.	Old N.B.
13317.	Bluffton.	First N.B.
13378.	Franklin.	Franklin N.B.
13503.	Poseyville.	Bozeman Waters First N.B.
13531.	East Chicago.	First N.B.
13532.	East Chicago.	Union N.B. of Indiana Harbor.
13542.	New Harmony.	New Harmony N.B.
13580.	Logansport.	N.B. of Logansport.
13643.	Martinsville.	N.B. of Martinsville.
13717.	Marion.	First N.B.
13729.	Marion.	Marion N.B.
13759.	Indianapolis.	American N.B.
13788.	Bedford.	Stone City N.B.
13816.	New Castle.	First N.B.
13818.	Fort Wayne.	Fort Wayne N.B.
13862.	Swayzee.	First N.B.
13888.	Wabash.	First N.B.
13938.	Terre Haute.	Merchants N.B.
13977.	Flora.	Bright N.B.
13987.	South Bend.	City N.B.
13988.	Greensburg.	Decatur County N.B.
14047.	New Albany.	Union N.B.
14075.	Franklin.	Johnson County N.B.
14113.	Goshen.	First N.B.
14175.	La Fayette.	La Fayette N.B.
14218.	Boonville.	Boonville N.B.
14226.	Butler.	Knisely N.B.
14258.	Linton.	Citizens N.B.
14288.	Rensselaer.	Farmers and Merchants N.B.
14292.	Greenwood.	N.B. of Greenwood.

IOWA

Charter Number	City	Name of Bank
15.	Davenport.	First N.B.
18.	Iowa City.	First N.B.
66.	Lyons.	First N.B.
80.	Koekuk.	First N.B.
107.	Ottumwa.	First N.B.
117.	Marion.	First N.B.
147.	Oskaloosa.	First N.B.
195.	Ottumwa.	Second N.B.
299.	Mount Pleasant.	First N.B.
317.	Dubuque.	First N.B.
323.	McGregor.	First N.B.
337.	Centerville.	First N.B.
351.	Burlington.	First N.B.
389.	Des Moines.	First N.B.
398.	Washington.	First N.B.
405.	Lansing.	First N.B.
411.	Marshalltown.	First N.B.
483.	Cedar Rapids.	City N.B.
485.	Des Moines.	Second N.B.
493.	Decorah.	First N.B.
500.	Cedar Rapids.	First N.B.
650.	Newton.	First N.B.
692.	Muscatine.	Muscatine N.B.
751.	Burlington.	Nat. State Bank.
792.	Waterloo.	First N.B.
846.	Dubuque.	Merchants' N.B.
848.	Davenport.	Davenport N.B.
922.	Mount Pleasant.	Nat. State Bank.
950.	Des Moines.	Nat. State Bank.
977.	Iowa City.	Iowa City N.B.
994.	Clinton.	Clinton N.B.
999.	Maquoketta.	First N.B.
1101.	Oskaloosa.	Nat. State Bank.
1299.	Bloomfield.	First N.B.
1403.	Winterset.	First N.B.
1441.	Koekuk.	State N.B.
1475.	Fairfield.	First N.B.
1479.	Council B.	First N.B.
1581.	Independence.	First N.B.
1593.	Vinton.	First N.B.

Charter Number	City	Name of Bank
1611.	Fort Madison.	Fort Madison N.B.
1618.	Osage.	Osage N.B.
1629.	Grinnell.	First N.B.
1661.	Fort Dodge.	First N.B.
1671.	Davenport.	Citizens' N.B.
1684.	Council Bluffs.	Pacific N.B.
1696.	Leon.	First N.B.
1724.	Chariton.	First N.B.
1726	Ottumwa.	Iowa N.B.
1744.	Burlington.	Merchants' N.B.
1757.	Sioux City.	First N.B.
1762.	Washington.	Washington N.B.
1776.	Osceola.	First N.B.
1786.	Sigourney.	First N.B.
1799.	Albia.	First N.B.
1801.	Dubuque.	Commercial N.B.
1810.	Charles City.	First N.B.
1811.	Indianola.	First N.B.
1813.	Anarnosa.	First N.B.
1815.	E[kader.	First N.B.
1836.	Atlantic.	First N.B.
1862.	Glenwood.	Mills County N.B.
1871.	Knoxville.	Knoxville N.B.
1874.	Webster City.	First N.B.
1880.	Tama.	First N.B.
1891.	Pella.	First N.B.
1943.	Wyoming.	First N.B.
1947.	Fort Dodge.	Merchants' N.B.
1970.	Des Moines.	Citizens N.B.
1976.	Sioux City.	Citizens' N.B.
1986.	Knoxville.	Marion County N.B.
1992.	Keokuk.	Keokuk N.B.
2002.	Winterset.	Citizens' N.B.
2012.	Belle Plaine.	First N.B.
2015.	West Union.	Fayette County N.B.
2028.	Clarinda.	First N.B.
2032.	Columbus Junction.	Louisa County N.B.
2033.	Brighton.	Brighton N.B.
2051.	Boone.	First N.B.
2063.	Pella.	Pella N.B.
2080.	Monticello.	Monticello N.B.
2115.	Marshalltown.	Farmers' N.B.
2130.	Red Oak.	First N.B.
2177.	Cedar Falls.	First N.B.
2182.	Lisbon.	First N.B.
2187.	Independence.	People's N.B.
2191.	Allerton.	First N.B.
2197.	Centerville.	Farmers' N.B.
2215.	Monroe.	First N.B.
2230.	Red Oak.	Valley N.B.
2247.	Malvern.	First N.B.
2298.	Bedford.	First N.B.
2307.	Des Moines.	Iowa N.B.
2326.	Afton.	First N.B.
2327.	Dubuque.	Second N.B.
2363.	Shenandoah.	First N.B.
2364.	Hamburg.	First N.B.
2411.	Nashua.	First N.B.
2417.	Oskaloosa.	Oskaloosa N.B.
2469.	Clinton.	City N.B.
2484.	Marengo.	First N.B.
2511.	Cedar Rapids.	Merchants' N.B.
2535.	Sioux City.	Sioux N.B.
2555.	Nevada.	First N.B.
2573.	Hampton.	First N.B.
2574.	Mason City.	First N.B.
2579.	Charles City.	Charles City N.B.
2583.	Des Moines.	Des Moines N.B.
2586.	Creston.	First N.B.
2588.	New Hampton.	First N.B.
2595.	Storm Lake.	First N.B.
2621.	Ottumwa.	Ottumwa N.B.
2631.	Des Moines.	Merchants' N.B.
2644.	Newton.	First N.B.
2656.	Washington.	First N.B.
2679.	Shenandoah.	Shenandoah N.B.
2695.	Davenport.	First N.B.
2721.	Stuart.	First N.B.
2728.	Le Mars.	First N.B.
2733.	Lyons.	First N.B.
2738.	Iowa City.	First N.B.
2753.	Marion.	First N.B.
2762.	Atlantic.	Atlantic N.B.
2763.	Fort Dodge.	Fort Dodge N.B.
2766.	Villisca.	First N.B.
2818.	Le Mars.	Le Mars N.B.
2821.	Iowa City.	Iowa City N.B.
2833.	Creston.	Creston N.B.
2841.	Centerville.	Centerville N.B.
2856.	Jesup.	First N.B.
2886.	Des Moines.	Valley N.B.
2895.	Oskaloosa.	Farmers and Traders' N.B.
2910.	Waterloo.	Commercial N.B.
2936.	Corning.	First N.B.
2953.	Grinnell.	Merchants' N.B.
2961.	Montezuma.	First N.B.
2971.	Marshalltown.	Commercial N.B.
2983.	Tipton.	First N.B.
2984.	Webster City.	Hamilton County N.B.
3012.	Albia.	Albia N.B.
3017.	Ames.	Union N.B.
3026.	Perry.	First N.B.
3048.	Griswold.	First N.B.
3049.	Cherokee.	First N.B.
3053.	Rockford.	First N.B.
3055.	Red Oak.	Red Oak N.B.
3071.	Greene.	First N.B.
3105.	Waverly.	First N.B.
3112.	Clarinda.	Clarinda N.B.

Charter Number	City	Name of Bank
3124.	Sioux City.	Security N.B.
3140.	Dubuque.	Dubuque N.B.
3153.	Rock Rapids.	First N.B.
3182.	De Witt.	First N.B.
3189.	Missouri Valley.	First N.B.
3192.	What Cheer.	First N.B.
3197.	Algona.	First N.B.
3225.	Grundy Center.	First N.B.
3226.	Panora.	Guthrie County N.B.
3252.	Iowa Falls.	First N.B.
3263.	Independence.	First N.B.
3273.	Boone.	First N.B.
3284.	Brooklyn.	First N.B.
3320.	Sibley.	First N.B.
3337.	Emmetsburg.	First N.B.
3396.	Grundy Center.	Grundy Center N.B.
3420.	Webster City.	Farmers' N.B.
3427.	Council Bluffs.	Council Bluffs N.B.
3439.	Eagle Grove.	First N.B.
3455.	Manning.	First N.B.
3618.	Sutherland.	First N.B.
3643.	Cedar Rapids.	Cedar Rapids N.B.
3736.	Clinton.	Merchants' N.B.
3788.	Clarion.	Wright County N.B.
3796.	Clarion.	First N.B.
3848.	Sheldon.	First N.B.
3871.	Cedar Falls.	Cedar Falls N.B.
3898.	Spencer.	First N.B.
3930.	Ida Grove.	First N.B.
3940.	Sioux City.	American N.B.
3968.	Sioux City.	Iowa State N.B.
3969.	Carroll.	First N.B.
3974.	Fort Madison.	First N.B.
4022.	Davenport.	Iowa N.B.
4114.	Laporte City.	First N.B.
4139.	Dunlap.	First N.B.
4155.	Primghar.	First N.B.
4209.	Sioux City.	Merchants' N.B.
4221.	Manchester.	First N.B.
4235.	Sioux City.	Corn Exchange N.B.
4268.	Corning.	N.B. of Corning.
4359.	Marshalltown.	City N.B.
4376.	Charter Oak.	First N.B.
4431.	Sioux City.	N.B. of Sioux City.
4450.	Sac City.	First N.B.
4510.	Sioux City.	Sioux N.B.
4511.	Odebolt.	First N.B.
4536.	Lyons.	Citizens' N.B.
4553.	Holstein.	First N.B.
4566.	Fort Dodge.	Commercial N.B.
4587.	Mason City.	City N.B.
4594.	Hawarden.	First N.B.
4601.	Peterson.	First N.B.
4609.	Tabor.	First N.B.
4630.	Sioux City.	Commercial N.B.
4633.	Knoxville.	Citizens' N.B.
4677.	Charles City.	Citizens' N.B.
4694.	Eagle Grove.	First N.B.
4696.	Anamosa.	Anamosa N.B.
4700.	Estherville.	First N.B.
4745.	Woodbine.	First N.B.
4754.	Belle Plaine.	Citizens' N.B.
4758.	Spirit Lake.	First N.B.
4761.	Nora Springs.	First N.B.
4784.	Denison.	First N.B.
4789.	Marathon.	First N.B.
4794.	Ireton.	First N.B.
4795.	Laurens.	First N.B.
4810.	Garner.	First N.B.
4814.	Glidden.	First N.B.
4824.	Sanborn.	First N.B.
4834.	Malvern.	Farmers' N.B.
4881.	Hartley.	First N.B.
4885.	Osage.	Farmers' N.B.
4889.	Forest City.	First N.B.
4891.	Audubon.	First N.B.
4902.	Blanchard.	First N.B.
4921.	Waukon.	First N.B.
4954.	Rolfe.	First N.B.
4966.	Lake City.	First N.B.
5011.	Forest City.	Forest City N.B.
5020.	Britt.	First N.B.
5022.	Sioux City.	Live Stock N.B.
5054.	Thompson.	First N.B.
5081.	Decorah.	N.B. of Decorah.
5088.	Vinton.	Farmers' N.B.
5113.	Cedar Rapids.	Citizens' N.B.
5120.	Waterloo.	Leavitt and Johnson N.B.
5123.	Lake Mills.	First N.B.
5135.	Traer.	First N.B.
5140.	Eldora.	First N.B.
5145.	Sidney.	N.B. of Sidney.
5154.	Buffalo Center.	First N.B.
5165.	Bedford.	Bedford N.B.
5185.	Rockwell City.	First N.B.
5200.	Rock Valley.	First N.B.
5207.	Harlan.	First N.B.
5302.	Dayton.	First N.B.
5305.	Crystal Lake.	First N.B.
5319.	Moulton.	First N.B.
5334.	Greenfield.	First N.B.
5342.	Eldon.	First N.B.
5366.	Clutier.	First N.B.
5372.	Dike.	First N.B.
5373.	Goldfield.	First N.B.
5402.	Lost Nation .	First N.B.
5412.	Chelsea.	First N.B.
5420.	New London.	First N.B.
5424.	Guthrie.	First N.B. Center.

Charter Number	City	Name of Bank
5442.	Armstrong.	First N.B.
5457.	Wesley.	First N.B.
5461.	Gladbrook.	First N.B.
5464.	Garden Grove.	First N.B.
5479.	Ayrshire.	First N.B.
5489.	Leon.	Exchange N.B.
5507.	Cedar Falls.	Citizens' N.B.
5514.	Coon Rapids.	First N.B.
5517.	Lenox.	First N.B.
5539.	Milford.	First N.B.
5540.	Hedrick.	First N.B.
5541.	Ruthven.	First N.B.
5554.	Brighton.	N.B. of Brighton.
5564.	Pleasantville.	First N.B.
5571.	Graettinger.	First N.B.
5576.	Dougherty.	First N.B.
5579.	Farmington.	First N.B.
5585.	Williams.	First N.B.
5597.	Titonka.	First N.B.
5611.	Richland.	First N.B.
5616.	Melvin.	First N.B.
5637.	Swea City.	First N.B.
5643.	Bancroft.	First N.B.
5659.	Hudson.	First N.B.
5685.	Burt.	First N.B.
5700.	Waterloo.	Waterloo N.B.
5703.	Burt.	Burt N.B.
5707.	Gowrie.	First N.B.
5738.	Essex.	First N.B.
5743.	Jewel Jct., Jewell.	First N.B.
5775.	Corwith.	First N.B.
5778.	Oelwein.	First N.B.
5803.	Essex.	Commercial N.B.
5817.	Odebolt.	Farmers N.B.
5838.	Council Bluffs.	Commercial N.B.
5868.	Lehigh.	First N.B.
5873.	Manifla.	First N.B.
5891.	Valley Junction.	First N.B.
5912.	Prescott.	First N.B.
5934.	Dysart.	First N.B.
5979.	Charles City.	Commercial N.B.
6014.	Chariton.	Chariton N.B.
6017.	Hamburg.	Farmers' N.B.
6033.	Osceola.	Osceola N.B.
6041.	Manifla.	Manilla N.B.
6056.	Red Oak.	Farmers' N.B.
6063.	Pomeroy.	First N.B.
6080.	Coon Rapids.	Coon Rapids N.B.
6122.	Washington.	Citizens' N.B.
6132.	Orange City.	First N.B.
6303.	Pocahontas.	First N.B.
6432.	Toledo.	First N.B.
6434.	Stanton.	First N.B.
6435.	Radcliffe.	First N.B.
6550.	Fonda.	First N.B.
6610.	Grafton.	First N.B.
6611.	Gilmore, Gilmore City.	First N.B.
6650.	Primghar.	Farmere N.B.
6659.	Klemme.	First N.B.
6700.	Farragut.	First N.B.
6705.	Deep River.	First N.B.
6722.	Dunkerton.	First N.B.
6737.	Churdan.	First N.B.
6750.	Lime Springs.	First N.B.
6755.	Prairie City.	First N.B.
6760.	Tipton.	City N.B.
6764.	Doon.	First N.B.
6771.	Logan.	First N.B.
6838.	Boone.	Boone N.B.
6852.	Macksburg.	Macksburg N.B.
6854.	Waterloo.	Black Hawk N.B.
6857.	Elliott.	First N.B.
6870.	Exira.	First N.B.
6880.	Greene.	Merchants' N.B.
6936.	Harvey.	First N.B.
6941.	Spencer.	Citizens' N.B.
6949.	Harris.	First N.B.
6953.	Hull.	First N.B.
6975.	Remsen.	First N.B.
6995.	Bagley.	First N.B.
7061.	Fontanelle.	First N.B.
7089.	Rock Rapids.	Lyon County N.B.
7108.	Aurelia.	First N.B.
7114.	Colfax.	First N.B.
7126.	Alta.	First N.B.
7137.	Linn Grove.	First N.B.
7189.	Sioux Rapids.	First N.B.
7261.	Lineville.	First N.B.
7287.	Norway.	First N.B.
7294.	Havelock.	First N.B.
7304.	Inwood.	First N.B.
7309.	Colin.	First N.B.
7322.	Akron.	First N.B.
7357.	Monroe.	Monroe N.B.
7369.	Sioux Center.	First N.B.
7382.	Henderson.	Farmers' N.B.
7401.	Sioux City.	City N.B.
7439.	Grinnell.	Citizens' N.B.
7469.	Montour.	First N.B.
7506.	Villisca.	Villisca N.B.
7521.	Iowa Falls.	State N.B.
7585.	Olin.	First N.B.
7607.	New Hampton.	Second N.B.
7609.	Rippey.	First N.B.
7682.	Clarence.	First N.B.
7736.	Guthrie.	Citizens N.B. Center.
7828.	Everly.	First N.B.
7833,	Randolph.	First N.B.

Charter Number	City	Name of Bank
7843.	Hampton.	Citizens' N.B.
7869.	Clear Lake.	First N.B.
7880.	Sheldon.	Sheldon N.B.
7988.	Renwick.	First N.B.
8032.	Spirit Lake.	Spirit Lake N.B.
8035.	Emmetsburg.	Emmetsburg N.B.
8047.	Pella.	Farmers' N.B.
8057.	Malvern.	Malvern N.B.
8076.	Oskaloosa.	Farmers' N.B.
8099.	Casey.	Abram Rutt N.B.
8100.	Corning.	Farmers' N.B.
8119.	Little Rock.	First N.B.
8198.	Sumner.	First N.B.
8211.	Blockton.	First N.B.
8247.	Seymour.	First N.B.
8257.	Inwood.	Farmers' N.B.
8262.	Jefferson.	First N.B.
8273.	Preston.	First N.B.
8277.	Humboldt.	First N.B.
8295.	Imogene.	First N.B.
8340.	Thornton.	First N.B.
8352.	New London.	New London N.B.
8367.	Garner.	Farmers' N.B.
8373.	Northwood.	First N.B.
8442.	Riceville.	First N.B.
8603.	Albia.	People's N.B.
8699.	Adair.	First N.B.
8725.	Corning.	Okey-Vernon N.B.
8748.	Belmond.	First N.B.
8762.	Ackley.	First N.B.
8900.	Hawkeye.	First N.B.
8915.	Griswold.	Griswold N.B.
8931.	State Center.	First N.B.
8950.	New Sharon.	First N.B.
8970.	Hubbard.	First N.B.
8971.	Shenandoah.	Commercial N.B.
8981.	Adel.	First N.B.
8986.	Fairfield.	Fairfield N.B.
9014.	Cambridge.	First N.B.
9015.	Northboro.	First N.B.
9017.	Story City.	First N.B.
9018.	Kanawha.	First N.B.
9024.	Chariton.	Lucas County N.B.
9069.	Strawberry Point.	First N.B.
9116.	Kingsley.	Farmers' N.B.
9125.	Diagonal.	First N.B.
9168.	Cedar Rapids.	Commercial N.B.
9231.	Allerton.	Farmers' N.B.
9233.	Eldora.	Hardin County N.B.
9298.	Milford.	Milford N.B.
9303.	Bloomfield.	N.B. of Bloomfield.
9306.	Council Bluffs.	City N.B.
9447.	Sonrad.	First N.B.
9549.	Clearfield.	First N.B.
9555.	Dyersville.	First N.B.
9585.	Sioux Rapids.	First N.B.
9592.	Fayette.	First N.B.
9619.	Kimballton.	Landmands N.B.
9664.	Arlington.	American N.B.
9723.	Shannon City.	First N.B.
9724.	Aurelia.	Farmers' N.B.
9737.	Grand River.	First N.B.
9819.	Marcus.	First N.B.
9821.	Floyd.	First N.B.
9846.	Parkersburg.	First N.B.
9853.	Crystal Lake.	Farmers' N.B.
9910.	George.	First N.B.
10030.	Dexter.	First N.B.
10034.	Storm Lake.	Citizens' First N.B.
10123.	Jefferson.	Farmers and Mqrchants' N.B.
10130.	Perry.	Perry N.B.
10139.	Sioux City.	Toy N.B.
10146.	Corydon.	First N.B.
10191.	Newell.	First N.B.
10207.	Waukon.	People's N.B.
10217.	Rockwell.	First N.B.
10222.	Story City.	Story City N.B.
10223.	Storm Lake.	Commercial N.B.
10238.	Terril.	First N.B.
10243.	Milton.	N.B. of Milton.
10354.	Harlan.	Harlan N.B.
10371.	Bode.	First N.B.
10395.	Royal.	Citizens' N.B.
10408.	Ames.	Ames N.B.
10428.	Mason City.	Security N.B.
10501.	Galva.	First N.B.
10518.	Sioux City.	Continental N.B.
10541.	Fredericksburg.	First N.B.
10562.	Mallard.	First N.B.
10599.	Lawler.	First N.B.
10640.	Winfield.	Farmers' N.B.
10684.	Saint Ansgar.	First N.B.
10701.	Mapleton.	First N.B.
10711.	Cherokee.	Security N.B.
10726.	Newton.	Clark N.B.
10729.	Rembrandt.	First N.B.
10812.	Paullina.	First N.B.
10848.	Derby.	First N.B.
10861.	Whiting.	First N.B.
10877.	Orange City.	Orange City N.B.
10889.	Merrill.	First N.B.
11162.	Webb.	Citizene N.B.
11210.	Seymour.	Seymour N.B.
11249.	Roland.	First N.B.
11295.	College Springs.	First N.B.
11304.	Fort Dodge.	Webster County N.B.
11582.	Rockwell City.	Rockwell City N.B.
11588.	Shenandoah.	Farmers' N.B.
11604.	Ogden.	First N.B.

Charter Number	City	Name of Bank
11644.	Ashton.	First N.B.
11735.	Rake.	Farmers' First N.B.
11907.	Farnhamville.	First N.B.
12248.	Lorimor.	First N.B.
12303.	Bellevue.	First N.B.
12430.	Sheffield.	First N.B.
12544.	Pocahontas.	First N.B.
12610.	Hamburg.	First N.B.
12636.	Creston.	First N.B.
12645.	Lake Park.	First N.B.
12656.	Hedrick.	Hedrick N.B.
12849.	Knoxville.	Knoxville N.B. and Trust Co.
12883.	Ashton.	First N.B.
12950.	Shenandoah.	Shenandoah N.B.
12998.	New Hampton.	New First N.B.
13020.	Spirit Lake.	First N.B.
13059.	Emmetsburg.	N.B. of Emmetsburg.
13073.	Toledo.	N.B. of Toledo.
13083.	Nevada.	Nevada N.B.
13109.	Corydon.	Commercial N.B.
13112.	Spencer.	Clay County N.B.
13188.	Independence.	Buchanan County N.B.
13232.	Tipton.	Tipton N.B.
13263.	Vinton.	Farmers N.B.
13321.	Des Moines.	Central N.B. & Trust Co.
13400.	Sioux Rapids.	First N.B.
13458.	Chariton.	N.B. & Trust Co.
13473.	Grimmell.	Poweshiek County N.B.
13495.	Seymour.	N.B. of Seymour.
13508.	Dyersville.	Dyersville N.B.
13538.	Sioux City.	First N.B.
13609.	Newton.	Newton N.B.
13686.	Colfax.	First N.B.
13694.	Burlington.	First N.B.
13697.	Iowa City.	First Capital N.B.
13702.	Waterloo.	N.B. of Waterloo.
13707.	Knoxville.	Community N.B. and Trust Co.
13766.	Humboldt.	First N.B.
13785.	Red Oak.	Montgomery County N.B.
13817.	Boone.	Citizens' N.B.
13842.	Hampton.	First N.B.
13849.	Washington.	N.B. of Washington.
13890.	Rockwell City.	N.B. of Rockwell City.
13939.	Hawarden.	First N.B.
13978.	West Union.	First N.B.
13991.	Fairfield.	First N.B.
14028.	Council Bluffs.	First N.B.
14036.	Garner.	Hancock County N.B.
14040.	Lenox.	First N.B.
14041.	Villisca.	Nodaway Valley N.B.
14057.	Shenandoah.	City N.B.
14065.	Nevada.	Nevada N.B.
14066.	Grundy Center.	Grundy N.B.
14069.	Belle Plaine.	Citizens' N.B.
14085.	Clear Lake.	First N.B.
14129.	Winterset.	Farmers and Merchants N.B.
14143.	What Cheer.	First N.B.
14158.	Bellevue.	First N.B.
14172.	Traer.	First N.B.
14253.	Le Mars.	First N.B.
14286.	Eldora.	Hardin County N.B.
14309.	Keokuk.	Keokuk N.B.
14326.	Glidden.	First N.B.

KANSAS

Charter Number	City	Name of Bank
182.	Leavenworth.	First N.B.
1448.	Leavenworth.	Second N.B.
1590.	Lawrence.	N.B. of Lawrence.
1660.	Topeka.	First N.B.
1672.	Atchison.	First N.B.
1718.	Ottawa.	First N.B.
1732.	Lawrence.	Second N.B.
1763.	Fort Scott.	First N.B.
1828.	Olathe.	First N.B.
1838.	Baxter Springs.	First N.B.
1840.	Wyandotte.	First N.B.
1864.	Paola.	First N.B.
1902.	Chetopa.	First N.B.
1910.	Ottawa.	People's N.B.
1913.	Wichita.	First N.B.
1915.	Emporia.	First N.B.
1927.	Fort Scott.	Merchants' N.B.
1945.	Topeka.	Topeka N.B.
1951.	Parsons.	First N.B.
1957.	El Dorado.	First N.B.
1977.	Junction City.	First N.B.
1979.	Burlington.	Burlington N.B.
1983.	Emporia.	Empbria N.B.
2001.	Council Grove.	First N.B.
2082.	Atchison.	Atchison N.B.
2094.	Manhattan.	First N.B.
2192.	Topeka.	State N.B.
2427.	Abilene.	First N.B.
2538.	Salina.	First N.B.
2589.	Hiawatha.	First N.B.
2640.	Cawker City.	First N.B.
2646.	Topeka.	First N.B.
2666.	Larned.	First N.B.
2758.	Atchison.	Exchange N.B.
2764.	Cottonwood Falls.	Chase County N.B.
2777.	Newton.	First N.B.
2782.	Wichita.	First N.B.
2786.	Wichita.	Wichita N.B.
2791.	Marysville.	First N.B.
2809.	Frankfort.	First N.B.
2879.	Wellington.	First N.B.
2912.	Washington.	First N.B.
2952.	Seneca.	First N.B.
2954.	Sabetha.	First N.B.

Charter Number	City	Name of Bank
2973.	Garnett.	First N.B.
2990.	Sabetha.	Citizens' N.B.
3002.	Strong City.	Strong City N.B.
3018.	Marion.	First N.B.
3021.	Independence.	First N.B.
3033.	Leavenworth.	Leavenworth N.B.
3035.	El Dorado.	N.B. of El Dorado.
3038.	Oswego.	First N.B.
3061.	Holton.	First N.B.
3066.	Concordia.	First N.B.
3072.	Clay Center.	First N.B.
3078.	Topeka.	Central N.B.
3090.	Concordia.	Concordia N.B.
3091.	Wellington.	First N.B.
3108.	Yates Center.	Woodson N.B.
3115.	Clyde.	First N.B.
3134.	Peabody.	First N.B.
3148.	Eureka.	First N.B.
3167.	Washington.	Washington N.B.
3170.	Burlington.	People's N.B.
3175.	Fort Scott.	Citizens' N.B.
3180.	Hutchinson.	First N.B.
3194.	Leavenworth.	Metropolitan N.B.
3199.	Hutchinson.	Hutchinson N.B.
3207.	Sterling.	First N.B.
3213.	El Dorado.	Exchange N.B.
3216.	Girard.	First N.B.
3218.	Winfield.	First N.B.
3231.	Beloit.	First N.B.
3242.	Howard.	First N.B.
3249.	Ellsworth.	First N.B.
3253.	Medicine Lodge.	First N.B.
3265.	Harper.	First N.B.
3277.	Cherryvale.	First N.B.
3297.	Newton.	Newton N.B.
3304.	Westmoreland.	First N.B.
3319.	Osborne.	First N.B.
3324.	Coffeyville.	First N.B.
3345.	Clay Center.	People's N.B.
3350.	Paola.	Miami County N.B.
3351.	Winfield.	Winfield N.B.
3353.	Minneapolis.	First N.B.
3360.	Arkansas City.	First N.B.
3363.	Great Bend.	First N.B.
3374.	Saint Mary's.	First N.B.
3384.	Anthony.	Harper County N.B.
3385.	Anthony.	First N.B.
3386.	Belleville.	First N.B.
3394.	Anthony.	Anthony N.B.
3431.	Harper.	Harper N.B.
3434.	Wamego.	First N.B.
3440.	Stockton.	First N.B.
3443.	Halstead.	Halstead N.B.
3447.	Ellsworth.	Central N.B.
3448.	Garden City.	First N.B.
3454.	Kirwin.	First N.B.
3463.	Pittsburg.	First N.B.
3464.	Lincoln.	First N.B.
3467.	Saint John.	First N.B.
3472.	Osborne.	Exchange N.B.
3473.	Newton.	German N.B.
3475.	Pittsburg.	N.B. of Pittsburg.
3509.	Kingman.	First N.B.
3511.	Oberlin.	First N.B.
3512.	Colby.	First N.B.
3521.	McPherson.	First N.B.
3524.	Wichita.	State N.B.
3531.	Salina.	Salina N.B.
3542.	Ness City.	First N.B.
3543.	Junction City.	First N.B.
3546.	Smith Center.	First N.B.
3559.	Kingman.	Kingman N.B.
3563.	Downs.	Exchange N.B.
3564.	Wellington.	State N.B.
3567.	Greenleaf.	First N.B.
3569.	Downs.	First N.B.
3577.	Lyons.	First N.B.
3584.	Lawrence.	Merchants' N.B.
3589.	Lindsborg.	First N.B.
3591.	Jewell.	First N.B.
3594.	Medicine Lodge.	Citizens' N.B.
3596.	Dodge City.	First N.B.
3601.	Phillipsburg.	First N.B.
3612.	Atchison.	United States N.B.
3630.	Smith Center.	Smith County N.B.
3649.	Pratt.	First N.B.
3657.	Russell.	First N.B.
3658.	Caldwell.	First N.B.
3667.	Greensburg.	First N.B.
3683.	Wichita.	Fourth N.B.
3687.	Norton.	First N.B.
3695.	Meade Center.	First N.B.
3703.	Coldwater.	First N.B.
3706.	Kansas City .	First N.B.
3710.	Ashland.	First N.B.
3720.	Olathe.	First N.B.
3726.	Kansas City.	Wyandotte N.B.
3731.	Minneapolis.	Minneapolis N.B.
3737.	Kingman.	Citizens' N.B.
3745.	Mankato.	First N.B.
3748.	Concordia.	Citizens' N.B.
3751.	Cimarron.	First N.B.
3756.	Wichita.	West Side N.B.
3758.	Hill City.	First N.B.
3759.	Kinsley.	First N.B.
3769.	Alma.	First N.B.
3775.	Russell Springs.	First N.B.
3776.	Wakeeney.	First N.B.
3777.	Abilene.	Abilene N.B.
3779.	Belleville.	N.B. of Belleville.

Charter Number	City	Name of Bank
3782.	Manhattan.	First N.B.
3787.	Pratt.	Pratt County N.B.
3790.	Topeka.	Kansas N.B.
3791.	McPherson.	Second N.B.
3794.	Howard.	Howard N.B.
3795.	Paola.	N.B. of Paola.
3803.	McPherson.	McPherson N.B.
3805.	Jetmore.	First N.B.
3807.	Humboldt.	Humboldt First N.B.
3810.	Horton.	First N.B.
3812.	Mankato.	Jewell County N.B.
3813.	Osage City.	First N.B.
3819.	Chanute.	First N.B.
3824.	Centralia.	First N.B.
3833.	El Dorado.	Merchants' N.B.
3835.	Fredonia.	First N.B.
3844.	Leoti.	First N.B.
3849.	Lawrence.	Lawrence N.B.
3852.	Stafford.	First N.B.
3853.	Meade Center.	Meade County N.B.
3855.	Sedan.	First N.B.
3861.	Hutchinson.	N.B. of Commerce.
3865.	Wellington.	Sumner N.B.
3880.	Burr Oak.	First N.B.
3881.	Lawrence.	Watkins N.B.
3885.	Hays City.	First N.B.
3888.	Dighton.	First N.B.
3900.	Garden City.	Finney County N.B.
3908.	Leavenworth.	Manufacturers' N.B.
3909.	Topeka.	Merchants' N.B.
3928.	Marion.	Cottonwood Valley N.B.
3963.	Erie.	First N.B.
3970.	La Crosse.	First N.B.
3991.	Paola.	People's N.B.
3992.	Arkansas City.	American N.B.
4008.	Manhattan.	Union N.B.
4032.	Garnett.	Anderson County N.B.
4036.	Chanute.	Chanute N.B.
4040.	Burlingame.	First N.B.
4058.	Herington.	First N.B.
4136.	Pittsburg.	Manufacturers' N.B.
4150.	Sedan.	Sedan N.B.
4284.	Junction City.	Central N.B.
4288.	Cherryvale.	Cherryvale N.B.
4317.	Salina.	American N.B.
4381.	Kansas City.	Inter-State N.B.
4487.	Arkansas City.	Home N.B.
4499.	Independence.	Commercial N.B.
4556.	Winfield.	Cowley County N.B.
4592.	Independence.	Citizens-First N.B.
4618.	Cawker City.	Farmers and Merchants' N.B.
4619.	Saint Mary's.	N.B. of Saint Mary's.
4626.	Sabetha.	N.B. of Sabetha.
4640.	Arkansas City.	Farmers' N.B.
4642.	Oberlin.	Oberlin N.B.
4742.	Salina.	Farmers' N.B.
4749.	Cherryvale.	Montgomery County N.B.
4798.	Galena.	Galena N.B.
4860.	Newton.	Midland N.B.
4931.	Minneapolis.	Citizens' N.B.
4945.	Salina.	N.B. of America.
4981.	El Dorado.	Farmers and Merchants' N.B.
5041.	Holton.	N.B. of Holton.
5101.	Seneca.	N.B. of Seneca.
5104.	Alma.	Alma N.B.
5169.	Wichita.	N.B. of Commerce.
5287.	Iola.	Northrup N.B.
5292.	Garnett.	N.B. of Commerce.
5349.	Caney.	Caney Valley N.B.
5353.	Lyons.	Lyons N.B.
5359.	Nortonville.	First N.B.
5386.	Ashland.	Stockgrowers' N.B.
5447.	Cherokee.	First N.B.
5498.	Emporia.	Citizens' N.B.
5506.	Havensville.	First N.B.
5516.	Caney.	Home N.B.
5529.	Madison.	First N.B.
5559.	Mount Hope.	First N.B.
5608.	Cedar Vale.	Cedar Vale N.B.
5655.	Eureka.	Citizens' N.B.
5687.	Hoxie.	First N.B.
5705.	Great Bend.	Citizens' N.B.
5757.	Council Grove.	Council Grove N.B.
5799.	Lebanon.	First N.B.
5810.	Kinsley.	N.B. of Kinsley.
5834.	Osborne.	Farmers' N.B.
5952.	Baxter Springs.	Baxter N.B.
6039.	Goodland.	First N.B.
6072.	Chanute.	N.B. of Chanute.
6101.	Waverly.	First N.B.
6103.	Columbus.	First N.B.
6120.	Hillsboro.	First N.B.
6149.	Leroy.	First N.B.
6229.	Pratt.	First N.B.
6311.	Kansas City.	Commercial N.B.
6326.	Yates Center.	Yates Center N.B.
6333.	Caldwell.	Caldwell N.B.
6392.	Wichita.	N.B. of Wichita.
6494.	El Dorado.	El Dorado N.B.
6530.	Cedarvale.	Citizens' N.B.
6590.	Cottonwood Falls.	Exchange N.B.
6643.	Augusta.	First N.B.
6672.	Lincoln.	Farmers N.B.
6701.	Beloit.	Union N.B.
6720.	Liberal.	First N.B.
6752.	Anthony.	Citizens' N.B.
6767.	Coldwater.	Coldwater N.B.
6797.	Coffeyville.	Condon N.B.
6817.	Mankato.	Mankato N.B.
6819.	Toronto.	First N.B.

Charter Number	City	Name of Bank
6841.	Logan.	First N.B.
6895.	Neodesha.	Neodesha N.B.
6914.	Neodesha.	First N.B.
6932.	Hamilton.	First N.B.
6955.	Burlington.	Farmers' N.B.
6963.	Humboldt.	Humboldt N.B.
6970.	Gaylord.	First N.B.
7125.	Larned.	Moffet Brothers N.B.
7178.	Clifton.	First N.B.
7192.	Meade.	First N.B.
7195.	Overbrook.	First N.B.
7218.	Fredonia.	Fredonia N.B.
7222.	Lyndon.	First N.B.
7226.	La Harpe.	First N.B.
7285.	Dodge City.	First N.B.
7298.	Oberlin.	Farmers' N.B.
7302.	Burr Oak.	Jewell County N.B.
7303.	Eureka.	Home N.B.
7313.	Plainville.	First N.B.
7318.	Moline.	First N.B.
7383.	Cherryvale.	People's N.B.
7412.	Kingman.	Farmers' N.B.
7416.	Goff.	First N.B.
7493.	Kensington.	First N.B.
7532.	Delphos.	First N.B.
7535.	Sedan.	People's N.B.
7561.	Lucas.	First N.B.
7590.	Edna.	First N.B.
7646.	Garden City.	Garden City N.B.
7683.	Glasco.	First N.B.
7815.	Stockton.	Stockton N.B.
7844.	Saint John.	Saint John N.B.
7882.	Goodland.	Farmers' N.B.
7907.	Topeka.	Capital N.B.
7911.	Marion.	Marion N.B.
7970.	White City.	First N.B.
8081.	Ness City.	Citizens' N.B.
8107.	Mound Valley.	First N.B.
8114.	Syracuse.	First N.B.
8142.	Ness City.	N.B. of Ness City.
8145.	Elk City.	First N.B.
8162.	Troy.	First N.B.
8197.	Hartford.	Hartford N.B.
8220.	Kiowa.	First N.B.
8255.	Almeria.	First N.B.
8274.	Stockton.	Nat. State Bank.
8290.	Norcatur.	First N.B.
8307.	Harper.	First N.B.
8308.	Harper.	Security N.B.
8339.	Norton.	N.B. of Norton.
8357.	Alma.	Commercial N.B.
8369.	Moline.	Moline N.B.
8379.	Abilene.	Farmers' N.B.
8396.	Barnard.	First N.B.
8399.	Wellington.	N.B. of Commerce.
8418.	Pittsburg.	N.B. of Commerce.
8430.	Hutchinson.	Commercial N.B.
8467.	Conway Springs.	First N.B.
8525.	Longton.	First N.B.
8596.	Formoso.	First N.B.
8602.	Kansas City.	Bankers N.B.
8708.	Elk City.	People's N.B.
8796.	Fort Leavenworth.	Army N.B.
8803.	Pleasanton.	First N.B.
8808.	Scott City.	First N.B.
8883.	Stafford.	Farmers' N.B.
8974.	Wetmore.	First N.B.
9097.	Englewood.	First N.B.
9136.	Highland.	First N.B.
9157.	Burlingame.	Burlingame N.B.
9160.	Edmond.	First N.B.
9197.	Bonner Springs.	First N.B.
9225.	Dexter.	First N.B.
9232.	Hoisington.	First N.B.
9309.	Kansas City.	People's N.B.
9373.	Prairie View.	First N.B.
9384.	Natoma.	First N.B.
9465.	Thayer.	First N.B.
9559.	Belleville.	People's N.B.
9595.	Fowler.	First N.B.
9695.	Gypsum.	Gypsum Valley N.B.
9758.	Union Stock Yards, Wichita.	Union Stock Yards N.B.
9773.	Dighton.	First N.B.
9794.	Solomon.	Solomon N.B.
9911.	Longton.	Home N.B.
9934.	Mayetta.	First N.B.
10041.	Oakley.	First N.B.
10065.	Luray.	First N.B.
10161.	Spearville.	First N.B.
10195.	Alma.	Farmers' N.B.
10359.	Attica.	First N.B.
10390.	Topeka.	Farmers' N.B.
10557.	Greensburg.	Farmers' N.B.
10575.	Medicine Lodge.	First N.B.
10587.	Beattie.	First N.B.
10644.	Atwood.	Farmers' N.B.
10746.	Arkansas City.	Security N.B.
10749.	Victoria.	First N.B.
10765.	Hutchinson.	American N.B.
10776.	Phillipsburg.	Farmers' N.B.
10789.	Greenleaf.	Citizens' N.B.
10863.	Lewis.	First N.B.
10888.	Augusta.	American N.B.
10902.	Americus.	Farmers' N.B.
10918.	Dodge City.	Southwest N.B.
10971.	Summerfield.	First N.B.
10980.	Marion.	Farmers and Drovers' N.B.
10982.	Quinter.	First N.B.

Charter Number	City	Name of Bank
10987.	Ellis.	First N.B.
10994.	Potwin.	First N.B.
11010.	Wichita.	Union N.B.
11047.	Colby.	Citizens' N.B.
11056.	Baxter Springs.	American N.B.
11107.	Fairview.	Farmers' N.B.
11145.	Caldwell.	Home N.B.
11154.	Towanda.	First N.B.
11177.	Beaver, Quinter.	Farmers' N.B.
11186.	Saint Marys.	Farmers' N.B.
11187.	Elkhart.	First N.B.
11222.	Green.	First N.B.
11300.	Hugoton.	First N.B.
11310.	Axtell.	First N.B.
11316.	Pretty Prairie.	Farmers' N.B.
11318.	Downs.	Downs N.B.
11374.	Chetopa.	N.B. of Chetopa.
11398.	Topeka.	Kaw Valley N.B.
11405.	Atchison.	City N.B.
11464.	Haviland.	First N.B.
11488.	Coats.	First N.B.
11531.	Colony.	First N.B.
11536.	Mankato.	Farmers' N.B.
11537.	Parsons.	Farmers' N.B.
11576.	Oswego.	First N.B.
11707.	Great Bend.	Farmers' N.B.
11728.	Richmond.	First N.B.
11738.	Frankfort.	Citizens' N.B.
11773.	Florence.	First N.B.
11775.	Clyde.	Exchange N.B.
11781.	Emporia.	Commercial N.B. and Trust Co.
11796.	Holyrood.	First N.B.
11798.	Louisburg.	First N.B.
11811.	Hanover.	First N.B.
11816.	Valley Falls.	First N.B.
11822.	Harveyville.	First N.B.
11828.	Penalosa.	Farmers' N.B.
11855.	Collyer.	First N.B.
11857.	Saint Francis.	First N.B.
11860.	Kanorado.	First N.B.
11887.	Randall.	Randall N.B.
11889.	Wellington.	Farmers' N.B.
11916.	Frankfort.	First N.B.
11933.	Agra.	Farmers' N.B.
11945.	Bendena.	Farmers' N.B.
11968.	Palco.	First N.B.
12168.	Tribune.	First N.B.
12191.	McCune.	First N.B.
12346.	Wichita.	Southwest N.B.
12353.	Onaga.	First N.B.
12384.	Hope.	First N.B.
12439.	Osawatomie.	First N.B.
12442.	Fort Scott.	Fort Scott N.B.
12457.	Eureka.	First N.B.
12490.	Wichita.	Fourth N.B.
12694.	Hoisington.	Hokington N.B.
12740.	Topeka.	N.B. of Topeka.
12791.	Cunningham.	First N.B.
12821.	Tonganoxie.	First N.B.
12935.	Towanda.	Towanda N.B.
13033.	Neodesha.	Union N.B.
13076.	Colby.	Thomas County N.B.
13106.	Hutchinson.	Exchange N.B.
13329.	Cimarron.	First N.B.
13347.	Girard.	Girard N.B.
13406.	Liberal.	Peoples N.B.
13492.	Independence.	Security N.B.
13601.	Alma.	First N.B.
13801.	Kansas City.	Security N.B.
13924.	Independence.	Citizens N.B.
13990.	Garden City.	Garden N.B.
14048.	Lyons.	Chandler N.B.
14163.	Goodland.	First N.B.
14329.	Eureka.	Citizens N.B.

KENTUCKY

Charter Number	City	Name of Bank
109.	Louisville.	First N.B.
718.	Covington.	First N.B.
760.	Lexington.	First N.B.
777.	Louisville.	Second N.B.
788.	Louisville.	Louisville City N.B.
790.	Louisville.	Planters' N.B.
906.	Lexington.	First and City N.B.
995.	Winchester.	Clark County N.B.
1204.	Stanford.	N.B. of Stanford.
1309.	Richmond.	Farmers' N.B.
1493.	Lancaster.	N.B. of Lancaster.
1599.	Paducah.	First N.B.
1600.	Danville.	Central N.B.
1601.	Danville.	First N.B.
1615.	Henderson.	Henderson N.B.
1694.	Lebanon.	N.B. of Lebanon.
1702.	Maysville.	N.B. of Maysville.
1705.	Stanford.	Farmers' N.B.
1720.	Lexington.	Fayette N.B.
1728.	Richmond.	First N.B.
1748.	Somerset.	N.B. of Somerset.
1760.	Franklin.	First N.B.
1767.	Springfield.	First N.B.
1790.	Richmond.	Madison N.B.
1807.	Harrodsburg.	First N.B.
1831.	Nicholasville.	First N.B.
1835.	Versailles.	Commercial N.B.
1847.	Covington.	Liberty N.B.
1859.	Covington.	Covington City N.B.
1900.	Cynthiana.	N.B. of Cynthiana.
1908.	Louisville.	Kentucky N.B.
1931.	Monticello.	N.B. of Monticello.

Charter Number	City	Name of Bank
1963.	Owenton.	N.B. of Owen.
2010.	Ashland.	Ashland N.B.
2062.	Louisville.	German N.B.
2070.	Paducah.	American German N.B.
2093.	Paducah.	City N.B.
2148.	Winchester.	Citizens' N.B.
2149.	Bowling Green.	Nat Southern Kentucky Bank.
2150.	Lebanon.	Marion N.B.
2161.	Louisville.	Merchants' N.B.
2164.	Louisville.	Citizens Union Bank.
2169.	Russellville.	Logan County N.B.
2171.	Louisville.	Third N.B.
2185.	Mount Sterling.	Mount Sterling N.B.
2190.	Lawrenceburg.	Anderson County N.B.
2196.	New Castle.	N.B. of New Castle.
2206.	Caverna.	Caverna N.B.
2209.	Morganfield.	N.B. of Union City.
2216.	Mount Sterling.	Farmers' N.B.
2245.	Mayfield.	First N.B.
2276.	Newport.	First N.B.
2323.	Flemingsburg.	Fleming County N.B.
2374.	Richmond.	Second N.B.
2393.	Lexington.	Nat. Exchange Bank.
2409.	Danville.	Farmers' N.B.
2467.	Maysville.	First N.B.
2531.	Harrodsburg.	Mercer N.B.
2560.	Cynthiana.	Farmers' N.B.
2576.	Owtnsboro.	First N.B.
2592.	Carrollton.	First N.B.
2663.	Maysville.	State N.B.
2722.	Covington.	Farmers and Traders' N.B.
2726.	Newport.	American N.B.
2740.	Catlettsburg.	Catlettsburg N.B.
2784.	Louisville.	Fourth N.B.
2788.	Stanford.	First N.B.
2868.	Owenton.	First N.B.
2888.	Lancaster.	Citizens' N.B.
2901.	Lexington.	Second N.B.
2917.	Hustonville.	N.B. of Hustonville.
2927.	Georgetown.	First N.B.
2931.	Henderson.	Planters' N.B.
2968.	Owenton.	Farmers' N.B.
3042.	Elizabethtown.	First N.B.
3052.	Lexington.	Phoenix and Third N.B.
3064.	Princeton.	First N.B.
3074.	Carrollton.	Carrollton N.B.
3290.	Winchester.	Winchester N.B.
3317.	Danville.	Boyle N.B.
3381.	Danville.	Citizens' N.B.
3832.	Somerset.	First N.B.
3856.	Hopkinsville.	First N.B.
3942.	Lexington.	Phoenix N.B.
3943.	London.	First N.B.
3944.	Ashland.	Second N.B.
3954.	Stanford.	Lincoln N.B.
3988.	Lebanon.	Citizens' N.B.
4006.	Owensboro.	Nat. Deposit Bank.
4090.	Frankfort.	State N.B.
4091.	Frankfort.	Frankfort N.B.
4145.	Louisville.	Union N.B.
4200.	Catlettsburg.	Big Sandy N.B.
4201.	Middlesborough.	First N.B.
4217.	Clay City.	Clay City N.B.
4260.	Covington.	Citizens' N.B.
4271.	Lebanon.	Farmers' N.B.
4356.	Greenville.	First N.B.
4430.	Richmond.	Richmond N.B.
4465.	Hickman.	Farmers and Merchants' N.B.
4559.	Ashland.	Merchants' N.B.
4563.	Fulton.	First N.B.
4598.	Pineville.	First N.B.
4612.	Augusta.	Farmers' N.B.
4616.	Augusta.	First N.B.
4765.	Newport.	Newport N.B.
4819.	Glasgow.	First N.B.
4956.	Louisville.	American-Southern N.B.
5033.	Mayfield.	City N.B.
5132.	Stanford.	Lincoln County N.B.
5161.	Louisville.	Louisville N.B.
5195.	Louisville.	Southern N.B.
5257.	Princeton.	Farmers' N.B.
5312.	Louisville.	N.B. of Kentucky.
5314.	Leitchfield.	Grayson County N.B.
5323.	Ludlow.	First N.B.
5376.	Frankfort.	Nat. Branch Bank of Kentucky.
5443.	Wickliffe.	First N.B.
5468.	Somerset.	Somerset Nat. Banking Co.
5486.	Glasgow.	Trigg N.B.
5792.	Hartford.	First N.B.
5881.	Somerset.	Farmers' N.B.
5900.	Bowling Green.	Citizens' N.B.
5959.	Carlisle.	First N.B.
6028.	Elizabethtown.	First Hardin N.B.
6100.	Paintsville.	Paintsville N.B.
6129.	Mount Sterling.	Traders' N.B.
6160.	Mount Sterling.	Montgomery N.B.
6167.	Fulton.	City N.B.
6244.	Sturgis.	First N.B.
6248.	Latonia.	First N.B.
6262.	Barbourville.	First N.B.
6323.	Paris.	First N.B.
6342.	Campbellsville.	Taylor N.B.
6419.	Monticello.	Citizens' N.B.
6546.	Russellville.	Citizens' N.B.
6622.	Pikesville.	First N.B.
6769.	Columbia.	First N.B.
6834.	Mayfield.	Farmers N.B.

Charter Number	City	Name of Bank
6872.	Glasgow.	Third N.B.
6894.	Hodgenville.	Farmers' N.B.
7012.	Dry Ridge.	First N.B.
7030.	Pikeville.	Pikeville N.B.
7037.	Greenup.	First N.B.
7086.	Middlesborough.	N.B. of Middleborough.
7110.	Louisa.	First N.B.
7122.	Louisa.	Louisa N.B.
7164.	Paintsville.	Citizens' N.B.
7174.	Williamsburg.	First N.B.
7215.	Pineville.	Bell N.B.
7242.	Sebree.	First N.B.
7254.	Prestonsburg.	First N.B.
7281.	Olive Hill.	Olive Hill N.B.
7284.	Barbourville.	N.B.of John A. Black.
7402.	Franklin.	Farmers and Merchants' N.B.
7457.	Louisville.	Continental N.B.
7490.	Morganfield.	Morganfield N.B.
7492.	Eddyville.	First N.B.
7497.	Lawrenceburg.	Lawrenceburg N.B.
7544.	Corbin.	First N.B.
7593.	Morehead.	Lenora N.B.
7602.	Horse Cave.	First N.B.
7605.	Manchester.	First N.B.
7653.	Richmond.	Citizens' N.B.
7751.	Beatyville.	N.B. of Beatyville.
7804.	Bowling Green.	Bowling Green N.B.
7890.	London.	N.B. of London.
7891.	Cannel City.	Morgan County N.B.
7916.	West Liberty.	First N.B.
7919.	Cave City.	H. Y. Davis N.B.
8110.	Covington.	Merchants' N.B.
8229.	Central City.	First N.B.
8258.	Hazard.	First N.B.
8331.	Bardwell.	First N.B.
8386.	Madisonville.	Morton N.B.
8435.	Berea.	Berea N.B.
8439.	Glasgow.	Citizens' N.B.
8451.	Madisonville.	Farmers' N.B.
8564.	Covington.	Commercial N.B.
8579.	Georgetown.	Georgetown N.B.
8599.	Scottsville.	First N.B.
8604.	Lawrenceburg.	Anderson N.B.
8622.	Uniontown.	First N.B.
8792.	Russell.	First N.B.
8814.	Adairville.	First N.B.
8830.	Brooksville.	First N.B.
8862.	Lawrenceburg.	Witherspoon N.B.
8903.	Burnside.	First N.B.
8905.	Salyersville.	Salyersville N.B.
8943.	Clay.	Farmers' N.B.
9098.	Clinton.	First N.B.
9241.	Louisville.	N.B. of Commerce.
9320.	Jackson.	First N.B.
9356.	Scottsville.	Allen County N.B.
9365.	Bowling Green.	American N.B.
9456.	Owensboro.	United States N.B.
9561.	Maysville.	N.B. of Maysville Assn.
9602.	Catlettsburg.	Kentucky N.B.
9634.	Corbin.	Whitley N.B.
9708.	Providence.	Union N.B.
9722.	Glasgow.	Farmers' N.B.
9791.	Harlan.	First N.B.
9832.	Richmond.	Southern N.B.
9842.	Russellville.	Nat. Deposit Bank.
9843.	Hodgenville.	La Rue N.B.
9880.	Wilmore.	First N.B.
10062.	Jenkins.	First N.B.
10254.	East Bernstadt.	First N.B.
10433.	Whitesburg.	First N.B.
10448.	Bowling Green.	Warren N.B.
10779.	Murray.	First N.B.
11336.	Munfordville.	N.B. of Munfordville.
11348.	Russell Springs.	First N.B.
11538.	Buffalo.	First N.B.
11544.	Somerset.	Citizens' N.B.
11548.	Dawson Springs.	First N.B.
11589.	Bowling Green.	Liberty N.B.
11890.	Stone.	First N.B.
11944.	Pikeville.	Day and Night N.B.
11947.	Falmouth.	First N.B.
11988.	Fleming.	First N.B.
12202.	Wallins Creek.	Wallins N.B.
12243.	Harlan.	Citizens' N.B.
12293.	Ashland.	Third N.B.
12295.	Harlan.	Harlan N.B.
12456.	Scottsville.	Farmers' N.B.
12649.	Lynch.	Lynch N.B.
12961.	Paducah.	Peoples N.B.
12982.	Grayson.	First N.B.
13023.	Paintsville.	Second N.B.
13024.	Elizabethtown.	Union N.B.
13248.	Hazard.	First N.B.
13479.	Hodgenville.	Lincoln N.B.
13612.	Harrodsburg.	Mercer County N.B.
13651.	Glasgow.	New Farmers N.B.
13757.	Henderson.	First N.B.
13763.	Paintsville.	First N.B.
13906.	Barbourville.	Union N.B.
13983.	Henderson.	Ohio Valley N.B.
14026.	Owenton.	First N.B.
14039.	Stanford.	First N.B.
14076.	Paris.	N.B. and Trust Co.
14138.	Owensboro.	National Deposit Bank.
14259.	Clinton.	First N.B.
14320.	Louisville.	Liberty N.B. and Trust Co.

LOUISIANA

Charter Number	City	Name of Bank
162.	New Orleans.	First N.B.
1591.	New Orleans.	Germania N.B.
1626.	New Orleans.	Louisiana N.B.
1747.	New Orleans.	Teutonia N.B.
1774.	New Orleans.	State N.B.
1778.	New Orleans.	New Orleans N.B.
1796.	New Orleans.	Union N.B.
1825.	New Orleans.	New Orleans N.B. Assn.
1898.	New Orleans.	Mutual N.B.
1937.	New Orleans.	Crescent City N.B.
2086.	New Orleans.	Hibernia N.B.
2633.	Baton Rouge.	First N.B.
3069.	New Orleans.	Whitney-Central N.B.
3595.	Shreveport.	First N.B.
3606.	Shreveport.	Commercial N.B.
3671.	New Iberia.	New Iberia N.B.
3692.	Monroe.	Ouachita N.B.
3978.	New Orleans.	American N.B.
4082.	Monroe.	Monroe N.B.
4154.	Lake Charles.	First N.B.
4216.	Homer.	Homer N.B.
4337.	New Orleans.	Southern N.B.
4340.	Opelousas.	First N.B.
4524.	New Iberia.	People's N.B.
4555.	Franklin.	First N.B.
5021.	Alexandria.	First N.B.
5023.	Lafayette.	First N.B.
5157.	Lake Charles.	Calcasieu N.B.
5520.	Crowley.	First N.B.
5649.	New Orleans.	Canal-Commercial N.B.
5752.	Shreveport.	Citizens' N.B.
5807.	Abbeville.	First N.B.
5843.	Patterson.	First N.B.
5844.	Shreveport.	Shreveport N.B.
5966.	Jennings.	First N.B.
6088.	Lake Charles.	Lake Charles N.B.
6264.	Leesville.	First N.B.
6291.	Lake Providence.	First N.B. of Lake Providence.
6360.	Welsh.	First N.B.
6418.	Welsh.	Welsh N.B.
6801.	Morgan City.	First N.B.
6858.	New Iberia.	State N.B.
6920.	Opelousas.	Opelousas N.B.
7047.	Lake Arthur.	First N.B.
7169.	New Roads.	First N.B.
7232.	Mansfield.	First N.B.
7476.	Arcadia.	First N.B.
7498.	New Orleans.	People's N.B.
7765.	Jennings.	State N.B.
7768.	Jeanerette.	First N.B.
7876.	New Orleans.	German American N.B.
8440.	Shreveport.	American N.B.
8654.	Monroe.	Ouachita N.B.
8677.	Eunice.	First N.B.
8734.	New Orleans.	Hibernia N.B.
8959.	Bogalusa.	First N.B.
9237.	De Ridder.	First N.B.
9834.	Baton Rouge.	Louisiana N.B.
9872.	Opelousas.	Planters' N.B.
10049.	Gibsland.	First N.B.
10153.	Monroe.	Union N.B.
10544.	Minden.	First N.B.
10588.	Ville Platte.	First N.B.
10700.	Crowley.	First N.B. of Acadia Parish.
10761.	Winnfield.	First N.B.
10836.	Lake Charles.	Calcasieu N.B. of S.W. La.
10870.	Shreveport.	City N.B.
10912.	Delhi.	Macon Ridge N.B.
11242.	Monroe.	Citizens' N.B.
11254.	Longville.	First N.B.
11324.	Oberlin.	First N.B.
11450.	Jennings.	Jennings N.B.
11521.	Shreveport.	Exchange N.B.
11541.	Elton.	First N.B.
11621.	Homer.	American N.B.
11638.	Homer.	Commercial N.B.
11650.	Oak Grove.	First N.B.
11669.	Mansfield.	American N.B.
11795.	Ruston.	First N.B.
11977.	Hammond.	Citizens' N.B.
12523.	Crowley.	First N.B.
12527.	Pineville.	First N.B.
12923.	Tallulah.	Madison N.B.
13169.	Gibsland.	First N.B.
13209.	Lafayette.	Commercial N.B.
13345.	Thibodaux.	Lafourche N.B.
13573.	Lake Charles.	Calcasieu N.B.
13648.	Shreveport.	Commercial N.B.
13655.	Monroe.	Ouachita N.B.
13688.	New Orleans.	Hibernia N.B.
13689.	New Orleans.	N.B. of Commerce.
13732.	Gretna.	First N.B. of Jefferson Parish.
13737.	Baton Rouge.	City N.B.
13839.	Norco.	St. Charles N.B.
13851.	Morgan City.	Citizens' N.B.
14086.	Hammond.	Citizens' N.B.
14168.	De Riddef.	First N.B.
14225.	Delhi.	First N.B.
14228.	Lake Charles.	Calcasieu-Marine N.B.
14281.	Donaldson.	First N.B.
14328.	Arcadia.	First N.B.

MAINE

Charter Number	City	Name of Bank
61.	Bath.	First N.B.
112.	Bangor.	First N.B.
154.	Auburn.	First N.B.
192.	Brunswick.	First N.B.
221.	Portland.	First N.B.
239.	Skowhegan.	First N.B.
298.	Skowhegan.	Second N.B.
306.	Bangor.	Second N.B.
310.	Hallowell.	First N.B.
330.	Lewiston.	First N.B.
367.	Augusta.	First N.B.
406.	Augusta.	Freeman's N.B.
446.	Damariscotta.	First N.B.
494.	Bath.	Bath N.B.
498.	Augusta.	First Nat Granite Bank.
518.	Bangor.	Kenduskeag N.B.
532.	Hallowell.	Northern N.B.
553.	Winthrop.	N.B. of Winthrop.
624.	Hallowell.	American N.B.
662.	Richmond.	First N.B.
740.	Gardiner.	Oakland N.B.
744.	Waldoboro.	Waldoboro N.B.
761.	Bath.	Lincoln N.B.
762.	Waterville.	Ticonic N.B.
782.	Bath.	Marine N.B.
798.	Waterville.	Waterville N.B.
840.	Belfast.	Belfast N.B.
878.	Portland.	Second N.B.
880.	Waterville.	People's N.B.
890.	Thomaston.	Thomaston N.B.
901.	Farmington.	Sandy River N.B.
909.	Richmond.	Richmond N.B.
939.	Gardiner.	Cubbossee N.B.
941.	Portland.	Canal N.B.
944.	Bowdoinham.	Nat. Village Bank.
953.	Damariscotta.	Newcastle N.B.
959.	South Berwick.	South Berwick N.B.
1023.	Portland.	Merchants' N.B.
1041.	Bath.	Sagadahock N.B.
1060.	Portland.	Casco N.B.
1079.	Bucksport.	Bucksport N.B.
1089.	Biddeford.	First N.B.
1095.	Bangor.	Traders' N.B.
1108.	Waldoboro.	Medomak N.B.
1118.	Brunswick.	Union N.B.
1134.	Orono.	Orono N.B.
1142.	Thomaston.	Georges N.B.
1174.	Gardiner.	Gardiner N.B.
1254.	Kennebunk.	Ocean N.B.
1315.	Brunswick.	Pejebscot N.B.
1425.	Calais.	Calais N.B.
1437.	Bangor.	Merchants' N.B.
1446.	Rockland.	Rockland N.B.
1451.	Portland.	Nat. Traders' Bank.
1495.	Eastport.	Frontier N.B.
1511.	Portland.	Cumberland N.B.
1523.	North Berwick.	North Berwick N.B.
1528.	Saco.	York N.B.
1535.	Saco.	Saco N.B.
1549.	Wiscasset.	First N.B.
1575.	Biddeford.	Biddeford N.B.
1687.	Bangor.	Farmers' N.B.
1956.	Norway.	Norway N.B.
2089.	Bangor.	Veazie N.B.
2097.	Rockland.	Lime Rock N.B.
2175.	Fairfield.	First N.B.
2231.	Oakland.	Messalonskee N.B.
2259.	Dexter.	First N.B.
2260.	Lewiston.	Manufacturers' N.B.
2267.	Phillips.	Union N.B.
2270.	Auburn.	Nat. Shoe and Leather Bank.
2306.	Waterville.	Merchants' N.B.
2311.	Camden.	Camden N.B.
2371.	Rockland.	North N.B.
2642.	Searsport.	Searsport N.B.
2743.	Bath.	First N.B.
2749.	Houlton.	First N.B.
2785.	Limerick.	Limerick N.B.
3219.	Gardiner.	Merrhants' N.B.
3247.	Hallowell.	Hallowell N.B.
3271.	Augusta.	Augusta N.B.
3690.	Dover.	Kineo N.B.
3804.	Ellsworth.	Liberty N.B.
3814.	Ellsworth.	First N.B.
3827.	Presque Isle.	Presque Isle N.B.
3941.	Bar Harbor.	First N.B.
4128.	Portland.	Portland N.B.
4188.	Pittsfield.	Pittsfield N.B.
4252.	Houlton.	Farmers' N.B.
4459.	Farmington.	First N.B.
4647.	Madison.	First N.B.
4780.	Guilford.	First N.B.
4781.	Fort Fairfield.	Fort Fairfield N.B.
4806.	Belfast.	People's N.B.
4844.	York Village.	York County N.B.
4868.	Portland.	Chapman N.B.
4957.	Phillips.	Phillips N.B.
4973.	Fairfield.	N.B. of Fairfield.
5050.	Sanford.	Sanford N.B.
5598.	Boothbay Harbor.	First N.B.
5861.	Farmington.	People's N.B.
6190.	Caribou.	Caribou N.B.
6231.	Camden.	Megunticook N.B.
6287.	Rumford.	Rumford N.B.
7586.	Belfast.	City N.B.
7613.	Bethel.	Bethel N.B.
7835.	Springvale.	Springvale N.B.
9181.	Bridgton.	Bridgton N.B.
9609.	Gardiner.	N.B. of Gardiner.
9826.	Kezar Falls.	Kezar Falls N.B.
10628.	Van Buren.	First N.B.
11403.	Fort Kent.	First N.B.
11462.	Machias.	Machias N.B.
13710.	Portland.	N.B. of Commerce.
13716.	Portland.	First N.B.
13730.	Springvale.	Springvale N.B.
13734.	Rockland.	First N.B.
13750.	Norway.	Norway N.B.

Charter Number	City	Name of Bank
13762.	Belfast.	First N.B.
13768.	Presque Isle.	Northern N.B.
13769.	Waterville.	First N.B.
13777.	Pittsfield.	First N.B.
13786.	Calais.	N.B. of Calais.
13827.	Houlton.	Farmers N.B.
13843.	Fort Fairfield.	First N.B.
14224.	Fort Kent.	First N.B.
14303.	Ellsworth.	Liberty N.B.

MARYLAND

Charter Number	City	Name of Bank
204.	Baltimore.	First N.B.
381.	Cumberland.	First N.B.
414.	Baltimore.	Second N.B.
742.	Westminster.	First N.B.
747.	New Windsor.	First N.B.
814.	Baltimore.	Third N.B.
826.	Baltimore.	Traders' N.B.
1109.	Baltimore.	Nat. Exchange Bank.
1138.	Frederick.	Central N.B.
1211.	Port Deposit.	Cecil N.B.
1236.	Elkton.	N.B. of Elkton.
1244.	Annapolis.	Farmers N.B.
1252.	Baltimore.	Nat. Farmers and Planters' Bank.
1267.	Frederick.	Farmers and Mechanics' N.B.
1303.	Baltimore.	Commercial and Farmers' N.B.
1325.	Baltimore.	Western N.B.
1336.	Baltimore.	Merchants N.B.
1337.	Baltimore.	Farmers and Merchants' N.B.
1384.	Baltimore.	Citizens' N.B.
1412.	Frostburg.	First N.B.
1413.	Baltimore.	Merchants' N.B.
1431.	Hagerstown.	First N.B.
1432.	Baltimore.	N.B. of Baltimore.
1434.	Easton.	Easton N.B. of Maryland.
1449.	Frederick.	Frederick County.
1489.	Baltimore.	Nat. Union Bank
1500.	Chestertown.	Kent N.B.
1519.	Cumberland.	Second N.B.
1526.	Westminster.	Farmers and Mechanics' N.B.
1551.	Williamsport.	Washington County N.B.
1589.	Frederick.	First N.B.
1596.	Westminster.	Union N.B.
1797.	Baltimore.	Central N.B.
2341.	Centreville.	Centreville N.B. of Md.
2416.	Cumberland.	Third N.B.
2453.	Baltimore.	Nat. Marine Bank.
2481.	Rising Sun.	N.B. of Rising Sun.
2498.	Cambridge.	N.B. of Cambridge.
2499.	Baltimore.	Drovers and Mechanics' N.B.
2547.	Denton.	Denton N.B.
2623.	Baltimore.	Manufacturers' N.B.
2797.	Bel Air.	Harford N.B.
3010.	Havre de Grace.	First N.B.
3187.	Rockville.	Montgomery County N.B.
3205.	Centreville.	Queen Anne's N.B.
3250.	Salisbury.	Salisbury N.B.
3305.	Chestertown.	Chestertown N.B.
3476.	Frederick.	Citizens' N.B.
3585.	Ellicott City.	Patapsco N.B.
3588.	Towson.	Towson N.B.
3783.	Snow Hill.	First N.B.
3933.	Bel Air.	Second N.B.
4046.	Easton.	Farmers and Mechanics' N.B.
4049.	Hagerstown.	Second N.B.
4085.	Cambridge.	Dorchester N.B.
4149.	Frostburg.	First N.B.
4162.	Elkton.	Second N.B.
4191.	Pocomoke City.	Pocomoke City N.B.
4218.	Baltimore.	Nat. Howard Bank
4285.	Baltimore.	N.B. of Commerce.
4327.	Chestertown.	Second N.B.
4364.	Laurel.	Citizens' N.B.
4496.	Cockeysville.	N.B. of Cockeysville.
4518.	Baltimore.	American N.B.
4530.	Baltimore.	Equitable N.B.
4533.	Baltimore.	Continental N.B.
4608.	Gaithersburg.	First N.B.
4634.	Aberdeen.	First N.B.
4799.	Canton,Baltimore.	Canton N.B.
4856.	Hagerstown.	People's N.B.
4926.	Frostburg.	Citizens' N.B.
5093.	Catonsville.	First N.B.
5122.	Denton.	People's N.B.
5331.	Midland.	First N.B.
5332.	Cumberland.	Citizens' N.B.
5445.	Havre de Grace.	Citizens' N.B.
5471.	Upper Marlboro.	First N.B. of Southern Maryland.
5561.	Sandy Spring.	First N.B.
5610.	Port Deposit.	N.B. of Port Deposit.
5623.	Oakland.	First N.B.
5776.	Oakland.	Maryland N.B.
5829.	Thurmont.	Thurmont N.B.
5831.	Westernport.	Citizens' N.B.
5880.	Cambridge.	Farmers and Merchants' N.B.
5943.	Grantsville.	First N.B.
5984.	Baltimore.	Old Town N.B.
6144.	Mount Savage.	First N.B.
6196.	Friendsville.	First N.B.
6202.	Pocomoke.	Citizens' N.B.
6297.	Snow Hill.	Commercial N.B.
6399.	Barton.	First N.B.
6588.	Oakland.	Garrett N.B.
6606.	Leonardtown.	First N.B. of Saint Mary's.
6761.	Salisbury.	People's N.B.
6845.	Chesapeake City.	N.B. of Chesapeake City.
7064.	North East.	First N.B.
7160.	Mount Airy.	First N.B.
7519.	Hyattsville.	First N.B.
7732.	Lonaconing.	First N.B.
7859.	Hancock.	First N.B.
8244.	Brunswick.	Pdople's N.B.
8272.	Kitzmillerville.	Blaine N.B.
8302.	Kitzmiller, Kitzmillerville.	First N.B.
8319.	Berlin.	First N.B.
8381.	Towson.	Second N.B.
8456.	La Plata.	Southern Maryland N.B.
8578.	Sykesville.	First N.B.
8587.	Sykesville.	Sykesville N.B.
8799.	Woodbine.	Woodbine N.B.
8860.	Poolesville.	Poolesville N.B.
8867.	Pikesville.	Pikesville N.B.
9066.	Union Bridge.	First N.B.
9238.	Monrovia.	First N.B.
9429.	Mechanicsville.	N.B. of Mechanicsville.
9444.	Parkton.	First N.B.
9469.	White Hall.	White Hall N.B.
9474.	Bel Air.	Farmers and Merchants' N.B.
9639.	Baltimore.	Nat. City Bank.
9699.	Clear Spring.	Clear Spring N.B.
9744.	Chestertown.	Third N.B.
9755.	Hampstead.	First N.B.
9830.	Silver Spring.	Silver Spring N.B.
10210.	Healdsburg.	First N.B.
11193.	Perryville.	N.B. of Perryville.
11207.	Baltimore.	Nat. Central Bank
12443.	Mount Rainier.	First N.B.
12590.	Hagerstown.	Nicodemus N.B.
13147.	Catonsville.	Catonsville N.B.
13680.	Bel Air.	First N.B.
13745.	Baltimore.	Baltimore N.B.
13747.	Frederick.	Frederick County N.B.
13773.	Ellicott City.	Patapsco N.B.
13776.	Oakland.	Garrett N.B.
13798.	Chestertown.	First N.B.
13840.	Port Deposit.	Cecil N.B.
13853.	Hancock.	Peoples N.B.
13867.	Parkton.	First N.B.
13979.	Frostburg.	Frostburg N.B.
14044.	Brunswick.	Peoples N.B.
14106.	Pocomoke City.	Citizens N.B.

MASSACHUSETTS

Charter Number	City	Name of Bank
14.	Springfield.	First N.B.
79.	Worcester.	First N.B.
96.	Barre.	First N.B.
156.	Dorchester.	First N.B.
158.	Marlboro.	First N.B.
181.	Springfield.	Second N.B.
188.	Grafton.	First N.B.
190.	Westfield.	First N.B.
200.	Boston.	First N.B.
256.	Fall River.	First N.B.
261.	New Bedford.	First N.B.
268.	Merrimac.	First N.B.
279.	Newburyport.	First N.B.
308.	Springfield.	Third N.B.
322.	Boston.	Second N.B.
327.	Winchendon.	First N.B.
331.	Lowell.	First N.B.
359.	Boston.	Third N.B.
379.	Boston.	N.B. of the Republic.
383.	Northampton.	First N.B.
393.	Amherst.	First N.B.
407.	Salem.	First N.B.
408.	Boston.	Boston N.B.
416.	Easton, N. Easton.	First N.B.
418.	Northampton.	Hampshire County N.B.
421.	Westborcr.	First N.B.
428.	Easthampton.	First N.B.
433.	Cambridge.	First N.B.
439.	Fall River.	Second N.B.
440.	Clinton.	First N.B.
442.	Worcester.	Worcester N.B.
449.	East Cambridge.	Cambridge N.B.
455.	Worcester.	Central N.B.
460.	Boston.	Nat. Hide and Leather Bank.
462.	Adams.	First N.B.
474.	Greenfield.	First N.B.
475.	Boston.	Merchants N.B.
476.	Worcester.	City N.B.
481.	Haverhill.	First N.B.
484.	Haverhill.	Haverhill N.B.
488.	Newton.	First N.B.
490.	Fairhaven.	N.B. of Fairhaven.
503.	Monson.	Monson N.B.
505.	Boston.	Market N.B.
506.	Lowell.	Merchants' N.B.
510.	Weymouth.	Union N.B.
513.	Leominster.	First N.B.
514.	Boston.	Blackstone N.B.
515.	Boston.	N.B. of Redemption.
516.	Yarmouth, Yarmouth Port.	First N.B.
517.	Quincy.	Nat. MountBank
524.	Boston.	Continental N.B.
525.	Boston.	North N.B.
528.	Framingham.	Framingham N.B.
529.	Boston.	Nat. Exchange Bank.
533.	Chelsea.	First N.B.
536.	Boston.	Eliot N.B.
545.	Boston.	Boylston N.B.
549.	Gloucester.	First N.B.
551.	Boston.	Broadway N.B.
554.	Boston.	N.B. of Commerce.
558.	Randolph.	Randolph N.B.
572.	Millbury.	Millbury N.B.
578.	Boston.	Howard N.B.
582.	Boston.	Shawmut N.B.
583.	Clinton.	Lancaster N.B.
584.	Newburyport.	Mechanicks' N.B.
588.	Maiden.	First N.B.
589.	Haverhill.	Essex N.B.
590.	Fall River.	Fall River N.B.
594.	Danvers.	First N.B.
595.	Boston.	People's N.B.
601.	Boston.	Washington N.B.
603.	Boston.	New England N.B.
609.	Boston.	Nat. City Bank.
612.	Fall River.	Massasoit N.B.
614.	East Cambridge.	Lechmere N.B.
615.	Boston.	Nat. Rockland Bank of Roxbury.
616.	Peabody.	Warren N.B.
618.	South Weymouth.	First N.B.
625.	Boston.	Tremont N.B.
626.	Hopkinton.	Hopkinton N.B.
628.	Ware.	Ware N.B.
629.	Boston.	Suffolk N.B.
633.	Haverhill.	Merrimack N.B.
634.	Boston.	Asiatic N.B.
635.	Boston.	Bunker Hill N.B. Charlestown.
638.	Lynn.	First N.B.
643.	Boston.	Fourth Atlantic N.B.
646.	Boston.	Shoe and Leather N.B.
647.	Salem.	Naumkeag N.B.
654.	Boston.	Atlas N.B.
663.	Canton.	Neponset N.B.
665.	Boston.	Freeman's N.B.
669.	Dedham.	Dedham N.B.
672.	Boston.	N.B. of North America.
676.	Marblehead.	Nat. Granite Bank.
677.	Boston.	Maverick N.B.
679.	Fall River.	Pocasset N.B.
684.	Milton.	Blue Hill N.B.
688.	Waltham.	Waltham N.B.
690.	New Bedford.	N.B. of Commerce.
691.	Salem.	Mercantile N.B.
697.	Lynn.	Nat. City Bank
702.	Fitchburg.	Rollstone N.B.
704.	Salem.	Salem N.B.
708.	Athol.	Millers River N.B.
712.	Harwich.	Cape Cod N.B.
714.	Nantucket.	Pacific N.B.
716.	Boston.	Mount Vernon N.B.
726.	Salem.	Merchants' N.B.
731.	Cambridge.	Charles River N.B.
736.	Provincetown.	First N.B.
743.	New Bedford.	Mechanics' N.B.
746.	Woburn.	First N.B.
753.	Lowell.	Railroad N.B.
764.	Oxford.	Oxford N.B.
765.	Worcester.	Citizens' N.B.
766.	Taunton.	Bristol County N.B.
767.	Marblehead.	Marblehead N.B.
769.	Whitinsville.	Whitinsville N.B.
770.	Cambridge.	Nat. City Bank.
778.	Boston.	Hamilton N.B.
779.	Plymouth.	Plymouth N.B.
781.	Lowell.	Wimesit N.B.
789.	Newton.	Newton N.B.
799.	New Bedford.	Merchants' N.B.
802.	Holliston.	Holliston N.B.
805.	Townsend.	Townsend N.B.
806.	Boston.	Nat. Market Bank of Brighton.
817.	Salem.	Nat. Exchange Bank
824.	Grafton.	Grafton N.B.
832.	Quincy.	Nat. Granite Bank.
833.	Concord.	Concord N.B.
847.	Boston.	Faneuil Hall N.B.
866.	Milford.	Milford N.B.
884.	Gardner.	First N.B.
885.	Lee.	Lee N.B.
895.	Conway.	Conway N.B.
899.	Gloucester.	Cape Ann N.B.
918.	Leicester.	Leicester N.B.
920.	Greenfield.	Franklin County N.B.
924.	Fall River.	Metacomet N.B.
932.	Boston.	Mechanics' N.B.
934.	Southbridge.	Southbridge N.B.
936.	Boston..	Globe N.B.
947.	Taunton.	Machinists' N.B.
957.	Taunton.	Taunton N.B.
958.	Peabody.	South Danvers N.B.
960.	Lowell.	Prescott N.B.
969.	Beverly.	Beverly N.B.
974.	Boston.	Massachusetts N.B.
982.	Springfield.	John Hancock N.B.
985.	Boston.	Nat. Union Bank.
986.	Lowell.	Appleton N.B.
987.	Springfield.	Pynchon N.B.
988.	Springfield.	Chicopee N.B.
993.	Boston.	Nat. Eagle Bank.
996.	Plymouth.	Old Colony N.B.
1005.	Boston.	Monument N.B.
1011.	Newburyport.	Ocean N.B.
1014.	Lawrence.	Bay State N.B.
1015.	Boston.	Old Boston N.B.
1018.	Northampton.	Northampton N.B.
1022.	Uxbridge.	Blackstone N.B.
1028.	Boston.	State N.B.

Charter Number	City	Name of Bank
1029.	Boston.	Columbian N.B.
1047.	Newburyport.	Merchants' N.B.
1048.	Lawrence.	Nat. Pemberton Bank.
1049.	Amesbury.	Powow River N.B.
1055.	Springfield.	Agawam N.B.
1056.	Chicopee.	First N.B.
1073.	Worcester.	Quinsigamond N.B.
1077.	Fitchburg.	Fitchburg N.B.
1082.	Pittsfield.	Agricultural N.B.
1085.	Wrentham.	N.B. of Wrentham.
1099.	Boston.	N.B. of Brighton.
1107.	Hyannis.	First N.B.
1119.	Hingham.	Hingham N.B.
1129.	Andover.	Andover N.B.
1135.	Worcester.	Mechanics' N.B.
1144.	Shellburne Falls.	Shellburne Falls N.B.
1162.	Gloucester.	Gloucester N.B.
1170.	Stockbridge.	Housatonic N.B.
1194.	Rockport.	Rockport N.B.
1201.	Lynn.	Central N.B.
1203.	Great Barrington.	Nat. Mahaiwe Bank.
1207.	Franklin.	Franklin N.B.
1210.	North Adams.	North Adams N.B.
1228.	Cambridge.	Cambridgeport N.B.
1246.	Holyoke.	Hadley Falls N.B.
1260.	Pittsfield.	Pittsfield N.B.
1274.	Tisbury, Vineyard Haven.	Martha's Vineyard N.B.
1279.	Northborough.	Northborough N.B.
1288.	Fall River.	Nat. Union Bank.
1295.	Boston.	Nat. Revere Bank.
1320.	Falmouth.	Falmouth N.B.
1329.	Lowell.	Old Lowell N.B.
1367.	Westfield.	Hampton N.B.
1386.	Abington.	Abington N.B.
1439.	Adams.	Berkshire N.B.
1440.	Wareham.	N.B. of Wareham.
1442.	Boston.	Hancock N.B.
1455.	Wakefield.	Wakefield N.B.
1469.	Boston.	Everett N.B.
1485.	Methuen.	N.B. of Methuen.
1527.	Boston.	Webster and Atlas N.B.
1604.	Attleborough, N. Attleborough.	Attleborough N.B.
1675.	Boston.	Nat. Security Bank.
1699.	Boston.	Kidder Nat. Gold Bank.
1827.	Boston.	N.B. of the Commonwealth.
1939.	Holyoke.	Holyoke N.B.
1962.	Lawrence.	Lawrence N.B.
1993.	Boston.	Eleventh Ward N.B.
2058.	Turners Falls.	Crocker N.B.
2103.	Boston.	Central N.B.
2107.	Natick.	Natick N.B.
2108.	Watertown.	Union Market N.B.
2111.	Boston.	Manufacturers' N.B.
2112.	Boston.	First Ward N.B.
2113.	Ashburnham.	First N.B.
2152.	Brockton.	Home N.B.
2153.	Fitchburg.	Safety Fund N.B.
2172.	Athol, Athol Center.	Athol N.B.
2232.	Attleboro.	First N.B.
2255.	Orange.	Orange N.B.
2262.	New Bedford.	Citizens' N.B.
2264.	Greenfield.	Packard N.B.
2265.	Fitchburg.	Wachusett N.B.
2273.	Worcester.	Security N.B.
2275.	Milford.	Home N.B.
2277.	Boston.	Fourth N.B.
2284.	GaFdner.	Westminster N.B.
2288.	Spencer.	Spencer N.B.
2289.	Boston.	Metropolitan N.B.
2292.	Gloucester.	City N.B.
2297.	Georgetown.	Georgetown N.B.
2304.	Boston.	Winthrop N.B.
2312.	Webster.	First N.B.
2324.	Palmer.	Palmer N.B.
2347.	Lawrence.	Pacific N.B.
2373.	Boston.	Pacific N.B.
2396.	North Adams.	Berkshire N.B.
2404.	Marlborough.	People's N.B.
2430.	Holyoke.	City N.B.
2433.	Springfield.	City N.B.
2435.	Springfield.	Chapin N.B.
2485.	South Framingham.	South Framingham N.B.
2504.	Brockton.	Brockton N.B.
2525.	Pittsfield.	Third N.B.
2563.	Lynn.	Nat. Security Bank.
2618.	Hudson.	Hudson N.B.
2685.	Barre.	First N.B.
2699.	Worcester.	First N.B.
2770.	Marlboro.	First N.B.
2846.	Boston.	Lincoln N.B.
2929.	Amesbury.	Amesbury N.B.
3073.	Ayer.	First N.B.
3092.	Williamstown.	Williamstown N.B.
3128.	Holyoke.	Home N.B.
3204.	Leominster.	Leominster N.B.
3365.	North Attleborough.	North Attleborough N.B.
3429.	Lynn.	Lynn N.B.
3510.	Haverhill.	Second N.B.
3553.	Brookline.	Brookline N.B.
3598.	Newton.	First N.B. of West Newton.
3868.	Rockland.	First N.B.
3923.	Boston.	Commercial N.B.
3977.	Lawrence.	Merchants' N.B.
3994.	Middleborough.	Middleborough N.B.
4013.	Lenox.	Lenox N.B.

Charter Number	City	Name of Bank
4074.	Chelsea.	Winnisimmet N.B.
4202.	Boston.	South End N.B.
4240.	Stoneham.	Stoneham N.B.
4300.	Lawrence.	Arlington N.B.
4488.	Reading.	First N.B.
4562.	Adams.	Greylock N.B.
4580.	Lynn.	Manufacturers' N.B.
4660.	Whitman.	Whitman N.B.
4664.	Arlington.	First N.B.
4703.	Holyoke.	Park N.B.
4753.	Lowell.	Traders' N.B.
4769.	Melrose.	Melrose N.B.
4771.	Somerville.	Somerville N.B.
4774.	Ipswich.	First N.B.
4833.	Haverhill.	Merchants' N.B.
4907.	Springfield.	Springfield N.B.
5071.	Winchester.	Middlesex County N.B.
5155.	Boston.	Nat. Shawmut Bank.
5158.	Boston.	Nat. Hamilton Bank.
5163.	Boston.	Colonial N.B.
5247.	Medford.	Medford N.B.
5840.	Boston.	American N.B.
5944.	Mansfield.	First N.B.
5964.	Pepperell, East Pepperell.	First N.B.
6077.	Lowell.	Union N.B.
6104.	Boston.	Nat. Suffolk Bank.
6821.	Fall River.	Massasoit-Pocasset N.B.
7297.	Wellesley.	Wellesley N.B.
7452.	Danvers.	Danvers N.B.
7550.	Woburn.	Woburn N.B.
7595.	Worcester.	Merchants' N.B.
7675.	North Attleboro.	Jewelers' N.B.
7920.	Hyde Park.	Hyde Park N.B.
7957.	Edgartown.	Edgartown N.B.
8150.	South Deerfield.	Produce N.B.
8474.	Norwood.	Norwood N.B.
9086.	North Attleborough.	Manufacturers N.B.
9426.	Foxborough.	Foxboro N.B.
9579.	Boston.	Mutual N.B.
9651.	Chelsea.	Broadway N.B.
10059.	Leominster.	Merchants' N.B.
10165.	Barre.	Second N.B.
10924.	Boston.	Roxbury N.B.
10955.	North Brookfield.	North Brookfield N.B.
11014.	Maiden.	Second N.B.
11067.	Woburn.	Tanners' N.B.
11068.	Boston.	Back Bay N.B.
11103.	Winchester.	Winchester N.B.
11137.	Boston.	Mattapan N.B.
11152.	Cambridge.	Manufacturers' N.B.
11169.	Lynn.	State N.B.
11236.	Webster.	Webster N.B.
11270.	Chelsea.	Nat. City Bank.
11339.	Boston.	Citizens' N.B.
11347.	Braintree.	Braintree N.B.
11388.	Southbridge.	People's N.B.
11510.	Everett.	Everett N.B.
11567.	Warren.	First N.B.
11790.	Boston.	Haymarket N.B.
11859.	Boston.	Oceanic N.B.
11868.	Arlington.	Arlington N.B.
11903.	Boston.	Boston N.B.
12336.	Boston.	Federal N.B.
12343.	Lowell.	Middlesex N.B.
12359.	Boston.	South Boston N.B.
12362.	Lynn.	State N.B.
12377.	Boston.	Commonwealth N.B.
12396.	Boston.	International N.B.
12405.	New Bedford.	Safe Deposit N.B.
12481.	Springfield.	Atlas N.B.
12540.	Boston.	Brotherhood of Locomotive Engineers N.B.
12567.	Dedham.	Dedham N.B.
12800.	Methuen.	Methuen N.B.
12862.	Boston.	Massachusetts N.B.
12979.	Medford.	First N.B.
13060.	Cambridge.	Cambridge N.B.
13152.	Revere.	First N.B.
13172.	Northfield.	Northfield N.B.
13222.	Buzzards Bay.	Buzzards Bay N.B.
13241.	Needham.	Needham N.B. for Savings & Trusts.
13252.	Newton.	Newton N.B.
13283.	Cohasset.	Cohasset N.B.
13386.	Barre.	Second N.B.
13387.	North Brookfield.	North Brookfield N.B.
13391.	Boston.	Old Colony N.B.
13394.	Spencer.	Spencer N.B.
13395.	Hyannis.	Barnstable County N.B.
13411.	Webster.	First N.B.
13558.	Reading.	First N.B.
13604.	Gloucester.	Gloucester N.B.
13733.	Athol.	First N.B.
13780.	Webster.	Webster N.B.
13796.	Reading.	First N.B.
13835.	Millbury.	Millbury N.B.
13933.	Pepperell.	First N.B.
14033.	Woburn.	Tanners N.B.
14087.	Chelsea.	Lincoln N.B.
14152.	Revere.	First N.B.
14266.	Haverhill.	Northern N.B.

MICHIGAN

Charter Number	City	Name of Bank
22.	Ann Arbor.	First N.B.
81.	Fenton.	First N.B.
97.	Detroit.	First N.B.
116.	Detroit.	Second N.B.
155.	Ypsilanti.	First N.B.
168.	Hillsdale.	First N.B.
191.	Kalamazoo.	First N.B.
232.	Lansing.	First N.B.
264.	Lansing.	Second N.B.
275.	Ionia.	First N.B.
294.	Grand Rapids.	First N.B.
354.	Romeo.	First N.B.
390.	Marquette.	First N.B.
410.	Bay City.	First N.B.
434.	Pontiac.	First N.B.
600.	Three Rivers.	First N.B.
637.	East Saginaw.	First N.B.
812.	Grand Rapids.	City N.B.
813.	Constantine.	First N.B.
825.	Sturgis.	First N.B.
1063.	Tecumseh.	N.B. of Tecumseh.
1065.	Jackson.	First N.B.
1205.	Battle Creek.	First N.B.
1235.	Coldwater.	Coldwater N.B.
1247.	Houghton.	First N.B.
1256.	Corunna.	First N.B.
1280.	Lowell.	Lowell N.B.
1359.	Kalamazoo.	Michigan N.B.
1433.	Detroit.	Nat. Insurance Bank.
1470.	Hillsdale.	Second N.B.
1515.	Marshall.	First N.B.
1518.	Marshall.	N.B. of Michigan.
1521.	Paw Paw.	First N.B.
1533.	Jackson.	People's N.B.
1539.	Saint Johns.	First N.B.
1542.	Detroit.	American N.B.
1544.	Albion.	Nat. Exchange Bank.
1550.	East Saginaw.	Merchants' N.B.
1573.	Owosso.	First N.B.
1574.	Pontiac.	Second N.B.
1587.	Monroe.	First N.B.
1588.	Flint.	First N.B.
1625.	Dowagiac.	First N.B.
1722.	Decatur.	First N.B.
1725.	Schoolcraft.	First N.B.
1730.	Muskegon.	Muskegon N.B.
1731.	Lapeer.	First N.B.
1745.	Hastings.	Hastings N.B.
1752.	Holly.	First N.B.
1758.	Charlotte.	First N.B.
1761.	Niles.	First N.B.
1764.	Mason.	First N.B.
1768.	Saginaw.	First N.B.
1780.	Flint.	Citizens' N.B.
1789.	Saint Clair.	First N.B.
1812.	Cassopolis.	First N.B.
1823.	South Haven.	First N.B.
1826.	Union City.	Union City N.B.
1829.	Allegan.	First N.B.
1832.	Big Rapids.	Northern N.B.
1849.	Grand Haven.	First N.B.
1857.	Port Huron.	First N.B.
1866.	Saint Joseph.	First N.B.
1886.	Niles.	Citizens' N.B.
1916.	Plymouth.	First N.B.
1918.	Saginaw.	Second N.B.
1919.	Three Rivers.	Manufacturers' N.B.
1924.	Coldwater.	Southern Michigan N.B.
1953.	Lansing.	Lansing N.B.
1965.	Holly.	Merchants' N.B.
1973.	Adrian.	First N.B.
2008.	Ionia.	Second N.B.
2017.	Muir.	First N.B.
2023.	Marshall.	Nat. City Bank.
2046.	Buchanan.	First N.B.
2054.	Greenville.	First N.B.
2081.	Muskegon.	Lumbermans' N.B.
2084.	Ishpeming.	First N.B.
2085.	Negaunee.	First N.B.
2095.	Centerville.	First N.B.
2143.	Hancock.	First N.B.
2145.	Bay City.	Second N.B.
2162.	Leslie.	First N.B.
2186.	Romeo.	Citizens' N.B.
2211.	Constantine.	Farmers' N.B.
2214.	Mount Clemens.	First N.B.
2365.	Detroit.	Merchants and Manufacturers' N.B.
2367.	Eaton Rapids.	First N.B.
2372.	Union City.	Farmers' N.B.
2379.	Milford.	First N.B.
2429.	Whitehall.	First N.B.
2460.	Grand Rapids.	Grand Rapids N.B.
2492.	Saginaw.	Citizens' N.B.
2539.	Manistee.	First N.B.
2550.	Quincy.	First N.B.
2591.	Detroit.	Commercial N.B.
2606.	Manistee.	Manistee N.B.
2607.	Pontiac.	First N.B.
2611.	Grand Rapids.	Fourth N.B.
2707.	Detroit.	First N.B.
2708.	Flushing.	First N.B.
2714.	Ann Arbor.	First N.B.
2761.	East Saginaw.	Home N.B.
2773.	Ludington.	First N.B.
2847.	Alpena.	Alpena N.B.
2853.	Bay City.	First N.B.
2855.	Midland City.	First N.B.
2870.	Detroit.	Detroit N.B.
2890.	Grand Rapids.	Old N.B.
2914.	Stanton.	First N.B.
2944.	Big Rapids.	Big Rapids N.B.
2987.	Vassar.	First N.B.
3034.	Charlotte.	Merchants' N.B.
3088.	Muskegon.	Merchants' N.B.

Charter Number	City	Name of Bank
3095.	Ishpeming.	Ishpeming N.B.
3109.	Plymouth.	Plymouth N.B.
3123.	East Saginaw.	East Saginaw N.B.
3133.	Three Rivers.	Three Rivers N.B.
3210.	Kalamazoo.	City N.B.
3211.	Kalamazoo.	Kalamazoo N.B.
3215.	Mount Pleasant.	First N.B.
3217.	Ithaca.	First N.B.
3235.	Cheboygan.	First N.B.
3239.	Saint Louis.	First N.B.
3243.	Greenville.	City N.B.
3251.	Concord.	First N.B.
3256.	Menominee.	First N.B.
3264.	Ovid.	First N.B.
3276.	Sturgis.	Sturgis N.B.
3293.	**Grand Rapids.**	**Grand Rapids National City Bank.**
3314.	Battle Creek.	N.B. of Battle Creek.
3316.	Albion.	First N.B.
3325.	Traverse City.	First N.B.
3334.	Houghton.	N.B. of Houghton.
3357.	Detroit.	American Exchange N.B.
3361.	Flint.	First N.B.
3378.	Saint John's.	Saint John's N.B.
3388.	Pontiac.	Pontiac N.B.
3410.	Owosso.	Second N.B.
3457.	Calumet.	First N.B.
3487.	Detroit.	Union N.B.
3488.	Grand Rapids.	Fifth N.B.
3513.	Lansing.	City N.B.
3514.	Detroit.	Third N.B.
3547.	Sault Ste. Marie.	First N.B.
3717.	Negaunde.	First N.B.
3730.	Detroit.	Preston N.B.
3747.	Sault Ste. Marie.	Sault Ste. Marie N.B.
3761.	Escanaba.	First N.B.
3806.	Iron Mountain.	First N.B.
3886.	Saint Ignace.	First N.B.
3896.	Battle Creek.	Merchants' N.B.
3911.	Saginaw.	Commercial N.B.
3925.	Buchanan.	First N.B.
3947.	Bessemer.	First N.B.
3948.	Lake Linden.	First N.B.
3971,	Ironwood.	First N.B.
4125.	Muskegon.	Union N.B.
4261.	Benton Harbor.	First N.B.
4398.	Muskegon.	Hackley N.B.
4413.	Reed City.	First N.B.
4446.	Port Huron.	First Nat. Exchange Bank.
4454.	Menominee.	Lumbermen's N.B.
4527.	White Pigeon.	First N.B.
4578.	Grand Haven.	N.B. of Grand Haven.
4649.	Plymouth.	First Nat. Exchange Bank.
4840.	Muskegon.	Nat. Lumberman's Bank.
4953.	Bay City.	Old Second N.B.
5199.	Rockland.	First N.B.
5348.	Manistique.	First N.B.
5415.	Durand.	First N.B.
5482.	Yale.	First N.B.
5594.	Saint Joseph.	Commercial N.B.
5607.	Petoskey.	First N.B.
5668.	Ishpeming.	Miners' N.B.
5669.	Morenci.	First N.B.
5789.	Ionia.	N.B. of Ionia.
5896.	Houghton.	Citizens' N.B.
6003.	Marquette.	Marquette N.B.
6485.	Ithaca.	Ithaca N.B.
6492.	Detroit.	Old Detroit N.B.
6727.	Hart.	First N.B.
6820.	Ontonagon.	First N.B.
6863.	Norway.	First N.B.
7013.	Battle Creek.	Central N.B.
7525.	Crystal Falls.	Iron County N.B.
7552.	Albion.	Albion N.B.
7589.	Battle Creek.	Old N.B.
7664.	Flint.	N.B. of Flint.
7676.	Houghton.	Houghton N.B.
8148.	Lansing.	Capital N.B.
8496.	Escanaba.	Escanaba N.B.
8545.	Iron River.	First N.B.
8598.	Laurium.	First N.B.
8703.	Detroit.	Guardian N.B.
8723.	Vassar.	Vassar N.B.
9000.	Munising.	First N.B. of Alger Co.
9020.	Boyne City.	First N.B.
9087.	Hancock.	Superior N.B.
9099.	Richland.	Farmers' N.B.
9218.	Rochester.	First N.B.
9359.	Hubbell.	First N.B.
9421.	Adrian.	N.B. of Commerce.
9497.	Buff Oak.	First N.B.
9509.	L'Anse.	Baraga County N.B.
9517.	Ironwood.	Gogebic N.B.
9556.	Negaunee.	Negaunce N.B.
9654.	Ithaca.	Commercial N.B.
9704.	Bronson.	People's N.B.
9792.	Croswell.	First N.B.
9854.	Hartford.	Olney N.B.
9874.	Birmingham.	First N.B.
10073.	Dowagiac.	Dowagiac: N.B.
10143.	Benton Harbor.	American N.B.
10498.	Watervliet.	First N.B.
10527.	Detroit.	First and Old Detroit N.B.
10529.	Benton.	Farmers and Merchants N.B.
10600.	Detroit.	Merchants' N.B.
10601.	Alpha.	First N.B.
10631.	Capac.	First N.B.
10632.	Saint Clair Heights.	Michigan N.B.
10673.	Gladwin.	First N.B.

Charter Number	City	Name of Bank
10742.	Richmond.	First N.B.
10753.	Carsonvifle.	First N.B.
10790.	Avoca.	First N.B.
10886.	Gladstone.	First N.B.
10997.	Flint.	First N.B.
11082.	Hamtramck.	People's N.B.
11260.	Marine City.	Liberty N.B.
11289.	Jackson.	Nat. Union Bank
11305.	Wakefield.	First N.B.
11454.	Chesaning.	First N.B.
11469.	Ironwood.	Iron N.B.
11547.	Crystal Falls.	Crystal Falls N.B.
11549.	Pontiac.	N.B. of Pontiac.
11586.	Howell.	First N.B.
11802.	Caspian.	Caspian N.B.
11813.	Blissfield.	First N.B.
11843.	Greenville.	Greenville N.B.
11852.	Battle Creek.	City N.B.
11929.	Iron Mountain.	N.B. of Iron Mountain.
11954.	Hermansville.	First N.B.
12027.	Marquette.	Union N.B.
12084.	Lawton.	First N.B.
12108.	Grand Rapids.	City N.B.
12288.	Pontiac.	First N.B.
12387.	Ironwood.	Merchants and Miners' N.B.
12436.	Ypsilanti.	People's N.B.
12474.	Reed City.	Reed City N.B.
12561.	Evart.	First N.B.
12616.	Wyandotte.	First N.B.
12657.	Royal Oak.	First N.B.
12661.	L'Anse Creuse.	First N.B.
12697.	Mason.	Dart N.B.
12793.	Almont.	First N.B.
12826.	Utica.	First N.B.
12847.	Detroit.	Griswold N.B.
12869.	Brighton.	First N.B.
12878.	Inkster.	Inkster N.B.
12944.	Algonac.	First N.B.
12953.	Plymouth.	First N.B.
12971.	Mount Clemens.	First N.B.
12989.	Dearborn.	First N.B.
12999.	Lincoln Park.	Lincoln Park N.B.
13072.	Jackson.	East Side Nat. U Bank.
13240.	Centerline.	First N.B.
13307.	Niles.	City N.B. & Trust Co.
13328.	Grand Rapids.	American N.B.
13434.	Grand Rapids.	Security N.B.
13513.	Manistique.	First N.B.
13522.	Cheboygan.	Citizens N.B.
13600.	Pontiac.	First N.B.
13607.	Bessemer.	Bessemer N.B.
13622.	Bay City.	N.B. of Bay City.
13671.	Detroit.	N.B. of Detroit.
13703.	Birmingham.	Birmingham N.B.
13738.	Detroit.	Manufacturers N.B.
13739.	Pontiac.	Community N.B.
13741.	Jackson.	N.B. of Jackson.
13753.	Niles.	First N.B.
13758.	Grand Rapids.	N.B. of Grand Rapids.
13793.	Richmond.	N.B. of Richmond.
13799.	Grand Rapids.	Peoples N.B.
13807.	Ypsilanti.	N.B. of Ypsilant.
13820.	Kalamazoo.	American N.B.
13821.	Adrian.	N.B. of Adrian.
13824.	Hubbell.	First N.B.
13833.	Benton Harbor	Farmers & Merchants N.B.
13841.	Rochester.	Rochester N.B.
13857.	Hastings.	N.B. of Hastings.
13858.	Battle Creek.	Central N.B.
13874.	Wyandotte.	N.B. of Wyandotte.
13929.	Ontonagon.	First N.B.
13931.	Ishpeming.	Miners First N.B.
13976.	Flint.	N.B. of Flint.
13995.	Eaton Rapids.	N.B. of Eaton Rapids.
14009.	Marshall.	First N.B.
14016.	Ludington.	N.B. of Ludington.
14022.	Utica.	Utica N.B.
14032.	Lansing.	Lansing N.B.
14062.	Hillsdale.	Hillsdale Count N.B.
14102.	Iron River.	Iron River N.B.
14111.	Gladstone.	First N.B.
14116.	Coldwater.	Coldwater N.B.
14144.	Howell.	First N.B.
14185.	Battle Creek.	Security N.B.
14187.	Ionia.	Ionia County N.B.
14249.	Hancock.	National Metals N.B.
14269.	Crystal Falls.	First N.B.
14280.	Manistique.	First N.B.

MINNESOTA

Charter Number	City	Name of Bank
203.	Saint Paul.	First N.B.
496.	Hastings.	First N.B.
550.	Winona.	First N.B.
579.	Rochester.	First N.B.
631.	New Ulm.	First N.B.
710.	Minneapolis.	First N.B.
719.	Minneapolis.	Nat. Exchange Bank.
725.	Saint Paul.	Second N.B.
1258.	Saint Paul.	Nat. Marine Bank.
1487.	Red Wing.	First N.B.
1514.	Stillwater.	First N.B.
1538.	Hastings.	Merchants' N.B.
1597.	Shakopee.	First N.B.
1623.	Minneapolis.	State N.B.
1643.	Winona.	United N.B.
1683.	Mankato.	First N.B.
1686.	Faribault.	First N.B.
1690.	Austin.	First N.B.
1740.	Lake City.	First N.B.

Charter Number	City	Name of Bank
1782.	Winona.	Winona Deposit.
1783.	Stillwater.	Lumbermen's N.B.
1794.	Saint Peter.	First N.B.
1830.	Minneapolis.	Merchants' N.B.
1842.	Winona.	Second N.B.
1863.	Faribault.	Citizens' N.B.
1911.	Owatonna.	First N.B.
1954.	Duluth.	First N.B.
2005.	Mankato.	Citizens' N.B.
2006.	Minneapolis.	Northwestern N.B.
2020.	Saint Paul.	Merchants' N.B.
2030.	Fergus Falls.	First N.B.
2073.	Northfield.	First N.B.
2088.	Rochester.	Union N.B.
2122.	Owatonna.	Farmer's N.B.
2159.	Kasson.	First N.B.
2268.	Winona.	Merchants' N.B.
2316.	Rochester.	Rocnester N.B.
2318.	New Ulm.	Citizens' N.B.
2387.	Cannon Falls.	First N.B.
2567.	Crookston.	First N.B.
2569.	Moorhead.	First N.B.
2571.	Glencoe.	First N.B.
2590.	Brainerd.	First N.B.
2648.	Fergus Falls.	Fergus Falls N.B.
2674.	Stillwater.	First N.B.
2768.	Duluth.	Duluth N.B.
2790.	Saint Cloud.	First N.B.
2795.	Minneapolis.	Union N.B.
2800.	Anoka.	First N.B.
2933.	Morris.	First N.B.
2934.	Fergus Falls.	Citizens' N.B.
2943.	Saint Paul.	Nat. German Am Bank.
2959.	Saint Paul.	Saint Paul N.B.
2995.	Alexandria.	First N.B.
3000.	Anoka.	Anoka N.B.
3009.	Saint Cloud.	German America N.B.
3039.	Shakopee.	First N.B.
3098.	Minneapolis.	Manufacturers N.B.
3100.	Wabasha.	First N.B.
3127.	Shakopee.	Merchants and Farmers' N.B.
3145.	Minneapolis.	Nicollet N.B.
3155.	Sauk Center.	First N.B.
3206.	Minneapolis.	N.B. of Commerce.
3224.	Winona.	First N.B.
3233.	Saint Paul.	Third N.B.
3262.	Crookston.	Merchants' N.B.
3426.	Detroit.	First N.B.
3428.	Lu Verne.	First N.B.
3453.	Duluth.	Merchants' N.B.
3550.	Worthington.	First N.B.
3560.	Albert Lea.	First N.B.
3562.	Mankato.	Mankato N.B.
3626.	Duluth.	First N.B.
3659.	Red Lake Falls.	First N.B.
3689.	Saint Paul.	Commercial N.B.
3784.	Minneapolis.	Flour City N.B.
3924.	Tower.	First N.B.
3982.	Pipestone.	First N.B.
4001.	Duluth.	N.B. of Commerce.
4034.	Little Falls.	First N.B.
4131.	Austin.	Austin N.B.
4302.	New Brighton.	Twin City N.B.
4421.	Duluth.	Marine N.B.
4509.	Lake Benton.	First N.B.
4595.	Marshall.	Lyon County N.B.
4614.	Marshall.	First N.B.
4617.	Elbow Lake.	First N.B.
4638.	East Grand Forks.	First N.B.
4644.	Breckenridge.	First N.B.
4655.	Little Falls.	American N.B.
4669.	Wells.	First N.B.
4702.	Albert Lea.	Albert Lea N.B.
4713.	Moorhead.	Moorhead N.B.
4727.	Mankato.	Nat. Citizens' Bank.
4739.	Minneapolis.	Columbia N.B.
4750.	New Duluth.	New Duluth N.B.
4797.	Saint Cloud.	Merchants' N.B.
4807.	Princeton.	First N.B.
4821.	Wadena.	First N.B.
4831.	Appleton.	First N.B.
4847.	Austin.	Citizens' N.B.
4859.	Saint James.	First N.B.
4916.	Wadena.	Merchants' N.B.
4928.	Owatonna.	Nat. Farmers' Bank.
4936.	Fairmont.	First N.B.
4951.	Minneapolis.	Swedish-American N.B.
4959.	Barnesville.	First N.B.
4969.	Kasson.	N.B. of Kasson.
4992.	Tracy.	First N.B.
5063.	Windom.	First N.B.
5256.	Slayton.	First N.B.
5301.	Wilmont.	First N.B.
5301.	Stewartville.	First N.B.
5362.	West Concord.	First N.B.
5374.	Eyota.	First N.B.
5377.	Elmore.	First N.B.
5383.	Heron Lake.	First N.B.
5393.	Blue Earth.	First N.B.
5405.	Cloquet.	First N.B.
5406.	Winnebago City.	First N.B.
5423.	Fairmont.	Martin County N.B.
5453.	Ada.	First N.B.
5542.	Park Rapids.	First N.B.
5553.	Eveleth.	First N.B.
5568.	Staples.	First N.B.
5570.	Ellsworth.	First N.B.
5582.	Bemidji.	First N.B.
5706.	Lyle.	First N.B.

Charter Number	City	Name of Bank
5745.	Hibbing.	First N.B.
5826.	Redwood Falls.	First N.B.
5852.	Jackson.	First N.B.
5859.	Alexandria.	Farmers' N.B.
5866.	Warren.	First N.B.
5892.	Ruthton.	First N.B.
5894.	Thief River Falls.	First N.B.
5895.	Northfield.	Northfield N.B.
5907.	Argyle.	First N.B.
5910.	Worthington.	Citizens' N.B.
5969.	Chokio.	First N.B.
5988.	Fertile.	First N.B.
6022.	Verndale.	First N.B.
6029.	Ceylon.	First N.B.
6035.	Wheaton.	First N.B.
6054.	Fulda.	First N.B.
6098.	Barnesville.	Barnesville N.B.
6118.	Litchfield.	First N.B.
6128.	Albert Lea.	Citizens' N.B.
6151.	Willmar.	First N.B.
6154.	Benson.	First N.B.
6199.	Hills.	First N.B.
6203.	Tyler.	First N.B.
6204.	Minnesota Lake.	First N.B.
6208.	Long Prairie.	First N.B.
6237.	Saint Charles.	First N.B.
6259.	Campbell.	First N.B.
6266.	Eagle Bend.	First N.B.
6276.	Perham.	First N.B.
6279.	Preston.	First N.B.
6285.	Hanley Falls.	First N.B.
6293.	Plainview.	First N.B.
6304.	Two Harbors.	First N.B.
6310.	Morris.	Morris N.B.
6316.	Spring Valley.	First N.B.
6321.	Dawson.	First N.B.
6331.	Welcome.	Welcome N.B.
6335.	Breckenridge.	Breckenridge N.B.
6348.	Sherburn.	Sherburn N.B.
6349.	Pelican Rapids.	First N.B.
6352.	Cass Lake.	First N.B.
6364.	Truman.	Truman N.B.
6366.	Canby.	First N.B.
6387.	Sleepy Eye.	First N.B.
6396.	Windom.	Windom N.B.
6401.	Twin Valley.	First N.B.
6412.	Westbrook.	First N.B.
6413.	Minneota.	First N.B.
6417.	Sauk Center.	Merchants' N.B.
6431.	Albert Lea.	Security N.B.
6436.	Rushford.	First N.B.
6448.	Clarkfield.	First N.B.
6449.	Minneapolis.	Minnesota N.B.
6459.	Ortonville.	First N.B.
6467.	Ivanhoe.	First N.B.
6468.	Hendricks.	First N.B.
6478.	Bricelyn.	First N.B.
6488.	McIntosh.	First N.B.
6519.	Mankato.	N.B. of Commerce.
6520.	Duluth.	City N.B.
6523.	Jasper.	First N.B.
6527.	Virginia.	First N.B.
6532.	Minnesota Lake.	Farmers' N.B.
6537.	Lakefield.	First N.B.
6544.	Waseca.	First N.B.
6563.	Grand Rapids.	First N.B.
6571.	Boyd.	Boyd N.B.
6583.	Renville.	First N.B.
6584.	Cottonwood.	First N.B.
6608.	Chatfield.	First N.B.
6623.	Dodge Center.	Farmers' N.B.
6631.	Alden.	First N.B.
6637.	Ivanhoe.	Ivanhoe N.B.
6661.	Parkers Prairie.	First N.B.
6682.	Dodge Center.	First N.B.
6693.	Fertile.	Citizens' N.B.
6696.	Lake Benton.	Nat. Citizens' Bank.
6704.	Cannon Falls.	Farmers and Merchants' N.B.
6731.	Royalton.	First N.B.
6732.	South Saint Paul.	Stockyards N.B.
6738.	Dunnell.	First N.B.
6747.	Ortonville.	Citizens' N.B.
6775.	Blooming Prairie.	First N.B.
6783.	Roseau.	First N.B.
6784.	Emmons.	First N.B.
6787.	Mapleton.	First N.B.
6788.	Wells.	Wells N.B.
6795.	Madison.	First N.B.
6803.	Aitkin.	First N.B.
6813.	Bagley.	First N.B.
6828.	Saint Paul.	American N.B.
6837.	Osakis.	First N.B.
6840.	Balaton.	First N.B.
6860.	Montevideo.	First N.B.
6862.	Rushmore.	First N.B.
6889.	Fosston.	First N.B.
6906.	Henning.	First N.B.
6917.	Minneota.	Farmers and Merchants' N.B.
6918.	Lake Crystal.	First N.B.
6921.	LeSueur Center.	First N.B.
6933.	Grand Meadow.	First N.B.
6934.	Hallock.	First N.B.
6954.	Rush City.	First N.B.
6973.	Carlton.	First N.B.
6991.	Eveleth.	Miners' N.B.
6992.	Jackson.	Jackson N.B.
6996.	Hancock.	First N.B.
7014.	Winthrop.	First N.B.
7021.	Saint James.	Citizens' and Security N.B.
7024.	Frazee.	First N.B.

Charter Number	City	Name of Bank
7033.	Hancock.	Hancock N.B.
7080.	Long Prairie.	People's N.B.
7081.	Ulen.	First N.B.
7092.	New Prague.	First N.B.
7100.	Madelia.	First N.B.
7109.	Le Roy.	First N.B.
7128.	Iona.	First N.B.
7143.	Lake Park.	First N.B.
7161.	Clinton.	First N.B.
7184.	Elgin.	First N.B.
7196.	Hatstad.	First N.B.
7199.	Le Sueur.	First N.B.
7213.	Graceville.	First N.B.
7221.	Lamberton.	First N.B.
7227.	Browerville.	First N.B.
7268.	Deer Creek.	First N.B.
7273.	Belle Plaine.	First N.B.
7283.	Waterville.	First N.B.
7292.	Mora.	First N.B.
7307.	Red Wing.	Goodhue County N.B.
7341.	Browns Valley.	First N.B.
7373.	Bertha.	First N.B.
7380.	International Falls.	First N.B.
7387.	Braharn.	First N.B.
7427.	Canby.	Nat. Citizens' Bank.
7428.	Cambridge.	First N.B.
7438.	Beardsley.	First N.B.
7508.	Caledonia.	First N.B.
7566.	Melrose.	First N.B.
7603.	Goodhue.	First N.B.
7625.	Woodstock.	First N.B.
7641.	Blue Earth.	Farmers' N.B.
7647.	Chisholm.	First N.B.
7708.	Princeton.	First N.B.
7742.	Glenwood.	First N.B.
7764.	Motley.	First N.B.
7770.	Lu Verne.	Farmers' N.B.
7772.	Hawley.	First N.B.
7797.	Jackson.	Brown N.B.
7933.	Foley.	First N.B.
7958.	Hopkins, W. Minneapolis.	First N.B.
7960.	Adrian.	First N.B.
8049.	Herman.	First N.B.
8050.	Raymond.	First N.B.
8051.	Cold Spring.	First N.B.
8059.	Adams.	First N.B.
8108.	Saint Paul.	Capital N.B.
8122.	Detroit.	Merchants' N.B.
8241.	Bemidji.	Northern N.B.
8269.	Springfield.	First N.B.
8322.	Coleraine.	First N.B.
8378.	Chaska.	First N.B.
8416.	Granite Falls.	First N.B.
8476.	Walker.	First N.B.
8523.	Staples.	City N.B.
8551.	Fairmont.	Fairmont N.B.
8592.	Ely.	First N.B.
8683.	Harmony.	First N.B.
8697.	Biwabik.	First N.B.
8720.	Minneapolis.	Security N.B.
8726.	Mahnomen.	First N.B.
8729.	Grey Eagle.	First N.B.
8756.	Battle Lake.	First N.B.
8757.	Elk River.	First N.B.
8813.	Appleton.	First N.B.
8977.	Lu Verne.	N.B. of Lu Verne.
8989.	Worthington.	Worthington N.B.
8993.	Wheaton.	N.B. of Wheaton.
9031.	Mabel.	First N.B.
9033.	Adrian.	N.B. of Adrian.
9050.	Milaca.	First N.B.
9059.	Preston.	N.B. of Preston.
9063.	Olivia.	People's First N.B.
9064.	Stephen.	First N.B.
9131.	Deer River.	First N.B.
9147.	Blackduck.	First N.B.
9253.	Waseca.	Farmers' N.B.
9262.	Gilbert.	First N.B.
9267.	Mountain Lake.	First N.B.
9321.	Beaver Creek.	First N.B.
9327.	Duluth.	Northern N.B.
9374.	Duluth.	American Exchange N.B.
9409.	Minneapolis.	Midland N.B.
9442.	Minneapolis.	Metropolitan N.B.
9457.	Hendricks.	Farmers' N.B.
9464.	Sandstone.	First N.B.
9596.	Starbuck.	First N.B.
9703.	Deerwood.	First N.B.
9771.	Fairfax.	First N.B.
9775.	Amboy.	First N.B.
9837.	Red Lake Falls.	Farmers' N.B.
9838.	Crosby.	First N.B.
9903.	Delano.	First N.B.
10147.	Hutchinson.	Farmers' N.B.
10261.	Minneapolis.	Nat. City Bank.
10382.	Ironton.	First N.B.
10393.	Winnebago.	Blue Earth Valley N.B.
10475.	Saint Paul.	N.B. of Commerce.
10507.	Lanesboro.	First N.B.
10554.	Isanti.	First N.B.
10570.	Atwater.	First N.B.
10580.	Kasson.	N.B. of Dodge County.
10603.	Kiester.	First N.B.
10642.	New Richland.	First N.B.
10665.	Ada.	Ada N.B.
10710.	Baudette.	First N.B.
10736.	Nashwauk.	First N.B.
10740.	Lakeville.	First N.B.
10783.	Aitkin.	Farmers' N.B.

Charter Number	City	Name of Bank
10824.	Swanville.	First N.B.
10830.	Gonvick.	First N.B.
10841.	Aitkin.	N.B. of Aitkin.
10862.	Brandon.	First N.B.
10865.	Winona.	Winona N.B.
10898.	Wendell.	First N.B.
10903.	Keewatin.	First N.B.
10936.	Pipestone.	Pipestone N.B.
10940.	Saint Paul.	Nat. Exchange Bank
10946.	Brewster.	First N.B.
11023.	Buffalo.	First N.B.
11042.	Kasson.	Nat. Farmers' Bank
11054.	Bovey.	First N.B.
11090.	Fairmont.	Citizens' N.B.
11125.	Proctor.	First N.B.
11167.	Minneapolis.	Bankers' N.B.
11173.	Erskine.	First N.B.
11178.	Minneapolis.	Lincoln N.B.
11212.	Hastings.	Hastings N.B.
11215.	Montgomery.	First N.B.
11218.	Jordan.	First N.B.
11224.	Avoca.	First N.B.
11261.	Barnesville.	Farmers' N.B.
11267.	Pequot.	First N.B.
11286.	Warren.	Warren N.B.
11288.	Hanska.	First N.B.
11293.	Lake Wilson.	First N.B.
11332.	Paynesville.	First N.B.
11345.	Aurora.	First N.B.
11356.	Lancaster.	First N.B.
11365.	Kerkhoven.	First N.B.
11392.	Clearbrook.	First N.B.
11401.	Lake Crystal.	American N.B.
11410.	Waconia.	First N.B.
11500.	Virginia.	American Exchange N.B.
11550.	Motordale.	First N.B.
11552.	Good Thunder.	First N.B.
11563.	Pine River.	First N.B.
11575.	Kilkenny.	First N.B.
11579.	Nashwauk.	American N.B.
11581.	Pine City.	First N.B.
11606.	Granaada.	First N.B.
11608.	Marble.	First N.B.
11611.	Big Lake.	First N.B.
11622.	Buhl.	First N.B.
11627.	Ivanhoe.	Farmers and Merchants' N.B.
11652.	Forest Lake.	First N.B.
11668.	Faribault.	Security N.B.
11685.	Shakopee.	People's N.B.
11687.	Farmington.	First N.B.
11709.	Rice.	First N.B.
11710.	Rice.	Rice N.B.
11717.	Mahnomen.	Farmers' N.B.
11724.	Holland.	First N.B.
11740.	Menahga.	First N.B.
11741.	Saint Paul.	Twin Cities N.B.
11761.	Barnum.	First N.B.
11770.	Saint Paul.	Wabash N.B.
11776.	Rosemount.	First N.B.
11777.	Watertown.	First N.B.
11778.	Minneapolis.	Minneapolis N.B.
11810.	Duluth.	Minnesota N.B.
11815.	Warroad.	First N.B.
11818.	Saint Cloud.	American N.B.
11848.	Roseau.	Roseau County N.B.
11861.	Minneapolis.	Payday N.B.
11863.	Littlefork.	First N.B.
11974.	Proctor.	People's N.B.
11987.	White Bear Lake.	First N.B.
12032.	Farwell.	First N.B.
12115.	Richfield.	Richfield N.B.
12140.	Duluth.	Duluth N.B.
12282.	Minneapolis.	Transportation Brotherhoods N.B.
12357.	Two Harbors.	First N.B.
12395.	Cokato.	First N.B.
12507.	Wadena.	First N.B.
12518.	West Minneapolis, Hopkins.	Minneapolis, Security N.B.
12568.	Hibbing.	Hibbing N.B.
12607.	Grey Eagle.	N.B. of Grey Eagle.
12634.	Luverne.	First and Farmers' N.B.
12844.	Lamberton.	New First N.B.
12859.	Litchfield.	First N.B.
12864.	Alexandria.	Farmers' N.B.
12922.	Saint Paul.	Nat. Exchange Bank
12941.	Mahnomen.	First N.B.
12947.	Moose Lake.	First N.B.
12959.	Buffalo.	Buffalo N.B.
12972.	Minneapolis.	Bloomington-Lake N.B.
13066.	Minneapolis.	Fourth Northwestern N.B.
13075.	Detroit Lakes.	Becker County N.B.
13078.	Duluth.	Pioneer N.B.
13081.	Olivia.	Citizens N.B.
13086.	Montevideo.	Security N.B.
13095.	Jackson.	First N.B.
13096.	Minneapolis.	Minnehaha N.B.
13108.	Minneapolis.	Central N.B.
13114.	Columbia Heights.	Columbia N.B.
13116.	Duluth.	Western N.B.
13127.	Minneapolis.	Third Northwestern N.B.
13131.	St. Paul.	Midway N.B.
13140.	Minneapolis.	Fifth Northwestern N.B.
13167.	St. Paul.	St. Paul N.B.
13204.	Lakefield.	First N.B.
13242.	Amboy.	First N.B.
13255.	Winnebago.	First N.B.
13269.	Jackson.	Jackson N.B.
13297.	Moorhead.	First N.B.
13303.	Deer Creek.	First N.B.

Charter Number	City	Name of Bank
13350.	Northfield.	Northfield N.B. & Trust Co.
13353.	Little Falls.	American N.B.
13396.	Red Wing.	Security N.B. & Trust Co.
13397.	Benson.	N.B. of Benson.
13399.	Pipestone.	Pipestone N.B.
13401.	Willmar.	Security N.B.
13405.	East Grand Forks.	Minnesota N.B.
13422.	Albert Lea.	Freeborn County N.B. and Trust Co.
13468.	Ivanhoe.	Farmers and Merchants N.B.
13486.	Litchfield.	Northwestern N.B.
13518.	Paynesville.	First N.B.
13544.	Luverne.	Luverne N.B.
13547.	Anoka.	First N.B.
13556.	Wheaton.	First N.B.
13561.	Madison.	Klein N.B.
13564.	Dawson.	Northwestern N.B.
13615.	Stewartville.	Stewartville N.B.
13692.	Park Rapids.	Citizens N.B.
13713.	Cannon Falls.	First N.B.
13784.	Madelia.	Citizens N.B.
13972.	Lake Crystal.	Lake Crystal N.B.
13973.	St. Charles.	First N.B.
14042.	Winthrop.	First N.B.
14068.	Amboy.	Security N.B.
14167.	West Concord.	First N.B.
14216	Hutchinson.	First N.B.
14220.	Mankato.	N.B. of Commerce.
14296.	St. James.	First N.B.
14311.	Buffalo.	Oakley N.B.

MISSISSIPPI

Charter Number	City	Name of Bank
803.	Vicksburg.	N.B. of Vicksburg.
1610.	Jackson.	First N.B.
2638.	Columbus.	First N.B.
2891.	West Point.	First N.B.
2957.	Meridian.	First N.B.
3176.	Meridian.	Meridian N.B.
3258.	Vicksburg.	First N.B.
3332.	Jackson.	First N.B.
3430.	Vicksburg.	Merchants' N.B.
3566.	Yazoo City.	First N.B.
3656.	Aberdeen.	First N.B.
3688.	Starkville.	First N.B.
3701.	Natchez.	First N.B.
3765.	Greenville.	First N.B.
4521.	Tupelo.	First N.B.
5176.	Hattiesburg.	First N.B.
5177.	Hattiesburg.	First N.B.
5613.	Lumberton.	First N.B.
5715.	Port Gibson.	Mississippi N.B.
6121.	Vicksburg.	American N.B.
6188.	Gulfport.	First N.B.
6305.	Natchez.	N.B. of Commerce.
6595.	Clarksdale.	First N.B.
6646.	Jackson.	Capital N.B.
6681.	Laurel.	First N.B.
6847.	Canton.	First N.B.
6923.	Laurel.	Laurel N.B.
7200.	Shaw.	First N.B.
7216.	Greenwood.	First N.B.
7266.	Meridian.	Citizens' N.B.
7461.	McComb.	First N.B.
7507.	Vicksburg.	Citizens' N.B.
8514.	New Albany.	First N.B.
8593.	Moss Point.	Pascagoula N.B.
8719.	Poplarville.	N.B. of Poplarville.
9040.	Pontotoc.	First N.B.
9041.	Philadelphia.	First N.B.
9094.	Corinth.	First N.B.
9196.	Okolona.	First N.B.
9204.	Ripley.	First N.B.
9251.	Ackerman.	First N.B.
9728.	Collins.	First N.B.
9751.	Corinth.	Citizens' N.B.
9753.	Summit.	N.B. of Summit.
9865.	Oxford.	First N.B.
10154.	Iuka.	First N.B.
10326.	Columbia.	Citizens' N.B.
10338.	Summit.	Progressive N.B.
10361.	Columbus.	N.B. of Commerce.
10463.	Jackson.	State N.B.
10494.	Brookhaven.	First N.B.
10523.	Jackson.	Jackson-State N.B.
10555.	Aberdeen.	Aberdeen N.B.
10576.	Biloxi.	First N.B.
10688.	Itta Bena.	First N.B.
10738.	Columbus.	Columbus N.B.
10745.	Rosedale.	First N.B.
10873.	Holly Springs.	First N.B.
11898.	Laurel.	Commercial N.B. and Trust Co.
12073.	Rosedale.	Rosedale N.B.
12222.	Clarksdale.	Planters' N.B.
12478.	Hattiesburg.	Commercial N.B.
12499.	Vicksburg.	Nat. People's Savings Bank andTrust Co.
12501.	Vicksburg.	Nat. City Savings Bank and Trust Co.
12537.	Natchez.	Britton and Koontz N.B.
12587.	Yazoo City.	Delta N.B.
12822.	Columbus.	First N.B.
13156.	Gulfport.	N.B. of Gulfport.
13313.	Lexington.	First N.B.
13403.	Greenville.	Commercial N.B.
13413.	Waynesboro.	First N.B.
13551.	Meridian.	First N.B.
13553.	Gulfport.	First N.B.
13708.	Jackson.	Capital N.B.
13722.	Natchez.	Britton and Koontz N.B.
14176.	Waynesboro.	First N.B.

MISSOURI

Charter Number	City	Name of Bank
67.	Columbia.	First N.B.
89.	Saint Louis.	First N.B.
139.	Saint Louis.	Second N.B.
170.	Saint Louis.	First N.B.
260.	Saint Charles.	First N.B.
283.	Saint Louis.	Fourth N.B.
454.	Carondelet.	First N.B.
1112.	Saint Louis.	Saint Louis N.B.
1381.	Saint Louis.	Union N.B.
1467.	Columbia.	Exchange N.B.
1501.	Saint Louis.	Merchants' N.B.
1529.	Independence.	First N.B.
1571.	Hannibal.	First N.B.
1580.	Saint Joseph.	First N.B.
1584.	Boonville.	Central N.B.
1612.	Kansas City.	First N.B.
1627.	Sedalia.	First N.B.
1665.	Saint Louis.	N.B. of the State of Missouri.
1667.	Saint Joseph.	State N.B.
1677.	Springfield.	Greene County N.B.
1701.	Springfield.	First N.B.
1711.	Shelbina.	First N.B.
1712.	California.	Moniteau N.B.
1735.	Palmyra.	First N.B.
1751.	Pleasant Hill.	First N.B.
1770.	Columbia.	Boone County N.B.
1803.	Paris.	First N.B.
1809.	Jefferson City.	First N.B.
1839.	La Grange.	First N.B.
1843.	Butler.	Bates County N.B.
1856.	Warrensburg.	First N.B.
1858.	Saint Louis.	Valley N.B.
1865.	Rolla.	N.B. of Rolla.
1877.	Knob Noster.	First N.B.
1901.	Kansas City.	Kansas City N.B.
1940.	Clinton.	First N.B.
1966.	Trenton.	First N.B.
1971.	Sedalia.	Citizens' N.B.
1995.	Kansas City.	Commercial N.B.
2013.	Carthage.	First N.B.
2055.	Jefferson City.	Nat. Exchange Bank.
2218.	Lancaster.	First N.B.
2356.	Platte City.	Farmers' N.B.
2432.	Memphis.	Scotland County N.B.
2440.	Kansas City.	Merchants N.B.
2561.	Butler.	Butler N.B.
2613.	Kansas City.	Citizens N.B.
2636.	Appleton City.	First N.B.
2713.	Kirksvilit.	First N.B.
2835.	Saint Louis.	Fifth N.B.
2862.	Macon.	First N.B.
2881.	Mexico.	First N.B.
2884.	Marshall.	First N.B.
2898.	Saint Joseph.	Sexton N.B.
2919.	Sedalia.	Third N.B.
2970.	Saint Joseph.	N.B. of Saint Joseph.
2979.	Palmyra.	First N.B.
3005.	Carthage.	First N.B.
3068.	Unionville.	Marshall N.B.
3079.	Tar-kio.	First N.B.
3103.	Louisiana.	Exchange N.B.
3110.	Milan.	First N.B.
3111.	Louisiana.	Mercantile N.B.
3137.	Unionville.	N.B. of Unionville.
3268.	Maryville.	First N.B.
3322.	Paris.	N.B. of Paris.
3380.	Grant City.	First N.B.
3456.	Kansas City.	First N.B.
3489.	Kansas City.	N.B. of Kansas City.
3544.	Kansas City.	American N.B.
3637.	Kansas City.	Union N.B.
3686.	Chillicothe.	First N.B.
3712.	Liberty.	First N.B.
3718.	Springfield.	Central N.B.
3754.	Harrisonville.	First N.B.
3760.	Kansas City.	N.B. of Commerce.
3793.	Kansas City.	German American N.B.
3841.	Joplin.	First N.B.
3863.	Kansas City.	Nat. Exchange Bank.
3904.	Kansas City.	Midland N.B.
3946.	Trenton.	Grundy County N.B.
3957.	Trenton.	First N.B.
3959.	Nevada.	First N.B.
4000.	Moberly.	First N.B.
4010.	Hannibal.	First N.B.
4048.	Saint Louis.	Continental N.B.
4053.	Saint Joseph.	Schuster-Hax N.B.
4057.	Lamar.	First N.B.
4079.	Carrollton.	First N.B.
4083.	Brunswick.	First N.B.
4111.	Chillicothe.	Citizens' N.B.
4141.	Odessa.	N.B. of Odessa.
4151.	Hamilton.	First N.B.
4157.	Independence.	First N.B.
4160.	Stewartsville.	First N.B.
4174.	Hopkins.	First N.B.
4178.	Saint Louis.	N.B. of Commerce.
4215.	Plattsburg.	First N.B.
4225.	Pierce City.	First N.B.
4228.	Saint Joseph.	State N.B.
4232.	Saint Louis.	N.B. of the Republic.
4243.	Maryville.	Maryville N.B.
4251.	Kansas City.	Aetna N.B.
4259.	Cameron.	First N.B.
4262.	Saint Louis.	Laclede N.B.
4329.	Platte City.	First N.B.
4360.	Springfield.	American N.B.
4373.	King City.	First N.B. and Trust Co.
4381.	Kansas City.	Inter-State N.B.
4392.	Sedalia.	Sedalia N.B.
4409.	Aurora.	First N.B.
4425.	Joplin.	Joplin N.B.
4441.	Carthage.	Central N.B.
4464.	Kansas City.	Metropolitan N.B.
4475.	Cartbrville.	First N.B.
4494.	Kansas City.	Missouri N.B.
4575.	Saint Louis.	Chemical N.B.
4611.	Cape Girardeau.	First N.B.
4786.	Kansas City.	Continental N.B.
4815.	Carthage.	Carthage N.B.
4933.	Trenton.	Trenton N.B.
4939.	Saint Joseph.	First N.B.
5002.	Saint Louis.	Merchants-Laclede N.B.
5036.	West Plains.	First N.B.
5082.	Springfield.	Nat. Exchange Bank
5107.	Kirksvile.	N.B. of Kirksville.
5138.	Kansas City.	New England N.B.
5156.	Warrensburg.	People's N.B.
5172.	Saint Louis.	State N.B.
5209.	Springfield.	Union N.B.
5250.	Kansas City.	City N.B.
5388.	Washington.	First N.B.
5515.	Sarcoxie.	First N.B.
5544.	Lathrop.	First N.B.
5780.	Savannah.	First N.B.
5788.	Saint Louis.	Mechanics' N.B.
5794.	Paris.	Paris N.B.
5827.	Gallatin.	First N.B.
5871.	Kirksville.	Baird N.B.
5973.	Monett.	First N.B.
6242.	Burlington Junction.	First N.B.
6272.	Saint Joseph.	Tootle-Lacy N.B.
6343.	Harrisonville.	Citizens' N.B.
6369.	Jasper.	First N.B.
6382.	Neosho.	First N.B.
6383.	King City.	Citizens' N.B.
6405.	Butler.	Bates N.B.
6549.	Ridgeway.	First N.B.
6635.	Hannibal.	Hannibal N.B.
6773.	Saint Louis.	Washington N.B.
6875.	Centralia.	First N.B.
6885.	Campbell.	First N.B.
6926.	Cowgill.	First N.B.
7066.	Marceline.	First N.B.
7094.	Liberal.	First N.B.
7154.	Pleasant Hill.	Farmers' N.B.
7179.	Saint Louis.	Bankers Worlds Fair N.B.
7205.	Albany.	First N.B.
7256.	Versailles.	First N.B.
7271.	Bolivar.	First N.B.
7282.	Mountain Grove.	First N.B.
7351.	Braymer.	First N.B.
7460.	Jamesport.	First N.B.
7494.	Jackson.	People's N.B.
7570.	Saint Louis.	American Exchange N.B.
7573.	Bosworth.	First N.B.
7643.	Manchester.	First N.B.
7656.	Seneca.	First N.B.
7684.	Golden City.	First N.B.
7715.	Saint Louis.	Mechanics-American N.B.
7729.	Canton.	First N.B.
7741.	Excelsior Springs.	First N.B.
7806.	Clinton.	Clinton N.B.
7808.	Saint Louis.	City N.B.
7853.	Linn Creek.	First N.B.
7884.	Polo.	First N.B.
7900.	Ludlow.	First N.B.
7921.	Salem.	First N.B.
8009.	Bethany.	First N.B.
8011.	Wellston.	First N.B.
8016.	Webb City.	N.B. of Webb City.
8021.	Saint Joseph.	Burnes N.B.
8276.	Kirksville.	Citizens' N.B.
8358.	Fulton.	First N.B.
8359.	Salisbury.	Farmers and Merchants' N.B.
8363.	Salisbury.	First N.B.
8407.	Cainesville.	First N.B.
8455.	Saint Louis.	Central N.B.
8509.	Clinton.	People's N.B.
8570.	Green City.	American N.B.
8657.	Ludlow.	Farmers' N.B.
8660.	Kansas City.	Central N.B.
8738.	Kansas City.	N.B. of the Republic.
8877.	Cabool.	First N.B.
8914.	Steelville.	First N.B.
8916.	Fairview.	First N.B.
8947.	Joplin.	Cunningham N.B.
8979.	Cassville.	First N.B.
9029.	Green City.	City N.B.
9042.	Saint Joseph.	American N.B.
9137.	Shelbina.	Shelbina N.B.
9172.	Kansas City.	Security N.B.
9236.	Kansas City.	Traders' N.B.
9297.	Saint Louis.	Mercantile N.B.
9311.	Kansas City.	Southwest N.B.
9315.	Springfield.	Merchants' N.B.
9382.	Nevada.	Thornton N.B.
9383.	Kansas City.	Park N.B.
9404.	Kansas City.	Gate City N.B.
9460.	Saint Louis.	Broadway N.B.
9490.	Edina.	First N.B.
9519.	Windsor.	First N.B.
9560.	Kansas City.	Drovers N.B.
9677.	Kansas Citv.	Nat. Reserve Bank.

Charter Number	City	Name of Bank
9928.	Chaffee.	First N.B.
9932.	Seymour.	People's N.B.
10009.	Marshfield.	First N.B.
10039.	Kansas City.	Commonwealth N.B.
10055.	El Dorado Springs.	First N.B.
10074.	Springfield.	McDaniel N.B.
10122.	Purdy.	First N.B.
10231.	Kansas City.	N.B. of Commerce.
10367.	Harlem, North Kansas City.	N.B. of Harlem.
10375.	Adrian.	First N.B.
10384.	Holden.	First N.B.
10413.	Kansas City.	Stock Yards N.B.
10633.	Golden City.	Citizens' N.B.
10695.	Lebanon.	First N.B.
10784.	Cartithersville.	First N.B.
10892.	Kansas City.	Midwest N.B. and Trust Co.
10915.	Boonville.	Boonville N.B.
11037.	Kansas City.	Nat. City Bank.
11235.	Montgomery City.	First N.B.
11320.	Dexter.	First N.B.
11344.	Kansas City.	Fidelity N.B. and Trust Co.
11366.	Saint Louis.	Saint Louis N.B.
11372.	Sweet Springs.	First N.B.
11377.	Kansas City.	Continental N.B. of Jackson Co.
11402.	Perryville.	First N.B.
11467.	Stoutland.	First N.B.
11472.	Kansas City.	Columbia N.B.
11491.	Kansas City.	Central Exchange N.B.
11919.	Cardwell.	First N.B.
11973.	Saint Louis.	Republic N.B.
11989.	Saint Louis.	Nat. City Bank.
12010.	Purdy.	Purdy N.B.
12066.	Saint Louis.	Security N.B. Savings and Trust Co.
12216.	Saint Louis.	Saint Louis N.B.
12220.	Saint Louis.	Grand N.B.
12260.	Kansas City.	Continental N.B. and Trust Co.
12329.	Clayton.	Clayton N.B.
12333.	Clayton.	First N.B.
12389.	Saint Louis.	Telegraphers' N.B.
12413.	Adrian.	N.B. of Adrian.
12452.	Steele.	First N.B.
12491.	Saint Louis.	Twelfth Street N.B.
12506.	Saint Louis.	American Exchange N.B.
12643.	Saint Louis.	Cherokee N.B.
12674.	Ridgeway.	Farmers' N.B.
12686.	Kansas City.	New England N.B. and Trust Co.
12770.	Springfield.	New First N.B.
12781.	Webster Grove.	First N.B.
12794.	Kansas City.	Drovers N.B.
12815.	Parkville.	First N.B.
12820.	Brookfield.	First N.B.
12907.	Oran.	First N.B.
12916.	Saint Louis.	Boatmen's N.B.
12955.	Maplewood.	Citizens N.B.
13142.	Jefferson City.	Exchange N.B.
13162.	Joplin.	Conqueror First N.B.
13264.	St. Louis.	South Side N.B.
13268.	Unionville.	N.B. of Unionville.
13270.	St. Louis.	Vandeventer N.B.
13293.	Ludlow.	Ludlow N.B.
13367.	Versailles.	First N.B.
13376.	St. Louis.	Plaza N.B.
13481.	Clayton.	Clayton N.B.
13504.	Mount Vernon.	First N.B.
13514.	Luxemburg.	Lafayette N.B. and Trust Co.
13546.	Cowgill.	First N.B.
13690.	North Kansas City	N.B. in North Kansas City.
13726.	St. Louis.	American Exchange N.B.
13736.	Kansas City.	Union N.B.
13875.	Liberty.	National Commercial Bank.
13936.	Kansas City.	City N.B. and Trust Co.
14092.	Caruthersville.	N.B. of Caruthersville.
14119.	Butler.	First N.B.
14128.	St. Louis.	South Side N.B.
14196.	Lamar.	First N.B.

MONTANA

Charter Number	City	Name of Bank
1649.	Helena.	First N.B.
1960.	Helena.	Montana N.B.
1975.	Deer Lodge.	First N.B.
2027.	Bozeman.	First N.B.
2105.	Helena.	People's N.B.
2106.	Missoula.	First N.B.
2476.	Great Falls.	Northwestern N.B.
2566.	Butte.	First N.B.
2732.	Helena.	Merchants' N.B.
2752.	Miles City.	First N.B.
2757.	Helena.	Second N.B.
2803.	Bozeman.	Bozeman N.B.
2813.	Helena.	Montana N.B.
3006.	Livingston.	First N.B.
3075.	Bozeman.	Gallatin Valley N.B.
3097.	Billings.	First N.B.
3120.	Dillon.	First N.B.
3173.	Dillon.	Dillon N.B.
3275.	Miles City.	Stock Growers' N.B.
3375.	White Suphur Springs.	First N.B.
3525.	Great Falls.	First N.B.
3605.	Livingston.	Nat. Park Bank.
3965.	Anaconda.	First N.B.
3995.	Missoula.	Western Montana N.B.
4117.	Livingston.	Livingston N.B.
4194.	Fort Benton.	Stockmen's N.B.
4283.	Butte City.	Silver Bow N.B.
4323.	Boulder.	First N.B.
4396.	Helena.	American N.B.
4406.	Helena.	Helena N.B.
4434.	Great Falls.	Merchants' N.B.
4541.	Great Falls.	Great Falls N.B.
4572.	Castle.	First N.B.
4586.	Kalispell.	First N.B.
4590.	Big Timber.	First N.B.
4593.	Billings.	Yellowstone N.B.
4600.	Neihart.	First N.B.
4651.	Kalispell.	Globe N.B.
4658.	Philipsburg.	First N.B.
4803.	Kalispell.	Conrad N.B.
4843.	Philipsburg.	Merchants and Miners' N.B.
4932.	Big Timber.	Big Timber N.B.
4968.	Bozeman.	Commercial N.B.
5015.	Miles City.	Commercial N.B.
5671.	Helena.	N.B. of Montana.
5676.	Havre.	First N.B.
6097.	Chinook.	First N.B.
7101.	Glendive.	First N.B.
7172.	Plains.	First N.B.
7274.	Lewistown.	First N.B.
7320.	Forsyth.	First N.B.
7441.	Bozeman.	N.B.of Gallatin Valley.
7644.	Harlem.	First N.B.
7990.	Glasgow.	First N.B.
8055.	Glendive.	Merchants' N.B.
8168.	Culbertson.	First N.B.
8259.	Wibaux.	First N.B.
8539.	Moore.	First N.B.
8589.	Whitefish.	First N.B.
8635.	Kalispell.	Kalispell N.B.
8655.	Glasgow.	Glasgow N.B.
8669.	Laurel.	First N.B.
8716.	Laurel.	Citizens' N.B.
9004.	Sidney.	First N.B.
9103.	Ismay.	First N.B.
9165.	Roundup.	First N.B.
9215.	Hardin.	First N.B.
9270.	Harlowton.	First N.B.
9337.	Three Forks.	First N.B.
9355.	Billings.	Merchants' N.B.
9396.	Columbus.	First N.B.
9440.	Havre.	Citizens' N.B.
9449.	Poison.	First N.B.
9486.	Hamilton.	First N.B.
9520.	Valier.	First N.B.
9574.	Cut Bank.	First N.B.
9583.	Anaconda.	Anaconda N.B.
9594.	Libby.	First N.B.
9738.	Malta.	First N.B.
9759.	Conrad.	First N.B.
9782.	Havre.	Havre N.B.
9789.	Saco.	First N.B.
9841.	Red Lodge.	United States N.B.
9864.	Ronan.	First N.B.
9899.	Deer Lodge.	United States N.B.
9982.	Townsend.	First N.B.
10053.	Chinook.	Farmers' N.B.
10438.	Plentywood.	First N.B.
10443.	Baker.	First N.B.
10530.	Great Falls.	Commercial N.B.
10539.	Sidney.	Yellowstone Valley N.B.
10552.	Sidney.	Farmers' N.B.
10625.	Stanford.	First N.B.
10675.	Roundup.	Roundup N.B.
10709.	Stevensville.	First N.B.
10715.	Hobson.	First N.B.
10769.	Bridger.	First N.B.
10803.	Geraldine.	First N.B.
10809.	Broad View.	First N.B.
10819.	Denton.	First N.B.
10838.	Scobey.	First N.B.
10881.	Richey.	First N.B.
10883.	Browning.	First N.B.
10884.	Miles City.	Miles City N.B.
10885.	Poplar.	First N.B.
10907.	Judith Gap.	First N.B.
10910.	Winsdale.	First N.B.
10917.	Baylor.	First N.B.
10922.	Pompey's Pillar.	First N.B.
10926.	Sidney.	Sidney N.B.
10928.	Intake.	First N.B.
10929.	Joplin.	First N.B.
10933.	Billings.	Montana N.B.
10934.	Carlyle.	First N.B.
10937.	Choteau.	First N.B.
10939.	Grass Range.	First N.B.
10942.	Forsyth.	American N.B.
10952.	Geyser.	First N.B.
10953.	Shelby.	First N.B.
10985.	Bainville.	First N.B.
10986.	Reserve.	First N.B.
10991.	Roy.	First N.B.
10995.	Carter.	First N.B.
10996.	Three Forks.	American N.B.
11000.	Livingston.	Northwestern N.B.
11004.	Big Sandy.	First N.B.
11006.	Winifred.	First N.B.
11008.	Twin-Bridges.	First N.B.
11013.	Mott, Stickley.	First N.B.
11017.	Rapelje, Lake Basin.	First N.B.
11024.	Whitehall.	First N.B.
11026.	Hysham.	First N.B.
11027.	Brockton.	First N.B.
11030.	Brady.	First N.B.
11032.	Savage.	First N.B.
11036.	Wolf Point.	First N.B.
11040.	Malta.	Malta N.B.
11048.	Nashua.	First N.B.
11061.	Froid.	First N.B.
11063.	Big Sandy.	Farmers' N.B.
11066.	Absarokee.	Stillwater Valley N.B.
11070.	Hardin.	Stockmen's N.B.
11074.	Plevna.	First N.B.
11075.	Wolf Point.	Citizens' N.B.
11077.	Havre.	Montana N.B.
11078.	Raymond.	First N.B.
11085.	Harlowton.	Farmers' N.B.
11086.	Dodson.	First N.B.
11089.	Galata.	First N.B.
11095.	Raynesford.	Stockmen's N.B.
11096.	Fresno.	First N.B.
11097.	Opheim.	First N.B.
11098.	Scobey.	Merchants N.B.
11101.	Circle.	First N.B.
11105.	Chester.	First N.B.
11131.	Highwood.	First N.B.
11134.	Oswego.	First N.B.
11160.	Lodge Grass.	First N.B.
11165.	Charlo.	First N.B.
11176.	Lambert.	First N.B.
11199.	Savoy.	First N.B.
11203.	Rudyard.	First N.B.
11209.	Westby.	First N.B.
11220.	Columbus.	Stockmen's N.B.
11269.	Musselshell.	First N.B.
11298.	Bridger.	American N.B.
11307.	Fairfield.	First N.B.
11334.	Reed Point.	First N.B.
11335.	Wilsall.	First N.B.
11350.	Antelope.	First N.B.
11382.	Ekalaka.	First N.B.
11391.	Winhett.	First N.B.
11418.	Broadus.	First N.B.
11429.	Great Falls.	Northern N.B.
11437.	Rosebud.	First N.B.
11465.	Ingomar.	First N.B.
11475.	McCabe.	First N.B.
11492.	Lima.	Security N.B.
11493.	Jordan.	First N.B.
11673.	Belt.	First N.B.
11696.	Billings.	American N.B.
12015.	Fairview.	First N.B.
12361.	Three Forks.	Labor N.B. of Montana.
12407.	Billings.	Midland N.B.
12536.	Miles City.	First N.B.
12542.	Anaconda.	N.B. of Anaconda.
12585.	Hysham.	First N.B.
12608.	Lewistown.	N.B. of Lewistown.
12679.	Sidney.	Richland N.B.
13384.	Livingston.	National Park Bank.
13417.	Harlowton.	Continental N.B.
13837.	Chinook.	Farmers N.B.
14334.	Butte.	Miners N.B.

NEBRASKA

Charter Number	City	Name of Bank
209.	Omaha.	First N.B.
1417.	Nebraska City.	Otoe County N.B.
1633.	Omaha.	Omaha N.B.
1679.	Omaha.	Central N.B.
1798.	Lincoln.	First N.B.
1846.	Brownville.	First N.B.
1855.	Nebraska City.	Nebraska City N.B.
1899.	Lincoln.	State N.B.
1914.	Plattsmouth.	First N.B.
1974.	Fremont.	First N.B.
2121.	Ashland.	First N.B.
2357.	Beatrice.	First N.B.
2528.	Hastings.	First N.B.
2536.	Nebraska City.	Merchants' N.B.
2665.	Omaha.	Nebraska N.B.
2683.	York.	First N.B.
2706.	Crete.	First N.B.
2724.	Blair.	First N.B.
2746.	Falls City.	First N.B.
2750.	Lincoln.	Lincoln N.B.
2756.	Hebron.	First N.B.
2771.	Seward.	First N.B.
2774.	Norfolk.	First N.B.
2775.	Omaha.	Merchants' N.B.
2778.	Schuyler.	First N.B.
2779.	Grand Island.	First N.B.
2780.	Wahoo.	First N.B.
2806.	Kearney.	First N.B.
2807.	Columbus.	First N.B.
2811.	Red Cloud.	First N.B.
2825.	Pawnee City.	First N.B.
2848.	Fremont.	Fremont N.B.
2871.	Central City.	First N.B.
2897.	Aurora.	First N.B.
2902.	David City.	First N.B.
2921.	Ashland.	N.B. of Ashland.
2955.	Tecumseh.	First N.B.
2960.	Friend.	First N.B.
2964.	Fullerton.	First N.B.
2978.	Omaha.	United States N.B.
2988.	Lincoln.	Capital N.B.
2991.	Wilber.	First N.B.
2994.	Fairbury.	First N.B.
3057.	Minden.	First N.B.
3059.	North Bend.	First N.B.
3060.	Seward.	Jones N.B.
3081.	Beatrice.	Beatrice N.B.
3083.	Syracuse.	First N.B.
3086.	Hastings.	Exchange N.B.
3099.	Hastings.	City N.B.
3101.	Grand Island.	Citizens' N.B.

Charter Number	City	Name of Bank	Charter Number	City	Name of Bank	Charter Number	City	Name of Bank
3117.	Exeter.	Exeter N.B.	4632.	South Omaha.	Union Stock Yards N.B.	8760.	Hay Springs.	First N.B.
3118.	Wahoo.	Saunders County N.B.	4791.	Pender.	First N.B.	8797.	Creighton.	Creighton N.B.
3121.	Exeter.	First N.B.	4820.	Crete.	Crete N.B.	8811.	Utica.	First N.B.
3126.	Saint Paul.	First N.B.	4890.	Gothenburg.	First N.B.	8812.	Curtis.	First N.B.
3129.	Saint Paul.	Saint Paul N.B.	4895.	De Witt.	First N.B.	8823.	McCook.	McCook N.B.
3152.	Schuyler.	Schuyler N.B.	4935.	York.	City N.B.	8851.	Lawrence.	First N.B.
3162.	York.	York N.B.	5180.	Columbus.	Commercial N.B.	8863.	Bancroft.	First N.B.
3163.	Omaha.	Commercial N.B.	5189.	Genoa.	First N.B.	8885.	Lincoln.	Central N.B.
3181.	Red Cloud.	Red Cloud N.B.	5213.	Lincoln.	City N.B.	8888.	Harrison.	First N.B.
3188.	Fremont.	Farmers and Merchants' N.B.	5281.	Weeping Water.	City N.B.	8949.	South Omaha.	Live Stock N.B.
3201.	Kearney.	Kearney N.B.	5282.	Newman Gorve.	First N.B.	8975.	Campbell.	First N.B.
3208.	Holdrege.	First N.B.	5297.	Hooper.	First N.B.	8988.	Decature.	First N.B.
3230.	Fairmont.	First N.B.	5308.	Pender.	Pender N.B.	8992.	Ainsworth.	N.B. of Ainsworth.
3238.	Humboldt.	First N.B.	5337.	Humphrey.	First N.B.	8995.	Fairbury.	Bonham N.B.
3240.	Sutton.	First N.B.	5346.	Saint Edward.	First N.B.	9056.	Aurora.	Aurora N.B.
3292.	Lexington.	First N.B.	5368.	Wakefield.	First N.B.	9092.	Amherst.	First N.B.
3302.	Arapahoe.	First N.B.	5384.	Fullerton.	Fullerton N.B.	9138.	Wymore.	City N.B.
3339.	Ord.	First N.B.	5397.	Superior.	Superior N.B.	9191.	Rushville.	Stockmen's N.B.
3340.	West Point.	West Point N.B.	5400.	Hartington.	Hartington N.B.	9200.	Shelton.	Shelton N.B.
3342.	Orleans.	First N.B.	5419.	Loomis.	First N.B.	9217.	Tilden.	First N.B.
3343.	Auburn.	First N.B.	5440.	Elgin.	First N.B.	9223.	Adams.	First N.B.
3347.	Norfolk.	Norfolk N.B.	5657.	Alliance.	Alliance N.B.	9244.	Wayne.	Citizens' N.B.
3364.	Stanton.	First N.B.	5690.	Neligh.	Neligh N.B.	9258.	Callaway.	First N.B.
3370.	West Point.	First N.B.	5770.	O'Neill.	O'Neill N.B.	9395.	Grand Island.	Grand Island N.B.
3373.	Loup City.	First N.B.	5787.	Elmwood.	First N.B.	9400.	Minden.	Minden Exchange N.B.
3379.	McCook.	First N.B.	5793.	Saint Edward.	Smith N.B.	9436.	McCook.	Citizens' N.B.
3390.	Dorchester.	First N.B.	5937'.	Pilger.	First N.B.	9448.	Bristow.	First N.B.
3392.	Wayne.	First N.B.	5941.	Pilger.	Farmers' N.B.	9466.	Omaha.	City N.B.
3403.	Greenwood.	First N.B.	5957.	Carroll.	First N.B.	9504.	Plainview.	First N.B.
3419.	Blue Hill.	First N.B.	5995.	Broken Bow.	Custer N.B.	9581.	Scottsbluff.	Scottsbluff N.B.
3424.	O'Neill.	First N.B.	6166.	Tecumseh.	Citizens' N.B.	9591.	Craig.	First N.B.
3445.	Broken Bow.	Custer County N.B.	6201.	Nebr. Sidney.	First N.B.	9623.	Butte.	First N.B.
3449.	Broken Bow.	First N.B.	6221.	Lyons.	First N.B.	9653.	Morrill.	First N.B.
3481.	Ord.	Ord N.B.	6240.	Ecottsbluff.	First N.B.	9665.	Naper.	First N.B.
3483.	Indianola.	First N.B.	6282.	Gothenburg.	Gothenburg N.B.	9666.	Bayard.	First N.B.
3493.	Fairfield.	First N.B.	6378.	Valentine.	First N.B.	9671.	Winnebago.	First N.B.
3495.	Nelson.	First N.B.	6415.	Wilber.	N.B. of Wilber.	9694.	Gering.	Gering N.B.
3496.	North Platte.	First N.B.	6464.	Anoka.	Anoka N.B.	9711.	Bridgeport.	First N.B.
3516.	Omaha.	Union N.B.	6489.	Atkinson.	First N.B.	9730.	Omaha.	Corn Exchange N.B.
3523.	Weeping Water.	First N.B.	6493.	Osceola.	First N.B.	9731.	Crete.	City N.B.
3526.	Kearney.	Buffalo County N.B.	6503.	Bloomfield.	First N.B.	9741.	Lodge Pole.	First N.B.
3529.	Superior.	First N.B.	6506.	Cambridge.	First N.B.	9762.	Imperial.	First N.B.
3549.	Franklin.	First N.B.	6541.	Pawnee City.	N.B. of Pawnee City.	9772.	Havelock.	First N.B.
3571.	Lincoln.	German N.B.	6600.	Kearney.	Central N.B.	9785.	Lynch.	First N.B.
3574.	Clay Center.	First N.B.	6805.	Genoa.	Genoa N.B.	9790.	Chappell.	First N.B.
3580.	Alma.	First N.B.	6818.	Beemer.	First N.B.	9793.	Laurel.	First N.B.
3603.	Omaha.	State N.B.	6866.	Wisner.	Citizens' N.B.	9796.	Coleridge.	First N.B.
3611.	South Omaha.	South Omaha N.B.	6900.	Crawford.	First N.B.	9816.	Walthill.	Walthill N.B.
3619.	Beaver City.	First N.B.	6901.	Scribner.	First N.B.	9831.	Lehigh.	First N.B.
3627.	Ponca.	First N.B.	6939.	Clarks.	First N.B.	9908.	South Omaha.	Stock Yards N.B.
3628.	Auburn.	Carson N.B.	6947.	Stuart.	First N.B.	9979.	Laurel.	Laurel N.B.
3652.	Ogallala.	First N.B.	7026.	Mitchell.	First N.B.	9984.	Wakefield.	Farmers' N.B.
3653.	Sutton.	Sutton N.B.	7065.	Humboldt.	N.B. of Humboldt.	9994.	Wausa.	First N.B.
3674.	Rulo.	First N.B.	7204.	Elwood.	First N.B.	10011.	Tilden.	Tilden N.B.
3725.	Tobias.	First N.B.	7239.	Lincoln.	N.B. of Commerce.	10017.	Wausa.	Commercial N.B.
3732.	Hastings.	Nebraska N.B.	7277.	Loup City.	First N.B.	10021.	Madison.	Madison N.B.
3741.	Norfolk.	Citizens' N.B.	7325.	Spencer.	First N.B.	10022.	Oakland.	Farmers and Merchants' N.B.
3773.	Madison.	First N.B.	7329.	Norfolk.	Nebraska N.B.	10023.	Coleridge.	Coleridge N.B.
3801.	David City.	Central Nebraska N.B.	7333.	Dodge.	First N.B.	10025.	Belden.	First N.B.
3823.	Chadron.	First N.B.	7340.	Burwell.	First N.B.	10033.	Brunswick.	First N.B.
3875.	Holdrege.	Holdrege N.B.	7355.	Diller.	First N.B.	10081.	Oshkosh.	First N.B.
3891.	Saint Paul.	Citizens' N.B.	7384.	Sargent.	First N.B.	10242.	Hemingford.	First N.B.
3921.	Gibbon.	First N.B.	7393.	Ansley.	First N.B.	10340.	Fairbury.	Farmers and Merchants' N.B.
3927.	Broken Bow.	Central Nebraska N.B.	7421.	Randolph.	First N.B.	10970.	Hershey.	First N.B.
3934.	David City.	City N.B.	7425.	Emerson.	First N.B.	11071.	Valentine.	Farmers' N.B.
3939.	Wood River.	First N.B.	7449.	North Bend.	N.B. of North Bend.	11426.	Basisett.	First N.B.
3958.	Kearney.	City N.B.	7477.	Randolph.	Security N.B.	11829.	Omaha.	Peters N.B.
3960.	Albion.	First N.B.	7520.	Oxford.	First N.B.	11835.	South Sioux City.	First N.B.
3999.	Elm Creek.	First N.B.	7574.	Spalding.	First N.B.	12225.	Unadilla.	First N.B.
4024.	North Platte.	North Platte N.B.	7578.	Tobias.	Tobias N.B.	12342.	Lincoln.	Lincoln State N.B.
4029.	Wisner.	First N.B.	7622.	Greeley.	First N.B.	12495.	Herningford.	Citizens' N.B.
4042.	Shelton.	First N.B.	7737.	University.	First N.B. Place.	12552.	Harrison.	Sioux N.B.
4043.	Ravenna.	First N.B.	7821.	York.	Farmers' N.B.	12625.	Morrill.	First N.B.
4052.	Geneva.	First N.B.	7836.	Stanton.	Stanton N.B.	12626.	Mitchell.	First N.B.
4078.	Pawnee City.	Farmers' N.B.	7861.	Wilcox.	First N.B.	13013.	Kearney.	City N.B.
4080.	Liberty.	First N.B.	7881.	Atkinson.	Atkinson N.B.	13017.	Lincoln.	City N.B.
4087.	Omaha.	American N.B.	7925.	Overton.	First N.B.	13101.	Osmond.	First N.B.
4089.	Ainsworth.	First N.B.	7949.	Shelby.	First N.B.	13138.	Springviiw.	First N.B.
4110.	Neligh.	First N.B.	8027.	Blair.	Blair N.B.	13139.	Ainsworth.	Commercial N.B.
4129.	Harvard.	First N.B.	8031.	Hayes Center.	First N.B.	13148.	Central City.	Farmers N.B.
4148.	Beatrice.	German N.B.	8062.	Gering.	First N.B.	13158.	Arcadia.	First N.B.
4161.	Lexington.	Dawson County N.B.	8093.	Litchfield.	First N.B.	13176.	Shelton.	First N.B.
4163.	Sterling.	First N.B.	8097.	Bradshaw.	First N.B.	13182.	Laurel.	Security N.B.
4165.	Cozad.	First N.B.	8105.	Benedict.	First N.B.	13189.	Exeter.	Wallace N.B.
4170.	Grant.	First N.B.	8113.	Gothenburg.	Citizens' N.B.	13243.	Exeter.	Exeter N.B.
4173.	Albion.	Albion N.B.	8161.	Johnson.	First N.B.	13244.	Primrose.	First N.B.
4176.	Rushville.	First N.B.	8172.	Gresham.	First N.B.	13271.	Lyman.	First N.B.
4185.	Beatrice.	Nebraska N.B.	8183.	Henderson.	First N.B.	13281.	Wakefield.	Wakefield N.B.
4210.	Wymore.	First N.B.	8186.	Crofton.	First N.B.	13316.	Minatare.	First N.B.
4226.	Alliance.	First N.B.	8218.	Trenton.	First N.B.	13322.	Minden.	Nebraska N.B.
4242.	Creighton.	First N.B.	8246.	Aurora.	Fidelity N.B.	13333.	Lincoln.	Continental N.B.
4245.	York.	Nebraska N.B.	8282.	Cedar Rapids.	First N.B.	13339.	Oakdale.	First N.B.
4270.	Omaha.	N.B. of Commerce.	8285.	Hampton.	First N.B.	13408.	Fremont.	Stephens N.B.
4276.	Tecumseh.	Tecumseh N.B.	8286.	Strornsburg.	First N.B.	13415.	Wayne.	State N.B.
4280.	Pierce.	First N.B.	8317.	Madison.	Farmers' N.B.	13419.	Grant.	Farmers N.B.
4324.	Tekamah.	First N.B.	8328.	Columbus.	Central N.B.	13420.	Kimball.	American N.B.
4345.	Holdrege.	City N.B.	8335.	Wynot.	First N.B.	13423.	Lewellen.	First N.B.
4354.	Wayne.	Wayne N.B.	8372.	Allen.	First N.B.	13424.	Grand Island.	Nebraska N.B.
4357.	Grand Island.	Security N.B.	8383.	Johnson.	German N.B.	13425.	Sidney.	American N.B.
4435.	Lincoln.	Columbia N.B.	8385.	Central City.	Central City N.B.	13426.	Cozad.	First N.B.
4484.	Geneva.	Geneva N.B.	8400.	Marquette.	First N.B.	13429.	Bushnell.	First N.B.
4504.	Fremont.	Commercial N.B.	8413.	Wolbach.	First N.B.	13431.	Seward.	Cattle N.B.
4528.	Hartington.	First N.B.	8466.	Bertrand.	First N.B.	13433.	Glenvil.	First N.B.
4557.	South Sioux City.	First N.B.	8469.	Brazile Mills.	First N.B.	13435.	Ashland.	Farmers & Merchants N.B.
4583.	Arlington.	First N.B.	8521.	Gordon.	First N.B.	13440.	Kimball.	Kimball N.B.
4588.	Atiburn.	Farmers and Merchants' N.B.	8533.	Polk.	First N.B.	13446.	Overton.	Overton N.B.
4589.	South Omaha.	Packers' N.B.	8567.	Orleans.	Citizens' N.B.	13453.	Pilger.	Farmers N.B.
4606.	Lincoln.	American Exchange N.B.	8651.	Kearney.	Commercial N.B.	13456.	Doniphan.	N.B. of Doniphan.
4610.	Oakland.	First N.B.	8685.	Walthill.	First N.B.	13461.	Greeley.	City N.B.

Charter Number	City	Name of Bank
13462.	St. Paul.	Citizens N.B.
13463.	St. Paul.	St. Paul N.B.
13464.	Tobias.	Citizens N.B.
13515.	Hastings.	Hastings N.B.
13557.	Ord.	First N.B.
13568.	Neligh.	N.B. of Neligh.
13582.	Norfolk.	De Lay N.B.
13591.	Creighton.	American N.B.
13617.	Alliance.	Nebraska N.B.
13620.	Loup City.	First N.B.
13953.	Hastings.	City N.B.
14004.	Omaha.	City N.B.
14017.	Aurora.	Packers N.B.
14018.	Grand Island.	Overland N.B.
14073.	Exeter.	First N.B.
14083.	Superior.	Security N.B.
14174.	Ashland.	Citizens N.B.
14194.	David City.	City N.B.
14256.	Scribner.	First N.B.
14282.	Wymore.	Wymore N.B.
14308.	West Point.	Farmers & Merchants N.B.
14339.	Norfolk.	N.B. of Norfolk.
14340.	Grand Island.	Commercial N.B.

NEVADA

Charter Number	City	Name of Bank
1331.	Austin.	First N.B. of Nevada.
2478.	Reno.	First N.B.
3575.	Winnemucca.	First N.B.
7038.	Reno.	Farmers and Merchants' N.B.
7654.	Lovelock.	First N.B.
7743.	Elko.	First N.B.
8424.	Reno.	Reno N.B.
8530.	Tonopah.	Nevada First N.B.
8561.	Ely.	First N.B.
8686.	Rhyolite.	First N.B.
9078.	Goldfield.	First N.B.
9242.	Carson City.	First N.B.
9310.	Ely.	Ely N.B.
9452.	McGill.	McGill N.B.
9578.	East Ely.	Copper N.B.
11784.	Eureka.	Farmers and Merchants' N.B.

NEW HAMPSHIRE

Charter Number	City	Name of Bank
19.	Portsmouth.	First N.B.
84.	Nashua.	First N.B.
318.	Concord.	First N.B.
401.	Portsmouth.	Nat. Mechanics' Traders' Bank.
499.	Derry.	Derry N.B.
537.	Charlestown.	Connecticut River N.B.
559.	Keene.	Cheshire N.B.
574.	Manchester.	Arnoskeag N.B.
576.	Francestown.	First N.B.
596.	Claremont.	Claremont N.B.
758.	Concord.	Nat. State Capital Bank
808.	Lebanon.	N.B. of Lebanon.
838.	Gonic.	First N.B.
877.	Keene.	Keene N.B.
887.	Winchester.	Winchester N.B.
888.	Newport.	First N.B.
946.	Keene.	Ashuelot N.B.
1020.	Pittsfield.	Pittsfield N.B.
1025.	Portsmouth.	Rockingham N.B.
1043.	Dover.	Dover N.B.
1052.	Portsmouth.	New Hampshire N.B.
1059.	Manchester.	Manchester N.B.
1070.	Milford.	Souhegan N.B.
1071.	Sandwich.	Carroll County N.B.
1087.	Dover.	Cochecho N.B.
1145.	Hanover.	Dartmouth N.B.
1147.	Exeter.	Nat. Granite Stat Bank.
1153.	Manchester.	First N.B.
1179.	Peterborough.	First N.B.
1180.	Somersworth.	First N.B.
1183.	Somersworth.	Somersworth N.B.
1242.	East Jaffrey.	Monadnock N.B.
1310.	Nashua.	Indian Head N.B.
1330.	New Market.	New Market N.B.
1333.	Tilton.	Citizens' N.B.
1353.	Dover.	Strafford N.B.
1486.	Wolfborough.	Lake N.B.
1520.	Manchester.	Merchants' N.B.
1645.	Laconia.	Laconia N.B.
1674.	Warner.	Kearsarge N.B.
1688.	Hillsborough.	First N.B.
1885.	Littleton.	Littleton N.B.
2022.	Farmington.	Farmington N.B.
2138.	Rochester.	Rochester N.B.
2240.	Nashua.	Second N.B.
2299.	Keene.	Citizens' N.B.
2362.	Manchester.	Second N.B.
2443.	Franklin.	Franklin N.B.
2447.	Concord.	Mechanicks' N.B.
2587.	Plymouth.	Pemigewasset N.B.
2600.	Lancaster.	Lancaster N.B.
2672.	Portsmouth.	First N.B.
2741.	Nashua.	First N.B.
3404.	Newport.	Citizens' N.B.
4037.	Laconia.	People's N.B.
4041.	Colebrook.	Colebrook N.B.
4523.	Berlin.	Berlin N.B.
4693.	Manchester.	N.B.of the Commonwealth.
4740.	Lakeport.	Lakeport N.B.
4793.	Claremont.	People's N.B.
5092.	Woodsville.	Woodsville N.B.
5151.	Bristol.	First N.B.
5183.	Colebrook.	Farmers and Traders' N.B.
5258.	Gorham.	Gorham N.B.
5274.	Dover.	Merchants' N.B.

Charter Number	City	Name of Bank
5317.	Groveton.	Coos County N.B.
5622.	Berlin.	City N.B.
8038.	West Derry.	First N.B.
8147.	Wolfeboro.	Wolfeboro N.B.
9001.	Gorham.	White Mountain N.B.
12889.	Exeter.	Rockingham N.B.
13247.	Wilton.	Wilton N.B.
13764.	Farmington.	Farmington N.B.
13808.	Groveton.	Groveton N.B. Bank.
13829.	Claremont.	Claremont N.B.
13861.	Rochester.	New Public N.B.
14100.	Berlin.	Berlin N.B.

NEW JERSEY

Charter Number	City	Name of Bank
52.	Newark.	First N.B.
208.	New Brunswick.	First N.B.
281.	Trenton.	First N.B.
288.	Jamesburg.	First N.B.
329.	Paterson.	First N.B.
362.	Newark.	Second N.B.
370.	Vincetown.	First N.B.
374.	Jersey City.	First N.B.
395.	Somerville.	First N.B.
399.	Woodstown.	First N.B.
431.	Camden.	First N.B.
445.	Red Bank.	First N.B.
447.	Plainfield.	First N.B.
452.	Freehold.	First N.B.
487.	Elizabeth.	First N.B.
587.	New Brunswick.	N.B. of New Jersey.
695.	Jersey City.	Second N.B.
810.	Paterson.	Second N.B.
860.	Washington.	First N.B.
876.	Newton.	Merchants' N.B.
881.	Rahway.	Union N.B.
892.	Flemington.	Hunterdon County N.B.
896.	Rahway.	N.B. of Rahway.
925.	Newton.	Sussex N.B.
951.	Freehold.	Freehold Nat. Banking Company.
1096.	Belvidere.	Belvidere N.B.
1113.	Morristown.	Nat. Iron Bank.
1114.	Clinton.	Clinton N.B.
1168.	Mount Holly.	Farmers N.B. of New Jersey.
1182.	Jersey City.	Hudson County N.B.
1188.	Morristown.	First N.B.
1191.	Medford.	Burlington County N.B.
1199.	Woodbury.	First N.B.
1209.	Camden.	Nat. State Bank.
1217.	Newark.	Essex County N.B.
1220.	Newark.	Newark City N.B.
1221.	Sussex.	Farmers' N.B.
1222.	Burlington.	Mechanics' N.B.
1239.	Phillipsburg.	Phillipsburg N.B.
1251.	Newark.	Mechanics' N.B.
1259.	Hackettstown.	Hackettstown N.B.
1270.	Millville.	Millville N.B.
1272.	Lambertville.	Lambertville N.B.
1316.	Newark.	Nat. Newark & Essex Banking Co.
1317.	Orange.	Orange N.B.
1326.	Salem.	Salem N.B.
1327.	Trenton.	Mechanics' N.B.
1346.	Bridgeton.	Cumberland N.B.
1356.	Mount Holly.	Mount Holly N.B.
1400.	Toms River.	Ocean County N.B.
1436.	Elizabeth.	Nat. State Bank.
1444.	Hoboken.	First N.B.
1452.	Newark.	Nat. State Bank.
1459.	Frenchtown.	Union N.B.
1681.	Princeton.	Princeton N.B.
1737.	Hightstown.	First N.B.
1759.	Hightstown.	Central N.B.
1818.	Newark.	Merchants and Manufacturers' N.B.
1905.	Hackensack.	First N.B.
2040.	Newark.	Manufacturers' N.B.
2045.	Newark.	Union N.B.
2076.	Dover.	Nat. Union Bank.
2083.	Newark.	North Ward N.B.
2243.	Plainfield.	City, N.B.
2246.	Clinton.	First N.B.
2257.	Red Bank.	Second N.B.
2271.	Bloomsbury.	Bloomsbury N.B.
2331.	Flemington.	Flemington N.B.
2339.	Lambertville.	Arnwell N.B.
2343.	Mount Holly.	Union N.B.
2399.	Vineland.	Vineland N.B.
2509.	Toms River.	First N.B.
2527.	Atlantic City.	Atlantic City N.B.
2551.	Madison.	First N.B.
2918.	Vineland.	Vineland N.B.
2923.	Swedesboro.	Swedesboro N.B.
2999.	Bridgeton.	Bridgeton N.B.
3040.	Manasquan.	First N.B.
3164.	Keyport.	First N.B.
3168.	Cranbury.	First N.B.
3372.	Camden.	Camden N.B.
3387.	Moorestown.	Moorestown N.B.
3451.	Asbury Park.	First N.B.
3501.	Allentown.	Farmers' N.B.
3572.	Passaic.	Passaic N.B.
3621.	Atlantic City.	Second N.B.
3680.	Jersey City.	Third N.B.
3697.	New Brunswick.	People's N.B.
3709.	Trenton.	Broad Street N.B.
3716.	Woodbury.	Farmers and Mechanics' N.B.
3744.	Hoboken.	Second N.B.
3792.	Asbury Park.	Asbury Park N.B.
3843.	Glassboro.	First N.B.

Charter Number	City	Name of Bank
3866.	BouN.B.ook.	First N.B.
3878.	South Amboy.	First N.B.
3922.	Salem.	City N.B.
3936.	Gloucester.	Gloucester City N.B.
3996.	Haddonfield.	Haddonfield N.B.
4056.	Bloomfield.	Bloomfield N.B.
4072.	Paterson.	Paterson N.B.
4119.	Atlantic.	Atlantic Highlands Highlands N.B.
4138.	LoN.B.anch.	First N.B.
4147.	Keyport.	People's N.B.
4182.	Freehold.	Central N.B.
4254.	Hopewell.	Hopewell N.B.
4274.	Boonton.	Boonton N.B.
4365.	Englewood.	Citizens' N.B.
4420.	Atlantic City.	Union N.B.
4535.	Red Bank.	Navesink N.B.
4719.	Westfield.	First N.B.
4724.	Orange.	Second N.B.
4766.	East Orange.	East Orange N.B.
4872.	Princeton.	First N.B.
4942.	Somerville.	Second N.B.
4980.	Belvidere.	Warren County N.B.
5005.	Rutherford.	Rutherford N.B.
5061.	Summit.	First N.B.
5121.	Washington.	Washington N.B.
5136.	Dover.	People's N.B.
5205.	Ridgewood.	First N.B.
5208.	Millville.	Mechanics' N.B.
5215.	Perth Amboy.	First N.B.
5232.	Lakewood.	First N.B.
5260.	Rahway.	Rahway N.B.
5333.	High Bridge.	First N.B.
5363.	Belmar.	First N.B.
5387.	Penn's Grove.	Penn's Grove N.B.
5403.	Ocean Grove.	Ocean Grove N.B.
5416.	Carlstadt.	Carlstadt N.B.
5556.	Phillipsburg.	Second N.B.
5621.	Blairstown.	First N.B.
5712.	Point. Pleasant.	Ocean County N.B. of
5718.	Pennington.	First N.B.
5730.	Spring Lake, Spring Lake Beach.	First N.B.
5830.	Cape May.	First N.B.
5884.	Atlantic City.	Chelsea N.B.
5921.	Hackensack.	Hackensack N.B.
5926.	Seabright.	First N.B.
5981.	Paulsboro.	First N.B.
6038.	Long Branch.	Citizens' N.B.
6060.	Ocean City.	First N.B.
6179.	South River.	First N.B.
6278.	Wildwood.	Marine N.B.
6440.	Matawan.	Farmers and Merchants N.B.
6508.	Pleasantville.	First N.B.
6673.	Asbury Park.	Seacoast N.B.
6692.	Netcong.	Citizens' N.B.
6707.	Elmer.	First N.B.
6728.	Mullica Hill.	Farmers' N.B.
6823.	Riverside.	Riverside N.B.
6912.	Butler.	First N.B.
6960.	Bernardsville.	Bernardsville N.B.
7131.	Caldwell.	Caldwell N.B.
7171.	Cranford.	Cranford N.B.
7223.	Englishtown.	First N.B.
7265.	Williamstown.	First N.B.
7291.	Lakewood.	People's N.B.
7364.	Branchville.	First N.B.
7436.	Freehold.	Nat. Freehold Banking Co.
7754	Metuchen.	Metuchen N.B.
7799.	Hackensack.	People's' N.B.
7945.	Cape May Court House.	First N.B.
7981.	Irvington.	Irvington N.B.
7983.	Collingswood.	Collingswood N.B.
8007.	Pedricktown.	First N.B.
8129.	Pemberton.	People's N.B.
8227.	Hamburg.	Hardyston N.B.
8254.	New Egypt.	First N.B.
8267.	Hackettstown.	People's N.B.
8299.	Woodbridge.	First N.B.
8323.	Merchantville.	First N.B.
8382.	Belleville.	First N.B.
8390.	Guttenberg.	First N.B.
8394.	Closter.	Closter N.B.
8401.	Edgewater.	First N.B.
8437.	Roosevelt, Chrome.	First N.B.
8454.	Bayonne.	First N.B.
8462.	Garfield.	First N.B.
8483.	Roselle.	First N.B.
8484.	Riverton.	Cinnaminson N.B.
8497.	Barnegat.	First N.B.
8500.	Pitman.	Pitman N.B.
8501.	Dunellen.	First N.B.
8512.	Bound Brook	Bound Brook N.B.
8566.	Rockaway.	First N.B.
8582.	Mays Landing.	First N.B.
8614.	Tenafly.	First N.B.
8623.	Westfield.	People's N.B.
8627.	Arlington.	First N.B.
8661.	Millburn.	First N.B.
8681.	Tuckahoe.	Tuckahoe N.B.
8704.	Beverly.	First N.B.
8777.	Westwood.	First N.B.
8779.	Milford.	First N.B.
8800.	Atlantic City.	Boardwalk N.B.
8829.	Little Falls.	Little Falls N.B.
8874.	Fort Lee.	First N.B.

Charter Number	City	Name of Bank
9061.	White House Station.	First N.B.
9213.	Manasquan.	Manasquan N.B.
9229.	Jersey City.	Merchants' N.B.
9260.	Califon.	Califon N.B.
9268.	Bordentown.	First N.B.
9285.	Cape May.	Merchants' N.B.
9339.	Montclair, Upper Montclair.	First N.B.
9367.	Ramsey.	First N.B.
9380.	Secaucus.	First N.B.
9391.	North Plainfield.	Borough N.B.
9413.	Haddon Heights.	Haddon Heights N.B.
9420.	Lodi.	First N.B.
9498.	Bridgeton.	Farmers and Merchants' N.B.
9542.	West Orange.	First N.B.
9544.	Town of Union, Weehawken.	First N.B.
9577.	Montclair.	Essex N.B.
9597.	Blackwood.	First N.B.
9605.	Newark.	American N.B.
9612.	Caldwell.	Citizens' N.B.
9661.	East Newark.	First N.B.
9779.	Berlin.	Berlin N.B.
9780.	Ridgefield Park.	First N.B.
9833.	Blairstown.	People's N.B.
9867.	West Hoboken.	N.B. of North Hudson.
9912.	Newark.	Broad and Market N.B.
10036.	Port Norris.	First N.B.
10110.	Eatontown.	First N.B.
10118.	Hope.	First N.B.
10142.	Westfield.	N.B. of Westfield.
10224.	Bradley Beach.	First N.B.
10248.	Ventnor City, Atlantic City.	Ventnor City N.B.
10376.	Keansburg.	Keansburg N.B.
10417.	Lyndhurst.	First N.B.
10430.	Westville.	First N.B.
10440.	Minotola.	First N.B.
10471.	Clayton.	Clayton N.B.
10712.	Bloomsbury.	Citizens' N.B.
10787.	Pompton Lakes.	First N.B.
10823.	Absecon.	Tirst N.B.
10831.	Florence.	First N.B.
10840.	Farmingdale.	First N.B.
10919.	Verona.	Verona N.B.
10932.	Asbury Park.	Merchants' N.B.
10935.	Milltown.	First N.B.
11081.	Wrightstown.	First N.B.
11147.	Clementon.	Clementon N.B.
11351.	Perth Amboy.	City N.B.
11361.	Dumont.	Dumont N.B.
11368.	Bergenfield.	Bergenfield N.B.
11409.	Nutley.	First N.B.
11428.	Fords.	Fords N.B.
11446.	Audubon.	Audubon N.B.
11543.	Bogota.	Bogota N.B.
11545.	Linden.	Linden N.B.
11553.	Red Bank.	Broad Street N.B.
11607.	Collingswood.	Memorial N.B.
11618.	Cliffside Park.	Cliffside Park N.B.
11620.	Roebling.	First N.B.
11658.	Beach Haven.	Beach Haven N.B.
11727.	Hillside, Elizabeth	Hillside N.B.
11734.	Woodstown.	Woodstown N.B.
11744.	Elizabeth.	People's N.B.
11759.	Ridgewood.	Citizens' N.B.
11793.	Palmyra.	Palmyra N.B.
11847.	South Plainfield.	First N.B.
11888.	Woodbridge.	Woodbridge N.B.
11909.	Palisades Park.	Palisades Park N.B.
11943.	Chatham.	First N.B.
11950.	Leonia.	First N.B.
11979.	Paterson.	Nat. Trust Bank.
11983.	Clifton.	First N.B.
12002.	Peapack-Gladstone.	Peapack-Gladstone N.B.
12014.	Hackensack.	City N.B.
12019.	Belleville.	People's N.B. an Trust Co.
12022.	Laurel Springs.	Laurel Springs N.B.
12033.	North Arlington.	North Arlington N.B.
12037.	Ridgefield.	Ridgefield N.B.
12064.	West New York, Weehawken.	First N.B.
12145.	Newfield.	First N.B.
12167.	Paterson.	Totowa N.B.
12195.	Park Ridge.	First N.B.
12205.	Passaic.	Passaic N.B. and Trust Co.
12228.	East Rutherford.	First N.B.
12255.	Jersey City.	Journal Square N.B.
12263.	Cranford.	First N.B.
12269.	Montclair.	Montclair N.B.
12272.	Wyckoff.	First N.B.
12279.	Sea Isle City.	First N.B.
12297.	Garwood.	First N.B.
12301.	Jersey City.	Union Trust and of Hudson Co.
12338.	East Orange.	First N.B.
12354.	Seaside Heights.	Coast N.B.
12367.	Bayonne.	Bayonne N.B.
12378.	Little Ferry.	Little Ferry N.B.
12383.	Paterson.	N.B. of America.
12397.	Jersey City.	Franklin N.B.
12402.	West Englewood.	West Englewood N.B.
12422.	Avon-by-the-Sea.	First N.B.
12425.	Union Center, Union.	Union Center N.B.
12428.	Maple Shade.	Maple Shade N.B.
12465.	Fairview.	First N.B.
12468.	New Brunswick.	Citizens' N.B.

Charter Number	City	Name of Bank
12497.	Palisade.	Palisade N.B. of Fort Lee.
12510.	Pleasantville.	Pleasantville N.B.
12519.	Westmont.	Westmont N.B.
12520.	Red Bank.	Nat. Bank and Co.
12521.	Ocean City.	Ocean City N.B.
12524.	Perth Amboy.	Perth Amboy N.B.
12559.	Somers Point.	First N.B.
12560.	Paterson.	Labor Co-Opera N.B.
12570.	Newark.	Lincoln N.B.
12571.	Lakehurst.	First N.B.
12576.	Newark.	Citizens' N.B. an Trust Co.
12598.	Highland Park.	First N.B.
12603.	Midland Park.	First N.B.
12604.	Newark.	Forest Hill N.B.
12606.	Yardville.	Yardville N.B.
12609.	Glen Rock.	First N.B.
12617.	Atco.	Atco N.B.
12618.	Mount Ephraim.	Mount Ephraim N.B.
12621.	Oaklyn.	Oaklyn N.B.
12631.	Newark.	South Side N.B. and Trust Co.
12646.	Hamilton Square.	First N.B.
12660.	Bloomingdale.	First N.B.
12663.	Hawthorne.	First N.B.
12675.	Montclair.	People's N.B.
12690.	Clifton.	Clifton N.B.
12706.	Allendale.	First N.B.
12726.	Paterson.	Broadway N.B.
12732.	North Bergen.	First N.B.
12749.	Union City.	Union City N.B.
12750.	Nutley.	Franklin N.B.
12771.	Newark.	Labor Co-Operative N.B.
12806.	Guttenberg.	Liberty N.B.
12823.	Alpha.	Alpha N.B.
12828.	Rahway.	Citizens' N.B.
12829.	Weehawken.	Hamilton N.B.
12830.	Springfield.	First N.B.
12834.	Passaic.	American N.B.
12848.	West Paterson.	Westside N.B.
12854.	Haledon.	Haledon N.B.
12861.	Prospect Park.	Prospect Park N.B.
12876.	Irvington.	People's N.B.
12886.	Atlantic City.	Pacific Avenue N.B.
12891.	Allenhurst.	Allenhurst N.B.
12894.	Woodlynne.	Woodlynne N.B.
12895.	Paterson.	Columbus N.B.
12901.	Paterson.	Eastside N.B.
12902.	Hillsdale.	Hillsdale N.B.
12903.	North Merchantville.	Pennsauken Township N.B.
12917.	Mantua.	N.B. of Mantua.
12939.	Jersey City.	Labor N.B.
12942.	Manville.	Manville N.B.
12946.	Newark.	Port Newark N.B.
12949.	Trenton.	Prospect N.B.
12964.	Newark.	Peoples N.B.
12977.	Woodbine.	Woodbine N.B.
12978.	Stone Harbor.	First N.B.
12981.	Teaneck.	Teaneck N.B.
12984.	Riverside.	First N.B.
12990.	Bayonne.	Mechanics N.B.
13012.	Tenafly.	Northern Valley N.B.
13034.	Harrison.	Harrison N.B.
13039.	Trenton.	Security N.B.
13043.	Newark.	Hayes Circle Nat. Bank & Trust Co.
13047.	Wharton.	First N.B.
13058.	Newark.	Mount Prospect N.B.
13065.	Bay Head.	Bay Head N.B.
13117.	Oradell.	First N.B.
13120.	Camden.	American N.B.
13123.	Passaic.	Lincoln N.B.
13125.	Marlton.	First N.B.
13129.	Livingston.	Livingston N.B.
13136.	Cedar Grove.	First N.B.
13164.	Lodi.	First N.B.
13166.	Columbus.	First N.B.
13173.	Whippany.	First N.B.
13174.	Plainfield.	Plainfield N.B.
13203.	Camden.	Third N.B. & Trust Co.
13215.	Point Pleasant Beach.	Point Pleasant Beach N.B.
13265.	Woodridge.	Woodridge N.B.
13337.	Leonia.	Central N.B.
13363.	Asbury Park.	Asbury Park N.B. & Trust Co.
13364.	Hackensack.	Bergen County N.B.
13369.	Sayreville.	First N.B.
13530.	Haddon Heights.	First N.B.
13537.	Kearny.	Kearny N.B.
13540.	Linden.	Linden N.B.
13552.	Sea Bright.	First N.B.
13560.	Avon-by-the-Sea.	First N.B.
13574.	Rockaway.	First N.B.
13628.	Belvidere.	First N.B.
13629.	Plainfield.	Fourth N.B.
13834.	Orange.	Orange First N.B.
13848.	Belmar.	Belmar N.B.
13855.	Branchville.	Branchville N.B.
13893.	Edgewater.	Edgewater N.B.
13898.	Spring Lake.	First N.B.
13910.	New Egypt.	First N.B.
13916.	Metuchen.	Metuchen N.B.
13946.	Garfield.	First N.B.
13969.	Collingswood.	Citizens N.B.
14006.	Clementon.	N.B. of Clementon.
14014.	Guttenberg.	Liberty N.B.
14084.	Lakewood.	Peoples N.B.
14088.	Palisades Park.	N.B. of Palisades Park.

Charter Number	City	Name of Bank
14145.	Ocean City.	N.B. of Ocean City.
14151.	Secaucus.	Peoples N.B.
14153.	Carteret.	First N.B.
14162.	Cliffside Park.	United N.B.
14177.	Sea Bright.	Sea Bright N.B.
14189.	Tuckahoe.	First N.B.
14240.	Newfield.	First N.B.
14287.	Fort Lee.	First N.B.
14289.	Pleasantville.	Mainland N.B.
14305.	West New York.	N.B. of West New York.
14321.	Paterson.	National Union Bank.

NEW MEXICO

Charter Number	City	Name of Bank
1750.	Sante Fe.	First N.B.
2024.	Sante Fe.	Second N.B. of New Mexico.
2436.	Las Vegas.	First N.B.
2454.	Las Vegas.	San Miguel N.B.
2614.	Albuquerque.	First N.B.
2627.	Socorro.	First N.B.
3160.	Deming.	First N.B.
3222.	Albuquerque.	Albuquerque N.B.
3539.	Silver City.	Silver City N.B.
3554.	Silver City.	First N.B.
4455.	Eddy.	First N.B.
4485.	Socorro.	New Mexico N.B.
4574.	Socorro.	Socorro N.B.
4734.	Raton.	First N.B.
4746.	Deming.	N.B. of Deming.
5220.	Roswell.	First N.B.
5244.	Alamogordo.	First N.B.
5487.	Carlsbad.	First N.B.
5713.	Clayton.	First N.B.
6081.	Santa Rosa.	First N.B.
6183.	Farmington.	First N.B.
6187.	Portales.	First N.B.
6288.	Tucumcari.	First N.B.
6363.	Raton.	Citizens' N.B.
6597.	Belen.	First N.B.
6714.	Roswell.	American N.B.
6777.	Roswell.	Citizens' N.B.
6884.	Carlsbad.	N.B. of Carlsbad.
6974.	Deming.	Deming N.B.
7043.	Artesia.	First N.B.
7186.	Albuquerque.	State N.B.
7503.	Hagerman.	First N.B.
7720.	Las Cruces.	First N.B.
8098.	Raton.	N.B. of New Mexico.
8120.	Raton.	Raton N.B.
8132.	Silver City.	American N.B.
8173.	Texico.	First N.B.
8315.	Alamogordo.	Citizens' N.B.
8348.	Elida.	First N.B.
8364.	Portales.	Citizens' N.B.
8391.	Texico.	Texico N.B.
8397.	Melrose.	First N.B.
8584.	Lake Arthur.	First N.B.
8617.	Fort Sumner.	First N.B.
8662.	Cutter.	First N.B.
8663.	Nara Visa.	First N.B.
8767.	Clovis.	Clovis N.B.
8782.	Lakewood.	Lakewood N.B.
8784.	Clovis.	First N.B.
8880.	Lordsburg.	First N.B.
9151.	Farmington.	San Juan County N.B.
9292.	Cimarron.	First N.B.
9441.	Hope.	First N.B.
9468.	Artesia.	State N.B.
9988.	Gallup.	First N.B.
10268.	Magdalena.	First N.B.
10594.	Tucumcari.	American N.B.
10962.	Carlsbad.	State N.B.
10963.	Carrizozo.	First N.B.
11011.	Hot Springs.	First N.B.
11029.	Lovington.	First N.B.
11102.	Taos.	First N.B.
11136.	Clayton.	Clayton N.B.
11329.	Willard.	First N.B.
11442.	Albuquerque.	Citizens' N.B.
11449.	Columbus.	First N.B.
11565.	Springer.	First N.B.
11711.	Loving.	First N.B.
11746.	Grady.	First N.B.
11900.	Gallup.	N.B. of Gallup.
11958.	Roy.	First N.B.
12485.	Albuquerque.	Albuquerque N.B.
12514.	Farmington.	People's N.B.
12522.	Clovis.	First N.B.
12569.	Carlsbad.	Carlsbad N.B.
12710.	Silver City.	New First N.B.
12879.	Hatch.	First N.B.
12924.	Raton.	First N.B.
13438.	Hot Springs.	Hot Springs N.B.
13488.	New Hobbs.	First N.B.
13814.	Albuquerque.	First N.B.
14081.	Tucumcari.	First-American N.B.

NEW YORK

Charter Number	City	Name of Bank
6.	Syracuse.	First N.B.
29.	New York.	First N.B.
34.	Rondout.	First N.B.
35.	Beacon, Fishkill-on-the Hudson.	Fishkill N.B.
45.	Ellenville.	First N.B.
62.	New York.	Second N.B.
71.	Adams.	First N.B.
73.	Watertown.	First N.B.
75.	Dansville.	First N.B.
87.	New York.	Third N.B.
94.	Port Jervis.	First N.B.

Charter Number	City	Name of Bank
99.	Moravia.	First N.B.
102.	Seneca Falls.	First N.B.
103.	South Worcester.	First N.B.
119.	Elmira.	First N.B.
120.	Utica.	First N.B.
140.	Syracuse.	Second N.B.
149.	Elmira.	Second N.B.
151.	New Berlin.	First N.B.
159.	Syracuse.	Third N.B.
163.	Troy.	First N.B.
165.	Bath.	First N.B.
166.	Albion.	First N.B.
167.	Geneva.	First N.B.
169.	Penn Yan.	First N.B.
179.	Chittenango.	First N.B.
184.	Sandy Hill.	First N.B.
185.	Utica.	Second N.B.
193.	Hobart.	First N.B.
199.	Attica.	First N.B.
202.	Binghamton.	First N.B.
211.	Lockport.	First N.B.
217.	Leonardsville.	First N.B.
222.	Ithaca.	First N.B.
223.	Cooperstown.	Second N.B.
226.	Cortland.	First N.B.
229.	Medina.	First N.B.
231.	Auburn.	First N.B.
235.	Buffalo.	First N.B.
245.	Morrisville.	First N.B.
254.	New York.	Sixth N.B.
255.	Oswego.	First N.B.
259.	Canandaigua.	First N.B.
262.	Hornell.	First N.B.
265.	Friendship.	First N.B.
266.	Plattsburg.	First N.B.
267.	Albany.	First N.B.
273.	Oxford.	First N.B.
280.	Cooperstown.	First N.B.
282.	Franklin.	First N.B.
285.	Whitehall.	First N.B.
290.	New York.	Fourth N.B.
292.	Baldwinsville.	First N.B.
295.	Palmyra.	First N.B.
296.	Oswego.	Second N.B.
297.	Waverly.	First N.B.
301.	Havana.	First N.B.
302.	Andes.	First N.B.
303.	Skaneateles.	First N.B.
304.	Clyde.	First N.B.
307.	New York.	Tenth N.B.
314.	Warwick.	First N.B.
316.	Champlain.	First N.B.
321.	Plattsburg.	Vilas N.B.
334.	Greenport.	First N.B.
340.	Batavia.	First N.B.
341.	New York.	Fifth N.B.
342.	Union Springs.	First N.B.
343.	Havana.	Havana N.B.
345.	Now York.	Irving N.B.
348.	Lowville.	First N.B.
349.	Newark.	First N.B.
353.	Candor.	First N.B.
358.	Penn Yan.	First N.B.
364.	Tarrytown.	First N.B.
368.	Waterloo.	First N.B.
375.	Saint Johnsville.	First N.B.
376.	New York.	Central N.B.
382.	Brockport.	First N.B.
384.	New York.	Eighth N.B.
387.	New York.	Ninth N.B.
396.	Hudson.	First N.B.
402.	Port Chester.	First N.B.
412.	Aurora.	First N.B.
420.	Oneonta.	First N.B.
444.	New York.	Nat. Currency Bank.
451.	Kingston.	First N.B.
453.	Buffalo.	Farmers and Mechanics' N.B.
456.	Watkins.	Watkins N.B.
461.	Cobleskill.	First N.B.
465.	Poughkeepsie.	First N.B.
467.	Fort Plain.	Nat. Fort Plain Bank.
468.	Newburgh.	N.B. of Newburgh.
471.	Ossining.	First N.B.
472.	Deposit.	Deposit N.B.
504.	Westfield.	First N.B.
519.	Oneida.	First N.B.
523.	Middletown.	First N.B.
527.	Rochester.	First N.B.
548.	Jamestown.	First N.B.
564.	Angelica.	First N.B.
598.	Malone.	Farmers' N.B.
621.	Troy.	Nat. Exchange Bank.
639.	Lockport.	Niagara County N.B.
640.	Troy.	Troy City N.B.
653.	Yonkers.	First N.B.
658.	Brooklyn.	Nassau N.B.
659.	Poughkeepsie.	Fallkill N.B.
671.	Watertown.	Second N.B.
687.	New York.	Nat. Broadway Bank.
706.	Amenia.	First N.B.
721.	Troy.	Manufacturers' N.B.
729.	Ithaca.	Merchants and Farmers' N.B.
733.	New York.	N.B. of Commerce.
737.	Warsaw.	Wyoming County N.B.
739.	Albany.	Nat. Albany Exchange Bank.
750.	New York.	American N.B.
752.	Red Hook.	First N.B.
801.	West Winfield.	First N.B.
811.	Elmira.	Chemung Canal N.B.
821.	Oswego.	Nat. Marine Bank.

Charter Number	City	Name of Bank
822.	Dover, Dover Plains.	Dover Plains N.B.
830.	South East.	Croton River N.B.
841.	Fredonia.	Fredonia N.B.
842.	Castleton.	N.B. of Castleton.
850.	Buffalo.	Third N.B.
862.	Owego.	Tioga N.B.
868.	Potsdam.	N.B. of Potsdam.
886.	Geneseo.	Genesee Valley N.B.
891.	New York.	Nat. Park Bank.
893.	Saratoga Springs.	Saratoga N.B.
904.	Troy.	Merchants and Mechanics N.B.
905.	New York.	Tradesmen's N.B.
914.	Malone.	N.B. of Malone.
917.	New York.	Nat. Shoe and Leather Bank.
923.	Brooklyn.	First N.B.
929.	Kinderhook.	Nat. Union Bank.
937.	Le Roy.	First N.B.
938.	Jamestown.	City N.B.
940.	Troy.	United N.B.
949.	Geneva.	Geneva N.B.
954.	Ballston Spa.	First N.B.
955.	Kingston.	State of New York N.B.
963.	Troy.	Union N.B.
964.	New York.	Market and Fulton N.B.
968.	Fulton.	First N.B.
971.	Fishkill.	N.B. of Fishkill.
972.	New York.	Saint Nicholas N.B.
976.	Carmel.	Putnam County N.B.
980.	Glens Falls.	First N.B.
981.	Pine Plains.	Stissing N.B.
990.	Hudson.	Farmers' N.B.
991.	Troy.	Nat. State Bank.
992.	Troy.	Mutual N.B.
998.	New York.	Seventh N.B.
1000.	New York.	N.B. of the Republic.
1012.	Troy.	Central N.B.
1019.	Owego.	First N.B.
1026.	Kinderhook.	N.B. of Kinderhook.
1027.	Lyons.	Lyons N.B.
1039.	Lockport.	Nat. Exchange Bank
1040.	Saugerties.	First N.B.
1045.	Albany.	Merchants' N.B.
1050.	Kingston.	Nat. Ulster County Bank.
1067.	New York.	Mercantile N.B.
1072.	Rochester.	Farmers and Merchants' N.B.
1074.	Batavia.	N.B. of Genesee.
1075.	New York.	Wall Street N.B.
1080.	New York.	Atlantic N.B.
1083.	Groton.	First N.B.
1090.	Oneida.	Oneida Valley N.B.
1091.	Hudson.	Nat. Hudson River Bank.
1104.	Rochester.	Traders' N.B.
1105.	New York.	East River N.B.
1106.	Newburgh.	Highland N.B.
1110.	Fayetteville.	N.B. of Fayetteville.
1116.	New York.	New York County N.B.
1120.	Kingston.	Rondout N.B.
1121.	New York.	Metropolitan N.B.
1122.	Canajoharie.	Canajoharie N.B.
1123.	Albany.	Union N.B.
1127.	Salem.	N.B. of Salem.
1130.	Mohawk.	Nat. Mohawk Valley Bank.
1136.	Cherry Valley.	Nat. Central Bank.
1143.	Cuba.	Cuba N.B.
1149.	Kingston.	Kingston N.B.
1157.	Rhinebeck.	First N.B.
1160.	Whitehall.	Old N.B.
1166.	Sherburne.	Sherburne N.B.
1178.	Fulton.	Citizens' N.B.
1186.	New Paltz.	Huguenot N.B.
1189.	Binghamton.	City N.B.
1192.	Waverly.	Waverly N.B.
1196.	New York.	Leather Manufacturers' N.B.
1198.	Catskill.	Tanners' N.B.
1208.	Saugerties.	Saugerties N.B.
1212.	Fonda.	Nat. Mohawk River Bank.
1213.	Newburgh.	Quassaick N.B.
1215.	New York.	Marine N.B.
1218.	Fort Edward.	N.B. of Fort Edward.
1223.	Brooklyn.	Farmers and Citizens' N.B.
1224.	New York.	Pacific N.B.
1226.	Schenectady.	Mohawk N.B.
1227.	Saratoga Springs.	Commercial N.B.
1229.	Waterford.	Saratoga County N.B.
1231.	New York.	Importers and Traders' N.B.
1232.	New York.	Ocean N.B.
1240.	Seneca Falls.	Nat. Exchange Bank
1250.	New York.	Mechanics and Metals N.B.
1253.	Ballston Spa.	Ballston Spa N.B.
1257.	Canajoharie.	Nat. Spraker Bank.
1261.	New York.	Nat. Butchers and Drovers' Bank.
1262.	Albany.	New York State N.B.
1264.	Vernon.	N.B. of Vernon.
1265.	Watervliet.	N.B. of Watervliet.
1266.	Greenwich.	Washington County N.B.
1269.	Pawling.	N.B. of Pawling.
1271.	Cazenovia.	N.B. of Cazenovia.
1275.	Cambridge.	Cambridge Valley N.B.
1276.	Middletown.	Middletown N.B.
1278.	New York.	Union N.B.
1282.	Rochester.	Nat. Union Bank.
1285.	Auburn.	Auburn City N.B.
1286.	Nyack.	Rockland County N.B.
1287.	Syracuse.	Salt Springs N.B.
1289.	Albany.	Nat. Mechanics and Farmers' Bank.
1290.	New York.	Citizens N.B.

Charter Number	City	Name of Bank
1291.	Albany.	Albany City N.B.
1293.	Glens Falls.	Glens Falls N.B.
1294.	Catskill.	Catskill N.B.
1297.	New York.	Bowery N.B.
1298.	Schuylerville.	N.B. of Schuylerville.
1301.	Albany.	Nat. Commercial Bank and Trust Co.
1304.	Somers.	Farmers and Drovers' N.B.
1305.	Poughkeepsie.	City N.B.
1306.	Poughkeepsie.	Poughkeepsie N.B.
1307.	Amsterdam.	First N.B.
1308.	Utica.	Utica N.B.
1311.	Owego.	Nat. Union Bank.
1312.	Poughkeepsie.	Farmers and Manufacturers' N.B.
1323.	Delhi.	Delaware N.B.
1324.	New York.	Gallatin N.B.
1334.	Hamilton.	Nat. Hamilton Bank.
1335.	Amsterdam.	Farmers' N.B.
1341.	Syracuse.	Syracuse N.B.
1342.	Syracuse.	Merchants' N.B.
1344.	Little Falls.	Herkimer County N.B.
1345.	Auburn.	Cayuga County N.B.
1347.	Cohoes.	N.B. of Cohoes.
1348.	North Granville.	North Granville N.B.
1349.	Chester.	Chester N.B.
1350.	Auburn.	N.B. of Auburn.
1351.	Auburn.	Nat. Exchange Bank.
1352.	New York.	Hanover N.B.
1354.	Norwich.	N.B. of Norwich.
1355.	Oswego.	Lake Ontario N.B.
1357.	New York.	Irving N.B.
1361.	Waterville.	N.B. of Waterville.
1362.	Rochester.	Flour City N.B.
1363.	Port Jervis.	N.B. of Port Jervis.
1370.	New York.	Merchants' N.B.
1371.	New York.	Grocers' N.B.
1372.	New York.	N.B. of Commonwealth.
1373.	New York.	N.B. of North America.
1374.	New York.	Phenix N.B.
1375.	New York.	Chatham and Phenix N.B.
1376.	Rome.	Central N.B.
1380.	Poughkeepsie.	Merchants' N.B.
1388.	New York.	Atlantic N.B.
1389.	New York.	Continental N.B.
1391.	Elmira.	N.B. of Chemung.
1392.	Utica.	Oneida N.B.
1393.	New York.	Bank of NY Nat. Banking Assn.
1394.	New York.	American Exchange N.B.
1395.	Utica.	First N.B.
1397.	Rochester.	Clarke N.B.
1398.	Coxsackie.	N.B. of Coxsackie.
1399.	Goshen.	N.B. of Orange County.
1401.	Syracuse.	Mechanics' N.B.
1408.	Goshen.	Goshen N.B.
1410.	Rome.	Fort Stanwix N.B.
1414.	Rome.	First N.B.
1416.	Mount Morris.	Genesee River N.B.
1422.	Peekskill.	West Chester County N.B.
1426.	Lansingburg.	N.B. of Lansingburg.
1443.	Brooklyn.	Manufacturers' N.B.
1458.	Whitestown.	N.B. of Whitestown.
1461.	New York.	Nat. City Bank.
1463.	Unadilla.	Nat. Unadilla Bank.
1473.	Middletown.	Walkill N.B.
1474.	Gloversville.	Nat. Fulton County Bank.
1476.	New York.	N.B. of the State of New York.
1490.	Watertown.	Jefferson County N.B.
1491.	Brooklyn.	Atlantic N.B.
1496.	Pulaski.	Pulaski N.B.
1497.	New York.	Fulton N.B.
1499.	New York.	Chemical N.B.
1503.	Monticello.	Nat. Union Bank.
1507.	Watertown.	Nat. Union Bank.
1508.	Watertown.	N.B. and Loan Co.
1509.	Albion.	Orleans County N.B.
1510.	Schoharie.	Schoharie County N.B.
1513.	Binghamton.	Nat. Broome County Bank.
1525.	Canastota.	Canastota N.B.
1531.	Adams.	Hungerford N.B.
1534.	Lansingburg.	Nat. Exchange Bank.
1543.	Brooklyn.	Nat. City Bank.
1556.	New York.	Croton N.B.
1561.	Ithaca.	Tompkins County N.B.
1563.	Jamestown.	Chautauqua County N.B.
1569.	Syracuse.	Fourth N.B.
1624.	New York.	Mechanics and Traders' N.B.
1655.	Newport.	N.B. of Newport.
1670.	Ilion.	Ilion N.B.
1691.	New York.	Union Square N.B.
1697.	Port Henry.	First N.B.
1753.	Keeseville.	Keeseville N.B.
1887.	Olean.	First N.B.
1938.	Gloversville.	N.B. of Gloversville.
2074.	Yonkers.	Citizens' N.B.
2117.	Ellenville.	Home N.B.
2136.	Binghamton.	Merchants' N.B.
2151.	Oneonta.	Wilber N.B.
2224.	Nunda.	First N.B.
2225.	Brewsters.	First N.B.
2229.	Haverstraw.	N.B. of Haverstraw.
2233.	Whitehall.	Merchants' N.B.
2239.	Amsterdam.	Manufacturers' N.B.
2272.	Cortland.	N.B. of Cortland.
2294.	Granville.	N.B. of Granville.
2320.	Boonville.	First N.B.
2345.	Franklinville.	First N.B.
2348.	Walden.	Walden N.B.

Charter Number	City	Name of Bank
2353.	Moravia.	Moravia N.B.
2370.	New York.	Chase N.B.
2376.	Olean.	Exchange N.B.
2378.	Nyack.	Nyack N.B.
2383.	Rochester.	Commercial N.B.
2398.	Homer.	First N.B.
2400.	Little Falls.	Nat. Herkimer County Bank.
2401.	Oneida.	Nat. State Bank.
2405.	Penn Yan.	Yates County N.B.
2406.	Little Falls.	Little Falls N.B.
2410.	Rome.	Farmers' N.B.
2418.	Johnstown.	First N.B.
2421.	Batavia.	Genesee County N.B.
2426.	Lowville.	Black River N.B.
2437.	Attica.	Attica N.B.
2441.	Poland.	Poland N.B.
2442.	Carthage.	First N.B.
2446.	Ogdensburg.	N.B. of Ogdensburg.
2448.	Camden.	First N.B.
2451.	Cuba.	First N.B.
2463.	Dundee.	Dundee N.B.
2468.	Clyde.	Briggs N.B.
2471.	Hoosick Falls.	First N.B.
2472.	Salamanca.	First N.B.
2487.	Middleburgh.	First N.B.
2493.	Roundout.	First N.B.
2507.	New York.	United States N.B.
2510.	Gouverneur.	First N.B.
2517.	Greenwich.	First N.B.
2522.	Hornell.	Citizens' N.B.
2534.	Plattsburg.	Iron N.B.
2543.	Bainbridge.	First N.B.
2553.	Richburg.	First N.B.
2598.	New York.	Garfield N.B.
2602.	Stamford.	N.B. of Stamford.
2608.	New York.	Lincoln N.B.
2610.	Salamanca.	Salamanca N.B.
2615.	Saratoga Springs.	Citizens' N.B.
2619.	Dunkirk.	Merchants' N.B.
2626.	Tarrytown.	Tarrytown N.B.
2632.	Friendship.	Citizens' N.B.
2651.	Richfield Springs.	First N.B.
2655.	Corning.	First N.B. and Trust Co.
2657.	Watertown.	Watertown N.B.
2661.	Millerton.	Millerton N.B.
2668.	New York.	Second N.B.
2755.	Franklinville.	Union N.B.
2765.	Canandaigua.	Ontario County N.B.
2827.	Cortland.	Second N.B.
2838.	Sandy Hill.	N.B. of Sandy Hill.
2845.	Adams.	Adams N.B.
2850.	Wellsville.	First N.B.
2860.	Fort Plain.	Fort Plain N.B.
2869.	Fultonville.	Fultonville N.B.
2873.	Troy.	N.B. of Troy.
2892.	Springville.	First N.B.
2916.	Dunkirk.	Lake Shore N.B.
2920.	Amsterdam.	Merchants' N.B.
2976.	New York.	Sprague N.B.
2996.	Owego.	Owego N.B.
3011.	Norwich.	Chenango N.B.
3047.	Watkins.	First N.B.
3154.	Granville.	Farmers' N.B.
3166.	Westfield.	N.B. of Westfield.
3171.	Mechanicsville.	First N.B.
3174.	Plattsburg.	Merchants' N.B.
3183.	Herkimer.	First N.B.
3186.	Homer.	Homer N.B.
3193.	Marathon.	First N.B.
3232.	Greenport.	People's N.B.
3244.	Hudson Falls.	People's N.B.
3245.	Salem.	People's N.B.
3282.	Albany.	Nat. Exchange Bank.
3283.	Le Roy.	N.B. of Le Roy.
3307.	Malone.	People's N.B.
3309.	Salem.	First N.B.
3312.	Gloversville.	Fulton County N.B.
3329.	Seneca Falls.	Exchange N.B.
3330.	Fort Edward.	First N.B.
3333.	Middletown.	Merchants' N.B.
3359.	New York.	Southern N.B.
3366.	Malone.	Third N.B.
3415.	New York.	Seaboard N.B.
3444.	Now Brighton.	First N.B. of Staten Island.
3582.	Frankfort.	First N.B.
3672.	Carthage.	Carthage N.B.
3681.	Edmeston.	First N.B.
3696.	Canton.	First N.B.
3700.	New York.	Western N.B.
3771.	New York.	N.B. of Deposit.
3797.	Clayton.	First N.B.
3800.	Painted Post.	Bronson N.B.
3817.	Canandaigua.	Canandaigua N.B.
3822.	Sidney.	Sidney N.B.
3846.	Jamestown.	Jamestown N.B.
4061.	Adams.	Farmers' N.B.
4103.	Adams.	Citizens' N.B.
4105.	Elmira.	Elmira N.B.
4152.	New York.	Interstate N.B.
4211.	Amsterdam.	Amsterdam City N.B.
4223.	Poland.	N.B. of Poland.
4230.	Riverhead.	Suffolk County N.B.
4296.	Watertown.	City N.B.
4335.	New York.	Washington N.B.
4416.	Cold Spring.	N.B. of Cold- Spring-on-Hudson.
4419.	Canastota.	First N.B.
4482.	Dansville.	Merchants and Farmers' N.B.
4491.	Ticonderoga.	First N.B.
4493.	Eariville.	First N.B.
4495.	Walton.	First N.B.
4497.	Hobart.	N.B. of Hobart.
4512.	New York.	Columbus N.B.
4519.	Perry.	First N.B.
4567.	New York.	Western N.B. of the U.S.
4581.	New York.	N.B. of North America.
4645.	New York.	Liberty N.B.
4711.	Schenectady.	Union N.B.
4741.	Buffalo.	Columbia N.B.
4846.	Glens Falls.	Merchants' N.B.
4855.	New York.	Franklin N.B.
4858.	Port Henry.	Citizens' N.B.
4869.	Tonawanda.	First N.B.
4870.	Morris.	First N.B.
4880.	Hempstead.	First N.B.
4898.	New York.	Nat. Union Bank.
4899.	Niagara Falls.	First N.B.
4906.	Babylon.	Babylon N.B.
4914.	Beacon, Matteawan.	Matteawan N.B.
4925.	Liberty.	Sullivan County N.B.
4962.	Schenevus.	Schenevus N.B.
4985.	Granville.	Granville N.B.
4986.	Medina.	Medina N.B.
4988.	Wellsville.	Citizens' N.B.
4998.	Albion.	Citizens' N.B.
5003.	New York.	Standard N.B.
5026.	Mount Kisco.	Mount Kisco N.B.
5037.	Mechanicville.	Manufacturers' N.B.
5053.	Walden.	N.B. of Walden.
5068.	Port Jefferson.	First N.B.
5072.	Saranac Lake.	Adirondack N.B.
5108.	Clayton.	Nat. Exchange Bank.
5112.	New York.	Astor N.B.
5137.	Elmira.	Merchants' N.B.
5141.	Herkimer.	Herkimer N.B.
5174.	Buffalo.	City N.B.
5178.	Addison.	First N.B.
5186.	Sayville.	Oysterman's N.B.
5196.	Wayland.	First N.B.
5210.	Milford.	Milford N.B.
5228.	Potsdam.	Citizens' N.B.
5237.	New York.	Nat. Commercial Bank.
5271.	Mount Vernon.	First N.B.
5284.	Alexandria Bay.	First N.B. of the Thousand Islands.
5286.	Syracuse.	American Exchange N.B.
5293.	Mexico.	First N.B.
5299.	Holland Patent.	First N.B.
5336.	Highland.	First N.B.
5360.	Skaneateles.	N.B. of Skaneateles.
5390.	Spring Valley.	First N.B.
5407.	Falconer.	First N.B.
5411.	Mamaroneck.	First N.B.
5465.	Syracuse.	N.B. of Syracuse.
5605.	Hermon.	First N.B.
5631.	Akron.	Wickware N.B.
5648.	Caledonia.	First N.B.
5662.	Rye.	Rye N.B.
5675.	Cazenovia.	Cazenovia N.B.
5746.	Tully.	First N.B.
5783.	New York.	New Amsterdam N.B.
5785.	Plattsburg.	Plattsburg N.B. and Trust Company.
5816.	Castleton.	Nat. Exchange Bank
5846.	Suffern.	Suffern N.B.
5851.	South Glens Falls.	First N.B.
5867.	Gainesville.	Gainesville N.B.
5874.	Hoosick Falls.	People's N.B.
5924.	Margaretville.	People's N.B.
5928.	Wolcott.	First N.B.
5936.	Northport.	First N.B.
5990.	New York.	United N.B.
6019.	Larchmont.	Larchmont N.B.
6087.	Le Roy.	Le Roy N.B.
6094.	Carthage.	Nat. Exchange Bank
6148.	Silver Springs.	Silver Springs N.B.
6184.	Buffalo.	Marine N.B.
6186.	Buffalo.	Manufacturers and Traders' N.B.
6198.	Port Richmond.	Port Richmond N.B.
6253.	New York.	Northern N.B.
6284.	New York.	Equitable N.B.
6330.	Springville.	Citizens' N.B.
6351.	White Plains.	First N.B.
6371.	Irvington.	Irvington N.B.
6386.	Ripley.	First N.B.
6425.	New York.	Nat. Reserve Bank
6427.	New Rochelle.	Nat. City Bank
6441.	New York.	Thirty-Fourth Street N.B.
6447.	Dolgeville.	First N.B.
6470.	Hudson Falls.	Sandy Hill N.B.
6479.	Corinth.	Corinth N.B.
6482.	Remsen.	First N.B.
6487.	Dryden.	First N.B.
6552.	Ossining.	Ossining N.B.
6562.	Stapleton.	Stapleton N.B.
6587.	Huntington.	First N.B.
6613.	Plattsburg.	City N.B.
6630.	Oriskany Falls.	First N.B.
6694.	Massena.	First N.B.
6785.	Patchogue.	Citizens' N.B.
6802.	Newark.	Arcadia N.B.
6809.	North Tonawanda.	State N.B.
6964.	Lackawanna.	Lackawanna N.B.
6965.	Syracuse.	Commercial N.B.
7009.	Allegany.	First N.B.
7102.	Olean.	Citizens' N.B.
7107.	New York.	Maiden Lane N.B.
7203.	New York.	Coal and Iron N.B.
7233.	Philmont.	First N.B.
7255.	Granville.	Washington County N.B.
7290.	Stapleton.	Richmond Borough N.B.
7305.	Cooperstown.	Cooperstown N.B.
7344.	Cornwall.	First N.B.
7447.	New York.	Battery Park N.B.
7450.	New York.	Aetna N.B.
7479.	Lyons.	Gavitt N.B.
7483.	West Winfield.	West Winfield N.B.
7485.	Hunter.	Greene County N.B.
7512.	Sharon Springs.	First N.B.
7541.	Trumansburg.	First N.B.
7563.	Monroe.	Monroe N.B.
7588.	Salem.	Salem N.B.
7612.	Troy.	Nat. City Bank.
7618.	Grand Gorge.	First N.B.
7630.	Fort Edward.	Fort Edward N.B.
7678.	Roxbury.	N.B. of Roxbury.
7679.	Whitney Point.	First N.B.
7699.	Glens Falls.	N.B. of Glens Falls.
7703.	Freeport.	First N.B.
7733.	Saint Regis Falls.	Saint Regis Falls N.B.
7763.	East Hampton.	East Hampton N.B.
7774.	South Otselic.	Otselic Valley N.B.
7813.	Lestershire.	First N.B.
7823.	Buffalo.	Central N.B.
7840.	Ovid.	First N.B.
7850.	Whitesville.	First N.B.
7878.	Downsville.	First N.B.
7939.	Bayside.	Bayside N.B.
7982.	Montgomery.	N.B. of Montgomery.
8022.	Boonville.	Nat. Exchange Bank
8026.	Rochester.	Lincoln N.B.
8058.	Greenwood.	First N.B.
8111.	Rochester.	N.B. of Commerce.
8146.	Andover.	Burrows N.B.
8153.	Tupper Lake.	Tupper Lake N.B.
8157.	Franklinville.	People's N.B.
8158.	Theresa.	Farmers' N.B.
8191.	Roscoe.	First N.B.
8194.	Mariner Harbor.	Mariner Harbor N.B.
8240.	Bronxville.	Gramatan N.B.
8268.	Jamaica.	First N.B.
8297.	Hudson Falls.	Hudson Falls N.B.
8301.	Horseheads.	First N.B.
8334.	Tottenville.	Tottenville N.B.
8343.	Argyle.	First N.B.
8371.	Morristown.	Frontier N.B.
8388.	Whitehall.	N.B. of Whitehall.
8398.	Peekskill.	Peekskill N.B.
8453.	Jamestown.	Nat. Chautauqua County Bank.
8463.	Dexter.	First N.B.
8513.	Sidney.	People's N.B.
8516.	Mount Vernon.	Mount Vernon N.B.
8531.	Canton.	Saint Lawrence County N.B.
8586.	Hastings upon Hudson.	First N.B.
8613.	Hancock.	First N.B.
8634.	New York.	Beaver N.B.
8665.	New York.	Nat. Copper Bank.
8717.	Clifton Springs.	Ontario N.B.
8793.	Lake George.	First N.B.
8794.	Islip.	First N.B.
8833.	Lindenhurst.	First N.B.
8834.	Marlboro.	First N.B.
8838.	Highland Falls.	Citizens' N.B.
8847.	Fleischmanns, Griffin Corners.	First N.B.
8850.	Highland Falls.	First N.B.
8853.	Corona.	First N.B.
8865.	Ozone Park, New York.	First N.B.
8872.	Rockville Centre.	First N.B.
8873.	Amityville.	First N.B.
8882.	Farmingdale.	First N.B.
8893.	Chateaugay.	First N.B.
8920.	Oneonta.	Citizens' N.B.
8922.	New York.	Sherman N.B.
8923.	Lynbrook.	Lynbrook N.B.
8926.	New York.	Bronx N.B.
8935.	Saranac Lake.	Saranac Lake N.B.
8957.	Whitestone.	First N.B.
9019.	Fredonia.	N.B. of Fredonia.
9060.	East Worcester.	East Worcester N.B.
9065.	Washingtonville.	First N.B.
9109.	Ilion.	Manufacturers' N.B.
9135.	Warrensburgh.	Emerson N.B.
9171.	Croton on Hudson.	First N.B.
9187.	Mineola.	First N.B.
9206.	Middleport.	First N.B.
9219.	Brooklyn.	People's N.B.
9271.	Far Rockaway.	N.B. of Far Rockaway.
9276.	Union.	Farmers' N.B.
9305.	Gloversville.	City N.B.
9322.	East Islip.	First N.B.
9326.	Wappingers Falls.	N.B.of Wappingers Falls.
9360.	New York.	Union Exchange N.B.
9399.	Nichols.	Nichols N.B.
9405.	Westport.	Lake Champlain N.B.
9414.	Ridgewood, Brooklyn.	Ridgewood N.B.
9415.	Windsor.	Windsor N.B.
9418.	Sodus.	First N.B.
9427.	Callicoon.	Callicoon N.B.
9434.	Deposit.	Farmers' N.B.
9482.	Brown Station.	Ashokan N.B.
9516.	Unadilla.	Unadilla N.B.

Charter Number	City	Name of Bank
9529.	Ravena.	First N.B.
9569.	New York.	Audubon N.B.
9643.	Brushton.	First N.B.
9644.	Belfast.	First N.B.
9669.	Bridgehampton.	Bridgehampton N.B.
9691.	Flushing.	Flushing N.B.
9716.	North Creek.	North Creek N.B.
9717.	New York.	Gotham N.B.
9748.	Jamestown.	American N.B.
9804.	Poland.	Citizens' N.B.
9820.	Smithtown Branch.	N.B.of Smithtown Branch.
9822.	Olean.	Olean N.B.
9825.	Yonkers.	Yonkers N.B.
9839.	Phelps:.	Phelps N.B.
9857.	Cato.	First N.B.
9866.	Altamont.	First N.B.
9869.	Marcellus.	First N.B.
9900.	Ticonderoga.	Ticonderoga N.B.
9921.	Genoa.	First N.B.
9939.	New York.	Nat. Nassau Bank.
9940.	Pine Bush	Pine Bush N.B.
9950.	East Aurora.	First N.B.
9955.	New York.	Harriman N.B.
9956.	Florida.	Florida N.B.
9977.	Watkins.	Glen N.B.
9990.	Central Valley.	Central Valley N.B.
10016.	North Rose.	First N.B.
10029.	Bay Shore.	First N.B.
10037.	Liberty.	N.B. of Liberty.
10043.	Livingston Manor.	Livingston Manor N.B.
10046.	Holcomb.	Hamlin N.B.
10047.	Canandaigua.	County N.B.
10054.	Brooklyn.	Greenpoint N.B.
10077.	Copenhagen.	Copenhagen N.B.
10084.	Cornwall.	Cornwall N.B.
10109.	Central Square.	First N.B.
10111.	Newark Valley.	First N.B.
10126.	Barker.	Somerset N.B.
10141.	East Rochester.	First N.B.
10155.	Wallkill.	Wallkill N.B.
10159.	Silver Creek.	First N.B.
10175.	Lacona.	First N.B.
10185.	Southampton.	First N.B.
10199.	New Berlin.	N.B. of New Berlin.
10216.	Hammond.	Citizens' N.B.
10235.	Bath.	Bath N.B.
10258.	Silver Creek.	Silver Creek N.B.
10295.	Clinton.	Hayes N.B.
10329.	Long Island city.	Commercial N.B.
10351.	Frankfort.	Citizens' N.B.
10358.	Babylon.	Babylon N.B.
10374.	Redwood.	Redwood N.B.
10410.	Arcade.	First N.B.
10444.	Forestville.	First N.B.
10446.	Heuvelton.	First N.B.
10456.	Jeffersonville.	First N.B.
10477.	Sparkill.	First N.B.
10481.	Cherry Creek.	Cherry Creek N.B.
10497.	Montour Falls.	Montour N.B.
10525.	Tuckahoe.	First N.B.
10526.	Pearl River.	First N.B.
10546.	Marion.	First N.B.
10569.	Edwards.	Edwards N.B.
10623.	Gasport.	First N.B.
10747.	Winthrop.	First N.B.
10754.	Bliss.	Bliss N.B.
10755.	Lake Placid.	Lake Placid N.B.
10767.	Harrisville.	First N.B.
10778.	New York.	Chatham and Phenix N.B.
10781.	Red Creek.	Red Creek N.B.
10788.	Pulaski.	People's N.B.
10816.	Lisle.	First N.B.
10855.	Kerhonkson.	Kerhonkson N.B.
10856.	Athens.	Athens N.B.
10869.	Fairport.	Fairport N.B.
10895.	Norfolk.	First N.B.
10923.	Walden.	Third N.B.
10930.	Conewango.	Conewango Valley N.B.
10943.	Brasher Falls.	Brasher Falls N.B.
10948.	Croghan.	Croghan N.B.
10964.	Old Forge.	First N.B.
11020.	Weedsport.	First N.B.
11033.	Rockville Centre.	Nassau County N.B.
11034.	New York.	Public N.B.
11055.	Friendship.	Union N.B.
11057.	Tannersville.	Mountains N.B.
11059.	Woodridge, Centerville Sta.	First N.B.
11072.	Bellmore.	First N.B.
11087.	Hicksville.	Long Island N.B.
11238.	Trenton, Barneveld.	First N.B.
11243.	Andes.	N.B. of Andes.
11277.	Clayville.	N.B. of Clayville.
11284.	Whitesboro.	Whitestown N.B.
11292.	Port Washington.	Port Washington N.B.
11319.	Buffalo.	Broadway N.B.
11349.	Savona.	Savona N.B.
11360.	Jamestown.	Liberty N.B.
11375.	Hempstead.	Second N.B.
11404.	Tuxedo.	Tuxedo N.B.
11435.	Buffalo.	Lafayette N.B.
11448.	Unionville.	First N.B.
11474.	Baldwin.	Baldwin N.B.
11489.	Niagara Falls.	Falls N.B.
11511.	East Setauket.	Tinker N.B.
11513.	Afton.	First N.B.
11514.	Afton.	Afton N.B.
11518.	Freeport.	Citizens' N.B.
11583.	Angola.	Evans N.B.
11603.	Lynbrook.	People's N.B.

Charter Number	City	Name of Bank
11626.	Albany.	Union N.B. and Trust Co.
11639.	New York.	New York Nat. Irving.Bank.
11649.	Milton.	First N.B.
11655.	New York.	Richmond Hill N.B.
11656.	Middleville.	Middleville N.B.
11657.	Hartwick.	Hartwick N.B.
11686.	New York.	Nat. American Bank.
11708.	Scarsdale.	Scarsdale N.B.
11713.	New York.	New York Produce Exchange N.B.
11730.	Westbury.	Wheatley Hills N.B.
11739.	Romulus.	Romulus N.B.
11742.	Port Leyden.	Port Leyden N.B.
11747.	Mount Vernon.	American N.B.
11755.	Long Be.ach.	N.B. of Long Beach.
11768.	Buffalo.	Community N.B.
11785.	New Hartford.	First N.B.
11809.	South Fallsburg.	South Fallsburg N.B.
11836.	Buffalo.	Merchants' N.B.
11844.	New York.	Progress N.B.
11854.	Cedarhurst.	Peninsula N.B.
11881.	Valley Stream.	Valley Stream N.B.
11883.	Buffalo.	Amherst N.B.
11897.	Malone.	Citizens' N.B.
11912.	Lancaster.	Citizens' N.B.
11924.	Manhasset.	First N.B.
11927.	Maybrook.	Maybrook N.B.
11951.	Pelham.	Pelham N.B.
11953.	Roosevelt.	First N.B.
11956.	Painted Post.	Painted Post N.B.
11965.	New York.	Commercial Exchange N.B.
11969.	Rouses Point.	First N.B.
11971.	Willsboro.	Essex County N.B.
12017.	Hamden.	First N.B.
12018.	Lisbon.	First N.B.
12021.	New York.	Metropolitan N.B.
12071.	Atlanta.	Atlanta N.B.
12122.	Syracuse.	Liberty N.B.
12123.	New York.	Seaboard N.B.
12164.	Windham.	First N.B.
12174.	Greene.	First N.B.
12208.	Kenmore.	First N.B.
12213.	New York.	Capitol N.B.
12214.	New York.	Lebanon N.B.
12224.	New York.	Lincoln N.B.
12242.	Germantown.	Germantown N.B.
12252.	New York.	Rockaway Beach N.B.
12280.	New York.	Ozone Park N.B.
12284.	Niagara Falls.	Cataract N.B.
12294.	Woodmere.	Hewlett-Woodmere N.B.
12300.	New York.	Hamilton N.B.
12313.	Buffalo.	South Side N.B.
12337.	Buffalo.	Genesee N.B.
12344.	New York.	N.B. of Bay Ridge.
12352.	New York.	Liberty N.B.
12370.	New York.	Franklin N.B.
12375.	Jordan.	Jordan N.B.
12379.	Central Islip.	Central Islip N.B.
12398.	Corona, New York.	Queensboro N.B.
12406.	New York.	United N.B.
12417.	Trumansburg.	State N.B.
12419.	Brooklyn.	Bushwick N.B.
12445.	Buffalo.	Riverside N.B.
12449.	Floral Park.	First N.B.
12450.	Geneva.	N.B. of Geneva.
12458.	Oceanside.	Oceanside N.B.
12460.	Inwood.	First N.B.
12473.	Bellport.	Bellport N.B.
12476.	Westfield.	Grape Belt N.B.
12489.	Kings Park.	Kings Park N.B.
12494.	Macedon.	First N.B.
12496.	Narrowsburg.	First N.B.
12503.	Merrick.	First N.B.
12512.	Little Neck.	Little Neck N.B.
12515.	North Tarrytown.	First N.B.
12516.	New York.	Commercial N.B.
12535.	Pittsford.	Pittsford N.B.
12538.	Rochester.	N.B. of Rochester.
12548.	New Rochelle.	Central N.B.
12549.	Hankins.	First N.B.
12550.	New York.	Jamaica N.B.
12551.	Cutchogue.	First N.B.
12553.	New York.	Grace N.B.
12574.	White Plains.	People's N.B.
12586.	Cairo.	First N.B.
12592.	Port Byron.	N.B. of Port Byron.
12593.	East Northport.	Citizens' N.B.
12601.	Harrison.	First N.B.
12632.	New York.	Metropolitan N.B and Trust Co.
12659.	Great Neck Station.	First N.B. of Great Neck.
12705.	Hartsdale.	Hartsdale N.B.
12746.	Chappaqua.	Chappaqua N.B.
12757.	New York.	Pacific N.B.
12773.	Rensselaer.	N.B. of Rensselaer.
12785.	Newburgh.	Broadway N.B.
12788.	Patchogue.	People's N.B.
12810.	Savannah.	N.B. of Savannah.
12811.	Pleasantville.	First N.B.
12818.	East Rockaway.	East Rockaway.
12825.	New York.	Fordham N.B.
12836.	Lyons Falls.	Lyons Falls N.B.
12837.	New York.	Bowery N.B.
12874.	New York.	Central N.B.
12884.	Sherrill.	First N.B.
12885.	New York, Astoria.	Long Island N.B.
12892.	New York.	Lafayette N.B. of Brooklyn.
12897.	New York.	N.B. of Ridgewiew.
12900.	Melrose.	Melrose N.B.
12925.	West Seneca,	

Charter Number	City	Name of Bank
	Buffalo.	Seneca N.B.
12932.	New York.	Peoples Trust Co. of Brooklyn. Nat. Banking Assn.
12938.	North Syracuse.	North Syracuse N.B.
12940.	Tuckahoe.	Crestwood N.B.
12948.	New York.	Rugby N.B. of Brooklyn.
12951.	Central Park.	Central Park N.B.
12954.	Waverly.	Citizens N.B.
12956.	Elmsford.	First N.B.
12957.	New York.	Woodside N.B.
12958.	Fair Haven.	Fair Haven N.B.
12963.	Seaford.	Seaford N.B.
12965.	New York.	N.B. of Yorkville.
12970.	New York.	Traders N.B. of Brooklyn.
12980.	New York.	Granit N.B. of Brooklyn.
12987.	Hampton Bays.	Hampton Bays N.B.
12992.	Ardsley.	First N.B.
12997.	Franklin Square.	Franklin Square N.B.
13000.	New York.	Flatbush N.B. of Brooklyn.
13004.	Endicott.	Endicott N.B.
13006.	Livonia.	Stewart N.B.
13025.	New York.	Discount N.B.
13027.	New York.	Claremont N.B.
13035.	New York.	Elmhurst N.B.
13037.	Interlaken.	Wheeler N.B.
13045.	New York.	Seward N.B.
13049.	White Plains.	Plaza N.B.
13051.	New York.	Greenwich N.B.
13055.	New York.	Prospect N.B. of Brooklyn.
13062.	Baldwin.	Sunrise N.B.
13063.	New York.	Bedford N.B. of Brooklyn.
13074.	LoN.B.ach.	Nat. City Bank.
13080.	New York.	Bensonhurst N.B. of Brooklyn.
13085.	Buffalo.	Frontier N.B.
13088.	New York.	Bay Parkway N.B. of Brooklyn.
13089.	Bolton Landing.	Bolton N.B.
13104.	West Hempstead.	West Hempstead N.B.
13105.	New York.	College Point N.B.
13115.	New York.	Douglaston N.B.
13121.	Mahopac.	Mahopac N.B.
13122.	New York.	Guardian N.B.
13124.	East Williston.	Williston N.B. of Williston Park.
13126.	Glen Head.	First N.B.
13130.	Lake Ronkonkoma.	N.B. of Lake Ronkonkoma.
13132.	New York.	Mutual N.B.
13143.	Glen Cove.	First N.B.
13145.	Webster.	Webster N.B.
13149.	New York.	Springfield Garde N.B.
13163.	New York.	Longacre N.B.
13193.	New York.	Bank of America Nat. Ass'n.
13194.	New York.	Commercial Exchange N.B.
13207.	New York.	Industrial N.B.
13219.	Buffalo.	Lincoln N.B.
13229.	Wyoming.	N.B. of Wyoming.
13234.	Bellerose.	First N.B.
13237.	New York.	Dunbar N.B.
13239.	Yonkers.	Bryn Mawr-Nepperhan N.B.
13242.	New York.	Forest Hills N.B.
13246.	Bolivar.	First N.B.
13250.	New York.	Commercial N.B. and Trust Co.
13254.	New York.	Straus N.B. and Trust Co.
13260.	New York.	Lefcourt Normandie N.B.
13289.	Wells.	Hamilton County N.B.
13292.	New York.	Brooklyn N.B.
13295.	New York.	Sterling N.B. and Trust Co.
13296.	New York.	N.B. of Queens County.
13301.	New York.	Blair N.B.
13304.	New York.	Kingsboro N.B. of Brooklyn.
13310.	Port Washington.	Harbor N.B.
13314.	Nanuet.	Nanuet N.B.
13319.	Yonkers.	Central N.B.
13326.	Roslyn.	Roslyn N.B. and Trust Co.
13327.	New York.	Broadway N.B. and Trust Co.
13330.	Rochester.	First N.B. and Trust Co.
13334.	New York.	N.B. of Bayside.
13346.	New York.	Fort Greene N.B.
13360.	New York.	Washingston Square N.B.
13365.	La Fargeville.	First N.B.
13377.	Elmira.	Southside N.B.
13379.	New York.	Newtown N.B.
13393.	Syracuse.	Lincoln N.B. and Trust Co.
13404.	Mineola.	Central N.B.
13441.	Buffalo.	Niagara N.B.
13442.	New York.	National Exchange Bank and Trust Co.
13445.	Mattituck.	Mattituck N.B. and Trust Co.
13476.	Minoa.	First N.B.
13493.	Odessa.	First N.B.
13521.	Argyle.	N.B. of Argyle.
13528.	Middletown.	First Merchants N.B. and Trust Co.
13545.	Washingtonville.	First N.B.
13548.	Plattsburg.	Merchants N.B.
13559.	Montgomery.	First N.B.
13563.	Sidney.	First N.B.
13567.	Highland Falls.	First N.B.
13575.	Greene.	First N.B.
13583.	Montour Falls.	Montour N.B.
13584.	Carthage.	Carthage National Exchange Bank.
13590.	Callicoon.	First N.B.
13592.	Mamaroneck.	First N.B.
13664.	Painted Post.	First N.B.
13748.	Cherry Valley.	Otsego County N.B.
13822.	Kingston.	National Ulster County Bank.
13825.	Florida.	N.B. of Florida.

Charter Number	City	Name of Bank
13876.	Canajoharie.	National Spraker Bank
13882.	Yonkers.	First N.B.
13889.	Tuckahoe.	Crestwood N.B.
13895.	Tuxedo.	N.B. of Tuxedo.
13909.	Andover.	Andover N.B.
13911.	Gouverneur.	First N.B.
13913.	Washingtonville.	Central N.B.
13945.	Philmont.	Philmont N.B.
13952.	Buffalo.	Lincoln-East Side N.B.
13955.	New Rochelle.	First N.B.
13956.	Middletown.	N.B. of Middletown.
13959.	New York.	Fidelity N.B.
13960.	Pine Bush.	N.B. of Pine Bush.
13962.	Windham.	N.B. of Windham.
13965.	Brockport.	Brockport N.B.
14019.	Kings Park.	N.B. of Kings Park.
14025.	Oxford.	N.B. of Oxford.
14078.	Cherry Creek.	Cherry Creek N.B.
14267.	Phelps.	N.B. of Phelps.

NORTH CAROLINA

Charter Number	City	Name of Bank
1547.	Charlotte.	First N.B.
1557.	Raleigh.	Raleigh N.B. of N.C.
1632.	New Berne.	N.B. of New Berne.
1656.	Wilmington.	First N.B.
1659.	Salem.	First N.B.
1682.	Raleigh.	State N.B.
1756.	Fayetteville.	Fayetteville N.B.
1766.	Raleigh.	Citizens' N.B.
1781.	Charlotte.	Merchants and Farmers' N.B.
2003.	Fayetteville.	People's N.B.
2135.	Charlotte.	Commercial N.B.
2314.	Charlotte.	Traders' N.B.
2319.	Winston.	First N.B.
2321.	Wilson.	First N.B.
2322.	Greensboro.	N.B. of Greensboro.
2425.	Winston.	Wachovia N.B.
2981.	Salisbury.	First N.B.
3389.	Raleigh.	N.B. of Raleigh.
3418.	Asheville.	First N.B.
3490.	High Point.	First N.B.
3682.	Statesville.	First N.B.
3811.	Durham.	First N.B.
3903.	Concord.	Concord N.B.
4094.	Asheville.	N.B. of Asheville.
4292.	Winston, Winston-Salem.	People's N.B.
4377.	Gastonia.	First N.B.
4568.	High Point.	Commercial N.B.
4597.	Hickory.	First N.B.
4628.	Elizabeth City.	First and Citizens' N.B.
4726.	Wilmington.	Atlantic N.B.
4896.	Mount Airy.	First N.B.
4947.	Wadesboro.	First N.B.
4960.	Wilmington.	N.B. of Wilmington.
4997.	Washington.	First N.B.
5031.	Greensboro.	Greensboro N.B.
5048.	Goldsboro.	N.B. of Goldsboro.
5055.	Charlotte.	Charlotte N.B.
5110.	Asheville.	Blue Ridge N.B.
5168.	Greensboro.	City N.B.
5182.	Wilmington.	Murchison N.B.
5450.	Morganton.	First N.B.
5451.	Kings Mountain.	First N.B.
5651.	Laurinsburg.	First N.B.
5673.	Elkin.	Elkin N.B.
5677.	Fayetteville.	N.B. of Fayetteville.
5698.	Lexington.	First N.B.
5767.	Roanoke Rapids.	First N.B.
5885.	Oxford.	First N.B.
6075.	Newton.	Shuford N.B.
6095.	Marion.	First N.B.
6554.	Waynesville.	First N.B.
6616.	Lillington.	N.B. of Lillington.
6744.	Lincolnton.	First N.B.
6776.	Shelby.	First N.B.
7188.	Dunn.	First N.B.
7362.	Rocky Mount.	First N.B.
7398.	Lumberton.	First N.B.
7536.	Gastonia.	Citizens' N.B.
7554.	Louisburg.	First N.B.
7564.	Henderson.	First N.B.
7698.	Durham.	Citizens' N.B.
7913.	Wilmington.	Southern N.B.
7959.	Shelby.	Shelby N.B.
8160.	Greenville.	N.B. of Greenville.
8184.	Lincolnton.	County N.B.
8356.	Tarboro.	First N.B.
8445.	Lenoir.	First N.B.
8571.	West Jefferson.	First N.B.
8649.	Burlington.	First N.B.
8682.	Fayetteville.	Fourth N.B.
8712.	Monroe.	First N.B.
8772.	Asheville.	American N.B.
8788.	Thomasville.	First N.B.
8837.	Hendersonville.	First N.B.
8844.	Graham.	N.B. of Alamance.
8902.	Creedmoor.	First N.B.
8953.	Asheboro.	First N.B.
8996.	Oxford.	N.B. of Granville.
9044.	Kinston.	N.B. of Kinston.
9067.	Raleigh.	Commercial N.B.
9076.	Salisbury.	People's N.B.
9085.	Kinston.	First N.B.
9123.	Greensboro.	Commercial N.B.
9124.	Wilmington.	American N.B.
9164.	Charlotte.	Union N.B.
9203.	Forest City.	First N.B.
9335.	Statesville.	Commercial N.B.

Charter Number	City	Name of Bank
9458.	Murphy.	First N.B.
9471.	Raleigh.	Merchants' N.B.
9531.	Mooresville.	First N.B.
9548.	Cherryville.	First N.B.
9571.	Hendersonville.	People's N.B.
9916.	Winston.	Merchants' N.B.
10112.	Greensboro.	American Exchange N.B.
10260.	Louisburg.	Farmers' N.B.
10502.	Smithfield.	First N.B.
10608.	Rocky Mount.	Planters' N.B.
10610.	Lumberton.	N.B. of Lumberton.
10614.	Goldsboro.	Wayre N.B.
10629.	Mount Olive.	First N.B.
10630.	Rocky Mount.	N.B. of Rocky Mount.
10662.	Spencer.	First N.B.
10734.	Hendersonville.	Citizens' N.B.
10739.	Selma.	First N.B.
10792.	Ayden.	Farmers' and Merchants' N.B.
10851.	Hamlet.	First N.B.
10876.	Hertford.	Farmers' N.B.
10887.	Snow Hill.	First N.B.
11091.	Albemarle.	First N.B.
11211.	Roxboro.	First N.B.
11229.	Reidsville.	First N.B.
11431.	Spring Hope.	First N.B.
11440.	Smithfield.	Citizens' N.B.
11477.	Gastonia.	Third N.B.
11551.	Murfreesboro.	First N.B.
11697.	Mebane.	First N.B.
11767.	Warsaw.	First N.B.
12009.	Fairmont.	First N.B.
12176.	Wilmington.	Commercial N.B.
12244.	Asheville.	N.B. of Commerce.
12259.	Leaksville.	First N.B.
12278.	Winston-Salem.	Farmers' N.B. and Trust Co.
12461.	Forest City.	N.B. of Forest City.
12614.	Benson.	First N.B.
12633.	La Grange.	N.B. of La Grange.
12772.	Snow Hill.	N.B. of Snow Hill.
12896.	Cherryville.	Cherryville N.B.
13168.	Fayetteville.	Cumberland N.B.
13298.	New Bern.	First N.B.
13306.	Tarboro.	Edgecombe N.B.
13500.	Forest City.	First N.B.
13523.	Lenoir.	Union N.B.
13554.	Ayden.	First N.B.
13613.	Burlington.	N.B. of Burlington.
13626.	Wilson.	N.B. of Wilson.
13636.	Henderson.	First N.B.
13657.	Durham.	Depositors N.B.
13721.	Asheville.	First N.B. & Trust Co.
13761.	Greensboro.	Security N.B.
13779.	Gastonia.	Citizens' N.B.
13791.	Sanford.	N.B. of Sanford.
13859.	Oxford.	Union N.B.
13896.	Oxford.	Oxford N.B.
13985.	Greensboro.	Guilford N.B.
14147.	Winston.	First N.B. Salem.
14229.	Cherryville.	Cherryville N.B.
14291.	Gastonia.	N.B. of Commerce.

NORTH DAKOTA

Charter Number	City	Name of Bank
2377.	Fargo.	N. Dak. First N.B.
2434.	Bismarck.	First N.B.
2514.	Fargo.	Red River Valley N.B.
2548.	Valley City.	First N.B.
2564.	Grand Forks.	First N.B.
2570.	Grand Forks.	First N.B.
2578.	Jamestown.	First N.B.
2580.	Jamestown.	James River N.B.
2585.	Mandan.	First N.B.
2624.	Wahpeton.	First N.B.
2650.	Valley City.	Farmers and Merchants' N.B.
2677.	Bismarck.	Bismarck N.B.
2792.	Casselton.	First N.B.
2840.	Grafton.	First N.B.
2854.	Larimore.	First N.B.
2986.	Bismarck.	Capital N.B.
3096.	Grafton.	Grafton N.B.
3169.	Bismarck.	Merchan& N.B.
3301.	Grand Forks.	Grand Forks N.B.
3331.	Jamestown.	Jamestown N.B.
3397.	Devil's Lake.	First N.B.
3400.	Hillsboro.	First N.B.
3411.	Hillsboro.	Hillsboro N.B.
3436.	Park River.	First N.B.
3438.	Pembina.	First N.B.
3504.	Grand Forks.	Second N.B.
3602.	Fargo.	Citizens' N.B.
3669.	Lisbon.	First N.B.
3673.	Mayville.	First N.B.
3714.	Devil's Lake.	Merchants' N.B.
4009.	Minot.	First N.B.
4106.	Wahpeton.	N.B. of Wahpeton.
4143.	Lakota.	First N.B.
4256.	Fargo.	N.B. of North Dakota.
4372.	Grand Forks.	Union N.B.
4384.	Dickinson.	First N.B.
4537.	Bathgate.	First N.B.
4550.	Saint Thomas.	First N.B.
4552.	Wahpeton.	Citizens' N.B.
4561.	Jamestown.	Lloyds N.B.
4802.	Langdon.	First N.B.
4812.	Grand Forks.	Merchants' N.B.
5087.	Fargo.	Fargo N.B.
5364.	Valley City.	American N.B.
5375.	Cooperstown.	First N.B.
5408.	Fessenden.	First N.B.

Charter Number	City	Name of Bank
5455.	Lakota.	N.B. of Lakota.
5488.	Harvey.	First N.B.
5500.	Minnewaukon.	First N.B.
5551.	Carrington.	First N.B.
5567.	Williston.	First N.B.
5772.	Lidgerwood.	First N.B.
5798.	Cando.	First N.B.
5886.	Devil's Lake.	Ramsey County N.B.
5893.	Hope.	First N.B.
5980.	Northwood.	First N.B.
6064.	Kenmare.	First N.B.
6085.	Bottineau.	First N.B.
6157.	Rolla.	First N.B.
6210.	Courtenay.	First N.B.
6218.	Hankinson.	First N.B.
6225.	Drayton.	First N.B.
6255.	Fairmount.	First N.B.
6286.	Larimore.	N.B. of Larimore.
6312.	Leeds.	First N.B.
6315.	Minot.	Minot N.B.
6327.	Washburn.	First N.B.
6337.	Churchs Ferry.	First N.B.
6341.	Rugby.	First N.B.
6393.	New Rockford.	First N.B.
6397.	Starkweather.	First N.B.
6398.	Ellendale.	First N.B.
6407.	Crary.	First N.B.
6428.	New Salem.	First N.B.
6429.	Minot.	Second N.B.
6457.	Oakes.	First N.B.
6463.	Page.	First N.B.
6474.	Forman.	First N.B.
6475.	Omemee.	First N.B.
6486.	Enderlin.	First N.B.
6518.	Milton.	First N.B.
6555.	Kenmare.	Kenmare N.B.
6557.	Tower City.	First N.B.
6559.	Buffalo.	First N.B.
6601.	Edmore.	First N.B.
6690.	Lamoure.	First N.B.
6712.	Wimbledon.	First N.B.
6733.	Bisbee.	First N.B.
6743.	Hatton.	First N.B.
6766.	Willow City.	First N.B.
6898.	Knox.	First N.B.
6977.	Sheldon.	First N.B.
6985.	Hunter.	First N.B.
6988.	Oakes.	Oakes N.B.
7008.	Mohall.	First N.B.
7116.	Bowbells.	First N.B.
7142.	Casselton.	Cass County N.B.
7162.	Westhope.	First N.B.
7166.	Wyndmere.	First N.B.
7234.	Osnabrock.	First N.B.
7295.	Fingal.	First N.B.
7315.	Carpio.	First N.B.
7324.	Finley.	First N.B.
7332.	Willow City.	Merchants' N.B.
7377.	Cando.	Cando N.B.
7569.	Munich.	First N.B.
7650.	Hampden.	First N.B.
7663.	Dickinson.	Dakota N.B.
7689.	Minot.	Union N.B.
7693.	Portland.	First N.B.
7695.	Wahpeton.	German American N.B.
7727.	Hannaford.	First N.B.
7810.	Tolley.	First N.B.
7820.	Jamestown.	Citizens' N.B.
7846.	McCumber.	First N.B.
7852.	Adams.	First N.B.
7855.	Antler.	First N.B.
7857.	Mylo.	First N.B.
7866.	Rolette.	First N.B.
7872.	Egeland.	First N.B.
7879.	Bottineau.	Bottineau N.B.
7905.	Hatton.	Farmers and Merchants' N.B.
7914.	Edgeley.	First N.B.
7918.	Crystal.	First N.B.
7943.	Kensal.	First N.B.
7955.	Towner.	First N.B.
8019.	Rock Lake.	First N.B.
8029.	Kramer.	First N.B.
8077.	Goodrich.	First N.B.
8084.	Hankinson.	Citizens' N.B.
8096.	Overly.	First N.B.
8124.	McHenry.	First N.B.
8170.	Fargo.	Merchants' N.B.
8187.	Lansford.	First N.B.
8201.	Dickinson.	Merchants' N.B.
8226.	Maddock.	First N.B.
8230.	Lidgerwood.	Farmers' N.B.
8264.	Milnor.	Milnor N.B.
8265.	Binford.	First N.B.
8280.	Milnor.	First N.B.
8298.	Litchville.	First N.B.
8324.	Williston.	Citizens N.B.
8395.	Hope.	Hope N.B.
8419.	Abercrombie.	First N.B.
8448.	Sanborn.	First N.B.
8502.	Brinsmade.	First N.B.
8821.	Turtle Lake.	First N.B.
8881.	McClusky.	First N.B.
8886.	Sheyenne.	First N.B.
8917.	Wimbledon.	Merchants' N.B.
8976.	Bowman.	First N.B.
8991.	Hettinger.	First N.B.
8997.	Steele.	First N.B.
9005.	Sharon.	First N.B.
9016.	Glen Ullin.	First N.B.

Charter Number	City	Name of Bank
9075.	Langdon.	Cavalier County N.B.
9082.	Marmarth.	First N.B.
9133.	Walhalla.	First N.B.
9161.	Marion.	First N.B.
9214.	Ryder.	First N.B.
9287.	Nome.	First N.B.
9386.	Ambrose.	First N.B.
9390.	Anamoose.	Anamoose N.B.
9412.	Anamoose.	First N.B.
9472.	Stanley.	First N.B.
9484.	Beach.	First N.B.
9489.	Mott.	First N.B.
9521.	Ellendale.	Farmers' N.B.
9524.	Drake.	First N.B.
9539.	Belfield.	First N.B.
9590.	Linton.	First N.B.
9622.	Bismarck.	City N.B.
9631.	Ellendale.	Ellendale N.B.
9684.	Reeder.	First N.B.
9689.	Plaza.	First N.B.
9698.	Yates.	First N.B.
9714.	La Moure.	Farmers' N.B.
9754.	Northwood.	Citizens' N.B.
9776.	New England.	First N.B.
9778.	Garrison.	First N.B.
10116.	Cavalier.	First N.B.
10405.	Scranton.	First N.B.
10425.	East Fairview, Fairview, Mont.	First N.B.
10495.	Jamestown.	Farmers and Merchants' N.B.
10496.	Reynolds.	First N.B.
10519.	Crosby.	Citizens' N.B.
10581.	Medina.	First N.B.
10596.	Crosby.	First N.B.
10604.	Mandan.	Merchants' N.B.
10706.	Sentinel Butte.	First N.B.
10721.	McVille.	First N.B.
10724.	Streeter.	First N.B.
10741.	Hebron.	First N.B.
10814.	Buxton.	First N.B.
10820.	Kilideer.	First N.B.
10864.	Ashley.	First N.B.
10896.	Portland.	Farmers' N.B.
10921.	Taylor.	First N.B.
10966.	Van Hook.	First N.B.
11069.	Kulm.	La Moure County First N.B.
11110.	Neche.	First N.B.
11112.	Bathgate.	Bathgate N.B.
11142.	Grand Forks.	Northwestern N.B.
11166.	Streeter.	Citizens' N.B.
11184.	Makoti.	First N.B.
11185.	Petersburg.	First N.B.
11217.	Fullerton.	First N.B.
11226.	Parshall.	First N.B.
11272.	Underwood.	First N.B.
11297.	Alexander.	First N.B.
11311.	Aneta.	First N.B.
11338.	Tuttle.	First N.B.
11346.	Golva.	First N.B.
11353.	Woodworth.	First N.B.
11378.	Napoleon.	First N.B.
11417.	Valley City.	Security N.B.
11494.	Montpelier.	First N.B.
11555.	Fargo.	Security N.B.
11599.	Thompson.	First N.B.
11605.	Mooreton.	First N.B.
11641.	Fairmount.	N.B. of Fairmount.
11665.	Linton.	City N.B.
11677.	Hettinger.	Live Stock N.B.
11712.	Wilton.	First N.B.
11719.	Max.	First N.B.
11786.	Fargo.	Northern N.B.
12003.	Edgeley.	Security N.B.
12023.	Michigan City.	Lamb's N.B.
12026.	Fargo.	Dakota N.B.
12046.	Cavalier.	Merchants' N.B.
12258.	Donnybrook.	First N.B.
12393.	Drake.	First N.B.
12401.	Dickinson.	Liberty N.B.
12464.	Whitman.	First N.B.
12502.	Taylor.	Security N.B.
12743.	Lidgerwood.	Farmers' N.B.
12776.	Lidgerwood.	First N.B.
12817.	Valley City.	First N.B.
12853.	Gackle.	First N.B.
12875.	Wahpeton.	N.B. of Wahpeton.
13041.	Hope.	Security N.B.
13053.	Langdon.	First N.B.
13190.	Finnley.	Steele County N.B.
13323.	Fargo.	Merchants N.B. & Trust Co.
13324.	Valley City.	N.B. of Valley City.
13344.	Jamestown.	N.B. & Trust Co. of Jamestown.
13357.	Grand Forks.	Red River N.B. & Trust Co.
13362.	Cooperstown.	First N.B.
13385.	Valley City.	American N.B. & Trust Co.
13398.	Bismarck.	Dakota N.B. & Trust Co.
13410.	Glen Ullin.	First N.B.
13436.	Neche.	First N.B.
13454.	Carson.	First N.B.
13455.	Minot.	Union N.B. & Trust Co.
13501.	Garrison.	First N.B.
13594.	Portland.	First & Farmers N.B.
13790.	Grand Forks.	First N.B.
14080.	Mott.	First N.B.
14275.	Williston.	First & Commercial N.B.

OHIO

Charter Number	City	Name of Bank
3.	Youngstown.	First N.B.
5.	Fremont.	First N.B.
7.	Cleveland.	First N.B.
9.	Dayton.	First N.B.
10.	Dayton.	Second N.B.
13.	Cleveland.	Second N.B.
16.	Sandusky.	First N.B.
20.	Cincinnati.	Fifth-Third N.B.
24.	Cincinnati.	First N.B.
27.	Akron.	First N.B.
32.	Cincinnati.	Second N.B.
36.	Findlay.	First N.B.
40.	Akron.	Second N.B.
43.	Salem.	First N.B.
46.	McConnels.	First N.B. ville.
53.	Lodi.	First N.B.
56.	Hamilton.	First N.B.
59.	Troy.	First N.B.
68.	Portsmouth.	First N.B.
72.	Oberlin.	First N.B.
74.	Warren.	First N.B.
76.	Canton.	First N.B.
86.	Germantown.	First N.B.
90.	Upper Sandusky.	First N.B.
91.	Toledo.	First N.B.
92.	Logan.	First N.B.
93.	Cincinnati.	Fourth N.B.
98.	Ironton.	First N.B.
100.	Cadiz.	First N.B.
101.	Greenfield.	First N.B.
106.	Ravenna.	First N.B.
118.	Circleville.	First N.B.
123.	Columbus.	First N.B.
127.	Cardington.	First N.B.
128.	Chillicothe.	First N.B.
131.	Zanesville.	Second N.B.
132.	Pomeroy.	First N.B.
133.	Beverly.	First N.B.
136.	Gallipolis.	First N.B.
137.	Lancaster.	First N.B.
141.	Cambridge.	First N.B.
142.	Marietta.	First N.B.
153.	Geneva.	First N.B.
164.	Zanesville.	First N.B.
171.	South Charleston.	First N.B.
172.	Circleville.	Second N.B.
183.	Ashland.	First N.B.
210.	Sandusky.	Second N.B.
214.	Bridgeport.	First N.B.
215.	Norwalk.	First N.B.
216.	Massillon.	First N.B.
220.	Painesville.	First N.B.
233.	Athens.	First N.B.
237.	Bryan.	First N.B.
238.	Springfield.	First N.B.
242.	Ironton.	Second N.B.
243.	Delaware.	First N.B.
248.	Toledo.	Second N.B.
257.	Sidney.	First N.B.
258.	Mount Gilead.	First N.B.
263.	Springfield.	Second N.B.
274.	Delphos.	First N.B.
277.	Xenia.	Second N.B.
284.	Washington C.H.	First N.B.
287.	Marion.	First N.B.
289.	Ripley.	First N.B.
315.	Saint Clairsville.	First N.B.
350.	Ravenna.	Second N.B.
365.	Wilmington.	First N.B.
369.	Xenia.	First N.B.
378.	Cuyahoga Falls.	First N.B.
388.	Granville.	First N.B.
419.	Galion.	First N.B.
422.	Van Wert.	First N.B.
427.	Jefferson.	First N.B.
436.	Mansfield.	First N.B.
438.	Elyria.	First N.B.
443.	Bucyrus.	First N.B.
463.	Canton.	Second N.B.
464.	Wellington.	First N.B.
480.	Mansfield.	Richland N.B.
492.	Mount Pleasant.	First N.B.
501.	Smithfield.	First N.B.
530.	Eaton.	First N.B.
591.	Columbus.	Nat. Exchange Bank.
599.	Columbus.	Franklin N.B.
607.	Toledo.	Toledo N.B.
620.	Cincinnati.	Central N.B.
630.	Cincinnati.	Ohio N.B.
652.	Kent.	Kent N.B.
715.	Batavia.	First N.B.
738.	Franklin.	First N.B.
773.	Cleveland.	Merchants' N.B.
786.	Cleveland.	Nat. City Bank.
787.	Hillsborough.	First N.B.
800.	Mansfield.	Farmers' N.B.
807.	Cleveland.	Commercial N.B.
809.	Toledo.	Northern N.B.
828.	Wooster.	Wayne County N.B.
829.	Hamilton.	Second N.B.
844.	Cincinnati.	Merchants' N.B.
853.	Delaware.	Delaware County N.B.
858.	Newark.	First N.B.
859.	Marietta.	Marietta N.B.
863.	Urbana.	Citizens N.B.
898.	Dayton.	Dayton N.B.
900.	Tiffifi.	First N.B.
907.	Tiffin.	Nat. Exchange Bank.
908.	Mount Vernon.	First N.B.
911.	Barnesville.	First N.B.
916.	Urbana.	Champaign N.B.
931.	Norwalk.	Norwalk N.B.
933.	Ripley.	Farmers' N.B.
935.	Portsmouth.	Portsmouth N.B.
973.	Salem.	Farmers' N.B.
975.	Ashtabula.	Farmers' N.B.
1006.	Piqua.	Piqua N.B.
1044.	Wellsville.	First N.B.
1051.	Mount Vernon.	Knox County N.B.
1061.	Piqua.	Citizens N.B.
1062.	Steubenville.	Jefferson N.B.
1064.	London.	Madison N.B.
1068.	New Richmond.	First N.B.
1088.	Portsmouth.	Farmers' N.B.
1092.	Greenville.	Farmers' N.B.
1146.	Springfield.	Mad River N.B.
1164.	Steubenville.	First N.B.
1172.	Chillicothe.	Ross County N.B.
1185.	Cincinnati.	Commercial N.B.
1230	Zanesville.	Muskingum N.B.
1238.	Lebanon.	First N.B.
1241.	Lancaster.	Hocking Valley N.B.
1277.	Chillicothe.	Chillicothe N.B.
1318.	Massillon.	Union N.B.
1447.	Cadiz.	Harrison N.B.
1545.	Middletown.	First N.B.
1578.	Warren.	Trumbull N.B.
1689.	Cleveland.	Ohio N.B.
1784.	Bellefontaine.	Bellefontaine N.B.
1788.	Dayton.	Merchants' N.B.
1895.	Toledo.	Merchants' N.B.
1903.	Jackson.	First N.B.
1904.	Plymouth.	First N.B.
1906.	Defiance.	Defiance N.B.
1912.	Wooster.	N.B. of Wooster.
1917.	Napoleon.	First N.B.
1920.	Coshocton.	First N.B.
1923.	Millersburg.	First N.B.
1929.	Shelby.	First N.B.
1930.	Minerva.	First N.B.
1942.	Cambridge.	Guernsey N.B.
1944.	Bellaire.	First N.B.
1948.	Portsmouth.	Iron N.B.
1958.	Portsmouth.	Kinney N.B.
1972.	Washington C.H.	Fayette County N.B.
1980.	Pomeroy.	Pomeroy N.B.
1981.	New London.	First N.B.
1982.	Manchester.	Manchester N.B.
1984.	Galion.	Citizens' N.B.
1989.	Quaker City.	Quaker City N.B.
1997.	Wilmington.	Clinton County N.B.
1999.	New Philadelphia	Citizens' N.B.
2004.	Berea.	First N.B.
2025.	Middletown.	First and Merchants' N.B.
2026.	Jefferson.	Second N.B.
2031.	Ashtabula.	Ashtabula N.B.
2034.	Garrettsville.	First N.B.
2035.	Lima.	First N.B.
2036.	McArthur.	Vinton County N.B.
2037.	Green Spring.	First N.B.
2039.	Hillsborough.	Citizens' N.B.
2041.	Alliance.	First N.B.
2052.	Malta.	Malta N.B.
2053.	Medina.	First N.B.
2056.	New Lexington.	First N.B.
2061.	Sandusky.	Third N.B.
2071.	Urbana.	Third N.B.
2091.	Medina.	Phoenix N.B.
2098.	Springfield.	Lagonda N.B.
2102.	Caldwell.	Noble County N.B.
2146.	East Liverpool.	First N.B.
2160.	Steubenville.	Nat. Exchange Bank
2181.	Thurman.	Centreville N.B.
2203.	New Lisbon.	First N.B.
2210.	Middleport.	First N.B.
2217.	Youngstown.	Second N.B.
2219.	Batesville.	First N.B.
2220.	Waynesville.	Waynesville N.B.
2282.	Franklin.	Farmers' N.B.
2296.	Toledo.	Commercial N.B.
2302.	Bellevue.	First N.B.
2315.	Cincinnati.	Nat. La Fayette Bank
2325.	Mechanicsburg.	Farmers' N.B.
2350.	Youngstown.	Mahoning N.B.
2360.	Lebanon.	Lebanon N.B.
2389.	Hubbard.	Hubbard N.B.
2423.	Columbus.	Fourth N.B.
2438.	Monroeville.	First N.B.
2444.	Cadiz.	Farmers and Mechanics' N.B.
2449.	Hillsborough.	Merchants' N.B.
2459.	Mount Gilead.	Morrow County N.B.
2474.	Bryan.	Farmers' N.B.
2479.	Warren.	Second N.B.
2480.	Bellefontaine.	People's N.B.
2482.	Youngstown.	Commercial N.B.
2488.	Saint Paris.	First N.B.
2489.	Canton.	City N.B.
2495.	Cincinnati.	Citizens' N.B.
2496.	Granville.	First N.B.
2497.	Lima.	Merchants' N.B.
2500.	Kenton.	First N.B.
2516.	Defiance.	Merchants' N.B.
2524.	Cincinnati.	Lincoln N.B.
2529.	Zanesville.	Citizens' N.B.
2542.	Cincinnati.	Metropolitan N.B.
2544.	East Liverpool.	Potters' N.B.
2549.	Cincinnati.	Union N.B.
2575.	Xenia.	Citizens' N.B.
2577.	Mansfield.	Citizens' N.B.
2582.	Uhrichsville.	Farmers and Merchants' N.B.
2604.	Dayton.	Winters N.B.
2605.	Columbus.	Commercial N.B.

Charter Number	City	Name of Bank
2616.	Cincinnati.	Exchange N.B.
2620.	Springfield.	Springfield N.B.
2625.	Lorain.	First N.B.
2628.	Van Wert.	Van Wert N.B.
2662.	Cleveland.	N.B. of Commerce.
2664.	Cincinnati.	Second N.B.
2678.	Dayton.	Third N.B.
2690.	Cleveland.	First N.B.
2691.	Salem.	First N.B.
2693.	Youngstown.	First N.B.
2698.	Akron.	First N.B.
2703.	Fremont.	First N.B.
2705.	Georgetown.	First N.B.
2712.	McConnelsville.	First N.B.
2716.	Akron.	Second N.B.
2718.	Oberlin.	Citizens' N.B.
2719.	Geneva.	First N.B.
2727.	Troy.	First N.B.
2730.	Cincinnati.	Third N.B.
2754.	South Charleston.	Farmers' N.B.
2798.	Cincinnati.	Fifth-Third N.B.
2810.	Sandusky.	Moss N.B.
2817.	Circleville.	Third N.B.
2831.	Fostoria.	First N.B.
2837.	Ripley.	Ripley N.B.
2842.	Painesville.	Painesville N.B.
2859.	Lima.	Lima N.B.
2861.	Cambridge.	Old N.B.
2863.	Elyria.	First N.B.
2866.	Wellington.	First N.B.
2872.	Cambridge.	Central N.B.
2874.	Dayton.	City N.B.
2882.	Felicity.	First N.B.
2885.	Delphos.	Delphos N.B.
2908.	Barnesville.	People's N.B.
2922.	Cincinnati.	Cincinnati N.B.
2932.	Xenia.	Xenia N.B.
2942.	West Liberty.	Logan N.B.
2946.	Akron.	City N.B.
2956.	Cleveland.	Cleveland N.B.
2992.	Greenville.	Second N.B.
2993.	Chillicothe.	Central N.B.
3004.	Tippecanoe City.	Tipp N.B.
3077.	Kinsman.	Kinsman N.B.
3141.	Sandusky.	Citizens' N.B.
3157.	Wapakoneta.	First N.B.
3177.	Flushing.	First N.B.
3191.	Newark.	People's N.B.
3202.	Cleveland.	Union N.B.
3234.	Milford.	Milford N.B.
3272.	Cleveland.	Mercantile N.B.
3274.	Bucyrus.	Second N.B.
3291.	Ripley.	Citizens' N.B.
3310.	Steubenville.	Steubenville N.B.
3315.	Tiffin.	Tiffin N.B.
3328.	Mount Vernon.	Knox N.B.
3362.	Warren.	Western Reserve N.B.
3461.	Cincinnati.	Fidelity N.B.
3477.	Findlay.	Buckeye N.B.
3492.	Conneaut.	First N.B.
3505.	Kenton.	Kenton N.B.
3519.	Leetonia.	First N.B.
3535.	Wapakoneta.	People's N.B.
3545.	Cleveland.	Euclid Park N.B.
3565.	Wellston.	First N.B.
3581.	Galion.	Galion N.B.
3606.	Cincinnati.	Ohio Valley N.B.
3610.	Columbus.	Clinton N.B.
3639.	Cincinnati.	Atlas N.B.
3642.	Cincinnati.	Market N.B.
3654.	Canfield.	Farmers' N.B.
3707.	Cincinnati.	Equitable N.B.
3720.	Alliance.	First N.B.
3729.	Findlay.	American N.B.
3750.	Piqua.	Third N.B.
3772.	Lima.	Ohio N.B.
3820.	Toledo.	N.B. of Commerce.
3821.	Dayton.	Fourth N.B.
3825.	Troy.	Troy N.B.
3840.	Hamilton.	Miami Valley N.B.
3876.	Miamisburg.	First N.B.
3889.	Eaton.	Preble County N.B.
3950.	Cleveland.	State N.B.
4045.	Bowling Green.	First N.B.
4054.	Dayton.	American N.B.
4133.	Lockland.	First N.B.
4164.	Marietta.	Citizens' N.B.
4190.	Niles.	First N.B.
4197.	Clyde.	First N.B.
4219.	Saint Marys.	First N.B.
4239.	Lebanon.	Citizens' N.B.
4286.	Massillon.	Merchants' N.B.
4293.	Dover.	Exchange N.B.
4298.	Zanesville.	Union N.B.
4318.	Cleveland.	Central N.B. Savings and Trust Co.
4331.	Dover.	First N.B.
4336.	Ironton.	Citizens' N.B.
4347.	North Baltimore.	First N.B.
4443.	Columbus.	First N.B.
4472.	Middleport.	Middleport N.B.
4506.	Ashtabula.	Marine N.B.
4579.	Columbus.	Deshler N.B.
4585.	Toledo.	N.B. of Toledo.
4599.	Oxford.	First N.B.
4657.	Wooster.	Wooster N.B.
4661.	Defiance.	First N.B.
4671.	Chardon.	First N.B.
4697.	Columbus.	Hayden-Clinton N.B.
4712.	New London.	New London N.B.
4763.	Washington C.H.	Midland N.B.
4772.	Cortland.	First N.B.
4778.	Huron.	First N.B.
4782.	Cleveland.	Western Reserve N.B.
4792.	Sandusky.	Third Nat. Exchange Bank.
4805.	Urbana.	N.B. of Urbana.
4822.	Miamisburg.	Citizens' N.B.
4839.	Arcanum.	First N.B.
4842.	Medina.	Old Phoenix N.B.
4853.	Cadiz.	Fourth N.B.
4864.	Belmont.	First N.B.
4867.	Hicksville.	First N.B.
4884.	Girard.	First N.B.
4961.	Akron.	Citizens' N.B.
4970.	Youngstown.	Wick N.B.
4977.	Niles.	City N.B.
4993.	Saint Clairsville.	Second N.B.
5006.	Cleveland.	Park N.B.
5029.	Columbus.	Merchants and Manufacturers' N.B.
5039.	Steubenville.	Commercial N.B.
5065.	Columbus.	Ohio N.B.
5075.	Ashtabula.	N.B. of Ashtabula.
5090.	Cleveland.	American Exchange N.B.
5098.	East Liverpool.	Citizens' N.B.
5099.	Crestline.	First N.B.
5100.	Franklin.	Franklin N.B.
5103.	Coshocton.	Coshocton N.B.
5125.	Lima.	American N.B.
5139.	Medina.	Medina County N.B.
5144.	Dresden.	First N.B.
5152.	Cleveland.	Colonial N.B.
5160.	Springfield.	Citizens' N.B.
5191.	Cleveland.	Coal and Iron N.B.
5194.	Cleveland.	Bank of Commerce Nat. Assn.
5197.	Scio.	Farmers and Producers' N.B.
5212.	Marietta.	Central N.B.
5214.	Sidney.	First Nat. Exchange Bank.
5218.	Napoleon.	First N.B.
5230.	Barberton.	First N.B.
5251.	Mount Gilead.	N.B. of Morrow County.
5259.	McConnelsville.	Citizens' N.B.
5262.	Newcomerstown.	First N.B.
5277.	College Corner.	First N.B.
5315.	Montpelier.	First N.B.
5329.	Lowell.	First N.B.
5341.	Montpelier.	Montpelier N.B.
5344.	Minerva.	First N.B.
5350.	Cleveland.	Century N.B.
5370.	Mantua.	First N.B.
5371.	Lorain.	N.B. of Commerce.
5382.	Mount Sterling.	First N.B.
5396.	Carrollton.	First N.B.
5414.	Woodsfield.	First N.B.
5425.	Ada.	First N.B.
5427.	Tiffin.	City N.B.
5448.	Upper Sandusky.	Commercial N.B.
5522.	Plain City.	Farmers' N.B.
5523.	Celina.	First N.B.
5530.	Covington.	Citizens' N.B.
5552.	Chesterhill.	First N.B.
5555.	Roseville.	First N.B.
5577.	Delta.	Farmers' N.B.
5602.	Bethesda.	First N.B.
5618.	Dillonvale.	First N.B.
5626.	Bluffton.	First N.B.
5627.	Bethel.	First N.B.
5634.	Chillicothe.	Citizens' N.B.
5635.	Waverly.	First N.B.
5640.	Fredericktown.	First N.B.
5641.	Byesville.	First N.B.
5650.	Marion.	City N.B.
5653.	Cleveland.	Metropolitan N.B.
5678.	Cleveland.	Market N.B.
5694.	Mingo Junction.	First N.B.
5760.	Zanesville.	Old Citizens' N.B.
5762.	Clarington.	First N.B.
5769.	Zanesville.	Commercial N.B.
5802.	Hicksville.	Hicksville N.B.
5805.	Cleveland.	Bankers' N.B.
5819.	Barberton.	American N.B.
5828.	Wadsworth.	First N.B.
5862.	Paulding.	Paulding N.B.
5870.	Wadsworth.	Wadsworth N.B.
5917.	Paulding.	First N.B.
5996.	Georgetown.	People's N.B.
5999.	New Matarnoras.	First N.B.
6016.	Adena.	People's N.B.
6059.	Oxford.	Oxford N.B.
6068.	Fairport Harbor.	First N.B.
6119.	Carey.	First N.B.
6147.	Youngstown.	Old N.B.
6227.	Port Clinton.	First N.B.
6249.	Burton.	First N.B.
6280.	Delphos.	N.B. of Delphos.
6289.	Warren.	New N.B.
6296.	Columbiana.	First N.B.
6308.	Marion.	Marion N.B.
6314.	Elmwood Place.	First N.B.
6322.	Norwood.	First N.B.
6345.	Wellsville.	People's N.B.
6353.	Warren.	Union N.B.
6362.	Orrville.	Orrville N.B.
6372.	Dalton.	First N.B.
6379.	Orrville.	First N.B.
6391.	Belmont.	Belmont N.B.
6455.	Sandusky.	Commercial N.B.
6458.	Caldwell.	Citizens' N.B.
6466.	Ravenna.	Ravenna N.B.
6505.	New Lexington.	Citizens' N.B.
6515.	Butler.	First N.B.
6529.	Dresden.	Dresden N.B.
6565.	Leipsic.	First N.B.
6566.	Cambridge.	N.B. of Cambridge.
6593.	East Palestine.	First N.B.
6594.	New Carlisle.	First N.B.
6620.	Mount Gilead.	Mount Gilead N.B.
6621.	Barnesville.	N.B. of Barnesville.
6624.	Bridgeport.	Bridgeport N.B.
6628.	Dunkirk.	First N.B.
6632.	Oak Harbor.	First N.B.
6640.	Mount Pleasant.	Mount Pleasant N.B.
6652.	Dunkirk.	Woodruff N.B.
6656.	Weston.	First N.B.
6657.	Loudonville.	First N.B.
6662.	Summerfield.	First N.B.
6667.	Mount Pleasant.	People's N.B.
6675.	La Rue.	Campbell N.B.
6763.	Akron.	Nat. City Bank.
6770.	Elmore.	First N.B.
6779.	Loveland.	Loveland N.B.
6816.	Loveland.	First N.B.
6827.	Grove City.	First N.B.
6836.	Dennison.	Twin City N.B.
6843.	Dennison.	Dennison N.B.
6892.	Coshocton.	Commercial N.B.
6943.	Watertown.	First N.B.
6976.	New Concord.	First N.B.
7001.	Greenwich.	First N.B.
7006.	Ottawa.	First N.B.
7017.	Lodi.	Exchange N.B.
7025.	Beillsville.	First N.B.
7035.	Plymouth.	People's N.B.
7039.	Piketon.	Piketon N.B.
7074.	Kalida.	First N.B.
7091.	Wauseon.	First N.B.
7130.	Greenville.	Greenville N.B.
7187.	New Holland.	First N.B.
7235.	Amesville.	First N.B.
7237.	Somerset.	First N.B.
7248.	Mount Vernon.	Farmers and Merchants' N.B.
7327.	Bellaire.	Farmers and Merchants' N.B.
7370.	Clarksville.	Farmers' N.B.
7391.	Newton Falls.	First N.B.
7399.	Senecaville.	First N.B.
7403.	Mason.	First N.B.
7456.	Cleves.	Hamilton County N.B.
7486.	Bowerston.	First N.B.
7487.	Cleveland.	Nat. Commercial Bank.
7505.	Delaware.	Delaware N.B.
7517.	Lancaster.	Fairfield N.B.
7518.	Forest.	First N.B.
7542.	New Richmond.	New Richmond N.B.
7557.	Eaton.	Eaton N.B.
7584.	Columbus.	Union N.B.
7596.	Utica.	First N.B.
7621.	Columbus.	N.B. of Commerce.
7631.	Buckeye City.	First N.B.
7638.	Mount Vernon.	New Knox N.B.
7639.	Baltimore.	First N.B.
7649.	Logan.	N.B. of Logan.
7661.	Mount Healthy.	First N.B.
7670.	Wooster.	Citizens' N.B.
7671.	Westerville.	First N.B.
7688.	Steubenville.	People's N.B.
7711.	Sardis.	First N.B.
7744.	Athens.	Athens N.B.
7745.	Columbus.	Huntington N.B.
7759.	Powhatan.	First N.B.
7781.	Portsmouth.	Central N.B.
7787.	Newark.	Franklin N.B.
7790.	Rock Creek.	First N.B.
7795.	Tiffin.	Commercial N.B.
7800.	Sardinia.	First N.B.
7818.	Columbus.	City N.B.
7851.	New Bremen.	First N.B.
7862.	Sidney.	Citizens' N.B.
7896.	Spring Valley.	Spring Valley N.B.
7947.	Monroe.	Monroe N.B.
7984,	Somerton.	First N.B.
8000.	Franklin.	Warren N.B.
8017.	Convoy.	First N.B.
8042.	Stockport.	First N.B.
8127.	Saint Paris.	Central N.B.
8175.	Coolville.	Coolville N.B.
8182.	Centerburg.	First N.B.
8188.	Milford.	Citizens' N.B.
8228.	Harrison.	First N.B.
8251.	Wilmington.	Citizens' N.B.
8300.	Camden.	First N.B.
8411.	Sabina.	First N.B.
8420.	Belpre.	First N.B.
8423.	Glouster.	First N.B.
8438.	Cincinnati.	American N.B.
8441.	Middleport.	Citizens' N.B.
8478.	Cheviot.	First N.B.
8488.	Carthage.	First N.B.
8505.	Norwood.	Norwood N.B.
8507.	Lebanon.	Farmers and Merchants' N.B.
8536.	Jackson Center.	First N.B.
8557.	Madisonville, Cincinnati.	First N.B.
8588.	Blanchester.	First N.B.
8701.	Lima.	Old N.B.
8705.	Toronto.	First N.B.
8709.	Morrow.	First N.B.

Charter Number	City	Name of Bank
8741.	Morrow.	Morrow N.B.
8826.	Toronto.	N.B. of Toronto.
8839.	Tippecanoe City.	Citizens' N.B.
8978.	Lewisville.	First N.B.
9062.	West Milton.	First N.B.
9091.	Manchester.	Farmers' N.B.
9095.	Mount Sterling.	Citizens' N.B.
9163.	Bradford.	First N.B.
9179.	Newark.	Park N.B.
9192.	Fostoria.	Union N.B.
9194.	Ansonia.	First N.B.
9199.	Richwood.	First N.B.
9211.	New Paris.	New Paris N.B.
9221.	Hudson.	N.B. of Hudson.
9243.	Hillsboro.	Farmers and Traders' N.B.
9255.	Arcanum.	Farmers' N.B.
9274.	Mendon.	First N.B.
9282.	Columbus.	Central N.B.
9284.	Logan.	Rempel N.B.
9336.	Versailles.	First N.B.
9394.	Higginsport.	First N.B.
9446.	Springfield.	Farmers' N.B.
9450.	Okeana.	First N.B.
9487.	West Union.	First N.B.
9518.	Seven Mile.	Farmers' N.B.
9536.	Kingston.	First N.B.
9547.	Lancaster.	Lancaster N.B.
9553.	Brookville.	First N.B.
9563.	Pitsburg.	First N.B.
9630.	Louisville.	First N.B.
9675.	Osborn.	First N.B.
9761.	Mount Washington.	First N.B.
9768.	Bremen.	First N.B.
9799.	Neffs.	Neffs N.B.
9815.	Racine.	First N.B.
9859.	Somerville.	Somerville N.B.
9930.	Williamsburg.	First N.B.
9953.	Akron.	First-Second N.B.
9961.	Wapakoneta.	Auglaize N.B.
10058.	Gettysburg.	Citizens' N.B.
10101.	New London.	Third N.B.
10105.	Greenfield.	People's N.B.
10267.	Williamsport.	Farmers' N.B.
10373.	London.	Central N.B.
10436.	Haviland.	Farmers' N.B.
10479.	Athens.	N.B. of Athens.
10677.	Lodi.	People's N.B.
10692.	Mount Orab.	Brown County N.B.
10947.	New Vienna.	First N.B.
11141.	Cleveland.	Union Commerce N.B.
11216.	Freeport, Prairie Depot.	Prairie Depot N.B.
11252.	Chagrin Falls.	First N.B.
11275.	Norwalk.	Citizens' N.B.
11343.	Pandora.	First N.B.
11363.	Cumberland.	First N.B.
11376.	Cleveland.	Northern N.B.
11383.	Sycamore.	First N.B.
11573.	Bluffton.	Citizens' N.B.
11598.	Kansas.	First N.B.
11614.	Middleport.	Mutual N.B.
11617.	Harveysburg.	Harveysburg N.B.
11714.	Carrollton.	First N.B.
11723.	Antwerp.	First N.B.
11726.	Bellefontaine.	People's N.B.
11733.	West Alexandria.	First N.B.
11772.	Lynchburg.	First N.B.
11803.	Rockford.	First N.B.
11804.	Rockford.	Rockford N.B.
11831.	Marion.	Nat. City Bank an Trust Co.
11851.	Edon.	Farmers' N.B.
11862.	Cleveland.	Brotherhood of Locomotive Engineers Co-Operative N.B.
11878.	Cleveland.	Superior N.B. and Trust Co.
11948.	Mineral City.	First N.B.
11994.	Willoughby.	First N.B.
12008.	Flushing.	Community N.B.
12013.	Sardinia.	Farmers' N.B.
12034.	Alliance.	Alliance N.B..
12196.	Delphos.	Old N.B.
12321.	Wellington.	First N.B.
12332.	Youngstown.	Second N.B.
12347.	Rocky River.	First N.B.
12350.	Columbus.	Columbus N.B.
12365.	Port Clinton.	Magruder N.B.
12446.	Cincinnati.	Brotherhood of Railway Clerks N.B.
13150.	Jewett.	First N.B.
13154.	Caldwell.	Noble County N.B.
13171.	Smithfield.	First N.B.
13198.	West Union.	N.B. of Adams County.
13256.	Toledo.	West Toledo N.B.
13318.	Painesville.	Painesville N.B. Trust Co.
13457.	Defiance.	N.B. of Defiance.
13490.	Washington Court House.	First N.B.
13535.	Delaware.	Delaware County N.B.
13569.	Chardon.	Central N.B.
13586.	Youngstown.	Union N.B.
13596.	New Lexington.	Peoples N.B.
13687.	Massilon.	First N.B.
13715.	Lakewood.	Peoples N.B.
13740.	Bryan.	Citizens N.B.
13742.	Orrville.	N.B. of Orrville.
13749.	Bellefontaine.	Bellefontaine N.B.
13767.	Lima.	N.B. of Lima.
13774.	Cleves.	Cleves N.B.
13797.	Van Wert.	Van Wert N.B.
13802.	Dennison.	First N.B.
13832.	Portsmouth.	N.B. of Portsmouth.
13836.	Kinsman.	First N.B.
13844.	Caldwell.	First N.B.
13847.	Woodsfield.	Citizens N.B.
13850.	East Palestine.	First N.B.
13883.	Carrollton.	First N.B.
13899.	Bryan.	First N.B.
13905.	Cambridge.	Central N.B.
13912.	Montpelier.	N.B. of Montpelier.
13914.	Bellaire.	First N.B.
13920.	Mansfield.	Mansfield Savings Trust N.B.
13922.	St. Clairsville.	First N.B.
13923.	Coshocton.	Coshocton N.B.
13944.	Greenville.	Greenville N.B.
13971.	Marietta.	New First N.B.
13989.	Port Clinton.	Port Clinton N.B.
13996.	Bellaire.	Farmers & Merchants N.B.
13997.	Fremont.	N.B. of Fremont.
14011.	Dillonvale.	First N.B.
14030.	Toledo.	N.B. of Toledo.
14050.	Bridgeport.	Bridgeport N.B.
14077.	Bradford.	Bradford N.B.
14105.	Springfield.	Lagonda N.B.
14132.	St. Marys.	First N.B.
14141.	Brookville.	Brookville N.B.
14183.	Mingo Junction.	Mingo N.B.
14188.	Arcanum.	Arcanum N.B.
14192.	Mt. Healthy.	Mt. Healthy N.B.
14203.	Oak Harbor.	N.B. of Oak Harbor.
14232.	Painesville.	First N.B.
14261.	Bethesda.	Goshen N.B.
14264.	West Milton.	Citizens N.B.
14290.	Lorain.	N.B. of Lorain.
14294.	New Bremen.	First N.B.
14300.	Paulding.	N.B. of Paulding.
14316.	Camden.	First N.B.
14323.	Mt. Gilead.	First N.B. B.

OKLAHOMA

Charter Number	City	Name of Bank
4348.	Guthrie.	First N.B.
4383.	Guthrie.	N.B. of Guthrie.
4385.	Muskogee.	First N.B.
4393.	Ardmore.	First N.B.
4402.	Oklahoma City.	First N.B.
4636.	Purcell.	Purcell N.B.
4704.	Vinita.	First N.B.
4705.	Guthrie.	Capitol N.B.
4723.	Ardmore.	City N.B.
4756.	Purcell.	Chickasaw N.B.
4770.	Oklahoma City.	Oklahoma N.B.
4830.	El Reno.	First N.B.
4862.	Oklahoma.	First N.B. City.
4987.	Claremore-.	First N.B.
5016.	Wagoner.	First N.B.
5052.	McAlester.	First N.B.
5083.	Vinita.	Vinita N.B.
5091.	Pauls Valley.	First N.B.
5095.	Shawnee.	First N.B.
5115.	Shawnee.	Shawnee N.B.
5126.	Wynnewood.	First N.B.
5128.	Checotah.	First N.B.
5129.	Durant.	First N.B.
5159.	Oklahoma.	Western N.B. City.
5171.	Tulsa.	First N.B.
5206.	Stillwater.	First N.B.
5224.	Pawnee.	First N.B.
5236.	Muskogee.	Commercial N.B.
5246.	Caddo.	Choctaw N.B.
5248.	Norman.	First N.B.
5252.	Miami.	First N.B.
5270.	Holdenville.	First N.B.
5272.	Newkirk.	First N.B.
5298.	Davis.	First N.B.
5310.	Bartlesville.	First N.B.
5328.	Kingfisher.	First N.B.
5335.	Enid.	First N.B.
5345.	Marietta.	First N.B.
5347.	Stillwater.	Stillwater N.B.
5352.	Weatherford.	First N.B.
5354.	Chandler.	First N.B.
5378.	Tecumseh.	First N.B.
5379.	Duncan.	First N.B.
5401.	Nowata.	First N.B.
5404.	Madill.	First N.B.
5417.	Roff.	First N.B.
5418.	Okmulgee.	First N.B.
5431.	Chickasha.	First N.B.
5436.	Stillwater.	N.B. of Commerce.
5460.	Blackwell.	First N.B.
5462.	Lexington.	First N.B.
5473.	Hennessey.	First N.B.
5474.	Ponca City.	First N.B.
5478.	Tahlequah.	First N.B.
5492.	Pawnee.	Arkansas Valley N.B.
5508.	Mangum.	First N.B.
5537.	South McAlester.	State N.B.
5546.	Pryor Creek.	First N.B.
5547.	Chickasha.	Citizens' N.B.
5575.	Woodward.	First N.B.
5587.	Alva.	First N.B.
5590.	Durant.	Durant N.B.
5596.	Sallisaw.	First N.B.
5612.	Norman.	Cleveland County N.B.
5620.	Ada.	First N.B.
5633.	Ada.	Ada N.B.
5647.	Coalgate.	First N.B.
5656.	Mountain View.	First N.B.
5716.	Oklahoma.	American N.B. City.
5724.	Marlow.	First N.B.
5731.	Wynnewood.	Southern N.B.
5732.	Tulsa.	City N.B.
5735.	Holdenville.	N.B. of Holdenville.
5740.	Kingfisher.	Kingfisher N.B.
5748.	Sulphur.	First N.B.
5753.	Lawton.	City N.B.
5755.	Lehigh.	Lehigh N.B.
5758.	Weatherford.	Nat. Exchange Bank.
5766.	Elk City.	First N.B.
5790.	Kingfisher.	People's N.B.
5791.	Atoka.	Atoka N.B.
5796.	Medford.	First N.B.
5800.	Ryan.	First N.B.
5804.	Watonga.	First N.B.
5809.	Tishomingo.	First N.B.
5811.	Mangum.	Mangum N.B.
5860.	Vinita.	Cherokee N.B.
5875.	Shawnee.	Oklahoma N.B.
5887.	Okeene.	First N.B.
5902.	Eufaula.	First N.B.
5905.	Anadarko.	First N.B.
5911.	Cleveland.	First N.B.
5914.	Lawton.	First N.B.
5915.	Hobart.	Hobart N.B.
5922.	Ardmore.	Ardmore N.B.
5923.	Anadarko.	N.B. of Anadarko.
5935.	Weturnka.	First N.B.
5950.	Wapanucka.	First N.B.
5951.	Sapulpa.	First N.B.
5954.	Hobart.	First N.B.
5955.	Chelsea.	First N.B.
5958.	Marietta.	Marietta N.B.
5960.	Billings.	First N.B.
5961.	Pawhuska.	First N.B.
5967.	Eufaula.	Eufaula N.B.
5982.	Wakita.	First N.B.
5985.	El Reno.	Citizens' N.B.
6048.	Wagoner.	Wagoner N.B.
6052.	Cordell.	First N.B.
6058.	Sayre.	First N.B.
6061.	Ponca City.	Farmers' N.B.
6111.	Hennessey.	Hennessey N.B.
6113.	Altus.	First N.B.
6130.	Hugo.	First N.B.
6138.	Collinsville.	First N.B.
6142.	Chandler.	Chandler N.B.
6156.	Edmond.	First N.B.
6159.	Yukon.	First N.B.
6161.	Cashion.	First N.B.
6163.	Geary.	First N.B.
6164.	Elk City.	Elk City N.B.
6171.	Lindsay.	First N.B.
6230.	McAlester.	American N.B.
6232.	Ralston.	First N.B.
6241.	Okmulgee.	Citizens' N.B.
6254.	Wewoka.	First N.B.
6257.	Clinton.	Farmers' N.B.
6258.	Bartlesville.	First N.B.
6260.	Bristow.	First N.B.
6263.	Mounds.	First N.B.
6267.	Hobart.	City N.B.
6269.	Chandler.	Union N.B.
6299.	Comanche.	First N.B.
6306.	Stroud.	First N.B.
6307.	Anadarko.	Citizens' N.B.
6324.	Weleetka.	First N.B.
6358.	Hobart.	Farmers and Merchants' N.B.
6365.	Madill.	Madill N.B.
6367.	Nowata.	Nowata N.B.
6406.	McAlester.	City N.B.
6414.	Tahlequah.	Cherokee N.B.
6416.	Shawnee.	State N.B.
6450.	Norman.	City N.B.
6477.	Okemah.	First N.B.
6490.	Alva.	Alva N.B.
6511.	Boynton.	First N.B.
6517.	Quinton.	First N.B.
6539.	Fort Gibson.	First N.B.
6540.	Holdenville.	N.B. of Commerce.
6570.	Temple.	First N.B.
6578.	Mannsville.	First N.B.
6602.	Vinita.	Farmers N.B.
6612.	Walters.	First N.B.
6639.	Pants Valley.	N.B. of Commerce.
6641.	Wanette.	First N.B.
6647.	Cordell.	City N.B.
6655.	Pond Creek.	First N.B.
6660.	McLoud.	First N.B.
6669.	Tulsa.	Farmers' N.B.
6677.	Cherokee.	First N.B.
6678.	Oklahoma City.	Oklahoma City N.B..
6683.	Bokchito.	First N.B.
6689.	Weleetka.	Weleetka N.B.
6702.	Kingfisher.	Farmers' N.B.
6710.	Lindsay.	Lindsay N.B.
6717.	Muldrow.	First N.B.
6719.	Carmen.	First N.B.
6736.	Foss.	First N.B.
6753.	Harrison.	First N.B.
6804.	Dustin.	First N.B.
6844.	Carmen.	Carmen N.B.
6851.	Clinton.	Clinton N.B.
6855.	Okmulgee.	Okmulgee N.B.
6867.	Henryetta.	First N.B.
6868.	Beggs.	First N.B.
6879.	Coweta.	First N.B.
6890.	Wilburton.	First N.B.
6893.	Cushing.	First N.B.
6911.	Muskogee.	City N.B.
6916.	Blackwell.	Blackwell N.B.
6928.	Durant.	FarmersN.B.
6940.	Clinton.	First N.B.

Charter Number	City	Name of Bank
6972.	Perry.	First N.B.
6980.	Calvin.	First N.B.
6981.	Oklahoma City.	Commercial N.B.
7019.	Taloga.	First N.B.
7032.	Bartlesville.	American N.B.
7042.	Tishomingo.	American N.B.
7050.	Hartshorne.	First N.B.
7053.	Calvin.	Citizens' N.B.
7054.	Stonewall.	First N.B.
7071.	Ada.	Citizens' N.B.
7085.	Tulsa.	Tulsa N.B.
7099.	Bennington.	First N.B.
7103.	Pond Creek.	N.B. of Pond Creek.
7104.	Poteau.	N.B. of Poteau.
7115.	Broken Arrow.	First N.B.
7117.	Fairview.	First N.B.
7118.	Poteau.	First N.B.
7127.	Apache.	First N.B.
7159.	Altus.	Altus N.B.
7177.	Prague.	First N.B.
7185.	Francis.	First N.B.
7197.	Mill Creek.	First N.B.
7207.	Lexington.	Farmers' N.B.
7209.	Berwyn.	First N.B.
7217.	Stigler.	First N.B.
7238.	Weatherford.	Liberty N.B.
7251.	Ramona.	First N.B.
7278.	Thomas.	First N.B.
7289.	Duncan.	Duncan N.B.
7293.	Norman.	Farmers' N.B.
7299.	Guthrie.	N.B. of Commerce.
7321.	Coalgate.	Coalgate N.B.
7328.	Mangum.	City N.B.
7368.	Caddo.	Caddo N.B.
7386.	Cleveland.	Cleveland N.B.
7389.	Byars.	First N.B.
7420.	Cornish.	First N.B.
7432.	Stigler.	American N.B.
7442.	Davis.	Merchants and Planters' N.B.
7444.	Tonkawa.	First N.B.
7499.	Bokchito.	Bokchito N.B.
7571.	Sallisaw.	First N.B.
7583.	Blackwell.	State N.B.
7600.	Broken Affow.	Arkansas Valley N.B.
7611.	Pawnee.	Pawnee N.B.
7615.	Porter.	First N.B.
7619.	Holdenville.	American N.B.
7628.	Wagoner.	City N.B.
7633.	Konawa.	First N.B.
7651.	Boswell.	First N.B.
7666.	Atoka.	Citizens' N.B.
7667.	Antlers.	First N.B.
7677.	Okemah.	Okemah N.B.
7697.	Purcell.	Union N.B.
7706.	Centralia.	First N.B.
7707.	Woodville.	First N.B.
7723.	Madill.	City N.B.
7724.	Weturnka.	American N.B.
7747.	Hugo.	Hugo N.B.
7756.	Tecumseh.	Farmers' N.B.
7771.	Thomas.	Thomas N.B.
7780.	Talihina.	First N.B.
7783.	Lamont.	First N.B.
7788.	Sapulpa.	American N.B.
7811.	Walters.	Walters N.B.
7822.	Haskell.	First N.B.
7842.	Milburn.	First N.B.
7883.	Pawhuska.	Citizens' N.B.
7892.	Pauls Valley.	Pauls Valley N.B.
7893.	Kingston.	First N.B.
7927.	Hominy.	First N.B.
7950.	Sterrett.	First N.B.
7962.	Colbert.	First N.B.
7964.	Owasso.	First N.B.
7967.	Waukomis.	First N.B.
7972.	Fairfax.	First N.B.
7976.	Ravia.	First N.B.
7996.	Terral.	First N.B.
8010.	Erick.	First N.B.
8024.	Webbers Falls.	First N.B.
8052.	Wewoka.	Farmers' N.B.
8056.	Hollis.	Hollis N.B.
8061.	Hollis.	First N.B.
8078.	Fort Towson.	First N.B.
8079.	Fort Gibson.	Farmers' N.B.
8082.	Antlers.	Citizens' N.B.
8126.	Eldorado.	First N.B.
8137.	Okla. Wapanucka.	People's N.B.
8138.	Guymon.	First N.B.
8140.	Frederick.	First N.B.
8144.	Cement.	First N.B.
8159.	Prague.	Prague N.B.
8177.	Keota.	First N.B.
8189.	Lehigh.	Merchants' N.B.
8202.	Fairfax.	Fairfax N.B.
8203.	Chickasha.	Chickasha N.B.
8206.	Frederick.	City N.B.
8209.	Hastings.	First N.B.
8210.	Hastings.	N.B. of Hastings.
8213.	Konawa.	Konawa N.B.
8214.	Newkirk.	Farmers' N.B.
8231.	Enid.	Enid N.B.
8270.	Dewey.	First N.B.
8278.	Marietta.	Farmers' N.B.
8294.	Maud.	First N.B.
8304.	Wanette.	State N.B.
8310.	Temple.	Farmers' N.B.
8313.	Pawhuska.	American N.B.
8316.	Olustee.	First N.B.
8336.	Rush Springs.	First N.B.
8342.	Granite.	First N.B.
8349.	Helena.	First N.B.
8353.	Boswell.	Boswell N.B.
8354.	Ardmore.	Bankers' N.B.
8361.	Comanche.	Citizens' N.B.
8366.	Comanche.	Comanche N.B.
8375.	Lawton.	Lawton N.B.
8472.	Oklahoma City.	Security N.B.
8475.	Tuttle.	First N.B.
8479.	Porum.	First N.B.
8486.	Idabel.	First N.B.
8524.	Stratford.	First N.B.
8543.	Gage.	First N.B.
8546.	Mill Creek.	Merchants and Planters' N.B.
8552.	Tulsa.	Central N.B.
8553.	Kiefer.	First N.B.
8563.	Luther.	First N.B.
8577.	Kaw City.	First N.B.
8595.	Tonkawa.	Tonkawa N.B.
8609.	Tupelo.	First N.B.
8615.	Seiling.	First N.B.
8616.	Duncan.	City N.B.
8638.	Kiowa.	First N.B.
8644.	Minco.	First N.B.
8668.	Davenport.	First N.B.
8676.	Porter.	Porter N.B.
8687.	Shattuck.	First N.B.
8702.	Blanchard.	First N.B.
8715.	Waurika.	Citizens' N.B.
8727.	Custer City, Custer.	First N.B.
8730.	Cushing.	Farmers' N.B.
8744.	Waurika.	First N.B.
8754.	Olustee.	Farmers' N.B.
8759.	Verden.	First N.B.
8775.	Altus.	City N.B.
8790.	Afton.	First N.B.
8809.	Warner.	First N.B.
8825.	Hollis.	First N.B.
8852.	Texhoma.	First N.B.
8859.	Verden.	N.B. of Verden.
8861.	Waurika.	Waurika N.B.
8876.	Morris.	First N.B.
8896.	Buffalo.	First N.B.
8944.	Eldorado.	Farmers and Merchants' N.B.
8994.	Atoka.	American N.B.
8999.	Maysville.	First N.B.
9008.	Cherokee.	Alfalfa County N.B.
9011.	Newkirk.	Eastman N.B.
9023.	Muskogee.	Muskogee N.B.
9032.	Mulhall.	First N.B.
9046.	Sulphur.	Park N.B.
9275.	Spiro.	First N.B.
9514.	Seminole.	First N.B.
9564.	Oklahoma City.	Farmers' N.B.
9567.	Bartlesville.	Union N.B.
9584.	Capitol Hill.	First N.B.
9586.	Enid.	First N.B.
9616.	Ponca City.	Germania N.B.
9620.	Allen.	First N.B.
9658.	Tulsa.	Exchange N.B.
9696.	Okmulgee.	Farmers' N.B.
9701.	Muskogee.	American N.B.
9709.	Waynoka.	First N.B.
9767.	Fairview.	Farmers and Merchants' N.B.
9801.	Ponca City.	Farmers' N.B.
9835.	Bokchito.	First N.B.
9856.	Oklahoma City.	Oklahoma Stock Yards N.B..
9881.	Kingston.	First N.B.
9884.	Cherokee.	Farmers' N.B.
9888.	Heavener.	First N.B.
9920.	Milburn.	First N.B.
9937.	Noble.	First N.B.
9938.	Chickasha.	Oklahoma N.B.
9942.	Tulsa.	N.B. of Commerce.
9943.	Tulsa.	Oklahoma N.B.
9944.	Hydro.	First N.B.
9946.	Marlow.	State N.B.
9947.	Okmulgee.	Exchange N.B.
9948.	Nowata.	Producers' N.B.
9949.	Nowata.	Commercial N.B.
9951.	Lenapah.	Lenapah N.B.
9952.	Elk City.	First N.B.
9954.	Kingfisher.	People's N.B.
9959.	Sayre.	First N.B.
9960.	Olustee.	First N.B.
9962.	Lawton.	Lawton N.B.
9963.	Eldorado.	First N.B.
9964.	Guymon.	City N.B.
9965.	Collinsville.	First N.B.
9967.	Temple.	Temple N.B.
9968.	Cordell.	Farmers' N.B.
9969.	Skiatook.	First N.B.
9970.	Stilwell.	First N.B.
9971.	Cordell.	Cordell N.B.
9972.	Cordell.	State N.B.
9973.	Sallisaw.	Farmers' N.B.
9974.	Lahoma.	First N.B.
9975.	Muldrow.	First N.B.
9976.	Sayre.	Beckham County N.B.
9980.	Harrah.	First N.B.
9981.	Custer City.	People's State N.B.
9983.	Wellston.	First N.B.
9985.	Clinton.	Oklahoma State N.B.
9986.	Dewey.	Security N.B.
9987.	Shattuck.	Shattuck N.B.
9991.	Terlton.	First N.B.
9992.	Valliant.	First N.B.
9993.	Canadian.	First N.B.
9995.	Sentinel.	First N.B.
9998.	Shawnee.	N.B. of Commerce.
10001.	Addington.	First N.B.
10002.	Hominy.	N.B. of Commerce.
10003.	Braman.	First N.B.
10005.	Pond Creek.	Farmers' N.B.
10006.	Grandfield.	First N.B.
10007.	Stuart.	First N.B.
10010.	Caddo.	Security N.B.
10012.	Tishomingo.	Tishomingo N.B.
10013.	Holdenville.	State N.B.
10014.	Yale.	First N.B.
10015.	Oktaha.	First N.B.
10019.	Miami.	Ottawa County N.B.
10020.	Geary.	First N.B.
10031.	Coweta.	N.B. of Commerce.
10032.	Tyrone.	First N.B.
10051.	Checotah.	People's N.B.
10063.	Checotah.	Commercial N.B.
10075.	Kaw City.	First N.B.
10094.	Hastings.	N.B. of Hastings.
10095.	Frederick.	N.B. of Commerce.
10096.	Lone Wolf.	First N.B.
10104.	Kenefic.	First N.B.
10113.	Muskogee.	Oklahoma N.B.
10115.	Bristow.	Bristow N.B.
10117.	Claremore.	N.B. of Claremore.
10119.	Grove.	First N.B.
10151.	Edmond.	Citizens' N.B.
10158.	Westville.	First N.B.
10160.	Haskell.	Haskell N.B.
10170.	Wilburton.	Latimer County N.B.
10172.	Roff.	Farmers and Merchants' N.B.
10193.	Alex.	First N.B.
10196.	Yukon.	Yukon N.B.
10202.	Enid.	Enid N.B.
10203.	Carmen.	Carmen N.B.
10205.	Marlow.	N.B. of Marlow.
10209.	Hennessey.	Farmers and Merchants' N.B.
10226.	Calvin.	Calvin N.B.
10227.	Waukomis.	Waukomis N.B.
10239.	Heavener.	State N.B.
10240.	Hollis.	N.B. of Commerce.
10244.	Duncan.	First N.B.
10249.	Hollis.	State N.B.
10255.	Broken Arrow.	Citizens' N.B.
10262.	Tulsa.	Liberty N.B.
10277.	Washington.	First N.B.
10280.	Collinsville.	Collinsville N.B.
10283.	Maysville.	Farmers' N.B.
10286.	Madill.	Madill N.B.
10288.	Hobart.	City N.B.
10298.	Keota.	Keota N.B.
10304.	Tecumseh.	Tecumseh N.B.
10311.	Snyder.	Kiowa N.B.
10314.	Sasakwa.	First N.B.
10317.	Snyder.	First N.B.
10321.	Muskogee.	Exchange N.B.
10332.	Cushing.	Farmers' N.B.
10339.	Afton.	First N.B.
10342.	Tulsa.	American N.B.
10343.	Bennington.	Bennington N.B.
10347.	Achille.	First N.B.
10349.	Henryetta.	Miners' N.B.
10356.	Foraker.	First N.B.
10363.	Boswell.	State N.B.
10366.	Soper.	First N.B.
10368.	Blair.	First N.B.
10380.	Achille.	Farmers and Merchants' N.B.
10381.	Colbert.	First N.B.
10385.	Aylesworth.	Fir:st N.B.
10388.	Eufaula.	State N.B.
10389.	Gotebo.	First N.B.
10394.	Ardmore.	State N.B.
10402.	Kaw City.	N.B. of Kaw City.
10424.	Broken Bow.	First N.B.
10431.	Tishomingo.	Farmers' N.B.
10437.	Braggs.	First N.B.
10442.	Hydro.	Farmers' N.B.
10454.	Francis.	Francis N.B.
10464.	Skiatook.	Oklahoma N.B.
10467.	Bixby.	First N.B.
10468.	Tahlequah.	Central N.B.
10474.	Sallisaw.	Citizens' N.B.
10482.	Beggs.	Farmers' N.B.
10487.	Fairland.	First N.B.
10500.	Haworth.	First N.B.
10513.	Ada.	Merchants and Planters' N.B.
10515.	Kiowa.	People's N.B.
10520.	Hulbert.	First N.B.
10521.	Hammon.	Farmers' N.B.
10531.	Tupelo.	Farmers' N.B.
10538.	Durant.	State N.B.
10548.	Ringling.	First N.B.
10561.	Fort Gibson.	Citizens' N.B.
10563.	Dustin.	American N.B.
10566.	Hooker.	First N.B.
10573.	Vian.	First N.B.
10574.	New Wilson.	First N.B.
10595.	Drurnright.	First N.B.
10612.	Arcadia.	First N.B.
10615.	Stroud.	Stroud N.B.
10627.	Blue Jacket.	First N.B.
10649.	Porum.	N.B. of Commerce.
10659.	Holdenville.	Farmers' N.B.
10672.	Talihina.	First N.B.
10689.	Commerce.	First N.B.
10722.	Yale.	Farmers' N.B.
10737.	Rosston.	First N.B.

Charter Number	City	Name of Bank
10804.	Beaver.	First N.B.
10849.	Bristow.	American N.B.
10875.	Erick.	First N.B.
10904.	Tulsa.	Planters' N.B.
10906.	Tulsa.	Union N.B.
10913.	Okeene.	N.B. of Okeene.
10960.	Pocasset.	First N.B.
10967.	Kusa.	First N.B.
10981.	Butler. Okla.	First N.B.
11001.	Okmulgee.	Central N.B.
11016.	Sulphur.	Farmers' N.B.
11018.	Healdton.	First N.B.
11052.	Tipton.	First N.B.
11064.	Hartshorne.	Hartshorne N.B.
11084.	Boise City.	First N.B.
11093.	Ardmore.	Exchange N.B.
11129.	Oilton.	First N.B.
11149.	Allen.	Allen N.B.
11157.	Quapaw.	First N.B.
11181.	Valliant.	American N.B.
11182.	Calera.	Calera N.B.
11190.	Boswell.	Farmers and Merchants' N.B.
11192.	Madill.	Marshall County N.B.
11194.	Picher.	First N.B.
11219.	Billings.	N.B. of Billings.
11230.	Oklahoma City.	Liberty N.B.
11232.	Fovrgan.	First N.B.
11246.	Idabel.	American N.B.
11256.	Fort Towson.	American N.B.
11306.	Nash.	First N.B.
11314.	Pawhuska.	Liberty N.B.
11315.	Stuart.	Liberty N.B.
11384.	Temple.	Security N.B.
11394.	Goltry.	First N.B.
11396.	Wynona.	First N.B.
11397.	Tonkawa.	Farmers' N.B.
11419.	Byron.	First N.B.
11436.	Lenapah.	Citizens' N.B.
11459.	Valliant.	Citizens' N.B.
11460.	Bigheart.	First N.B.
11481.	Oklahoma City.	Southwest N.B.
11485.	Tahlequah.	Guaranty N.B.
11498.	Byars.	American N.B.
11535.	Devol.	First N.B.
11551.	Hanna.	First N.B.
11568.	Porum.	Guaranty N.B.
11584.	Enid.	American N.B.
11612.	Caney.	First N.B.
11624.	Picher.	Picher N.B.
11628.	Oklahoma City.	Tradesmen's N.B.
11648.	Terral.	First N.B.
11654.	Davidson.	First N.B.
11661.	Depew.	Depew N.B.
11676.	Coalgate.	City N.B.
11680.	Lawton.	Security N.B.
11688.	Bartlesville.	Exchange N.B.
11705.	Chattanooga.	First N.B.
11763.	Carnegie.	First N.B.
11771.	Comanche.	State N.B.
11788.	Paden.	Paden N.B.
11791.	Jennings.	First N.B.
11824.	Paden.	First N.B.
11837.	Bartlesville.	Central N.B.
11842.	Durant.	Commercial N.B.
11891.	Laverne.	First N.B.
11894.	Okarche.	First N.B.
11913.	Idabel.	Idabel N.B.
11920.	Checotah.	Commercial N.B.
11932.	Morris.	Morris N.B.
11940.	Boswell.	Citizens' N.B.
11963.	Okmulgee.	Union N.B.
11982.	Slick.	First N.B.
12012.	Boley.	First N.B.
12016.	Oklahoma City.	Fidelity N.B.
12035.	Moore.	First N.B.
12036.	Norman.	Security N.B.
12038.	Blackwell.	Blackwell N.B.
12039.	Enid.	Garfield N.B.
12040.	Blackwell.	Security N.B.
12041.	Billings.	First N.B.
12042.	Tulsa.	Producers' N.B.
12043.	Tulsa.	Security N.B.
12044.	Enid.	Central N.B.
12045.	Billings.	Billings N.B.
12048.	Okmulgee.	American N.B.
12049.	Cherokee.	Cherokee N.B.
12050.	Clinton.	Security N.B.
12051.	Duncan.	Oklahoma N.B.
12052.	Wynona.	Wynona N.B.
12053.	Ardmore.	American N.B.
12054.	Cushing.	Oklahoma N.B.
12059.	Carnegie.	Farmers' N.B.
12060.	Chandler.	Farmers' N.B.
12065.	Duncan.	Security N.B.
12067.	Lawton.	American N.B.
12068.	Kingfisher.	Citizens' N.B.
12069.	Hominy.	Hominy N.B.
12074.	Weleetka.	State N.B.
12076.	Barnsdall.	Barnsdall N.B.
12078.	Wellston.	Wellston N.B.
12079.	Sand Springs.	First N.B.
12081.	Helena.	Helena N.B.
12082.	Stillwater.	American N.B.
12086.	Putnam.	First N.B.
12087.	Holdenville.	American N.B.
12088.	Hitchcock.	First N.B.
12089.	Tahlequah.	Liberty N.B.
12093.	Elk City.	Farmers' N.B.
12094.	Waurika.	Farmers' N.B.
12095.	Stroud.	State N.B.
12099.	Weturnka.	N.B. of Commerce.
12102.	Kenefick.	First N.B.
12103.	Locust Grove.	First N.B.
12104.	Depew.	State N.B.
12106.	Idabel.	State N.B.
12107.	Hinton.	First N.B.
12109.	Leedey.	First N.B.
12111.	Coweta.	Security N.B.
12113.	Aline.	Clarks N.B.
12116.	Centrahorna.	First N.B.
12117.	Pryor Creek, Pryor.	American N.B.
12118.	Walters.	American N.B.
12120.	Apache.	American N.B.
12125.	Texhoma.	Farmers' N.B.
12126.	Durant.	American N.B.
12128.	Hooker.	Farmers and Merchants' N.B.
12129.	Marlow.	First N.B.
12130.	Blair.	First N.B.
12131.	Brinkharn.	First N.B.
12133.	Binger.	First N.B.
12134.	Purcell.	McClain County N.B.
12135.	Poteau.	LeFlore County N.B.
12136.	Hugo.	City N.B.
12141.	Fletcher.	First N.B.
12142.	Granite.	First N.B.
12144.	Ada.	Security N.B.
12147.	Carter.	First N.B.
12148.	Coyle.	First N.B.
12149.	Davis.	City N.B.
12150.	Hastings.	Oklahoma N.B.
12152.	Alva.	Central N.B.
12155.	Altus.	Altus N.B.
12157.	Norman.	City N.B.
12158.	Poteau.	Central N.B.
12161.	Kemp City.	First N.B.
12163.	Tyrone.	Farmers' N.B.
12165.	Shidler.	First N.B.
12169.	Wheatland.	First N.B.
12171.	Dustin.	First N.B.
12173.	Ninnekah.	First N.B.
12177.	Shidler.	Shidler N.B.
12179.	Guymon.	Texas County N.B.
12185.	Custer City.	People's N.B.
12188.	Mill Creek.	Mill Creek N.B.
12200.	Calumet.	First N.B.
12203.	Beggs.	American N.B.
12206.	Newkirk.	Security N.B.
12207.	Enick.	Farmers' N.B.
12211.	Bokchito.	First N.B.
12212.	Pawhuska.	N.B. of Commerce.
12215.	Pauls Valley.	Exchange N.B.
12218.	Snyder.	Kiowa N.B.
12221.	Loco.	First N.B.
12223.	Britton.	First N.B.
12230.	Chickasha.	Farmers' N.B.
12237.	Hollis.	Farmers' N.B.
12239.	Kiefer.	First N.B.
12245.	Cheyenne.	First N.B.
12265.	Boynton.	American N.B.
12277.	Muskogee.	Muskogee-Security N.B.
12298.	Sentinel.	Security N.B.
12299.	Cordell.	First N.B.
12302.	Cordell.	Cordell N.B.
12310.	Castle.	First N.B.
12312.	Paden.	State N.B.
12315.	Carney.	First N.B.
12318.	Gracemont.	First N.B.
12322.	Jones.	First N.B.
12330.	Marietta.	Love County N.B.
12331.	Stigler.	Security N.B.
12334.	Wynnewood.	State N.B.
12335.	Cement.	First N.B.
12339.	Shawnee.	Federal N.B.
12356.	Tonkawa.	American N.B.
12368.	Wagoner.	American N.B.
12369.	Bennington.	American N.B.
12376.	Helena.	Farmers' N.B.
12388.	Slick.	Slick N.B.
12394.	Porter.	Merchants and Planters' N.B.
12441.	Shawnee.	N.B. of Commerce.
12472.	Ardmore.	First N.B.
12486.	Syre.	American N.B.
12498.	Carmen.	First N.B.
12529.	Coalgate.	First N.B.
12555.	Sallisaw.	American N.B.
12591.	Ada.	First N.B.
12629.	Henryetta.	People's N.B.
12801.	Hugo.	N.B. of Commerce.
12812.	Duncan.	First N.B.
12827.	Wilson.	First N.B.
12890.	Muskogee.	Commercial N.B.
12908.	Tishomingo.	First N.B.
12918.	Muskogee.	Citizens' N.B.
13018.	Durant.	Durant N.B.
13021.	Madill.	First N.B.
13100.	Hartshorne.	Hartshorne N.B.
13276.	Oklahoma City.	South Oklahoma N.B.
13355.	Pawhuska.	First N.B.
13361.	Skiatook.	Oklahoma First N.B.
13480.	Tulsa.	Fourth N.B.
13527.	Pawhuska.	Citizens-First N.B.
13677.	Ardmore.	First N.B.
13679.	Tulsa.	N.B. of Tulsa.
13751.	Okmulgee.	Citizens N.B.
13756.	Altus.	N.B. of Cornmerce.
13760.	Frederick.	First N.B.
13770.	McAlester.	N.B. of McAlester.
13891.	Ponca City.	First N.B.
13930.	Shawnee.	American N.B.
14005.	Durant.	First N.B.
14020.	Perry.	First N.B.
14108.	Walters.	Walters N.B.
14131.	Antlers.	First N.B.
14278.	Blackwell.	First N.B.
14304.	Pawhuska.	N.B. of Commerce.
14315.	Enid.	Security N.B.
14322.	Weturnka.	American N.B.

OREGON

Charter Number	City	Name of Bank
1553.	Portland.	First N.B.
2630.	Pendleton.	First N.B.
2816.	Salem.	First N.B.
2865.	Baker City.	First N.B.
2928.	Albany.	First N.B.
2947.	Union.	First N.B.
3025.	East Portland.	First N.B.
3184.	Portland.	Portland N.B.
3313.	Island City.	First N.B.
3399.	McMinnville.	First N.B.
3402.	Portland.	Ainsworth N.B.
3405.	Salem.	Capital N.B.
3422.	Portland.	Commercial N.B.
3441.	The Dalles.	First N.B.
3458.	Eugene.	First N.B.
3486.	Astoria.	First N.B.
3534.	Dalles City.	The Dalles N.B.
3536.	Portland.	Merchants' N.B.
3655.	La Grande.	La Grande N.B.
3665.	Pendleton.	Pendleton N.B.
3676.	Arlington.	First N.B.
3719.	Portland.	Oregon N.B.
3774.	Heppner.	First N.B.
3851.	Prineville.	First N.B.
3857.	McMinnville.	McMinnville N.B.
3912.	Enterprise.	Wallowa N.B.
3918.	Arlington.	Arlington N.B.
3953.	Heppner.	N.B. of Heppner.
3966.	Hillsboro.	First N.B.
3972.	Independence.	First N.B.
3979.	Independence.	Independence N.B.
3986.	Eugene City.	Eugene N.B.
4168.	Grant's Pass.	First N.B. of Southern Oregon.
4206.	Baker City.	Baker City N.B.
4249.	Pendleton.	N.B. of Pendleton.
4301.	Corvallis.	First N.B.
4326.	Albany.	Linn County N.B.
4403.	Astoria.	Astoria N.B.
4452.	La Grande.	Farmers and Traders' N.B.
4514.	Portland.	United States N.B.
4516.	Athena.	First N.B.
4624.	Roseburg.	First N.B.
5642.	Cottage .B.	First N.B.
5747.	Ashland.	First N.B.
5822.	Ontario.	First N.B.
6295.	Burns.	First N.B.
6491.	Canyon City.	First N.B. of Grant County.
6547.	Sumpter.	First N.B.
6644.	Elgin.	First N.B.
6768.	Baker City.	Citizens' N.B.
6849.	Coquille.	First N.B.
7059.	Condon.	First N.B.
7072.	Dallas.	First N.B.
7167.	Klamath Falls.	First N.B.
7244.	Lakeview.	First N.B.
7272.	Hood River.	First N.B.
7301.	Pendleton.	Commercial N.B.
7472.	Dallas.	Dallas N.B.
7475.	Marshfield.	First N.B. of Coos Bay.
7537.	Newberg.	First N.B.
7701.	Medford.	First N.B.
8036.	Forest Grove.	First N.B.
8048.	Joseph.	First N.B.
8236.	Medford.	Medford N.B.
8261.	Condon.	Condon N.B.
8387.	Union.	Union N.B.
8528.	Vale.	First N.B.
8554.	Forest Grove.	Forest Grove N.B.
8556.	Oregon City.	First N.B.
8574.	Tillamook.	First N.B.
8691.	Burns.	Harney County N.B.
8721.	Sheridan.	First N.B.
8750.	Corvallis.	Benton County N.B.
8941.	Springfield.	First N.B.
8955.	Roseburg.	Roseburg N.B.
9002.	Wallowa.	Stockgrowers and Farmers' N.B.
9021.	Salem.	United States N.B.
9047.	Saint Johns.	First N.B.
9127.	Lebanon.	First N.B.
9146.	Harrisburg.	First N.B.
9180.	Portland.	Lumbermen's N.B.
9201.	Milton.	First N.B.
9228.	Pendleton.	American N.B.
9281.	Hermiston.	First N.B.
9314.	La Grande.	United States N.B.
9328.	North Bend.	First N.B.
9348.	Ontario.	Ontario N.B.
9358.	Newberg.	United States N.B.
9363.	Bend.	First N.B.
9423.	Roseburg.	Douglas N.B.
9431.	Ashland.	United States N.B.
9496.	Vale.	United States N.B.
9718.	Bandon.	First N.B.
9763.	Prairie City.	First N.B.
9806.	McMinnville.	United States N.B.
9917.	Hillsboro.	Hillsboro N.B.
9923.	Hillsboro.	American N.B.
10056.	Merrill.	First N.B.
10071.	Monmouth.	First N.B.

Charter Number	City	Name of Bank
10103.	Portland.	Peninsula N.B.
10164.	Lebanon.	Lebanon N.B.
10218.	Junction City.	First N.B.
10300.	Portland.	Northwestern N.B.
10345.	Eugene.	United States N.B.
10432.	Paisley.	Paisley N.B.
10534.	Linton.	First N.B.
10619.	Canby.	First N.B.
10676.	Gardiner.	First N.B.
10992.	Scappoose.	First N.B.
11007.	Heppner.	Farmers and Stock Growers' N.B.
11106.	Silverton.	First N.B.
11121.	Lakeview.	Commercial N.B.
11200.	Saint Helen.	First N.B.
11271.	Molalla.	First N.B.
11294.	Redmond.	First N.B.
11302.	Redmond.	Redmond N.B.
11466.	Halfway.	First N.B.
11691.	Madres.	First N.B.
11758.	Clatskanie.	First N.B.
11801.	Klamath Falls.	American N.B.
11807.	Dalles City.	Citizens' N.B.
11885.	Harrisburg.	Harrisburg N.B.
11906.	Woodburn.	First N.B.
11917.	Stayton.	First N.B.
11937.	Toledo.	First N.B.
11975.	Aurora.	First N.B.
12077.	Marshfield.	Coos Bay N.B.
12193.	Mount Angel.	First N.B.
12262.	Vale.	Vale N.B.
12427.	Wheeler.	First N.B.
12470.	Portland.	West Coast N.B.
12557.	Portland.	Portland N.B.
12613.	Portland.	Brotherhood Co-Operative N.B.
12655.	Prineville.	Prineville N.B.
13093.	Bend.	Lumbermens N.B.
13192.	Tillamook.	Tillamook N.B.
13294.	Portland.	Central N.B.
13299.	Portland.	Citizens N.B.
13354.	Astoria.	N.B. of Commerce.
13576.	Pendleton.	First Inland N.B.
13602.	La Grande.	First N.B.
13633.	Milton.	Valley N.B.
13771.	Medford.	Medford N.B.
14001.	Clatskanie.	First N.B.
14054.	North Bend.	North Bend N.B.
14241.	Condon.	First N.B.
14306.	Toledo.	National Security Bank.

PENNSYLVANIA

Charter Number	City	Name of Bank
1.	Philadelphia.	First N.B.
12.	Erie.	First N.B.
21.	Carlisle.	First N.B.
25.	Marietta.	First N.B.
30.	Wilkes-Barre.	First N.B.
31.	Huntingdon.	First N.B.
39.	Towanda.	First N.B.
42.	Strasburg.	First N.B.
48.	Pittsburgh.	First N.B.
49.	Scranton.	Second N.B.
51.	Johnstown.	First N.B.
54.	Girard.	First N.B.
57.	Hollidaysburg.	First N.B.
60.	Newville.	First N.B.
69.	Kittanning.	First N.B.
77.	Scranton.	First N.B.
104.	Wilkes-Barre.	Second N.B.
110.	Union Mills, Union City.	First N.B.
115.	Meadville.	First N.B.
125.	Reading.	First N.B.
135.	Brownsville.	First N.B.
138.	Bethlehem.	First N.B.
143.	Conneautville.	First N.B.
148.	West Chester.	First N.B.
161.	Allentown.	First N.B.
173.	Oil City.	First N.B.
174.	Mifflinburg.	First N.B.
175.	Williamsport.	First N.B.
187.	Hanover.	First N.B.
189.	Franklin.	First N.B.
197.	York.	First N.B.
198.	Allegheny.	First N.B.
201.	Harrisbur.	First N.B.
213.	Philadelphia.	Second N.B.
234.	Philadelphia.	Third N.B.
240.	Lebanon.	First N.B.
244.	Waynesboro.	First N.B.
246.	Wrightsville.	First N.B.
247.	Altoona.	First N.B.
249.	Greenville.	First N.B.
252.	Pittsburgh.	First N.B.
253.	Milton.	First N.B.
270.	Uniontown.	First N.B.
272.	Norristown.	First N.B.
286.	Philadelphia.	Fourth N.B.
291.	Pittsburgh.	Third N.B.
293.	Bloomsburg.	First N.B.
300.	Curwensville.	First N.B.
305.	Waynesburg.	First N.B.
309.	Butler.	First N.B.
311.	Gettysburg.	First N.B.
312.	Media.	First N.B.
313.	Indiana.	First N.B.
324.	Newtown.	First N.B.
325.	Danville.	First N.B.
326.	Mechanicsburg.	Second N.B.
328.	Wellsborough.	First N.B.
332.	Chester.	First N.B.
333.	Lancaster.	First N.B.
338.	Downington.	First N.B.
352.	Philadelphia.	Sixth N.B.
355.	Chester.	Delaware County N.B.
357.	Selinsgrove.	First N.B.
371.	Columbia.	First Columbia N.B.
373.	Allentown.	Second N.B.
380.	Mechanicsburg.	First N.B.
386.	Mount Pleasant.	First N.B.
392.	Mercer.	First N.B.
403.	Ashland.	First N.B.
413.	Philadelphia.	Seventh N.B.
423.	Minersville.	First N.B.
430.	Lansdale.	First N.B.
432.	Pittsburgh.	Fourth N.B.
435.	Glen Rock.	First N.B.
437.	Mauch Chunk.	First N.B.
459.	Bellefonte.	First N.B.
469.	Mauch Chunk.	Second N.B.
478.	Pittston.	First N.B.
507.	Lock Haven.	First N.B.
520.	Warren.	First N.B.
521.	Providence.	First N.B.
522.	Philadelphia.	Eighth N.B.
535.	Erie.	Keystone N.B.
538.	Philadelphia.	Farmers and Mechanics' N.B.
539.	Philadelphia.	Philadelphia N.B.
540.	Philadelphia.	Penn N.B.
541.	Philadelphia.	N.B. of Northern Liberties.
542.	Philadelphia.	Corn Exchange N.B.
543.	Philadelphia.	City N.B.
544.	Philadelphia.	Kensington N.B.
546.	Philadelphia.	N.B. of Germantown.
547.	Philadelphia.	N.B. of Commerce.
552.	West Chester.	N.B. of Chester County.
556.	Philadelphia.	Commercial Manufacturers N.B.
560.	Philadelphia.	Southwark N.B.
561.	Philadelphia.	Consolidation N.B.
562.	New Castle.	First N.B.
563.	Philadelphia.	Union N.B.
566.	Northumberland.	First N.B.
567.	Mahanoy City.	First N.B.
568.	Berwick.	First N.B.
569.	Corry.	Corry N.B.
570.	Philadelphia.	Tradesmen's N.B.
573.	Doylestown.	Doylestown N.B.
575.	Coatesville.	N.B. of Chester Valley.
580.	Harrisburg.	Harrisburg N.B.
585.	Middletown.	N.B. of Middletown.
586.	Washington.	First N.B.
592.	Philadelphia.	Girard N.B.
593.	Chambersburg.	N.B. of Chambersburg.
597.	Lancaster.	Farmers' N.B.
602.	Philadelphia.	Bank of North America.
604.	York.	York N.B.
605.	Corry.	First N.B.
606.	Erie.	Second N.B.
608.	Pottstown.	N.B. of Pottstown.
610.	Philadelphia.	Mechanics' N.B.
611.	Gettysburg.	Gettysburg N.B.
613.	Pittsburgh.	Merchants and Manufacturers' N.B.
619.	Pittsburgh.	Citizens' N.B.
622.	Titusville.	First N.B.
623.	Philadelphia.	Commonwealth N.B.
632.	New Brighton.	N.B. of Beaver County.
641.	Columbia.	Columbia N.B.
644.	Honesdale.	Honesdale N.B.
648.	Brownsville.	Monongahela N.B.
649.	Pottsville.	Miners' N.B.
655.	Lebanon.	Valley N.B.
656.	Philadelphia.	Western N.B.
661.	Downington, E. Downington.	Downington N.B.
664.	Carbondale.	First N.B.
667.	Mount Joy.	First N.B.
668.	Pittsburgh.	Pittsburgh N.B. of Commerce.
674.	Phoenixville.	N.B. of Phoenixville.
675.	Pittsburgh.	Iron City N.B.
678.	Pittsburgh.	Tradesmen's N.B.
680.	Lebanon.	Lebanon N.B.
681.	Uniontown.	N.B. of Fayette County.
683.	Lancaster.	Lancaster County N.B.
685.	Pittsburgh.	Farmers' Deposit N.B.
689.	Shamokin.	Northumberland County N.B.
693.	Reading.	Nat. Union Bank.
694.	York.	York County N.B.
696.	Reading.	Farmers' N.B.
700.	Pittsburgh.	Mechanics' N.B.
705.	Pittsburgh.	Union N.B.
707.	Plymouth.	First N.B.
711.	Milton.	Milton N.B.
717.	Bristol.	Farmers' N.B. of Bucks County.
722.	Pittsburgh.	Allegheny N.B.
723.	Philadelphia.	Central N.B.
727.	Pittsburgh.	People's N.B.
728.	Oxford.	N.B. of Oxford.
732.	Wilkes-Barre.	Wyoming N.B.
734.	Williamsport.	Lumberman's N.B.
741.	North East.	First N.B.
745.	Lewisburg.	Lewisburg N.B.
755.	Philadelphia.	Nat. Exchange Bank
757.	Pittsburgh.	German N.B.
768.	Clearfield.	First N.B.
774.	Clarion.	First N.B.
776.	Allegheny.	Second N.B.
784.	Lewisburg.	Union N.B.
797.	Tremont.	First N.B.
834.	Shippensburg.	First N.B.
835.	Tunkhannock.	Wyoming N.B.
837.	Muncy.	First N.B.
839.	Waynesburg.	Farmers and Drovers' N.B.
854.	Plumer.	First N.B.
855.	Clearfield.	County N.B.
867.	Blairsville.	First N.B.
870.	Erie.	Marine N.B.
871.	Meadville.	Merchants' N.B.
879.	Titusville.	Second N.B.
897.	Brookville.	First N.B.
912.	Manheim.	Manheirn N.B.
926.	Pittsburgh.	First N.B. of Birmingham.
1053.	Susquehanna.	First N.B.
1057.	Pittsburgh.	Exchange N.B.
1078.	Danville.	Danville N.B.
1081.	Greencastle.	First N.B.
1094.	Athens.	First N.B.
1124.	Meadville.	N.B. of Crawford County.
1148.	Norristown.	Montgomery N.B.
1152.	Pottsville.	Government N.B.
1156.	New Castle.	N.B. of Lawrence County.
1171.	Easton.	First N.B.
1176.	Franklin.	Venango N.B.
1219.	Tamaqua.	First N.B.
1233.	Easton.	Easton N.B.
1237.	Sunbury.	First N.B.
1273.	Lock Haven.	Lock Haven N.B.
1322.	Allentown.	Allentown N.B.
1411.	Catasauqua.	N.B. of Catasauqua.
1435.	Pittston.	Pittston N.B.
1464.	Williamsport.	Williamsport N.B.
1505.	Williamsport.	West Branch N.B.
1516.	Mount Joy.	Union Nat., Mount Joy Bank.
1579.	Lewiston.	Mifflin County N.B.
1647.	Philadelphia.	N.B. of the Republic.
1654.	Kittanning.	Kittanning N.B.
1663.	Pottsville.	Pennsylvania N.B.
1676.	Honeybrook.	First N.B.
1685.	Sharon.	First N.B.
1743.	Philadelphia.	Nat. Security Bank
1875.	Reading.	Keystone N.B.
1894.	Pittsburgh.	Fifth N.B.
1936.	Phoenixville.	Farmers and Mechanics' N.B.
1946.	Scranton.	Third N.B.
2018.	Spring City.	N.B. of Spring City.
2050.	Bethlehem.	Lehigh Valley N.B.
2078.	Conshohocken.	First N.B.
2131.	Green Lane.	Green Lane N.B.
2137.	Boyertown.	N.B. of Boyertown.
2139.	Williamsport.	City N.B.
2142.	Schwenksville.	N.B. of Schwenksville.
2195.	Pittsburgh.	City N.B.
2222.	McKeesport.	First N.B.
2223.	Montrose.	First N.B.
2226.	Warren.	Citizens' N.B.
2227.	Williamsport.	Lycoming N.B.
2228.	York.	Farmers' N.B.
2235.	Allegheny.	Third N.B.
2236.	Pittsburgh.	Diamond N.B.
2237.	Pittsburgh.	Marine N.B.
2241.	Millerstown.	German N.B.
2244.	Sharon.	Sharon N.B.
2249.	Jenkintown.	Jenkintown N.B.
2251.	Greenville.	Greenville N.B.
2252.	Millersburg.	First N.B.
2253.	Hatboro.	Hatboro N.B.
2256.	Mercer.	Farmers and Mechanics' N.B.
2258.	Meyersdale.	First N.B.
2261.	Allegheny.	German N.B.
2278.	Pittsburgh.	Duquesne N.B.
2279.	Pittsburgh.	Metropolitan N.B.
2280.	Ashland.	Citizens' N.B.
2281.	Pittsburgh.	Smithfield N.B.
2285.	Tarenturn.	First N.B.
2286.	Freeport.	First N.B.
2291.	Philadelphia.	Keystone N.B.
2293.	Slatington.	N.B. of Slatington.
2301.	Permsburg.	Perkiomen N.B.
2303.	York.	Western N.B.
2308.	Lehighton.	First N.B.
2317.	Philadelphia.	Centennial N.B.
2329.	Connellsville.	First N.B.
2333.	Souderton.	Union N.B.
2334.	Permsburg.	FarmersN.B.
2335.	Harmony.	Harmony N.B.
2337.	Towanda.	Citizens' N.B.
2366.	Quakertown.	Quarkertown N.B.
2384.	Arinville.	Arinville N.B.
2385.	Easton.	Northampton County N.B.
2392.	Brookville.	Jefferson County N.B.
2397.	Dillsburg.	Dillsburg N.B.
2408.	Burgettstown.	Burgettstown N.B.
2415.	Pittsburgh.	Fort Pitt N.B.
2428.	Bradford.	Bradford N.B.
2452.	Lititz.	Lititz N.B.
2457.	Brownsville.	Nat. Deposit Bank.
2462.	Philadelphia.	Merchants' N.B.
2464.	Parkesburg.	Parkesburg N.B.
2466.	Titusville.	Hyde N.B.
2470.	Bradford.	First N.B.
2473.	Reading.	Commercial N.B.
2483.	Watsontown.	Watsontown N.B.
2505.	Canton.	First N.B.

Charter Number	City	Name of Bank
2515.	Ephrata.	Ephrata N.B.
2526.	Kennett Square.	N.B. of Kennett Square.
2530.	New Holland.	New Holland N.B.
2552.	Reading.	Second N.B.
2558.	Greensburg.	First N.B.
2562.	Greensburg.	Merchants and Farmers' N.B.
2581.	Norristown.	People's N.B.
2609.	Saltsburg.	First N.B.
2634.	Lancaster.	Fulton N.B.
2654.	Kittanning.	N.B. of Kittanning.
2659.	Bangor.	First N.B.
2667.	Sellersville.	Sellersville N.B.
2669.	West Grove.	N.B. of West Grove.
2671.	Conshohocken.	Tradesmen's N.B.
2673.	Brownsville.	Second N.B.
2697.	Scranton.	First N.B.
2700.	Strasburg.	First N.B.
2710.	Marietta.	First N.B.
2711.	Pittsburgh.	Commercial N.B.
2731.	Philadelphia.	First N.B.
2736.	Wilkes-Barre.	First N.B.
2739.	Johnstown.	First N.B.
2744.	Hollidaysburg.	First N.B.
2745.	Pittsburgh.	First N.B.
2781.	Altoona.	Second N.B.
2787.	Stroudsburg.	First N.B.
2799.	Braddock.	First N.B.
2822.	Hummelstown.	Hummelstown N.B.
2828.	Braddock.	Braddock N.B.
2834.	Titusville.	Roberts N.B.
2849.	Christiana.	N.B. of Christiana.
2852.	Mauch Chunk.	Linderman N.B.
2857.	West Chester.	Farmers' N.B.
2864.	Gap.	Gap N.B.
2899.	Reading.	Penn N.B.
2900.	Boyertown.	Farmers' N.B.
2904.	Chester.	Chester N.B.
2906.	Oxford.	Farmers' N.B.
2958.	York.	Drovers and Mechanics' N.B.
2969.	Du Bois.	First N.B. of Du Bois City.
2977.	Rochester.	First N.B.
3030.	Punxsutawney.	First N.B.
3044.	Clarion.	Second N.B.
3045.	Shamokin.	First N.B.
3051.	Brookville.	N.B. of Brookville.
3063.	Langhorne.	People's N.B.
3067.	Quarryville.	Quarryville N.B.
3085.	Philadelphia.	Independence N.B.
3089.	Bedford.	First N.B.
3104.	Kittanning.	Farmers' N.B.
3143.	Shenandoah.	First N.B.
3144.	Susquehanna.	City N.B.
3147.	Malvern.	N.B. of Malvern.
3198.	Lincoln.	Lincoln N.B.
3220.	Ambler.	First N.B.
3255.	Emporium.	First N.B.
3259.	New Brighton.	N.B. of New Brighton.
3335.	Elizabethtown.	Elizabethtown N.B.
3356.	Beaver Falls.	First N.B.
3358.	Topton.	Topton N.B.
3367.	Lancaster.	Northern N.B.
3371.	Philadelphia.	Ninth N.B.
3383.	Washington.	Citizens' N.B.
3423.	Philadelphia.	Tenth N.B.
3459.	Watsontown.	Farmers' N.B.
3468.	Philadelphia.	Spring Garden N.B.
3480.	Muncy.	Citizens' N.B.
3491.	Philadelphia.	Northwestern N.B.
3494.	Pottstown.	Nat. Iron Bank.
3498.	Philadelphia.	Southwestern N.B.
3507.	Philadelphia.	Produce N.B.
3551.	Royersford.	N.B. of Royersford.
3557.	Philadelphia.	Fourth Street N.B.
3599.	Steelton.	Steelton N.B.
3604.	Philadelphia.	Manayunk N.B.
3632.	Stroudsburg.	Stroudsburg N.B.
3635.	Manheim.	Keystone N.B.
3650.	Lancaster.	People's N.B.
3666.	Media.	Charter N.B.
3684.	Philadelphia.	Market Street N.B.
3705.	Williamsport.	Merchants' N.B.
3713.	Harrisburg.	Merchants' N.B.
3723.	Philadelphia.	Chestnut Street N.B.
3763.	Renovo.	First N.B.
3766.	Bryn Mawr.	Bryn Mawr N.B.
3808.	Mountville.	Mountville N.B.
3829.	Homestead.	First N.B.
3831.	Latrobe.	First N.B.
3850.	Beaver.	First N.B.
3873.	Columbia.	Central N.B.
3874.	Pittsburgh.	Monongahela N.B.
3877.	Port Allegany.	First N.B.
3893.	Hazleton.	First N.B.
3902.	Hughesville.	First N.B.
3905.	Birdsboro.	First N.B.
3910.	Latrobe.	Citizens' N.B.
3938.	Wellsborough.	Wellsborough N.B.
3945.	Berwyn.	Berwyn N.B.
3955.	Nanticoke.	First N.B.
3961.	Bethlehem.	Bethlehem N.B.
3980.	Mount Carmel.	First N.B.
3987.	Lancaster.	Conestoga N.B.
3990.	Coatesville.	N.B. of Coatesville.
3997.	Mahanoy City.	Union N.B.
4011.	East Stroudsburg.	East Stroudsburg N.B.
4039.	Mifflintown.	First N.B.
4050.	Philadelphia.	Quaker City N.B.
4063.	Hyndman.	N.B. of South Pennsylvania.
4092.	Jeannette.	First N.B.
4098.	Scottdale.	First N.B.
4100.	Somerset.	First N.B.
4142.	Duncannon.	Duncannon N.B.
4156.	Middleburgh.	First N.B.
4181.	Washington.	Farmers and Mechanics' N.B.
4183.	Scranton.	Traders' N.B.
4192.	Philadelphia.	Northern N.B.
4199.	Bradford.	Commercial N.B.
4204.	Hazleton.	Hazleton N.B.
4205.	Delta.	First N.B.
4207.	Yardley.	Yardley N.B.
4212.	Johnstown.	Citizens' N.B.
4222.	Pittsburgh.	Pennsylvania N.B.
4227.	Somerset.	Somerset County N.B.
4255.	Claysville.	N.B. of Claysville.
4267.	Waynesburg.	Citizens' N.B.
4272.	Chambersburg.	Valley N.B.
4273.	Claysville.	First N.B.
4330.	North Wales.	North Wales N.B.
4339.	Pittsburgh.	Liberty N.B.
4352.	Pen Argyl.	First N.B.
4355.	Tyrone.	First N.B.
4367.	Delta.	Miles N.B.
4374.	Butler.	Butler County N.B.
4408.	Orwigsburg.	First N.B.
4422.	Girardville.	First N.B.
4428.	Darby.	First N.B.
4444.	Carlisle.	Merchants' N.B.
4445.	Waynesboro.	People's N.B.
4453.	Tarentum.	N.B. of Tarentum.
4462.	Sewickley.	First N.B.
4479.	Corry.	Citizens' N.B.
4481.	Connellsville.	Second N.B.
4505.	Dashore.	First N.B.
4513.	Bangor.	Merchants' N.B.
4534.	Charleroi.	First N.B.
4538.	Reedsville.	Reedsville N.B.
4543.	Bloomsburg.	Farmers' N.B.
4544.	Johnsonburg.	Johnsonburg N.B.
4546.	Shenandoah.	Merchants' N.B.
4548.	Catawissa.	First N.B.
4549.	New Brighton.	Union N.B.
4560.	Avondale.	N.B. of Avondale.
4570.	Canonsburg.	First N.B.
4615.	Ernlenton.	First N.B.
4622.	California.	First N.B.
4625.	McKeesport.	N.B. of McKeesport.
4665.	Stewartstown.	First N.B.
4673.	Dawson.	First N.B.
4676.	New Castle.	Citizens' N.B.
4698.	Irwin.	First N.B.
4714.	Pottstown.	Citizens' N.B.
4728.	Wilkinsburg.	First N.B.
4730.	Duquesne.	First N.B.
4751.	Royersford.	Home N.B.
4752.	McDonald.	First N.B.
4762.	Carnegie.	First N.B.
4818.	Ellwood City.	First N.B.
4823.	Corry.	N.B. of Corry.
4832.	Philipsburg.	First N.B.
4836.	Clearfield.	Clearfield N.B.
4850.	Belle Vernon.	First N.B.
4857.	Patton.	First N.B.
4861.	Connellsville.	Yough N.B.
4875.	Mount Pleasant.	Citizens' N.B.
4876.	McKeesport.	Citizens' N.B.
4877.	Verona.	First N.B.
4879.	Warren.	Warren N.B.
4883.	Pittsburgh.	Lincoln N.B.
4887.	Reading.	Reading N.B.
4892.	Mount Pleasant.	Farmers and Merchants N.B.
4894.	Bcaver Falls.	Farmers' N.B.
4908.	Reynoldsville.	First N.B.
4909.	Mercer.	Mercer County N.B.
4910.	Pittsburgh.	Columbia N.B.
4913.	New Kensington.	First N.B.
4915.	Athens.	Farmers' N.B.
4917.	Newport.	First N.B.
4918.	Pittsburgh.	Western N.B.
4919.	Blairsville.	Blairsville N.B.
4923.	Ephrata.	Farmers' N.B.
4927.	North East.	First N.B.
4938.	Meadville.	New First N.B.
4948.	Coudersport.	First N.B.
4955.	Lebanon.	People's N.B.
4965.	Huntingdon.	Union N.B.
4971.	Cochranton.	First N.B.
4974.	Greensburg.	Westmoreland N.B.
4978.	New Bethlehem.	First N.B.
4979.	Lebanon.	Farmers' N.B.
4984.	Troy.	First N.B.
4991.	Allegheny.	Enterprise N.B.
5000.	Wilmerding.	East Pittsburgh N.B.
5007.	Blossburg.	Miners' N.B.
5010.	West Newton.	First N.B.
5014.	Ridgway.	Elk County N.B.
5017.	Pittsburgh.	United States N.B.
5019.	Du Bois.	Deposit N.B.
5025.	Kane.	First N.B.
5034.	Uniontown.	Second N.B.
5038.	Tionesta.	Forest County N.B.
5040.	Tionesta.	Citizens' N.B.
5042.	Beaver.	Beaver N.B.
5043.	Elkland.	Pattison N.B.
5044.	Grove City.	First N.B.
5051.	New Bethlehem.	Citizens' N.B.
5058.	McDonald.	People's N.B.
5059.	Johnstown.	Cambria N.B.
5066.	Philipsburg.	Moshannon N.B.
5069.	Coraopolis.	Coraopolis N.B.
5073.	Kittanning.	Merchants' N.B.
5077.	Nazareth.	Nazareth N.B.
5080.	Vandergrift.	First N.B.
5084.	Ebensburg.	First N.B.
5085.	Waynesburg.	People's N.B.
5102.	Kutztown.	Kutztown N.B.
5114.	Elizabeth.	First N.B.
5118.	Easton.	Northampton N.B.
5130.	Ford City.	First N.B.
5131.	Union City.	N.B. of Union City.
5133.	New Bloomfield.	First N.B.
5142.	McKees Rocks.	First N.B.
5147.	Mifflintown.	Juniata Valley N.B.
5166.	East Greenville.	Perkiomen N.B.
5170.	Rochester.	Rochester N.B.
5184.	Red Lion.	Red Lion First N.B.
5198.	Delta.	People's N.B.
5202.	Athens.	Athens N.B.
5204.	Glen Campbell.	First N.B.
5211.	Bloomsburg.	Bloomsburg N.B.
5216.	Schuylkill Haven.	First N.B.
5221.	Franklin.	Lamberton N.B.
5225.	Pittsburgh.	Bank of Pittsburg Nat. Assn.
5227.	Northampton.	Cement N.B. of Siegfried.
5234.	Lansford.	First N.B.
5240.	Oil City.	Oil City N.B.
5241.	Myerstown.	Myerstown N.B.
5242.	Windber.	Windber N.B.
5245.	Newport.	Perry County N.B.
5253.	Monessen.	First N.B.
5255.	Irwin.	Citizens' N.B.
5265.	Wilkinsburg.	Central N.B.
5289.	Lewistown.	Citizens' N.B.
5306.	Belleville.	Belleville N.B.
5307.	Confluence.	First N.B.
5311.	Smithton.	First N.B.
5321.	East Brady.	First N.B.
5327.	Oakdale.	First N.B.
5339.	Wyalusing.	First N.B.
5340.	Rockwood.	First N.B.
5351.	Tarenturn.	People's N.B.
5356.	East Brady.	People's N.B.
5365.	Homestead.	Homestead N.B.
5389.	Millville.	First N.B.
5391.	Butler.	Farmers' N.B.
5429.	Meshoppen.	First N.B.
5441.	Masontown.	First N.B.
5444.	Bath.	First N.B.
5452.	Somerset.	Farmers' N.B.
5454.	Freedom.	Freedom N.B.
5459.	Philadelphia.	Franklin N.B.
5481.	Emlenton.	Farmers' N.B.
5495.	Roscoe.	First N.B.
5496.	Milford.	First N.B.
5497.	Brickway.	First N.B.
5501.	Grove City.	Grove City N.B.
5502.	Leechburg.	First N.B.
5509.	Bellevue.	Bellevue N.B.
5518.	Forest City.	First N.B.
5527.	Jeannette.	Jeannette N.B.
5531.	Littlestown.	First N.B.
5563.	Elizabethville.	First N.B.
5565.	Oil City.	Lamberton N.B.
5573.	Shickshinny.	First N.B.
5574.	Montgomery.	First N.B.
5578.	East Stroudsburg.	Monroe County N.B.
5599.	Mars.	Mars N.B.
5601.	Halifax.	Halifax N.B.
5615.	Ashland.	Ashland N.B.
5625.	Shamokin.	Market Street N.B.
5646.	Fayette City.	First N.B.
5666.	Sayre.	First N.B.
5667.	Big Run.	Citizens' N.B.
5682.	Stoystown.	First N.B.
5684.	Sayre.	N.B. of Sayre.
5686.	Nazareth.	Second N.B.
5702.	Punxsutawney.	Punxsutawney N.B.
5708.	Glassport.	Glassport N.B.
5723.	Apollo.	First N.B.
5727.	Marienville.	Gold Standard N.B.
5729.	Natrona.	First N.B.
5736.	Perkasie.	First N.B.
5742.	Dayton.	First N.B.
5744.	Latrobe.	People's N.B.
5768.	Cresson.	First N.B.
5773.	Lititz.	Farmers' N.B.
5777.	Beaver Springs.	First N.B.
5784.	Carmichaels.	First N.B.
5801.	Meyersdale.	Second N.B.
5818.	Barnesboro.	First N.B.
5823.	Berlin.	First N.B.
5832.	Waynesboro.	Citizens' N.B.
5833.	Meyersdale.	Citizens' N.B.
5835.	Donora.	First N.B.
5837.	New Salem.	Delmont N.B.
5848.	Pitcairn.	First N.B.
5855.	Carrolltown.	First N.B.
5857.	Greencastle.	Citizens' N.B.
5878.	Monaca.	Monaca N.B.
5879.	Monaca.	Citizens' N.B.
5899.	Ellwood City.	Ellwood City N.B.
5908.	Houston.	First N.B.
5913.	Johnstown.	United States N.B.
5920.	Fredericktown.	First N.B.
5945.	Ridgway.	Ridgway N.B.
5948.	West Alexander.	West Alexander N. B.
5956.	Monessen.	People's N.B.
5965.	Punxsutawney.	Farmers' N.B.
5968.	Monongahela City.	First N.B.
5974.	Scottdale.	Broadway N.B.
5977.	Sheraden.	First N.B.

Charter Number	City	Name of Bank
6010.	Crafton.	First N.B.
6023.	Pittsburgh.	Federal N.B.
6037.	Denver.	Denver N.B.
6045.	Parkers Landing.	First N.B.
6049.	Herndon.	First N.B.
6051.	Slatington.	Citizens' N.B.
6066.	Port Allegany.	Citizens' N.B.
6083.	Rural Valley.	Rural Valley N.B.
6090.	Huntingdon.	Standing Stone N.B.
6105.	Waynesburg.	American N.B.
6106.	Salisbury, Elk Lick.	First N.B.
6108.	Weatherly.	First N.B.
6109.	Swissvale.	First N.B.
6114.	Point Marion.	First N.B.
6117.	Tower City.	Tower City N.B.
6127.	Kittanning.	Nat. Kittanning Bank.
6131.	Minersville.	Union N.B.
6135.	Bolivar.	Bolivar N.B.
6141.	Zelienople.	First N.B.
6153.	Pittsburgh.	Republic N.B.
6155.	Jersey Shore.	N.B. of Jersey Shore.
6158.	Jermyn.	First N.B.
6162.	Berwick.	Berwick N.B.
6165.	Tremont.	Tremont N.B.
6174.	Carnegie.	Carnegie N.B.
6175.	Freeland.	First N.B.
6182.	Edenburg, Knox.	Clarion County N.B.
6193.	Sheffield.	Sheffield N.B.
6209.	Ebensburg.	American N.B.
6216.	Pittsburgh.	Cosmopolitan N.B.
6220.	Everett.	First N.B.
6250.	Hooversville.	First N.B.
6270.	Sutersville.	First N.B.
6275.	Clifton Heights.	First N.B.
6281.	Ligonier.	First N.B.
6301.	Pittsburgh.	Mellon N.B.
6325.	Wilmerding.	Wilmerding N.B.
6328.	Benton.	Columbia County N.B.
6344.	Perryopolis.	First N.B.
6350.	Le Raysville.	First N.B.
6373.	West Elizabeth.	First N.B.
6384.	Falls Creek.	First N.B.
6408.	Connellsville.	Union N.B.
6411.	Mount Union.	First N.B.
6420.	Finleyville.	First N.B.
6438.	Tunkhannock.	Citizens' N.B.
6442.	Gallitzin.	First N.B.
6444.	Stewartstown.	People's N.B.
6445.	Hawley.	First N.B.
6452.	Connellsville.	Citizens' N.B.
6453.	Etna, Pittsburgh, Sharpsburg.	First N.B.
6456.	Manor.	Manor N.B.
6465.	Quakertown.	Merchants' N.B.
6483.	Slippery Rock.	First N.B.
6495.	Clairton.	Clairton N.B.
6499.	Tyrone.	Farmers and Merchants' N.B.
6500.	Youngwood.	First N.B.
6501.	Osceola, Osceola Mills.	First N.B.
6507.	Hays.	Hays N.B.
6512.	Berlin.	Philson N.B.
6516.	Tyrone.	Blair County N.B.
6528.	Masontown.	Masontown N.B.
6531.	Lehighton.	Citizens' N.B.
6533.	Cambridge Springs.	First N.B.
6534.	Mauch Chunk.	Mauch Chunk N.B.
6536.	Spring Grove.	First N.B.
6560.	Sharon.	Merchants and Manufacturers' N.B.
6567.	Pittsburgh.	Colonial N.B.
6568.	Turtle Creek.	N.B. of Turtle Creek.
6569.	Rimersburg.	Rimersburg N.B.
6573.	South Fork.	First N.B.
6574.	Turtle Creek.	First N.B.
6580.	New Alexandria.	New Alexandria N.B.
6581.	Pleasant Unity.	Pleasant Unity N.B.
6589.	Saint Marys.	Saint Marys N.B.
6599.	New Salem.	First N.B.
6603.	Boswell.	First N.B.
6615.	Hyndman.	Hoblitzell N.B.
6626.	Midway.	Midway N.B.
6636.	Bridgeville.	First N.B.
6638.	Stoneboro.	First N.B.
6642.	Smithfield.	First N.B.
6645.	Allentown.	Merchants' N.B.
6648.	Dallastown.	First N.B.
6654.	Chester.	Pennsylvania N.B.
6664.	Wampum.	First N.B.
6665.	Portland.	Portland N.B.
6676.	Rimersburg.	First N.B.
6695.	Houtzdale.	First N.B.
6708.	Red Lion.	Farmers and Merchants' N.B.
6709.	Addison.	First N.B.
6715.	New Freedom.	First N.B.
6725.	Pittsburgh.	Washington N.B.
6739.	Summerville.	Union N.B.
6741.	Garrett.	First N.B.
6746.	Montrose.	Farmers' N.B.
6756.	Derry.	First N.B.
6794.	Wilson.	First N.B.
6796.	Braddock.	Union N.B.
6799.	Shingle House.	First N.B.
6800.	Fayette City.	Fayette City N.B.
6806.	Pittsburgh.	Industrial N.B.
6829.	Sharpsville.	First N.B.
6832.	Ligonier.	N.B. of Ligonier.
6848.	Windber.	Citizens' N.B.
6859.	Harrisville.	First N.B.
6874.	Hollidaysburg.	Citizens' N.B.
6877.	Sunbury.	Sunbury N.B.
6878.	East Berlin.	East Berlin N.B.
6881.	Plymouth.	Plymouth N.B.
6887.	Coalport.	First N.B.
6891.	Conneaut Lake.	First N.B.
6913.	West Middlesex.	First N.B.
6929.	Ellsworth.	N.B. of Ellsworth.
6937.	Webster.	First N.B.
6942.	Shamokin.	N.B. of Shamokin.
6944.	Burgettstown.	Washington N.B.
6946.	Shippensburg.	People's N.B.
6948.	Clintonville.	First N.B.
6950.	Ringtown.	First N.B.
6962.	Trafford City.	First N.B.
6969.	Curwensville.	Citizens' N.B.
6971.	Williamsburg.	First N.B.
6979.	East Conemaugh.	First N.B.
6983.	Mount Morris.	Farmers and Merchants' N.B.
6997.	Montoursville.	First N.B.
7000.	Cherry Tree.	First N.B.
7003.	Swineford.	First N.B.
7005.	Northumberland.	Northumberland N.B.
7051.	Lansford.	Citizens' N.B.
7056.	Atglen.	Atglen N.B.
7076.	Cecil.	First N.B.
7078.	Christiana.	Christiana N.B.
7090.	Rices Landing.	Rices Landing N.B.
7112.	Wehrum.	First N.B.
7139.	Emaus.	Emaus N.B.
7156.	Millerstown.	First N.B.
7181.	Spangler.	First N.B.
7193.	Swarthmore.	Swarthmore N.B.
7229.	Saxton.	First N.B.
7262.	Scenery Hill.	First N.B.
7263.	Washington.	Old N.B.
7280.	Galeton.	First N.B.
7286.	Tamaqua.	Tamaqua N.B.
7310.	Millsboro.	First N.B.
7312.	Edinboro.	First N.B.
7334.	Winburne.	Bituminous N.B.
7343.	Girard.	N.B. of Girard.
7349.	New Cumberland.	New Cumberland N.B.
7353.	Marysville.	First N.B.
7356.	Bellwood.	First N.B.
7363.	Parnassus.	Parnassus N.B.
7366.	Freeport.	Farmers' N.B.
7367.	Portage.	First N.B.
7395.	New Brighton.	Old N.B.
7400.	Madera.	Madera N.B.
7405.	Hickory.	Farmers' N.B.
7406.	Nanticoke.	Nanticoke N.B.
7409.	Zelienople.	People's N.B.
7430.	Curwensville.	Curwensville N.B.
7445.	Connellsville.	Colonial N.B.
7448.	Catawissa.	Catawissa N.B.
7453.	Du Bois.	Du Bois N.B.
7465.	Johnstown.	Union N.B.
7471.	Fredonia.	Fredonia N.B.
7473.	Mount Jewett.	Mount Jewett N.B.
7488.	Sykesville.	First N.B.
7511.	State College.	First N.B.
7522.	Philadelphia.	Textile N.B.
7528.	Economy.	People's N.B.
7559.	McKeesport.	Union N.B.
7560.	Pittsburgh.	Keystone N.B.
7576.	Dunbar.	First N.B.
7581.	Pittsburgh.	American N.B.
7594.	Avonmore.	First N.B.
7610.	Mahaffey.	Mahaffey N.B.
7620.	Reynoldsville.	People's N.B.
7624.	Export.	First N.B.
7642.	Oakmont.	First N.B.
7702.	Hallstead.	First N.B.
7710.	Pen Argyl.	Pen Argyl N.B.
7716.	Newport.	Citizens' N.B.
7722.	Trevorton.	First N.B.
7735.	Lansdale.	Citizens' N.B.
7749.	Rochester.	People's N.B.
7769.	McClure.	First N.B.
7785.	Peckville.	Peckville N.B.
7792.	Jeannette.	People's N.B.
7816.	Vandergrift.	Citizens' N.B.
7819.	Marion Center.	Marion Center N.B.
7826.	Middletown.	Citizens' N.B.
7854.	Avella.	Lincoln N.B.
7856.	York Springs.	First N.B.
7860.	Frackville.	First N.B.
7873.	Sharpsville.	Sharpsville N.B.
7874.	Shippenville.	First N.B.
7887.	Plumville.	First N.B.
7897.	New Berlin.	First N.B.
7910.	Nicholson.	First N.B.
7917.	Biglerville.	Biglerville N.B.
7929.	Philadelphia.	Nat. Deposit Bank.
7931.	Danielsville.	Danielsville N.B.
7935.	Benson, Hollsopple.	First N.B.
7974.	Martinsburg.	First N.B.
7993.	Indiana.	Citizens' N.B.
8045.	Quarryville.	Farmers' N.B.
8083.	McConnellsburg.	First N.B.
8092.	Tioga.	Grange N.B.
8131.	Wernersville.	Wernersville N.B.
8141.	Spring Grove.	People's N.B.
8151.	Pine Grove.	Pine Grove N.B.
8164.	Dallas.	First N.B.
8165.	Youngsville.	First N.B.
8185.	Beaver.	Fort McIntosh N.B.
8190.	Canderbilt.	First N.B.
8196.	Bentleyville.	First N.B.
8223.	Topton.	N.B. of Topton.
8233.	Patton.	Grange N.B.
8235.	Scranton.	People's N.B.
8238.	Juniata.	First N.B.
8245.	Fairchance.	First N.B.
8263.	Reynoldsville.	Citizens' N.B.
8283.	Catasauqua.	Lehigh N.B.
8311.	Midland.	First N.B.
8320.	Springdale.	Springdale N.B.
8326.	Liverpool.	First N.B.
8329.	Bridgeport.	Bridgeport N.B.
8344.	Richland.	Richland N.B.
8380.	Hazelhurst.	Hazelhurst N.B.
8393.	Mount Carmel.	Union N.B.
8404.	Collegeville.	Collegeville N.B.
8405.	Lemasters.	Lemasters N.B.
8410.	Exchange.	Farmers' N.B.
8421.	Blue Ball.	Blue Ball N.B.
8428.	Blacklick.	First N.B.
8446.	East Mauch Chunk.	Citizens' N.B.
8450.	Lilly.	First N.B.
8459.	Ambridge.	First N.B.
8464.	Clearfield.	Farmers and Traders' N.B.
8493.	Mount Holly Springs.	First N.B.
8494.	Avoca.	First N.B.
8498.	Wellsville.	Wellsville N.B.
8499.	New Holland.	Farmers' N.B.
8503.	New Castle.	Union N.B.
8517.	Wyoming.	First N.B.
8576.	Lyndora.	Lyndora N.B.
8590.	Aliquippa.	First N.B.
8591.	Smethport.	Grange N.B. of McKean Co.
8619.	McAdoo.	First N.B.
8633.	Edwardsville.	First N.B.
8646.	Downingtown.	Grange N.B. of Chester Co.
8653.	Selinsgrove.	Farmers' N.B.
8656.	Ashley, Wilkes-Barre.	First N.B.
8678.	Ellwood City.	People's N.B.
8724.	Slippery Rock.	Citizens' N.B.
8737.	Scranton.	Union N.B.
8739.	Ulysses.	Grange N.B. of Potter Co.
8761.	Bellevue.	Citizens' N.B.
8764.	Sharon.	McDowell N.B.
8773.	McVeytown.	McVeytown N.B.
8778.	Duncannon.	People's N.B.
8783.	Fredericksburg.	First N.B.
8795.	Munhall.	First N.B.
8806.	Olyphant.	First N.B.
8810.	Mansfield.	First N.B.
8824.	Aspinwall.	First N.B.
8831.	Mansfield.	Grange N.B.
8845.	Laceyville.	Grange N.B. of Wyoming Co.
8849.	Troy.	Grange N.B. of Bradford Co.
8854.	Evans City.	Citizens' N.B.
8855.	Homer City.	Homer City N.B.
8858.	Oley.	First N.B.
8866.	Montgomery.	Farmers and Citizens' N.B.
8879.	Union City.	Home N.B.
8890.	West Conshohocken.	People's N.B.
8901.	Somerfield.	First N.B.
8913.	Bernville.	First N.B.
8919.	Bruin.	First N.B.
8921.	Luzerne.	Luzerne N.B.
8924.	Hughesville.	Grange N.B. of Lycoming Co.
8930.	Palmerton.	First N.B.
8938.	West York, York.	Industrial N.B.
8939.	Fleetwood.	First N.B.
8946.	Sligo.	Sligo N.B.
8954.	West Alexander.	People's N.B.
8960.	New Milford.	Grange N.B. of Susquehanna Co.
8962.	Schaefferstown.	First N.B.
8964.	Pottsville.	Merchants' N.B.
8968.	Mohnton.	Mohnton N.B.
8969.	Mechanicsburg.	Mechanicsburg N.B.
8973.	New Albany.	First N.B.
8985.	Orbisonia.	First N.B.
9026.	Brownstown.	Brownstown N.B.
9028.	Hamburg.	First N.B.
9034.	Coopersburg.	First N.B.
9058.	Bentleyville.	Farmers and Miners' N.B.
9072.	Goldsboro, Etters.	First N.B.
9084.	Green Lane.	Valley N.B.
9107.	Hegins.	First N.B.
9110.	Spartansburg.	Grange N.B.
9113.	Coplay.	Coplay N.B.
9114.	Bendersville.	Bendersville N.B.
9128.	Castle Shannon.	First N.B.
9130.	Factoryville.	First N.B.
9139.	Ardentsville.	N.B. of Ardentsville.
9149.	North East.	N.B. of North East.
9154.	Clintonville.	People's N.B.
9198.	Mount Pleasant.	People's N.B.
9202.	Riegelsville.	First N.B.
9207.	Littlestown.	Littlestown N.B.
9216.	Intercourse.	First N.B.
9235.	Wilkes-Barre.	Luzerne County N.B.
9240.	Auburn.	First N.B.
9247.	Shenandoah.	Citizens' N.B.
9248.	Forest City.	Farmers and Miners' N.B.
9249.	Howard.	First N.B.
9256.	Fairfield.	First N.B.
9257.	Telford.	Telford N.B.
9259.	Millersville.	Millersville N.B.
9264.	Bainbridge.	First N.B.
9290.	Leechburg.	Farmers' N.B.

Charter Number	City	Name of Bank
9307.	Claysville.	Farmers' N.B.
9312.	Landisville.	First N.B.
9316.	Terre Hill.	Terre Hill N.B.
9317.	Canton.	Farmers' N.B.
9318.	Cressona.	First N.B.
9330.	Mercersburg.	First N.B.
9340.	Moscow.	First N.B.
9344.	Penbrook.	Penbrook N.B.
9345.	Loganton.	Loganton N.B.
9361.	Mount Wolf.	Union N.B.
9362.	Dover.	Dover N.B.
9364.	Akron.	Akron N.B.
9385.	Fawn Grove.	First N.B.
9392.	Williamsburg.	Farmers and Merchants' N.B.
9402.	Bally.	First N.B.
9416.	Eldred.	First N.B.
9422.	Lititz.	Lititz Springs N.B.
9430.	Cambridge Springs.	Springs N.B.
9461.	Maytown.	Maytown N.B.
9473.	Gratz.	First N.B.
9480.	Fryburg.	First N.B.
9495.	Leesport.	First N.B.
9503.	Point Marion.	People's N.B.
9505.	Ulster.	First N.B.
9507.	Seven Valleys.	Seven Valleys N.B.
9508.	Ralston.	First N.B.
9511.	Millheim.	Farmers' N.B.
9513.	Westfield.	Farmers and Traders' N.B.
9526.	McAlisterville.	Farmers' N.B.
9528.	Laporte.	First N.B.
9534.	Albion.	First N.B.
9541.	Harleysville.	Harleysville N.B.
9543.	Freedom.	Saint Clair N.B.
9552.	Mildred.	First N.B.
9554.	New Wilmington.	First N.B.
9569.	Centralia.	First N.B.
9588.	Newville.	Farmers' N.B.
9600.	Jessup.	First N.B.
9638.	Hopewell.	Hopewell N.B.
9647.	Hop Bottom.	Hop Bottom N.B.
9656.	New Tripoli.	New Tripoli N.B.
9660.	Jefferson, Codorus.	Codorus N.B.
9668.	Glenside.	Glenside N.B.
9678.	Patterson, Mifflin.	People's N.B.
9702.	Lawrenceville.	First N.B.
9706.	York.	Central N.B.
9727.	Grantham.	Grantham N.B.
9739.	Coaldale.	First N.B.
9752.	Myerstown.	Farmers' N.B.
9769.	Rockwood.	Farmers and Merchants' N.B.
9783.	Genesee.	First N.B.
9803.	Turbotville.	Turbotville N.B.
9814.	Butler.	Merchants' N.B.
9851.	Dickson City.	Dickson City N.B.
9862.	Edwardsville, Wilkes-Barre.	People's N.B.
9863.	Punxsutawney.	County N.B.
9868.	Dunmore.	First N.B.
9886.	Lake Ariel, Ariel.	First N.B.
9898.	Clymer.	Clymer N.B.
9901.	Washington.	People's N.B.
9902.	Aliquippa.	Aliquippa N.B.
9905.	Ardmore.	Ardmore N.B.
9978.	Knoxville.	First N.B.
9996.	Delmont.	People's N.B.
10027.	Waterford.	Ensworth N.B.
10042.	East Smithfield.	First N.B.
10128.	Belleville.	Farmers' N.B.
10183.	Three Springs.	First N.B.
10188.	Herminie.	First N.B.
10206.	Mount Union.	Central N.B.
10211.	Thompsontown.	Farmers' N.B.
10214.	Weissport.	Weissport N.B.
10232.	Claysburg.	First N.B.
10246.	Rome.	Farmers' N.B.
10251.	Nesquehoning.	First N.B.
10313.	Petersburg.	First N.B.
10335.	Orbisonia.	Orbisonia N.B.
10353.	New Florence.	New Florence N.B.
10383.	Clarks Summit.	Abington N.B.
10415.	Farrell.	First N.B.
10452.	Strausstown.	Strausstown N.B.
10466.	Republic.	First N.B.
10493.	Russellton.	First N.B.
10506.	Lewistown.	Russell N.B.
10590.	Johnstown.	N.B. of Johnstown.
10606.	Wyalusing.	N.B. of Wyalusing.
10666.	Schel I burg.	First N.B.
10704.	Cairnbrook.	First N.B.
10707.	Marietta.	Exchange N.B.
10775.	Elverson.	Elverson N.B.
10811.	Dry Run.	Citizens' N.B.
10837.	Elysburg.	First N.B.
10839.	Ambridge.	Ambridge N.B.
10847.	Ridley Park.	Ridley Park N.B.
10899.	Fannettsburg.	Fannettsburg N.B.
10950.	Lemasters.	People's N.B.
10951.	Woodlawn.	First N.B.
11015.	New Hope.	Solebury N.B.
11058.	Orangeville.	Farmers' N.B.
11062.	Lykens.	First N.B.
11115.	Irvona.	First N.B.
11127.	Liberty.	Farmers' N.B.
11188.	Coaldale, Six Mile Run, Bedford Co.	Broad Top N.B.
11204.	Timblin.	First N.B.
11213.	Spring Mills.	First N.B.
11227.	Hastings.	First N.B.
11244.	Mapleton, Mapleton Depot.	First N.B.

Charter Number	City	Name of Bank
11257.	Burnham.	First N.B.
11263.	Alexandria.	First N.B.
11317.	Beaverdale.	First N.B.
11369.	Port Royal.	First N.B.
11370.	Jefferson.	First N.B.
11373.	Port Royal.	Port Royal N.B.
11386.	Lansdowne.	Lansdowne N.B.
11393.	Springville.	First N.B.
11407.	Davidsville.	First N.B.
11413.	Hooversville.	Citizens' N.B.
11476.	Philadelphia.	Drovers and Merchants' N.B.
11482.	Philadelphia.	N.B. of Commerce.
11487.	Monessen.	Citizens' N.B.
11505.	Marcus Hook.	Marcus Hook N.B.
11512.	Dauphin.	Dauphin N.B.
11524.	Loysville.	First N.B.
11539.	Philadelphia.	Broad Street N.B.
11570.	Ellwood City.	Citizens' N.B.
11593.	Allenwood.	Allenwood N.B.
11643.	Picture Rocks.	Picture Rocks N.B.
11692.	Lock Haven.	County N.B.
11757.	Bakerton, Elmora.	First N.B.
11760.	Butler.	South Side N.B.
11789.	Rebersburg.	Rebersburg N.B.
11834.	Volant.	First N.B.
11841.	Shoemakersville.	First N.B.
11849.	Sipesville.	First N.B.
11865.	Pittston.	Liberty N.B.
11866.	Waynesboro.	First N.B.
11892.	Pitcairn.	People's N.B.
11896.	Arnold.	Arnold N.B.
11899.	Seward.	First N.B.
11902.	Burnside.	Burnside N.B.
11908.	Philadelphia.	N.B. of North Philadelphia.
11910.	Saegertown.	First N.B.
11938.	Koppel.	First N.B.
11966.	Osceola Mills.	People's N.B.
11967.	Central City.	Central City N.B.
11981.	Numidia.	Valley N.B.
11993.	West.	Citizens' N.B. Alexander.
11995.	North Belle Vernon Belle Vernon.	People's N.B.
12029.	Jerome.	First N.B.
12063.	Windsor.	First N.B.
12098.	Johnstown.	Moxham N.B.
12137.	Philadelphia.	Rittenhouse N.B.
12159.	Nescopeck.	Nescopeck N.B.
12189.	Conneautville.	First N.B.
12192.	Centre Hall.	First N.B.
12197.	Penbrook.	N.B. of Penbrook.
12261.	State College.	People's N.B.
12281.	Blue Ridge Summit.	First N.B.
12304.	Roaring Spring.	First N.B.
12305.	York.	Eastern N.B.
12326.	Indian Head.	First N.B.
12327.	Girardville.	Liberty N.B.
12349.	Mocanaqua.	First N.B.
12355.	Bolivar.	Citizens' N.B.
12358.	Paoli.	Paoli N.B.
12363.	North Girard.	First N.B.
12380.	Camp Hill.	Camp Hill N.B.
12414.	Pittsburgh.	Highland N.B.
12459.	Dickson City.	Liberty N.B.
12471.	Neffs.	Neffs N.B.
12500.	Uniontown.	Uniontown N.B. and Trust Co.
12504.	Wayne.	Main Line N.B.
12526.	Cheltenham.	Cheltenham N.B.
12530.	Jenkintown.	Citizens' N.B.
12562.	Austin.	First N.B.
12563.	Nuremburg.	First N.B.
12573.	Philadelphia.	Overbrook N.B.
12582.	Chalfont.	Chalfont N.B.
12588.	Saint Michael.	Saint Michael N.B.
12595.	Narberth.	Narberth N.B.
12597.	Monroeton.	First N.B.
12602.	Wehrum.	N.B. of Wehrum.
12688.	Hershey.	Hershey N.B.
12695.	Bala-Cynwyd.	Bala-Cynwyd N.B.
12720.	Cassandra.	First N.B.
12805.	Shamokin.	West End N.B.
12808.	Yukon.	First N.B.
12858.	Oakmont, Upper Darby.	Oakmont N.B.
12860.	Philadelphia.	Queen Lane N.B.
12911.	Newfoundland.	First N.B.
12912.	Derry.	First N.B.
12921.	Kingston.	First N.B.
12931.	Philadelphia.	N.B. of Olney.
12933.	Wilcox.	Wilcox.N.B.
12934.	Carnegie.	Union N.B.
12967.	Dale.	Date N.B.
12975.	Fogelsville.	Fogelsville N.B.
12994.	Monessen.	N.B. and Trust Co.
13002.	Roseto.	First N.B.
13003.	Philadelphia.	Tioga N.B.
13005.	Waynesboro.	Waynesboro N.B. and Trust Co.
13009.	Burgettstown.	Peoples N.B.
13011.	Seward.	Citizens' N.B.
13015.	Morton.	Morton N.B.
13026.	Hatfield.	Hatfield N.B.
13030.	Elkins Park.	Elkins Park N.B.
13031.	Springfield.	Springfield N.B.
13032.	Philadelphia.	Erie N.B.
13040.	Scranton.	County N.B.
13064.	Friedens.	First N.B.
13084.	Kensington.	Union N.B.
13087.	Ambridge.	Economy N.B.
13113.	Philadelphia.	N.B. of Mt. Airy.

Charter Number	City	Name of Bank
13118.	Bellafonte.	Farmers N.B.
13133.	Dublin.	Dublin N.B.
13134.	Waynesboro.	First N.B. and Trust Co.
13141.	Roslyn.	Roslyn N.B.
13151.	Lansdowne.	N.B. of Lansdowne.
13153.	Pittsburgh.	Forbes N.B.
13160.	Glen Lyon.	Glen Lyon N.B.
13175.	Philadelphia.	Northeast N.B. of Holmesburg.
13177.	Exeter.	First N.B.
13180.	Philadelphia.	City N.B. and Trust Co.
13186.	Leola.	Leola N.B.
13196.	Highland Park.	State Road N.B.
13197.	Jersey Shore.	Union N.B.
13205.	Beech Creek.	Beech Creek N.B.
13225.	Scranton.	Hyde Park N.B.
13251.	Souderton.	Peoples N.B.
13325.	Philadelphia.	North Broad N.B.
13341.	Philadelphia.	Lehigh N.B.
13371.	Erie.	Lawrence Park N.B.
13381.	Blossburg.	Citizens N.B. and Trust Co.
13392.	Conyngham.	Conyngham N.B.
13432.	Ligonier.	Ligonier N.B.
13447.	Butler.	Union N.B.
13485.	Uniontown.	Third N.B.
13491.	Connellsville.	N.B. and Trust Co.
13494.	Lemoyne.	West Shore N.B.
13496.	Sewickley.	Union N.B.
13524.	Nanticoke.	Miners N.B.
13533.	Gallitzin.	First N.B.
13566.	Brockway.	First N.B.
13571.	New Kensington.	Logan N.B.
13585.	Charleroi.	N.B. of Charleroi.
13606.	Portland.	Portland N.B.
13618.	Mansfield.	First N.B.
13619.	Shenandoah.	Miners N.B.
13644.	Donora.	Union N.B.
13658.	Ligonier.	First N.B.
13663.	Bentleyville.	Citizens N.B.
13699.	Sewickley.	First N.B.
13700.	Latrobe.	First N.B.
13701.	Pittsburgh.	Pitt N.B.
13754.	Peckville.	First N.B.
13765.	McConnellsburg.	Fulton County N.B.
13772.	Scottdale.	First N.B.
13781.	Johnstown.	United States N.B.
13794.	Derry.	First N.B.
13803.	Sharon.	First N.B.
13812.	Harrisville.	First N.B.
13813.	Canonsburg.	First N.B.
13823.	Wilkinsburg.	First N.B.
13826.	Freeport.	First N.B.
13845.	New Wilmington.	Depositors N.B.
13846.	Mercer.	Farmers N.B.
13852.	Wilkes-Barre.	Miners N.B.
13860.	Crafton.	Crafton N.B.
13863.	Strausston.	Strausston N.B.
13866.	Braddock.	First N.B.
13868.	Blairsville.	Blairsville N.B.
13869.	Finleyville.	First N.B.
13871.	Albion.	First N.B.
13873.	Waynesburg.	Union N.B.
13884.	Fredonia.	Fredonia N.B.
13887.	New Freedom.	First N.B.
13900.	Somerset.	Peoples N.B.
13907.	New Florence.	New Florence N.B.
13908.	Rural Valley.	Peoples N.B.
13917.	Birdsboro.	First N.B.
13927.	Fleetwood.	First N.B.
13937.	Dickson City.	First N.B.
13940.	Tarentum.	First N.B.
13942.	Conneautville.	Farmers N.B.
13947.	Scranton.	Scranton N.B.
13950.	Yardley.	Yardley N.B.
13957.	Reynoldsville.	Peoples N.B.
13967.	McKeesport.	Union N.B.
13970.	Freeland.	First N.B.
13980.	Conneaut Lake.	First N.B.
13982.	Herndon.	Herndon N.B.
13992.	Frackville.	First N.B.
13994.	Heggins.	First N.B.
13998.	Clearfield.	County N.B.
13999.	Berwyn.	Berwyn N.B.
14007.	Bethlehem.	Bethlehem N.B.
14023.	Kingston.	Kingston N.B.
14029.	Cambridge Springs.	Springs-First N.B.
14031.	Tower City.	Tower City N.B.
14037.	Ambler.	Ambler N.B.
14043.	Clarion.	First N.B.
14049.	Dover.	Dover N.B.
14051.	Export.	First N.B.
14055.	Greensburg.	First N.B.
14067.	Rockwood.	Union N.B.
14070.	Koppel.	First N.B.
14071.	Jefferson.	Codorus N.B.
14079.	Olyphant.	N.B. of Olyphant.
14082.	Windber.	Citizens N.B.
14089.	Stoystown.	First N.B.
14091.	East Berlin.	East Berlin N.B.
14093.	Union City.	N.B. of Union City.
14094.	Cecil.	First N.B.
14098.	Indiana.	First N.B.
14107.	McKees Rocks.	First N.B.
14112.	Wampum.	First N.B.
14117.	Beaver Falls.	First N.B.
14120.	Philadelphia.	N.B. of Olney.
14121.	Mount Wolf.	Union N.B.
14122.	Clifton Heights.	Clifton Heights N.B.
14123.	Charleroi.	First N.B.
14133.	Latrobe.	Commercial N.B.

Charter Number	City	Name of Bank
14139.	Narberth.	N.B. of Narberth.
14155.	Ford City.	N.B. of Ford City.
14156.	Hooversville.	Hooversville N.B.
14169.	Sykesville.	First N.B.
14170.	Bangor.	First N.B.
14171.	Philadelphia.	South Philadelphia N.B.
14181.	Gallitzin.	First N.B.
14182.	Williamsburg.	First N.B.
14191.	Girard.	Girard N.B.
14197.	Philadelphia.	Northwestern N.B.
14201.	Delta.	Delta N.B.
14205.	Forest City.	First and Farmers N.B.
14210.	Pittsburgh.	Keystone N.B.
14214.	Green Lane.	First N.B.
14215.	Zelienople.	Union N.B.
14219.	Erie.	N.B. and Trust Co.
14239.	Bedford.	Hartley N.B.
14250.	Hamburg.	N.B. of Hamburg.
14251.	Bridgeville.	Bridgeville N.B.
14262.	Pottsville.	City N.B.
14263.	Patton.	First N.B.
14271.	Pittsburgh.	N.B. of America.
14274.	Oil City.	Oil City N.B.
14276.	Marietta.	Exchange N.B.
14277.	Reading.	Union N.B.
14284.	Bedford.	First N.B.
14293.	Shenandoah.	Union N.B.
14301.	Gratz.	Gratz N.B.
14333.	Masontown.	Second N.B.
14344.	Wilkes-Barre.	Hanover N.B.
14345.	Youngsville.	Youngsville N.B.

PORTO RICO

Charter Number	City	Name of Bank
6484.	San Juan.	First N.B. of Porto Rico.

RHODE ISLAND

Charter Number	City	Name of Bank
134.	Providence.	First N.B.
565.	Providence.	Second N.B.
636.	Providence.	Third N.B.
673.	Warren.	First N.B.
772.	Providence.	Fourth N.B.
823.	Westerly.	Nat. Niantic Bank.
843.	Pawtucket.	First N.B.
856.	Pawtucket.	Slater N.B.
948.	Providence.	Phenix N.B.
952.	Westerly.	Washington N.B.
970.	Woonsocket.	Citizens' N.B.
983.	Providence.	Rhode Island N.B.
1002.	Providence.	Fifth N.B.
1007.	Providence.	Mechanics' N.B.
1008.	Warren.	Nat. Hope Bank.
1021.	Newport.	First N.B.
1030.	Providence.	Nat. Eagle Bank.
1035.	Slatersville, Smithfield.	First N.B.
1036.	Providence.	N.B. of North America.
1054.	Hopkinton.	First N.B.
1058.	Woonsocket.	Woonsocket N.B.
1126.	Providence.	Globe N.B.
1131.	Providence.	Merchants' N.B.
1150.	Ashaway.	Ashaway N.B.
1151.	Providence.	Old N.B.
1158.	Kingston.	Nat. Landholders' Bank.
1161.	Anthony.	Coventry N.B.
1169.	Westerly.	Nat. Phenix Bank.
1173.	Providence.	Weybosset N.B.
1206.	Wakefield.	Wakefield N.B.
1283.	Providence.	Manufacturers' N.B.
1284.	West Warwick.	Centreville N.B. of Warwick.
1292.	Bristol.	First N.B.
1302.	Providence.	Providence N.B.
1319.	Providence.	Commercial N.B.
1328.	Providence.	Blackstone Canal N.B.
1339.	Providence.	Nat. Exchange Bank.
1366.	Providence.	N.B. of Commerce.
1369.	Providence.	Lime Rock N.B.
1396.	Providence.	Traders' N.B.
1401.	Woonsocket.	First N.B.
1404.	Cumberland.	Cumberland N.B.
1405.	East Greenwich.	Greenwich N.B.
1409.	Woonsocket.	Nat. Union Bank.
1419.	Warren.	Nat. Warren Bank.
1421.	Woonsocket.	Producers' N.B.
1423.	Woonsocket.	Nat. Globe Bank.
1429.	Providence.	City N.B.
1460.	Phenix.	Phenix N.B.
1472.	Providence.	American N.B.
1492.	Newport.	Newport N.B.
1498.	Greenville.	Nat. Exchange Bank.
1506.	Providence.	Roger Williams N.B.
1512.	Pascoag.	Pascoag N.B.
1532.	Newport.	N.B. of Rhode Island.
1546.	Newport.	Aquidneck N.B.
1552.	Scituate, North Scituate.	Scituate N.B.
1554.	Wakefield.	Nat. Exchange Bank.
1562.	Bristol.	Nat. Eagle Bank.
1565.	Newport.	Nat. Exchange Bank.
1592.	Wickford.	Wickford N.B.
1616.	Pawtucket.	Pacific N.B.
2554.	Newport.	Union N.B.
2913.	Providence.	Atlantic N.B.
5925.	Providence.	United N.B.
13901.	Providence.	Rhode Island Hospital N.B.
13981.	Providence.	Columbus N.B.

SOUTH CAROLINA

Charter Number	City	Name of Bank
1621.	Charleston.	Peoples' N.B.
1622.	Charleston.	First N.B.
1680.	Columbia.	Carolina N.B.
1765.	Columbia.	Central N.B.
1804.	Chester.	N.B. of Chester.
1844.	Newberry.	N.B. of Newberry.
1848.	Spartanburg.	First N.B.
1935.	Greenville.	First N.B.
2044.	Charleston.	N.B. of Charleston Assn.
2060.	Union.	Merchants and Planters' N.B.
2072.	Anderson.	N.B. of Anderson.
2087.	Winnsboro.	Winnsboro N.B.
2512.	Darlington.	Darlington N.B.
3082.	Sumter.	N.B. of Sumter.
3421.	Abbeville.	N.B. of Abbeville.
3540.	Laurens.	N.B. of Laurens.
3616.	Rock Hill.	First N.B.
3809.	Sumter.	First N.B.
4996.	Spartanburg.	Central N.B.
5004.	Greenville.	City N.B.
5064.	Gaffney.	First N.B.
5134.	Rock Hill.	Nat. Union Bank.
5269.	Orangeburg.	First N.B.
5595.	Batesburg.	First N.B.
6102.	Whitmire.	First N.B.
6385.	Bennettsville.	Planters' N.B.
6658.	Spartanburg.	American N.B.
6871.	Columbia.	Nat. Loan and Exchange Bank.
6931.	York.	First N.B.
6994.	Prosperity.	People's N.B.
7027.	Greenwood.	Nat. Loan and Exchange Bank.
7858.	Lancaster.	First N.B.
8041.	Clinton.	First N.B.
8133.	Columbia.	Palmetto N.B.
8471.	Chester.	Nat. Exchange Bank.
8766.	Greenville.	Norwood N.B.
9057.	Leesville.	N.B. of Leesville.
9083.	Camden.	First N.B.
9104.	Anderson.	Citizens' N.B.
9190.	Greenville.	Fourth N.B.
9296.	Lexington.	Home N.B.
9342.	Cheraw.	First N.B.
9407.	Rock Hill.	People's N.B.
9533.	Sharon.	First N.B.
9650.	Aiken.	First N.B.
9687.	Columbia.	Liberty N.B. of S.C.
9690.	Conway.	First N.B.
9742.	Union.	Citizens' N.B.
9747.	Florence.	First N.B.
9849.	Walterboro.	First N.B.
9876.	Mullins.	First N.B.
9941.	Fort Mill.	First N.B.
9999.	Darlington.	Carolina N.B.
10085.	Marion.	Marion N.B.
10129.	Sumter.	City N.B.
10137.	Hartsville.	First N.B.
10263.	Bishopville.	First N.B.
10315.	Columbia.	Nat. State Bank.
10485.	Wagener.	First N.B.
10536.	Conway.	Conway N.B.
10537.	Conway.	People's N.B.
10543.	Charleston.	Commercial N.B.
10586.	Springfield.	First N.B.
10593.	Woodruff.	First N.B.
10597.	Columbia.	People's N.B.
10605.	Laurens.	Enterprise N.B.
10635.	Greenville.	People's N.B.
10650.	Orangeburg.	Edisto N.B.
10651.	Saint Matthews.	Saint Matthews N.B.
10652.	Laurens.	Laurens N.B.
10655.	Gaffney.	Merchants and Planters' N.B.
10660.	Sumter.	N.B. of South Carolina.
10663.	Chester.	People's N.B.
10670.	Sumter.	N.B. of Sumter.
10674.	Orangeburg.	Orangeburg N.B.
10679.	Elloree.	First N.B.
10680.	Holly Hill.	First N.B.
10681.	Lake City.	Farmers and Merchants' N.B.
10699.	Chester.	Citizens' N.B.
10708.	Charleston.	Atlantic N.B.
10743.	Bennettsville.	People's N.B.
10748.	Olanta.	First N.B.
10798.	Saluda.	First N.B.
10802.	Saluda.	Planters' N.B.
10815.	Batesburg.	Citizens' N.B.
10832.	Brunson.	First N.B.
10859.	Laurens.	Farmers' N.B.
10872.	Bishopville.	Bishopville N.B.
10908.	Dillon.	First N.B.
10979.	Fairf ax.	First N.B.
11080.	Lamar.	Lamar N.B.
11111.	Allendale.	First N.B.
11153.	Clio.	First N.B.
11155.	Manning.	First N.B.
11189.	Norway.	Farmers' N.B.
11287.	Barnwell.	First N.B.
11439.	Clover.	First N.B.
11499.	Greenville.	Woodside N.B.
11562.	Bowman.	N.B. of Bowman.
11704.	Bamberg.	First N.B.
11914.	North.	First N.B.
12025.	Greer.	First N.B.
12146.	Spartanburg.	Carolina N.B.
12175.	Anderson.	Carolina N.B.
12233.	Saint George.	First N.B.
12273.	Charleston.	Dime N.B.
12381.	Honea Path.	N.B. of Honea Path.
12412.	Columbia.	Columbia N.B.
12668.	Fairfax.	Nat. Security Bank.
12702.	Charleston.	Exchange N.B.
12774.	Prosperity.	Citizens' N.B.
12799.	Florence.	First N.B.
12865.	Charleston.	Norwood-Carolina N.B.
13720.	Columbia.	First N.B.
13918.	Orangeburg.	First N.B.
14135.	Orangeburg.	Southern N.B.
14211.	Spartanburg.	Commercial N.B.
14341.	Mullins.	Davis N.B.

SOUTH DAKOTA

Charter Number	City	Name of Bank
2068.	Yankton.	First N.B.
2391.	Deadwood.	First N.B.
2461.	Deadwood.	Merchants' N.B.
2465.	Sioux Falls.	First N.B.
2645.	Mitchell.	First N.B.
2819.	Huron.	First N.B.
2823.	Sioux Falls.	Sioux Falls N.B.
2830.	Canton.	First N.B.
2843.	Sioux Falls.	Dakota N.B.
2911.	Chamberlain.	First N.B.
2935.	Watertown.	First N.B.
2941.	Pierre.	First N.B.
2980.	Aberdeen.	First N.B.
2989.	Huron.	Beadle County N.B.
3087.	Brookings.	First N.B.
3130.	Plankinton.	First N.B.
3149.	Madison.	First N.B.
3151.	Madison.	Citizens' N.B.
3237.	Rapid City.	First N.B.
3267.	Huron.	Huron N.B.
3326.	Aberdeen.	Aberdeen N.B.
3349.	Watertown.	Citizens' N.B.
3352.	Columbia.	First N.B.
3393.	Sioux Falls.	Minnehaha N.B.
3398.	Redfield.	First N.B.
3401.	Rapid City.	Black Hills N.B.
3414.	Watertown.	Watertown N.B.
3435.	De Smet.	First N.B.
3437.	Ashton.	First N.B.
3479.	Clark.	First N.B.
3508.	Dell Rapids.	First N.B.
3522.	Redfield.	Merchants' N.B.
3552.	Deadwood.	Deadwood N.B.
3578.	Mitchell.	Mitchell N.B.
3586.	Sioux Falls.	Citizens' N.B.
3597.	Madison.	Madison N.B.
3636.	Huron.	N.B. of Dakota.
3675.	Parker.	First N.B.
3739.	Sturgis.	First N.B.
3932.	Aberdeen.	Northwestern N.B.
4104.	Pierre.	Pierre N.B.
4237.	Fort Pierre.	First N.B.
4279.	Pierre.	N.B. of Commerce.
4282.	Chamberlain.	Chamberlain N.B.
4370.	Hot Springs.	First N.B.
4448,	Custer City.	First N.B.
4603.	Vermillion.	First N.B.
4613.	Yankton.	Yankton N.B.
4629.	Sioux Falls.	Union N.B.
4631.	Lead.	First N.B.
4637.	Canton.	N.B. of Canton.
4874.	Spearfish.	First N.B.
4983.	Deadwood.	American N.B.
5355.	De Smet.	De Smet N.B.
5428.	Sisseton.	First N.B.
5477.	Centerville.	First N.B.
5854.	Flandreau.	First N.B.
5898.	Salem.	First N.B.
5901.	Elk Point.	First N.B.
5916.	Arlington.	First N.B.
5918.	Alexandria.	First N.B.
5946.	Woonsocket.	First N.B.
6000.	Castlewood.	First N.B.
6073.	Britton.	First N.B.
6099.	Volga.	First N.B.
6124.	Waubay.	First N.B.
6181.	Freeman.	First N.B.
6185.	White Rock.	First N.B.
6256.	Redfield.	Redfield N.B.
6294.	White.	First N.B.
6339.	Hot Springs.	Hot Springs N.B.
6357.	Clear Lake.	First N.B.
6368.	Elkton.	First N.B.
6381.	Toronto.	First N.B.
6395.	Sisseton.	Citizens' N.B.
6409.	Clark.	Clark County N.B.
6446.	Wessington Springs	First N.B.
6462.	Brookings.	Farmers' N.B.
6473.	Milbank.	First N.B.
6502.	Webster.	First N.B.
6561.	Belle Fourche.	First N.B.
6585.	Howard.	First N.B.
6688.	Colman.	First N.B.
6789.	Miller.	First N.B.
6792.	Tyndall.	First N.B.
6925.	Bridgewater.	First N.B.
6990.	Sturgis.	Commercial N.B.
7048.	Scotland.	First N.B.
7134.	White.	Farmers' N.B.
7252.	Egan.	First N.B.
7335.	Hudson.	First N.B.
7352.	Vermillion.	Vermillion N.B.
7426.	Bridgewater.	Farmers' N.B.
7455.	Mitchell.	Western N.B.
7504.	Watertown.	Security N.B.
7582.	Mount Vernon.	First N.B.
7597.	Vienna.	First N.B.
7662.	Parkston.	First N.B.

Charter Number	City	Name of Bank
7686.	South Shore.	First N.B.
7755.	Garretson.	First N.B.
7794.	Highmore.	First N.B.
7885.	Groton.	First N.B.
7968.	Wakonda.	First N.B.
8012.	Armour.	First N.B.
8125.	Redfield.	American N.B.
8248.	Spearfish.	American N.B.
8291.	White Lake.	First N.B.
8325.	Wessington.	First N.B.
8332.	White Lake.	United States N.B.
8480.	Bristol.	First N.B.
8550.	Chamberlain.	Brule N.B.
8559.	Webster.	Farmers and Merchants' N.B.
8600.	Gregory.	First N.B.
8624.	Frederick.	First N.B.
8642.	Aberdeen.	Dakota N.B.
8698.	Milbank.	Farmers and Merchants' N.B.
8711.	Fairfax.	First N.B.
8776.	Gettysburg.	First N.B.
8781.	Huron.	City N.B.
8841.	Huron.	N.B. of Huron.
8942.	Springfield.	First N.B.
9166.	Hot Springs.	People's N.B.
9188.	Letcher.	First N.B.
9269.	Lemmon.	First N.B.
9283.	McIntosh.	First N.B.
9301.	Chamberlain.	Whitbeck N.B.
9376.	Selby.	First N.B.
9377.	Gregory.	Gregory N.B.
9393.	Gary.	First N.B.
9445.	Yankton.	Dakota N.B.
9587.	Fort Pierre.	Fort Pierre N.B.
9679.	Hecla.	First N.B.
9693.	Dell Rapids.	Home N.B.
9817.	Morristown.	First N.B.
9858.	Veblen.	First N.B.
9915.	Sioux Falls.	American N.B.
9958.	Pukwana.	First N.B.
10098.	Kennebec.	First N.B.
10187.	Alexandria.	Security N.B.
10256.	Oldham.	First N.B.
10416.	Henry.	First N.B.
10553.	Sioux Falls.	Scandinavian- American N.B.
10592.	Sioux Falls.	Security N.B.
10636.	Madison.	Lake County N.B.
10637.	Midland.	First N.B.
10683.	Frankfort.	First N.B.
10714.	Lake Norden.	First N.B.
10744.	Mobridge.	First N.B.
10758.	Lake Preston.	First N.B.
10772.	Bryant.	First N.B.
10773.	Lake Preston.	Farmers' N.B.
10774.	Florence.	First N.B.
10780.	Howard.	Howard N.B.
10797.	Goodwin.	First N.B.
10800.	Hayti.	First N.B.
10808.	Viborg.	First N.B.
10813.	Beresford.	First N.B.
10818.	Alcester.	Farmers and Merchants' N.B.
10822.	Alcester.	Alcester N.B.
10833.	Carthage.	First N.B.
10846.	Gary.	N.B. of Gary.
10868.	Bristol.	Citizens' N.B.
10893.	Brandt.	First N.B.
10961.	Faulkton.	First N.B.
11031.	Scotland.	Corn Belt N.B.
11119.	Winner.	First N.B.
11237.	Pollock.	First N.B.
11323.	Menno.	First N.B.
11341.	Sisseton.	Security N.B.
11399.	Wilmot.	First N.B.
11441.	Wetonka.	First N.B.
11456.	Farmer.	First N.B.
11457.	Davis.	First N.B.
11506.	Eden.	First N.B.
11527.	Eureka.	First N.B.
11558.	Garden City.	First N.B.
11585.	Onida.	First N.B.
11590.	Mobridge.	Security N.B.
11637.	Tyndall.	Citizens' N.B.
11653.	Yankton.	N.B. of Commerce.
11689.	South Shore.	Farmers' N.B.
11812.	Emery.	Security N.B.
12024.	Winner.	Winner N.B.
12325.	Fairfax.	Farmers' N.B.
12374.	Webster.	Dakota N.B.
12488.	Sherman.	First N.B.
12547.	Saint Lawrence.	First N.B.
12611.	Alexandria.	First N.B.
12620.	Wessington Springs.	N.B. of Wessington Springs.
12662.	Oldham.	Oldham N.B.
12777.	Onida.	Onida N.B.
12784.	Salem.	McCook County N.B.
12838,	Brookings.	Security N.B.
12857.	Lemmon.	New First N.B.
12872.	Dell Rapids.	New First N.B.
12877.	Clear Lake.	Deuel County N.B.
12881.	Sioux Falls.	Citizens' N.B.
12888.	Wessington.	Citizens' N.B.
12920.	Howard.	New First N.B.
13061.	Ree Heights.	First N.B.
13181.	Brookings.	Brookings N.B.
13221.	Lake Norden.	Lake Norden N.B.
13282.	Mount Vernon.	First N.B.
13286.	Arlington.	First N.B.
13302.	Fairfax.	Farmers N.B.
13346.	Vermillion.	First N.B. and Trust Co.
13407.	Milbank.	Farmers and Merchants N.B.
13430.	Philip.	First N.B.
13459.	Leola.	First N.B.
13460.	Britton.	First N.B.
13466.	Hyron.	Security N.B.
13467.	Mobridge.	First N.B.
13477.	Bison.	First N.B.
13483.	Chamberlain.	First N.B. and Trust Co.
13517.	Madison.	Northwestern N.B.
13549.	Ethan.	First N.B.
13589.	Viborg.	Security N.B.
14099.	Rapid City.	Rapid City N.B.
14252.	Pierre.	First N.B.

TENNESSEE

Charter Number	City	Name of Bank
150.	Nashville.	First N.B.
336.	Memphis.	First N.B.
391.	Knoxville.	First N.B.
771.	Nashville.	Second N.B.
1225.	Memphis.	Tennessee N.B.
1296.	Nashville.	Third N.B.
1407.	Memphis.	Merchants' N.B.
1603.	Clarksville.	First N.B.
1606.	Chattanooga.	First N.B.
1636.	Memphis.	German N.B.
1664.	Lebanon.	N.B. of Lebanon.
1666.	Cleveland.	Cleveland N.B.
1669.	Nashville.	Fourth and First N.B.
1692.	Murfreesboro.	First N.B.
1707.	Gallatin.	First N.B.
1708.	Lebanon.	Second N.B.
1713.	Columbia.	First N.B.
1727.	Pulaski.	N.B. of Pulaski.
1746.	Chattanooga.	City N.B.
1834.	Franklin.	N.B. of Franklin.
1990.	Pulaski.	Giles N.B.
2000.	Murfreesboro.	Stones River N.B.
2019.	Springfield.	Springfield N.B.
2049.	Knoxville.	East Tennessee N.B.
2096.	Memphis.	Fourth N.B.
2114.	Fayetteville.	First N.B.
2127.	Memphis.	Central State N.B.
2167.	Bristol.	First N.B.
2168.	Jackson.	First N.B.
2198.	Shelbyville.	N.B. of Shelbyville.
2200.	Nashville.	Mechanics' N.B.
2221.	McMinnville.	First N.B.
2513.	Nashville.	Merchants' N.B.
2559.	Chattanooga.	Third N.B.
2568.	Columbia.	Second N.B.
2593.	McMinnville.	People's N.B.
2635.	Pulaski.	People's N.B.
2658.	Knoxville.	Mechanics' N.B.
2720.	Clarksville.	Clarksville N.B.
2796.	Bristol.	First N.B.
3032.	Nashville.	American N.B.
3062.	Franklin.	Farmers' N.B.
3107.	Tullahoma.	First N.B.
3228.	Nashville.	Commercial N.B.
3241.	Clarksville.	Farmers and Merchants' N.B.
3288.	Centreville.	First N.B.
3341.	Athens.	First N.B.
3432.	Morristown.	First N.B.
3530.	Shelbyville.	People's N.B.
3576.	Jackson.	Second N.B.
3614.	Sparta.	First N.B.
3633.	Memphis.	Memphis N.B.
3660.	South Pittsburg.	First N.B.
3691.	Chattanooga.	Chattanooga N.B.
3702.	Fayetteville.	Elk N.B.
3708.	Knoxville.	Third N.B.
3837.	Knoxville.	City N.B.
3919.	Union City.	First N.B.
3951.	Johnson City.	First N.B.
4015.	Rogersville.	Rogersville N.B.
4020.	Tullahoma.	Traders' N.B.
4060.	Chattanooga.	Fourth N.B.
4102.	Knoxville.	State N.B.
4169.	Rockwood.	First N.B.
4177.	Greeneville.	First N.B.
4236.	Gallatin.	First N.B.
4303.	Cardiff.	First N.B.
4307.	Memphis.	Continental N.B.
4362.	Dayton.	First N.B.
4442.	Union City.	Farmers and Merchants' N.B.
4456.	Chattanooga.	Merchants' N.B.
4501.	Harriman.	First N.B.
4648.	Knoxville.	Holston N.B.
4654.	Harriman.	Manufacturers' N.B.
4679.	Pulaski.	Citizens' N.B.
4715.	Jonesboro.	First N.B.
4849.	Columbia.	Maury N.B.
5056.	Memphis.	N.B. of Commerce.
5263.	Dyersburg.	First N.B.
5528.	Manchester.	First N.B.
5536.	Gainesboro.	First N.B.
5545.	Gallatin.	First and People's N.B.
5617.	Martin.	First N.B.
5679.	Dayton.	American N.B.
5754.	Lebanon.	American N.B.
5888.	Johnson City.	Unaka N.B.
5963.	Waverly.	First N.B.
6042.	Brownsville.	First N.B.
6076.	Pulaski.	Nat. People's Bank.
6093.	Lawrenceburg.	First N.B.
6189.	Springfield.	People's N.B.
6236.	Johnson City.	Unaka and City N.B.
6729.	Nashville.	Merchants' N.B.
6930.	Dickson.	First N.B.
7225.	La Follette.	N.B. of La Follette.
7314.	Tracy City.	First N.B.
7397.	Decherd.	First N.B. of Franklin Co.
7636.	Jellico.	N.B. of Jellico.
7665.	Jellico.	First N.B.
7740.	Tazewell.	Claiborne N.B.
7817.	Chattanooga.	American N.B.
7834.	McMinnville.	American N.B.
7848.	Chattanooga.	Hamilton N.B.
7870.	Columbia.	Phoenix N.B.
7912.	Sparta.	American N.B.
7928.	Carthage.	First N.B.
8025.	Morristown.	City N.B.
8039.	Oneida.	First N.B.
8292.	Dickson.	Citizens' N.B.
8406.	Trenton.	First N.B.
8443.	Franklin.	Harpeth N.B.
8506.	Camden.	First N.B.
8555.	Fayetteville.	Elk N.B.
8558.	Lynnville.	First N.B.
8601.	Huntland.	First N.B.
8631.	Winchester.	American N.B.
8640.	Winchester.	Farmers' N.B.
8673.	Lenoir City.	First N.B.
8714.	Lebanon.	Lebanon N.B.
8836.	Selmer.	First N.B.
8889.	Savannah.	First N.B.
8934.	Lewisburg.	First N.B.
9027.	Copperhill.	First N.B. of Polk Co.
9089.	Woodbury.	First N.B.
9112.	Martin.	City N.B.
9162.	Etowah.	First N.B.
9176.	Chattanooga.	Citizens' N.B.
9184.	Memphis.	Nat. City Bank.
9239.	Union City.	Third N.B.
9319.	Mount Pleasant.	First N.B.
9331.	Waverly.	Citizens' N.B.
9334.	Paris.	First N.B.
9470.	Spring City.	First N.B.
9532.	Nashville.	Tennessee- Hermitage N.B.
9558.	Elizabethton.	First N.B.
9565.	Ducktown.	First N.B.
9627.	Wartrace.	First N.B.
9629.	Union City.	Old N.B.
9632.	Newport.	First N.B.
9659.	Nashville.	Cumberland Valley N.B.
9667.	Cookeville.	First N.B.
9692.	Cookeville.	Cookeville N.B.
9720.	Erwin.	First N.B.
9774.	Nashville.	Broadway N.B.
9807.	Smyrna.	First N.B.
9809.	Crossville.	First N.B.
9827.	Centerville.	Citizens' N.B.
10028.	Coal Creek.	First N.B.
10181.	Linden.	First N.B.
10190.	Doyle.	First N.B.
10192.	Huntsville.	First N.B.
10198.	Fayetteville.	Farmers' N.B.
10306.	Petersburg.	First N.B.
10327.	Knoxville.	American N.B.
10334.	Jackson.	Security N.B.
10401.	Knoxville.	Union N.B.
10404.	Kenton.	First N.B.
10449.	Ripley.	First N.B.
10470.	Pikeville.	First N.B.
10491.	Covington.	First N.B.
10508.	Russellville.	First N.B.
10540.	Memphis.	Mercantile N.B.
10542.	Maryville.	First N.B.
10577.	Dickson.	Dickson N.B.
10583.	Erwin.	Erwin N.B.
10622.	Nashville.	Tennessee N.B.
10735.	Athens.	Citizens' N.B.
10785.	Shelbyville.	Farmers' N.B.
10842.	Kingsport.	First N.B.
10976.	Elizabethton.	Holston N.B.
11202.	Sweetwater.	First N.B.
11479.	Jefferson City.	First N.B.
11839.	Johnson City.	Tennessee N.B.
11915.	Harriman.	Harriman N.B.
11985.	Hohenwald.	First N.B.
11998.	Oliver Springs.	Tri-County N.B.
12031.	Harriman.	First N.B.
12080.	Loudon.	First N.B.
12257.	Rockwood.	Rockwood N.B.
12264.	Rockwood.	City N.B.
12276.	Nashville.	Central N.B.
12319.	Kingston.	First N.B.
12324.	Lexington.	First N.B.
12348.	Memphis.	Southern N.B.
12438.	Trenton.	Citizens' N.B.
12440.	Sevierville.	First N.B.
12467.	La Follette.	People's N.B.
12469.	Johnson City.	Washington County N.B.
12484.	La Follette.	Farmers' N.B.
12639.	Springfield.	First N.B.
12790.	Jackson.	N.B. of Commerce.
13056.	Smithville.	First N.B.
13077.	Big Sandy.	First N.B.
13103.	Nashville.	Third N.B.
13349.	Memphis.	Union Planters N.B. and Trust Co.
13482.	Greeneville.	Citizens N.B.
13539.	Knoxville.	Hamilton N.B.
13635.	Johnson City.	Hamilton N.B.
13640.	Bristol.	First N.B.
13654.	Chattanooga.	Chattanooga N.B.
13681.	Memphis.	N.B. of Commerce.
13746.	Chattanooga.	Commercial N.B.
13948.	Fayetteville.	Union N.B.
14231.	Rockwood.	First N.B.
14279.	Maryville.	Blount N.B.

Charter Number	City	Name of Bank
		TEXAS
1566.	Galveston.	First N.B.
1642.	Galveston.	N.B. of Texas.
1644.	Houston.	First N.B.
1657.	San Antonio.	San Antonio N.B.
1777.	Jefferson.	N.B. of Jefferson.
2092.	Houston.	Nat. Exchange Bank.
2099.	Denison.	First N.B.
2118.	Austin.	First N.B.
2157.	Dallas.	First N.B.
2189.	Waco.	First N.B.
2349.	Fort Worth.	First N.B.
2359.	Fort Worth.	City N.B.
2455.	Dallas.	City N.B.
2477.	Weatherford.	First N.B.
2486.	Laredo.	Milmo N.B.
2521.	El Paso.	State N.B.
2532.	El Paso.	First N.B.
2617.	Austin.	State N.B.
2689.	Fort Worth.	Traders' N.B.
2723.	Weatherford.	Citizens' N.B.
2729.	McKinney.	First N.B.
2735.	Belton.	First N.B.
2767.	San Angelo.	First N.B.
2801.	Colorado.	Colorado N.B.
2802.	Gainesville.	Gainesville N.B.
2812.	Denton.	First N.B.
2836.	Gainesville.	First N.B.
2867.	Honey Grove.	First N.B.
2883.	San Antonio.	Traders' N.B.
2893.	Colorado.	First N.B.
2909.	McKinney.	Collin County N.B.
2937.	Brownwood.	First N.B.
2939.	Ennis.	Ennis N.B.
2940.	Decatur.	First N.B.
2949.	Denton.	Exchange N.B.
2974.	Waxahachie.	First N.B.
2982.	Cleburne.	First N.B.
2998.	Greenville.	First N.B.
3007.	Burnet.	First N.B.
3008.	Dallas.	Dallas N.B.
3014.	Mexia.	First N.B.
3015.	Brenham.	First N.B.
3016.	Greenville.	Hunt County N.B.
3022.	Henrietta.	Henrietta N.B.
3027.	Taylor.	First N.B.
3046.	Hillsboro.	Hill County N.B.
3058.	Denison.	State N.B.
3065.	Texarkana.	First N.B.
3094.	Bonham.	First N.B.
3113.	Marshall.	First N.B.
3131.	Fort Worth.	Fort Worth N.B.
3132.	Dallas.	American N.B.
3135.	Waco.	Citizens' N.B.
3159.	Sherman.	Merchants and Planters' N.B.
3165.	Montague.	First N.B.
3195.	Abilene.	First N.B.
3200.	Wichita Falls.	First N.B.
3212.	Waxahachie.	Citizens' N.B.
3221.	Fort Worth.	State N.B.
3227.	Temple.	First N.B.
3229.	Gainesville.	Red River N.B.
3248.	Alban .	First N.B.
3260.	San Angelo.	San Angelo N.B.
3261.	Lampasas.	First N.B.
3286.	Baird.	First N.B.
3289.	Austin.	City N.B.
3295.	Belton.	Belton N.B.
3298.	San Antonio.	Texas N.B.
3336.	Abilene.	Abilene N.B.
3344.	San Marcos.	Wood N.B.
3346.	San Marcos.	First N.B.
3433.	Coleman.	First N.B.
3446.	Bryan.	First N.B.
3466.	Sulphur Springs.	First N.B.
3506.	Corsicana.	First N.B.
3517.	Houston.	Commercial N.B.
3532.	Ennis.	People's N.B.
3533.	Ballinger.	First N.B.
3561.	Comanche.	First N.B.
3608.	El Paso.	El Paso N.B. of Texas.
3623.	Dallas.	American Exchange N.B.
3624.	Farmersville.	First N.B.
3631.	Fort Worth.	Merchants' N.B.
3638.	Paris.	First N.B.
3644.	Alvarado.	First N.B.
3645.	Corsicana.	Corsicana N.B.
3646.	Greenville.	Greenville N.B.
3651.	Tyler.	First N.B.
3664.	Dallas.	State N.B.
3694.	Palestine.	First N.B.
3727.	Granbury.	First N.B.
3738.	San Antonio.	Lockwood N.B.
3742.	Calvert.	First N.B.
3762.	Hillsboro.	Farmers' N.B.
3764.	Plano.	Plano N.B.
3785.	Texarkana.	Texarkana N.B.
3786.	Hillsboro.	Sturgis N.B.
3816.	Terrell.	First N.B.
3834.	Dallas.	North Texas N.B.
3836.	Kaufman.	First N.B.
3858.	Temple.	Temple N.B.
3859.	Taylor.	Taylor N.B.
3890.	Rockwall.	First N.B.
3901.	Waco.	American N.B.
3906.	La Grange.	First N.B.
3915.	Corsicana.	City N.B.
3973.	Clarksville.	First N.B.
3975.	Weatherford.	Merchants and Farmers' N.B.
3984.	Wolfe City.	Wolfe City N.B.
3985.	Dallas.	N.B. of Commerce.
3989.	Sulphur Springs.	City N.B.
3998.	Texarkana.	Interstate N.B.
4004.	Fort Worth.	Farmers and Mech N.B.
4014.	Forney.	N.B. of Forney.
4016.	Meridian.	First N.B.
4017.	Beaumont.	First N.B.
4021.	Commerce.	First N.B.
4028.	Houston.	Houston N.B.
4030.	Lockhart.	First N.B.
4033.	Vernon.	First N.B.
4035.	Cleburne.	N.B. of Cleburne.
4062.	Dublin.	First N.B.
4065.	Vernon.	Vernon N.B.
4070.	Bryan.	City N.B.
4076.	McGregor.	First N.B.
4077.	Longview.	First N.B.
4081.	Stephenville.	Erath County N.B.
4086.	Cameron.	First N.B.
4093.	Bastrop.	First N.B.
4095.	Stephenville.	First N.B.
4097.	Gatesville.	First N.B.
4101.	Marshall.	Marshall N.B.
4112.	Honey Grove.	Planters' N.B.
4116.	Decatur.	Wise County N.B.
4118.	Orange.	First N.B.
4127.	Dallas.	Central N.B.
4130.	Vernon.	State N.B.
4134.	Cisco.	First N.B.
4140.	Cuero.	First N.B.
4144.	Quanah.	First N.B.
4146.	Laredo.	Rio Grande N.B.
4153.	Galveston.	Galveston N.B.
4166.	Abilene.	Farmers and Merchants N.B.
4167.	Belton.	Citizens' N.B.
4175.	Rockdale.	First N.B.
4179.	Flatonia.	First N.B.
4184.	Victoria.	First N.B.
4193.	Ballinger.	Ballinger N.B.
4198	Brady.	First N.B.
4208.	Huntsville.	Gibbs N.B.
4213.	Dallas.	Bankers and Merchants' N.B.
4214.	Amarillo.	First N.B.
4231.	Bowie.	Bowie N.B.
4238.	Beeville.	First N.B.
4241.	Bellville.	First N.B.
4246.	Comanche.	Comanche N.B.
4248.	Wichita Falls.	City N.B. of Commerce.
4253.	Navasota.	First N.B.
4263.	Seymour.	First N.B.
4265.	Bowie.	First N.B.
4266.	Luling.	First N.B.
4269.	Groesbeeck.	Groesbeeck N.B.
4278.	Athens.	First N.B.
4289.	Van Alstyne.	First N.B.
4291.	Fairfield.	First N.B.
4294.	Georgetown.	First N.B.
4295.	New Braunfels.	First N.B.
4306.	Big Springs.	First N.B.
4308.	Austin.	Austin N.B.
4309.	Waco.	Provident N.B.
4311.	Ladonia.	First N.B.
4316.	Llano.	First N.B.
4321.	Galveston.	American N.B.
4322.	Austin.	American N.B.
4333.	Haskell.	First N.B.
4338.	Halletsville.	First N.B.
4344.	Brownwood.	Merchants' N.B.
4346.	Rusk.	First N.B.
4349.	Waco.	Farmers and Merchants' N.B.
4350.	Houston.	South Texas N.B.
4353.	Tyler.	City N.B.
4361.	Quanah.	City N.B.
4363.	Yoakum.	First N.B.
4366.	Hico.	First N.B.
4368.	Midland.	First N.B.
4371.	Llano.	Iron City N.B.
4379.	Waxahachie.	Waxahachie N.B.
4386.	Cleburne.	Farmers and Merchants' N.B.
4388.	Gatesville.	Citizens' N.B.
4389.	Grand View.	First N.B.
4391.	Graham.	First N.B.
4395.	Colorado.	Citizens' N.B.
4404.	Temple.	Bell County N.B.
4405.	Nacogdoches.	First N.B.
4410.	Giddings.	First N.B.
4411.	Paris.	City N.B.
4415.	Dallas.	Ninth N.B.
4418.	Graham.	First N.B.
4423.	Corpus Christi.	Corpus Christi N.B.
4436.	Palestine.	Palestine N.B.
4438.	Rockport.	First N.B.
4447.	Denison.	N.B. of Denison.
4451.	Hamilton.	Hamilton N.B.
4461.	Itasca.	First N.B.
4463.	Houston.	Planters and Mechanics' N.B.
4466.	Eastland.	Eastland N.B.
4474.	Haskell.	Haskell N.B.
4483.	Jacksboro.	First N.B.
4490.	Eagle Pass.	First N.B.
4492.	Kaufman.	Citizens' N.B.
4500.	Cooper.	First N.B.
4515.	Ladonia.	Weldon N.B.
4517.	Uvalde.	First N.B.
4525.	San Antonio.	Alamo N.B.
4540.	Bonham.	Bonham N.B.
4545.	Marble Falls.	First N.B.
4565.	Goliad.	First N.B.
4571.	Quanah.	Quanah N.B.
4577.	Brownsville.	First N.B.
4621.	Nocoma.	First N.B.
4659.	San Angelo.	Citizens' N.B.
4662.	Velasco.	Velasco N.B.
4682.	Detroit.	First N.B.
4683.	Coleman.	Coleman N.B.
4684.	Crockett.	First N.B.
4687.	Goldthwaite.	First N.B.
4692.	Whitewright.	First N.B.
4695.	Brownwood.	First N.B.
4701.	Daingerfield.	N.B. of Daingerfield.
4706.	Marlin.	First N.B.
4707.	Dallas.	Mercantile N.B.
4708.	Denton.	Denton County N.B.
4710.	Amarillo.	Amarillo N.B.
4717.	Rockwall.	Farmers and Merchants' N.B.
4721.	Jefferson.	State N.B.
4722.	Mount Pleasant.	First N.B.
4732.	Gatesville.	City N.B.
4747.	Tyler.	Tyler N.B.
4748.	San Antonio.	Fifth N.B.
4768.	Blooming Grove.	First N.B.
4777.	Pilot Point.	Pilot Point N.B.
4785.	Bowie.	City N.B.
4848.	Fort Worth.	American N.B.
4863.	Pittsburg.	First N.B.
4865.	Dublin.	Dublin N.B.
4866.	Beeville.	Commercial N.B.
4900.	Hillsboro.	Citizens' N.B.
4903.	Wharton.	First N.B.
4905.	Hempstead.	Farmers' N.B.
4911.	Rockwall.	Rockwall County N.B.
4922.	Atlanta.	First N.B.
4924.	Itasca.	Citizens' N.B.
4946.	Fort Worth.	Nat. Live Stock Bank.
4950.	Colorado.	People's N.B.
4976.	Hearne.	First N.B.
4982.	Clarksville.	Red River N.B.
4990.	Terrell.	American N.B.
5001.	Laredo.	Laredo N.B.
5008.	Hubbard.	First N.B.
5018.	Wills Point.	First N.B.
5035.	Greenville.	City N.B.
5060.	Eagle Pass.	Simpson N.B.
5078.	Dallas.	N.B. of Dallas.
5079.	Paris.	Paris N.B.
5097.	Seguin.	First N.B.
5109.	Leonard.	First N.B.
5127.	Mineola.	First N.B.
5146.	Bonham.	Fannin County N.B.
5175.	Uvalde.	Uvalde N.B.
5179.	San Antonio.	Frost N.B.
5181.	Eagle Pass.	Border N.B.
5190.	Navasota.	Citizens' N.B.
5192.	Sherman.	Grayson County N.B.
5201.	Beaumont.	Beaumont N.B.
5203.	Vernon.	Waggoner N.B.
5217.	San Antonio.	City N.B.
5238.	Canyon.	First N.B.
5239.	El Paso.	Lowdon N.B.
5275.	Taylor.	City N.B.
5276.	Colorado.	City N.B.
5288.	Gilmer.	First N.B.
5294.	Del Rio.	First N.B.
5324.	Celeste.	First N.B.
5325.	Saint Jo.	First N.B.
5338.	Nocona.	Nocona N.B.
5343.	Tyler.	Citizens' N.B.
5367.	Port Lavaca.	First N.B.
5399.	Moulton.	First N.B.
5409.	Mount Vernon.	First N.B.
5422.	Bartlett.	First N.B.
5439.	Grapevine.	Grapevine N.B.
5463.	Clarendon.	First N.B.
5466.	Sonora.	First N.B.
5475.	Plainview.	First N.B.
5483.	Wylie.	First N.B.
5484.	Cameron.	Citizens' N.B.
5485.	Port Arthur.	First N.B.
5491.	Lockhart.	Lockhart N.B.
5493.	Baird.	Home N.B.
5504.	McGregor.	Citizens' N.B.
5511.	Mineral Wells.	First N.B.
5513.	Rosebud.	First N.B.
5533.	Cooper.	Delta N.B.
5543.	West.	First N.B.
5549.	Venus.	First N.B.
5560.	Stamford.	First N.B.
5569.	Petty.	First N.B.
5580.	Snyder.	First N.B.
5581.	Jacksonville.	First N.B.
5589.	Iowa Park.	First N.B.
5604.	Hereford.	First N.B.
5606.	Marlin.	Marlin N.B.
5614.	Karnes City.	Karnes County N.B.
5628.	Shiner.	First N.B.
5636.	New Boston.	First N.B.
5645.	Lampasas.	Lampasas N.B.
5660.	De Leon.	First N.B.
5661.	Merkel.	First N.B.
5663.	Italy.	First N.B.
5665.	Decatur.	City N.B.
5670.	Howe.	Farmers' N.B.
5674.	Winnsboro.	First N.B.
5680.	Albany.	Albany N.B.
5681.	Howe.	First N.B.
5692.	Plano.	Farmers and Merchants' N.B.
5696.	Grand Saline.	N.B. of Grand Saline.

Charter Number	City	Name of Bank
5697.	Mexia.	Citizens' N.B.
5704.	Rogers.	First N.B.
5710.	Roxton.	First N.B.
5711.	Archer City.	First N.B.
5719.	Cumby.	First N.B.
5721.	Nevada.	First N.B.
5722.	Grand Saline.	First N.B.
5728.	Dodd City.	First N.B.
5733.	Blossom.	First N.B.
5737.	Trenton.	First N.B.
5739.	Ladonia.	Ladonia N.B.
5741.	Gilmer.	Farmers and Merchants' N.B.
5749.	Itasca.	Itasca N.B.
5750.	Killeen.	First N.B.
5759.	Gordon.	First N.B.
5761.	Lacksboro.	Citizens' N.B.
5765.	Hondo.	First N.B.
5774.	Moody.	First N.B.
5781.	Sweetwater.	First N.B.
5786.	Aspermont.	First N.B.
5795.	Glen Rose.	First N.B.
5797.	Lufkin.	Lufkin N.B.
5806.	Arlington.	Citizens' N.B.
5808.	Granbury.	City N.B.
5824.	Crandall.	First N.B.
5825.	Beaumont.	American N.B.
5836.	Dublin.	Citizens' N.B.
5841.	Beaumont.	Citizens' N.B.
5847.	Whitesboro.	First N.B.
5850.	Mart.	First N.B.
5853.	Llano.	Llano N.B.
5858.	Houston.	Merchants' N.B.
5864.	Sherman.	Commercial N.B.
5865.	Roby.	First N.B.
5882.	Thorndale.	First N.B.
5897.	Graham.	Graham N.B.
5904.	Seymour.	Favis N.B.
5932.	Kemp.	First N.B.
5938.	Crandall.	Citizens' N.B.
5953.	Crockett.	Farmers and Merchants' N.B.
5971.	Center.	First N.B.
5972.	Quanah.	State N.B.
5991.	Nacogdoches.	Commercial N.B.
5992.	Childress.	City N.B.
6001.	Throckmorton.	First N.B.
6009.	Lufkin.	Angelina County N.B.
6011.	Farmersville.	Farmers and Merchants' N.B.
6024.	Childress.	Childress N.B.
6040.	Center Point.	First N.B.
6043.	Longview.	Citizens' N.B.
6046.	Celina.	First N.B.
6050.	Orange.	Orange N.B.
6062.	Bay City.	First N.B.
6067.	Alvord.	Alvord N.B.
6069.	Blum.	First N.B.
6071.	Wills Point.	Van Zandt County N.B.
6078.	Forney.	City N.B.
6091.	Anson.	First N.B.
6092.	Goldthwaite.	Goldthwaite N.B.
6107.	Memphis.	First N.B.
6112.	El Campo.	First N.B.
6115.	Cisco.	Citizens' N.B.
6134.	Jasper.	First N.B.
6139.	Mount Pleasant.	State N.B.
6140.	Mesquite.	First N.B.
6150.	Gatesville.	Gatesville N.B.
6152.	Carthage.	Merchants and Farmers' N.B.
6168.	Winnsboro.	Farmers' N.B.
6169.	Livingston.	First N.B.
6176.	Henderson.	First N.B.
6177.	Timpson.	First N.B.
6195.	Lubbock.	First N.B.
6197.	Carthage.	First N.B.
6212.	Troupe.	First N.B.
6214.	San Augustine.	First N.B.
6223.	Lott.	First N.B.
6224.	Commerce.	Planters and Merchants' N.B.
6234.	Tyler.	Jester N.B.
6245.	San Augustine.	San Augustine N.B.
6247.	Morgan.	First N.B.
6271.	Enloe.	First N.B.
6277.	Gonzales.	Gonzales N.B.
6292.	Gainesville.	Lindsay N.B.
6298.	Tulia.	First N.B.
6300.	Collinsville.	First N.B.
6313.	Wharton.	Wharton N.B.
6317.	Temple.	City N.B.
6320.	Floresville.	First N.B.
6329.	Groveton.	First N.B.
6338.	Beaumont.	Gulf N.B.
6346.	Frisco.	First N.B.
6356.	Madisonville.	First N.B.
6361.	Granger.	First N.B.
6376.	Ferris.	Ferris N.B.
6390.	Sealy.	Sealy N.B.
6394.	Conroe.	First N.B.
6400.	Athens.	Athens N.B.
6402.	Crowell.	First N.B.
6404.	Gunter.	First N.B.
6410.	Midland.	Midland N.B.
6422.	Mabank.	First N.B.
6430.	Deport.	First N.B.
6461.	Groesbeck.	Citizens' N.B.
6471.	Italy.	Citizens' N.B.
6476.	Abilene.	Citizens' N.B.
6522.	Runge.	Runge N.B.
6551.	Royse.	First N.B.
6553.	Ferris.	Citizens' N.B.
6572.	Waco.	Nat. City Bank.
6596.	Nederland.	First N.B.
6605.	Lone Oak.	First N.B.
6607.	Caldwell.	Caldwell N.B.
6614.	Caldwell.	First N.B.
6627.	Nacogdoches.	Stone Fort N.B.
6668.	Big Springs.	West Texas N.B.
6679.	Rockwall.	Citizens' N.B.
6686.	Wortham.	First N.B.
6703.	Rockwall.	Rockwall N.B.
6757.	Ballinger.	Citizens' N.B.
6762.	Dalhart.	First N.B.
6780.	Henderson.	Farmers and Merchants' N.B.
6791.	Cleburne.	Citizens' N.B.
6807.	San Angelo.	Western and Lando N.B.
6810.	Sour Lake.	First N.B.
6812.	Hereford.	Western N.B.
6814.	Emory.	First N.B.
6822.	Fort Worth.	Stockyards N.B.
6826.	Canadian.	First N.B.
6831.	Uvalde.	Commercial N.B.
6856.	Sour Lake.	Sour Lake N.B.
6865.	Amarillo.	N.B. of Commerce.
6883.	Jacksonville.	Citizens' N.B.
6896.	Alba.	Alba N.B.
6915.	Whitewright.	Planters' N.B.
6922.	Hughes Springs.	First N.B.
6935.	Miles.	Miles N.B.
6956.	San Antonio.	N.B. of Commerce.
6966.	Burnet.	Burnet N.B.
6968.	Frost.	First N.B.
6987.	Yorktown.	First N.B.
6989.	Pearsall.	Pearsall N.B.
7002.	Brownsville.	Merchants' N.B.
7010.	Vernon.	Herring N.B.
7016.	Van Alstyne.	Farmers' N.B.
7028.	Abilene.	American N.B.
7041.	Smithville.	First N.B.
7045.	Floydada.	First N.B.
7052.	Dallas.	Texas N.B.
7055.	Blooming Grove.	Citizens' N.B.
7070.	Alvin.	First N.B.
7075.	El Paso.	Nat. Exchange Bank
7096.	Daingerfield.	Citizens' N.B.
7098.	Mason.	Mason N.B.
7105.	Comanche.	Farmers and Merchants' N.B.
7106.	Munday.	First N.B.
7113.	Dallas.	Gaston N.B.
7119.	Llano.	Home N.B.
7123.	Claude.	First N.B.
7129.	Jefferson.	Rogers N.B.
7140.	Garlend.	First N.B.
7144.	Lewisville.	First N.B.
7146.	Manor.	Farmers' N.B.
7147.	Covington.	First N.B.
7149.	Kyle.	Kyle N.B.
7157.	Hico.	Hico N.B.
7165.	Fort Worth.	Western N.B.
7170.	Palestine.	Royall N.B.
7183.	Eastland.	City N.B.
7194.	Naples.	Morris Co. N.B.
7201.	Mansfield.	First N.B.
7212.	Devine.	Adams N.B.
7214.	Alpine.	First N.B.
7231.	Coolidge.	First N.B.
7243.	Cotulla.	Stockmen's N.B.
7245.	Clifton.	First N.B.
7249.	Center.	Farmers' N.B.
7257.	Annona.	First N.B.
7269.	Grandview.	Farmers and Merchants' N.B.
7316.	San Antonio.	Woods N.B.
7317.	Bartlett.	Bartlett N.B.
7331.	Ennis.	Citizens' N.B.
7337.	Anderson.	First N.B.
7345.	Arlington.	Arlington N.B.
7348.	Campbell.	Campbell N.B.
7360.	Cisco.	Merchants and Farmers' N.B.
7376.	Pittsburg.	Pittsburg N.B.
7378.	Merit.	First N.B.
7392.	Texarkana.	City N.B.
7394.	Lampasas.	City N.B.
7407.	Hubbard.	Farmers' N.B.
7410.	Gorman.	First N.B.
7413.	McLean.	First N.B.
7414.	Miles.	Runnels County N.B.
7422.	Breckenridge.	First N.B.
7433.	Del Rio.	Del Rio N.B.
7466.	Merkel.	Merkel N.B.
7481.	Merkel.	Farmers and Merchants' N.B.
7482.	Seymour.	Farmers' N.B.
7495.	Aubrey.	First N.B.
7509.	Belton.	Belton N.B.
7510.	Greenville.	Commercial N.B.
7514.	El Paso.	City N.B.
7515.	Tyler.	Farmers and Merchants' N.B.
7524.	Bells.	First N.B.
7529.	Kerens.	First N.B.
7530.	El Paso.	American N.B.
7534.	Eagle Lake.	First N.B.
7546.	Mart.	Farmers and Merchants' N.B.
7548.	Goliad.	Commercial N.B.
7553.	De Leon.	Farmers and Merchants' N.B.
7572.	Lampasas.	People's N.B.
7599.	McGregor.	McGregor N.B.
7617.	Nocona.	Farmers and Merchants' N.B.
7623.	Frankston.	First N.B.
7635.	Snyder.	Snyder N.B.
7640.	Stamford.	Citizens' N.B.
7645.	Savoy.	First N.B.
7657.	Lone Oak.	Farmers' N.B.
7668.	Corpus Christi.	City N.B.
7669.	Benjamin.	First N.B.
7674.	Mount Vernon.	Merchants and Planters' N.B.
7694.	Atlanta.	Atlanta N.B.
7700.	San Saba.	First N.B.
7714.	Tioga.	First N.B.
7731.	Valley View.	First N.B.
7748.	Ozona.	Ozona N.B.
7753.	Bay City.	Bay City N.B.
7775.	Midlothian.	First N.B.
7798.	Venus.	Farmers and Merchants' N.B.
7807.	Sabinal.	Sabinal N.B.
7814.	Jacksboro.	Jacksboro N.B.
7825.	Haskell.	Farmers' N.B.
7827.	Brady.	Brady N.B.
7838.	Franklin.	First N.B.
7875.	Whitney.	First N.B.
7886.	Sanger.	First N.B.
7906.	Rising Star.	First N.B.
7915.	Whitney.	Citizens' N.B.
7924.	New Braunfels.	Cornal N.B.
7944.	Abilene.	Commercial N.B.
7953.	Knox City.	First N.B.
7956.	Lindale.	First N.B.
7961-	Canyon.	Canyon N.B.
7977.	Delhart.	Delhart N.B.
7989.	Garland.	State N.B.
8001.	Tolar.	First N.B.
8005.	Memphis.	Hall County N.B.
8008.	Holland.	First N.B.
8013.	Kenedy.	Kenedy N.B.
8018.	Stratford.	First N.B.
8034.	Schulenburg.	First N.B.
8037.	Mineola.	Mineola N.B.
8054.	Stephenville.	Farmers' N.B.
8066.	Rosebud.	Planters' N.B.
8068.	Galveston.	Merchants' N.B.
8070.	Galveston.	Seawall N.B.
8071.	Alvord.	Farmers and Merchants' N.B.
8072.	Ranger.	First N.B.
8094.	Stanton.	First N.B.
8102.	Wellington.	First N.B.
8103.	Pleasanton.	First N.B.
8106.	Clyde.	First N.B.
8109.	Santa Ana.	First N.B.
8112.	Stanton.	Stanton N.B.
8123.	Edna.	Allen N.B.
8130.	Walnut Springs.	First N.B.
8134.	Blanco.	Blanco N.B.
8156.	Elgin.	Elgin N.B.
8169.	Odessa.	Citizens' N.B.
8176.	Santo.	First N.B.
8178.	Wolfe City.	Citizens' N.B.
8179.	Higgins.	First N.B.
8195.	Teague.	First N.B.
8200.	Goree.	First N.B.
8204.	Rockwall.	Farmers' N.B.
8208.	Lubbock.	Citizens' N.B.
8215.	Munday.	Citizens' N.B.
8239.	West.	N.B. of West.
8242.	Rule.	First N.B.
8249.	Higgins.	Citizens' N.B.
8252.	Hamlin.	First N.B.
8287.	North Fort Worth.	Exchange N.B.
8288.	Houston.	Nat. City Bank.
8303.	Dickens.	First N.B.
8306.	Paint Rock.	First N.B.
8312.	Brownwood.	Citizens' N.B.
8318.	Grapevine.	Farmers' N.B.
8327.	May.	First N.B.
8330.	Bowie.	N.B. of Bowie.
8355.	Toyah.	First N.B.
8392.	Gonzales.	Farmers' N.B.
8402.	Saint Jo.	Citizens' N.B.
8427.	Hamlin.	Hamlin N.B.
8431.	Farwell.	First N.B.
8449.	De Kalb.	First N.B.
8465.	Seminole.	Seminole N.B.
8515.	Crosbyton.	Citizens' N.B.
8518.	Belton.	People's N.B.
8519.	Floresville.	City N.B.
8522.	New Boston.	New Boston N.B.
8526.	Hemphill.	First N.B.
8535.	Hawley.	First N.B.
8538.	Thornton.	First N.B.
8542.	Paris.	American N.B.
8562.	Cuero.	Buchel N.B.
8565.	Karnes City.	City N.B.
8568.	Midlothian.	Farmers' N.B.
8573.	Brady.	Commercial N.B.
8575.	El Dorado.	First N.B.
8581.	Greenville.	Greenville Nat. Exchange Bank.
8583.	Cross Plains.	Farmers' N.B.
8585.	Naples.	Naples N.B.
8597.	Tahoka.	First N.B.
8606.	Falls City.	Falls City N.B.
8610.	Nocona.	City N.B.
8611.	Princeton.	First N.B.
8621.	Lorena.	First N.B.
8641.	Bronte.	First N.B.
8645.	Houston.	Lumbermen's N.B.
8659.	Robert Lee.	First N.B.
8664.	Dallas.	Commonwealth N.B.
8672.	Bellevue.	First N.B.
8674.	Marfa.	Marfa N.B.
8690.	Sanger.	Sanger N.B.
8693.	Rotan.	First N.B.
8694.	Yoakum.	Yoakum N.B.
8706.	Burkburnett.	First N.B.
8731.	Bridgeport.	First N.B.
8742.	Lovelady.	First N.B.

Charter Number	City	Name of Bank
8769.	Perryton.	First N.B.
8770.	Jefferson.	Commercial N.B.
8771.	Pecos.	First N.B.
8780.	Clyde.	Clyde N.B.
8787.	Byers.	First N.B.
8807.	Oakville.	First N.B.
8816.	Silverton.	First N.B.
8817.	Moore.	Moore N.B.
8818.	Waco.	Exchange N.B.
8843.	Turnersville.	First N.B.
8884.	Grand Saline.	Citizens' N.B.
8891.	Canton.	First N.B.
8897.	Anson.	Farmers and Merchants' N.B.
8899.	Galveston.	City N.B.
8911.	Ochiltree.	Ochiltree N.B.
8925.	Odessa.	Western N.B.
8928.	Gatesville.	Farmers' N.B.
8965.	Cresson.	Cresson N.B.
8982.	Olney.	First N.B.
9053.	Stanton.	Home N.B.
9081.	Plainview.	Citizens' N.B.
9126.	Lockney.	First N.B.
9142.	Pampa.	First N.B.
9148.	Valley Mills.	First N.B.
9155.	El Paso.	N.B. of Commerce.
9178.	Crowell.	Foard County N.B.
9193.	Lockney.	Lockney N.B.
9205.	Kosse.	First N.B.
9226.	Houston.	American N.B.
9245.	Dallas.	Union N.B.
9341.	Dallas.	Trinity N.B.
9353.	Houston.	Houston Nat. Exchange Bank.
9357.	Beaumont.	Commercial N.B.
9369.	Forney.	Farmers' N.B.
9485.	Post City.	First N.B.
9611.	Spur.	Spur N.B.
9625.	Hutto.	Hutto N.B.
9637.	Caddo Mills.	First N.B.
9712.	Houston.	Union N.B.
9749.	Putnam.	First N.B.
9781.	San Saba.	San Saba N.B.
9802.	Plainview.	Third N.B.
9805.	Wellington.	City N.B.
9810.	Mertzon.	First N.B.
9812.	Brownwood.	Coggin N.B.
9813.	Sterling City.	First N.B.
9828.	Waco.	Central Texas N.B.
9845.	Jayton.	First N.B.
9848.	Fort Stockton.	First N.B.
9906.	Quanah.	Citizens' N.B.
9931.	Como.	First N.B.
9936.	Texas City.	First N.B.
9989.	Crosbyton.	First N.B.
10008.	Melissa.	Melissa N.B.
10040.	Texas City.	Texas City N.B.
10044.	Menard.	First N.B.
10050.	Electra.	First N.B.
10052.	Merkel.	Southern N.B.
10076.	Ganado.	First N.B.
10078.	Trinity.	Trinity N.B.
10090.	Mission.	First N.B.
10140.	El Paso.	Commercial N.B.
10148.	San Antonio.	Groos N.B.
10152.	Houston.	South Texas Commercial N.B.
10163.	Bonita.	First N.B.
10169.	Pharr.	First N.B.
10182.	Maud.	Maud N.B.
10189.	La Coste.	La Coste N.B.
10220.	Waco.	Central N.B.
10225.	Houston.	N.B. of Commerce.
10229.	Strawn.	First N.B.
10230.	Paducah.	First N.B.
10241.	Gregory.	First N.B.
10266.	Kingsbury.	First N.B.
10274.	Aransas Pass.	First N.B.
10275.	Normangee.	First N.B.
10276.	Cleveland.	First N.B.
10297.	Mount Calm.	First N.B.
10320.	Poth.	First N.B.
10323.	Lometa.	First N.B.
10331.	Dallas.	Merchants' N.B.
10350.	Richmond.	First N.B.
10360.	Victoria.	Victoria N.B.
10398.	Sealy.	Farmers' N.B.
10400.	Crawford.	First N.B.
10403.	Malakoff.	First N.B.
10411.	Cleburne.	Home N.B.
10418.	Krum.	First N.B.
10420.	Freeport.	Freeport N.B.
10426.	Omaha.	First N.B.
10472.	Newcastle.	First N.B.
10473.	Campbell.	Campbell Nat. Exchange Bank.
10476.	Linden.	First N.B.
10478.	Jasper.	Citizens' N.B.
10483.	Bogata.	First N.B.
10488.	Winfield.	First N.B.
10509.	Rhome.	First N.B.
10547.	Wichita Falls.	N.B. of Commerce.
10549.	Bynum.	First N.B.
10564.	Dallas.	Security N.B.
10598.	Lipan.	First N.B.
10607.	Sherman.	Commercial N.B.
10617.	Honey Grove.	State N.B.
10624.	Edgewood.	First N.B.
10626.	Cooper.	Farmer's and Merchants N.B.
10634.	Whitesboro.	City N.B.
10638.	Avery.	First N.B.
10639.	Bogata.	Bogata N.B.
10643.	Clarksville.	City N.B.
10645.	Allen.	First N.B.
10646.	Quitman.	First N.B.
10647.	Petty.	Citizens' N.B.
10657.	Bagwell.	First N.B.
10661.	Newsome.	First N.B.
10664.	San Angelo.	Central N.B.
10668.	Eddy.	First N.B.
10678.	Bardwell.	First N.B.
10682.	Nixon.	First N.B.
10694.	Dawson.	First N.B.
10703.	Spur.	City N.B.
10713.	Irene.	First N.B.
10717.	Winters.	First N.B.
10728.	Hawkins.	First N.B.
10757.	Kaufman.	Farmers and Merchants' N.B.
10782.	Texline.	First N.B.
10793.	San Antonio.	State N.B.
10806.	San Saba.	City N.B.
10845.	Junction.	First N.B.
10860.	Brenham.	Farmers' N.B.
10871.	Spearman.	First N.B.
10874.	Moran.	First N.B.
10927.	Purdon.	First N.B.
10941.	Martindale.	Martindale N.B.
10949.	Channing.	First N.B.
10954.	Fayetteville.	Farmers' N.B.
10956.	Schwertner.	First N.B.
10957.	McLean.	American N.B.
10965.	Dallas.	Tenison N.B.
10974.	El Paso.	Border N.B.
11002.	Matador.	First N.B.
11003.	Lubbock.	Farmers' N.B.
11019.	Tom Bean.	First N.B.
11021.	Sour Lake.	Citizens' N.B.
11022.	Corsicana.	State N.B.
11138.	Turkey.	First N.B.
11140.	Waco.	Liberty N.B.
11143.	Godley.	Citizens' N.B.
11158.	Follett.	Farmers' N.B.
11163.	Larnesa.	First N.B.
11171.	Grand Prairie.	First N.B.
11175.	McAllen.	First N.B.
11223.	Stratford.	Sherman County N.B.
11239.	Dawson.	Liberty N.B.
11258.	Eastland.	American N.B.
11279.	San Juan.	First N.B.
11291.	Victoria.	People's N.B.
11301.	Wichita Falls.	American N.B.
11325.	Collinsville.	Collinsville N.B.
11357.	Cisco.	American N.B.
11379.	Woodsboro.	First N.B.
11400.	Booker.	First N.B.
11406.	Menard.	Menard N.B.
11408.	Booker.	Edwards N.B.
11411.	Kerens.	Kerens N.B.
11414.	Menard.	Bevans N.B.
11415.	Brownfield.	First N.B.
11423.	Lancaster.	First N.B.
11430.	Fort Worth.	N.B. of Commerce.
11447.	Groom.	First N.B.
11452.	Desdemona.	First N.B.
11453.	West Columbia.	First N.B.
11486.	Wichita Falls.	Exchange N.B.
11503.	Jakehamon.	First N.B.
11519.	Bertram.	First N.B.
11525.	Sipe Springs.	First N.B.
11591.	Rio Grande.	First N.B.
11595.	Perryton.	Perryton N.B.
11625.	Caddo.	First N.B.
11629.	Amarillo.	City N.B.
11630.	Eastland.	Citizens' N.B.
11632.	Rice.	First N.B.
11634.	Rocksprings.	First N.B.
11642.	Granger.	Granger N.B.
11647.	White Deer.	First N.B.
11659.	Necessity.	First N.B.
11700.	Fabens.	First N.B.
11706.	Quitaque.	First N.B.
11722.	Canadian.	Southwest N.B.
11749.	Dallas.	Dallas N.B.
11762.	Wichita Falls.	Security N.B.
11792.	Falfurrias.	First N.B.
11799.	Port Neches.	First N.B.
11800.	Hamilton.	Perry N.B.
11814.	Bandera.	First N.B.
11838.	Mathis.	First N.B.
11874.	Bangs.	First N.B.
11879.	Mercedes.	First N.B.
11928.	Electra.	Security N.B.
11930.	Clifton.	Clifton N.B.
11931.	Arlington.	Farmers' N.B.
11959.	Nocona.	People's N.B.
11964.	Mexia.	City N.B.
11970.	Quinlan.	First N.B.
11996.	Dallas.	Southwest N.B.
11997.	Fort Worth.	Continental N.B.
12005.	Farwell.	Farwell N.B.
12055.	Houston.	Public N.B.
12062.	Houston.	Guaranty N.B.
12070.	Houston.	State N.B.
12091.	Port Arthur.	Merchants' N.B.
12101.	Follett.	Follett N.B.
12110.	Ennis.	First N.B.
12119.	Harlingen.	First N.B.
12138.	Beaumont.	Texas N.B.
12162.	San Antonio.	Commercial N.B.
12166.	Wellington.	City N.B.
12182.	Kenedy.	First N.B.
12186.	Dallas.	Republic N.B.
12187.	Kenedy.	Nichols N.B.
12190.	Mexia.	Prendergast-Smith N.B.
12199.	Beaumont.	City N.B.
12235.	Corpus Christi.	State N.B.
12236.	Brownsville.	State N.B.
12241.	Buda.	Farmers' N.B.
12247.	Corrigan.	Corrigan N.B.
12266.	Swenson.	Swenson N.B.
12287.	Texas.	First N.B.
12289.	Alpine.	State N.B.
12307.	Quanah.	First N.B.
12308.	Quanah.	Security N.B.
12309.	Taft.	First N.B.
12371.	Fort Worth.	Texas N.B.
12382.	Leonard.	Leonard N.B.
12390.	Nordheirn.	First N.B.
12408.	Rowena.	First N.B.
12409.	Bridgeport.	Bridgeport N.B.
12411.	Longview.	Rembert N.B.
12415.	Norton.	First N.B.
12416.	Paradise.	First N.B.
12421.	La Porte.	First N.B.
12423.	Streetman.	First N.B.
12424.	Perrin.	First N.B.
12434.	Galveston.	South Texas N.B.
12437.	Graford.	First N.B.
12448.	Eastland.	Exchange N.B.
12462.	Refugio.	First N.B.
12463.	Llano.	Citizens' N.B.
12475.	Galveston.	United States N.B.
12487.	El Paso.	Nat. Border Bank
12505.	Winfield.	Winfield N.B.
12508.	Richland.	First N.B.
12513.	Chillicothe.	First N.B.
12543.	Big Spring.	State N.B.
12554.	Robstown.	First N.B.
12556.	Palestine.	East Texas N.B.
12566.	Houston.	Seaport N.B.
12580.	Alvin.	First N.B.
12583.	Wylie.	Wylie N.B.
12589.	Goldthwaite.	First N.B.
12612.	Bishop.	First N.B.
12619.	Amherst.	First N.B.
12622.	Plano.	Farmers' N.B.
12627.	Wheeler.	First N.B.
12641.	Weslaco.	First N.B.
12648.	Richmond.	Fort Bend N.B.
12650.	Dallas.	Central N.B.
12651.	Paris.	Liberty N.B.
12652.	Oglesby.	First N.B.
12654.	Rowlett.	First N.B.
12664.	Alvord.	First N.B.
12666.	Childress.	First N.B.
12669.	Mineral Wells.	State N.B.
12670.	Wills Point.	State N.B.
12671.	Alvord.	Alvord N.B.
12672.	Childress.	City N.B.
12676.	Olney.	City N.B.
12677.	Clint.	First N.B.
12680.	Georgetown.	City N.B.
12681.	Como.	Como N.B.
12682.	Lubbock.	First N.B.
12683.	Lubbock.	Lubbock N.B.
12684.	Sylvester.	First N.B.
12685.	Milford.	First N.B.
12687.	Millsap.	First N.B.
12689.	Karnes City.	State N.B.
12691.	Windom.	First N.B.
12692.	Floydala.	Floyd County N.B.
12696.	Handley.	First N.B.
12698.	Kilgore.	Kilgore N.B.
12699.	Bonham.	State N.B.
12700.	Hamlin.	Farmers and Merchants' N.B.
12701.	Italy.	Farmers' N.B.
12703.	Marshall.	State N.B.
12707.	Dallas.	Mercantile N.B.
12708.	Grapevine.	Tarrant County N.B.
12709.	Odell.	First N.B.
12711.	Valley View.	Valley View N.B.
12712.	West.	State N.B.
12713.	Thornton.	Farmers' N.B.
12714.	Grand Prairie.	City N.B.
12715.	Reagan.	First N.B.
12717.	Clifton.	First N.B.
12718.	Needville.	First N.B.
12719.	Cumby.	First N.B.
12722.	Blackwell.	First N.B.
12723.	Bronte.	First N.B.
12724.	Josephine.	First N.B.
12725.	Sudan.	First N.B.
12727.	Moran.	Moran N.B.
12728.	Denison.	Citizens' N.B.
12729.	Robstown.	State N.B.
12730.	Stephenville.	Farmers-First N.B.
12731.	Bowie.	Security N.B.
12733.	Terrell.	State N.B.
12734.	Mineral Wells.	City N.B.
12736.	Dallas.	North Texas N.B.
12737.	Marlin.	Citizens' N.B.
12738.	Collinsville.	Security N.B.
12739.	Evant.	First N.B.
12741.	Bailey.	First N.B.
12742.	Groom.	State N.B.
12744.	Hale Center.	First N.B.
12745.	Grand Saline.	State N.B.
12747.	La Feria.	First N.B.
12748.	Paducah.	Security N.B.

Charter Number	City	Name of Bank
12752.	Melvin.	First N.B.
12753.	Robstown.	Gouger N.B.
12756.	Rosenberg.	First N.B.
12758.	Dublin.	Fariners' N.B.
12759.	Enihouse.	First N.B.
12760.	Lone Oak.	Citizens' N.B.
12761.	Quinlan.	Quinlan N.B.
12762.	Weatherford.	Parker County N.B.
12763.	Kaufman.	Citizens' N.B.
12767.	Larnesa.	State N.B.
12768.	Santa Ana.	State N.B.
12769.	El Paso.	El Paso N.B.
12775.	Strawn.	Strawn N.B.
12778.	Commerce.	Citizens' N.B.
12782.	Nixon.	Nixon N.B.
12783.	Celina.	Farmers and Merchants' N.B.
12786.	Ireland.	First N.B.
12789.	Raymondville.	First N.B.
12792.	Brownsville.	First N.B.
12795.	Cisco.	First N.B.
12796.	Rochelle.	Rochelle N.B.
12798.	Levelland.	First N.B.
12803.	Lovelady.	State N.B.
12809.	Conroe.	First N.B.
12824.	Littlefield.	First N.B.
12831.	O'Donnell.	First N.B.
12835.	Lakeview.	First N.B.
12840.	Houston.	Harrison N.B.
12843.	Blossom.	Farmers' N.B.
12845.	Sulphur.	First N.B. Springs.
12850.	Liberty.	First-Liberty N.B.
12855.	Dickinson.	First N.B.
12867.	Anna.	First N.B.
12898.	Newton.	First N.B.
12899.	Roscoe.	First N.B.
12915.	Pickton.	First N.B.
12919.	George West.	First N.B.
12927.	Ralls.	First N.B.
12928.	Meadow.	First N.B.
12936.	Caddo Mills.	State N.B.
12943.	Lott.	Lott N.B.
12968.	Kingsville.	First N.B.
12969.	Post.	Citizens N.B.
12995.	Hebbronville.	First N.B.
13014.	Borger.	First N.B.
13019.	Honey Grove.	American N.B.
13022.	West.	State N.B.
13046.	Cooper.	First N.B.
13048.	Farmersville.	Farmersville N.B.
13052.	Blossom.	Blossom N.B.
13067.	Teague.	Teague N.B.
13070.	Panhandle.	First N.B.
13107.	Cleburne.	City N.B.
13110.	Tyler.	Peopies N.B.
13111.	Lamesa.	Larnesa N.B.
13170.	Glen Rose.	First N.B.
13183.	McAllen.	First N.B.
13191.	Lorena.	Lorena N.B.
13199.	Wolfe City.	Wolfe City N.B.
13206.	Temple.	First N.B.
13211.	Cushing.	First N.B.
13238.	Odessa.	Odessa N.B.
13249.	Wellington.	First N.B.
13257.	Mount Pleasant.	First N.B.
13259.	Detroit.	Planters' N.B.
13266.	Pecan Gap.	Pecan Gap N.B.
13272.	Valley Mills.	First N.B.
13277.	Farmersville.	First N.B.
13279.	Kosse.	Kosse N.B.
13284.	Electra.	First N.B.
13285.	Rhome.	First N.B.
13287.	Terrell.	State N.B.
13291.	Parnpa.	Pampa N.B.
13315.	Edinburg.	First N.B.
13402.	Rockwall.	First N.B.
13416.	Honey Grove.	First N.B.
13427.	McKinney.	First N.B.
13428.	Clarksville.	Red River N.B.
13443.	Henderson.	Citizens N.B.
13450.	Jefferson.	Commercial N.B.
13475.	Houtto.	First N.B.
13489.	Plainview.	First N.B.
13507.	Frost.	Frost N.B.
13511.	Plano.	First N.B.
13516.	Waxahachie.	Citizens N.B.
13519.	Saint Jo.	Citizens N.B.
13526.	Hemphill.	First N.B.
13541.	Paris.	Liberty N.B.
13555.	Blooming Grove.	First N.B.
13562.	Colorado.	Colorado N.B.
13572.	Pearsall.	Pearsall N.B.
13578.	San Antonio.	N.B. of Fort Sam Houston.
13587.	San Angelo.	San Angelo N.B.
13588.	Brownwood.	Citizens N.B.
13593.	Munday.	First N.B.
13595.	Coleman.	First Coleman N.B.
13598.	Stamford.	First N.B.
13608.	Odessa.	First N.B.
13610.	Fredericksburg.	Fredericksburg N.B.
13614.	Iowa Park.	State N.B.
13623.	Decatur.	First N.B.
13642.	Pleasanton.	First N.B.
13647.	Lott.	First N.B.
13649.	Whitney.	First N.B.
13653.	Sulphur Springs.	First N.B.
13656.	Kerens.	First N.B.
13661.	Orange.	First N.B.
13665.	Wichita Falls.	City N.B.
13667.	Ennis.	Citizens N.B.
13668.	Burkburnett.	First N.B.

Charter Number	City	Name of Bank
13669.	Mount Calm.	First N.B.
13670.	Midlothian.	First N.B.
13675.	Valley Mills.	First N.B.
13676.	Wichita Falls.	Wichita N.B.
13678.	Brenham.	Farmers N.B.
13683.	Houston.	First N.B.
13698.	Gainesville.	Gainesville N.B.
13706.	Trinity.	First N.B.
13727.	Abilene.	Citizens N.B.
13731.	Cameron.	First N.B.
13743.	Dallas.	Mercantile N.B.
13778.	Temple.	First N.B.
13810.	Belton.	Farmers N.B.
13815.	Henrietta.	First N.B.
13854.	Santa Anna.	Santa Anna N.B.
13919.	Luling.	First N.B.
13925.	Houston.	San Jacinto N.B.
13926.	Austin.	Capital N.B.
13934.	Lockhart.	First-Lockhart N.B.
13935.	West.	West N.B.
13943.	Houston.	City N.B.
13951.	Cleburne.	Cleburne N.B.
13964.	Alto.	First N.B.
13974.	Clarksville.	First N.B.
13984.	Big Spring.	First N.B.
14012.	George West.	First N.B.
14015.	Plainview.	City N.B.
14027.	Breckenbridge.	First N.B.
14072.	Falfurrias.	First N.B.
14090.	Canyon.	First N.B.
14101.	Goose Creek.	First N.B.
14104.	Groveton.	First N.B.
14114.	Marlin.	Marlin N.B.
14124.	Edinburg.	First N.B.
14126.	Groesbeck.	Citizens N.B.
14149.	Haskell.	Haskell N.B.
14154.	Newcastle.	Farmers N.B.
14157.	Robstown.	Robstown N.B.
14164.	Cuero.	Bouchel N.B.
14165.	McLean.	American N.B.
14179.	San Antonio.	South Texas N.B.
14199.	Dalhart.	First N.B.
14204.	Angleton.	First N.B.
14206.	Amarillo.	Amarillo N.B.
14207.	Pampa.	First N.B.
14208.	Lubbock.	First N.B.
14212.	Farmersville.	First N.B.
14227.	Comanche.	State N.B.
14236.	McKinney.	Central N.B.
14270.	Snyder.	Snyder N.B.
14272.	White Deer.	Farmers N.B.
14273.	Brownwood.	Citizens N.B.
14283.	San Antonio.	Bexar County N.B.
14299.	Eastland.	Eastland N.B.
14302.	Cotulla.	Stockmens N.B.
14312.	De Kalb.	First N.B.
14330.	Junction.	Junction N.B.

UTAH

Charter Number	City	Name of Bank
1646.	Salt Lake City.	Miners' N.B. of Salt Lake.
1695.	Salt Lake City.	First N.B. of Utah.
1921.	Salt Lake City.	Salt Lake City N.B. of Utah.
2059.	Salt Lake City.	Deseret N.B.
2597.	Ogden.	First N.B.
2641.	Provo.	First N.B.
2880.	Ogden.	Utah N.B.
3139.	Ogden.	Commercial N.B.
3306.	Salt Lake City.	Union N.B.
3537.	Nephi.	First N.B.
4051.	Salt Lake City.	Commercial N.B.
4310.	gait Lake City.	N.B. of the Republic.
4341.	Salt Lake City.	Utah State N.B.
4432.	Salt Lake City.	American N.B.
4486.	Provo City.	N.B. of Commerce.
4564.	Park City.	First N.B.
4670.	Logan.	First N.B.
6012.	Price.	First N.B.
6036.	Brigham City.	First N.B.
6558.	Murray.	First N.B.
6958.	Morgan.	First N.B.
7296.	Ogden.	N.B. of Commerce.
7685.	Layton.	First N.B.
7696.	Coalville.	First N.B.
8508.	Nephi.	Nephi N.B.
9111.	Spanish Fork.	First N.B.
9119.	Beaver City, Beaver.	First N.B.
9403.	Salt Lake City.	Continental N.B.
9652.	Salt Lake City.	Nat. Copper Bank.
10135.	Smithfield.	Commercial N.B.
10308.	Salt Lake City.	Nat. City Bank.
10925.	Moab.	First N.B.
11228.	Magna.	First N.B.
11266.	Monticello.	First N.B.
11529.	Delta.	First N.B.
11631.	Bingham Canyon.	First N.B.
11702.	Myton.	First N.B.
11725.	Gunnison.	Gunnison City N.B.

VERMONT

Charter Number	City	Name of Bank
122.	Springfield.	First N.B.
130.	Bennington.	First N.B.
194.	North Bennington.	First N.B.
228.	Orwell.	First N.B.
269.	Saint Albans.	First N.B.
278.	Brandon.	First N.B.
344.	Fair Haven.	First N.B.
404.	Brandon.	Brandon N.B.
470.	Brattleboro.	First N.B.
489.	Saint Johnsbury.	First N.B.

Charter Number	City	Name of Bank
748.	Montpelier.	First N.B.
816.	Windsor.	Ascutney N.B.
820.	Rutland.	Rutland County N.B.
857.	Montpelier.	Montpelier N.B.
861.	Burlington.	First N.B.
962.	Bethel.	Nat. White River Bank.
1004.	Chelsea.	Orange County N.B.
1133.	Woodstock.	Woodstock N.B.
1140.	Lyndon.	N.B. of Lyndon.
1163.	Hyde Park.	Lamoille County N.B.
1195.	Middlebury.	N.B. of Middlebury.
1197.	Burlington.	Merchants' N.B.
1200.	Poultney.	N.B. of Poultney.
1364.	Vergennes.	N.B. of Vergennes.
1368.	Derby Line.	N.B. of Derby Line.
1383.	Proctorsville.	Nat. Black River Bank.
1406.	Wells River.	N.B. of Newbury.
1430.	Brattleboro.	Vermont N.B.
1450.	Rutland.	N.B. of Rutland.
1462.	Waterbury.	Waterbury N.B.
1488.	Manchester.	Battenkill N.B.
1541.	Irasburg.	Irasburg N.B. of Orleans.
1564.	Jamaica.	West River N.B.
1576.	Danville.	Caledonia N.B.
1583.	Saint Albans.	Vermont N.B.
1598.	Castleton.	Castleton N.B.
1634.	Swanton.	Nat. Union Bank.
1638.	Northfield.	Northfield N.B.
1653.	Bellows Falls.	N.B. of Bellows Falls.
1673.	Royalton.	N.B. of Royalton.
1698.	Burlington.	Howard N.B.
1700.	Rutland.	Baxter N.B.
2109.	Barre.	N.B. of Barre.
2120.	Chelsea.	First N.B.
2263.	Newport.	N.B. of Newport.
2274.	Randolph.	Randolph N.B.
2290.	Barton.	Barton N.B.
2295.	Saint Johnsbury.	Merchants' N.B.
2305.	Brattleboro.	People's N.B.
2395.	Bennington.	County N.B.
2422.	Fairhaven.	Allen N.B.
2475.	Vergennes.	Farmers' N.B.
2537.	Rutland.	Clement N.B.
2545.	Poultney.	First N.B.
2905.	Rutland.	Killington N.B.
2950.	Rutland.	Clement N.B.
3080.	Manchester Center.	Factory Point N.B.
3150.	Middletown Springs.	Gray N.B.
3158.	Lyndonville.	Lyndonville N.B.
3257.	Windsor.	Windsor N.B.
3311.	Rutland.	Merchants' N.B.
3482.	Saint Albans.	Welden N.B.
3484.	White River Junction.	First N.B.
4258.	Swanton.	Ferris N.B.
4275.	Island Pond.	Island Pond N.B.
4380.	Chester.	N.B. of Chester.
4929.	Chelsea.	N.B. of Orange County.
4943.	Swanton.	People's N.B.
6252.	Bristol.	First N.B.
7068.	Barre.	People's N.B.
7267.	Bradford.	Bradford N.B.
7614.	Enosburg Falls.	First N.B.
7721.	Windsor.	State N.B.
9108.	White River Junction.	Hartford N.B.
9824.	Poultney.	Citizens' N.B.
11615.	Richford.	Richford N.B.
13261.	Poultney.	First N.B.
13685.	Windsor.	Windsor County.
13712.	Brandon.	Brandon N.B.
13755.	Bethel.	National White River Bank.
13800.	St. Albans.	Welden N.B.
13894.	Bellows Falls.	Windham N.B.
13915.	Montpelier.	Montpelier N.B.
13986.	Enosburg Falls.	Enosburg Falls N.B.
14234.	Poultney.	Poultney N.B.

U.S. VIRGIN ISLANDS

Charter Number	City	Name of Bank
14335.	St. Thomas.	Virgin Islands N.B.

VIRGINIA

Charter Number	City	Name of Bank
271.	Norfolk.	First N.B.
651.	Alexandria.	First N.B.
1111.	Richmond.	First N.B.
1125.	Richmond.	N.B. of Virginia.
1137.	Norfolk.	Exchange N.B.
1155.	Richmond.	Nat. Exchange Bank
1378.	Petersburg.	First N.B.
1468.	Charlottesville.	Charlottesville N.B.
1548.	Petersburg.	Merchants' N.B.
1558.	Lynchburg.	First N.B.
1570.	Richmond.	Farmers' N.B.
1572.	Harrisonburg.	First N.B.
1582.	Fredericksburg.	N.B. of Fredericks.
1585.	Staunton.	First N.B.
1609.	Danville.	First N.B.
1620.	Staunton.	Nat. Valley Bank.
1628.	Richmond.	Planters' N.B.
1635.	Winchester.	Shenandoah Valley N.B.
1658.	Clarksville.	First N.B.
1704.	Norfolk.	People's N.B.
1716.	Alexandria.	Citizens' N.B.
1738.	Leesburg.	Loudoun N.B.
1742.	Charlottesville.	Citizens' N.B.
1754.	Richmond.	Merchants' N.B.
1769.	Petersburg.	Commercial N.B.
1824.	Salem.	Farmers' N.B.
1985.	Danville.	First N.B.
2269.	Staunton.	Augusta N.B.
2506.	Lynchburg.	Nat. Exchange Bank

Charter Number	City	Name of Bank
2594.	Charlottesville.	People's N.B.
2737.	Roanoke.	First N.B.
2760.	Lynchburg.	People's N.B.
2907.	Roanoke.	Roanoke N.B.
2967.	Front Royal.	Front Royal N.B.
3209.	Mount Jackson.	Mount Jackson N.B.
3368.	Norfolk.	Norfolk N.B.
3515.	Petersburg.	N.B. of Petersburg.
3570.	Culpeper.	Farmers' N.B.
3917.	Leesburg.	People's N.B.
4026.	Roanoke.	Commercial N.B.
4027.	Roanoke.	Nat. Exchange Bank.
4047.	Suff olk.	First N.B.
4071.	Pulaski.	Pulaski N.B.
4257.	Bedford City, Liberty.	First N.B.
4314.	Lexington.	First N.B.
4460.	Buchanan.	First N.B.
4477.	Bristol.	Dominion N.B.
4503.	Covington.	Covington N.B.
4531.	Roanoke.	Citizens' N.B.
4635.	Newport News.	First N.B.
4743.	Norfolk.	City N.B.
4940.	Onancock.	First N.B.
5032.	Manassas.	N.B. of Manassas.
5150.	Abingdon.	First N.B.
5229.	Richmond.	American N.B.
5261.	Harrisonburg.	Rockingham N.B.
5268.	Fredericks, Conway, Gordonburg.	Garnett N.B.
5290.	Irvington.	Lancaster N.B.
5326.	Covington.	Citizens' N.B.
5394.	Culpeper.	Second N.B.
5438.	Orange.	N.B. of Orange.
5449.	Woodstock.	Shenandoah N.B.
5532.	Orange.	American N.B.
5591.	Culpeper.	Culpeper N.B.
5683.	Farmville.	First N.B.
5725.	Scottsville.	Scottsville N.B.
5872.	South Boston.	First N.B.
6005.	Charlottesville.	Jefferson N.B.
6008.	Clifton Forge.	First N.B.
6018.	Purcellville.	Purcellville N.B.
6031.	Luray.	First N.B.
6032.	Norfolk.	N.B. of Commerce.
6084.	Winchester.	Farmers and Merchants' N.B.
6123.	Tazewell.	Tazewell N.B.
6126.	Warrenton.	Fauquier N.B.
6206.	Luray.	Page Valley N.B.
6235.	Norton.	First N.B.
6246.	Parksley.	Parksley N.B.
6389.	Fairfax.	N.B. of Fairfax.
6443.	Washington.	Rappahannock N.B.
6666.	Broadway.	First N.B.
6685.	Rocky Mount.	First N.B.
6748.	Manassas.	People's N.B.
6778.	Hampton.	Merchants' N.B.
6781.	Newport News.	Newport News N.B.
6782.	Radford, East Radford.	First N.B.
6798.	Roanoke.	People's N.B.
6839.	Marion.	Marion N.B.
6842.	Hampton.	First N.B.
6886.	Lebanon.	First N.B.
6899.	Coeburn.	First N.B.
6903.	Staunton.	Staunton N.B.
7093.	Alexandria.	Alexandria N.B.
7135.	Gate City.	People's N.B.
7150.	Orange.	Citizens' N.B.
7173.	Lexington.	People's N.B.
7206.	Martinsville.	First N.B.
7208.	Gate City.	First N.B.
7258.	Onley.	Farmers and Merchants' N.B.
7308.	Lynchburg.	American N.B.
7338.	Berryville.	First N.B.
7587.	Waynesboro.	First N.B.
7659.	Hallwood.	Hallwood N.B.
7709.	Petersburg.	Virginia N.B.
7782.	Graham.	First N.B.
7847.	Pocahontas.	First N.B.
7937.	Christiansburg.	First N.B.
8003.	Esmont.	Esmont N.B.
8091.	Pearisburg.	First N.B.
8152.	Roanoke.	City N.B.
8362.	Clintwood.	Citizens' N.B.
8384.	Jonesville.	People's N.B.
8389.	Rosslyn.	Arlington N.B.
8414.	South Boston.	Boston N.B.
8547.	Saint Paul.	Saint Paul N.B.
8643.	South Boston.	Planters and Manufacturers N.B.
8666.	Richmond.	Nat. State and City Bank.
8688.	Emporia.	First N.B.
8722.	Hot Springs.	Bath County N.B.
8746.	Strasburg.	People's N.B.
8753.	Strasburg.	Massanutten N.B.
8791.	Galax.	First N.B.
8819.	Abingdon.	People's N.B.
8875.	Chilhowie.	N.B. of Chilhowie.
8984.	Rocky Mount.	People's N.B.
9012.	Wytheville.	First N.B.
9043.	Monterey.	First N.B. of Highland.
9177.	Clifton Forge.	Clifton Forge N.B.
9222.	Farmville.	People's N.B.
9224.	Blackstone.	First N.B.
9246.	Charlottesville.	Albemarle N.B.
9261.	Waynesboro.	Waynesboro N.B.
9291.	Chase City.	First N.B.
9295.	Altavista.	First N.B.

Charter Number	City	Name of Bank
9300.	Portsmouth.	First N.B.
9343.	Danville.	American N.B.
9375.	Buchanan.	Buchanan N.B.
9379.	Appalachia.	First N.B.
9433.	Lawrenceville.	First N.B.
9455.	Crewe.	First N.B.
9475.	Danville.	N.B. of Danville.
9635.	Herndon.	N.B. of Herndon.
9642.	Warrenton.	People's N.B.
9663.	Richmond.	Manchester N.B.
9732.	Emporia.	Planters' N.B.
9733.	Suffolk.	N.B. of Suffolk.
9746.	Norton.	N.B. of Norton.
9764.	Troutville.	First N.B.
9847.	Martinsville.	People's N.B.
9861.	Hamilton.	Farmers and Merchants' N.B.
9885.	Norfolk.	Virginia N.B.
9890.	Buena Vista.	First N.B.
9924.	Jonesville.	Powell Valley N.B.
10061.	Rural Retreat.	First N.B.
10080.	Richmond.	Central N.B.
10156.	Danville.	Virginia N.B.
10194.	Norfolk.	Seaboard N.B.
10252.	Honaker.	First N.B.
10253.	Marshall.	Marshall N.B.
10287.	Gordonsville.	N.B. of Gordonsville.
10325.	Fredericksburg.	Planters' N.B.
10344,	Richmond.	Broadway N.B.
10524.	New Market.	Citizens' N.B.
10532.	Roanoke.	American N.B.
10568.	New Market.	First N.B.
10611.	Wise.	Wise County N.B.
10618.	Charlottesville.	N.B. of Charlottesville.
10621.	Bedford.	Citizens' N.B.
10658.	Gloucester.	First N.B.
10696.	Lexington.	Rockbridge N.B.
10821.	Chatham.	First N.B.
10827.	Reedville.	Commonwealth N.B.
10834.	Independence.	Grayson County N.B.
10835.	Brookneal.	First N.B.
10850.	Richlands.	First N.B.
10857.	Richlands.	Richlands N.B.
10866.	Hopewell.	N.B. of Hopewell.
10882.	Williamsburg.	First N.B.
10914.	Waverly.	First N.B.
10968.	Louisa.	First N.B.
10973.	Stanley.	Farmers and Merchants' N.B.
10993.	Newcastle.	First N.B.
11028.	Newport News.	Schmelz N.B.
11133.	Shenandoah.	First N.B.
11174.	Penniman.	First N.B.
11191.	Roanoke.	Liberty N.B.
11205.	Appomattox.	Farmers' N.B.
11265.	Saltville.	First N.B.
11313.	Abingdon.	Citizens' N.B.
11328.	Bedford.	People's N.B.
11364.	Newport News.	Nat. Mechanic's Bank.
11381.	Portsmouth.	American N.B.
11387.	Pulaski.	People's N.B.
11444.	Narrows.	First N.B.
11480.	Dillwyn.	First N.B.
11501.	Dillwyn.	Merchants and Planters' N.B.
11517.	Charlottesville.	Farmers and Merchants' N.B.
11533.	Tazewell.	Farmers' N.B.
11554.	Yorktown.	First N.B.
11569.	Round Hill.	Round Hill N.B.
11690.	Radford, East Radford	Farmers and Merchants N.B.
11694.	Harrisonburg.	N.B. of Harrisonburg.
11698.	Grundy.	First N.B.
11718.	Marion.	People's N.B.
11764.	Vienna.	Vienna N.B.
11765.	Big Stone Gap.	First N.B.
11797.	Flint Hill.	First N.B.
11817.	Roanoke.	Colonial N.B.
11858.	Pennington Gap.	First N.B.
11901.	Stuart.	First N.B.
11911.	Vinton.	First N.B.
11941.	Woodstock.	N.B. of Woodstock.
11946.	Charlottesville.	Commerce N.B.
11957.	Lovingston.	First N.B. of Nelson County.
11960.	Brookneal.	People's N.B.
11976.	Bassett.	First N.B.
11978.	Ashland.	First N.B.
11990.	Troutdale.	First N.B.
12092.	Poquoson, Odd.	First N.B.
12151.	Norfolk.	Continental N.B.
12183.	Victoria.	First N.B.
12204.	Leesburg.	Leesburg Upperville N.B.
12229.	Blacksburg.	N.B. of Blacksburg.
12240.	Emporia.	Citizens' N.B.
12251.	Kenbridge.	First N.B.
12267.	Phoebus.	Old Point N.B.
12290.	Fries.	First N.B.
12311.	Ferrum.	First N.B.
12451.	Ashland.	Hanover N.B.
12477.	Quantico.	First N.B.
12539.	Middleburg.	Middleburg N.B.
12599.	Wytheville.	Wythe County N.B.
12966.	Warrenton.	Fauquier N.B.
13275.	Front Royal.	Citizens N.B.
13343.	Norfolk.	Colonial N.B.
13502.	Gate City.	Peoples N.B.
13603.	Fredericksburg.	Planters N.B.
13775.	Hampton.	Citizens N.B.
13792.	Petersburg.	Citizens N.B.
13878.	Onancock.	First N.B.
13880.	Honaker.	First N.B.
14052.	Crewe.	N.B. of Crewe.

Charter Number	City	Name of Bank
14180.	Clifton Forge.	Mountain N.B.
14190.	Onley.	Farmers & Merchants N.B.
14223.	Abingdon.	Washington County N.B.
14325.	Herndon.	Citizens N.B.
14337.	Victoria.	Peoples N.B.

WASHINGTON

Charter Number	City	Name of Bank
2380.	Walla Walla.	First N.B.
2520.	Dayton.	First N.B.
2772.	Dayton.	Columbia N.B.
2783.	Seattle.	First N.B.
2805.	Spokane.	First N.B.
2876.	Yakima.	First N.B.
2924.	Tacoma.	Tacoma N.B.
2948.	Port Townsend.	First N.B.
2966.	Seattle.	Puget Sound N.B.
2985.	Seattle.	Merchants' N.B.
3024.	Olympia.	First N.B.
3031.	Vancouver.	First N.B.
3037.	Ellensburg.	First N.B.
3076.	Colfax.	First N.B.
3119.	Colfax.	Second N.B.
3172.	Tacoma.	Merchants' N.B.
3355.	Yakima.	First N.B.
3409.	Spokane.	Traders' N.B.
3417.	Tacoma.	N.B. of Tacoma.
3460.	Pomeroy.	First N.B.
3528.	Spokane.	Fidelity N.B.
3789.	Tacoma.	N.B. of Commerce.
3799.	Dayton.	N.B. of Dayton.
3838.	Spokane Falls, Spokane.	Spokane N.B.
3862.	Yakima.	Yakima N.B.
3867.	Ellensburg.	Kittitas Valley N.B.
3887.	Snohomish.	First N.B.
3956.	Walla Walla.	Baker-Boyer N.B.
3976.	New Whatcom.	Bellingham Bay N.B.
4002.	Davenport.	Big Bend N.B.
4005.	Spokane Falls.	Citizens' N.B.
4018.	Tacoma.	Washington N.B.
4025.	Spokane, Spokane Falls.	Browne N.B.
4031.	Goldendale.	First N.B.
4044.	Spokane.	Exchange N.B.
4059.	Seattle.	Washington N.B.
4069.	Tacoma.	Citizens' N.B.
4099.	Whatcom.	First N.B.
4122.	Oakesdale.	First N.B.
4124.	Seattle.	Boston N.B.
4171.	New Whatcom.	Bennett N.B.
4186.	Palouse City.	First N.B.
4203.	Chehalis.	First N.B.
4224.	Puyallup.	First N.B.
4229.	Seattle.	Seattle N.B.
4277.	Spokane Falls.	Washington N.B.
4290.	Port Townsend.	Port Townsend N.B.
4297.	Olympia.	Capital N.B.
4315.	Port Angeles.	First N.B.
4351.	New Whatcom.	Columbia N.B.
4375.	Seattle.	N.B. of Commerce.
4387.	Fairhaven.	Fairhaven N.B.
4390.	Hoquiam.	Hoquiam N.B.
4397.	Seattle.	Commercial N.B.
4407.	Aberdeen.	First N.B.
4426.	Tacoma.	N.B. of the Republic.
4427.	Hoquiam.	First N.B.
4439.	Centralia.	First N.B.
4457.	Slaughter.	First N.B.
4458.	Anacortes.	First N.B.
4467.	South Bend.	First N.B.
4470.	Blaine.	First N.B.
4471.	Blaine.	Blaine N.B.
4473.	Dayton.	Citizens' N.B.
4526.	Snohomish.	Snohomish N.B.
4529.	Mount Vernon.	First N.B.
4532.	Waterville.	First N.B.
4542.	Cheney.	First N.B.
4623.	Tacoma.	Columbia N.B.
4668.	Spokane.	Old N.B.
4681.	Waitsburg.	First N.B.
4686.	Everett.	First N.B.
4699.	Pullman.	First N.B.
4738.	Everett.	Everett N.B.
4779.	Montesano.	First N.B.
4788.	Colton.	First N.B.
4796.	Everett.	Puget Sound N.B.
5243.	Fairhaven.	Citizens' N.B.
5472.	Montesano.	Montesano N.B.
5652.	Olympia.	Olympia N.B.
5751.	Ritzville.	First N.B.
6006.	Tacoma.	Lumbermen's N.B.
6013.	Vancouver.	Vancouver N.B.
6053.	Everett.	American N.B.
6074.	Port Angeles.	First N.B.
6742.	Clarkston.	First N.B.
7095.	Colfax.	Colfax N.B.
7372.	Bellingham.	First N.B.
7474.	Bellingham.	Bellingham N.B.
7489.	Prosser.	First N.B.
7527.	Davenport.	Davenport N.B.
7767.	Toppenish.	First N.B.
7908.	Sedro-Woolley.	First N.B.
8064.	Wenatchee.	First N.B.
8090.	Dayton.	Dayton N.B.
8104.	Colville.	First N.B.
8279.	Oroville.	First N.B.
8481.	Sunnyside.	First N.B.
8639.	Kelso.	First N.B.
8736.	Centralia.	United States N.B.

Charter Number	City	Name of Bank
8743.	Ritzville.	Pioneer N.B.
8789.	Chewelah.	First N.B.
8828.	Newport.	First N.B.
8895.	Waitsburg.	First N.B.
8948.	Kennewick.	First N.B.
8958.	Connell.	Connell N.B.
8987.	Vancouver.	Citizens' N.B.
9030.	Medical Lake.	First N.B.
9052.	Odessa.	First N.B.
9054.	Washtucna.	First N.B.
9068.	Walla Walla.	Third N.B.
9070.	Bellingham.	Northwestern N.B.
9079.	Ellensburg.	Washington N.B.
9080.	Cheney.	N.B. of Cheney.
9101.	Lind.	First N.B.
9102.	Quincy.	First N.B.
9129.	Wapato.	First N.B.
9144.	Cheney.	Security N.B.
9150.	Oakesdale.	N.B. of Oakesdale.
9170.	Brewster.	First N.B.
9182.	Hillyard.	First N.B.
9185.	Garfield.	Garfield N.B.
9210.	Harrington.	First N.B.
9265.	Pasco.	First N.B.
9273.	Rosalia.	Whitman County N.B.
9280.	Bremerton.	First N.B.
9351.	Malden.	First N.B.
9372.	Monroe.	First N.B.
9389.	Chehalis.	First N.B.
9411.	Okanogan.	First N.B.
9417.	Prosser.	Benton County N.B.
9443.	Dayton.	Broughton N.B.
9478.	Monroe.	Monroe N.B.
9499.	Palouse.	Farmers' N.B.
9535.	Aberdeen.	United States N.B.
9576.	Zillah.	First N.B.
9589.	Spokane.	N.B. of Commerce.
9646.	Vancouver.	United States N.B.
9662.	Seattle.	Mercantile N.B.
9757.	Mabton.	First N.B.
9798.	Seattle.	Dexter Horton N.B.
9808.	Burlington.	First N.B.
10000.	White Salmon.	First N.B.
10026.	Seattle.	Nat. City Bank.
10174.	Kent.	First N.B.
10407.	Tonasket.	First N.B.
10469.	Cle Elum.	First N.B.
10499.	Reardan.	Reardan N.B.
10511.	Colfax.	Farmers' N.B.
10585.	Auburn.	First N.B.
10602.	Mount Vernon.	Mount Vernon N.B.
10648.	Burlington.	Burlington N.B.
10686.	Camas.	First N.B.
11045.	Ellensburg.	N.B. of Ellensburg.
11146.	Seattle.	Seaboard N.B.
11172.	Saint John.	First N.B.
11247.	Ephrata.	First N.B.
11280.	Seattle.	Union N.B.
11285.	Poulsbo.	First N.B.
11416.	Pomeroy.	Farmers' N.B.
11546.	Grandview.	First N.B.
11667.	Ferndale.	First N.B.
11672.	Raymond.	First N.B.
11674.	Selah.	First N.B.
11693.	Everett.	Security N.B.
11750.	Goldendale.	N.B. of Goldendale.
11751.	Aberdeen.	Aberdeen N.B.
11805.	Camp Lewis.	Army N.B.
11808.	Lynden.	First N.B.
11832.	Seattle.	Metropolitan N.B.
11856.	Seattle.	Marine N.B.
11864.	Kirkland.	First N.B.
11935.	Stanwood.	First N.B.
11984.	Conway.	First N.B.
12007.	Seattle.	Horton Nat. Trust and Savings Bank.
12085.	Auburn.	Auburn N.B.
12114.	Enumclaw.	First N.B.
12121.	Redmond.	First N.B.
12143.	Enumclaw.	Enumclaw N.B.
12153.	Seattle.	University N.B.
12154.	Mount Vernon.	Skagit N.B.
12170.	Odessa.	First N.B.
12180.	Sprague.	First N.B.
12181.	Sunnyside.	Sunnyside N.B.
12184.	Palouse.	Security N.B.
12217.	Kent.	Kent N.B.
12231.	Garfield.	State N.B.
12234.	Bellingham.	American N.B.
12246.	Yakima.	West Side N.B.
12269.	Ilwaco.	First N.B.
12292.	Tacoma.	Puget Sound N.B.
12392.	Longview.	First N.B.
12399.	Renton.	First N.B.
12419.	Spokane.	Brotherhood's Co-Operative N.B.
12509.	Cosmopolis.	First N.B.
12667.	Tacoma.	Brotherhood Co-Operative N.B.
12704.	Aberdeen.	Grays Harbor N.B.
12851.	Greenwood, Seattle.	Greenwood N.B.
13057.	Gig Harbor.	First N.B.
13091.	Aberdeen.	American N.B.
13099.	Centralia.	First N.B.
13137.	Vancouver.	Washington N.B.
13201.	Hoquiam.	Lumbermans N.B. & Trust Co.
13230.	Seattle.	Pacific N.B.
13233.	Elma.	First N.B.
13290.	Everett.	Citizens N.B. & Trust Co.
13331.	Spokane.	First National Trust & Savings Bank.
13351.	Port Townsend.	American N.B.
13374.	Stanwood.	Stanwood N.B.
13439.	East Stanwood.	N.B. of East Stanwood.
13444.	Reardan.	First N.B.
13470.	Seattle.	Central N.B. of Commerce.
13471.	Seattle.	Washington N.B. of Commerce.
13581.	Seattle.	Ballard First N.B.
13662.	Olympia.	Washington N.B.
13723.	Shelton.	First N.B.
13724.	Colville.	Colville Valley N.B.
14038.	Auburn.	Auburn N.B.
14166.	Tonasket.	First N.B.
14186.	Vancouver.	Vancouver N.B.

WEST VIRGINIA

Charter Number	City	Name of Bank
180.	Parkersburg.	First N.B.
360.	Wheeling.	First N.B.
864.	Parkersburg.	Second N.B.
961.	Fairmont.	First N.B.
1343.	Wheeling.	Merchants' N.B. of West Va.
1387.	Wellsburg.	First N.B.
1424.	Wheeling.	N.B. of West Virginia.
1427.	Parkersburg.	Parkersburg N.B.
1502.	Morgantown.	Merchants' N.B. of West Va.
1504.	Point Pleasant.	Merchants' N.B.
1524.	Martinsburg.	N.B. of Martinsburg.
1530.	Clarksburg.	Merchants' N.B. of West Va.
1594.	Wheeling.	Nat. Savings Bank.
1607.	Weston.	Nat. Exchange Bank.
1608.	Kingwood.	N.B. of Kingwood.
1795.	Charleston.	First N.B.
1868.	Charlestown.	First N.B. of Jefferson.
1883.	Piedmont.	N.B. of Piedmont.
1884.	Wellsburg.	Wellsburg N.B.
2144.	Martinsburg.	People's N.B.
2445.	Grafton.	First N.B.
2458.	Morgantown.	Second N.B.
2649.	Parkersburg.	Citizens' N.B.
3029.	Moorefield.	South Branch Valley N.B.
3106.	Huntington.	First N.B.
3236.	Charleston.	Charleston N.B.
3629.	Piedmont.	First N.B.
4088.	Piedmont.	Davis N.B.
4412.	Charleston.	Citizens' N.B.
4569.	Clarksburg.	Traders' N.B.
4607.	Huntington.	Huntington N.B.
4643.	Bluefield.	First N.B.
4667.	Charleston.	Kanawha N.B.
4718.	Elkins.	Elkins N.B.
4760.	Buckhannon.	Traders' N.B.
4775.	Ceredo.	First N.B.
4811.	Martinsburg.	Citizens' N.B.
4828.	Davis.	N.B. of Davis.
5012.	Mannington.	First N.B.
5027.	Sistersville.	First N.B.
5028.	Sistersville.	Farmers and Producers' N.B.
5164.	Wheeling.	Nat. Exchange Bank.
5226.	Saint Marys.	First N.B.
5266.	New Martinsville.	First N.B.
5280.	Ronceverte.	First N.B.
5320.	Parkersburg.	Farmers and Mechanics' N.B.
5434.	Fayetteville.	Fayetteville N.B.
5562.	Hinton.	First N.B.
5583.	Morgantown.	Citizens' N.B.
5691.	Montgomery.	Montgomery N.B.
5701.	Point Pleasant.	Point Pleasant N.B.
5717.	Moundsville.	First N.B.
5814.	Friendly.	First N.B.
5903.	Alderson.	First N.B.
5939.	Glenville.	First N.B.
6020.	Cameron.	First N.B.
6170.	Middlebourne.	First N.B.
6205.	Keyser.	First N.B.
6213.	Sutton.	First N.B.
6226.	Ronceverte.	Ronceverte N.B.
6233.	Williamstown.	Williamstown N.B.
6283.	Martinsburg.	Old N.B.
6302.	Philippi.	First N.B.
6332.	Kingwood.	Kingwood N.B.
6377.	Philippi.	Citizens' N.B.
6424.	West Union.	First N.B.
6510.	Madison.	Madison N.B.
6538.	Marlinton.	First N.B.
6548.	Sistersville.	People's N.B.
6582.	New Cumberland	First N.B.
6618.	Belington.	Citizens' N.B.
6619.	Belington.	First N.B.
6634.	Belington.	Belington N.B.
6674.	Bluefield.	Flat Top N.B.
6735.	Beckley.	First N.B.
6790.	Harrisville.	First N.B.
6830.	Williamson.	First N.B.
6984.	Chester.	First N.B.
6999.	Terra Alta.	First N.B.
7029.	Clarksburg.	Empire N.B.
7060.	Elkins.	Randolph N.B.
7191.	Pennsboro.	First N.B.
7246.	Permsboro.	Citizens' N.B.
7250.	Salem.	First N.B.
7270.	Charles Town.	Nat. Citizens' Bank.
7275.	Clendenin.	First N.B.
7359.	Huntington.	West Virginia N.B.
7545.	Monogah.	First N.B.
7626.	Newburg.	First N.B.
7672.	Pineville.	First N.B.
7681.	Clarksburg.	Union N.B.
7734.	Bluefield.	American N.B.
7845.	Hendricks.	First N.B.
7998.	Hinton.	N.B. of Summers.
8136.	Logan.	First N.B.
8171.	Hamlin.	Lincoln N.B.
8219.	Princeton.	First N.B.
8309.	Northfork.	First N.B.
8333.	Gary.	Gary N.B.
8345.	Fayetteville.	Fayette County N.B.
8360.	Webster Springs.	First N.B.
8376.	Elkins.	People's N.B.
8434.	Richwood.	First N.B.
8569.	Charleston.	Nat. City Bank
8749.	Pineville.	Citizens' N.B.
8751.	Gormania.	First N.B.
8904.	Ansted.	Ansted N.B.
8983.	Elm Grove.	First N.B. and Trust Company.
8998.	Thurmond.	N.B. of Thurmond.
9038.	Beckley.	People's N.B.
9048.	Welch.	First N.B.
9071.	Welch.	McDowell County N.B.
9288.	Rowlesburg.	First N.B.
9453.	Shinnston.	First N.B.
9462.	Fairmont.	N.B. of Fairmont.
9523.	Alderson.	Alderson N.B.
9598.	Huntington.	American N.B.
9604.	Sutton.	Home N.B.
9610.	Parsons.	First N.B.
9640.	Saint Albans.	First N.B.
9645.	Fairmont.	People's N.B.
9721.	Peterstown.	First N.B.
9740.	Montgomery.	Merchants' N.B.
9766.	Romney.	First N.B.
9850.	Winona.	Winona N.B.
9909.	Berwind.	Berwind N.B.
9913.	Kenova.	First N.B.
10067.	Williamson.	N.B. of Commerce.
10097.	Griffithsville.	Oil Field N.B.
10127.	Spencer.	First N.B.
10157.	Clark, Northfork.	Clark N.B.
10219.	Fairview.	First N.B.
10250.	Rowlesburg.	People's N.B.
10285.	Reedy.	First N.B.
10348.	Hinton.	Citizens' N.B.
10369.	Keystone.	First N.B.
10370.	Matewan.	Matewan N.B.
10392.	Anawalt.	First N.B.
10450.	Worthington.	First N.B.
10455.	Wheeling.	Citizens' N.B.
10480.	Albright.	First N.B.
10559.	Cowen.	First N.B.
10589.	Beckley.	Beckley N.B.
10759.	Ravenswood.	First N.B.
10762.	Ripley.	First N.B.
11049.	Mount Hope.	First N.B.
11109.	Bluefield.	Bluefield N.B.
11264.	Matoaka.	First N.B.
11268.	Jaeger.	First N.B.
11340.	South Charleston.	First N.B.
11483.	Williamstown.	Farmers and Mechanics' N.B.
11502.	Kimball.	First N.B.
11664.	Bayard.	Bayard N.B.
11670.	Hurricane.	Hurricane N.B.
11877.	Bridgeport.	First N.B.
12075.	Oak Hill.	Oak Hill N.B.
12270.	Mullens.	First N.B.
12283.	Beckley.	Nat. Exchange Bank.
12372.	Jaeger.	Tug River N.B.
12483.	Elkins.	Citizens' N.B.
12565.	East Rainelle.	First N.B.
12765.	Milton.	Milton N.B.
12839.	Matoaka.	Matoaka N.B.
13231.	Point Pleasant.	Citizens N.B.
13484.	Kimball.	Kimball N.B.
13505.	Gary.	Gary N.B.
13509.	Charleston.	N.B. of Commerce.
13512.	Welch.	McDowell County N.B.
13621.	Parkersburg.	Peoples N.B.
13627.	Richwood.	Cherry River N.B.
13634.	Weston.	Weston N.B.
13646.	Buckhannon.	Central N.B.
13783.	Marlinton.	First N.B.
13811.	Fairmont.	First N.B.
13830.	Ronceverte.	First N.B.
13831.	Keyser.	N.B. of Keyser.
13881.	West Union.	First N.B.
13885.	Oak Hill.	Merchants & Miners N.B.
13954.	Logan.	N.B. of Logan.
14002.	Elkins.	Tygarts Valley N.B.
14013.	Webster Springs.	Webster Springs N.B.
14034.	Oak Hill.	First N.B.
14053.	Philippi.	First N.B.
14136.	Salem.	First N.B.
14142.	Moundsville.	First N.B.
14198.	Berkeley Springs.	Citizens N.B.
14295.	Wellsburg.	Wellsburg N.B.
14318.	Ansted.	N.B. of Ansted.

WISCONSIN

Charter Number	City	Name of Bank
64.	Milwaukee.	First-Wisconsin N.B.
83.	Janesville.	First N.B.
95.	Hudson.	First N.B.
124.	Whitewater.	First N.B.
144.	Madison.	First N.B.
157.	Fort Atkinson.	First N.B.
178.	Columbus.	First N.B.
212.	Kenosha.	First N.B.
218.	Oshkkosh.	First N.B.
230.	Monroe.	First N.B.
400.	Berlin.	First N.B.

Charter Number	City	Name of Bank
425.	Ripon.	First N.B.
426.	Fox Lake.	First N.B.
457.	Racine.	First N.B.
555.	Fond du Lac.	First-Fond du Lac N.B.
749.	Janesville.	Rock County N.B.
836.	Beloit.	Beloit N.B.
851.	Beaver Dam.	N.B. of Beaver Dam.
852.	Manitowoc.	First N.B.
873.	Elkhorn.	First N.B.
874.	Green Bay.	First N.B.
1003.	Milwaukee.	Nat. Exchange Bank
1009.	Green Bay.	City N.B.
1010.	Watertown.	Wisconsin N.B.
1017.	Milwaukee.	Milwaukee N.B. of Wisconsin.
1076.	Jefferson.	N.B. of Jefferson.
1086.	Waukesha.	Waukesha N.B.
1115.	Sparta.	First N.B.
1159.	Waukesha.	Farmers' N.B.
1248.	Delavan.	N.B. of Delavan.
1313.	La Crosse.	First N.B.
1415.	Cedarburg.	First N.B.
1438.	Milwaukee.	Merchants' N.B.
1483.	Milwaukee.	Nat. City Bank.
1568.	Oshkosh.	Commercial N.B.
1602.	Neenah.	First N.B.
1650.	Appleton.	Appleton N.B.
1710.	Brodhead.	First N.B.
1714.	Menasha.	N.B. of Menasha.
1729.	Evansville.	First N.B.
1749.	Appleton.	First N.B.
1771.	Boscobel.	First N.B.
1787.	Oshkosh.	Union N.B.
1802.	Racine.	Manufacturers' N.B.
1819.	Green Bay.	N.B. of Commerce.
1820.	Appleton.	Manufacturers' N.B.
1933.	Burlington.	First N.B.
1998.	Wisconsin Rapids.	First N.B.
2069.	Eau Claire.	First N.B.
2079.	Baraboo.	First N.B.
2123.	Sheboygan.	First N.B.
2125.	Chippewa Falls.	First N.B.
2132.	Green Bay.	Kellogg N.B.
2133.	De Pere.	First N.B.
2163.	Beloit.	First N.B.
2344.	La Crosse.	La Cross N.B.
2407.	Beloit.	Citizens' N.B.
2557.	Racine.	Union N.B.
2565.	Appleton.	Commercial N.B.
2603.	Neenah.	Manufacturers' N.B.
2647.	Waukesha.	Nat. Exchange Bank
2653.	Superior.	First N.B.
2715.	Milwaukee.	First N.B.
2725.	Beloit.	Second N.B.
2748.	Janesville.	First N.B.
2759.	Eau Claire.	Eau Claire N.B.
2820.	Wausau.	First N.B.
2851.	Menomonie.	First N.B.
2877.	Oshkosh.	N.B. of Oshkosh.
2925.	Whitewater.	Citizens' N.B.
3001.	Stevens Point.	First N.B.
3125.	Lake Geneva.	First N.B.
3146.	Ripon.	Ripon N.B.
3161.	Darlington.	First N.B.
3196.	Ashland.	Ashland N.B.
3203.	Mineral Point.	First N.B.
3270.	Beaver Dam.	First N.B.
3308.	Darlington.	Citizens' N.B.
3391.	Waupun.	First N.B.
3412.	La Crosse.	Union N.B.
3541.	Oconto.	Oconto N.B.
3590.	Ashland.	First N.B.
3607.	Ashland.	Northern N.B.
3609.	Baraboo.	First N.B.
3641.	Kaukauna.	First N.B.
3685.	Fond du Lac.	Fond du Lac N.B.
3704.	Merrill.	First N.B.
3724.	Menasha.	First N.B.
3778.	Chippewa Falls.	Lumbermen's N.B.
3884.	Green Bay.	Citizens' N.B.
3897.	Black River Falls.	First N.B.
3926.	Superior.	First N.B.
4055.	Shullsburg.	First N.B.
4123.	Marinette.	First N.B.
4137.	Marinette.	Stephenson N.B.
4196.	Oshkosh.	German N.B.
4234.	Portage.	First N.B.
4304.	Hurley.	First N.B.
4305.	Ripon.	American N.B.
4312.	Rhinelander.	First N.B.
4399.	Superior, West Superior.	Keystone N.B.
4414.	Waupaca.	First N.B.
4424.	Waupaca.	Old N.B.
4508.	Oshkosh.	Nat. Union Bank.
4573.	Marshfield.	First N.B.
4602.	Beaver Dam.	American N.B.
4620.	Berlin.	First N.B.
4639.	Wisconsin Rapids.	Wood County N.B.
4641.	Berlin.	Berlin N.B.
4650.	Platteville.	First N.B.
4680.	Superior, West Superior.	Superior N.B.
4736.	Merrill.	N.B. of Merrill.
4744.	Wausau.	American N.B.
4783.	Green Bay.	McCartney N.B.
4816.	Milwaukee.	Central N.B.
4817.	Milwaukee.	Wisconsin N.B.
4878.	Superior,	

Charter Number	City	Name of Bank
	W. Superior.	Northwestern N.B.
4893.	South Milwaukee.	South Milwaukee N.B.
4912.	Stevens Point.	Citizens' N.B.
4937.	Appleton.	Citizens' N.B.
4975.	Manitowoc.	N.B. of Manitowoc.
5013.	New London.	First N.B.
5047.	La Crosse.	N.B. of La Crosse.
5143.	Antigo.	First N.B.
5222.	Stoughton.	First N.B.
5437.	Marshfield.	American N.B.
5446.	Tigerton.	First N.B.
5458.	Milwaukee.	Marine N.B.
5469.	Shawano.	First N.B.
5505.	Oconomowoc.	First N.B.
5521.	Oconto.	Citizens' N.B.
5535.	Ladysmith.	First N.B.
5557.	Oshkosh.	Commercial N.B.
5566.	Omro.	First N.B.
5592.	Lake Geneva.	Farmers' N.B.
5632.	Cuba City.	First N.B.
5658.	Peshtigo.	Peshfigo N.B.
5695.	Medford.	First N.B.
5779.	Mondovi.	First N.B.
5933.	Chilton.	Chilton N.B.
5942.	Antigo.	Langlade N.B.
5947.	Sheboygan Falls.	Dairymen's N.B.
5978.	Princeton.	First N.B.
6015.	Fond du Lac.	Commercial N.B.
6034.	Neenah.	Nat. Manufacturers' Bank.
6222.	Campbellsport.	First N.B.
6273.	Clintonville.	First N.B.
6403.	Shawano.	Wisconsin N.B.
6469.	De Pere.	N.B. of De Pere.
6575.	Seymour.	First N.B.
6604.	Oshkosh.	Old Commercial N.B.
6663.	Rice Lake.	First N.B.
6698.	Dodgeville.	First N.B.
6711.	Rib Lake.	First N.B.
6853.	Milwaukee.	N.B. of Commerce.
6908.	West Allis.	First N.B.
7007.	Lancaster.	First N.B.
7040.	Edgerton.	First N.B.
7087.	River Falls.	First N.B.
7136.	Wautorna.	First N.B.
7158.	Bayfield.	First N.B.
7224.	Brillion.	First N.B.
7264.	Fairchild.	First N.B.
7347.	La Crosse.	Batavian N.B.
7434.	Phillips.	First N.B.
7462.	Beaver Dam.	Old N.B.
7470.	Weyauwega.	First N.B.
7831.	Hayward.	First N.B.
7898.	Waupun.	N.B. of Waupun.
7901.	Richland Center.	First N.B.
7966.	Ladysmith.	Ladysmith N.B.
8118.	Dale.	First N.B.
8281.	Eau Claire.	Union N.B.
8338.	Alma.	First N.B.
8444.	Grantsburg.	First N.B.
8491.	Frederic.	First N.B.
8529.	Viroqua.	First N.B.
8632.	Rio.	First N.B.
8671.	Hartford.	First N.B.
8689.	Wauwatosa.	First N.B.
8710.	Manawa.	First N.B.
8887.	Marion.	German American N.B.
9003.	Watertown.	Merchants' N.B.
9140.	Superior.	United States N.B.
9153.	Madison.	Commercial N.B.
9304.	Stoughton.	Citizens' N.B.
9347.	Oshkosh.	City N.B.
9387.	Crandon.	First N.B.
9419.	Port Washington.	First N.B.
9522.	Fennimore.	First N.B.
9606.	Neillsville.	First N.B.
10106.	Baldwin.	First N.B.
10176.	Merrill.	Citizens' N.B.
10322.	Stone Lake.	First N.B.
10330.	Wisconsin Rapids.	Citizens' N.B.
10489.	Park Falls.	First N.B.
10510.	Hudson.	N.B. of Hudson.
10522.	Prescott.	First N.B.
10620.	Oregon.	First N.B.
10653.	Mayville.	First N.B.
10667.	Blair.	First N.B.
10725.	Pepin.	First N.B.
10733.	Nelson.	First N.B.
10791.	Durand.	First N.B.
10880.	Highland.	First N.B.
10890.	Barron.	First N.B.
10938.	Racine.	American N.B.
11051.	Niagara.	First N.B.
11060.	West Bend.	First N.B.
11083.	Glenwood City.	Farmers' N.B.
11104.	Horicon.	First N.B.
11114.	Blanchardville.	First N.B.
11128.	Boyceville.	First N.B.
11150.	Sheboygan.	Security N.B.
11245.	Knapp.	First N.B.
11412.	New Richmond.	First N.B.
11432.	Maiden Rock.	First N.B.
11463.	Sparta.	Farmers' N.B.
11526.	Saint Croix Falls.	First N.B.
11577.	Deerfield.	First N.B.
11594.	Hurley.	Hurley N.B.
11646.	Rhinelander.	Oneida N.B.
11783.	Burlington.	Burlington N.B.
11826.	Ladysmith.	Pioneer N.B.
11986.	Bruce.	First N.B.

Charter Number	City	Name of Bank
12124.	Eagle River.	First N.B.
12286.	Marion.	First N.B.
12351.	Kenosha.	United States N.B.
12482.	Milwaukee.	American N.B.
12534.	Washburn.	First N.B.
12541.	Kenosha.	Brown N.B.
12564.	Milwaukee.	Northwestern N.B.
12575.	Princeton.	Farmers-Merchants' N.B.
12628.	Milwaukee.	Grand and Sixth N.B.
12644.	Hayward.	People's N.B.
12814	Crandon	Crandon N.B.
12816.	Milwaukee.	Mechanics' N.B.
13165.	Superior.	N.B. of Commerce.
13184.	Milwaukee.	Second Wisconsin N.B.
13202.	Bangor.	First N.B.
13308.	Soldiers Grove.	First N.B.
13366.	Madison.	University Avenue N.B.
13487.	Phillips.	First N.B.
13529.	Durand.	First N.B.
13599.	Fennimore.	First N.B.
13616.	Oconomowoc.	Oconomowoc N.B.
13645.	Eau Claire.	American N.B. & Trust Co.
13806.	Oshkosh.	Oshkosh N.B.
13870.	Ashland.	Union N.B.
13879.	Fond du Lac.	National Exchange Bank.
13904.	Princeton.	Farmers-Merchants' N.B.
13921.	Manitowoc.	Manitowoc N.B.
13932.	Edgerton.	N.B. of Edgerton.
14058.	Viroqua.	First N.B.
14059.	Mayville.	First N.B.
14060.	Baraboo.	First N.B.
14063.	Waupaca.	First N.B.
14064.	Watertown.	Wisconsin N.B.
14095.	Durand.	Security N.B.
14109.	Superior.	Union N.B.
14125.	Marshfield.	Citizens N.B.
14130.	Marion.	First N.B.
14150.	Tigerton.	First N.B.
14184.	Darlington.	First N.B.
14200.	Neillsville.	First N.B.
14233.	Oconto.	First N.B.
14242.	Clintonville.	Clintonville N.B.
14314.	Shawano.	Shawano N.B.
14336.	Wauwatosa.	First N.B.

WYOMING

Charter Number	City	Name of Bank
1800.	Cheyenne.	First N.B.
2110.	Laramie.	Wyoming N.B.
2518.	Laramie.	Laramie N.B.
2652.	Cheyenne.	Stockgrowers' N.B.
3299.	Buffalo.	First N.B.
3416.	Cheyenne.	Cheyenne N.B.
3556.	Douglas.	First N.B.
3615.	Laramie.	Albany N.B.
3920.	Rock Springs.	First N.B.
4320.	Rawlins.	First N.B.
4343.	Sundance.	First N.B.
4604.	Sheridan.	First N.B.
4720.	Lander.	First N.B.
4755.	Rock Springs.	Rock Springs N.B.
4989.	Laramie.	First N.B.
5295.	Guernsey.	First N.B.
5413.	Rawlins.	Rawlins N.B.
5480.	Kemmerer.	First N.B.
5949.	Thermopolis.	First N.B.
6340.	Meeteetse.	First N.B.
6850.	Casper.	Casper N.B.
7083.	Casper.	Stockmen's N.B.
7198.	Newcastle.	First N.B.
7319.	Cody.	First N.B.
7978.	Shoshoni.	First N.B.
8020.	Cody.	Shoshone N.B.
8087.	Douglas.	Douglas N.B.
8089.	Cheyenne.	Citizens' N.B.
8232.	Shoshoni.	Wind River N.B.
8253.	Worland.	First N.B.
8275.	Sheridan.	Sheridan N.B.
8432.	Wheatland.	First N.B.
8534.	Evanston.	First N.B.
8612.	Evanston.	Evanston N.B.
8961.	Saratoga.	First N.B.
9289.	Torrington.	First N.B.
9557.	Rawlins.	Stock Growers' N.B.
10265.	Powell.	First N.B.
10533.	Casper.	Wyoming N.B.
10565.	Powell.	Powell N.B.
10698.	Green River.	First N.B.
10810.	Greybull.	First N.B.
10844.	Lovell.	First N.B.
10858.	Bason.	First N.B.
11079.	Newcastle.	Newcastle N.B.
11132.	Torrington.	Citizens' N.B.
11231.	Lingle.	First N.B.
11309.	Torrington.	Torrington N.B.
11342.	Rock River.	First N.B.
11352.	Manville.	First N.B.
11380.	Cheyenne.	American N.B.
11390.	Lusk.	First N.B.
11490.	Casper.	N.B. of Commerce.
11666.	Hanna.	First N.B.
11683.	Casper.	Citizens' N.B.
12558.	Parco.	First N.B.
12638.	Thermopolis.	First N.B.
14103.	Riverton.	First N.B.

APPENDIX

I. THE SIGNATURES OF UNITED STATES CURRENCY

The following table (courtesy of the Treasury Department and W. A Philpott, Jr.) shows the exact period of time during which each two of the various signers of our currency were in office concurrently.

Register of the Treasury	Treasurer of the U.S.	Combined Tenure Began	Combined Tenure Ended	Length of Time Years	Length of Time Months	Length of Time Days *
Lucius E. Chittenden	F. E. Spinner	4-17-1861	8-10-1864	3	3	23
S. B. Colby	F. E. Spinner	8-11-1864	9-21-1867	3	1	10
Noah L. Jeffries	F. E. Spinner	10-5-1867	3-15-1869	1	5	10
John Allison	F. E. Spinner	4-3-1869	6-30-1875	6	2	27
John Allison	John C. New	6-30-1875	7-1-1676	1	-	1
John Allison	A. U. Wyman	7-1-1876	6-30-1877	-	11	29
John Allison	James Gilfillan	7-1-1877	3-23-1878	-	8	22
Glenni W. Scofield	James Gilfillan	4-1-1878	5-20-1881	3	1	19
Blanche K. Bruce	James Cilfillan	5-21-1881	3-31-1883	1	10	10
Blanche K. Bruce	A. U. Wyman	4-1-1883	4-30-1885	2	-	29
Blanche K. Bruce	Conrad N. Jordan	5-1-1885	6-5-1885	-	1	4
William S. Rosecrans	Conrad N.Jordan	6-8-1885	5-23-1887	1	11	15
William S. Roseerans	James W. Hyatt	5-24-1887	5-10-1889	1	11	16
William S. Rarecrans	J. N. Huston	5-11-1889	4-21-1891	1	11	13
William S. Rosecrans	Enos H. Nebeker	4-25-1891	5-31-1893	2	1	6
William S. Rosecrans	Daniel N. Morgan	6-1-1893	6-19-1893	-	-	18
James F. Tillman	Daniel N. Morgan	7-1-1893	6-30-1897	3	11	29
James F. Tillman	Ellis H.Roberts	7-1-1897	12-21897	-	5	1
Blanche K. Bruce	Ellis H. Roberts	12-3-1897	5-17-1898	-	3	14
Judson W. Lyons	Ellis H. Roberts	4-7-1898	6-30-1905	7	2	23
Judson W. Lyons	Charles H. Treat	7-1-1905	4-1-1906	-		-
William T. Vernon	Charles H. Treat	6-12-1906	10-30-1909	3	9	18
William T. Vernon	Lee McClung	11-1-1909	3-14-1911	1	4	13
James C. Napier	Lee McClung	8-15-1911	11-21-1912	1	4	6
James C. Napier	Carmi A. Thompson	11-22-1912	3-31-1913	-	8	9
James C. Napier	John Burke	4-1-1913	9-30-1913	-	4	29
Gabe E. Parker	John Burke	10-1-1913	12-31-1914	1	5	30
Houston B.Teehee	John Burke	3-24-1915	11-20-1919	4	2	26
William S. Elliott	John Burke	11-21-1919	1-5-1921	1	7	14
William S. Elliott	Frank White	5-2-1921	1-261922	-	1	22
Harley V. Speelman	Frank White	1-25-1922	9-30-1927	5	8	5
Walter O. Woods	Frank White	10-1-1927	5-1-1928	-	7	-
Walter O. Woods	H. T. Tate	5-31-1928	1-17-1929	-	7	16
Edward E. Jones	Walter O. Woods	1-22-1929	5-31-1933	4	4	9
Secretary of the Treasury						
William G. McAdoo	John Burke	4-1-1913	12-15-1918	5	8	14
Carter Glass	John Burke	12-18-1918	2-1-1920	1	1	15
D. F. Houston	John Burke	2-2-1920	1-5-1921	-	11	3
A. W. Mellon	Frank White	5-2-1921	5-1-1928	6	11	29
A. W. Mellon	H. T. Tate	4-30-1928	1-17-1929	-	8	16
A. W. Mellon	Walter O. Woods	1-18-1929	2-12-1932	3	-	25
Ogden L. Mills	Walter O. Woods	2-13-1932	3-3-1933	1	-	18
W. H. Woodin	Walter O. Woods	3-4-1933	5-31-1933	-	2	27
W. H. Woodin	W. A. Julian	6-1-1933	12-31-1933	-	7	-
Henry Morgenthau, Jr.	W. A. Julian	1-1-1934	7-22-1945	11	6	22
Fred M. Vinson	W. A. Julian	7-23-1945	7-23-1946	1	-	-
John W. Snyder	W. A. Julian	1-25-1946	5-29-1949	2	10	4
John W. Snyder	Georgia Neese Clark	6-21-1949	1-20-1953	3	7	-
George M. Humphrey	Ivy Baker Priest	1-28-1953	7-28-1957	4	6	-
Robert B. Anderson	Ivy Baker Priest	7-29-1957	1-20-1961	3	5	23
C. Douglas Dillon	Elizabeth Rudel Smith	1-30-1961	4-13-1962	1	3	14
C. Douglas Dillon	Kathryn O'Hay Granahan	1-3-1963	3-31-1965	2	2	28
Henry Fowler	Kathryn O'Hay Granahan	4-1-1965	10-13-1966	1	6	13
Joseph Barr	*Kathryn O'Hay Granahan	12-23-1968	1-20-1969	-	-	28
David Kennedy	Dorothy Andrews Elston	5-8-1969	9-16-1970	1	4	8
David Kennedy	‡Dorothy Andrews Kabis	9-17-1970	2-1-1971	-	4	15
John B. Connally	Dorothy Andrews Kabis	2-8-1971	7-3-1971	-	44	25
John B. Connally	Romana Acosta Banuelos	12-17-1971	6-12-1973	-	5	26
George P. Shultz	Romana Acosta Banuelos	6-12-1972	2-14-1974	1	8	2
William E. Simon	Francine I. Neff	6-21-1974	1-19-1977	2	6	28
W. Michael Blumenthal	Azie Taylor Morton	9-12-1977	8-4-1979	1	10	24
G. William Miller	Azie Taylor Morton	8-6-1979	1-20-1981	1	5	15
Donald T. Regan	Angela Marie Buchanan	3-17-1981	7-5-1983	2	3	18
Donald T. Regan	Katherine Davalos Ortega	9-22-1983	2-3-1985	1	4	12
James A. Baker	Katherine Davalos Ortega	2-4-1985	8-18-1988	3	6	13
Nicholas F. Brady	Katherine Davalos Ortega	9-15-88	6-30-1989	-	9	15
Nicholas F. Brady	Catalina Vasquez Villalpando	11-20-1989	1-20-1993	3	2	1
Lloyd M. Bentsen	Mary Ellen Withrow	3-1-1994	12-22-1994	-	9	22
Robert E. Rubin	Mary Ellen Withrow	10-1-1995	7-2-1999	3	9	1
Lawrence F. Summers	Mary Ellen Withrow	7-2-1999				

Although no longer Treasurer, Kathryn Granahan's signature continued in use until Dorothy Elston was named to replace her.

‡ When Dorothy Elston married Walter Kabis on September 17, 1970, it was the first time the signature of a Treasurer was changed during the term of office.

II. DATES OF ISSUE FOR SMALL SIZE NOTES

The following table (compiled by David L. Ganz and with the cooperation of the Bureau of Engraving and Printing) shows the dates between which the Bureau printed each series of small size notes ($5 and up). When available, both the first and last dates of printing are given. If both dates could not be located the reader should assume dates close to those listed under "Combined Tenure" for each signature combination listed in Appendix I.

With the knowledge that a dollar bill remains in circulation for approximately 18 months, and that higher denominations circulate for a longer time in direct relation to the value, i.e., up to four years for a twenty dollar note and to between seven and eight years for fifty and hundred dollar notes; by using this table, the reader can determine the approximate length of time each issue of small size currency remained in circulation.

$5 FEDERAL RESERVE NOTES

Catalog Number	Signatures	Series	First Delivered	Last Delivered	
1950	Mellon-Tate	1928	4-30-28	1-17-29	
1951	Mellon-Woods	1928A	1-18-29		
1952	Mellon-Woods	1928B	2-12-32		
1953	Mills-Woods	1928C	2-13-32	3-3-33	
1954	Woodin-Woods	1928D	3-5-33	5-31-33	
1955-1956	Morgenthau-Julian	1934	11-2-34	No Record	
1957	Morgenthau-Julian	1934A	No Record	4-2-47	
2301	Vinson-Julian	1934	6-8-42		(Overprinted
2302	Vinson-Julian	1934A		5-30-44	"HAWAII")
1958	Vinson-Julian	1934B	11-19-45	4-1-47	
1959	Julian-Snyder	1934C	9-31-46	7-3-50	
1960-1961	Snyder-Clark	1934D, 1950	11-7-50	9-1-53	
1962	Humphrey-Priest	1950A	7-14-53	9-10-57	
1963	Anderson-Priest	1950B	9-25-57	6-14-61	
1964	Dillon-Smith	1950C	3-3-61	3-13-63	
1965	Dillon-Granahan	1950D	1-5-63	8-31-65	
1966	Fowler-Granahan	1950E	9-9-65	7-2-67	
1967	Dillon-Granahan	1963	9-16-64	7-15-65	
1968	Fowler-Granahan	1963A	6-7-65	9-9-69	
1969	Kennedy-Elston	1969	8-4-69	11-10-71	
1970	Connally-Kabis	1969A	6-28-71	5-2-73	
1971	Connally-Banuelos	1969B	5-2-73	2-13-73	
1972	Shultz-Banuelos	1969C	10-24-72	12-10-74	
1973	Simon-Neff	1974	9-27-74	4-12-78	
1974	Blumenthal-Morton	1977	10-20-77	6-10-80	
1975	Miller-Morton	1977A	12-21-79	12-10-81	
1976i	Regan-Buchanan	1981	6-3-81	7-2-84	
1977	Regan-Ortega	1981A	4-17-84	7-11-85	
1978	Baker-Ortega	1985	6-26-85		

$5 UNITED STATES NOTES

Catalog Number	Signatures	Series	First Delivered	Last Delivered
1525	Mellon-Woods	1928	5-21-29	12-19-30
1526	Mills-Woods	1928A	1-8-31	No Record
1527	Morgenthau-Julian	1928B	No Record	6-18-34
1528	Morgenthau-Julian	1928C	6-19-34	2-25-46
1529	Vinson-Julian	1928D	3-11-46	9-19-46
1530	Snyder-Julian	1928E	9-20-46	3-21-50
1531	Snyder-Clark	1928F	3-21-50	4-27-53
1532	Humphrey-Priest	1953	5-6-53	8-28-57
1533	Anderson-Priest	1953A	2-10-58	1-13-61
1534	Dillon-Smith	1953B	10-5-61	2-25-63
1535	Dillon-Granahan	1953C	2-26-63	11-8-63
1536	Dillon-Granahan	1963	3-2-64	11-27-67

$5 SILVER CERTIFICATES

Catalog Number	Signatures	Series	First Delivered	Last Delivered	
1650	Morgenthau-Jullian	1934	7-20-34	1-26-38	
1651	Morgenthau-Julian	1934A	1-27-38	2-6-46	
2307	Morgenthau-Julian	1934A	9-4-42	5-8-44	WW II
1652	Vinson-Julian	1934B	2-6-46	12-16-46	
1653	Snyder-Julian	1934C	12-19-46	10-24-49	
1654	Snyder-Clark	1934D	10-25-49	10-1-53	
1655	Humphrey-Priest	1953	5-12-53	8-21-57	
1656	Anderson-Priest	1953A	12-9-57	3-17-61	
1657	Dillon-Smith	1953B	3-28-61	4-25-62	
1658	Dillon-Granahan	1953C	11-12-63	8-31-64	

$5 FEDERAL RESERVE BANK NOTES
(National Currency)

Catalog Number	Signatures	Series	First Delivered	Last Delivered
1800, 1850	Jones-Woods	1929	3-11-33	1-11-34

$10 FEDERAL RESERVE NOTES

Catalog Number	Signatures	Series	First Delivered	Last Delivered	
2000	Mellon-Tate	1928	4-30-28	1-11-29	
2001	Mellon-Woods	1928A	1-18-29	No Record	
2002	Mellon-Woods	1928B	No Record	2-12-32	
2003	Mills-Woods	1928C	2-13-32	3-3-33	
2004-2005	Morgenthau-Julian	1934	10-17-34	12-13-35	
2006	Morgenthau-Julian	1934A	6-8-42	7-12-44	
2303	Mortgenthau-Julian	1934A	6-8-42	8-12-46	(Overprinted
2007	Vinson-Julian	1934B	11-23-45	6-3-47	"HAWAII")
2008	Snyder-Julian	1934C	10-22-46	1-19-50	
2009	Snyder-Clark	1934D	9-28-49	1-31-51	
2010	Snyder-Clark	1950	11-7-50	10-1-53	
2011	Humphrey-Priest	1950A	4-3-53	9-12-57	
2012	Anderson-Priest	1950B	9-25-57	5-15-61	
2013	Dillon-Smith	1950C	10-23-59	3-14-63	
2014	Dillon-Granahan	1950D	2-19-63	8-30-65	
2015	Fowler-Granahan	1950E	9-13-65	9-16-68	
2016	Dillon-Granahan	1963	4-24-64	7-8-65	
2017	Fowler-Granahan	1963A	5-12-65	7-28-69	
2018	Kennedy-Elston	1969	8-4-69	10-4-71	
2019	Connally-Kabis	1969A	7-9-71	4-25-73	
2020	Connally-Banuelos	1969B	6-5-72	9-5-73	
2021	Shultz-Banuelos	1996C	11-6-72	12-10-74	
2022	Simon-Neff	1974	9-3-74	6-14-78	
2023	Biumenthal-Morton	1977	1-4-77	2-11 -8	
2024	Miller-Morton	1977 A	4-10-77	3-1-82	
2025	Regan-Buchanan	1981	3-23-82	4-17-84	
2026	Regan-Ortega	1981A	4-17-84	1-7-86	
2027	Baker-Ortega	1985	9-10-85		

$10 FEDERAL RESERVE BANK NOTES
(National Currency)

Catalog Number	Signatures	Series	First Delivered	Last Delivered
1801, 1860	Jones-Woods	1929	3-10-33	11-18-33

$10 SILVER CERTIFICATES

Catalog Number	Signatures	Series	First Delivered	Last Delivered	
1700	Woodin-Julian	1933	1-5-34	2-27-34	
1700-a	Morgenthau-Julian	1933A	2-27-34	4-2-34	
2308	Morgenthau-Julian	1934	9-4-42		WW II
2309	Morgenthau-Julian	1934A		5-8-44	WW II
1703	Morgenthau-Julian	1934	4-17-34	4-1-35	
1702	Morgenthau-Julian	1934A	4-2-35	9-4-46	
1703	Vinson-Julian	1934B	9-4-46	8-5-47	
1704	Snyder-Julian	1934C	8-5-47	7-12-50	
1705	Snyder-Clark	1934D	7-12-50	4-14-53	
1706	Humphrey-Priest	1953	5-12-53	8-27-57	
1707	Anderson-Priest	1953A	2-13-58	2-17-56	
1708	Dillon-Smith	19538	2-2-62	3-14-62	

Catalog Number	Signatures	Series	First Delivered	Last Delivered

$20 FEDERAL RESERVE NOTES

Catalog Number	Signatures	Series	First Delivered	Last Delivered
2050	Mellon-Tate	1928	4-30-28	1-17-29
2051	Mellon-Woods	1928A	1-18-29	No Record
2052	Mellon-Woods	1928B	No Record	2-12-32
2053	Mills-Woods	1928C	2-13-32	3-3-33
2304	Vinson-Julian	1934	6-8-42	(Overprinted
2305	Vinson-Julian	1934A		7-18-44 "HAWAII")
2054	Morgenthau-Julian	1934	2-2-35	No Record
2055	Morgenthau-Julian	1934A	No Record	2-4-46
2056	Vinson-Julian	1934B	11-29-45	10-22-47
2057	Julian-Snyder	1934C	1-7-47	4-3-50
2058	Snyder-Clark	1934D	1-13-50	1-29-51
2059	Snyder-Clark	1950	11-7-50	8-31-53
2060	Humphrey-Priest	1950A	8-19-53	8-30-57
2061	Anderson-Priest	1950B	9-23-57	6-16-61
2062	Dillon-Smith	1950C	2-28-61	3-21-63
2063	Dillon-Granahan	1950D	2-12-63	11-30-63
2064	Dillon-Granahan	1950E	9-1-65	7-13-66
2065	Dillon-Granahan	1963	10-7-64	7-2-65
2066	Fowler-Granahan	1963A	6-8-65	8-29-69
2067	Kennedy-Elston	1969	7-30-69	9-15-71
2068	Connally-Kabis	1969A	6-15-71	3-21-73
2069	Connally-Banuelos	1969B	6-6-72	4-25-73
2070	Shultz-Banuelos	1969C	9-27-72	11-14-74
2071	Simon-Neff	1974	9-11-74	7-19-78
2072	Blumenthal-Morton	1977	4-27-78	1-27-82
2073	Regan-Buchanan	1981	11-17-81	7-9-84
2074	Regan-Ortega	1981A	5-22-84	12-2-85
2075	Baker-Ortega	1985	10-25-85	

$20 FEDERAL RESERVE BANK NOTES
(National Currency)

Catalog Number	Signatures	Series	First Delivered	Last Delivered
1802, 1870	Jones-Woods	1929	3-11-33	12-22-33

$50 FEDERAL RESERVE NOTES

Catalog Number	Signatures	Series	First Delivered	Last Delivered
2100	Mellon-Woods	1928	6-13-29	No Record
2101	Mellon-Woods	1928A	No Record	12-10-34
2102	Morgenthau-Julian	1934	3-9-35	No Record
2103	Morgenthau-Julian	1934A	No Record	7-13-46
2104	Vinson-Julian	1934B	7-11-46	8-19-47
2105	Snyder-Julian	1934C	8-12-47	1-11-51
2106	Snyder-Clark	1934D	7-21-50	1-11-51
2107	Snyder-Clark	1950	2-21-51	8-28-57
2108	Humphrey-Priest	1950A	12-7-54	8-20-57
2109	Anderson-Priest	1950B	10-14-57	12-8-60
2110	Dillon-Smith	1950C	7-12-61	12-4-62
2111	Dillon-Granahan	1950D	7-19-63	8-27-65
2112	Fowler-Granahan	1950E	9-10-65	11-30-65
2113	Fowler-Granahan	1963A	11-8-66	7-1-69
2114	Kennedy-Elston	1969	7-9-69	9-20-72
2115	Connally-Kabis	1969A	8-11-71	8-1-73
2116	Connally-Banuelos	1969B	9-5-72	12-5-73
2117	Shultz-Banuelos	1969C	11-2-72	12-11-74
2118	Simon-Neff	1974	8-29-74	1-6-81
2119	Blumenthal-Morton	1977	8-16-76	1-11-83
2120	Regan-Buchanan	1981	5-3-81	2-25-85
2121	Regan-Ortega	1981A	10-23-84	11-5-85
2122	Baker-Ortega	1985	10-24-85	

$50 FEDERAL RESERVE BANK NOTES
(National Currency)

Catalog Number	Signatures	Series	First Delivered	Last Delivered
1803, 1880	Jones-Woods	1929	3-11-33	8-30-33

$100 FEDERAL RESERVE NOTES

Catalog Number	Signatures	Series	First Delivered	Last Delivered
2130	Mellon-Woods	1928	8-30-29	No Record
2151	Mellon-Woods	1928A	No Record	12-6-34
2152	Morgenthau-Julian	1934	3-9-35	No Record
2153	Morgenthau-Julian	1934A	No Record	1-19-51
2154	Vinson-Julian	1934B	7-13-49	8-4-47
2155	Snyder-Julian	1934C	12-31-46	1-18-31
2156	Snyder-Clark	1934D	7-24-50	1-17-51
2157	Snyder-Clark	1950	5-9-51	9-9-53
2158	Humphrey-Priest	1950A	12-8-54	8-20-57
2159	Anderson-Priest	1950B	9-4-37	12-9-60
2160	Dillon-Smith	1950C	9-12-61	12-14-62
2161	Dillon-Granahan	1950D	7-23-63	8-30-65
2162	Fowler-Granahan	1950E	9-3-65	7-27-66
2163	Fowler-Granahan	1963A	9-27-66	12-24-66
2164	Kennedy-Elston	1969	7-9-69	11-9-71
2165	Kennedy-Kabis	1969A	8-9-71	12-4-73
2166	Shultz-Banuelos	1969C	10-3-72	10-31-74
2167	Simon-Neff	1974	10-15-74	7-18-78
2168	Blumenthal-Morton	1977	8-8-78	11-29-83
2169	Regan-Buchanan	1981	5-15-81	7-15-85
2170	Regan-Ortega	1981A	11-6-84	11-20-85
2171	Baker-Ortega	1985	11-20-85	

$100 UNITED STATES NOTES

Catalog Number	Signatures	Series	First Delivered	Last Delivered
1550	Fowler-Granahan	1966	10-14-68	11-5-68
1551	Kennedy-Elston	1966A	1-26-71	1-26-71

$100 FEDERAL RESERVE BANK NOTES
(National Currency)

Catalog Number	Signatures	Series	First Delivered	Last Delivered
1804, 1890	Jones-Woods	1929	3-11-33	3-30-33

$500 FEDERAL RESERVE NOTES

Catalog Number	Signatures	Series	First Delivered	Last Delivered
2200	Mellon-Woods	1928	11-14-29	3-18-33
2201	Morgenthau-Julian	1934	12-23-35	7-21-45

$1000 FEDERAL RESERVE NOTES

Catalog Number	Signatures	Series	First Delivered	Last Delivered
2210	Mellon-Woods	1928	11-14-29	7-26-33
2211	Morgenthau-Julian	1934	12-17-35	11-17-43
2212	Morgenthau-Julian	1934A	3-30-42	7-21-45

III. UNCUT SHEETS OF SMALL SIZE NOTES

Small size notes were printed in sheets of twelve from 1928 to 1952 and were sold to the public starting in 1935. Sheets made from 1928 to 1934 were made for presentation only and are rare.

A small additional number were released upon the introduction of eighteen subject sheets in 1953, but the practice was discontinued soon thereafter. Although thirty-two subject sheets were first printed in 1957, it was not until 1981that, as part of the Bureau of Engraving and Printing's Public Affairs Program, they were made available for sale to the public.

Listed below, by catalog number, are only those sheets for which a record of issue is known. There are also records of sheets of Federal Reserve Notes, Series of 1928, in denominations from $5 to $50; and of $10 and $20 Federal Reserve Bank Notes, Series of 1929. Since these sheets were most likely issued for official purposes only, and are extremely rare, they are not listed individually.

LEGAL TENDER NOTES

No. & Denomination		Series	Sheet Size	No. Issued	Value
1500	$1	1928	12	11	Rare
1501	$2	1928	12	5	Rare
1504	$2	1928C	12	25	$1,500.00
1505	$2	1928D	12	50	$1,400.00
1506	$2	1928E	12	50	$1,400.00
1507	$2	1928F	12	100	$1,400.00
1508	$2	1928G	12	100	$1,300.00
1509	$2	1953	18	100	$1,850.00
1525	$5	1928	12	5	Rare
1529	$5	1928D	12	25	$2,750.00
1530	$5	1928E	12	100	$2,500.00
1532	$5	1963	18	100	$3,250.00

SILVER CERTIFICATES

No. & Denomination		Series	Size	No. Issued	Value
1600	$1	1928	12	80	$3,000.00
1602	$1	1928B	12	6	Rare
1603	$1	1928C	12	11	Rare
1604	$1	1928D	12	60	$3,000.00
1605	$1	1928E	12	25	$15,000.00
1606	$1	1934	12	25	$3,000.00
1607	$1	1935	12	100	$1,250.00
1608	$1	1935A	12	100	$1,000.00
1611	$1	1935B	12	100	$1,000.00
1612	$1	1935C	12	100	$1,850.00
1613	$1	1935D	12	300	$1,250.00
1613	$1	1935D	18	102	$1,300.00
1614	$1	1935E	18	400	$1,250.00

Sheet No. & Denomination		Series	Size	No. Issued	Value
1650	$5	1934	12	25	$2,750.00
1652	$5	1934B	12	20	$3,250.00
1653	$5	1934C	12	100	$2,250.00
1654	$5	1934D	12	100	$2,250.00
1655	$5	1953	18	100	$2,000.00
1700	$10	1933	12	1	Rare
1700A	$10	1933A	12	1	Rare
1701	$10	1934	12	10	$5,250.00
1706	$10	1953	18	100	$5,000.00

NATIONAL BANK NOTES

These notes were printed in sheets of 12 but only delivered in sheets of six. Valuations are for the most common banks and for Type I Notes. Others command higher prices.

1800	$5	1929	6		$900.00
1801	$10	1929	6		$950.00
1802	$20	1929	6		$1,000.00
1803	$50	1929	6		$5,000.00
1804	$100	1929	6		$6,000.00

WORLD WAR II EMERGENCY ISSUES

2300	$1 HAWAII	1935A	12	25	$7,500.00
2306	$1 YELLOW SEAL	1935A	12	25	$9,000.00

FEDERAL RESERVE NOTES

1911	$1	1981	32		50.00
1911	$1	1981	16		27.50
1911	$1	1981	4		12.50
1912	$1	1981A	32		50.00
1912	$1	1981A	16		27.50
1912	$1	1981A	4		12.50
1913	$1	1985	32		50.00
1913	$1	1985	16		27.50
1913	$1	1985	4		12.50
1914	$1	1985	32		50.00
1914	$1	1985	16		27.50
1914	$1	1985	4		12.50
1921	$1	1995	32		50.00
1921	$1	1995	16		31.00
1921	$1	1995	8		20.00
1921	$1	1995	4		15.00
1935*	$2	1976	32		50.00
1935*	$2	1976	16		27.50
1936	$2	1995	32		85.00
1936	$2	1995	16		48.00
1936	$2	1995	8		28.00
1936	$2	1995	4		19.00
1984	$5	1995	32		195.00
1984	$5	1995	16		105.00
1984	$5	1995	8		58.00
1984	$5	1995	4		35.00
2032*	$10	1995	16		249.00

IV. PRICE APPRECIATION RECORD OF UNCIRCULATED LARGE SIZE TYPE NOTES

The following listing records the market values of Large Size type notes in uncirculated condition for the past forty-five years. The values used are the prices taken from the 1953, 1964, 1975, 1992 and present edition of this book. The comparison shows with clarity the steadily rising popularity of these issues. Although it is not exhaustive, the editors have tried to include at least one note of each design for which prices have been shown in the past. Scarce early issues, which are infrequently available, are not included.

The notes selected are not rarities, but rather, "type" notes i.e. notes selected to represent each design issued by the Government. While some collectors acquire every signature combination or variety available, type note collectors acquire the most common, least expensive note in a series. Also, "type" note collectors acquire notes in the best condition they can afford. When the collection is complete, it includes a specimen of every different type of note issued by the United States.

No.	1953	1964	1975	1992	2001	No.	1953	1964	1975	1992	2001
16	25.00	85.00	325.00	650.00	1,850.00	358	27.50	200.00	400.00	1,100,00	3,500.00
18	40.00	110.00	335.00	1,200.00	2,250.00	361	80.00	450.00	900.00	2,500.00	4,250.00
34	20.00	50.00	175.00	400.00	1,000.00	362	40.00	210.00	500.00	750.00	2,200.00
40	5.00	45.00	115.00	235.00	525.00	368	60.00	500.00	1,100.00	2,750.00	6,000.00
41	37.50	250.00	485.00	1,850.00	3,500.00	371	50.00	285.00	475.00	1,500.00	7,500.00
42	40.00	325.00	750.00	2,200.00	5,000.00	374	100.00	950.00	3,250.00	10,000.00	17,500.00
57	10.00	32.50	60.00	235.00	475.00	375	75.00	1,500.00	3,600.00	15,000.00	20,000.00
64	45.00	82.50	275.00	1,100.00	2,500.00	380	40.00	160.00	500.00	1,000.00	1,600.00
91	17.50	27.50	60.00	225.00	600.00	391	60.00	525.00	1,450.00	2,750.00	4,000.00
93	85.00	300.00	550.00	2,350.00	6,000.00	394	75.00	260.00	600.00	1,500.00	1,500.00
95	65.00	210.00	525.00	2,200.00	3,500.00	409	100.00	275.00	850.00	3,500.00	3,000.00
96	65.00	250.00	700.00	1,850.00	4,500.00	466	27.50	75.00	160.00	850.00	800.00
113	50.00	125.00	250.00	850.00	1,500.00	479	35.00	90.00	175.00	750.00	900.00
122	35.00	75.00	350.00	1,750.00	3,400.00	493	60.00	150.00	300.00	1,000.00	1,250.00
123	45.00	385.00	1,200.00	3,000.00	4,750.00	507	150.00	440.00	800.00	4,500.00	6,500.00
124	125.00	425.00	950.00	7,500.00	10,000.00	519	250.0	250.00	250.00	5,500.00	8,500.00
127	125.00	1,200.00	2,250.00	5,000.00	9,500.00	532	30.00	120.00	275.00	700.00	800.00
147	750.00	150.00	300.00	950.00	2,000.00	539	40.00	140.00	325.00	850.00	900.00
148	200.00	1,850.00	4,250.00	Rare	Rare	550	60.00	175.00	350.00	1,100.00	1,100.00
151	750.00	4,500.00	8,500.00	20,000.00	70,000.00	558	160.00	500.00	850.00	4,500.00	5,000.00
164	200.00	500.00	1,200.00	4,500.00	13,000.00	566	250.00	675.00	2,000.00	6,000.00	5,500.00
165	400.00	2,750.00	5,500.00	32,500.00	Rare	573	50.00	275.00	700.00	1,000.00	1,100.00
168	400.00	4,250.00	8,500.00	27,500.00	85,000.00	577	50.00	250.00	500.00	1,400.00	1,400.00
181	300.00	725.00	1,550.00	9,000.00	16,000.00	580	85.00	500.00	1,200.00	2,600.00	2,250.00
221	50.00	240.00	500.00	1,100.00	1,700.00	598	15.00	22.00	70.00	250.00	300.00
223	15.00	65.00	225.00	900.00	1,500.00	624	27.50	32.50	80.00	300.00	300.00
225	25.00	90.00	300.00	950.00	1,900.00	650	47.50	55.00	110.00	300.00	350.00
236	4.50	18.00	42.50	150.00	425.00	675	120.00	190.00	250.00	1,950.00	1,950.00
237	3.50	15.00	37.50	52.50	100.00	698	200.00	275.00	385.00	2,300.00	2,300.00
240	27.50	125.00	325.00	1,250.00	2,500.00	708	10.00	42.50	57.50	150.00	300.00
245	35.00	300.00	700.00	2,400.00	4,250.00	747	17.50	70.00	110.00	425.00	1,300.00
247	55.00	330.00	800.00	2,500.00	4,000.00	782	25.00	90.00	150.00	370.00	750.00
258	8.00	32.50	135.00	450.00	750.00	813	60.00	335.00	775.00	1,850.00	2,400.00
259	50.00	285.00	1,200.00	3,400.00	7,500.00	822	85.00	575.00	900.00	2,750.00	6,500.00
267	30.00	160.00	475.00	2,600.00	4,250.00	832	35.00	115.00	180.00	400.00	1,800.00
268	55.00	380.00	1,300.00	4,250.00	7,500.00	844	17.50	20.00	35.00	90.00	240.00
281	20.00	60.00	275.00	1,100.00	2,700.00	892	60.00	165.00	250.00	600.00	2,000.00
282	27.50	135.00	375.00	1,250.00	2,500.00	904	27.50	30.00	42.50	120.00	240.00
286	150.00	750.00	1,500.00	4,250.00	4,750.00	952	60.00	200.00	275.00	800.00	2,250.00
289	100.00	475.00	1,000.00	3,750.00	7,500.00	964	45.00	47.50	57.50	175.00	300.00
291	75.00	285.00	600.00	4,500.00	9,000.00	1012	135.00	375.00	500.00	2,000.00	5,500.00
304	40.00	190.00	425.00	1,500.00	4,000.00	1024	125.00	130.00	145.00	850.00	1,150.00
308	200.00	1,200.00	2,000.00	10,000.00	10,000.00	1036	125.00	130.00	145.00	850.00	1,150.00
309	200.00	675.00	1,750.00	6,500.00	15,000.00	1072	225.00	450.00	550.00	2,200.00	8,000.00
313	120.00	800.00	1,750,00	9,500.00	25,000.00	1084	200.00	210.00	240.00	850.00	2,000.00
320	75.00	250.00	550.00	3,000.00	7,000.00	1166	500.00	1,800.00	2,800.00	Rare	Rare
330	175.00	600.00	1,100.00	Rare	Rare						
343	300.00	1,150.00	2,750.00	Rare	Rare						
347	70.00	300.00	650.00	1,750.00	4,000.00						
350	20.00	85.00	200.00	500.00	1,400.00						
353	75.00	500.00	1,000.00	2,500.00	6,500.00						

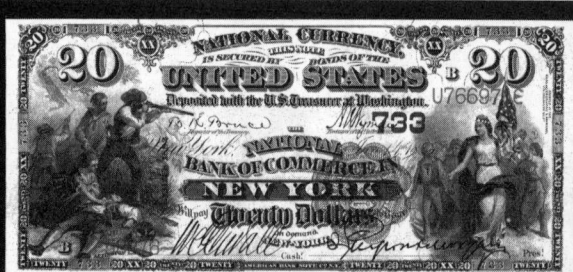

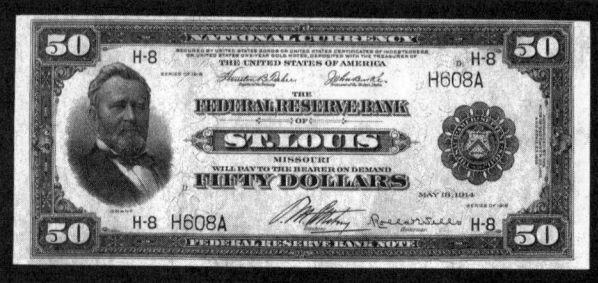

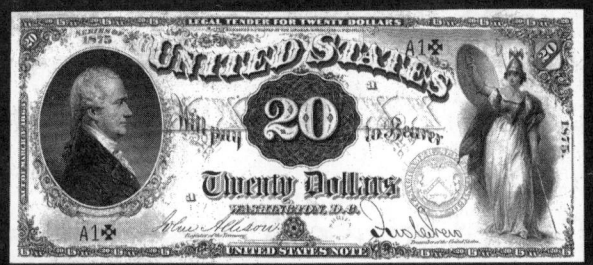

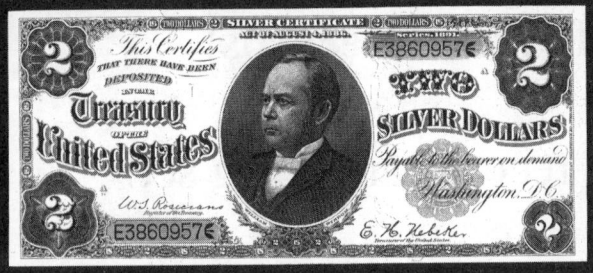

RECORDS, LIKE CURRENCY, COME IN THREE SIZES

Record price paid for a Large Size Note: $935,000*
SOLD by CAA in our January, 2000 AUCTION
*Fr. 1218d 1882 Gold Certificate

Record price paid for a Small Size Note: $126,500*
SOLD by CAA in our May, 1998 AUCTION
*Fr. 2230-E $10,000 1928 Federal Reserve Note

Record price paid for a piece of Fractional Currency: $39,600*
SOLD by CAA in our January, 1997 AUCTION
*Fr. 1255a 10c Third Issue

One Company — All Three Records!

Sell your currency where records are being set!

CURRENCY AUCTIONS OF AMERICA, INC.

Allen Mincho
P.O. Box 700
Spicewood, TX 78669
(830) 693-7590   Fax (830) 693-1283

Charter Member

Leonard Glazer
P.O. Box 111
Forest Hills, NY 11375
(718) 268-3221

Charter Member

RONALD J. GILLIO

WANTS TO BUY ALL NATIONAL BANKNOTES OF CALIFORNIA & NEVADA

PAYING TOP DOLLAR

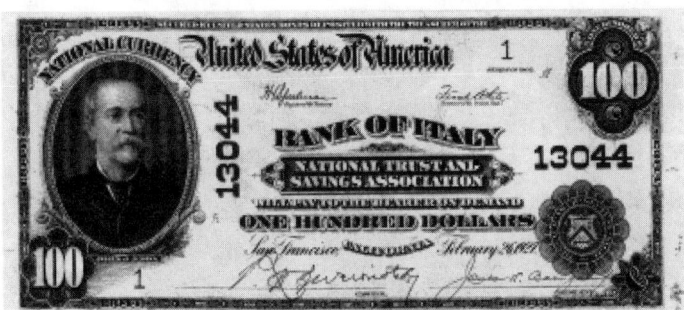
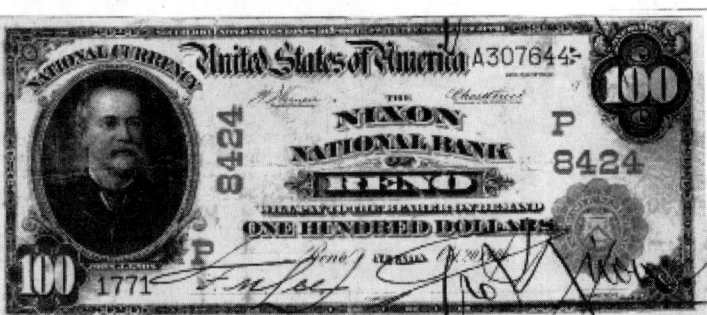

I HAVE BEEN BUYING CALIFORNIA & NEVADA NATIONAL BANKNOTES QUIETLY FOR THE PAST 35 YEARS

I AM THE ULTIMATE BUYER PAYING COLLECTOR'S PRICES BECAUSE I AM A COLLECTOR - I WILL TRAVEL TO BUY
NO DEAL IS TOO SMALL OR TOO BIG
GIVE ME A TRY

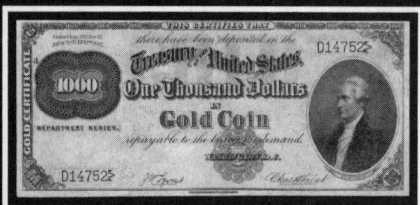

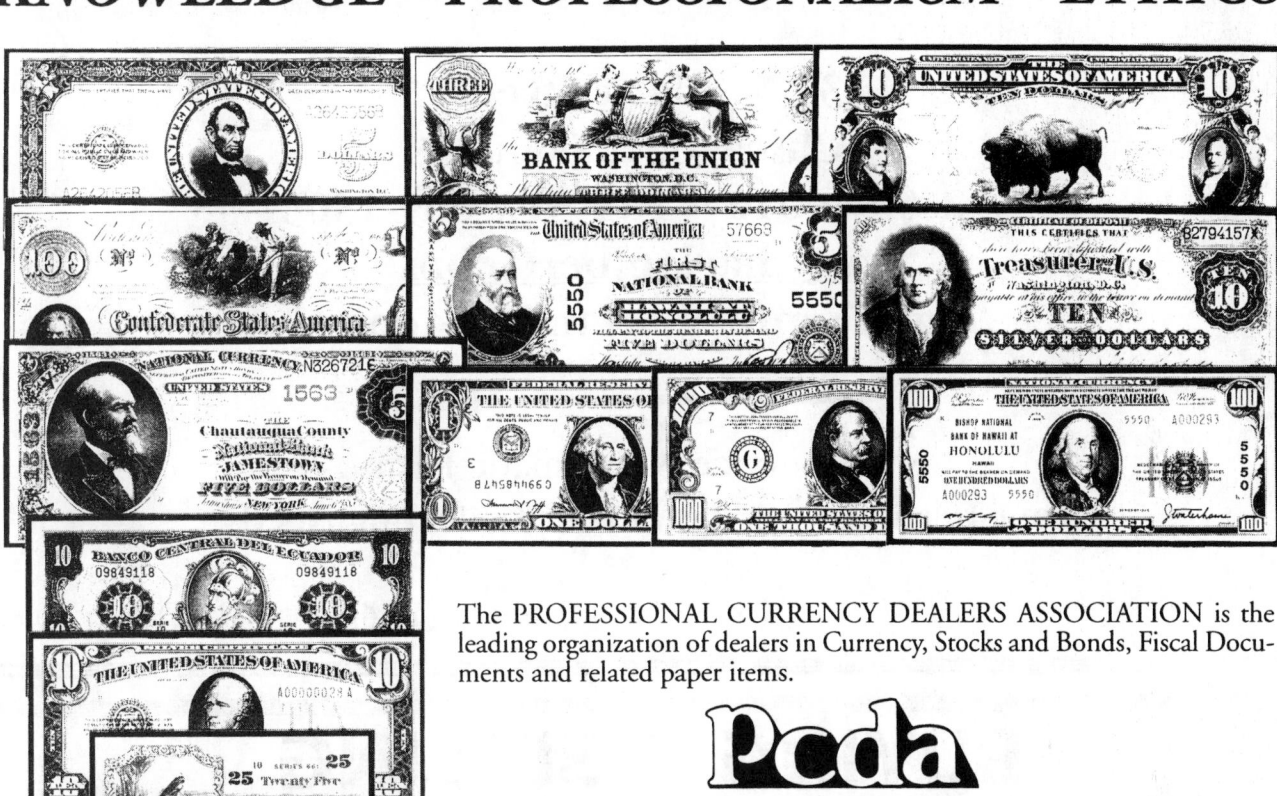

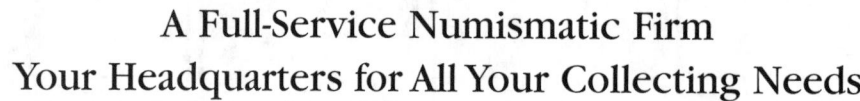

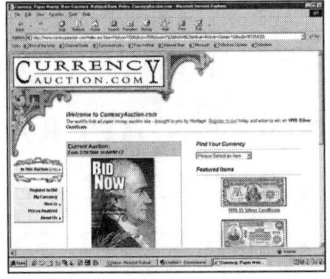

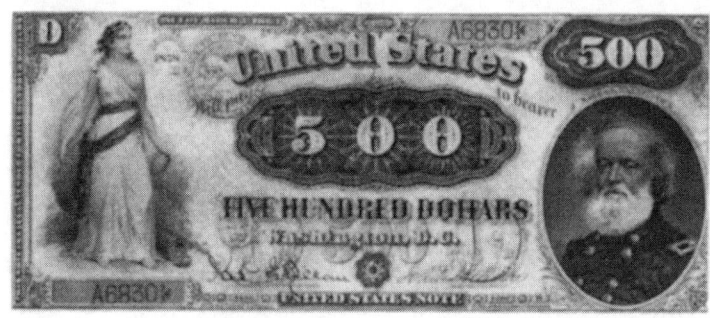

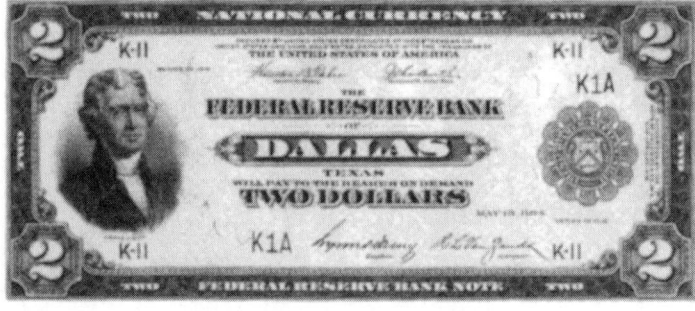

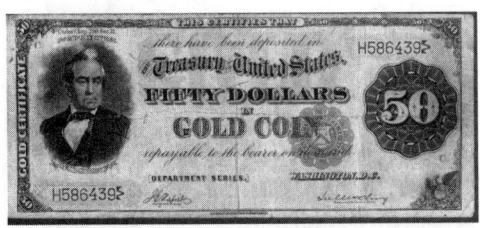

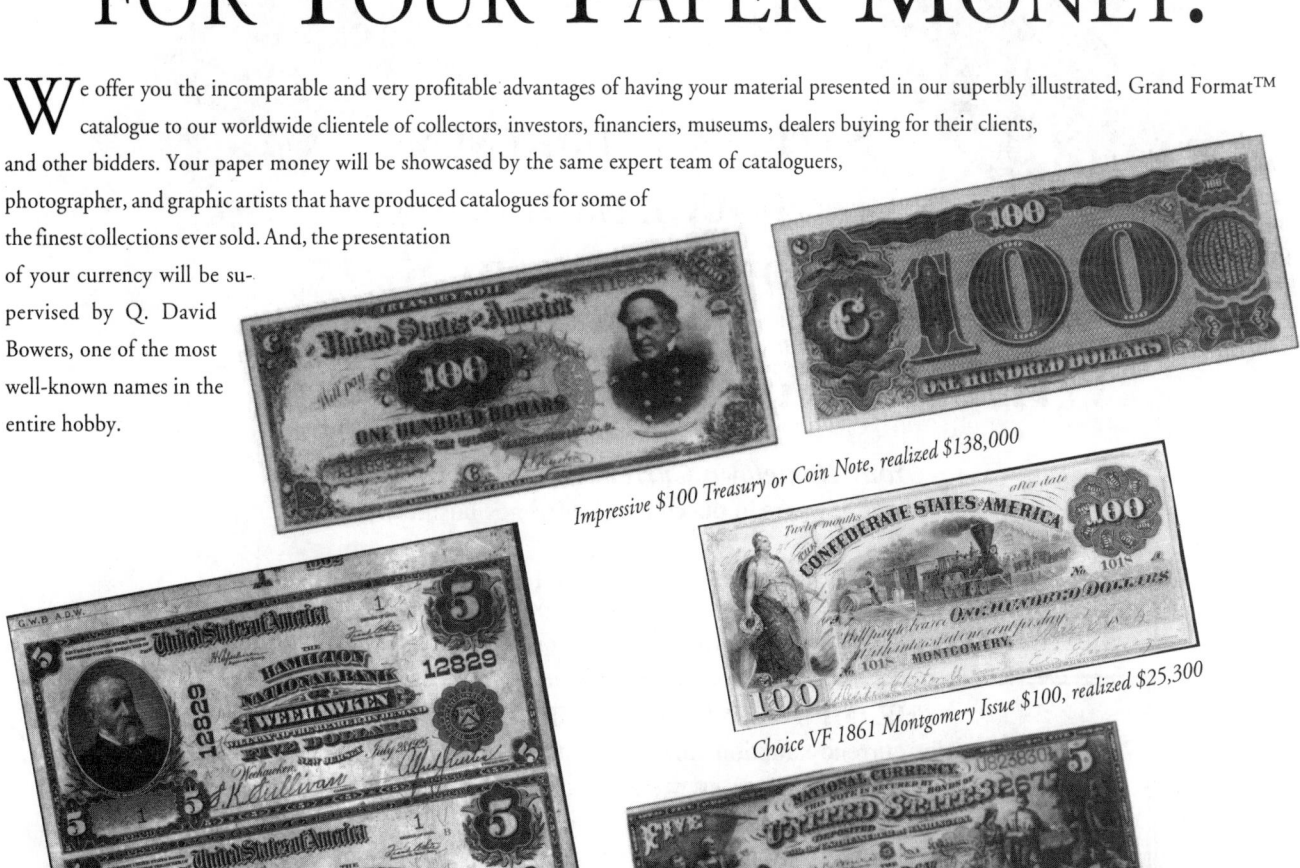

  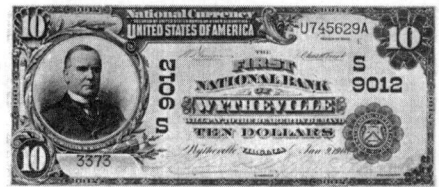

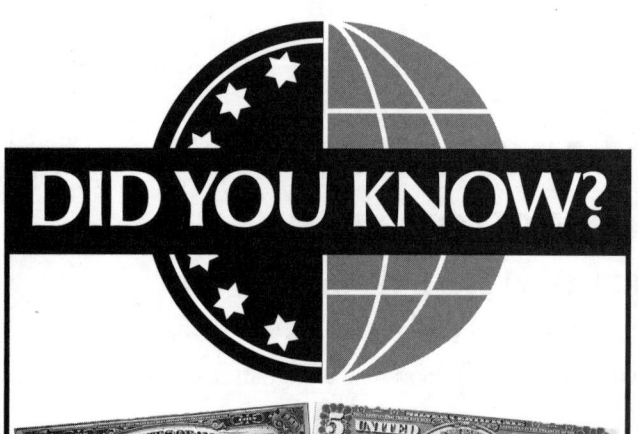
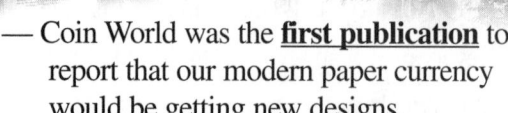

Design No. 1. Note 3. $5 Demand Note of 1861.

Design No. 2. Note 6. $10 Demand Note of 1861.

Design No. 3. Note 11. $20 Demand Note of 1861.
This is a cancelled specimen.

Design No. 5. Note 18. $1 Legal Tender Note of 1869.
Because of their intense coloring, the 1869 Legal Tender
issues are known as *"Rainbow Notes."*

Design No. 6. Note 22. $1 Legal Tender Note of 1875.
The *"Sawhorse"* Reverse.

Design No. 7. Note 40. $1 Legal Tender Note of 1923.
The *"Cogwheel"* Reverse.

Design No. 8. Note 41. $2 Legal Tender Note of 1862.

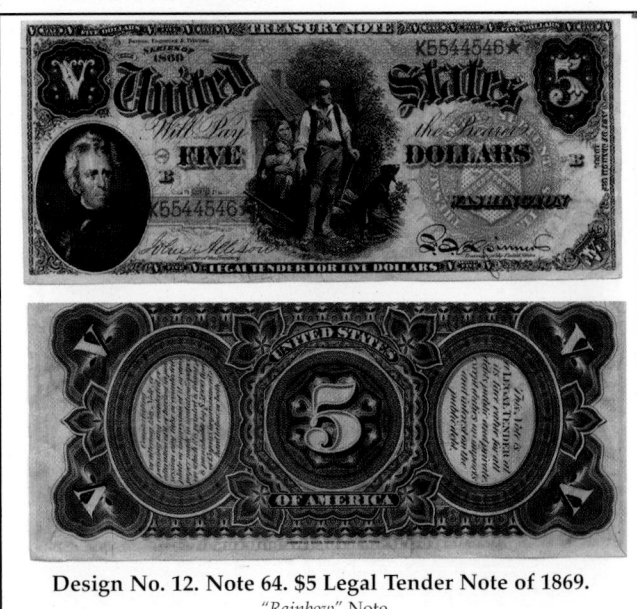

Design No. 12. Note 64. $5 Legal Tender Note of 1869.
"Rainbow" Note

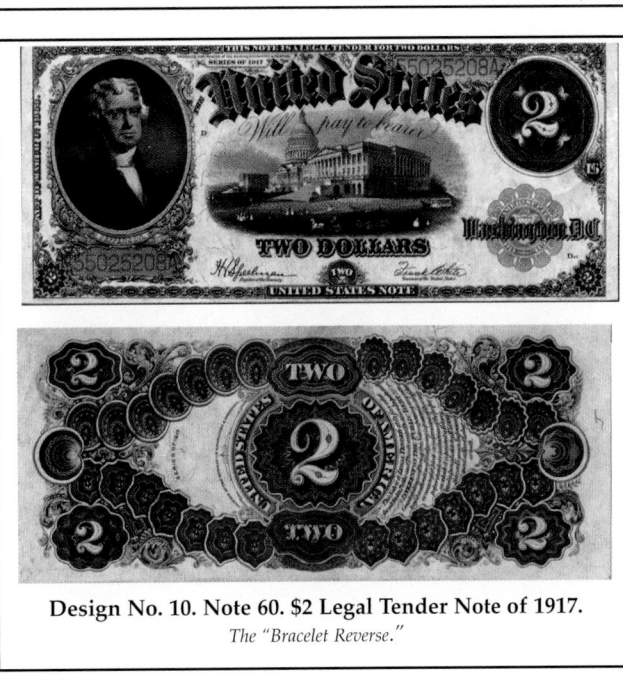

Design No. 10. Note 60. $2 Legal Tender Note of 1917.
The "Bracelet Reverse."

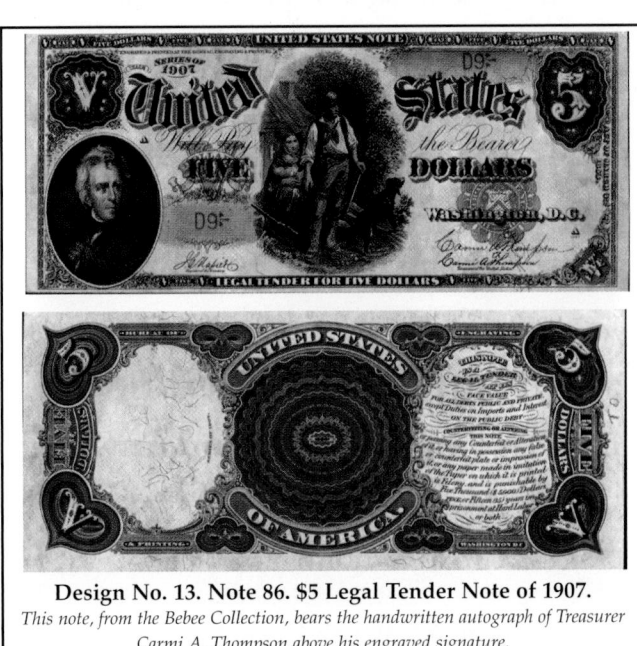

Design No. 13. Note 86. $5 Legal Tender Note of 1907.
This note, from the Bebee Collection, bears the handwritten autograph of Treasurer Carmi A. Thompson above his engraved signature.

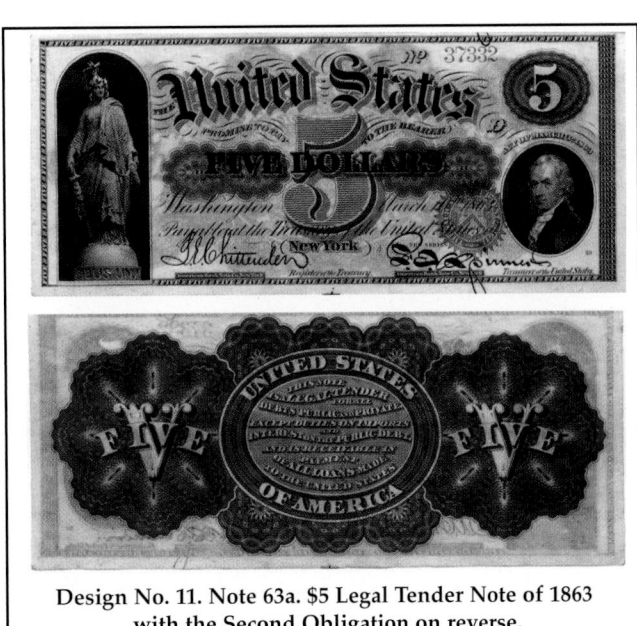

Design No. 11. Note 63a. $5 Legal Tender Note of 1863
with the Second Obligation on reverse.

Design No. 14. Note 93. $10 Legal Tender Note of 1862
with the First Obligation on reverse.

Design No. 14a. Note 95b. $10 Legal Tender Note of 1863 with the Second Obligation on reverse.

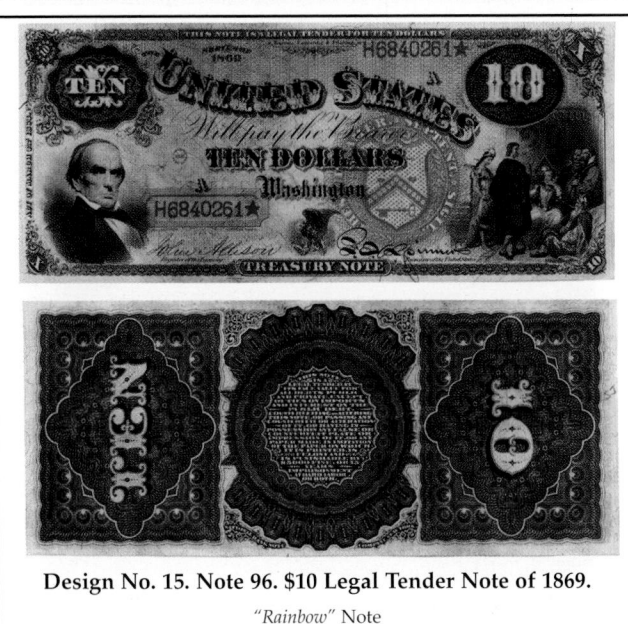

Design No. 15. Note 96. $10 Legal Tender Note of 1869.

"Rainbow" Note

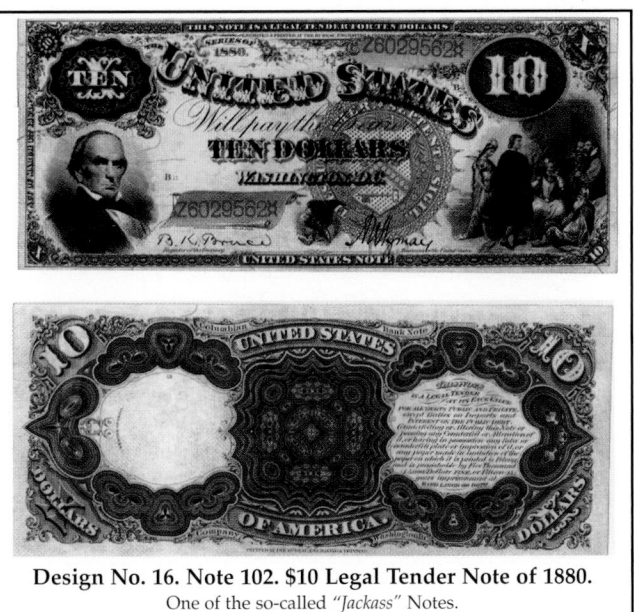

Design No. 16. Note 102. $10 Legal Tender Note of 1880.

One of the so-called *"Jackass"* Notes.

Design No. 17. Note 120. $10 Legal Tender Note of 1901.

The *"Bison"* Note.

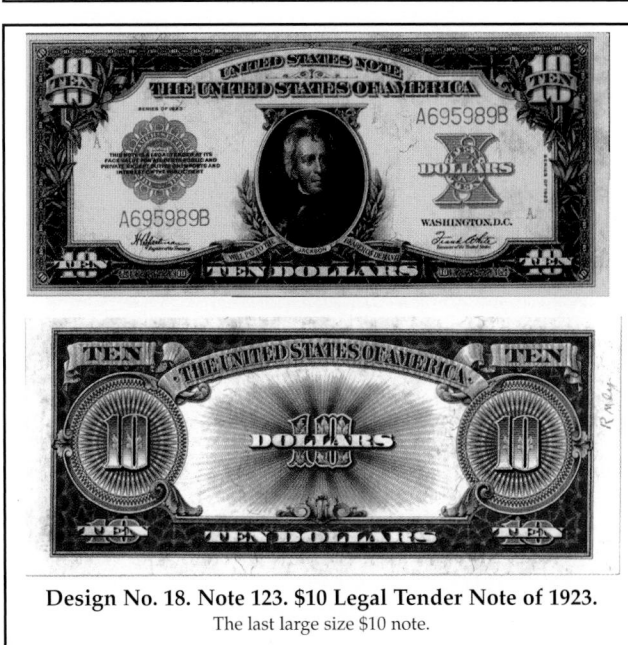

Design No. 18. Note 123. $10 Legal Tender Note of 1923.

The last large size $10 note.

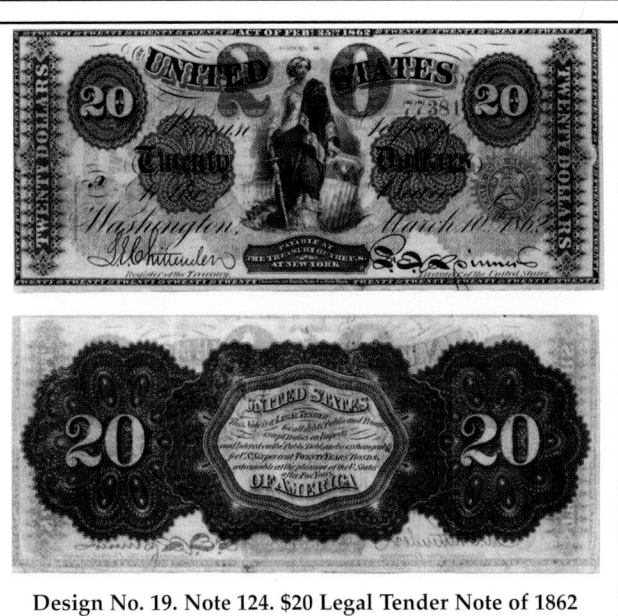

Design No. 19. Note 124. $20 Legal Tender Note of 1862 with First Obligation on reverse.

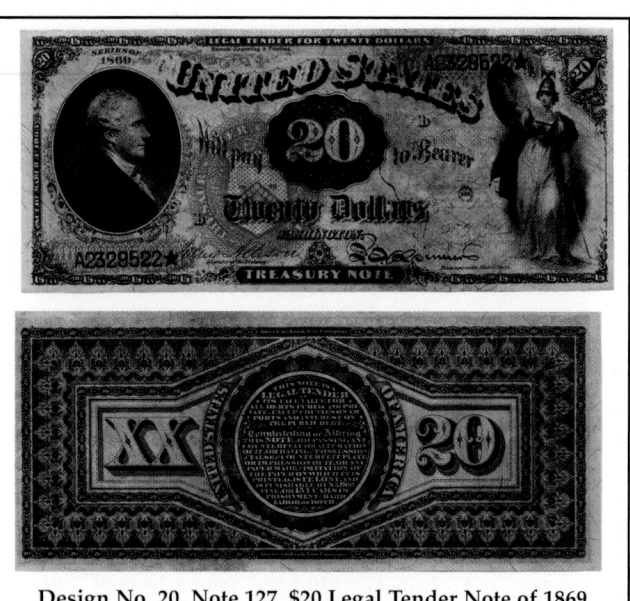

Design No. 20. Note 127. $20 Legal Tender Note of 1869
"Rainbow" Note.

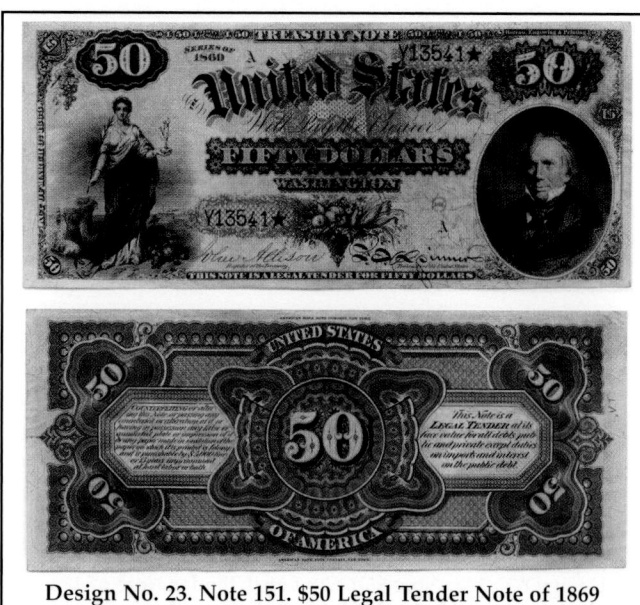

Design No. 23. Note 151. $50 Legal Tender Note of 1869

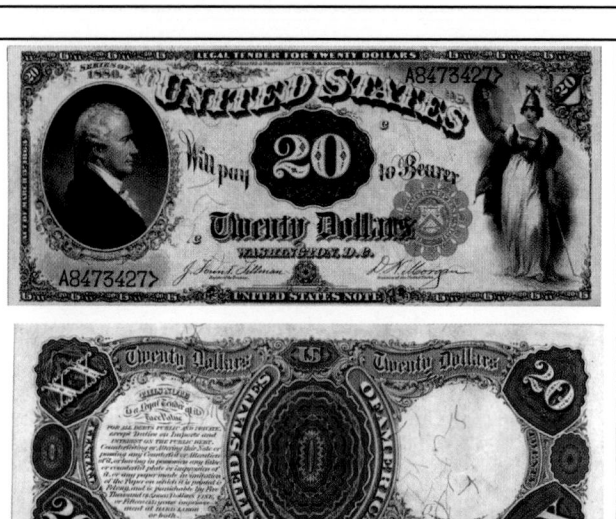

Design No. 21. Note 141. $20 Legal Tender Note of 1880.

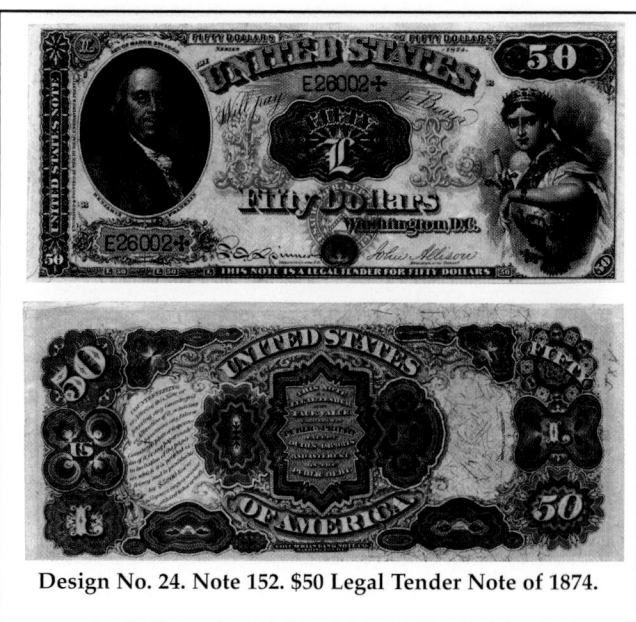

Design No. 24. Note 152. $50 Legal Tender Note of 1874.

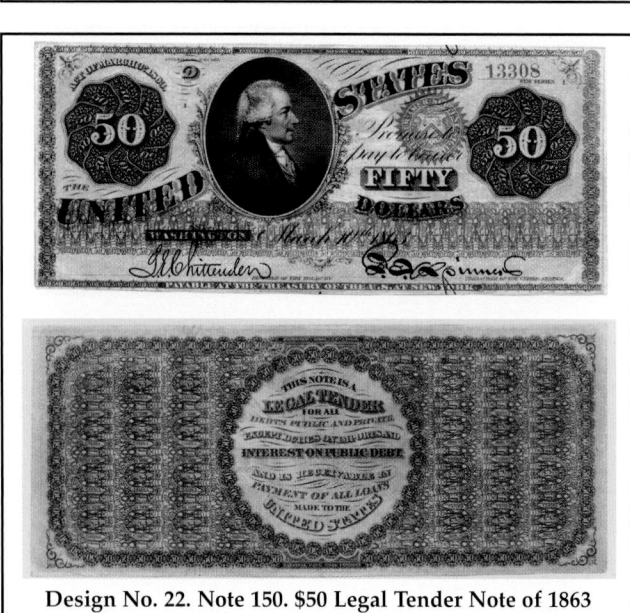

Design No. 22. Note 150. $50 Legal Tender Note of 1863
with the Second Obligation on the reverse.

Design No. 25. Note 167-a. $100 Legal Tender Note of 1863.

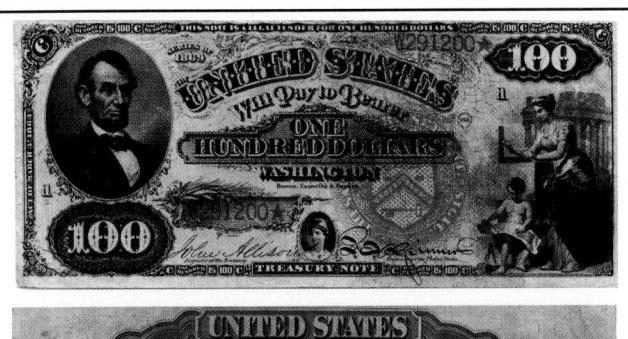

Design No. 26. Note 168. $100 Legal Tender Note of 1869.
"Rainbow" Note.

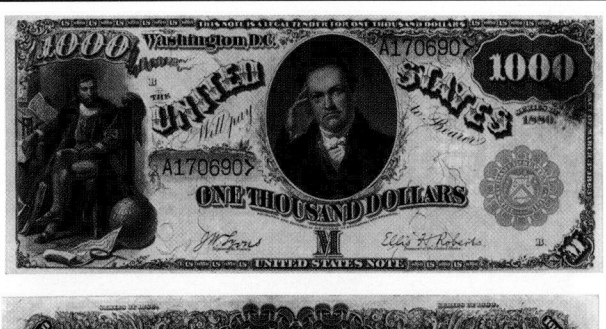

Design No. 32. Note 187-j. $1,000 Legal Tender Note of 1880.

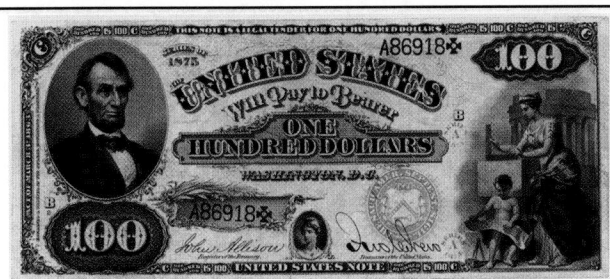

Design No. 27. Note 169. $100 Legal Tender Note of 1875.

Design No. 35. Note 190-b. $10 Compound Interest
Treasury Note of 1864.

Design No. 30. Note 185-m. $500 Legal Tender Note of 1880.

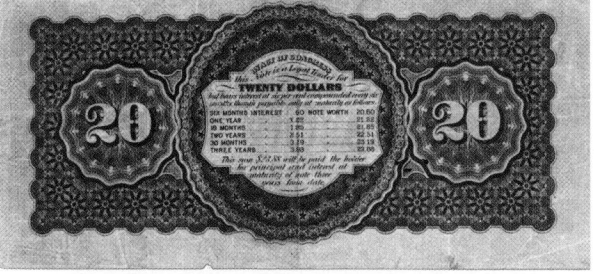

Design No. 36. Note 191-a. $20 Compound Interest
Treasury Note of 1864.

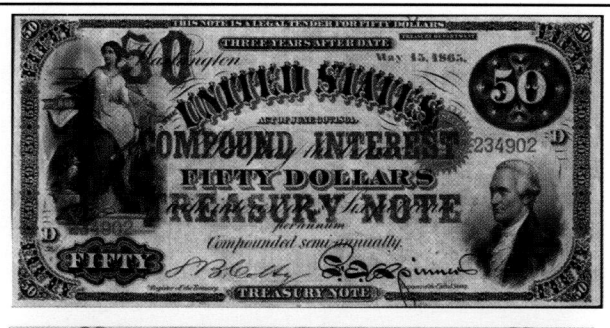

Design No. 37. Note 192-b. $50 Compound Interest
Treasury Note of 1864.

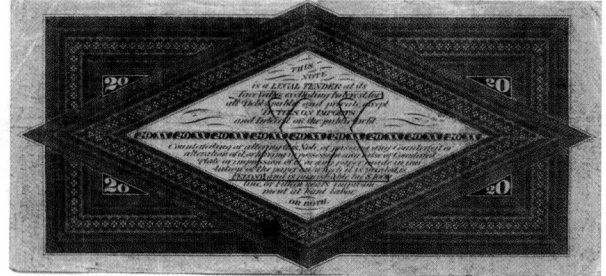

Design No. 42. Note 197-a. $20 One Year Interest
Bearing Note of 1863.

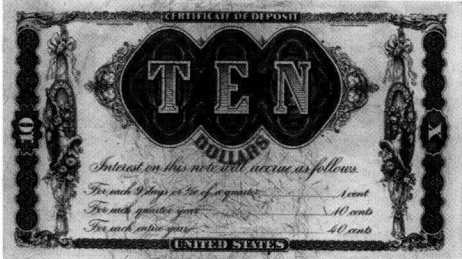

Design No. 58-b. $10 Refunding Certificate of 1879.

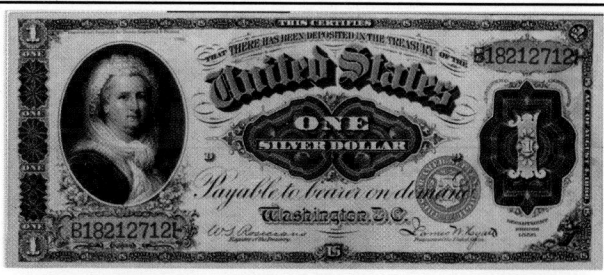

Design No. 59. Note 216. Silver Certificate of 1886.

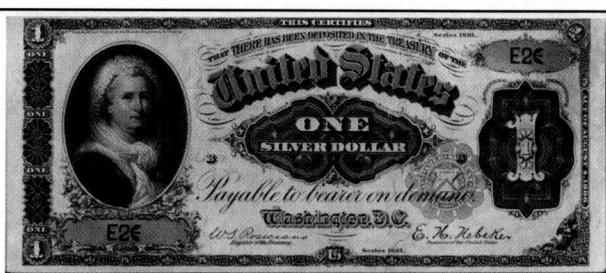

Design No. 60. Note 222. Silver Certificate of 1891.

Design No. 61. Note 224. $1 Silver Certificate of 1896.
The One Dollar Note in the *Educational Series.*

Design No. 62. Note 231. $1 Silver Certificate of 1899.

Design No. 63. Note 239. $1 Silver Certificate of 1923.

Design No. 64. Note 244. $2 Silver Certificate of 1886.

Design No. 65. Note 245. $2 Silver Certificate of 1891.

Design No. 66. Note 247. $2 Silver Certificate of 1896.
The Two Dollar Note in the *"Educational Series."*

Design No. 67. Note 254. $2 Silver Certificate of 1899.
*This note, from the Bebee Collection, bears the handwritten autograph of Treasurer
Carmi A. Thompson above his engraved signature.*

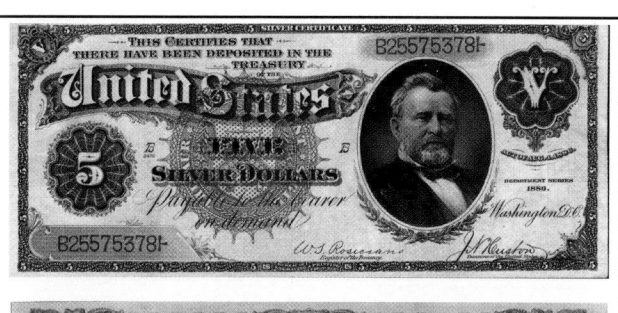

Design No. 68. Note 262. $5 Silver Certificate of 1886.
The "Silver Dollar Back."

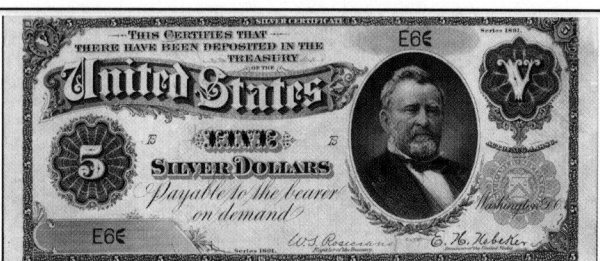

Design No. 69. Note. 266. $5 Silver Certificate of 1891.

Design No. 70. Note 270. $5 Silver Certificate of 1896.
The Five Dollar (and final) Note in the *"Educational Series."*

Design No. 71. Note 276. $5 Silver Certificate of 1899.
Commonly known as the *"Indian Chief"* or *"Oncpapa"* Note.

Design No. 72. Note 282. $5 Silver Certificate of 1923.
The *"Porthole"* Note.

**Design No. 73. Note 285-a. $10 Silver Certificate of 1878
with engraved countersignature of A.U. Wyman.**

Design No. 75. Note. 298. $10 Silver Certificate of 1891.
The so-called *"Tombstone"* Note.

Design No. 76-a. Note 310. $20 Silver Certificate of 1880.

Design No. 77. Note 313. $20 Silver Certificate of 1886.

Design No. 79. Note 324. $50 Silver Certificate of 1878.

Design No. 81. Note 337. $100 Silver Certificate of 1878.
Countersigned by R.M. Anthony and payable at San Francisco.
This is the only specimen known to exist.

Design No. 82. Note 344. $100 Silver Certificate of 1891.

Design No. 85. Note 347. $1 Treasury Note of 1890.

This note, from the Bebee Collection, bears the handwritten autograph of Treasurer J.N. Huston with the notation "Treasurer US 1889-1891."

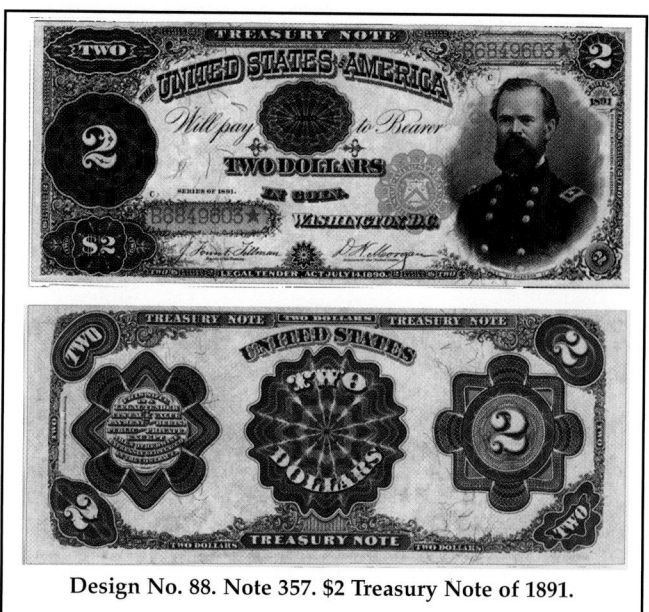

Design No. 88. Note 357. $2 Treasury Note of 1891.

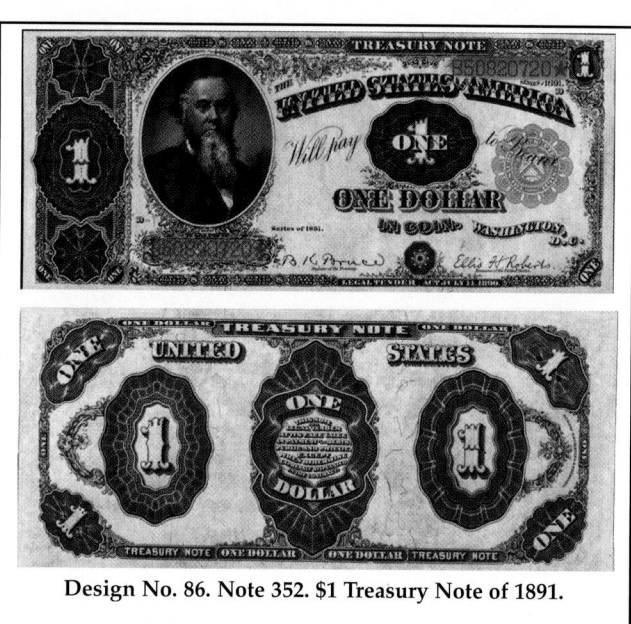

Design No. 86. Note 352. $1 Treasury Note of 1891.

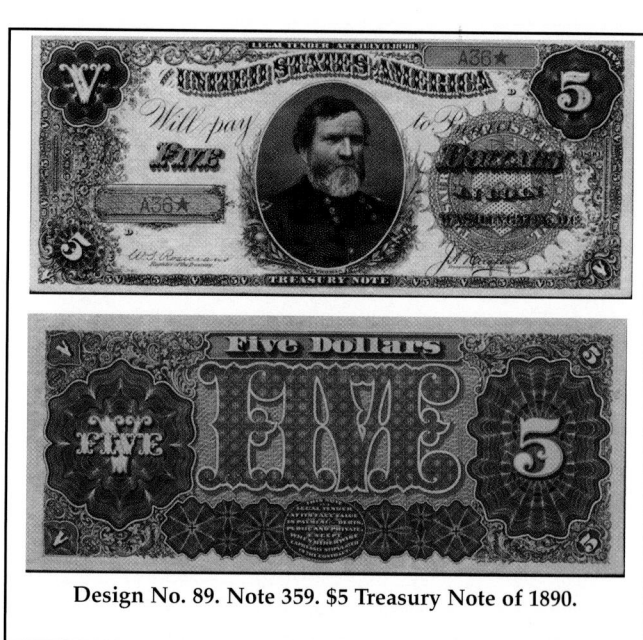

Design No. 89. Note 359. $5 Treasury Note of 1890.

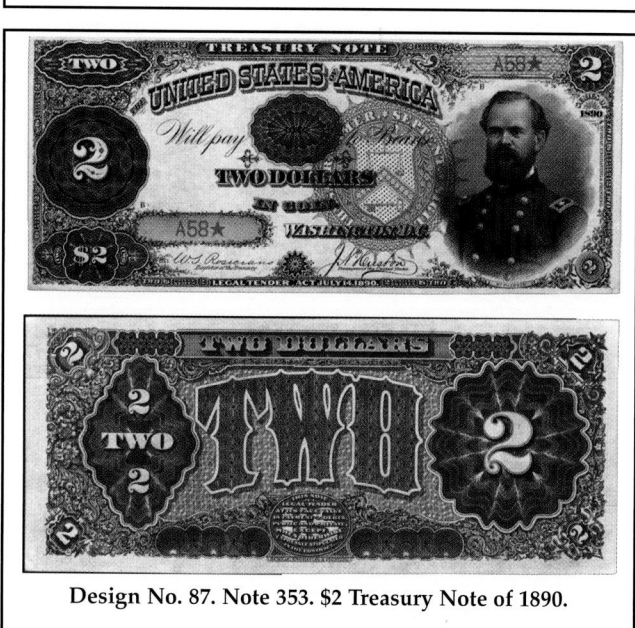

Design No. 87. Note 353. $2 Treasury Note of 1890.

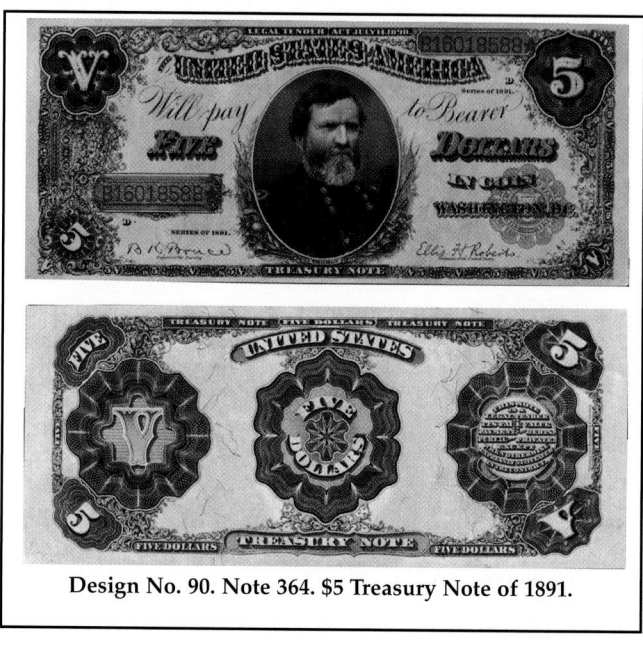

Design No. 90. Note 364. $5 Treasury Note of 1891.

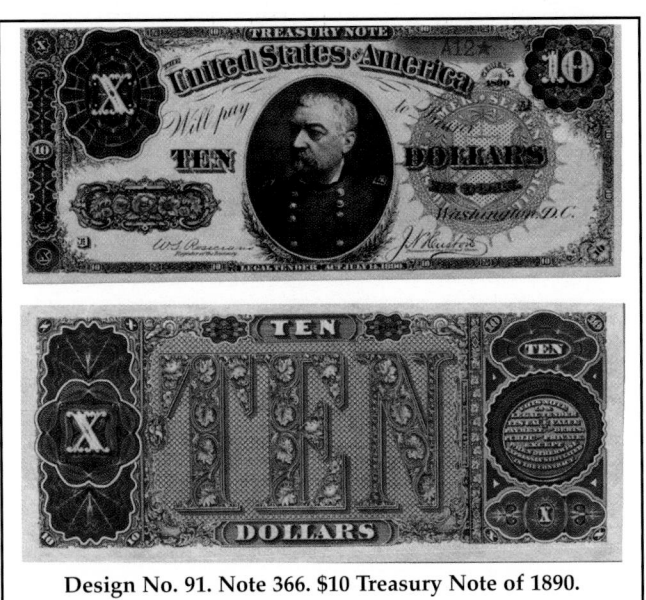

Design No. 91. Note 366. $10 Treasury Note of 1890.

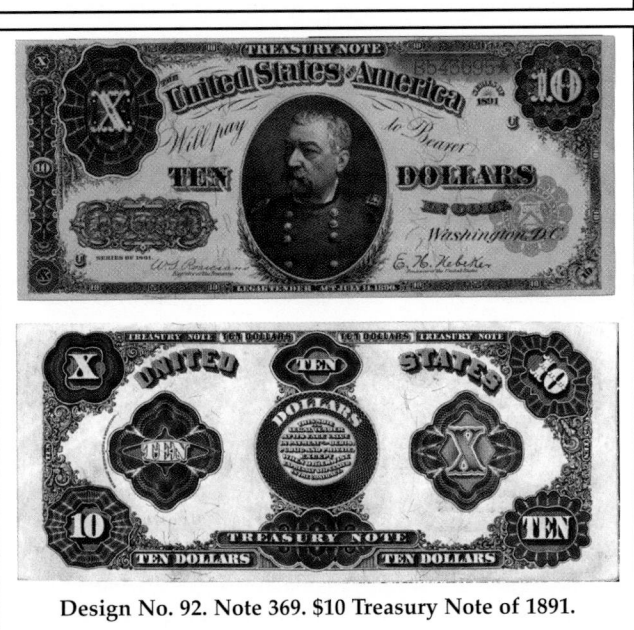

Design No. 92. Note 369. $10 Treasury Note of 1891.

Design No. 93. Note 372. $20 Treasury Note of 1890.

Design No. 94. Note 375. $20 Treasury Note of 1891.

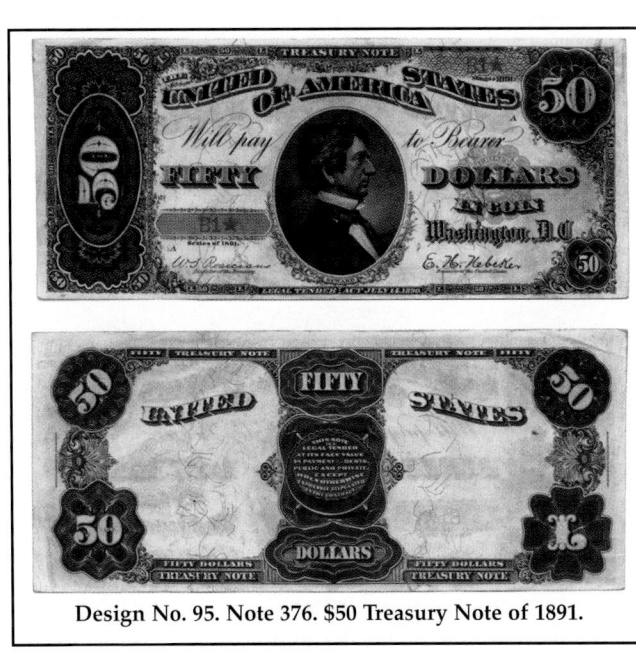

Design No. 95. Note 376. $50 Treasury Note of 1891.

Design No. 96. Note 377. $100 Treasury Note of 1890.

The "Watermelon" Note.

Design No. 99. Note 382. $1 National Bank Note.
Original Series. First Charter Period.

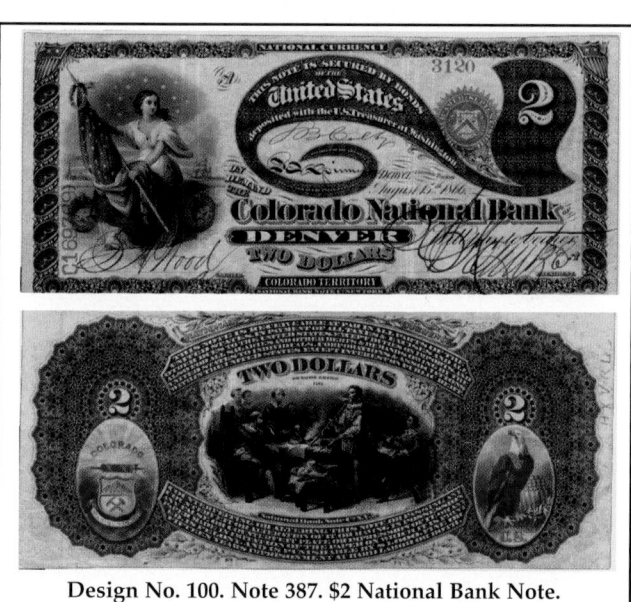

Design No. 100. Note 387. $2 National Bank Note.
Original Series. First Charter Period.
The "Lazy Deuce."

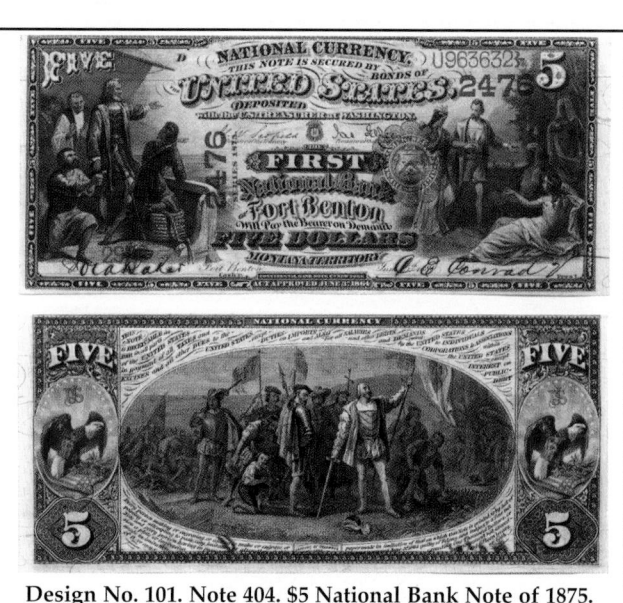

Design No. 101. Note 404. $5 National Bank Note of 1875.
First Charter Period.

Design No. 102. Note 419. $10 National Bank Note of 1875.
First Charter Period.

Design No. 103. Note 431. $20 National Bank Note of 1875.
First Charter Period.

Design No. 104. Note 447. $50 National Bank Note of 1875.
First Charter Period.

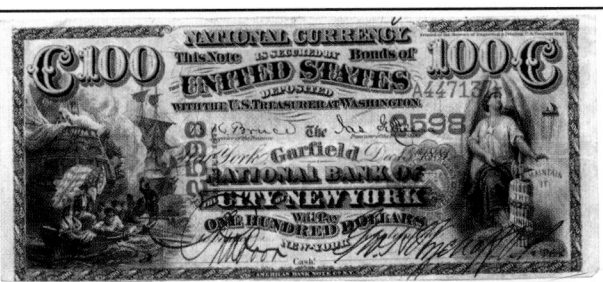

Design No. 105. Note 460. $100 National Bank Note of 1875.
First Charter Period.

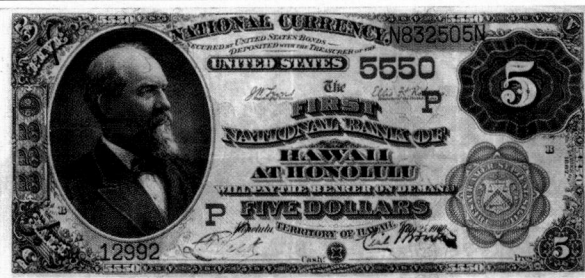

Design No. 108. Note 477. $5 National Bank Note of 1882.
Second Charter Period. First Issue. Brown Back.

Design No. 109. Note 490. $10 National Bank Note of 1882.
Second Charter Period. First Issue. Brown Back.

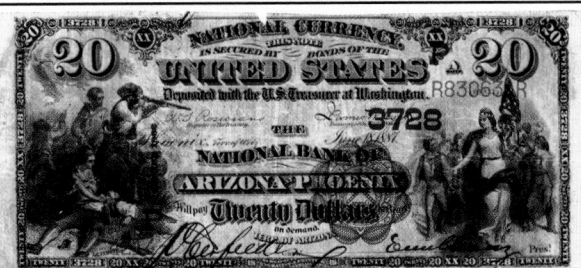

Design No. 110. Note 497. $20 National Bank Note of 1882.
Second Charter Period. First Issue. Brown Back.

Design No. 111. Note 518. $50 National Bank Note of 1882.
Second Charter Period. First Issue. Brown Back.

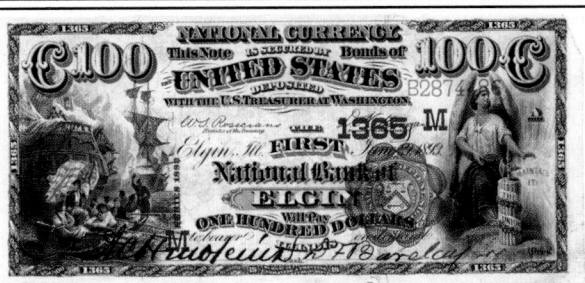

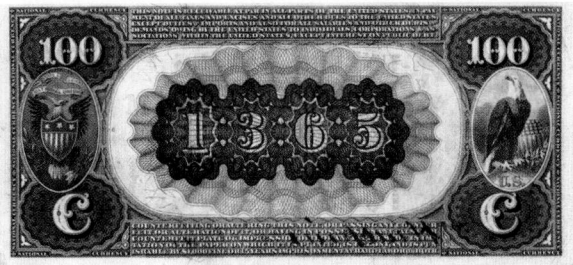

Design No. 112. Note 526. $100 National Bank Note of 1882.
Second Charter Period. First Issue. Brown Back.

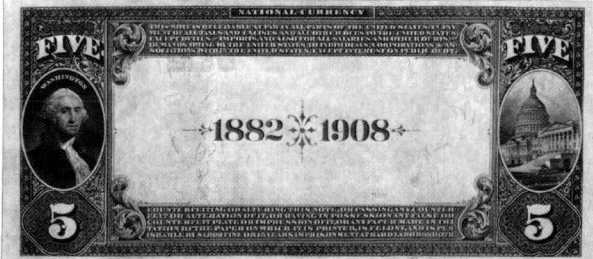

No. 113. Note 537. $5 National Bank Note of 1882.
Second Charter Period. Second Issue. Date on Back.

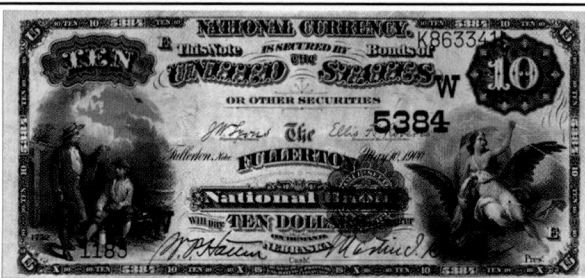
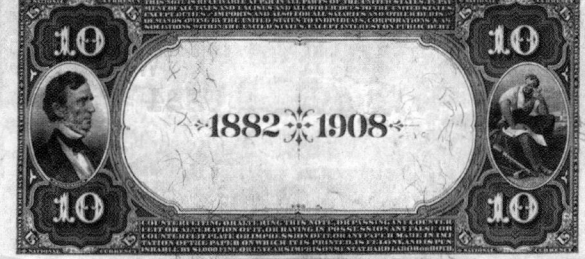

Design No. 114. Note 545. $10 National Bank Note of 1882.
Second Charter Period. Second Issue. Date on Back.

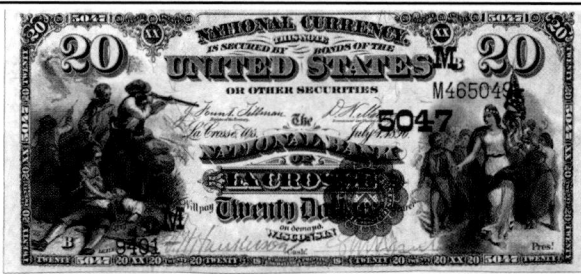
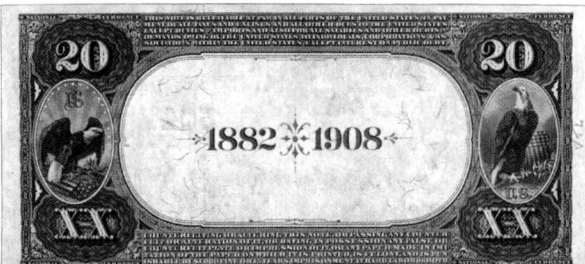

Design No. 115. Note 552. $20 National Bank Note of 1882.
Second Charter Period. Second Issue. Date on Back.

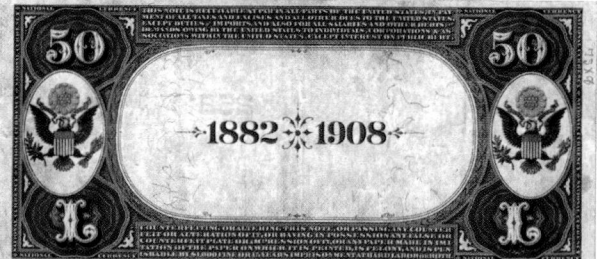

Design No. 116. Note 563. $50 National Bank Note of 1882.
Second Charter Period. Second Issue. Date on Back.

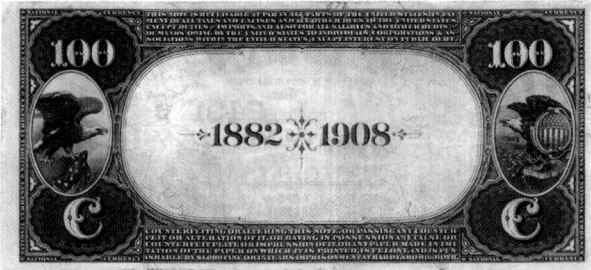

Design No. 117. Note 572. $100 National Bank Note of 1882.
Second Charter Period. Second Issue. Date on Back.

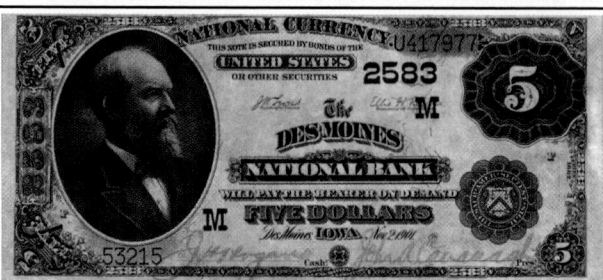

Design No. 118. Note 574. $5 National Bank Note of 1882.
Second Charter Period. Third Issue. Value on Back.

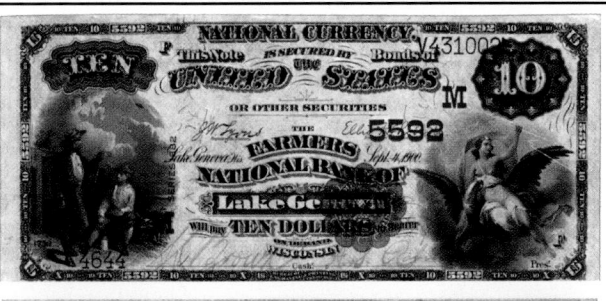

Design No. 119. Note 577. $10 National Bank Note of 1882.
Second Charter Period. Third Issue. Value on Back.

Design No. 122-b. Note 607. $5 National Bank Note of 1902.
Third Charter Period. Third Issue. Blue Seal. No Date on Back.

Design No. 122. Note 587. $5 National Bank Note of 1902.
Third Charter Period. First Issue. Red Seal.

Design No. 123. Note 613. $10 National Bank Note of 1902.
Third Charter Period. First Issue. Red Seal.

Design No. 122-a. Note 591. $5 National Bank Note of 1902.
Third Charter Period. Second Issue. Blue Seal. Date on Back.

Design No. 123-b. Note 624. $10 National Bank Note of 1902.
Third Charter Period. Third Issue. Blue Seal. No Date on Back.

Design No. 124-a. Note 645. $20 National Bank Note of 1902.
Third Charter Period. Second Issue. Blue Seal. Date on back.

Design No. 126-a. Note 691. $100 National Bank Note of 1902.
Third Charter Period. Second Issue. Blue Seal, Date on Back

Design No. 124-b. Note 654. $20 National Bank Note of 1902.
Third Charter Period. Third Issue. Blue Seal. No Date on Back.

Design No. 126-b. Note 698. $100 National Bank Note of 1902.
Third Charter Period. Third Issue. Blue Seal. No Date on Back.

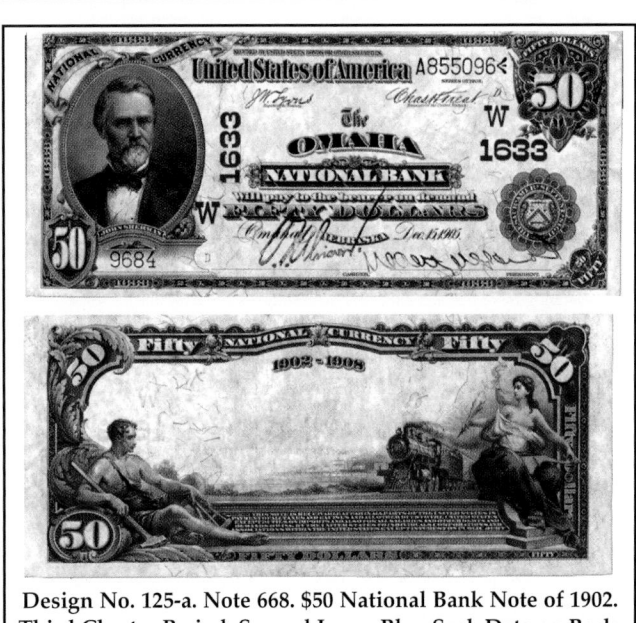

Design No. 125-a. Note 668. $50 National Bank Note of 1902.
Third Charter Period. Second Issue. Blue Seal. Date on back.

Design No. 127. Note 714.
$1 Federal Reserve Bank Note of 1918.

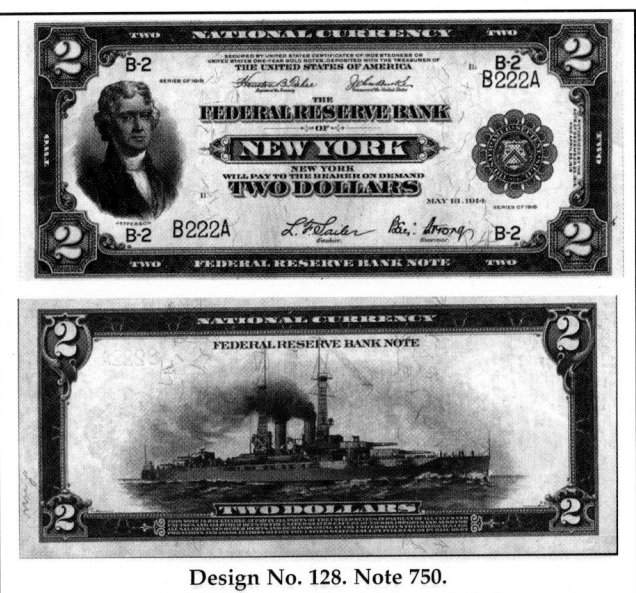

Design No. 128. Note 750.
$2 Federal Reserve Bank Note of 1918.

Design No. 131. Note 824.
$20 Federal Reserve Bank Note of 1915.

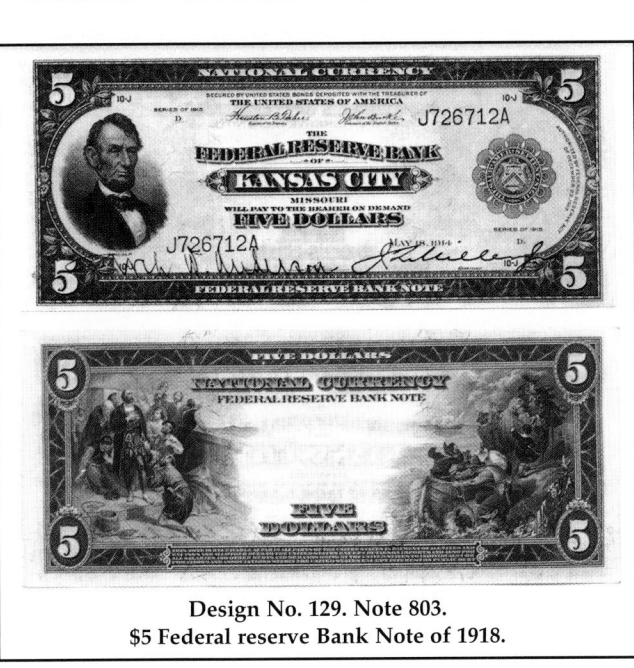

Design No. 129. Note 803.
$5 Federal reserve Bank Note of 1918.

Design No. 132. Note 831.
$50 Federal Reserve Bank Note of 1918.

Design No. 130. Note 814.
$10 Federal Reserve Bank Note of 1918.

Design No. 133. Note 871-a.
$5 Federal Reserve Note of 1914 with Blue Seal.

Design No. 134. Note 893-a.
$10 Federal Reserve Note of 1914 with Red Seal.

Design No. 136. Note 1053.
$50 Dollar Federal Reserve Note of 1914 with Blue Seal.

Design No. 135. Note 1008.
$20 Federal Reserve Note of 1914 with Blue Seal.

Design No. 137. Note 1073a.
$100 Federal Reserve Note of 1914 with Red Seal.

Design No. 136. Note 1014.
$50 Dollar Federal Reserve Note of 1914 with Red Seal.

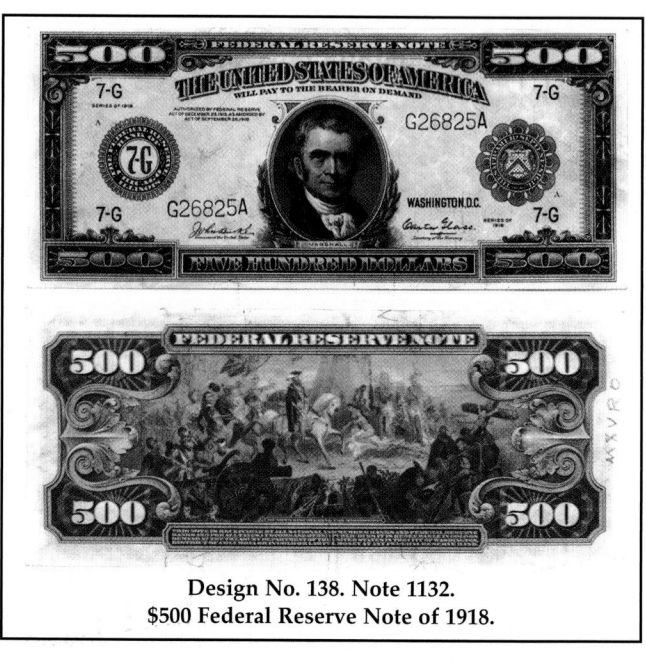

Design No. 138. Note 1132.
$500 Federal Reserve Note of 1918.

Design No. 142. Note 1136.
$5 National Gold Bank Note of 1870.

Design No. 145. Note 1160.
$50 National Gold Bank Note of 1870.

Design No. 143. Note 1142.
$10 National Gold Bank Note of 1870.

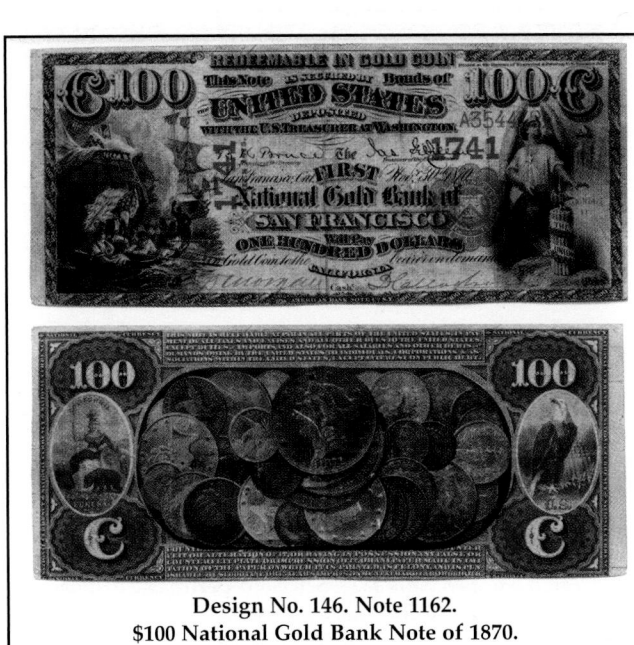

Design No. 146. Note 1162.
$100 National Gold Bank Note of 1870.

Design No. 144. Note 1152.
$20 National Gold Bank Note of 1870.

Design No. 147. Note 1170. $10 Gold Certificate of 1907.

Design No. 148. Note 1176. $20 Gold Certificate of 1882.

Design No. 151. Note 1198. $50 Gold Certificate of 1913.

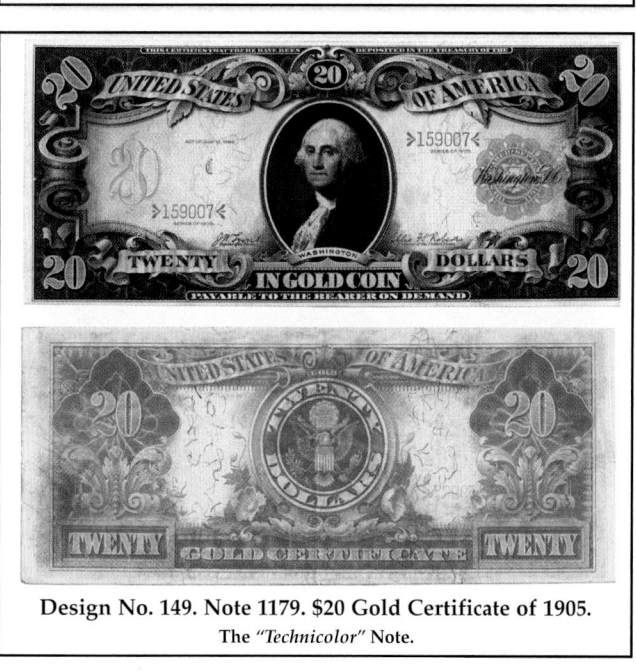

Design No. 149. Note 1179. $20 Gold Certificate of 1905.
The *"Technicolor"* Note.

Design No. 152. Note 1215. $100 Gold Certificate of 1922.

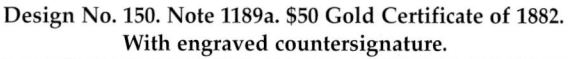

Design No. 150. Note 1189a. $50 Gold Certificate of 1882.
With engraved countersignature.

Design No. 153. Note 1216. $500 Gold Certificate of 1882.